Media Law

Media Law

Rex S. Heinke

Gibson, Dunn & Crutcher
Los Angeles, California

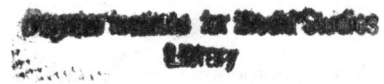

The Bureau of National Affairs, Inc., Washington, D.C.

Copyright © 1994
The Bureau of National Affairs, Inc.

Library of Congress Cataloging-in-Publication Data

Heinke, Rex S.
    Media law / Rex S. Heinke.
      p. cm.
    Includes index.
    ISBN 0-87179-800-X
    1. Press law—United States. 2. Freedom of the press—United States. 3. Mass media—Law and legislation—United States.
I. Title.
KF2750.H45   1994
342.73′0853—dc20
[347.302853]
                                                                                                                            94-25572
                                                                                                                                  CIP

Authorization to photocopy items for internal or personal use, or the internal or personal use of specific clients, is granted by BNA Books for libraries and other users registered with the Copyright Clearance Center (CCC) Transactional Reporting Service, provided that $1.00 per page is paid directly to CCC, 27 Congress St., Salem, MA 01970. 0-87179-800-X/94/$0 + 1.00.

Published by BNA Books
1250 23rd St., N.W., Washington, D.C. 20037-1165
International Standard Book Number: 0-87179-800-X

PREFACE

This is a book about the law on the gathering and publishing of information by the media. It discusses the free speech and free press clauses of the First Amendment,[1] as well as comparable state constitutional provisions, and their application to the news gathering and publishing/broadcasting activities of the media. It also discusses statutes and court decisions that have a direct impact on the media's news gathering and publishing/broadcasting activities.

This book is not a general treatise on the First Amendment or on all laws that affect the media—e.g., antitrust, tax, or labor laws—except to the extent they directly affect information gathering and dissemination. It is, however, a book that should be useful to everyone interested in the legal problems that arise from the media's gathering and distribution of information.

Like any such project, this book is the result of the labor of many people. First, there are my present and former colleagues at Gibson, Dunn & Crutcher who were instrumental in helping me write many of this book's chapters: Chapter 1, Susan Erburu Reardon; Chapter 2, Kelli L. Sager and Sheila R. Caudle; Chapter 3, Diane A. Golden; Chapter 4, Kurt L. Schmalz; Chapter 5, A. Randall Farnsworth; Chapter 6, Cynthia Edson Libby and Vivienne A. Vella; Chapter 7, Ragnhild Reif; Chapter 10, Susan E. Abitanta and Richard Pachter; Chapter 11, Phillip H. Rudolph and Karen N. Frederiksen; Chapter 12, Lester E. Greenman; Chapter 13, Jeri C. Okamoto; and Chapter 14, David Lopez.

In addition, there are many others who helped with the writing of one or more chapters: Alicia J. Bentley; Timothy L. Alger; Allison A. Arabian; Eileen M. Decker; June R. McIvor; Marci Lerner; Shauna Weeks; Robin Goldstein; Nancy Gillespie; Howard Bashman; Mary Donlevy; Jane H. Farr; Antoinette D. Paglia; and Lila Rogers, who also worked diligently on the galley proofs. Richard J. Tofel also read and commented on some of the chapters.

There are also the people who got me through the extended ordeal of writing this book: my wife, Margaret A. Nagle, who taught me how to write; Anne Scott, who skillfully shepherded the book through BNA's editing process; and my secretaries Lynn B. Weatherwax and Sharon L. Cooper, who along with our paralegals Amanda Robertson-Bora and Vicki S. Rousopoulos,

---

[1] "As everyone knows—with the glaring exception of the law review editors—it is the First Amendment, not the first amendment." NIMMER ON FREEDOM OF SPEECH vii (1984).

performed perhaps the hardest work on this book. Finally, there is my partner, Robert S. Warren, who taught me what I know about media law.

Of course, I am responsible for the ultimate result and any errors. If you find errors, please write to me and they will be corrected in the next supplement.

REX S. HEINKE

Los Angeles, California
May 1994

SUMMARY TABLE OF CONTENTS

		Page
Preface		v
Chapter 1.	News Gathering	1
Chapter 2.	Defamation	69
Chapter 3.	False Light	141
Chapter 4.	Private Facts	157
Chapter 5.	Intrusion, Trespass, Wiretapping, and Related Problems	185
Chapter 6.	Appropriation and the Right of Publicity	211
Chapter 7.	Media Liability for False Advertisements and Other Similar Statements	241
Chapter 8.	Imitation and Incitement	255
Chapter 9.	Applicability of General Laws to the Media	269
Chapter 10.	Prior Restraints	299
Chapter 11.	Commercial Speech	335
Chapter 12.	Time, Place, and Manner Restrictions	377
Chapter 13.	Access to the Media	407
Chapter 14.	Confidential Sources and Related Problems	469
Table of Cases		517
Index		591

DETAILED TABLE OF CONTENTS

    Page

PREFACE v

CHAPTER 1. NEWS GATHERING 1

§1.1	Introduction		1
§1.2	Overview of Supreme Court Decisions		1
	§1.2(A)	The Constitutional Right of Access	2
		§1.2(A)(i) *Gannett Co. v. DePasquale*	2
		§1.2(A)(ii) *Richmond Newspapers v. Virginia*	4
		§1.2(A)(iii) *Globe Newspaper Co. v. Superior Court*	5
		§1.2(A)(iv) *Press-Enterprise I*	6
		§1.2(A)(v) *Waller v. Georgia*	7
		§1.2(A)(vi) *Press-Enterprise II*	8
	§1.2(B)	The Common Law Right of Access	11
§1.3	Procedural Requirements for Closure		11
§1.4	Access to Criminal Pretrial and Posttrial Proceedings		13
	§1.4(A)	Pretrial Suppression Hearings	13
	§1.4(B)	Preliminary Hearings and Other Pretrial Proceedings	17
	§1.4(C)	Bail and Related Hearings	18
	§1.4(D)	Mental Competency Hearings	19
	§1.4(E)	Posttrial Hearings	21
§1.5	Access to Criminal Trial Proceedings		21
	§1.5(A)	Trials	22
	§1.5(B)	Voir Dire	24
	§1.5(C)	Juvenile Proceedings	26
§1.6	Access to Civil Pretrial and Trial Proceedings		29
§1.7	Access to Administrative and Quasi-Judicial Proceedings and Records		30
§1.8	Inspecting and Copying Court Records and Evidence		32
	§1.8(A)	Criminal Records	33
	§1.8(B)	Civil Records	42

		§1.8(B)(i) Civil Discovery Materials	42
		§1.8(B)(ii) Sealed Civil Records	48
§1.9	Access to People and Places		49
	§1.9(A)	Prisoners and Executions	49
	§1.9(B)	Jurors	54
	§1.9(C)	Public Employees, Migrant Workers, and Students	54
	§1.9(D)	Disaster, Crime, and Military Operation Sites	55
	§1.9(E)	Legislative and Political Proceedings	56
	§1.9(F)	Public Sporting Facilities	57
	§1.9(G)	Polling Places and Exit Polls	57
	§1.9(H)	Court Buildings	59
§1.10	Electronic Coverage of Court and Other Proceedings		60
§1.11	Open Meetings and Public Records Laws		66

CHAPTER 2. DEFAMATION 69

§2.1	The Common Law of Defamation		69
§2.2	Impact of the First Amendment on Defamation Law		70
§2.3	Elements of a Defamation Claim		78
§2.4	Purposes of Defamation Law		79
§2.5	Defamatory Meaning		79
	§2.5(A)	Defamatory Meaning and Implications	82
	§2.5(B)	Pleading All the Defamatory Words	83
	§2.5(C)	The Innocent Construction Rule	83
	§2.5(D)	The Single Instance Rule	83
	§2.5(E)	Insults, Epithets, Jokes, and Cartoons	84
	§2.5(F)	Necessity of Injury to Reputation	85
	§2.5(G)	Inducement, Innuendo, and Colloquium	85
	§2.5(H)	Libel and Slander	85
	§2.5(I)	Per Se and Per Quod Libel and Slander	86
	§2.5(J)	The Four Slander Per Se Categories	88
	§2.5(K)	Defamation Per Se and the First Amendment	90
§2.6	Publication		90
	§2.6(A)	Individual Liability	91
	§2.6(B)	Republication	92
	§2.6(C)	The Single Publication Rule	92
§2.7	Fact Versus Opinion		93
§2.8	Fair Comment		97
§2.9	Falsity		98
§2.10	Permissible Plaintiffs		99
	§2.10(A)	Of and Concerning the Plaintiff	100
	§2.10(B)	Defamation of Groups	101
§2.11	Fault		102
	§2.11(A)	Public Officials	102
		§2.11(A)(i) Official Conduct	103

		§2.11(A)(ii) Public Officials and Absolute Privilege	104
		§2.11(A)(iii) Mentioning the Plaintiff's Public Official Status	104
	§2.11(B)	Public Figures	104
	§2.11(C)	Limits on the Public Official and Public Figure Rules	109
		§2.11(C)(i) Nonmedia Defendants	109
		§2.11(C)(ii) Passage of Time	110
	§2.11(D)	Criticism of the Public Official and Public Figure Doctrine	110
	§2.11(E)	Actual Malice	111
		§2.11(E)(i) Actual Malice and Misinterpretation	115
		§2.11(E)(ii) The "Clear and Convincing Evidence" Requirement	116
	§2.11(F)	Private Figures: Negligence and Other Fault Standards	116
	§2.11(G)	Wire Service Defense	117
	§2.11(H)	Fault by Broadcasters	118
	§2.11(I)	Liability of Individual and Corporate Defendants	118
	§2.11(J)	Waiver of First Amendment Protection	119
§2.12	Matter of Public or Private Concern		120
§2.13	Absolute Privileges		121
	§2.13(A)	Consent	121
	§2.13(B)	Statements Made in Judicial, Legislative, Executive, and Administrative Proceedings	121
	§2.13(C)	Publications Required by Law	122
	§2.13(D)	Miscellaneous Absolute Privileges	122
§2.14	Conditional Privileges		123
	§2.14(A)	The Interested Party Privilege	123
	§2.14(B)	Abuse of a Conditional Privilege	124
§2.15	Conditional Absolute Privileges		124
	§2.15(A)	The Accurate Summary Privilege	124
	§2.15(B)	The Neutral Report Privilege	127
§2.16	Damages		128
	§2.16(A)	Effect of *Gertz* on Damages	128
	§2.16(B)	"Libel-Proof" Plaintiffs and Incremental Harm	130
	§2.16(C)	Correction and Retraction Statutes	131
	§2.16(D)	Damages for Loss of Political Office	132
	§2.16(E)	Reforming the Damages Remedy	133
§2.17	Injunctive Relief		133
§2.18	Statutes of Limitations		133
§2.19	Conflicts of Laws		134
§2.20	Personal Jurisdiction		135
§2.21	Motions to Dismiss and Summary Judgment		137
§2.22	Countersuits by the Media and Recovery of Attorneys' Fees		137
§2.23	Related Causes of Action		138
§2.24	Criminal Libel		139

§2.25	Searching Appellate Review	139
§2.26	Statistics on the Outcomes of Defamation Litigation	140

CHAPTER 3. FALSE LIGHT ... 141

§3.1	Introduction		141
§3.2	Definition of False Light		141
§3.3	Defamation and False Light Compared		142
§3.4	The Uneasy Coexistence of Defamation and False Light		142
§3.5	Elements of a False Light Claim		144
	§3.5(A)	Proper Plaintiff	144
	§3.5(B)	Identification of the Plaintiff	144
	§3.5(C)	Publicity	145
	§3.5(D)	Oral Statements	146
	§3.5(E)	The "Highly Offensive" Requirement	146
	§3.5(F)	Falsity	149
	§3.5(G)	Opinion	149
	§3.5(H)	The First Amendment and Fault	150
§3.6	Privileges and Consent		152
§3.7	Supreme Court Cases		152
§3.8	Application of Defamation Principles in False Light Cases		154

CHAPTER 4. PRIVATE FACTS ... 157

§4.1	Introduction			157
§4.2	Origin of the Right of Privacy			157
§4.3	History of the Private Facts Tort			159
	§4.3(A)	The Warren-Brandeis Approach		159
	§4.3(B)	The Restatement (Second) of Torts		160
§4.4	Plaintiffs			160
	§4.4(A)	The Plaintiff Must Be Identifiable		160
	§4.4(B)	The Plaintiff Must Be Living		162
	§4.4(C)	Family Members As Plaintiffs		162
	§4.4(D)	Legal Entities As Plaintiffs		162
§4.5	Oral Disclosure			163
§4.6	Elements of the Private Facts Cause of Action			163
	§4.6(A)	Truth		163
	§4.6(B)	Publicity		163
	§4.6(C)	Private Information		164
		§4.6(C)(i)	Public Records and Confidential Information	166
		§4.6(C)(ii)	Ordinary News Gathering Techniques and Confidential Information	168
		§4.6(C)(iii)	Unauthorized Disclosures by the Government	171

		§4.6(C)(iv)	Expunged Records	172
		§4.6(C)(v)	Passage of Time	172
	§4.6(D)	The "Highly Offensive to a Reasonable Person" Requirement		174
	§4.6(E)	Issues of Legitimate Public Concern		175
		§4.6(E)(i)	Question of Law or Fact	175
		§4.6(E)(ii)	Newsworthiness	176
		§4.6(E)(iii)	Public Figures	177
		§4.6(E)(iv)	The Newsworthiness of Names	179
§4.7	Standard of Fault			180
§4.8	Infliction of Emotional Distress			181
§4.9	Defenses			182
	§4.9(A)	Waiver, Consent, and Estoppel		182
	§4.9(B)	Defamation Privileges		183
	§4.9(C)	The First Amendment		183
§4.10	Remedies			183

CHAPTER 5. INTRUSION, TRESPASS, WIRETAPPING, AND RELATED PROBLEMS ... 185

§5.1	Introduction			185
§5.2	Elements of Intrusion			185
	§5.2(A)	Intentional Acts		186
	§5.2(B)	Intrusive Acts		186
	§5.2(C)	Private Affairs		187
	§5.2(D)	The "Highly Offensive to a Reasonable Person" Requirement		189
	§5.2(E)	Publication of Information Obtained by the Media's Intrusion and the First Amendment		189
	§5.2(F)	Possession and Ownership		193
	§5.2(G)	Defenses		193
		§5.2(G)(i)	Government Invitations	193
		§5.2(G)(ii)	Consent	196
		§5.2(G)(iii)	Public Interest/Newsworthiness	196
		§5.2(G)(iv)	The First Amendment and Criminal Trespass	197
	§5.2(H)	Damages		198
	§5.2(I)	Question of Law		198
§5.3	Trespass			198
§5.4	Conversion and Trespass to Chattels			199
	§5.4(A)	Publication of Stolen Information		199
	§5.4(B)	Privilege to Disclose Illegal Acts		202
§5.5	Wiretapping, Bugging, and Eavesdropping			203
	§5.5(A)	The Fourth Amendment		203
	§5.5(B)	Federal Statutes		204
		§5.5(B)(i)	Title III of the Omnibus Crime Control Act of 1968	204

		§5.5(B)(ii) 47 U.S.C. Section 605	207
	§5.5(C)	Federal Administrative Regulations	208
	§5.5(D)	State Statutory Law	209
	§5.5(E)	State Common Law	209

CHAPTER 6. APPROPRIATION AND THE RIGHT OF PUBLICITY 211

§6.1	Introduction	211
§6.2	Development of Appropriation and Publicity Law	211
§6.3	The Cause of Action	213
	§6.3(A) Plaintiffs	213
	§6.3(B) Is Celebrity or Public Status Required?	213
	§6.3(C) Must the Use Be for Advertising or Trade Purposes?	214
	§6.3(D) What Must Be Used?	216
	§6.3(D)(i) Names	216
	§6.3(D)(ii) Likenesses and Look-Alikes	217
	§6.3(D)(iii) Voice, Gestures, Mannerisms, or Live Shows	218
	§6.3(E) Fault	218
	§6.3(F) Relief	219
	§6.3(F)(i) Damages	219
	§6.3(F)(ii) Injunctions	220
	§6.3(F)(iii) Attorneys' Fees	220
§6.4	Defenses	220
	§6.4(A) The First Amendment	220
	§6.4(B) Fiction, Docudramas, and Biographies	223
	§6.4(C) Incidental Use	224
	§6.4(D) Advertisements of the Media's Contents	225
	§6.4(E) Federal Preemption	225
	§6.4(F) Consent	228
	§6.4(G) Privileges	228
§6.5	Statutes	229
	§6.5(A) New York	229
	§6.5(B) California	230
	§6.5(C) The Lanham Act	231
§6.6	Survival of the Cause of Action	232
	§6.6(A) California	234
	§6.6(A)(i) Common Law	234
	§6.6(A)(ii) Statutory Law	235
	§6.6(B) Tennessee	236
	§6.6(B)(i) Common Law	236
	§6.6(B)(ii) Statutory Law	236
	§6.6(C) New York	237
	§6.6(C)(i) Common Law	237
	§6.6(C)(ii) Statutory Law	238
	§6.6(D) Other Jurisdictions	238

Chapter 7. Media Liability for False Advertisements and Other Similar Statements 241

§7.1	Introduction...	241
§7.2	Liability to Advertisers for Errors in Advertisements	241
§7.3	Liability to Readers or Viewers for False Advertisements and Other False Statements	242
	§7.3(A) Intentional False Statements	242
	§7.3(B) Negligent False Statements	243
	§7.3(C) Strict Liability	246
	§7.3(D) Impact of the First Amendment	247
§7.4	Liability for the Publication of Maps	249
§7.5	Liability for Endorsing Advertised Products	250
§7.6	Statutory Liability for False Advertising	251
§7.7	Liability for Advertising Illegal Acts	253

Chapter 8. Imitation and Incitement 255

§8.1	Introduction	255
§8.2	The General Rule: No Media Liability	255
	§8.2(A) No Duty of Care	258
	§8.2(B) First Amendment Barriers	259
§8.3	The Exception: Incitement of Imminent Lawless Action	262
§8.4	Rejection of the Constitutional Actual Malice Test	266

Chapter 9. Applicability of General Laws to the Media 269

§9.1	Introduction	269
§9.2	Federal Antitrust Law	269
	§9.2(A) No Automatic Exemption	269
	§9.2(B) The Newspaper Preservation Act's Constitutionality	271
§9.3	Civil Rights Law	272
	§9.3(A) Section 1983	272
	§9.3(A)(i) The "Under Color of State Law" Requirement	273
	§9.3(A)(ii) Federal Right Requirement and Defamation	273
	§9.3(A)(iii) Federal Right Requirement and Privacy	275
	§9.3(B) Section 1985: State Action, Class-Based Animus, and Federal Rights	276
	§9.3(C) Section 1986	279
	§9.3(D) Section 1981	279
	§9.3(E) Civil Rights Suits by the Media	280
§9.4	Federal Election Law	280

§9.5	Federal Labor Law	282
§9.6	Federal Securities Law	283
	§9.6(A) Rule 10b-5	283
	§9.6(B) Scalping	284
	§9.6(C) Investment Advisers Act	287
	§9.6(D) Proxy Solicitation	290
§9.7	Taxation	291
§9.8	"Son of Sam" Antiprofit Statutes	295
§9.9	Postal Rates	297

CHAPTER 10. PRIOR RESTRAINTS ... 299

§10.1	Introduction	299
§10.2	History and Nature of Prior Restraints	299
§10.3	Theory and Rationales	303
§10.4	Presumptive Unconstitutionality and Heavy Burden of Justification	306
§10.5	The Collateral Bar Rule	307
§10.6	National Security	310
	§10.6(A) The "Pentagon Papers Case"	311
	§10.6(B) Government Contracts for Prepublication Approval	314
§10.7	Criminal and Other Trials	317
	§10.7(A) Gag Orders on the Press	317
	§10.7(B) Gag Orders on Trial Participants	323
§10.8	Privacy	327
§10.9	Defamation	328
§10.10	Business Interests: Trade Secrets, Trademarks, and Copyrights	329
§10.11	Student and Prison Newspapers	331
§10.12	Procedural Issues	331

CHAPTER 11. COMMERCIAL SPEECH ... 335

§11.1	Introduction	335
§11.2	Defining Commercial Speech	335
§11.3	Early Evolution of the Commercial Speech Doctrine in the Supreme Court	341
§11.4	*Central Hudson*'s Four-Part Test	346
§11.5	*Posadas*—Diminishing Protection for Commercial Speech	349
§11.6	Specific Types of Advertising	356
	§11.6(A) Liquor	356
	§11.6(B) Tobacco	362
	§11.6(C) Gambling and Lotteries	366
	§11.6(D) Abortion, Contraception, and Family Planning	371
	§11.6(E) Public Utilities	372

§11.6(F)	Drug Paraphernalia		373
§11.6(G)	Brothels and Escort Services		374
§11.6(H)	Housing and Employment		374
§11.6(I)	Professional Advertising		375

CHAPTER 12. TIME, PLACE, AND MANNER RESTRICTIONS 377

§12.1	Introduction		377
§12.2	The Test for Time, Place, and Manner Restrictions		377
	§12.2(A)	Content Neutrality and Standardless Discretion	377
	§12.2(B)	"Narrowly Tailored to Serve a Significant Governmental Interest"	378
	§12.2(C)	"Ample Alternative Means of Communication"	381
§12.3	Time Restrictions		382
§12.4	Place Restrictions		383
	§12.4(A)	Traditional Public Forums: Parks and Streets	384
	§12.4(B)	Nontraditional or Limited Forums: Public Property	384
	§12.4(C)	Public Property Not Regarded As a Public Forum	386
	§12.4(D)	Private Property, Shopping Malls, and the Home	386
§12.5	Manner Restrictions		388
	§12.5(A)	Handbills and Pamphlets	388
	§12.5(B)	Door-to-Door Solicitation	389
	§12.5(C)	News Racks and Vending Machines	391
	§12.5(D)	Billboards and Other Signs	395
	§12.5(E)	Sound Trucks and Loudspeakers	399
	§12.5(F)	Anonymous Communications	400
	§12.5(G)	Cable Television Distribution and Satellite Dishes	401
	§12.5(H)	Telephones	405

CHAPTER 13. ACCESS TO THE MEDIA 407

§13.1	Introduction		407
§13.2	The Constitutionality of Government-Mandated Access to the Broadcast and Print Media		407
	§13.2(A)	Government-Mandated Access to the Broadcast Media	407
	§13.2(B)	Government-Mandated Access to the Print Media	413
	§13.2(C)	The Supreme Court's Uneasy Dichotomy of the Print and Broadcast Media	415
§13.3	Access Regulations Imposed on the Broadcast Media		417
	§13.3(A)	The Equal Time/Opportunities Rule	417
		§13.3(A)(i) What Constitutes a "Use"?	418
		§13.3(A)(ii) Who Is a "Legally Qualified Candidate"?	420

			§13.3(A)(iii) The "No Censorship" Provision	420
			§13.3(A)(iv) What Constitutes an "Equal Opportunity"?	420
		§13.3(B)	The Reasonable Access Rule	421
		§13.3(C)	The Fairness Doctrine	423
			§13.3(C)(i) Development and Scope of the Doctrine	423
			§13.3(C)(ii) The Fairness Doctrine Compared With Other Broadcast Access Regulations	426
		§13.3(D)	The Personal Attack Rule	427
		§13.3(E)	The Political Editorializing Rule	428
		§13.3(F)	The Decline of Government-Mandated Access to the Broadcast Media: Demise of the Fairness Doctrine	428
§13.4		Access to the Print Media		430
	§13.4(A)	The Publisher's General Right to Refuse Advertisements		431
	§13.4(B)	Antitrust Laws and the Publisher's Right to Refuse Advertisements		432
		§13.4(B)(i) Section 1 Violations		432
		§13.4(B)(ii) Section 2 Violations		433
	§13.4(C)	Contractual Rights and the Publisher's Right to Refuse Advertisements		435
	§13.4(D)	Antidiscrimination Laws and the Publisher's Right to Refuse Advertisements		436
§13.5		Access to Government-Controlled Media		437
	§13.5(A)	The Public Forum Theory		438
	§13.5(B)	The Government As Publisher		440
		§13.5(B)(i) Prison Publications		440
		§13.5(B)(ii) School-Sponsored Publications		445
	§13.5(C)	The Government As Broadcaster		451
	§13.5(D)	Other Government-Related Media		455
§13.6		Access to Cable Television		457
	§13.6(A)	Introduction		457
	§13.6(B)	The Historical Analogy to Broadcasting		458
	§13.6(C)	Cable Access Requirements at the Local Level: Continuing the Analogy to Broadcasting		462
	§13.6(D)	The Cable Act: Legislative Recognition of Cable Regulation		464
	§13.6(E)	The Shift Away From the Cable/Broadcasting Analogy		464

CHAPTER 14. CONFIDENTIAL SOURCES AND RELATED PROBLEMS 469

§14.1	Introduction	469
§14.2	*Branzburg v. Hayes*	469
§14.3	Sources of Protection	474

§14.3(A)	The First Amendment and State Constitutions		474
§14.3(B)	The Fifth Amendment		479
§14.3(C)	Department of Justice Guidelines		480
§14.3(D)	Federal Rules of Criminal Procedure		481
§14.3(E)	Federal Rules of Civil Procedure		482
§14.3(F)	Federal Rules of Evidence		483
§14.3(G)	Federal Common Law		484
§14.3(H)	State Law		486
	§14.3(H)(i)	Alabama	486
	§14.3(H)(ii)	Alaska	487
	§14.3(H)(iii)	Arizona	487
	§14.3(H)(iv)	Arkansas	487
	§14.3(H)(v)	California	487
	§14.3(H)(vi)	Colorado	488
	§14.3(H)(vii)	Delaware	489
	§14.3(H)(viii)	District of Columbia	489
	§14.3(H)(ix)	Georgia	489
	§14.3(H)(x)	Illinois	489
	§14.3(H)(xi)	Indiana	490
	§14.3(H)(xii)	Kentucky	490
	§14.3(H)(xiii)	Louisiana	490
	§14.3(H)(xiv)	Maryland	491
	§14.3(H)(xv)	Michigan	491
	§14.3(H)(xvi)	Minnesota	492
	§14.3(H)(xvii)	Montana	492
	§14.3(H)(xviii)	Nebraska	492
	§14.3(H)(xix)	Nevada	493
	§14.3(H)(xx)	New Jersey	493
	§14.3(H)(xxi)	New Mexico	494
	§14.3(H)(xxii)	New York	495
	§14.3(H)(xxiii)	North Dakota	496
	§14.3(H)(xxiv)	Ohio	496
	§14.3(H)(xxv)	Oklahoma	497
	§14.3(H)(xxvi)	Oregon	497
	§14.3(H)(xxvii)	Pennsylvania	497
	§14.3(H)(xxviii)	Rhode Island	498
	§14.3(H)(xxix)	South Carolina	499
	§14.3(H)(xxx)	Tennessee	499
§14.4	Common Issues		499
§14.4(A)	Who Is Protected?		499
§14.4(B)	Who Holds the Privilege?		500
§14.4(C)	Waiver		501
§14.4(D)	What Information and Materials Are Protected?		502
§14.4(E)	Sanctions for Failure to Disclose		503
§14.4(F)	Alternatives to Full Disclosure		504
§14.4(G)	Choice of Law		505
§14.5	Civil Cases		507
§14.5(A)	The Reporter As Plaintiff		507

	§14.5(B)	The Reporter As Defendant	507
	§14.5(C)	The Reporter As Third Party	509
§14.6	Criminal Cases		510
	§14.6(A)	Grand Jury Subpoenas and Prosecutor Requests	510
	§14.6(B)	Criminal Defendant Requests	511
§14.7	Breach of Promise Actions Against Reporters		512
§14.8	Search and Seizure of Press Facilities		514

TABLE OF CASES 517

INDEX 591

CHAPTER 1

NEWS GATHERING

§1.1 INTRODUCTION

This chapter discusses news gathering: the media's right of access to government proceedings, documents, people, and places.[1] It focuses on direct restrictions on news gathering, such as closed court proceedings, rather than on other restraints, such as damage actions.[2] In particular, this chapter reviews the U.S. Supreme Court cases in which the First Amendment and common law rights of access evolved; discusses the access given to various stages of criminal and civil judicial proceedings, as well as quasi-judicial and other government proceedings; analyzes the media's right to inspect and copy evidence and other government records; examines access to identifiable groups of people and public places; examines electronic coverage of government proceedings; and briefly discusses open meeting and public record laws.

§1.2 OVERVIEW OF SUPREME COURT DECISIONS

After *Nebraska Press Association v. Stuart*,[3] in which the U.S. Supreme Court held that the media ordinarily could not be enjoined from publishing information obtained during open judicial proceedings, courts began instead to close judicial proceedings—usually at the request of criminal defendants.[4] This resulted in a series of Supreme Court decisions[5] that created and then expanded a First Amendment right of access to judicial proceedings. It also resulted in a Supreme Court decision that recognized a common law right of access.[6]

---

[1] Branzburg v. Hayes, 408 U.S. 665, 707, 1 Media L. Rep. 2617, 2634 (1972) ("news gathering is not without its First Amendment protections"). For a more detailed discussion of *Branzburg*, which is largely concerned with reporters' privilege, see Chapter 14. *See generally* Note, *The Rights of the Public and the Press to Gather Information*, 87 HARV. L. REV. 1505 (1974).
[2] *See, e.g.,* Chapter 5. There is substantial overlap between these two chapters.
[3] 427 U.S. 539, 1 Media L. Rep. 1064 (1976). This case is discussed at length in Chapter 10.
[4] *See, e.g., infra* §1.2(A)(i), (ii), (iv), and (vi).
[5] *See infra* §§1.2(A)(i)–(vi).
[6] *See infra* §1.2(B).

§1.2(A) The Constitutional Right of Access

§1.2(A)(i) Gannett Co. v. DePasquale

The Supreme Court did not immediately accept a constitutional right of access to criminal proceedings. In *Gannett Co. v. DePasquale*,[7] the trial court granted the criminal defendants' motion to close a hearing on their motion to suppress statements they made to the police about the murder of their fishing companion. Although a reporter was present at the time of the closure, there was no objection to closure by the media. Only after the suppression hearing was completed did the trial court permit a hearing on the media's request for immediate access to the suppression hearing transcript. The trial court denied that request, finding that the defendants' fair trial rights outweighed the media's interest in access.[8]

In affirming the trial court's closure order, the Supreme Court reasoned that pretrial publicity could interfere with the defendants' Sixth Amendment right to a fair trial by prejudicing the jury pool.[9] This risk was greater during pretrial suppression hearings where possibly inadmissible evidence, such as confessions, was discussed, than during a trial where an already impaneled jury could be shielded from prejudicial publicity.[10]

The Court then held that neither the public nor the press had a Sixth Amendment right of access: the Sixth Amendment's guarantee of a public trial belongs to the accused.[11] While the Sixth Amendment did not give the defendants the right to *compel* a private trial, when the judge, the prosecutor, and the defendants agreed to it, such a hearing could be closed.[12] The Court also stated that the Sixth Amendment did not incorporate the common law tradition of open trials and, in any event, there was no common law tradition of public attendance at *pretrial* proceedings, which usually were private.[13]

As to the First Amendment, even assuming that there was such a right of access to a pretrial suppression hearing,[14] the Court found that the trial court properly balanced the defendants' Sixth Amendment rights with any First

---

[7] 443 U.S. 368, 5 Media L. Rep. 1337 (1979).

[8] *Id.* at 371–76, 5 Media L. Rep. at 1338–40. In *Gannett*, there was an "opinion of the Court," authored by Justice Stewart and joined in by Chief Justice Burger and Justices Powell, Rehnquist, and Stevens. *Id.* at 370, 5 Media L. Rep. at 1338. There were also separate concurrences by Justices Burger, Powell, and Rehnquist, as well as a concurrence in part and dissent in part by Justice Blackmun, in which Justices Brennan, White, and Marshall joined. *Id.* at 394, 397, 403, 406, 5 Media L. Rep. at 1348, 1351, 1352, 1353. Because the Court was so badly fractured, a detailed analysis of the Justices' opinions is necessary.

[9] *Id.* at 378–79, 5 Media L. Rep. at 1341–42.

[10] *Id.* at 378, 5 Media L. Rep. at 1341.

[11] *Id.* at 379–81, 5 Media L. Rep. at 1342 (citing In re Oliver, 333 U.S. 257 (1948) and Estes v. Texas, 381 U.S. 532, 1 Media L. Rep. 1187 (1965)). For a detailed discussion of *Estes,* see *infra* §1.12.

[12] 443 U.S. at 384–91, 5 Media L. Rep. at 1344–47. *Compare* Waller v. Georgia, 467 U.S. 39, 47–49, 10 Media L. Rep. 1714, 1718–19 (1984), discussed *infra* §1.2(A)(v).

[13] 443 U.S. at 382–93, 5 Media L. Rep. at 1343–47 (citing original New York Field Code of Criminal Procedure, published in 1850, which permitted closure of pretrial proceedings at defendant's request). Compare the Court's analysis of this issue in *Waller,* 461 U.S. 39, discussed *infra* §1.2(A)(v), and *Press-Enterprise II,* 478 U.S. 1, 12–13, 106, 13 Media L. Rep. 1001, 1006–07 (1986), discussed *infra* §1.2(A)(vi).

[14] 443 U.S. at 392, 5 Media L. Rep. at 1347 ("We need not decide in the abstract, however, whether there is any such constitutional right."). The Court acknowledged that some of its members had found a First Amendment access right in Pell v. Procunier, 417 U.S. 817, 1 Media L. Rep. 2379 (1974); Saxbe v. Washington Post Co., 417 U.S. 843, 850, 1 Media L. Rep. 2314, 2316 (1974) (Powell, J., dissenting); and Houchins v. KQED, 438 U.S. 1, 16, 3 Media L. Rep. 2521, 2526 (1978) (Stewart, J., concurring), *id.* at 19, 3 Media L. Rep. at 2527 (Stevens, J., dissenting). For a detailed discussion of these cases, see *infra* §1.9.

Amendment rights that might exist, especially since the media were given a hearing on closure and the denial of access was only temporary, because a transcript of the hearing was later released.[15]

Gannett produced four other opinions. Justice Lewis Powell's concurrence recognized a qualified First Amendment right of access to suppression hearings, noting that such hearings are often as important as trials.[16] He also indicated that the trial court should determine the appropriateness of closure using standards similar to those for "gag orders."[17] Justice Powell also noted that the media and public representatives present at the time of any closure motion should be given the opportunity to be heard.[18] Having set forth these standards, Justice Powell joined in the Court's opinion because he concluded that the trial court had complied with these requirements.[19]

Justice William Rehnquist's concurrence found no constitutional right of access.[20] Chief Justice Warren Burger's concurrence emphasized that the Court was dealing with a pretrial proceeding, not a trial.[21]

Justice Harry Blackmun, joined by Justices William Brennan, Byron White, and Thurgood Marshall, concurred only in the Court's holding that the case was not moot because the closure orders were "capable of repetition, yet evading review."[22] In dissent, Justice Blackmun stated that the Sixth Amendment's "public trial" guarantee, while phrased as a right of the accused, was based on the common law tradition of public trials and thus included a public right of access to trials.[23] He reasoned that since a pretrial suppression hearing may be decisive to the outcome of a case, it was enough like a criminal trial that the Sixth Amendment public trial guarantee applied.[24] Justice Blackmun concluded that defendants seeking closure must show a substantial probability that irreparable damage to their fair trial rights would result without closure,[25] that alternatives to closure would not adequately protect their fair trial rights,[26] and that closure would be effective in protecting against the perceived harm.[27]

By seeming to sanction court closures, *Gannett* triggered a wave of court closures that soon reached the Supreme Court.

---

[15] 443 U.S. at 391–93, 5 Media L. Rep. at 1347–48.

[16] *Id.* at 397 n.1, 5 Media L. Rep. at 1348 n.1 (Powell, J., concurring). *Compare* Press-Enterprise II, 478 U.S. 1, 13 Media L. Rep. 1001 (1986), discussed *infra* §1.2(A)(vi).

[17] 443 U.S. at 399–401, 5 Media L. Rep. at 1349–50 (Powell, J., concurring) (citing Nebraska Press Ass'n v. Stuart, 427 U.S. 539, 1 Media L. Rep. 1064 (1976)).

[18] *Id.* at 401, 5 Media L. Rep. at 1350 (Powell, J., concurring).

[19] *Id.* at 403, 5 Media L. Rep. at 1350–51 (Powell, J., concurring).

[20] *Id.* at 403–06, 5 Media L. Rep. at 1351–52 (Rehnquist, J., concurring).

[21] *Id.* at 394–97, 5 Media L. Rep. at 1352–53 (Burger, C.J., concurring). But see Chief Justice Burger's majority opinion in *Press-Enterprise II,* where he found that there was a "tradition of accessibility to preliminary hearings of the type conducted in California," and held that "[f]rom *Burr* until the present day, the near uniform practice of state and federal courts has been to conduct preliminary hearings in open court." Press-Enterprise II, 478 U.S. 1, 10, 13 Media L. Rep. 1001, 1005 (1986), discussed *infra* §1.2(A)(vi).

[22] 443 U.S. at 406, 5 Media L. Rep. at 1353 (Blackmun, J., concurring and dissenting) (referring to part II of Court's opinion, 443 U.S. at 377, 5 Media L. Rep. at 1341).

[23] *Id.* at 433–39, 5 Media L. Rep. at 1364–66 (Blackmun, J., concurring and dissenting).

[24] *Id.*

[25] *Id.* at 441–42, 5 Media L. Rep. at 1367–68 (Blackmun, J., concurring and dissenting).

[26] *Id.* (giving as examples of alternatives that should be considered: "continuance, severance, change of venue, change of venire, *voir dire,* peremptory challenges, sequestration, and admonition of the jury").

[27] 443 U.S. at 441–42, 5 Media L. Rep. at 1367–68 (Blackmun, J., concurring and dissenting). Justice Blackmun concluded that a defendant must demonstrate "a strict and inescapable necessity for closure." *Id.* at 443, 5 Media L. Rep. at 1368. Compare Press-Enterprise II, 478 U.S. 1, 14, 13 Media L. Rep. 1001, 1007 (1986), discussed *infra* §1.2(A)(vi), where the Court held that California should have applied a "substantial probability" rather than a "reasonable likelihood" standard for closure of a preliminary hearing.

§1.2(A)(ii) Richmond Newspapers v. Virginia

The Supreme Court first explicitly recognized a First Amendment right of access to criminal trials in *Richmond Newspapers v. Virginia*,[28] where the Court reviewed an order that completely closed an entire criminal trial. The defendant was facing his fourth trial for the murder of a hotel manager three years earlier.[29] The trial court judge, having presided over the defendant's first three trials, all of which ended in mistrials, closed the trial at the defendant's request; the prosecutor did not object. No objections were recorded on behalf of the media.[30] Later, when the media moved to vacate the closure order, the trial court held a closed hearing where, without making evidentiary findings and without considering any alternatives to closure, it refused to open the trial.[31] The closed trial resumed, and the court later publicly announced that the defendant had been found not guilty.

A fragmented Supreme Court reversed.[32] Chief Justice Burger's "judgment of the Court" distinguished the closure of the trial from the closure of the pretrial suppression hearing in *Gannett*.[33] Without evidence that closure is required to protect the "superior right to a fair trial" or "some other overriding consideration," a trial court cannot close a criminal trial.[34] Justice Burger's opinion stated that, due to history and tradition, criminal trials were presumptively open proceedings under the First Amendment, absent some "overriding interest articulated in findings."[35] Since the trial judge made no findings, failed to recognize any constitutional right to attend the trial, and did not consider alternatives to closure, closure was improper.[36] The opinion recognized, however, that a trial court may establish "time, place, and manner" restrictions on access to avoid an overcrowded courtroom.[37]

There were four separate concurring opinions. Justice White filed a brief concurrence restating his belief that there was a Sixth Amendment right of access to "criminal proceedings."[38] In their concurrence, Justices Brennan and Marshall analyzed the historical tradition and functional purposes of open trials, concluding that the Virginia statute that permitted the trial closure violated the First Amendment.[39] Their opinion also recognized that there may be "counter-

---

[28] 448 U.S. 555, 6 Media L. Rep. 1833 (1980).
[29] *Id.* at 559, 6 Media L. Rep. at 1835.
[30] *Id.* at 560, 6 Media L. Rep. at 1835.
[31] *Id.* at 560–61, 6 Media L. Rep. at 1835–36.
[32] In *Richmond Newspapers*, there was no opinion of the Court. Chief Justice Burger announced the "judgment of the Court," in which Justices White and Stevens joined. *Id.* at 558, 6 Media L. Rep. at 1835. Justices White and Stevens also filed separate concurring opinions. *Id.* at 581–82, 6 Media L. Rep. at 1845. Justices Brennan, Marshall, Stewart, and Blackmun concurred in the judgment of the Court in three separate opinions. *Id.* at 584, 598, 601, 6 Media L. Rep. at 1846, 1852, 1853. Justice Rehnquist dissented. *Id.* at 604, 6 Media L. Rep. at 1854. Justice Powell did not participate. *Id.* at 558, 6 Media L. Rep. at 1835.
[33] 448 U.S. at 564, 6 Media L. Rep. at 1837.
[34] *Id.*
[35] *Id.* at 563–81, 6 Media L. Rep. at 1837–44. For a discussion of access to criminal trials, see *infra* §1.5(A).
[36] 448 U.S. at 581, 6 Media L. Rep. at 1844.
[37] *Id.* at 581–82 n.18, 6 Media L. Rep. at 1844–45 n.18. *See generally* Note, *What Ever Happened to "The Right to Know"?: Access to Government-Controlled Information Since Richmond Newspapers*, 73 VA. L. REV. 111 (1987). Time, place, and manner restrictions are also discussed in Chapter 12.
[38] 448 U.S. at 581–82, 6 Media L. Rep. at 1845 (White, J., concurring). Justice White's use of this term and his reference to *Gannett* both suggest that he did not accept the pretrial/trial distinction in Chief Justice Burger's opinion.
[39] *Id.* at 598, 6 Media L. Rep. at 1852 (Brennan and Marshall, JJ., concurring).

vailing interests" that are "sufficiently compelling to reverse this presumption of openness."[40]

Justice Potter Stewart's concurrence recognized a First Amendment right of access to "civil as well as criminal" trials.[41] He carefully distinguished this right from a right of access to pretrial proceedings, such as the suppression hearing in *Gannett,* an issue that in his view the Court had not decided in *Gannett* or *Richmond Newspapers.*[42] Justice Blackmun reiterated his continuing belief in the Sixth Amendment right of access that he identified in *Gannett* while nonetheless accepting the First Amendment right of access found by the Court.[43] Justice Rehnquist, as the lone dissenter, adhered to his *Gannett* view that there is no First Amendment right of access.[44]

Richmond Newspapers marked the Court's first recognition of a First Amendment right of access to government-controlled information: a criminal trial. Which interests might overcome that right was soon tested.

§1.2(A)(iii) Globe Newspaper Co. v. Superior Court

Two years after *Richmond Newspapers,* the Supreme Court decided *Globe Newspaper Co. v. Superior Court.*[45] The Court considered whether closure should be permitted to protect juvenile rape victims testifying in a criminal trial.[46]

The Globe Newspaper Company had sought relief from trial court orders that closed hearings on certain preliminary motions in a trial involving the rape of three minor girls. Despite the prosecution's waiver of the victims' statutory rights to exclude the media, the Massachusetts Supreme Judicial Court denied relief.[47] Nine months after the criminal trial concluded, that court also held that a Massachusetts statute required mandatory closure of all rape and sexual assault trials during the testimony of minor victims.[48]

Globe sought review in the U.S. Supreme Court, which remanded the case for further consideration in light of *Richmond Newspapers.*[49] On remand, Massachusetts' highest court held that *Richmond Newspapers* did not require it to invalidate the Massachusetts statute, because rape trials were a recognized exception to the history of open criminal trials and Massachusetts' interest in protecting minor victims from public rape and sexual assault trials would be defeated if courts made case-by-case determinations.[50]

---

[40]*Id.* The concurrence listed, as an example, "national security concerns about confidentiality." *Id.* at 598 n.24, 6 Media L. Rep. at 1852 n.24 (Brennan and Marshall, JJ., concurring). It also stated that the First Amendment right should not prevent the use of sidebar or in-chambers conferences during a trial, which are permissible devices used in the "interests of decorum." *Id.* at 598 n.23, 6 Media L. Rep. at 1852 n.23 (Brennan and Marshall, JJ., concurring). *See also infra* note 222.

[41]*Id.* at 599, 6 Media L. Rep. at 1852 (Stewart, J., concurring in judgment). *Accord id.* at 580 n.17, 6 Media L. Rep. at 1844 n.17 ("Whether the public has a right of access to attend trials of civil cases is a question not raised by this case, but we note that historically both civil and criminal cases have been presumptively open."). For a discussion of access to civil proceedings, see *infra* §1.6.

[42]448 U.S. at 599, 6 Media L. Rep. at 1852.

[43]*Id.* at 603 & n.3, 6 Media L. Rep. at 1854 & n.3 (Blackmun, J., concurring in judgment).

[44]*Id.* at 604–06, 6 Media L. Rep. at 1854–55 (Rehnquist, J., dissenting).

[45]457 U.S. 596, 8 Media L. Rep. 1689 (1982).

[46]*Id.* at 598, 8 Media L. Rep. at 1690. For a discussion of access to criminal trials, see *infra* §1.5(A).

[47]457 U.S. at 599–600, 8 Media L. Rep. at 1690–91.

[48]*Id.* at 600, 8 Media L. Rep. at 1691.

[49]Globe Newspaper Co. v. Superior Ct., 449 U.S. 894 (1980).

[50]Globe Newspaper Co. v. Superior Ct., 423 N.E.2d 773, 7 Media L. Rep. 1626 (Mass. 1981), *rev'd,* 457 U.S. 596, 8 Media L. Rep. 1689 (1982).

On appeal for the second time, the U.S. Supreme Court confirmed *Richmond Newspapers'* holding that the public and the media have a First Amendment right of access to criminal trials.[51] Justice Brennan, writing for the Court, explained that this right was based on the historically open nature of criminal trials and on the function of public access to a criminal trial that "enhances the quality and safeguards the integrity of the fact finding process ... fosters an appearance of fairness ... [and] permits the public to participate in and serve as a check upon the judicial process."[52] The Court expressly rejected the Massachusetts Supreme Judicial Court's holding that rape trials can be closed because they are not part of the same tradition of openness as other criminal trials, stating that "the First Amendment right of access to criminal trials ... depends not on the historical openness of that type of criminal trial but rather on the state interests assertedly supporting the restriction."[53]

Although recognizing a constitutional right of access, the Court held that such access rights are not absolute.[54] A trial may be closed if the party seeking closure demonstrates a compelling government interest, but the restrictions on access must be narrowly tailored to serve that interest.[55]

The Court held that Massachusetts' mandatory closure rule was not "narrowly tailored" because the state's interest in protecting minor victims of rape and sexual assault could adequately be served by a case-by-case determination of whether the victim's testimony needed to be closed.[56] The Court also found that the Massachusetts statute was overbroad because minor victims of sex crimes were not the only crime victims who might be reluctant to testify, yet other crime victims were not entitled to mandatory closure.[57] For these reasons the Court held that the Massachusetts statute violated the First Amendment.[58]

Not only did *Globe Newspaper Co.* confirm a First Amendment access right, it made clear that mandatory closure of trials or portions of trials cannot withstand constitutional scrutiny: a case-by-case assessment is constitutionally required.

§1.2(A)(iv) Press-Enterprise I

Two years later, the Supreme Court further expanded the First Amendment right of access. In *Press-Enterprise Co. v. Superior Court (Press-Enterprise I),*[59] the Court reviewed a trial court's decision to close a six-week voir dire of the potential jurors for a trial about the rape and murder of a teenage girl.

---

[51] 457 U.S. at 603, 8 Media L. Rep. at 1692.
[52] *Id.* at 606, 8 Media L. Rep. at 1693–94. This two-pronged analysis of history and public policy has become a staple of access decisions. *See also infra* text at note 82.
[53] *Id.* at 605 n.13, 8 Media L. Rep. at 1693 n.13.
[54] *Id.* at 606–07, 8 Media L. Rep. at 1694.
[55] *Id.*
[56] 457 U.S. at 608, 8 Media L. Rep. at 1694. The Court listed the "factors to be weighed" during this case-by-case determination as "the minor victim's age, psychological maturity, and understanding, the nature of the crime, the desires of the victim, and the interests of parents and relatives." The Court noted that "the names of the minor victims were already in the public record, and the record indicates that the victims may have been willing to testify despite the presence of the press." Therefore, on a case-by-case determination, "closure might well have been deemed unnecessary." *Id.* at 608–09, 8 Media L. Rep. at 1694–95.
[57] *Id.* at 609–10, 8 Media L. Rep. at 1695–96.
[58] *Id.* at 610–11, 8 Media L. Rep. at 1696.
[59] 464 U.S. 501, 10 Media L. Rep. 1161 (1984).

Despite the newspaper's request to open the voir dire, the trial court had granted the prosecution's request for closure on the grounds that if the media attended, potential jurors' responses to questions would lack the candor necessary to ensure a fair trial.[60] The trial court also refused to release the transcript of the voir dire either after the jury was impaneled or after the defendant had been convicted and sentenced, on the grounds that release of such a transcript would violate the jurors' rights of privacy and the "implied promise of confidentiality" that the prosecutor represented he had given prospective jurors.[61]

After reviewing historical accounts of open jury selection,[62] the Supreme Court, without dissent, held that the "presumption of openness" with respect to a voir dire examination "may be overcome only by an overriding interest based on findings that closure is essential to preserve higher values and is narrowly tailored to serve that interest."[63] Such a government interest must be set forth along with specific findings so a reviewing court can determine whether closure was proper.[64]

The Court concluded that the Sixth Amendment and juror privacy interests did not warrant closure because there were no findings showing that an "open proceeding in fact threatened those interests" and because the trial court had failed to consider any alternatives that would have protected the jurors' privacy interests.[65] While acknowledging that privacy interests "may, in some circumstances, give rise to a compelling interest,"[66] the Court suggested as an alternative that the trial court could ask general voir dire questions in open court to see if any member of the venire had something embarrassing or private that they wished to present in camera.[67] The Court also held that the trial court erred by failing to unseal nonconfidential parts of the voir dire transcript, particularly when the trial court itself had admitted that " 'most of the information' in the transcript was 'dull and boring.' "[68]

Press-Enterprise I established that the First Amendment right of access was not limited to trials, but precisely how far that right extended was unclear. The next case to reach the Court raised that issue, although in a Sixth Amendment context.

§1.2(A)(v) Waller v. Georgia

In *Waller v. Georgia*,[69] the Court again expanded rights of access to criminal proceedings by unanimously holding that a criminal defendant's Sixth Amendment right to a public trial extends to a pretrial suppression hearing.[70]

---

[60]*Id.* at 503, 10 Media L. Rep. at 1162.
[61]*Id.* at 504, 10 Media L. Rep. at 1162.
[62]*Id.* at 505–08, 10 Media L. Rep. at 1163–64.
[63]*Id.* at 510, 10 Media L. Rep. at 1165.
[64]464 U.S. at 510, 10 Media L. Rep. at 1165.
[65]*Id.* at 510–11, 10 Media L. Rep. at 1165–66. For a discussion of access to voir dire in criminal cases, see *infra* §1.5(B).
[66]464 U.S. at 511, 10 Media L. Rep. at 1166.
[67]*Id.* at 512, 10 Media L. Rep. at 1166.
[68]*Id.* at 513, 10 Media L. Rep. at 1166. As another alternative, the Court suggested releasing the transcript with the affected juror's name deleted. *Id.*
[69]467 U.S. 39, 10 Media L. Rep. 1714 (1984).
[70]*Id.* at 43, 10 Media L. Rep. at 1716. For a discussion of access to suppression hearings, see *infra* §1.4(A).

Closure could be ordered over the defendant's objection only if "the party seeking to close the hearing ... advance[s] an overriding interest that is likely to be prejudiced, the closure [is] no broader than necessary to protect that interest, the trial court ... consider[s] reasonable alternatives ..., and it ... make[s] findings adequate to support the closure."[71] The Court found that the trial court's order, which completely closed a seven-day suppression hearing, was improper where the privacy interests that the trial court sought to protect related to only 2½ hours of wiretap audiotapes played during the hearing.[72] The transcript of the suppression hearing, which the trial court released to the public only after an open trial had resulted in the defendant's partial acquittal, revealed that most of the hearing concerned the procedures for making the tapes and allegations of police and prosecutorial misconduct.[73]

Because the defendant and not the media challenged the closure order in *Waller*, the Court did not have to and chose not to reconsider the issue of the media's right of access to pretrial suppression hearings under either the Sixth or First Amendments. *Waller* strongly suggested, however, that the Court would find a constitutional right of access to pretrial criminal proceedings, and the Court was soon faced with this issue.

§1.2(A)(vi) Press-Enterprise II

In *Press-Enterprise Co. v. Superior Court (Press-Enterprise II)*,[74] the defendant, a nurse charged with murdering twelve patients, had moved to close his preliminary hearing to the media and the public. A magistrate granted his unopposed motion, finding that the case "had attracted national publicity and 'only one side may get reported in the media.' "[75] The Court then conducted a 41-day preliminary hearing entirely in secret. The prosecution presented mostly medical and scientific testimony, while the defendant introduced no evidence; instead, his attorneys "vigorous[ly]" cross-examined the prosecution's witnesses.[76] At the hearing's conclusion, the magistrate sealed the tran-

---

[71]467 U.S. at 48, 10 Media L. Rep. at 1718.
[72]*Id.* at 48–49, 10 Media L. Rep. at 1718–19.
[73]*Id.* at 42–43, 10 Media L. Rep. at 1716. The Court noted that the public "has a strong interest in exposing substantial allegations of police misconduct." *Id.* at 47, 10 Media L. Rep. at 1718.
[74]478 U.S. 1, 13 Media L. Rep. 1001 (1986). *See generally* Wynne, *Closed to the Media: The Defendant's Right of Privacy in the Preliminary Examination*, 5 COMM./ENT. L.J. 317 (1983).
To understand the issues decided by the U.S. Supreme Court in *Press-Enterprise II*, its predecessor case, San Jose Mercury-News v. Superior Ct., 638 P.2d 655, 7 Media L. Rep. 2522 (Cal. 1982), which did not reach the U.S. Supreme Court, must be discussed. In *San Jose Mercury-News*, the California Supreme Court traced the history of constitutional rights of access, in particular *Gannett* and *Richmond Newspapers*, *id.* at 657–60, 7 Media L. Rep. at 2523–25, specifically noting that in *Gannett*, the U.S. Supreme Court described preliminary hearings as "traditionally private at common law." *Id.* at 659, 7 Media L. Rep. at 2524. The California Supreme Court concluded that *Gannett* and *Richmond Newspapers* did not represent any "consensus that there is a right to attend preliminary hearings." *Id.* at 659, 7 Media L. Rep. at 2525. The court did acknowledge, however, that an open preliminary hearing has many of the "societal benefits" that public trials and pretrial suppression hearings have. *Id.* at 662, 7 Media L. Rep. at 2527. Nevertheless, the California Supreme Court ultimately approved the California statute's provision for mandatory closure solely at a defendant's request based on the peculiar features of preliminary hearings, primarily the fear that the public will erroneously conclude that a defendant bound over for a trial is guilty and the concern that a defendant will be unable to show that a public preliminary hearing will be prejudicial, since such hearings are held so soon after an arrest and evidence of prejudice may not be available at that early stage. *Id.* at 663–65, 7 Media L. Rep. at 2528–29. The California Legislature then amended the statute to require a defendant to show "a reasonable likelihood of substantial prejudice" to his or her rights before closure could be granted. It was this version of the statute that reached the U.S. Supreme Court in *Press-Enterprise II*.
[75]478 U.S. at 4, 13 Media L. Rep. at 1003.
[76]*Id.*

script, rejecting the newspaper's request for access.[77] Later, the trial court denied a similar request, made by both the media and the prosecution, despite a finding that the transcript was factual and noninflammatory.[78]

In analyzing the propriety of the proceedings, the Supreme Court elaborated on the guiding principles enunciated in its earlier access opinions. The Court stated that "[t]he right to an open public trial is a shared right of the accused and the public, the common concern being the assurance of fairness."[79] The Court cited *Waller* as recognizing that "the First Amendment right of access would in most instances attach to [pretrial suppression hearings]."[80] The Court then rejected the pretrial/trial distinction "because the First Amendment question cannot be resolved solely on the label [the court] give[s] the event, *i.e.*, 'trial' or otherwise, particularly where the preliminary hearing functions much like a full scale trial."[81]

To determine whether "a qualified First Amendment right of public access attaches" to any type of criminal proceeding, a court must consider "whether the place and process has historically been open to the press and general public.... [and] whether public access [has] play[ed] a significant positive role in the functioning of the particular process in question."[82] The qualified First Amendment right of access can be " 'overcome only by an overriding interest based on findings that closure is essential to preserve higher values and is narrowly tailored to serve that interest.' "[83]

Applying these principles to "preliminary hearings as conducted in California," the Court concluded that there is a First Amendment right of access to such proceedings.[84] First, the Court found a "tradition of accessibility" based on "the near uniform practice of state and federal courts ... to conduct preliminary hearings in open court."[85] The Court then distinguished its contrary observation in *Gannett*, that there was no common law tradition of access to pretrial proceedings. It pointed out that in many states that follow New York's Field Code,[86] which permitted such hearings to be closed on the defendant's

---

[77]*Id.* at 5, 13 Media L. Rep. at 1003.
[78]*Id.*
[79]*Id.* at 7, 13 Media L. Rep. at 1004.
[80]*Id. Compare* Gannett Co. v. DePasquale, 443 U.S. 368, 379–81, 5 Media L. Rep. 1337, 1342 (1979), discussed *supra* §1.2(A)(i), where the Court held that the public trial right belongs to the accused, not the public.
[81]478 U.S. at 7, 13 Media L. Rep. at 1004. Compare *Gannett*, 443 U.S. at 392, 5 Media L. Rep. at 1347, discussed *supra* §1.2(A)(i), where the Court did not decide whether there was any First Amendment right of access to a pretrial suppression hearing.
[82]478 U.S. at 8–9, 13 Media L. Rep. at 1004–05. Compare *Gannett*, 443 U.S. at 394–97, 5 Media L. Rep. at 1352–53, discussed *supra* §1.2(A)(i), where Chief Justice Burger's concurrence emphasized the distinction between trial and pretrial proceedings, finding no common law tradition of access to pretrial hearings. However, there is no absolute requirement that the proceeding be one that has historically been open. *See infra* §§1.4(A) and (C). The historical or experience issue is to be determined by the experience of the entire country rather than the experience of a particular jurisdiction. El Vocero de Puerto Rico v. Puerto Rico, 113 S. Ct. 2004, 21 Media L. Rep. 1440, 1441 (1993). For a list of the policy reasons for access, see text at *infra* note 135; see also *supra* note 52 and *infra* notes 93 and 94 and accompanying text.
[83]478 U.S. at 9, 13 Media L. Rep. at 1005 (quoting Press-Enterprise Co. v. Superior Ct. (Press-Enterprise I), 464 U.S. 501, 510, 10 Media L. Rep. 1161, 1165 (1984), discussed *supra* §1.2(A)(iv)).
[84]*Id.* at 10, 13 Media L. Rep. at 1005. The Supreme Court has made it clear that its ruling is not limited by any peculiarities of California preliminary hearing procedure. *El Vocero de Puerto Rico*, 113 S. Ct. 2004, 1 Media L. Rep. 1440. *See generally infra* §1.4(B).
[85]478 U.S. at 10 & n.3, 13 Media L. Rep. at 1005 & n.3.
[86]*Id.* at 11, 13 Media L. Rep. at 1006. *See Gannett*, 443 U.S. at 390–91, 5 Media L. Rep. at 1346, discussed *supra* §1.2(A)(i).

motion, "the proceedings are presumptively open to the public and are closed only for cause shown."[87]

Second, the Court found that access had a "positive" role to play in the functioning of preliminary hearings.[88] The California preliminary hearing was "sufficiently like a trial" to make access "essential to the proper functioning of the criminal justice system."[89] Those trial-like features include the accused's "right to personally appear at the hearing, to be represented by counsel, to cross-examine hostile witnesses, to present exculpatory evidence, and to exclude illegally obtained evidence."[90] The Court noted that once probable cause has been found at this type of hearing, the defendant pleads guilty in "the majority of cases" and the preliminary hearing frequently "provides 'the sole occasion for public observation of the criminal justice system.' "[91] Thus, "[b]ecause of its extensive scope, the preliminary hearing is often the final and most important in the criminal proceeding."[92]

The Court also noted that the absence of a jury at such a hearing makes public access "even more significant," because there is no jury to check the prosecutor or the judge.[93] Also, there is a " 'community therapeutic value' of openness," especially where "certain violent crimes" are involved.[94]

Having firmly established a First Amendment access right, the Court rejected the California Supreme Court's holding that a preliminary hearing could be closed " 'upon finding a reasonable likelihood of substantial prejudice.' "[95] Instead, the Court set forth the following standard for closure if a defendant's fair trial rights are asserted:

> The preliminary hearing shall be closed only if specific findings are made demonstrating that, first, there is a substantial probability that the defendant's right to a fair trial will be prejudiced by publicity that closure would prevent and, second, reasonable alternatives to closure cannot adequately protect the defendant's fair trial rights.[96]

Explaining this standard, the Court noted that the "risk of prejudic[ial pretrial publicity] does not automatically justify refusing public access to hearings on every *motion to suppress.*"[97]

With *Press-Enterprise II,* the Supreme Court had come full circle from *Gannett.*[98] A First Amendment right of access was established and extended

---

[87]478 U.S. 1, 11 & n.4, 13 Media L. Rep. 1001, 1006 & n.4.
[88]*Id.* at 12, 13 Media L. Rep. at 1006.
[89]*Id.*
[90]*Id.* at 11–12, 13 Media L. Rep. at 1006.
[91]*Id.* (quoting San Jose Mercury-News v. Municipal Ct., 638 P.2d 655, 663 (Cal. 1982)).
[92]478 U.S. at 12, 13 Media L. Rep. at 1006.
[93]*Id.* at 12–13, 13 Media L. Rep. at 1006.
[94]*Id.* at 13, 13 Media L. Rep. at 1006.
[95]*Id.* at 14, 13 Media L. Rep. at 1007 (quoting Press-Enterprise Co. v. Superior Ct., 691 P.2d 1026, 1032 (Cal. 1984)).
[96]*Id. See generally* Frasca, *Estimating the Occurrence of Trials Prejudiced by Press Coverage,* 72 JUDICATURE 162 (Oct./Nov. 1988); Pratte, *What Effect Does Pretrial News Coverage Have on Jurors?* 72 JUDICATURE 168 (Oct./Nov. 1988).
[97]478 U.S. at 15, 13 Media L. Rep. at 1007 (emphasis added). It is not entirely clear whether, with this cryptic comment, the Court meant to extend the First Amendment right of access to pretrial suppression hearings as well as preliminary hearings. The lower courts have readily concluded, however, that such an extension is appropriate. *See infra* §1.4(A).
[98]As a result of this change in Supreme Court rulings, cases that deny access and that were decided before *Press-Enterprise II* are not reliable authority.

to pretrial and trial criminal proceedings. This right can only be overcome by specific findings that closure is essential to preserve a compelling or overriding state interest, that any closure is narrowly tailored to serve that interest, and that there are no adequate alternatives to closure.

§1.2(B) The Common Law Right of Access

The Supreme Court has also recognized a common law right of access to judicial records.[99]

§1.3 PROCEDURAL REQUIREMENTS FOR CLOSURE

In *Gannett,* the Supreme Court concluded that the trial court had acted properly in denying media access to a pretrial suppression hearing because, among other things, the trial court had given the media an opportunity to be heard.[100]

In his concurrence and dissent, Justice Blackmun set forth certain safeguards required for a court to order closure: (1) those public and media representatives removed from the court must have a reasonable opportunity to be heard;[101] (2) the court must make findings in support of closure;[102] and (3) neither the public nor the media need demonstrate that the interest in an open proceeding is legitimate.[103]

It was not until *Press-Enterprise II,* however, that the Supreme Court set forth procedural standards for closure.[104] The Court concluded that closure could be ordered only if specific findings were made demonstrating that "first, there is a substantial probability that the defendant's right to a fair trial will be prejudiced by publicity that closure would prevent and, second, reasonable alternatives to closure cannot adequately protect the defendant's fair trial rights."[105] From this beginning, other courts have amplified and expanded the procedural requirements for closures.[106]

Ordinarily, a public hearing on the question of access is required.[107] All closure motions must be made in open court unless the party seeking closure can demonstrate that, without closure of the hearing on the closure motion, it would not be able to argue its position.[108] If a closure motion is initially made

---

[99]Nixon v. Warner Communications, 435 U.S. 589, 597, 3 Media L. Rep. 2074, 2077 (1978), discussed *infra* §1.8(A).

[100]Gannett Co. v. DePasquale, 443 U.S. 368, 391–93, 5 Media L. Rep. 1337, 1347–48 (1979).

[101]*Id.* at 445–46, 5 Media L. Rep. at 1369 (Blackmun, J., concurring and dissenting). *See also id.* at 401, 5 Media L. Rep. at 1350 (Powell, J., concurring). Justice Powell expressly refused to require that notice be given to any member of the public who was not present before any closure hearing. *Id.*

[102]*Id.* at 446, 5 Media L. Rep. at 1369 (Blackmun, J., concurring and dissenting).

[103]*Id.* at 443–44, 5 Media L. Rep. at 1368 (Blackmun, J., concurring and dissenting).

[104]478 U.S. 1, 14, 13 Media L. Rep. 1001, 1007 (1984). On proper procedures, *see generally* In re Knight Pub'g Co., 743 F.2d 231, 10 Media L. Rep. 2379 (4th Cir. 1984). Procedural issues are also discussed in other sections of this chapter in the context of particular types of hearings.

[105]478 U.S. at 14, 13 Media L. Rep. at 1007.

[106]*See infra* notes 107–122.

[107]*See, e.g.,* Capital Cities Broadcasting Corp. v. Tenth Dist. Judge, 283 N.W.2d 779, 5 Media L. Rep. 2058 (Mich. Ct. App. 1979); Patuxent Pub'g Corp. v. State, 429 A.2d 554, 7 Media L. Rep. 1349 (Md. Spec. Ct. App. 1981).

[108]*See, e.g.,* State v. Burak, 431 A.2d 1246, 7 Media L. Rep. 1318 (Conn. Super. Ct. 1981).

in closed court, it must be renewed in open court.[109] In addition, all closure motions must be immediately docketed.[110]

Even if a hearing is closed by court order, the court must, within a reasonable time, hold a hearing at which media and public representatives can move for access to the sealed transcript of the closed hearing.[111] The transcripts should be made available as soon as possible.[112]

Only members of the media who are present are entitled to a preclosure hearing.[113] The court is not required to give personal notice to the media or other interested parties.[114]

The media have the right to intervene in ongoing civil and criminal actions in order to seek access;[115] indeed, intervention is sometimes required.[116] If the intervening media organization's request for access is denied, that nonparty can immediately appeal the denial of access in most jurisdictions.[117]

In issuing an order denying access, the court's order must specify the reasons for the closure.[118] Where the reasons for denying access are not specified, the order will be reversed.[119] Where a common law right of access is asserted, the standard of review is abuse of discretion, but where a constitutional right of access is asserted, the standard of review is "an independent examination of the whole record."[120]

While opposition to closure of a trial or a hearing must be made at the time the court closes the proceeding (or at least before it concludes), access to transcripts, evidence, and court documents need not be sought in as timely a fashion.[121] The termination of the underlying action to which the media sought access will not moot an appeal of an order denying access.[122]

---

[109] United States v. Raffoul, 826 F.2d 218, 14 Media L. Rep. 1534 (3d Cir. 1987).

[110] *Id.;* United States v. Haller, 837 F.2d 84, 87, 14 Media L. Rep. 2166, 2168–69 (2d Cir. 1988) (immediate docketing required unless there are "extraordinary circumstances"); Gannett River States Pub'g Co. v. Hand, 571 So. 2d 941, 18 Media L. Rep. 1516 (Miss. 1990).

[111] *Raffoul,* 826 F.2d 218.

[112] *Burak,* 431 A.2d 1246.

[113] *Raffoul,* 826 F.2d 218.

[114] *Id.*

[115] Hearst Corp. v. State, 484 A.2d 292, 11 Media L. Rep. 1195 (Md. Ct. Spec. App. 1984); Gannett Co. v. State, 565 A.2d 895, 16 Media L. Rep. 2358 (Del. 1989); State v. Tallman, 537 A.2d 422, 15 Media L. Rep. 1344 (Vt. 1987); *Gannett River States,* 571 So. 2d 941. *Contra* In re Grand Jury Investig., 587 F.2d 598, 4 Media L. Rep. 1713 (3d Cir. 1978) (court based holding that media cannot intervene at appellate level to request unsealing of grand jury witness' affidavit on local criminal procedure rule requiring intervention or challenge by separate action in district court).

[116] Public Citizen v. Liggett Group, 858 F.2d 775, 15 Media L. Rep. 2129 (1st Cir. 1988), *cert. denied,* 488 U.S. 1030 (1989); Courier-Journal & Louisville Times Co. v. Peers, 747 S.W.2d 125, 15 Media L. Rep. 1051 (Ky. 1988).

[117] News Am. Div., Hearst Corp. v. State, 447 A.2d 1264, 8 Media L. Rep. 2088 (Md. 1982); *Gannett Co.,* 565 A.2d 895, 16 Media L. Rep. 2358; In re Subpoena to Testify Before Grand Jury Directed to Custodian Records, 864 F.2d 1559, 16 Media L. Rep. 1165 (11th Cir. 1989); United States v. Haller, 837 F.2d 84, 14 Media L. Rep. 2166 (2d Cir. 1988). However, other courts have required a writ to be sought or have adopted some other procedure. United States v. Chagra, 701 F.2d 354, 358–60, 9 Media L. Rep. 1409, 1412–14 (5th Cir. 1983) (extensive citations on various approaches).

[118] *See supra* §1.2(A)(iv), note 64; *Subpoena to Testify Before Grand Jury,* 864 F.2d 1559; *Haller,* 837 F.2d 84; *Gannett River States,* 571 So. 2d 941.

[119] People v. Perez, 417 N.Y.S.2d 487, 5 Media L. Rep. 1590 (N.Y. App. Div. 1979); United States v. Kooistra, 796 F.2d 1390, 13 Media L. Rep. 1175 (11th Cir. 1986).

[120] In re Capital Cities/ABC's Application, 913 F.2d 89, 92, 18 Media L. Rep. 1049, 1051 (3d Cir. 1990) (quoting Bose Corp. v. Consumers Union, 466 U.S. 485, 499 (1984)).

[121] C.L. v. Edson, 409 N.W.2d 417, 14 Media L. Rep. 1145 (Wis. Ct. App. 1987) (intervention timely nine months after judgment where newspaper first sought access to documents four months after judgment and intervention would not prejudice parties).

[122] Gannett Co. v. DePasquale, 443 U.S. 368, 377, 5 Media L. Rep. 1337, 1341 (1979) (issue of access to suppression hearing not moot but " 'capable of repetition, yet evading review' ") (quoting South Pac. Terminal Co. v. Interstate Commerce Comm'n, 219 U.S. 498, 515 (1911)); *Haller,* 837 F.2d 84; Anderson

§1.4 ACCESS TO CRIMINAL PRETRIAL AND POSTTRIAL PROCEEDINGS

This section discusses access to various pretrial and posttrial proceedings. A constitutional right of access to such proceedings is now well recognized.

§1.4(A) Pretrial Suppression Hearings

Before *Gannett,* several courts considered whether a trial court could close a pretrial suppression hearing to the media and the public. Using various theories, some courts upheld such closures,[123] while others favored open proceedings.[124] However, in *Gannett,* the Supreme Court held that the public and the media had no right of access under the Sixth Amendment to pretrial suppression hearings[125] and that any First Amendment right was overcome by the defendant's showing of possible prejudice to his or her fair trial rights.[126] This left the status of any constitutional right of access to pretrial criminal proceedings quite unclear.

In *Waller v. Georgia,* the Supreme Court began to clear up the confusion by unanimously holding that a criminal defendant's Sixth Amendment right to a public trial extends to *pretrial* suppression hearings.[127] Two years later, in *Press-Enterprise II,* the Court suggested that the First Amendment right of access extended to pretrial suppression hearings, though it actually ruled that this right applied to another type of pretrial criminal proceeding: preliminary hearings.[128] Thus, while the Supreme Court has not explicitly ruled on the existence of a First Amendment right of access to pretrial suppression hearings, such a right is now well established.[129] In all of these cases, the courts established procedural as well as substantive prerequisites to closure, in particular

---

v. Cryovac, Inc., 805 F.2d 1, 13 Media L. Rep. 1721 (1st Cir. 1986) (nonparty newspaper's appeal of protective order not moot despite settlement of case); KPNX Broadcasting Co. v. Superior Ct. of Maricopa County, 678 P.2d 431, 10 Media L. Rep. 1289 (Ariz. 1984); Lexington Herald-Leader Co. v. Meigs, 660 S.W.2d 658, 9 Media L. Rep. 2153 (Ky. 1983); In re Times World Corp., 373 S.E.2d 484, 15 Media L. Rep. 2210 (Va. Ct. App. 1988); State v. Tallman, 537 A.2d 422, 15 Media L. Rep. 1344 (Vt. 1987); Sioux Falls Argus Leader v. Young, 455 N.W.2d 864, 868, 18 Media L. Rep. 1044, 1046–47 (S.D. 1990). *But see* State ex rel. Pulitzer Pub'g Co. v. Lohmar, 633 S.W.2d 195, 8 Media L. Rep. 1417 (Mo. Ct. App. 1982) (moot because later open hearing was held).

[123]*See, e.g.,* In re Merola, 415 N.Y.S.2d 992, 5 Media L. Rep. 1033 (N.Y. App. Div.) (closure upheld where thirteen-year-old defendant tried for murder under new juvenile law and there was extensive publicity immediately before suppression hearing), *aff'd,* 393 N.E.2d 1038, 5 Media L. Rep. 1371 (N.Y. 1979) (trial court's decision complied with *Gannett*), *cert. denied,* 448 U.S. 910 (1980); Philadelphia Newspapers v. Jerome, 387 A.2d 425, 3 Media L. Rep. 2185 (Pa. 1978) (upholding closure because of concerns about pretrial publicity), *appeal dismissed,* 443 U.S. 913, 5 Media L. Rep. 1304 (1979).

[124]*See, e.g.,* United States v. Cianfrani, 573 F.2d 835, 852–54, 3 Media L. Rep. 1961, 1971–72 (3d Cir. 1978) (relying on Sixth Amendment, majority found closure proper only if "strictly and inescapably necessary"); Gore Newspapers Co. v. Reasbeck, 363 So. 2d 609, 4 Media L. Rep. 1751 (Fla. Dist. Ct. App. 1978) (improper for court to permit defendant to swear reporters as "witnesses" and then sequester them to avoid need for closure); Hearst Corp. v. Cholakis, 386 N.Y.S.2d 892, 2 Media L. Rep. 2085 (N.Y. App. Div. 1976) (closure orders annulled).

[125]*Gannett,* 443 U.S. at 383–84, 5 Media L. Rep. at 1343–44.

[126]*Id.* at 392–93, 5 Media L. Rep. at 1347.

[127]467 U.S. 39, 43, 10 Media L. Rep. 1714, 1716 (1984), discussed *supra* §1.2(A)(v).

[128]*See supra* text accompanying notes 80 and 97.

[129]In re Herald Co., 734 F.2d 93, 10 Media L. Rep. 1673 (2d Cir. 1984); United States v. Brooklier, 685 F.2d 1162, 8 Media L. Rep. 2177 (9th Cir. 1982); United States v. Criden (Criden II), 675 F.2d 550, 8 Media L. Rep. 1297 (3d Cir. 1982). *See also* In re New York Times Co., 828 F.2d 110, 114, 14 Media L. Rep. 1625, 1627 (2d Cir. 1987) (documents filed in connection with suppression hearing), *cert. denied,* 485 U.S. 977 (1988); United States v. Cortese, 568 F. Supp. 114, 9 Media L. Rep. 1912 (M.D. Pa. 1983) (suppression hearing to determine admissibility of wiretap evidence should be public except to extent tapes are played or transcripts are read, and they should be made available if found admissible).

requiring that all closure motions be docketed to give the media and the public a reasonable opportunity to object to closure.[130]

In *United States v. Criden (Criden II)*,[131] the Third Circuit based its analysis on *Gannett* and *Richmond Newspapers*. After stating that "[n]either case is controlling here" and explicitly rejecting *Richmond Newspapers'* "historical analysis" as irrelevant to evaluating access to a criminal pretrial proceeding, the court held that there was a First Amendment right of access and vacated the district court's sealing orders.[132] The court emphasized the growth of the "relative importance of pretrial procedure to that of trial"[133] and relied exclusively on the second prong of *Richmond Newspapers'* analysis: examining the "societal interests in open pretrial criminal proceedings."[134] The Third Circuit identified at least six "societal interests" discussed in *Richmond Newspapers'* various opinions that apply with equal force to "pre-trial criminal proceedings": (1) promoting informed discussion of government affairs by providing the public with a more complete understanding of the judicial system; (2) assuring that the proceedings are conducted fairly and thus promote the public's "perception of fairness"; (3) providing an "outlet for community concern, hostility, and emotion," which has a "significant community therapeutic value"; (4) serving as a check on corrupt judicial practices; (5) enhancing the performance of all participants in a judicial proceeding; and (6) discouraging perjury.[135]

Similarly, the Second Circuit found a First Amendment right of access to pretrial suppression hearings in *In re Herald Co.*[136] by making a painstaking analysis of the various opinions in *Gannett, Richmond Newspapers, Globe Newspaper Co.,* and *Press-Enterprise I,* which it described as "nose-count jurisprudence."[137] After reviewing the standards that other courts have used to determine the constitutionality of closure orders,[138] the court held that closure could only be ordered upon a showing of "a significant risk of prejudice to the defendant's right to a fair trial or of danger to persons, property, or the integrity of significant activities entitled to confidentiality, such as ongoing undercover investigations or detection devices," and remanded for application of these standards.[139]

---

[130]*Herald Co.*, 734 F.2d at 102–03, 10 Media L. Rep. at 1680; *Brooklier*, 685 F.2d at 1168, 8 Media L. Rep. at 2180 (court, however, refused to establish any "inflexible rule" on notice, while noting with approval the docketing requirement in *Criden II*); *Criden II*, 675 F.2d at 557–60, 8 Media L. Rep. at 1302–04. *See also supra* §1.3.

[131]675 F.2d 550, 8 Media L. Rep. 1297 (3d Cir. 1982).

[132]*Id.* at 554–55, 8 Media L. Rep. at 1300. The Third Circuit did acknowledge, however, that its holding of a Sixth Amendment right of access in United States v. Cianfrani, 573 F.2d 835, 3 Media L. Rep. 1961 (3d Cir. 1978), was "implicitly overruled" by *Gannett*. 675 F.2d at 556, 8 Media L. Rep. at 1301.

[133]675 F.2d at 555, 8 Media L. Rep. at 1300.

[134]*Id.* at 555–57, 8 Media L. Rep. at 1300–1301.

[135]*Id.* at 556, 8 Media L. Rep. at 1301.

[136]734 F.2d 93, 10 Media L. Rep. 1673 (2d Cir. 1984).

[137]*Id.* at 98 n.3, 10 Media L. Rep. at 1676 n.3.

[138]*Id.* at 99, 10 Media L. Rep. at 1677–78 (relying on *Criden II* standard that closure is appropriate only on findings that " 'other means will be insufficient to preserve the defendant's rights and that closure is necessary to protect effectively against the perceived harm' " (quoting Criden II, 675 F.2d 550, 561–62, 8 Media L. Rep. 1297, 1305 (3d Cir. 1982)) and *Brooklier* standard that closure must be " 'strictly and inescapably necessary in order to protect the fair-trial guarantee' " (quoting United States v. Brooklier, 685 F.2d 1162, 1167, 8 Media L. Rep. 2177, 2179 (9th Cir. 1982))).

[139]734 F.2d at 100, 10 Media L. Rep. at 1678. For a discussion of cases involving undercover investigation or detection devices, see *infra* §1.5(A).

In *United States v. Brooklier*,[140] the Ninth Circuit held that, based on its reading of *Gannett, Richmond Newspapers,* and *Globe Newspaper Co.*, a First Amendment right of access to pretrial suppression hearings existed and had been violated.[141] Because the suppression hearing in *Brooklier* began before trial but continued during trial, the Ninth Circuit noted the "impracticability" of allowing access to depend on whether a proceeding was characterized as a pretrial or trial proceeding.[142]

Many state courts also have considered whether closing a pretrial suppression hearing was appropriate. These courts sometimes failed to find any *federal* constitutional right of access, especially if the cases were decided early in the Supreme Court's evolution of a constitutional right of access; instead, these courts often chose to rely on state constitutional or statutory guarantees of open courts as the basis for a right of access.[143] Some courts have found it unnecessary to specify a single basis for access, referring to both state and federal constitutional provisions, as well as other laws, as the basis for access rights.[144]

Likewise, the standards for permitting closure that state courts initially adopted varied widely. Some earlier decisions adopted the American Bar Association's Fair Trial-Free Press Guidelines,[145] and others created their own rules and procedures.[146]

---

[140] 685 F.2d 1162, 8 Media L. Rep. 2177 (9th Cir. 1982).

[141] *Id.* at 1170, 8 Media L. Rep. at 2182.

[142] *Id. Compare* Poughkeepsie Newspapers v. Rosenblatt, 463 N.E.2d 1222, 10 Media L. Rep. 1560 (N.Y. 1984) (closed hearing to determine admissibility of evidence during trial proper) *with* Houston Chronicle Pub'g Co. v. Shaver, 630 S.W.2d 927, 8 Media L. Rep. 1314 (Tex. Crim. App. 1982) (Texas Constitution and statutes guarantee access to midtrial hearing on admissibility of confession).

[143] Shiras v. Britt, 589 S.W.2d 18, 5 Media L. Rep. 2020 (Ark. 1979) (Arkansas statute provided for public sittings of court); Miami Herald Pub'g Co. v. Lewis, 426 So. 2d 1, 8 Media L. Rep. 2281 (Fla. 1982) (Florida precedent "supportive of open government"); Iowa Freedom of Info. Council v. Wifvat, 328 N.W.2d 920, 9 Media L. Rep. 1194 (Iowa 1983) (Iowa Const. art. I, §7 provides rights analogous to First Amendment); State v. Birdsong, 422 So. 2d 1135, 9 Media L. Rep. 1010 (La. 1982) (La. Const. art. I, §22 provides for "open" courts); Keene Pub'g Corp. v. Cheshire County Super. Ct., 406 A.2d 137, 5 Media L. Rep. 1626 (N.H. 1979) (N.H. Const. pt. I, art. 22 provides right to gather news unaffected by *Gannett*); Commonwealth v. Hayes, 414 A.2d 318, 328, 334, 6 Media L. Rep. 1273, 1281, 1286, 1290 (Pa.) (concurring opinions found right of access under Pa. Const. art. I, §11), *cert. denied*, 449 U.S. 992 (1980); Herald Ass'n v. Ellison, 419 A.2d 323, 6 Media L. Rep. 1638 (Vt. 1980) (Vermont tradition of open proceedings relied upon); Federated Pubns. v. Swedberg, 633 P.2d 74, 7 Media L. Rep. 1865 (Wash. 1981) (Wash. Const. art. I, §10 guarantees open administration of justice), *cert. denied*, 456 U.S. 984 (1982); State ex rel. Herald Mail Co. v. Hamilton, 267 S.E.2d 544, 6 Media L. Rep. 1343 (W. Va. 1980) (W. Va. Const. art. III, §§14 and 17 provide for rights analogous to Sixth Amendment and for open courts, respectively).

[144] Arkansas Television Co. v. Tedder, 662 S.W.2d 174, 10 Media L. Rep. 1617 (Ark. 1983) (relying on First Amendment, Arkansas case law, and Arkansas statute); Kansas City Star Co. v. Fossey, 630 P.2d 1176, 7 Media L. Rep. 2250 (Kan. 1981) (no constitutional basis for access specified); Journal Newspapers v. State, 456 A.2d 963, 9 Media L. Rep. 1392 (Md. Ct. Spec. App.) (First Amendment and Md. Const. Decl. of Rts. art. 40 referred to), *aff'd*, 465 A.2d 426, 9 Media L. Rep. 2233 (Md. 1983); State ex rel. Smith v. District Ct. of Eighth Judicial Dist., 654 P.2d 982, 8 Media L. Rep. 2608 (Mont. 1982) (First Amendment and Montana Constitution's "right to know" provision both relied upon); Kearns-Tribune Corp. v. Lewis, 685 P.2d 515, 10 Media L. Rep. 1737 (Utah 1984) (right of access found under both First Amendment and Utah Const. art. I, §15).

[145] Kansas City Star Co., 630 P.2d at 1180–84, 7 Media L. Rep. at 2254–56; *State ex rel. Smith*, 654 P.2d at 986–88, 8 Media L. Rep. at 2611–12; *see also Swedberg*, 633 P.2d at 76–78, 7 Media L. Rep. at 1867–68 (Washington Bench-Bar-Press Guidelines followed). For a discussion of the ABA Guidelines and other "voluntary fair trial/free press agreements," see Riemer, *Television Coverage of Trials: Constitutional Protection Against Absolute Denial of Access in the Absence of a Compelling Interest*, 30 Vill. L. Rev. 1267, 1277–78 & nn.41–43 (1985). *See also United States Judicial Conference Guidelines on Fair Trial/Free Press*, 6 Media L. Rep. (BNA) 1897 (1980).

[146] *Miami Herald Pub'g Co.*, 426 So. 2d at 6, 8 Media L. Rep. at 2285 (closure only if "necessary to prevent a serious and imminent threat to the administration of justice"); *Birdsong*, 422 So. 2d at 1138, 9 Media L. Rep. at 1012 ("reasonable likelihood of substantial prejudice to . . . right to a fair trial"); *Kearns-Tribune Corp.*, 685 P.2d at 523, 10 Media L. Rep. at 1742 ("realistic likelihood of prejudice") (citing

Some courts followed the standards in *Gannett* and *Richmond Newspapers,* while more recent decisions follow *Press-Enterprise II.*[147] Virtually all courts have incorporated certain basic concepts found in the leading Supreme Court opinions: (1) requiring the trial court's consideration of alternatives to closure;[148] (2) providing the public, or more specifically the media, with notice and an opportunity to be heard before closure;[149] and (3) requiring the trial court to articulate its reasons for denying or ordering closure.[150] In any event, after *Press-Enterprise II,* it is well established that the media and the public have a constitutional right of access to pretrial suppression hearings and that *Press-Enterprise II*'s requirements are controlling.[151]

State v. Williams, 459 A.2d 641, 656, 9 Media L. Rep. 1585, 1596 (N.J. 1983)); *Herald Mail Co.,* 267 S.E.2d at 551, 6 Media L. Rep. at 1350 ("clear likelihood that there will be irreparable damage to defendant's right to a fair trial").

[147]*Arkansas Television Co.,* 662 S.W.2d at 176–77, 10 Media L. Rep. at 1619 (following first two prongs of Justice Blackmun's *Gannett* standards); *Iowa Freedom of Info. Council,* 328 N.W.2d at 924–25, 9 Media L. Rep. at 1198 (following Blackmun's *Gannett* standards); *Journal Newspapers,* 456 A.2d at 970, 9 Media L. Rep. at 1397 (same); Commonwealth v. Buehl, 462 A.2d 1316, 9 Media L. Rep. 1896 (Pa. Super. Ct. 1983) (following *Richmond Newspapers,* to close criminal pretrial proceeding notice to public must be provided, hearing must be held if any public representative appears to oppose closure, alternatives must be considered, and if closure is granted, reasons must be stated on record for rejecting alternatives); Federated Pubns. v. Kurtz, 615 P.2d 440, 446–47, 6 Media L. Rep. 1577, 1582 (Wash. 1980) (following Justice Powell's *Gannett* standards); State v. Drake, 701 S.W.2d 604, 12 Media L. Rep. 1488 (Tenn. 1985) (criminal pretrial hearings may only be closed, even if no opposition to closure, on showing of overriding interest likely to be prejudiced by open hearing and only if court considers reasonable alternatives, makes closure no broader than necessary, and issues adequate findings); Mississippi Pubrs. Corp. v. Coleman, 515 So. 2d 1163, 14 Media L. Rep. 2005 (Miss. 1987) (closure of pretrial suppression hearing allowed where findings tracked *Press-Enterprise II*); State v. Tallman, 537 A.2d 422, 428, 15 Media L. Rep. 1344, 1349 (Vt. 1987) (adopting test from *Press-Enterprise II*).

[148]United States v. Ellis, 8 Media L. Rep. 1868 (D. Mass. 1982) (closure of suppression hearing improper where trial court found defendant's fair trial rights could be protected by appropriate voir dire); *Arkansas Television Co.,* 662 S.W.2d at 176–77, 10 Media L. Rep. at 1619; State v. Couture, 435 A.2d 369, 7 Media L. Rep. 1408 (Conn. Super. Ct. 1981); *Iowa Freedom of Info. Council,* 328 N.W.2d at 924–25, 9 Media L. Rep. at 1198; *Kansas City Star Co.,* 630 P.2d at 1182–84, 7 Media L. Rep. at 2255–57; *Journal Newspapers,* 456 A.2d at 970, 9 Media L. Rep. at 1397; Buzbee v. Journal Newspapers, 465 A.2d 426, 9 Media L. Rep. 2233 (Md. Ct. App. 1983) (alternatives must be considered for closure to be proper); *Smith,* 654 P.2d at 986–88, 8 Media L. Rep. at 2611–12; Commonwealth v. Hayes, 414 A.2d 318, 323–24, 6 Media L. Rep. 1273, 1277–78 (Pa.), *cert. denied,* 449 U.S. 992 (1980); *Kearns-Tribune Corp.,* 685 P.2d at 522–24, 10 Media L. Rep. at 1742–43; *Swedberg,* 633 P.2d at 76–77, 7 Media L. Rep. at 1867; *Kurtz,* 615 P.2d at 446–47, 6 Media L. Rep. at 1582; *Herald Mail Co.,* 267 S.E.2d at 551, 6 Media L. Rep. at 1349 (noting that, as alternative to closing pretrial suppression hearing, "procedural methods applied by law enforcement officials in obtaining the questioned material" rather than "the substantive content of the evidence to be suppressed" should and often would be subject of hearing). For one list of alternatives, see *supra* note 26. *But see Miami Herald Pub'g Co.,* 426 So. 2d at 6, 8 Media L. Rep. at 2285 (expressly excluding change of venue as closure alternative); *Herald Ass'n,* 419 A.2d at 326, 6 Media L. Rep. at 1640–41 (change of venue "should not lightly be resorted to").

[149]United States v. Baker, 5 Media L. Rep. 1417 (W.D. Wash. 1979); *Miami Herald Pub'g Co.,* 426 So. 2d at 7–9, 8 Media L. Rep. at 2286–87; *Iowa Freedom of Info. Council,* 328 N.W.2d at 925–26, 9 Media L. Rep. at 1199 (procedure suggested but not "obligatory"); Oneonta Star v. Mogavero, 434 N.Y.S.2d 781, 6 Media L. Rep. 2271 (N.Y. App. Div. 1980); Merola v. Warner, 427 N.Y.S.2d 808, 6 Media L. Rep. 1250 (N.Y. App. Div. 1980); *Kearns-Tribune Corp.,* 685 P.2d at 523–24, 10 Media L. Rep. at 1743; *Kurtz,* 625 P.2d at 446–47, 6 Media L. Rep. at 1582.

[150]Miami Herald Pub'g Co., 426 So. 2d at 7–8, 8 Media L. Rep. at 2286; *Iowa Freedom of Info. Council,* 328 N.W.2d at 925–26, 9 Media L. Rep. at 1199 (findings suggested but not "obligatory"); *Kansas City Star Co.,* 630 P.2d at 1183–84, 7 Media L. Rep. at 2256; *Journal Newspapers,* 465 A.2d at 966–67, 9 Media L. Rep. at 1394; *Smith,* 654 P.2d at 988, 8 Media L. Rep. at 2613; Associated Press v. Bell, 510 N.E.2d 313, 14 Media L. Rep. 1156 (N.Y. 1987) (closure only possible where specific findings demonstrate substantial probability that defendant's fair trial rights would be prejudiced and no reasonable alternatives to closure existed); *Kearns-Tribune Corp.,* 685 P.2d at 523–24, 10 Media L. Rep. at 1743; *Herald Mail Co.,* 267 S.E.2d at 551, 6 Media L. Rep. at 1350.

[151]*See, e.g.,* State v. Tallman, 537 A.2d 422, 15 Media L. Rep. 1344 (Vt. 1987) (First Amendment right of access to pretrial suppression hearings); Gannett Westchester Rockland Newspapers v. La Cava, 551 N.Y.S.2d 261, 18 Media L. Rep. 1397 (N.Y. App. Div. 1990) (mere possibility of prejudicial pretrial publicity cannot justify closure of suppression hearing). See also *supra* §1.2(A)(vi) on *Press-Enterprise II*'s requirements.

§1.4(B) Preliminary Hearings and Other Pretrial Proceedings

Unlike a pretrial suppression hearing, the purpose of a preliminary hearing is not to make evidentiary rulings but to determine whether the prosecution has met its burden of showing probable cause for bringing a defendant to trial. Courts that considered closure of a preliminary hearing before *Press-Enterprise II* were deeply split on whether there was a right of access and, if it existed, how it was to be applied.[152]

Whether courts permitted closure of a preliminary hearing often depended on how effective the court considered the alternatives to closure (e.g., change of venue, searching jury voir dire, cautionary jury instructions, and augmenting the jury pool by use of "foreign" jurors).[153] Likewise, courts that found closure unnecessary based their decisions on the availability of an alternative to closure.[154] In contrast, courts that permitted closure found such alternatives unsatisfactory.[155] In *Press-Enterprise II,* however, the Supreme Court ended the dispute, holding that there is a First Amendment right of access to preliminary hearings.[156]

While courts before *Press-Enterprise II* were badly split on access to preliminary hearings, they nonetheless generally disfavored closure of other pretrial hearings, particularly when broad closure orders covering all pretrial proceedings were entered.[157] Courts have also granted access to arraign-

---

[152] *Cases Holding That Preliminary Hearing Should Be Open:* United States v. Dean, 5 Media L. Rep. 2595 (S.D. Ga. 1980); State v. Anonymous, 479 A.2d 1244, 10 Media L. Rep. 2214 (Conn. Super. Ct. 1984); Keene Pub'g Corp v. Keene Dist. Court, 380 A.2d 261, 3 Media L. Rep. 1595 (N.H. 1977); State v. Williams, 459 A.2d 641, 9 Media L. Rep. 1585 (N.J. 1983); Minot Daily News v. Holum, 380 N.W.2d 347, 12 Media L. Rep. 1812 (N.D. 1986); Ex parte South Carolina Press Ass'n, 314 S.E.2d 321, 10 Media L. Rep. 1495 (S.C. 1984); Steinle v. Lollis, 307 S.E.2d 230, 10 Media L. Rep. 1255 (S.C. 1983); Rapid City Journal Co. v. Circuit Ct. of Eighth Judicial Cir. (Bradenburg), 286 N.W.2d 125, 5 Media L. Rep. 2365 (S.D. 1979).

Cases Upholding Closure or Partial Closure of Preliminary Hearing: San Jose Mercury-News v. Municipal Ct., 638 P.2d 655, 7 Media L. Rep. 2522 (Cal. 1982); Gannett Pac. Corp. v. Richardson, 580 P.2d 49, 3 Media L. Rep. 2575 (Haw. 1978); Dickinson Newspapers v. Jorgensen, 338 N.W.2d 72, 9 Media L. Rep. 2063 (N.D. 1983); State ex rel. Feeney v. District Ct. of Seventh Judicial Dist., 607 P.2d 1259, 6 Media L. Rep. 1174 (Wyo. 1980); In re Midland Pub'g Co., 362 N.W.2d 580, 11 Media L. Rep. 1337 (Mich. 1984) (no First Amendment or Michigan constitutional right of access to pretrial criminal proceedings).

[153] *See, e.g., Williams,* 459 A.2d 641.

[154] *Anonymous,* 479 A.2d at 1248–49, 10 Media L. Rep. at 2217–18 (First Amendment right of access to probable cause hearings and all documents considered during hearing, except court held that defendant's statement was to remain sealed to protect privacy rights, since no probable cause found); *Keene Pub'g Corp.,* 380 A.2d at 263, 3 Media L. Rep. at 1597 (media voluntarily agreed not to publish names of juveniles disclosed during probable cause hearings).

[155] *See, e.g., Jorgensen,* 338 N.W.2d at 79–80, 9 Media L. Rep. at 2068.

[156] *See supra* §1.2(A)(vi). The Supreme Court has reaffirmed that there is a constitutional right of access to preliminary hearings. El Vocero de Puerto Rico v. Puerto Rico, 113 S. Ct. 2004, 21 Media L. Rep. 1440 (1993). *Accord* Booth Newspapers v. Twelfth Dist. Ct. Judge, 432 N.W.2d 400, 15 Media L. Rep. 2258 (Mich. Ct. App. 1988) (qualified First Amendment right of access to preliminary examinations); Capital Newspapers v. Lee, 530 N.Y.S.2d 872, 15 Media L. Rep. 1668 (N.Y. App. Div. 1988) (cannot close preliminary hearing without hearing and specific findings); Des Moines Register & Tribune Co. v. Iowa Dist. Ct., 426 N.W.2d 142 (Iowa 1988) (recognizing constitutional right of access to preliminary hearing and declaring contrary rule of criminal procedure unconstitutional); Cowles Pub'g Co. v. Magistrate Ct., 800 P.2d 640, 18 Media L. Rep. 1273 (Idaho 1990) (recognizing qualified First Amendment right of access to preliminary hearings). *But see* Mississippi Pubrs. Corp. v. Coleman, 515 So. 2d 1163, 14 Media L. Rep. 2005 (Miss. 1987) (order excluding press and public from all pretrial hearings and jury selection until murder trial begins upheld).

[157] United States v. Civella, 493 F. Supp. 786, 6 Media L. Rep. 1744 (W.D. Mo. 1980) (court denied defendants' motion to close all pretrial proceedings and to seal all pretrial motions); R.W. Page Corp. v. Lumpkin, 292 S.E.2d 815, 8 Media L. Rep. 1824 (Ga. 1982) (public trial guarantee in Georgia Constitution applies to pretrial, midtrial, and posttrial hearings; trial court had entered succession of orders closing various pretrial proceedings); Seattle Times Co. v. Ishikawa, 640 P.2d 716, 8 Media L. Rep. 1041 (Wash. 1982) (reversing closure).

ments[158] and other pretrial proceedings such as plea hearings[159] and pretrial motions.[160]

Pretrial discovery depositions in criminal cases, if allowed at all, have been closed to the media and public.[161] In addition, access has usually been denied to grand jury and some similar proceedings.[162]

§1.4(C) Bail and Related Hearings

Several federal circuit courts of appeal have recognized a First Amendment right of access to pretrial bail reduction and similar hearings, although closure of such hearings has sometimes been upheld.[163] In *United States v. Chagra,* the Fifth Circuit held that, even though there was no historical tradition of open bail hearings, there was a constitutional right of access.[164] The court then adopted Justice Powell's standards for closure in *Gannett:* if the defen-

---

[158]Palm Beach Newspapers v. Nourse, 413 So. 2d 467, 8 Media L. Rep. 1606 (Fla. Dist. Ct. App. 1982); Times-Union v. Harris, 423 N.Y.S.2d 263, 5 Media L. Rep. 2153 (N.Y. App. Div. 1979) (citing Westchester Rockland Newspapers v. Leggett, 399 N.E.2d 518, 523, 5 Media L. Rep. 2009, 2012 (N.Y. 1979), where court observed in dicta that there would be little justification for holding private arraignment), *appeal dismissed,* 407 N.E.2d 1349 (N.Y. 1980). For further discussion of *Westchester Rockland,* see *infra* §1.4(D), notes 173–79.

[159]New York Times Co. v. Demakos, 529 N.Y.S.2d 97, 15 Media L. Rep. 1524 (N.Y. App. Div. 1988) (error to exclude media from plea proceedings without hearing and specific findings); United States v. Haller, 837 F.2d 84, 14 Media L. Rep. 2166 (2d Cir. 1988) (First Amendment right of access to plea hearings and plea agreements but upholding redaction of one paragraph of plea agreement); In re Washington Post Co., 807 F.2d 383, 13 Media L. Rep. 1793 (4th Cir. 1986) (First Amendment right of access to plea hearings and documents filed in connection with such hearings); United States v. Kooistra, 796 F.2d 1390, 13 Media L. Rep. 1175 (11th Cir. 1986) (recognizing First Amendment and common law right of access). See also *infra* note 382.

[160]Oregonian Pub'g Co. v. O'Leary, 736 P.2d 173, 14 Media L. Rep. 1019 (Ore. 1987) (Oregon constitution requires public hearing on motion to compel testimony from witnesses who have claimed privilege against self-incrimination); In re Charlotte Observer, 882 F.2d 850, 16 Media L. Rep. 2032 (4th Cir. 1989) (First Amendment right of access to hearing on motion to change venue); Houston Chronicle Pub'g Co. v. Dean, 792 S.W.2d 273, 17 Media L. Rep. 2071 (Tex. Ct. App. 1990) (Texas statute required access to hearing on criminal defendant's motion to change venue); United States v. Pageau, 526 F. Supp. 1221, 1223 (N.D.N.Y. 1981) (access to entrapment hearing).

[161]Florida Freedom Newspapers v. McCrary, 520 So. 2d 32, 36, 14 Media L. Rep. 2374 (Fla. 1988) ("no first amendment right of access to pretrial discovery material"; statutory right of access to public records must be balanced with fair trial rights); Post-Newsweek Stations Fla. v. State, 474 So. 2d 344, 12 Media L. Rep. 1039 (Fla. Dist. Ct. App. 1985) (no constitutional right to attend criminal discovery depositions but permitting access to filed deposition transcripts), *approved,* 510 So. 2d 896 (Fla. 1987). Compare the decisions on civil depositions *infra* §1.6, notes 278 and 279.

[162]Press-Enterprise II, 478 U.S. 1, 9, 13 Media L. Rep. 1001, 1004 (1986) (describing grand jury as "government [operation] that would be totally frustrated if conducted openly"); In re Donovan, 801 F.2d 409, 13 Media L. Rep. 1233 (D.C. Cir. 1986) (no First Amendment right of access to federal grand jury materials because grand jury not pretrial criminal proceeding); In re Subpoena to Testify before Grand Jury Directed to Custodian of Records (Univ. of Fla. Athletic Program), 864 F.2d 1559, 1562–63, 16 Media L. Rep. 1165, 1166–67 (11th Cir. 1989) (no right of access to grand jury); In re Grand Jury, 528 So. 2d 51, 15 Media L. Rep. 1963 (Fla. Dist. Ct. App. 1988) (no right of access to hearings and motions to expunge grand jury presentment where there was no indictment). *See also* Troy Pub'g Co. v. Dwyer, 494 N.Y.S.2d 537, 12 Media L. Rep. 1306 (N.Y. App. Div. 1985) (no right of access under Judiciary Law §4 or First Amendment to pretrial hearing compelling suspect to provide hair and blood samples, analogizing proceeding to issuance of warrant or grand jury hearing, and holding that "investigatory process" is traditionally secret); *see also infra* §1.8(A). *But see* Eagle Printing Co. v. Delaney, 671 S.W.2d 883, 10 Media L. Rep. 2098 (Tex. Crim. App. 1984) (vacating closure of judicial court of inquiry to investigate prostitution); In re Rosahn, 671 F.2d 690, 8 Media L. Rep. 1187 (2d Cir. 1982) (reversing closure of contempt proceeding against grand jury witness who objected); In re P.R., 637 P.2d 346, 7 Media L. Rep. 2277 (Colo. 1981) (granting access to most of contempt proceeding against grand jury witness). *See also infra* notes 385–90.

[163]In re Globe Newspaper Co., 729 F.2d 47, 10 Media L. Rep. 1433 (1st Cir. 1984); United States v. Chagra, 701 F.2d 354, 9 Media L. Rep. 1409 (5th Cir. 1983). However, the tests for closure and their applications in these cases have been superseded by the more rigorous standards in later Supreme Court decisions—especially *Press-Enterprise II,* discussed *supra* §1.2(A)(vi). Seattle Times Co. v. United States Dist. Ct., 845 F.2d 1513, 1517, 15 Media L. Rep. 1273, 1275–76 (9th Cir. 1988) (finding right of access to pretrial release proceedings and documents and then applying "substantial probability" test).

[164]701 F.2d at 363–64, 9 Media L. Rep. at 1416.

dant's fair trial right will "likely be prejudiced," if alternatives to closure cannot adequately protect the defendant's fair trial right, and if closure will probably be effective in protecting that right, then closure is appropriate.[165] Applying these standards, the court found that the trial court properly ordered closure of the bail hearing because there had been extensive publicity regarding the defendants' alleged conspiracy to assassinate a federal judge.[166] Finally, the court expressly held that bail-setting procedures, which were not formally held before a magistrate in court, were not covered by its holding that there was a right of access, noting that "[t]hese informal procedures serve an important purpose. They allow the expeditious release of the defendant."[167]

The First Circuit also adopted Justice Powell's *Gannett* standards for closure in *In re Globe Newspaper Co.*[168] Although the court found that the facts would justify closure even under the stricter standard proposed in Justice Blackmun's *Gannett* dissent, "the less stringent standard produced a more equitable result, at least in the context of bail proceedings, where the court may receive evidence that is not admissible at trial and that consequently poses 'a serious threat to the defendant's fair trial right.' "[169] The First Circuit held that the defendant's Sixth Amendment fair trial rights and his statutory rights of privacy regarding wiretapped communications outweighed the First Amendment right of access in this case.[170] The court based its determination in part on its belief that

> [t]he interests of the press and the public weigh less heavily at this early point in the proceedings than they do later, both because the tradition of openness in bail hearings is not as strong and because the press and public will have later opportunities to examine the material admitted at those hearings. By contrast, the privacy and fair trial interests of the defendants are at their zenith during the bail hearings, since they have not yet had an opportunity to test the material admitted at the hearings.[171]

State courts reviewing the closure of bail hearings have also found a right of access.[172]

§1.4(D) Mental Competency Hearings

Several state courts have found that the media and the public have a right of access to pretrial mental competency hearings.[173] In *Westchester Rockland*

---

[165] *Id.* at 364–65, 9 Media L. Rep. at 1417. The court noted that the Justice Department also had adopted these standards, but the Justice Department standards were later revised and now require a showing of a substantial likelihood of injury. 28 C.F.R. §50.9 (1985).
[166] 701 F.2d at 363, 365, 9 Media L. Rep. at 1416, 1418.
[167] *Id.* at 363, 9 Media L. Rep. at 1416.
[168] 729 F.2d 47, 10 Media L. Rep. 1433 (1st Cir. 1984).
[169] *Id.* at 57, 10 Media L. Rep. at 1441.
[170] *Id.* at 52–56, 10 Media L. Rep. at 1437–39.
[171] *Id.* at 59, 10 Media L. Rep. at 1442.
[172] United States v. Edwards, 430 A.2d 1321, 7 Media L. Rep. 1324 (D.C. 1981) (closure violates First Amendment right of access; adopts Justice Powell's *Gannett* standards), *cert. denied,* 455 U.S. 1022 (1982); State ex rel. Post-Tribune Pub'g Co. v. Porter Super. Ct., 412 N.E.2d 748, 6 Media L. Rep. 2300 (Ind. 1980) (closure justified because trial court balanced interests and denied change of venue to assure defendant's speedy trial right); Williams v. Stafford, 589 P.2d 322, 4 Media L. Rep. 2073 (Wyo. 1979) (no closure without *closed* hearing to determine if "clear and present danger" to fair trial rights and no reasonable alternatives available; sealed record of closed hearing shall be kept with factual findings supporting closure and made available to media only at completion of trial).
[173] Westchester Rockland Newspapers v. Leggett, 399 N.E.2d 518, 5 Media L. Rep. 2009 (N.Y. 1979); Society of Prof. Journalists v. Bullock, 743 P.2d 1166, 14 Media L. Rep. 1737 (Utah 1987); Miami Herald

Newspapers v. Leggett,[174] the New York Court of Appeals vacated the closure of a pretrial mental competency hearing in a rape case, distinguishing it from a pretrial suppression hearing both because of its scope and its impact on the defendant's fair trial right. The court emphasized that the purpose of a pretrial mental competency hearing is narrowly limited to the defendant's *present* mental capacity and ability to assist in his or her own defense.[175] Relying on New York's statutory guarantee of a public trial, the court held that such a hearing is "presumptively open," although there is no absolute right of access.[176]

The extent of the access right granted in *Westchester Rockland* is uncertain. The court concluded that change of venue requires the defendant to waive the fundamental right of trial by a jury of peers from the locality, that a continuance interferes with the right to a speedy trial, and that sequestration is impractical at the pretrial stage where there are no jurors to sequester.[177] The court also noted that the public interest could "be preserved by making the transcript available to the media as soon as the danger of prejudice to the defendant has passed."[178] The court awarded the media this "alternative" relief, making a transcript available after the hearing.[179]

In *Miami Herald Publishing Co. v. Chappell*,[180] on the other hand, the Florida District Court of Appeal held that the trial court had erred in ordering closure of a criminal pretrial competency hearing because "the same reasoning that requires open trials mandates open competency proceedings."[181] The Florida court expressly found that the issues and testimony in a criminal competency proceeding are of a type unlikely to jeopardize the defendant's fair trial rights.[182] Unlike *Westchester Rockland,* the court in *Chappell* established a strict standard for closure: "(1) closure is necessary to prevent a serious and imminent threat to the administration of justice, (2) no less restrictive alternative measure is available, [and] (3) that closure will in fact achieve the court's

---

Pub'g Co. v. Chappell, 403 So. 2d 1342, 7 Media L. Rep. 1956 (Fla. Dist. Ct. App. 1981). *See also* In re Seegrist, 539 A.2d 799, 15 Media L. Rep. 1329 (Pa. 1988) (no error to deny closure of informal proceeding to determine whether defendant should undergo involuntary emergency psychiatric treatment where evidence had previously been produced at public hearing); State ex rel. Wisconsin State Journal v. Circuit Ct., 389 N.W.2d 73, 12 Media L. Rep. 2320 (Wis. Ct. App. 1986) (hearings to determine whether people found not guilty by reason of insanity should later be released presumptively open to public and media). *But see* Tribune Co. v. D.M.L., 566 So. 2d 1333, 18 Media L. Rep. 1076 (Fla. Dist. Ct. App. 1990) (because of state statute, no common law right of access to hearing on patient's continued involuntary commitment to mental health treatment center). The U.S. Supreme Court's most recent First Amendment access decisions simply reinforce the access right found in these cases. *See, e.g., supra* §1.2(A)(vi).

[174] 399 N.E.2d 518, 5 Media L. Rep. 2009 (N.Y. 1979).

[175] *Id.* at 524, 5 Media L. Rep. at 2013. The court noted that this "is not the same question that the jury may be called upon to decide if the defendant raises an insanity defense at trial."

[176] *Id.* at 522–23, 5 Media L. Rep. at 2011–12. The court refused to reach the issue of a right of access under the First Amendment or the New York Constitution.

[177] *Id.* at 526, 5 Media L. Rep. at 2015.

[178] *Id. Westchester Rockland*'s skepticism about alternatives to closure has been superseded by the U.S. Supreme Court's repeated command in its decisions after *Westchester Rockland* that such alternatives are viable options and can only be rejected if there is a specific finding that they are inadequate. *See supra* §1.2(A)(iv) and (vi).

[179] 399 N.E.2d at 526, 5 Media L. Rep. at 2015.

[180] 403 So. 2d 1342, 7 Media L. Rep. 1956 (Fla. Dist. Ct. App. 1981).

[181] *Id.* at 1344–45, 7 Media L. Rep. at 1957–58 (citing Richmond Newspapers v. Virginia, 448 U.S. 555, 6 Media L. Rep. 1833 (1980) and State ex rel. Miami Herald Pub'g Co. v. McIntosh, 340 So. 2d 904, 2 Media L. Rep. 1328 (Fla. 1977) (basing decision on Florida's commitment to open judicial proceedings)).

[182] *Id.* at 1344–45, 7 Media L. Rep. at 1958.

purpose."[183] This holding is more consistent with current Supreme Court rulings than is *Westchester Rockland*.[184]

§1.4(E) Posttrial Hearings

The courts have held that a variety of posttrial hearings—e.g, motions for postconviction sentence reduction,[185] sentencing hearings,[186] motions to set aside a guilty verdict,[187] postconviction habeas corpus proceedings,[188] probation revocation hearings,[189] expungement hearings,[190] and posttrial hearings regarding alleged juror misconduct[191]—must be conducted openly.

As the Ninth Circuit concluded in *CBS Inc. v. United States District Court*,[192] there is

> no principled basis for affording greater confidentiality to post-trial documents and proceedings than is given to pretrial matters .... The primary justifications for access to criminal proceedings, first that criminal trials historically have been open to the press and to the public, and, second, that access to criminal trials plays a significant role in the functioning of the judicial process and the governmental system, apply with as much force to post-conviction proceedings as to the trial itself.[193]

§1.5 ACCESS TO CRIMINAL TRIAL PROCEEDINGS

The Supreme Court expressly held in *Richmond Newspapers* and *Press-Enterprise I* that the public, including the media, has a First Amendment right of access to criminal trials and the voir dire of potential jurors, respectively.[194]

---

[183]*Id.* at 1345, 7 Media L. Rep. at 1958. *See also* Society of Prof. Journalists v. Bullock, 743 P.2d 1116, 14 Media L. Rep. 1737 (Utah 1987) (pretrial competency hearing can only be closed after hearing on closure and written findings that open hearing would have realistic likelihood of prejudice to fair trial rights; if hearing closed, transcript of closed proceeding must be released as soon as possible).

[184]*See supra* §1.2(A)(vi).

[185]CBS, Inc. v. United States Dist. Ct., 765 F.2d 823, 11 Media L. Rep. 2285 (9th Cir. 1985).

[186]In re Washington Post Co., 807 F.2d 383, 13 Media L. Rep. 1793 (4th Cir. 1986) (First Amendment right of access to sentencing hearings and documents filed in connection with such hearings); Palm Beach Newspapers v. Cook, 434 So. 2d 355 (Fla. Dist. Ct. App. 1983) (finding right of access but upholding closure because of "grave risk of harm" to persons and because of ongoing criminal investigation). *But see* Phoenix Newspapers v. Superior Ct., 680 P.2d 166, 10 Media L. Rep. 1659 (Ariz. 1984) (in camera hearing to modify defendant's sentence proper, but media must be granted access to transcript unless court determines it will interfere with pending criminal proceedings); Miami Herald Pub'g Co. v. State, 363 So. 2d 603, 4 Media L. Rep. 1681 (Fla. Dist. Ct. App. 1978) (closure of posttrial sentencing hearing upheld but case remanded for additional findings on length of time record should be sealed, whether there were alternatives to sealing, need to seal entire record, and whether subsequent events in case removed necessity for sealing).

[187]Gannett Co. v. Mark, 387 N.Y.S.2d 336, 2 Media L. Rep. 1189 (N.Y. App. Div. 1976).

[188]Houston Chronicle Pub'g Co. v. McMaster, 598 S.W.2d 864, 6 Media L. Rep. 1363 (Texas Ct. Crim. App. 1980).

[189]State ex rel. Great Falls Tribune Co. v. Montana Eighth Dist. Ct., 777 P.2d 345, 16 Media L. Rep. 2155 (Mont. 1989) (public and press right of access to probation revocation hearing but hearing may be closed when individual privacy demands).

[190]Shifflet v. Thomson Newspapers, 431 N.E.2d 1014, 8 Media L. Rep. 1199 (Ohio 1982). *See also infra* note 391.

[191]Globe Newspaper Co. v. Commonwealth, 556 N.E.2d 356, 17 Media L. Rep. 2195 (Mass. 1990) (recognizing right of access to posttrial hearing on whether court officer's remark improperly influenced jury). *See also* Times Pub'g Co. v. Penick, 433 So. 2d 1281, 9 Media L. Rep. 2185 (Fla. Dist. Ct. App. 1983) (trial court must give media notice and opportunity to be heard; court declined to rule on substantive propriety of closure order).

[192]765 F.2d 823, 825, 11 Media L. Rep. 2285, 2286 (9th Cir. 1985).

[193]*Id.* at 825, 11 Media L. Rep. at 2286 (citation omitted).

[194]*See supra* §1.2(A)(ii) and (iv). *But see* United States v. Edwards, 823 F.2d 111, 14 Media L. Rep. 1399 (5th Cir. 1987), *cert. denied*, 485 U.S. 934 (1988) (no First Amendment right of access to midtrial

Accordingly, the most important issue in this area is what showing will overcome that right.

§1.5(A) Trials

In *Richmond Newspapers,* the Supreme Court recognized two interests that could require closure: (1) the defendant's "superior right to a fair trial," or (2) "some other overriding consideration."[195] Before *Richmond Newspapers,* however, courts had already carved out certain exceptions to the right of access to criminal trials, such as the testimony of an undercover investigator or testimony about the use of secret government investigatory devices.[196] These appear to be the type of "overriding considerations" justifying closure that the Supreme Court had in mind.[197]

Whether such considerations actually justify closure depends on the facts of each case. In *United States ex rel. Lloyd v. Vincent,*[198] the Second Circuit upheld a limited trial closure during the testimony of an undercover narcotics agent. The court found that the witness was "actively engaged in ongoing narcotics investigations in an undercover capacity,"[199] and if required to testify in open court, the witness would become useless for other investigatory work and his life would be imperiled.[200] The court cautioned, however, that the "better course" for the trial court would have been to hold an evidentiary hearing to determine the necessity for closure.[201]

Other courts have refused to permit the closure of an undercover agent's trial testimony.[202] In *United States v. Powers,*[203] the Eighth Circuit upheld denial of a criminal *defendant's* motion to close his own trial testimony on the grounds that he was acting as a government informant at the time of his alleged crimes. The court held that his subjective fear that revelation of his actions as a government informant could endanger him and his family did not meet its standards for closure, which were modeled on those in Justice Blackmun's

---

hearing on alleged juror misconduct, but recognizing right of access to transcript of such proceedings as soon as jury renders verdict).

[195] Richmond Newspapers v. Virginia, 448 U.S. 555, 564, 6 Media L. Rep. 1833, 1837 (1980). A defendant's fair trial right is often raised as a basis for closure and is discussed throughout this chapter.

[196] *See, e.g.,* United States ex rel. Lloyd Vincent, 520 F.2d 1272 (2d. Cir.) (closure of trial testimony of undercover narcotics agent permitted), *cert. denied,* 423 U.S. 937 (1975); United States v. Bell, 464 F.2d 667 (2d Cir.) (closure of trial testimony about government's "hijacker profile" permitted), *cert. denied,* 409 U.S. 991 (1972).

[197] *Richmond Newspapers,* 448 U.S. at 598 n.24, 6 Media L. Rep. at 1852 n.24 (Brennan and Marshall, JJ., concurring) (citing "national security concerns about confidentiality" as justifying closure); Gannett Co. v. DePasquale, 443 U.S. 368, 401, 5 Media L. Rep. 1337, 1348 (1979) (Powell, J., concurring) ("preserv[ing] the confidentiality of sensitive information" can justify closure).

[198] 520 F.2d 1272, 1274 (2d Cir.), *cert. denied,* 423 U.S. 937 (1975).

[199] *Id.*

[200] *Id. See also* People v. Santos, 551 N.E.2d 1245 (N.Y. 1990) ("Active engagement in the community as an undercover agent is itself a compelling reason for excluding the public from the courtroom, at least when the fact of such engagement is elicited from the witness himself.").

[201] 520 F.2d at 1275.

[202] People v. Jones, 391 N.E.2d 1335, 5 Media L. Rep. 1262 (N.Y. 1979) (prosecutor's assertion that undercover agent would be in fear of his life inadequate), *cert. denied,* 444 U.S. 946 (1979); New York v. Cordero, 541 N.Y.S.2d 417, 16 Media L. Rep. 1732 (N.Y. App. Div. 1989) (reversible error to close trial to protect identity of undercover police officer absent any showing that open courtroom would jeopardize ongoing investigations or officer's safety), *aff'd,* 551 N.E.2d 103 (N.Y. 1989). *See also* People v. Cuevas, 409 N.E.2d 1360 (N.Y. 1980) (allowing access to court testimony of undercover police officer whose activities were ongoing).

[203] 622 F.2d 317, 6 Media L. Rep. 1161 (8th Cir.), *cert. denied,* 449 U.S. 837 (1980).

Gannett dissent.[204] The defendant had argued that his entire criminal trial should be closed so that he could present a defense that his criminal possession of counterfeit materials was part of his activities as a government informant, but refused to accept the trial court's suggestion that he stipulate with the prosecution that he was a government informant.[205]

Before the Second Circuit decided *Vincent,* it recognized a related but more specialized exception for closing testimony regarding a "hijacking profile" developed by the airlines and government to combat airline hijackings.[206] The court held in *United States v. Bell* that the "protection of the air travelling public" was sufficient justification for excluding the media and the public from testimony about the profile.[207] In a later case the court emphasized that closure should be narrowly limited to testimony actually describing the profile itself and should not be extended to more general testimony about the defendant's conduct.[208] Courts have also sometimes rejected closure requests by the prosecution to protect a witness whose life has allegedly been threatened.[209]

Sex crime cases have produced mixed results. The Supreme Court made it clear in *Globe Newspaper Co.* that a law mandating closure in all such cases was unconstitutional;[210] instead, a case-by-case determination is required.[211] Protection of reputation does not justify closure, however, so a defendant teacher's request for closure to protect his professional reputation and to prevent further incidents of teachers being accused of sexual misconduct by pupils has been denied.[212]

In *Douglas v. Wainwright,* the Eleventh Circuit held, both initially and on remand from the Supreme Court,[213] that the partial closure of the courtroom

---

[204]*Id.* at 321–23, 325, 6 Media L. Rep. 1163–65, 1166.

[205]*Id.* at 320–21, 6 Media L. Rep. at 1162.

[206]United States v. Ruiz-Estrella, 481 F.2d 723 (2d Cir. 1973) (closure improper because it covered more than testimony about "hijacking profile"; limited closure would have been appropriate); United States v. Clark, 475 F.2d 240 (2d Cir. 1973) (same). *See also* United States v. Slocum, 464 F.2d 1180 (3d Cir. 1972).

[207]464 F.2d 667, 670 (2d Cir.), *cert. denied,* 409 U.S. 901 (1972).

[208]*Ruiz-Estrella,* 481 F.2d at 726.

[209]Commonwealth v. Contakos, 453 A.2d 578, 9 Media L. Rep. 1038 (Pa. 1982) (plurality); State ex rel. New Mexico Press Ass'n v. Kaufman, 648 P.2d 300, 8 Media L. Rep. 1713 (N.M. 1982) (court cannot be closed because of mere speculation that press publication of murder trial jurors' names will expose them to intimidation). *But see* Commonwealth v. Stetson, 427 N.E.2d 926, 7 Media L. Rep. 2342 (Mass. 1981) (court did not abuse discretion in closing evidentiary hearing during testimony of minor sexual assault of witness fearing retaliation).

[210]*See supra* §1.2(A)(iii). Cases decided before *Globe Newspaper Co.* had often upheld exclusion orders in sex crime cases involving juvenile victims. State v. Burney, 276 S.E.2d 693, 7 Media L. Rep. 1411 (N.C. 1981) (not error for court to exclude all but certain people from seven-year-old rape victim's testimony); State v. Shepard, 438 A.2d 125, 7 Media L. Rep. 1140 (Conn. 1980) (error to exclude public but not press from juvenile witness' testimony in rape case). Of course, cases decided after *Globe Newspaper Co.* often reached a different result. *See, e.g.,* Eversole v. Superior Ct., 195 Cal. Rptr. 816, 9 Media L. Rep. 2436 (Cal. Ct. App. 1983) (trial court erred in closing preliminary hearing during testimony of minor sexual assault victim without considering specific alternatives to closure). *See also* WXYZ, Inc. v. Hand, 658 F.2d 420, 7 Media L. Rep. 1817 (6th Cir. 1981) (statute allowing for suppression of various information in sex offense cases unconstitutional).

[211]Lexington Herald Leader v. Tackett, 601 S.W.2d 905, 6 Media L. Rep. 1436 (Ky. 1980) (embarrassment and emotional trauma to juvenile witnesses in sodomy prosecution did not warrant closure); State v. Mounsey, 5 Media L. Rep. 2387 (Wash. Ct. App. 1979) (denial of exclusion of press from burglary/rape trial not improper). *But see* State v. Frazier, 440 A.2d 916, 7 Media L. Rep. 1854 (Conn. 1981) (not error to exclude public from courtroom during trial testimony of sexual assault victim), *cert. denied,* 458 U.S. 1112 (1982); People v. Jones, 422 N.Y.S.2d 999, 7 Media L. Rep. 2096 (N.Y. App. Div. 1981) (not error to exclude public from rape victim's trial testimony).

[212]Detroit Free Press v. Recorder's Ct. Judge, 294 N.W.2d 827, 6 Media L. Rep. 1586 (Mich. 1980).

[213]714 F.2d 1532, 9 Media L. Rep. 2457 (11th Cir.), *vacated and remanded for further reconsideration,* 468 U.S. 1206 (1984) (in light of Waller v. Georgia, 468 U.S. 1212 (1984) and Strickland v. Washington, 468 U.S. 1206 (1984)), *aff'd per curiam,* 739 F.2d 531 (11th Cir. 1984), *cert. denied,* 469 U.S. 1208 (1985).

to the public but not to the media during a key witness' trial testimony, in order to protect the witness from embarrassment in a sex crime and murder case, did not violate the defendant's Sixth Amendment right to a public trial.[214] The court held, however, that the trial court's other reason for permitting partial closure, "protection of the morality of the general public," did not qualify as a sufficient reason for even a partial closure of the trial.[215]

As with the closure of pretrial hearings,[216] many courts have found trial closures to be improper because the trial court refused to comply with the basic procedural safeguards set forth by the Supreme Court: notice and an opportunity to be heard, consideration of alternatives to closure, and making findings about the reasons for closure.[217] In *Sacramento Bee v. United States District Court*,[218] however, the Ninth Circuit held that, although the trial court did not consider all possible alternatives to closure and the closure order itself was improper,[219] the trial court's error was insufficient to warrant issuance of a writ of mandamus prohibiting further closure orders.[220]

One court concluded that, where the purpose was to prevent interruptions caused by people entering and leaving the courtroom, the trial court's order locking the courtroom during the charge to the jury did not violate any right of access.[221] Similarly, contemporaneous access by the public and the media to sidebar conferences may sometimes be denied, but transcripts of those proceedings must ordinarily be made available.[222]

§1.5(B) Voir Dire

In *Press-Enterprise I*,[223] the Supreme Court held without dissent that the voir dire examination of potential jurors is presumptively open to the public and the press.[224] Before *Press-Enterprise I*, several federal and state courts held, on a variety of rationales, that closing the voir dire of jurors was improper.[225]

---

[214] 714 F.2d at 1545, 9 Media L. Rep. at 2466, *aff'd*, 739 F.2d at 533.
[215] *Id.* at 1545, 9 Media L. Rep. at 2466.
[216] *See supra* §1.3.
[217] In re Knight Pub'g Co., 743 F.2d 231, 10 Media L. Rep. 2379 (4th Cir. 1984); Rovinsky v. McKaskle, 722 F.2d 197, 10 Media L. Rep. 1183 (5th Cir. 1984) (Sixth Amendment case); Detroit Free Press v. Macomb Circuit Judge, 275 N.W.2d 482, 4 Media L. Rep. 2180 (Mich. 1979); Capital Newspapers v. Clyne, 418 N.E.2d 1111, 8 Media L. Rep. 1712 (N.Y. 1982); Capital Newspapers Group v. Brown, 429 N.Y.S.2d 749, 6 Media L. Rep. 1494 (N.Y. App. Div. 1980).
[218] 656 F.2d 477, 7 Media L. Rep. 1929 (9th Cir. 1981), *cert. denied*, 456 U.S. 983 (1982).
[219] *Id.* at 482–83, 7 Media L. Rep. at 1932–33. The trial court considered only sequestration, admonition of jurors, and clipping the juror's newspapers; it failed to consider such alternatives as continuance, severance, change of venue and venire, intensive voir dire, and additional peremptory challenges.
[220] *Id.* at 483, 7 Media L. Rep. at 1933. Furthermore, the trial court did not hold any hearing with the media until after entering the closure orders. *Id.* at 480, 7 Media L. Rep. at 1930. This decision reflects more the limited scope of review the court applied than any agreement with what the trial court did. *Id.* at 483, 7 Media L. Rep. at 1933.
[221] People v. Colon, 521 N.E.2d 1075, 15 Media L. Rep. 1235 (N.Y.) (locking courtroom doors during jury instructions to prevent distraction of spectators entering or leaving was reasonable time, place, and manner restriction and did not violate right to public trial), *cert. denied*, 487 U.S. 1239 (1988).
[222] United States v. Smith, 787 F.2d 111, 114, 12 Media L. Rep. 1935, 1938 (3d Cir. 1986); In re Capital Cities/ABC's Application, 913 F.2d 89, 94–95, 18 Media L. Rep. 1049, 1053 (3d Cir. 1990). *See also* Rovinsky v. McKasle, 722 F.2d 197, 201 n.12, 10 Media L. Rep. 1183, 1186 n.12 (5th Cir. 1984). *See also supra* note 40.
[223] 464 U.S. 501, 10 Media L. Rep. 1161 (1984), discussed *supra* §1.2(A)(iv).
[224] *Id.* at 510–11, 10 Media L. Rep. at 1165.
[225] United States v. Brooklier, 685 F.2d 1162, 8 Media L. Rep. 2177 (9th Cir. 1982) (First Amendment

Since *Press-Enterprise I,* courts have reached different results depending on the facts before them. The Fourth Circuit, in *In re Greensboro News Co. (Greensboro News I)*[226] and *In re Greensboro News Co. (Greensboro News II),*[227] held that a trial court properly closed voir dire in a civil rights trial arising from a riot involving Ku Klux Klan and Nazi Party members. On rehearing, the court distinguished *Press-Enterprise I,* because unlike in *Press-Enterprise I,* fair trial issues had been raised, and the trial court's closure order had provided for release of the voir dire transcript as soon as a jury had been impaneled.[228] In *In re Dallas Morning News,* however, the Fifth Circuit held that *Press-Enterprise I* requires general questioning of the venire panel, as well as questioning of individual members of the venire, to be open to the public and press.[229]

In *Ukiah Daily Journal v. Superior Court,*[230] the California Court of Appeal vacated an order closing voir dire and expressly followed *Press-Enterprise I*'s observation that the procedures for "death-qualifying" a California jury do not require closing the voir dire to the press and the public but merely require conducting an individual voir dire of potential jurors outside the presence of other members of the venire.[231] *Ukiah Daily Journal* also fully adopted *Press-Enterprise I*'s standard for closure.[232]

In an unusual case, *In re Memphis Publishing Co.,* the Sixth Circuit held that the use of an electronic device that emitted white noise during voir dire, which prevented the media, public, and other jurors from hearing the questioning, violated *Press-Enterprise I.*[233] While no objection to the use of the device was initially made, on the second day of jury selection a reporter questioned its use, and the next day several media organizations sought to intervene to challenge the "closure."[234] The trial court denied their motion to open the voir dire on the ground that it "might well" undermine the defendant's right to a fair trial.[235] The Sixth Circuit concluded that this naked assertion, absent

---

right of access to voir dire, which is deemed part of trial); United States ex rel. Pulitzer Pub'g Co., 635 F.2d 676, 6 Media L. Rep. 2232 (8th Cir. 1980) (relying on *Richmond Newspapers* and *Gannett*); Commercial Printing Co. v. Lee, 553 S.W.2d 270, 2 Media L. Rep. 2352 (Ark. 1977) (relying on Arkansas statute permitting public to observe administration of justice); Rapid City Journal Co. v. Circuit Ct. (Tice), 283 N.W.2d 563, 5 Media L. Rep. 1706 (S.D. 1979) (relying on state tradition of open court proceedings); State ex rel. La Crosse Tribune v. Circuit Ct., 340 N.W.2d 460, 10 Media L. Rep. 1041 (Wis. 1983) (relying on legislative presumption of openness). *See also* Commonwealth v. Johnson, 455 A.2d 654, 9 Media L. Rep. 1649 (Pa. Super. Ct. 1982) (closure of jury selection violated defendant's right to public trial). *But see* Lexington Herald-Leader v. Meigs, 660 S.W.2d 658, 9 Media L. Rep. 2153 (Ky. 1983) (not error to close individual voir dire).

[226] 727 F.2d 1320, 10 Media L. Rep. 1239 (4th Cir.), *cert. denied,* 469 U.S. 829 (1984). This case was decided immediately before *Press-Enterprise I.*

[227] 727 F.2d 1326, 10 Media L. Rep. 1462 (4th Cir. 1984). This case was decided immediately after *Press-Enterprise I.*

[228] *Id.* at 1327–29, 10 Media L. Rep. at 1463–64. The safety of potential jurors also appeared to be a factor influencing this decision. *Greensboro News I,* 727 F.2d at 1325, 10 Media L. Rep. at 1245.

[229] 916 F.2d 205, 206, 18 Media L. Rep. 1333, 1334 (5th Cir. 1990). However, upon a proper showing, questioning of individuals can be closed. *Id.*

[230] 211 Cal. Rptr. 673, 11 Media L. Rep. 1676 (Cal. Ct. App. 1985).

[231] *Id.* at 675–76, 11 Media L. Rep. at 1678–79.

[232] *Id.* at 674–75, 676–77, 11 Media L. Rep. at 1677, 1679. *See also* United States v. Peters, 754 F.2d 753, 11 Media L. Rep. 1513 (7th Cir. 1985) (error to exclude public from criminal voir dire without making specific findings, without considering alternatives to closure, and without narrow tailoring of closure order); In re Times-World Corp., 373 S.E.2d 474, 15 Media L. Rep. 2210 (Va. Ct. App. 1988) (error to close voir dire without notice, hearing, and specific findings).

[233] 887 F.2d 646, 648–49, 16 Media L. Rep. 2384, 2386 (6th Cir. 1989).

[234] *Id.* at 647, 16 Media L. Rep. at 2385.

[235] *Id.* at 647–48, 16 Media L. Rep. at 2385.

any specific findings of fact that supported it, was insufficient to justify closure.[236]

Decisions involving requests for access to written information about jurors and potential jurors are not uniform.[237]

§1.5(C) Juvenile Proceedings

Without any controlling Supreme Court decision, requests for access to juvenile proceedings have produced conflicting decisions. Some courts have decided whether there is a statutory right of access to juvenile proceedings,[238] while others have considered whether there is a constitutional right of access to juvenile hearings.[239]

Cases in the former category include *Brian W. v. Superior Court*,[240] where the California Supreme Court upheld media access to a hearing to determine a juvenile's fitness to be tried as an adult. The court interpreted a state statute to include the media within the category of persons who have a "direct and legitimate interest in the particular case or the work of the court."[241] This statutory access right was discretionary, not mandatory.[242] However, the statute was "not inconsistent with the overall scheme of the juvenile court law," because "the judge can exercise control over disclosure of the juvenile's identity."[243]

---

[236]*Id.* at 648, 16 Media L. Rep. at 2386.

[237]*See infra* notes 523–26.

[238]In re T.R., 556 N.E.2d 439, 451, 17 Media L. Rep. 2241, 2250 (Ohio 1990) (in abuse, neglect, and custody proceeding, closure may be ordered if there is "a reasonable and substantial basis for believing that public access could harm the child or endanger the fairness of the proceeding, and . . . the potential for harm outweighs the benefits of public access"), *cert. denied,* 498 U.S. 958 (1990); Cheyenne K. v. Tuolomne County Super. Ct., 256 Cal. Rptr. 68, 16 Media L. Rep. 1411 (Cal. Ct. App. 1989) (public has statutory right of access to mental competency hearing of juvenile charged with murder unless juvenile establishes reasonable likelihood of substantial prejudice to fair trial rights); Tribune Newspapers West v. Superior Ct., 218 Cal. Rptr. 505 (Cal. Ct. App. 1985); Taylor v. State, 438 N.E.2d 275, 8 Media L. Rep. 2287 (Ind. 1982), *cert. denied,* 459 U.S. 1149 (1983); In re Welfare of K., 269 N.W.2d 367, 4 Media L. Rep. 1539 (Minn. 1978); Seattle Times v. County of Benton, 661 P.2d 964, 9 Media L. Rep. 1541 (Wash. 1983). *See generally* Katz, *The Grim Reality of Open Juvenile Delinquency Hearings,* 28 N.Y.L. SCH. L. REV. 101 (1983); Note, *The Public Right of Access to Juvenile Delinquency Hearings,* 81 MICH. L. REV. 1540 (1983).

[239]*See infra* text at notes 253–63.

[240]574 P.2d 788, 3 Media L. Rep. 1993 (Cal. 1978).

[241]*Id.* at 791, 3 Media L. Rep. at 1994–95 (interpreting CAL. WELF. & INST. CODE §676). *Accord* San Bernardino County v. Superior Ct., 283 Cal. Rptr. 332, 19 Media L. Rep. 1545 (Cal. Ct. App. 1991) (interpreting statute governing access to juvenile dependency proceedings). *See also* Wideman v. Garbarino, 770 P.2d 320, 16 Media L. Rep. 1253 (Ariz. 1989) (Arizona statute requiring hearing to determine whether juvenile should be tried as adult to be held in chambers does not require hearing to be private but confirms juvenile judge's discretion to admit media to hearing); News Group Boston v. Massachusetts, 568 N.E.2d 600, 18 Media L. Rep. 2102 (1991).

[242]574 P.2d at 790, 3 Media L. Rep. at 1994. *See also* Ohio ex rel. Fyffe v. Pierce, 531 N.E.2d 673, 15 Media L. Rep. 2431 (Ohio 1988) (juvenile court had statutory discretion to exclude press and public from juvenile proceedings, but closure not mandatory). *Compare* Stauffer Communications v. Mitchell, 789 P.2d 1153, 17 Media L. Rep. 1739 (Kan. 1990) (upholding closure of detention proceedings in juvenile case).

[243]574 P.2d at 791, 3 Media L. Rep. at 1995. Other courts considering a statutory access right have also emphasized the availability of alternate procedures to prevent identification of the juvenile. *See* In re Welfare of K., 269 N.W.2d 367, 369, 4 Media L. Rep. 1539, 1540 (Minn. 1978) (no abuse of discretion to permit reporter to attend juvenile hearing pursuant to statutory exception for those with "direct interest in the work of the [juvenile] Court" where media agreed not to identify juveniles); Seattle Times Co. v. County of Benton, 661 P.2d 964, 967–68, 9 Media L. Rep. 1541, 1543–44 (Wash. 1983) (reporter permitted access to juvenile records under statutory exception for "legitimate research" provided she satisfied other requirements of statute, including preservation of anonymity of persons identified in files). The *Brian W.* court recognized, however, that restrictions on the media's ability to identify juveniles could constitute an unconstitutional prior restraint and therefore expressly did not decide the extent to which such restrictions were permissible. 574 P.2d at 791 n.6, 3 Media L. Rep. at 1995 n.6. *See also infra* note 258.

While not relying on a constitutional right of access, *Brian W.* borrowed constitutional analyses from the U.S. Supreme Court's opinions in prior restraint cases[244] to respond to the juvenile's fair trial concerns. In particular, the court required consideration of alternatives to closure, such as sequestration or change of venue,[245] and approved the trial court's requirement that the juvenile establish "a reasonable likelihood" that without closure he would be unable to obtain a fair trial.[246] The court also noted that past media coverage relating to the case had been "neither excessive nor sensational," and the jury pool in that jurisdiction was large.[247]

More recently, in *Tribune Newspapers West v. Superior Court*,[248] the California Court of Appeal held that a juvenile court abused its discretion by closing a fitness hearing without holding a notice hearing at which (1) the juvenile met his burden to establish that there was a "reasonable likelihood of substantial prejudice" to his fair trial rights and (2) the media had the opportunity to prove by a preponderance of the evidence that there was no such "reasonable likelihood."[249] Although following *Brian W.*'s holding that the statute established a right of access,[250] the court expressly reviewed cases involving *constitutional* access rights in developing its standards for closure.[251] The court devoted a large part of its opinion to evaluating and identifying various alternatives to closure, an inquiry that has become an essential feature of constitutional access cases.[252]

When courts have addressed the media's right of access to juvenile hearings on purely constitutional grounds, many have decided that there is no such constitutional access right.[253] The Vermont Supreme Court, in *In re J.S.*,[254] held that there was no First Amendment right of access because there was no tradition of openness for juvenile hearings, since many states have laws to preserve the confidentiality of these proceedings.[255] The court concluded that

---

[244] 574 P.2d at 791 n.6, 3 Media L. Rep. at 1995 n.6. *Brian W.* was decided even before *Gannett,* the earliest of the Supreme Court "access" cases. *See supra* §1.2(A).

[245] 574 P.2d at 792, 3 Media L. Rep. at 1996.

[246] *Id.* at 792 & n.7, 3 Media L. Rep. at 1995 & n.7.

[247] *Id.* at 791, 3 Media L. Rep. at 1996.

[248] 218 Cal. Rptr. 505 (Cal. Ct. App. 1985).

[249] *Id.* at 509–10.

[250] *Id.* at 507–08.

[251] *Id.* at 508–10 (analyzing *Richmond Newspapers, Press-Enterprise I,* and California Supreme Court's decision, which was reversed in *Press-Enterprise II,* discussed *supra* §1.2(A)(vi)).

[252] *Id.* at 512–16. Furthermore, the court held that the increased cost of these alternatives should not be controlling in the closure decision. *Id.* at 514.

[253] F.T.P. v. Courier-Journal & Louisville Times Co., 774 S.W.2d 444, 16 Media L. Rep. 1921 (Ky. App. 1989) (no violation of state or federal constitutions to exclude press and public from court proceedings concerning whether juvenile defendant should be tried as adult since defendant was still juvenile and entitled to confidentiality until transferred); In re T.R., 556 N.E.2d 439, 451, 17 Media L. Rep. 2241, 2248–49 (Ohio) (acknowledging that there may be constitutional right of access to juvenile delinquency proceedings but holding that abuse, neglect, and dependency proceedings neither presumptively open nor presumptively closed), *cert. denied,* 498 U.S. 958 (1990); In re N.H.B., 769 P.2d 844 (Utah Ct. App. 1989) (statute that presumed juvenile proceedings were closed did not violate Utah or U.S. constitutions); San Bernardino County v. Superior Ct., 283 Cal. Rptr. 332, 19 Media L. Rep. 1545 (Cal. Ct. App. 1991) (interpreting statute governing access to juvenile dependency proceedings). *But see* Florida Pub'g Co. v. Morgan, 322 S.E.2d 233, 11 Media L. Rep. 1021 (Ga. 1984) (presumption that juvenile delinquency, deprivation, and unruliness hearings are closed cannot be conclusive). *Accord* New Jersey Div. of Youth & Family Servs. v. J.B., 576 A.2d 261, 17 Media L. Rep. 2183 (N.J. 1990) (proceedings to terminate parents' custody of children because of alleged child abuse presumptively closed, but presumption not mandatory).

[254] 438 A.2d 1125, 7 Media L. Rep. 2402 (Vt. 1981).

[255] *Id.* at 1127, 7 Media L. Rep. at 2404.

the "compelling interests in confidentiality" of juvenile proceedings override "any remaining First Amendment goals."[256] Similarly, the Rhode Island Supreme Court held in *Edward A. Sherman Publishing Co. v. Goldberg*[257] that the right of access to criminal trials, as established in *Richmond Newspapers,* did not apply to juvenile proceedings because "[t]he interests of the juvenile ... are most often best served by anonymity and confidentiality."[258]

Other courts have held that the media do have a right of access to juvenile proceedings. In *Capital Newspapers v. Moynihan,*[259] the New York Court of Appeals held that sentencing hearings of felons who had been granted youthful offender status were presumptively open to the press and public. Although closure was allowed by statute, the court stated that closure is proper only if the party seeking closure shows compelling reasons for it, the media are given an opportunity to be heard, and the trial court provides a statement of reasons for closure in open court.[260]

Similarly, in *Associated Press v. Bradshaw,* the South Dakota Supreme Court held that, before closing a juvenile proceeding, the juvenile court must consider (1) the nature and extent of press coverage, (2) whether coverage has been excessive or sensational, (3) whether the minor's name has been released to the public, (4) whether alternatives to closure exist, and (5) whether the closure of the proceedings will be temporary.[261] The juvenile court must then balance the juvenile's interest in confidentiality against the media's First Amendment rights.[262] If the proceedings are closed, the juvenile court must issue specific findings that closure is essential to preserve higher values and is narrowly tailored to serve that interest.[263]

---

[256]*Id.* *Compare* In re K.F., 559 A.2d 663, 16 Media L. Rep. 1984 (Vt. 1989) (juvenile charged with manslaughter not entitled to have arraignment and hearing on motion to transfer case to juvenile court closed because pretrial proceedings presumptively open and confidentiality only attaches if case is transferred to juvenile court).

[257]443 A.2d 1252, 8 Media L. Rep. 1489 (R.I. 1982).

[258]*Id.* at 1258, 8 Media L. Rep. at 1493. The court nonetheless struck down as a prior restraint a court order conditioning the media's attendance at such a hearing on its agreement not to publish the juvenile's name where the media learned that name from nonjudicial sources or records. *Id.* at 1257–58, 8 Media L. Rep. at 1492–93. *Accord* In re A Minor, 537 N.E.2d 292, 16 Media L. Rep. 1449 (Ill. 1989) (trial court's order prohibiting newspaper, which learned juvenile's name from nonjudicial sources, from publishing juvenile's name was unconstitutional prior restraint; order conditioning newspaper's attendance at future hearings on its agreement not to publish name also unconstitutional since name had been learned by lawful means); *San Bernardino County,* 283 Cal. Rptr. 332, 19 Media L. Rep. 1545. *Compare* In re A Minor, 595 N.E.2d 1052, 20 Media L. Rep. 1372 (Ill. 1992) (finding no constitutional problem with court order allowing media to attend juvenile court hearing contingent on them not publishing names of minors where identities of minors were discovered only through media's presence at proceedings); In re Hughes County Action No. JUV 90-3, 452 N.W.2d 128, 17 Media L. Rep. 1513 (S.D. 1990) (holding access could be conditioned on media's agreeing not to publish juveniles' and witnesses' names); In re VV Pub'g Corp., 577 A.2d 412, 417, 17 Media L. Rep. 2256, 2260 (N.J. 1990) (upholding order that conditioned access on media obeying order prohibiting disclosure of names of juvenile sexual abuse victims). *See also* In re J.D.C., 594 A.2d 70, 19 Media L. Rep. 1040 (D.C. 1991) (where one newspaper allegedly broke promise not to reveal juvenile's identity, all press should then be excluded). For a detailed discussion of prior restraints, see Chapter 10. *See also supra* note 243.

[259]519 N.E.2d 825, 14 Media L. Rep. 2262 (N.Y. 1988).

[260]*Id.* at 829–30, 14 Media L. Rep. at 2266.

[261]410 N.W.2d 577, 14 Media L. Rep. 1566 (S.D. 1987). *See also* State ex rel. Oregonian Pub'g Co. v. Deiz, 613 P.2d 23, 27, 6 Media L. Rep. 1369, 1371 (Or. 1980) (relying on OR. CONST. art. I, §10, providing for open administration of justice in finding access right).

[262]*Bradshaw,* 410 N.W.2d at 580–81, 14 Media L. Rep. at 1569. *But see* In re Hughes County Action No. JUV 90-3, 452 N.W.2d 128, 17 Media L. Rep. 1513 (S.D. 1990) (upholding closure of adjudicatory portion of juvenile hearing).

[263]Herald Co. v. Tormey, 537 N.Y.S.2d 978, 16 Media L. Rep. 1702 (N.Y. Sup. Ct.) (in criminal action against defendant eligible for youthful offender status, trial court erred in closing hearing on closure motion, sealing accusatory instrument, and closing arraignment and all further proceedings because there was no

§1.6 ACCESS TO CIVIL PRETRIAL AND TRIAL PROCEEDINGS

While *Richmond Newspapers* did not expressly decide that there is a constitutional right of access to civil proceedings, it strongly suggested that the constitutional right of access extended this far.[264] Not surprisingly then, the courts that have squarely considered this question have held there is a First Amendment right of access to civil proceedings.[265]

In *Newman v. Graddick*[266] and *In re Iowa Freedom of Information Council*,[267] the courts extended a First Amendment right of access to civil proceedings based on a very specific analysis of the similarities between a criminal proceeding and the type of civil proceedings before them. In *Newman*, the Eleventh Circuit held that the right of access should extend to pre- and posttrial hearings in civil class actions because the cases related to the release of convicted prisoners from overcrowded state prisons.[268] The court refused to decide whether the media had a First Amendment right of access to all civil trials.[269] Likewise, the Eighth Circuit also found a First Amendment right of access to a contempt hearing in *In re Iowa Freedom of Information Council* because such hearings are "a hybrid containing both civil and criminal characteristics."[270]

In *Publicker Industries v. Cohen*,[271] however, the Third Circuit held unequivocally that "the First Amendment does secure a right of access to civil proceedings."[272] After analyzing the Supreme Court's opinions in *Gannett*, *Richmond Newspapers*, and *Globe Newspaper Co.*, the court adopted the standard for closure enunciated in *Press-Enterprise I*.[273] Applying these standards to a stockholder proxy battle,[274] the court held that Publicker Industries' interest

---

record of any findings supporting closure), *aff'd*, 544 N.Y.S.2d 750 (N.Y. App. Div.), *appeal denied*, 547 N.E.2d 103 (N.Y. 1989).

[264] *See supra* note 41. *See generally* Note, *The First Amendment Right of Access to Civil Trials After Globe Newspaper Co. v. Superior Court*, 51 U. CHI. L. REV. 286 (1984).

[265] *See, e.g.*, Publicker Indus. v. Cohen, 733 F.2d 1059, 10 Media L. Rep. 1777 (3d Cir. 1984); In re Iowa Freedom of Info. Council, 724 F.2d 658, 10 Media L. Rep. 1120 (8th Cir. 1983); Newman v. Graddick, 696 F.2d 796, 9 Media L. Rep. 1104 (11th Cir. 1983). *See also* In re Astri Inv. & Sec. Corp., 88 Bankr. 730, 15 Media L. Rep. 1673 (D. Md. 1988) (recognizing right of access to bankruptcy creditors' meeting). *But see* Cincinnati Gas & Elec. Co. v. General Elec. Co., 854 F.2d 900, 15 Media L. Rep. 2020 (6th Cir. 1988) (no right of access to summary jury trial), *cert. denied*, 489 U.S. 1033 (1989).

[266] 696 F.2d 796, 9 Media L. Rep. 1104 (11th Cir. 1983).

[267] 724 F.2d 658, 10 Media L. Rep. 1120 (8th Cir. 1983).

[268] 696 F.2d at 801, 9 Media L. Rep. at 1107.

[269] *Id*.

[270] 724 F.2d at 661, 10 Media L. Rep. at 1122. The court nonetheless permitted closure of that portion of the hearing where a witness testified about trade secrets. *Id.* at 661–63, 10 Media L. Rep. at 1122–23 (Proctor & Gamble information concerning tampons used by toxic shock syndrome victim). *Accord* Standard & Poor's Corp. v. Commodity Exchange, 541 F. Supp. 1273, 8 Media L. Rep. 1755 (S.D.N.Y. 1982) (closure of "trade secret" testimony in civil injunction proceeding upheld). *See also* Webster Groves Sch. Dist. v. Pulitzer Pub'g Co., 898 F.2d 1371, 17 Media L. Rep. 1633 (8th Cit. 1990) (upholding closure of preliminary injunction hearing to prohibit handicapped child from attending school); Morgan v. Foretich, 528 A.2d 425, 14 Media L. Rep. 1342 (D.C. 1987) (upholding closure of civil contempt proceeding in child custody and visitation dispute to protect child).

[271] 733 F.2d 1059, 10 Media L. Rep. 1777 (3d Cir. 1984).

[272] *Id.* at 1061, 10 Media L. Rep. at 1777. *Accord* State v. Cottman Transmission Sys., 542 A.2d 859, 15 Media L. Rep. 1644 (Md. Ct. Spec. App. 1988); Brown & Williamson Tobacco Corp. v. Federal Trade Comm'n, 710 F.2d 1165, 1179 (6th Cir. 1983) ("[t]he policy considerations discussed in *Richmond Newspapers* apply to civil as well as criminal cases"), *cert. denied*, 465 U.S. 1100 (1984); In re Continental Ill. Sec. Litig., 732 F.2d 1302, 1308, 10 Media L. Rep. 1593, 1597 (7th Cir. 1984) ("the policy reasons for granting public access to criminal proceedings apply to civil cases as well").

[273] 733 F.2d at 1062, 10 Media L. Rep. at 1778.

[274] *Id.* at 1071–72, 10 Media L. Rep. at 1786.

in protecting allegedly confidential information was not a sufficiently "overriding interest" to justify closure.[275] The court found that the allegedly confidential nature of the information, which involved "poor management" and "bad business practices," could not overcome the "presumption of openness plus the policy interest in protecting unsuspecting people from investing in Publicker."[276]

State courts have likewise found a right of access to civil proceedings under various nonconstitutional rationales.[277] Cases regarding requests to attend civil depositions are in disagreement. Some courts have denied requests by the public and the media to attend civil depositions,[278] but other more recent decisions, influenced by the general trend in favor of access, have concluded that there is a right to attend civil depositions.[279]

§1.7 ACCESS TO ADMINISTRATIVE AND QUASI-JUDICIAL PROCEEDINGS AND RECORDS

Courts have upheld access to formal fact-finding hearings, such as those held by the Mine Safety and Health Administration to investigate the cause of a coal mine fire.[280] In *Society of Professional Journalists v. Secretary of Labor,* the court identified and followed the two-pronged analysis of *Globe Newspaper Co.* to decide whether there was a First Amendment access right to the mine safety investigation hearing,[281] first looking at "historical traditions" of access[282] and then at the functional considerations and the "procedural importance of openness."[283] While the court admitted that there was no historical tradition of access to (or even holding of) administrative hearings, it compared the formal fact-finding hearing to investigate a mine fire to a civil

---

[275]*Id.* at 1074, 10 Media L. Rep. at 1788. *See also Brown & Williamson Tobacco Corp,* 710 F.2d at 1179–80 (damage to reputation does not justify closure).

[276]733 F.2d at 1074, 10 Media L. Rep. at 1788.

[277]Barron v. Florida Freedom Newspapers, 531 So. 2d 113, 15 Media L. Rep. 1901 (Fla. 1988) (recognizing right of access to all civil proceedings); Sentinel Star v. Edwards, 387 So. 2d 367, 374–75, 6 Media L. Rep. 1603, 1609 (Fla. Ct. App. 1980) (media has common law right of access to posttrial hearing regarding juror misconduct in wrongful death case); KUTV, Inc. v. Conder, 635 P.2d 412, 7 Media L. Rep. 1915 (Utah 1981) (relying on "general proposition [that civil proceedings should] be open to the public," particularly when conduct of elected public official is challenged). *See also* FED. R. CIV. P. 43(a) and 77(b) (providing for trials "in open court").

[278]Westchester Rockland Newspapers v. Marbach, 413 N.Y.S.2d 411, 413, 4 Media L. Rep. 2256, 2257 (N.Y. App. Div. 1979) (no First Amendment right to attend civil depositions); Times Newspapers v. McDonnell Douglas Corp., 387 F. Supp. 189, 197, 1 Media L. Rep. 2346, 2352 (C.D. Cal. 1974) (same). *Compare supra* note 161. *See also* Kimberlin v. Quinlan, 145 F.R.D. 1 (D.D.C. 1992) (media have no right to attend civil depositions except in antitrust cases).

[279]United States v. Didrichsons, 15 Media L. Rep. 1869 (W.D. Wash. 1988); In re Texaco, 84 Bankr. 14, 15 Media L. Rep. 1201 (Bankr. S.D.N.Y. 1988); Avirgan v. Hull, 118 F.R.D. 252, 14 Media L. Rep. 2136 (D.D.C. 1987); Estate of Rosenbaum v. New York City, 21 Media L. Rep. 1987 (E.D.N.Y. 1993) (allowing four media representatives to attend civil deposition where deponents were public officials). *See also infra* note 427.

[280]Society of Prof. Journalists v. Secretary of Labor, 616 F. Supp. 569, 11 Media L. Rep. 2474 (D. Utah 1985) (First Amendment right of access found), *appeal dismissed,* 832 F.2d 1180, 14 Media L. Rep. 1827 (10th Cir. 1987). *See also* In re Nigris, 577 A.2d 1292, 1298, 18 Media L. Rep. 1422, 1426 (N.J. Super. Ct. App. Div. 1990) (right of access to exhibit admitted at Casino Control Commission hearing "may be of constitutional dimension").

[281]616 F. Supp. at 573–75, 11 Media L. Rep. at 2478.

[282]*Id.* at 575–76, 11 Media L. Rep. at 2478–79.

[283]*Id.* at 576–77, 11 Media L. Rep. at 2479–80. The court expressly rejected the government's contention that these hearings should be compared to grand jury proceedings, which are traditionally secret. *Id.* at 578, 11 Media L. Rep. at 2481.

trial, which historically has been open.[284] The court also held that an open hearing was important because the investigation of a disaster "can create an emotional catharsis."[285] However, the court limited this access right to the formal fact-finding sessions of an administrative body.[286]

Courts have also upheld access to other administrative proceedings, including a state attorney's inquiry,[287] an Immigration and Naturalization Service deportation hearing,[288] an attorney disciplinary proceeding,[289] a physician disciplinary proceeding,[290] and an unemployment benefits hearing.[291] Courts have also found either a common law or First Amendment right of access to municipal tax abatement records,[292] a state-owned legislative retrieval service's data base,[293] and certain congressional records,[294] though often on an equal protection rationale.[295]

In *First Amendment Coalition v. Judicial Inquiry & Review Board*,[296] however, the Third Circuit upheld a Pennsylvania constitutional provision denying access to hearings of a judicial inquiry and review board or its records unless the Board recommended that disciplinary action be taken.[297] Just as in *Society of Professional Journalists,* the court utilized the historical/functional analysis of *Richmond Newspapers* and *Globe Newspaper Co.* to determine

---

[284] *Id.* at 575, 11 Media L. Rep. at 2478–79.

[285] *Id.* at 576, 11 Media L. Rep. at 2479.

[286] *Id.* at 577, 11 Media L. Rep. at 2480 ("It is doubtful that the right of access would extend to informal interviews or internal agency deliberations.").

[287] KFGO Radio v. Rothe, 298 N.W.2d 505, 6 Media L. Rep. 2217 (N.D. 1980) (right of access under N.D. CONST. art. I, §22). *See also* Sheridan Newspapers v. City of Sheridan, 660 P.2d 785, 9 Media L. Rep. 2393 (Wyo. 1983) (recognizing statutory and constitutional right of access to certain police records); Houston Chronicle Pub'g Co. v. City of Houston, 531 S.W.2d 177 (Tex. Civ. App. 1975) (same), *writ of error refused,* 536 S.W.2d 559 (Tex. 1976).

[288] Pechter v. Lyons, 441 F. Supp. 115, 117–18, 3 Media L. Rep. 1445, 1446 (S.D.N.Y. 1977) (right of access based on application of discretionary federal regulation that court holds "is but one of countless manifestations of a public policy centuries old that judicial proceedings, especially those in which the life or liberty of an individual is at stake, should be subject to public scrutiny").

[289] Daily Gazette Co. v. Committee on Legal Ethics of W. Va. State Bar, 326 S.E.2d 705, 11 Media L. Rep. 1722 (W. Va. 1984) (right of access under West Virginia Constitution).

[290] Daily Gazette Co. v. West Virginia Bd. of Medicine, 352 S.E.2d 66, 13 Media L. Rep. 2125 (W. Va. 1986) (public has right of access under West Virginia Consititution to physician disciplinary proceedings after state board of medicine makes determination there is probable cause to proceed; if no probable cause found, there still is right of access to complaint and board's findings).

[291] Herald Co. v. Weisenberg, 455 N.Y.S.2d 413, 415, 8 Media L. Rep. 2450, 2452 (N.Y. App. Div. 1982) (Judiciary Law §4's right of access "should be applied with equal force to quasi-judicial proceedings"), *aff'd,* 452 N.E.2d 1190 (N.Y. 1983). *See also* Red Bank Register v. Board of Educ., 501 A.2d 985, 12 Media L. Rep. 1860 (N.J. Super. Ct. App. Div. 1985) (recognizing common law right of access to school curriculum reports); Asbury Park Press v. Seaside Heights, 586 A.2d 870, 18 Media L. Rep. 2264 (N.J. Super. Ct. Law. Div. 1990) (recognizing common law right of access to police incident reports and witness statements).

[292] McCoy v. Providence Journal Co., 190 F.2d 760 (1st Cir.) (common law right of access), *cert. denied,* 342 U.S. 894 (1951). *See also* Daily Gazette Co. v. Caryl, 380 S.E.2d 209, 16 Media L. Rep. 1908 (W. Va. 1989) (statutory right of access to tax liability compromises made by state tax commissioner).

[293] Legi-Tech v. Keiper, 766 F.2d 728, 11 Media L. Rep. 2482 (2d Cir. 1985).

[294] Schwartz v. United States Dep't of Justice, 435 F. Supp. 1203, 3 Media L. Rep. 1335 (D.D.C. 1977) (holding there is common law right of access to congressional records exempt from disclosure under federal Freedom of Information Act), *aff'd without opinion,* 596 F.2d 888 (D.C. Cir. 1979).

[295] *McCoy,* 190 F.2d at 763 (court upheld media plaintiff's equal protection claim because city officials gave competing newspaper access to municipal tax records); *Keiper,* 776 F.2d at 733–36, 11 Media L. Rep. at 2485–88 (challenged state statute only constitutional if private legislative information services have access to legislative documents on substantially equal basis as state-owned legislative retrieval service); Capital Cities Media v. Chester, 797 F.2d 1164 (3d Cir. 1986) (no First Amendment right of access to records of state environmental agency, but equal protection claim recognized). Of course, access to such proceedings and records may also be available by statute. *See infra* §1.11.

[296] 784 F.2d 467, 12 Media L. Rep. 1753 (3d Cir. 1986).

[297] *Id.* at 467–78, 12 Media L. Rep. at 1760–61. *See also* Nichols v. Gamso, 315 N.E.2d 770 (N.Y. 1974) (reaching similar result on statutory grounds); Herald Ass'n v. Judicial Conduct Bd., 544 A.2d 596, 15

whether a First Amendment access right existed.[298] After examining its history, the court concluded that the Board's hearings were like those of a grand jury, which are traditionally secret, but its recommendation of disciplinary action was like an indictment, a traditionally public document.[299]

In conducting its functional analysis, the court refused to accept the media's argument that the Board's hearings must be open simply because they involve the exercise of a governmental function.[300] Referring to Justice Brennan's caution in *Richmond Newspapers* that " 'the stretch of this protection is theoretically endless,' "[301] the court held that it must "[pay] heed to the circumstances in which [functional needs for the First Amendment access right] are invoked."[302] The court then concurred with the Pennsylvania Legislature's judgment, as set forth in the state constitution, that access was only appropriate if discipline was recommended.[303]

Other courts have also refused access to various administrative proceedings[304] or records.[305]

§1.8 INSPECTING AND COPYING COURT RECORDS AND EVIDENCE

The U.S. Supreme Court acknowledged the existence of a "common-law right of access to judicial records" in *Nixon v. Warner Communications*.[306]

Media L. Rep. 1078 (Vt. 1988) (no right of access to discovery materials not filed with judicial conduct board). *But see* In re Grand Jury Investig. Spring Term 1988, 543 So. 2d 757, 16 Media L. Rep. 1169 (Fla. Dist. Ct. App. 1989) (records of investigation of judge, who was not arrested or indicted, subject to disclosure to extent compiled independently of grand jury's inquiry).

[298]784 F.2d at 471–74, 12 Media L. Rep. at 1756–58.

[299]*Id.* at 472, 12 Media L. Rep. at 1757. The court further noted that "[t]hese administrative proceedings, unlike conventional criminal and civil trials, do not have a long tradition of openness" and rejected the media's argument that the board's hearings should be treated as "open impeachment hearings." *See also* Daily Gazette Co. v. West Virginia Bd. of Medicine, 352 S.E.2d 66, 13 Media L. Rep. 2125 (W. Va. 1986) (public has right of access under West Virginia Constitution to physician disciplinary proceedings after state board of medicine makes determination there is probable cause to proceed; if no probable cause is found, there is still right of access to complaint and board's findings). *But see generally* Note, *A First Amendment Right of Access to Judicial Disciplinary Proceedings*, 132 U. PA. L. REV. 1163 (1984).

[300]784 F.2d at 473–77, 12 Media L. Rep. at 1758–61.

[301]*Id.* at 474, 12 Media L. Rep. at 1758 (quoting Richmond Newspapers v. Virginia, 448 U.S. 555, 588, 6 Media L. Rep. 1833, 1847 (1980) (Brennan, J., concurring)).

[302]*Id.* at 473, 12 Media L. Rep. at 1758.

[303]*Id.* at 476–77, 12 Media L. Rep. at 1760–61.

[304]A.S. Abell Pub'g Co. v. Board of Regents of Univ. of Md., 514 A.2d 25, 13 Media L. Rep. 1359 (Md. Ct. Spec. App. 1986) (state university task force investigating student athlete's death); Johnson Newspaper Corp. v. Melino, 547 N.Y.S.2d 915, 17 Media L. Rep. 1060 (N.Y. App. Div. 1989) (no right of access to teacher disciplinary hearings), *aff'd*, 564 N.E.2d 1046, 18 Media L. Rep. 1551 (N.Y. 1990). *See also* Marion County Sheriff's Merit Bd. v. Peoples Broadcasting Corp., 547 N.E.2d 235, 17 Media L. Rep. 1521 (Ind. 1989) (no First Amendment right to attend deliberations of agency that had already held public hearing on disciplinary charges against sheriff's deputy).

[305]Nero v. Hyland, 386 A.2d 846, 3 Media L. Rep. 2367 (N.J. 1978) (any common law right of access to records of investigation of governor's nominee to lottery commission outweighed by need to effectively screen nominees); Gartner v. United States Info. Agency, 726 F. Supp. 1183 (S.D. Iowa 1989) (no First Amendment right to copy U.S. Information Agency documents where contents of documents had already been disclosed); Yeste v. Miami Herald Pub'g Co., 451 So. 2d 491, 10 Media L. Rep. 2298 (Fla. Dist. Ct. App. 1984) (rejecting First Amendment access right to cause of death portion of death certificate); Birmingham News Co. v. Roper, 4 Media L. Rep. 1075 (N.D. Ala. 1978) (weekly listing of births and deaths); Combined Communications Corp. v. Boger, 689 F. Supp. 1065, 15 Media L. Rep. 2365 (W.D. Okla. 1988) (no First Amendment right of access to NCAA letter to university about alleged rules violations); News & Observer Pub'g Co. v. State, 322 S.E.2d 133 (N.C. 1984) (no First Amendment access right to state police records); Calder v. Internal Revenue Serv., 890 F.2d 781, 17 Media L. Rep. 1283 (5th Cir. 1989) (no First Amendment right of access to IRS records relating to its tax investigation of Al Capone); Register Div. of Freedom Newspapers v. County of Orange, 205 Cal. Rptr. 92, 96 (Cal. Ct. App. 1984) ("a newspaper has no special constitutional right of access to [public records]"). *But see* ACLU of Miss. v. Mississippi, 911 F.2d 1066, 18 Media L. Rep. 1056 (5th Cir. 1990) (finding common law but rejecting First Amendment right of access to State Sovereignty Commission records).

[306]435 U.S. 589, 597, 608, 3 Media L. Rep. 2074, 2077, 2082 (1978). This case was decided before any of the Supreme Court's other access cases.

While some courts before and after *Nixon* have found a First Amendment right of access to inspect and copy criminal evidence,[307] other courts have relied solely on the common law right of access.[308]

§1.8(A) Criminal Records

In *Nixon v. Warner Communications,* Justice Powell's opinion for the Court framed the issue as whether the trial court should release to the media "certain ["Watergate"] tapes admitted into evidence," noting that the media wished "to copy the tapes for broadcasting and sale to the public."[309] In the Supreme Court, none of the criminal defendants sought to prevent media access to the audiotape evidence; instead, a nonparty, President Richard Nixon, objected to copying.[310] The Court noted that the audiotape evidence had been obtained through subpoenas issued by the Watergate Special Prosecutor on two separate occasions.[311] After the trial court had listened to the subpoenaed audiotapes in camera, it arranged to have copies made of only the "relevant and admissible portions";[312] these approximately 22 hours of edited tapes were played in open court for the jury and the public during the trial. Furthermore, everyone present in the courtroom received special earphones and transcripts prepared by the Special Prosecutor. These transcripts, unlike the audiotapes, were not admitted into evidence but were "widely reprinted" in the media.[313]

The media first filed a motion to inspect and copy the audiotapes six weeks after the trial had begun. The motion was transferred to another judge, Judge Gerhard Gesell, who granted the media's motion, holding that the "common-law privilege of public access to judicial records" permitted the media to inspect and copy the audiotapes.[314] Judge Gesell was dissatisfied with the proposed copying procedures he received and transferred disposition of the access requests back to the trial judge, Judge John Sirica, for handling.[315] Judge Sirica then denied without prejudice the media's petitions for immediate access to the tapes, reasoning that the "release of the transcripts had apprised the public of the tapes' contents, the public's 'right to know' did not . . . overcome the need to safeguard the defendant's [fair trial] rights on appeal."[316]

The media appealed this decision to the District of Columbia Circuit Court of Appeals, which reversed and remanded for development of a plan for release.[317]

---

[307] In re State-Record Co., 917 F.2d 124, 128, 18 Media L. Rep. 1286, 1289 (4th Cir. 1990) (substantial probability rather than reasonable likelihood is the test); Associated Press v. United States Dist. Ct., 705 F.2d 1143, 9 Media L. Rep. 1617 (9th Cir. 1983) (post-*Nixon*); United States v. Carpentier, 526 F. Supp. 292, 7 Media L. Rep. 2332 (E.D.N.Y. 1981) (post-*Nixon*); Northwest Pubns. v. Anderson, 259 N.W.2d 254, 3 Media L. Rep. 1302 (Minn. 1977) (pre-*Nixon*).

[308] *See, e.g.,* United States v. Criden (Criden III), 681 F.2d 919, 8 Media L. Rep. 2062 (3d. Cir. 1982); In re NBC (Jenrette), 653 F.2d 609, 7 Media L. Rep. 1193 (D.C. Cir. 1981); United States v. Criden (Criden I), 648 F.2d 814, 7 Media L. Rep. 1153 (3d. Cir. 1981); In re NBC (Myers), 635 F.2d 945, 6 Media L. Rep. 1961 (2d Cir. 1980). *See generally* Marburger, *In Defense of Broadcaster Access to Evidentiary Video and Audio Tapes,* 44 U. Pitt. L. Rev. 647 (1983); Note, *The Common Law Right to Inspect and Copy Judicial Records: In Camera or On Camera,* 16 Ga. L. Rev. 659 (1982).

[309] 435 U.S. at 591–96, 3 Media L. Rep. at 2074–77.
[310] *Id.* at 600–602, 3 Media L. Rep. at 2078–79.
[311] *Id.* at 591–92, 3 Media L. Rep. at 2075.
[312] *Id.* at 593, 3 Media L. Rep. at 2075.
[313] *Id.* at 592–93, 3 Media L. Rep. at 2075–76.
[314] 435 U.S. at 595, 3 Media L. Rep. at 2076.
[315] *Id.*
[316] *Id.* (quoting United States v. Mitchell, 386 F. Supp. 639, 641, 643–44 (D.D.C. 1974)).
[317] *Id.* at 595, 3 Media L. Rep. at 2076 (citing United States v. Mitchell, 397 F. Supp. 186, 188–89

The Supreme Court granted review and then squarely rejected the media's claim that there was either a First or Sixth Amendment right of access to the tapes.[318] However, the Court upheld a "common-law right of access to judicial records."[319] While recognizing the long-standing existence of this right,[320] the Court held that the right is "not absolute" and that "the decision as to access is one best left to the sound discretion of the trial court, a discretion to be exercised in light of the relevant facts and circumstances of the particular case."[321] The Court gave the following examples of circumstances in which courts exercising their "supervisory power over [their] own records and files" might deny the media their common law right to inspect and copy: to prevent court files (1) from being " 'used to gratify private spite or promote public scandal' through the publication of 'the painful and sometimes disgusting details of a divorce case,' " (2) from serving "as reservoirs of libelous statements for press consumption," and (3) from serving as "sources of business information that might harm a litigant's competitive standing."[322]

The Court gave no further guidance as to "the contours of the common-law right."[323] And, while setting forth both the media's and President Nixon's reasons for and against release of the audiotapes, the Court refused to decide "how the balance would be struck if the case were resolved only on the basis of [those] facts and arguments."[324] Thus, the Court did not decide (1) what kinds of third-party privacy and property interests in a witness' voice and conversations on tape overcome the common law right of access,[325] (2) what fair trial rights of a defendant yet to be tried or who may be retried will overcome the common law right of access,[326] and (3) whether the common law

---

(D.D.C. 1975), rev'd, 551 F.2d 1252, 2 Media L. Rep. 1097 (D.C. Cir. 1976), rev'd, 435 U.S. 589, 3 Media L. Rep. 2074 (1978)).

[318]Id. at 608–09, 3 Media L. Rep. at 2082–83. The Court held that there was no First Amendment right because the media "[were] permitted to listen to the tapes and report on what was heard." The only thing the media were denied was physical access to the tapes to copy them. Id. at 609, 3 Media L. Rep. at 2082. In addition, "the opportunity of members of the public and the press to attend the trial and to report what they have observed" satisfied the Sixth Amendment public trial guarantee. Id. at 610, 3 Media L. Rep. at 2083. However, a constitutional right of access to documents submitted in connection with criminal proceedings is now well established, based on more recent Supreme Court decisions. Globe Newspaper Co. v. Pokaski, 868 F.2d 497, 16 Media L. Rep. 1385 (1st Cir. 1989) (records in criminal cases ending with not guilty or no probable cause finding); Associated Press v. United States Dist. Ct., 705 F.2d 1143, 1145, 9 Media L. Rep. 1617, 1618 (9th Cir. 1983) (documents filed in pretrial proceedings); In re Washington Post Co., 807 F.2d 383, 390, 13 Media L. Rep. 1793, 1798 (4th Cir. 1986) (documents filed in connection with plea and sentencing hearings); In re New York Times Co., 828 F.2d 110, 114, 14 Media L. Rep. 1625, 1627 (2d Cir. 1987) (documents filed in connection with pretrial suppression hearings), cert. denied, 485 U.S. 977 (1988); United States v. Peters, 754 F.2d 753, 763, 11 Media L. Rep. 1513, 1520 (7th Cir. 1985) (trial exhibits); United States v. Smith, 776 F.2d 1104, 1111, 12 Media L. Rep. 1345, 1350 (3d Cir. 1985) (bill of particulars).

[319]435 U.S. at 597, 3 Media L. Rep. at 2077.
[320]Id. at 597 n.7, 3 Media L. Rep. at 2077 n.7.
[321]Id. at 598–99, 3 Media L. Rep. at 2077–78.
[322]Id. at 598, 3 Media L. Rep. at 2077–78.
[323]Id. at 599, 3 Media L. Rep. at 2078.
[324]435 U.S. at 603, 3 Media L. Rep. at 2079.
[325]Id. at 599–602, 3 Media L. Rep. at 2078–79 (recitation of Nixon's privacy/property interest arguments about use of tapes). Compare, e.g., United States v. Criden (Criden III), 681 F.2d 919, 8 Media L. Rep. 2062 (3d Cir. 1982) (selective redaction of tapes' references to third parties that will cause "serious harm," not "mere embarrassment," proper) with In re KSTP Television, 504 F. Supp. 360, 6 Media L. Rep. 2249 (D. Minn. 1980) (no access to videotape evidence of rape victim's treatment by defendant because victim's privacy rights outweigh any access right). This issue is discussed in greater detail infra notes 354, 359–63, and 378.

[326]435 U.S. at 602 n.14, 3 Media L. Rep. at 2079 n.14 (noting that defendants' fair trial rights, which were Judge Sirica's principal reason for refusing to release tapes, no longer at issue because defendants' appeals had been resolved). Compare, e.g., In re NBC (Jenrette), 653 F.2d 609, 7 Media L. Rep. 1193 (D.C.

right of access includes a right to inspect and copy evidence contemporaneously with its introduction and use at trial.[327]

Ultimately, the Court reversed the Court of Appeals because of the Presidential Recordings and Materials Preservation Act of 1974,[328] an issue that was neither advanced by the parties nor considered by the lower courts.[329] Therefore, the Court's final disposition of "this concededly singular case"[330] rested on the narrow holding that the "presence of an alternative means of public access [the procedures to be established under the Act] tips the scales in favor of denying release" of the tapes to the media despite their common law access right.[331]

In their dissenting opinion, Justices White and Brennan agreed with the majority of the Court that the Act was dispositive of the access issue;[332] interpreting the provisions of that Act differently, however, they concluded that the trial court should be ordered to surrender its copies of the tape evidence to the Administrator for disposition.[333] In contrast, Justice Thurgood Marshall's separate dissent felt that the Act "strongly indicates that the tapes should be released to the public as directed by the Court of Appeals."[334]

In his separate dissent, Justice John Paul Stevens characterized the majority's reliance on the Act as "ironic, to put it mildly,"[335] since the Act Administrator's latest regulations for copying Nixon's Watergate tapes deferred to the procedures established by the trial court.[336] Justice Stevens further echoed Justice Marshall's interpretation of the Act as "far from requiring the District Court to suppress these tapes, [it] manifests Congress' settled resolve 'to provide as much public access to the materials as is physically possible as quickly as possible.' "[337]

Just as the well-publicized Watergate affair created the first major opportunity for courts to decide the media's right of access to evidence admitted at trial, prosecutions arising out of the sweeping Federal Bureau of Investigation undercover "sting" operation known as "Abscam" spawned a series of opinions that recognized the media's common law right to copy videotaped evidence admitted and played during these trials.[338] In *In re NBC (Myers), In re*

Cir. 1981) (defendant's "hypothetical" retrial not sufficient to delay access) *with* Belo Broadcasting Corp. v. Clark, 654 F.2d 423, 7 Media L. Rep. 1841 (5th Cir. 1981) (trial court did not abuse discretion in finding access to tapes could prejudice fair trial rights of defendant yet to be tried). This issue is discussed in greater detail *infra* notes 338–42, 353, and 356–58.

[327]435 U.S. at 602–03, 3 Media L. Rep. at 2079–80 (discussion of timing of release of tapes). See also *id.* at 602–03, 3 Media L. Rep. at 2079, where the Court suggested that the trial court's responsibility as custodian of records "does not permit copying upon demand." Whether this reference indicated the Court's disapproval of contemporaneous access is uncertain. *See infra* notes 351 and 352.

[328]435 U.S. at 605–06, 3 Media L. Rep. at 2081.

[329]*Id.* at 603, 3 Media L. Rep. at 2080.

[330]*Id.* at 608, 3 Media L. Rep. at 2082.

[331]*Id.* at 606, 3 Media L. Rep. at 2081. Furthermore, the Court expressed its opinion that the Act's Administrator "remains free . . . to design such procedures for public access as he believes will advance the policies of the Act" and refused to consider the constitutionality and statutory validity of any procedures he had established under the Act. *Id.* at 607–08, 3 Media L. Rep. at 2081–82.

[332]*Id.* at 611, 3 Media L. Rep. at 2083.

[333]435 U.S. at 613–17, 3 Media L. Rep. at 2083–84 (White, J., dissenting).

[334]*Id.* at 613–15, 3 Media L. Rep. at 2084 (Marshall, J., dissenting).

[335]*Id.* at 616, 3 Media L. Rep. at 2086 (Stevens, J., dissenting).

[336]*Id.* at 616 n.5, 3 Media L. Rep. at 2085–86 n.5 (Stevens, J., dissenting).

[337]*Id.* at 615–16, 3 Media L. Rep. at 2085 (quoting S. REP. NO. 368, 94th Cong., 1st Sess. 13 (1975); H.R. REP. NO. 560, 94th Cong., 1st Sess. 16 (1975)) (Stevens, J., dissenting).

[338]United States v. Criden (Criden III), 681 F.2d 919, 8 Media L. Rep. 2062 (3d Cir. 1982); In re NBC (Jenrette), 653 F.2d 609, 7 Media L. Rep. 1193 (D.C. Cir. 1981); United States v. Criden (Criden I), 648

NBC (Jenrette), and *In re NBC (Criden I)*, the Second, District of Columbia, and Third Circuits, respectively, each found a strong presumption in favor of the common law right of access, because the Abscam cases involved issues of major public importance regarding the alleged misconduct of members of Congress and other public officials.[339]

In all of these cases the defendants opposed access, arguing that release of the tape evidence would prejudice their fair trial rights. In *Myers,* the Second Circuit held that such alleged prejudice to other defendants facing trial was too speculative and suggested that a careful voir dire be used if necessary to eliminate any potential jurors tainted by publicity from the prior trial.[340] In *Jenrette,* the District of Columbia Circuit held that possible prejudice to a defendant should his case be retried was too "hypothetical" to delay release of the tape evidence to the media.[341] Finally, in *Criden I,* the Third Circuit held that trial courts deciding such access requests must distinguish between "hypothetical" and "actual" prejudice caused by publicity.[342]

In *Criden I,* however, the court did hold that third-party privacy concerns could be a legitimate basis to deny permission to copy specific portions of audio and videotape evidence.[343] The Third Circuit considered this specific issue again in *Criden III,* holding that the district court, on remand from *Criden I,* should have personally reviewed and redacted the tapes for material regarding third parties that would cause "serious harm," not "mere embarrassment."[344] The court also held that permitting the government to excise all third-party references, whether innocuous or not, was improper.[345]

Many other courts also have acknowledged the media's common law right to copy audio and videotape evidence admitted during a criminal trial.[346] Although these cases recognized the media's right of access, the rationales for extending that right to a particular type of audio- or videotape material have varied widely. For example, in *In re ABC (Hinckley),*[347] the trial court adhered

---

F.2d 814, 7 Media L. Rep. 1153 (3d Cir. 1981); In re NBC (Myers), 635 F.2d 945, 6 Media L. Rep. 1961 (2d Cir. 1980). *See also* United States v. Carpentier, 526 F. Supp. 292, 7 Media L. Rep. 2332 (E.D.N.Y. 1981) (First Amendment right of access to Abscam audiotape evidence, although not played in court during public sentencing hearing).

[339]*Myers,* 635 F.2d at 951–53, 6 Media L. Rep. at 1965–66; *Jenrette,* 653 F.2d at 613–14, 7 Media L. Rep. at 1196; *Criden I,* 648 F.2d at 824–26, 7 Media L. Rep. at 1161–62.

[340]635 F.2d at 952–54, 6 Media L. Rep. at 1966–67.

[341]653 F.2d at 618–19, 7 Media L. Rep. at 1200. The court expressly relied on its discussion of fair trial rights in United States v. Mitchell, 551 F.2d 1252, 2 Media L. Rep. 1097 (D.C. Cir. 1976), *rev'd on other grounds,* 435 U.S. 589, 3 Media L. Rep. 2074 (1978).

[342]648 F.2d at 827, 7 Media L. Rep. at 1163 ("Accordingly, the danger to defendants' fair trial rights on a possible retrial is not based on the trial court's experience in this case, but rather on its conjecture about possible future difficulties.").

[343]*Id.* at 829, 7 Media L. Rep. at 1165.

[344]*Criden III,* 681 F.2d 919, 921–22, 8 Media L. Rep. 2062, 2064–65 (3d Cir. 1982).

[345]*Id.* The court noted that "[v]ery few of the references to third parties . . . rise to the level of 'intensified pain,' as distinguished from mere embarrassment . . . *particularly because the transcripts of these conversations are already public information." Id.* at 922, 8 Media L. Rep. at 2065 (emphasis added). *Accord* United States v. Thompson, 17 Media L. Rep. 1004, 1005–06 (D.C. Cir. 1989) (once evidence is known to public there is almost never justification for preventing its copying).

[346]United States v. Torres, 602 F. Supp. 1458, 11 Media L. Rep. 1661 (N.D. Ill. 1985); United States v. Mouzin, 559 F. Supp. 463, 9 Media L. Rep. 1357 (C.D. Cal. 1983); In re CBS (Shannon), 540 F. Supp. 769, 8 Media L. Rep. 1833 (N.D. Ill. 1982); United States v. Pageau, 535 F. Supp. 1031, 8 Media L. Rep. 1270 (N.D.N.Y. 1982); United States v Reiter, 7 Media L. Rep. 1927 (D. Md. 1981); United States v. Sanders, 611 F. Supp. 45, 11 Media L. Rep. 1666 (S.D. Fla. 1985) (access to videotapes upheld); In re ABC, 10 Media L. Rep. 1828 (N.D. Ill. 1984) (videotapes admitted into evidence in criminal trial can be copied), *application granted sub nom.* United States v. Wolfson, 10 Media L. Rep. 2047 (N.D. Ill. 1984).

[347]537 F. Supp. 1168, 8 Media L. Rep. 1441 (D.D.C. 1982).

to one criterion: whether the taped material was "evidence" to be offered to the jury. Using this criterion, the trial court permitted the media to copy audiotapes of actress Jodie Foster's conversations with Hinckley, which were to be played to the jury at trial, but denied access to a videotaped deposition of Foster.[348] In contrast, the district court in *In re CBS (Shannon)*[349] permitted the media to copy tape-recorded conversations involving the alleged corruption of a public agency, which were played in open court during a sentencing hearing but were not admitted in evidence, holding that "the policy behind the common law presumption of access is that what transpires in the courtroom is public property."[350]

Moreover, the Second Circuit in *Myers* held that only the "most extraordinary circumstances" justify prohibiting the media from copying taped evidence contemporaneously with its introduction at trial.[351] One court held, however, that the media need only have a right to copy such evidence, once admitted, on a daily basis, which did not include the right to install wires to record simultaneously the taped materials as they were played in court.[352]

Despite the numerous decisions granting the media access to taped evidence, courts have sometimes denied such access either to protect a defendant's fair trial rights[353] or to safeguard asserted third-party privacy interests.[354] Courts have occasionally denied access for other reasons.[355]

In *Belo Broadcasting Corp. v. Clark*,[356] the Fifth Circuit interpreted *Nixon* more narrowly than other circuits did in *Myers, Jenrette,* and *Criden I*. The

---

[348]*Id.* at 1170–71, 1173, 8 Media L. Rep. at 1442, 1444. *Accord* United States v. Miller, 579 F. Supp. 862, 10 Media L. Rep. 1321 (S.D. Fla. 1984) (common law right of access to audio- and videotapes played at trial but not to tapes that were not played); In re WFMJ Broadcasting Co., 566 F. Supp. 1036, 9 Media L. Rep. 1622 (N.D. Ohio 1983) (right to copy tapes only after jury has heard them). *Compare* In re CBS, Inc., 828 F.2d 958, 14 Media L. Rep. 1636 (2d Cir. 1987) (recognized right to copy videotaped deposition of criminal witness who was too ill to testify at trial).

[349]540 F. Supp. 769, 8 Media L. Rep. 1833 (N.D. Ill. 1982).

[350]*Id.* at 771 n.3, 8 Media L. Rep. at 1834 n.3. *Accord* United States v. Martin, 746 F.2d 964, 10 Media L. Rep. 2465 (3d Cir. 1984) (allowing access to transcripts of audiotapes where transcripts not admitted into evidence but provided to jury); State v. Grecco, 455 A.2d 485, 487, 8 Media L. Rep. 2645, 2646 (N.J. Super. 1982) (press granted access to transcripts of tapes played in open court, even though tapes not admitted into evidence, because they are "means to understand" what reporters listened to in open court).

[351]In re NBC (Myers), 635 F.2d 945, 951, 6 Media L. Rep. 1961, 1965 (2d Cir. 1980); *see also* Valley Broadcasting Co. v. United States Dist. Ct. (Spilotro), 798 F.2d 1289, 13 Media L. Rep. 1347 (9th Cir. 1986) (common law right to inspect and copy audio- and videotape exhibits as they are received into evidence during criminal trial; right can only be denied if strong presumption in favor of access overcome by articulated facts).

[352]United States v. Torres, 602 F. Supp 1458, 1462–64, 11 Media L. Rep. 1661, 1663–65 (N.D. Ill. 1985). The trial court based its denial on Judical Canon 3(A)(7) and a local court rule regarding the broadcasting of trial proceedings, thereby comparing this type of simultaneous access to the actual filming of a criminal trial, which is discussed in more detail *infra* §1.10. *Myers* also approved copying at the end of each court session. *Myers,* 635 F.2d at 952 n.7, 6 Media L. Rep. at 1966 n.7. *See also* United States v. Eaves, 685 F. Supp. 1243, 15 Media L. Rep. 1300 (N.D. Ga. 1988) (delaying release of tapes of defendant accepting bribe until close of evidence).

[353]United States v. Beckham, 789 F.2d 401, 12 Media L. Rep. 2073 (6th Cir. 1986); United States v. Edwards, 672 F.2d 1289, 8 Media L. Rep. 1145 (7th Cir. 1982); Belo Broadcasting Corp. v. Clark, 654 F.2d 423, 7 Media L. Rep. 1841 (5th Cir. 1981); United States v. Bolen, 8 Media L. Rep. 1048 (S.D. Fla. 1981).

[354]United States v. Hubbard, 650 F.2d 293, 6 Media L. Rep. 1909 (D.C. Cir. 1980); In re KSTP Television, 504 F. Supp. 360, 6 Media L. Rep. 2249 (D. Minn. 1980). *See also infra* note 447.

[355]*See, e.g.,* In re Post-Newsweek Stations, 722 F.2d 325, 10 Media L. Rep. 1087 (6th Cir. 1983) (contemporaneous access to videotapes during trial denied by appellate court because district court had not issued final decision); *Beckham,* 789 F.2d at 411, 12 Media L. Rep. at 2080 (denial of transcripts within trial court's discretion where "numerous errors in the transcripts" found). *Contra* United States v. Guzzino, 766 F.2d 302, 11 Media L. Rep. 2215 (7th Cir. 1985) (error to deny access to audiotapes admitted into evidence at criminal trial even though tapes were poor and might be misunderstood).

[356]654 F.2d 423, 7 Media L. Rep. 1841 (5th Cir. 1984).

court concluded that "the opinion in *Nixon v. Warner Communications* offers no basis from which one can derive the overpowering presumption in favor of access discovered by the Second and District of Columbia Circuits. The Supreme Court there neither drafted explicit limits nor assigned specific weight to this common law right of access."[357] The Fifth Circuit therefore concluded that decisions regarding the common law right of access can be reviewed only for abuse of discretion, and the trial court had not abused its discretion because it denied access to protect the fair trial rights of defendants still to be tried.[358]

In *United States v. Hubbard*,[359] the District of Columbia Circuit discovered a distinct right of privacy that might outweigh the common law right of access. The court stayed an order unsealing third-party documents of the Church of Scientology, introduced en masse under seal at a pretrial suppression hearing, to demonstrate the unlawfulness of a search and seizure conducted by the prosecution.[360] Quoting *Nixon*'s limited exceptions for denying access " 'where court files might have become a vehicle for improper purposes,' "[361] the court interpreted this language to extend to "where a third party's property and privacy rights are at issue."[362] The court held that these privacy rights were particularly strong because the Scientology documents had been introduced into evidence during a suppression hearing at which they proved to be neither relevant to the crimes charged by the prosecution nor necessary to the trial court's decision on the suppression motion.[363]

Courts have extended the common law right of access to types of criminal evidence beyond the audio- and videotape material involved in *Nixon* and the Abscam cases, permitting the media to inspect and copy hearing transcripts,[364] complete court files previously sealed under a "blanket" order,[365] plea agree-

---

[357]*Id.* at 433, 7 Media L. Rep. at 1848.

[358]*Accord Beckham*, 789 F.2d at 411, 12 Media L. Rep. at 2080 ("When weighing the Sixth Amendment right to a fair trial against the First Amendment right to be present at criminal trials and report on them, the justifications for barring access . . . must be compelling. [Citations omitted.] But here the Media's right at issue is the common-law right to inspect and copy public records. . . . Although we might have weighed the factors differently, we do not find that the district court's balancing process constituted an abuse of discretion."); United States v. Webbe, 791 F.2d 103, 12 Media L. Rep. 2193 (8th Cir. 1986) (same); United States v. Evans, 16 Media L. Rep. 1174 (N.D. Ga. 1989) (same); In re Pacific & S. Co., 361 S.E.2d 159, 14 Media L. Rep. 1764 (Ga. 1987) (media have no right to criminal trial evidence consisting of videotapes of crime scene and murder defendant's statement to police, even after conviction, because appeal process not complete). *But see* United States v. Finley, 16 Media L. Rep. 1735 (N.D. Ill. 1989) (criminal defendant's mere assertion that jury may be unduly prejudiced by disclosure of copies and transcripts of taped evidence at same time as submitted to jury does not justify denial of access).

[359]650 F.2d 293, 6 Media L. Rep. 1909 (D.C. Cir. 1980).

[360]*Id.* at 296–302, 6 Media L. Rep. at 1910–16.

[361]*Id.* at 314–15, 6 Media L. Rep. at 1927–28.

[362]*Id.* at 319, 6 Media L. Rep. at 1931.

[363]*Id.* at 321–22, 6 Media L. Rep. at 1933. *Compare* In re CBS, Inc., 828 F.2d 958, 14 Media L. Rep. 1636 (2d Cir. 1987) (recognizing right to copy videotaped deposition of criminal witness too ill to testify at trial; witness' privacy concerns not compelling).

[364]United States v. Brooklier, 685 F.2d at 1162, 1172–73, 8 Media L. Rep. 2177, 2183–84 (9th Cir. 1982) (First Amendment right of access to transcripts of three closed hearings); *see also* discussions of this case *supra* §1.4(A); Reilly v. McKnight, 439 N.Y.S.2d 727, 7 Media L. Rep. 1445 (N.Y. App. Div. 1981), *aff'd*, 430 N.E.2d 922 (N.Y. 1981) (access to preliminary hearing transcript); United States v. Posner, 594 F. Supp. 930, 11 Media L. Rep. 1560 (S.D. Fla. 1984) (recognizing First Amendment right to inspect and copy criminal defendant's income tax returns introduced into evidence at codefendant's trial). *But see* Honolulu Advertiser v. Takao, 580 P.2d 58, 4 Media L. Rep. 1423 (Haw. 1978) (order prohibiting access to preliminary hearing transcript upheld to protect fair trial rights of rape defendant; media had attended hearing).

[365]Associated Press v. United States Dist. Ct., 705 F.2d 1143, 9 Media L. Rep. 1617 (9th Cir. 1983) (First Amendment right of access to all court filings in DeLorean prosecution previously sealed under

ments,[366] documents related to attempts to recuse a judge and disqualify defense attorneys,[367] and *Brady*[368] materials.[369] On the other hand, some courts have denied access to bills of particulars, indictments, and informations,[370] while others have permitted access.[371] In one case, the court even permitted the sealing of the trial briefs.[372]

Several courts have recently considered whether the media are entitled to access to search warrants and related materials. While some courts have found that the media have a qualified First Amendment right of access to search warrant materials[373] or a common law right of access,[374] other courts have held

---

"blanket" order); Northwest Pubns. v. Anderson, 259 N.W.2d 254, 3 Media L. Rep. 1302 (Minn. 1977) (First Amendment right of access to sealed court files of pending murder prosecution). *See also* State v. Cianci, 496 A.2d 139, 11 Media L. Rep. 2403 (R.I. 1985) (protective order sealing all pretrial discovery documents in controversial criminal case against mayor of Providence improper unless (1) narrowly tailored, (2) only reasonable alternative, (3) access permitted to nonsensitive parts of record, and (4) made findings explaining need for sealing).

[366]United States v. Northrop Corp., 746 F. Supp. 1002, 17 Media L. Rep. 2262 (C.D. Cal. 1990) (exhibit to plea agreement listing matters government would not prosecute unsealed, rejecting claim that unsealing would compromise grand jury secrecy). *See also infra* note 382.

[367]In re NBC (Presser II), 828 F.2d 340, 14 Media L. Rep. 1417 (6th Cir. 1987) (finding First Amendment right of access but remanding for further proceedings on fair trial issues).

[368]*See* Brady v. Maryland, 373 U.S. 83 (1963) (dealing with evidence in possession of prosecution that is favorable to defendant).

[369]In re Storer Communications (Presser I), 828 F.2d 330, 14 Media L. Rep. 1429 (6th Cir. 1987) (finding First Amendment right of access but remanding for further proceedings on fair trial issues).

[370]United States v. Smith (Appeal of Patriot News Co.), 776 F.2d 1104, 12 Media L. Rep. 1345 (3d Cir. 1985) (privacy interests to be protected involved more than "mere embarrassment" of third parties; unsealing of documents might be "career-ending" for some unindicted coconspirators listed there). *See also* In re New York Times, 9 Media L. Rep. 2077 (N.D. Ga. 1983) (unsealing bill of particulars after trial and grand jury proceedings completed held proper, provided names of unindicted coconspirators redacted).

[371]Worrell Newspapers v. Westhafer, 570 F. Supp. 1447, 9 Media L. Rep. 2222 (S.D. Ind. 1983) (statute authorizing sealed indictments until indicted parties' arrests constitutional, given "compelling" interest in arresting suspects before flight), *rev'd,* 739 F.2d 1219, 10 Media L. Rep. 2088 (7th Cir. 1984), *aff'd,* 469 U.S. 1200 (1985); United States v. General Motors Corp., 352 F. Supp. 1071 (E.D. Mich. 1973) (no Sixth or First Amendment right to seal bill of particulars; unindicted third parties have no special privacy interests against embarrassment).

[372]United States v. Swindall, 16 Media L. Rep. 1990 (N.D. Ga. 1989) (sealing of trial briefs proper where they contained highly sensitive information previously undisclosed that if disclosed on eve of trial could expose potential jurors to possibly inadmissible but inflammatory material).

[373]In re Search Warrant for Secretarial Area Outside Office of Thomas Gunn (Gunn I), 855 F.2d 569, 15 Media L. Rep. 1969 (8th Cir. 1988) (qualified First Amendment right to affidavits and materials supporting search warrants in pre-indictment investigation), *cert. denied,* 488 U.S. 1009 (1989); In re Search Warrants Issued on June 11, 1988, 710 F. Supp. 701, 16 Media L. Rep. 1602 (D. Minn. 1989) (media have qualified First Amendment right to search warrant and wiretap materials but right may be overcome by government showing that disclosure would compromise ongoing investigation); In re Search Warrants Issued on May 21, 1987, 18 Media L. Rep. 1095, 1098 (D.D.C. 1990) (recognizing common law right of access after indictment); In re Sealed Documents, 15 Media L. Rep. 1983 (D.D.C. 1988) (recognizing both First Amendment and common law right of access). *See also* Commonwealth v. Fenstermaker, 530 A.2d 414, 14 Media L. Rep. 1555 (1987) (affidavits issued in support of executed arrest warrants are judicial records and presumptively open); Greenwood v. Wolchik, 544 A.2d 1156, 14 Media L. Rep. 2277 (Vt. 1988) (probable cause affidavits become public documents after judicial officer finds probable cause; "mere possibility" of prejudice to defendant's fair trial rights does not justify sealing).

[374]Baltimore Sun Co. v. Goetz, 886 F.2d 60, 16 Media L. Rep. 2295 (4th Cir. 1989) (affidavits supporting search warrants are judicial records to which qualified common law right of access attaches and can only be sealed upon specific findings that sealing is essential to preserve higher values and is narrowly tailored to serve that end); also referred to in In re Application and Affidavit for Search Warrant, 923 F.2d 324, 18 Media L. Rep. 1593 (4th Cir. 1991) (same, rejecting prejudicial pretrial publicity claim), *cert. denied,* 111 S.Ct. 2243 (1991); In re Newsday, 895 F.2d 74, 17 Media L. Rep. 1385 (2d Cir. 1990) (common law right of access to search warrant application, including wiretap material, where names of innocent third parties redacted and government admits need for secrecy is over), *cert. denied,* 496 U.S. 931 (1990); In re Sealed Documents, 15 Media L. Rep. 1983 (D.D.C. 1988) (recognizing both common law and First Amendment right of access); P.G. Pub'g Co. v. Commonwealth, 566 A.2d 857, 16 Media L. Rep. 2433 (Pa. Super. Ct. 1989) (recognizing common law right of access to search warrants and supporting affidavits, which can be overcome by showing that disclosure will seriously endanger ongoing police investigation).

that there is no First Amendment right of access.[375] Some courts have allowed access on other grounds.[376] The right of access can be overcome by the need to protect an ongoing investigation[377] or third-party privacy interests.[378] In such cases, redaction is the less restrictive alternative.[379] Similarly, cases on access to wiretapped conversations have produced a variety of results.[380]

---

[375]Times-Mirror Co. v. United States, 873 F.2d 1210, 16 Media L. Rep. 1513 (9th Cir. 1989) (no First Amendment right of access to search warrant proceedings and supporting documents while pre-indictment investigation ongoing since proceedings have not traditionally been open, public's legitimate interest in search warrant process is outweighed by substantial potential damage to criminal investigatory process, and significant privacy interests would be jeopardized; no common law right of access or right under FED. R. CRIM. P. 41(g)); Newspapers of New England v. Clerk-Magistrate, 531 N.E.2d 1261, 16 Media L. Rep. 1457 (Mass. 1988), cert. denied, 490 U.S. 1066 (1989) (no First Amendment right of access to search warrant affidavit before indictment); Seattle Times v. Eberharter, 713 P.2d 710, 12 Media L. Rep. 1794 (Wash. 1986) (no First Amendment or state constitutional right of access to search warrant affidavits in unfiled criminal cases). But see Cowles Pub'g Co. v. Murphy, 637 P.2d 966, 7 Media L. Rep. 2400 (Wash. 1981) (right of access to executed warrants and accompanying documents unless there is substantial threat to law enforcement or privacy interests); See Oberlander, A First Amendment Right of Access to Affidavits in Support of Search Warrants, 90 COLUM. L. REV. 2216 (1990). See also Oziel v. Superior Ct., 273 Cal. Rptr. 196, 18 Media L. Rep. 1113 (Cal. Ct. App. 1990) (no right of access to videotape of search warrant execution).

[376]In re Various Search Warrants, 441 N.W.2d 255, 16 Media L. Rep. 1534 (Wis. Ct. App. 1989) (access to search warrant information and subpoenaed materials granted for purpose of preparing action for disclosure of such information); In re Search Warrant for Second Floor Bedroom, 489 F. Supp. 207, 212, 6 Media L. Rep. 1420, 1424 (D.R.I. 1980) (finding access right under FED. R. CRIM. P. 41(g)); see also Baltimore Sun, 886 F.2d at 65, 16 Media L. Rep. at 2298 (basing common law right of access on FED. R. CRIM. P. 41(g)) and Newsday, 895 F.2d 74, 17 Media L. Rep. 1385. But see Times-Mirror Co., 873 F.2d 1210, 16 Media L. Rep. 1513 (no right of access under FED. R. CRIM. P. 41(g)); Seattle Times v. Eberharter, 713 P.2d 710, 12 Media L. Rep. 1794 (Wash. 1986) (no state constitutional right of access).

[377]Certain Interested Individuals v. Pulitzer Pub'g Co. (Gunn II), 895 F.2d 460, 17 Media L. Rep. 1364 (8th Cir.) (substantial probability that ongoing investigation would be severely compromised by release of documents), cert. denied, 498 U.S. 880 (1990); Search Warrants Issued on June 11, 1988, 710 F. Supp. 701, 16 Media L. Rep. 1602 (same); In re Sealed Documents, 15 Media L. Rep. 1983 (D.D.C. 1988) (government's compelling interest in ongoing investigation outweighed public's First Amendment and common law right of access to documents supporting executed search warrants). Compare United States v. Eastern Airlines, 923 F.2d 241, 18 Media L. Rep. 1714 (2d Cir. 1991) (where search warrant executed and government did not oppose disclosure, unsealing proper).

[378]Gunn II, 895 F.2d 460, 17 Media L. Rep. 1364 (privacy interests particularly compelling in pre-indictment phase); Search Warrants Issued on June 11, 1988, 710 F. Supp. at 704–05, 16 Media L. Rep. at 1604 (third-party privacy interests may be sufficiently compelling considering extent of public knowledge of material, accusatory nature of material, and need for public scrutiny of government operations disclosed in material).

[379]In re New York Times Co., 834 F.2d 1152, 1154, 14 Media L. Rep. 2013, 2015 (2d Cir. 1987) (redaction must be done even if it would render document "almost meaningless"), cert. denied, 485 U.S. 977 (1988). Contra Gunn I, 855 F.2d 569, 15 Media L. Rep. 1969 (8th Cir. 1988) (where line-by-line redaction of documents impracticable, sealing proper, but court could not seal docket sheet, which was public record).

[380]United States v. Rosenthal, 763 F.2d 1291, 11 Media L. Rep. 2237 (11th Cir. 1985) (Title III provisions and privacy interests alone cannot bar access to wiretap materials in evidence as legally intercepted communications; court must balance common law right of access against any competing interests); United States v. Dorfman, 690 F.2d 1230, 8 Media L. Rep. 2257 (7th Cir. 1982) (no unsealing of relevant wiretap materials obtained under Title III until admitted into evidence at trial); State ex rel. Bingaman v. Brennan, 645 P.2d 982, 8 Media L. Rep. 1629 (N.M. 1982) (no right of access to wiretap recordings not played in open court or received into evidence even if they resulted in indictments); In re Kansas City Star, 666 F.2d 1168, 7 Media L. Rep. 2353 (8th Cir. 1981) (wiretap material sealed when admitted into evidence during bond revocation hearing can be disclosed only on "good cause" showing); NBC v. United States Dep't of Justice, 735 F.2d 51, 10 Media L. Rep. 1866 (2d Cir. 1984) (NBC, defending libel charges, not permitted access to wiretap material under Title III because unable to make "good cause" showing under 18 U.S.C. §2518(8)(b); court distinguished between litigant seeking access to engage in discovery and media wishing to inspect and copy criminal evidence as part of news gathering activities); In re New York Times Co. (New York Times I), 828 F.2d 110, 14 Media L. Rep. 1625 (2d Cir. 1987) (qualified First Amendment right of access to motion papers cannot be overcome by simply citing Title III; remanding for analysis of Title III issue), cert. denied, 485 U.S. 977 (1988); In re Search Warrants Issued, 18 Media L. Rep. 1095, 1099–1100 (D.D.C. 1990) (recognizing First Amendment access right to Title III materials used to justify search warrants but redacting names of innocent third parties); In re Interception of Wire and Oral Communications (Kattar), 682 F. Supp. 669, 15 Media L. Rep. 1355 (D.N.H. 1988) (no First Amendment or common law right of access to Title III materials).

The cases on access to pre-sentence reports are split.[381] There is a First Amendment right of access to plea agreements and related documents, however.[382]

There is a constitutional right of access to documents concerning payments made to indigent criminal defendants' court-appointed counsel and experts.[383] There is also a constitutional right of access to records in criminal cases involving an acquittal, a dismissal, a nolle prosequi, or a finding of no probable cause, but not to such records if a grand jury does not indict.[384]

With respect to grand jury records, the courts' primary concern is preserving the traditional secrecy of grand jury proceedings, which has been codified in various state and federal rules of procedure.[385] This concern has not, however, prevented courts from granting access to some grand jury records, particularly "ministerial" records[386] or the grand jury's report, including any underlying documentary basis for the findings in that report.[387] While courts have based this access right on the common law[388] and various statutes pertaining to grand juries,[389] they have repeatedly rejected a First Amendment right of access to grand jury records.[390]

---

[381] United States v. Schelette, 854 F.2d 359 (9th Cir. 1988) (media have common law right of access to pre-sentence probation reports despite governmental claim that disclosure would dry up flow of information from informants). *Contra* United States v. Corbitt, 879 F.2d 224, 16 Media L. Rep. 1993 (7th Cir. 1989) (no First Amendment right of access to pre-sentence reports since historically closed and since access would interfere with functions of probation); United States v. Boesky, 674 F. Supp. 1128, 14 Media L. Rep. 2105 (S.D.N.Y. 1987) (nondisclosure of pre-sentence report justified by defendant's involvement in ongoing criminal investigation).

[382] Washington Post Co. v. Robinson, 935 F.2d 282, 18 Media L. Rep. 2027 (D.C. Cir. 1991) (recognizing First Amendment right of access to plea agreements); Oregonian Pub'g Co. v. United States Dist. Ct., 920 F.2d 1462, 18 Media L. Rep. 1504 (9th Cir. 1990), *cert. denied sub nom.* Wolsky v. Oregonian Pub'g Co., 111 St. Ct. 2809 (1991) (same); *see also supra* note 159.

[383] United States v. Suarez, 880 F.2d 626, 630–31, 16 Media L. Rep. 2283, 2286 (2d Cir. 1989) (holding that presumptive constitutional right of access to criminal proceedings extends to documents filed in such proceedings).

[384] Globe Newspaper Co. v. Pokaski, 868 F.2d 497, 509–11, 16 Media L. Rep. 1385, 1395–96 (1st Cir. 1989).

[385] *See, e.g.,* In re Subpoena to Testify Before Grand Jury (Univ. of Fla. Athletic Program), 864 F.2d 1559, 16 Media L. Rep. 1165 (11th Cir. 1989) (no First Amendment right of access to grand jury or related proceedings regarding dispute over compliance with grand jury subpoena); In re Special Grand Jury, 674 F.2d 778, 778–81, 8 Media L. Rep. 1422, 1424 (9th Cir. 1982) (referring to both doctrine of grand jury secrecy and FED. R. CRIM. P. 6(e)); Pigman v. Evansville Press, 537 N.E.2d 547, 16 Media L. Rep. 1688 (Ind. App. 1989) (grand jury subpoenas confidential under state statute). See Branzburg v. Hayes, 408 U.S. 665, 684–85, 1 Media L. Rep. 2617, 2624–25 (1972), which expressly mentioned grand jury proceedings as a recognized exception to the media's right to gather news. *See also supra* note 162.

[386] *Special Grand Jury,* 674 F.2d at 781, 8 Media L. Rep. at 1424 (records showing how grand jury impaneled and operated).

[387] Miami Herald Pub'g Co. v. Marko, 352 So. 2d 518, 3 Media L. Rep. 1542 (Fla. 1977) (access granted to grand jury report and findings critical of unindicted highway patrolman's conduct); In re Grand Jury Presentment, 548 So. 2d 721, 16 Media L. Rep. 2204 (Fla. Dist. Ct. App. 1989) (grand jury presentment that accompanied indictment public record to which right of access attached). *Contra* McClatchy Newspapers v. Superior Ct., 751 P.2d 1329, 15 Media L. Rep. 1529 (Cal. 1988) (court could prevent disclosure of part of proposed grand jury report and seal evidentiary materials gathered during secret investigation since disclosure exceeded grand jury's authority); In re Carey, 5 Media L. Rep. 1158 (N.Y. App. Div. 1979) (upholding trial court's decision not to release two volumes of grand jury report on Attica prison uprising that made reference to grand jury minutes and testimony); United States v. Gurney, 558 F.2d 1202, 1210–11, 3 Media L. Rep. 1081, 1086 (5th Cir. 1977) (upholding trial court's decision to excise from transcript portion of witness' grand jury testimony not read to jury during subsequent trial).

[388] *Special Grand Jury,* 674 F.2d at 780–82, 8 Media L. Rep. at 1423–24 (citing *Nixon*). *See also* State v. Mecham, 15 Media L. Rep. 2151 (Ariz. Super. Ct. 1988) (citing *Press-Enterprise II,* disclosure of transcripts of grand jury proceedings that led to indictment of governor warranted due to interest in having public examine grand jury process).

[389] In re Grand Jury Investig. by Curran, 561 A.2d 974, 16 Media L. Rep. 2238 (Conn. App. Ct. 1989) (under statute media entitled to hearing on request for disclosure of records of grand jury investigation); *Marko,* 352 So. 2d at 520–23, 3 Media L. Rep. at 1544–46 (interpreting Florida statute permitting "repression" of "improper and unlawful" statements included in grand jury report); *Carey,* 5 Media L. Rep. at 1160–63 (interpreting statutes regarding grand jury secrecy).

[390] In re Subpoena to Testify Before Grand Jury, 864 F.2d 1559, 16 Media L. Rep. 1165 (11th Cir. 1989)

Courts have also upheld various expungement statutes, which permit government record-keeping bodies to seal certain arrest and conviction information either after a certain lapse of time or once an individual has obtained permission to have that information removed or "expunged" from his or her record.[391] In these cases, the courts did not base their holdings on a determination that there was no right of access to this type of information: whatever right of access existed, whether under the common law or the First Amendment, was satisfied by the availability of these records to the media and the public before expungement.[392]

Barring a particular reporter from access to court documents is of course impermissible.[393]

§1.8(B) Civil Records

This section discusses the media's right to inspect and copy records from civil proceedings.

§1.8(B)(i) Civil Discovery Materials

In *Seattle Times Co. v. Rhinehart*,[394] the U.S. Supreme Court considered the rights of a media defendant to disclose information that it had obtained through civil discovery procedures that was subject to a protective order[395]

(no First Amendment right of access to grand jury proceedings); Globe Newspaper Co. v. Pokaski, 868 F.2d 497, 16 Media L. Rep. 1385 (1st Cir. 1989) (no First Amendment right of access to grand jury records in cases where no bill issued); *Marko,* 352 So. 2d at 519–21, 3 Media L. Rep. at 1543–44 (refusing to base decision on media's claim of First Amendment access rights).

[391]Herald Co. v. McNeal, 511 F. Supp. 269, 7 Media L. Rep. 1248 (E.D. Mo. 1981); Stephens v. Van Arsdale, 608 P.2d 972, 6 Media L. Rep. 1142 (Kan. 1980). *See also* New Bedford Standard-Times Pub'g Co. v. Clerk of Third Dist. Ct., 387 N.E.2d 110, 4 Media L. Rep. 2393 (Mass. 1979) (statute preventing access to *alphabetical* index of criminal cases and convictions upheld against First Amendment challenge). *Contra Pokaski,* 868 F.2d 497, 16 Media L. Rep. 1385. *See also supra* note 190.

[392]*McNeal,* 511 F. Supp. at 272–73, 7 Media L. Rep. at 1251 ("The information which plaintiff seeks is not totally shielded from public view"; court found no First Amendment violation where arrest records expunged of those persons not charged within 30 days of arrest, not convicted within one year of arrest, acquitted, or against whom charges are dismissed or nolle prossed); *Van Arsdale,* 608 P.2d at 981–85, 6 Media L. Rep. at 1149–52 ("legislative policy to expunge criminal records after the lapse of a considerable period of time and after an appropriate judicial proceeding has been conducted" does not violate common law right of access). *See also New Bedford Standard-Times,* 387 N.E.2d at 116, 4 Media L. Rep. at 2397 (access to same records available through chronological index).

[393]United States v. Peters, 754 F.2d 753, 763, 11 Media L. Rep. 1513, 1520 (7th Cir. 1985) (judge could not bar particular reporter from access to trial exhibits available to other members of press). *See also infra* note 429.

[394]467 U.S. 20, 10 Media L. Rep. 1705 (1984). *See generally* Cohen, *Access to Pretrial Documents Under the First Amendment,* 84 COLUM. L. REV. 1813 (1984); Note, *Protective Orders and Commercial Information—Is Good Cause Enough?* 59 ST. JOHN'S L. REV. 103 (1984).

[395]Federal Rule of Civil Procedure 26(c), on protective orders, states:
Upon motion by a party or by the person from whom discovery is sought, and for good cause shown, the court in which the action is pending or alternatively, on matters relating to deposition, the court in the district where the deposition is to be taken may make any order which justice requires to protect a party or person from annoyance, embarrassment, oppression, or undue burden or expense, including one or more of the following: (1) that the discovery not be had; (2) that the discovery may be had only on specified terms and conditions, including a designation of the time or place; (3) that the discovery may be had only by a method of discovery other than that selected by the party seeking discovery; (4) that certain matters not be inquired into, or that the scope of the discovery be limited to certain matters; (5) that discovery be conducted with no one present except persons designated by the court; (6) that a deposition after being sealed be opened only by order of the court; (7) that a trade secret or other confidential research, development, or commercial information not be disclosed or be disclosed only in a designated way; (8) that the parties simultaneously file specified documents or information enclosed in sealed envelopes to be opened as directed by the court.

entered for "good cause."[396] The Court granted certiorari in *Seattle Times* to "resolve the conflict"[397] between the Washington Supreme Court's upholding of the protective order and the holdings of two federal circuit courts of appeal in *In re Halkin*[398] and *In re San Juan Star Co.*[399]

In *In re Halkin,* the plaintiffs had sought damages and equitable relief against the Central Intelligence Agency and the National Security Agency for alleged unlawful surveillance of their activities opposing the Vietnam War.[400] The defendants obtained a protective order barring the disclosure of documents produced during discovery, including disclosure to the press.[401] The Court of Appeals reversed, concluding that "First Amendment rights attach to materials made available through the discovery process."[402]

In *In re San Juan Star Co.,* the court reviewed a protective order entered in a civil rights action that barred the parties' attorneys from disclosing any information learned through depositions taken after the order's entry; the ban on disclosure extended not only to the press and third parties, but to the attorneys' clients as well.[403] The court established a standard it described as " 'good cause' that incorporates a 'heightened sensitivity' to the First Amendment concerns at stake."[404] Applying this standard, the court upheld the protective order except for that portion of the trial court's order that prohibited counsel from disclosing the depositions' contents to their clients.[405]

In *Seattle Times Co. v. Rhinehart,* the Supreme Court rejected both the strict First Amendment scrutiny of *Halkin* and the looser "heightened sensitivity" standard of *San Juan Star.*[406] Instead, the Court held that, "[w]here ... a protective order is entered on a showing of good cause as required by [Federal Rule of Civil Procedure] 26(c), is limited to the context of pretrial civil discovery, and does not restrict the dissemination of the information gained from other sources, it does not offend the First Amendment."[407]

Seattle Times involved a libel suit brought against the *Seattle Times* and the *Walla Walla Union-Bulletin* for a series of articles about the spiritual leader of a religious group, the Aquarian Foundation.[408] After the lawsuit was filed, the newspaper defendants propounded interrogatories and document production requests asking for, among other things, "the identity of the Foundation's donors during the preceding ten years, and a list of its members during that period."[409] In response to the plaintiff's objections, the media

---

[396] 467 U.S. at 23–25, 10 Media L. Rep. at 1708.
[397] *Id.* at 29, 10 Media L. Rep. at 1709.
[398] 598 F.2d 176, 4 Media L. Rep. 2025 (D.C. Cir. 1979).
[399] 662 F.2d 108, 7 Media L. Rep. 2144 (1st Cir. 1981).
[400] 598 F.2d at 179–80, 4 Media L. Rep. at 2025–26.
[401] *Id.* at 180–82, 4 Media L. Rep. at 2025–28.
[402] *Id.* at 190, 4 Media L. Rep. at 2035. *See also id.* at 188, 4 Media L. Rep. at 2033 (distinguishing International Prods. Corp. v. Koons, 325 F.2d 403 (2d Cir. 1963), as not standing for "extreme proposition" that "plaintiffs voluntarily waived any First Amendment rights in discovery materials when they entered into the discovery process").
[403] 662 F.2d at 111, 7 Media L. Rep. at 2145.
[404] *Id.* at 116, 7 Media L. Rep. at 2149.
[405] *Id.* at 118, 7 Media L. Rep. at 2151. *See also* Doe v. District of Columbia, 697 F.2d 1115 (D.C. Cir. 1983) (protective order prohibiting disclosure of deposition results to clients impermissibly restricted attorney-client relationship).
[406] 467 U.S. at 34–37 & n.23, 10 Media L. Rep. at 1712–13 & n.23.
[407] *Id.* at 37, 10 Media L. Rep. at 1713.
[408] *Id.* at 23, 10 Media L. Rep. at 1706.
[409] *Id.* at 24, 10 Media L. Rep. at 1707.

defendants moved for an order compelling this discovery. The plaintiffs opposed the motion on the grounds that supplying this information would "violate the First Amendment rights of members and donors to privacy, freedom of religion, and freedom of association."[410] Because the defendants had indicated that they intended to use information obtained through discovery to write future articles about the plaintiffs and their lawsuit, the plaintiffs sought a protective order that would prevent the media defendants from disseminating this information.[411]

The trial court granted both the defendants' motion to compel and the plaintiff's motion for a protective order.[412] However, the protective order did not apply to "information gained by means other than the discovery process."[413] The Supreme Court of Washington affirmed, rejecting the newspapers' argument that such an order entered using a "good cause" standard was a "prior restraint" and holding that the plaintiffs had "a recognizable privacy interest" in the information shielded by the protective order.[414]

Justice Lewis Powell's opinion for the U.S. Supreme Court held that a protective order, which limited a litigant's dissemination of information obtained only through use of court processes in a lawsuit, "implicate[d] the First Amendment rights of the restricted party to a far lesser extent than would restraints on dissemination of [other] information."[415] The opinion described discovery as "a matter of legislative grace," concluding that "continued court control over the discovered information does not raise the same spectre of government censorship that such control might suggest in other situations."[416] The Court observed that pretrial depositions and interrogatories are usually conducted in private and "are not public components of a civil trial."[417] The Court also noted that there was no First Amendment problem in this case, at least in part because a party subject to this protective order "may disseminate the identical information covered by the protective order as long as the information is gained through means independent of the court's processes."[418]

Finally, the Court held that trial courts could grant protective orders using the "good cause" standard of Rule 26(c), because that rule "furthers a substantial governmental interest unrelated to the suppression of expression."[419] That "substantial governmental interest" was the encouragement of "[l]iberal discovery ... for the sole purpose of assisting in the preparation and trial, or the settlement, of litigated disputes."[420] Protective orders, according to the Court, are necessary to prevent abuse of the courts' processes that could result when litigants publicly release information "that not only is irrelevant but ... could be damaging to reputation and privacy."[421] The Court noted that "the trial

---

[410] *Id.*
[411] 467 U.S. at 24, 10 Media L. Rep. at 1707.
[412] *Id.* at 25–27, 10 Media L. Rep. at 1707–08.
[413] *Id.* at 26–27, 10 Media L. Rep. at 1707–08.
[414] *Id.* at 28–29, 10 Media L. Rep. at 1709.
[415] *Id.* at 33–34, 10 Media L. Rep. at 1711–12.
[416] 467 U.S. at 33–34, 10 Media L. Rep. at 1711–12 (citing Judge Wilkey's dissenting opinion in In re Halkin, 598 F.2d 176, 206–07, 4 Media L. Rep. 2025, 2047–48 (D.C. Cir. 1979)).
[417] *Id.* (citing Gannett Co. v. DePasquale, 443 U.S. 368, 5 Media L. Rep. 1337 (1979)).
[418] *Id.* at 33–34, 10 Media L. Rep. at 1711–12.
[419] *Id.* at 34–35, 10 Media L. Rep. at 1712.
[420] *Id.*
[421] 467 U.S. at 34–35, 10 Media L. Rep. at 1712.

court[s] have substantial latitude to fashion protective orders" under Rule 26(c), and held that trial courts should be permitted to exercise that latitude without being required to make "burdensome evidentiary findings" or to face "time-consuming interlocutory appeals" that would result from the "heightened First Amendment scrutiny" that *Halkin* and *San Juan Star* required.[422]

The concurring justices found the protective order appropriate for reasons alluded to by the majority opinion, namely the plaintiffs' "interests in privacy and religious freedom."[423] Justices Brennan and Marshall found these interests "sufficient . . . to overcome the protections afforded free expression by the First Amendment."[424] Their concurring opinion described the majority's holding as recognizing that "pre-trial protective orders, designed to limit the dissemination of information gained through the civil discovery process, are subject to scrutiny under the First Amendment."[425]

Before *Seattle Times,* many state and federal courts reviewed the propriety of protective orders either barring a media litigant from disseminating discovery materials or prohibiting the media from inspecting or copying discovery materials from a case; *Seattle Times* rejected the rationales used to decide some of those cases.[426] In other cases, access was granted because the documents subject to the protective order had later been admitted into evidence and therefore had become the kind of documents that both functionally and historically should be considered public records to which the media have a right of access.[427]

---

[422]*Id.* at 36 & n.23, 10 Media L. Rep. at 1713 & n.23.

[423]*Id.* at 38, 10 Media L. Rep. at 1713–14. *Compare* the opinion of the Court, *id.* at 36–37 & n.24, 10 Media L. Rep. at 1713–14 & n.24.

[424]*Id.*

[425]*Id.* at 37, 10 Media L. Rep. at 1713. *See* Plaquemines Comm'n Council Parish v. Delta Dev. Co., 472 So. 2d 560, 11 Media L. Rep. 2353 (La. 1985) (court held pursuant to Louisiana Constitution provision for open courts that protective orders subject to scrutiny if they infringe First Amendment interests, citing same language in *Seattle Times'* opinion relied on in concurrence).

[426]Koster v. Chase Manhattan Bank, 93 F.R.D. 471, 475–80, 8 Media L. Rep. 1155, 1158–62 (S.D.N.Y. 1982) (court refused to enter broad protective order in sexual harassment case, using "good cause" standard that recognized limited First Amendment interest under *Halkin* and *San Juan Star*); Reliance Ins. Co. v. Barron's, 428 F. Supp. 200, 204–05, 2 Media L. Rep. 1641, 1643–45 (S.D.N.Y. 1977) (court found that protective order would act as "prior restraint" on media defendant's rights to use discovery material produced in libel suit; protective order would be impossible to enforce without necessity for impermissibly inquiring in every instance whether media had obtained information from sources outside litigation); Houston Chronicle Pub'g Co. v. Hardy, 678 S.W.2d 495, 10 Media L. Rep. 1841 (Tex. Civ. App. 1984) (court upheld protective order but recognized some First Amendment interest in disseminating information from discovery (citing *Halkin* and *San Juan Star*)), *cert. denied,* 470 U.S. 1052 (1985). *See also* Georgia Gazette Pub'g Co. v. Ramsey, 284 S.E.2d 386, 7 Media L. Rep. 2249 (Ga. 1981) (relying on state constitution and citing *Halkin,* protective order issued against media defendant in invasion of privacy action held to be prior restraint). *But see* In re Agent Orange Prod. Liab. Litig., 96 F.R.D. 582, 583–85, 9 Media L. Rep. 1083, 1084–85 (E.D.N.Y. 1983) (media have no access right to discovery materials and no standing to challenge protective order where litigants have not asserted any interest in disseminating documents).

[427]In re Continental Ill. Sec. Litig., 732 F.2d 1302, 10 Media L. Rep. 1593 (7th Cir. 1984) (media have common law right of access to special litigation committee report admitted into evidence, which was subject to protective order, on corporation's motion to end derivative actions; not reasonable for corporation to assume protective order would extend to using report as evidence in "adjudicative hearing"); Joy v. North, 692 F.2d 880, 894 (2d Cir. 1982) (court reversed trial court's protective order sealing special litigation committee report after court, relying in part on report, entered summary judgment), *cert. denied,* 460 U.S. 1051 (1983); In re Coordinated Pretrial Proceedings in Petroleum Prods. Antitrust Litig, 101 F.R.D. 34, 10 Media L. Rep. 1300 (C.D. Cal. 1984) (court unsealed some documents subject to "umbrella" protective order, such as summary judgment evidence, because of common law right of access, commenting that many documents never would have met "good cause" standard or because of passage of time no longer met standard); In re Agent Orange Prod. Liab. Litig., 98 F.R.D. 539, 9 Media L. Rep. 2001 (E.D.N.Y. 1983) (court decided to release documents subject to "blanket" protective order once they were introduced as exhibits to summary judgment motion, citing media's common law right of access; court mentioned *Halkin*

Since *Seattle Times,* some courts have refused to allow access to discovery materials, concluding that good cause for a protective order had been shown.[428] Other courts have concluded that good cause for a protective order was not shown.[429]

When discovery documents are used as parts of motions, access to them is usually granted,[430] even if they were produced subject to a protective order.[431] However, one leading court has reached the opposite conclusion[432] despite an articulate dissent.[433]

Blanket protective orders covering most discovery and entered into on the parties' stipulation with a judge's perfunctory consent have been successfully

---

and *San Juan Star,* but no First Amendment scrutiny used); Cianci v. New Times Pub'g Co., 88 F.R.D. 562, 6 Media L. Rep. 2502 (S.D.N.Y. 1980) (protective order sealing deposition of plaintiff in libel suit against media vacated because deposition used as evidence in defendant's motion to dismiss); Thomson v. Cash, 377 A.2d 135, 3 Media L. Rep. 1095 (N.H. 1977) (deposition transcript in libel action filed in connection with summary judgment motion); Carter v. Utah Power & Light Co., 800 P.2d 1095, 1098, n.6, 18 Media L. Rep. 1497, 1499 n.6 (Utah 1990) (holding that filed depositions presumptively public but noting split in authorities). *See also supra* notes 278 and 279 and *infra* notes 430 and 452.

[428]Anderson v. Cryovac, Inc., 805 F.2d 1, 13 Media L. Rep. 1721 (1st Cir. 1986) (prejudicial pretrial publicity justified protective order); In re Alexander Grand & Co. Litig., 820 F.2d 352, 355–56, 14 Media L. Rep. 1370, 1373 (11th Cir. 1987) ("fear of adverse publicity, intimidation or other outside forces that could interfere with the free flow of information" constituted good cause); In re Korean Air Lines Disaster, 597 F. Supp. 621, 622, 10 Media L. Rep. 2494, 2495 (D.D.C. 1984) (protective order needed to create "a climate of free exchange with respect to the ongoing pretrial discovery"); Coalition Against Police Abuse v. Superior Ct., 216 Cal. Rptr. 614 (Cal. Ct. App. 1985) (upholding protective order prohibiting dissemination of names of nonparty individuals and organizations contained in discovery material); Courier-Journal v. Marshall, 828 F.2d 361, 14 Media L. Rep. 1561 (6th Cir. 1987) (protective order in civil rights action restricting disclosure of names found on Ku Klux Klan membership list constitutional); Krause v. Rhodes, 535 F. Supp. 338 (N.D. Ohio 1979) (requiring deletion of names of third-party witnesses and investigators to protect privacy rights), *aff'd,* 671 F.2d 212, 8 Media L. Rep. 1130 (6th Cir.), *cert. denied,* 459 U.S. 823 (1982); Pioneer Hi-Bred Int'l v. Holden's Found. Seeds, 105 F.R.D. 76 (N.D. Ind. 1985) (trade secret).

[429]Cipollone v. Liggett Group, 785 F.2d 1108, 1121 (3d Cir. 1986) ("a business will have to show with some specificity that the embarrassment resulting from dissemination of the information would cause a significant harm to its competitive and financial position"), *on remand,* 113 F.R.D. 86 (D.N.J. 1986) (rejecting various justifications for protective order); *North,* 692 F.2d at 894 (protective order denied where only argument for it that disclosure would injure banks' reputation), *cert. denied,* 460 U.S. 1051 (1983); In re Texaco, 84 Bankr. 14, 15 Media L. Rep. 1201 (Bankr. S.D.N.Y. 1988) (extensive previous publicity of similar information defeated request for protective order); Avirgan v. Hall, 118 F.R.D. 252, 254, 14 Media L. Rep. 2136, 2138 (D.D.C. 1987) (requiring "specific facts showing 'clearly defined and serious injury' resulting from [disclosure of] discovery"; "merely conclusory statements" not enough); In re Agent Orange Prod. Liab. Litig., 96 F.R.D. 582, 584, 9 Media L. Rep. 1083, 1084 (E.D.N.Y. 1983) (protective order cannot limit disclosure of information not learned through discovery). Giving access to only one media entity is completely improper, however. *See Cryovac, Inc.,* 805 F.2d at 9, 13 Media L. Rep. at 1727; *supra* note 393. The courts have also been particularly willing to deny protective orders where the lawsuit concerns a matter of public interest. *See, e.g.,* In re Agent Orange Prod. Liab. Litig., 821 F.2d 139, 146 (2d Cir.), *cert. denied,* 484 U.S. 953 (1987); Courier-Journal and Louisville Times Co. v. Peers, 747 S.W.2d 125, 130, 15 Media L. Rep. 1051, 1055 (Ky. 1988) (lawsuit against county officials).

[430]Rushford v. New Yorker Magazine, 846 F.2d 249, 15 Media L. Rep. 1437 (4th Cir. 1988) (recognizing First Amendment right of access to documents attached to summary judgment motion, which is substitute for trial); Littlejohn v. BIC Corp., 851 F.2d 673, 15 Media L. Rep. 1841 (3d Cir. 1988) (noting waiver due to admission of documents at trial). Cases on attachments to discovery motions are split, however. *Compare Cryovac, Inc.,* 805 F.2d at 11–12, 13 Media L. Rep. at 1729–30 (no access in part because of lack of history of access to such motions) *with* Mokhiber v. Davis, 537 A.2d 1100, 1112, 14 Media L. Rep. 2313, 2322 (D.C. 1988) (upholding access and rejecting lack of history of access: "[i]t would make little sense to shut off access for what is, practically speaking, a new kind of judicial process just because that particular procedure did not exist at common law").

[431]*Rushford,* 846 F.2d 249, 15 Media L. Rep. 1437.

[432]In re Reporters Comm. for Freedom of the Press, 773 F.2d 1325, 12 Media L. Rep. 1073 (D.C. Cir. 1985) (authored by Judge (now Justice) Antonin Scalia) (no First Amendment right of access to summary judgment and trial exhibits until judgment entered; refusing to decide common law right of access issue).

[433]*Id.* at 1342, 12 Media L. Rep. at 1087–88 (Wright, J., dissenting) (arguing that there was common law right of access and that First Amendment holding "unnecessary" and "advisory").

attacked,[434] although there is authority supporting them.[435] These orders have been overturned despite arguments that they were relied upon[436] and that they may only be modified if an extraordinary change in circumstances is shown.[437] Indeed, blanket protective orders have been modified even after judgment was entered.[438]

Despite *Seattle Times,* some courts have concluded that the First Amendment must be considered when a protective order is sought;[439] others have reached the opposite conclusion.[440] Some courts have now held that their rules of civil procedure create a presumptive right of access to discovery materials,[441] and in some jurisdictions there are now explicit rules to this effect.[442]

Intervention is the way for the media to raise their objections to protective orders if they are not parties,[443] although failure to formally intervene is not fatal.[444] Third parties may intervene to oppose disclosure,[445] but intervention by the media has sometimes been denied.[446]

---

[434]Public Citizen v. Liggett Group, 858 F.2d 775, 790–91 (1st Cir. 1988), *cert. denied,* 488 U.S. 1030 (1989); In re Coordinated Pretrial Proceedings in Petroleum Prods. Antitrust Litig., 101 F.R.D. 34, 10 Media L. Rep. 1300, 1307 (C.D. Cal. 1984); Sharjah Inv. Co. v. P.C. Telemart, 107 F.R.D. 81, 11 Media L. Rep. 2383 (S.D.N.Y. 1985) (court refused to enforce stipulated protective order because parties had not made "good cause" showing required by FED. R. CIV. P. 26 (c)).

[435]In re Alexander Grant & Co. Litig., 820 F.2d 352, 14 Media L. Rep. 1370 (11th Cir. 1987); Houston Chronicle Pub'g Co. v. Hardy, 678 S.W.2d 495 (Tex. Ct. App. 1984), *cert. denied,* 470 U.S. 1052 (1985); Zenith Radio Corp. v. Matsushita Elec. Indus., 529 F. Supp. 866 (E.D. Pa. 1981).

[436]Brown & Williamson Tobacco Corp. v. Federal Trade Comm'n, 710 F.2d 1165, 1180 (6th Cir. 1983) ("[t]he confidentiality agreement between the parties does not bind the court in any way"); In re Continental Ill. Sec. Litig., 732 F.2d 1302, 1311, 10 Media L. Rep. 1593, 1599–1600 (7th Cir. 1984) (vacating protective order despite claim of prior confidentiality agreement); In re Agent Orange Prod. Liab. Litig., 98 F.R.D. 539, 544, 9 Media L. Rep. 2001, 2005 (E.D.N.Y. 1983) ("[t]he mere fact that a document was submitted under seal does not protect it forever from disclosure"); United States v. Kentucky Utils. Co., 124 F.R.D. 146, 151 (E.D. Ky. 1989) (stipulated protective orders endorsed by court not binding when later challenged by access motion). *But see* In re Consumers Power Co. Sec. Litig., 109 F.R.D. 45, 50 (E.D. Mich. 1985).

[437]Wilk v. American Medical Ass'n, 635 F.2d 1295, 1299–1300 (7th Cir. 1980) (distinguishing contrary cases); Public Citizen v. Liggett Group, 858 F.2d 775, 791, 15 Media L. Rep. 2129, 2142–43 (1st Cir. 1988), *cert. denied,* 488 U.S. 1030 (1989). *See generally* Annot., *Modification of Protective Order Entered Pursuant to Rule 26(c), Federal Rules of Civil Procedure,* 85 A.L.R. FED. 538 (1987).

[438]*Public Citizen,* 858 F.2d at 782, 15 Media L. Rep. at 2135; In re Agent Orange Prod. Liab. Litig., 821 F.2d 139, 147–48 (2d Cir.) (even though disclosure revised "incidental" terms of settlement agreement), *cert. denied,* 484 U.S. 953 (1987); Krause v. Rhodes, 671 F.2d 212, 8 Media L. Rep. 1130 (6th Cir.), *cert. denied,* 459 U.S. 823 (1982). *See also Kentucky Utils. Co.,* 927 F.2d 252, 18 Media L. Rep. 1877 (requiring extraordinary circumstances to justify revision of judgment that provided for destruction of discovery materials). After judgment, however, a court cannot require parties to file previously unfiled discovery requests. *Public Citizen,* 858 F.2d at 781, 15 Media L. Rep. at 2134. *See also infra* note 457.

[439]*See, e.g.,* Anderson v. Cryovac, Inc., 805 F.2d 1, 7, 13 Media L. Rep. 1721, 1725 (1st Cir. 1986) ("[p]rotective discovery orders are subject to first amendment scrutiny, but that scrutiny must be made within the framework of Rule 26(c)'s requirement of good cause").

[440]*See, e.g.,* Cipollone v. Liggett Group, 785 F.2d 1108, 1118–20 (3d Cir. 1986).

[441]*Public Citizen,* 858 F.2d at 790, 15 Media L. Rep. at 2141; *Agent Orange Prod. Liab. Litig.,* 821 F.2d at 145–46.

[442]TEX. R. CIV. P. 76a; FLA. STAT. ch. 69.081; VA. CODE. ANN. §8.01–420.01; N.Y. CIV. PRAC L. & R. §3103 (Consol. 1994). The Texas rule is discussed in detail in Doggett & Mucchetti, *Public Access to the Courts: Discouraging Secrecy in the Public Interest,* 69 TEX. L. REV. 643 (1991).

[443]*Public Citizen,* 858 F.2d at 783, 15 Media L. Rep. at 2135–36.

[444]*Id.* at 784, 15 Media L. Rep. at 2136; In re Beef Indus. Antitrust Litig., 589 F.2d 786, 788–89 (5th Cir. 1979).

[445]In re Coordinated Pretrial Proceedings in Petroleum Prods. Antitrust Litig., 101 F.R.D. 34, 44–45, 10 Media L. Rep. 1300, 1307–08 (C.D. Cal. 1984).

[446]Oklahoma Hosp. Ass'n v. Oklahoma Pub'g Co., 748 F.2d 1421, 11 Media L. Rep. 1325 (10th Cir. 1984) (press lacks standing to challenge protective order regarding civil discovery documents because (1) parties would not disseminate documents even if protective order lifted and (2) documents not filed with court), *cert. denied,* 473 U.S. 905 (1985); Booth Newspapers v. Midland Circuit Judge, 377 N.W.2d 868, 12 Media L. Rep. 1519 (Mich. Ct. App. 1985) (press lacks standing to seek access to civil discovery), *appeal denied,* 384 N.W.2d 767 (Mich. 1986), *cert. denied,* 479 U.S. 1031 (1987).

§1.8(B)(ii) Sealed Civil Records

Whether relying on the First Amendment or the common law, courts have usually refused to seal court records in civil proceedings. Thus, courts have refused to seal prejudgment documents;[447] motions and supporting evidence;[448] the record in administrative proceedings subject to judicial review;[449] hearing transcripts of pretrial motions;[450] and pleadings,[451] briefs, and other trial records.[452] Courts have been particularly reluctant to seal an entire court file.[453]

Divorce cases have spawned a variety of disputes.[454] There has also been considerable litigation over access to settlement documents—access has usually been granted,[455] although there are exceptions.[456] A court can grant access

---

[447] Atlanta Journal & Const. v. Long, 369 S.E.2d 755, 15 Media L. Rep. 1821 (Ga. 1988) (relying on state procedural rules; mere embarrassment not enough to justify closure), *modified*, 377 S.E.2d 150 (Ga. 1989). *But see* State ex rel. KOIN-TV v. Olsen, 711 P.2d 966, 12 Media L. Rep. 1625 (Or. 1985) (denial of request to copy videotape of civil defendant's trial testimony played in open court, marked as exhibit, and received into evidence does not violate federal or state constitution or common law). *See also supra* notes 346–55.

[448] Mokhiber v. Davis, 537 A.2d 1100, 14 Media L. Rep. 2313 (D.C. 1988) (discovery motions and motions for continuance); Bank of Am. Nat'l Trust & Sav. Ass'n v. Hotel Rittenhouse Assocs., 800 F.2d 339, 13 Media L. Rep. 1450 (3d Cir. 1986) (motion to enforce settlement).

[449] Brown & Williamson Tobacco Corp. v. Federal Trade Comm'n, 710 F.2d 1165, 1179–80 (6th Cir. 1983) (even though documents originally submitted to FTC subject to promise of confidentiality), *cert. denied*, 465 U.S. 1100 (1984); State ex rel. Bilder v. Delavan, 334 N.W.2d 252, 9 Media L. Rep. 2294 (Wis. 1983) (sealed disciplinary records about police chief's suspension submitted as part of his case against town).

[450] Publicker Indus. v. Cohen, 733 F.2d 1059, 1066–71, 10 Media L. Rep. 1777, 1782–85 (3d Cir. 1984).

[451] Charlottesville Newspapers v. Berry, 206 S.E.2d 267 (Va. 1974); Willie Nelson Music Co. v. Commissioner, 85 T.C. 914, 12 Media L. Rep. 1657 (T.C. 1985) (allegations of undue notoriety insufficient to overcome public interest in access to pleadings, depositions, exhibits, and filings in tax case).

[452] Wilson v. American Motors Corp., 759 F.2d 1568, 11 Media L. Rep. 2008 (11th Cir. 1985) (entire court file; damage to reputation does not justify sealing); Pratt & Whitney Can. v. United States, 14 Cl. Ct. 268, 15 Media L. Rep. 1033 (Cl. Ct. 1988) (refusing to seal judicial records on whether there were violations of protective orders despite privacy claims and potential harm to attorneys' reputations, but redacting trade secrets).

[453] Barron v. Florida Freedom Newspapers, 531 So. 2d 113, 15 Media L. Rep. 1901 (Fla. 1988) (affirming reversal of order sealing entire court file; requiring use of "least restrictive closure procedure necessary to accomplish its purpose"); Shenandoah Pub'g House v. Fanning, 368 S.E.2d 253, 15 Media L. Rep. 1659 (Va. 1988) (least restrictive test adopted); *Wilson*, 759 F.2d 1568, 11 Media L. Rep. 2008 (unsealing court file). *See also* S.E.N. v. R.L.B., 699 P.2d 875, 11 Media L. Rep. 2278 (Alaska 1985) (unconstitutional to seal court file, close all hearings, and ban all extrajudicial communications in child custody case).

[454] *Barron*, 531 So. 2d 113, 15 Media L. Rep. 1901 (affirming reversal of order sealing court file in divorce of prominent state senator); George W. Prescott Pub'g Co. v. Register of Probate for Norfolk County, 479 N.E.2d 658, 11 Media L. Rep. 2331 (Mass. 1985) (in divorce cases confidential discovery materials can be sealed on privacy grounds, but "overriding necessity" required when public official involved). *But see* Katz v. Katz, 514 A.2d 1374, 13 Media L. Rep. 1296 (Pa. Super. Ct. 1986) (access to divorce hearing to divide property may be denied on showing that disclosure would result in clearly defined serious injury), *appeal denied*, 527 A.2d 542 (Pa. 1987).

[455] Bank of Am. Nat'l Trust & Sav. Ass'n v. Hotel Rittenhouse Assocs., 800 F.2d 339, 13 Media L. Rep. 1450 (3d Cir. 1986) (common law right of access not overridden by judicial policy of promoting settlement and does not justify denying public access to settlement agreement filed under seal in civil action nor to motions to enforce agreement); *Wilson*, 759 F.2d at 1571–72 n.4, 11 Media L. Rep. at 2011 n.4 (payment for sealing order as part of settlement of personal injury action not "even entitled to consideration in deciding whether or not to seal a record"); C.L. v. Edson, 409 N.W.2d 417, 14 Media L. Rep. 1145 (Wis. Ct. App. 1987) (cannot seal settlement documents absent showing that public interest favoring secrecy outweighs strong presumption favoring public disclosure of court records; failure to make showing warrants disclosure with redaction of minor plaintiff's identity); *Shenandoah Pub'g House*, 368 S.E.2d 253, 15 Media L. Rep. 1659 (recognizing public's interest in learning whether settlements are equitable and courts have properly approve them); Society of Prof. Journalists v. Briggs, 675 F. Supp. 1308, 14 Media L. Rep. 2273 (D. Utah 1987) (recognizing First Amendment right of access to settlement agreement resolving lawsuit involving allegations of government misconduct). *See also* Federal Trade Comm'n v. Standard Fin. Mgmt. Corp., 830 F.2d 404, 14 Media L. Rep. 1750 (1st Cir. 1987) (financial records submitted for court's consideration in deciding whether to approve settlement are judicial records; "only the most compelling reasons can justify non-disclosure").

[456] H.S. Gere & Sons v. Frey, 509 N.E.2d 271, 14 Media L. Rep. 1791 (Mass. 1987) (statutory rape case); Doe v. Roe, 495 A.2d 1235, 12 Media L. Rep. 1219 (Me. 1985) (denying intervention to seek unsealing of personal injury settlement).

to a case's records even after the case has come to an end, at least if the court still has physical custody of the records in question.[457] Before access can be denied, notice and an opportunity to be heard must be given, findings to justify closure must be made, and a court must consider less dramatic alternatives.[458]

§1.9 ACCESS TO PEOPLE AND PLACES

§1.9(A) Prisoners and Executions

The Supreme Court has considered the media's access rights to prisoners in two cases: *Pell v. Procunier*[459] and *Saxbe v. Washington Post Co.*[460] The Court decided *Pell* and *Saxbe* on the same day.[461] In *Pell*, the Court reviewed a California regulation forbidding media interviews with inmates selected by the media;[462] in *Saxbe,* the Court considered a virtually identical federal rule.[463] Because there was an "apparent conflict in approach" in the lower courts, the Supreme Court granted certiorari.[464]

In *Pell*, prisoners and three professional journalists challenged the constitutionality of a California prison regulation that prohibited the media from specifying which inmates they wanted to interview.[465] While the prisoners contended that the regulation violated their First Amendment free speech rights,[466] the media claimed that their First Amendment news gathering right had been unconstitutionally limited.[467] The district court held that the regulation infringed the prisoners' First Amendment rights, but not those of the media, because the regulation had always given the media sufficient access, including " 'the freedom to enter the California institutions and interview at random'."[468]

The Supreme Court reversed the district court's ruling regarding the prisoners,[469] holding that, due to the alternative channels of communication open to prison inmates, the restriction of "one manner in which prisoners can communicate with persons outside of prison" was not unconstitutional.[470] Since the restriction operated in a content-neutral manner, it was a valid regulation of the prisoner's conduct and did not interfere with any First Amendment

---

[457]Littlejohn v. BIC Corp., 851 F.2d 673, 683, 15 Media L. Rep. 1841, 1847–48 (3d Cir. 1988). *See also supra* note 438. *But see* Ashpole v. Millard, 778 S.W.2d 169, 16 Media L. Rep. 2302 (Tex. Ct. App. 1989) (court has no jurisdiction to unseal record after case dismissed).
[458]Stone v. Univ. of Md. Medical Sys., 855 F.2d 178, 15 Media L. Rep. 2375 (4th Cir. 1988). *See generally supra* §1.3.
[459]417 U.S. 817, 1 Media L. Rep. 2379 (1974).
[460]417 U.S. 843, 1 Media L. Rep. 2314 (1974). In Houchins v. KQED, Inc., 438 U.S. 1, 3 Media L. Rep. 2521 (1978), discussed *infra,* the Court considered the media's right of access to a place: a prison.
[461]Both cases were decided on June 24, 1974.
[462]417 U.S. at 819, 1 Media L. Rep. at 2380.
[463]417 U.S. at 844, 846–47, 1 Media L. Rep. at 2314–15, 2315–16. This prohibition only extended to inmates of medium and maximum security prisons. *Id.*
[464]*Saxbe,* 417 U.S. at 846, 1 Media L. Rep. at 2315. Justice Stewart wrote both opinions of the Court, in which Chief Justice Burger and Justices White, Blackmun, and Rehnquist joined. *Pell,* 417 U.S. at 818, 1 Media L. Rep. at 2380; *Saxbe,* 417 U.S. at 844, 1 Media L. Rep. at 2314.
[465]417 U.S. at 819, 1 Media L. Rep. at 2380.
[466]*Id.* at 820–21, 1 Media L. Rep. at 2380–81.
[467]*Id.* at 821, 1 Media L. Rep. at 2380–81.
[468]*Id.* (quoting Hillery v. Procunier, 364 F. Supp. 196, 200 (N.D. Cal. 1973).
[469]*Id.* at 835, 1 Media L. Rep. at 2386. *See generally* Donovan, *Constitutionality of Regulations Restricting Prisoner Correspondence With the Media,* 56 FORDHAM L. REV. 1151 (1988). *See* Chapter 13, §13.5(B)(i).
[470]417 U.S. at 823, 1 Media L. Rep. at 2382.

right retained by the prisoners.[471] The regulation was a " 'reasonable time, place and manner [regulation] ... necessary to further significant governmental interests' " in prison security.[472]

The Court also rejected the media's First Amendment claim of a "right to gather news without governmental interference ... includ[ing] a right of access to the sources of what is regarded as newsworthy information."[473] The challenged regulation was "not part of an attempt ... to frustrate the press' investigation and reporting of ... [the] conditions in [the state's prisons]."[474] The Court further noted that, under existing prison regulations, the media "enjoy[ed] access to California prisons that is not available to other members of the public."[475] With respect to face-to-face prisoner interviews, the Court found that "the press is granted the same access ... as is accorded any member of the general public."[476] Quoting its views on news gathering in *Branzburg v. Hayes*,[477] the Court held that "[t]he First and Fourteenth Amendments ... [do] not, however, require government to accord the press special access to information not shared by members of the public generally."[478]

In *Saxbe*, both the district court and the District of Columbia Circuit Court overturned the Federal Bureau of Prisons' Policy Statement absolutely banning face-to-face prisoner interviews, holding that media requests for such interviews could only be rejected "on an individual basis ... 'where it is the judgment of the administrator directly concerned ... that the interview presents a serious risk of administrative or disciplinary problems.' "[479]

The Supreme Court reversed, noting that the ban on "prearranged press interviews with individually designated inmates was motivated by the same disciplinary and administrative considerations ... [reviewed] in *Pell v. Procunier*."[480] The Supreme Court concluded that "this case [is] constitutionally indistinguishable from *Pell* ... and thus fully controlled by the holding in that case."[481]

Justice William Douglas wrote a single dissent for both *Pell* and *Saxbe*,[482] arguing that the regulation violated the constitutional rights of both the prison-

---

[471]*Id.* at 827–28, 1 Media L. Rep. at 2383.

[472]*Id.* at 826–27, 1 Media L. Rep. at 2383 (quoting Grayned v. City of Rockford, 408 U.S. 104, 115 (1972)).

[473]*Id.* at 829–30, 1 Media L. Rep. at 2384–85.

[474]*Id.* at 830, 1 Media L. Rep. at 2384–85. Justice Stewart noted that there were regular public tours of California prisons during which the media could "stop and speak about any subject to any inmates whom they might encounter." *Id.* at 830, 1 Media L. Rep. at 2385. Furthermore, the regulation permitted the media to interview inmates selected at random by prison officials or inmate participants in any prison group program on which they were reporting. *Id.*

[475]417 U.S. at 830–31, 1 Media L. Rep. at 2384–85. Justice Stewart characterized the challenged regulation as "merely eliminat[ing] a special privilege formerly given to representatives of the press *vis-a-vis* members of the public generally." He described the privilege as having been eliminated

in response to a violent episode that the Department of Corrections felt was at least partially attributable to the former policy ... [which] had resulted in press attention being concentrated on a relatively small number of inmates who ... gained a disproportionate degree of notoriety and influence among their fellow inmates [and] ... often became the source of severe disciplinary problems.

Id. at 831–82, 1 Media L. Rep. at 2385.

[476]*Id.* at 831 n.8, 1 Media L. Rep. at 2385 n.8.

[477]*Id.* at 833–34, 1 Media L. Rep. at 2385–86 (quoting Branzburg v. Hayes, 408 U.S. 665, 681, 684–85, 707, 1 Media L. Rep. 2617, 2623, 2624–25, 2633–34 (1972)).

[478]*Id.* at 834, 1 Media L. Rep. at 2386.

[479]*Saxbe*, 417 U.S. 843, 845–46, 1 Media L. Rep. 2314, 2315 (1974) (quoting Washington Post. Co. v. Kleindiest, 494 F.2d 994, 1006–07 (D.C. Cir. 1974)).

[480]*Id.* at 848, 1 Media L. Rep. at 2316.

[481]*Id.* at 850, 1 Media L. Rep. at 2317.

[482]*Pell*, 417 U.S. at 836, 1 Media L. Rep. at 2387–89 (Douglas, J., dissenting).

ers[483] and the media[484] and stating that the regulation was an overbroad limitation on the prisoners' free speech rights, regardless of the existence of alternative means of expression.[485] The media should have " 'a preferred position in our constitutional scheme . . . bring[ing] fulfillment to the public's right to know.' "[486]

The dissent then argued that this "preferred position" was particularly important here, because "[t]he average citizen is most unlikely to inform himself about the operation of the prison system by requesting an interview with a particular inmate with whom he has no prior relationship. He is likely instead . . . to rely upon the media for information."[487] While the dissent conceded that prison officials could impose reasonable time, place, and manner restrictions on interviews, it stated that the prisons' legitimate interest in discipline did not justify the "complete ban on interviews."[488]

Justice Powell concurred in the Court's opinion in *Pell* on prisoners' rights but dissented on the issue of the media's rights.[489] In his dissent in *Saxbe*, he commented that the majority would accept "any governmental restriction on access to information, no matter how severe . . . so long as it does not single out the media for special disabilities not applicable to the public at large."[490] While Justice Powell agreed with the majority that the media do not have "constitutional rights superior to those enjoyed by ordinary citizens,"[491] he stated that *Branzburg* "did not hold that the government is wholly free to restrict press access to newsworthy information."[492] Because, in his opinion, the interview ban was "categorical in nature," it "preclude[d] accurate and effective reporting on prison conditions and inmate grievances . . . [and] substantially impair[ed] a core value of the First Amendment."[493]

Like Justice Douglas, Justice Powell noted that the media "act as [agents] of the public at large," thereby performing "a crucial function in effecting the societal purpose of the First Amendment."[494] He also joined with Justice Douglas in observing that prison officials "may enforce reasonable time, place, and manner restrictions."[495] Unlike Justice Douglas, Justice Powell did not feel that a prison official had to evaluate each interview request separately;[496] instead, prison officials could fulfill their constitutional duty by establishing new regulations that "would enable the Bureau to safeguard its legitimate interests without incurring the risks associated with administration of a wholly *ad hoc* interview policy."[497]

---

[483]*Pell*, 417 U.S. at 836–39, 1 Media L. Rep. at 2387–88 (Douglas, J., dissenting).
[484]*Id.* at 839–42, 1 Media L. Rep. at 2388–89 (Douglas, J., dissenting).
[485]*Id.* at 838, 1 Media L. Rep. at 2387–88 (Douglas, J., dissenting).
[486]*Id.* at 840, 1 Media L. Rep. at 2388 (Douglas, J., dissenting) (quoting Branzburg v. Hayes, 408 U.S. 665, 721, 1 Media L. Rep. 2617, 2639 (1972)).
[487]*Id.* at 841, 1 Media L. Rep. at 2389 (Douglas, J., dissenting).
[488]*Pell*, 417 U.S. at 840–41, 1 Media L. Rep. at 2388–89 (Douglas, J., dissenting).
[489]*Id.* at 835–36, 1 Media L. Rep. at 2386–87 (Powell, J., concurring in part and dissenting in part).
[490]*Saxbe*, 417 U.S. 843, 857, 1 Media L. Rep. 2314, 2320 (1974) (Powell, J., dissenting).
[491]*Id.*
[492]*Id.* at 859, 1 Media L. Rep. at 2321 (Powell, J., dissenting).
[493]*Id.* at 860–61, 1 Media L. Rep. at 2321–22 (Powell, J., dissenting).
[494]*Id.* at 863, 1 Media L. Rep. at 2322 (Powell, J., dissenting).
[495]*Saxbe*, 417 U.S. at 873, 1 Media L. Rep. at 2326 (Powell, J., dissenting).
[496]*Id.*
[497]*Id.* According to Justice Powell, such regulations could include limitations on the number of interviews of any given inmate within a certain time period (so as to avoid the notoriety concerns mentioned in

Courts that have considered media requests for access to prisoners since *Pell* and *Saxbe* have generally followed those cases.[498]

The Supreme Court considered the media's right of access to prisons in *Houchins v. KQED*.[499] There was no opinion of the Court; Chief Justice Burger instead announced the "judgment of the Court" and identified the issue as "whether the news media have a constitutional right of access to a county jail, over and above that of other persons, to interview inmates and make sound recordings, films, and photographs for publication and broadcasting by newspapers, radio and television."[500]

Public television station KQED in San Francisco had sued for relief under 42 U.S.C. Section 1983 after being denied permission to film inside a portion of a county jail where a prisoner had committed suicide. After the suit was filed, the sheriff established a formal access policy (there had been none before), including a program of monthly public tours. The jail's policy, however, did not permit the use of cameras or tape recorders on tours, and the public tour did not include the part of the jail where the suicide occurred.[501] The district court granted KQED's motion for a preliminary injunction, prohibiting officials from denying KQED camera access to the entire jail.[502] The Ninth Circuit affirmed, holding that, despite *Pell* and *Saxbe,* the media had a "First and Fourteenth Amendment right of access to prisons and jails."[503]

The Supreme Court reversed.[504] Chief Justice Burger stated that

> [t]he public importance of conditions in penal facilities and the media's role of providing information afford no basis for reading into the Constitution a right of the public or the media to enter these institutions, with camera equipment, and take moving and still pictures of inmates for broadcast purposes. This Court has never intimated a First Amendment guarantee of a right of access to all sources of information within government control.[505]

He also stated that "[t]he right to *receive* ideas and information is not the issue in this case"—the media were instead claiming a "special privilege of access" beyond what was available to the public, which was "not essential to

---

Pell), the right to refuse interviews with a prisoner in solitary confinement, and the right to suspend press interviews in any "institutional emergency."

[498] Jersawitz v. Hanberry, 783 F.2d 1532, 12 Media L. Rep. 1842 (11th Cir. 1986) (upholding prison regulation permitting only FCC-licensed media to interview inmates for broadcast), *cert. denied,* 479 U.S. 883 (1986); Mann v. State's Attorney for Montgomery County, 468 A.2d 124, 10 Media L. Rep. 1114 (Md. Ct. App. 1983) (upholding Maryland law prohibiting interviews with criminal defendant found competent to stand trial awaiting trial in maximum security facility for treatment of criminally insane). *See also* Times Pub'g Co. v. Florida Dep't of Corrections, 375 So. 2d 304, 5 Media L. Rep. 1510 (Fla. Dist. Ct. App.) (court struck down, without reaching constitutional issue, prison's emergency rule prohibiting media interviews with death row inmates once death warrant issued; rule-making procedures not followed and rule not sufficiently justified), *modified,* 375 So. 2d 307, 5 Media L. Rep. 1861 (Fla. Dist. Ct. App. 1979); United States v. Fort, 14 Media L. Rep. 1942 (N.D. Ill. 1987) (media have right of access to interview incarcerated defendants in pending criminal case who have indicated their willingness even though defense counsel opposes it).

[499] 438 U.S. 1, 3 Media L. Rep. 2521 (1978). For a discussion on access to various judicial proceedings, see *supra* §1.2.

[500] 438 U.S. at 4–7, 3 Media L. Rep. at 2521. Chief Justice Burger was joined by Justices White and Rehnquist; Justices Marshall and Blackmun did not participate in the decision.

[501] *Id.* at 4–7, 3 Media L. Rep. at 2521–22.

[502] *Id.*

[503] *Id.* at 7, 3 Media L. Rep. at 2523.

[504] *Id.* at 16, 3 Media L. Rep. at 2526.

[505] 438 U.S. at 7, 3 Media L. Rep. at 2523.

guarantee the freedom to communicate or publish,"[506] and had been rejected in *Pell* and *Saxbe*. Further, the Chief Justice noted, the legislature, not the Court, should decide whether prisons and jails would be opened in the way requested by KQED.[507] Accordingly, Chief Justice Burger concluded that the press has no right of access "different from or greater than that afforded the public generally" and remanded the case for further proceedings.[508]

Justice Stewart provided the decisive swing vote, concurring in the judgment that reversed the preliminary injunction. He felt that the preliminary injunction was overly broad in giving KQED access to parts of the jail that the public could not see on the monthly tours and in giving it the right to interview randomly encountered inmates.[509] He also felt, however, that KQED was entitled to some injunctive relief, namely more access than the monthly public tours and the use of cameras and recording equipment.[510] He concluded that Chief Justice Burger's concept, that the media were only entitled to "equal access" with the public, should not mean "access that is identical in all respects," but must be interpreted with "more flexibility in order to accommodate the practical distinctions between the press and the general public."[511] He stated therefore that, on remand, the district court could also grant further injunctive relief "depend[ing] upon the extent of access then permitted the public."[512]

Justice Stevens, in his dissent, which was joined by Justices Brennan and Powell, argued that neither *Pell* nor *Saxbe* controlled. Unlike *Pell,* the challenged prison policy did not give the press a greater right of access than that afforded the public.[513] Justice Stevens faulted the majority for considering the prison access implemented after KQED filed suit (prison tours) instead of the policy before it filed suit (no formal policy at all).[514] In addition, because the Court in *Pell* specifically found that prison officials had not concealed conditions, the "no-access policy" in *Houchins* required an entirely different type of constitutional scrutiny.[515] Rather than waiting for the general public "who may also have been injured by petitioner's unconstitutional access policy" to vindicate their rights, the press should be able to seek relief.[516] Thus, the special concerns of the media required a different remedy than for potential public litigants.[517] Justice Stevens also argued that there are "reasons which militate in favor of providing special protection to the flow of information to the public about prisons"—in particular "the unique function they perform in a democratic society."[518]

---

[506]*Id.* at 12, 3 Media L. Rep. at 2525.
[507]*Id.*
[508]*Id.* at 16, 3 Media L. Rep. at 2526.
[509]*Id.* (Stewart, J., concurring in judgment).
[510]438 U.S. at 16, 3 Media L. Rep. at 2526 (Stewart, J., concurring in judgment).
[511]*Id.* Among these "practical distinctions," Justice Stewart noted that "if a television reporter is to convey the jail's sights and sounds to those who cannot personally visit the place, he must use cameras and sound equipment." *Id.* at 17, 3 Media L. Rep. at 2526–27.
[512]*Id.* at 19, 3 Media L. Rep. at 2527.
[513]*Id.* at 23–26, 3 Media L. Rep. at 2530 (Stevens, J., dissenting).
[514]*Id.*
[515]438 U.S. at 29–30, 3 Media L. Rep. at 2532.
[516]*Id.* at 25, 3 Media L. Rep. at 2530.
[517]*Id.* at 31–32, 3 Media L. Rep. at 2533. *See generally id.* at 30–38, 3 Media L. Rep. at 2532–36.
[518]*Id.* at 36, 3 Media L. Rep. at 2535.

Before *Houchins,* courts had decided, relying on *Pell* and *Saxbe,* that the media have no First Amendment right to attend[519] or film[520] a prison execution.[521] *Pell* and *Saxbe* continue to be followed in access to execution cases.[522]

§1.9(B) Jurors

The *Pell* and *Saxbe* rationale has not been followed by courts considering media requests for access to many other groups of people. In general, courts have recognized the media's First Amendment right to interview jurors regarding their verdict or deliberations.[523] This right has been qualified, however, to prohibit repeated contact with any juror who has expressed a desire not to be interviewed or to protect disclosure of the ballots of other jurors.[524] The issue of access to the names and addresses of jurors has produced conflicting results. Most courts have granted access;[525] others have not.[526]

§1.9(C) Public Employees, Migrant Workers, and Students

Courts have also rejected as violating the First Amendment orders or policies prohibiting public employees from speaking with the media about their

---

[519]Kearns-Tribune Corp. v. Utah Bd. of Corrections, 2 Media L. Rep. 1353 (D. Utah 1977) (upholding Utah statute that denied access to all but involved officials and witnesses selected by condemned prisoner, here, Gary Gilmore; general public as well as media had no right to attend).

[520]Garrett v. Estelle, 556 F.2d 1274, 2 Media L. Rep. 2265 (5th Cir. 1977) (no right to film execution where both public and media had right to observe), *cert. denied,* 438 U.S. 914 (1978).

[521]*See generally* Note, *The Executioner's Song: Is There a Right to Listen?* 69 VA. L. REV. 373 (1983).

[522]Halquist v. Department of Corrections, 783 P.2d 1065, 17 Media L. Rep. 1250 (Wash. 1989) (post-*Houchins* case) (no right under Washington state constitution to attend and videotape execution).

[523]Journal Pub'g Co. v. Mechem, 801 F.2d 1233, 13 Media L. Rep. 1391 (10th Cir. 1986) (posttrial order prohibiting press interviews of jurors in civil case impermissibly broad); United States v. Sherman, 581 F.2d 1358, 4 Media L. Rep. 1433 (9th Cir. 1978) (postverdict order prohibiting media from contacting and interviewing jurors violated First Amendment right to gather news; recognizing First Amendment right to interview jurors regarding verdict or deliberations); In re Express News Corp., 695 F.2d 807, 9 Media L. Rep. 1001 (5th Cir. 1982) (court rule forbidding interviews of jurors except with court's permission unconstitutional, but noting jurors have no obligation to talk to media). See also *supra* §1.5(B) on access to voir dire and Chapter 10, §10.7(B) on prior restraints on jurors.

[524]United States v. Harrelson (El Paso Times), 713 F.2d 1114, 1117–18, 9 Media L. Rep. 2113, 2115–16 (5th Cir. 1983) (court rules (1) prohibiting repeated attempts to interview juror after juror expresses desire not to be interviewed and (2) preventing inquiry into vote of jurors other than interviewee held not an abuse of discretion), *cert. denied,* 465 U.S. 1041 (1984). Contacting prospective murder trial jurors who are under court order not to discuss the case with anyone may constitute contempt. In re Stone, 703 P.2d 1319, 11 Media L. Rep. 2209 (Colo. Ct. App. 1985).

[525]Des Moines Register & Tribune Co. v. Osmundson, 248 N.W.2d 493, 2 Media L. Rep. 1321 (Iowa 1976) (order preventing disclosure of jurors' identities is unconstitutional prior restraint violating First Amendment because jury list is public record; based on interpretation of Iowa's freedom of information act); In re Baltimore Sun Co., 841 F.2d 74, 14 Media L. Rep. 2379 (4th Cir. 1988) (recognizing right of access to names and addresses of jurors chosen and not chosen after jury seated; also concluding that United States v. Gurney, 558 F.2d 1202, 3 Media L. Rep. 1081 (5th Cir. 1977), is wrongly decided); In re Globe Newspaper Co., 920 F.2d 88, 18 Media L. Rep. 1401 (1st Cir. 1990) (recognizing federal statutory right of access where trial had concluded); Newsday v. Goodman, 552 N.Y.S.2d 965, 17 Media L. Rep. 1725 (N.Y. App. Div. 1990) (recognizing right of access to questionnaires completed by jurors but upholding deletion of their identities); Pantos v. City & County of San Francisco, 198 Cal. Rptr. 489, 10 Media L. Rep. 1279 (Cal. Ct. App. 1984) (list of potential jurors by name and address is judicial record open to inspection and copying); Lesher Communications v. Superior Ct., 274 Cal. Rptr. 154, 18 Media L. Rep. 1331 (Cal. Ct. App. 1990) (recognizing First Amendment right of access to confidential jury voir dire questionnaires but refusing access to questionnaires of jurors never called into jury box); Copley Press v. Superior Ct., 278 Cal. Rptr. 443, 18 Media L. Rep. 1800 (Cal. Ct. App. (same), *cert. denied,* 112 S. Ct. 304 (1991).

[526]United States v. Gurney, 558 F.2d 1202, 1210 n.12, 3 Media L. Rep. 1081, 1086 n.12 (5th Cir. 1977) (upholding trial court order refusing to release jury list containing private information about jurors not announced in open court), *cert. denied,* 435 U.S. 968 (1978); Gannett Co. v. State, 571 A.2d 735 (Del.) (no First Amendment right of access to names of prospective jurors), *cert. denied,* 495 U.S. 918 (1990). *See also* United States v. Edwards, 823 F.2d 111, 14 Media L. Rep. 1399 (5th Cir. 1987), *cert. denied sub nom.*

jobs.[527] These cases have not been based on the media's news gathering rights; instead, courts have found these policies to be unconstitutionally overbroad restraints on the *employees'* freedom of speech.[528]

One court has upheld the media's right of access to migrant laborers, subject to reasonable restrictions, by relying on state constitutional guarantees.[529] Another court based its similar decision on federal constitutional guarantees.[530]

The Second Circuit has held, however, that high school officials can prevent student newspaper reporters from "interviewing" fellow students by distributing and collecting a questionnaire on sexual attitudes.[531] The court framed the constitutional issue as the First Amendment right to *collect information,* distinguishing it from the media's right to *communicate* information.[532]

§1.9(D) Disaster, Crime, and Military Operation Sites

For various reasons, courts have upheld the denial of press passes that would give the bearers special access to crime and disaster scenes, holding that there was no absolute First Amendment right of media access.[533] A later decision found a right to such passes, however.[534] One court also relied on *Houchins* to overturn a regulation of the National Transportation Safety Board that limited the media's access to an airline crash site to one hour per day,

---

Times-Picayune Pub'g Corp. v. Edwards, 485 U.S. 934 (1988) (upholding redaction of juror names from transcript of midtrial proceedings on possible juror misconduct). *Compare* United States v. Doherty, 675 F. Supp. 719, 14 Media L. Rep. 1406 (D. Mass. 1987) (seven-day delay in releasing juror's names and addresses after verdict in criminal trial permissible).

[527]Pickering v. Board of Educ., 391 U.S. 563 (1968) (school teacher fired for sending letter critical of school board policy to local newspaper); Mt. Healthy City Bd. of Educ. v. Doyle, 429 U.S. 274 (1977) (school board refused to renew teacher's contract in part because teacher complained to media about school board's policy); Grady v. Blair, 529 F. Supp. 370, 7 Media L. Rep. 2543 (N.D. Ill. 1981) (fire department order prohibiting on- or off-duty employees from speaking with media about department activities); Rossi v. City of Milwaukee, 7 Media L. Rep. 2265 (E.D. Wis. 1981) (city planning department policy requiring employees to obtain department approval before responding to media inquiries); Atlanta Prof. Firefighters v. Brown, 7 Media L. Rep. 2263 (N.D. Ga. 1981) (city public safety commissioner's order requiring public employees to obtain express written permission before assisting or consulting with media). *See also* Donovan v. R.D. Andersen Constr. Co., 552 F. Supp. 249 (D. Kan. 1982) (Occupational Safety and Health Act protects employee communications to news media about working conditions).

[528]*Grady,* 529 F. Supp. at 372, 7 Media L. Rep. at 2544; *Rossi,* 7 Media L. Rep. at 2267; *Atlanta Prof. Firefighters,* 7 Media L. Rep. at 2264.

[529]Freedman v. New Jersey State Police, 343 A.2d 148 (N.J. Super. Ct. Law Div. 1975) (access recognized under N.J. CONST. art. 1, ¶6).

[530]Franceschina v. Morgan, 346 F. Supp. 833 (S.D. Ind. 1972) (right to communicate with migrant workers may be protected by action against company operating migrant worker camp).

[531]Trachtman v. Anker, 563 F.2d 512, 519–20, 3 Media L. Rep. 1041, 1047 (2d Cir.) ("The First Amendment right to express one's views does not include the right to importune others to respond to questions when there is reason to believe that such importuning may result in harmful consequences."), *cert. denied,* 435 U.S. 925 (1978). *See generally* the discussion of *Trachtman* in Comment, *Behind the Schoolhouse Gate: Sex and the Student Pollster,* 54 N.Y.U. L. REV. 161 (1979); *see also* Comment, *Student Editorial Discretion, the First Amendment, and Public Access to the Campus Press,* 16 U.C. DAVIS L. REV. 1089 (1983).

[532]*Trachtman,* 563 F.2d at 516 n.2, 3 Media L. Rep. at 1044 n.2.

[533]Watson v. Cronin, 384 F. Supp. 652 (D. Colo. 1974) (denial of press credentials to person with criminal record upheld as reasonable restriction on qualified news gathering right); Los Angeles Free Press v. Los Angeles, 88 Cal. Rptr. 605 (Cal. Ct. App. 1970) (denial of press passes to reporters without regular crime beat responsibilities upheld as reasonable classification), *cert. denied,* 401 U.S. 982 (1971). *See also* Mintz v. Director, Dep't of Motor Vehicles, 691 F.2d 507, 9 Media L. Rep. 1301 (9th Cir. 1982) (upholding denial of special press license plates because photographer not "regularly employed or engaged as a bona fide . . . photographer"), *cert. denied,* 460 U.S. 1071 (1983).

[534]Sherrill v. Knight, 569 F.2d 124, 3 Media L. Rep. 1514 (D.C. Cir. 1977) (First Amendment right of access and Fifth Amendment procedural due process to White House press passes). *See also infra* note 539.

holding that such a restriction, established without any showing of overriding need, violated the qualified First Amendment news gathering right.[535]

In *Flynt v. Weinberger*,[536] the media challenged the Reagan administration's "blackout" on coverage of the United States' invasion of Grenada. The court declined to rule on the merits, however, finding the case moot because the invasion was a unique event and there was "no 'reasonable expectation' that the ... controversy will recur."[537] In dicta, however, the court said that it would not restrain the government from limiting press access to future military operations, because such an injunction "would limit the range of options available to the commanders in the field in the future, possibly jeopardizing the success of military operations and the lives of military personnel and thereby gravely damaging the national interest."[538]

§1.9(E) Legislative and Political Proceedings

Courts also have upheld the media's First Amendment right of access to various legislative proceedings;[539] public officials' news conferences;[540] a political candidate's campaign headquarters[541] and a city council meeting,[542] both of which only union-member television camerapersons had been permitted to

---

[535]Westinghouse Broadcasting Co. v. National Transp. Safety Bd., 8 Media L. Rep. 1177, 1184 (D. Mass. 1982). *See also* Connell v. Hudson, 733 F. Supp. 465, 17 Media L. Rep. 1803 (D.N.H. 1990) (police violated photographer's right to gather news by ordering him not to take pictures of accident); Channel 10 v. Gunnarson, 337 F. Supp. 634 (D. Minn. 1972) (confiscation of camera from photographer who took pictures of inside of store from public sidewalk using his light improper). *But see* Leiserson v. City of San Diego, 229 Cal. Rptr. 22 (Cal. Ct. App. 1986) (applying CAL. PENAL CODE §409.5(d), court found sufficient evidence to support trial court's finding that disaster site also scene of possible crime and thus outside scope of access statute); Opinion of Attorney General No. 84-802, 67 Op. Att'y Gen. 535 (Cal. 1984) (based on interpretation of CAL. PENAL CODE §409.5(d), media cannot be denied access to earthquake site; no First Amendment right of access, however, citing *Pell*); City of Oak Creek v. King, 436 N.W.2d 285, 16 Media L. Rep. 1273 (Wis. 1989) (news photographer had no First Amendment right of access to airplane crash beyond that of general public). *See generally* Chapter 5.

[536]588 F. Supp. 57, 10 Media L. Rep. 1978 (D.D.C. 1984), *aff'd on other grounds and vacated*, 762 F.2d 134, 11 Media L. Rep. 2118 (D.C. Cir. 1985).

[537]*Id.* at 59, 10 Media L. Rep. at 1979.

[538]*Id.* at 60, 10 Media L. Rep. at 1980. *See also* Nation Magazine v. United States Dep't of Defense, 762 F. Supp. 1558, 19 Media L. Rep. 1257 (S.D.N.Y. 1991).

[539]Lewis v. Baxley, 368 F. Supp. 768, 1 Media L. Rep. 2525 (M.D. Ala. 1973) (statute restricting media's access to legislature's galleries unless reporters fill out financial interest questionnaires held unconstitutional). *Accord* Opinion of Justices to the Senate, 392 N.E.2d 849, 5 Media L. Rep. 2059 (Mass. 1979); Kovach v. Maddux, 238 F. Supp. 835, 1 Media L. Rep. 2367 (M.D. Tenn. 1965) (exclusion of newspaper and its representatives from floor of Tennessee Senate unconstitutional); WJW-TV v. City of Cleveland, 686 F. Supp. 177, 15 Media L. Rep. 1351 (N.D. Ohio 1988) (recognizing First Amendment right of access to city council meeting, *vacated as moot*, 878 F.2d 906, 16 Media L. Rep. 2328 (6th Cir.), *cert. denied*, 493 U.S. 819 (1989). *See also* Note, *Mr. Smith Comes Home: The Constitutional Presumption of Openness in Local Legislative Meetings*, 40 CASE W. RES. L. REV. 227 (1989–90). *But see* Moffit v. Willis, 459 So. 2d 1018 (Fla. 1984) (denial of access to secret legislative committee meetings upheld on separation of powers grounds); Consumers Union v. Periodical Correspondents' Ass'n, 515 F.2d 1341 (D.C. Cir. 1975) (refusal to give *Consumer Reports* credentials for access to periodical press galleries in Congress upheld on separation of powers grounds), *cert. denied*, 423 U.S. 1051 (1976). *See also supra* notes 533 and 534.

[540]Times-Picayune Pub'g Co. v. Lee, 15 Media L. Rep. 1713 (E.D. La. 1988) (sheriff's decision to exclude one reporter from news conference violated First Amendment); Borreca v. Fasi, 369 F. Supp. 906, 1 Media L. Rep. 2410 (D. Haw. 1974) (injunction granted against mayor barring one reporter from news conference).

[541]American Broadcasting Cos. v. Cuomo, 570 F.2d 1080 (2d Cir. 1977) (network entitled to send nonunion camera crew to cover candidate's campaign headquarters on election night on same basis as other networks).

[542]Westinghouse Broadcasting Co. v. Dukakis, 409 F. Supp. 895 (D. Mass. 1976) (nonunion camera crew entitled to equal access to "official news sources" under both First Amendment and equal protection analyses). *But see* National Broadcasting Co. v. Communications Workers of Am., 860 F.2d 1022, 16 Media L. Rep. 1356 (11th Cir. 1988) (labor union's exclusion of network from its convention held in city-owned convention center not state action and thus did not violate First Amendment); *infra* note 638.

attend; White House events covered on a "pool" basis;[543] and presidential and vice-presidential election debates covered on a "pool" basis.[544]

§1.9(F) Public Sporting Facilities

Several courts have considered the media's right of access to sporting facilities. One court upheld a female reporter's right of access to the New York Yankees' locker room;[545] another court concluded that a state racing association could not prohibit an employee of a horse-racing newspaper from taking a camera into the paddock area of the race track because the restriction was content-based and did not apply to any other journalist.[546] However, another court refused to enter a preliminary injunction to permit a local television station equal camera access to a world skating championship held in a civic arena for which a television network had purchased exclusive coverage rights.[547] Similarly, another court found no First Amendment violation in denying an independent photojournalist access to a rock music concert to take photos.[548]

§1.9(G) Polling Places and Exit Polls

The media's practice of approaching voters after they leave a polling place and asking them questions about their backgrounds and the reasons they voted as they did has created substantial litigation. Since at least 1980, such exit polls have been an important part of the media's coverage of elections.[549] Exit polls allow journalists to report not only who won, but also to report and analyze the constituencies a candidate carried and the factors that voters considered important.[550] Moreover, because exit polls are taken as voters leave the polls, television networks may be able to recognize trends and report likely results even before the polls have closed. This effect is magnified in a national election where significant trends in Eastern voting may be reported before large numbers of Westerners have voted.[551] Some studies have indicated that, because

---

[543]Cable News Network v. American Broadcasting Cos., 518 F. Supp. 1238, 7 Media L. Rep. 2053 (N.D. Ga. 1981) (White House's exclusion of all television media representatives from events at which only "pool" coverage allowed in effort to coerce television networks to resolve "pool" dispute violated television networks' First Amendment access rights).

[544]WPIX Inc. v. League of Women Voters, 595 F. Supp. 1484, 1491–93, 10 Media L. Rep. 2433, 2435–38, 2441 (S.D.N.Y. 1984) (independent television station's demand for access to presidential debates without using "pool" arrangement denied, but court recognized possible First Amendment right to "equal access to important public events").

[545]Ludtke v. Kuhn, 461 F. Supp. 86, 4 Media L. Rep. 1625 (S.D.N.Y. 1978) (policy denying newswomen access violated equal protection and due process clauses of Fourteenth Amendment).

[546]Stevens v. New York Racing Ass'n, 665 F. Supp. 164, 14 Media L. Rep. 1641 (E.D.N.Y. 1987) (granting preliminary injunction).

[547]Post-Newsweek Stations-Conn. v. Travelers Ins. Co., 510 F. Supp. 81, 6 Media L. Rep. 2540 (D. Conn. 1981) (citing *Houchins,* court held that local station had no First Amendment right of access greater than public).

[548]D'Amario v. Providence Civic Center Auth., 639 F. Supp. 1538, 13 Media L. Rep. 1769 (D.R.I. 1986), *aff'd without op.,* 815 F.2d 692 (1st Cir.), *cert. denied,* 484 U.S. 859 (1987).

[549]*See generally* Copple, *Early Election Projections: A Conflict of Democratic Values,* 65 ORE. L. REV. 593 (1986); Note, *Exit Polls and the First Amendment,* 98 HARV. L. REV. 1927, 1928–30 (1985); Note, *Clearing CBS, Inc. v. Smith From the Path to the Polls: A Proposal to Legitimate States' Interests in Restricting Exit Polls,* 74 IOWA L. REV. 737 (1989).

[550]Daily Herald Co. v. Munro, 838 F.2d 380, 388, 14 Media L. Rep. 2332 (9th Cir. 1988) (noting that *New York Times* used exit polling to report that 1980 presidential election result was " 'a rejection of President Carter more than a conservative revolution' ").

[551]Note, *supra* note 549, 98 HARV. L. REV. at 1929 (based on exit polling, NBC predicted Ronald Reagan's 1980 presidential victory at 5:15 p.m. Pacific time).

Ronald Reagan was declared the winner so early in the 1980 presidential race, many Western Democrats did not vote at all, which possibly affected the results in tight local races.[552]

Congress has passed a nonbinding resolution asking the media to delay broadcasting election-night projections.[553] Bills making such a rule mandatory, as well as others that would establish a uniform national closing time for polls or prohibit the release of vote results before the polls close, have also been considered by Congress.[554] Several states have passed statutes that forbid exit polling, and many others have considered such laws.[555]

In *Brown v. Hartlage,* the Supreme Court noted that "[s]tates have a legitimate interest in preserving the integrity of their electoral processes."[556] This interest includes maintaining proper order and decorum in and around polling places.[557] State laws that forbid exit polling are generally couched in terms of protecting orderly polling and are usually defended by the states without direct reference to exit polls or their alleged evils.[558] The statutes prevent exit polling by banning all voter solicitation or polling within a specified distance of any polling place. By the time voters have dispersed this far, potential exit pollers can no longer distinguish voters from passersby.[559]

In the leading case on exit polls and the First Amendment, *Daily Herald v. Munro,*[560] the Ninth Circuit emphatically rejected a Washington statute that forbade any polling of voters within 300 feet of a polling place. The court found that, because the statute regulated a specific subject matter—the discussion of voting—it was content-based and therefore could not be a valid time, place, and manner restriction.[561] Applying a "compelling interest" standard, the court found that the statute was not narrowly tailored to the state's interest in maintaining decorum at the polls because it forbade all exit polling, even when it caused no disruption.[562] The court also found that less restrictive alternatives, such as reducing the restricted area or having separate entrances and exits at

---

[552]Calmes, *Exit Polls Targeted: Method Sought to Restrict Broadcast Vote Predictions,* 42 CONG. Q. WEEKLY REP. 565, 566 (1984) (quoting Rep. Don Edwards of California: "California gets screwed on this, especially the poor people and the working people who have no choice but to vote after they get off work."); Comment, *Restricting the Broadcast of Election-Day Projections: A Justifiable Protection of the Right to Vote,* 9 DAYTON L. REV. 297, 298–300 (1984).

[553]H.R. Con. Res. 321, 98th Cong., 2d Sess., 130 CONG. REC. H6023 (daily ed. June 18, 1984). The three major television networks have sent letters to Congress promising not to broadcast election results in any state until that state's polls have closed. Note, *supra* note 549, 98 HARV. L. REV. at 1942–43 and n.90. *See* Swift, *The Congressional Concern About Early Calls,* 49 PUB. OPINION Q. 2 (1985).

[554]Note, *supra* note 549, 98 HARV. L. REV. at 1927–28.

[555]Calmes, *supra* note 552, at 566.

[556]456 U.S. 45, 52 (1982).

[557]Mills v. Alabama, 384 U.S. 214, 218, 1 Media L. Rep. 1334, 1335–36 (1966); Clean-Up '84 v. Heinrich, 759 F.2d 1511, 1514 (11th Cir. 1985) ("the state has a significant interest in . . . ensur[ing] its voters that they may exercise their franchise without distraction, interruption, or harassment").

[558]Daily Herald Co. v. Munro, 838 F.2d 380, 386–87, 14 Media L. Rep. 2332, 2336–37 (9th Cir. 1988) (state argued that banning exit polls was not purpose of statute but that barring early projections based on such polls is significant government interest); CBS, Inc. v. Smith, 681 F. Supp. 794, 15 Media L. Rep. 1251 (S.D. Fla. 1988) (state offered several justifications not including desire to halt exit polling). *Compare* Abrams, *Press Practices, Polling Restrictions, Public Opinion and First Amendment Guarantees,* 49 PUB. OPINION Q. 15, 16 (1985) (bar on polling within 300 feet of polling place is "end run" around First Amendment).

[559]*See Smith,* 681 F. Supp. at 799, 800, 15 Media L. Rep. at 1255.

[560]838 F.2d 380, 14 Media L. Rep. 2332 (9th Cir. 1988).

[561]*Id.* at 385, 14 Media L. Rep. at 2335.

[562]*Id.*

polls, made this statute unconstitutionally overbroad.[563] Like other courts that have considered broad restrictions on exit polling voters near a polling place, the Ninth Circuit held that the statute's reach, which included the banning of exit polling in traditional public forums such as streets and parks, made it an unconstitutional restraint on free expression.[564]

Courts have repeatedly held that exit polling is news gathering, which is protected by the First Amendment.[565] They have further concluded that exit polling involves political discussion, which is at the core of protected First Amendment speech.[566] States retain the power to ban disruptive politicking, however, particularly within the polling place.[567]

§1.9(H) Court Buildings

Courts have also rejected orders that exclude sketch artists from the courtroom.[568] The Fifth Circuit struck down as vague rules that prohibited media access to "halls and hallways" in a criminal court building,[569] while the Fourth Circuit overruled an order that barred the media from "mingling" with trial participants to the extent that the order applied to sidewalks adjacent to the courthouse.[570]

---

[563]*Id.*

[564]*Id.* at 384–85, 14 Media L. Rep. at 2334–35; *Smith,* 681 F. Supp. at 802–06; *Clean-Up '84,* 759 F.2d at 1513–14 (statute overbroad because it included private homes and businesses within 100 yards of polling place). *See also* CBS, Inc. v. Growe, 15 Media L. Rep. 2275 (D. Minn. 1988) (Minnesota statute specifically prohibiting exit polls unconstitutional because it was content-based restriction not narrowly tailored to serve compelling governmental interest).

[565]*Daily Herald Co.,* 838 F.2d at 384, 14 Media L. Rep. at 2334 ("the First Amendment protects the media's right to gather news"); *Clean-Up '84,* 759 F.2d at 1513 (exit polling is First Amendment activity); National Broadcasting Co. v. Cleland, 697 F. Supp. 1204, 15 Media L. Rep. 2265 (N.D. Ga. 1988) (Georgia statute prohibiting exit poll within 250 feet of polling place violates First Amendment, but state can prohibit such polls within 25 feet of polling place exit); CBS, Inc. v. Smith, 681 F. Supp. 794, 803, 15 Media L. Rep. 1251, 1258 (S.D. Fla. 1988) (Florida statute prohibiting all solicitation of voters within 150 feet of polling place violates First Amendment by restricting news gathering; "[s]imply put, newsgathering is a basic right protected by the First Amendment"); Firestone v. News-Press Pub'g Co., 538 So. 2d 457, 16 Media L. Rep. 1265 (Fla. 1989) (Florida statute prohibiting nonvoters from coming within 50 feet of open polling place violates First Amendment because concern with interference with orderly voting process insufficient to overcome chilling effect); National Broadcasting Co. v. Colburg, 699 F. Supp. 241, 16 Media L. Rep. 1267 (D. Mont. 1988) (Montana statute prohibiting exit polls within 200 feet of polling place violates First Amendment).

[566]*See, e.g., Colburg,* 699 F. Supp. at 242, 16 Media L. Rep. at 1268 ("Free discussion of governmental affairs is clearly protected as political speech. Gathering and dissemination of information concerning why and how people vote constitutes speech which is protected by the first amendment").

[567]*Firestone,* 538 So. 2d 457, 16 Media L. Rep. 1265 (can exclude nonvoters from polling room).

[568]State v. Palm Beach Newspapers, 395 So. 2d 544, 546 n.2, 7 Media L. Rep. 1021, 1022 n.2 (Fla. 1981) (no basis for excluding sketch artists from courtroom during murder trial); United States v. Columbia Broadcasting Sys., 497 F.2d 102, 19 Media L. Rep. 1351 (5th Cir. 1974) (revising order restricting making and broadcasting sketches). *See also* Central S.C. Chapter, Soc'y of Prof. Journalists v. Martin, 556 F.2d 706, 708, 2 Media L. Rep. 2146, 2148 (4th Cir. 1977) (court questioned order prohibiting sketching), *cert. denied,* 434 U.S. 1022 (1978); KPNX Broadcasting Co. v. Superior Ct., 678 P.2d 431, 10 Media L. Rep. 1289 (Ariz. 1984) (court review of sketches of jury was prior restraint); KCST-TV Channel 39 v. Municipal Ct., 246 Cal. Rptr. 869, 16 Media L. Rep. 1026 (Cal. Ct. App. 1988) (order prohibiting television station from exhibiting drawing of defendant's face made during arraignment was unconstitutional prior restraint). *Contra* Tsokalas v. Partill, 756 F. Supp. 89, 18 Media L. Rep. 1737 (D. Conn. 1991). *See also infra* §1.10.

[569]Angelico v. Louisiana, 593 F.2d 585, 5 Media L. Rep. 1026 (5th Cir. 1979). *Accord* Dorfman v. Meiszner, 430 F.2d 558, 1 Media L. Rep. 2396 (7th Cir. 1970). *But see* Mazzetti v. United States, 518 F.2d 781 (10th Cir. 1975) (distinguishing Dorfman v. Meiszner, 430 F.2d 558, 1 Media L. Rep. 2396 (7th Cir. 1970)).

[570]556 F.2d at 708, 2 Media L. Rep. at 2148.

§1.10 ELECTRONIC COVERAGE OF COURT AND OTHER PROCEEDINGS

On two occasions the Supreme Court has considered the propriety of electronic media coverage of criminal trials: in *Estes v. Texas*[571] and *Chandler v. Florida*.[572] In the sixteen years that separate these decisions, the Court's willingness to permit state experimentation with televised court proceedings has increased significantly,[573] at least partially as a result of major technological improvements in such coverage. On the other hand, despite the Court's refusal to declare such experiments per se unconstitutional in *Chandler v. Florida*,[574] it has both implicitly[575] and explicitly, as the rule-making authority for all federal courts,[576] refused to endorse such experiments.

Nonetheless, an ever-increasing number of states have implemented experimental or permanent court rules that permit televised coverage of trials.[577] This section will not attempt to catalog the current status or individual features of each of those court experiments;[578] rather, after discussing *Estes* and *Chandler*, this section will review cases in which courts, following those decisions, have upheld the constitutionality of experimental broadcasting programs[579] but have also refused to find any absolute First or Sixth Amendment right to insist that a court proceeding be televised.[580]

In *Estes*, the issue before the Court was whether the convicted criminal defendant had been "deprived of his right under the Fourteenth Amendment to due process by the televising and broadcasting of his trial."[581] Justice Tom

---

[571] 381 U.S. 532, 1 Media L. Rep. 1187 (1965). *See generally* Zimmerman, *Overcoming Future Shock: Estes Revisited, or a Modest Proposal for the Constitutional Protection of the News-Gathering Process*, 1980 DUKE L.J. 641 (1980).

[572] 449 U.S. 560, 7 Media L. Rep. 1041 (1981).

[573] Compare the discussion of *Estes* in the text accompanying *infra* notes 581–613 with the discussion of *Chandler* in the text accompanying *infra* notes 614–634.

[574] 449 U.S. at 582–83, 7 Media L. Rep. at 1050.

[575] *Id.* ("[T]here is no reason for this Court either to endorse or to invalidate Florida's experiment. In this setting, because this Court has no supervisory authority over state courts, our review is confined to whether there is a constitutional violation.").

[576] Federal Rule of Criminal Procedure 53 provides: "The taking of photographs in the court room during the progress of judicial proceedings or radio broadcasting of judicial proceedings from the court room shall not be permitted by the court." Likewise, local federal court rules often prohibit cameras in federal courtrooms, including the Supreme Court's chambers. Riemer, *Television Coverage of Trials: Constitutional Protection Against Absolute Denial of Access in the Absence of a Compelling Interest*, 30 VILL. L. REV. 1267, 1275 nn.30–32 (1985). However, even the federal courts finally have begun to experiment with televised judicial proceedings. In re Judicial Conference Guidelines, 18 Media L. Rep. 1270 (1990).

[577] Forty-five states now allow for some form of radio and television coverage of their courts, and 39 states allow media coverage with cameras and microphones in both trial and appellate courts. *RTNDA Report on Cameras in Courts*, EDITOR & PUBLISHER, Feb. 8, 1992, at p.20 (citing Radio-Television News Directors Association (RTNDA) report, *News Media Coverage of Judicial Proceedings With Cameras and Microphones: A Survey of the States*, Jan. 1, 1992).

[578] *See, e.g.*, In re Permitting Media Coverage for an Indefinite Period, 539 A.2d 976, 15 Media L. Rep. 1473 (R.I. 1988) (Rhode Island Supreme Court extended experimental program for electronic media coverage of court proceedings but amended guidelines to permit courts, by nonreviewable order, to exclude media).

[579] *See, e.g.*, State ex rel. Grinnell Communications Corp. v. Love, 406 N.E.2d 809, 6 Media L. Rep. 1615 (Ohio 1980) (relying on *Estes*).

[580] *See infra* note 637.

[581] 381 U.S. 532, 534–35, 1 Media L. Rep. 1187, 1188 (1965). Justice Clark wrote the opinion of the Court, in which Justice Harlan concurred "subject to the reservations and to the extent indicated in his concurring opinion." *Id.* at 534, 1 Media L. Rep. at 1188. Justice Harlan's concurrence appears *id.* at 587, 1 Media L. Rep. at 1207. Chief Justice Warren wrote a separate concurrence, in which Justices Douglas and Goldberg joined. *Id.* at 552, 1 Media L. Rep. at 1194. Leading the dissenters, Justice Stewart submitted an opinion in which Justices Black, Brennan, and White joined. *Id.* at 601, 1 Media L. Rep. at 1213. Justice White also wrote a separate dissenting opinion in which Justice Brennan joined; Justice Brennan also included a brief separate opinion. *Id.* at 617, 1 Media L. Rep. at 1219–20.

Clark, writing for the Court, described the case as one in which there had been "massive pretrial publicity" leading to "national notoriety" even before the defendant moved for an order preventing television and radio coverage, as well as still photography, of his trial.[582] The hearing on this motion, which lasted two days, was broadcast live on radio and television. All parties "conceded that the activities of the television crews and news photographers led to considerable disruption of the hearings."[583] Despite this, the trial judge denied the defendant's motion, instead granting a month's continuance of the trial date and ordering the construction of a booth at the courtroom's rear to which the court restricted all cameras and photographers.[584]

During the trial, the court made various rules governing coverage that "changed as the exigencies of the situation seemed to require."[585] As a result, there was very little live coverage of the trial. For example, at the defendant's request, the media did not film his attorneys. Therefore, the public saw only the state's side of the case, usually as film clips on "regularly scheduled newscasts."[586]

The Court decided that this media coverage had deprived the defendant of his due process rights and reversed his conviction.[587] In reaching this conclusion, Justice Clark set forth the following principles:

(1) The pretrial publicity, namely, the televised two-day hearing on whether to exclude the media, was relevant to whether the defendant had been deprived of his due process rights.[588]

(2) The media have no First Amendment right to televise from a courtroom, and courts do not discriminate between the print and electronic media so long as representatives of both can attend the trial. With the present state of television technology, the "hazards to a fair trial" are such that a defendant's fair trial rights must prevail over a claim of a right to televise.[589]

(3) Because "reporters of all media" could attend the trial, the public's "right to know" was satisfied.[590]

(4) Regardless of whether the defendant demonstrated actual prejudice to his due process rights, his conviction should be reversed because the state used a procedure "inherently lacking in due process."[591]

(5) Televising a criminal trial "might cause actual unfairness"[592] by (a) improperly influencing jurors regarding the notoriety of the defendant;[593] (b) impairing the trial witnesses' testimony;[594] (c) distracting the trial

---

[582]*Id.* at 535, 1 Media L. Rep. at 1188. The defendant already had been granted a venue change.

[583]*Id.* at 536, 1 Media L. Rep. at 1188. Both venire members and trial witnesses atttended the hearing, although the court released the venire members once the defendant received a trial continuance. *Id.* When a new jury was impaneled, four of the jurors had seen the televised hearings. *Id.* at 538, 1 Media L. Rep. at 1189.

[584]*Id.* at 536–37, 1 Media L. Rep. at 1188–89.

[585]*Id.* at 537, 1 Media L. Rep. at 1189.

[586]381 U.S. at 537, 1 Media L. Rep. at 1189. *See also id.* at 551, 1 Media L. Rep. at 1194.

[587]*Id.* at 535, 1 Media L. Rep. at 1188.

[588]*Id.* at 536, 1 Media L. Rep. at 1188.

[589]*Id.* at 539–40, 1 Media L. Rep. at 1189–90.

[590]*Id.* at 541, 1 Media L. Rep. at 1190.

[591]381 U.S. at 542–43, 1 Media L. Rep. at 1190–91.

[592]*Id.* at 545, 1 Media L. Rep. at 1192.

[593]*Id.* at 545–46, 1 Media L. Rep. at 1192.

[594]*Id.* at 547–48, 1 Media L. Rep. at 1192–93.

judge, particularly if he or she is an elected official;[595] and (d) placing pressure on the defendant and his relationship with his attorney.[596] Justice Clark noted that many of these factors had manifested themselves during the *Estes* trial.[597]

Chief Justice Warren's concurrence set forth his "additional views" on why "the televising of criminal trials is inherently a denial of due process."[598] It contained much stronger and more absolute language, referring to "our condemnation of televised criminal trials" and "our conclusion that this is the appropriate time to make a definitive appraisal of television in the courtroom."[599]

Furthermore, the Chief Justice indicated that televised criminal trials violate the Sixth Amendment fair trial guarantee, because television coverage (1) "diverts the trial from its proper purpose," (2) "gives the public the wrong impression about the purpose of trials," and (3) "singles out certain defendants and subjects them to trials under prejudicial conditions not experienced by others."[600] And, foreshadowing the Court's holding in *Gannett Co. v. DePasquale,* Chief Justice Warren noted that the Sixth Amendment's public trial guarantee is a right of the accused, not something conferring a "special benefit" on the media.[601]

In contrast, Justice John Harlan, while joining in the majority's conclusion that the defendant's due process rights had been violated by permitting television coverage during "a notorious criminal trial such as this one,"[602] stated that he did not wish to establish an absolute rule "preventing the States from pursuing a novel course of procedural experimentation."[603] Although he also joined in the majority holding that "[n]o constitutional provision guarantees a right to televise trials,"[604] Justice Harlan refused to concede that television's impact on trial fairness would be the same in every case, whether of "wide popular interest," like *Estes,* or merely "run-of-the-mill."[605] Having raised this distinction, however, he then stated that he was "by no means prepared to say that the constitutional issue should ultimately turn upon the nature of the particular case involved."[606]

Concluding an opinion that was as flexible as the Chief Justice's concurrence was absolute, Justice Harlan observed that

> [if the day arrives] when television will have become so commonplace an affair in the daily life of the average person as to dissipate all reasonable likelihood that

---

[595] *Id.* at 548–49, 1 Media L. Rep. at 1193.
[596] 381 U.S. at 549–50, 1 Media L. Rep. at 1193–94.
[597] *Id.* at 550–51, 1 Media L. Rep. at 1194. Specifically, Justice Clark observed that voir dire required an entire week, while the trial lasted only three days, and "the trial judge was . . . harassed." *Id.* at 551, 1 Media L. Rep. at 1194.
[598] *Id.* at 552, 1 Media L. Rep. at 1194 (Warren, C.J., concurring).
[599] *Id.*
[600] *Id.* at 565, 1 Media L. Rep. at 1199 (Warren, C.J., concurring). *See generally id.* at 565–83, 1 Media L. Rep. at 1199–1206 (Warren, C.J., concurring).
[601] 381 U.S. at 583, 1 Media L. Rep. at 1206 (Warren, C.J., concurring). *See* the discussion of *Gannett supra* §1.2(A)(i).
[602] *Id.* at 587, 1 Media L. Rep. at 1208 (Harlan, J., concurring).
[603] *Id.*
[604] *Id.* at 588, 1 Media L. Rep. at 1208 (Harlan, J., concurring).
[605] *Id.* at 590, 1 Media L. Rep. at 1209 (Harlan, J., concurring).
[606] 381 U.S. at 590, 1 Media L. Rep. at 1209 (Harlan, J., concurring).

its use in courtrooms may disparage the judicial process ... the constitutional judgment called for now would of course be subject to re-examination in accordance with the traditional workings of the Due Process Clause.[607]

Although Justice Stewart clearly dissented from the majority's conclusion that the defendant's due process rights had been violated,[608] the remainder of his opinion essentially echoed Justice Harlan's views. He felt that "the introduction of television into a courtroom is, at least in the present state of the art, an extremely unwise policy,"[609] but stated his unwillingness to translate "this personal view into a *per se* constitutional rule,"[610] noting that with changing television broadcast technology, "any *per se* rule ... might serve to stifle or abridge true First Amendment rights."[611]

Justice White's separate dissent likewise expressed his concern "that it is premature to promulgate such a broad constitutional principle ["a flat ban on the use of cameras in the courtroom"] at the present time."[612]

Finally, Justice Brennan noted in his brief separate opinion a fact that became the basis for *Chandler v. Florida* sixteen years later: "[O]nly four of the five Justices voting to reverse rest on the proposition that televised criminal trials are constitutionally infirm, whatever the circumstances .... Thus today's decision is *not* a blanket constitutional prohibition against the televising of state criminal trials."[613]

Like *Estes*,[614] the criminal defendants in *Chandler* challenged the constitutionality of Canon 3A(7) of Florida's Code of Judicial Conduct.[615] This provision, basically modeled after Canon 3A(7) of the American Bar Association's Code of Judicial Conduct, which was adopted in 1972,[616] set forth Florida's guidelines for a program permitting electronic media coverage of all its judicial proceedings. This program was initially experimental,[617] but in 1979 the Florida Supreme Court promulgated a revised Canon 3A(7) that was accompanied by implementing guidelines for permanent electronic media coverage.[618]

In *Chandler,* the U.S. Supreme Court held that Florida's Canon 3A(7) was not per se unconstitutional; it was only unconstitutional if the defendants

---

[607]*Id.* at 595–96, 1 Media L. Rep. at 1211 (Harlan, J., concurring).
[608]*Id.* at 601, 1 Media L. Rep. at 1213 (Stewart, J., dissenting). *See generally id.* at 604–11, 1 Media L. Rep. at 1214–17 (Stewart, J., dissenting).
[609]*Id.* at 601, 1 Media L. Rep. at 1213 (Stewart, J., dissenting).
[610]*Id.* at 601–02, 1 Media L. Rep. at 1213–14 (Stewart, J., dissenting).
[611]381 U.S. at 604, 1 Media L. Rep. at 1214 (Stewart, J., dissenting).
[612]*Id.* at 615, 1 Media L. Rep. at 1219 (White, J., dissenting).
[613]*Id.* at 617, 1 Media L. Rep. at 1219–20 (Brennan, J., dissenting).
[614]In *Estes,* the defendant "recite[d] his claim in the framework of Canon 35 of the Judicial Canons of the American Bar Association," which was the predecessor to Canon 3A(7). Canon 35 set forth the ABA's view at the time that the "broadcasting, televising, and photographing of court proceedings" should be prohibited. In Texas, however, it had "no binding effect on the courts." Estes v. Texas, 381 U.S. 532, 535, 1 Media L. Rep. 1187, 1188 (1965).
[615]Chandler v. Florida, 449 U.S. 560, 567, 7 Media L. Rep. 1041, 1044 (1981).
[616]*Id.* at 563, 7 Media L. Rep. at 1042.
[617]*Id.* at 562–65, 7 Media L. Rep. at 1042–43. The original text of Florida's Canon 3(A)(7) appears *id.* at 564 n.2, 7 Media L. Rep. at 1042 n.2. *See* In re Post-Newsweek Stations, Fla., 327 So. 2d 1 (Fla.) (announcing experimental program for televising one civil and one criminal trial), *amended,* 337 So. 2d 804 (Fla. 1976), *amended,* 347 So. 2d 402, 2 Media L. Rep. 1832 (Fla. 1977) (supplementing earlier opinion and establishing one-year pilot program for covering all judicial proceedings without necessity for trial parties' consent).
[618]*Chandler,* 449 U.S. at 564–66, 7 Media L. Rep. at 1043 (setting out text of revised Canon 3A(7)). *See* In re Post-Newsweek Stations, 370 So. 2d 764, 778–79, 5 Media L. Rep. 1039, 1050–51 (Fla. 1979) (setting forth permanent guidelines for electronic media coverage).

showed that actual prejudice had resulted when the court permitted broadcast coverage of the trial over their objections.[619] The Court based its opinion on a careful reading of *Estes'* "six separate opinions."[620] In particular, the Court focused on Justice Harlan's concurrence, observing that because he "provided the fifth vote necessary in support of the judgment," his opinion was "fundamental to an understanding of the ultimate holding of *Estes.*"[621] After "parsing" that opinion, the Court concluded that

> *Estes* is not to be read as announcing a constitutional rule barring still photographic, radio and television coverage in all cases and under all circumstances. It does not stand as an absolute ban on state experimentation with an evolving technology, which, in terms of modes of mass communication, was in its relative infancy in 1964, and is, even now, in a state of continuing change.[622]

Having decided that *Estes* did not control its decision, the Court refused to establish a per se "constitutional ban on all broadcast coverage," including Florida's program.[623] The Court set forth several reasons for this, including:

(1) the lack of "unimpeachable" empirical data "sufficient to establish that the mere presence of the broadcast media inherently has an adverse effect on [the judicial] process";[624]

(2) changes both in "television technology" and "safeguards [that] have been built into the experimental programs in state courts, and into the Florida program, to avoid some of the most egregious problems envisioned by the six opinions in the *Estes* case";[625] and

(3) encouraging the "concept of federalism" by permitting the states to experiment with their own broadcasting programs.[626]

Finally, the Court held that the defendants had failed to meet their burden of proving that broadcast coverage had denied them due process at their trial, specifically noting that neither defendant had "show[n] that the media's coverage of his case ... compromised the ability of the jury to judge him fairly" nor that "coverage ... had an adverse impact on the trial participants sufficient to constitute a denial of due process."[627]

Justices Stewart and White both indicated in their concurrences that *Estes* should be overruled.[628] Justice Stewart noted that "the restrictions on television in the *Estes* trial were not significantly different from those in the trial of these

---

[619]449 U.S. at 577, 582–83, 7 Media L. Rep. at 1048, 1050. Chief Justice Burger wrote the opinion of the Court, in which five other Justices joined: Brennan, Marshall, Blackmun, Powell, and Rehnquist. *Id.* at 562–63, 7 Media L. Rep. at 1042. Both Justices Stewart and White wrote separate concurring opinions, with Stewart concurring in "the result" and White in "the judgment." *Id.* at 561, 583, 586, 7 Media L. Rep. at 1042, 1051, 1052. Justice Stevens did not take part in the case. *Id.* at 562–63, 583, 7 Media L. Rep. at 1042, 1051.

[620]*Id.* at 570–71, 7 Media L. Rep. at 1045.
[621]*Id.*
[622]*Id.* at 573–74, 7 Media L. Rep. at 1046–47.
[623]*Id.* at 574–75, 7 Media L. Rep. at 1047.
[624]449 U.S. at 576 & n.11, 578–79, 7 Media L. Rep. at 1048 & n.11, 1049.
[625]*Id.* at 576–77, 7 Media L. Rep. at 1048. The Court noted in this regard that the criminal defendants had not made use of Florida's procedural safeguards, neither requesting "an evidentiary hearing to show adverse impact or injury" nor making "anything more than generalized allegations of prejudice."
[626]*Id.* at 579–81, 7 Media L. Rep. at 1049–50.
[627]*Id.* at 581, 7 Media L. Rep. at 1050.
[628]*Id.* at 583, 7 Media L. Rep. at 1051 (Stewart, J., concurring in result); *id.* at 587, 7 Media L. Rep. at 1052 (White, J., concurring in judgment).

appellants."[629] He concluded that *Estes* could not be distinguished from *Chandler* on that basis, and therefore that "[t]oday the Court reaches precisely the opposite conclusion [from *Estes*]. I have no great trouble in agreeing with the Court today, but I would acknowledge our square departure from precedent."[630]

Justice White emphasized that he had been one of the *Estes* dissenters.[631] He felt that the Court's opinion in *Chandler* had "effectively eviscerate[d] *Estes*"[632] even if *Estes* was read narrowly "as forbidding the televising of only widely publicized and sensational criminal trials."[633] He pointed out that "[t]he Florida rule has no exception for the sensational or widely publicized case."[634]

Even before *Chandler,* a variety of courts had upheld the constitutionality of their states' programs for electronic media coverage of judicial proceedings, whether experimental or permanent.[635] After *Chandler,* courts were even more willing to uphold such experiments.[636]

Even after *Chandler,* however, courts have refused to find any First or Sixth Amendment right to insist on broadcast coverage of a judicial proceeding. Thus, challenges to Federal Rule of Criminal Procedure 53, which prohibits electronic media coverage of federal proceedings, have failed,[637] as have some

---

[629]449 U.S. at 583, 7 Media L. Rep. at 1051 (Stewart, J., concurring in result).
[630]*Id.* at 586, 7 Media L. Rep. at 1052 (Stewart, J., concurring in result).
[631]*Id.* at 587, 7 Media L. Rep. at 1052 (White, J., concurring in judgment).
[632]*Id.* at 588, 7 Media L. Rep. at 1053 (White, J., concurring in judgment).
[633]*Id.* at 587, 7 Media L. Rep. at 1052 (White, J., concurring in judgment). Justice White based this narrow interpretation of *Estes* on Justice Harlan's concurrence.
[634]449 U.S. at 588, 7 Media L. Rep. at 1053 (White, J., concurring in judgment).
[635]Trinidad v. Stettin, 5 Media L. Rep. 1171, 1173–74 (S.D. Fla. 1979) (court found nothing unconstitutional about Florida's Canon 3A(7) on its face, citing Justice Harlan's concurrence in *Estes* and commenting that trials at issue not well-publicized); State ex rel. Grinnell Communications Corp. v. Love, 406 N.E.2d 809, 811, 6 Media L. Rep. 1615, 1617 (Ohio 1980) (trial court cannot rely on *Estes* to prevent media coverage pursuant to Ohio rules, which make broadcast coverage mandatory); State v. Wampler, 569 P.2d 46, 3 Media L. Rep. 1639 (Or. Ct. App. 1977) (trial court's order permitting use of television cameras and lights in hallway outside courtroom not per se unconstitutional, citing *Estes*), *cert. denied,* 436 U.S. 960 (1978). *See also* Lyles v. State, 330 P.2d 734, 739, 742 (Okla. Crim. App. 1958) (pre-*Estes* decision permitting television cameras and still photography in courtroom under equal access concept; court criticized Canon 35 as "fabricated out of sheer implication and not hammered out on the anvil of experience").
[636]*See, e.g.,* State v. Newsome, 426 A.2d 68, 71–73, 7 Media L. Rep. 1308, 1310–12 (N.J. Super. Ct. App. Div. 1981) (television coverage of murder trial pursuant to New Jersey's experimental program did not per se violate defendant's due process and fair trial rights, citing *Estes* and *Chandler* and specifically noting that New Jersey guidelines for electronic media prevent evils of *Estes*); State v. Hanna, 378 S.E.2d 640, 645, 17 Media L. Rep. 1411, 1414 (W. Va. 1989) (upholding criminal conviction despite claim that noise from cameras interfered with fair trial rights: "the defendant has the burden of showing with specificity the deleterious effect of the media coverage on his trial"); Georgia Television Co. v. Napper, 365 S.E.2d 275, 14 Media L. Rep. 2382 (Ga. 1988) (error to deny television coverage of judicial proceeding about whether local government had to open meeting to press and public on grounds that judicial proceeding not newsworthy and such coverage would " 'stifle, inhibit, frustrate or prevent' the Socratic dialogue beneficial to the free exchange of ideas between court and counsel"); People v. Spring, 200 Cal. Rptr. 849 (Cal. Ct. App. 1984) (in murder case, defendant failed to show with specificity that presence of television camera impaired jury's ability to decide case or that television camera adversely affected any trial participants). *But see* Georgia Television Co. v. State, 363 S.E.2d 528, 14 Media L. Rep. 2143 (Ga. 1988) (no abuse of discretion to deny television coverage of pretrial proceedings in criminal case where previous conviction set aside because of pretrial publicity).
[637]Conway v. United States, 852 F.2d 187, 15 Media L. Rep. 1967 (6th Cir.) (FED. R. CRIM. P. 53 and analogous local rule absolutely prohibiting broadcasting, telecasting, and photographing do not violate First Amendment right of access to judicial proceedings), *cert. denied,* 488 U.S. 943 (1988); United States v. Edwards, 785 F.2d 1293, 12 Media L. Rep. 1997 (5th Cir. 1986) (same); United States v. Kerley, 753 F.2d 617, 620–22, 11 Media L. Rep. 1572, 1574–76 (7th Cir. 1985) (defendant had no First or Sixth Amendment right to have criminal trial broadcast where prohibited by FED. R. CRIM. P. 53); Westmoreland v. Columbia Broadcasting Sys., 752 F.2d 16, 21–24, 11 Media L. Rep. 1013, 1016–19 (2d Cir. 1984) (no First Amendment right to televise civil trial where local federal court rule prohibited coverage, citing *Estes* and *Chandler*), *cert. denied,* 472 U.S. 1017 (1985); United States v. Hastings, 695 F.2d 1278, 1282–84, 8 Media L. Rep. 2617, 2620–22 (11th Cir.) (FED. R. CRIM. P. 53 and local federal rule prohibiting broadcast coverage of criminal trial did not violate First or Sixth Amendment, citing *Estes* and *Chandler*), *cert. denied,* 461 U.S. 931 (1983).

challenges to restrictions on electronic coverage of government meetings.[638] In a similar vein, challenges to bans on the use of tape recorders have also been unsuccessful, although it is hard to see what substantial objection there is to the use of such devices.[639]

Finally, various state court rules and procedures require an evidentiary hearing on any motion about electronic coverage as well as findings that justify any exclusion.[640] Various categories of cases or testimony have also been suggested as justifying the exclusion or limitation of cameras in the courtroom.[641] Once electronic access is granted, however, a court cannot reserve the right to edit what will be broadcast.[642]

§1.11 Open Meetings and Public Records Laws

The federal legislation that addresses these issues are the Freedom of Information Act (FOIA),[643] which provides for public disclosure and access to records maintained by various federal agencies, departments, and bodies; and the Government in the Sunshine Act,[644] which requires many of the same entities to conduct their decision-making meetings openly. No attempt is made here to explain the intricacies of these two acts, which by themselves have received lengthy examinations.[645] Similar state public records laws[646] and open

---

[638] Johnson v. Adams, 629 F. Supp. 1563, 12 Media L. Rep. 1973 (E.D. Tex. 1986) (county board's refusal to allow videotaping upheld). *See also* Combined Communications Corp. v. Finesilver, 672 F.2d 818, 821, 8 Media L. Rep. 1233, 1234 (10th Cir. 1982) (no First Amendment right to televise court-ordered settlement negotiations taking place at courthouse, citing *Estes*). *But see supra* notes 541–545.

[639] United States v. Yonkers Bd. of Educ., 747 F.2d 111, 10 Media L. Rep. 2521 (2d Cir. 1984) (relying on local court rule); Sigma Delta Chi v. Speaker, Md. House of Delegates, 310 A.2d 156, 1 Media L. Rep. 2375 (Md. 1973) (prohibition against tape recorders on legislature's floor upheld).

[640] Multimedia WMAZ v. State, 353 S.E.2d 173, 13 Media L. Rep. 2069 (Ga. 1987) (Georgia rules require notice, hearing, and specific findings before exclusion of electronic media); Ohio ex rel. Miami Valley Broadcasting Corp. v. Kessler, 413 N.E.2d 1203, 1204–05, 6 Media L. Rep. 2341, 2343 (Ohio 1980) (under Ohio procedures, court must give media notice of hearing if defendants dispute broadcast coverage, including opportunity at that hearing to cross-examine defendant's witnesses and adduce proof regarding impact of coverage); State v. Palm Beach Newspapers, 395 So. 2d 544, 548–49, 7 Media L. Rep. 1021, 1023–24 (Fla. 1981) (under Florida's Canon 3A(7), trial court must conduct evidentiary hearing before prohibiting broadcast coverage of murder trial testimony; witness' "bare asssertion of fear" should not be sufficient to bar cameras); State ex rel. New Mexico Press Ass'n v. Kaufman, 648 P.2d 300, 304 (N.M. 1982) (notice, hearing, and findings required). *See also* KFMB-TV Channel 8 v. Municipal Ct., 271 Cal. Rptr. 109, 112–13, 17 Media L. Rep. 2294, 2297 (Cal. Ct. App. 1990) (court should explain its reasons for denying access).

[641] State v. Green, 395 So. 2d 532, 537, 7 Media L. Rep. 1025, 1027 (Fla. 1981) (categories of witnesses or cases that may justify exclusion of cameras in courtroom: (1) undercover officers or informants, (2) witnesses with new identities, (3) incarcerated witnesses who fear reprisal when they return to prison, (4) rape victims, and (5) child custody proceedings; upholding ban on electronic coverage based on finding it would render plaintiff incompetent); Ladone v. Lerner, 521 N.Y.S.2d 760, 14 Media L. Rep. 2110 (N.Y. App. Div. 1987) (no error to deny broadcast coverage of summations and jury charge in criminal case because of case's emotionally charged and highly volatile nature).

[642] *KFMB-TV Channel 8*, 271 Cal. Rptr. at 112, 17 Media L. Rep. at 2296 ("Once the proceedings have been recorded there is nothing in the rule authorizing the court to refuse, limit, or terminate the later broadcasting of such proceeding.").

[643] 5 U.S.C. §552, Pub. L. 89-554 §1, 80 Stat. 383 (1966).

[644] 5 U.S.C. §552b, Pub. L. 94-409 §3(a), 90 Stat. 1241 (1976).

[645] *See, e.g.*, J. O'Reilly, Federal Information Disclosure: Procedures, Forms and the Law (1990); Allen Adler, Litigation Under the Federal Open Government Laws (17th ed. 1992).

[646] Ala. Code §36-12-40 *et seq.*; Alaska Stat. §09.25.110; Ariz. Rev. Stat. Ann. §39-121; Ark. Stat. Ann. §25-19-101 *et seq.*; Cal. Gov't Code §6250 *et seq.*; Colo. Rev. Stat. §24-72-201 *et seq.*; Conn. Gen. Stat. §1-19; Del. Code Ann. tit. 29, §10001 *et seq.*; D.C. Code Ann. §1-1521 *et seq.*; Fla. Stat. §119.01 *et seq.*; Ga. Code §50-18-70 *et seq.*; Hawaii Rev. Stat. §92F-11 *et seq.*; Idaho Code §9-338 *et seq.*; Ill. Rev. Stat. ch. 116, §43.4 *et seq.*; Ind. Code §5-14-3-1 *et seq.*; Iowa Code §22.1 *et seq.*; Kan. Stat. Ann. §45-215 *et seq.*; Ky. Rev. Stat. §61.870 *et seq.*; La. Rev. Stat. Ann. §10-611; Me. Rev. Stat. tit. 1, §401 *et seq.*;

meetings laws also exist.[647] They are important avenues to information about the government, but review of their provisions is beyond the scope of this book.

MD. ANN. CODE art. 76A, §1 et seq.; MASS. GEN. LAWS ANN. ch. 66, §10; MICH. COMP. LAWS §15.231 et seq.; MINN. STAT. ANN. §13.03; MISS. CODE ANN. §25-61-1 et seq.; MO. REV. STAT. §610 et seq.; MONT. REV. CODE ANN. §2-6-101 et seq.; NEB. REV. STAT. §84-712 et seq.; NEV. REV. STAT. §239.010 et seq.; N.H. REV. STAT. ANN. §91-A:1 et seq.; N.J. STAT. ANN. §47:1A-1 et seq.; N.M. STAT. ANN. §14-2-1 et seq.; N.Y. PUB. OFF. LAW §84 et seq.; N.C. GEN. STAT. §132-1 et seq.; N.D. CENT. CODE §44-04-18; OHIO REV. CODE ANN. tit. 1, §149.43; OKLA. STAT. ANN. tit. 51, §24A.1 et seq.; OR. REV. STAT. §192.410 et seq.; PA. STAT. ANN. tit. 65, §66.1 et seq.; R.I. GEN. LAWS §38-2-1 et seq.; S.C. CODE ANN. §30-4-10 et seq.; S.D. COMP. LAWS ANN. §1-27-1 et seq.; TENN. CODE ANN. §10-7-503; TEX. REV. CIV. STAT. ANN. tit. 110A, art. 6252-17A; UTAH STAT. ANN. §63-2-59 et seq.; VT. STAT. ANN. tit. 1, §315 et seq.; VA. CODE §2.1-340 et seq.; WASH. REV. CODE ANN. §42.17.260 et seq.; W. VA. CODE §29B-1-1 et seq.; WIS. STAT. §19.21; WYO. STAT. §16-4-201 et seq.

[647]ALA. CODE §13A-14-2; ALASKA STAT. §44.62.310; ARIZ. REV. STAT. ANN. §38-431 et. seq.; ARK. STAT. ANN. §25-19-101 et seq.; CAL. GOV'T CODE §54953; COLO. REV. STAT. §29-9-101; CONN. GEN. STAT. §1-21; DEL. CODE ANN. tit. 29, §10001 et seq.; D.C. CODE ANN. §1-1504; FLA. STAT. §286.011; GA. CODE §50-14-1 et seq.; HAWAII REV. STAT. §92-1 et seq.; IDAHO CODE §67-2340 et seq.; ILL. REV. STAT. ch. 102, §41 et seq.; IND. CODE §5-14-1.5-1 et seq.; IOWA CODE §21.1 et seq.; KAN. STAT. ANN. §75-4317 et seq.; KY. REV. STAT. §61.805 et seq.; LA. REV. STAT. ANN. §42:5; ME. REV. STAT. tit. 1, §401 et seq.; MD. ANN. CODE §10-501 et seq.; MASS. GEN. LAWS ANN. ch. 30A, §11A1/2; MICH. COMP. LAWS §15.261 et seq.; MINN. STAT. ANN. §471.705; MISS. CODE ANN. §25-41-1 et seq.; MO. REV. STAT. §610 et seq.; MONT. REV. CODE ANN. §2-3-201 et seq.; NEB. REV. STAT. §84-1408 et seq.; NEV. REV. STAT. §241.020 et seq.; N.H. REV. STAT. ANN. §91-A:1 et seq.; N.J. STAT. ANN. §10:4-7 et seq.; N.M. STAT. ANN. §10-15-1 et seq.; N.Y. PUB. OFF. LAW §100 et seq.; N.C. GEN. STAT. §143-318.9 et seq.; N.D. CENT. CODE §44-04-19; OHIO REV. CODE ANN. tit. 1, §121.22; OKLA. STAT. ANN. tit. 25, §301 et seq.; OR. REV. STAT. §192.610 et seq.; PA. STAT. ANN. tit. 65, §271 et seq.; R.I. GEN. LAWS §42-46-1 et seq.; S.C. CODE ANN. §30-4-10 et seq.; S.D. COMP. LAWS ANN. §1-25-1 et seq.; TENN. CODE ANN. §8-44-101 et seq.; TEX. REV. CIV. STAT. ANN. tit. 110A, art. 6252-17; UTAH CODE ANN. §52-4-1 et seq.; VT. STAT. ANN. tit. 1, §311 et seq.; VA. CODE §2.1-340 et seq.; WASH. REV. CODE ANN. §42.30.010 et seq.; W. VA. CODE §6-9A-1 et seq.; WIS. STAT. §19.81 et. seq.; WYO. STAT. §16-4-401 et seq.

Chapter 2

DEFAMATION

§2.1 The Common Law of Defamation

At common law, the elements of defamation were the publication[1] of a defamatory statement[2] of and concerning the plaintiff.[3] Liability could be premised on a statement of the defendant's opinion.[4] In those instances, where defamatory statements were actionable per se, general damages were presumed.[5] It also was presumed that the statement was false, so the defendant had the burden of proving its truth.[6] The defendant's fault was presumed as well,[7] as was malice.[8] Thus, at common law, defamation was a strict liability tort.[9] Unless there was an applicable privilege, it was not necessary to show any fault on the defendant's part to prevail.

---

[1] McGuire v. Adkins, 226 So. 2d 659, 661 (Ala. 1969); Gaetano v. Sharon Herald Co., 231 A.2d 753, 755 (Pa. 1967); Almy v. Kvamme, 387 P.2d 372, 374 (Wash. 1963).

[2] Kimmerle v. New York Evening Journal, 186 N.E. 217, 218 (N.Y. 1933) (defining defamation as "words which tend to expose one to public hatred, shame, obloquy, contumely, odium, contempt, ridicule, aversion, ostracism, degradation, or disgrace, or to induce an evil opinion of one in the minds of right-thinking persons, and to deprive one of their confidence and friendly intercourse in society"). For cases using the more modern definition provided in the Restatement (Second) of Torts §559 (1977) [hereinafter Restatement (Second)] ("[a] communication is defamatory if it tends so to harm the reputation of another as to lower him in the estimation of the community or to deter third persons from associating or dealing with him"), see Morrison v. National Broadcasting Co., 227 N.E.2d 572, 574 (N.Y. 1967); Beecher v. Montgomery Ward & Co., 517 P.2d 667, 669 (Or. 1973); Cosgrove Studio & Camera Shop v. Pane, 182 A.2d 751, 753 (Pa. 1962). *See also infra* §2.5.

[3] Gnapinsky v. Goldyn, 128 A.2d 697, 702–03 (N.J. 1957); Brodsky v. Journal Pub'g Co., 42 N.W.2d 855, 857 (N.D. 1950); Ryan v. Hearst Pub'g, 100 P.2d 24, 25 (Wash. 1940).

[4] Smith v. Levitt, 227 F.2d 855 (9th Cir. 1955); Lowe v. Brown, 235 P. 272 (Or. 1925).

[5] Layne v. Tribune Co., 146 So. 234, 236 (Fla. 1933); Roth v. Greensboro News Co., 6 S.E.2d 882, 888 (N.C. 1940); Lavdati v. Stea, 117 A. 422, 424 (R.I. 1922). Where a statement was not actionable per se, the plaintiff was required to plead and prove special damages. Life Printing & Pub'g Co. v. Field, 58 N.E.2d 307, 311 (Ill. App. Ct. 1944); Walker v. Tucker, 295 S.W. 138, 139 (Ky. 1927); Gaare v. Melbostad, 242 N.W. 466, 467 (Minn. 1932). For a discussion of when defamatory statements are actionable per se, see *infra* §§2.5(I), (J), and (K).

[6] Age-Herald Pub'g Co. v. Waterman, 81 So. 621, 626 (Ala. 1919); Rhynas v. Adkisson, 159 N.W. 877, 880 (Iowa 1916); Owens v. Scott Pub'g Co., 284 P.2d 296, 303–04 (Wash. 1955), *cert. denied*, 350 U.S. 968 (1956). The original common law rule held that truth was not a defense. Garrison v. Louisiana, 379 U.S. 64, 72, 1 Media L. Rep. 1548, 1551 (1964). Indeed, at one time the rule was that "the greater the truth, the greater the libel." W. Prosser & P. Keeton, Handbook on the Law of Torts §116 at 840 n.6 (5th ed. 1984) (attributed to Lord Mansfield); *see also* L.W. Levy, Legacy of Suppression: Freedom of Speech and Press in Early American History 13 (1960).

[7] Upton v. Times-Democrat Pub'g Co., 28 So. 970, 971 (La. 1901); *Roth*, 6 S.E.2d at 887; Corrigan v. Bobbs-Merrill Co., 126 N.E. 260, 262 (N.Y. 1920).

[8] State v. Clyne, 35 P. 789, 791 (Kan. 1894); *Waterman*, 81 So. at 626; Burnett v. National Enquirer, 144 Cal. App. 3d 991, 1007, 193 Cal. Rptr. 206, 9 Media L. Rep. 1921 (Cal. Ct. App. 1983), *appeal dismissed*, 465 U.S. 1014 (1984).

[9] Gertz v. Robert Welch, Inc., 418 U.S. 323, 346, 1 Media L. Rep. 1633 (1974); Peck v. Tribune Co.,

Because of these common law presumptions, a prima facie case of defamation was easily proved. Professor Lawrence H. Eldredge recommended that the plaintiff put the defendant publisher on the stand, authenticate the offending article, have it admitted into evidence, establish the newspaper's circulation (if it was impressive), and rest.[10] All the common law elements of defamation—the publication of a defamatory statement about the plaintiff—would have been shown.[11] It was then up to the defendant to prove truth or demonstrate a privilege to avoid liability. In short, the common law of defamation strongly favored plaintiffs. The constitutionalization of defamation, discussed next, has reversed many of these presumptions.

§2.2 IMPACT OF THE FIRST AMENDMENT ON DEFAMATION LAW

Before 1964, the U.S. Supreme Court refused to apply the First Amendment in defamation cases.[12] Beginning in 1964, however, with its seminal opinion in *New York Times Co. v. Sullivan*,[13] the Supreme Court revolutionized the common law of defamation by applying the First Amendment to many such cases. In *Sullivan*, the plaintiff, one of the three elected commissioners for the city of Montgomery, Alabama, with responsibility for its police department, brought a libel action based on a paid advertisement that was critical of the Montgomery Police Department's treatment of blacks. The defendants were four black Alabama clergymen, who allegedly prepared the ad, and *The New York Times*, which published it.[14]

In accord with the common law, the trial judge instructed the jury that the statements were not privileged, and that because the statements were libelous per se, malice, falsity, and general damages were presumed; the plaintiff only had to prove that the statements were published and were of and concerning him.[15]

The Supreme Court[16] noted that the history of the United States has been marked by "a profound national commitment to the principle that debate on

---

214 U.S. 185, 189 (1909). *But see* Summit Hotel Co. v. National Broadcasting Co., 8 A.2d 302, 306–8 (Pa. 1939) (rejecting strict liability for any personal injury tort, including defamation).

[10]Eldredge, *Practical Problems in Preparation and Trial of Libel Cases,* 15 VAND. L. REV. 1085, 1089–90 (1962).

[11]This assumes that the statement in question is libelous on its face and there is no dispute that the publication is about the plaintiff. *Id.* at 1089.

[12]New York Times Co. v. Sullivan, 376 U.S. 254, 268 & n.6, 1 Media L. Rep. 1527, 1532–33 & n.6 (1964).

[13]376 U.S. 254, 1 Media L. Rep. 1527 (1964). This decision and *Gertz,* 418 U.S. 323, 1 Media L. Rep. 1633, are so important to an understanding of modern defamation law that they should be read by anyone interested in this subject.

[14]376 U.S. at 256, 1 Media L. Rep. at 1528.

[15]*Id.* at 262, 1 Media L. Rep. at 1530.

[16]Initially, the Court rejected two arguments against the application of the First Amendment. First, the Court held that there was sufficient state action to justify application of the First Amendment via the Fourteenth Amendment, because the Alabama courts had utilized state power in deciding this case. *Id.* at 265, 1 Media L. Rep. at 1531. The Court also rejected the argument that the First Amendment applies only to the federal government and not to the states. *Id.* at 276–78, 1 Media L. Rep. at 1536–37. Second, the Court held that the then-existing commercial speech exception to the First Amendment did not apply, even though a paid advertisement was at the heart of this case. *Id.* at 265, 1 Media L. Rep. at 1531–32. While the advertisement was in a sense commercial, "[i]t communicated information, expressed opinion, recited grievances, protested claimed abuses, and sought financial support on behalf of a movement whose existence and objectives are matters of the highest public interest and concern." *Id.* at 266, 1 Media L. Rep. at 1532. The Court held that it was also irrelevant that *The New York Times* was paid for the advertisement, because

public issues should be uninhibited, robust, and wide-open, and that it may well include vehement, caustic, and sometimes unpleasantly sharp attacks on government and public officials."[17] It then reversed the $500,000 judgment in favor of the commissioner.[18] In its key holding, the Court ruled that the First Amendment requires

> a federal rule that prohibits a public official from recovering damages for a defamatory falsehood relating to his official conduct unless he proves that the statement was made with "actual malice"—that is, with knowledge that it was false or with reckless disregard of whether it was false or not.[19]

In reaching this conclusion, the Court found that "erroneous statement is inevitable in free debate, and that it must be protected if the freedoms of expression are to have the 'breathing space' that they 'need ... to survive.' "[20] Thus, the fact that a statement is false cannot eliminate First Amendment protection. Similarly, injury to officials' reputations by defamatory statements cannot eliminate First Amendment protection: "Criticism of their official conduct does not lose its constitutional protection merely because it is effective criticism and hence diminishes their official reputations."[21]

Nor can the combination of these two items—false statements that damage reputations—eliminate First Amendment protection. As the Court stated, "[t]his is the lesson to be drawn from the great controversy over the Sedition Act of 1798."[22] That law had essentially transplanted the English common law of seditious libel[23] to the United States by making it a crime to defame the U.S. government or any of its top officials. After reviewing the history of the Sedition Act, including the conclusions of Congress, President Thomas Jefferson, various Supreme Court justices, and legal commentators that the Act was unconstitutional, the Court found that "the attack upon its [constitutional] validity has carried the day in the court of history."[24]

Finally, the Court found that the defense of truth was inadequate to prevent self-censorship:[25]

> Under such a rule, would-be critics of official conduct may be deterred from voicing their criticism, even though it is believed to be true and even though it is in fact true, because of doubt whether it can be proved in court or fear of the expense of having to do so.[26]

---

any other conclusion would shut off editorial advertisements. *Id.* For a discussion of the commercial speech doctrine, see Chapter 11.

[17]*Id.* at 270, 1 Media L. Rep. at 1533–34.

[18]One commentator has described this decision as " 'an occasion for dancing in the streets.' " Kalven, *The New York Times Case: A Note on "The Central Meaning of the First Amendment,"* 1964 SUP. CT. REV. 191, 221 (quoting Alexander Meiklejohn).

[19]376 U.S. at 279–80, 1 Media L. Rep. at 1537. Justices Black, Douglas, and Goldberg concurred on the grounds that the First Amendment prevented *any* defamation claims in such circumstances. *Id.* at 293–305, 1 Media L. Rep. at 1545–48. For a discussion of this issue, see *infra* §2.11(A)(ii).

[20]*Id.* at 271–72, 1 Media L. Rep. at 1534 (quoting NAACP v. Button, 371 U.S. 415, 433 (1963)).

[21]*Id.* at 273, 1 Media L. Rep. at 1534–35.

[22]*Id.*, 1 Media L. Rep. at 1535.

[23]For a discussion of the English law, see LEVY, *supra* note 6, at 7–17. Levy also discusses the passage and application of the Sedition Act of 1798. *Id.* at 198–214.

[24]376 U.S. at 276, 1 Media L. Rep. at 1536.

[25]*Id.* at 278, 1 Media L. Rep. at 1536.

[26]*Id.* at 279, 1 Media L. Rep. at 1537. Numerous other decisions have also expressed concern with the "chilling effect" on the exercise of free speech and press rights that can result from defamation suits. As the Supreme Court noted in Dombrowski v. Pfister, 380 U.S. 479, 487 (1965): "The chilling effect upon the exercise of First Amendment rights may derive from the fact of the prosecution, unaffected by the prospects

Having established the fault standard to be applied in defamation actions involving public official plaintiffs, the Court made " 'an independent examination of the whole record' " to determine whether the evidence presented showed with convincing clarity that the defendants had acted with actual malice.[27] As to the four individual defendants, there was no evidence that they knew or had reason to know that anything in the advertisement was false, so the judgment as to them was reversed.[28]

As to *The New York Times,* the Court held that its failure to retract the statements as to the plaintiff commissioner and its correction as to the governor of Alabama did not show actual malice at the time of publication.[29] There was also evidence introduced at trial showing that the *Times* did not verify the accuracy of the advertisement by comparing it to news stories contained in its own files.[30] The Court ruled that this did not establish that the *Times* acted with actual malice.[31] While the failure to verify the accuracy of statements contained in the advertisement may have constituted negligence, that failure was insufficient to show that the people at the *Times* who were responsible for the publication actually "knew" that the advertisement contained false statements.[32]

The *Sullivan* decision also constitutionalized the common law rule that a defamatory statement must be "of and concerning" the plaintiff. While the advertisement referred to the Montgomery Police Department, it contained no reference to the plaintiff, either by name or by official position.[33] The Court held that the First Amendment precluded recovery by a public official for impersonal defamatory remarks that were critical of government operations.[34] A contrary holding would have subjected the press to liability whenever it exercised its constitutional right to publish remarks critical of the government.[35]

In its next important defamation decision, which addressed two consolidated cases, *Curtis Publishing Co. v. Butts* and *Associated Press v. Walker,*[36] the Supreme Court held that the actual malice rule also applied to defamatory statements about plaintiffs who were *public figures* rather than *public officials.* Plaintiff Wally Butts was the athletic director for the University of Georgia,

---

of its success or failure." *Accord* Ollman v. Evans, 750 F.2d 970, 993, 11 Media L. Rep. 1433 (D.C. Cir. 1984), *cert. denied,* 471 U.S. 1127 (1985) (libel actions "may threaten the public and constitutional interest in free, and frequently rough, discussion") (Bork, J., concurring); Franchise Realty Interstate Corp. v. San Francisco Local Joint Exec. Bd. of Culinary Workers, 542 F.2d 1076, 1083 (9th Cir. 1976), *cert. denied,* 430 U.S. 940 (1977) (noting that where First Amendment guarantees are at issue, there is "danger that the mere pendency of the action will chill the exercise of First Amendment rights"). *See also infra* §2.21.

The Court also noted that public officials are protected by an absolute privilege when they are sued for defamation by those they criticize. The Court concluded that the actual malice rule, which protects individuals who criticize public officials, would counterbalance this advantage of public officials. 376 U.S. at 282, 1 Media L. Rep. at 1538.

[27] 376 U.S. at 285, 1 Media L. Rep. at 1540 (quoting Edwards v. South Carolina, 372 U.S. 229, 235 (1963)). For a discussion of the standards for appellate review, see *infra* §2.25.
[28] 376 U.S. at 285–86, 1 Media L. Rep. at 1540.
[29] *Id.* at 286–87, 1 Media L. Rep. at 1540.
[30] *Id.* at 287, 1 Media L. Rep. at 1540.
[31] *Id.*
[32] *Id.* at 287–88, 1 Media L. Rep. at 1540–41.
[33] 376 U.S. at 288, 1 Media L. Rep. at 1541.
[34] *Id.* at 292, 1 Media L. Rep. at 1542–43. *See also infra* §2.10(A).
[35] 376 U.S. at 292, 1 Media L. Rep. at 1542–43. The Court also recognized that government entities cannot sue for libel. *Id.* at 291, 1 Media L. Rep. at 1542.
[36] 388 U.S. 130, 1 Media L. Rep. 1568 (1967). Before this decision, the Court decided the important false light case of Time, Inc. v. Hill, 385 U.S. 374, 1 Media L. Rep. 1791 (1967), which is discussed in Chapter 3.

although he was actually employed by a private corporation rather than the state of Georgia;[37] plaintiff Edwin Walker was a retired army general who actively opposed the use of federal troops to enforce school desegregation and who had received wide publicity for his statements opposing such federal action.[38]

The article about Butts accused him of trying to "fix" a football game between the University of Georgia and the University of Alabama;[39] the article about Walker accused him of personally leading a crowd to attack federal marshals enforcing a court decree ordering the enrollment of an African American, James Meredith, as a student at the University of Mississippi.[40]

Chief Justice Earl Warren reasoned that the actual malice rule should apply to public figures, because no real distinction between public officials and public figures exists:

> To me, differentiation between "public figures" and "public officials" and adoption of separate standards of proof for each have no basis in law, logic, or First Amendment policy. Increasingly, in this country, the distinctions between governmental and private sectors are blurred. Since the depression of the 1930's and World War II there has been a rapid fusion of economic and political power, a merging of science, industry and government, and a high degree of interaction between the intellectual, governmental, and business worlds. Depression, war, international tensions, national and international markets and the surging growth of science and technology have precipitated national and international problems that demand national and international solutions. While these trends and events have occasioned a consolidation of governmental power, power has also become more organized in what we have commonly considered to be the private sector.
>
> In many situations, policy determinations which traditionally were channeled through formal political institutions are now originated and implemented through a complex array of boards, committees, commissions, corporations, and associations, some only loosely connected with the Government. This blending of positions and power has also occurred in the case of individuals so that many who do not hold public office at the moment are nevertheless intimately involved in the resolution of important public questions or, by reason of their fame, shape events in areas of concern to society at large.[41]

Justice William Brennan, joined by Justice Byron White, agreed that the actual malice rule applied to public figures for the reasons set forth by the Chief Justice.[42] Justice Hugo Black, joined by Justice William Douglas, reluctantly acceded to the Chief Justice's view that the actual malice rule applied to public figures, but only so the Court could agree on a disposition of the case.[43] Accordingly, a majority of the Court agreed that the actual malice rule applies to public figure plaintiffs.[44]

---

[37] 388 U.S. at 135–36, 1 Media L. Rep. at 1569.
[38] *Id.* at 140, 1 Media L. Rep. at 1571.
[39] *Id.* at 135, 1 Media L. Rep. at 1569.
[40] *Id.* at 140, 1 Media L. Rep. at 1571.
[41] *Id.* at 163–64, 1 Media L. Rep. at 1580 (Warren, C.J., concurring).
[42] 388 U.S. at 173, 1 Media L. Rep. at 1584 (Brennan, J., concurring and dissenting).
[43] *Id.* at 170, 1 Media L. Rep. at 1583 (Black, J., dissenting). Justices Black and Douglas adhered to their view that the First Amendment bars all libel actions. *Id.* at 170–72, 1 Media L. Rep. at 1583–84.
[44] *Id.* at 155, 1 Media L. Rep. at 1577; *see also* Wolston v. Reader's Digest Ass'n, 443 U.S. 157, 163–64, 5 Media L. Rep. 1273 (1979). All members of the Court agreed that the verdict for Walker had to be reversed and the case remanded for further proceedings. 388 U.S. at 162. As to Butts, while Chief Justice Warren and Justices Brennan, White, Black, and Douglas agreed that the actual malice rule applied to public figures,

Justice John Harlan, writing for a plurality of four members of the Court, proposed a standard for public figures that was less demanding than the actual malice rule. He would have allowed a public figure to recover damages "for a defamatory falsehood whose substance makes substantial danger to reputation apparent, on a showing of highly unreasonable conduct constituting an extreme departure from standards of investigation and reporting ordinarily adhered to by responsible publishers."[45] This standard has never been accepted by the Supreme Court.[46]

In its next important decision, *Rosenbloom v. Metromedia*,[47] the Court considered whether the actual malice rule applied to a plaintiff who was neither a public official nor a public figure, but who was involved in a matter of public interest.[48] In *Rosenbloom*, the plaintiff, a distributor of nudist magazines, brought an action against a radio station and claimed that news reports concerning his arrest were defamatory.[49]

In a plurality decision containing five separate opinions, the Court reversed a judgment in favor of the plaintiff. Justice Brennan, joined by Chief Justice Warren Burger and Justice Harry Blackmun, favored extending the actual malice rule to all instances in which the media were reporting on a private individual's involvement "in an event of public or general concern."[50] They reasoned that information about any matter of public or general interest was important to the First Amendment's design to facilitate self-governance[51] and that, in any event, the First Amendment was not limited to information bearing directly on self-government.[52] Justice Black concurred in the reversal but reiterated his view that the First Amendment absolutely bars recovery in defamation

---

they did not agree on the dispostion of *Butts*. The Chief Justice felt that Butts had proved actual malice. *Id.* at 170, 1 Media L. Rep. at 1583 (Warren, C.J., concurring). Justice Brennan, joined by Justice White, would have remanded for a jury determination of actual malice. *Id.* at 174, 1 Media L. Rep. at 1584 (Brennan, J., concurring). Justice Black, joined by Justice Douglas, voted to reverse the jury's verdict for Butts. *Id.* at 170–71, 1 Media L. Rep. at 1583 (Black, J., concurring and dissenting). Nevertheless, *Butts* was affirmed because Justice Harlan and the three justices who concurred in his opinion (Justices Clark, Stewart, and Fortas) voted to affirm the jury's verdict, 388 U.S. at 156, 161–62, as did the Chief Justice.

[45]*Id.* at 155, 1 Media L. Rep. at 1577. Justice Harlan felt that *Butts* and *Walker* were similar in some respects to cases involving public officials, because both Butts and Walker commanded substantial public interest—Butts due to his position and Walker because he thrust himself into the vortex of an important public controversy. *Id.* at 155, 1 Media L. Rep. at 1577. Justice Harlan stated that the public interest in *Butts* and *Walker* was no less than that concerning public officials, and concluded that the common law defamation rules therefore did not provide sufficient protection against defamation actions by public figures. *Id.* However, Justice Harlan felt that *Butts* and *Walker* were also different from defamation actions brought by public officials. First, because a libel recovery by a public official could be viewed as a vindication of government policy, Justice Harlan concluded that a libel action by a public official was analogous to a prosecution for seditious libel, which should not be permitted. Public figures hold no government positions, however, so he felt that a libel recovery by a public figure could not be viewed as a vindication of government policy. *Id.* at 153–54, 1 Media L. Rep. at 1576. Second, public officials also enjoy a privilege against being sued for defamation that is largely neutralized by the actual malice rule's protection of their detractors. Because public figures such as Butts and Walker are entitled to no such privilege, Justice Harlan felt no offsetting rule was necessary. *Id.* at 154, 1 Media L. Rep. at 1576–77.

[46]*See, e.g.*, Harte-Hanks Communications v. Connaughton, 491 U.S. 657, 666, 16 Media L. Rep. 1881, 1885 (1989) (reiterating rejection of this standard: "[t]oday there is no question that public figure libel cases are controlled by the *New York Times* standard and not by the professional standards rule, which never commanded a majority of this Court").

[47]403 U.S. 29, 1 Media L. Rep. 1597 (1971). This decision is the Supreme Court's broadest application of the constitutional actual malice rule.

[48]*Id.* at 31–32, 1 Media L. Rep. at 1598.
[49]*Id.* at 32–34, 1 Media L. Rep. at 1598–99.
[50]*Id.* at 52, 1 Media L. Rep. at 1605–06.
[51]*Id.* at 41, 1 Media L. Rep. at 1601.
[52]403 U.S. at 42, 1 Media L. Rep. at 1602.

actions against the news media, even where actual malice is shown.[53] Justice Douglas took no part in the case.[54] Justice White concluded that the actual malice rule applied because the newscast described government activities, namely the actions of police officers.[55]

Justice Harlan and Justice Thurgood Marshall, who were joined by Justice Potter Stewart, filed dissenting opinions. Their dissents agreed that, in defamation cases involving private individuals, states should be free to define the standard of fault so long as they did not impose liability without fault; actual damages should be a prerequisite to recovery; and jury verdicts should be confined to ascertainable limits.[56] Justice Harlan would have allowed punitive damages on a showing of "express malice," but only where the punitive damages bore a reasonable and purposeful relationship to the actual harm done.[57] Justice Marshall, however, stated that damages should be restricted to actual losses.[58]

The *Rosenbloom* plurality's conclusion, that the actual malice rule should extend to all cases in which the media reported on matters of public concern, was rejected in the 5-4 decision of *Gertz v. Robert Welch, Inc.*[59] There, the family of a young man who had been shot and killed by a Chicago police officer had retained attorney Elmer Gertz to represent them in civil litigation against the police officer.[60] Gertz sued a publication of the John Birch Society for libel after it printed an article that labeled him a communist and implied that he had a criminal record.[61]

At the outset, the Court stated that statements of pure opinion cannot serve as the basis for a defamation action: "However pernicious an opinion may seem, we depend for its correction not on the conscience of judges or juries but on the competition of other ideas. But there is no constitutional value in false statements of fact."[62]

The Court then held that application of the actual malice rule should be limited to cases involving public officials and public figures.[63] For the Court, Justice Lewis Powell identified two factors to support this holding: First, public

---

[53] *Id.* at 57, 1 Media L. Rep. at 1608 (Black, J., concurring).
[54] *Id.*
[55] *Id.* at 62, 1 Media L. Rep. at 1609 (White, J., concurring).
[56] *Id.* at 64, 1 Media L. Rep. at 1610 (Harlan, J., dissenting); *id.* at 85–87, 1 Media L. Rep. at 1618–19 (Marshall, J., dissenting).
[57] 403 U.S. at 77, 1 Media L. Rep. at 1615 (Harlan, J., dissenting).
[58] *Id.* at 87, 1 Media L. Rep. at 1619 (Marshall, J., dissenting).
[59] 418 U.S. 323, 1 Media L. Rep. 1633 (1974). The opinion was written by Justice Powell and was joined in by Justices Stewart, Marshall, Rehnquist, and Blackmun. Justice Blackmun, who had joined Justice Brennan's plurality opinion in *Rosenbloom*, stated that he felt the actual malice rule should apply to situations involving an event of public interest. He joined the Court's opinion to eliminate the uncertainty caused by the fractionalized *Rosenbloom* decision, however. *Id.* at 353–54, 1 Media L. Rep. at 1645 (Blackmun, J., concurring).
[60] *Id.* at 325, 1 Media L. Rep. at 1634.
[61] *Id.* at 326–37, 1 Media L. Rep. at 1634–35.
[62] *Id.* at 339–40, 1 Media L. Rep. at 1640 (footnote omitted). *But see* New York Times Co. v. Sullivan, 376 U.S. 254, 279 n.19, 1 Media L. Rep. 1527, 1537 n.19 (1964) ("Even a false statement may be deemed to make a valuable contribution to public debate, since it brings about 'the clearer perception and livelier impression of truth, produced by its collision with error.'" (quoting J.S. MILL, ON LIBERTY 15 (1947)). The Court went on to note that "[t]he First Amendment requires that we protect some falsehood in order to protect speech that matters." 418 U.S. at 341, 1 Media L. Rep. at 1640. For a discussion of the opinion doctrine, see *infra* §2.7.
[63] 418 U.S. at 343, 1 Media L. Rep. at 1641.

figures and public officials typically enjoy significantly greater access to channels of communication than do private individuals, and they therefore have a better opportunity to respond to false statements about themselves.[64] Second, public officials and public figures have voluntarily exposed themselves to the risk of injury from defamatory falsehoods.[65] Because private individuals have neither accepted public office nor assumed an "influential role in ordering society," no such assumption applies to them.[66] As a consequence of seeking government office, public officials run the risk of closer public scrutiny than might otherwise be the case.[67] According to the Court, public figures stand in a similar position:

> Hypothetically, it may be possible for someone to become a public figure through no purposeful action of his own, but the instances of truly involuntary public figures must be exceedingly rare. For the most part those who attain this status have assumed roles of especial prominence in the affairs of society. Some occupy positions of such persuasive power and influence that they are deemed public figures for all purposes. More commonly, those classed as public figures have thrust themselves to the forefront of particular public controversies in order to influence the resolution of the issues involved. In either event, they invite attention and comment.[68]

The Court then held that no such assumption is proper as to private figures who have not voluntarily exposed themselves to public attention and who have no ready access to the media.[69] "Thus, private individuals are not only more vulnerable to injury than public officials and public figures; they are also more deserving of recovery."[70] Accordingly, the Court held that the First Amendment does not require private figure plaintiffs to prove actual malice to prevail in defamation actions.[71]

Having held that the actual malice rule applies only to public officials and public figures, the Court determined that Gertz was not a public official.[72] The defendant argued that Gertz's appearance at the coroner's inquest rendered him a de facto public official, but the Court summarily dismissed this argument because it would sweep all lawyers under the actual malice rule and distort the meaning of the public official category beyond all recognition.[73]

The Court also found that Gertz was not a public figure.[74] In so holding, the Court identified two types of voluntary public figures. One may become a "general purpose" public figure where one achieves "such pervasive fame or notoriety that he becomes a public figure for all purposes and in all contexts."[75]

---

[64] *Id.* at 344, 1 Media L. Rep. at 1641. *Accord* Wolston v. Reader's Digest Ass'n, 443 U.S. 157, 164 (1979).

[65] 418 U.S. at 344–45, 1 Media L. Rep. at 1641–42. The Court went on to say that, even if this is not always the case, the media are entitled to operate on the assumption that it is true. *Id.* at 345, 1 Media L. Rep. at 1642.

[66] *Id. Accord Wolston,* 443 U.S. at 164.

[67] 418 U.S. at 344, 1 Media L. Rep. at 1641.

[68] *Id.* at 345, 1 Media L. Rep. at 1642. This statement has been repeatedly quoted with approval by the Court. *See, e.g.,* Time, Inc. v. Firestone, 424 U.S. 448, 453, 1 Media L. Rep. 1665 (1976); *Wolston,* 443 U.S. at 164.

[69] 418 U.S. at 345, 1 Media L. Rep. at 1642.

[70] *Id.*

[71] *Id.* at 348, 1 Media L. Rep. at 1643.

[72] *Id.* at 351, 1 Media L. Rep. at 1644.

[73] *Id.*

[74] 418 U.S. at 352, 1 Media L. Rep. at 1644.

[75] *Id.* at 351, 1 Media L. Rep. at 1644.

More commonly, one may become a "limited purpose" or "vortex" public figure where one "voluntarily injects himself or is drawn into a particular public controversy and thereby becomes a public figure for a limited range of issues. . . . In either case such persons assume special prominence in the resolution of public questions."[76]

The Court held that Gertz was not a general purpose public figure: None of the jurors had ever heard of Gertz, and there was no evidence that this was atypical.[77] Although Gertz had been active in community and professional affairs and was well-known in some circles, this was not sufficient to establish "clear evidence of general fame or notoriety in the community, and pervasive involvement in the affairs of society."[78]

The Court also found that Gertz was not a limited purpose public figure:[79] His role at the coroner's inquest related solely to the representation of his private client, he took no part in the criminal prosecution of the police officer, and he did not discuss the criminal or civil litigation with the press.[80] Such activity was insufficient to establish that Gertz had thrust himself into the vortex of the controversy at issue or that he engaged the public's attention in an attempt to influence the controversy's outcome.[81]

While *Gertz* refused to extend the actual malice rule to private individuals, it did find that the common law gave the media insufficient protection against defamation actions brought by private figures. Because the common law presumed fault as well as damages, the media could be required to pay substantial verdicts even though they had done everything within their power to ensure that their news stories were accurate. For this reason, the Court announced two additional limitations on state libel laws: The first was that "so long as they do not impose liability without fault, the States may define for themselves the appropriate standard of liability for a publisher or broadcaster of defamatory falsehood injurious to a private individual."[82] The second limitation was that a state cannot permit recovery of presumed or punitive damages absent a showing of actual malice.[83] Where such a showing cannot be made, the only compensation available is for actual injury.[84] While the Court declined to define actual injury, it did state that actual injury included impairment of reputation and standing in the community, personal humiliation, and mental anguish and suffering.[85]

The effect of these and other Supreme Court decisions was to radically alter the common rules of defamation.[86] As a matter of federal constitutional law:

---

[76]*Id.*
[77]*Id.* at 352, 1 Media L. Rep. at 1644.
[78]*Id.* at 351–52, 1 Media L. Rep. at 1644.
[79]418 U.S. at 351–52, 1 Media L. Rep. at 1644.
[80]*Id.*
[81]*Id.* at 352, 1 Media L. Rep. at 1644.
[82]*Id.* at 347, 1 Media L. Rep. at 1642 (footnote omitted).
[83]*Id.* at 349–50, 1 Media L. Rep. at 1643–44.
[84]418 U.S. at 349–50, 1 Media L. Rep. at 1643–44. *But see* Dun & Bradstreet v. Greenmoss Builders, 472 U.S. 749, 761, 11 Media L. Rep. 2417 (1985) (First Amendment does not require showing of actual malice for recovery of punitive or presumed damages where speech does not involve matter of public concern); *see also infra* §2.12.
[85]418 U.S. at 350, 1 Media L. Rep. at 1643.
[86]*See supra* §2.1. No attempt is made here to discuss the closely related tort of injurious falsehood, which includes slander of title and trade libel. RESTATEMENT (SECOND) §623A. Usually, however, this tort is

(1) Whether statements are defamatory is subject to review under the First Amendment.[87]

(2) The rule that statements must be published to a third party to be actionable is unchanged.[88]

(3) Only statements of fact can be actionable; statements that cannot be reasonably interpreted as stating or implying actual facts or statements that cannot be objectively proven to be true or false are not actionable.[89]

(4) The plaintiff ordinarily has the burden of proving falsity rather than the defendant having the burden of proving truth.[90]

(5) Whether statements are about the plaintiff is subject to review under the First Amendment.[91]

(6) Ordinarily, presumed fault, which created strict liability, is no longer permissible; to be actionable the statement must be published with the requisite degree of fault, e.g., negligence or actual malice, depending on whether the plaintiff is a private figure, a public official, or a public figure.[92]

(7) Presumed and punitive damages are not permissible in cases involving speech on matters of public concern, at least unless the defendant is shown to have acted with actual malice.[93]

(8) The plaintiff still must be a defamable plaintiff.[94]

§2.3 ELEMENTS OF A DEFAMATION CLAIM

A good working definition of actionable defamation is:[95]
(1) a statement that has a defamatory meaning;[96]
(2) that is published;[97]
(3) that is an objectively verifiable statement of fact;[98]
(4) that is false;[99]
(5) that is of and concerning the plaintiff;[100]
(6) that is published with the requisite degree of fault;[101]

---

more difficult to prove than defamation, because it requires proof of intent to harm, constitutional actual malice, and pecuniary loss. *Id.*

[87] Rosenblatt v. Baer, 383 U.S. 75, 1 Media L. Rep. 1558 (1966); *see infra* §2.5.
[88] *See infra* §2.6.
[89] Milkovich v. Lorain Journal Co., 497 U.S. 1, 17 Media L. Rep. 2009 (1990); *see also* Gertz v. Robert Welch, Inc., 418 U.S. 323, 1 Media L. Rep. 1633 (1974); Old Dominion Branch No. 496, Nat'l Ass'n of Letter Carriers v. Austin, 418 U.S. 264 (1974); *see infra* §2.7.
[90] Philadelphia Newspapers v. Hepps, 475 U.S. 767, 768–69, 12 Media L. Rep. 1977 (1986); Cianci v. New Times Pub'g Co., 639 F.2d 54, 59, 6 Media L. Rep. 1625 (2d Cir. 1980); Rinaldi v. Holt, Rinehart & Winston, 366 N.E.2d 1299, 1305, 2 Media L. Rep. 2169 (N.Y. 1977); *see infra* §2.9. The Supreme Court has not expressly decided whether this rule applies to cases involving private figures and speech that is of purely private concern. *Hepps,* 475 U.S. at 775–76, 12 Media L. Rep. at 1980–82.
[91] New York Times Co. v. Sullivan, 376 U.S. 254, 1 Media L. Rep. 1527 (1964); *see infra* §2.10.
[92] *Gertz,* 418 U.S. 323, 1 Media L. Rep. 1633; *see infra* §2.11.
[93] *Gertz,* 418 U.S. 323, 1 Media L. Rep. 1633. However, these rules do not apply if the speech involves a matter of private concern. Dun & Bradstreet v. Greenmoss Builders, 472 U.S. 749, 761, 11 Media L. Rep. 2417 (1985); *see infra* §2.12.
[94] *See infra* §§2.10 and 2.16(B).
[95] American defamation law sometimes differs widely from jurisdiction to jurisdiction. No attempt is made here to note every such difference.
[96] *See infra* §2.5.
[97] *See infra* §2.6.
[98] *See infra* §§2.7 and 2.8.
[99] *See infra* §2.9.
[100] *See infra* §2.10.
[101] *See infra* §2.11.

(7) that causes actual injury, and in some circumstances, special damages;[102]

(8) to a defamable plaintiff.[103]

In addition, privileged statements are not actionable.[104]

§2.4 Purposes of Defamation Law

The tort of defamation allows a plaintiff to vindicate his or her reputation by prevailing in a court action.[105] It also compensates the plaintiff for any injuries suffered.[106] In addition, it punishes the defendant by making him or her compensate the plaintiff for injuries suffered, deterring the defendant from again defaming the plaintiff or others.[107]

Some courts have suggested that defamation law also protects the plaintiff's interest in privacy—the right to be let alone.[108] However, this misapprehends the purpose of defamation law, which is to protect a plaintiff's good reputation, not his or her interest in lack of public attention.[109] This latter interest is protected by the intrusion and private facts torts.[110]

Against these concerns is opposed the public's interest in a free flow of information about all topics of human endeavor.[111] Not only does this assist the public in governing our democracy,[112] it contributes to peaceful social change through education[113] and leads to individual self-fulfillment.[114] It is primarily the continuing conflict between these two sets of interests that has made defamation law so complex.

§2.5 Defamatory Meaning

Whether a statement is defamatory is initially a question of law for the court.[115] Only if a court determines that a statement is susceptible to a defamatory meaning may the case go to a jury to determine whether it was actually

---

[102] *See infra* §2.16(A).
[103] *See infra* §2.16(B).
[104] *See infra* §§2.13, 2.14, and 2.15.
[105] L. Eldredge, The Law of Defamation §3, at 4–5 (1978); Rosenblatt v. Baer, 383 U.S. 75, 86, 1 Media L. Rep. 1558, 1562 (1966) ("Society has a pervasive and strong interest in preventing and redressing attacks upon reputation"); Gaetano v. Sharon Herald Co., 231 A.2d 753, 755 (Pa. 1967) (vindication is primary purpose of defamation action).
[106] Gertz v. Robert Welch, Inc., 418 U.S. 323, 341, 1 Media L. Rep. 1633 (1974).
[107] Restatement (Second) §623 n. Punitive damages also serve this purpose. *See infra* §2.16(A).
[108] Rancho La Costa v. Superior Ct., 165 Cal. Rptr. 347, 360, 6 Media L. Rep. 1351 (Cal. Ct. App. 1980), *cert. denied*, 450 U.S. 902 (1981).
[109] Kimmerle v. New York Evening Journal, 186 N.E. 217, 218 (N.Y. 1933) (no right of privacy).
[110] See Chapters 4 and 5.
[111] Thornhill v. Alabama, 310 U.S. 88, 95 (1940) ("The safeguarding of those rights to the ends that men may speak as they think on matters vital to them and that falsehoods may be exposed through the processes of education and discussion is essential to free government.").
[112] Stromberg v. California, 283 U.S. 359, 369 (1931) ("The maintenance of the opportunity for free political discussion to the end that government may be responsive to the will of the people and that changes may be obtained by lawful means, an opportunity essential to the security of the Republic, is a fundamental principle of our constitutional system.").
[113] Blasi, *The Checking Value in First Amendment Theory*, 1977 Am. B. Found. Res. J. 521; *see also Thornhill*, 310 U.S. at 95.
[114] T. Emerson, The System of Freedom of Expression 6–9 (1970).
[115] Restatement (Second) §614; Corman v. Blanchard, 211 Cal. App. 2d 126, 131–32, 27 Cal. Rptr. 327 (Cal. Ct. App. 1962); Mendoza v. Gallup Indep. Co., 764 P.2d 492, 494, 15 Media L. Rep. 2319 (N.M. Ct. App. 1988). Whether a statement is defamatory is not to be determined by declarations, but by the court. San Francisco Bay Guardian v. Superior Ct., 21 Cal. Rptr. 2d 464, 21 Media L. Rep. 1791 (Cal. Ct. App. 1993).

defamatory.[116] As a result, numerous defamation cases are dismissed at an early stage—usually after a demurrer or motion to dismiss for failure to state a claim—because the offending statement is not susceptible to a defamatory interpretation.

A defamatory communication has been defined as one that "tends so to harm the reputation of another as to lower him in the estimation of the community or to deter third persons from associating or dealing with him."[117] To be defamatory, a statement does not have to defame a person in the eyes of all members of a community. However, it must injure a person's reputation in the eyes of a substantial minority of the community. This requirement prevents small groups from defining what is defamatory.[118]

That minority must also be a respectable, or, as some courts have said, a "right-thinking" minority of the community.[119] This requirement prevents antisocial groups from defining what is acceptable conduct. For example, to say a person is a "snitch" may be one of the worst things that can be said of a convict, because it will surely injure his reputation in prison. Such a statement is not defamatory, however, because convicts are neither a substantial nor respectable minority of the community.[120]

It is also well established that a statement is not defamatory simply because it is unpleasant, hostile, annoying, or embarrassing to the plaintiff.[121]

Whether a statement is defamatory is to be determined by the standard of the average reader[122] applying its ordinary meaning.[123] Its meaning must be determined from the words used when construed in the context of the article or broadcast.[124] The extrinsic circumstances surrounding the article or statement must also be considered.[125]

---

[116]RESTATEMENT (SECOND) §614, cmt. b; Yorty v. Chandler, 13 Cal. App. 3d 467, 475, 91 Cal. Rptr. 709 (Cal. Ct. App. 1970).

[117]RESTATEMENT (SECOND) §559.

[118]*Id.* §559(e); Peck v. Tribune Co., 214 U.S. 185, 189–90 (1909); Burns v. McGraw-Hill Broadcasting Co., 659 P.2d 1351, 1357, 9 Media L. Rep. 1257 (Colo. 1983).

[119]Burrascano v. Levi, 452 F. Supp. 1066, 1072 (D. Md. 1978), *aff'd,* 612 F.2d 1306 (4th Cir. 1979). *See also Peck,* 214 U.S. at 189–90; Grant v. Reader's Digest Ass'n, 151 F.2d 733, 735 (2d Cir.), *cert. denied,* 326 U.S. 797 (1945); Herrmann v. Newark Morning Ledger Co., 140 A.2d 529, 530 (N.J. Super. Ct. App. Div. 1958).

[120]*Burrascano,* 452 F. Supp. at 1072; *Peck,* 214 U.S. at 189–90.

[121]Gang v. Hughes, 111 F. Supp. 27, 29–30 (S.D. Cal.), *aff'd,* 218 F.2d 432 (9th Cir. 1954) ("[i]t is not sufficient, standing alone, that the language is unpleasant and annoys or irks plaintiff, and subjects him to jests or banter, so as to affect his feelings"); *see also* Western Broadcast Co. v. Times Mirror Co., 14 Cal. App. 2d 120, 125, 57 P.2d 977 (Cal. Ct. App. 1936); Pierce v. Capital Cities Communications, 576 F.2d 495, 503–04, 3 Media L. Rep. 2259 (3d Cir.), *cert. denied,* 439 U.S. 861 (1978). Thus, for example, it is not defamatory to inaccurately associate the plaintiff with a particular political party. Cox v. Hatch, 761 P.2d 556, 562, 16 Media L. Rep. 1366 (Utah 1988).

[122]Lorentz v. RKO Radio Pictures, 155 F.2d 84, 87 (9th Cir.), *cert. denied,* 329 U.S. 727 (1946); Sullivan v. Warner Bros. Theatres, 109 P.2d 760, 762 (Cal. Ct. App. 1941); *Western Broadcast Co.,* 57 P.2d at 978.

[123]World Pub'g Co. v. Mullen, 61 N.W. 108, 108 (Neb. 1894); Cafferty v. Southern Tier Pub'g Co., 123 N.E. 76, 78 (N.Y. 1919).

[124]RESTATEMENT (SECOND) §563, cmt. d; MacRae v. Afro-Am. Co., 172 F. Supp. 184, 186–87 (E.D. Pa. 1959), *aff'd,* 274 F.2d 287 (3d Cir. 1960); Hoffman v. Washington Post Co., 433 F. Supp. 600, 602 n.1, 3 Media L. Rep. 1143 (D.D.C. 1977), *aff'd,* 578 F.2d 442, 3 Media L. Rep. 2546 (D.C. Cir. 1978); Corman v. Blanchard, 211 Cal. App. 2d 126, 131–32, 27 Cal. Rptr. 327 (Cal. Ct. App. 1962). *See infra* §2.5(A).

[125]RESTATEMENT (SECOND) §563, cmt. e; Greyhound Sec. v. Greyhound Corp., 207 N.Y.S.2d 383, 386–87 (N.Y. App. Div. 1960) ("the climate of publication and the character and relationship of the audience to plaintiff must be taken into consideration"). For example, in Dworkin v. Hustler Magazine, 867 F.2d 1188, 16 Media L. Rep. 1113 (9th Cir.), *cert. denied,* 493 U.S. 812 (1989), the court, in a libel case brought by a well-known feminist against *Hustler Magazine,* took into account the extremity of the statements and the nature of the publication in determining that the statements on which the suit was based were not defamatory.

Headlines can create special problems. Some jurisdictions hold that headlines are actionable without reference to the article they concern;[126] others have reached the opposite result and require the article and headline to be construed together.[127] At the very least, headlines are not actionable unless, standing alone, they meet all the requirements for a defamatory statement.[128]

What is defamatory at one time may not be defamatory later, or vice versa. For example, it was once illegal for lawyers to advertise. Thus, to say a lawyer advertised would have been defamatory, because it would have amounted to a claim that the lawyer violated the law. Since most prohibitions on lawyer advertising are now unconstitutional, however, it ordinarily would not be defamatory to say a lawyer advertises.[129] Similarly, the defamatory nature of the statement that a plaintiff is a communist or is associated with the Communist Party has changed over time.[130]

At least one court has suggested that any statement in the mass media that is even arguably susceptible to a defamatory meaning must be found to have a defamatory meaning,[131] the rationale being that at least some people in a large audience will think the statement is defamatory.[132] More recent cases have refused to adopt such an approach because this lenient test would make virtually every statement defamatory.[133] Where a statement is susceptible to a defamatory meaning, the jury decides the statement's reasonable interpretation.[134]

---

[126]Schermerhorn v. Rosenberg, 426 N.Y.S.2d 274, 283, 6 Media L. Rep. 1376 (N.Y. App. Div. 1980); Gustin v. Evening Press Co., 137 N.W. 674, 675 (Mich. 1912).

[127]*See, e.g.,* Fernandes v. Tenbruggencate, 649 P.2d 1144, 1148, 8 Media L. Rep. 2577 (Haw. 1982); Naked City v. Chicago Sun-Times, 395 N.E.2d 1042, 1044, 5 Media L. Rep. 1806 (Ill. App. Ct. 1979); Hrlsky v. Globe Democrat Pub'g Co., 152 S.W.2d 119, 121–22 (Mo. 1941); Bray v. Providence Journal Co., 220 A.2d 531, 535 (R.I. 1966). One court stated that the test in determining which rule to apply was whether the article was likely to be read with the headline. Gambuzza v. Time, Inc., 239 N.Y.S.2d 466, 469–70 (N.Y. App. Div. 1963). Another considered whether the plaintiffs were specifically named in the headline. Ledger-Enquirer Co. v. Brown, 105 S.E.2d 229, 231–32 (Ga. 1958). The Delaware Supreme Court took the middle road, stating that a headline could be defamatory by itself or could be cured by the article following it, depending on the circumstances of the particular case. Reardon v. News-Journal Co., 164 A.2d 263, 265–66 (Del. 1960); *see also* Contemporary Mission v. New York Times Co., 842 F.2d 612, 15 Media L. Rep. 1180 (2d Cir.), *cert. denied,* 488 U.S. 856 (1988) (inaccurate subheading cured by text immediately following it).

[128]*See, e.g., Schermerhorn,* 426 N.Y.S.2d at 283 (if headline read independently, "general principles of libel" should be applied to determine if it is actionable).

[129]*See* Chapter 11.

[130]Early cases held that such statements were not defamatory. *See, e.g.,* Harris v. Curtis Pub'g Co., 121 P.2d 761, 766 (Cal. Ct. App. 1942); Hays v. American Defense Soc'y, 169 N.E. 380, 382–83 (N.Y. 1929); McAndrew v. Scranton Republican Pub'g Co., 72 A.2d 780, 784–85 (Pa. 1950). Later cases have almost universally held such statements to be defamatory. *See, e.g.,* MacLeod v. Tribune Pub'g Co., 343 P.2d 36, 41 (Cal. 1959); Joopanenko v. Gavagan, 67 So. 2d 434, 438 (Fla. 1953); Herrmann v. Newark Morning Ledger Co., 138 A.2d 61, 71 (N.J. Super. Ct. App. Div. 1958); Toomey v. Farley, 138 N.E.2d 221, 225 (N.Y. 1956). *See also* Lasky v. ABC, 631 F. Supp. 962, 971, 13 Media L. Rep. 1379 (S.D.N.Y. 1986) (defamatory meaning found in statement that plaintiff, during McCarthy era, accused another individual of being a communist).

It also used to be defamatory to falsely refer to someone as a Negro or black. Natchez Times Pub'g Co. v. Dunigan, 72 So. 2d 681, 684 (Miss. 1954); Hargrove v. Oklahoma Press Pub'g Co., 265 P. 635, 636 (Okla. 1928); Bowen v. Independent Pub'g Co., 96 S.E.2d 564, 566 (S.C. 1957). In the wake of the civil rights movement, it is unlikely that this rule would be followed.

[131]*MacLeod,* 343 P.2d at 43–44. *See also* Wandt v. Hearst's Chicago Am., 109 N.W. 70, 71 (Wis. 1906) (libel found where plaintiff may be damaged in estimation of *some*).

[132]*MacLeod,* 343 P.2d at 43.

[133]*See, e.g.,* Forsher v. Bugliosi, 608 P.2d 716, 723, 6 Media L. Rep. 1097 (Cal. 1980) ("the fact that some person might, with extra sensitive perception, understand such a meaning cannot compel this court to establish liability at so low a threshold").

[134]MacRae v. Afro-Am. Co., 172 F. Supp. 184, 186 (E.D. Pa. 1959), *aff'd,* 274 F.2d 287 (3d Cir. 1960); Clark v. Pearson, 248 F. Supp. 188, 192 (D.D.C. 1965); Eadie v. Pole, 221 A.2d 547, 549 (N.J. Super. Ct.

An almost endless number of cases hold that particular words are or are not defamatory.[135]

§2.5(A) Defamatory Meaning and Implications

A defamatory meaning can arise out of what is implied as well as what is expressly stated.[136] However, the implication must be one that is apparent to the reasonable reader, not simply one that some readers could divine.[137] In addition, the implication must be a specific one; it cannot be based on the tenor or tone of an article or broadcast.[138] Implications often are not actionable because they are not statements of verifiable fact.[139] Several recent decisions have held that public officials and public figures cannot sue over implications.[140]

App. Div. 1966); Rovira v. Boget, 148 N.E. 534, 535 (N.Y. 1925) (whether defendant, in calling plaintiff "coquette," meant prostitute or poached egg was question for jury).

[135]*Defamatory:* Manale v. New Orleans Dep't of Police, 673 F.2d 122 (5th Cir. 1982) ("gay" and "fruit" to describe police officer); Brewer v. Memphis Pub'g Co., 626 F.2d 1238, 6 Media L. Rep. 2025 (5th Cir. 1980), *cert. denied,* 452 U.S. 962 (1981) (divorced or cuckolded); Makofsky v. Cunningham, 576 F.2d 1223 (5th Cir. 1978) (in default on contract); Diplomat Elec. v. Westinghouse Elec. Supply Co., 378 F.2d 377 (5th Cir. 1967) (delinquent account); Belli v. Orlando Daily Newspapers, 389 F.2d 579 (5th Cir. 1967), *cert. denied,* 393 U.S. 825 (1968) (lawyer had "taken" organization); Mid-America Food Serv. v. ARA Serv., 578 F.2d 691, 698 (8th Cir. 1978) (statements that food service establishment in financial difficulty and almost closed by health department); Michigan Microtech v. Federated Pubns., 466 N.W.2d 717, 18 Media L. Rep. 2131, 2133 (Mich. Ct. App. 1991) (statement that plaintiff discontinuing sales of satellite dishes found to have potentially negative effect on business reputation); Smith v. McMullen, 589 F. Supp. 642, 10 Media L. Rep. 2250 (S.D. Tex. 1984) (baseball team's general manager "is a despicable human being").

Not Defamatory: Chuy v. Philadelphia Eagles Football Club, 595 F.2d 1265, 4 Media L. Rep. 2537 (3d Cir. 1979) (statement that plaintiff suffered from fatal disease); Church of Scientology v. Cazares, 638 F.2d 1272, 1289, 7 Media L. Rep. 1668 (5th Cir. 1981) ("money motivated rip-off"); Southard v. Forbes, Inc., 588 F.2d 140, 142, 4 Media L. Rep. 2019 (5th Cir.), *cert. denied,* 444 U.S. 832 (1979) (suggestion antique car investment program would be investigated by Securities and Exchange Commission if it was stock); Curtis Pub'g Co. v. Birdsong, 360 F.2d 344, 348 (5th Cir. 1966) ("those bastards"); Littlefield v. Ft. Dodge Messenger, 614 F.2d 581, 582 n.2, 5 Media L. Rep. 2325 (8th Cir.), *cert. denied,* 445 U.S. 945 (1980) (plaintiff's "present whereabouts are not known"); Kaplan v. Newsweek, 10 Media L. Rep. 2142 (N.D. Cal. 1984), *aff'd without opinion,* 776 F.2d 1053, 12 Media L. Rep. 1277 (9th Cir. 1985) (description of professor's class as "gut" course); Lawrence v. Evans, 573 So. 2d 695, 18 Media L. Rep. 1524 (Miss. 1990) (libel plaintiff's lawyer's statements that "[w]hatever defense they are using, a defense that they are not using is that the statements they made were true"); Golub v. Esquire Pub'g, 508 N.Y.S.2d 188, 13 Media L. Rep. 1687 (N.Y. App. Div. 1986) (description of attorney as "loose-tongued lawyer" who "revealed his innermost thoughts").

[136]RESTATEMENT (SECOND) §563, cmt. c; *see also* Tavoulareas v. Piro, 817 F.2d 762, 780, 13 Media L. Rep. 2377 (D.C. Cir.) (en banc), *cert. denied,* 484 U.S. 870 (1987); Church of Scientology of Cal. v. Flynn, 744 F.2d 694, 696 (9th Cir. 1984).

[137]*See, e.g.,* White v. Fraternal Order of Police, 909 F.2d 512, 519, 17 Media L. Rep. 2137, 2142 (D.C. Cir. 1990); *Forsher,* 608 P.2d at 723, 6 Media L. Rep. at 1102 (defamatory meaning in context of whole book "must be one that can be reasonably inferred"). Some courts have also required an affirmative showing that the defendant intended or endorsed the defamatory implication for it to be deemed actionable. *See, e.g., White,* 909 F.2d at 520, 17 Media L. Rep. at 2143.

[138]*See, e.g.,* Herbert v. Lando, 603 F. Supp. 983, 991, 11 Media L. Rep. 1692, 1698 (S.D.N.Y. 1985), *aff'd in part and rev'd in part on other grounds,* 781 F.2d 298, 307–08, 12 Media L. Rep. 1593 (2d Cir. 1986); Sassone v. Elder, 626 So. 2d 345, 22 Media L. Rep. 1049 (La. 1993) (if libel by implication permissible at all, implication must be principal one that would be drawn, even if plaintiff is private figure).

[139]Janklow v. Newsweek, 788 F.2d 1300, 12 Media L. Rep. 1961 (8th Cir.) (en banc), *cert. denied,* 479 U.S. 883 (1986); Price v. Viking Penguin, 881 F.2d 1426, 1439–40, 16 Media L. Rep. 2169, 2179 (8th Cir. 1989), *cert. denied,* 493 U.S. 1036 (1990). *See also* Locricchio v. Evening News Ass'n, 476 N.W.2d 112, 133–34, 20 Media L. Rep. 1065 (Mich. 1991), *cert. denied,* 112 S. Ct. 1267 (1992) (assuming claim can be made for defamatory implications, plaintiff still has burden of proving alleged implications are false).

[140]Mihalik v. Duprey, 417 N.E.2d 1238, 1241, 7 Media L. Rep. 1258 (Mass. App. Ct. 1981); Schaefer v. Lynch, 406 So. 2d 185, 7 Media L. Rep. 2302 (La. 1981); Strada v. Connecticut Newspapers, 477 A.2d 1005, 10 Media L. Rep. 2165 (Conn. 1984); DeFalco v. Anderson, 506 A.2d 1280, 12 Media L. Rep. 2125 (N.J. Super Ct. App. Div. 1986); Pietrafeso v. DPI, Inc., 757 P.2d 1113, 15 Media L. Rep. 1736 (Colo. Ct. App. 1988). *But see* Saenz v. Playboy Enters., 841 F.2d 1309, 1313–14, 15 Media L. Rep. 1043 (7th Cir. 1988) (rejecting rule that public figures/officials can never sue for defamatory implications).

§2.5(B) Pleading All the Defamatory Words

It is a well-established rule that all of the libelous or slanderous words must be set forth in the complaint, if known, or their substance must be pled if the exact wording is not known.[141] This rule is a necessary corollary to the rule that the court should in the first instance decide whether the statements in question are susceptible to a defamatory meaning,[142] and to the newer rule that the court in the first instance should decide whether the statements in question are verifiable statements of fact.[143] The court cannot make either of these determinations without knowing the language that is at issue. This common law rule now appears to be mandated by the First Amendment.[144]

§2.5(C) The Innocent Construction Rule

Under the innocent construction rule, a statement susceptible to both a defamatory and an innocent interpretation is not actionable.[145] Illinois may be the only state that follows this rule;[146] many other jurisdictions have specifically rejected it.[147]

§2.5(D) The Single Instance Rule

It has been held that a statement only accusing someone of making a mistake or error on one occasion is not actionable, unless special damages are pled and proved.[148] Of course, if it is charged that the misconduct is continuous

---

[141] Asay v. Hallmark Cards, 594 F.2d 692, 698–99 (8th Cir. 1979) (required as matter of federal common law); Small v. American Broadcasting Cos., 10 Media L. Rep. 2391, 2392 (N.D. Iowa 1984); Herbert v. Lando, 603 F. Supp. 983, 990, 11 Media L. Rep. 1692, 1697, 1698 (S.D.N.Y. 1985), *aff'd in part and rev'd in part*, 781 F.2d 298 (2d Cir.), *cert. denied*, 476 U.S. 1182 (1986); Des Granges v. Crall, 149 P. 777, 777–78 (Cal. Ct. App. 1915); Haub v. Friermuth, 82 P. 571, 571 (Cal. Ct. App. 1905); Schulze v. Coykendall, 545 P.2d 392, 397 (Kan. 1976). *But see* Foster v. Turner Broadcasting, 844 F.2d 955, 958 n.3, 15 Media L. Rep. 1225, 1227 n.3 (2d Cir.), *cert. denied*, 488 U.S. 994 (1988) (pleading of exact words no longer required in Second Circuit).

[142] *See supra* §2.5.

[143] *See infra* §2.7.

[144] New York Times Co. v. Sullivan, 376 U.S. 254, 284, 1 Media L. Rep. 1527 (1964); Franchise Realty Interstate Corp. v. San Francisco Local Joint Exec. Bd. of Culinary Workers, 542 F.2d 1076, 1082–83 (9th Cir. 1976), *cert. denied*, 430 U.S. 940 (1977). Second Circuit cases dispensing with the exact wording rule have relied on the liberal pleading standard of Federal Rule of Civil Procedure 8 and have not addressed First Amendment issues. *See* Kelly v. Schmidberger, 806 F.2d 44, 46 (2d Cir. 1986); Geisler v. Petrocelli, 616 F.2d 636, 639–40 (2d Cir. 1980).

[145] John v. Tribune Co., 24 Ill. 2d 437, 442, 181 N.E.2d 105 (Ill.), *cert. denied*, 371 U.S. 877 (1962). However, the innocent interpretation must be a reasonable one. Chapski vi. Copley Press, 442 N.E.2d 195, 199, 8 Media L. Rep. 2403 (Ill. 1982); *see also* Sweeney v. Sengstacke Enters., 536 N.E.2d 823, 825, 16 Media L. Rep. 1506, 1508 (Ill. App. Ct. 1989) (law does not permit "forced and strained interpretation" of article in order to find innocent construction).

[146] *See, e.g.*, Haberstroh v. Crain Pubns., 545 N.E.2d 295, 298, 16 Media L. Rep. 2423, 2424–25 (Ill. App. Ct. 1989); Altman v. Amoco Oil Co., 406 N.E.2d 142, 144 (Ill. App. Ct. 1980); Dauw v. Field Enters., 397 N.E.2d 41, 43, 5 Media L. Rep. 1893 (Ill. App. Ct. 1979). *But see* England v. Automatic Canteen Co. of Am., 349 F.2d 989 (6th Cir. 1965) (innocent construction rule applied to defamation action brought in Ohio); Capobianco v. Pulitzer Pub'g Co., 812 S.W.2d 852, 855, 18 Media L. Rep. 2290, 2292 (Mo. Ct. App. 1991) ("in a libel per se action, words must be read 'in their most innocent sense' to determine whether they are 'unequivocally' libelous") (quoting Walters v. Kansas City Star Co., 406 S.W.2d 44, 51 (Mo. 1966)).

[147] *See, e.g.*, Macrae v. Afro-Am. Co., 172 F. Supp. 184, 187 (E.D. Pa. 1959), *aff'd*, 274 F.2d 287 (3d Cir. 1960); Okun v. Superior Ct., 629 P.2d 1369, 1373 (Cal.), *cert. denied sub nom.* Maple Properties v. Superior Ct. of Los Angeles County, 454 U.S. 1099 (1981); Boyer v. Pitt Pub'g Co., 188 A. 203, 204 (Pa. 1936); Memphis Pub'g Co. v. Nichols, 569 S.W.2d 412, 419 n.7, 4 Media L. Rep. 1573 (Tenn. 1978). *See also* James v. Garrett Co., 353 N.E.2d 834, 837–38 (N.Y. 1976) (jury must decide whether statements likely to be understood by average reader as defamatory).

[148] Bowes v. Magna Concepts, 561 N.Y.S.2d 16, 18 Media L. Rep. 1303 (N.Y. App. Div. 1990);

or has happened frequently, then the single instance rule does not apply.[149] The theory behind the rule appears to be that everyone is fallible, so little or no harm is done by saying that someone on one occasion did something wrong.[150]

§2.5(E) Insults, Epithets, Jokes, and Cartoons

Statements are not defamatory simply because they offend someone or make them upset or angry[151]—to be defamatory, they must damage a person's reputation.[152] Thus, the use of insults and epithets is not actionable as defamation.[153]

Similarly, jokes, satire, parody, and other abuse usually are not actionable defamation because they do not damage a person's reputation or do not involve verifiable statements of fact.[154] Where such ridicule is factual, however, it may be actionable.[155]

In a similar vein, political cartoons, colorful language, and other hyperbole generally are not actionable as defamation.[156] Some cases reach this result on the ground that such statements have no defamatory meaning,[157] while others reach this result on the ground that they are nonactionable statements of opinion.[158]

November v. Time, Inc., 194 N.E.2d 126, 128 (N.Y. 1963). *See also* Britton v. Winfield Pub. Library, 428 N.E.2d 650, 652–53 (Ill. App. Ct. 1981) (applying innocent construction rule to single instance area).

[149]Twiggar v. Ossining Printing & Pub'g Co., 146 N.Y.S. 529, 530 (N.Y. App. Div. 1914), *appeal dismissed,* 116 N.E. 1080 (N.Y. 1917).

[150]As one court stated, "there is no physician, however eminent, who is not liable to mistake the symptoms of a particular disease, nor any attorney who may not misunderstand the complicated nature and legal consequences of a particular litigation." Mattice v. Wilcox, 42 N.E. 270, 272 (N.Y. 1895).

[151]Sellers v. Time, Inc., 423 F.2d 887, 891 (3d Cir.), *cert. denied,* 400 U.S. 830 (1970); Phoenix Printing Co. v. Robertson, 195 P. 487, 489 (Okla. 1921); Scott-Taylor, Inc. v. Stokes, 229 A.2d 733, 734 (Pa. 1967).

[152]Cohen v. New York Times Co., 138 N.Y.S. 206, 210 (N.Y. App. Div. 1912).

[153]Old Dominion Branch No. 496, Nat'l Ass'n of Letter Carriers v. Austin, 418 U.S. 264, 282–83 (1974) (including plaintiff's name in "List of Scabs" that defined scab as traitor to God, country, family and class nonactionable rhetoric); Curtis Pub'g Co. v. Birdsong, 360 F.2d 344, 348 (5th Cir. 1966) (calling highway patrolmen "bastards" nonactionable vituperation); Tokmakian v. Fritz, 67 A.2d 834, 836 (R.I. 1949) (calling neighbor "drunk driver" during heated argument nonactionable epithet); Blovin v. Anton, 431 A.2d 489, 7 Media L. Rep. 1714 (Vt. 1981) (calling opponent "horse's ass," "jerk," and "idiot" nonactionable hyperbole). *See also* Hayden v. Bracy, 744 F.2d 1338, 1344 n.4 (8th Cir. 1984) ("negative comment").

[154]Polygram Records v. Superior Ct., 170 Cal. App. 3d 543, 547, 556, 216 Cal. Rptr. 252, 11 Media L. Rep. 2363 (Cal. Ct. App. 1985) (statements by comedian Robin Williams about plaintiff's wine not actionable); Arno v. Stewart, 54 Cal. Rptr. 392, 394 (Cal. Ct. App. 1966) (calling entertainer "singing member of Mafia" not actionable); Lane v. Arkansas Valley Pub'g Co., 675 P.2d 747, 751, 9 Media L. Rep. 1726 (Colo. Ct. App.), *cert. denied,* 467 U.S. 1252 (1984) (tongue-in-cheek article not libelous); Werber v. Klopfer, 272 A.2d 631, 635–37 (Md. 1971) (lampoon of professor not libelous). *See also* Embrey v. Holly, 429 A.2d 251, 259 (Md. Ct. Spec. App. 1981) (whether harmless joke or defamation is jury question), *rev'd in part,* 442 A.2d 966, 8 Media L. Rep. 1409 (Md. 1982).

[155]*See, e.g.,* Burton v. Crowell Pub'g Co., 82 F.2d 154, 156 (2d Cir. 1936); Megarry v. Norton, 290 P.2d 571, 573 (Cal. Ct. App. 1955); Farnsworth v. Hyde, 512 P. 1003, 1004–05 (Or. 1973). The fact that the statement was intended as a jest does not necessarily prevent liability. *See, e.g.,* Powers v. Durgin-Snow Pub'g Co., 144 A.2d 294, 296–97 (Me. 1958); Triggs v. Sun Printing & Pub'g Ass'n, 71 N.E. 739, 742–43 (N.Y. 1904); State v. Elder, 143 P. 482, 485 (N.M. 1914).

[156]Greenbelt Coop. Pub'g Ass'n v. Bresler, 398 U.S. 6, 14, 1 Media L. Rep. 1589 (1970) (use of term "blackmail" nonactionable hyperbole); Redco v. CBS, Inc., 758 F.2d 970, 972 (3d Cir. 1985) (report that "multi-piece tire rims kill people" nonactionable opinion even though no one had died in accidents involving plaintiff's brand of rims); Yorty v. Chandler, 91 Cal. Rptr. 709 (Cal. Ct. App. 1970) (cartoon not actionable); Reaves v. Foster, 200 So. 2d 453, 456 (Miss. 1967) (cartoon not actionable); Capital-Gazette Newspapers v. Stack, 445 A.2d 1038, 1045, 8 Media L. Rep. 1704 (Md.), *cert. denied,* 459 U.S. 989 (1982) (political hyperbole not actionable); Flip Side v. Chicago Tribune Co., 564 N.E.2d 1244, 1253–56, 18 Media L. Rep. 1409, 1416 (Ill. App. Ct. 1990), *appeal denied,* 571 N.E.2d 147 (Ill. 1991) (comic strip not actionable).

[157]*See, e.g., Bresler,* 398 U.S. at 14; Palm Beach Newspapers v. Early, 334 So. 2d 50, 53 (Fla. Dist. Ct. App. 1976), *cert. denied and appeal dismissed,* 354 So. 2d 351, 3 Media L. Rep. 2183 (Fla. 1977), *cert. denied,* 439 U.S. 910, 4 Media L. Rep. 1592 (1978) (cartoons not actionable).

[158]*See, e.g., Chandler,* 13 Cal. App. 3d at 476–77; Miskovsky v. Oklahoma Pub'g Co., 654 P.2d 587, 594, 7 Media L. Rep. 2607 (Okla. 1982); Reaves v. Foster, 200 So. 2d 453, 456 (Miss. 1967). Cartoons may be found actionable under some circumstances, for example, if a cartoon "maliciously presents as fact defamatory material which is false." *Chandler,* 13 Cal. App. 3d at 472. *See infra* §2.7.

§2.5(F) Necessity of Injury to Reputation

In *Time, Inc. v. Firestone*,[159] the Supreme Court held that it was constitutional for a plaintiff in a defamation action to waive her claim for injury to reputation and still recover damages for mental pain and suffering.[160] This was not inconsistent with the rules established by *Gertz* on damages,[161] but a number of jurisdictions bar recovery for defamation unless a plaintiff's reputation is injured.[162]

§2.5(G) Inducement, Innuendo, and Colloquium

In determining whether there is a defamatory meaning, three technical terms are important: inducement, innuendo, and colloquium. The "inducement" consists of the extra, extrinsic facts that must be pled to make the statement defamatory;[163] the "innuendo" is a statement of what the initial words plus the inducement were understood to mean;[164] and the "colloquium" is an allegation that a statement is of and concerning the plaintiff.[165]

For example, the statement that Mr. and Mrs. A had twins is not defamatory. However, if the inducement—that they have only been married two months—is also pled, then the innuendo is that they conceived the twins out of wedlock.[166]

The innuendo cannot add to or change the meaning of the allegedly defamatory words[167] and cannot beget a defamation action.[168] Its sole purpose is to explain what the words were understood to mean by their recipients.[169]

§2.5(H) Libel and Slander

Instead of being a single tort, defamation is actually two closely related torts: libel and slander.[170] In general, libel consists of written communications,

---

[159] 424 U.S. 448, 1 Media L. Rep. 1665 (1976).

[160] *Id.* at 460, 1 Media L. Rep. at 1669.

[161] *Id.* ("In [*Gertz*] we made it clear that States could base awards on elements other than injury to reputation, specifically listing 'personal humiliation, and mental anguish and suffering' as examples of injuries which might be compensated consistently with the Constitution upon a showing of fault.").

[162] *See, e.g.,* Miles v. Perry, 529 A.2d 199, 202, 14 Media L. Rep. 1985 (Conn. App. Ct. 1987) (harm to reputation is "necessary element . . . of the defamation cause of action"); Dresbach v. Doubleday & Co., 518 F. Supp. 1285, 1293, 7 Media L. Rep. 2105 (D.D.C. 1981) ("injury to reputation must be shown on the libel claim"); Gobin v. Globe Pub'g Co., 649 P.2d 1239, 1243, 8 Media L. Rep. 2191 (Kan. 1982) ("[u]nless injury to reputation is shown, plaintiff has not established a valid claim for defamation"). *Contra* Melton v. Bow, 247 S.E.2d 100 (Ga.), *cert. denied,* 439 U.S. 985 (1978) (no burden to plead or prove harm to reputation); Littlefield v. Fort Dodge Messenger, 481 F. Supp. 919 (N.D. Iowa 1978), *aff'd,* 614 F.2d 581, 5 Media L. Rep. 2325 (8th Cir.), *cert. denied,* 445 U.S. 945 (1980) (plaintiff may be compensated for injuries other than damage to reputation).

[163] RESTATEMENT (SECOND) §563, cmt. f; *see also* Penry v. Dozier, 49 So. 909, 913 (Ala. 1909).

[164] RESTATEMENT (SECOND) §563, cmt. f; *see also Penry,* 49 So. at 913; Kee v. Armstrong, Byrd & Co., 182 P. 494, 498–99 (Okla. 1919); Pfeifly v. Henry, 112 A. 768, 769 (Pa. 1921).

[165] RESTATEMENT (SECOND) §563, cmt. f; McLaughlin v. Fisher, 24 N.E. 60, 62 (Ill. 1890); Carey v. Evening Call Pub'g Co., 62 A.2d 327, 329–30 (R.I. 1948).

[166] This example is taken from an actual case, Morrison v. Richie & Co., 39 Scot. L. Rep. 432 (1902).

[167] RESTATEMENT (SECOND) §563, cmt. f; Lorentz v. RKO Radio Pictures, 155 F.2d 84, 87 (9th Cir.), *cert. denied,* 329 U.S. 727 (1946); Sellers v. Time, Inc., 423 F.2d 887, 890 (3d Cir.), *cert. denied,* 400 U.S. 830 (1970); Wilder v. Johnson Pub'g Co., 551 F. Supp. 622, 625, 9 Media L. Rep. 1145 (E.D. Va. 1982); Corman v. Blanchard, 211 Cal. App. 2d 126, 138, 27 Cal. Rptr. 327 (Cal. Ct. App. 1962).

[168] Grice v. Holk, 108 So. 2d 359, 361 (Ala. 1959); Okun v. Superior Ct., 29 Cal. 3d 442, 449–50, 629 P.2d 1369 (Cal.), *cert. denied sub nom.* Maple Properties v. Superior Ct., 454 U.S. 1099 (1981); Reece v. Grissom, 267 S.E.2d 839, 841 (Ga. Ct. App. 1980).

[169] *Grice,* 108 So. 2d at 361; Bates v. Campbell, 2 P.2d 383, 385 (Cal. 1931); McNamara v. Goldan, 87 N.E. 440, 442 (N.Y. 1909).

[170] Parkman v. Hastings, 531 S.W.2d 481, 482–83 (Ark. 1976); Spence v. Funk, 396 A.2d 967, 970, 4 Media L. Rep. 1981 (Del. 1978); Martin v. Outboard Marine Corp., 113 N.W.2d 135, 138 (Wis. 1962).

while slander consists of oral communications.[171] Sometimes the defamatory statements are a combination of written and oral communications, e.g., when an oral statement is given to a newspaper reporter and the statement is then published by the newspaper.[172] To determine whether such statements are libel or slander, the courts look to how widely the communication was disseminated and how long it will persist.[173] The stronger these factors are, the more likely a statement will be found to be libel rather than slander.[174]

The most important issue in this area for the media is whether radio and television broadcasts are libel or slander. The majority view is that both are libel.[175] However, several states have statutes providing that such communications are slander.[176]

The distinctions between libel and slander arose out of the jurisdictional conflict between the English common law and ecclesiastical courts in the Middle Ages.[177] Given this origin, it is probably not surprising that many commentators have not had anything good to say about the bifurcation of defamation into libel and slander.[178]

Policy considerations help to explain the distinction between libel and slander, however. Libelous statements tend to be more damaging than slanderous statements, because written comments are more permanent and more likely to be given a wide circulation. Nevertheless, it is easy to imagine situations where this generalization is wrong. A slanderous speech to a thousand members of a plaintiff's profession is clearly more damaging to the plaintiff's reputation than a single libelous letter to one member of a plaintiff's profession. In any event, the distinction between libel and slander persists.[179]

§2.5(I) Per Se and Per Quod Libel and Slander

A statement is libelous per se if the statement is defamatory on its face, i.e., without resort to additional facts not mentioned in the statement;[180] it is

---

[171]RESTATEMENT (SECOND) §568; *Parkman*, 531 S.W.2d at 482–84; Molt v. Public Indem. Co., 161 A. 346, 346 (N.J. 1932); Locke v. Gibbons, 299 N.Y.S. 188, 192 (N.Y. Sup. Ct. 1937), *aff'd*, 2 N.Y.S.2d 1015 (N.Y. App. Div. 1938).

[172]RESTATEMENT (SECOND) §568, cmt. f; *see* Newton v. Family Fed. Sav. & Loan Ass'n, 616 P.2d 1213, 1215 (Or. Ct. App. 1980) ("[a]n oral slanderous statement made to a newspaper reporter, which is then published, is a libel"). *See also* Gambrill v. Schooley, 48 A. 730, 732 (Md. 1901) (dictation taken down by stenographer constitutes libel); Ostrowe v. Lee, 175 N.E. 505, 506 (N.Y. 1931) (same).

[173]RESTATEMENT (SECOND) §568, cmt. d; *see* Hartmann v. Winchell, 73 N.E.2d 30, 32 (N.Y. 1947); *Locke*, 299 N.Y.S. at 192 (same).

[174]RESTATEMENT (SECOND) §568, cmt. h.

[175]*Id.* §568A; First Indep. Baptist Church v. Southerland, 373 So. 2d 647, 650 (Ala. 1979); Charles Parker Co. v. Silver City Crystal Co., 116 A.2d 440, 443 (Conn. 1955); Sorensen v. Wood, 243 N.W. 82, 85 (Neb. 1932), *appeal dismissed*, 290 U.S. 599 (1933); Shor v. Billingsley, 158 N.Y.S.2d 476 (N.Y. Sup. Ct.), *aff'd*, 169 N.Y.S.2d 416 (N.Y. App. Div. 1957); Gibler v. Houston Post Co., 310 S.W.2d 377, 385 (Tex. 1958).

[176]RESTATEMENT (SECOND) §568A, cmt. b. *See, e.g.,* CAL. CIV. CODE §46 (West 1954); N.D. REV. CODE §12-2815 (1943). *See also* American Broadcasting-Paramount Theatres v. Simpson, 126 S.E.2d 873, 879–80 (Ga. Ct. App. 1962) (creating new category of defamation, "defamacast").

[177]RESTATEMENT (SECOND) §568, cmt. b.

[178]*See, e.g.,* PROSSER & KEETON, *supra* note 6, §111, at 771–73; ELDREDGE, *supra* note 105, §12, at 77.

[179]However, Illinois and Virginia have abolished these distinctions between libel and slander; in both jurisdictions, actions for libel are treated as actions for slander for purposes of the per se/per quod distinction. Brown & Williamson Tobacco Corp. v. Jacobson, 713 F.2d 262, 267, 9 Media L. Rep. 1936 (7th Cir. 1983); Fleming v. Moore, 275 S.E.2d 632, 635, 7 Media L. Rep. 1313 (Va. 1981).

[180]RESTATEMENT (SECOND) §569, cmt. b; Thompson v. Upton, 146 A.2d 880, 883–84 (Md. 1958); Bernstein v. Dun & Bradstreet, 368 P.2d 780, 783 (Colo. 1962); Shaw Cleaners & Dyers v. Des Moines Dress Club, 245 N.W. 231, 233 (Iowa 1932). At common law, because fault and damages were presumed

libelous per quod if additional facts are necessary to understand its defamatory meaning.[181]

For example, if a newspaper writes that a married man and a married woman had sexual intercourse, the statement is not libelous per se, because if they are married to each other there is no adultery and thus no defamation. However, if additional facts—that they are not married to each other (the inducement)—and their meaning—that they engaged in adultery (the innuendo)—are pled and proved, the statement becomes defamatory. Such a statement is libel per quod. Whether a statement is libelous per se or libelous per quod is a question of law for the court.[182]

If a statement is libelous per se, then the plaintiff does not have to plead and prove special damages, i.e., actual out-of-pocket losses.[183] If a statement is libelous per quod, then to prevail the plaintiff must plead and prove special damages as a result of the libel[184] as well as the inducement and innuendo. When this has been done, a plaintiff may recover any damages that are otherwise available.[185]

In a majority of jurisdictions, the libel per se/per quod distinction is the rule;[186] in a minority of jurisdictions, the distinction is without significance.[187]

The libel per se/per quod distinction attempts to balance two competing interests: a defamed person's interest in recovering damages and a speaker's

---

(see *supra* §2.1), if a statement was libelous per se, that also meant that malice and damages did not need to be proven. This is no longer accurate. Mid-Florida Television v. Boyles, 467 So. 2d 282–83, 11 Media L. Rep. 1774, 1774–75 (Fla. 1985). Now, to say that a statement is libelous per se simply means that it is libelous on its face. *Id.*

[181]*Bernstein*, 368 P.2d at 783; *see also* the discussion in RESTATEMENT (SECOND) §569 app.; Winehoilt v. Westinghouse Elec. Corp., 476 A.2d 217, 219, 10 Media L. Rep. 2005 (Md. Ct. Spec. App.), *cert. denied*, 483 A.2d 38 (Md. 1984).

[182]*See, e.g.*, Kleir Advertising v. Premier Pontiac, 921 F.2d 1036, 1044, 18 Media L. Rep. 1529, 1535 (10th Cir. 1990).

[183]RESTATEMENT (SECOND) §569, cmt. c; *see also* Newson v. Henry, 443 So. 2d 817, 824, 10 Media L. Rep. 1421 (Miss. 1983); Marcone v. Penthouse Int'l, 533 F. Supp. 353, 361, 8 Media L. Rep. 1444 (E.D. Pa. 1982), *cert. denied*, 474 U.S. 864 (1985); Brockman v. Detroit Diesel Allison Div., Gen. Motors Corp., 366 N.E.2d 1201, 1203 n.2 (Ind. Ct. App. 1977).

[184]*Marcone*, 533 F. Supp. at 361; *Bernstein*, 368 P.2d at 782; Moore v. P.W. Pub'g Co., 209 N.E.2d 412, 415 (Ohio 1965), *cert. denied*, 382 U.S. 978 (1966). Detailed pleading and proof of special damages is required.

Adequate: Continental Nut Co. v. Robert L. Berner Co., 345 F.2d 395, 397 (7th Cir. 1965) (detailed gross sales figures alleged); Fleck Bros. Co. v. Sullivan, 423 F.2d 155, 156–57 (7th Cir. 1970) (allegation that two suppliers changed terms of credit).

Inadequate: Grzelak v. Calumet Pub'g Co., 543 F.2d 579, 583 (7th Cir. 1975) (allegations of harm to reputation and emotional distress); Brown & Williamson Tobacco Corp. v. Jacobson, 713 F.2d 262, 270, 9 Media L. Rep. 1936 (7th Cir. 1983) (allegations of sales decreases, damage to reputation for honesty, and damage to advertising efforts).

[185]*See, e.g.*, PROSSER & KEETON, *supra* note 6, at 794. *But see* Shaw Cleaners & Dyers v. Des Moines Dress Club, 245 N.W. 231, 234 (Iowa 1932) (*only* entitled to special damages for libel per quod).

[186]*See, e.g.*, Schaeffer v. Zekman, 554 N.E.2d 988, 991, 17 Media L. Rep. 1931, 1933 (Ill. App. Ct. 1990); Winehoilt v. Westinghouse Elec. Corp., 476 A.2d 217, 219, 10 Media L. Rep. 2005 (Md. Ct. Spec. App.), *cert. denied*, 483 A.2d 38 (Md. 1984); *Brockman*, 366 N.E.2d at 1203; Croton v. Gillis, 304 N.W.2d 820, 821–22 (Mich. Ct. App. 1981); Knight v. Neodesha Police Dep't, 620 P.2d 837, 846 (Kan. Ct. App. 1980); Winters v. Morgan, 576 P.2d 1152, 1154, 3 Media L. Rep. 2021 (Okla. 1978); Charles Parker Co. v. Silver City Crystal Co., 116 A.2d 440, 443–44 (Conn. 1955); *Shaw Cleaners & Dyers*, 245 N.W. at 233–35; *Moore*, 209 N.E.2d at 415; Brodsky v. Journal Pub'g Co., 42 N.W.2d 855, 856 (S.D. 1950); Dun & Bradstreet v. Robinson, 345 S.W.2d 34, 40 (Ark. 1961); Langworthy v. Pulitzer Pub'g Co., 368 S.W.2d 385, 388 (Mo. 1963).

[187]*See, e.g.*, Lent v. Huntoon, 470 A.2d 1162, 1169, 9 Media L. Rep. 2547 (Vt. 1983); Spence v. Funk, 396 A.2d 967, 971, 4 Media L. Rep. 1981 (Del. 1978); Newton v. Family Fed. Sav. & Loan Ass'n, 616 P.2d 1213, 1215 (Or. Ct. App. 1980); Memphis Pub'g Co. v. Nichols, 569 S.W.2d 412, 419, 4 Media L. Rep. 1573 (Tenn. 1978); Martin v. Outboard Marine Corp., 113 N.W.2d 135, 139 (Wis. 1962). *See also* RESTATEMENT (SECOND) §569. At least one commentator claims that this is actually the majority view. ELDREDGE, *supra* note 105, §24, at 157–74.

interest in being free of liability for making statements that did not appear to be defamatory. Thus, at common law, if a defamed person could show that his or her injury was real, by pleading and proving special damages that person could pursue a libel action even though the libeler was without fault. On the other hand, if the allegedly defamed person could not plead and prove special damages, then the interest in not imposing liability on an innocent defendant outweighed any interest in protecting reputation, so no recovery was allowed.

A statement is slanderous per se if it falls into one of four categories: (1) charges any person with a serious crime, (2) charges any person with having a loathsome disease, (3) charges any person with serious sexual misconduct, or (4) indicates that any person is unfit for his or her office, trade, profession, or business.[188] Any slanderous statement that does not fall within one of these four per se categories is slander per quod.[189]

Just as with libel, if a statement is slander per se, then the plaintiff does not have to plead and prove special damages.[190] If a statement is slander per quod, then the plaintiff must plead and prove special damages as a result of the slander.[191] When this has been done, a plaintiff may recover any damages that are otherwise available.[192]

The differences between libel per se/per quod and slander per se/per quod have often confused judges and lawyers. This is not surprising, because the same words are used—per se and per quod—and because, if a statement is libel per quod or slander per quod, special damages must be pled and proved. There, however, the similarity ends.

For libel, the per se/per quod distinction depends on whether the defamatory statement is libelous on its face. For slander, the per se/per quod distinction depends on whether the slanderous statement falls into one of the four per se categories. Whether a statement is libel per se or per quod does not depend on whether it falls in one of the four per se categories. Similarly, whether a statement is slander per se or per quod does not depend on whether it is slanderous on its face.

Some courts have ignored these differences and created the new categories of defamation per se or per quod.[193] Still other courts have held that a statement not libelous on its face is still libelous per se if it falls in one of the four slander per se categories.[194]

§2.5(J) The Four Slander Per Se Categories

There are four slander per se categories. First, charges of criminal conduct are slander per se if the crime is punishable by imprisonment in a federal or

---

[188]*See infra* §2.5(J); *see also* RESTATEMENT (SECOND) §570; *Spence,* 396 A.2d at 970; Bradshaw v. Swagerty, 563 P.2d 511, 513 (Kan. Ct. App. 1977); CAL. CIV. CODE §46 (1990).

[189]*See, e.g.,* Campbell v. Jacksonville Kennel Club, 66 So. 2d 495, 497 (Fla. 1953); *Bradshaw,* 563 P.2d at 514; Dunnebacke v. Williams, 381 S.W.2d 909, 913 (Tenn. 1964).

[190]*Croton,* 304 N.W.2d at 821; Waechter v. Carnation Co., 485 P.2d 1000, 1004 (Wash. Ct. App. 1971); Swagman v. Swift & Co., 152 N.W.2d 562, 563 (Mich. Ct. App.), *remanded,* 387 N.W.2d 912 (Mich. 1967).

[191]Henderson v. Ripperger, 594 P.2d 251, 255 (Kan. Ct. App. 1979); Baum v. Gillman, 667 P.2d 41, 42 (Utah 1983).

[192]*See, e.g.,* PROSSER & KEETON, *supra* note 6, at 794.

[193]Brown & Williamson Tobacco Corp. v. Jacobson, 713 F.2d 262, 267–69, 9 Media L. Rep. 1936 (7th Cir. 1983); Fleming v. Moore, 275 S.E.2d 632, 635, 7 Media L. Rep. 1313 (Va. 1981); Grein v. La Poma, 340 P.2d 766, 769 (Wash. 1959).

[194]Sauerhoff v. Hearst Corp. 538 F.2d 588 (4th Cir. 1976); Belli v. Orlando Daily Newspapers, 389

state institution or if the crime involves moral turpitude.[195] Thus, only the charge of serious criminal conduct is slander per se;[196] minor offenses do not fall in this category.[197] Unfortunately, the line between serious and minor crimes is not always clear. Courts try to distinguish between criminal offenses that seriously damage reputation and those that do not, which is the real guide to whether a charge of criminal conduct is serious enough to be slander per se.

Second, statements that someone has an existing venereal disease or other loathsome and communicable disease are slanderous per se.[198] This includes charges that someone has syphilis, gonorrhea, leprosy, and probably typhoid and the plague.[199] Charges that someone has previously had these diseases, however, are not slanderous per se.[200]

Third, the most important per se category involves charges that someone is unfit for his or her occupation or office. The occupation or office involved may be profit-making or nonprofit, governmental or nongovernmental, or for business or pleasure, but it must be lawful.[201] In addition, the slanderous statement must directly defame the plaintiff in his or her occupation or office, or it must impugn a particular skill or ability that is necessary for the occupation or office.[202] Thus, a charge that a public official engaged in misconduct while in office is not slanderous per se if he is no longer in public office.[203] Similarly, a charge that a clerk consorts with prostitutes is not slanderous per se, although it is slanderous per se to say that a lawyer is ignorant and unqualified to practice law.[204]

General disparagement is not slanderous per se. The disparagement must affect the plaintiff in a way that is especially harmful to someone in that office or occupation.[205] Thus, saying that a clerical employee does not pay his or her bills is not slanderous per se, because it does not affect that person's reputation

---

F.2d 579 (5th Cir. 1967), *cert. denied,* 393 U.S. 825 (1968). *See also* Raboya v. Shrybman & Assocs., 777 F. Supp. 58, 19 Media L. Rep. 1669 (D.D.C. 1991).

[195]RESTATEMENT (SECOND) §571; Taylor v. Gumpert, 131 S.W. 968 (Ark. 1910); Dunnebacke v. Williams, 381 S.W.2d 909, 911–12 (Tenn. 1964).

[196]Deese v. Collins, 133 S.E. 92, 92–93 (N.C. 1926); Privitera v. Town of Phelps, 435 N.Y.S.2d 402, 404–05, 6 Media L. Rep. 2470 (N.Y. App. Div. 1981); Stevens v. Wilber, 300 P. 329, 330–31 (Or. 1931). *See also* Starobin v. Northridge Lakes Dev. Co., 287 N.W.2d 747, 753–54 (Wis. 1980) (charge of disorderly conduct "serious" enough to be defamation per se).

[197]Shaw v. Killingsworth, 106 So. 138, 139 (Ala. 1925) (charge of misdemeanor not actionable per se); Amick v. Montross, 220 N.W. 51, 54 (Iowa 1928) (charge of drunkenness not actionable per se); *Dunnebacke,* 381 S.W.2d at 912 (charge of altering minutes not actionable per se).

[198]RESTATEMENT (SECOND) §572.

[199]*See id.* §572, cmt. b (leprosy); *id.* §572, cmt. c (typhoid); *see also* Lewis v. Hayes, 132 P. 1022, 1023 (Cal. 1913) (leprosy); McDonald v. Nugent, 98 N.W. 506, 507 (Iowa 1904) (venereal disease); Sally v. Brown, 295 S.W. 890, 891 (Ky. 1927) (venereal disease).

[200]RESTATEMENT (SECOND) §572, cmt. d; Hamilton v. Nance, 74 S.E. 627, 628 (N.C. 1912); Lowe v. DeHoog, 193 S.W. 969, 971 (Mo. 1917).

[201]RESTATEMENT (SECOND) §573; *id.* §573, cmt. b (unlawful occupation not included); Correia v. Santos, 191 Cal. App. 2d 844, 854–55, 13 Cal. Rptr. 132 (Cal. Ct. App. 1961) (nonprofit association); Hargan v. Purdy, 20 S.W. 432, 433 (Ky. 1892) (no slander per se of "doctor" illegally practicing medicine); Lloyd v. Harris, 194 N.W. 101, 102 (Minn. 1923) (tenant farmer).

[202]Korry v. International Tel. & Tel. Corp., 444 F. Supp. 193, 196 (S.D.N.Y. 1978); *Correia,* 191 Cal. App. 2d at 853; Swagman v. Swift & Co., 152 N.W.2d 562, 564 (Mich. Ct. App.), *remanded,* 387 N.W.2d 912 (Mich. 1967).

[203]RESTATEMENT (SECOND) §573, cmt. c; *see also Korry,* 444 F. Supp. 193.

[204]RESTATEMENT (SECOND) §573, illus. 2 & 4; *see also* High v. Supreme Lodge of the World, 7 N.W.2d 675, 677–78 (Minn. 1943) (charging attorney with lack of integrity and misconduct actionable per se); Buck v. Savage, 323 S.W.2d 363, 369 (Tex. Civ. App. 1959) (not actionable per se to call drug house operator "queer").

[205]RESTATEMENT (SECOND) §573, cmt. e; Smith v. Fielden, 326 S.W.2d 476, 480 (Tenn. 1959) (not actionable per se to call newspaperman "drunk"); Dorr v. C.B. Johnson, Inc., 660 P.2d 517, 520 (Colo. Ct. App. 1983) (actionable per se to charge employee truck driver with drunkenness).

as a clerk; but the same statement about a businessperson is slanderous per se because it affects his or her reputation as a businessperson.[206]

A statement that someone has made a single mistake or on one occasion has engaged in misconduct is not slander per se.[207] It is slanderous per se, however, to charge someone with a course of such conduct or to say that he or she does such things repeatedly.[208]

Fourth, statements that a woman is unchaste are also slanderous per se.[209] This rule may apply to men as well.[210]

§2.5(K) Defamation Per Se and the First Amendment

The libel per se/per quod distinction was an attempt to partially mitigate the harsh impact of the common law's rule that defamation was a no-fault tort.[211] Before the libel per se/per quod rule was adopted, a person could make a statement that did not appear to be libelous and then be held absolutely liable even though he or she did not know that the statement was libelous.[212]

In *Gertz,* the Supreme Court suggested that the libel per se/per quod rule may be constitutionally required in defamation cases.[213] Because *Gertz* abolishes the common law rule of strict liability in most defamation actions, it seems unlikely that in such cases a publisher could constitutionally be liable for defamatory statements that were not defamatory on their face, at least so long as the publisher does not have independent knowledge of their defamatory nature.[214] Otherwise, the publisher would be liable without fault, which is exactly what *Gertz* prohibits.

§2.6 PUBLICATION

It is essential to a defamation claim that the defamatory statement has been published to at least one third party.[215] Publication is a technical term

---

[206]RESTATEMENT (SECOND) §573, illus. 7 & 8; Walter v. Duncan, 153 N.Y.S.2d 916, 918 (N.Y. App. Div. 1956) (slanderous per se to say businessman does not pay bills); Liebel v. Montgomery Ward & Co., 62 P.2d 667, 671 (Mont. 1936) (not slanderous per se to say stenographer does not pay bills). *See also* Hruby v. Kalina, 424 N.W.2d 130, 15 Media L. Rep. 1559 (Neb. 1988) ("you crooked bastard" and "you're crooked" not slanderous per se, but "you stole the money" is).

[207]RESTATEMENT (SECOND) §573, cmt. d; *see also* Mason v. Sullivan, 271 N.Y.S.2d 314, 316 (N.Y. App. Div. 1966); Blende v. Hearst Pubns., 93 P.2d 733, 735 (Wash. 1939); *but see High,* 7 N.W.2d at 678 (charge of single mistake still defamatory per se). *See also supra* §2.5(D).

[208]RESTATEMENT (SECOND) §573, cmt. d; *see also Mason,* 271 N.Y.S.2d at 316.

[209]RESTATEMENT (SECOND) §574; *see also* Hollman v. Brady, 233 F.2d 877, 878 (9th Cir. 1956); Gnapinsky v. Goldyn, 128 A.2d 697, 701–02 (N.J. 1957); Crellin v. Thomas, 247 P.2d 264, 264 (Utah 1952).

[210]RESTATEMENT (SECOND) §574, cmt. c. *But see* Sauerhoff v. Hearst Corp., 388 F. Supp. 117, 124 (D. Md. 1974) (no per se claim where male's chastity impugned), *vacated on other grounds,* 538 F.2d 588 (4th Cir. 1976); Moricoli v. Schwartz, 361 N.E.2d 74 (Ill. App. Ct. 1977) (calling plaintiff "fag" not actionable per se).

[211]PROSSER & KEETON, *supra* note 6, at 795–96.

[212]*See* cases cited *supra* note 7.

[213]Gertz v. Robert Welch, Inc., 418 U.S. 323, 349–50, 1 Media L. Rep. 1633 (1974).

[214]*Id.* at 347–48 & n.10. *See also* Gazette, Inc. v. Harris, 325 S.E.2d 713, 11 Media L. Rep. 1609 (Va. 1985) (actual malice must be shown if defamatory statement does not make substantial damage to reputation apparent).

[215]RESTATEMENT (SECOND) §577; *see id.* at cmt. b. *See also* Gaetano v. Sharon Herald Co., 231 A.2d 753, 755 (Pa. 1967); Almy v. Kvamme, 387 P.2d 372, 374 (Wash. 1963).

meaning dissemination, not publication, in a book or magazine.[216] If there is no such publication, there has been no defamation no matter how damaging the statement may otherwise be,[217] because the tort of defamation seeks to protect reputation. If there is no dissemination to a third party, then there can be no damage to reputation.

While some unusual problems may arise when the only dissemination is to a single third party, e.g., a stenographer,[218] in the usual case publication is not an issue. This is obviously true where a statement is in a newspaper or in a television broadcast.[219]

Of course, the greater the dissemination, the greater the possible damages. Correspondingly, while dissemination to one third party is actionable, the damage it causes may be trivial or nonexistent depending on who receives the statement.[220]

Finally, each separate repetition of a defamation is a separate publication that is actionable.[221]

§2.6(A) Individual Liability

Each participant in the defamation—a reporter and an editor, for example—can be liable if they were sufficiently involved in the publication.[222] Now that the First Amendment usually requires that some level of fault be shown before there is liability, each alleged participant in the defamation must be examined to determine whether the standard of fault that applies to him or her has been met, and whether any privileges apply to his or her publication.[223]

---

[216]*Black's Law Dictionary* defines publication as follows: "Law of Libel: The Act of making the defamatory matter known publicly, of disseminating it, or communicating it to one or more persons (i.e., to third person or persons)." BLACK'S LAW DICTIONARY 1105 (5th ed. 1979). *See also* Ostrowe v. Lee, 175 N.E. 505 (N.Y. 1931) ("In the law of defamation, 'publication' is a term of art.").

[217]*See supra* note 215.

[218]RESTATEMENT (SECOND) §577, cmt. h. *See also Ostrowe,* 175 N.E. 505; Rickbeil v. Grafton Deaconess Hosp., 23 N.W.2d 247, 251–52 (N.D. 1946). *But see* Satterfield v. McLellan Stores Co., 2 S.E.2d 709, 711 (N.C. 1939) (stenographer is not third person for purposes of publication requirement); Watson v. Wannamaker, 57 S.E.2d 477, 478 (S.C. 1950) (same for secretary).

[219]*See, e.g.,* A. HANSON, LIBEL AND RELATED TORTS §70, at 64 (1969); ELDREDGE, *supra* note 105, §36, at 206.

[220]*See, e.g.,* Laskowski v. County of Nassau, 394 N.Y.S.2d 442, 444 (N.Y. App. Div. 1977) (damage award of $4500 excessive where only one person heard slanderous remarks).

[221]RESTATEMENT (SECOND) §577A(1); Dixson v. Newsweek, 562 F.2d 626, 631, 3 Media L. Rep. 1123 (10th Cir. 1977); Lininger v. Knight, 226 P.2d 809, 812 (Colo. 1951); Cox Enters. v. Gilreath, 235 S.E.2d 633, 634 (Ga. Ct. App. 1977). *But see infra* §2.6(C).

[222]Fairbanks Pub'g Co. v. Pitka, 376 P.2d 190, 196 (Alaska 1962) (corporate owner and publisher of newspaper liable; corporation president not liable); Davis v. Hearst, 116 P. 530, 541 (Cal. 1911) (newspaper owner liable); World Pub'g Co. v. Minahan, 173 P. 815, 817–18 (Okla. 1918) (managing editor liable); Tavoulareas v. Piro, 93 F.R.D. 11 (D.D.C. 1981) (chairman of publishing company not liable); Dworkin v. Hustler Magazine, 634 F. Supp. 727, 12 Media L. Rep. 2162 (D. Wyo. 1986) (magazine distributor not liable); Catalfo v. Jensen, 628 F. Supp. 1453, 12 Media L. Rep. 1867 (D.N.H. 1986) (free-lance photographer not liable); Cubby, Inc. v. Compuserve, 776 F. Supp. 135, 19 Media L. Rep. 1525 (S.D.N.Y. 1991) (operator of on-line electronic database not liable). *See also infra* §2.11(I).

[223]RESTATEMENT (SECOND) §578, cmt. b. *See, e.g.,* Schiavone Constr. Co. v. Time, Inc., 735 F.2d 94, 96–97, 10 Media L. Rep. 1831 (3d Cir. 1984) (applying privilege analysis to republisher); *Dixson,* 562 F.2d at 630–31 (applying fault analysis to republisher); Chang v. Michiana Telecasting Corp., 900 F.2d 1085, 17 Media L. Rep. 1768 (7th Cir. 1990) (republishing television station did not act with actual malice); Lewis v. Time, Inc., 83 F.R.D. 455, 463, 5 Media L. Rep. 1790 (E.D. Cal. 1979), *aff'd,* 710 F.2d 549, 9 Media L. Rep. 1984 (9th Cir. 1983) (distributor cannot be held liable without fault). *See also* Phoenix Newspapers v. Church, 537 P.2d 1345, 1360 (Ariz. Ct. App. 1975), *cert. denied and appeal dismissed,* 425 U.S. 908 (1976) ("an individual defendant cannot be liable unless the jury finds that the individual himself has been activated by actual malice (knowledge of falsity)"); Karaduman v. Newsday, 416 N.E.2d 557, 6 Media L. Rep. 2345 (N.Y. 1980) (analyzing liability of reporters, editor, book publisher, and newspaper).

§2.6(B) Republication

At common law, where there was strict liability for all defamatory statements, a republisher was as liable as the original defamer.[224]

A person who publishes a defamatory statement may be liable for its foreseeable republication as well as the original publication. Thus, a person who speaks to a reporter or broadcaster may be liable for his or her initial statements as well as for their accurate republication.[225]

Liability for republication cannot be avoided by qualifying the republication, for example, by saying that "Mr. X told me that Mr. Y is a child molester."[226] Such qualifications may be raised in mitigation of damages, however.[227] In addition, more modern cases hold that, where the historical fact that certain allegations were made is accurately reported and the allegations are not joined in, there is no liability.[228]

§2.6(C) The Single Publication Rule

While in general each separate publication, whether to the same person or to a new person, creates a new cause of action for defamation, the single publication rule limits a plaintiff to only one cause of action for the same communication in the mass media.[229] Thus, under this rule, a single publication

---

[224] RESTATEMENT (SECOND) §578; *see* Oklahoma Pub'g Co. v. Givens, 67 F.2d 62, 64–65 (10th Cir. 1933); Utah State Farm Bureau Fed'n v. National Farmers Union Serv. Corp., 198 F.2d 20, 23 (10th Cir. 1952); Nance v. Flaugh, 253 S.W.2d 207, 208 (Ark. 1952). The rule for mere distributors of defamatory material required that the distributor "know or should have known" of the defamation. *See* Sexton v. American News Co., 133 F. Supp. 591, 593 (N.D. Fla. 1955); Hartmann v. American News Co., 171 F.2d 581, 585 (7th Cir. 1948), *cert. denied,* 337 U.S. 907 (1949); Church of Scientology v. Minnesota State Medical Ass'n Found., 264 N.W.2d 152, 156, 3 Media L. Rep. 2177 (Minn. 1978). *But see* Layne v. Tribune Co., 146 So. 234, 238–39 (Fla. 1933) (newspapers not liable without fault for republication of defamatory material received from news agency).

[225] Davis v. National Broadcasting Co., 320 F. Supp. 1070, 1072 (E.D. La. 1970) (TV station may be liable for foreseeable republication by newspaper), *aff'd,* 447 F.2d 981 (5th Cir. 1971); Moore v. Allied Chem. Corp., 480 F. Supp. 364, 376 (E.D. Va. 1979) (speaker may be liable for republication of statements originally broadcast); Luster v. Retail Credit Co., 575 F.2d 609, 613–14 (8th Cir. 1978) (mercantile agency liable for foreseeable republication of defamatory report); Cormier v. Blake, 198 So. 2d 139, 144 (La. Ct. App. 1967) (person liable for newspaper republishing grand jury report in criminal suit if statements made in filing criminal charges not made in good faith); Campo v. Paar, 239 N.Y.S.2d 494, 498 (N.Y. App. Div. 1963) (person giving statement to newspaper liable for subsequent publication). *But see Karaduman,* 416 N.E.2d at 561 (must show original defamer participated in or approved of republication); Rinaldi v. Viking Penguin, 438 N.E.2d 377, 7 Media L. Rep. 1202 (N.Y. 1981) (must show original author participated in or approved of republication). *See also* Osmond v. EWAP, Inc., 200 Cal. Rptr. 674 (Cal. Ct. App. 1984) (author of nondefamatory statement not liable for modified republication containing defamatory statements).

[226] RESTATEMENT (SECOND) §578, cmt. b; *see also* Maloof v. Post Pub'g Co., 28 N.E.2d 458, 459 (Mass. 1940) (preceding defamatory statement with "it is alleged" no defense); Cobbs v. Chicago Defender, 31 N.E.2d 323, 325 (Ill. App. Ct. 1941) (attributing defamatory remarks to "rumor" no defense); Cepeda v. Cowles Magazine and Broadcasting, 328 F.2d 869 (9th Cir.), *cert. denied,* 379 U.S. 844, 13 L. Ed. 2d 50, 85 (1964) (attributing defamatory remarks to third person no defense). Similarly, liability in such circumstances cannot be avoided by claiming a quote is "true." It is not enough that the attribution of the quote is accurate—the information in the quote itself must be true. RESTATEMENT (SECOND) §581A, cmt. e.

[227] *See, e.g.,* Goodrow v. New York Am., 252 N.Y.S. 140, 145 (N.Y. App. Div. 1931); *see also* ELDREDGE, *supra* note 105, §97, at 582–83.

[228] Basilius v. Honolulu Pub'g Co., 711 F. Supp. 548, 551–52, 16 Media L. Rep. 1759 (D. Haw.) (accurate report of contents of anonymous letter precluded defamation liability regardless of truth or falsity of allegations), *aff'd without opinion,* 888 F.2d 1394 (9th Cir. 1989); In re United Press Int'l, 106 B.R. 323, 16 Media L. Rep. 2401 (D.D.C. 1989) (wire service's accurate report of newspaper article not actionable).

[229] RESTATEMENT (SECOND) §577A. *See also* Wheeler v. Dell Pub'g Co., 300 F.2d 372, 375 (7th Cir. 1962); Backus v. Look, 39 F. Supp. 662 (S.D.N.Y. 1941); Gregoire v. G.P. Putnam's Sons, 81 N.E.2d 45, 47 (N.Y.), *reh'g denied,* 83 N.E.2d 152 (N.Y. 1948).

of a newspaper, book, or magazine, a single radio or television broadcast, or a single exhibition of a film creates only one cause of action for defamation.[230]

There are several reasons for this rule: (1) it prevents a multiplicity of suits based on the same act—without it, a plaintiff could bring a separate action for every person who saw a national television program or read a daily newspaper, which would needlessly burden the courts with duplicative litigation;[231] (2) it protects defendants from the harassment of multiple suits;[232] (3) it prevents the recovery of excessive damages by requiring that all damages for each edition be awarded in one action;[233] and (4) it upholds the integrity of statutes of limitations, because without the rule a new claim would accrue each time someone read a defamatory publication.[234]

If there is more than one edition of each newspaper, or if there is a rebroadcast of a television or radio show, a new cause of action accrues.[235] However, the continued distribution of the same edition of a book, newspaper, or magazine is not a separate publication.[236]

The plaintiff may recover all damages suffered in all jurisdictions from the single publication. However, the decision in the plaintiff's initial action bars any other action in any jurisdiction by the same plaintiff against the same defendant for the same publication.[237]

Most jurisdictions now follow the single publication rule.[238]

§2.7 FACT VERSUS OPINION

While the rule at common law was that statements of fact and statements of opinion were actionable as defamation, it is now clear that only verifiable

---

[230]RESTATEMENT (SECOND) §577A; *see also* Ettore v. Philco Television Broadcasting Corp., 229 F.2d 481, 494–95 (3d Cir.), *cert. denied*, 351 U.S. 926 (1956) (broadcast); Ogden v. Association of U.S. Army, 177 F. Supp. 498, 499–501 (D.D.C. 1959) (book).

[231]Keeton v. Hustler Magazine, 465 U.S. 770, 79 L. Ed. 2d 790, 799, 10 Media L. Rep. 1405 (1984); Mattox v. News Syndicate Co., 176 F.2d 897, 905 (2d Cir.), *cert. denied*, 338 U.S. 858 (1949).

[232]*Keeton*, 79 L. Ed. 2d at 799; *see also* RESTATEMENT (SECOND) §577A, cmt. b; Gaetano v. Sharon Herald Co., 231 A.2d 753, 756 (Pa. 1967); Graham v. Today's Spirit, 468 A.2d 454, 457–58, 10 Media L. Rep. 1337 (Pa. 1983).

[233]RESTATEMENT (SECOND) §577A, cmt. b.

[234]Cases involving the single publication rule frequently involve statutes of limitations issues. *See, e.g.*, Carroll City/County Hosp. v. Cox Enters., 256 S.E.2d 443, 444 (Ga. 1979); Church of Scientology v. Minnesota State Medical Ass'n Found., 264 N.W.2d 152, 155, 3 Media L. Rep. 2177 (Minn. 1978); *Graham*, 468 A.2d at 457–58.

[235]*See, e.g.*, Kanarek v. Bugliosi, 108 Cal. App. 3d 327, 332–33, 166 Cal. Rptr. 526, 6 Media L. Rep. 1864 (Cal. Ct. App. 1980) (publication of paperback after publication of hardcover created new cause of action); Foretich v. Glamour, 753 F. Supp. 955, 960–61, 18 Media L. Rep. 1256, 1259–60 (D.D.C. 1990) (reprint of magazine article is new publication); Cox Enters. v. Gilreath, 235 S.E.2d 633, 3 Media L. Rep. 1031 (Ga. Ct. App. 1977) (new edition of newspaper). *Compare* Belli v. Roberts Bros. Furs, 49 Cal. Rptr. 625, 628 (Cal. Ct. App. 1966) (six editions of newspaper over two days comprised "a single integrated publication").

[236]*Kanarek*, 166 Cal. Rptr. 526, 6 Media L. Rep. 1864.

[237]RESTATEMENT (SECOND) §577A, cmt. f.

[238]*See, e.g.*, Keeton v. Hustler Magazine, 465 U.S. 770, 777 n.8 (1984); Morrissey v. William Morrow & Co., 739 F.2d 962, 10 Media L. Rep. 2305 (4th Cir. 1984), *cert. denied*, 469 U.S. 1216 (1985); Spears Free Clinic and Hosp. for Poor Children v. Maier, 261 P.2d 489, 491–92 (Colo. 1953); *Carroll City/County Hosp.*, 256 S.E.2d at 444–45; Forman v. Mississippi Pub'g Corp., 14 So. 2d 344, 347 (Miss. 1943); *Church of Scientology*, 264 N.W.2d at 155; *Cox Enters.*, 235 S.E.2d at 634.

Several states have adopted the law proposed by the National Conference of Commissions on Uniform State Laws. *See* 14 U.L.A. 351–55 (1980 & Supp. 1985). The states adopting most or all of the uniform act include Arizona (ARIZ. REV. STAT. ANN. §12-651 (1956 & Supp. 1984)), California (CAL. CIV. CODE §§3425.1–.5 (West 1954)), Idaho (IDAHO CODE §6-702 (1949)), Illinois (ILL. REV. STAT. ch. 126, ¶¶11–15 (1983)), New

statements of fact are actionable as defamation.[239] The evolution of this new doctrine began with *Gertz,* where the Supreme Court seemed to hold that statements of opinion were not actionable.[240] Following *Gertz,* a large body of case law rapidly developed that interpreted *Gertz* as holding that statements of opinion were not actionable.[241]

But in *Milkovich v. Lorain Journal Co.,* the Supreme Court held that statements of opinion are not protected by the First Amendment.[242] The Court also held, however, that hyperbole, rhetoric, loose or figurative language, and statements that are not verifiable statements of fact are protected by the First Amendment.[243] Whether *Milkovich* really changes the rule or simply the labels is not completely clear,[244] although its practical effect has not been significant.[245] Ultimately, *Milkovich* seems to have done little to affect the substance of the debate: under *Milkovich,* if a statement is one of verifiable fact, it is actionable; if it is not a statement of verifiable fact or is hyperbole, rhetoric, or loose or figurative speech, it is not actionable.[246]

Whether a statement is a verifiable statement of fact does not depend on the plaintiff's status (i.e., whether he or she is a public official or a public figure)[247] or on the defendant's status (i.e., whether the defendant is part of the media).[248] How unreasonable or derogatory the statement is and the defendant's motive in making it are also irrelevant.[249] The rule that only verifiable statements of fact are actionable also applies to claims other than defamation.[250]

Mexico (N.M. STAT. ANN. §§41-7-1 to 41-7-5 (1978)), North Dakota (N.D. CENT. CODE §14-02-10 (1981 & Supp. 1983)), and Pennsylvania (42 PA. CONS. STAT. ANN. §8341 (Supp. 1985)). *See also* NEV. REV. STAT. §20-209 (1977) (statute similar to Uniform Act).

[239]Milkovich v. Lorain Journal Co., 497 U.S. 1, 17 Media L. Rep. 2009 (1990). *See also* Old Dominion Branch No. 496, Nat'l Ass'n of Letter Carriers v. Austin, 418 U.S. 264, 284 (1974); Greenbelt Coop. Pub'g Ass'n v. Bresler, 398 U.S. 6, 14, 1 Media L. Rep. 1589 (1970).

[240]Gertz v. Robert Welch, Inc., 418 U.S. 323, 339–40, 1 Media L. Rep. 1663 (1974); *see also* Bose Corp. v. Consumers Union of U.S., 466 U.S. 485, 504, 10 Media L. Rep. 1625 (1984).

[241]*See, e.g.,* Gregory v. McDonnell Douglas Corp., 552 P.2d 425 (Cal. 1976); Lewis v. Time, Inc., 710 F.2d 549, 553, 9 Media L. Rep. 1984 (9th Cir. 1983); Woods v. Evansville Press Co., 791 F.2d 480, 487, 12 Media L. Rep. 2179, 2185 (7th Cir. 1986); Ollman v. Evans, 750 F.2d 970, 974–75, 11 Media L. Rep. 1433 (D.C. Cir. 1984) (en banc), *cert. denied,* 471 U.S. 1127, 11 Media L. Rep. 2015 (1985); MacConnell v. Mitten, 638 P.2d 689, 692 (Ariz. 1981); Chaves v. Johnson, 335 S.E.2d 97, 101–03 (Va. 1985); Owen v. Carr, 497 N.E.2d 1145, 1148 (Ill. 1986).

[242]497 U.S. at 21.

[243]*Id.* at 17.

[244]*See* Warren, Heinke & Sager, *Not As Bad As It Looks,* NAT'L L.J. (July 30, 1990).

[245]Many courts have concluded that *Milkovich* has not substantially changed the law. *See, e.g.,* Moyer v. Amador Valley Joint Union High Sch. Dist., 275 Cal. Rptr. 494, 18 Media L. Rep. 1602 (Cal. Ct. App. 1990); Weinberg v. Pollock, No. CV 89 02 77 735, 1991 Conn. Super. LEXIS 1435, 19 Media L. Rep. 1442 (Conn. Super. Ct. 1991); Lester v. Powers, 596 A.2d 65 (Me. 1991); Huyen v. Driscoll, 479 N.W.2d 76 (Minn. 1991). Other courts have found that it has changed the law, but then reached the same result on other grounds. *See, e.g.,* Unelko v. Rooney, 912 F.2d 1049, 1053, 1055–57, 17 Media L. Rep. 2317 (9th Cir. 1990), *cert. denied,* 111 S. Ct. 1586 (1991) (plaintiff failed to prove falsity); Immuno AG v. Moor-Jankowski, 567 N.E.2d 1270, 1276, 18 Media L. Rep. 1625 (N.Y.), *cert. denied,* 111 S. Ct. 2261 (1991) (on remand from U.S. Supreme Court in light of *Milkovich,* court held plaintiff failed to show falsity). Reliance has also been placed on state constitutions to hold that statements of opinion are protected despite *Milkovich. See, e.g., Immuno AG,* 567 N.E.2d at 1277–82.

[246]It is hard to see how this is substantially different from the way the issue was phrased before *Milkovich,* namely, Is this a nonactionable statement of opinion or an actionable statement of fact?

[247]Lewis v. Time, Inc., 710 F.2d 549, 553, 9 Media L. Rep. 1984 (9th Cir. 1983); Ollman v. Evans, 750 F.2d 970, 11 Media L. Rep. 1433 (D.C. Cir. 1984) (en banc), *cert. denied,* 471 U.S. 1127, 11 Media L. Rep. 2015 (1985); Deupree v. Iliff, 860 F.2d 300, 15 Media L. Rep. 2225 (8th Cir. 1988).

[248]Henry v. Halliburton, 690 S.W.2d 775, 784, 11 Media L. Rep. 2185, 2191 (Mo. 1985).

[249]Hotchner v. Castillo-Puche, 551 F.2d 910, 913, 2 Media L. Rep. 1545 (2d Cir.), *cert. denied,* 434 U.S. 834, 8 Media L. Rep. 1128 (1977).

[250]*See, e.g.,* Unelko Corp. v. Rooney, 912 F.2d 1049, 1058, 17 Media L. Rep. 2317 (9th Cir. 1990), *cert. denied,* 111 S. Ct. 1586 (1991). This is consistent with the rule that First Amendment protection cannot be

Whether a statement is factual is an issue to be decided by the court in the first instance.[251] Because of this, many defamation cases are dismissed on motion. If the court is unable to determine whether a statement is factual, however, then that determination is made by the trier of fact—usually a jury.[252]

As with the issue of whether a statement has a defamatory meaning, the difficult question is how to determine whether a statement is a verifiable statement of fact. While no bright-line test exists to resolve every case, several guidelines exist.

A verifiable statement of fact is one that can be proven true or false. A statement that cannot be proven to be true or false is not actionable.[253] If statements that could not be verified were actionable, then the jury or other fact finder would be free to punish speech not because it was false, but simply because the fact finder did not like it.

Many cases have applied a multifactor analysis in trying to determine whether a statement is actionable as a verifiable fact. Thus, the actual language used, the contents of the entire article or broadcast, the context in which the statement was made, and the use of qualifiers about the speaker's belief in the statement all have been considered.[254] The D.C. Circuit synthesized these guidelines into this test: examine (1) the language involved to see whether it "has a precise core of meaning or ... whether [it] is indefinite and ambiguous";[255] (2) "the statement's verifiability—is the statement capable of being objectively verified true or false";[256] (3) "the full context of the statement—the entire article or column";[257] and (4) "the broader context or setting in which the statement was made."[258]

First, the initial focus must be on the language itself. Some statements by their very nature appear to be factual; others do not.[259] Second, especially in light of *Milkovich,* whether a statement is verifiable is central to determining whether a statement is actionable defamation.[260] Third, the context of a statement is also important. Thus, statements on editorial pages and in reviews of restaurants, books, theaters, movies, and the like are usually found not to be factual.[261] Finally, statements issued in the heat of a political campaign, a labor

---

evaded by relabeling a defamation claim. Hustler Magazine v. Falwell, 485 U.S. 46, 57, 14 Media L. Rep. 2281 (1988). *But see* S & W Seafoods Co. v. Jacor Broadcasting of Atlanta, 390 S.E.2d 228, 17 Media L. Rep. 1340 (Ga. Ct. App. 1989) (5-4 decision upholding dismissal of defamation, false light, and interference with business relations claims because statements at issue were opinion, but allowing intentional infliction of emotional distress claim to proceed).

[251]RESTATEMENT (SECOND) §566, cmt. c; Lauderback v. American Broadcasting Cos., 741 F.2d 193, 196 n.6, 10 Media L. Rep. 2241 (8th Cir. 1984), *cert. denied,* 469 U.S. 1190 (1985); Silsdorf v. Levine, 449 N.E.2d 716, 9 Media L. Rep. 1815 (N.Y. 1983), *cert. denied,* 464 U.S. 831 (1983).

[252]Yetman v. English, 811 P.2d 323, 332 (Ariz. 1991); Good Gov't Group v. Superior Ct., 586 P.2d 572, 4 Media L. Rep. 2082 (Cal. 1978), *cert. denied,* 441 U.S. 961 (1979).

[253]Milkovich v. Lorain Journal Co., 497 U.S. 1, 17 Media L. Rep. 2009 (1990); *Hotchner,* 551 F.2d at 913 ("[a]n assertion that cannot be proved false cannot be held libelous").

[254]*Milkovich,* 497 U.S. at 9, 17 Media L. Rep. at 2012–13; Ollman v. Evans, 750 F.2d 970, 979, 11 Media L. Rep. 1433, 1440 (D.C. Cir. 1984) (en banc), *cert. denied,* 471 U.S. 1125, 11 Media L. Rep. 2015 (1985).

[255]*Ollman,* 750 F.2d at 979, 11 Media L. Rep. at 1440.
[256]*Id.*
[257]*Id.*
[258]*Id.*
[259]*See infra* notes 267 and 268.
[260]*Id.*
[261]Mr. Chow of N.Y. v. Ste. Jour Azur, 759 F.2d 219, 11 Media L. Rep. 1713 (2d Cir. 1985) (restaurant review); Mashburn v. Collin, 355 So. 2d 879, 3 Media L. Rep. 1673 (La. 1977) (restaurant review); Myers v. Boston Magazine Co., 403 N.E.2d 376, 6 Media L. Rep. 1241 (1980) ("Best and Worst" column); Greer

strike, or election; a battle for control of a corporation; or other similar disputes often are found not to be factual.[262] In all of these situations, readers or viewers are likely to treat defamatory statements as nonfactual.

Courts also look to the way a statement is phrased to determine whether it is verifiable fact. Thus, statements phrased in terms of apparency—"I believe" or "it is my opinion"— are more likely to be nonfactual statements. This does not mean that liability can be avoided by simply saying that "I saw the plaintiff in the bank yesterday, he had a gun, and he demanded money from the teller, so I believe he is a bank robber." Nor can liability be avoided merely by placing the same statements on a newspaper's editorial page.

Nonfactual statements that disclose the facts on which they rely are not actionable,[263] although not all facts favorable to the plaintiff have to be disclosed.[264] The rationale for this rule is that when the facts on which a nonfactual statement is based are disclosed or otherwise known, the listener can choose whether to accept or reject the statement.[265]

Statements of the underlying facts may themselves be actionable defamation, however. Assume, for example, that you say that you have arrived home from work every Friday for the last three months, that you have seen your neighbor on his patio drinking a beer, and that he is an alcoholic. Since the basis for your statement is disclosed, your conclusion that your neighbor is an alcoholic is a nonfactual statement, and the facts that underlie it are not actionable because they do not have a defamatory meaning.

Next, assume that these same statements were made, except that instead of a single beer you say that you saw your neighbor drink a fifth of scotch on each occasion, that you have seen him do the same thing on 50 other occasions in the last year, and that on each occasion he was so drunk he could not walk. Here again, the conclusion that your neighbor is an alcoholic is not a factual statement, but the underlying factual statements could be defamatory if false.

Finally, assume that you say that you have arrived home every Friday for the last three months, that you have seen your neighbor drinking on his patio, and that he is an alcoholic. The conclusion that your neighbor is an alcoholic is actionable because it implies undisclosed, defamatory facts, namely that the drinking you saw justifies your conclusion that he is an alcoholic.

The qualification, that nonfactual statements of opinion can be actionable if they imply facts that have not been disclosed, is one that must not be applied too broadly. Almost any statement suggests that it has some basis. Thus, this qualification could swallow up the rule that nonfactual statements are not

---

v. Columbus Monthly Pub'g Corp., 448 N.E.2d 157, 161, 8 Media L. Rep. 2129 (Ohio Ct. App. 1982) (play, movie, and restaurant reviews); Phantom Touring v. Affiliated Pubns., 953 F.2d 724, 19 Media L. Rep. 1786 (1st Cir.), *cert. denied,* 112 S. Ct. 2942 (1992) (theater review).

[262]Information Control Corp. v. Genesis One Computer Corp., 611 F.2d 781 (9th Cir. 1980) (fight for corporate control); Gregory v. McDonnell Douglas Corp., 552 P.2d 425 (Cal. 1976) (union dispute).

[263]RESTATEMENT (SECOND) §566; Lewis v. Time, Inc., 710 F.2d 549, 553, 9 Media L. Rep. 1984 (9th Cir. 1983).

[264]Lauderback v. American Broadcasting Cos., 741 F.2d 193, 198, 10 Media L. Rep. 2241 (8th Cir. 1984), *cert. denied,* 469 U.S. 1190 (1985).

[265]Hotchner v. Castillo-Puche, 551 F.2d 910, 913, 2 Media L. Rep. 1545 (2d Cir. 1977), *cert. denied,* 434 U.S. 834, 8 Media L. Rep. 1128 (1977); Silsdorf v. Levine, 462 N.Y.S.2d 822, 825, 449 N.E.2d 716, 9 Media L. Rep. 1815 (N.Y. 1983), *cert. denied,* 464 U.S. 831 (1983).

actionable, unless it is interpreted to apply only when a statement clearly implies that undisclosed facts exist.[266]

Numerous statements have been found to be nonfactual,[267] while others have been found to be ones of verifiable fact[268] or ones that a jury could find were statements of verifiable fact.[269]

§2.8 Fair Comment

At common law there was a qualified privilege for comments on matters of public concern—for example, the public conduct of public officers and employees, candidates and applicants for such positions, and government contractors;[270] the operation of educational, religious, and charitable organizations;[271] and scientific, artistic, literary, and dramatic productions and exhibitions.[272]

---

[266] Redco Corp. v. CBS, Inc., 758 F.2d 970, 972, 11 Media L. Rep. 1861 (3d Cir. 1985), *cert. denied*, 474 U.S. 843 (1985).

[267] Greenbelt Coop. Pub'g Ass'n v. Bresler, 398 U.S. 6, 14, 1 Media L. Rep. 1589 (1970) ("blackmail"); Old Dominion Branch No. 496, Nat'l Ass'n of Letter Carriers v. Austin, 418 U.S. 264, 284 (1974) ("unfair," "fascist," and "scab"); Buckley v. Littell, 539 F.2d 882, 893, 1 Media L. Rep. 1762, 1770–71 (2d Cir. 1976), *cert. denied*, 429 U.S. 1062 (1977) ("fellow traveler" and "fascist"); Avins v. White, 627 F.2d 637, 643 (3d Cir.), *cert. denied*, 449 U.S. 982 (1980) (comments on law school, e.g., "academic ennui"); National Found. for Cancer Research v. Council of Better Business Bureaus, 705 F.2d 98, 100–101, 9 Media L. Rep. 1915, 1917 (4th Cir.), *cert. denied*, 464 U.S. 830 (1983) (evaluation of plaintiff's use of charitable contributions); Time, Inc. v. Johnston, 448 F.2d 378, 384 (4th Cir. 1971) ("destroyed" is hyperbole when used to describe how one basketball player outplayed another); Orr v. Argus-Press Co., 586 F.2d 1108, 1115, 4 Media L. Rep. 1593, 1598 (6th Cir. 1978), *cert. denied*, 440 U.S. 960, 4 Media L. Rep. 2536 (1979) ("fraud," "alleged swindle," and "phony shopping mall investment scheme"); *Lauderback*, 741 F.2d at 196, 10 Media L. Rep. 2245 (taken as whole, broadcast's portrayal of plaintiff "as a less than scrupulous and honest insurance agent" was opinion); Pring v. Penthouse Int'l, 695 F.2d 438, 443, 8 Media L. Rep. 2409, 2412 (10th Cir. 1982), *cert. denied*, 462 U.S. 1132 (1983) (statement that plaintiff levitated men by fellatio was pure fantasy); Rinsley v. Brandt, 700 F.2d 1304, 1309, 9 Media L. Rep. 1225, 1228 (10th Cir. 1983) ("A theory [psychiatry] to which they were willing to sacrifice a child's life."); Edwards v. National Audubon Soc'y, 556 F.2d 113, 121, 2 Media L. Rep. 1849, 1855 (2d Cir.), *cert. denied*, 434 U.S. 1002, 10 Media L. Rep. 1365 (1977) ("the epithet 'liar,' standing by itself, merely expressed . . . opinion"); Caron v. Bangor Pub'g Co., 470 A.2d 782, 785, 10 Media L. Rep. 1365, 1367 (Me. 1984) (remark that plaintiff was too overweight to be effective cop), *cert. denied*, 467 U.S. 1241 (1984); O'Loughlin v. Patrolmen's Benevolent Ass'n, 576 N.Y.S.2d 858, 859, 19 Media L. Rep. 1735, 1736 (N.Y. App. Div. 1991) ("have no feelings" and "are a disgrace"); Moyer v. Amador Valley Joint Union High Sch. Dist., 275 Cal. Rptr. 494, 497–98, 18 Media L. Rep. 1602, 1604–05 (Cal. Ct. App. 1990) ("babbler" and "the worst teacher").

[268] Gertz v. Robert Welch, Inc., 418 U.S. 323, 331 n.4, 1 Media L. Rep. 1663 (1974) ("Leninist" and "communist-fronter"); Cianci v. New Times Pub'g Co., 639 F.2d 54, 6 Media L. Rep. 1625 (2d Cir. 1980) (charges that mayor was rapist and obstructer of justice); Buckley v. Littell, 539 F.2d 882, 1 Media L. Rep. 1762 (2d Cir. 1976), *cert. denied*, 429 U.S. 1062 (1977) (comparison of plaintiff with known libeler); *Edwards*, 556 F.2d at 117 (accusation of being paid to lie); Ball v. E.W. Scripps Co., 801 S.W.2d 684, 687, 18 Media L. Rep. 1545, 1547 (Ky. 1990), *cert. denied*, 111 S. Ct. 1622 (1991) (statement about prosecutor: "they [criminals] couldn't have a better friend"); Kahn v. Bower, 284 Cal. Rptr. 244, 19 Media L. Rep. 1236 (Cal. Ct. App. 1991) (letter accusing social worker of incompetence and hostility toward handicapped children).

[269] Good Gov't Group v. Superior Ct., 586 P.2d 572, 4 Media L. Rep. 2082 (Cal. 1978), *cert. denied*, 441 U.S. 961 (1979).

[270] Restatement (First) of Torts §607 (1938) [hereinafter Restatement (First)]; Julian v. American Business Consultants, 155 N.Y.S.2d 1, 137 N.E.2d 1 (N.Y. 1956) (political activities of actor); Orr v. Argus-Press Co., 586 F.2d 1108, 1113, 4 Media L. Rep. 1593 (6th Cir. 1978), *cert. denied*, 440 U.S. 960, 4 Media L. Rep. 2536 (1979); Beauharnais v. Pittsburgh Courier Pub'g Co., 243 F.2d 705, 708 (7th Cir. 1957); A.S. Abell Co. v. Kirby, 176 A.2d 340, 341 (Md. 1961).

[271] Restatement (First) §608; Klos v. Zahorik, 84 N.W. 1046, 1047 (Iowa 1901).

[272] Restatement (First) §608; Brewer v. Hearst Pub'g Co., 185 F.2d 846, 850 (7th Cir. 1950 (scientific research); Potts v. Dies, 132 F.2d 734, 735 (D.C. Cir. 1942) (literary work), *cert. denied*, 319 U.S. 762 (1943); Conkwright v. Globe News Pub'g Co., 398 S.W.2d 385, 386 (Tex. Civ. App. 1965).

The majority view was that only statements of opinion were protected by this privilege, and only if the facts on which they were based were disclosed or already known.[273] If the facts disclosed were defamatory, they also had to be true, privileged, or not actionable for some other reason; otherwise, such facts could be the basis for a defamation action.[274] In addition, the statements could not have been made solely to inflict harm.[275]

Under this majority view, fair comment appeared to have been supplanted by the opinion rule derived from *Gertz,* because that rule could not be overcome by showing malice,[276] as could the majority view of fair comment. Whether the fair comment doctrine will be reinvigorated by *Milkovich* remains to be seen.

The minority view of the fair comment privilege was that it protected comments on matters of public concern so long as the speaker did not know or have reason to know that the facts disclosed as the basis of the comments were false.[277] This view is essentially the same as the constitutional actual malice rule, but it is broader because it applies to all cases involving matters of public concern, while the constitutional actual malice rule applies only to cases where the plaintiff is a public official or figure.[278] Thus, the minority view of the fair comment doctrine may have a role to play where the plaintiff is a private figure and the standard of fault is not actual malice.[279]

§2.9 FALSITY

In early English law, truth was not a defense to a defamation claim. As the infamous Star Chamber said in 1606, "the greater the truth, the greater the libel."[280] Starting with the famous trial of John Zenger in 1734,[281] truth came to be accepted as a defense in American common law. Thus, the defendant must plead and prove truth if he or she wants to assert it as a defense, at least according to the common law.

However, this rule was called into question as a result of decisions by the U.S. Supreme Court holding that most defamation plaintiffs have to prove fault

---

[273]RESTATEMENT (FIRST) §606; *Julian,* 155 N.Y.S.2d at 8–9; Venn v. Tennessean Newspapers, 201 F. Supp. 47, 56 (M.D. Tenn. 1962), *aff'd,* 313 F.2d 639 (6th Cir.), *cert. denied,* 374 U.S. 830 (1963); Kelly v. Hoffman, 74 A.2d 922, 927 (N.J. Super. Ct. App. Div. 1950).

[274]RESTATEMENT (FIRST) §606; *Venn,* 201 F. Supp. at 57; Fisher v. Washington Post Co., 212 A.2d 335, 337 (D.C. 1965); *Kirby,* 176 A.2d at 343.

[275]RESTATEMENT (FIRST) §606(1)(c) and (2); *see also Brewer,* 185 F.2d at 850; *Potts,* 132 F.2d at 735; Beauharnais v. Pittsburgh Courier Pub'g Co., 243 F.2d 705, 708 (7th Cir. 1957).

[276]Yerkie v. Post-Newsweek Stations, Mich., 470 F. Supp. 91, 94, 4 Media L. Rep. 2566 (D. Md. 1979); Hoffman v. Washington Post Co., 433 F. Supp. 600, 603, 3 Media L. Rep. 1143 (D.D.C. 1977), *aff'd without opinion,* 578 F.2d 442, 3 Media L. Rep. 2546 (1978). *But see* Wehringer v. Newman, 400 N.Y.S.2d 533, 537, 3 Media L. Rep. 1708 (N.Y. App. Div. 1978) (maintaining common law privilege in addition to constitutional one).

[277]Coleman v. MacLennan, 98 P. 281 (Kan. 1908); Orr v. Argus-Press Co., 586 F.2d 1108, 1113, 4 Media L. Rep. 1593 (6th Cir. 1978), *cert. denied,* 440 U.S. 960, 4 Media L. Rep. 2536 (1979); Pearson v. Fairbanks Pub'g Co., 413 P.2d 711, 714 (Alaska 1966). Indeed, the Supreme Court expressly relied on *Coleman* when it adopted the actual malice rule. New York Times v. Sullivan, 376 U.S. 254, 1 Media L. Rep. 1527 (1964).

[278]*See infra* §2.11.

[279]*See infra* §2.11(F).

[280]De Libellis Farnosis, 77 Eng. Rep. 250 (1606). This remark has also been attributed to Lord Mansfield. PROSSER & KEETON, *supra* note 6, §116, at 840 n.6; *see also* LEVY, *supra* note 6, at 13.

[281]For a discussion of the Zenger trial, see LEVY, *supra* note 6, at 132–34.

to prevail.[282] Fault cannot be proven in the abstract; there has to be fault as to something. That something in defamation actions is falsity. The defendant has to be at fault as to falsity—if the actual malice rule applies, the defendant has to have published the statement knowing it was false or with substantial doubts about its truthfulness; if the applicable standard of fault is negligence, then the defendant must have been negligent in determining whether the statement was true or false.[283] As a result, courts have held that plaintiffs in such cases must plead and prove falsity.[284]

The Supreme Court adopted this rule in *Philadelphia Newspapers v. Hepps*,[285] where the Court held, in a 5-4 decision, that even a private figure suing a media defendant about a matter of public concern has the burden of pleading and proving falsity.[286] The Court did not decide whether this rule applies when the defendant is not a member of the media or when a matter of private concern is involved,[287] nor did it decide whether a plaintiff must prove falsity by clear and convincing evidence or simply by a preponderance of the evidence.[288]

For a statement to be true, it need not be *literally* true—only the "gist" or "sting" of the statement needs to be true.[289] Similarly, for a statement to be true it does not have to contain all information that is favorable to the plaintiff.[290]

At common law, even true statements could be actionable if they were made for improper motives, but the modern rule in most jurisdictions was that true statements were not actionable no matter what the motivation for the statement.[291] This rule is now constitutionally compelled in most and possibly all cases.[292]

§2.10 Permissible Plaintiffs

Defamation suits may be brought by individuals, corporations, unions, and partnerships.[293] The real effect of a plaintiff not being an individual is to

---

[282]For a discussion of the Supreme Court cases, see *supra* §2.2.
[283]Wilson v. Scripps-Howard Broadcasting Co., 642 F.2d 371, 375, 7 Media L. Rep. 1169, 1171 (6th Cir.), *cert. dismissed,* 454 U.S. 1130 (1981).
[284]Garrison v. Louisiana, 379 U.S. 64, 73, 1 Media L. Rep. 1548 (1964); *Wilson,* 642 F.2d at 375–76, 7 Media L. Rep. at 1171, *cert. granted,* 454 U.S. 962 (1981) *and cert. dismissed,* 454 U.S. 1130 (1981); Hunt v. Liberty Lobby, 720 F.2d 631, 651, 10 Media L. Rep. 1097 (11th Cir. 1983). *But see* Golden Bear Distrib. Sys. v. Chase Revel, Inc., 708 F.2d 944, 948–49, 9 Media L. Rep. 1857 (5th Cir. 1983). *See also* Restatement (Second) §581A, cmt. b; *id.* §613, cmt. j.
[285]475 U.S. 767, 12 Media L. Rep. 1977 (1986).
[286]*Id.* at 776.
[287]*Id.* at 775–76. *See also infra* §§2.11(C)(i) and 2.12.
[288]475 U.S. at 779.
[289]Wehling v. Columbia Broadcasting Sys., 721 F.2d 506, 509, 10 Media L. Rep. 1125 (5th Cir. 1983); Brueggemeyer v. Associated Press, 609 F.2d 825, 5 Media L. Rep. 2369 (5th Cir. 1980); Simonson v. United Press Int'l, 654 F.2d 478, 7 Media L. Rep. 1737 (7th Cir. 1981) ("raped" instead of "sexually assaulted" and "ruled" instead of "commented from the bench"); Rinsley v. Brandt, 700 F.2d 1304, 9 Media L. Rep. 1225 (10th Cir. 1983) (instituted lawsuit instead of consulting with lawyer about filing suit); Redco Corp. v. CBS, Inc., 758 F.2d 970, 972, 11 Media L. Rep. 1861 (3d Cir. 1985) (where there had been numerous accidents, product was dangerous), *cert. denied,* 474 U.S. 843 (1985); Read v. Phoenix Newspapers, 819 P.2d 939, 19 Media L. Rep. 1563 (1991).
[290]*Redco Corp.,* 758 F.2d at 972.
[291]Garrison v. Louisiana, 379 U.S. 64, 70–72, 78, 1 Media L. Rep. 1548, 1550–51, 1553–54 (1964).
[292]*Id.* at 73, 1 Media L. Rep. at 1552 (where plaintiff is public figure or official); Philadelphia Newspapers v. Hepps, 475 U.S. 767, 12 Media L. Rep. 1977 (1986) (private figure plaintiff, media defendant, and matter of public concern).
[293]Eason Pub'g v. Atlanta Gazette, 233 S.E.2d 232, 232–33 (Ga. 1977) (corporation); Vogel v. Bushnell,

limit the available damages—legal entities, unlike individuals, cannot sue for emotional distress because they cannot suffer such injury.[294]

In addition, the defamation must involve a characteristic that an entity can have. For example, to say a corporation has syphilis cannot defame it, because only human beings can have syphilis. On the other hand, to say that a corporation regularly cheats its customers is something that a corporation can do, so a defamation action can be based on such a charge.[295]

Some plaintiffs cannot sue for defamation. Government entities cannot, because such actions would prevent speech about how the government operates.[296] Deceased persons cannot sue for defamation, because their reputations die with them.[297] However, if a person dies while his libel case is pending, the action may survive, in whole or in part, depending on the survival statute in that jurisdiction.[298]

§2.10(A) Of and Concerning the Plaintiff

As a matter of common and now constitutional law, a defamatory statement must be of and concerning a plaintiff to be actionable, i.e., the statement must be about the plaintiff.[299] The plaintiff need not be mentioned by name—it is sufficient if the plaintiff can be identified by other statements in the broadcast or article or by extrinsic facts known to viewers or readers.[300]

Defamation actions by relatives of the defamed person are not allowed. By defaming Mr. *A,* a defendant does not defame Mrs. *A,* Mr. and Mrs. *A*'s children, the parents of Mr. *A,* or other members of Mr. *A*'s family.[301] Similarly, defamation of a corporation does not defame its officers, directors, or shareholders.[302]

---

221 S.W. 819, 822–23 (Mo. Ct. App. 1920) (partnership); Kirkman v. Westchester Newspapers, 24 N.Y.S.2d 860, 862 (N.Y. App. Div. 1941), *aff'd in relevant part,* 39 N.E.2d 919, 920–21 (N.Y. 1942) (unions). See also Daniels v. Sanitarium Ass'n, 381 P.2d 652, 657 (Cal. 1963).

[294]*See* cases cited in preceding note.

[295]*Eason Pub'g,* 233 S.E.2d at 232–33 (corporation can be libeled with respect to business reputation); Converters Equip. Corp. v. Condes Corp., 258 N.W.2d 712, 715 (Wis. 1977); Golden Palace v. National Broadcasting Co., 386 F. Supp. 107, 109 (D.D.C. 1974), *aff'd without opinion,* 530 F.2d 1094 (D.C. Cir. 1976).

[296]New York Times Co. v. Sullivan, 376 U.S. 254, 291, 1 Media L. Rep. 1527, 1542 (1964).

[297]RESTATEMENT (SECOND) §560; Lee v. Weston, 402 N.E.2d 23, 26–27 (Ind. 1980); Gruschus v. Curtis Pub'g Co., 342 F.2d 775, 776 (10th Cir. 1965).

[298]*Compare* Kelly v. Johnson Pub'g Co., 160 Cal. App. 2d 718, 723, 325 P.2d 659 (Cal. Ct. App. 1958) (cause of action does not survive) *with* Moore v. Washington, 311 N.Y.S.2d 310 (N.Y. App. Div. 1970) (cause of action survives).

[299]RESTATEMENT (SECOND) §564; *Sullivan,* 376 U.S. 254, 1 Media L. Rep. 1527; Geisler v. Petrocelli, 616 F.2d 636, 637, 6 Media L. Rep. 1023 (2d Cir. 1980); Farber v. Cornils, 487 P.2d 689, 691 (Idaho 1971).

[300]Cosgrove Studio & Camera Shop v. Pane, 182 A.2d 751, 753 (Pa. 1962); Harwood Pharmacal Co. v. National Broadcasting Co., 174 N.E.2d 602, 603 (N.Y. 1961). However, an indirect reference to a plaintiff cannot be the basis for liability. *Sullivan,* 376 U.S. 254, 1 Media L. Rep. 1527 (references to police not of and concerning county commissioner who supervised police). Furthermore, failure to mention a plaintiff is not actionable. Blatty v. New York Times Co., 42 Cal. 3d 1033, 1044, 728 P.2d 1177, 13 Media L. Rep. 1928 (Cal. 1986), *cert. denied,* 485 U.S. 934 (1988).

[301]Lee v. Weston, 402 N.E.2d 23, 27 (Ind. Ct. App. 1980) (detailed discussion of rule's rationale); Hughes v. New Eng. Newspaper Pub'g Co., 43 N.E.2d 657, 658 (Mass. 1942) (husband and wife); Louisville Times Co. v. Emrich, 66 S.W.2d 73, 75 (Ky. 1933) (same); Ryan v. Hearst Pub'g, 100 P.2d 24 (Wash. 1940) (wife, husband, and kids); Saucer v. Giroux, 54 Cal. App. 732, 733, 202 P. 887 (Cal. Ct. App. 1921) (brother and mother); *Kelly,* 160 Cal. App. 2d at 723 (brother and sisters).

[302]Cohn v. National Broadcasting Co., 414 N.Y.S.2d 906, 909, 4 Media L. Rep. 2533 (N.Y. App. Div. 1979) (law firm not defamed by defamation of partner in firm), *aff'd,* 408 N.E.2d 672, 6 Media L. Rep. 1398 (N.Y.), *cert. denied,* 449 U.S. 1022 (1980); AIDS Counseling & Testing Ctrs. v. Group W Television,

Fictitious works create special problems, because someone may be inadvertently defamed.[303] At common law, liability could be imposed even if the author of a work did not intend to refer to the plaintiff, so long as it was reasonable to conclude that it was the plaintiff to whom the author referred. This was true even if the work included a disclaimer stating that the work was fictional and that no reference to any actual persons was intended, although such disclaimers were important in determining whether it was reasonable to conclude that the work referred to the plaintiff.[304] Because such strict liability is no longer permissible under the First Amendment, a defendant must be shown to have acted with the requisite degree of fault before liability may be imposed in such circumstances.[305]

§2.10(B) Defamation of Groups

Courts generally have refused to allow any member of a group to sue for defamation that refers to an entire group if the group consists of more than 25 people.[306] There are two rationales for this rule: First, defamatory statements do little damage to the reputation of any member of a group larger than 25 if the defamation refers to all members of the group. For example, a statement that all police officers in Los Angeles are corrupt is extremely unlikely to have any effect on the reputation of any given officer. Second, the price to be paid by making such statements actionable is simply too high. The discussion of many matters of great importance would be stifled if every teacher in Chicago could sue for defamation over a statement that all Chicago teachers are incompetent, or if all doctors could sue because someone said all doctors "gouge" their clients by agreeing to fix their fees. Numerous cases illustrate these principles.[307]

Once the number in a group falls below 25, however, the danger to any group member's reputation begins to increase, while the need to allow impersonal criticism of groups begins to decrease. The smaller the group and the clearer it is that the defamatory statements refer to every member of the group,

---

903 F.2d 1000, 17 Media L. Rep. 1893 (4th Cir. 1990) (investors in company could not sue for statements about company); Dexter's Hearthside Restaurant v. Whitehall Co., 508 N.E.2d 113, 14 Media L. Rep. 1664 (Mass. Ct. App. 1987).

[303]Bindrim v. Mitchell, 155 Cal. Rptr. 29, 5 Media L. Rep. 1113 (Cal. Ct. App.), *cert. denied*, 444 U.S. 984 (1979); Aguilar v. Universal City Studios, 219 Cal. Rptr. 819, 12 Media L. Rep. 1485 (Cal. Ct. App. 1985).

[304]Corrigan v. Bobbs-Merrill Co., 126 N.E. 260, 262 (N.Y. 1920).

[305]*Bindrim*, 155 Cal. Rptr. 29, *cert. denied*, 444 U.S. 984; Pring v. Penthouse Int'l, 695 F.2d 438, 440, 8 Media L. Rep. 2409 (10th Cir. 1982), *cert. denied*, 462 U.S. 1132 (1983).

[306]*Cases Articulating "25-Person" Rule:* Barger v. Playboy Enters., 564 F. Supp. 1151, 1153, 9 Media L. Rep. 1656 (N.D. Cal. 1983), *aff'd*, 732 F.2d 163, 10 Media L. Rep. 1527 (9th Cir.), *cert. denied*, 469 U.S. 853 (1984); Schuster v. U.S. News & World Report, 459 F. Supp. 973, 977, 4 Media L. Rep. 1911 (D. Minn. 1978), *aff'd*, 602 F.2d 850, 5 Media L. Rep. 1773 (8th Cir. 1979); O'Brien v. Williamson Daily News, 735 F. Supp. 218, 222–23, 18 Media L. Rep. 1037, 1039–40 (E.D. Ky. 1990), *aff'd without opinion*, 931 F.2d 893 (6th Cir. 1991).

[307]*Cases Finding Group Too Large:* Granger v. Time, Inc., 568 P.2d 535, 539, 3 Media L. Rep. 1021 (Mont. 1977) (204 persons); Michigan United Conservation Clubs v. CBS News, 665 F.2d 110, 112, 7 Media L. Rep. 2331 (6th Cir. 1981) (over 1 million persons); Neiman-Marcus v. Lait, 13 F.R.D. 311 (D.N.Y. 1952) (382 persons); Ajay Nutrition Foods v. Food & Drug Admin., 378 F. Supp. 210, 218 (D.N.J. 1974), *aff'd without opinion*, 513 F.2d 625 (3d Cir. 1975) (entire industry of sellers and distributors of health food products). *But see* Brady v. Ottaway Newspapers, 445 N.Y.S.2d 786, 8 Media L. Rep. 1671 (N.Y. App. Div. 1981) (group of 53); Fawcett Pubns. v. Morris, 377 P.2d 42, 52 (Okla. 1962) (article referring to football team), *cert. denied and appeal dismissed*, 376 U.S. 513 (1964).

the more likely the statements will be found to be of and concerning a member of the group. This is the rule of "small and all."[308]

If a statement refers to fewer than all members of a group, then it can be of and concerning that smaller group. For example, a statement that "all cops are killers, and Ms. *Y* is a prime example of that" is certainly of and concerning Ms. *Y* though not all police officers. Because defamation of government entities is not actionable, however, a defamatory reference to a small group of public officials that does not single out any particular official or clearly refer to all members of a small group is not actionable, because this would effectively allow recovery for defamation of government entities.[309]

Class actions for defamation are inappropriate both because the group membership would have to exceed 25 to justify the use of the cumbersome class action device and because the individual issues in a class action for defamation would outweigh the common issues of law and fact.[310]

§2.11 Fault

New York Times,[311] *Butts/Walker,*[312] and *Gertz*[313] established two constitutional rules as to fault:

(1) public official[314] and public figure[315] plaintiffs must prove, by clear and convincing evidence, that the defendant acted with actual malice; and

(2) private figure plaintiffs must show some kind of fault, usually at least negligence, by the defendant.[316]

Thus, it usually is essential in any defamation action to determine whether the plaintiff is a public official, public figure, or private figure, because this will determine what level of federal constitutional fault the plaintiff must prove to prevail.

§2.11(A) Public Officials

Like the determination of defamatory meaning,[317] whether a statement constitutes a verifiable fact,[318] and public figure status,[319] public official status is an issue to be decided by the court in the first instance.[320]

---

[308]Restatement (Second) §564, cmt. b; Hansen v. Stoll, 636 P.2d 1236, 1240–41, 8 Media L. Rep. 1204 (Ariz. Ct. App. 1981) (seven people); Montgomery Ward & Co. v. Skinner, 25 So. 2d 572, 579–80 (Miss. 1946) (three people); American Broadcasting-Paramount Theatres v. Simpson, 126 S.E.2d 873, 881–82 (Ga. Ct. App. 1962) (two people); Cushman v. Day, 602 P.2d 327, 331–32 (Or. Ct. App. 1979) (13 people); *Lait*, 13 F.R.D. 311 (25 people). *But see* Arcand v. Evening Call Pub'g Co., 567 F.2d 1163, 1165, 3 Media L. Rep. 1748 (1st Cir. 1977) (statement referred to one unidentified member of 21-member group; held no member of group could sue).

[309]*See supra* §2.10; *see also* Wainman v. Bowler, 576 P.2d 268, 270–71, 3 Media L. Rep. 2044 (Mont. 1978); Rosenblatt v. Baer, 383 U.S. 75, 79–83, 1 Media L. Rep. 1558 (1966).

[310]Los Angeles Fire & Police Protective League v. Rodgers, 86 Cal. Rptr. 623 (Cal. Ct. App. 1970).

[311]New York Times Co. v. Sullivan, 376 U.S. 254, 1 Media L. Rep. 1537 (1964).

[312]Curtis Pub'g Co. v. Butts *and* Associated Press v. Walker, 388 U.S. 130, 1 Media L. Rep. 1568 (1967).

[313]Gertz v. Robert Welch, Inc., 418 U.S. 323, 1 Media L. Rep. 1663 (1974).

[314]*Sullivan,* 376 U.S. at 279–80, 1 Media L. Rep. at 1537–38.

[315]*Butts,* 388 U.S. at 155.

[316]*Gertz,* 418 U.S. at 335–37. However, if the defamatory statement is about a matter of private rather than public concern, this rule may not apply. *See infra* §2.12.

[317]*See supra* §2.5.

[318]*See supra* §2.7.

[319]*See infra* §2.11(B).

[320]Rosenblatt v. Baer, 383 U.S. 75, 88, 1 Media L. Rep. 1558 (1966); Kahn v. Bower, 284 Cal. Rptr. 244, 19 Media L. Rep. 1236 (Cal. Ct. App. 1991).

The Supreme Court's most comprehensive definition of the term "public official" is "that the 'public official' designation applies at the very least to those among the hierarchy of government employees who have, or appear to the public to have, substantial responsibility for or control over the conduct of government affairs."[321] No more comprehensive definition has been given by the Supreme Court, although the Court has noted that the term "public official" "cannot be thought to include all public employees."[322]

The meaning of "public official" is defined by federal law standards rather than state standards.[323] Although one justification for applying the actual malice rule to public officials is that they often have an absolute privilege to defame others, public official status is not dependent on the existence of such a privilege.[324]

A variety of people have been found to be public officials,[325] others have been found not to be public officials,[326] and in some areas the cases are in conflict.[327]

§2.11(A)(i) Official Conduct

The Supreme Court has held that statements protected by the actual malice rule must relate to the official conduct of a public official.[328] While this holding might appear to severely limit the scope of the actual malice rule, this is not the case. The Court has held that "anything which might touch on an official's fitness for office is relevant"[329] to his or her official conduct. This includes "dishonesty, malfeasance, or improper motivation, even though these characteristics may also affect the official's private character."[330] The Court has also

---

[321] 383 U.S. at 85.
[322] *Id.* at 84.
[323] Hutchinson v. Proxmire, 443 U.S. 111, 119 n.8, 5 Media L. Rep. 1279 (1979).
[324] *Rosenblatt*, 383 U.S. at 84–85 n.10. For a discussion of such privileges, *see infra* §2.13.
[325] *Rosenblatt*, 383 U.S. at 77 (supervisor of county recreation area); Ocala Star-Banner Co. v. Damron, 401 U.S. 295, 299, 1 Media L. Rep. 1624 (1971) (mayor); Monitor Patriot Co. v. Roy, 401 U.S. 265, 271, 1 Media L. Rep. 1619 (1971) (candidates for elective office, but suggesting candidates are more appropriately described as public figures); Simonson v. United Press Int'l, 654 F.2d 478, 7 Media L. Rep. 1737 (7th Cir. 1981) (judges); Meiners v. Moriarity, 563 F.2d 343 (7th Cir.) (FBI agents); Fadell v. Minneapolis Star & Tribune Co., 557 F.2d 107, 2 Media L. Rep. 2198 (7th Cir.), *cert. denied*, 434 U.S. 966, 3 Media L. Rep. 1432 (1977) (tax assessors); Arnheiter v. Random House, 578 F.2d 804, 4 Media L. Rep. 1174 (9th Cir. 1978) (commander of naval vessel during war); Britton v. Koep, 470 N.W.2d 518, 19 Media L. Rep. 1208 (Minn. 1991) (county probation officer).
[326] Gertz v. Robert Welch, Inc., 418 U.S. 323, 335–37, 1 Media L. Rep. 1663 (1974) (lawyers); Jenoff v. Hearst Corp., 644 F.2d 1004, 7 Media L. Rep. 1081 (4th Cir. 1981) (police informant); Arctic Co. v. Loudoun Times Mirror, 624 F.2d 518, 6 Media L. Rep. 1433 (4th Cir. 1980), *cert. denied*, 449 U.S. 1102 (1981) (government contractor who agreed to do historical and archeological research on proposed water project); Furgason v. Clausen, 785 P.2d 242, 249–50, 18 Media L. Rep. 1369, 1374–75 (N.M. Ct. App. 1989) (member of mayoral advisory committee); Jones v. Palmer Communications, 440 N.W.2d 884, 894–95, 16 Media L. Rep. 2137, 2143 (Iowa 1989) (low-ranking firefighter).
[327] *Compare, e.g.,* Franklin v. Benevolent & Protective Order of Elks, 159 Cal. Rptr. 131, 5 Media L. Rep. 1977 (Cal. Ct. App. 1979) (teacher not public official) *and* Richmond Newspapers v. Lipscomb, 362 S.E.2d 32, 14 Media L. Rep. 1953 (Va. 1987), *cert. denied*, 486 U.S. 1023 (1988) (same) *with* Basarich v. Rodeghero, 321 N.E.2d 739, 742 (Ill. App. Ct. 1974) (teacher is public official) *and* Johnston v. Corinthian Television Corp., 583 P.2d 1101, 1102–03, 3 Media L. Rep. 2518 (Okla. 1978) (same). Police officers have almost always been held to be public officials. Reed v. Northwestern Pub'g Co., 530 N.E.2d 474, 15 Media L. Rep. 2233 (Ill. 1988), *cert. denied*, 489 U.S. 1067 (1989) (police officer on beat). *But see* Nash v. Keene Pub'g Co., 498 A.2d 348, 12 Media L. Rep. 1025 (N.H. 1985) (whether police officer is public official is question of fact for jury).
[328] New York Times Co. v. Sullivan, 376 U.S. 254, 264, 1 Media L. Rep. 1527, 1531 (1964).
[329] Garrison v. Louisiana, 379 U.S. 64, 77, 1 Media L. Rep. 1548, 1553 (1964).
[330] *Id.* at 77, 1 Media L. Rep. at 1553 (quoted with approval in Monitor Patriot Co. v. Roy, 401 U.S. 265, 273–74, 1 Media L. Rep. 1619 (1971)); *see also* Ocala Star-Banner Co. v. Damron, 401 U.S. 295, 300 (1971) (charge of indictment for perjury).

held that the "official conduct" requirement essentially ceases to exist in the context of election campaigns.[331]

In any event, the scope of this requirement is not to be determined by "the customary meaning of the phrase 'official conduct.' "[332] It is also clear "as a matter of constitutional law that a charge of criminal conduct, no matter how remote in time or place, can never be irrelevant to an official's or a candidate's fitness for office."[333]

§2.11(A)(ii) Public Officials and Absolute Privilege

Some defamation defendants have argued that they are entitled to an absolute privilege under the First Amendment if the plaintiff is a public official and if the defamatory statements relate to the official's performance of the duties of his or her office.[334] In essence, it has been contended that officials' performance of their duties is indistinguishable from the government's performance, and since the government cannot sue for defamation, neither should high government officials. To date this argument has not found favor with the courts.[335]

§2.11(A)(iii) Mentioning the Plaintiff's Public Official Status

It has sometimes been contended that, unless the plaintiff's public official status is mentioned in the defamatory publication, the actual malice rule does not apply.[336] The Supreme Court has never ruled on that contention.[337] At the very least, such a requirement makes no sense if the plaintiff's status is already known to many of those who read or hear the defamatory statement.

§2.11(B) Public Figures

Public figure status, like public official status,[338] is an issue to be decided by the court in the first instance.[339] Several Supreme Court cases discuss public figure status; the first of these are the decisions in *Butts* and *Walker*.[340] The Court found that Butts, the athletic director of the University of Georgia[341] and

---

[331] Monitor Patriot Co. v. Roy, 401 U.S. 265, 274–75, 1 Media L. Rep. 1619 (1971) ("it is by no means easy to see what statements about a candidate might be altogether without relevance to his fitness for the office he seeks").

[332] *Id.* at 274.

[333] *Id.* at 277.

[334] Sharon v. Time, Inc., 599 F. Supp. 538, 553–54, 11 Media L. Rep. 1153, 1163–64 (S.D.N.Y. 1984).

[335] *Id.*

[336] *See, e.g.,* Bufalino v. Associated Press, 692 F.2d 266, 273, 8 Media L. Rep. 2384 (2d Cir. 1982), *cert. denied,* 462 U.S. 1111 (1983). *See also* Guinn v. Texas Newspapers, 738 S.W.2d 303, 16 Media L. Rep. 1024 (Tex. Ct. App. 1987), *cert. denied,* 488 U.S. 1041 (1989). *Contra* Stone v. Essex County Newspapers, 330 N.E.2d 161, 171 (Mass. 1975) (newspaper's failure to identify plaintiff's public capacity "not crucial" in determining whether to apply actual malice rule).

[337] Ocala Star-Banner Co. v. Darmon, 401 U.S. 295, 300 n.4 (1971) (theory abandoned in Supreme Court).

[338] *See supra* note 320.

[339] *See, e.g.,* Rosenblatt v. Baer, 383 U.S. 75, 88, 1 Media L. Rep. 1558 (1966); Lewis v. Coursolle Broadcasting of Wis., 377 N.W.2d 166, 12 Media L. Rep. 1641 (Wis. 1985); Weingarten v. Block, 102 Cal. App. 3d 129, 134–35, 5 Media L. Rep. 2585 (Cal. Ct. App.), *cert. denied,* 449 U.S. 899 (1980); Rebozo v. Washington Post Co., 637 F.2d 375, 379, 6 Media L. Rep. 2505 (5th Cir.), *cert. denied,* 454 U.S. 964 (1981).

[340] Curtis Pub'g Co. v. Butts *and* Associated Press v. Walker, 388 U.S. 130, 1 Media L. Rep. 1568 (1967).

[341] *Id.* at 135.

a "well-known and respected figure in coaching ranks,"[342] was a public figure.[343] It also found that Walker, a former U.S. Army officer who had commanded federal troops during the integration of Little Rock's schools and who later made a number of strong, widely publicized statements against such federal intervention, "could fairly be deemed a man of some political prominence."[344]

A plurality of the Court concluded that Butts probably attained his public figure status by his position alone,[345] while Walker attained his by thrusting himself into the vortex of a public controversy.[346] The plurality also noted that both Butts and Walker commanded continuing public attention and had sufficient media access to respond to their critics.[347] This method of analysis has been carried forward in later cases.[348]

In *Gertz,* the Court held, as a matter of federal constitutional law, that while public figures and public officials must prove constitutional actual malice to prevail in a defamation action, private figures do not have to prove actual malice to recover compensatory damages.[349] The Court gave two reasons for the distinction: (1) public figures and officials usually have greater access to the media to rebut charges against them than do private figures;[350] and (2) public figures and officials, unlike private figures, have voluntarily exposed themselves to the risk of defamatory falsehoods.[351]

The *Gertz* Court then identified three types of public figures: involuntary, voluntary all-purpose, and voluntary limited-purpose.[352] It noted that "the instances of truly involuntary public figures must be exceedingly rare."[353]

As to voluntary public figures, the Court said that voluntary all-purpose public figures are ones that "occupy positions of such persuasive power and influence that they are deemed public figures for all purposes" or are ones that achieve "such pervasive fame or notoriety" that they become "public figure[s] for all purposes and in all contexts."[354]

According to the Court, voluntary limited-purpose public figures are ones who "have thrust themselves to the forefront of particular public controversies in order to influence the resolution of the issues involved."[355] Such limited-purpose or vortex public figures are ones who "voluntarily inject" themselves or are "drawn into a particular public controversy and thereby [become] ... public figure[s] for a limited range of issues."[356] In any event, voluntary public figures are ones who "invite attention and comment."[357]

---

[342]*Id.* at 154–55, 162.
[343]*Id.* at 136.
[344]*Id.* at 140.
[345]388 U.S. at 155.
[346]*Id.*
[347]*Id.* at 154–55, 162.
[348]*See infra* notes 349–98 and accompanying text.
[349]418 U.S. 323, 337, 347, 1 Media L. Rep. 1663 (1974). *Gertz* is discussed in greater length *supra* §2.2.
[350]418 U.S. at 344.
[351]*Id.* at 344–45.
[352]*Id.* at 345.
[353]*Id.*
[354]*Id.* at 351.
[355]418 U.S. at 345.
[356]*Id.* at 351.
[357]*Id.* at 345.

In *Gertz,* the plaintiff was held to be neither an all-purpose public figure nor a limited-purpose public figure.[358] He was not well-known enough to be an all-purpose public figure, and he had not done enough to attract the public's attention to be a limited-purpose public figure.[359]

Several Supreme Court cases since *Gertz* have applied these rules. The first was *Time, Inc. v. Firestone.*[360] *Time Magazine* published an erroneous report on the sensational divorce proceedings of plaintiff Mary Alice Firestone and Russell Firestone, an heir to the Firestone tire fortune.[361] The Court held that the plaintiff was not a public figure:[362] She had no special prominence in the affairs of society, and she had not thrust herself into any particular public controversy.[363]

While the Court agreed that the plaintiff's divorce had become a "cause celebre," it said that this did not make it a public controversy.[364] Similarly, the Court said that the plaintiff had no choice but to go to court if she wanted a divorce, so she had not "freely chose[n] to publicize issues."[365] The Court even held that the plaintiff's use of press conferences to answer questions about the divorce action did not make her a public figure, because they should have had no effect on the outcome of the divorce action.[366]

In the companion cases of *Hutchinson v. Proxmire*[367] and *Wolston v. Reader's Digest Association,*[368] the Supreme Court found that neither of the plaintiffs was a public figure. In *Hutchinson,* plaintiff Ronald Hutchinson, a research behavioral scientist, sued U.S. Senator William Proxmire and his legislative aide for defamation, because Proxmire gave the "Golden Fleece" award for wasteful government spending to the federal agencies that sponsored the plaintiff's research.[369]

Since it was not contended that the plaintiff was an all-purpose public figure, the Court considered only whether he was a limited-purpose public figure with respect to commentary on his receipt of federal funds for his research.[370] The Court concluded that neither the plaintiff's applications for federal funds and the publicity about them nor his access to the media after the Golden Fleece award demonstrated that he was a public figure.[371] According to the Court, the plaintiff "did not have the regular and continuing access to the media that is one of the accoutrements of a public figure."[372]

---

[358] *Id.* at 352.
[359] *Id.* at 351–52.
[360] 424 U.S. 448, 1 Media L. Rep. 1665 (1976).
[361] *Id.* at 450. The judgment in the divorce proceeding stated:
According to certain testimony in behalf of the defendant [husband], extramarital escapades of the plaintiff [wife] were bizarre and of an amatory nature which would have made Dr. Freud's hair curl. Other testimony, in plaintiff's [wife's] behalf, would indicate that defendant [husband] was guilty of bounding from one bed partner to another with the erotic zest of a satyr.
Id. at 450–451.
[362] *Id.* at 453.
[363] *Id.*
[364] *Id.* at 454.
[365] 424 U.S. at 454.
[366] *Id.* at 454–55 and n.3 The Court also refused to extend the actual malice rule to cover all reports of the judicial proceedings. *Id.* at 455–57.
[367] 443 U.S. 111, 5 Media L. Rep. 1279 (1979).
[368] 443 U.S. 157, 5 Media L. Rep. 1273 (1979).
[369] *Id.* at 114.
[370] *Id.* at 134.
[371] *Id.* at 134–35.
[372] *Id.* at 136.

The Court also held that the plaintiff had not invited public attention by applying for federal grants or by the articles on his research that he wrote for professional publications.[373] The plaintiff had not thrust himself into any particular public controversy, although there was a general concern over government expenditures.[374] Finally, the Court noted that defendants cannot, by their own actions, confer public figure status on someone.[375]

In *Wolston,* the plaintiff sued because he had been accused in the defendant's book of being a Soviet agent.[376] In the late 1950s, a special federal grand jury in New York City investigated the activities of Soviet agents in the United States.[377] After the plaintiff's aunt and uncle pled guilty to espionage, the plaintiff traveled from his home in the District of Columbia to New York City in response to grand jury subpoenas.[378]

In July 1958, however, the plaintiff failed to respond to a grand jury subpoena, and a federal judge issued a show cause order regarding contempt.[379] The plaintiff appeared at the contempt hearing, offered to testify, and when that offer was refused, contended that his mental depression prevented him from previously attending.[380] When his pregnant wife became hysterical on the witness stand, however, he pled guilty to the contempt charge.[381] Fifteen newspaper stories were published about these events.[382]

After reiterating the two factors set forth in *Gertz* to determine public figure status, namely the plaintiff's access to the media to rebut defamatory statements and whether the plaintiff voluntarily exposed him- or herself to the risk of defamatory falsehoods, the Court quoted the *Gertz* definitions of public figures, namely people who " 'occupy positions of such persuasive power and influence that they are deemed public figures for all purposes' " or " '[m]ore commonly, those ... [who] have thrust themselves to the forefront of particular public controversies in order to influence the resolution of the issues involved.' "[383]

The Court noted that no one contended that the plaintiff had "such 'persuasive power and influence' that he could be deemed one of the small groups of individuals who are public figures for all purposes."[384] As to limited-purpose public figure status, the Court rejected the lower courts' conclusion that the plaintiff had thrust himself into the forefront of a public controversy about Soviet espionage in the United States by not appearing before the grand jury.[385] The Court held that, even though the plaintiff may have known that his failure to appear before the grand jury might generate publicity, this was not decisive: "[T]he simple fact that these events attracted media attention ... is not conclusive of the public-figure issue."[386]

---

[373] 443 U.S. at 135.
[374] *Id.* The Court also said that receipt of public grants did not automatically make one a public figure. *Id.*
[375] *Id.*
[376] *Id.* at 159.
[377] *Id.* at 161.
[378] 443 U.S. at 162.
[379] *Id.*
[380] *Id.* at 162–63.
[381] *Id.* at 163.
[382] *Id.*
[383] 443 U.S. at 164.
[384] *Id.* at 165.
[385] *Id.* at 166.
[386] *Id.* at 167.

Similarly, the Court stated, the plaintiff's failure to appear before the grand jury was not an attempt "to invite public comment or influence the public with respect to any issue."[387] The plaintiff did not use the contempt citation to attract attention or to generate a public debate about any issue.[388] The plaintiff thus did not relinquish his interest in the protection of his name.[389]

The Court's decisions appear to take a narrow view of who is a voluntary limited-purpose public figure and look particularly to whether a plaintiff has assumed the risk of defamatory comment by actively participating in the public debate over some issue. The Court also looks to the plaintiff's access to the media in determining limited-purpose public figure status.

In practice, however, the lowers courts have found it difficult to decide such cases with any consistency. For example, in *Vegod Corp. v. ABC*,[390] the California Supreme Court held that a corporation that conducted a "closing out" sale for a "landmark store" was not a public figure, even though the destruction of the store was controversial.[391] A year later, however, the Third Circuit held that the advertising and selling of discount steaks created public figure status.[392] Similarly, while one court held that "Miss Wyoming" was not a public figure for purposes of a fictional article about beauty contests,[393] another court held that a "Playboy Playmate" was a public figure with respect to a satire on *Playboy Magazine*.[394]

Numerous plaintiffs have been found to be general- or limited-purpose public figures,[395] while many others have not.[396] The case law on corporations

---

[387]*Id.* at 168.
[388]443 U.S. at 168.
[389]*Id.* The Court also said that simply engaging in criminal conduct did not automatically make one a public figure for comment even on the limited range of issues relating to such conduct. *Id.*
[390]25 Cal. 3d 763, 603 P.2d 14, 5 Media L. Rep. 2043 (Cal. 1979), *cert. denied,* 449 U.S. 886 (1980).
[391]*Id.* at 765.
[392]Steaks Unlimited v. Deaner, 623 F.2d 264, 273–74, 6 Media L. Rep. 1229 (3d Cir. 1980).
[393]Pring v. Penthouse Int'l, 7 Media L. Rep. 1101, 1104 (D. Wyo. 1984).
[394]Vitale v. National Lampoon, 449 F. Supp. 442, 3 Media L. Rep. 2223 (E.D. Pa. 1978). *Compare* Lloyds v. United Press Int'l, 311 N.Y.S.2d 373, 376 (N.Y. Sup. Ct. 1970) (trainer of standard bred horses is public figure) *with* Wheeler v. Green, 593 P.2d 777, 787–88, 5 Media L. Rep. 1132 (1978) (trainer of Appaloosa race horses not public figure). *Compare* Rancho La Costa v. Superior Ct., 165 Cal. Rptr. 347, 356, 6 Media L. Rep. 1351 (Cal. Ct. App. 1980) (alleged organized crime figures not public figures) *with* Bufalino v. Detroit Magazine, Nos. 125458, 125459, 1990 Mich. App. LEXIS 525, at 2, 18 Media L. Rep. 1491, 1493 (Mich. Ct. App. 1990) (organized crime figure is public figure).
[395]*General Purpose:* Greenbelt Coop. Pub'g Ass'n v. Bresler, 398 U.S. 6, 7–9, 1 Media L. Rep. 1589 (1970) (prominent local real estate developer and member of Maryland House of Delegates from neighboring district involved in substantial zoning controversy); Monitor Patriot Co. v. Roy, 401 U.S. 265, 271, 1 Media L. Rep. 1619 (1971) (candidates for elective office); Carson v. Allied News Co., 529 F.2d 206, 210 (7th Cir. 1976) (entertainer Johnny Carson).

Limited Purpose: Lerman v. Flynt Distrib. Co., 745 F.2d 123, 137, 10 Media L. Rep. 2497 (2d Cir. 1984) (author of nine novels); Yiamouyiannis v. Consumers Union of U.S., 619 F.2d 932, 939, 6 Media L. Rep. 1065 (2d Cir.), *cert. denied,* 499 U.S. 839 (1980) (fluoridation opponent); Chuy v. Philadelphia Eagles Football Club, 595 F.2d 1265, 4 Media L. Rep. 2537 (3d Cir. 1979) (guard on football team); Fitzgerald v. Penthouse Int'l, 691 F.2d 666, 8 Media L. Rep. 2340 (4th Cir. 1982), *cert. denied,* 460 U.S. 1024 (1983) (expert on dolphins); Rebozo v. Washington Post Co., 637 F.2d 375, 6 Media L. Rep. 2505 (5th Cir.), *cert. denied,* 454 U.S. 964 (1981) (friend and adviser of President Richard Nixon); Miller v. Transamerican Press, 621 F.2d 721, 6 Media L. Rep. 1598 (5th Cir.), *modified on rehearing,* 628 F.2d 932, 6 Media L. Rep. 2252 (5th Cir. 1980), *cert. denied,* 450 U.S. 1041 (1981) (high official of Teamsters union); Vandenburg v. Newsweek, 441 F.2d 378 (5th Cir. 1971), *cert. denied,* 404 U.S. 864 (1971) (state university track coach); Dacey v. Florida Bar, 427 F.2d 1292 (5th Cir. 1970) (author of *How to Avoid Probate*); Orr v. Argus-Press Co., 586 F.2d 1108, 4 Media L. Rep. 1593 (6th Cir. 1978), *cert. denied,* 440 U.S. 960 (1979) (lawyer indicted when shopping mall proposal collapsed); Arnheiter v. Random House, 578 F.2d 804, 4 Media L. Rep. 1174 (9th Cir. 1978) (commander of navy vessel who turned dismissal from command into "cause celebre"); Waldbaum v. Fairchild Pub'g, 627 F.2d 1287, 1300, 5 Media L. Rep. 2629 (D.C. Cir.), *cert. denied,* 449 U.S. 898 (1980) ("mover and shaker of many . . . controversial actions" in supermarket business); Knudsen v. Kansas Gas and Elec. Co., 807 P.2d 71, 78, 18 Media L. Rep. 1900 (Kan. 1991) (free-lance writer who wrote article that created public controversy).

[396]*General Purpose:* Gertz v. Robert Welch, Inc., 418 U.S. 323, 351, 1 Media L. Rep. 1633 (1974)

Ch. 2 Defamation

is unclear.[397] A few plaintiffs have even been found to be involuntary public figures.[398]

§2.11(C) Limits on the Public Official and Public Figure Rules

The following sections discuss whether the constitutional actual malice rule applies when there is a nonmedia defendant or when there has been a substantial passage of time since the plaintiff was a public official or figure.

§2.11(C)(i) Nonmedia Defendants

For many years, the Supreme Court did not explicitly decide whether the actual malice rule or other First Amendment rules apply to defamation cases against nonmedia defendants.[399] In several cases, however, without discussing the issue, the Supreme Court applied the actual malice rule to nonmedia defendants.[400]

The issue probably would not have arisen if *Gertz* had not been repeatedly, and presumably intentionally, phrased in terms of media defendants.[401] As a result, the cases were split on whether First Amendment limits applied where the defendant was not a member of the media.[402]

(lawyer); Avins v. White, 627 F.2d 637 (3d Cir. 1980), *cert. denied,* 449 U.S. 982 (1980) (dean of law school).

Limited Purpose: Gertz, 418 U.S. at 352 (lawyer); Time, Inc. v. Ragano, 427 F.2d 219 (5th Cir. 1970) (lawyer for purported organized crime figures); Levine v. CMP Pubns., 738 F.2d 660, 10 Media L. Rep. 2337 (5th Cir. 1984), *reh'g denied,* 753 F.2d 1341 (1985) (en banc) (businessman involved in trade secret litigation and campaign to prevent state judge who handled case from becoming federal judge); Braun v. Flynt, 726 F.2d 245, 10 Media L. Rep. 1497 (5th Cir.), *cert. denied sub nom.* Chic Magazine v. Braun, 469 U.S. 883 (1984) (entertainer who performed act with diving pig at amusement park); Golden Bear Distrib. Sys. of Tex. v. Chase Revel. Inc., 708 F.2d 944, 9 Media L. Rep. 1857 (5th Cir. 1983) (corporation that advertised its services); Wilson v. Scripps-Howard Broadcasting Co., 642 F.2d 371, 7 Media L. Rep. 1169 (6th Cir.), *cert. dismissed per stipulation,* 454 U.S. 1130 (1981) (cattleman); Littlefield v. Fort Dodge Messenger, 614 F.2d 581, 584, 5 Media L. Rep. 2325 (8th Cir.), *cert. denied,* 455 U.S. 945 (1980) (lawyer involved in license suspension hearings); Lawrence v. Moss, 639 F.2d 634, 6 Media L. Rep. 2377 (10th Cir.), *cert. denied,* 451 U.S. 1031 (1981) (campaign aide and former government official); Ryder v. Time, Inc., 557 F.2d 824, 824–25, 2 Media L. Rep. 1221 (D.C. Cir. 1976) (former member of Virginia House of Delegates and unsuccessful candidate for Virginia State Senate); Blake v. Gannett Co., 529 So. 2d 595, 15 Media L. Rep. 1561 (Miss. 1988) (farmer who received allegedly controversial loans from government).

[397]Bruno & Stillman, Inc. v. Globe Newspaper Co., 633 F.2d 583, 6 Media L. Rep. 2057 (1st Cir. 1980) (corporation not automatically public figure). *But see* Brown & Williamson Tobacco Corp. v. Jacobson, 713 F.2d 262, 9 Media L. Rep. 1936 (7th Cir. 1983) (suggesting large corporations not private figures).

[398]Meeropol v. Nizer, 560 F.2d 1061, 1066, 2 Media L. Rep. 2269 (2d Cir. 1977), *cert. denied,* 434 U.S. 1013 (1978) (children of Julius and Ethel Rosenberg); Carson v. Allied News Co., 529 F.2d 206 (7th Cir. 1976) (wife of famous entertainer); Dameron v. Washington Magazine, 779 F.2d 736, 12 Media L. Rep. 1509 (D.C. Cir. 1985), *cert. denied,* 476 U.S. 1141 (1986) (air traffic controller).

[399]Bose Corp v. Consumers Union of U.S., 466 U.S. 485, 492–93 n.8, 10 Media L. Rep. 1625 (1984).

[400]New York Times Co. v. Sullivan, 376 U.S. 254, 1 Media L. Rep. 1557 (1964) (Alabama clergymen); St. Amant v. Thompson, 390 U.S. 727, 1 Media L. Rep. 1586 (1968) (defeated candidate for U.S. Senate); Linn v. Plant Guard Workers, 383 U.S. 53 (1966) (union); Garrison v. Louisiana, 379 U.S. 64, 1 Media L. Rep. 1548 (1964) (criminal libel action against district attorney).

[401]*Gertz* framed the issue as "whether *a newspaper or broadcaster* that publishes defamatory falsehoods about an individual who is neither a public official nor a public figure may claim a constitutional privilege against liability for the injury inflicted by those statements." Gertz v. Robert Welch, Inc., 418 U.S. 323, 332, 1 Media L. Rep. 1633, 1637 (1974) (emphasis added). *See also id.* at 340, 341, 343, 347.

[402]*Applies:* Avins v. White, 627 F.2d 637 (3d Cir. 1980), *cert. denied,* 449 U.S. 982 (1980) (constitutional protections apply to nonmedia defendants at least where statement is made in public and recipients have strong interest in subject matter).

Does Not Apply: Grove v. Dun & Bradstreet, 438 F.2d 433, 437–38 (3d Cir.), *cert. denied,* 404 U.S. 898 (1971) (credit report); Wheeler v. Green, 593 P.2d 777, 784, 5 Media L. Rep. 1132 (Or. 1979) (constitutional protections apply to nonmedia defendants only if plaintiff is public figure or public official).

The Supreme Court appears to have resolved this issue, indicating that the media or nonmedia status of a defendant is irrelevant in determining the First Amendment protections available.[403] Subsequent decisions are in accord.[404]

§2.11(C)(ii) Passage of Time

The Supreme Court has not yet decided whether a substantial passage of time can alter an individual's status as a public figure or public official.[405] It is settled, however, that merely leaving public office does not end public official status.[406] Moreover, several courts have held that the passage of time does not end public figure status.[407]

§2.11(D) Criticism of the Public Official and Public Figure Doctrine

The Supreme Court's rejection of the *Rosenbloom* plurality's application of the constitutional actual malice rule to statements about all matters of public interest or concern[408] and the Court's limits on the scope of the public figure doctrine[409] are based on a balancing of First Amendment interests against the interest in protecting reputation. In particular, the Supreme Court has held that limited-purpose public figures should be determined by two factors: (1) whether the plaintiff has assumed the risk of defamatory comments, and (2) whether the plaintiff has access to the media to rebut defamatory statements, although the latter is less important than the former.[410] Thus, assumption of risk and self-help reduce the interest in reputation so that the relative importance of First Amendment interests requires application of the actual malice rule.

---

[403]Dun & Bradstreet v. Greenmoss Builders, 464 U.S. 959, 11 Media L. Rep. 2417 (1983). *Accord* Nodar v. Galbreath, 462 So. 2d 803, 11 Media L. Rep. 1521 (Fla. 1984). There are at least two reasons why it makes no sense to distinguish between media and nonmedia defendants in applying First Amendment limits in defamation actions. First, no public policy would be furthered by only providing First Amendment protection to the media in defamation cases. Surely being a member of the media does not mean that one's comments are any more important, valuable, or correct than those of someone who is not a member of the media. Second, the line between the media and the nonmedia is easily crossed. For example, a speech to an organization's members would be a nonmedia publication, but the same information published as an article in the organization's monthly magazine and distributed to its members would be a media publication protected by the First Amendment. To distinguish on this basis would be a triumph of form over substance.

[404]Culliton v. Mize, 403 N.W.2d 853, 14 Media L. Rep. 1122 (Minn. Ct. App. 1987); Miller v. Nestande, 192 Cal. App. 3d 191, 200 n.7, 237 Cal. Rptr. 359, 14 Media L. Rep. 1233, 1237 n.7 (Cal. Ct. App. 1987) (disapproving contrary language in earlier case); Casso v. Brand, 776 S.W.2d 551, 554 & n.2, 16 Media L. Rep. 1929 (Tex. 1989) (citing numerous cases).

[405]Wolston v. Reader's Digest Ass'n, 443 U.S. 157, 166 n.7, 5 Media L. Rep. 1273 (1979).

[406]Rosenblatt v. Baer, 383 U.S. 75, 87 n.14, 1 Media L. Rep. 1558 (1966); Zerangue v. TSP Newspapers, 814 F.2d 1066, 1069–70, 13 Media L. Rep. 2438, 2440–41 (5th Cir. 1987) (passage of six years did not return former public officials to private figure status. *Compare* Crane v. Arizona Republic, 729 F. Supp. 698, 708, 17 Media L. Rep. 1353, 1361–62 (C.D. Cal. 1989), *modified on other grounds*, 972 F.2d 1511 (9th Cir. 1992) (actual malice rule does not apply to article about activities of former public official occurring after he left office).

[407]Time, Inc. v. Johnston, 448 F.2d 378 (4th Cir. 1971) (former professional basketball player did not lose public figure status even though described incident occurred 12 years before article); Street v. National Broadcasting Co., 645 F.2d 1227, 7 Media L. Rep. 1001 (6th Cir.), *cert. dismissed per stipulation*, 454 U.S. 1095 (1981) (key witness in famous rape trial of nine black youths—"Scottsboro Boys"—in Alabama in the 1930s); Perry v. Columbia Broadcasting Sys., 499 F.2d 797 (7th Cir.), *cert. denied*, 419 U.S. 883 (1974) (1930s film star who had not made film in several decades). *See also* Mosesian v. McClatchy Newspapers, 285 Cal. Rptr. 430, 19 Media L. Rep. 1815 (Cal. Ct. App. 1991) (even though licensing controversy subsided for several months, plaintiff was still public figure), *cert. denied*, 112 S. Ct. 1946 (1992).

[408]Gertz v. Robert Welch, Inc., 418 U.S. 323, 346, 1 Media L. Rep. 1633 (1974); *see supra* §2.2.

[409]*See supra* §2.11(A).

[410]*Gertz*, 418 U.S. at 344–45.

Similarly, general-purpose public figures are defined, at least in part, by whether they have assumed the risk of defamatory comments.[411] Thus, central to current public figure doctrine is assumption of risk.

On the other hand, the Supreme Court has recognized that there are involuntary public figures, albeit indicating that such figures are rare.[412] The Court has yet to explain why such figures exist or how they are to be recognized. What is clear, however, is that the Court's recognition of involuntary public figures is in direct conflict with the very heart of the current public figure doctrine—the voluntary assumption of the risk of defamatory statements. Voluntary and involuntary public figures are mutually exclusive categories; it is hard to see how both can exist, yet that is the current state of the law.

It is possible, of course, that involuntary public figures can be defined simply as those who have access to the media, but the Supreme Court has not suggested this definition, and the cases that have found people to be involuntary public figures do not turn on this rationale.[413] This leaves only the *Rosenbloom* rationale. Involuntary public figures appear to be those who are involved in matters of public concern, even though they have not assumed the risk of defamatory statements and may not have access to the media to help themselves.[414]

The Supreme Court's reason for requiring public officials to meet the actual malice test is much the same. Public officials have substantial control over government affairs and, consequently, their activities are matters of public concern.[415] While some public officials have regular access to the media to answer charges against them, many do not. Thus, establishing public official status is not based on access to the media but on the public's interest in the person's activities.

Similarly, while many public officials have assumed the risk of defamatory comments by, for example, running for election, many other public officials, such as police officers, do not appear to have assumed such risks. Like involuntary public figures, public officials are defined not by their assumption of risk or their access to the media but by the public's interest in their activities. Yet this is the position of the *Rosenbloom* plurality (which *Gertz* rejected)— plaintiffs must meet the actual malice test if the comments about them involve a matter of public concern.

Thus, the Supreme Court's application of the actual malice rule lacks any consistent rationale. As a result, the Court must someday confront the contradiction in its recognition of both voluntary and involuntary public figures and must develop a consistent rationale for application of the actual malice rule.

§2.11(E) Actual Malice

The Supreme Court initially defined actual malice as a publication made with "knowledge that [the offending statement] was false or with reckless

---

[411] *Id.* at 345.
[412] *Id.*
[413] *See supra* note 398.
[414] *Gertz,* 418 U.S. at 345.
[415] *See supra* §2.11(A).

disregard of whether it was false or not."[416] While the Court has retained the first part of this definition, in later cases it largely has moved away from references to reckless disregard and instead refers to "those false statements made with a high degree of awareness of their probable falsity."[417] Apparently, the Court made this shift to avoid actual malice being equated with gross negligence.

In *St. Amant v. Thompson*,[418] the Supreme Court made this clear by defining "actual malice" so that it could not be equated with gross negligence:

> These cases are clear that reckless conduct is not measured by whether a reasonably prudent man would have published, or would have investigated before publishing. There must be sufficient evidence to permit the conclusion that the defendant in fact entertained serious doubts as to the truth of his publication. Publishing with such doubts shows reckless disregard for truth or falsity and demonstrates actual malice.
>
> It may be said that such a test puts a premium on ignorance, encourages the irresponsible publisher not to inquire, and permits the issue to be determined by the defendant's testimony that he published the statement in good faith and unaware of its probable falsity. Concededly the reckless disregard standard may permit recovery in fewer situations than would a rule that publishers must satisfy the standard of the reasonable man or the prudent publisher.[419]

The Court went on to say that

> [t]he defendant in a defamation action brought by a public official cannot, however, automatically insure a favorable verdict by testifying that he published with a belief that the statements were true. The finder of fact must determine whether the publication was indeed made in good faith. Professions of good faith will be unlikely to prove persuasive, for example, where a story is fabricated by the defendant, is the product of his imagination, or is based wholly on an unverified anonymous telephone call. Nor will they be likely to prevail when the publisher's allegations are so inherently improbable that only a reckless man would have put them in circulation. Likewise, recklessness may be found where there are obvious reasons to doubt the veracity of the informant or the accuracy of his reports.[420]

This controlling definition of actual malice[421] is the same whether the plaintiff is a public official or a public figure.[422]

Actual malice cannot be shown by demonstrating that a speaker lacked a reasonable belief in the truth of his statements.[423] The Supreme Court has also made it clear that actual malice does not mean "hatred, ill will, spite, enmity, or a wanton desire to injure"[424] and that actual malice cannot be proven by

---

[416]New York Times Co. v. Sullivan, 376 U.S. 254, 280, 1 Media L. Rep. 1527 (1964).

[417]Garrison v. Louisiana, 379 U.S. 64, 78–79, 1 Media L. Rep. 1548 (1964); Monitor Patriot Co. v. Roy, 401 U.S. 265, 272, 1 Media L. Rep. 1619 (1971).

[418]390 U.S. 727, 1 Media L. Rep. 1586 (1968).

[419]*Id.* at 731.

[420]*Id.* at 732 (footnote omitted).

[421]*See, e.g.,* McCoy v. Hearst Corp., 727 P.2d 711, 13 Media L. Rep. 2169 (Cal. 1986), *cert. denied,* 481 U.S. 1041 (1987). *Contra* Sible v. Lee Enters., 729 P.2d 1271, 13 Media L. Rep. 1738 (Mont. 1986), *cert. denied,* 483 U.S. 1011 (1987).

[422]Greenbelt Coop. Pub'g Ass'n v. Bresler, 398 U.S. 6, 11, 1 Media L. Rep. 1589 (1970). *See also* Rosenbloom v. Metromedia, 403 U.S. 29, 52 n.18, 1 Media L. Rep. 1597 (1971) (Brennan, J.). However, the actual malice rule may not apply to commercial speech. U.S. Healthcare v. Blue Cross of Greater Phila., 898 F.2d 914, 17 Media L. Rep. 1681 (3d Cir.), *cert. denied,* 498 U.S. 816.

[423]Garrison v. Louisiana, 379 U.S. 64, 78, 1 Media L. Rep. 1548, 1553–54 (1964).

[424]*Id.* at 78, 1 Media L. Rep. at 1553; Henry v. Collins, 380 U.S. 356, 357 (1965); Rosenblatt v. Baer, 383 U.S. 75, 84, 1 Media L. Rep. 1558 (1966); *Bresler,* 398 U.S. at 10. *See also* Tavoulareas v. Piro, 817 F.2d 762, 13 Media L. Rep. 2377 (D.C. Cir.) (en banc) (actual malice not shown by reporter's "adversarial

showing that the defendant failed to investigate or was negligent in investigating the truth of the statements before publishing them,[425] although a deliberate effort to avoid the truth can be evidence of actual malice.[426]

Similarly, the repulsive or defamatory nature of the speech itself cannot establish actual malice.[427] The defendant's profit motive is equally irrelevant.[428] Moreover, the failure to follow professional journalistic standards does not constitute actual malice.[429] However, a plaintiff is entitled to try to prove a defendant's state of mind of actual malice through circumstantial evidence of these items, "[a]lthough courts must be careful not to place too much reliance on such factors."[430]

The plaintiff's denial of the defamatory statement's truth does not establish actual malice; otherwise, actual malice would almost always exist, because people seldom admit the truth of such statements.[431] Minor embellishments and fictionalizations do not constitute actual malice,[432] nor does the use of strong language.[433] Even the repetition of defamatory charges to provoke a response does not amount to actual malice.[434]

An important and recurring issue is what sources may be reasonably relied on. Sources that have proved reliable in the past can be relied on,[435] as can sources who are friends[436] and even sources who are known to be biased.[437]

---

stance" and newspaper's management's pressure to produce high impact, investigative stories), *cert. denied sub nom.* Tavoulareas v. Washington Post Co., 484 U.S. 870 (1987); Fletcher v. San Jose Mercury News, 264 Cal. Rptr. 699, 705, 17 Media L. Rep. 1321, 1326 (Cal. Ct. App. 1990), *cert. denied,* 498 U.S. 813 (1990) (reporter's prior "highly critical" article about plaintiff, "slick" and "devious" interviewing style, hostility toward plaintiff, and lack of objectivity in article did not constitute actual malice).

[425]379 U.S. at 79, 1 Media L. Rep. at 1554; *Rosenblatt,* 383 U.S. at 83–84; Beckley Newspapers Corp. v. Hanks, 389 U.S. 81, 84–85, 1 Media L. Rep. 1585 (1967); St. Amant v. Thompson, 390 U.S. 727, 733 (1968); Old Dominion Branch No. 496, Nat'l Ass'n of Letter Carriers v. Austin, 418 U.S. 264, 281–82 (1974). *But see* Hunt v. Liberty Lobby, 720 F.2d 631, 645, 10 Media L. Rep. 1097 (11th Cir. 1983) (if not "hot news," then actual malice may be inferred from grossly inadequate investigation).

[426]Harte-Hanks Communications v. Connaughton, 491 U.S. 657, 16 Media L. Rep. 1881 (1989).

[427]Linn v. United Plant Guard Workers, 383 U.S. 53, 63 (1966); *Bresler,* 398 U.S. at 10; Contemporary Mission v. New York Times Co., 842 F.2d 612, 15 Media L. Rep. 1180 (2d Cir.), *cert. denied sub nom.* O'Reilly v. New York Times Co., 488 U.S. 856 (1988).

[428]*Connaughton,* 491 U.S. 657, 16 Media L. Rep. 1881.

[429]*Id.* at 666.

[430]*Id.* at 668. *Accord* Bandido's Inc. v. Journal Gazette Co., No. 57A03-9012-CV-00533, 1991 Ind. App. LEXIS 1653, 19 Media L. Rep. 1479 (Ind. Ct. App. 1991).

[431]Edwards v. National Audubon Soc'y, 556 F.2d 113, 121, 2 Media L. Rep. 1849 (2d Cir.), *cert. denied,* 434 U.S. 1002, 3 Media L. Rep. 1560 (1977) ("such denials are so commonplace in the world of polemical charge and countercharge that, in themselves, they hardly alert the conscientious reporter to the likelihood of error"). *See also* Reader's Digest Ass'n v. Superior Ct., 37 Cal. 3d 244, 259, 690 P.2d 610, 11 Media L. Rep. 1065, 1071 (Cal. 1984) (failure to contact plaintiff does not prove actual malice). Any other rule also would discourage reporters from contacting potential plaintiffs to get their side of a story.

[432]Meeropol v. Nizer, 560 F.2d 1061, 1065, 2 Media L. Rep. 2269 (2d Cir. 1977), *cert. denied,* 434 U.S. 1013 (1978); Miller v. News Syndicate Co., 445 F.2d 356, 358 (2d Cir. 1971); Hotchner v. Castillo-Puche, 551 F.2d 910, 914, 2 Media L. Rep. 1545 (2d Cir.), *cert. denied,* 434 U.S. 834, 3 Media L. Rep. 1128 (1977). *Compare* Varnish v. Best Medium Pub'g Co., 405 F.2d 608, 612 (2d Cir. 1968), *cert. denied,* 394 U.S. 987 (1969) ("substantial" falsity finding upheld).

[433]Ryan v. Brooks, 634 F.2d 726, 733, 6 Media L. Rep. 2155 (4th Cir. 1980).

[434]Dickey v. CBS, Inc., 583 F.2d 1221, 1225, 1227–29, 4 Media L. Rep. 1353 (3d Cir. 1978).

[435]*Ryan,* 634 F.2d at 732. *See also infra* note 475.

[436]Brewer v. Memphis Pub'g Co., 626 F.2d 1238, 1258–59, 6 Media L. Rep. 2025 (5th Cir. 1980), *cert. denied,* 452 U.S. 962 (1981) (source was friend of reporter's sister).

[437]Vandenburg v. Newsweek, 441 F.2d 378 (5th Cir. 1971), *cert. denied,* 404 U.S. 864 (1971) (biased sources and reporter's personal observations); Reuber v. Food Chem. News, 925 F.2d 703, 715, 18 Media L. Rep. 1689, 1698 (4th Cir. 1991) (en banc), *cert. denied,* 111 S. Ct. 2814 (1991) ("Self-interest (and the related desire to place opposing views and persons in an unfavorable light) motivates many news sources; if dealing with such persons were to constitute evidence of actual malice on the part of a reporter, much newsgathering would be severly chilled."); Silvester v. ABC, 839 F.2d 1491, 15 Media L. Rep. 1138 (11th Cir. 1988) (reliance on source that law enforcement officers regarded as unreliable upheld).

Other media reports can also be relied on.[438] Reliance on a single anonymous and unverified telephone call, however, may constitute actual malice.[439] One court has even held that a dispute over what a reporter knew or had been told will not establish actual malice.[440]

A failure to retract a statement does not show actual malice.[441] However, there may be actual malice where a newspaper republishes the defamatory statements after receiving a retraction demand and making a correction.[442] Failure to include remarks that "balance" the defamatory statements does not constitute actual malice,[443] nor do factual inaccuracies that are not part of the defamatory statements.[444]

The deliberate alteration of quotes can constitute actual malice if it creates a materially false change in meaning.[445] The deliberate destruction of notes may also create an inference of actual malice if there is no other evidence to support the defamatory statements other than the destroyed notes.[446] In addition, the actual malice rule has often defeated defamation-by-implication claims.[447]

A variety of cases have found that actual malice was[448] or was not[449] shown. Others have concluded that the issue should be resolved at trial.[450]

Adoption of the term "actual malice" was a mistake. As commonly understood, the word "malice" means spite, hatred, ill will, or a desire to harm someone. Yet, as demonstrated above, it is absolutely clear that actual malice does not mean any of these things.

---

[438] Rosanova v. Playboy Enters., 580 F.2d 859, 862, 4 Media L. Rep. 1550 (5th Cir. 1978).

[439] St. Amant v. Thompson, 390 U.S. 727, 732, 1 Media L. Rep. 1586 (1968). But reliance on a single source is permissible. Chang v. Michiana Telecasting Corp., 900 F.2d 1085, 1089, 17 Media L. Rep. 1768, 1772 (7th Cir. 1990); Liberty Lobby v. Anderson, No. 81-2240, 1990 U.S. Dist. LEXIS 19587, at 14, 19 Media L. Rep. 1011, 1015 (D.D.C. 1990).

[440] Long v. Arcell, 618 F.2d 1145, 6 Media L. Rep. 1430 (5th Cir. 1980), cert. denied, 449 U.S. 1083 (1981).

[441] New York Times Co. v. Connor, 365 F.2d 567, 577 (5th Cir. 1966); Hurley v. Northwest Pub'g, 273 F. Supp. 967, 974 (D. Minn. 1967), aff'd without opinion, 398 F.2d 346 (8th Cir. 1968). See also New York Times Co. v. Sullivan, 376 U.S. 254, 286, 1 Media L. Rep. 1527, 1540 (1964).

[442] Zerangue v. TSP Newspapers, 814 F.2d 1066, 13 Media L. Rep. 2438 (5th Cir. 1987). See also Dombey v. Phoenix Newspapers, 724 P.2d 562, 13 Media L. Rep. 1282 (Ariz. 1986).

[443] Brown v. Herald Co., 698 F.2d 949, 951, 9 Media L. Rep. 1149 (8th Cir. 1983); Berry v. National Broadcasting Co., 480 F.2d 428, 433 (8th Cir. 1973), cert. dismissed, 418 U.S. 911 (1974).

[444] Berry, 480 F.2d at 433.

[445] Masson v. New Yorker Magazine, 111 S. Ct. 2419, 18 Media L. Rep. 2241 (1991). See also Dunn v. Gannett N.Y. Newspapers, 833 F.2d 446, 14 Media L. Rep. 1871 (3d Cir. 1987).

[446] Compare Brown & Williamson Tobacco Corp. v. Jacobson, 827 F.2d 1119, 1134–36, 14 Media L. Rep. 1497 (7th Cir. 1987) with Chang v. Michiana Telecasting Corp., 900 F.2d 1085, 1090, 17 Media L. Rep. 1768, 1772 (7th Cir. 1990).

[447] Newton v. National Broadcasting Co., 930 F.2d 662, 18 Media L. Rep. 1001 (9th Cir. 1990), cert. denied, 112 S. Ct. 192 (1991); Saenz v. Playboy Enters., 841 F.2d 1309, 15 Media L. Rep. 1043 (7th Cir. 1988).

[448] See, e.g., Harte-Hanks Communications v. Connaughton, 491 U.S. 657, 667, 16 Media L. Rep. 1881 (1989); Goldwater v. Ginzburg, 414 F.2d 324, 339–40, 1 Media L. Rep. 1737 (2d Cir. 1969), cert. denied, 369 U.S. 1049 (1970); Appleyard v. Transamerican Press, 539 F.2d 1026, 1029 (4th Cir. 1976), cert. denied, 429 U.S. 1041 (1977); Alioto v. Cowles Communications, 623 F.2d 616, 620, 6 Media L. Rep. 1573 (9th Cir. 1980), cert. denied, 449 U.S. 1102 (1981); Ball v. E.W. Scripps Co., 801 S.W.2d 684, 18 Media L. Rep. 1545 (Ky. 1990).

[449] See, e.g., Hotchner v. Castillo-Puche, 551 F.2d 910, 913–24, 2 Media L. Rep. 1545 (2d Cir. 1977), cert. denied, 434 U.S. 834, 3 Media L. Rep. 1128 (1977) (reversing jury verdict); Hardin v. Santa Fe Reporter, 745 F.2d 1323, 1326, 11 Media L. Rep. 1026 (10th Cir. 1984) (reliance on unverified word of one informant with no special access to information about plaintiff "perilously close" to actual malice).

[450] See, e.g., Masson v. New Yorker Magazine, 111 S. Ct. 2419, 18 Media L. Rep. 2241 (1991); Warford v. Lexington Herald-Leader Co., 789 S.W.2d 758, 17 Media L. Rep. 1785 (Ky. 1990), cert. denied, 111 S. Ct. 754 (1991); Foretich v. Advance Magazine Pubrs., 765 F. Supp. 1099, 1110, 18 Media L. Rep. 2280, 2288–90 (D.D.C. 1991).

The term "actual malice" is particularly confusing for juries unschooled in the law who must be instructed that actual malice does not mean what it appears to mean. Even if a jury gets over the problem of understanding that words mean not what they *seem* to mean but what the court *says* they mean, it may still have to grapple with two meanings of malice. One is "actual malice"; the other is "common law malice"—spite, hatred, ill will, or a desire to harm, which still may be relevant to defeating a qualified privilege or punitive damages. The jury should be spared the conundrum of having to deal with two different concepts that masquerade under the same name. Unfortunately, the term "actual malice" is now so deeply imbedded in the law that probably only the Supreme Court can eradicate it. The Court has now made a partial attempt to do this.[451]

Some early cases refer to the actual malice rule as a privilege.[452] This, however, is a misnomer, because the actual malice rule really establishes a constitutional rule setting forth the degree of the defendant's fault that the plaintiff must prove. Characterizing the actual malice rule as a privilege wrongly suggests that the defendant has the burden of pleading and proving actual malice, which is not the case.[453] To help eliminate this confusion, the actual malice rule should be renamed, possibly as the "constitutional fault" or "scienter" rule, thereby alleviating some of the difficulties caused by the term "actual malice."

§2.11(E)(i) Actual Malice and Misinterpretation

Difficult problems arise when actual malice is alleged because the person reporting something misinterpreted or misunderstood it. In *Time, Inc. v. Pape*,[454] *Time Magazine* published an article about a report of the U.S. Civil Rights Commission. *Time* repeated charges in the report that came from a civil complaint, but it omitted any reference to the term "alleged."[455] Because the report itself equivocated as to whether it agreed with the charges in the civil complaint,[456] the Court refused to find that the omission of the word "alleged" amounted to actual malice:[457]

> Time's omission of the word "alleged" amounted to the adoption of one of a number of possible rational interpretations of a document that bristled with ambiguities. The deliberate choice of such an interpretation, though arguably reflecting a misconception, was not enough to create a jury issue of "malice" under *New York Times*. To permit the malice issue to go to the jury because of the omission of a word like "alleged," despite the context of that word in the Commission Report and the external evidence of the Report's overall meaning,

---

[451]*Masson*, 111 S. Ct. at 2429–30, 18 Media L. Rep. at 2248 ("in place of the term actual malice, it is better practice that jury instructions refer to publication of a statement with knowledge of falsity or reckless disregard as to truth or falsity").
[452]*See, e.g.,* New York Times Co. v. Sullivan, 376 U.S. 254, 282, 1 Media L. Rep. 1527 (1964).
[453]*See infra* §2.11(E)(ii).
[454]401 U.S. 279, 1 Media L. Rep. 1627 (1971).
[455]*Id.* at 283.
[456]*Id.* at 286–89.
[457]The Court cautioned that this did not mean that the word "alleged" could always be omitted. *Id.* at 292.

would be to impose a much stricter standard of liability on errors of interpretation or judgment than on errors of historic fact.[458]

This decision is particularly important to the media because they often report not what they saw happen, but what others *say they* saw happen. *Pape* makes it clear that errors of judgment in interpreting ambiguous information cannot constitute actual malice.[459]

§2.11(E)(ii) The "Clear and Convincing Evidence" Requirement

The plaintiff must prove constitutional actual malice by "clear and convincing evidence,"[460] or as it is sometimes described, by evidence with "convincing clarity."[461] Clear and convincing evidence has been described as "that degree of belief greater than the usually imposed burden of proof by a fair preponderance of the evidence, but less than the burden of proof beyond a reasonable doubt imposed in criminal cases."[462]

§2.11(F) Private Figures: Negligence and Other Fault Standards

After the Supreme Court's decision in *Gertz v. Robert Welch, Inc.*,[463] the states were invited to establish their own fault standards for private figure plaintiffs.[464] The Court made it clear that usually some degree of fault must be shown before a plaintiff could recover.[465]

Most states opted to require private figure plaintiffs to show negligence.[466] In these jurisdictions, a private figure plaintiff may recover compensatory

---

[458]*Id.* at 290. The Court also noted that the report's ambiguity meant that the truthfulness or accuracy of *Time*'s article could not be determined. To allow such an issue to go to a jury would "put the publisher virtually at the mercy of the unguided discretion of a jury." *Id.* at 291.

[459]401 U.S. at 292. *See also* Bose Corp. v. Consumers Union of U.S., 466 U.S. 485, 512–13, 10 Media L. Rep. 1625 (1984), *reh'g denied,* 467 U.S. 1267 (1984) (description of loudspeaker system as causing sound to "wander about the room" instead of "across" room, while imprecise use of language, did not establish actual malice). *Accord* McBride v. Merrell Dow Pharmaceuticals, 800 F.2d 1208, 1212, 13 Media L. Rep. 1386 (D.C. Cir. 1986) ("Ambiguity of a statement's subject matter may be probative evidence negating a finding of actual malice."). *Compare* DiSalle v. P.G. Pub'g Co., 544 A.2d 1345, 1351–54, 15 Media L. Rep. 1873, 1877–79 (Pa. Super. Ct. 1988), *cert. denied,* 492 U.S. 906 (1989).

[460]*See, e.g.,* Anderson v. Liberty Lobby, 477 U.S. 242, 244, 12 Media L. Rep. 2297 (1986); *see also* Gertz v. Robert Welch, Inc., 418 U.S. 323, 342, 1 Media L. Rep. 1633 (1974) ("clear and convincing proof").

[461]In New York Times Co. v. Sullivan, 376 U.S. 254, 1 Media L. Rep. 1527 (1964), the Court referred to this standard as "the convincing clarity which the constitutional standard demands." *Id.* at 285–86. *See also* Rosenbloom v. Metromedia, 403 U.S. 29, 50–52, 1 Media L. Rep. 1597 (1971); Goldwater v. Ginzburg, 414 F.2d 324, 341–42, 1 Media L. Rep. 1737 (2d Cir. 1969), *cert. denied,* 396 U.S. 1049 (1970); Dacey v. Connecticut Bar Ass'n, 368 A.2d 125, 133–34 (Conn. 1976), *appeal after remand,* 441 A.2d 49 (Conn. 1981); Callahan v. Westinghouse Broadcasting Co., 363 N.E.2d 240, 241–42, 2 Media L. Rep. 2226 (Mass. 1977); Stone v. Essex County Newspapers, 330 N.E.2d 161, 174–75 (Mass. 1975).

[462]*Stone,* 330 N.E.2d at 175. *See also Dacey,* 368 A.2d at 134 (evidence that "induces in the mind of the trier a reasonable belief that the facts asserted are highly probably true, that the probability that they are true or exist is substantially greater than the probability that they are false or do not exist"); *Callahan,* 363 N.E.2d at 242 (proof must be "strong, positive and free from doubt" and "full, clear and decisive").

[463]418 U.S. 323, 1 Media L. Rep. 1633 (1973).

[464]*Id.* at 347. *See also* Dun & Bradstreet v. Greenmoss Builders, 472 U.S. 749, 761–63, 11 Media L. Rep. 2417 (1985).

[465]*Gertz,* 418 U.S. 323. *See also* Time, Inc. v. Firestone, 424 U.S. 448, 461–64, 1 Media L. Rep. 1665 (1976). The failure to make a finding of fault requires a new trial. 424 U.S. at 461–64.

[466]*See, e.g.,* Troman v. Wood, 340 N.E.2d 292 (Ill. 1975) ("reasonable grounds" standard); *Stone,* 330 N.E.2d 161 (ordinary negligence standard); Denny v. Mertz, 318 N.W.2d 141, 8 Media L. Rep. 1369 (Wis.), *cert. denied,* 459 U.S. 883 (1982) (negligence standard applies whether or not defendant is media defendant. *See generally* DiSabatino, *State Constitutional Protection of Allegedly Defamatory Statements Regarding Private Individual,* 33 A.L.R.4th 212 (1984). *See also* Ashby v. Hustler Magazine, 802 F.2d 856, 13 Media L. Rep. 1416 (6th Cir. 1986) (negligence was jury question).

damages on a showing that the publisher of the defamatory material did so without the exercise of reasonable care.[467]

A few jurisdictions require private figure plaintiffs to demonstrate actual malice if the case involves a matter of public concern.[468] New York has adopted a gross irresponsibility standard for such cases,[469] and Louisiana simply requires a showing of "fault."[470] Some decisions indicate that, where the plaintiff is a private figure and the matter is a wholly private one, the common law rule of strict liability is constitutional.[471]

§2.11(G) Wire Service Defense

In a defamation action where someone has relied on information obtained from a reputable wire service or similar source, courts have found the defendants not negligent.[472] Absent any indication on the face of the wire service report that the information contained there is erroneous, the defendant who republishes that information, either verbatim or in summary, cannot be held liable for defamation.[473] Under these circumstances there is no independent duty to verify or investigate.[474] Where the actual malice rule applies, reliance on a wire service or other reputable source is often a successful defense.[475]

---

[467]*See, e.g.,* Miles v. Perry, 529 A.2d 199, 14 Media L. Rep. 1985 (Conn. App. Ct. 1987) (negligence need only be shown by preponderance of evidence); Phillips v. Evening Star Newspaper Co., 424 A.2d 78, 6 Media L. Rep. 2191 (D.D.C. 1980), *cert. denied,* 451 U.S. 989 (negligence standard). Whether a malpractice standard applies if negligence is the applicable fault standard is uncertain. *Not Applicable:* Kassel v. Gannett Co., 875 F.2d 935, 942–43, 16 Media L. Rep. 1814, 1820 (1st Cir. 1989); Michigan Microtech v. Federated Pubns., 466 N.W.2d 717, 721–22, 18 Media L. Rep. 2131, 2134–35 (Mich. Ct. App. 1991). *Applicable:* Simon, *Libel As Malpractice: News Media Ethics and the Standard of Care,* 53 FORDHAM L. REV. 449 (1984).

[468]*See, e.g.,* AAFCO Heating & Air Conditioning Co. v. Northwest Pub'g, 321 N.E.2d 580, 586, 1 Media L. Rep. 1683 (Ind. Ct. App. 1974), *cert. denied,* 424 U.S. 913 (1976) (public interest extended to all matters that "affect our efforts to live and work together in a free society"); Diversified Mgmt. v. Denver Post, 653 P.2d 1103, 8 Media L. Rep. 2505 (Colo. 1982) (what is matter of public or general concern is question of law for court).

[469]Chappadeau v. Utica Observer-Dispatch, 341 N.E.2d 569, 1 Media L. Rep. 1693 (N.Y. 1975) (to be liable, where matter is one of public concern, defendant must have acted in grossly irresponsible manner without regard for ordinary standards of information gathering and disemination). *Compare* Dalbec v. Gentleman's Companion, 828 F.2d 921, 14 Media L. Rep. 1705 (2d Cir. 1987) (gross irresponsibility shown) *with* Gaeta v. New York News, 465 N.E.2d 892, 10 Media L. Rep. 1966 (N.Y. 1984) (gross irresponsibility not shown).

[470]*See, e.g.,* WHC, Inc. v. Tri-State Road Boring, 468 So. 2d 764 (La. Ct. App. 1985) (plaintiff need only establish "fault"; fault is not defined, however).

[471]*See* Denny v. Mertz, 318 N.W.2d 141, 8 Media L. Rep. 1369 (Wis. 1982), *cert. denied,* 459 U.S. 883 (1982) (strict liability applied to nonmedia defendant); Coleman v. Collins, 384 So. 2d 229 (Fla. Dist. Ct. App. 1980) (defendant not member of news media). *See also* Dun & Bradstreet v. Greenmoss Builders, 472 U.S. 749, 11 Media L. Rep. 2417 (1985).

[472]Nelson v. Associated Press, 667 F. Supp. 1468, 14 Media L. Rep. 1577 (S.D. Fla. 1987) (newspaper's and magazine's republication of reputable wire service report was defense to libel and slander action); Brown v. Courier Herald Pub'g Co., 700 F. Supp. 534, 15 Media L. Rep. 2350 (S.D. Ga. 1988) (adopting wire service defense); Gay v. Williams, 486 F. Supp. 12, 5 Media L. Rep. 1785 (D. Alaska 1979) (no liability under Alaska law for republication of reputable wire service report); Lovett v. Caddo, 584 So. 2d 1197, 19 Media L. Rep. 1670 (La. Ct. App. 1991) (reliance on authorized police source); McKinney v. Avery Journal, 393 S.E.2d 295, 18 Media L. Rep. 1204 (N.C. Ct. App. 1990) (reliance on other newspaper reports and sheriff).

[473]*See* cases cited *supra* note 472. *See also* Waskow v. Associated Press, 462 F.2d 1173 (D.C. Cir. 1972); Appleby v. Daily Hampshire Gazette, 478 N.E.2d 721, 11 Media L. Rep. 2372 (1985).

[474]*Appleby,* 478 N.E.2d at 725. *See also* Zetes v. Richman, 447 N.Y.S.2d 889 (N.Y. App. Div. 1982) (reliance on wire service did not amount to gross irresponsibility). The rationale is that to impose such a duty on the news media would impermissibly interfere with their ability to disseminate information. *Appleby,* 478 N.E.2d 721, 11 Media L. Rep. 2372; *Gay,* 486 F. Supp. 12, 5 Media L. Rep. 1785.

[475]*Gay,* 486 F. Supp. 12, 5 Media L. Rep. 1785; *Waskow,* 462 F.2d 1173; Davis v. Costa-Gavras, 580 F. Supp. 1082, 10 Media L. Rep. 1257 (S.D.N.Y. 1984) (reliance on hardcover book publisher); Ortiz v. Valdescastilla, 478 N.Y.S.2d 895, 10 Media L. Rep. 2193 (N.Y. App. Div. 1984) (free-lancer). *See also*

§2.11(H) Fault by Broadcasters

Because of the common law rule of strict liability for defamatory statements, the National Association of Broadcasters prepared a model statute to protect against liability for defamatory statements made on the air by someone who did not work for the broadcaster.[476] The model statute (1) limits liability to those situations where the broadcaster fails to exercise "due care" in preventing such broadcasts, (2) completely bars liability where a station carries the broadcast of a network, and (3) bars any liability if the broadcaster is prohibited from censoring the broadcast by the provisions of any federal statute or regulation of the Federal Communications Commission.[477] This model statute and similar statutes have been adopted in several states.[478]

The importance of the model statute's first provision has decreased because the common law's strict liability rule has been abolished in most situations.[479] The second provision's absolute bar on liability could be of importance in the limited situation it covers, while the final provision is the law anyway.[480]

§2.11(I) Liability of Individual and Corporate Defendants

Active participation in a publication is a prerequisite to the liability of an individual defendant.[481] Traditional tort theories of vicarious liability, such as respondeat superior, can also be the basis for imposing liability.[482]

Mehau v. Gannett Pac. Corp., 658 P.2d 312, 9 Media L. Rep. 1337 (Haw. 1983) (actual malice by wire service does not raise question of fact as to newspapers' actual malice); *supra* notes 435–40.

[476]Remmers, *Recent Legislative Trends in Defamation by Radio,* 64 HARV. L REV. 727, 740–41 (1951); *see also* ELDREDGE, *supra* note 105, §14, at 89–90.

[477]The text of the model statute is set out in Remmers, *supra* note 476, at 741.

[478]*See, e.g.,* CAL. CIV. CODE §48.5 (West 1982); FLA. STAT. ANN. §770.04 (West 1986); GA. CODE ANN. §105-712 (Hamison 1991); N.C. GEN. STAT. ANN. §99-5 (Michie 1985); NEB. REV. STAT. §§86-601 to 86-603 (1992).

[479]*See supra* §2.11.

[480]*See infra* §2.13(C).

[481]*See, e.g.,* Tavoulareas v. Piro, 759 F.2d 90, 136–37, 11 Media L. Rep. 1777 (D.C. Cir. 1985), *vacated in part on other grounds,* 817 F.2d 762, 13 Media L. Rep. 2377 (D.C. Cir.) (en banc), *cert. denied sub nom.* Tavoulareas v. Washington Post Co., 484 U.S. 870 (1987) (to be liable for defamation, defendant must have published or knowingly participated in publication); Industrial Equip. Co. v. Emerson Elec. Co., 554 F.2d 276, 289 (6th Cir. 1977) (no liability absent ratification, approval, encouragement, or adoption of libelous statement); Skeoch v. Ottley, 377 F.2d 804, 808 (3d Cir. 1967). *See also* Fairbanks Pub'g Co. v. Pitka, 376 P.2d 190 (Alaska 1962) (owner/publisher held not liable for defamation statements because duties did not extend to actual publication of libel); Cahill v. Hawaiian Paradise Park Corp., 543 P.2d 1356 (Haw. 1975) (corporate officers may not be held personally liable for statements made by corporate agents unless there is evidence of active participation); Lewis v. Time, Inc., 83 F.R.D. 455, 463, 5 Media L. Rep. 1790 (E.D. Cal. 1979), *aff'd,* 710 F.2d 549, 9 Media L. Rep. 1984 (9th Cir. 1983) (no liability without direct participation in or knowledge of libelous publication). *But see* Goudy v. Dayton Newspaper, 237 N.E.2d 909, 914 (Ohio Ct. App. 1967) (managing editor responsible for libel even without actual knowledge). *See also supra* §2.6(A).

[482]*See* Cantrell v. Forest City Pub'g Co., 419 U.S. 245, 1 Media L. Rep. 1815 (1974). *See also* Sprague v. Walter, 516 A.2d 706, 13 Media L. Rep. 1177 (Pa. Super. Ct. 1986), *aff'd,* 543 A.2d 1078, 15 Media L. Rep. 1625 (Pa.), *appeal dismissed,* 488 U.S. 988 (1988) (newspaper liable for defamatory statements of employee reporter whose work was reviewed by executive editor prior to publication); Tinley v. Davis, 609 P.2d 1252 (N.M. 1980) (employer liable even if statements unauthorized or unratified so long as they fall within scope of employment). Some jurisdictions distinguish between libel and slander in imposing vicarious liability. *See* Mulherin v. Globe Oil Co., 328 S.E.2d 406, 407–08 (Ga. Ct. App. 1985) (restating rule in Georgia that employer is liable for libelous statements of employees; with respect to slander, no vicarious liability absent showing that employer directed or authorized statement). *But see* Cooper v. Alabama Farm Bureau Mut. Casualty Ins. Co., 385 So. 2d 630 (Ala. 1980) (overruling 73 years of prior law to hold employer liable for slander under doctrine of respondeat superior). Acts of an independent contractor do not result in vicarious liablility. *See* Nader v. DeToledano, 408 A.2d 31, 5 Media L. Rep. 1550 (D.C. 1979), *cert. denied,* 444 U.S. 1078 (1980); Martin Marietta Corp. v. Evening Star Newspaper Co., 417 F. Supp. 947, 951–52

In those cases where a showing of fault is constitutionally required,[483] the requisite degree of fault must also be established as to each individual defendant.[484] Moreover, a number of jurisdictions hold that the liability does not extend to punitive damages awards absent a showing of authorization or ratification of the offending publication.[485]

Actual malice cannot be established by showing that somewhere within a newspaper's possession there is information contrary to what was published.[486] Instead, it must be shown that the individuals who actually published the article knew this information.[487] Respondeat superior, however, appears to satisfy this requirement.[488]

§2.11(J) Waiver of First Amendment Protection

In *Curtis Publishing Co. v. Butts*,[489] a plurality of the Supreme Court held that failure to raise a First Amendment-based defense in the trial court constitutes a waiver only if the defense was a "known right."[490] Furthermore, proof that the right was "known" must be "clear and compelling," because a finding of waiver under the circumstances might impose on a "freedom which is the 'matrix, the indispensable condition, of nearly every other form of freedom.'"[491]

In *Butts,* the publisher of the *Saturday Evening Post* did not request that the jury be instructed that the plaintiff was a public official who must prove actual malice to prevail in his defamation action.[492] On appeal, the publisher pointed out that *New York Times Co. v. Sullivan* had not been decided at the time of trial.[493] The plaintiff responded that the publisher waived any such First Amendment argument because its lawyers should have seen "the handwriting on the wall" and because the publisher's lawyers were involved in the *Sullivan* case and thus well aware of the First Amendment claims raised there.[494]

(D.D.C. 1976). For a discussion of independent contractor status, *see* Kassell v. Gannett Co., 875 F.2d 935, 16 Media L. Rep. 1814 (1st Cir. 1989).

[483]*See supra* §2.11.

[484]*See* Murray v. Bailey, 613 F. Supp. 1276, 1281, 11 Media L. Rep. 1369 (N.D. Cal. 1985) (actual malice must be demonstrated for each defendent individually); Phoenix Newspapers v. Church, 537 P.2d 1345, 1360 (Ariz. Ct. App. 1975), *cert. denied and appeal dismissed,* 425 U.S. 908 (1976); Reed v. Northwestern Pub'g Co., 530 N.E.2d 474, 15 Media L. Rep. 2233 (Ill. 1988), *cert. denied,* 489 U.S. 1067 (1989).

[485]*See, e.g.,* Mercury Motors Express v. Smith, 393 So. 2d 545 (Fla. 1981). *See also* Slaughter v. Valleydale Packers, 94 S.E.2d 260, 263 (Va. 1956) (punitive damages not available against employer without express ratification or authorization). This also is the Restatement view. *See* RESTATEMENT (SECOND) §909.

[486]New York Times Co. v. Sullivan, 376 U.S. 254, 287, 1 Media L. Rep. 1527, 1540 (1964).

[487]*Id.;* Reed, 530 N.E.2d 474, 15 Media L. Rep. 2233; Speer v. Ottoway Newspapers, 828 F.2d 475, 14 Media L. Rep. 1601 (8th Cir. 1987), *cert. denied,* 485 U.S. 970 (1988); Rust Communications Group v. 70 State Street Travel Serv., 504 N.Y.S.2d 927, 13 Media L. Rep. 1063 (N.Y. App. Div. 1986).

[488]Cantrell v. Forest City Pub'g Co., 419 U.S. 245, 253–54, 1 Media L. Rep. 1815, 1818 (1974).

[489]388 U.S. 130, 1 Media L. Rep. 1568 (1967).

[490]*Id.* at 145. Although the four justices in the plurality concluded that no waiver had occurred, they went on to determine that the defendant publisher's conduct was not constitutionally protected. *Id.* at 161. In dissenting, four justices also implicitly found that there was no waiver, concluding that the verdict for the plaintiff should be reversed and the case retried using the appropriate constitutional standards. *See id.* at 170 (Black, J., concurring and dissenting); *id.* at 172 (Brennan, J., concurring and dissenting). Only Chief Justice Warren, in a separate opinion that concurred in the plurality's ultimate result, found that the publisher had waived its First Amendment rights. *Id.* at 165–66 (Warren, C.J., concurring in result).

[491]*Id.* at 145 (quoting Palko v. Connecticut, 302 U.S. 319, 327 (1937)).

[492]*Id.* at 137, 144–45.

[493]*Id.* at 143–44. The Supreme Court held, in New York Times Co. v. Sullivan, 376 U.S. 254, 1 Media L. Rep. 1527 (1967), that public officials must prove constitutional "actual malice" to recover damages for defamation. *See supra* §§2.2 and 2.11.

[494]388 U.S. at 143–44.

The plurality, led by Justice Harlan, held that no waiver had occurred.[495] Justice Harlan observed that it was "inadvisable" to determine whether a right was "known" by a litigant by looking outside the record, and he noted that the seditious libel arguments in *Sullivan* were inapplicable to the *Butts* facts.[496] Furthermore, the defendant publisher raised the actual malice issue promptly after the *Sullivan* decision, both the trial court and an appellate court had an opportunity to consider the issue, and the plaintiff had not been prejudiced by the defendant's failure to raise the defense earlier.[497]

There is no waiver "if the error is so fundamental that the failure to recognize it will result in a miscarriage of justice."[498]

§ 2.12 MATTER OF PUBLIC OR PRIVATE CONCERN

In *Rosenbloom v. Metromedia*,[499] a plurality of the Supreme Court held that the actual malice rule applied to all publications involving matters of public concern.[500] However, in *Gertz v. Robert Welch, Inc.*,[501] the Supreme Court rejected this view, holding that the actual malice rule only applies if the plaintiff is a public official or public figure.[502]

In *Gertz* the Court also held that a defamation plaintiff cannot recover presumed or punitive damages, at least unless the plaintiff proves that the defendant acted with constitutional actual malice.[503] The question then arose whether these damage rules applied to all defamation cases. The Supreme Court addressed this question in *Dun & Bradstreet v. Greenmoss Builders*.[504]

In *Greenmoss*, the plaintiff, a real estate developer and contractor, was a private figure. The defendant was a credit reporting agency whose defamatory report was found to have caused the bankruptcy of the plaintiff. The Court held that the *Gertz* damage rules did not apply because the publication was about a matter of private, not public, concern.[505] Thus, *Greenmoss* resurrected *Rosenbloom*'s focus on whether speech was about a matter of public or private concern, but used it to limit rather than expand federal constitutional protection.

Courts have interpreted the public concern requirement broadly, usually concluding that a publication does involve a matter of public concern.[506] The

---

[495] *Id.*
[496] *Id.* at 144–45.
[497] *Id.* at 145. The publisher first raised the issue in its motion for a new trial, but the judge held that the *Sullivan* actual malice standard was inapplicable. *Id.* at 138–39, 145 n.10. The Fifth Circuit held that the publisher had waived the defense. *Id.* at 139; *see* Curtis Pub'g Co. v. Butts, 351 F.2d 702, 713 (5th Cir. 1965). The Supreme Court plurality found that the plaintiff was not prejudiced by the defendant's delay becauses "it is almost certain that [the trial judge] would have rebuffed any effort to interpose general constitutional defenses at the time of trial." Butts, 388 U.S. at 145 & n.10.
[498] *See, e.g.*, Hunt v. Liberty Lobby, 720 F.2d 631, 647, 10 Media L. Rep. 1097 (11th Cir. 1983) (although jury instruction not objected to it was nonetheless grounds for reversal of jury verdict).
[499] 403 U.S. 29, 1 Media L. Rep. 1597 (1971).
[500] *Id.* at 52, 1 Media L. Rep. at 1605–06.
[501] 418 U.S. 323, 1 Media L. Rep. 1633 (1974).
[502] *Id.* at 345–46, 1 Media L. Rep. at 1642. The impact of *Rosenbloom* and *Gertz* on the actual malice rule is discussed in greater detail *supra* § 2.2.
[503] 418 U.S. at 349.
[504] 472 U.S. 749, 11 Media L. Rep. 2417 (1985).
[505] *Id.* at 761.
[506] Weiner v. Doubleday & Co., 549 N.E.2d 453, 17 Media L. Rep. 1165 (N.Y. 1989), *cert. denied*, 495 U.S. 930 (1990) (statements in book about emotional turmoil of woman convicted of murdering father that concerned her relationship with psychiatrist); Jones v. Palmer Communications, 440 N.W.2d 884, 16 Media

public/private concern distinction has not been applied where the plaintiff is a public figure or a public official.[507] Whether speech is about a matter of public or private concern is an issue of law for a court.[508]

§ 2.13 ABSOLUTE PRIVILEGES

An absolute privilege is just what its name implies—a privilege that exists even if the defamatory statement was known to be false when made and was published for no other reason than to injure the plaintiff.[509] Such a privilege can only be defeated by showing that it does not apply to the situation at hand.[510]

§ 2.13(A) Consent

Consent to the publication of a defamatory statement creates an absolute privilege.[511] This is nothing more than a specialized application of the general rule that consent is a complete defense in tort actions. Ordinarily, the key issue is the scope of the consent.[512] Consent is not usually an important defense in defamation cases, however.[513]

§ 2.13(B) Statements Made in Judicial, Legislative, Executive, and Administrative Proceedings

Defamatory statements made by participants—judges, attorneys, parties, witnesses, and jurors[514]—in judicial proceedings are absolutely privileged[515] so long as they have some relation to the judicial proceeding in which they are made.[516] However, such statements need not be relevant or material to any issue in the judicial proceeding.[517]

L. Rep. 2137 (Iowa 1989) (statements about dismissal of firefighter); Wiemer v. Rankin, 790 P.2d 347, 17 Media L. Rep. 1753 (Idaho 1990) (statements asserting plaintiff killed wife and lied about it); Carney v. Santa Cruz Women Against Rape, 271 Cal. Rptr. 30, 18 Media L. Rep. 1123 (Cal. Ct. App. 1990) (newsletter addressing sexual assault and harassment). *Compare* Phyfer v. Fiona Press, 12 Media L. Rep. 2211 (N.D. Miss. 1986) (publication of woman's nude photo with sexually suggestive quote matter of private concern).

[507]Dworkin v. Hustler Magazine, 867 F.2d 1188, 16 Media L. Rep. 1113 (9th Cir. 1989), *cert. denied*, 493 U.S. 812 (1989).

[508]Connick v. Myers, 461 U.S. 138, 147–48 n.7 (1983).

[509]*See* RESTATEMENT (SECOND) §611, cmt. b. *See also* Read v. News-Journal Co., 474 A.2d 119, 120–21, 10 Media L. Rep. 1399 (Del. 1984) (absolute immunity renders publisher's motive irrelevant).

[510]*See id.*

[511]RESTATEMENT (SECOND) §892A, cmt. f, and §583; Litman v. Massachusetts Mut. Life Ins. Co., 739 F.2d 1549, 1556 (11th Cir. 1984) (by giving permission to prospective employer to contact ex-employer, plaintiff consented to defamation). One commentator has suggested that it is improper to classify consent as a "privilege"; if consent is given, no tort has occurred. ELDREDGE, *supra* note 105, §61, at 317.

[512]*See, e.g.,* Kelly v. William Morrow & Co., 186 Cal. App. 3d 1625, 1633, 231 Cal. Rptr. 497 (Cal. Ct. App. 1986); Sharman v. C. Schmidt & Sons, 216 F. Supp. 401, 405–07 (E.D. Pa. 1963).

[513]*See* Live Oak Pub'g Co. v. Cohagan, 286 Cal. Rptr. 198 (Cal. Ct. App. 1991) (newspaper that published ad for defendant could not base libel action on ad).

[514]Smith v. Hatch, 271 Cal. App. 2d 39, 46, 76 Cal. Rptr. 350 (Cal. Ct. App. 1969) (privilege extended to judges, attorneys, parties in private litigation, judicial officers, witnesses, and jurors).

[515]*See* RESTATEMENT (SECOND) §§585–89; Silberg v. Anderson, 50 Cal. 3d 205, 220, 786 P.2d 365 (Cal. 1990); Petty v. General Accident Fire & Life Ins. Corp., 365 F.2d 419, 421 (3d Cir. 1966).

[516]*Silberg,* 50 Cal. 3d at 220; Mock v. Chicago, Rock Island & Pac. R.R. Co., 454 F.2d 131, 135 (8th Cir. 1972).

[517]*See, e.g., Hatch,* 271 Cal. App. 2d at 46 ("the defamatory matter need not be relevant, pertinent or material to any issue before the court, it need only have some connection or some relation to the judicial proceeding").

This privilege is particularly broad, covering even defamatory statements made before the institution of judicial action if the action is being seriously contemplated in good faith.[518] Quasi-judicial proceedings are also covered by the privilege.[519] However, the case law is split on whether the dissemination of complaints and press releases containing a complaint's allegations are protected by this absolute privilege.[520]

Legislators, whether federal, state, or local, are absolutely privileged to make defamatory statements in the performance of their legislative duties.[521] Federal[522] as well as state[523] officials have an absolute privilege to make defamatory statements in the course of their official duties. These privileges are not ordinarily of great importance to the media, but there are exceptions.[524]

§2.13(C) Publications Required by Law

Where publication is required by law, there is an absolute privilege for any defamation that occurs.[525] The most important application of this rule to the media is under the Federal Communications Act,[526] where broadcasters are required by law to carry certain broadcasts. The Supreme Court has made clear that such conduct is absolutely privileged.[527] No other result seems reasonable, because it would be grossly unfair to require someone to carry a broadcast, to punish them if they do not carry it, yet to permit them to be punished if they do.

§2.13(D) Miscellaneous Absolute Privileges

Other absolute privileges are occasionally at issue in defamation cases, including sovereign immunity,[528] the Act of State doctrine,[529] and the Eleventh Amendment.[530]

---

[518]ITT Telecom Prods. Corp. v. Dooley, 214 Cal. App. 3d 307, 313, 262 Cal. Rptr. 773 (Cal. Ct. App. 1989) (statements made by consultant to aid in potential litigation); Lerette v. Dean Witter Org., 131 Cal. Rptr. 592, 594–95 (Cal. Ct. App. 1976) (demand letter prior to complaint).

[519]McDonald v. Smith, 472 U.S. 479 (1985) (recognizing actual malice rule applies to petitioning government for redress of grievances), *on remand,* Smith v. McDonald, 895 F.2d 147, 17 Media L. Rep. 1499 (4th Cir. 1990) (applying absolute privilege under North Carolina law to quasi-judicial proceeding).

[520]*Not Privileged:* Green Acres Trust v. London, 688 P.2d 617 (Ariz. 1984); Asay v. Hallmark Cards, 594 F.2d 692, 697–98 (8th Cir. 1979) (complaint given to news services); Kennedy v. Cannon, 182 A.2d 54 (Md. Ct. App. 1962).

Privileged: Susan A. v. Sonoma County, 3 Cal. Rptr. 2d 27, 31, 19 Media L. Rep. 1889, 1891 (1991); McNally v. Yarnall, 764 F. Supp. 853 (S.D.N.Y. 1991); Johnston v. Cartwright, 355 F.2d 32, 37–38 (8th Cir. 1966). *See also* Marrero v. Hialeah, 625 F.2d 499 (5th Cir. 1980), *cert. denied,* 450 U.S. 913 (1981).

[521]*See* Brubaker v. Board of Educ., 502 F.2d 973, 991 (7th Cir. 1974), *cert. denied,* 421 U.S. 965 (1975) (school board members who passed allegedly defamatory resolutions).

[522]*See, e.g.,* Barr v. Matteo, 360 U.S. 564, 569–70 (1959) (federal administrative law judges); Scherer v. Morrow, 401 F.2d 204, 205 (7th Cir. 1968), *cert. denied,* 393 U.S. 1084 (1969) (secret service agent); Stepanian v. Addis, 699 F.2d 1046, 1048 (11th Cir. 1983) (federal prosecutor).

[523]Colaizzi v. Walker, 542 F.2d 969, 974 (7th Cir. 1976) (director of investigations for executive branch of state government), *cert. denied,* 430 U.S. 960 (1977).

[524]*See, e.g.,* McClatchy Newspapers v. Superior Ct., 234 Cal. Rptr. 702, 13 Media L. Rep. 2281 (Cal. Ct. App. 1987) (defamatory statements by reporter during deposition privileged).

[525]RESTATEMENT (SECOND) §592A.

[526]*See* 27 U.S.C.S. §315 (1981).

[527]Farmers Educ. & Coop. Union v. WDAY, Inc., 360 U.S. 525, 531 (1959).

[528]Davis v. Littell, 398 F.2d 83, 85 (9th Cir. 1968), *cert. denied,* 393 U.S. 1018 (1969) (general counsel of Native American tribe).

[529]DeRoburt v. Gannett Co., 733 F.2d 701, 703–04, 10 Media L. Rep. 1898 (9th Cir. 1984), *cert. denied,* 469 U.S. 1159 (1985).

[530]Ronwin v. Shapiro, 657 F.2d 1071, 1073, 7 Media L. Rep. 2100 (9th Cir. 1981) (Arizona State Board of Regents as publisher of *Arizona Law Review*).

§2.14 Conditional Privileges

A conditional or qualified privilege is just what its name implies—a privilege that can be overcome by a proper showing of abuse of the privilege.[531] This, of course, distinguishes it from an absolute privilege, which cannot be overcome by a showing that it was abused.[532]

§2.14(A) The Interested Party Privilege

Three conditional privileges cover communications between parties that have an interest in the communication. First, a person who publishes a defamatory statement is conditionally privileged to do so if he or she makes the statement to protect a lawful interest of his or her own.[533]

Second, a person who publishes a defamatory statement is conditionally privileged to do so if he or she makes the statement to protect a lawful interest of the recipient or a third person.[534] Thus, people who provide information to reporters at the reporters' request may be conditionally privileged to do so.[535] The availability of a conditional privilege for credit reporting agencies is not entirely clear.[536]

Third, a person who publishes a defamatory statement to others who have an interest in the subject matter of the communication—for example, partners, co-tenants, family members, shareholders, employees of an entity, members of a labor union, a religious organization, or a club[537]—is conditionally privileged to do so.[538] This rule has been applied to organizations that circulate newsletters, newspapers, and other similar publications to their members as well as to publications circulated to people with an interest in a particular subject.[539] This privilege has usually not been applied to general circulation publications that discuss matters of interest to the public, but the cases are not uniform.[540]

---

[531] Restatement (Second) §593.
[532] *See supra* §2.13.
[533] Restatement (Second) §594; Shenkman v. O'Malley, 157 N.Y.S.2d 290, 297–300 (N.Y. App. Div. 1956) (defense to defamatory attack); Faber v. Byrle, 229 P.2d 718, 723 (Kan. 1951); Haycox v. Dunn, 104 S.E.2d 800, 810–11 (Va. 1958).
[534] Restatement (Second) §595; Gasbarro v. Lever Bros. Co., 490 F.2d 424, 426 (7th Cir. 1973) (employee health insurance manager's comments to employees about plaintiff's doctor's allegedly outrageous fees); Zuschek v. Whitmoyer Labs, 430 F. Supp. 1163, 1165–66 (E.D. Pa. 1977), *aff'd*, 571 F.2d 573 (3d Cir. 1978); Coopersmith v. Williams, 468 P.2d 739, 741 (Colo. 1970).
[535] Restatement (Second) §595, cmt. i; Stevenson v. Baltimore Baseball Club, 243 A.2d 533, 536 (Md. 1968), *overruled on other grounds*, 387 A.2d 1129 (Md. 1978).
[536] *Cases Granting Limited Privilege:* Anderson v. Dun & Bradstreet, 543 F.2d 732, 736 (10th Cir. 1976); ABC Needlecraft Co. v. Dun & Bradstreet, 245 F.2d 775, 777 (2d Cir. 1957); Koral Sales v. Dun & Bradstreet, 389 F. Supp. 985, 985–86 (E.D. Wis. 1975). *But see* Pacific Packing Co. v. Bradstreet Co., 139 P. 1007, 1010 (Idaho 1914) (credit reports not privileged). *See also* 15 U.S.C. §1681h(e) (1982) (limiting liability for erroneous consumer credit reports).
[537] Creswell v. Pruitt, 239 S.W.2d 165, 168 (Tex. Civ. App. 1951) (religious organization); Rankin v. Phillippe, 211 A.2d 56, 58 (Pa. Super. Ct. 1965) (same); Zito v. American Fed'n of Musicians, 401 N.Y.S.2d 929, 931 (N.Y. App. Div. 1978) (union); Mick v. American Dental Ass'n, 139 A.2d 570, 578 (N.J. Super. Ct. App. Div.), *cert. denied*, 141 A.2d 318 (N.J. 1958) (dental association); Reininger v. Prickett, 137 P.2d 595, 597 (Okla. 1943) (fraternal order); Ward v. Painter's Local Union, 252 P.2d 253, 257 (Wash. 1953) (union); Chambers v. Leiser, 86 P. 627, 628 (Wash. 1906) (stockholders).
[538] Restatement (Second) §596; Straitwell v. National Steel Corp., 869 F.2d 248, 16 Media L. Rep. 1329 (4th Cir. 1989) (press release to community about results of company's investigation into practices of certain management personnel).
[539] *See, e.g., Mick*, 139 A.2d at 578; Maidman v. Jewish Pubns., 355 P.2d 265 (Cal. 1960); *Zito*, 401 N.Y.S.2d at 931.
[540] Brown v. Kelly Broadcasting Co., 771 P.2d 460, 16 Media L. Rep. 1625 (Cal. 1989) (no privilege for media for communications relating to matters of public interest); Rouch v. Enquirer & News of Battle

§2.14(B) Abuse of a Conditional Privilege

A conditional privilege may be lost in a number of ways. If the publication is made with constitutional actual malice, the conditional privilege will be lost.[541] The constitutional actual malice rule is the primary test for overcoming conditional privileges.[542] If the publication is made solely out of spite or ill will or solely to harm the plaintiff, the privilege will be lost.[543] However, people seldom act solely for one reason. Thus, for example, if the speaker is motivated by the ill will he or she would naturally feel for the plaintiff's apparent misconduct, there has been no abuse of the privilege.[544]

While there is some authority that excessive publication of a defamatory statement abuses a conditional privilege,[545] this view is analytically unsound. To say that a publication is excessive means simply that some of the communication is protected by the privilege and some of it is not. Thus, the publication is not actionable to the extent it was within a privilege, and is actionable to the extent that it was outside any privilege. The privilege is not lost by the excessive publication, however: it simply does not apply to the part of the communication that is not privileged.[546] Similarly, adding defamatory statements not within a privilege to those statements within a privilege does not abuse the privilege: statements within the privilege are not actionable; those outside it are.[547]

§2.15 CONDITIONAL ABSOLUTE PRIVILEGES

Besides absolute and conditional privileges, conditional absolute privileges, i.e., privileges that are absolute so long as certain conditions are met,[548] are also available. Two such privileges are important to the operation of the media: the accurate summary privilege and the neutral report privilege.

§2.15(A) The Accurate Summary Privilege

At common law, there was strict liability for republications. Thus, reports in the media about contested government proceedings—court cases, or legislative battles, for example—could easily result in liability for defamation. Ac-

---

Creek, 398 N.W.2d 245, 13 Media L. Rep. 2201 (Mich. 1986) (same). *But see* Seegmiller v. KSL, Inc., 626 P.2d 968, 977–79, 7 Media L. Rep. 1012 (Utah 1981) (recognizing privilege in some circumstances); Crump v. Beckley Newspapers, 320 S.E.2d 70, 81, 10 Media L. Rep. 2225, 2231–32 (W. Va. 1984) (remanding for reconsideration of qualified privilege issue).

[541]Jolly v. Valley Pub'g Co., 388 P.2d 139, 142 (Wash. 1964); Marchesi v. Franchino, 387 A.2d 1129, 1131–33 (Md. 1978).

[542]RESTATEMENT (SECOND) §600.

[543]*Id.* §603, cmt. a; Powers v. Carvalho, 368 A.2d 1242, 1249 (R.I. 1977); *Maidman,* 355 P.2d at 270–71.

[544]Craig v. Wright, 76 P.2d 248, 250 (Okla. 1938); Boston Mut. Life Ins. Co. v. Varone, 303 F.2d 155, 159 (1st Cir. 1962); De Mott v. Amalgamated Meat Cutters, 320 P.2d 50 (Cal. Ct. App. 1958).

[545]Galvin v. New York, New Haven and Hartford Ry. Co., 168 N.E.2d 262, 266 (Mass. 1960); Kruse v. Rabe, 79 A. 316, 317 (N.J. 1911) (excessive publication implies malice); *see also* Porter v. Eyster, 294 F.2d 613, 618–19 (4th Cir. 1961) (finding no excessive publication); Oberman v. Dun & Bradstreet, 586 F.2d 1173, 4 Media L. Rep. 2137 (7th Cir. 1978) (no excessive publication).

[546]*See* RESTATEMENT (SECOND) §599, cmt. b and §604, cmt. c (supporting idea of severability).

[547]*Id.* §605A, cmt. b.

[548]*See, e.g.,* Catalano v. Pechous, 419 N.E.2d 350, 6 Media L. Rep. 2511 (Ill. 1980), *cert. denied,* 451 U.S. 911 (1981) (fair report privilege not lost because of malice). However, some jurisdictions only recognize a qualified fair report privilege. *See, e.g.,* Doe v. Doe, 941 F.2d 280, 19 Media L. Rep. 1705 (5th Cir. 1991) (Louisiana).

cordingly, the common law has long recognized a privilege for accurate summaries of government proceedings or public meetings on matters of public concern.[549]

The accurate summary privilege is necessary because the public needs information on such proceedings. No one, not even a person who can devote all of her or his time to it, can personally attend every official proceeding or every public meeting. The media and others have to be the public's eyes and ears at such events.

Similarly, those who report on such proceedings must be able to summarize them, so long as the summaries are reasonably accurate. The public is no more able to read transcripts of all official proceedings and public meetings than it is able to attend them.

To fall within the accurate summary privilege, a report need not be a complete report of everything that happened—the media are not transcription services. However, the report must give a substantially accurate summary of what occurred—literal accuracy is not required, and a certain degree of literary license is allowed.[550] All that is necessary is that the "gist" or "sting" of what is reported be accurate.[551] Whether a report is an accurate summary is usually a question of law.[552]

Official events covered by the accurate summary privilege include judicial,[553] legislative,[554] administrative,[555] and executive[556] proceedings. Also included are reports on the contents of government documents.[557] This privilege is broadly interpreted and has been extended to reports of secret official proceedings[558] as well as to preliminary steps in proceedings before there is any official action,[559] although there is contrary authority on both points.[560]

---

[549]RESTATEMENT (SECOND) §611.

[550]Jennings v. Telegram-Tribune Co., 164 Cal. App. 3d 119, 125, 210 Cal. Rptr. 485, 11 Media L. Rep. 1419 (Cal. Ct. App. 1985); Holy Spirit Ass'n for Unification of World Christianity v. New York Times Co., 424 N.Y.S.2d 165, 167, 399 N.E.2d 1185, 5 Media L. Rep. 2219 (N.Y. 1979).

[551]*Holy Spirit Ass'n,* 399 N.E.2d at 1187; Binder v. Triangle Pubns., 275 A.2d 53, 58 (Pa. 1971); Mattson v. Chronicle Pub'g Co., 509 N.E.2d 150, 14 Media L. Rep. 1185 (Ill. App. Ct. 1987).

[552]McClatchy Newspapers v. Superior Ct., 189 Cal. App. 3d 961, 976, 234 Cal. Rptr. 702, 13 Media L. Rep. 2281 (Cal. Ct. App. 1987); Easton v. Public Citizens, 19 Media L. Rep. 1882, 1884 (S.D.N.Y. 1991), *aff'd without opinion,* No. 92-7173, 1992 U.S. App. LEXIS 14403 (2d Cir. 1992).

[553]Lowenschuss v. West Pub'g Co., 542 F.2d 180, 185–86 (3d Cir. 1976) (publication of judicial decision by legal publisher); Taylor v. West Pub'g Co., 693 F.2d 837, 838 (8th Cir. 1982) (same); Ronwin v. Shapiro, 657 F.2d 1071, 1075, 7 Media L. Rep. 2100 (9th Cir. 1981) (report in law review of statement in Arizona Supreme Court decision). *See also* Dorsey v. National Enquirer, 952 F.2d 250, 19 Media L. Rep. 1673, 1677 (9th Cir. 1991) (privilege applied to out-of-court statements related to judicial proceeding).

[554]Nusbaum v. Newark Morning Ledger Co., 206 A.2d 185, 187 (N.J. Super. Ct. App. Div. 1965), *cert. denied,* 209 A.2d 138 (N.J. 1965) (congressional hearing); Bray v. Providence Journal Co., 220 A.2d 531, 535 (R.I. 1966) (school committee meeting); Leininger v. New Orleans Item Pub'g Co., 101 So. 411, 412 (La. 1924) (proceedings of municipal council).

[555]Briarcliff Lodge Hotel v. Citizen-Sentinel Pub'g, 183 N.E. 193, 197–98 (N.Y. 1932) (water board).

[556]Sciandra v. Lynett, 187 A.2d 586, 588 (Pa. 1963) (report by governor); Brandon v. Gazette Pub'g Co., 352 S.W.2d 92, 93–94 (Ark. 1961) (statements by governor).

[557]Medico v. Time, Inc., 643 F.2d 134, 139, 6 Media L. Rep. 2529 (3d Cir.), *cert. denied,* 454 U.S. 836 (1981) (privilege applies to preliminary FBI reports).

[558]Reeves v. American Broadcasting Cos., 719 F.2d 602, 607–08, 9 Media L. Rep. 2289 (2d Cir. 1983) (grand jury proceedings); White v. Fraternal Order of Police, 909 F.2d 512, 527, 17 Media L. Rep. 2137, 2149 (D.C. Cir. 1990); *see also* RESTATEMENT (SECOND) §611.

[559]Campbell v. New York Evening Post, 157 N.E. 153, 155 (N.Y. 1927) (filing of pleadings in judicial proceeding); Newell v. Field Enters., 415 N.E.2d 434, 6 Media L. Rep. 2450 (Ill. App. Ct. 1980) (thorough discussion of issue); Cox v. Lee Enters., 723 P.2d 238, 13 Media L. Rep. 1230 (Mont. 1986) (privilege applies to court documents even if not acted on). *See generally* Theuman, *Libel and Slander: Reports of Pleadings As Within Privilege for Reports of Judicial Proceedings,* 20 A.L.R.4th 577 (1983).

[560]*See, e.g.,* Sibley v. Holyoke-Telegram Pub'g Co., 461 N.E.2d 823, 825–26, 10 Media L. Rep. 1557,

Public meetings covered by this privilege include political meetings and conventions, shareholder meetings, and meetings to complain about government policy.[561] Meetings not open to the public, however, are apparently not within this privilege.[562] The privilege also covers press conferences,[563] although there appears to be no authority on whether it covers interviews with the press. In some jurisdictions the statutory privilege is only available for reports in the media.[564]

Whether the official proceedings or public meeting must be mentioned to make the accurate summary privilege applicable is unclear.[565] This seems to be a sensible limitation, however, because the reader or viewer then understands that what is being reported is a government proceeding or public meeting. Courts adopting this limitation have concluded that it furthers the policy behind the privilege—to inform the public of what happens at such events.[566] Nevertheless, this limitation should not be mechanically or rigidly applied. If it is reasonably apparent, from the context of the statement or because of other things the public should know, that the information came from government proceedings or public meetings, no explicit statement to that effect should be required.[567]

The privilege will not come into play if the person reporting on the official proceedings or public meetings takes sides on the merits of what is happening in a particular proceeding or expresses his or her own point of view.[568] Even in that instance, if portions of the report are an accurate abridgement of what happened, those portions would be privileged.[569] Portions of the report containing the reporter's personal commentary would not be within the privilege, however, although they may not be actionable for other reasons.[570]

1558–59 (Mass. 1984) (report of proceeding before any action taken not within privilege); Danziger v. Hearst Corp., 107 N.E.2d 62, 64 (N.Y. 1952) (closed judicial proceedings not within privilege).

[561] See, e.g., Phoenix Newspapers v. Choisser, 312 P.2d 150 (Ariz. 1957) (chamber of commerce forum).

[562] RESTATEMENT (SECOND) §611, cmt. i; Kimball v. Post Pub'g Co., 85 N.E. 103, 105 (Mass. 1908); see also Danziger, 107 N.E.2d at 64 (closed judicial proceedings not within privilege).

[563] Kilgore v. Younger, 30 Cal. 3d 770, 777, 640 P.2d 793, 8 Media L. Rep. 1886 (Cal. 1982); Coleman v. Newark Morning Ledger Co., 149 A.2d 193, 200–201 (N.J. 1959).

[564] See, e.g., CAL. CIV. CODE §47(d) (West 1994); TEX. REV. CIV. STAT. ANN. art. 5432 (1958).

[565] See, e.g., White v. Fraternal Order of Police, 909 F.2d 512, 527–29 (D.C. Cir. 1990) (applying privilege to newspaper article attributing information to secret government proceedings but denying privilege to television broadcast attributing same information to "police sources"); Bufalino v. Associated Press, 692 F.2d 266, 271 & n.4, 8 Media L. Rep. 2384 (2d Cir. 1982) (reporter must actually rely on public records and properly attribute information to records in order to claim privilege), cert. denied, 462 U.S. 1111 (1983). But see Medico v. Time, Inc., 643 F.2d 134, 146–47 (3d Cir. 1981) (applying privilege because FBI documents supported article's claims), cert. denied, 454 U.S. 836 (1981); Mathis v. Philadelphia Newspapers, 455 F. Supp. 406, 416 (E.D. Pa. 1978) (applying privilege because context made clear that law enforcement agencies supplied information, although not explicitly stated). In any event, the information published does not have to be obtained from the proceeding; it can be obtained indirectly. See, e.g., Binder v. Triangle Pubns., 275 A.2d 53 (Pa. 1971); McCracken v. Evening News Ass'n, 141 N.W.2d 694 (Mich. 1966).

[566] White, 909 F.2d at 528; Bufalino, 692 F.2d at 271, 8 Media L. Rep. at 2389.

[567] Dameron v. Washington Magazine, 779 F.2d 736, 739, 12 Media L. Rep. 1508 (D.C. Cir. 1985), cert. denied, 476 U.S. 1141 (1986). See also Hayward v. Watsonville Register-Pajaronian & Sun, 265 Cal. App. 2d 255, 259, 71 Cal. Rptr. 295 (Cal. Ct. App. 1965) (article attributing information to "police sources" privileged); Village of Grafton v. American Broadcasting Cos., 435 N.E.2d 1131, 1137 (Ohio Ct. App. 1980) (news report based on "government sources" privileged).

[568] Dameron, 779 F.2d at 739–40, 12 Media L. Rep. at 1508.

[569] Schuster v. U.S. News & World Report, 602 F.2d 850, 854 & n.8, 5 Media L. Rep. 1773 (8th Cir. 1979) (liberal construction of media's privilege).

[570] See, e.g., Easton v. Public Citizen, 19 Media L. Rep. 1882, 1888 (S.D.N.Y. 1991), aff'd without opinion, 969 F.2d 1043 (2d Cir. 1992).

There is some authority for the proposition that the accurate summary privilege does not apply to the proceedings of foreign governments.[571] A constitutional accurate summary privilege has also been recognized.[572]

§2.15(B) The Neutral Report Privilege

The common law rule that publishers are responsible for defamatory statements that they republish creates particular problems for the media, which often repeat the statements of others provided in press releases, speeches, and interviews. The problem is particularly acute when charges and countercharges are made by contending groups and not all of them can be true.

Republishing such statements is protected by the accurate summary report privilege[573] to some extent, but that privilege does not prevent liability in all such situations. This is illustrated by the case that first created the neutral report privilege, *Edwards v. National Audubon Society*,[574] where prominent scientists and university professors brought a libel action against the officers of an environmental organization who claimed that the plaintiffs were "being paid to lie, or . . . [were] parroting something [they knew] little about."[575] They also sued a newspaper that published an article on this controversy that included the environmental defendants' charges.[576] The article discussed the controversy surrounding the use of the pesticide DDT and contained the responses of several of the plaintiffs to the environmental defendants' charges.[577] The court held that

> [s]uccinctly stated, when a responsible, prominent organization like the National Audubon Society makes serious charges against a public figure, the First Amendment protects the accurate and disinterested reporting of those charges, regardless of the reporter's private views regarding their validity. . . . What is newsworthy about such accusations is that they were made. We do not believe that the press may be required under the First Amendment to suppress newsworthy statements merely because it has serious doubts regarding their truth. Nor must the press take up cudgels against dubious charges in order to publish them without fear of liability for defamation.[578]

The Second Circuit has subsequently reaffirmed the privilege of neutral reportage but has indicated that the privilege only applies if (1) the publisher does not concur in or espouse the defamatory statements; (2) the statements are made by a responsible, prominent entity; (3) the statements relate to a public controversy; and (4) the statements are made against a public official or figure.[579] Other courts have declined to adopt the privilege, holding that

---

[571]Lee v. Dong-A Ilbo, 849 F.2d 876, 15 Media L. Rep. 1593 (4th Cir. 1988) (2-1 decision), *cert. denied*, 489 U.S. 1067 (1989).

[572]Cox Broadcasting v. Cohn, 420 U.S. 469, 1 Media L. Rep. 1819 (1975); Levine v. CMP Pubns., 738 F.2d 660, 10 Media L. Rep. 2337 (5th Cir. 1984); Liberty Lobby v. Dow Jones & Co., 838 F.2d 1287, 14 Media L. Rep. 2249 (D.C. Cir.), *cert. denied*, 488 U.S. 825 (1988). *See also* Sowle, *Defamation and the First Amendment: The Case for a Constitutional Privilege of Fair Report*, 54 N.Y.U. L. Rev. 469 (1979).

[573]*See supra* §2.15(A).

[574]556 F.2d 113, 3 Media L. Rep. 1849 (2d Cir.), *cert. denied*, 434 U.S. 1002 (1977).

[575]*Id.* at 117

[576]*Id.*

[577]*Id.* at 120.

[578]*Id.* (citations omitted).

[579]Cianci v. New Times Pub'g Co., 639 F.2d 54, 68, 6 Media L. Rep. 1625 (2d Cir. 1980). Other courts have interpreted the privilege more broadly. Price v. Viking Penguin, 881 F.2d 1426, 16 Media L. Rep. 2169 (8th Cir. 1989), *cert. denied*, 493 U.S. 1036 (1990); Barry v. Time, Inc., 584 F. Supp. 1110, 1126–27, 10 Media L. Rep. 1809 (N.D. Cal. 1984); In re United Press Int'l, 16 Media L. Rep. 2401 (D.D.C. 1989).

such a broad grant of immunity where the publisher has "serious doubts" as to the truthfulness of the defamatory charges is inconsistent with the actual malice rule.[580]

This issue has also generated substantial academic commentary.[581] Whether the privilege exists and what its precise elements are remain unsettled.

§2.16 DAMAGES

In a defamation action, nominal, general, special, and punitive damages can be recovered. Nominal damages are very small in amount, usually $1, and their main function is to vindicate the plaintiff's reputation by showing that he or she has prevailed. They are awarded when the plaintiff has been unable to prove any substantial injury to his or her reputation.[582]

General damages, including damages to reputation, are at the heart of every defamation case. At common law, they included not only damages to reputation that were proved but also damages that were assumed to naturally flow from the defamation, commonly known as presumed damages.[583] General damages may also be recovered for emotional distress and bodily harm that results from the defamatory publication.[584]

Special damages, i.e., actual out-of-pocket economic losses, are also recoverable.[585] Punitive or exemplary damages are also available to punish the defendant for misconduct and to deter any future repetition of it.[586]

§2.16(A) Effect of *Gertz* on Damages

In *Gertz v. Robert Welch, Inc.*, the Supreme Court held that presumed and punitive damages were unconstitutional, at least unless constitutional actual malice was demonstrated.[587] As to presumed damages, the Court reasoned that the common law presumption of injury from publication alone allowed juries

---

[580]*See, e.g.,* Dickey v. CBS, Inc., 583 F.2d 1221, 1225, 4 Media L. Rep. 1353 (3d Cir. 1978). *But see* Medico v. Time, Inc., 643 F.2d 134, 145, 6 Media L. Rep. 2529 (3d Cir.), *cert. denied,* 454 U.S. 836 (1981) (stating that *Dickey*'s comments on neutral report privilege are dicta, so issue remains open in Third Circuit). *See also* McCall v. Courier-Journal & Louisville Times Co., 623 S.W.2d 882, 886–87, 7 Media L. Rep. 2118 (Ky. 1981), *cert. denied,* 456 U.S. 975 (1982); Janklow v. Viking Press, 378 N.W.2d 875, 881, 12 Media L. Rep. 1534 (S.D. 1985).

[581]*See, e.g.,* Note, *The Developing Privilege of Neutral Reportage,* 69 VA. L. REV. 853 (1983); Note, *Price v. Viking Penguin, Inc.: The Neutral Reportage Privilege and Robust, Wide Open Debate,* 75 MINN. L. REV. 157 (1990).

[582]*See, e.g.,* RESTATEMENT (SECOND) §620; Walkon Carpet Corp. v. Klapprodt, 231 N.W.2d 370, 373–34 (N.D. 1975); Elliott v. Roach, 409 N.E.2d 661, 684 (Ind. Ct. App. 1980); Kraisinger v. Liggett, 592 P.2d 477, 479–80 (Kan. Ct. App. 1979) (plaintiff entitled to nominal damages but failure to award not reversible error).

[583]RESTATEMENT (SECOND) §621. *See also* Bock v. Plainfield Courier-News, 132 A.2d 523, 527 (N.J. Super. Ct. App. Div. 1957) (general damages presumed at common law); Dalton v. Meister, 188 N.W.2d 494, 497 (Wis. 1971) (same), *cert. denied,* 405 U.S. 934 (1972).

[584]RESTATEMENT (SECOND) §623. *See also* Luster v. Retail Credit Co., 575 F.2d 609, 614 (8th Cir. 1978); Braman v. Walthall, 225 S.W.2d 342, 348–49 (Ark. 1949); Pettengill v. Booth Newspapers, 278 N.W.2d 682, 684, 5 Media L. Rep. 1326 (Mich. Ct. App. 1979).

[585]RESTATEMENT (SECOND) §622. *See also* Korry v. International Tel. & Tel. Corp., 444 F. Supp. 193, 197 (S.D.N.Y. 1978) (court found proof of special damages inadequate); Stuempges v. Parke, Davis & Co., 297 N.W.2d 252, 258–59 (Minn. 1980).

[586]RESTATEMENT (SECOND) §621, cmt. d (1977); Davis v. Schuchat, 510 F.2d 731, 738 (D.C. Cir. 1975); Appleyard v. Transamerican Press, 539 F.2d 1026, 1030 (4th Cir. 1976), *cert. denied,* 429 U.S. 1041 (1977).

[587]Gertz v. Robert Welch, Inc., 418 U.S. 323, 349, 1 Media L. Rep. 1633 (1974).

to award substantial sums without any proof of actual harm.[588] This inhibits the exercise of First Amendment rights and invites juries to punish unpopular speech rather than compensating individuals for their actual injury. States have no substantial interest in securing such "gratuitous awards far in excess of any actual injury."[589]

The Court declined to give a comprehensive definition of "actual injury," noting that "actual injury" includes out-of-pocket economic loss, "impairment of reputation and standing in the community, personal humiliation, and mental anguish and suffering."[590] All such awards must be based on appropriate jury instructions and supported by competent evidence, although the evidence does not have to assign an actual dollar amount to the injury.[591]

Similarly, as to punitive damages, the Court noted that they are awarded in wholly unpredictable amounts that bear no relationship to the actual harm that occurred.[592] Like presumed damages, punitive damages can be used to punish speech the jury dislikes, because they do not have to bear any relationship to any actual harm. Accordingly, the Court held that punitive damages cannot be recovered unless the plaintiff at least proves actual malice.[593]

Nominal damages may also be unconstitutional in those cases where the *Gertz* damage rules apply,[594] because *Gertz* limits damages to recovery for actual injury, at least unless it is proven that the defamatory statement was made with constitutional actual malice. By definition, nominal damages are not compensation for actual injury. If there was actual injury, more than nominal damages would be appropriate.

It can be argued that the rationale behind the actual injury requirement established by *Gertz*—to prevent juries from punishing speech they disagreed with by arbitrarily awarding substantial damages unrelated to actual damages—has limited application to nominal damages because they are small in amount. However, this ignores the enormous costs of defending such cases, which may be direct (e.g., attorneys' fees) and indirect (e.g., lost time from reporting).

The effect of *Gertz* on damage awards should be quite dramatic. In many defamation cases plaintiffs cannot show any out-of-pocket losses; nor can they show that anyone thinks less of them because of the defamatory statement: their most likely witnesses on this point—family, friends, and business associates—are unlikely to believe defamatory statements about their spouse, golfing partner, or co-worker. Consequently, apart from the emotional distress that may result from the defamatory statement, there often is no injury.

Under the doctrine of presumed damages, however, plaintiffs were able to leave it to the jury to decide what their case was worth. This is exactly what *Gertz* condemned.

---

[588]*Id.*
[589]*Id.* at 349.
[590]*Id.* at 350.
[591]*Id. See also* Linn v. United Plant Guard Workers, 383 U.S. 53, 65–66 (1966) ("If the amount of damages awarded is excessive, it is the duty of the trial judge to require a remittitur or a new trial.") (quoted with approval in Old Dominion Branch No. 496, Nat'l Ass'n of Letter Carriers v. Austin, 418 U.S. 264, 287 n.17 (1974)); Lerman v. Flynt Distrib. Co., 745 F.2d 123, 141, 10 Media L. Rep. 2497, 2509 (2d Cir. 1984), *cert. denied,* 471 U.S. 1054 (1985) (warning against "mega-verdicts").
[592]418 U.S. at 350.
[593]*Id.*
[594]For a discussion of the cases in which the *Gertz* damage rules apply, *see supra* §2.12.

Courts are now beginning to understand that *Gertz* not only abolishes presumed damages in most cases but requires real proof of actual injury. A good example of this is *A.H. Belo Corp. v. Rayzor*,[595] where the Texas Court of Appeals held that the plaintiff's evidentiary burden was not met where the only proffered evidence was the plaintiff's own testimony that he had suffered embarrassment and humiliation as a result of the alleged defamation.[596]

Whether presumed or punitive damages are ever permissible in defamation cases is a question the Supreme Court has yet to resolve. In *Gertz* the Court seemed to intentionally leave the question open by saying that such damages were not available "at least" until constitutional actual malice was shown.[597] If the Court had not meant to leave the issue open, it could easily have dropped "at least" from that statement.

Courts that have considered the availability of punitive damages in defamation cases when actual malice is shown are split.[598] The availability of presumed damages when actual malice is shown has not been as thoroughly litigated.[599] In any event, before punitive damages can be awarded, the applicable state law requirements must also be met.[600]

§2.16(B) "Libel-Proof" Plaintiffs and Incremental Harm

Evidence that a plaintiff's general reputation was tarnished or his or her reputation for a given characteristic was poor prior to the publication of the allegedly defamatory material is admissible to mitigate damages.[601] Where a

---

[595] 644 S.W.2d 71, 85, 8 Media L. Rep. 2425 (Tex. Ct. App. 1982).

[596] *Id. See also Linn*, 383 U.S. at 66 ("likewise, the defamed party must establish that he has suffered some sort of compensable harm as a prerequisite to the recovery of additional punitive damages."); Littlefield v. Fort Dodge Messenger, 614 F.2d 581, 5 Media L. Rep. 2325 (8th Cir. 1980), *cert. denied*, 445 U.S. 945 (1980) (although plaintiff lost job he could not prove any actual damages because he could not prove that supervisor who fired him believed defamatory statement). Several cases have severely restricted the recovery of damages in defamation cases, although there are exceptions. Nevada Indep. Broadcasting Corp. v. Allen, 664 P.2d 337, 346, 9 Media L. Rep. 1769, 1775–76 (Nev. 1983) (damages reduced from $675,000 to $50,000, even though plaintiff was "politically assassinated"); Newton v. NBC, 677 F. Supp. 1066, 14 Media L. Rep. 1914 (D. Nev. 1987), *rev'd on other issues*, 930 F.2d 662 (9th Cir. 1990) ($5 million award for damage to reputation reduced to $50,000); Burnett v. National Enquirer, 7 Media L. Rep. 1321 (Cal. Super. Ct. 1981), *aff'd*, 193 Cal. Rptr. 206, 9 Media L. Rep. 1921 (1983) (reducing $300,000 general damage award to $50,000 despite distribution of 16 million copies of publication); Douglass v. Hustler Magazine, 769 F.2d 1128, 1144 (7th Cir. 1985), *cert. denied*, 475 U.S. 1094 (1986) ("$300,000 for emotional distress is an absurd figure.... we will not allow plaintiffs to throw themselves on the generosity of the jury; if they want damages they must prove them.... Modest compensatory damages are, as they should be, the norm in these cases."). *But see* Brown & Williamson Tobacco Corp. v. Jackson, 827 F.2d 1119, 14 Media L. Rep. 1497 (7th Cir. 1987), *cert. denied*, 485 U.S. 993 (1988) (upholding award of $5,050,000).

[597] 418 U.S. at 349.

[598] *Allowed:* Goldwater v. Ginzburg, 414 F.2d 324, 1 Media L. Rep. 1737 (2d Cir. 1969), *cert. denied*, 396 U.S. 1049 (1970); Appleyard v. Transamerican Press, 539 F.2d 1026 (4th Cir. 1976), *cert. denied*, 429 U.S. 1041 (1977) (but court warned that punitive damages must not be excessive in relation to actual harm suffered); Hunt v. Liberty Lobby, 720 F.2d 631, 650 n.34, 10 Media L. Rep. 1097 (11th Cir. 1983) (same).

Not Allowed: Taskett v. King Broadcasting Co., 546 P.2d 81, 86, 1 Media L. Rep. 1716 (Wash. 1976); Stone v. Essex County Newspapers, 330 N.E.2d 161, 169 (Mass. 1975).

[599] *Allowed:* Gertz v. Robert Welch, Inc., 680 F.2d 527, 8 Media L. Rep. 1769 (7th Cir. 1982), *cert. denied*, 459 U.S. 1226 (1983); Brown & Williamson Tobacco Corp. v. Jacobson, 713 F.2d 262, 273, 9 Media L. Rep. 1936 (7th Cir. 1983).

Not Allowed: Maheu v. Hughes Tool Co., 569 F.2d 459, 3 Media L. Rep. 1847 (9th Cir. 1977) (assumed to be unavailable after *Gertz*); Spence v. Funk, 396 A.2d 967, 970, 4 Media L. Rep. 1981 (Del. 1978) (ruled out by implication); Little Rock Newspapers v. Dodrill, 660 S.W.2d 933, 10 Media L. Rep. 1063 (Ark. 1983) (damage to reputation cannot be presumed in any case).

[600] Burnett v. National Enquirer, 193 Cal. Rptr. 206, 9 Media L. Rep. 1921 (Cal. Ct. App. 1983), *appeal dismissed*, 465 U.S. 1014 (1984).

[601] Marcone v. Penthouse Int'l Magazine for Men, 754 F.2d 1072, 11 Media L. Rep. 1577 (3d Cir.), *cert. denied*, 474 U.S. 864, *reh'g denied*, 474 U.S. 1014 (1985); *Dodrill*, 660 S.W.2d 933, 10 Media L. Rep. 1063.

plaintiff's reputation is so notorious and tarnished that any further assault cannot bring it any lower in the estimation of the public, that plaintiff is "libel-proof" and may not recover damages as a matter of law.[602] Most often the libel-proof plaintiff doctrine is invoked where the defamatory material concerns the plaintiffs' criminal activities.[603] The doctrine has also been applied in noncriminal cases where the claimed damage is to the plaintiff's business or personal reputation.[604]

Some courts have recognized the separate but related doctrine of incremental harm. In these cases, damage done to the plaintiff's reputation by the defamatory material is slight or de minimis compared to that done by other nonactionable statements.[605] Thus, where the bulk of the defendant's statements are not actionable, e.g., because they are privileged or true, and the actionable remainder does no substantial harm beyond that done by the nonactionable statements, a plaintiff may not recover damages for defamation.[606]

The Supreme Court, in *Masson v. New Yorker Magazine*,[607] rejected the argument that the incremental harm doctrine was "compelled as a matter of First Amendment protection for speech."[608] Each state, however, was left free to adopt the incremental harm doctrine.[609]

§2.16(C) Correction and Retraction Statutes

There is great diversity among American correction and retraction statutes.[610] These statutes are premised on the logical assumption that much of the

---

[602]*See, e.g.,* Jackson v. Longcope, 476 N.E.2d 617, 11 Media L. Rep. 2282 (Mass. 1985); Ray v. Time, Inc., 452 F. Supp. 618 (W.D. Tenn. 1976), *aff'd without opinion,* 582 F.2d 1280 (6th Cir. 1978).

[603]*See, e.g.,* Logan v. District of Columbia, 447 F. Supp. 1328, 1332, 3 Media L. Rep. 2094 (D.D.C. 1978) (inaccurate publication regarding plaintiffs' drug use not actionable due to plaintiffs' long history of drug abuse and drug-related criminal activity). *See also* Cofield v. Advertiser Co., 486 So. 2d 434, 12 Media L. Rep. 2039 (Ala. 1986) (libel plaintiff, by virtue of life as habitual criminal, unlikely to recover more than nominal damages as matter of law); Cardillo v. Doubleday & Co., 518 F.2d 638 (2d Cir. 1975) (same). *But see* Brooks v. American Broadcasting Cos., 737 F. Supp. 431, 17 Media L. Rep. 2041 (N.D. Ohio 1990), *modified,* 932 F.2d 495, 18 Media L. Rep. 2121 (6th Cir. 1991) (summary judgment for defendant vacated and case remanded to determine factual issue of whether plaintiff was "libel-proof"); Liberty Lobby v. Anderson, 746 F.2d 1563, 1569, 11 Media L. Rep. 1001 (D.C. Cir. 1984) (declining to apply libel-proof doctrine), *vacated on other grounds,* 477 U.S. 242 (1986).

[604]*See, e.g.,* Guccione v. Hustler Magazine, 800 F.2d 298, 13 Media L. Rep. 1316 (2d Cir. 1986), *cert. denied,* 479 U.S. 1091 (1987) (publisher held libel-proof as matter of law with respect to reputation for adultery); Wynberg v. National Enquirer, 564 F. Supp. 924, 928, 8 Media L. Rep. 2398 (C.D. Cal. 1982) (plaintiff's past conduct, criminal convictions, and reputation for taking advantage of women generally rendered him libel-proof with respect to lack of truth, honesty, and fair dealing in personal and business matters).

[605]*See, e.g.,* Simmons Ford, Inc. v. Consumers Union of U.S., 516 F. Supp. 742, 17 Media L. Rep. 1776 (S.D.N.Y. 1981) (damage attributable to misstatement in defendants' article miniscule in light of nonactionable portions).

[606]*See, e.g.,* Pastet v. Jackson Newspapers, 17 Media L. Rep. 1776 (Conn. Super. Ct. 1990) (misstatement in newspaper that plaintiff killed six people not actionable because plaintiff convicted and sentenced to death for killing one person); Herbert v. Lando, 781 F.2d 298, 311, 12 Media L. Rep. 1593 (2d Cir. 1986), *cert. denied,* 476 U.S. 1182 (1986) (two inaccurate statements held not actionable in light of nine accurate statements and ample evidence supporting defendants' conclusion that plaintiff lied about reporting war crimes).

[607]111 S. Ct. 2419, 18 Media L. Rep. 2241 (1991).

[608]*Id.* at 2436.

[609]*Id. Compare* Haynes v. Alfred A. Knopf, Inc., 8 F.3d 1222, 1227, 21 Media L. Rep. 2161, 2165 (7th Cir. 1993) ("The rule of substantial truth is based on a recognition that falsehoods which do no incremental damage to the plaintiff's reputation do not injure the only interest that the law of defamation protects.") *with* Masson v. New Yorker Magazine, 960 F.2d 896, 899, 20 Media L. Rep. 1009, 1012 (9th Cir. 1992) ("we conclude that the incremental harm doctrine is not an element of California libel law").

[610]At the one extreme, some state statutes preclude a civil suit for damages altogether unless notice is given or a retraction demand is made. *See, e.g.,* FLA. STAT. §770.01 (1990); N.C. GEN. STAT. ANN. §§99-1,

damage from defamatory statements can be cured by a correction of the defamatory statements. In jurisdictions where no retraction statute is in effect, evidence of a retraction is admissible to mitigate damages.[611] The constitutionality of such statutes has often been upheld, although that is not always the case.[612]

Limits on the scope of correction statutes have generated considerable litigation.[613] Many such statutes contain strict time limits for the plaintiff and the defendant.[614]

Plaintiffs are usually obliged to specify the exact statements that they complain about.[615] Defendants' corrections usually have to be more or less as conspicuous as their original offending statements, although an apology is not always required.[616] A timely and adequate correction will usually reduce the plaintiff's damages substantially.[617]

§2.16(D) Damages for Loss of Political Office

Courts have been reluctant to allow damages to be recovered for the loss of a political office.[618] They have understandably been concerned about the difficulty of proving such claims, since elections can be won or lost for a variety of reasons.[619] They have also been concerned about the need to violate the sanctity of the secret ballot to resolve such questions.[620]

99-2 (Michie 1990); WIS. STAT. §895.05(2) (1989–90). Others limit a plaintiff's recovery to special damages. *See, e.g.,* CAL. CIV. CODE §48a (West 1982). Most statutes, however, limit the availability of punitive or exemplary damages to situations where a retraction demand has been refused or there is a finding of actual malice, or both. *See, e.g.,* KY. REV. STAT. ANN. §411.051(b) (Baldwin 1991); MICH. COMP. LAWS §600.2911(2)(b) (1991); NEV. REV. STAT. ANN. §41.336–.338 (Michie 1975); UTAH CODE ANN. §§45-2-1, 45-2-1.5 (Michie 1991). Other statutes merely view the retraction as evidence of mitigation. *See, e.g.,* TEX. CIV. PRAC. & REM. CODE ANN. §73.003 (West 1991). Some statutes offer special provisions for candidates for public office. *See, e.g.,* MISS. CODE ANN. §95-1-5 (1990); N.D. CENT. CODE §14-02-08 (1991).

[611]*See, e.g.,* Di Lorenzo v. New York News, 432 N.Y.S.2d 483, 6 Media L. Rep. 2136 (N.Y. App. Div. 1981); Coffman v. Spokane Chronicle Pub'g Co., 117 P. 596 (Wash. 1911).

[612]*Constitutional:* Davidson v. Rogers, 574 P.2d 624, 626, 3 Media L. Rep. 2030 (Or. 1978); Holden v. Pioneer Broadcasting Co., 365 P.2d 845, 848 (Or. 1961), *cert. denied and appeal dismissed,* 370 U.S. 157 (1962); Werner v. Southern Cal. Associated Newspapers, 216 P.2d 825, 828 (Cal. 1950).
Unconstitutional: Byers v. Meridian Printing Co., 95 N.E. 917, 919 (Ohio 1911); Madison v. Yunker, 589 P.2d 126, 131, 4 Media L. Rep. 1337 (Mont. 1978) (violates state constitution); Boswell v. Phoenix Newspapers, 730 P.2d 186, 13 Media L. Rep. 1785 (Ariz. 1986), *cert. denied,* 481 U.S. 1029 (1987) (retraction statute violates abrogation clause of state constitution).

[613]*See, e.g.,* Pridonoff v. Balokovich, 228 P.2d 6, 8 (Cal. 1951) (statute covers author of newspaper article); Ross v. Gore, 48 So. 2d 412, 413 (Fla. 1950) (editorial writer within statute). *See also* White v. Valenta, 44 Cal. Rptr. 241 (Cal. Ct. App. 1965) (slanderous remarks made during plaintiff's live commercial not within statute); Morris v. National Fed'n of the Blind, 13 Cal. Rptr. 336 (Cal. Ct. App. 1961) (magazine not within statute).

[614]Under the California statute, for example, the plaintiff must demand a correction within 20 days of knowledge of the offending publication; the defendant must then publish the correction within three weeks to receive the statutory protection. CAL. CIV. CODE §48a (West 1982). Other statutes have much shorter time limits. *See, e.g.,* FLA. STAT. §770.01 (1990) (retraction or correction must be within 10 days of *receipt of notice* to limit plaintiffs' recovery to actual damages); ALA. CODE §6-5-185 (Michie 1990) (retraction or correction must be within 10 days of offending *publication* to limit plaintiffs' recovery). The Connecticut statute specifies only that the retraction be made within a "reasonable time." *See* CONN. GEN. STAT. §52-237 (1990).

[615]Mahnke v. Northwest Pubns., 124 N.W.2d 411, 415 (Minn. 1963) (sufficient if publisher can determine words complained of); Kapellas v. Kofman, 1 Cal. 3d 20, 35, 459 P.2d 912 (Cal. 1969).

[616]*See, e.g.,* Nevada Indep. Broadcasting Corp. v. Allen, 664 P.2d 337, 345, 9 Media L. Rep. 1769 (1983) (must be "full and unequivocal" retraction); Ellis v. Brockton Pub'g Co., 84 N.E. 1018, 1019 (Mass. 1908) (retraction printed in conspicuous place sufficient).

[617]Webb v. Call Pub'g Co., 180 N.W. 263, 264–65 (Wis. 1920) (retraction material to decrease damages); O'Connor v. Field, 41 N.Y.S.2d 492, 495 (N.Y. App. Div. 1943) (correction of article mitigates damages).

[618]Southwestern Pub'g Co. v. Horsey, 230 F.2d 319, 323 (9th Cir. 1956).

[619]*Id. See also* Lynch v. Republic Pub'g Co., 243 P.2d 636 (Wash. 1952); Gough v. Tribune-Journal Co., 275 P.2d 663 (Idaho 1954); Fisher v. Larsen, 188 Cal. Rptr. 216 (Cal. Ct. App. 1982), *cert. denied,* 464 U.S. 959 (1983). However, some courts have allowed recovery for injury to political reputation. *See, e.g.,* Allen, 664 P.2d 337, 9 Media L. Rep. 1769.

[620]Bush v. Head, 97 P. 512 (Cal. 1908).

§2.16(E) Reforming the Damages Remedy

Various proposals have been offered to modify or supplement the damages remedy.[621] Whatever their merits, none is likely to be widely adopted, because state legislatures do not appear to be seriously interested in the problem, and the courts are not well suited to undertaking a wholesale revision of defamation laws.

§2.17 INJUNCTIVE RELIEF

Prior restraints are not available.[622]

§2.18 STATUTES OF LIMITATIONS

A variety of statutes of limitations apply to defamation actions, although most of them are quite short.[623] These short statutes of limitations cannot be avoided by relabeling a defamation claim as something else.[624]

An important question is when the statute of limitations begins to run. In most cases it is the date on which the publication was first made.[625] However, some jurisdictions have held that, where the publication is not something that the plaintiff is likely to learn of immediately (e.g., a letter to a third person), the statute does not begin to run until the plaintiff knew of the publication or should have learned of it through the exercise of reasonable diligence.[626] This rule of discovery does not apply where the publication is in the media; there, knowledge of the publication is presumed.[627]

The common law rule is that each defamatory publication creates a separate cause of action. Thus, each publication will have a different limitations period.[628]

Defamatory statements in the media are subject to the single publication rule.[629] Under that rule there is only one cause of action for each edition of a

---

[621] Franklin, *Good Names and Bad Law: A Critique of Libel Law and a Proposal*, 18 U.S.F. L. REV. 1 (1983); National Conference of Commissioners on Uniform State Laws, Proposed Uniform Defamation Act (1992); Annenberg Washington Program of Northwestern University, Proposal for the Reform of Libel Law (1988) (on file with the Annenberg Program of Northwestern University, Washington, D.C.).

[622] *See* Chapter 10, §10.9.

[623] Many jurisdictions have a one-year statute of limitations. *See, e.g.*, ARIZ. REV. STAT. ANN. §12-541(1) (1981); CAL. CIV. PROC. CODE §340(3) (West 1982); KAN. STAT. ANN. §60-514 (1976); NEB. REV. STAT. §25-208 (Reissue 1979); UTAH CODE ANN. §78-12-29 (1953); VA. CODE §8.01-248 (1977 Repl. Vol.). New Hampshire appears to have the longest limitations period. In that state, suit must be brought within three years of the date the cause of action accrued, or six years if the cause of action accrued prior to August 28, 1981. *See* N.H. REV. STAT. ANN. §508.4 (1990).

[624] *See, e.g.*, Evans v. Philadelphia Newspapers, 601 A.2d 330, 19 Media L. Rep. 1868 (Pa. Super. Ct. 1991); Lashlee v. Sumner, 570 F.2d 107 (6th Cir. 1978).

[625] *See, e.g.*, Rinsley v. Brandt, 446 F. Supp. 850, 852 (D. Kan. 1977); Spears Free Clinic & Hosp. v. Maier, 261 P.2d 489, 491 (Colo. 1953).

[626] *See, e.g.*, Sears, Roebuck and Co. v. Ulman, 412 A.2d 1240, 1243 (Md. 1980). *But see* Patterson v. Renstrom, 195 N.W.2d 193, 194 (Neb. 1972) (ignorance of defamatory letters does not toll statute); Hawkins v. Justin, 311 N.W.2d 465, 466 (Mich. Ct. App. 1981) (knowledge of defamation irrelevant); Rainey v. Shaffer, 456 N.E.2d 1328, 1330 (Ohio Ct. App. 1983) (statute runs from date of slander whether plaintiff is aware of it or not).

[627] *See, e.g.*, Flynn v. Associated Press, 519 N.E.2d 1304, 15 Media L. Rep. 1265 (Mass. 1988) (statute runs from date of publication).

[628] Dorr v. C.B. Johnson, Inc., 660 P.2d 517, 520 (Colo. Ct. App. 1983); Walker v. Associated Press, 417 P.2d 486, 488 (Colo. 1966).

[629] *See supra* §2.6(C).

newspaper, book, magazine, or television or radio broadcast.[630] The limitations period begins to run upon dissemination of the publication or broadcast to a reasonable number of people for whom the publication was intended.[631] The date placed on the publication is not controlling; it is the actual date that the first general publication occurs that controls.[632]

§2.19 CONFLICTS OF LAWS

Where defamatory material is circulated in more than one state, choice of law questions can arise with respect to myriad issues.[633] The possible approaches are just as numerous.[634]

Many jurisdictions retain the traditional tort lex loci delecti rule, applying the law of the place where the injury occurred.[635] In a multistate defamation action, this may be the law of the plaintiff's domicile state, where it is presumed that the harm to reputation is the greatest, but this is not always the case.[636] Other states apply the "most significant relationship" test,[637] holding that the law of the state with the most significant relationship to the parties controls.[638]

These approaches focus predominantly on plaintiffs' interests. In contrast, California has adopted a "governmental interest" approach, applying the substantive law of the state whose policies would be most furthered by deciding the issues involved.[639] If no state is found to have a strong governmental interest in the litigation, the law of the forum is applied.[640]

Choice of law issues are often significant in determining what state's statute of limitations applies. Where one state's statute of limitations has expired, a plaintiff may be able to successfully bring a suit in another state with a longer limitations period.[641] Under traditional choice of law rules, the forum state's law governs such procedural matters.[642]

---

[630]*Id.*
[631]Morrissey v. William Morrow & Co., 739 F.2d 962, 967, 10 Media L. Rep. 2305 (4th Cir. 1984), *cert. denied*, 469 U.S. 1216 (1985).
[632]*Id.* at 967–68, 10 Media L. Rep. at 2305.
[633]RESTATEMENT (SECOND) OF CONFLICT OF LAWS §§149–50, cmt. b (1971). These issues include but are not limited to (1) whether or not a communication constitutes libel or slander, (2) whether proof of special damages is necessary, and (3) what matters constitute defenses or mitigation. *Id.*
[634]Prosser, *Interstate Publication,* 51 MICH. L. REV. 959, 971–78 (1953). *See generally* Annot., *Conflict of Laws With Respect to the "Single Publication" Rule as to Defamation, Invasion of Privacy, or Similar Tort,* 58 A.L.R.2d 650 (1958).
[635]*See, e.g.,* Sexton v. Ryder Truck Rental, 320 N.W.2d 843 (Mich. 1982) (lex loci applies unless Michigan has strong interest in applying Michigan law); Taylor v. Murray, 204 S.E.2d 747 (Ga. 1974) (applying substantive law of place where right accrues).
[636]For example, a plaintiff may be better known in another state, or if a plaintiff is a corporation, its business reputation may be harmed in a state other than the one that is its principal place of business. RESTATEMENT (SECOND) OF CONFLICT OF LAWS, *supra* note 633, at §150, cmts. e, f.
[637]*Id.* §150(1).
[638]In certain cases this may also be the law of the plaintiff's domicile. *See, e.g.,* Levine v. CMP Pubns., 738 F.2d 660, 10 Media L. Rep. 2337 (5th Cir. 1984), *reh'g denied*, 753 F.2d 1341 (5th Cir. 1985); Zimmerman v. Board of Pubns., 598 F. Supp. 1002, 11 Media L. Rep. 1545 (D. Colo. 1984).
[639]*See* Fleury v. Harper & Row, Pubrs., 698 F.2d 1022, 9 Media L. Rep. 1200 (9th Cir.), *cert. denied*, 464 U.S. 846 (1983); In re Yagman, 796 F.2d 1165, 13 Media L. Rep. 1545 (9th Cir. 1986), *cert. denied*, 484 U.S. 963 (1987).
[640]*Fleury,* 698 F.2d at 1025.
[641]*See* Keeton v. Hustler Magazine, 465 U.S. 770, 10 Media L. Rep. 1405 (1984).
[642]*See, e.g.,* Wood v. Hustler Magazine, 736 F.2d 1084, 10 Media L. Rep. 2113 (5th Cir. 1984), *cert. denied*, 469 U.S. 1107 (1985).

§2.20 PERSONAL JURISDICTION

Beginning with the Fifth Circuit's decision in *New York Times Co. v. Connor*, a body of case law developed holding that personal jurisdiction in cases involving First Amendment rights was limited by due process *and* First Amendment considerations.[643] The case law was by no means unanimous,[644] and the Restatement (Second) of Conflict of Laws did not take a position on whether the First Amendment affected the personal jurisdiction analysis.[645]

In two decisions decided on the same day, the Supreme Court made clear that the First Amendment is to play no role in the determination of such issues. In *Calder v. Jones*,[646] the Court considered a libel action brought in California by a California resident against the *National Enquirer*, a Florida corporation with its principal place of business in Florida; a *National Enquirer* reporter who wrote the offending article and who was a resident of Florida; and a *National Enquirer* editor who edited the article and who was also a resident of Florida.[647] The *National Enquirer*'s circulation was over 5 million copies, of which over 600,000 were distributed in California, making it the state with the largest circulation.[648]

The Court held that there was personal jurisdiction over all three defendants because "California is the focal point both of the story and of the harm suffered."[649] Accordingly, jurisdiction was proper because the effects of the defendants' conduct in California was to be anticipated.[650] "Under the circumstances, [the defendants] must 'reasonably anticipate being haled into court [in California]' to answer for the truth of the statements made in their article."[651]

The Court rejected "the suggestion that First Amendment concerns enter in the jurisdictional analysis,"[652] holding that "[t]he infusion of such concerns would needlessly complicate" the already imprecise jurisdictional inquiry; that constitutional limitations on substantive defamation law already protect against any chilling effect; and that to introduce such concerns at the jurisdictional stage would be a form of double counting in which the Court had previously refused to engage.[653]

In *Keeton v. Hustler Magazine*,[654] the Court considered a libel action brought in New Hampshire by a resident of New York against *Hustler Magazine*, an

---

[643] New York Times Co. v. Connor, 365 F.2d 567, 572 (5th Cir. 1966).

[644] *First Amendment Applicable:* Cox Enters. v. Holt, 678 F.2d 936, 937–38, 8 Media L. Rep. 1701, *modified on other grounds,* 691 F.2d 989 (11th Cir. 1982); McCabe v. Kevin Jenkins & Assocs., 531 F. Supp. 648, 654–55, 8 Media L. Rep. 1802 (E.D. Pa. 1982); Gonzales v. Atlanta Constitution, 4 Media L. Rep. 2146 (N.D. Ill. 1979).

First Amendment Not Applicable: Church of Scientology v. Adams, 584 F.2d 893, 899, 4 Media L. Rep. 1986 (9th Cir. 1978); Anselmi v. Denver Post, 552 F.2d 316, 324, 2 Media L. Rep. 1530 (10th Cir.), *cert. denied,* 432 U.S. 911 (1977); Buckley v. New York Post Corp., 373 F.2d 175, 182–83 (2d Cir. 1967).

[645] RESTATEMENT (SECOND) OF CONFLICT OF LAWS, *supra* note 633, at §§36, 37.

[646] 465 U.S. 783, 10 Media L. Rep. 1401 (1984).

[647] *Id.* at 785–86.

[648] *Id.* at 785.

[649] *Id.* at 789. The Court also noted that each defendant had to be evaluated separately on the basis of its own conduct. *Id.* at 790.

[650] *Id.*

[651] 465 U.S. at 790 (quoting World-Wide Volkswagen Corp. v. Woodson, 444 U.S. 286, 297 (1980)). The Court declined to decide whether the reporter's activities in California were sufficient to justify the assertion of jurisdiction over him. *Id.* at 810 n.6.

[652] *Id.* at 790.

[653] *Id.*

[654] 465 U.S. 770, 10 Media L. Rep. 1405 (1984).

Ohio corporation with its principal place of business in California.[655] *Hustler Magazine* sold between ten and fifteen hundred copies in New Hampshire each month.[656]

The Court held that there was personal jurisdiction over *Hustler Magazine* because "regular monthly sales of thousands of magazines cannot by any stretch of the imagination be characterized as random, isolated, or fortuitous."[657] The Court rejected each of the Court of Appeals' reasons for holding there was no jurisdiction.

First, the Court found that New Hampshire's interest in redressing injuries that occur there, even injuries to nonresidents; its interest in seeing that its residents are not misled by false and defamatory statements; and its interest in cooperating with other states in the application of the single publication rule[658] all justified requiring *Hustler Magazine* to appear in court in New Hampshire.[659]

Second, the Court held that just because New Hampshire had the longest statute of limitations in the country,[660] which made it the only jurisdiction where Keeton's claim was not time barred,[661] the state was not deprived of jurisdiction over *Hustler Magazine*.[662] Choice of law issues, like the applicable statute of limitations, did not affect the jurisdictional analysis.[663]

Third, while it was true that the plaintiff's contacts with New Hampshire were minimal, the Court refused to require the plaintiff to demonstrate her contacts with the forum,[664] noting that it had never required a plaintiff to make such a showing.[665]

As it had in *Calder*, the Court also held that the First Amendment is not relevant to the jurisdictional analysis[666] and that jurisdiction over each editor and reporter must be judged independently of jurisdiction over a publication.[667]

The results in *Calder* and *Keeton* are not very startling. Both publications had quite substantial sales in the jurisdictions in which they were sued. If that was not enough to sustain personal jurisdiction, then about the only place suit could have been brought would have been at the publications' principal places of business. That has never been the Supreme Court's view of personal jurisdiction under the Due Process Clause of the Fourteenth Amendment.

Even after *Calder* and *Keeton,* some limits still exist on personal jurisdiction. Some states do not exercise their jurisdiction to the full extent that is constitutional, choosing not to exercise jurisdiction based on the circulation of out-of-state publications.[668] In addition, where the out-of-state publication's

---

[655]*Id.* at 772.
[656]*Id.*
[657]*Id.* at 774.
[658]*See* the discussion *supra* §2.6(C).
[659]465 U.S. at 774–75.
[660]*Id.* at 773 (six years). New Hampshire has reduced its limitations period to three years for causes of action accruing *after* August 28, 1981. N.H. REV. STAT. ANN. §508:4 (Supp. 1983).
[661]465 U.S. at 773.
[662]*Id.*
[663]*Id.* at 778.
[664]*Id.* at 779–80.
[665]*Id.* at 779.
[666]465 U.S. at 780 n.12.
[667]*Id.* at 781 n.13.
[668]CONN. GEN. STAT. ANN. §52-596 (West Supp. 1970); GA. CODE ANN. §24-113.1(b) (1970); MINN. STAT. ANN. §543.19(1)(d)(3) (West Supp. 1984); N.Y. CIV. PRAC. LAW §302(a)(3) (McKinney 1972).

circulation in the forum is small, *Calder* and *Keeton* do not prevent a finding under the Due Process Clause that there is no personal jurisdiction.[669]

§2.21 MOTIONS TO DISMISS AND SUMMARY JUDGMENT

After the constitutional actual malice rule was created, a line of cases developed indicating that the summary disposition of defamation cases before trial, especially via motions for summary judgment, was the rule, not the exception.[670] These cases are based on the rationale that, even if a plaintiff prevailed, the expense of litigation could chill a defendant's exercise of his or her First Amendment rights.[671]

This rule has been questioned by the Supreme Court in dictum, although the Court did not explicitly reject it.[672] As a result, a number of courts then held that summary dispositions in First Amendment cases were neither favored nor disfavored.[673]

Other courts have adhered to the view that the summary disposition of cases invoking First Amendment rights is still favored.[674] Still other courts, while neither favoring nor disfavoring summary dispositions as a procedural matter, have noted that when a plaintiff must prove constitutional actual malice, it must be done by "clear and convincing" evidence; that this is a hard standard for a plaintiff to meet; and that, as a result, summary dispositions will often be appropriate.[675]

The Supreme Court has now resolved the issue by adopting this latter course,[676] although state courts sometimes follow their own rules.[677]

§2.22 COUNTERSUITS BY THE MEDIA AND RECOVERY OF ATTORNEYS' FEES

In recent years, the media have become more aggressive about seeking relief for what they view as groundless lawsuits meant only to harass and

---

[669]*See, e.g.,* Evangelize China Fellowship, Inc. v. Evangelize China Fellowship, 146 Cal. App. 3d 440, 449, 194 Cal. Rptr. 240 (Cal. Ct. App. 1983) (600 copies out of 8,500 per month).

[670]*See, e.g.,* Bon Air Hotel v. Time, Inc., 426 F.2d 858, 864–65 (5th Cir. 1970); Fadell v. Minneapolis Star & Tribune Co., 557 F.2d 107, 109, 2 Media L. Rep. 2198 (7th Cir. 1977), *cert. denied,* 434 U.S. 966 (1977); Adams v. Frontier Broadcasting Co., 555 P.2d 556, 566 & n.7, 2 Media L. Rep. 1166 (Wyo. 1976).

[671]Washington Post Co. v. Keogh, 365 F.2d 965, 968 (D.C. Cir. 1966), *cert. denied,* 385 U.S. 1011 (1967).

[672]Hutchinson v. Proxmire, 443 U.S. 111, 120 n.9, 5 Media L. Rep. 1279 (1979); *see also* Calder v. Jones, 465 U.S. 783, 791, 10 Media L. Rep. 1401 (1984) (*Hutchinson* implies that no special rules apply for summary judgments).

[673]Yiamouyiannis v. Consumers Union of U.S., 619 F.2d 932, 940, 6 Media L. Rep. 1065 (2d Cir. 1980), *cert. denied,* 449 U.S. 839 (1980) ("neutral approach"); Schultz v. Newsweek, 668 F.2d 911, 917, 7 Media L. Rep. 2552 (6th Cir. 1982) (same).

[674]Lauderback v. American Broadcasting Cos., 741 F.2d 193, 198, 10 Media L. Rep. 2241 (8th Cir. 1984), *cert. denied,* 469 U.S. 1190 (1985) ("may be 'particularly appropriate' in action for defamation"); Schuster v. U.S. News & World Report, 602 F.2d 850, 854–55, 5 Media L. Rep. 1773 (8th Cir. 1979) (noting that Supreme Court has said that cost of defending protracted lawsuit can chill First Amendment rights).

[675]Fadell v. Minneapolis Star & Tribune Co., 425 F. Supp. 1075, 1086, 2 Media L. Rep. 1961 (N.D. Ind. 1976), *aff'd,* 557 F.2d 107, 2 Media L. Rep. 2198 (7th Cir. 1977), *cert. denied,* 434 U.S. 966 (1977) ("absent proof [of actual malice] with 'convincing clarity' summary judgment must be granted to the defendant") (quoting New York Times Co. v. Sullivan, 376 U.S. 254 (1964)); Grzelak v. Calumet Pub'g Co., 543 F.2d 579, 581, 583 (7th Cir. 1975).

[676]Anderson v. Liberty Lobby, 477 U.S. 242, 255–56, 12 Media L. Rep. 2297 (1986).

[677]*Compare* Casso v. Brand, 776 S.W.2d 551, 16 Media L. Rep. 1929 (Tex. 1989) *with* Jones v. Palmer Communications, 440 N.W.2d 884, 16 Media L. Rep. 2137 (Iowa 1989).

intimidate them. Various theories of relief have been pursued against plaintiffs and their attorneys with varying degrees of success: malicious prosecution,[678] abuse of process,[679] Federal Rule of Civil Procedure 11,[680] 28 U.S.C. Section 1927,[681] 42 U.S.C. Section 1983,[682] bad faith,[683] the federal Constitution,[684] and state statutes.[685] However, until there is a fundamental change in the basic American rule that, absent a contract or statute, a party usually has to bear its own legal fees, no truly effective relief is in sight.

§2.23 RELATED CAUSES OF ACTION

In defamation suits other causes of action are frequently alleged, including intentional interference with contractual relations, prima facie tort, intentional infliction of emotional distress, negligent infliction of emotional distress, and invasion of privacy.[686] Where these related claims are based on the same derogatory speech as the defamation claim, they are often dismissed as surplusage that simply duplicates the defamation claim and attempts to avoid the common law, statutory, and constitutional restrictions on defamation claims.[687] In other cases, these claims have been subjected to the same restrictions as those for defamation actions and have been dismissed on that basis.[688]

---

[678]*See, e.g.*, Peisner v. Detroit Free Press, 242 N.W.2d 775 (Mich. Ct. App. 1976) (claim for malicious prosecution available after termination of prior suit in favor of defendant, but not as counterclaim in same action).

[679]*See, e.g.*, Edmonds v. Delta Democrat Pub'g Co., 93 So. 2d 171 (Miss. 1957) (defendant newspaper counterclaimed for abuse of process); *Peisner,* 242 N.W.2d 775 (same).

[680]*See, e.g.*, Willis v. Capital Cities Communications, 13 Media L. Rep. 1683 (D. Kan. 1986) (granted Rule 11 sanctions against plaintiff for frivolous filing of libel suit). *See also* Harrison v. Luse, 760 F. Supp. 1394 (D. Colo.) (pursuing defamation action with knowledge of statute of limitations defense warrants Rule 11 and Colorado statutory sanctions), *aff'd without opinion,* 951 F.2d 1259 (10th Cir. 1991).

[681]*See, e.g.*, National Ass'n of Gov't Employees v. National Fed'n of Fed. Employees, 844 F.2d 216 (5th Cir. 1988) (§1927 sanctions disallowed because court had repeatedly urged parties in defamation action to settle); LaRouche v. National Broadcasting Co., 780 F.2d 1134, 12 Media L. Rep. 1585 (4th Cir.), *cert. denied,* 479 U.S. 818 (1986) (denial of sanctions upheld); *Luse,* 760 F. Supp. 1394 (denied §1927 sanctions but upheld Rule 11 sanctions).

[682]*See, e.g.*, Jungherr v. San Francisco Unified Sch. Dist. Bd. of Educ., 923 F.2d 743 (9th Cir.), *cert. denied,* 112 S. Ct. 51 (1991) (institution of unsuccessful defamation action by local board of education president did not provide basis for action by defendant under 42 U.S.C. §1983).

[683]*See, e.g.*, Blanton v. Equitable Bank Nat'l Ass'n, 485 A.2d 694 (Md. Ct. Spec. App. 1985) (applying Maryland statute that awards costs and reasonable attorneys' fees for initiation, maintenance, or defense of lawsuit in bad faith); Nemeroff v. Abelson, 704 F.2d 652, 9 Media L. Rep. 1427 (2d Cir. 1983) (even under American rule, costs of litigation and attorneys' fees may be recovered by prevailing defendant if action is brought in bad faith).

[684]*See, e.g.*, Laxalt v. McClatchy, 622 F. Supp. 737, 12 Media L. Rep. 1377 (D. Nev. 1985) (dismissed defendants' federal constitution counterclaim against U.S. senator who brought defamation action on grounds of insufficient evidence that senator had acted under color of federal authority).

[685]*See, e.g.*, Kahn v. Bower, 284 Cal. Rptr. 244, 19 Media L. Rep. 1236 (Cal. Ct. App. 1991) (sanctions under CAL. CIV. PROC. CODE §128.5 denied where no indication on record that plaintiff in defamation action had acted in bad faith); Planned Protective Serv. v. Gorton, 245 Cal. Rptr. 790 (Cal. Ct. App. 1988) (limits application of CAL. CIV. PROC. CODE §1021.7 to peace officers and agencies). *But see* Kahn v. Bower, 284 Cal. Rptr. 244, 19 Media L. Rep. 1236 (Cal. Ct. App. 1991) (scope of §1021.7 remains open question).

[686]For a discussion of the four invasion of privacy torts, see Chapters 3–6.

[687]*See, e.g.*, Dworkin v. Hustler Magazine, 867 F.2d 1188, 1193 nn.2 & 3, 16 Media L. Rep. 1113 (9th Cir.), *cert. denied,* 493 U.S. 812 (1989); Boyles v. Mid-Florida Television Corp., 431 So. 2d 627, 636 (Fla. Dist. Ct. App. 1983), *aff'd,* 467 So. 2d 282, 11 Media L. Rep. 1774 (Fla. 1985). *See also* Flynn v. Higham, 197 Cal. Rptr. 145, 148 (Cal. Ct. App. 1983); Grimes v. Carter, 50 Cal Rptr. 808, 813 (Cal. Ct. App. 1966).

[688]Hustler Magazine v. Falwell, 485 U.S. 46, 14 Media L. Rep. 2281 (1988) (actual malice rule applied to intentional infliction of emotional distress claim); Fellows v. National Enquirer, 42 Cal. 3d 234, 13 Media L. Rep. 1305 (Cal. 1986) (libel per quod statute applies to false light claim); Blatty v. New York Times Co., 728 P.2d 1177, 13 Media L. Rep. 1928 (Cal. 1986), *cert. denied,* 485 U.S. 934 (1988) (of and concerning rule applies to intentional interference claim); Redco Corp. v. CBS, Inc., 758 F.2d 970, 973, 11 Media L.

The former approach is more sensible. The only purpose of such claims is to attempt to avoid the common law, statutory, and constitutional restraints on defamation actions simply by changing the title of a claim from defamation to some other tort. There is no reason to allow this; it only results in protracted and unproductive litigation over whether each of the rules in defamation actions applies to these duplicative claims.

§2.24 CRIMINAL LIBEL

In *Garrison v. Louisiana,* the Supreme Court held that where a defendant criticizes the official conduct of public officials, constitutional actual malice must be shown before there can be liability for criminal defamation.[689] The Court also held that truth is an absolute defense in such actions.[690] Finally, the Court suggested that criminal defamation statutes cannot be upheld unless they are necessary to prevent a clear and present danger of breach of the peace.[691]

Criminal libel statutes have also been struck down by the Supreme Court because they are often so vague that they give officials wide discretion to enforce such laws and thus punish unpopular speech.[692]

§2.25 SEARCHING APPELLATE REVIEW

In *New York Times Co. v. Sullivan,* the Supreme Court said that appellate courts "must 'make an independent review of the whole record' so as to assure ourselves that the judgment does not constitute a forbidden intrusion on the field of free expression."[693] The Court then applied this rule to hold that the plaintiff had failed to prove that the defendants acted with constitutional actual malice.[694] Numerous Supreme Court cases have repeated this rule in defamation cases.[695]

In *Bose Corp. v. Consumers Union of the United States,*[696] the Supreme Court was confronted with the argument that Federal Rule of Civil Procedure 52(a), which provides that "[f]indings of fact shall not be set aside unless clearly erroneous," conflicts with this rule. The Court held that, in an actual malice case, Rule 52(a) is not controlling; judges must conduct an independent review of the record to determine whether actual malice was shown with convincing clarity.[697] However, *Bose* left the exact scope of independent review uncertain.

Rep. 1861 (3d Cir.), *cert. denied,* 474 U.S. 843 (1985) (where defamation claims dismissed because statements were true or opinions, intentional interference with contractual relations claim also not actionable).

[689]379 U.S. 64, 78, 1 Media L. Rep. 1548, 1553 (1964). *Accord* People v. Ryan, 806 P.2d 935, 19 Media L. Rep. 1074 (Colo.), *cert. denied,* 112 S. Ct. 177 (1991).

[690]379 U.S. at 70–73, 1 Media L. Rep. at 1550–52.

[691]*Id.* at 69–70, 1 Media L. Rep. at 1550.

[692]*See* Ashton v. Kentucky, 384 U.S. 195, 200 (1966) and cases cited therein.

[693]376 U.S. 254, 285, 1 Media L. Rep. 1527, 1546 (1964) (quoting Edwards v. South Carolina, 372 U.S. 229, 235 (1963)).

[694]*Id.* at 285–86, 1 Media L. Rep. at 1527.

[695]Greenbelt Coop. Pub'g Ass'n v. Bresler, 398 U.S. 6, 11, 1 Media L. Rep. 1589 (1970); St. Amant v. Thompson, 390 U.S. 727, 732–33, 1 Media L. Rep. 1586 (1968); Time, Inc. v. Pape, 401 U.S. 279, 284, 1 Media L. Rep. 1627 (1971); Monitor Patriot Co. v. Roy, 401 U.S. 265, 277, 1 Media L. Rep. 1619 (1971).

[696]466 U.S. 485, 10 Media L. Rep. 1625 (1984).

[697]*Id.* at 514. The Court reversed the trial court's determination that actual malice had been shown. *Id.* at 511–12.

The Supreme Court again confronted this issue in *Harte-Hanks Communications v. Connaughton*,[698] where it held that a "reviewing court must consider the factual record in full."[699] According to the Court, the fact finder's (usually a jury's) credibility determinations ("historical facts") are to be reviewed under Rule 52(a)'s "clearly erroneous" standard, but the appellate court must still determine for itself the "constitutional fact" of whether there was actual malice.[700] The Court then relied on the facts that it concluded the jury must have found, rather than those it could have found, to find that actual malice had been shown.[701]

Connaughton did not fully resolve the question of precisely what scope of appellate review is proper. Some cases conclude that the scope of review is narrow;[702] others view it as quite broad.[703] The independent review test has also been applied to issues other than actual malice.[704]

§2.26 STATISTICS ON THE OUTCOMES OF DEFAMATION LITIGATION

Surveys examining the outcomes of defamation cases indicate that plaintiffs prevail more often at trial, while defendants are far more successful at securing pretrial relief, e.g., summary judgment or appellate relief in the form of a reversal or reduction in damages.[705] During 1980–1991, 189 of the 289 cases that went to trial (65 percent) ended in a verdict for the plaintiff.[706] Of those, 58 percent resulted in punitive damages, 36 percent resulted in awards over $1 million, and 5 percent resulted in awards over $10 million.[707] On appeal, however, only 30 percent of those judgments were affirmed as entered.[708]

Still, statistics covering the last few years show definite trends. Comparing 1980–1989 to 1990–1991, there has been no significant change in who wins jury trials.[709] However, average jury awards skyrocketed from $200,000 to $9 million.[710] While the results of many appeals were not yet available for cases tried in 1990–1991, many multimillion-dollar awards were settled for undisclosed amounts.[711]

---

[698] 491 U.S. 657, 16 Media L. Rep. 1881 (1989).
[699] *Id.* at 688.
[700] *Id.* at 688–89.
[701] *Id.* at 689–90.
[702] *See, e.g.,* Hinerman v. Daily Gazette Co., 423 S.E.2d 560, 20 Media L. Rep. 2169 (W. Va. 1992); Ball v. E.W. Scripps Co., 801 S.W.2d 684, 18 Media L. Rep. 1545 (Ky. 1990), *cert. denied,* 499 U.S. 976 (1991).
[703] *See, e.g.,* Newton v. National Broadcasting Co., 913 F.2d 652, 18 Media L. Rep. 1001 (9th Cir. 1990), *cert. denied,* 112 S. Ct. 192 (1991); Live Oak Pub'g Co. v. Cohagan, 234 Cal. App. 3d 1277 (Cal. Ct. App. 1991).
[704] Rouch v. Enquirer & News of Battle Creek, 487 N.W.2d 205, 211–12, 20 Media L. Rep. 2265 (Mich. 1992), *cert. denied,* 113 S. Ct. 1401 (1993); Locricchio v. Evening News Ass'n, 476 N.W.2d 112, 20 Media L. Rep. 1065 (Mich. 1991), *cert. denied,* 112 S. Ct. 1267 (1992) (falsity; private figure plaintiff).
[705] *See, e.g.,* Franklin, *Suing Media for Libel: A Litigation Study,* AM. BAR FOUND. RES. J. 795, 804 (1981); Franklin, *Winners and Losers and Why: A Study of Defamation Litigation,* AM. BAR FOUND. RES. J. 455, 494–96 (1980).
[706] *See* Libel Defense Resource Center, Bull. Special Issue B, at p.6 (July 31, 1992) (available from the Libel Defense Resource Center, New York, N.Y.).
[707] *Id.* at 8.
[708] *Id.* at 12 (data available for 1980–1989 only).
[709] *Id.* at 4.
[710] *Id.*
[711] *Id.* at 5.

Chapter 3

FALSE LIGHT

§3.1 Introduction

A member of the privacy family by birth,[1] false light has grown into the cousin of defamation. Although false light is still technically classified as an invasion of privacy action, its development has been so influenced by defamation principles that it has become almost identical to defamation.[2] Accordingly, in analyzing the tort of false light, this chapter focuses on the similarities and differences between false light and defamation. It also assumes that the reader is familiar with the basic principles of defamation.[3]

§3.2 Definition of False Light

Like many other legal concepts, false light may be easier to recognize than to define.[4] The Restatement (Second) of Torts states that "[t]he interest protected . . . is the interest of the individual in not being made to appear before the public in an objectionable false light or false position, or in other words, otherwise than as he is."[5] One of the few formulations that avoids defining false light by reference to itself provides that "[t]he essence of the term 'false light' is a major misrepresentation of a person's character, history, activities or beliefs which places that person in an objectionable false position before the party or parties to whom it is communicated."[6]

While false light claims arise in a variety of contexts, probably the most common type of false light claim involves the use of a plaintiff's photograph or likeness to illustrate an article, book, or broadcast. When the juxtaposition

---

[1]The history of the four invasion or privacy torts is discussed in Chapter 4. For a discussion of the other three branches of privacy, which often raise issues like those discussed in this chapter, see Chapters 4, 5, and 6.

[2]Crump v. Beckley Newspapers, 320 S.E.2d 70, 87, 10 Media L. Rep. 2225, 2237 (W. Va. 1983) ("courts and commentators have consistently treated false light privacy claims in essentially the same manner as they have treated defamation").

[3]*See generally* Chapter 2. Most of the issues in this chapter have counterparts in Chapter 2, which the reader should consult.

[4]Jacobellis v. Ohio, 378 U.S. 184, 197 (1964) (Stewart, J., concurring) (hard-core pornography may be "indefinable . . . . [b]ut I know it when I see it").

[5]Restatement (Second) of Torts §652E, cmt. b (1977) (hereinafter *Restatement (Second)*).

[6]Renwick v. News & Observer Pub'g Co., 312 S.E.2d 405, 415, 10 Media L. Rep. 1443, 1451 (N.C.) (Meyer, J., concurring in part and dissenting in part), *cert. denied,* 469 U.S. 858 (1984).

creates a false and usually unfavorable impression of the plaintiff, as where the photo of an honest taxi driver is used to illustrate an article about unscrupulous, cheating taxi drivers,[7] false light claims have been upheld.[8]

§3.3 DEFAMATION AND FALSE LIGHT COMPARED

False light arose to fill what was perceived to be a gap in the protection offered by defamation.[9] The main difference between defamation and false light turns on the interest sought to be protected: defamation is designed primarily to recompense injury to reputation, while false light is intended to afford recovery for injury to feelings.[10] While statements actionable as defamation are normally actionable as false light,[11] a false light action can sometimes exist even if a statement is not defamatory.[12]

§3.4 THE UNEASY COEXISTENCE OF DEFAMATION AND FALSE LIGHT

Whether there should be a separate claim for false light has been a matter of substantial debate, especially because of the enormous overlap of defamation and false light.[13] Many courts have recognized such a cause of action,[14] reasoning that (1) false light allows a court to ignore some of the limitations on defamation claims that may have no sound policy basis, e.g., the distinction between libel and slander; and (2) false light, by providing broader protection than defamation, "rests on an awareness that people who are made to seem pathetic or ridiculous may be shunned" even though they do not have a defamation claim.[15]

---

[7]Peay v. Curtis Pub'g Co., 78 F. Supp. 305 (D.D.C. 1948).

[8]Leverton v. Curtis Pub'g Co., 192 F.2d 974 (3d Cir. 1951) (affirming jury verdict for plaintiff on false light theory where photo of plaintiff being helped to her feet after almost being hit by car through no fault of her own used to illustrate article on pedestrian carelessness and traffic accidents). See also infra note 32 and accompanying text.

[9]In his treatise on torts, Dean Prosser wrote:
There has been a good deal of overlapping of defamation in the false light cases, and it seems clear that either action, or both, will very often lie. The privacy cases do go considerably beyond the narrow limits of defamation, and no doubt have succeeded in affording a needed remedy in a good many instances not covered by the other tort. But the question may well be raised, and is still unanswered, whether this branch of the tort is not capable of swallowing up and engulfing the whole law of defamation; and whether there is any false libel printed, for example, in a newspaper, which cannot be redressed upon the alternative ground.
W. PROSSER, THE LAW OF TORTS §117, at 813 (4th ed. 1971).

[10]Crump v. Beckley Newspapers, 320 S.E.2d 70, 87, 10 Media L. Rep. 2225, 2237 (W. Va. 1983) ("privacy actions involve injuries to emotions and mental suffering, while defamation actions involve injury to reputation"); Brink v. Griffith, 396 P.2d 793, 796 (Wash. 1964). However, in a defamation case, damages for emotional distress are also available (see Chapter 2, §2.16), while in a false light case, the injury to feelings may largely or exclusively arise from the unfavorable aspects of the publication. 396 P.2d at 796–97. Thus, the difference between the two torts is not great, assuming that it exists at all.

[11]PROSSER, supra note 9; Brink, 396 P.2d at 797.

[12]Cibenko v. Worth Pubrs., 510 F. Supp. 761, 7 Media L. Rep. 1298 (D.N.J. 1981) (prerequisite for false light invasion of privacy is falsity, but matter publicized need not be defamatory); McCall v. Courier-Journal & Louisville Times Co., 623 S.W.2d 882, 888 n.9, 7 Media L. Rep. 2118, 2122 n.9 (Ky. 1981), cert. denied, 456 U.S. 975 (1982) (same); Machleder v. Diaz, 801 F.2d 46, 57–58, 13 Media L. Rep. 1369, 1377 (2d Cir. 1986), cert. denied, 479 U.S. 1088 (1987) (same); RESTATEMENT (SECOND), supra note 5.

[13]See supra §3.3.

[14]See, e.g., McCall, 623 S.W.2d at 887–88, 7 Media L. Rep. at 2122–23; McCormack v. Oklahoma Pub'g Co., 613 P.2d 737, 739–41 (Okla. 1980). For an annually updated list of such jurisdictions, see Libel Defense Resource Center 50-State Survey—Current Developments in Media Libel and Invasion of Privacy (available from Libel Defense Resource Center, New York, N.Y.); see also Annot., False Light Invasion of Privacy—Cognizability and Elements, 57 A.L.R.4th 22 (1987).

[15]Douglass v. Hustler Magazine, 769 F.2d 1128, 1134, 11 Media L. Rep. 2264, 2267 (7th Cir. 1985), cert. denied, 475 U.S. 1094 (1986).

Even in jurisdictions where false light is recognized, however, it often has been subjected to a number of restrictions that largely render it nugatory. These restrictions are primarily of two sorts. Some courts hold that if there is a defamation claim based on the same publication, a false light claim is merely duplicative and should be dismissed as surplusage.[16] Other courts allow a false light claim to exist even if it is based on the same publication as the defamation claim but apply to the false light claim all the restrictions that apply to the defamation claim.[17] Either approach largely vitiates a false light claim.

More recently, some courts have refused to even recognize a false light cause of action,[18] although this trend is not universal.[19] These courts have reasoned that false light poses a severe threat to First Amendment values and that it wastes judicial resources because its recognition raises a host of new legal issues that the courts must address (especially whether some or all of the rules in defamation law apply to false light) without any offsetting gain, because most of the interests that false light is designed to protect are already protected by defamation.[20]

Academic reaction to false light has followed a similar path. False light initially received a largely favorable response from commentators.[21] More recently, however, false light has been subjected to severe academic criticism.[22]

Accordingly, there is now a substantial question of whether false light will survive as an independent tort. At the very least, recognition by many new

---

[16]Kapellas v. Kofman, 459 P.2d 912, 921 n.16 (1969) (false light invasion of privacy claim based on same publication as defamation claim is in substance equivalent to libel claim and is thus superfluous and should be dismissed when defamation claim also asserted).

[17]Jones v. Palmer Communications, 440 N.W.2d 884, 894, 16 Media L. Rep. 2137, 2143 (Iowa 1989) ("It is unreasonable to allow a party to evade the standards surrounding defamation law because the plaintiff has pled an alternative theory [false light]."); *see infra* §3.8. Indeed, in some areas, the restrictions on false light claims are more onerous than the comparable restrictions in defamation cases. *See infra* §§3.5(C) and (H).

[18]Renwick v. News & Observer Pub'g Co., 312 S.E.2d 405, 412, 10 Media L. Rep. 1443, 1448 (N.C. 1984); Sullivan v. Pulitzer Broadcasting Co., 709 S.W.2d 475, 478–80, 12 Media L. Rep. 2187, 2190–92 (Mo. 1986) (but court left open possibility it might recognize false light in "an appropriate case"); Angelotta v. ABC, 820 F.2d 806, 808, 14 Media L. Rep. 1185, 1187 (6th Cir. 1987) (holding that Ohio has expressly declined to recognize false light); Mitchell v. Random House, 865 F.2d 664, 617, 16 Media L. Rep. 1207, 1213 (5th Cir. 1989) (Mississippi has not and would not recognize false light). *See also* Eastwood v. Cascade Broadcasting Co., 722 P.2d 1295, 1298–99, 13 Media L. Rep. 1136, 1139 (Wash. 1986) (noting but not deciding whether to follow *Renwick* and *Sullivan*).

[19]Godbehere v. Phoenix Newspapers, 783 P.2d 781, 17 Media L. Rep. 1925 (Ariz. 1989) (recognizing false light claim).

[20]*Renwick*, 312 S.E.2d 405 (declining to recognize false light invasion of privacy in North Carolina because of threat to First Amendment values and reduction in judicial economy, given nearly identical nature of false light and defamation); *Sullivan*, 709 S.W.2d 475 (same). *See also* Kalian v. People Acting Through Community Effort, 408 A.2d 608, 5 Media L. Rep. 2174 (R.I. 1979) (recognition of false light is for legislature, not courts; legislature subsequently enacted false light statute, R.I. GEN. LAWS §9-1-28.1(a)(4)). Although the New York courts initially struggled with whether the state's civil rights laws encompassed a broader law of privacy than solely a right of publicity, *see, e.g.*, Arrington v. New York Times Co., 434 N.E.2d 1319, 1323, 8 Media L. Rep. 1351, 1354 (N.Y. 1982), *cert. denied*, 459 U.S. 1146 (1983) (3-3 decision) ("[t]here has been serious concern that, by sidestepping the safeguards which restrain the reach of traditional public defamation litigation, a false light approach would compromise the constitutional guarantee of freedom of the press"), New York's highest court recently reiterated that under New York law the right of privacy is governed exclusively by §§50 and 51 of New York's Civil Rights Law, which do not encompass a general common law of privacy. Howell v. New York Post Co., 612 N.E.2d 699, 703 (N.Y. 1993) (action against newspaper for invasion of privacy).

[21]Wade, *Defamation and the Right of Privacy*, 15 VAND. L. REV. 1120, 1122 (1962) (advocating adoption of false light as way to overcome "absurdities" of defamation); Nimmer, *The Right to Speak From Times to Time: First Amendment Theory Applied to Libel and Misapplied to Privacy*, 56 CAL. L. REV. 935, 963 (1968) (arguing that, despite many similarities between false light and defamation, certain false light cases more akin to classic invasion of privacy actions than to defamation and thus deserve different treatment).

[22]Zimmerman, *False Light Invasion of Privacy: The Light That Failed*, 64 N.Y.U. L. REV. 364, 366 (1989) ("False light invasion of privacy has caused enough theoretical and practical problems to make a compelling case for a stricter standard of birth control in the evolution of the common law.").

jurisdictions seems unlikely, and if it is recognized, false light will almost certainly be subjected to the restrictions of defamation law, which would deprive it of any true independent status.

§3.5 ELEMENTS OF A FALSE LIGHT CLAIM

The tort of false light invasion of privacy consists of (1) giving publicity to the matter (2) concerning the plaintiff (3) that is false and (4) that would be highly offensive to a reasonable person or a person of ordinary sensibilities.[23] The statement involved must also be one of fact, not opinion, and the defendant must have acted with the requisite degree of fault.[24]

§3.5(A) Proper Plaintiff

Because false light is supposed to protect feelings,[25] only living individuals can sue for false light;[26] legal entities cannot sue for false light because they have no feelings.[27] Relatives or friends of someone who has a false light claim also have no right to sue for false light.[28]

§3.5(B) Identification of the Plaintiff

A statement must be "of and concerning" the plaintiff for a false light claim to exist.[29] Courts frequently analyze this issue by reference to defamation

---

[23] *See generally* Annot., *supra* note 14.
[24] One who gives publicity to a matter concerning another that places the other before the public in a false light is subject to liability to the other for invasion of his privacy, if
    (a) the false light in which the other was placed would be highly offensive to a reasonable person, and
    (b) the actor had knowledge of or acted in reckless disregard as to the falsity of the publicized matter and the false light in which the other would be placed.
RESTATEMENT (SECOND), *supra* note 5, at §652E.
[25] *See supra* §3.3.
[26] Annot., *Invasion of Privacy by Publication Dealing with One Other Than Plaintiff*, 18 A.L.R.3d 873 (1968).
[27] Clinton Community Hosp. Corp. v. Southern Md. Medical Ctr., 374 F. Supp. 450, 456 (D. Md. 1974) ("[i]t is clear that corporations do not enjoy a right to privacy"), *aff'd*, 510 F.2d 1037 (4th Cir.), *cert. denied*, 422 U.S. 1048 (1975); J & C, Inc. v. Combined Communications Corp., 14 Media L. Rep. 2162, 2163 (Ky. Ct. App. 1987) ("corporations and business entities have no cause of action for the 'false light' tort"); Southern Air Transport v. ABC, 670 F. Supp. 38, 42, 14 Media L. Rep. 1683, 1686 (D.D.C. 1987) ("A corporation cannot be offended."), *on reconsideration summary judgment granted on other grounds*, 678 F. Supp. 8, 14 Media L. Rep. 2345 (D.D.C. 1988); RESTATEMENT (SECOND), *supra* note 5, at §652I, cmt. c; Annot., *False Light Invasion of Privacy—Defenses and Remedies*, 57 A.L.R.4th 244 (1987).
[28] *See, e.g.*, James v. Screen Gems, 344 P.2d 799 (Cal. Ct. App. 1959) (widow of Jesse James, Jr., could not sue for account of husband's life as son of famous outlaw); Weller v. Home News Pub'g Co., 271 A.2d 738 (N.J. Super. Ct. Law Div. 1970) (daughter and son-in-law could not maintain action based on use of deceased mother's photograph); Wood v. Hustler Magazine, 736 F.2d 1084, 1093, 10 Media L. Rep. 2113, 2120 (5th Cir. 1984) (husband could not recover where wife's privacy invaded by publication of nude photograph even though caption indicated husband took photograph), *cert. denied*, 469 U.S. 1107 (1985); Ritzmann v. Weekly World News, 614 F. Supp. 1336, 1341, 12 Media L. Rep. 1178, 1182 (N.D. Tex. 1985) (wife cannot recover for false description of estranged husband).
[29] Michigan United Conservation Clubs v. CBS News, 485 F. Supp. 893, 904, 5 Media L. Rep. 2566, 2574 (W.D. Mich. 1980) ("the publicity forming the basis for the false light claim [must] be reasonably capable of being understood as singling out, or pointing to, the plaintiff"), *aff'd*, 665 F.2d 110, 7 Media L. Rep. 2331 (6th Cir. 1981).

principles.[30] The group libel doctrine is also applicable to false light claims.[31] A common problem for the media is juxtaposing a videotape or photograph with commentary that might be interpreted to refer to individuals shown in the videotape or photograph, which can result in false light claims.[32]

The plaintiff has the burden of demonstrating that the statement is "of and concerning" him or her.[33] This burden can be a substantial one, particularly when the statement purports to be about a fictional character.[34] Depending on the circumstances, the identification issue may be a question of fact or a question of law.[35]

§3.5(C) Publicity

False light publicity requires "communication to the public in general or to a large number of persons as distinguished from one individual or a few."[36] By contrast, publication by the speaker to one individual other than

---

[30]Pring v. Penthouse Int'l, 695 F.2d 438, 8 Media L. Rep. 2409 (10th Cir. 1982) (resolution of identification issue same for libel and false light claims), *cert. denied,* 462 U.S. 1132 (1983); Geisler v. Petrocelli, 616 F.2d 636, 6 Media L. Rep. 1023 (2d Cir. 1980) ("of and concerning" requirement of libel applied to false light claim). See Chapter 2, §2.10.

[31]*Michigan United Conservation Clubs,* 485 F. Supp. at 899–900 (individual member of group cannot maintain false light action unless (1) group is small enough that publicity can be reasonably understood as referring to plaintiff or (2) circumstances reasonably support conclusion that there is particular reference to plaintiff).

[32]*See, e.g.,* Clark v. American Broadcasting Cos., 684 F.2d 1208, 1213–14, 8 Media L. Rep. 2049, 2051–52 (6th Cir. 1982), *cert. denied,* 460 U.S. 1040 (1983). This case was overruled on other grounds in Bichler v. Union Bank & Trust Co., 745 F.2d 1006, 10 Media L. Rep. 2393 (6th Cir. 1984) (en banc). Duncan v. WJLA-TV, 10 Media L. Rep. 1395 (D.D.C. 1984). *See also supra* notes 7 and 8.

[33]*Geisler,* 616 F.2d at 639, 6 Media L. Rep. at 1024 (plaintiff bears burden of proving statement is "of and concerning" him in defamation and false light actions).

[34]In *Geisler,* the plaintiff sued for libel and false light when the defendant, a casual business acquaintance, used the plaintiff's actual name and physical description for the protagonist, a female transsexual athlete, in the defendant's purportedly fictional book. Noting that the plaintiff's burden of proving identification "is not a light one," the court stated that the
> plaintiff must demonstrate that third parties apprehend the similarity between the real person and her literary cognate as something more than amusing coincidence or even conscious parallelism on a superficial plane. Rather, it is required that the reasonable reader must rationally suspect that the protagonist is in fact the plaintiff, notwithstanding the author's and publisher's assurances that the work is fictional. This points up the disturbing irony inherent in the scheme: the more virtuous the victim of the libel, the less likely it will be that she will be able to establish this essential confusion in the mind of the third party. Thus, the more deserving the plaintiff of recompense for the tarnishing of a spotless reputation, the less likely will be any actual recovery. Such a seeming contradiction is best resolved by the trier of fact since adjudication of the issue as a matter of law will seldom satisfy the expectation that legal holdings be consistent and logical.

616 F.2d at 639, 6 Media L. Rep. at 1025. *See also infra* §3.8.

[35]*See* Crump v. Beckley Newspapers, 320 S.E.2d 70, 90, 10 Media L. Rep. 2225, 2240 (W. Va. 1983) (reversing judgment of lower court granting summary judgment for defendant, holding that question of whether statements are "of and concerning" plaintiff is for jury). *Contra* Michigan United Conservation Clubs v. CBS News, 485 F. Supp. 893, 897, 5 Media L. Rep. 2566, 2568–69 (W.D. Mich. 1980) (rejecting plaintiffs' argument that summary judgment inappropriate because issue of identification is jury question; "it is for the court, in the first instance, to determine if the alleged libel is reasonably capable of bearing an application to the plaintiffs, and only if such a construction is possible will the case go to the jury for a determination of whether the publication did, in fact, concern the plaintiffs").

[36]Kinsey v. Macur, 165 Cal. Rptr. 608, 611 (Cal. Ct. App. 1980) (invasion of privacy must involve "publicity in the sense of communication to the public in general or to a large number of persons as distinguished from one individual or a few"); *Crump,* 320 S.E.2d at 87–88, 10 Media L. Rep. at 2237 (widespread publicity an essential ingredient); Moore v. Big Picture Co., 828 F.2d 270, 274–75, 14 Media L. Rep. 1865, 1868–69 (5th Cir. 1987) (publication to eight or fewer people does not meet publicity requirement); Rifkin v. Esquire Pub'g, 8 Media L. Rep. 1384, 1387 (C.D. Cal. 1982) (statements concerning plaintiff made to third parties by magazine reporters during prepublication attempts to gather information not "communication to the public in general"); RESTATEMENT (SECOND), *supra* note 5.

the plaintiff is sufficient to meet the publication requirement in defamation actions.[37]

§3.5(D) Oral Statements

While there is substantial contrary authority,[38] it is still the rule in a number of jurisdictions that there can be no actionable invasion of privacy for spoken as opposed to written words.[39]

§3.5(E) The "Highly Offensive" Requirement

In order for a plaintiff to recover for false light invasion of privacy, the publicity must be of a kind that would be "highly offensive" to a reasonable person or a person of ordinary sensibilities.[40] As one court has remarked:

> [T]he price of the license granted by the first amendment to the press to engage in robust activity is the necessity of every citizen of having some thickness of skin.... This requirement ensures that liability will not attach for the publication of information so innocuous that notice of potential harm would not be present. The childhood idiom "stick and stones may break my bones, but names can never hurt me" provides a cultural sense of the community standard on de minimus misrepresentations.[41]

The requisite offensiveness has been found in the inclusion of a plaintiff's photograph in a public "rogue's gallery" of convicted criminals when he had never been convicted of any crime;[42] the false attribution of statements about a movie star to the star's father;[43] the use of a photograph in a way that creates a false and unfavorable impression of a plaintiff;[44] and the failure to report portions of a wife's suicide note that said she killed herself to get away from

---

[37] *See* Chapter 2, §2.6.

[38] *See, e.g.,* Winegard v. Larsen, 260 N.W.2d 816, 819 (Iowa 1977) ("it is generally held today that the right of privacy can be violated by any means of communication"); Machleder v. Diaz, 801 F.2d 46, 56, 13 Media L. Rep. 1369, 1376 (2d Cir. 1986) ("false light law makes no distinction between oral or written words as defamation does"). *See generally* Annot., *Invasion of Right of Privacy by Merely Oral Declarations,* 19 A.L.R.3d 1318 (1968).

[39] *See, e.g.,* Grimes v. Carter, 50 Cal. Rptr. 808, 811 (Cal. Ct. App. 1966) ("California adheres to the proposition that the right of privacy may not be violated by word of mouth only"); Midwest Glass Co. v. Stanford Dev. Co., 339 N.E.2d 274, 277 (Ill. App. Ct. 1975) ("the general rule is that an invasion of privacy cannot be based merely on oral communications"). *But see* H & M Assocs. v. El Centro, 167 Cal. Rptr. 392, 400 (Cal. Ct. App. 1980) ("oral statements may ultimately receive wider coverage than printed statements.... The test should turn on the nature of the privacy invaded and not on the means of communication.").

[40] RESTATEMENT (SECOND), *supra* note 5, at §652E, cmt. c, states:

The plaintiff's privacy is not invaded when unimportant false statements are made, even when they are made deliberately. It is only when there is such a major misrepresentation of his character, history, activities or beliefs that serious offense may reasonably be expected to be taken by a reasonable man in his position, that there is a cause of action for invasion of privacy.

See also Winegard, 260 N.W.2d at 823 (citing RESTATEMENT (SECOND) in holding that minor variations between statements published and statements made by plaintiff are not actionable). The original Restatement required only that the statement be offensive, not highly offensive. Arrington v. New York Times Co., 434 N.E.2d 1319, 1323, 8 Media L. Rep. 1351, 1354 (N.Y. 1982).

[41] Crump v. Beckley Newspapers, 320 S.E.2d 70, 90, 10 Media L. Rep. 2225, 2239 (W. Va. 1983).

[42] Itzkovitch v. Whitaker, 39 So. 499 (La. 1905). *See also* Cantrell v. American Broadcasting Cos., 529 F. Supp. 746, 8 Media L. Rep. 1239 (N.D. Ill. 1981) (upholding plaintiff's false light claim based on portrayal of him by news reporter as somehow involved in arson-for-profit scheme).

[43] Selleck v. Globe Int'l, 212 Cal. Rptr. 838 (Cal. Ct. App. 1985). *But see* Jones v. Herald Post Co., 18 S.W.2d 972 (Ky. 1929) (attributing fictional quote to plaintiff about feelings toward her husband's murderers not actionable).

[44] *See supra* notes 7, 8, and 32.

her husband that, coupled with the false statement that she was the "happiest wife and mother in the neighborhood," implied that he was unperceptive and insensitive to her unhappiness.[45]

In contrast, the use of a photograph of plaintiffs at an airline counter standing near boxes of merchandise to illustrate an article on the large number of purchases made by Latin Americans in Miami and the highly profitable resale of such items in Latin America;[46] the portrayal of a plaintiff as intemperate, evasive, and thus seemingly responsible for illegal dumping of chemicals effectuated by the defendant news reporter's aggressive manner of interviewing the plaintiff on camera and "selective" editing;[47] and the use of a plaintiff's photo on the front cover of the *New York Times Magazine* to illustrate an article on the upward mobility of the black middle class[48] were all held not to be highly offensive. Even the portrayal of a plaintiff as a drug dealer when he was a possessor of drugs was held not to be highly offensive.[49]

A few decisions indicate that a sexually explicit publication's content may cast a false light on what would otherwise be an innocuous photograph and article.[50] However, most decisions have required that the photograph or article falsely imply that there was an "association" between the plaintiff and the publication so that a reasonable person would conclude that the plaintiff either consented to the use or endorsed the content of the publication.[51]

---

[45]Varnish v. Best Medium Pub'g Co., 405 F.2d 608 (2d Cir. 1968), *cert. denied,* 394 U.S. 987 (1969). This case takes an unreasonably broad view of what constitutes false light.

[46]Fogel v. Forbes, Inc., 500 F. Supp. 1081, 6 Media L. Rep. 1941 (E.D. Pa. 1980) (granting motion for summary judgment).

[47]Machleder v. Diaz, 801 F.2d 46, 58, 13 Media L. Rep. 1369, 1378 (2d Cir. 1986) ("in order to avoid a head-on collision with First Amendment rights, courts have narrowly construed the highly offensive standard."). *But see* Note, *The Ambush Interview: A False Light Invasion of Privacy?,* 34 CASE W. RES. L. REV. 72 (1983) ("The ambush [interview] does not discernibly further the goals of press freedom, and significantly compromises the privacy interests of subjects.").

[48]Arrington v. New York Times Co., 434 N.E.2d 1319, 1323, 8 Media L. Rep. 1351, 1354 (N.Y. 1982) (declining to decide whether false light invasion of privacy is cognizable in New York, court noted nonetheless that "by no means does this case measure up to this kind of criterion [high offensiveness]"). For cases holding that New York does not recognize false light, *see supra* note 20. *See also* Cefalu v. Globe Newspaper, 391 N.E.2d 935, 5 Media L. Rep. 1940 (Mass. App. Ct. 1979), *cert. denied and appeal dismissed,* 444 U.S. 1060 (1980) (photograph of plaintiff in unemployment line not actionable).

[49]Johnson v. Lexington Herald-Leader, 9 Media L. Rep. 1365, 1366 (Ky. Ct. App. 1983) ("We fail to perceive any false light in a situation where a person arrested for 'trafficking in cocaine' is later convicted of the lesser offense of possession of cocaine."). This case might also be analyzed as one holding that substantially true statements are not actionable as false light. *See infra* §3.5(F).

[50]Braun v. Flynt, 726 F.2d 245, 253–54, 10 Media L. Rep. 1497, 1503–04 (5th Cir.), *cert. denied,* 469 U.S. 883 (1984) (false light could be determined by reference to publication in which photograph appeared; mere use of plaintiff's photograph implied that she approved content of or consented to use of photograph in "magazine devoted exclusively to sexual exploitation and to disparagement of women"). *See also* Palmisano v. Modernismo Pubns., 470 N.Y.S.2d 196, 10 Media L. Rep. 1093 (N.Y. App. Div. 1983) (unauthorized publication of plaintiff's picture in homosexual magazine and attribution of imaginary statements to him stated cause of action for false light). *But see* Faloona v. Hustler Magazine, 799 F.2d 1000, 1006–07, 13 Media L. Rep. 1353 (5th Cir. 1986), *cert. denied,* 479 U.S. 1088 (1987) (photos of nude children reprinted for book review in sexually explicit magazine not actionable because "no tie to *Hustler* is claimed or suggested"; court held that its decision in *Braun* did not endorse evaluating entire publication but focused on immediate context of photograph or article). *Compare* Gill v. Curtis Pub'g Co., 239 P.2d 630 (Cal. 1952) (photo of happily married plaintiffs in affectionate pose used to illustrate article on evils of love based purely on sexual attraction actionable as false light) *with* Gill v. Hearst Pub'g Co., 253 P.2d 441 (Cal. 1953) (same photo published in different magazine to illustrate inoffensive article about love held not an invasion of plaintiffs' privacy).

[51]Fudge v. Penthouse Int'l, 840 F.2d 1012, 1019–20 (1st Cir.), *cert. denied,* 488 U.S. 821 (1988) (photo and story about schoolgirls included in adult magazine's "compendium of bizarre, idiotic, lurid and ofttimes witless" news items not actionable; context left "absolutely no room for the implication that *Penthouse* had in any way dealt with plaintiffs, or they with *Penthouse*"); Grimsley v. Guccione, 703 F. Supp. 903, 910, 16 Media L. Rep. 1659 (M.D. Ala. 1988) (photo and story about unexpected birth in same *Penthouse* news column not actionable "under either a 'consent to publication' theory or an 'endorsement of views' theory");

The authorities are split on whether the publication must be derogatory. Flattering statements have been held to be actionable,[52] but there is contrary authority.[53]

Whether a judge or jury is to determine if a publication is highly offensive is not entirely clear.[54] The rule appears to be that the issue is initially one of law, but close cases may be for the jury to decide.[55]

Because false light is a form of invasion of privacy, some cases hold that only statements involving matters of private concern are actionable as false light; statements about matters of public concern are not actionable.[56]

Douglass v. Hustler Magazine, 769 F.2d 1128, 1137–38, 11 Media L. Rep. 2264, 2270–71 (7th Cir. 1985) (plaintiff who consented to publication of her nude photos in *Playboy* had false light claim for publication of other photos from same sessions in *Hustler;* context and previous statements by publisher claiming that all magazine's subjects consented to photographs implied that plaintiff voluntarily associated with "unquestionably degrading" publication); Jackson v. Playboy Enters., 574 F. Supp. 10, 14, 9 Media L. Rep. 1575, 1578 (S.D. Ohio 1983) (photo of children with policewoman in common street scene published as part of article featuring photos of same policewoman, nude, not actionable); Faucheux v. Magazine Mgmt. Co., 5 Media L. Rep. 1697, 1700 (E.D. La. 1979) (use of widely reprinted photo in sexually explicit magazine of husband and wife police officers kissing while riding their police motorcycles not actionable; court declined to evaluate "taste" of publication); Easter Seal Soc'y v. Playboy Enters., 530 So. 2d 643, 647–50, 15 Media L. Rep. 2384 (La. Ct. App. 1988) (use in sexually explicit movie of stock footage of plaintiffs participating in Mardi Gras parade not actionable because "no suggestion, implication, or innuendo connecting any parade participant with the subject matter of the film"). *See also* Dempsey v. National Enquirer, 702 F. Supp. 927, 16 Media L. Rep. 1396 (D. Me. 1988), where the court evaluated false light claims against two tabloid newspapers under the rulings in *Fudge, Douglass,* and *Braun*. Both the *National Enquirer* and *Star* carried articles about a harrowing incident in which the plaintiff fell out of a small airplane in flight and then clung to the boarding ladder while his co-pilot brought the plane to a safe landing. The plaintiff contended that he had been cast in a false light because the publications were offensive. The court noted that the *National Enquirer* attributed the story to news sources other than the plaintiff, and dismissed the claim. *Id.* at 933. However, it refused to dismiss the claim against the *Star,* which had recounted the incident in first person and under the plaintiff's byline. "This unequivocal attribution creates a much closer question . . . [of whether] the plaintiff consented to publication or was portrayed 'otherwise than as he is,' the material falsity of the article as a whole, the false light created by association with the publication, and the degree of offensiveness to a reasonable person." *Id.* at 937.

[52]*See, e.g.,* Hill v. Hayes, 240 N.Y.S.2d 286 (N.Y. App. Div. 1963) (invasion of privacy where defendant portrayed plaintiff as heroic), *aff'd,* 207 N.E.2d 604 (N.Y. 1965), *rev'd on other grounds sub nom.* Time, Inc. v. Hill, 385 U.S. 374, 1 Media L. Rep. 1791 (1967); Spahn v. Julian Messner, Inc., 260 N.Y.S.2d 451, 456 (N.Y. App. Div. 1965) (laudatory though unauthorized fictionalized biography actionable), *aff'd,* 221 N.E.2d 543 (N.Y. 1966), *vacated and remanded,* 387 U.S. 239, *reaff'd on remand,* 233 N.E.2d 840 (N.Y. 1967); RESTATEMENT (SECOND), *supra* note 5, at illus. 9 (airline pilot portrayed as hero). *See also* Varnish v. Best Medium Pub'g Co., 405 F.2d 608 (2d Cir. 1968), *cert. denied,* 394 U.S. 987 (1969) and text accompanying *supra* note 45; *see generally* Annot., *False Light Invasion of Privacy—Neutral or Laudatory Depiction of Subject,* 59 A.L.R.4th 502 (1988).

[53]*See, e.g.,* Bernstein v. National Broadcasting Co., 129 F. Supp. 817, 835–36 (D.D.C. 1955) (holding that positive television portrayal would not be offensive to person of ordinary sensibilities), *aff'd,* 232 F.2d 369, 370 (D.C. Cir.), *cert. denied,* 352 U.S. 945 (1956); Jones v. Herald Post Co., 18 S.W.2d 972, 973 (Ky. 1929) (complimentary account of woman defending husband against assault not actionable).

[54]*Compare* Martin v. Municipal Pubns., 510 F. Supp. 255, 259 (E.D. Pa. 1981) (denying defendant's motion for summary judgment on ground that jury must decide whether publication of photo of plaintiff along with caption arguably depicting plaintiff as drunk and transvestite was highly offensive) *and* Dean v. Guard Pub'g Co., 744 P.2d 1296, 1298, 14 Media L. Rep. 2100, 2102 (Or. Ct. App. 1987) (jury question whether it was highly offensive to imply that alcoholic plaintiff was hospitalized and underwent aversion therapy for alcoholism) *with* Dempsey v. National Enquirer, 687 F. Supp. 692, 15 Media L. Rep. 2193 (D. Me. 1988) (deciding issue as matter of law as to one publication); Johnson v. Lexington Herald-Leader, 9 Media L. Rep. 1365, 1366 (Ky. Ct. App. 1983) (same); *and* Machleder v. Diaz, 801 F.2d 46, 58, 13 Media L. Rep. 1369, 1378 (2d Cir. 1986) (same).

[55]Romaine v. Kallinger, 537 A.2d 284, 290–91, 15 Media L. Rep. 1209, 1214 (N.J. 1988) (question is one of law for court, at least initially); *Easter Seal Soc'y,* 530 So. 2d at 648, 15 Media L. Rep. at 2387.

[56]*See, e.g.,* Godbehere v. Phoenix Newspapers, 783 P.2d 781, 789 (Ariz. 1989); Hardge-Harris v. Pleban, 741 F. Supp. 764, 776 (E.D. Mo. 1990) (dismissing plaintiffs' false light claim, finding that "the possible commission of a crime and the reporting of such suspicion to the appropriate authorities are matters of legitimate public interest"; "[T]he tort of false light invasion of privacy will not lie when the matter purportedly publicized is of legitimate public interest. 'It is for the court to say first whether the occasion or incident is one of proper public interest . . . . Where the operation of laws and activities of the police or other public bodies are involved, the matter is within the public interest.' " (quoting Hagler v. Democrat-News, 699 S.W.2d 96, 99 (Mo. Ct. App. 1985)). *See also* Neish v. Beaver Newspapers, 581 A.2d 619, 625,

§3.5(F) Falsity

As its name indicates, false light requires a showing of falsity.[57] This requirement distinguishes false light from the other branches of privacy and makes it very similar to defamation.[58] As with defamation, if the statement is true, there can be no false light and thus no actionable claim.[59] Similarly, there is no requirement that favorable comments about a plaintiff be included with the unfavorable comments, nor is there any requirement that the reporting be "balanced."[60] The plaintiff has the burden of proving falsity.[61]

§3.5(G) Opinion

Prior to *Milkovich v. Lorain Journal Co.*,[62] courts followed defamation holdings and rejected false light claims based on statements of opinion.[63] Courts are now likely to apply the Supreme Court's *Milkovich* analysis to false light actions.[64] Whether a statement constitutes fact or opinion is usually a question of law.[65]

---

18 Media L. Rep. 1251, 1255 (Pa. Super. Ct. 1990) (plaintiff waived false light claim by becoming public figure).

[57]Time, Inc. v. Hill, 385 U.S. 374, 386, 1 Media L. Rep. 1791, 1795–96 (1967) (stating New York requires "material and substantial falsification"); Winegard v. Larsen, 260 N.W.2d 816, 823 (Iowa 1977) (relying on Restatement for "material and substantial" falsity rule); Fogel v. Forbes, Inc., 500 F. Supp. 1081, 1088, 6 Media L. Rep. 1941, 1945 (E.D. Pa. 1980) ("matter published concerning the plaintiff [must] be untrue"); Brown v. Boney, 255 S.E.2d 784, 791, 5 Media L. Rep. 1395, 1400 (N.C. Ct. App. 1979) ("[i]f the plaintiff's case [for false light] is to succeed, he must show that the factual statements made concerning him and his actions were false"); RESTATEMENT (SECOND), *supra* note 5, at §652E, cmt. a.

[58]Rinsley v. Brandt, 700 F.2d 1304, 1308, 9 Media L. Rep. 1225, 1227–28 (10th Cir. 1983); *Machleder,* 801 F.2d at 52–53, 13 Media L. Rep. at 1373.

[59]*Rinsley,* 700 F.2d 1304, 9 Media L. Rep. 1225; *Machleder,* 801 F.2d at 54, 13 Media L. Rep. at 1374–75; Logan v. District of Columbia, 447 F. Supp. 1328, 3 Media L. Rep. 2094 (D.D.C. 1978).

[60]*Machleder,* 801 F.2d at 55, 13 Media L. Rep. at 1375 ("recovery for a false light tort may not be predicated on a rule that holds a media defendant liable for broadcasting truthful statements and actions because it failed to include additional facts which might have cast the plaintiff in a more favorable or balanced light"); Goodrich v. Waterbury Republican-Am., 448 A.2d 1317, 1331, 8 Media L. Rep. 2329, 2339 (Conn. 1982) (defendant not liable for false light because of "its decision to omit facts that may place the plaintiff under less harsh public scrutiny"); Alfego v. CBS, 7 Media L. Rep. 1075, 1076 (D. Mass. 1981) ("[t]he requirement of substantial accuracy does not . . . mandate the inclusion of every fact and detail sympathetic to each side of an issue").

[61]*Machleder,* 801 F.2d at 54, 13 Media L. Rep. at 1375.

[62]497 U.S. 1, 17 Media L. Rep. 2009 (1990).

[63]*See, e.g., Rinsley,* 700 F.2d at 1307, 9 Media L. Rep. at 1227; Cibenko v. Worth Pubrs., 510 F. Supp. 761, 767, 7 Media L. Rep. 1298, 1302 (D.N.J. 1981) (photo of white police officer prodding black man with nightstick to prevent him from sleeping in public, with caption posing rhetorical question whether officer would do same if man were white, constituted opinion); Fudge v. Penthouse Int'l, 840 F.2d 1012, 14 Media L. Rep. 2353 (1st Cir.), *cert. denied,* 488 U.S. 821 (1988) (photo of minor females with caption "Little Amazons Attack Boys" is opinion), *cert. denied,* 488 U.S. 821 (1988); Ault v. Hustler Magazine, 860 F.2d 877, 880–81, 15 Media L. Rep. 2205, 2207–08 (9th Cir. 1988) (characterizing plaintiff as "Asshole of the Month" is opinion), *cert. denied,* 489 U.S. 1080 (1989). For a discussion of the opinion rule in defamation actions, see Chapter 2, §2.7.

[64]In *Milkovich,* the Court held that statements of opinion may be defamatory if they imply an assertion of objective fact. 497 U.S. at 21–22, 17 Media L. Rep. at 2018. Statements that cannot reasonably be interpreted as stating actual facts, including "imaginative expression" and "rhetorical hyperbole," are not defamatory. *Id.* at 20; Hustler Magazine v. Falwell, 485 U.S. 46, 50 (1988). For a discussion of these standards, see Chapter 2, §2.7.

[65]*Rinsley,* 700 F.2d at 1307, 1309, 9 Media L. Rep. at 1227, 1228 (whether a given statement constitutes assertion of fact or opinion is question of law for court; " '[T]he distinction frequently is a difficult one, and what constitutes a statement of fact in one context may be treated as a statement of opinion in another, in light of the nature and content of the communication taken as a whole.' ") (quoting Gregory v. McDonnell Douglas Corp., 552 P.2d 425, 428, 131 Cal. Rptr. 641, 644 (Cal. 1976)). *Accord Ault,* 860 F.2d at 880–81, 15 Media L. Rep. at 2207.

§3.5(H) The First Amendment and Fault

In *Time, Inc. v. Hill*,[66] the U.S. Supreme Court extended the First Amendment's fault requirements, which are applicable in defamation actions, to false light invasion of privacy actions. In analyzing the plaintiffs' false light claim under the applicable New York privacy statute, the Court held that "the constitutional protections for speech and press preclude the application of the New York statute to redress false reports of matters of public interest in the absence of proof that the defendant published the report with knowledge of its falsity or in reckless disregard of the truth."[67] In other words, *all* plaintiffs, whether public officials, public figures, or private figures, must establish constitutional "actual malice"[68] in order to recover for false light invasion of privacy if the false publicity is about a matter of public interest.[69]

The somewhat erratic development of the constitutional actual malice doctrine in the defamation context has raised questions as to the continuing validity of *Hill*. Four years after *Hill* was decided, the Supreme Court decided *Rosenbloom v. Metromedia*,[70] where a plurality of the Court favored extending the actual malice requirement to all defamation cases involving matters of "public or general interest no matter what the plaintiff's status was."[71]

Three years later, in *Gertz v. Robert Welch, Inc.*,[72] the Court repudiated the plurality decision in *Rosenbloom* and returned to an approach based on the plaintiff's status. If a plaintiff is not a "public official" or a "public figure," i.e., is a "private figure," *Gertz* held that "[o]ur accommodation of the competing values at stake in defamation suits by private individuals allows the States to impose liability on the publisher or broadcaster of defamatory falsehood on a less demanding showing than that required by *New York Times [Co. v. Sullivan]*,"[73] even if the matter at issue is one of public interest or was newsworthy. Accordingly, the Court held that private figure plaintiffs could recover damages for actual injury if some degree of fault (e.g., negligence) was shown, leaving it to each state to determine what that degree of fault was.[74]

In contrast, under *Hill*, a private plaintiff who sues for false light must overcome the formidable actual malice barrier in order to recover if the false publicity concerns a matter of public interest. This dichotomy has led to uncertainty about the continuing validity of *Hill* when applied to private figure plaintiffs in false light cases that involve matters of public or general concern.[75]

There has been very little indication by the Supreme Court of the effect, if any, that it intended *Gertz* to have on *Hill*. *Gertz* twice cited *Hill* without

---

[66] 385 U.S. 374, 1 Media L. Rep. 1791 (1967).

[67] *Id.* at 387–88, 1 Media L. Rep. at 1796.

[68] For an analysis of the constitutional actual malice standard and its application in defamation actions, see Chapter 2, §2.11.

[69] RESTATEMENT (SECOND), *supra* note 5, at §652E, cmt. d. *See also Falwell*, 484 U.S. 46, 14 Media L. Rep. 2281 (public figure plaintiff must demonstrate constitutional actual malice in intentional infliction of emotional distress case).

[70] 403 U.S. 29, 1 Media L. Rep. 1597 (1971). This case was overruled in Gertz v. Robert Welch, Inc., 418 U.S. 323, 1 Media L. Rep. 1633 (1974) and Time, Inc. v. Firestone, 424 U.S. 448, 1 Media L. Rep. 1665 (1976). For a discussion of this case, see Chapter 2, §2.11.

[71] 403 U.S. at 31–32, 1 Media L. Rep. at 1597–98.

[72] 418 U.S. 323, 1 Media L. Rep. 1633. For a discussion of this case, see Chapter 2, §2.11.

[73] *Id.* at 348, 1 Media L. Rep. at 1643. For a discussion of who is a public official or public figure, see Chapter 2, §2.11.

[74] *Id.* at 347, 1 Media L. Rep. at 1642. See Chapter 2, §2.11.

[75] *See* RESTATEMENT (SECOND), *supra* note 5, at §652E, cmt. d.

ever intimating that it was overruled or even modified.[76] Shortly after *Gertz*, the Court decided *Cantrell v. Forest City Publishing Co.*,[77] in which this issue was expressly left open.[78] The following year, in *Cox Broadcasting Corp. v. Cohn*,[79] the Court noted the *Hill* holding but cited *Cantrell* for the proposition that the issue was still open.[80]

Many view the Supreme Court's failure to repudiate *Hill*, given three opportunities to do so, as confirmation that *Hill* is still valid, notwithstanding *Gertz* and Justice Lewis Powell's ambiguous concurring opinion in *Cox Broadcasting*.[81] The Restatement (Second) has concluded that *Hill* remains the governing authority, at least "[p]ending further enlightenment from the Supreme Court."[82] The lower courts are sharply divided on whether *Hill* is controlling.[83] The courts that follow *Hill* still must determine whether the false light statement is about a matter of public interest before the actual malice standard is applicable.[84]

---

[76]418 U.S. at 334 n.6, 348, 1 Media L. Rep. at 1638 n.6, 1643.
[77]419 U.S. 245, 1 Media L. Rep. 1815 (1974).
[78]Observing that neither party had objected to the imposition of the actual malice standard, the Court stated:
Consequently, this case presents no occasion to consider whether a State may constitutionally apply a more relaxed standard of liability for a publisher or broadcaster of false statements to a private individual under a false-light theory of invasion of privacy, or whether the constitutional standard announced in *Time, Inc. v. Hill* applies to all false-light cases.
Id. at 250–51, 1 Media L. Rep. at 1817.
[79]420 U.S. 469, 1 Media L. Rep. 1819 (1975).
[80]*Id.* at 490 n.19, 1 Media L. Rep. at 1827 n.19.
[81]Justice Powell stated:
The Court's abandonment of the "matter of general or public interest" standard as the determinative factor for deciding whether to apply the *New York Times* malice standard to defamation litigation brought by private individuals . . . *calls into question the conceptual basis of Time, Inc. v. Hill*. In neither *Gertz* nor our more recent decision in *Cantrell v. Forest City Publishing Co.* . . . , however, have we been called upon to determine whether a State may constitutionally apply a more relaxed standard of liability under a false-light theory of invasion of privacy.
Id. at 498 n.2, 1 Media L. Rep. at 1830 n.2 (Powell, J., concurring) (citations omitted, emphasis added).
[82]RESTATEMENT (SECOND), *supra* note 5, at §652E and cmt. d. In a caveat, the American Law Institute declined to take a position on whether negligence would ever be sufficient to impose liability for false light invasion privacy. *Id.*
[83]*Not Controlling:* Wood v. Hustler Magazine, 736 F.2d 1084, 1091–92, 10 Media L. Rep. 2113, 2118–19 (5th Cir. 1984); Crump v. Beckley Newspapers, 320 S.E.2d 70, 89, 10 Media L. Rep. 2225, 2239 (W. Va. 1983); Dresbach v. Doubleday & Co., 518 F. Supp. 1285, 1288–92, 7 Media L. Rep. 2105, 2106–10 (D.D.C. 1981) (applying negligence standard to false light action brought by private plaintiff); Rinsley v. Brandt, 446 F. Supp. 850 (D. Kan. 1977), *aff'd*, 700 F.2d 1304, 9 Media L. Rep. 1225 (10th Cir. 1983). *See also* Fitzgerald v. Penthouse Int'l, 525 F. Supp. 585, 602–03, 7 Media L. Rep. 2385, 2398 (D. Md. 1981) ("[a]lthough if presented with such a case this court might be inclined to hold, as a matter of constitutional law, that private individuals need show only negligence in a 'false light' suit . . . , the court need not reach that issue"), *aff'd in part and rev'd in part*, 691 F.2d 666, 8 Media L. Rep. 2340 (4th Cir. 1982), *cert. denied*, 460 U.S. 1024 (1983).
Controlling: McCall v. Courier-Journal & Louisville Times Co., 623 S.W.2d 882, 7 Media L. Rep. 2118 (Ky. 1981), *cert. denied*, 456 U.S. 975 (1982); Dodrill v. Arkansas Democrat Co., 590 S.W.2d 840, 845 n.9, 5 Media L. Rep. 1385, 1389 n.9 (Ark. 1979), *cert. denied*, 444 U.S. 1076 (1980); Dean v. Guard Pub'g Co., 699 P.2d 1158, 1160 n.4 (Or. Ct. App. 1985); Goodrich v. Waterbury Republican-Am., 448 A.2d 1317, 1330 n.22, 8 Media L. Rep. 2329, 2338 n.22 (Conn. 1982); McCammon & Assocs. v. McGraw-Hill Broadcasting Co., 716 P.2d 490, 12 Media L. Rep. 1846 (Colo. Ct. App. 1986); Colbert v. World Pub'g Co., 747 P.2d 286, 290–92, 14 Media L. Rep. 2188, 2192–93 (Okla. 1987); Lovgren v. Citizens First Nat'l Bank of Princeton, 534 N.E.2d 987, 991, 16 Media L. Rep. 1214, 1218 (Ill. 1989) (following *Hill* rule, but as matter of common, not constitutional, law); Machleder v. Diaz, 618 F. Supp. 1367, 1373–75, 12 Media L. Rep. 1193, 1197–99 (S.D.N.Y. 1985), *aff'd in part and rev'd in part on other grounds*, 801 F.2d 46, 13 Media L. Rep. 1369 (2d Cir. 1986), *cert. denied*, 479 U.S. 1088 (1987).
The commentators are also sharply divided. *Compare* Hill, *Defamation and Privacy Under the First Amendment*, 76 COLUM. L. REV. 1205, 1274 (1976) (*Hill* is not controlling) *and* Zimmerman, *False Light Invasion of Privacy: The Light That Failed*, 64 N.Y.U. L. REV. 364, 449–50 (1989) (*Hill* is controlling).
[84]*See, e.g., McCall*, 623 S.W.2d at 888 n.10, 7 Media L. Rep. at 2123 n.10. *See also* Roberts v. Dover, 525 F. Supp. 987, 995 n.9, 7 Media L. Rep. 2296, 2302 n.9 (M.D. Tenn. 1981). For a discussion of what constitutes a matter of public concern, see Chapter 2, §2.11.

In jurisdictions where *Hill* is not controlling, i.e., where the actual malice rule only applies to false light actions if the plaintiff is a public official or public figure, whether a plaintiff falls into one of these categories is decided by applying the tests used to decide these issues in defamation cases.[85] When the actual malice rule applies, the rules concerning its application in defamation cases also apply in false light cases, e.g., determining what does or does not constitute actual malice[86] and proving actual malice by clear and convincing evidence.[87]

If the actual malice rule is not applicable, then the court must determine what level of fault must be shown.[88]

§3.6 PRIVILEGES AND CONSENT

The absolute and conditional common law privileges that apply to defamation are also applicable in false light cases.[89] Consent also will defeat a false light claim.[90]

§3.7 SUPREME COURT CASES

Only two false light cases have been decided by the U.S. Supreme Court: *Time, Inc. v. Hill*[91] and *Cantrell v. Forest City Publishing Co.*[92] They both illustrate some of the problems false light cases raise.

---

[85]Rinsley v. Brandt, 446 F. Supp. 850, 856–58, 6 Media L. Rep. 1222, 1232–34 (D. Kan. 1977) (psychiatrist who wrote extensively about treating mentally ill and was director of state hospital was public official and public figure), *aff'd on other grounds,* 700 F.2d 1304, 9 Media L. Rep. 1225 (10th Cir. 1983); Braun v. Flynt, 726 F.2d 245, 249–50, 10 Media L. Rep. 1497, 1500 (5th Cir. 1984) (performer with "Ralph the Diving Pig" is not public figure); Brueggemeyer v. ABC, 684 F. Supp. 452, 455–58, 15 Media L. Rep. 1449, 1451–54 (N.D. Tex. 1985) (bulk meat retailer is limited-purpose public official); Cantrell v. American Broadcasting Cos., 529 F. Supp. 746, 758, 8 Media L. Rep. 1239, 1248 (N.D. Ill. 1981) (apartment manager is not public figure); *Roberts,* 525 F. Supp. at 990–91, 7 Media L. Rep. at 2297–98 (state highway patrol officer is public official). *See generally* Chapter 2, §2.11(A).

[86]*No Actual Malice:* Lerman v. Flynt Distrib. Co., 745 F.2d 123, 140–41, 10 Media L. Rep. 2497, 2509 (2d Cir. 1984); Berry v. National Broadcasting Co., 480 F.2d 428 (8th Cir. 1973), *cert. dismissed,* 418 U.S. 911 (1974); *Colbert,* 747 P.2d at 289–92, 14 Media L. Rep. at 2191–93; Logan v. District of Columbia, 447 F. Supp. 1328, 1336, 3 Media L. Rep. 2094, 2099–2100 (D.D.C. 1978); *Dodrill,* 590 S.W.2d at 845, 5 Media L. Rep. at 1388–89; *Roberts,* 525 F. Supp. at 995, 7 Media L. Rep. at 2302; Ashby v. Hustler Magazine, 802 F.2d 856, 860, 13 Media L. Rep. 1416, 1419–20 (6th Cir. 1986).

Actual Malice: Braun, 726 F.2d at 256–57, 10 Media L. Rep. at 1506–07.

[87]Douglass v. Hustler Magazine, 769 F.2d 1128, 1140, 11 Media L. Rep. 2264, 2273 (7th Cir. 1985) (reversible error to fail to give jury this instruction). For a discussion of the "clear and convincing evidence" standard, see Chapter 2, §2.11(E)(ii).

[88]*See, e.g.,* Nelson v. Globe Int'l, 626 F. Supp. 969, 980–81, 12 Media L. Rep. 1785, 1794 (S.D.N.Y. 1986) (applying New York's "gross departure from journalistic standards" test where plaintiff is private figure). For a discussion of such issues, see Chapter 2, §2.11(F).

[89]RESTATEMENT (SECOND), *supra* note 5, at §§652F & 652G; Crump v. Beckley Newspapers, 320 S.E.2d 70, 83 n.5, 10 Media L. Rep. 2225, 2233 n.5 (W. Va. 1983); McCall v. Courier-Journal & Louisville Times Co., 623 S.W.2d 882, 887, 7 Media L. Rep. 2118, 2122 (Ky. 1981); Bond v. Pecaut, 561 F. Supp. 1037 (N.D. Ill. 1983), *aff'd without opinion,* 734 F.2d 18 (7th Cir. 1984) (matter disclosed in judicial proceedings); Bichler v. Union Bank & Trust Co., 745 F.2d 1006, 1011, 10 Media L. Rep. 2393, 2396 (6th Cir. 1984) (en banc). For a discussion of the common law absolute and qualified privileges, see Chapter 2, §§2.13, 2.14, and 2.15.

[90]Faloona v. Hustler Magazine, 799 F.2d 1000, 1004–05, 13 Media L. Rep. 1353, 1356–57 (5th Cir. 1986); Faucheux v. Magazine Mgmt. Co., 5 Media L. Rep. 1697, 1701 (E.D. Pa. 1979). *But see Braun,* 726 F.2d at 255, 10 Media L. Rep. at 1505. *See generally* W. PROSSER & P. KEETON, HANDBOOK ON THE LAW OF TORTS 867–68 (5th ed. 1984).

[91]385 U.S. 374, 1 Media L. Rep. 1971 (1967).

[92]419 U.S. 245, 1 Media L. Rep. 1815 (1974).

In *Hill*, the defendant magazine contained an article concerning a play that was opening on Broadway. The play, based on a novel by the same author, depicted the experience of a family held hostage and violently beaten and abused in their own home by three escaped convicts. While neither the novel nor the play purported to be a true account, the defendant's article claimed that both works were inspired by the actual experience of James Hill, who, along with his family, had been held hostage at home by three escaped convicts. Contrary to the portrayal of the event in the book and play, however, the Hill family had not been subjected to any violence or abuse by their captors, nor had they engaged in the heroic acts described in the book and play.[93]

James Hill brought an action under New York's privacy statute[94] alleging that the article gave a false and damaging impression of the experience of his family. The New York courts held in favor of the plaintiff on the ground that the defendant fictionalized the plaintiffs' experience through material and substantial falsifications.[95] The Supreme Court set aside the judgment because the trial court's instructions to the jury did not specify clearly that fictionalization alone could not be the basis for liability; that the defendant acted with actual malice also had to be shown.[96]

In *Cantrell*, the plaintiffs brought a false light claim based on a newspaper article about them. The article sought to depict the impact on the community of a fatal bridge collapse by focusing on the experience of Mrs. Cantrell and her children, the family of one of the forty-four people killed in the disaster.[97] As research material for the article, the defendant reporter had visited Mrs. Cantrell's home and had talked with and photographed her children.[98]

Mrs. Cantrell objected to the article on the ground that it contained inaccuracies that cast her and her family in a false light and made them the objects of pity and ridicule.[99] Specifically, she objected to the article's emphasis on the family's poverty through the portrayal of their home as dirty and dilapidated and the attention focused on the old clothes worn by her children.[100] The article also falsely implied that the reporter had interviewed Mrs. Cantrell and claimed that "Margaret Cantrell will talk neither about what happened nor about how they are doing. She wears the same mask of non-expression she wore at the funeral," even though Mrs. Cantrell had been away during the entire time the reporter had been visiting her home.[101] The Court concluded from the "calculated falsehoods" in the article that the defendant reporter and newspaper

---

[93] 385 U.S. at 377–78, 1 Media L. Rep. at 1792.

[94] Although clearly a false light claim, the New York courts avoided labeling it as such and instead applied a judicial gloss to the statute to make fictionalization actionable. *Id.* at 381–82, 1 Media L. Rep. at 1793–94. *See also supra* note 20.

[95] *Id.* at 386, 1 Media L. Rep. at 1795–96. *See also* Spahn v. Julian Messner, Inc., 233 N.E.2d 840, 842 (N.Y. 1967) ("before recovery by a public figure may be had for unauthorized presentation of his life it must be shown, in addition to the other requirements of the statute, that the presentation is infected with material and substantial falsification . . . or with a reckless disregard for the truth"), *appeal dismissed*, 393 U.S. 1046 (1969).

[96] 385 U.S. at 396, 1 Media L. Rep. at 1799.

[97] The article in question was a "follow-up feature" written five months after the original prize-winning article about the disaster. 419 U.S. at 247, 1 Media L. Rep. at 1815.

[98] *Id.*

[99] *Id.* at 247–48, 1 Media L. Rep. at 1815–16.

[100] *Id.*

[101] *Id.*

publisher had published the article with the knowledge of its falsity or in reckless disregard of the truth, and upheld the judgment in favor of the plaintiffs.[102]

Hill and *Cantrell* both have been criticized for giving too little weight to First Amendment concerns: *Hill* because it did not consider the implications of allowing lawsuits for favorable, albeit inaccurate, descriptions of actual incidents;[103] and *Cantrell* because the information at issue was not obviously offensive.[104]

§3.8 APPLICATION OF DEFAMATION PRINCIPLES IN FALSE LIGHT CASES

False light is a relatively new and still-developing tort. One important aspect of this process is the extent to which established restrictions and limitations on defamation actions will be applied to false light claims.[105] The Restatement (Second) has concluded that

> [w]hen the false publicity is also defamatory so that either action may be maintained by the plaintiff, it is arguable that limitations of long standing that have been found desirable for the action for defamation should not be successfully evaded by proceeding upon a different theory of later origin . . . .[106]

The case law on this issue generally follows this approach, applying the limits on defamation claims to false light claims: the single publication rule and the Uniform Single Publication Act;[107] correction and retraction statutes;[108] the *Gertz* rule precluding recovery of presumed or punitive damages in defamation actions involving a matter of public concern, at least absent a showing of actual malice;[109] the requirement that special damages[110] be pleaded and proved by the plaintiff in "libel per quod" cases;[111] the rules on survival of claims

---

[102] 419 U.S. at 253, 1 Media L. Rep. at 1817–18. The Court distinguished such constitutional actual malice, defining it as "a term of art, created to provide a convenient shorthand expression for the standard of liability that must be established before a State may constitutionally permit public officials to recover for libel in actions brought against publishers," from common law malice, which "focus[es] on the defendant's attitude toward the plaintiff's privacy, not toward the truth or falsity of the material published." *Id.* at 251–52, 1 Media L. Rep. at 1817.

[103] Zimmerman, *False Light Invasion of Privacy: The Light That Failed,* 64 N.Y.U. L. REV. 364, 383–88 (1989).

[104] *Id.* at 388–89.

[105] This assumes that the relevant jurisdiction recognizes false light. *See supra* §3.4.

[106] RESTATEMENT (SECOND), *supra* note 5, at §652E, cmt. e.

[107] *See* 14 U.L.A. 375–80 (West 1990) (setting forth uniform act and listing jurisdictions where it has been adopted); Fleury v. Harper & Row, Pubrs., 698 F.2d 1022, 9 Media L. Rep. 1200 (9th Cir.), *cert. denied,* 464 U.S. 846 (1983). This case was overruled on other grounds in In re Complaint of McLinn, 739 F.2d 1395 (9th Cir. 1984) (en banc). Khaury v. Playboy Pubns., 430 F. Supp. 1342 (S.D.N.Y. 1977); Fouts v. Fawcett Pubns., 116 F. Supp. 535 (D. Conn. 1953).

[108] Kapellas v. Kofman, 459 P.2d 912 (1969); Werner v. Times-Mirror Co., 14 Cal. Rptr. 208, 215–16 (Cal. Ct. App. 1961); Magenis v. Fisher Broadcasting, 798 P.2d 1106, 1109–10, 18 Media L. Rep. 1229, 1232 (Or. Ct. App. 1990).

[109] RESTATEMENT (SECOND), *supra* note 5, at §652H, cmt. c; *see* Gertz v. Robert Welch, Inc., 418 U.S. 323, 349, 1 Media L. Rep. 1633, 1643 (1974). For a discussion of the rule as applied to libel claims, see Chapter 2, §2.16(A).

[110] Fellows v. National Enquirer, 721 P.2d 97, 108–09, 13 Media L. Rep. 1305, 1314–15 (Cal. 1986); Fogel v. Forbes, Inc., 500 F. Supp. 1081, 1088, 6 Media L. Rep. 1941, 1946 (E.D. Pa. 1980).

[111] "Libel per quod" refers to a statement whose defamatory nature is not apparent on its face, but rather requires knowledge of facts before its defamatory meaning is clear. For a discussion of libel per quod and libel per se, see Chapter 2, §2.5(I).

after a plaintiff's death;[112] statutes of limitations;[113] the rules on falsity;[114] and the "of and concerning" rule.[115]

---

[112]Frosch v. Grosset & Dunlap, Inc., 427 N.Y.S.2d 828, 6 Media L. Rep. 1272 (N.Y. App. Div. 1980) (holding estate of Marilyn Monroe could not sue for invasion of privacy based on biography published after Monroe's death). For a discussion of this issue in defamation cases, see Chapter 2, §2.10.

[113]Eastwood v. Cascade Broadcasting Co., 722 P.2d 1295, 1297–98, 13 Media L. Rep. 1136 (Wash. 1986) (but noting contrary cases); Gashgai v. Leibowitz, 703 F.2d 10, 13 (1st Cir. 1983); Weiner v. Superior Ct., 130 Cal. Rptr. 61, 63 (Cal. Ct. App. 1976); Smith v. Esquire, Inc., 494 F. Supp. 967, 970, 6 Media L. Rep. 1825, 1827 (D. Md. 1980); White v. Fawcett Pubns., 324 F. Supp. 403, 407–08 (W.D. Mo. 1971); Magenis v. Fisher Broadcasting, 798 P.2d 1106, 1109, 18 Media L. Rep. 1229 (Or. Ct. App. 1990). However, there is substantial contrary authority. Uhl v. Columbia Broadcasting Sys., 476 F. Supp. 1134, 1136, 5 Media L. Rep. 1801, 1801–02 (W.D. Pa. 1979) (defamation statute of limitations does not apply to false light claim where statutes make defamation and invasion of privacy "separate and distinct" torts, but favorably noting that statutory amendment had eliminated anomaly in future cases); Jensen v. Times Mirror Co., 634 F. Supp. 304, 315, 12 Media L. Rep. 2137, 2144 (D. Conn. 1986) (applying general tort statute of limitations of three years to false light claim rather than two-year statute of limitations for libel and slander), *on reconsideration certified for appeal on other grounds*, 647 F. Supp. 1525, 13 Media L. Rep. 2160 (D. Conn. 1986); Wood v. Hustler Magazine, 736 F.2d 1084, 1087–89, 10 Media L. Rep. 2113, 2115–16 (5th Cir. 1984) (applying general tort statute of limitations of two years to false light claim rather than one-year statute of limitations for libel and slander). *See generally* Annot., *Limitation of Actions: Invasion of Right of Privacy,* 33 A.L.R.4th 479 (1984).

[114]*See supra* §3.5(F).

[115]*See supra* §3.5(B).

CHAPTER 4

PRIVATE FACTS

§4.1 INTRODUCTION

This chapter discusses one of the four privacy torts—the public disclosure of true but highly offensive private facts. It also includes a brief overview of the development of privacy law.

§4.2 ORIGIN OF THE RIGHT OF PRIVACY

The right of privacy has its legal roots not in a judicial decision or legislative enactment, but in the publication of a law review article. In December 1890, the *Harvard Law Review* published "The Right to Privacy"[1] by Boston attorneys Samuel D. Warren II and Louis D. Brandeis. The article synthesized strands of the then-existing law of intellectual property, copyright, trade secrets, and contractual rights in confidential situations to create a legal framework for a new tort based on the "right to be let alone."[2]

In a frequently quoted passage, Warren and Brandeis (Brandeis later achieved distinction as a justice of the U.S. Supreme Court) fired the following salvo at turn-of-the-century American newspapers:

> The press is overstepping in every direction the obvious bounds of propriety and of decency. Gossip is no longer the resource of the idle and of the vicious, but has become a trade, which is pursued with industry as well as effrontery. To satisfy a prurient taste the details of sexual relations are spread broadcast in the columns of the daily papers. To occupy the indolent, column upon column is filled with idle gossip, which can only be procured by intrusion upon the domestic circle.[3]

The analysis in the Warren-Brandeis article was not immediately adopted by the courts, and indeed has yet to be adopted by all courts.[4] However, in

---

[1] Warren & Brandeis, *The Right to Privacy*, 4 HARV. L. REV. 193 (1890) (hereinafter *The Right to Privacy*).

[2] The phrase "the right to be let alone" was coined by Judge Cooley in his 19th-century treatise on torts, COOLEY ON TORTS 29 (2d ed. 1888). *The Right to Privacy, supra* note 1, at 195 n.4.

[3] *The Right to Privacy, supra* note 1, at 196. This view of the press has been criticized as exaggerated and inaccurate. Barron, *Demystifying a Landmark Citation*, 13 SUFFOLK U. L. REV. 875 (1979); D.R. PEMBER, PRIVACY AND THE PRESS: THE LAW, THE MASS MEDIA, AND THE FIRST AMENDMENT (1970).

[4] One of the earliest cases to consider the Warren-Brandeis proposal was Roberson v. Rochester Folding Box Co., 64 N.E. 442 (N.Y. 1902), in which the defendant used the photograph of a young woman on the label of its flour packages without her consent. She brought a privacy action against the advertisers alleging

1960, 70 years after publication of the Warren-Brandeis article, noted torts scholar William L. Prosser authored a law review article entitled "Privacy," which was a comprehensive review of the cases construing the Warren-Brandeis privacy analysis. In his article, Prosser concluded that the law of privacy actually consisted of four distinct causes of action:[5]

(1) intrusion on the plaintiff's seclusion or solitude, or into his private affairs (intrusion);

(2) public disclosure of embarrassing private facts about the plaintiff (private facts);

(3) publicity that places the plaintiff in a false light in the public eye (false light); and

(4) appropriation, for the defendant's advantage, of the plaintiff's name or likeness (appropriation or right of publicity).[6]

---

that she had suffered humiliation and emotional distress from the advertisements. The New York Court of Appeal, by a 4-3 vote, rejected her claim (and the Warren-Brandeis proposal), because "[a]n examination of the authorities leads us to the conclusion that the so-called 'right of privacy' has not as yet found an abiding place in our jurisprudence." *Id.* at 447. *Roberson* was widely criticized. *See* W. PROSSER & P. KEETON, THE LAW OF TORTS §117, at 850–51 (5th ed. 1984) (hereinafter LAW OF TORTS) (discussion of "storm of public disapproval" following *Roberson*). To answer critics, one of the concurring judges in *Roberson* wrote a law review article defending the decision. *See* O'Brien, *The Right of Privacy,* 2 COLUM. L. REV. 437 (1902). The New York Legislature responded to the criticism of *Roberson* by enacting a statute that made it both a misdemeanor and a tort to use the name, portrait, or picture of any person for advertising or trade purposes. *See* N.Y. CIV. RIGHTS LAW §§50–51 (McKinney 1992).

A few years later, in Pavesich v. New England Life Insurance Co., 50 S.E. 68 (Ga. 1905), the Georgia Supreme Court created a common law right of privacy similar to that espoused by Warren and Brandeis. In *Pavesich,* the plaintiff's picture was used in a newspaper advertisement as a commercial endorsement for life insurance without his consent. The Georgia Supreme Court held that *Roberson* had been wrongly decided:

So thoroughly convinced are we that the law recognizes, as a legal right, the right of privacy, and that the publication of one's picture without his consent by another as an advertisement, for the mere purpose of increasing the profits and gains of the advertiser, is an invasion of this right, that we venture to predict that the day will come that the American bar will marvel that a contrary view was ever entertained by judges of eminence and ability . . . .

Id. at 80–81. Both *Roberson* and *Pavesich* concern the privacy tort known as "appropriation" or "right of publicity." *See* Chapter 6. These cases might also have been brought as false light privacy claims, because the endorsements were false. *See* Chapter 3.

The private facts cause of action was also anticipated in *Pavesich,* along with the First Amendment concerns inherent in that branch of privacy:

The right of privacy is unquestionably limited by the right to speak and print. But there may arise cases where the speaking or printing of the truth might be considered an abuse of the liberty of speech and of the press, as in a case where matters of purely private concern, wholly foreign to a legitimate expression of opinion on the subject under discussion, are injected into the discussion for no other purpose and with no other motive than to annoy and harass the individual referred to. Such cases might be of rare occurrence, but if such should arise, the party aggrieved may not be without a remedy.

50 S.E. at 74. Today, most states recognize a tort cause of action for the public disclosure of highly offensive but true private facts. *See* LIBEL DEFENSE RESOURCE CENTER, 50-STATE SURVEY, CURRENT DEVELOPMENTS IN MEDIA LIBEL AND INVASION OF PRIVACY LAW (1992–93) (updated annually; available from the Libel Defense Resource Center, New York, N.Y.). Some jurisdictions recognize only a very limited cause of action. Anderson v. Fisher Broadcasting Co., 712 P.2d 803, 814 (Or. 1986); Hall v. Salisbury Post, 372 S.E.2d 711, 15 Media L. Rep. 2329 (N.C. 1988); *see also* Rutledge v. Phoenix Newspapers, 715 P.2d 1243, 12 Media L. Rep. 1969 (Ariz. Ct. App. 1986) (failure to state intentional infliction of emotional distress claim precludes private facts claim).

[5]Prosser, *Privacy,* 48 CAL. L. REV. 383 (1960). This taxonomy has been adopted by the Restatement (Second) of Torts §§652B–E (1977) [hereinafter RESTATEMENT (SECOND)]. *Compare* RESTATEMENT (FIRST), *infra* note 18. One commentator has disagreed with Prosser's division of the privacy tort into four branches, arguing instead that invasion of privacy should be a single tort based on an affront to human dignity and "an interference with individuality, an interference with the right of the individual to do what he will." Bloustein, *Privacy As an Aspect of Human Dignity: An Answer to Dean Prosser,* 39 N.Y.U. L. REV. 962, 1003 (1964).

[6]Prosser, *supra* note 5, at 389. Early cases, such as those cited *supra* note 4, did not distinguish between the privacy torts. Although each of the privacy torts has some similarities, the substantial differences among these actions require that they be treated distinctly. False light, like defamation, is essentially about false statements; it has little to do with a right to be let alone. Intrusion and private facts do concern the right to be let alone. Appropriation usually does not involve a desire to avoid publicity but a desire to get paid for the use of one's name or likeness. The private facts, intrusion, appropriation, and false light actions are

Although the Warren-Brandeis article contained strains of all four of these privacy torts, the authors' focus was on the need for a cause of action for public disclosure of embarrassing but true private facts. This chapter will examine the private facts cause of action in greater detail. The other three privacy torts are analyzed in other chapters.[7]

§4.3 History of the Private Facts Tort

§4.3(A) The Warren-Brandeis Approach

The privacy tort proposed by Warren and Brandeis was much broader than the private facts cause of action recognized today in most jurisdictions. Warren and Brandeis described their tort as follows:

> The design of the law must be to protect those persons with whose affairs the community has no legitimate concern, from being dragged into an undesirable and undesired publicity and to protect all persons, whatsoever; their position or station, from having matters which they may properly prefer to keep private, made public against their will. It is the unwarranted invasion of individual privacy which is reprehended, and to be, so far as possible, prevented.[8]

In effect, Warren and Brandeis applied a subjective standard to restrict "undesirable and undesired" publicity, gauged by the personal tastes and sensibilities of the prospective plaintiff. Thus, while some people might welcome a newspaper report of a party at their home, other people might abhor the publicity and find the report a matter "which they may properly prefer to keep private."[9] Over the years, however, the courts have replaced the subjective standard suggested by the Warren-Brandeis approach with an objective standard that requires the private facts disclosed to be "highly offensive to a reasonable person."[10]

Warren and Brandeis proposed some limitations on the privacy tort, including an exception for any "publication of matter which is of public or general interest,"[11] the use of privileges found in defamation law to excuse what could otherwise be a privacy invasion,[12] the defense of the plaintiff's consent to the publicity,[13] and waiver when the plaintiff made public facts that would ordinarily be private.[14]

---

separate and distinct torts. *Compare* Gill v. Hearst Pub'g Co., 40 Cal. 2d 224, 253 P.2d 441 (Cal. 1953) (published photograph of couple kissing in public place could not be basis for private facts action) *with* Gill v. Curtis Pub'g Co., 38 Cal. 2d 273, 239 P.2d 630 (Cal. 1952) (same plaintiffs could recover under false light theory for publication of same photograph with different article on shallowness of love at first sight). Unfortunately, many judges and lawyers talk about invasion of privacy as if it were one tort instead of four.

[7]False light is discussed in Chapter 3, intrusion in Chapter 5, and appropriation in Chapter 6.
[8]*The Right to Privacy, supra* note 1, at 214–15.
[9]*Id.* at 215. In this respect, the Warren-Brandeis approach contained strains of the appropriation branch of privacy where a person's private life was the property of that person and could not be disclosed to others without that person's permission. Zimmerman, *Requiem for a Heavyweight: A Farewell to Warren and Brandeis's Privacy Tort,* 68 Cornell L. Rev. 291, 295 (1983). As Warren and Brandeis wrote: "The right of property in its widest sense, including all possession, including all rights and privileges, and hence embracing the right to an inviolate personality, affords alone that broad basis upon which the protection which the individual demands can be rested." *The Right to Privacy, supra* note 1, at 211.
[10]Restatement (Second) §652D(a). *See infra* §4.6(D).
[11]*The Right to Privacy, supra* note 1, at 214–16. *See infra* §4.6(E).
[12]*The Right to Privacy, supra* note 1, at 216. *See infra* §4.9(B).
[13]*The Right to Privacy, supra* note 1, at 218. *See infra* §4.9(A).
[14]*The Right to Privacy, supra* note 1, at 218. *See infra* §4.9(A).

Truth was not a defense to the Warren-Brandeis privacy action.[15] Warren and Brandeis also wrote that a disclosure without malice was not a defense to their privacy tort.[16] Their proposed remedies included actions for damages, even in the absence of special damages; injunctive relief in a limited number of cases; and criminal penalties in special situations.[17]

§4.3(B) The Restatement (Second) of Torts

The Restatement (Second) of Torts §652D—"Publicity Given to Private Life"—describes the cause of action for private facts as follows:

> One who gives publicity to a matter concerning the private life of another is subject to liability to the other for invasion of his privacy, if the matter publicized is of a kind that:
> (a) would be highly offensive to a reasonable person, and
> (b) is not of legitimate concern to the public.[18]

Although some commentators disagree as to what constitutes a plaintiff's prima facie case, most courts use the Restatement (Second) as the definitive guide in determining what a plaintiff must show to recover for public disclosure of private facts.[19]

§4.4 PLAINTIFFS

§4.4(A) The Plaintiff Must Be Identifiable

In a private facts action, the offending disclosure of intimate facts must refer to, or be of and concerning, the plaintiff. Like the plaintiff in a defamation action, the private facts plaintiff must demonstrate that third parties would recognize that the offending disclosure refers to the plaintiff.[20]

---

[15]*The Right to Privacy, supra* note 1, at 218. *See infra* §4.6(A).

[16]*The Right to Privacy, supra* note 1, at 218. Warren and Brandeis used "malice" to mean spite or ill will. See *infra* §4.7 on whether there is a fault requirement in private facts cases.

[17]*The Right to Privacy, supra* note 1, at 219. *See infra* §4.10.

[18]The Restatement (First) of Torts included a section on "Interference with Privacy," which simply provided that "[a] person who unreasonably and seriously interferes with another's interest in not having his affairs known to others or his likeness exhibited to the public is liable to the other." RESTATEMENT (FIRST) OF TORTS §867 (1939).

Conspicuously absent from the Restatement (First) was any language limiting the cause of action on First Amendment grounds. Indeed, the examples set forth in §867 indicated a much broader liability for private facts than currently exists. The Restatement (Second) provides a much more detailed and sophisticated view of privacy, including a separate section for each of the four privacy torts.

[19]Prosser's view was that the plaintiff must show that (1) the disclosure was public, (2) the facts disclosed were private and not public, and (3) the matter made public would be highly offensive to a reasonable person of ordinary sensibilities. LAW OF TORTS, *supra* note 4, §117, at 856–57. In addition to these three elements, the Restatement (Second) requires that the plaintiff show that the public did not have a legitimate interest in the matter disclosed. The Prosser and Keeton treatise seems to favor an approach where the court examines how shocking the disclosure was and balances it against the nature of the publication and the extent of public interest in the matter disclosed. *Id.* at 857 and n.78 (citing Hill, *Defamation and Privacy Under the First Amendment*, 76 COLUM. L. REV. 1205, 1258–62 (1976)). This approach confuses the different elements of this tort and makes it impossible to apply the tort consistently or to analyze it logically. It is also, in effect, a call for content discrimination, which the First Amendment clearly forbids (see Chapter 12), because it requires an assessment of the value of the speech involved. Fortunately, the Restatement (Second) elements of the private facts action are the prevailing legal standard, especially after Cox Broadcasting v. Cohn, 420 U.S. 469 (1975), in which the Supreme Court extensively utilized the Restatement (Second) in analyzing that seminal private facts case. *See also infra* note 143.

[20]In defamation, this is referred to as the "of and concerning" requirement. Similarly, in privacy cases, the offending disclosure must be "of and concerning" the plaintiff. Branson v. Fawcett Pubns., 124 F. Supp. 429, 433 (E.D. Ill. 1954).

In most cases, the identification of the plaintiff by his or her full name or the depiction of the plaintiff in a clear photograph will satisfy this requirement.[21] Other fact patterns raise more difficult issues.

In one case, the Florida Supreme Court found that the reference in a novel to the plaintiff's first name, "Zelma," coupled with a detailed description of some of her personality traits, was enough to make the plaintiff "recognizable to herself and to her friends and acquaintances."[22] On the other hand, slight changes in the plaintiff's name or description of conduct associated with the plaintiff may be enough to keep the plaintiff from successfully asserting a private facts claim. In one case, the court found that an author's fictionalized account of a boyhood friend's exploits did not reasonably identify the friend when his name had been changed from "Esco Middlebrooks" to "Esco Brooks," and that the characteristics and exploits of the fictionalized character did not reasonably parallel those of the real person.[23]

Usually, the reference to a prior name of a plaintiff in the offending disclosure will not be sufficient identification, so long as the plaintiff's new name or identity is not revealed.[24] Similarly, courts generally have held that where the plaintiff is not identified by name, a depiction of a past event in which the plaintiff was a participant does not meet the identification requirement so long as the depiction does not identify the plaintiff in his or her present setting.[25]

Because the privacy right is personal in nature, references to a plaintiff's property, such as a house, car or horse,[26] or job title[27] generally will not sufficiently identify a plaintiff to sustain a private facts claim.

---

[21]Lambert v. Dow Chem. Co., 215 So. 673, 675 (La. 1968) (graphic photographs of plaintiff's severe on-the-job leg injury shown in safety meetings to fellow workers included plaintiff's name).

[22]Cason v. Baskin, 20 So. 2d 243 (Fla. 1944). *See also* Ross v. Midwest Communications, 870 F.2d 271 (5th Cir. 1989) (television documentary included plaintiff's first name and picture of plaintiff's residence).

[23]Middlebrooks v. Curtis Pub'g Co., 281 F. Supp. 1, 6 (D.S.C. 1968), *aff'd,* 413 F.2d 141 (4th Cir. 1969).

[24]*Compare* Meeropol v. Nizer, 560 F.2d 1061 (2d Cir. 1977), *cert. denied,* 434 U.S. 1013 (1978) *with* Melvin v. Reid, 112 Cal. App. 285, 297 P. 91 (Cal. Ct. App. 1931). *See infra* §4.6(E)(iv).

[25]In Bernstein v. National Broadcasting Co., 129 F. Supp. 817 (D.D.C.), *aff'd,* 232 F.2d 369 (D.C. Cir. 1955), *cert. denied,* 352 U.S. 945 (1956), the plaintiff's murder conviction and subsequent pardon for that crime were depicted on "The Big Story," a 1950s television show on fictionalized reenactments of actual news stories. Although the plaintiff's actual name was not used, he claimed that the actor who portrayed him bore a resemblance to him and that there were numerous similarities between the facts of his case and the facts broadcast, which made it possible for people to recognize him. The district court rejected the plaintiff's arguments and granted summary judgment for the defendant because, in addition to being a report on events of public interest, the identity of the plaintiff was so thoroughly disguised that it would be unreasonable for the average person to have recognized the plaintiff. The court noted that only those who already knew about the plaintiff's story could have possibly identified him, so there was no disclosure of any *private* facts. 129 F. Supp. at 833–37. *Accord* Miller v. National Broadcasting Co., 157 F. Supp. 240, 243 (D. Del. 1957) ("The Big Story" reenactment of plaintiff's past bank robbery did not use plaintiff's name or identify him in present setting); Smith v. National Broadcasting Co., 138 Cal. App. 2d 807, 292 P.2d 600, 603–04 (Cal. Ct. App. 1956) (televised story about plaintiff's false report of escaped panther did not identify plaintiff in present setting with past incident).

[26]Rawls v. Conde Nast Pubns., 446 F.2d 313 (5th Cir. 1971), *cert. denied,* 404 U.S. 1038 (1972), *reh'g denied,* 405 U.S. 969 (1972) (blurred photograph of plaintiff's house not sufficient identification of plaintiff); Branson v. Fawcett Pubns., 124 F. Supp. 429, 433 (E.D. Ill. 1954) (photograph of plaintiff's wrecked car not "of and concerning the plaintiff"); Bayer v. Ralston Purina Co., 484 S.W.2d 473, 475 (Mo. 1972) (photograph of Appaloosa horse used in defendant's advertisements did not identify plaintiff, horse's owner). *Contra* Motschenbacher v. R.J. Reynolds Tobacco Co., 498 F.2d 821 (9th Cir. 1974) (use of professional racer's distinctive car sufficient identification).

[27]For example, the reference in the movie *John Goldfarb, Please Come Home* to the president of Notre Dame University was not a sufficient identification of the school's current president to enable him to assert a privacy claim under New York's civil rights statute. University of Notre Dame Du Lac v. Twentieth Century Fox Film Corp., 256 N.Y.S.2d 301 (N.Y. App. Div.), *aff'd,* 207 N.E.2d 508 (N.Y. 1965).

§4.4(B) The Plaintiff Must Be Living

As in defamation, the private facts action only applies to a living plaintiff and will be extinguished with the death of the plaintiff,[28] unless the lawsuit was filed before the plaintiff's death.[29]

§4.4(C) Family Members As Plaintiffs

A deceased person's relatives may not maintain an action for invasion of privacy, either based on their own privacy interests or as a representative for the deceased, where the alleged invasion was directed primarily at the deceased.[30] Thus, a private facts action will not lie unless the relative is named in the disclosure and has an independent private facts claim based on the disclosure.[31] However, a few jurisdictions appear to recognize a "relational right" of privacy and allow family members to assert a private facts action based solely on publicity about a relative.[32]

§4.4(D) Legal Entities As Plaintiffs

Because emotional injury is at the heart of a private facts claim, the class of potential plaintiffs traditionally has been more limited than in defamation cases, where harm to reputation is the central issue. Thus, the right of privacy generally does not apply to a corporation, business association, or partnership, because these organizations do not have personal "feelings."[33] However, at least one appellate court has held that partnerships may state a cause of action for invasion of privacy.[34]

---

[28] Cordell v. Detective Pubns., 419 F.2d 989, 990 n.3 (6th Cir. 1969) (citing numerous authorities); Gruschus v. Curtis Pub'g Co., 342 F.2d 775, 776–77 (10th Cir. 1965); Reed v. Real Detective Pub'g Co., 162 P.2d 133, 138 (Ariz. 1945).

[29] At common law, actions for torts of a personal nature were extinguished upon the death of the plaintiff. Many states, however, have enacted statutes that prevent abatement of the privacy claim, and other personal torts, once the plaintiff has filed it, even if the plaintiff dies during the pendency of the action. *See, e.g.,* CAL. PROB. CODE §573 (Deering 1991); National Bank of Commerce v. Shaklee Corp., 503 F. Supp. 533, 539 (W.D. Tex. 1980). Special rules have evolved in this area in appropriation cases. *See* Chapter 6.

[30] *See Cordell,* 419 F.2d at 990 n.3 (citing numerous authorities); Metter v. Los Angeles Examiner, 35 Cal. App. 2d 304, 311–12 (Cal. Ct. App. 1939) (husband of woman who committed suicide could not assert cause of action for private facts because wife's right to privacy was personal and was extinguished by her death); Justice v. Belo Broadcasting, 472 F. Supp. 145 (N.D. Tex. 1979) (parents not actually named in report could not assert cause of action); Maritote v. Desilu Prods., 345 F.2d 418 (7th Cir.), *cert. denied,* 382 U.S. 883 (1965) (wife and son of gangster Al Capone could not assert privacy claim); *Gruschus,* 342 F.2d 775 (parents could not assert action for child); Werner v. Times-Mirror, 193 Cal. App. 2d 111, 14 Cal. Rptr. 208 (Cal. Ct. App. 1961) (spouse could not assert privacy action); Kelly v. Johnson Pub'g, 160 Cal. App. 2d 718, 325 P.2d 659 (Cal. Ct. App. 1958) (siblings could not assert privacy action).

[31] Boyd v. Thomson Newspaper Pub'g Co., 6 Media L. Rep. 1020 (W.D. Ark. 1980) (even though parents of deceased child were named in newspaper article about doctor on trial for malpractice, parents did not have private facts claim because claim was based on publicity about deceased child).

[32] For example, Georgia has allowed such derivative claims. Cox Broadcasting v. Cohn, 420 U.S. 469, 474 (1975); Bazemore v. Savannah Hosp., 155 S.E. 194 (Ga. 1930). At one time Alabama appeared to allow such claims, Smith v. Doss, 37 So. 2d 118, 121 (Ala. 1948), but it is now clear that it does not recognize them. Fitch v. Voit, 624 So. 2d 542, 543–44, 21 Media L. Rep. 1863, 1864 (Ala. 1993).

[33] CNA Fin. Corp. v. Teamsters Local 743, 515 F. Supp. 942, 946–47 (N.D. Ill. 1981) (corporation cannot maintain action for invasion of privacy in own name or in name of employees); Maysville Transit Co. v. Ort, 177 S.W.2d 369, 370 (Ky. 1943) (disclosure of confidential tax reports of corporation actionable under state statute; however, in absence of statute, corporation had no claim for invasion of privacy because it had no such rights).

[34] H & M Assocs. v. City of El Centro, 109 Cal. App. 3d 399, 410, 167 Cal. Rptr. 392 (Cal. Ct. App. 1980). *Contra* Ion Equip. Corp. v. Nelson, 168 Cal. Rptr. 361, 366 (Cal. Ct. App. 1980) (corporation has

§4.5 ORAL DISCLOSURE

In one respect, the Warren-Brandeis privacy tort was narrower than its modern counterpart—the authors restricted the tort to the printed word and noted that "[t]he injury resulting from . . . oral communications would ordinarily be so trifling that the law might well, in the interest of free speech, disregard it altogether."[35] Of course, Warren and Brandeis could not have anticipated the impact of motion pictures, radio, and television on privacy rights, and there is little doubt today that the tort applies to both oral and written disclosures.[36]

§4.6 ELEMENTS OF THE PRIVATE FACTS CAUSE OF ACTION

§4.6(A) Truth

The essential difference between a private facts claim and a defamation or false light claim is that the former involves true statements of fact, while the latter involves false statements of fact.[37] Whether, in light of the First Amendment, there can ever by any liability under a private facts theory, because only true statements are involved, is a question that the Supreme Court has expressly and repeatedly left open.[38] A negative answer would obliterate the private facts tort.

§4.6(B) Publicity

Another difference between a cause of action for defamation or false light and a cause of action for private facts is that the defamation action is triggered by a "publication" to a third party, while the private facts action requires "publicity."[39]

---

no "feelings" that may be injured by violation of privacy tort, although statutory claim for illegal eavesdropping may lie).

[35]*The Right to Privacy, supra* note 1, at 217.

[36]LAW OF TORTS, *supra* note 4, §117, at 858 & n.94 (citing Mau v. Rio Grande Oil, 28 F. Supp. 845 (N.D. Cal. 1939)); Strickler v. National Broadcasting Co., 167 F. Supp. 68 (S.D. Cal. 1958) (motion pictures); Ettore v. Philco Television Broadcasting Corp., 229 F.2d 481 (3d Cir.), *cert. denied,* 351 U.S. 926 (1956) (television).

[37]*See, e.g.,* Fellows v. National Enquirer, 42 Cal. 3d 234, 242, 721 P.2d 97 (Cal. 1986); Leidholdt v. LFP, Inc., 860 F.2d 890, 893, 15 Media L. Rep. 2201, 2204 (9th Cir. 1988), *cert. denied,* 489 U.S. 1080 (1989); Romaine v. Kallinger, 537 A.2d 284, 15 Media L. Rep. 1209, 1215 (N.J. 1988).

[38]Cox Broadcasting Corp. v. Cohn, 420 U.S. 469, 490–91, 1 Media L. Rep. 1819, 1827 (1975); Florida Star v. B.J.F., 491 U.S. 524, 530, 16 Media L. Rep. 1801 (1989); RESTATEMENT (SECOND) §652D ("It has not been established with certainty that liability of this nature [private facts] is consistent with the free-speech and free-press provisions of the First Amendment to the Constitution, as applied to state law through the Fourteenth Amendment."); *see also infra* §6(C)(i), (ii), and (iii).

Before *Florida Star,* some commentators concluded that *Cox Broadcasting* indicated a receptivity to private facts liability outside the public records context. LAW OF TORTS, *supra* note 4, §117, at 863 & n.54 (citing Hill, *Defamation and Privacy Under the First Amendment,* 76 COLUM. L. REV. 1205, 1268 (1976)). *See also* Time, Inc. v. Hill, 385 U.S. 374, 383 n.7 (1967) ("revelations may be so intimate and so unwarranted in view of the victim's position as to outrage the community's notion of decency"). Other commentators, however, concluded that *Cox Broadcasting* sounded the death knell for the private facts tort. Zimmerman, *supra* note 9, at 306. At least some members of the Supreme Court agree that the private facts tort is constitutional. *Florida Star,* 491 U.S. at 550–53 (White, Rehnquist, O'Connor, JJ., dissenting). In any event, the Court has not completely eliminated this tort, even though it has always ruled against private facts claims. *See Florida Star,* 491 U.S. at 530 ("[O]ur decisions have without exception upheld the press' right to publish").

[39]In defamation law, the publication requirement is usually satisfied by a communication from the defendant to a third party, even if that communication reaches only one person. RESTATEMENT (SECOND) §577. The

In the case of media defendants, the publicity requirement is easily met because the disclosure is usually contained in widely circulated articles or broadcasts. The publicity requirement becomes a more difficult concept to apply when nonmedia defendants are involved.[40] Some commentators have unsuccessfully argued against the publicity requirement on the grounds that "neighborhood gossip" and disclosures to a small circle of friends and family can be just as damaging to the victim as a public disclosure of the same information through the media.[41] Indeed, the failure to make such conduct actionable probably renders this tort unconstitutional.[42]

§4.6(C) Private Information

A plaintiff seeking recovery for public disclosure of highly offensive private facts must show that the facts disclosed are indeed "private" and not matters of public record or descriptions of something that have been left open to the public eye.[43] The Restatement (Second) suggests that private facts may include descriptions of a person's sexual relations, family quarrels, embarrassing illnesses, most intimate personal letters, and details of a person's home life or unsavory past.[44]

The conduct of a person in a public area, such as a street or store, is open to public commentary and even unauthorized photography. For example, in a frequently cited case, *Gill v. Hearst Publishing Co.*,[45] the California Supreme Court held that the publication of a photograph of a couple in a romantic pose at an ice cream stand in a public market did not constitute disclosure of a private

---

private facts publicity requirement, however, is only satisfied by a communication that reaches the public at large or reaches so many people that the matter is certain to become public knowledge. *Id.* §652D, cmt. a; Harris v. Easton Pub'g Co., 483 A.2d 1377, 1385–86, 11 Media L. Rep. 1209 (Pa. Super. Ct. 1984) (publication to 17 people met publicity requirement); Kinsey v. Macur, 165 Cal. Rptr. 608 (Cal. Ct. App. 1980) (publicity requirement met where spurned lover mailed negative letters to 20 close friends, family, and former spouse of plaintiff).

[40]The following cases illustrate the private facts publicity requirement: Brents v. Morgan, 299 S.W. 967 (Ky. 1927) (publicity requirement satisfied by defendant storekeeper who exhibited large sign in storefront window, which faced heavily traveled thoroughfare, naming plaintiff and stating that plaintiff had failed to pay accounts at store); Santiesteban v. Goodyear Tire & Rubber Co., 306 F.2d 9 (5th Cir. 1962) (publicity requirement met when defendant tire company removed tires from plaintiff's car, which was parked in parking lot of plaintiff's employer, a posh country club, where numerous persons saw tireless vehicle and plaintiff's co-workers subjected plaintiff to ridicule); Biederman's of Springfield v. Wright, 322 S.W.2d 892 (Mo. 1959) (bill collector's loud pronouncements about plaintiff's debts in public place constituted publicity of private facts); Voneye v. Turner, 240 S.W.2d 588 (Ky. 1951) (creditor's letters to plaintiff's employer did not constitute publicity because disclosure not publicly made); Beard v. Akzona, Inc., 517 F. Supp. 128, 132 (E.D. Tenn. 1981) (communication of private facts to small group of people with job-related connections to one of the plaintiffs not "publicity" of private fact); Porten v. University of San Francisco, 64 Cal. App. 3d 825, 134 Cal. Rptr. 839 (Cal. Ct. App. 1976) (under common law private facts claim, university's disclosure of contents of student's grade transcript to Scholarship and Loan Commission did not constitute publicity because it was not directed to public or large number of persons; however, publicity not required to state claim under state constitution).

[41]LAW OF TORTS, *supra* note 4, §117, at 857–58 ("There is considerable doubt about the necessity for a public disclosure."); Zimmerman, *supra* note 9, at 340–41 ("The distinction between press coverage and gossip may be important to our subjective sense of well-being, but it appears to be a dubious basis for imposing liability only on mass communicators of public facts, especially in light of the serious infringement on the press and free speech that such a limitation engenders."). Professor Zimmerman concludes that the probable reason for the publicity requirement is a social judgment that "back-fence" gossip is not suitable for legal control. *Id.* at 341. However, she argues that it is questionable policy to impose liability on the press for disclosures that, if made to a smaller audience, would be too insignificant an offense to warrant legal attention.

[42]*Florida Star*, 491 U.S. at 540–41.
[43]RESTATEMENT (SECOND) §652D, cmt. d.
[44]*Id.*
[45]253 P.2d 441 (Cal. 1953).

fact.[46] Although the photograph was taken without the plaintiffs' knowledge or authorization, the court noted that the picture was not surreptitiously snapped in a private area and that "[i]n short, the photograph did not disclose anything which until then had been private, but rather only extended knowledge of the particular incident to a somewhat larger public than had actually witnessed it at the time of occurrence."[47]

In addition, where allegedly private facts have already been published or broadcast by the media, they are no longer private, so the republisher or rebroadcaster cannot be liable on a private facts theory.[48]

Similarly, the "disclosure" in news articles that a former U.S. Marine who heroically foiled an assassination attempt on President Ford was a homosexual did not reveal private facts, because the plaintiff was publicly active in the gay community.[49] However, where a plaintiff took affirmative steps to conceal her sex-change operation, a news article revealing her past gender could constitute a public disclosure of a private fact.[50]

Moreover, a person who involuntarily becomes the subject of publicity while being in a public area does not have an action for private facts. Photographs or descriptions of accidents, suicides, or crimes do not violate a person's privacy rights so long as they occur in public.[51] For example, in *Harrison v. Washington Post Co.,*[52] a man mistakenly arrested as a bank robber was filmed by a television cameraman while he was being led away in handcuffs by police.[53] The court held that the broadcast of the film was not a disclosure of private facts, because the arrest and handcuffing took place in public view on a public sidewalk.[54] In another case, a fan at a football game who was photographed with his pants zipper down could not recover under the private facts tort because he was photographed in a public place.[55]

---

[46]*Id.* at 443.

[47]*Id.* at 444–45. However, the same plaintiffs were able to state a false light claim where the same photograph was used in a different article about the shallowness of love at first sight. Gill v. Curtis Pub'g Co., 239 P.2d 630 (1952).

[48]Heath v. Playboy Enters., 732 F. Supp. 1145, 1149 (S.D. Fla. 1990); Wolf v. Regardie, 553 A.2d 1213, 1219, 16 Media L. Rep. 1780, 1784 (D.C. 1989); Faloona v. Hustler Magazine, 799 F.2d 1000, 1006, 13 Media L. Rep. 1353, 1358 (5th Cir. 1986), *cert. denied,* 479 U.S. 1088 (1987); Sipple v. Chronicle Pub'g Co., 154 Cal. App. 3d 1040, 1047, 201 Cal. Rptr. 665, 668–69, 10 Media L. Rep. 1690 (Cal. Ct. App. 1984) (citing Sperry Rand Corp. v. Hill, 356 F.2d 181, 185 (1st Cir.), *cert. denied,* 384 U.S. 973 (1966)).

[49]*Sipple,* 154 Cal. App. 3d at 1047.

[50]Diaz v. Oakland Tribune, 139 Cal. App. 3d 118, 188 Cal. Rptr. 762 (1983). The article in *Diaz* stated that the first woman president of her class at Alameda College "was no lady." The plaintiff had changed her name from Antonio to Toni and had amended her driver's license, Social Security, and high school records to reflect the change in gender. 139 Cal. App. 3d at 123–24.

[51]Branson v. Fawcett Pubns., 124 F. Supp. 429 (E.D. Ill. 1954) (photograph of automobile accident); Metter v. Los Angeles Examiner, 95 P.2d 491 (1939) (suicide leap in public); Cape Pubns. v. Bridges, 423 So. 2d 426, 8 Media L. Rep. 2535 (Fla. Ct. App. 1982), *petition denied,* 431 So. 2d 988 (Fla.), *cert. denied,* 464 U.S. 893 (1983) (photograph of partially clad hostage); Berg v. Minneapolis Star & Tribune Co., 79 F. Supp. 957, 962–63 (D. Minn. 1948) (photograph of plaintiff in courtroom during recess not actionable where there was no court rule prohibiting photographs when court not in session).

[52]391 A.2d 781 (D.C. 1978).

[53]*Id.* at 783.

[54]*Id.* at 784. *See also* Jacova v. Southern Radio & Television Co., 83 So. 2d 34 (Fla. 1955) (innocent patron of cigar shop filmed while being detained by police in gambling raid at shop); Penwell v. Taft Broadcasting Co., 469 N.E.2d 1025, 1028, 10 Media L. Rep. 1550 (Ohio Ct. App. 1984) (television broadcast of innocent bystander arrested in drug bust at bar). *But see* Taylor v. KTVB Inc., 525 P.2d 984, 987–88 (Idaho 1974) (film of naked crime suspect being arrested outside his home actionable if disclosure made with "malice").

[55]Neff v. Time, Inc., 406 F. Supp. 858, 861 (W.D. Pa. 1976). *See also* McNamara v. Freedom Newspapers, 802 S.W.2d 901, 18 Media L. Rep. 1679 (Tex. Ct. App. 1991) (photograph taken during high school soccer game that showed plaintiff's exposed genitals not actionable).

However, where the publicized event occurs in an area that is not truly public, such as inside a private home or hospital room, a private facts claim may be asserted.[56] Cases involving prison inmates have reached different conclusions about whether a prison is a public or private place. Courts appear to distinguish between inmates photographed in private areas of a prison or in areas open to public view.[57]

At least one early decision held, however, on very questionable grounds, that when the public disclosure is highly offensive and the public interest in the publicized event is allegedly minimal, the published photograph of a person in a public place may constitute a disclosure of a private fact.[58]

§4.6(C)(i) Public Records and Confidential Information

Information contained in government records open to the public is not private by nature and, hence, use of information in such records cannot, as a matter of law, be the basis for a private facts action.[59]

In *Cox Broadcasting Corp. v. Cohn*, the Supreme Court cited the Warren-Brandeis article and Section 652D of the Restatement (Second), noting that "[i]n this sphere of collision between claims of privacy and those of the free press, the interests on both sides are plainly rooted in the traditions and significant concerns of our society."[60] The Court, in its first decision involving a private facts claim, reversed the Georgia Supreme Court, holding that "the First and Fourteenth Amendments command nothing less than that the states may not impose sanctions on the publication of truthful information contained in official court records open to public inspection."[61]

Before *Cox Broadcasting*, many courts had held that the accurately reported contents of public records were not actionable under the private facts tort.[62] *Cox Broadcasting* reinforced this view, which had its roots in the Warren-

---

[56]Dietemann v. Time, Inc., 449 F.2d 245 (9th Cir. 1971) (unauthorized filming by hidden camera of medical treatment inside private home actionable); Barber v. Time, Inc., 159 S.W.2d 291 (Mo. 1942) (photograph of plaintiff in hospital room actionable). These cases really involve intrusion claims. *See* Chapter 5.

[57]*Compare* Huskey v. National Broadcasting Co., 632 F. Supp. 1282, 12 Media L. Rep. 2105 (N.D. Ill. 1986) (unauthorized photograph of inmate plaintiff in prison exercise cage stated privacy claim) *with* Cox Communications v. Lowe, 328 S.E.2d 384, 386, 11 Media L. Rep. 2314 (Ga. Ct. App.), *cert. denied*, 474 U.S. 982 (1985) (unauthorized filming of prisoner walking in prison yard open to public view not actionable).

[58]In Daily Times Democrat v. Graham, 162 So. 2d 474 (Ala. 1964), the Alabama Supreme Court upheld a judgment against the defendant newspaper for publishing a photograph of a woman whose dress had been blown up by jets of air as she was entering a county fair "fun house." The court found that the photograph had no legitimate news value and was "offensive to modesty and decency." The court did not discuss the fact that the woman was photographed in a public place where she was seen by numerous people, and appeared to be swayed by what it called the "obscene" nature of the photograph. *Id.* at 477. Although the case is apparently good law in Alabama, it is unlikely that it would be followed today, because the photograph was of activity in a public place in public view. McNamara, 802 S.W.2d at 905, 18 Media L. Rep. at 1681–82 ("We do not find *Graham* persuasive .... because it did not discuss or analyze the availability of First Amendment protection for the newspaper."). *See* Zimmerman, *supra* note 9, at 348 n.297. Moreover, the court's characterization of the photograph as "obscene" undoubtedly would fail to meet the constitutional standard for obscenity. *See* Miller v. California, 413 U.S. 15 (1973).

[59]Cox Broadcasting v. Cohn, 420 U.S. 469 (1975). In *Cox Broadcasting,* the father of a murdered rape victim brought an action for damages against a television station that broadcast the victim's name in violation of a Georgia statute prohibiting public identification of rape victims. The television reporter learned the victim's name by reading the indictment of the victim's assailants and attending the trial of one of them. The Georgia Supreme Court had found that the plaintiff's complaint stated a cause of action for public disclosure of highly offensive private facts and that the First and Fourteenth Amendments did not require dismissal of the complaint. Cox Broadcasting v. Cohn, 200 S.E.2d 127, 130–32 (Ga. 1973).

[60]420 U.S. at 491.

[61]*Id.* at 495.

[62]Langford v. Vanderbilt Univ., 287 S.W.2d 32, 39 (Tenn. 1956) (no invasion of common law right of privacy where news report based on pleadings filed in libel lawsuit); Hubbard v. Journal Pub'g Co., 368

Brandeis article,[63] by giving constitutional protection to accurate reports of matters of public record.

Cox Broadcasting certainly did not answer all the questions regarding disclosure of private facts contained in public records. For example, is the *Cox Broadcasting* rule eliminated when the information from those records is embellished or sensationalized? Courts construing *Cox Broadcasting* have extended the protection to substantially accurate reports of the contents of public records and have granted defendants summary judgment even though their reports may have contained some embellishment.[64]

Although accurate reports based on the contents of public records will not give rise to an action for private facts, certain government records not open to public inspection may be the basis for a private facts action.[65] The Restatement (Second) indicates that "if the record is one not open to public inspection, as in the case of income tax returns, it is not public, and there is an invasion of privacy when it is made so."[66]

In some cases the public disclosure of government records is restricted by statute.[67] Statutes restricting dissemination of the identity of persons in a drug treatment program[68] and public disclosure of taxpayer records[69] have been held not to apply to the news media, however, and, hence, a private facts case against media defendants would not lie. In these cases, the news media constituted third parties that obtained the information from sources covered by the statutes. Action against those who disclosed the information to the press was still a possibility.[70]

One court has held that simply because a public record exists containing the alleged private fact does not necessarily excuse the public disclosure of the

---

P.2d 147, 148 (N.M. 1962) (disclosure of sexual assault victim's identity in news article based on juvenile court records open to public privileged); Bell v. Courier-Journal & Louisville Times Co., 402 S.W.2d 84, 88 (Ky. Ct. App. 1966) (report of judge's delinquent taxes based on public tax records not actionable invasion of privacy).

[63]The Warren-Brandeis article called for a privilege for any publication "made in a court of justice, in legislative bodies, or the committees of those bodies; in municipal assemblies, or the committees of such assemblies, or practically by any communication made in any other public body." *The Right to Privacy*, supra note 1, at 216. The authors would have extended a similar privilege to reports based on such proceedings. *Id.* at 217.

[64]Valentine v. CBS, Inc., 698 F.2d 430, 9 Media L. Rep. 1249 (11th Cir. 1983) (*Cox Broadcasting* rule extended to lyrics of popular song naming plaintiff in connection with highly publicized murder and trial where lyrics merely disclosed facts that were part of trial public record); Moloney v. Tribune Pub'g Co., 613 P.2d 1179, 1182 n.1, 6 Media L. Rep. 1426, 1428 n.1 (Wash. Ct. App. 1980). This case was overruled on other grounds in Bender v. City of Seattle, 664 P.2d 492, 9 Media L. Rep. 2101 (Wash. 1983) (use of term "streaked" to describe incident in which teenager ran from her home naked was "ill-chosen embellishment" but not material falsehood; report of teen's death contained in sheriff's investigation report). Even where the matter contained in the public record is untrue or a "farce," the *Cox Broadcasting* privilege has been held to apply to private facts claims. Honig v. Nashville Banner, 10 Media L. Rep. 2139, 2139–40 (Tenn. Ct. App. 1984) (public record of lawsuit in which there was claim for damages for placing "hex" on someone's sex life).

[65]*Cox Broadcasting*, 420 U.S. at 496.

[66]RESTATEMENT (SECOND) §652D, cmt. b. *But see infra* §4.6(C)(ii).

[67]In Patterson v. Tribune Co., 146 So. 2d 623 (Fla. Dist. Ct. App. 1962), *cert. denied,* 153 So. 2d 306 (Fla. 1963), a newspaper's "Suits Filed" column, compiled from a court docket, indicated that the plaintiff had been judicially committed as a narcotics addict. The appellate court reversed the summary judgment for the defendant because the portion of the court's docket dealing with such commitments was closed to public inspection pursuant to a statute. The appellate court further held that the statute imposed a duty on the newspaper not to publish the name of a committed narcotics user, even though the docket sheet from which it obtained the plaintiff's name was not sealed as required by statute. 146 So. 2d at 626. In light of later Supreme Court decisions, *Patterson* is not sound authority. *See infra* §6(C)(ii).

[68]Logan v. District of Columbia, 447 F. Supp. 1328 (D.D.C. 1978).

[69]Maysville Transit Co. v. Ort, 177 S.W.2d 369, 370 (Ky. 1943).

[70]Florida Star v. B.J.F., 491 U.S. 524, 534, 538, 16 Media L. Rep. 1801 (1989); *Logan,* 447 F. Supp. at 1333; *Ort,* 177 S.W.2d at 370.

private fact, at least when the defendant did not rely on the contents of the public record in making its report.[71] It would be more consistent with *Cox Broadcasting*, however to hold that once a private fact is placed in a public record, the fact is simply no longer private.[72]

Although legal rights can usually be waived, at least one court has held that a news reporter did not have authority to waive his newspaper's *Cox Broadcasting* right to report on matters of public record, because the right belonged to the newspaper's publisher.[73]

§4.6(C)(ii) Ordinary News Gathering Techniques and Confidential Information

Following its decision in *Cox Broadcasting*, the Supreme Court decided four cases that addressed important issues that further define the constitutional limits of liability for disclosure of truthful information. In *Oklahoma Publishing Co. v. District Court*,[74] the Court overturned an injunction by an Oklahoma state court that prohibited the publication of the name and picture of a juvenile who was being tried for second-degree murder.[75] The media had learned the identity of the boy during an open hearing in Juvenile Court—although an Oklahoma statute required juvenile hearings to be closed, the judge, prosecutor, and defense counsel had permitted the media to remain in the courtroom.[76] The Court held that the state could not prohibit the publication of information that had been lawfully obtained in open court.[77]

The next year, in *Landmark Communications v. Virginia*,[78] the Supreme Court reversed the criminal conviction of a newspaper owner for publishing confidential information about the proceedings of a judicial review commission.[79] The newspaper had violated state law by revealing the identity of a judge in an accurate news article about a pending investigation.[80] After noting that the case before it did not involve any contention that illegal means were used to secure the confidential information in question or that a state could not punish participants in confidential proceedings for revealing what had occurred, the Supreme Court held that a state could not impose criminal sanctions on nonparticipants, including the news media, for disclosing or publishing accu-

---

[71]Diaz v. Oakland Tribune, 139 Cal. App. 3d 118, 132 (1983). *Diaz* asserted that the *Cox Broadcasting* holding was narrow and stated that the "defendants did not rely on that document and cannot be heard to argue that the information contained therein is public." *Id.*

[72]Cox Broadcasting v. Cohn, 420 U.S. 469, 496 (1975) ("Once true information is disclosed in public court documents open to public inspection, the press cannot be sanctioned for publishing it."). *See also* Heath v. Playboy Enters., 732 F. Supp. 1145, 1148 (S.D. Fla. 1990) ("Facts taken from public records or proceedings are not private."); Alarcon v. Murphy, 201 Cal. App. 3d 1, 7, 248 Cal. Rptr. 26 (1988) (disclosure of facts in arrest and search warrant affidavit not actionable because public records involved, even though affidavit not available to public at time of disclosure).

[73]In Poteet v. Roswell Daily Record, 584 P.2d 1310, 4 Media L. Rep. 1749 (N.M. Ct. App. 1978), a prosecutor agreed not to attempt to close a preliminary hearing because a reporter allegedly agreed that he would not publish the name of a sexual assault victim who was to testify at this hearing. The court found that the right to publish the victim's name in connection with the hearing, which was derived from *Cox Broadcasting*, could only be waived by the publisher and not by the reporter. *Id.* at 1312–13, 4 Media L. Rep. at 175.

[74]430 U.S. 308, 2 Media L. Rep. 1456 (1977).
[75]*Id.* at 308–09.
[76]*Id.* at 311.
[77]*Id.* at 311–12.
[78]435 U.S. 829, 3 Media L. Rep. 2153 (1978).
[79]*Id.* at 845–46.
[80]*Id.* at 831.

rate information derived from a confidential judicial review proceeding.[81] Neither the state's interest in protecting the reputation of individual judges nor its interest in protecting the reputation of the judicial system justified criminal sanctions for speech about government affairs.[82]

The following year, in *Smith v. Daily Mail Publishing Co.*,[83] the Supreme Court reviewed a West Virginia statute that made it a misdemeanor for newspapers to publish the identity of alleged juvenile offenders without first obtaining a court order.[84] Two newspapers were charged under the statute for publishing articles identifying a youth suspected of shooting and killing a classmate at a junior high school.[85] The newspapers obtained the suspect's name at the school, immediately after the incident, by talking to police, eyewitnesses, and the prosecuting attorney.[86] The Supreme Court held that the statute was unconstitutional.[87]

Relying on *Landmark Communications, Cox Broadcasting,* and *Oklahoma Publishing,* the Court in *Daily Mail* found that "[i]f a newspaper lawfully obtains truthful information about a matter of public significance then state officials may not constitutionally punish publication of the information, absent a need to further a state interest of the highest order."[88] Because the state's interest in protecting the anonymity of juveniles charged with crimes was not an interest "of the highest order,"[89] it did not justify criminal sanctions for the newspapers' publications. That the published information came in part from nongovernment sources was irrelevant.[90]

Finally, in *Florida Star v. B.J.F.*,[91] the Court considered, for the first time since *Cox Broadcasting,* the media's civil liability in a private facts case. The

---

[81] *Id.* at 837–38.

[82] *Id.* at 838, 841. *See also* Nicholson v. McClatchy Newspapers, 177 Cal. App. 3d 509, 518, 223 Cal. Rptr. 58 (1986) (defendant newspaper published identity of candidate for judicial office who had been labeled not qualified by state judicial evaluation committee; civil liability could not be extended to newspaper because it obtained information lawfully, even though government source for information acted in violation of state law in releasing information to media).

These principles have been used to strike down several laws that prevented people, who appeared before or complained to government agencies, from revealing the information they gave the government. Butterworth v. Smith, 494 U.S. 624 (1990) (Florida statute prohibiting grand jury witnesses from disclosing their own testimony after termination of grand jury investigation); Baugh v. Judicial Inquiry & Review Comm'n, 907 F.2d 440, 17 Media L. Rep. 2092 (4th Cir. 1990) (complaints to judicial review commission); Doe v. Florida Judicial Qualifications Comm'n, 748 F. Supp. 1520, 18 Media L. Rep. 1433 (S.D. Fla. 1990) (ban on complainant disclosing complaint had been filed); Doe v. Supreme Ct. of Fla., 17 Media L. Rep. 1405 (S.D. Fla. 1990) (rule prohibiting disclosure of lawyer disciplinary hearings and writing or speaking about such complaints); Providence Journal Co. v. Newton, 723 F. Supp. 846, 17 Media L. Rep. 1033 (D.R.I. 1989) (rule prohibiting disclosure of contents of complaint against public officials and public discussion of same).

[83] 443 U.S. 97, 5 Media L. Rep. 1305 (1979).

[84] *Id.* at 98.

[85] *Id.* at 99–100.

[86] *Id.* at 99.

[87] *Id.* at 106.

[88] 443 U.S. at 103. The Court noted that its ruling did not involve privacy, prejudicial pretrial publicity, or unlawful press access to confidential judicial proceedings. *Id.* at 105.

[89] *Id.* The Court also found that West Virginia's asserted interest in protecting the anonymity of juvenile offenders was not accomplished by the statute because the law only applied to newspapers and not the electronic media. Moreover, the Court found that the imposition of criminal sanctions for violation of the statute was not necessary to protect the confidentiality of juvenile proceedings since all but five of the 50 states did not use criminal penalties to protect this state interest. *Id.*

[90] *Id.* at 103–4 ("That factor ["the government itself provided or made possible press access to the information"] is not controlling.... A free press cannot be made to rely solely on the sufferance of government to supply it with information.").

[91] 491 U.S. 524, 16 Media L. Rep. 1801 (1989).

newspaper defendant had published a rape victim's name, which it had obtained from a police report placed in the police press room, in a brief story about the crime.[92] There were no restrictions on access to the press room or on access to reports there,[93] but signs in the room made it clear that names of rape victims were not matters of public record and were not to be published.[94] Although the publication of the victim's name violated the newspaper's own internal policy,[95] it published the rape victim's name, and she sued. The trial court held that the publication constituted negligence per se because it violated a Florida statute that made it a misdemeanor to publish, or to cause or allow the publication of, the name, address, or other identifying information about a sexual assault victim.[96] The Supreme Court reversed,[97] holding that the appropriate test for determining liability was stated in *Daily Mail:* " '[i]f a newspaper lawfully obtains truthful information about a matter of public significance then state officials may not constitutionally punish publication of the information, absent a need to further a state interest of the highest order.' "[98]

The Court gave four reasons for applying the *Daily Mail* test: (1) the public interest in the dissemination of the truth; (2) the government's ability to keep information confidential by other means, including classifying information, adopting procedures to ensure that classified information is kept confidential, and providing a damage remedy against the government if it mishandles such information; (3) that punishing the press for publishing information that is already publicly available is quite unlikely to further any legitimate state interest; and (4) the risk of "timidity and self-censorship" that would result from punishing the press for publishing truthful information that it has received from the government.[99]

The Court then applied the *Daily Mail* test. First, it noted that there was no dispute that the published information was accurate.[100] Second, the Court

---

[92]*Id.* at 527.
[93]*Id.*
[94]*Id.* at 546 (White, J., dissenting).
[95]*Id.* at 528.
[96]491 U.S. at 526 n.1. *Compare* Dorman v. Aiken Communications, 398 S.E.2d 687, 18 Media L. Rep. 1394 (S.C. 1990) (similar South Carolina statute held not to create private cause of action).
[97]The same result had been reached by other courts even before this decision. *See, e.g.,* WXYZ, Inc. v. Hand, 658 F.2d 420, 426–27 (6th Cir. 1981) (statute that allowed courts to suppress identities of sex offense victims unconstitutional because state did not show that suppression furthered government interest of highest order); Doe v. Sarasota-Bradenton Fla. Television Co., 436 So. 2d 328, 329–30 (Fla. Dist. Ct. App. 1983) (First Amendment protects publication of rape victim's name when name obtained lawfully and state made no attempt to keep victim's name secret); State v. Stauffer Communications, 592 P.2d 891, 896 (Kan. 1979) (criminal sanctions provided by statute for publishing information in arrest warrants before their execution constitutionally may not be imposed for publication of truthful information lawfully obtained).
[98]491 U.S. at 533 (quoting Smith v. Daily Mail Pub'g Co., 443 U.S. 97, 103 (1979)). The Court had noted in *Daily Mail* that its ruling there did not involve privacy. 443 U.S. 97, 105 (1979). While some courts read this to mean that the *Daily Mail* test did not apply to private facts cases (*see* Times Mirror Co. v. Superior Ct., 198 Cal. App. 3d 1420, 1432, 244 Cal. Rptr. 556 (Cal. Ct. App.), *modified,* 199 Cal. App. 3d 1099e (Cal. Ct. App. 1988), *cert. dismissed,* 489 U.S. 1094 (1989); *see also* Hyde v. City of Columbia, 637 S.W.2d 251 (Mo. Ct. App. 1982), *cert. denied,* 459 U.S. 1226 (1983)), other cases rejected this view even before *Florida Star* was decided (Nicholson v. McClatchy Newspapers, 177 Cal. App. 3d 509, 518, 223 Cal. Rptr. 58 (Cal. Ct. App. 1986); Alim v. Superior Ct., 185 Cal. App. 3d 144, 153–54, 229 Cal. Rptr. 58 (Cal. Ct. App. 1986)). In any event, *Florida Star* settled this question by applying the *Daily Mail* test in a tort case for civil damages. *Florida Star,* 491 U.S. at 536. *See also* New York Times Co. v. Sullivan, 376 U.S. 254, 257, 1 Media L. Rep. 1527, 1528 (1964) (First Amendment protections apply whether or not sanction is criminal or civil; chilling effect of multimillion-dollar judgment may be far greater than that of small criminal fine).
[99]*Florida Star,* 491 U.S. at 533–36.
[100]*Id.* at 536.

concluded that the information was obtained lawfully, even though the police apparently had violated the Florida statute in question by placing their report with the victim's name in the press room.[101] Third, the Court held that the article was about a matter of public significance, even though it contained the plaintiff's name, because it involved the commission and investigation of a violent crime.[102]

The Court then analyzed whether, under the circumstances of this case, imposing liability on the newspaper would further a state interest of the highest order, noting that the interests that the plaintiff sought to protect—namely privacy of victims, physical safety of victims who may become targets of retaliation if their assailants learn their names, and encouraging victims to report crimes—were "highly significant interests."[103] The Court held, however, that these interests were undercut by (1) the failure of the police to comply with the applicable Florida statute, especially since the police report in question was, in essence, a press release; (2) the broad sweep of the trial court's holding that the publication was negligent per se, coupled with the lack of any scienter requirement; and (3) the facial underinclusiveness of the Florida statute, which only prohibited publications by the mass media but left anyone else free to disseminate the same information without liability.[104]

As a result of *Cox Broadcasting, Oklahoma Publishing, Landmark Communications, Daily Mail,* and *Florida Star,* few if any private facts cases against the media will be able to meet the rigorous requirements that the First Amendment imposes in this area.

§4.6(C)(iii) Unauthorized Disclosures by the Government

Because a private facts claim is extinguished by a finding that the information disclosed was contained in a public record, it is very important to determine whether the information is in such a record. Sometimes the government's internal use of information may make it a public record. For example, when an arguably confidential medical record was transferred to the governor's office for his review in connection with an investigation of a county home, the record became public.[105] More frequently, a government official accidentally or intentionally makes information public even though this is against the law. When

---

[101]*Id.* This part of the *Daily Mail* test raised the question of just what constitutes lawful newsgathering techniques. They at least include reliance on press releases or other information given to the press, even if the person releasing the information was bound by law not to release it, *id.*, as well as interviewing government and nongovernment witnesses for information, Smith v. Daily Mail Pub'g Co., 443 U.S. 97, 99, 103 (1979), and "asking persons questions, including those with confidential information or restricted information," *Nicholson,* 177 Cal. App. 3d at 519–20. *But see* State v. Heltzel, 552 N.E.2d 31 (Ind. 1990) (attempting to induce grand jurors to breach oath of secrecy constitutes unlawful activity unprotected by First Amendment; contempt improper, however, because grand jurors discharged two years earlier and reporters' actions did not impede administration of justice). *See also* Chapter 5.

[102]*Florida Star,* 491 U.S. at 536–37.

[103]*Id.* at 537.

[104]*Id.* at 537–40. This result appears to deprive cases like Times Mirror Co. v. Superior Court, 198 Cal. App. 3d 1420, 244 Cal. Rptr. 556, *modified,* 199 Cal. App. 3d 1099e (1988), *cert. dismissed,* 489 U.S. 1094 (1989) and Hyde v. City of Columbia, 637 S.W.2d 251 (Mo. Ct. App. 1982), *cert. denied,* 459 U.S. 1226 (1983) of any authority. *See also* Hood v. Naeter Bros. Pub'g Co., 562 S.W.2d 770 (Mo. Ct. App. 1978) (reaches result, on nonconstitutional grounds, irreconcilable with *Times Mirror* and *Hyde*).

[105]Howard v. Des Moines Register, 283 N.W.2d 289, 5 Media L. Rep. 1667 (Iowa 1979), *cert. denied,* 445 U.S. 904 (1980) (although recovery for plaintiff denied, court divided on whether disclosure subject to *Cox Broadcasting* privilege for public records or newsworthy as matter of law and thus not actionable).

this happens, the information is nonetheless "public," and no liability can attach for its publication.[106] Contrary decisions have been overturned.[107]

§4.6(C)(iv) Expunged Records

A once-public record of a criminal conviction that has since been expunged has been held to be a public record under *Cox Broadcasting,* so the press has a constitutional right to publish facts obtained from that record.[108] Similarly, an expungement statute that gives a person with an expunged criminal record the legal right to deny that the conviction ever occurred does not create a duty for members of the public who were aware of the conviction to pretend that the conviction did not exist, thereby foregoing disclosure of the expunged record.[109]

§4.6(C)(v) Passage of Time

One of the most frequently litigated aspects of the private facts tort has been whether and at what point public facts become private because of the passage of time. The prevailing general rule is that a lapse of time, even of a lengthy period, does not convert a public fact into a private fact.[110] Over the years, however, some courts, especially in California, have carved out a narrow exception to this general rule.

The passage-of-time exception arose early in the development of the private facts tort. In the celebrated case of *Melvin v. Reid,*[111] the plaintiff, a former prostitute who was tried and acquitted of murder, filed a private facts action alleging that the movie *The Red Kimono* had ruined her reformed life by revealing these events, which had occurred seven years earlier.[112] The movie used the plaintiff's maiden name and reenacted the murder trial.[113] The court held that use in the movie of past incidents in the plaintiff's life was not

---

[106]*Florida Star,* 491 U.S. 524 (disclosure of rape victim's name in violation of state law); Oklahoma Pub'g Co. v. District Ct., 430 U.S. 308 (1977) (disclosure of juvenile's name at trial in contravention of state law); Montesano v. Donrey Media Group, 668 P.2d 1081, 9 Media L. Rep. 2266 (Nev. 1983), *cert. denied,* 466 U.S. 959 (1984) (confidential juvenile records included in public court records became public records under *Cox Broadcasting*).

[107]Cape Pubns. v. Hitchner, 549 So. 2d 1374, 16 Media L. Rep. 2337, 2341 (Fla.), *appeal dismissed,* 493 U.S. 929 (1989) (state prosecutor showed reporter confidential file detailing plaintiffs' alleged child abuse in violation of state law); Boettger v. Loverro, 555 A.2d 1234, 1239, 16 Media L. Rep. 1467 (Pa. 1989), *vacated and remanded,* 493 U.S. 885 (1989), *aff'd,* 587 A.2d 712, 18 Media L. Rep. 2017 (1991) (Pennsylvania Supreme Court initially differentiated between records of wiretaps *intentionally* placed in court records, which were not actionable, and documents accidentally or inadvertently placed in same records, which were actionable; U.S. Supreme Court remanded for reconsideration in light of *Florida Star;* Pennsylvania Supreme Court then reversed itself, concluding that once wiretap transcripts were in court files, publication of their contents could not be actionable).

[108]Anonymous v. Dun & Bradstreet, 3 Media L. Rep. 2376 (N.D. Ill. 1978), *aff'd without opinion,* 594 F.2d 867 (7th Cir. 1979) (no private facts liability for publisher of credit rating report that disclosed past criminal record of corporate officer, even though convictions were more than 20 years old); Shifflet v. Thomson Newspapers, 431 N.E.2d 1014, 8 Media L. Rep. 1199 (Ohio 1982) (reference to expungement of 18-year-old indecent exposure conviction not actionable); Oden v. Cahill, 398 N.E.2d 1061 (Ill. App. Ct. 1979) (publication of arrest records, including expunged records, cannot be basis of private facts claim); Russell v. Miami Herald Pub'g Co., 570 So. 2d 979, 18 Media L. Rep. 2036 (Fla. Dist. Ct. App. 1990) (no contempt for publishing expunged criminal records).

[109]Bahr v. Statesman Journal Co., 624 P.2d 664 (Or. Ct. App. 1980).

[110]RESTATEMENT (SECOND) §652D, cmt. k.

[111]297 P. 91 (1931).

[112]*Id.* at 91.

[113]*Id.*

actionable, because the past incidents were based on public records.[114] Disclosing the plaintiff's new name in relation to those past incidents, however, was held to constitute an actionable disclosure of highly offensive private facts.[115]

Private facts plaintiffs had little success in getting courts to apply the *Melvin* passage-of-time exception until 1971,[116] when the California Supreme Court decided *Briscoe v. Reader's Digest Association.*[117] *Briscoe* breathed new life into *Melvin,* stating that it would be a "crass legal fiction that a matter once public never becomes private again."[118] *Briscoe* is not widely followed outside of California, and later California cases dealing with the passage-of-time issue indicate that *Briscoe* is restricted to its facts.[119]

The Restatement (Second) retains the passage-of-time exception merely as "a factor to be considered, with other facts, in determining whether the publicity goes to unreasonable lengths in revealing facts about one who has

---

[114]*Id.* at 93.
[115]*Id.*
[116]In another famous early case, Sidis v. F-R Publishing Corp., 113 F.2d 806 (2d Cir.), *cert. denied,* 311 U.S. 711 (1940), a magazine published a biographical sketch of the plaintiff who, 25 years earlier, had received publicity because he was a child prodigy. Since then, the plaintiff had avoided publicity and had remained out of the public eye until the article was published. The Second Circuit held that a private facts action would not lie, because the plaintiff's past accomplishments made his life, including certain private aspects of it, a continuing subject of public comment. 113 F.2d at 808–10.

Similarly, in Smith v. Doss, 37 So. 2d 118 (Ala. 1948), the Alabama Supreme Court refused to extend the *Melvin* passage-of-time exception. In *Doss,* the defendant broadcast the unusual but true story of John Lindgren, a local blacksmith, on a radio program called "Tuscaloosa Town Talks." Lindgren had disappeared in 1905 while on a trip to Birmingham to purchase stock for his business. By all appearances, Lindgren had been murdered, although his body was not found. A man who found Lindgren's mules and carriage was arrested for the murder and jailed for five months while awaiting trial. He was later acquitted. Twenty-five years later, Lindgren died of cancer in California, where he had been living since his disappearance. His will mentioned his Alabama family, and his body was returned to Tuscaloosa for burial. *Id.* at 118–20.

The broadcast of the Lindgren story occurred 16 years after his actual death. Lindgren's daughters brought a privacy action against the broadcaster. The Alabama Supreme Court affirmed the trial court's dismissal of the privacy complaint because "[b]y his own acts John Lindgren made himself a public character. The passage of time could not give privacy to his acts because the story of John Lindgren is part of the history of the community. It is embedded in the public record . . . ." *Id.* at 121.

In Barbieri v. News-Journal Co., 189 A.2d 773 (Del. 1963), the Delaware Supreme Court explicitly rejected *Melvin,* holding that a story about a bill to make whipping mandatory for certain crimes did not violate the plaintiff's privacy when it used the plaintiff's name to report that he was the last person to be whipped in Delaware nine years earlier. *Id.* at 776–77.

[117]4 Cal. 3d 529, 483 P.2d 34, 1 Media L. Rep. 1845 (Cal. 1971). In *Briscoe,* the plaintiff, a rehabilitated felon, filed a private facts action over an article about the crime of hijacking. The article mentioned that the plaintiff had been involved in a hijacking 11 years earlier. The California Supreme Court overruled the trial court's grant of a demurrer, holding that a jury should decide whether the plaintiff's rehabilitation made the belated report of the crime highly offensive to a reasonable person. 4 Cal. 3d at 543, 1 Media L. Rep. at 1852. *See infra* §4.6(E)(iv).

[118]4 Cal. 3d at 539. *Briscoe* was later removed to federal court, where the defendant won summary judgment on various grounds, including that the article was newsworthy. Briscoe v. Reader's Digest Ass'n, 1 Media L. Rep. 1852 (C.D. Cal. 1972). For a discussion of newsworthiness, *see infra* §4.6(E)(ii).

[119]Forsher v. Bugliosi, 26 Cal. 3d 792, 811, 608 P.2d 716 (Cal. 1980) (noting that *Briscoe* has not been extended to other facts and that it was exception to general rule that " 'once a man has become a public figure, or news, he remains a matter of legitimate recall to the public mind to the end of his days.' " (quoting Prosser, *Privacy,* 48 CAL. L. REV. 383, 418 (1960))). Many courts have also gone to great lengths to distinguish *Briscoe.* Wasser v. San Diego Union, 236 Cal. Rptr. 772 (Cal. Ct. App. 1987) (plaintiff's frequent filing of lawsuits kept him in or near public eye during 11 years following his acquittal); Beruan v. French, 128 Cal. Rptr. 869 (Cal. Ct. App. 1976) (disclosure of past criminal convictions of candidate for union office not actionable). *See also* Dresbach v. Doubleday & Co., 518 F. Supp. 1285, 1289–91, 7 Media L. Rep. 2105 (D.D.C. 1981) (son of parents killed in 1961 by second son has no private facts claim; *Briscoe* distinguished because rehabilitation of criminal not involved). Similarly, the publication of a 20-year-old juvenile conviction was held not actionable because it related to a topic of important public interest: police officers killed in the line of duty. Montesano v. Donrey Media Group, 668 P.2d 1081, 9 Media L. Rep. 2266 (Nev.), *cert. denied,* 466 U.S. 959 (1984). However, in Conklin v. Sloss, 150 Cal. Rptr. 121 (Cal. Ct. App. 1978), the court applied *Briscoe* to reverse the defendants' successful demurrer, where a newspaper reported that the plaintiff had been arrested for and convicted of murder 20 years earlier. 150 Cal. Rptr. at 122–24. Surprisingly, *Cox Broadcasting* was not discussed, so *Conklin* is dubious authority. Other courts that have confronted facts similar to *Conklin*'s have dismissed the private facts action. *See infra* note 121.

resumed the private, lawful and unexciting life led by the great bulk of the community."[120] The Supreme Court's decision in *Cox Broadcasting,* which held that accurate reports based on the contents of public records could not be the basis for a private facts claim, has abrogated the passage-of-time exception for information contained in public records.[121]

§4.6(D) The "Highly Offensive to a Reasonable Person" Requirement

Public disclosure of details of a person's private life, even if the disclosure is unauthorized and unwanted, does not give rise to a private facts action. A plaintiff must show, as part of his or her prima facie case, that the disclosure of private facts would be "highly offensive," not to the plaintiff, but to a reasonable person.[122] In an interesting case brought by a member of a Native American tribe that had a particular sensitivity to being photographed, *Bennaly v. Hundred Arrows Press,*[123] the court held that the plaintiff could not base his private facts claim on this special sensitivity, because the photograph would not be offensive to the reasonable person of ordinary sensitivity, even though the photograph was offensive to the plaintiff.[124]

Similarly, a private facts action could not be based on the disclosure that the plaintiff "has returned from a visit, gone camping in the woods or given a party at his house for his friends."[125] Even the disclosure of details of a person's private life that are embarrassing or annoying is not actionable.[126]

---

[120]RESTATEMENT (SECOND) §652D, cmt. k. Other factors in determining whether disclosure of a plaintiff's past unsavory conduct is actionable include whether the plaintiff has remained in the community where the past unsavory acts occurred, and whether the plaintiff has taken measures to conceal his or her identity by changing his or her name. Roshto v. Hebert, 439 So. 2d 428, 431 (La. 1983); Smith v. Doss, 37 So. 2d 118 (Ala. 1948).

[121]In *Roshto,* the Louisiana Supreme Court cited *Cox Broadcasting* and the Restatement (Second) in holding that the reproduction of a 25-year-old newspaper front page, which detailed the trial and conviction of the plaintiff for cattle rustling, was not an actionable disclosure of private facts. The court noted that the conviction occurred in the community in which the later article was published, the publishers made no effort to highlight or sensationalize the material, there was no "malice" on the publisher's part in printing the information, and the "Page from our Past" section of the newspaper in which the reproduction appeared satisfied a legitimate local interest in community history. 439 So. 2d at 430–31. Similarly, in Rawlins v. Hutchinson Publishing Co., 543 P.2d 988 (Kan. 1975), a "Looking Backward" newspaper column reported that a local police officer had been suspended and fired ten years previously for various improprieties. The column was held not to be actionable because the published information was public. 543 P.2d at 996. *See also Dresbach,* 518 F. Supp. at 1290 (passage of time case: "information in the public record is absolutely privileged"); Romaine v. Kallinger, 537 A.2d 284, 293, 295, 15 Media L. Rep. 1209 (N.J. 1988) ("*Briscoe* can[not] endure as a viable precedent in light of the absolute privilege . . . in *Cox Broadcasting*").

[122]RESTATEMENT (SECOND) §652D.

[123]614 F. Supp. 969, 12 Media L. Rep. 1356 (D.N.M. 1985), *overruled on other grounds,* 858 F.2d 618 (10th Cir. 1988).

[124]614 F. Supp. at 982.

[125]RESTATEMENT (SECOND) §652D, cmt. c ("The protection afforded to the plaintiff's interest in his privacy must be relative to the customs of the time and place, to the occupation of the plaintiff and to the habits of his neighbors and fellow citizens.").

[126]In Virgil v. Sports Illustrated, 424 F. Supp. 1286 (S.D. Cal. 1976), the disclosure of certain private facts about the plaintiff's personal eccentricities and past behavior in a magazine article about body surfing was found by the court to be "generally unflattering and perhaps embarrassing," but not actionable because, as a matter of law, these facts were not "highly offensive" to a reasonable person. Some of the facts reported were that the plaintiff put out cigarettes in his mouth, dove off stairs to impress women, injured himself to collect unemployment benefits so he could have time to body surf, engaged in gang fights as a youth, and frequently ate insects. *Id.* at 1286–87. *See also* Bisbee v. John C. Conover Agency, 452 A.2d 689, 9 Media L. Rep. 1298 (N.J. Super. Ct. App. Div. 1982) (newspaper article on sale of historic home that disclosed broker's name, home's purchase price, number of rooms within house, and purchaser's name and occupation could not be basis of private facts claim by purchaser because facts revealed could not, as matter of law, be offensive to reasonable person); Wolf v. Regardie, 553 A.2d 1213, 16 Media L. Rep. 1780 (D.C. 1989) (list of Washington, D.C.'s 100 richest individuals with description of plaintiff's real estate deals and holdings not highly offensive).

Professor Prosser suggested that the courts apply the "highly objectionable" standard as a kind of "mores" test under which liability is extended only for public disclosure of facts that would be viewed by the community as highly objectionable.[127] Thus, the disclosure that a plaintiff had been a child prodigy was not actionable because such a fact could not be viewed by the community as being highly objectionable,[128] and the disclosure that a plaintiff had found and returned a bag containing $240,000 in cash did not reveal any "unsavory" facts about the plaintiff and was also not actionable.[129]

§4.6(E) Issues of Legitimate Public Concern

The Restatement (Second) requires a private facts plaintiff to show not only that the defendant publicly disclosed highly offensive private facts, but that the disclosure of the private facts "is not of legitimate concern to the public."[130] Thus, the plaintiff, as part of his or her prima facie case, must show that the public has no legitimate interest in the disclosure.[131]

Where a media defendant is involved, the issue of legitimate public concern is usually discussed in terms of whether the disclosure was "newsworthy."[132] Where a nonmedia defendant is involved, the disclosure is generally not examined as to its newsworthiness; rather, the disclosure is examined to determine whether it furthers some public interest or policy.[133]

§4.6(E)(i) Question of Law or Fact

The case law is not entirely clear on whether the determination of "legitimate public concern" is a jury question or a matter of law for a judge.[134] Some cases require the trial judge to make a preliminary finding as to whether reasonable minds could differ about the newsworthiness of or public interest furthered by the disclosure. If a reasonable jury could determine that the disclosure was not newsworthy or in the public interest, then the judge should allow the case to go to the jury.[135]

---

[127] LAW OF TORTS, *supra* note 4, §117, at 857.
[128] Sidis v. F-R Pub'g Corp., 113 F.2d 806 (2d Cir.), *cert. denied*, 311 U.S. 711 (1940).
[129] Johnson v. Harcourt, Brace, Jovanovich, Inc., 118 Cal. Rptr. 370 (Cal. Ct. App. 1974).
[130] RESTATEMENT (SECOND) §652D, cmt. d; Cox Broadcasting v. Cohn, 420 U.S. 469 (1975).
[131] Diaz v. Oakland Tribune, 139 Cal. App. 3d 118, 133 (1983) (reversible error for trial court to fail to instruct jury that plaintiff had burden of proof that publicity not related to matter of legitimate public concern).
[132] For the most part, courts use "newsworthiness" and "matters of legitimate public concern" interchangeably.
[133] National Bonding Agency v. Demeson, 648 S.W.2d 748 (Tex. Ct. App. 1983) (no public interest served by bonding company's circulation of "wanted poster" depicting plaintiff, an alleged bail jumper, that disclosed certain intimate details of her sex life).
[134] *Compare* Sellers v. Henry, 329 S.W.2d 214 (Ky. 1959) (picture of dead girl's mutilated body taken by police after automobile accident and later published presented question of fact as to whether publication was in public interest) *and* Blount v. TD Pub'g Corp., 423 P.2d 421, 424 (N.M. 1966) (newsworthiness of article in detective magazine about murder of plaintiff's husband was question of fact: "[u]nless the source be a matter of public record ... news is a question of fact—a question answered daily by editors and publishers") *with* Virgil v. Sports Illustrated, 424 F. Supp. 1286, 1290 (S.D. Cal. 1976) (disclosure of plaintiff's eccentricities in article on body surfing did not appeal to public's morbid and sensational interests) *and* Gilbert v. Medical Economics Co., 665 F.2d 305 (10th Cir. 1981) (references to plaintiff's psychiatric and mental problems in article on medical malpractice and relationship of those problems to plaintiff's practice of medicine were of legitimate public concern because objective and reasonable minds could not differ on finding that article reported on issues of legitimate public interest).
[135] Capra v. Thoroughbred Racing Ass'n, 787 F.2d 463, 464–65 (9th Cir.), *cert. denied*, 479 U.S. 1017 (1986) ("[A] reasonable jury ... could find that the press release was not newsworthy as to one or more of

Strong First Amendment arguments support the view that this determination should be made by the judge, however. The standards for newsworthiness and matters of legitimate public concern are generally so vague and subjective that they would improperly allow jurors to punish speech because they disagree with its content.[136]

Moreover, decisions on this issue by juries rather than judges would lead to unpredictable and ad hoc results that would undoubtedly "invite timidity and self-censorship and very likely lead to the suppression of many items that would otherwise be published and that should be made available to the public."[137] In any event, since the Supreme Court has held that whether speech is of legitimate concern to the public is a question of law,[138] contrary cases appear to be wrongly decided.

§4.6(E)(ii) Newsworthiness

"News" is included within the issues generally considered to be matters of legitimate public concern.[139] The Supreme Court has indicated that news need not be informative, entertaining, timely, or important,[140] but should include discussion of "all issues about which information is needed or appropriate to enable the members of society to cope with the exigencies of their period."[141]

One court defined news as "that indefinable quality of information which arouses public attention."[142] Other courts weigh (1) the social value of the facts

---

the plaintiffs."); *Diaz*, 139 Cal. App. 3d at 133 ("Where reasonable minds could differ, we see no constitutional infirmity in allowing the jury to decide the issue of newsworthiness."); Times Mirror Co. v. Superior Ct., 198 Cal. App. 3d 1420, 1429, 244 Cal. Rptr. 556 (Cal. Ct. App.), *modified*, 199 Cal. App. 3d 1099e (Cal. Ct. App. 1988), *cert. dismissed*, 489 U.S. 1094 (1989) ("If there is room for differing views whether a publication would be newsworthy the question is one to be determined by the jury and not the court.").

[136]Hustler Magazine v. Falwell, 485 U.S. 46, 53–56 (1988) (allowing jurors to punish speech based on inherently subjective standard unconstitutional because it turns jury into censors). *Falwell* involved a claim brought by a well-known preacher for intentional infliction of emotional distress against a magazine for an off-color cartoon parody of the preacher. The jurors in *Falwell* were asked to determine whether the parody was "outrageous." *Id.* at 49. *See also* Anderson v. Fisher Broadcasting Co., 712 P.2d 803, 809 (Or. 1986) (newsworthiness "is not properly a community standard"); Romaine v. Kallinger, 537 A.2d 284, 293–94, 15 Media L. Rep. 1209 (N.J. 1988) ("it is for the court to determine whether a matter is of legitimate concern to the public interest").

[137]Cox Broadcasting v. Cohn, 420 U.S. 469, 496 (1975). *See also* Ross v. Midwest Communications, 870 F.2d 271, 275, 16 Media L. Rep. 1463, 1466 (5th Cir.), *cert. denied*, 493 U.S. 935 (1989) ("Exuberant judicial blue-pencilling after-the-fact would blunt the quills of even the most honorable journalists."). At the very least, jury decisions about newsworthiness must be closely scrutinized by the courts. *Diaz*, 139 Cal. App. 3d at 133.

[138]Connick v. Myers, 461 U.S. 138, 143 n.5, 148 n.7 (1983).

[139]The Restatement (Second) describes "news" as a term defined in large measure by publishers and broadcasters. It includes

publications concerning homicide and other crimes, arrests, police raids, suicides, marriages and divorces, accidents, fires, catastrophes of nature, a death from the use of narcotics, a rare disease, the birth of a child to a twelve-year-old girl, the reappearance of one supposed to have been murdered years ago, a report to the police concerning the escape of a wild animal and many other similar matters of genuine, even if more or less deplorable, popular appeal.

RESTATEMENT (SECOND) §625D, cmt. g.

[140]Time, Inc. v. Hill, 385 U.S. 374, 388 (1967).

[141]Thornhill v. Alabama, 310 U.S. 88, 102 (1940); Campbell v. Seabury Press, 614 F.2d 395, 397 (5th Cir. 1980); Van Straten v. Milwaukee Journal, 447 N.W.2d 105, 16 Media L. Rep. 2408 (Wis. Ct. App. 1989), *cert. denied*, 110 S. Ct. 2626 (1990) (story about suicide attempt of jail inmate who tested positive for AIDS is of legitimate public concern); White v. Fraternal Order of Police, 909 F.2d 512, 517, 17 Media L. Rep. 2137, 2141 (D.C. Cir. 1990) (whether police officers used drugs or were tested for drug use was matter of public concern).

[142]Sweenek v. Pathe News, 16 F. Supp. 746, 747 (E.D.N.Y. 1936); LAW OF TORTS, *supra* note 4, §117, at 860.

published, (2) the depth of the article's intrusion into ostensibly private affairs, and (3) the extent to which the party voluntarily acceded to a position of public notoriety.[143]

Thus, although they have not devised a precise definition of what is newsworthy, the courts, recognizing the First Amendment implications of the public's right to know what is going on in the community and the rest of the world, apply the definition broadly.[144]

The concept of newsworthiness, however is not limitless. The Restatement (Second) explains that "[t]he line is to be drawn when the publicity ceases to be the giving of information to which the public is entitled, and becomes a morbid and sensational prying into private lives for its own sake."[145] Accordingly, the publication of a photograph of a plaintiff sitting nude in a bathtub was not newsworthy, as a matter of law, because it was found to be a needless exposure of the plaintiff's private life to the public.[146]

It is unclear but quite doubtful that a disclosure would be actionable, even though newsworthy, because it revealed facts so offensive that they shocked the community's notion of decency.[147]

§4.6(E)(iii) Public Figures

In deciding whether publicity of private facts is actionable, the courts often examine whether the plaintiff is a public figure—"a person who, by his accomplishments, fame, mode of living, or accident has become a public personage."[148] The Restatement (Second) divides these public personages into "voluntary" and "involuntary" public figures.[149]

---

[143]Kapellas v. Kofman, 1 Cal. 3d 20, 36, 459 P.2d 912 (Cal. 1969); Briscoe v. Reader's Digest Ass'n, 4 Cal. 3d 529, 483 P.2d 34 (1971). This is an unsatisfactory approach. *See supra* notes 19, 136, and 137.

[144]LAW OF TORTS, *supra* note 4, §117, at 862. See *supra* §4.6(E) on what constitutes a matter of public concern.

[145]RESTATEMENT (SECOND) §652D, cmt. h.

[146]McCabe v. Village Voice, 550 F. Supp 525, 530, 8 Media L. Rep. 2580 (E.D. Pa. 1982). However, in Sipple v. Chronicle Publishing Co., 154 Cal. App. 3d 1040, 1049, 10 Media L. Rep. 1690 (Cal. Ct. App. 1984), the court found that the disclosure that the plaintiff, who heroically thwarted an assassination attempt on President Ford, was a homosexual was not so offensive as to shock the community notions of decency. Similarly, in Virgil v. Sports Illustrated, 424 F. Supp. 1286 (S.D. Cal. 1976), the court found that the revelation of the plaintiff's unorthodox behavior was not a disclosure "for its own sake" and constituted a "legitimate journalistic attempt to explain Virgil's extremely daring and dangerous style of body surfing at the Wedge." *Id.* at 1288–89.

[147]This notion seems to have had its origin in Sidis v. F-R Publishing Co., 113 F.2d 806 (2d Cir.), *cert. denied*, 311 U.S. 711 (1940), a case in which a magazine article published a detailed profile of a former child prodigy. Although the court in *Sidis* found that the article was newsworthy, albeit "merciless" in its detail, it stated in dictum that some "revelations may be so intimate and so unwarranted in view of the victim's position as to outrage the community's notions of decency." 113 F.2d at 809. This position, sometimes referred to as the "Sidis Principle," has been adopted in some subsequent cases, such as *Briscoe*. Commentators disagree on whether the Sidis Principle exists. *See* Hill, *Defamation and Privacy Under the First Amendment*, 76 COLUM. L. REV. 1205, 1263–64 (1976); LAW OF TORTS, *supra* note 4, §117, at 862–63. *See also infra* §4.8. It seems unlikely, however, that the Sidis Principle survives more recent Supreme Court decisions. *See supra* §6(C)(ii).

[148]LAW OF TORTS, *supra* note 4, §117, at 859–60 (quoting Cason v. Baskin, 30 So. 2d 635, 638 (Fla. 1947)). In defamation cases, the public figure concept is a constitutional standard to determine whether actual malice will be required to impose liability on the defendant for false statements. In private facts cases, the public figure analysis helps to determine whether there is liability for telling the truth. Thus, it can be a mistake to use public figure decisions in defamation cases to determine whether someone is a public figure in private facts cases.

[149]RESTATEMENT (SECOND) §652D, cmts. e, f.

Persons who voluntarily place themselves in the public eye by engaging in public activities are presumed to have surrendered their right to privacy for reports relating to those public activities and for certain private aspects of their lives that may not be directly related to their public activities.[150] Thus, the public disclosure of college students' academic standing may have involved publicity of private facts, but such a disclosure did not give rise to a private facts action because the disclosure involved the academic standing of varsity basketball players for a major university who were public figures.[151] On the other hand, a plaintiff who runs for and is elected to the presidency of her class at a small college may not be considered a voluntary public figure, as a matter of law, when the disclosure of private facts is about her sex change and not her public activities.[152] Similarly, when a hospital patient is photographed in her hospital bed and the photograph is published in a magazine under the caption "Starving Glutton" along with an article on her unusual eating disease, a private facts claim was found to exist since the patient did not expressly consent to the photograph and did not seek publicity.[153]

In other cases, a person neither seeks nor authorizes publicity but becomes part of a news event involuntarily. These "involuntary" public figures include victims of crime and accidents and even criminals, who often scrupulously avoid publicity. The Restatement (Second) notes that "[t]hese persons are regarded as properly subject to the public interest, and publishers are permitted to satisfy the curiosity of the public as to its heroes, leaders, villains and victims, and those who are closely associated with them."[154] Thus, a newspaper photograph showing a plaintiff who had been forced to disrobe escaping from a gunman who had held her hostage could not be the basis for a private facts damage award because the incident was a newsworthy event.[155]

Public figure status also extends to close relatives of public figures. So, for instance, the identification of the parents of a murder suspect was not actionable by the parents, even though the suspect was an adult and living away from his family, because naming the parents was reasonable in light of the seriousness of the crime and the fact that the parents' home was in close proximity to the murder site.[156]

The courts often examine whether a logical nexus exists between the plaintiff, usually a private person, and the newsworthy event. Thus, in the case of a civil rights leader's autobiography that described the author's close relationship with his brother, who had numerous personal problems, the author's

---

[150]*Id.*; Reuber v. Food Chem. News, 925 F.2d 703, 720, 18 Media L. Rep. 1689, 1702 (4th Cir. 1991) (en banc), *cert. denied*, 111 S. Ct. 2814 (1991) (because public is entitled to know about crime victims, who are involuntarily public figures, it is certainly entitled to know about private letter of reprimand issued to scientist who was public figure in malathion controversy).

[151]Bilney v. Evening Star Newspaper Co., 406 A.2d 652, 5 Media L. Rep. 1931 (Md. Ct. Spec. App. 1979).

[152]Diaz v. Oakland Tribune, 139 Cal. App. 3d 118 (1983).

[153]Barber v. Time, Inc., 159 S.W.2d 291, 294 (Mo. 1942).

[154]RESTATEMENT (SECOND) §652D, cmt. f; Tucker v. News Pub'g Co., 397 S.E.2d 499, 18 Media L. Rep. 1684 (Ga. Ct. App. 1990) (articles about vicious attack on high school student by other students not actionable).

[155]Cape Pubns. v. Bridges, 423 So. 2d 426, 8 Media L. Rep. 2535 (Fla. Dist. Ct. App. 1982), *petition denied*, 431 So. 2d 988 (Fla.), *cert. denied*, 464 U.S. 893 (1983).

[156]Strutner v. Dispatch Printing Co., 442 N.E.2d 129, 8 Media L. Rep. 2344 (Ohio Ct. App. 1982); RESTATEMENT (SECOND) §652D, cmt. i.

former sister-in-law was found to be sufficiently part of a matter of legitimate public interest to preclude her from asserting a private facts claim.[157]

§4.6(E)(iv) The Newsworthiness of Names

Some authority exists, predominantly in the California courts, to support the notion that even though the disclosure of certain facts about a person is not actionable because it is newsworthy, the identification of that person by name may not be constitutionally protected and is, hence, actionable.[158] However, *Cox Broadcasting,* which held that the publication of facts contained in a public record (including the name of a rape-murder victim) was constitutionally privileged, permits the identification of the plaintiff by name where the name was contained in a public record.[159]

Moreover, other courts have expressly rejected the view that identification of the plaintiff by name in an otherwise newsworthy report is actionable under a private facts theory. For example, the Iowa Supreme Court found that the identification of a plaintiff by name, in connection with her forced sterilization while she had been a patient in a state nursing home, was an important part of the news value of a newspaper article on conditions at the nursing home.[160] A plurality of the court stated that:

> In the sense of serving an appropriate news function, the disclosure contributed constructively to the impact of the article. It offered a personalized frame of reference to which the reader could relate, fostering perception and understanding. Moreover, it lent specificity and credibility to the report. In this way the disclosure served an effective means of accomplishing the intended news function. It had positive communicative value in attracting the reader's attention to the article's subject matter and in supporting expression of the underlying theme.[161]

---

[157]Campbell v. Seabury Press, 614 F.2d 395, 397, 5 Media L. Rep. 2612 (5th Cir. 1980). However, in Vassiliades v. Garfinckel's, Brooks Bros., 492 A.2d 580 (D.C. App. 1985), the court distinguished *Campbell* and found that "before and after" photographs of a plastic surgery patient used without the patient's consent in a department store promotion were actionable because they did not strengthen the impact or credibility of the public's awareness of plastic surgery. 492 A.2d at 589.

[158]Times Mirror Co. v. Superior Ct., 198 Cal. App. 3d 1420, 244 Cal. Rptr. 556, *modified,* 199 Cal. App. 3d 1099e (Cal. Ct. App. 1988), *cert. dismissed,* 489 U.S. 1094 (1989) (although newspaper report about murder was newsworthy per se, identification of eyewitness to murder by name was not); Briscoe v. Readers Digest Ass'n, 4 Cal. 3d 529, 541, 483 P.2d 34 (Cal. 1971) (summary judgment for defendant reversed because "a jury could find that publication of plaintiff's identity in connection with incidents of his past life was in this case of minimal social value"); Melvin v. Reid, 112 Cal. App. 285, 291, 297 P.91 (Cal. Ct. App. 1931) (although use in movie of past incidents in plaintiff's life not actionable because they were part of public record, film's reference to plaintiff by actual maiden name and new married name sufficient to state private facts claim); Deaton v. Delta Democrat Pub'g Co., 326 So. 2d 471 (Miss. 1976) (publication of names and photographs of retarded children in connection with article on state schools for retarded actionable even though issue of education for retarded was newsworthy and would not have been actionable absent identification of children); Barber v. Time, Inc., 159 S.W.2d 291, 295 (Mo. 1942) (although plaintiff's unusual ailment was of some public interest, published photograph and identification as "Starving Glutton" actionable).

[159]Cox Broadcasting Co. v. Cohn, 420 U.S. 469, 495 (1975); Williams v. New York Times, 462 So. 2d 38, 11 Media L. Rep. 1364 (Fla. Dist. Ct. App. 1984) (where rape victim's name was used at public trial there could be no liability for its publication despite claim that publication endangered victim's safety due to racial turmoil surrounding case). For a further discussion of *Cox Broadcasting,* see *supra* §4.6(C)(i).

[160]Howard v. Des Moines Register & Tribune Co., 283 N.W.2d 289 (Iowa 1979). The opinion was divided on whether the disclosure was permissible under the public record rule in *Cox Broadcasting* or on general newsworthiness grounds. *Id.* at 300–305.

[161]*Howard,* 283 N.W.2d at 303. Other cases holding that the identification of the plaintiff by name was not actionable are Gilbert v. Medical Economics Co., 665 F.2d 305, 308 (10th Cir. 1981) (publication of plaintiff's name "strengthens the impact and credibility of the physician's article" about physician's alleged malpractice); Ross v. Midwest Communications, 870 F.2d 271, 274, 16 Media L. Rep. 1463, 1466 (5th Cir.), *cert. denied,* 493 U.S. 935 (1989) (" 'photograph and name [of rape victim]' were 'substantially relevant to a newsworthy topic because they strengthen the impact and credibility of the article' " (quoting

Several other cases have reached a similar result.[162] This result now appears to be constitutionally compelled.[163]

§4.7 STANDARD OF FAULT

In defamation cases, the Supreme Court has eliminated strict liability and requires a finding of fault before imposing damages, at least if the subject matter of a publication is a matter of public concern.[164] In private facts cases, however, it is uncertain what fault standard applies, especially since the key to determining fault in defamation cases—the falsity of the statement—is not present in private facts actions.

Some courts have reworked the actual malice standard in defamation cases from "reckless disregard of or knowledge of falsity" to "reckless disregard of or knowledge of the offensiveness of the disclosure" in private facts cases.[165] Thus, one court found it "reasonable to require a plaintiff to prove, in each case, that the publisher invaded his privacy with reckless disregard for the fact that reasonable people would find the invasion highly offensive."[166]

Similarly, the Idaho Supreme Court found reversible error in a trial court's failure to instruct the jury on "malice" in a private facts case.[167] In that case, a television news program broadcast a plaintiff's arrest, in which he was taken from his home while nude.[168] The court reversed a judgment, notwithstanding the verdict for the defendant, and remanded, because the trial court did not instruct the jury to determine whether the disclosure was made for the purpose of embarrassing or humiliating the plaintiff or was made with reckless disregard of whether the disclosure would result in such embarrassment or humiliation.[169]

At least one case rejects any malice requirement,[170] but it appears to be wrongly decided.[171] What fault must be shown is an issue that remains unexplored in most jurisdictions, however.

Gilbert v. Medical Economics Co., 665 F.2d 305, 308 (10th Cir. 1981)); court questions whether names can ever be private facts).

[162]Meetze v. Associated Press, 95 S.E.2d 606, 610 (S.C. 1956) (use of name of 12-year-old who gave birth not actionable); McNutt v. New Mexico State Tribune Co., 538 P.2d 804, 808–09 (N.M. Ct. App.), cert. denied, 540 P.2d 248 (N.M. 1975) (report that included names and addresses of police officers involved in gun battle with members of black militant organization not actionable because it was newsworthy); Pasadena Star-News v. Superior Ct., 249 Cal. Rptr. 729, 731 (Cal. Ct. App. 1988) ("While articles on [newsworthy] topics sometimes avoid divulging the names of the individuals involved, no principle of tort law requires this journalistic approach"); Wolf v. Regardie, 553 A.2d 1213, 1220 n.12, 16 Media L. Rep. 1780, 1786 n.12 (D.C. 1989) ("The public has a right to know who owns the buildings in which they work or transact business, and who runs the banks in which they invest their money and deposit their savings."). In addition, since there is no claim at all unless the plaintiff is identified (see *supra* §4.4(A)), it is a strange rule that constitutional protection is lost by identifying the plaintiff and thus making out a prima facie case.

[163]Florida Star v. B.J.F., 491 U.S. 524, 536–37, 16 Media L. Rep. 1801, 1806–07 (1989).

[164]*See* Chapter 2.

[165]Briscoe v. Readers Digest Ass'n, 4 Cal. 3d 529, 483 P.2d 34 (Cal. 1971); Taylor v. K.T.V.B. TV, 525 P.2d 984 (Idaho 1974).

[166]*Briscoe*, 4 Cal. 3d at 542–43.

[167]*Taylor*, 525 P.2d at 988.

[168]*Id.* at 984.

[169]*Id.* at 987–88.

[170]Hawkins v. Multimedia, 344 S.E.2d 145, 12 Media L. Rep. 1878 (S.C.), cert. denied, 479 U.S. 1012 (1986) (plaintiff identified as teenage father in article on teen pregnancy; malice need only be shown when plaintiff seeks punitive damages).

[171]*See* Florida Star v. B.J.F., 491 U.S. 524, 539, 16 Media L. Rep. 1801 (1989) (noting that failure to impose scienter requirement in private facts cases "engender[s] the perverse result that truthful publications ... are less protected by the First Amendment than even the least protected defamatory falsehoods"). *See*

§4.8 INFLICTION OF EMOTIONAL DISTRESS

Because private facts plaintiffs frequently allege that the defendants' disclosure of intimate facts caused them extreme emotional distress, they sometimes include causes of action for intentional or negligent infliction of emotional distress with their private facts claims.[172] The courts, however, have been reluctant to extend liability for infliction of emotional distress to cases in which an action for private facts will not lie.[173]

It is unlikely that the publication of a truthful article or photograph of a person could constitute extreme and outrageous conduct when, as a matter of law, a private facts action will not lie.[174] Thus, an emotional distress claim will fall along with a dismissed private facts cause of action.[175] When the published report is based on events that occur at a public proceeding or in a public record, the emotional distress and private facts claims must be dismissed.[176]

The Supreme Court's decision in *Hustler Magazine v. Falwell*[177] will make it even more difficult to use emotional distress claims to circumvent the well-established constitutional protections afforded defamation and privacy defendants. In *Falwell*, the Supreme Court reversed a damage award for a public figure plaintiff, a well-known preacher, based on his claim for intentional

---

also Rutledge v. Phoenix Newspapers, 715 P.2d 1243, 1245, 12 Media L. Rep. 1969 (Ariz. Ct. App. 1986) (private facts claims must meet requirements of intentional infliction of emotional distress claim, including intent).

[172]To recover for intentional infliction of emotional distress, a plaintiff must prove the following four elements: "(1) extreme and outrageous conduct by the defendant; (2) defendant's injurious intent or reckless disregard for consequences of his acts; (3) causation, and (4) actual experience by plaintiff of severe emotional distress." RESTATEMENT (SECOND) §46.

[173]Fry v. Ionia Sentinel Standard, 300 N.W.2d 687, 6 Media L. Rep. 2497 (Mich. Ct. App. 1980); Ross v. Burns, 612 F.2d 271 (6th Cir. 1980); Cape Pubns. v. Bridges, 423 So. 2d 426, 8 Media L. Rep. 2535 (Fla. Dist. Ct. App. 1982), *petition denied,* 431 So. 2d 988 (Fla.), *cert. denied,* 464 U.S. 893 (1983); Doe v. Sarasota-Bradenton Television, 436 So. 2d 328, 9 Media L. Rep. 2074 (Fla. Dist. Ct. App. 1983).

[174]For example, in *Ross,* 612 F.2d 271, the Sixth Circuit overturned a jury verdict for an undercover vice squad officer who sued two reporters who photographed him and published the photograph in an article describing activities of "undercover narcs." The plaintiff brought actions against the reporters for invasion of privacy and intentional infliction of emotional distress, alllegeing that the publication of the photograph and article destroyed his cover and jeopardized his personal safety and effectiveness on the job, causing him to experience extreme emotional distress. The plaintiff was photographed in a public place outside a courthouse. The Sixth Circuit found that the plaintiff did not show that the publication of the article and photograph by the defendants constituted "extreme and outrageous conduct." *Id.* at 274. The court reviewed emotional distress cases construing the extreme and outrageous conduct requirements and stated that:

> Appellant's conduct in this case consisted of photographing an undercover police officer in a public place and publishing those photographs and the officer's identity in conjunction with "news articles" expressing strong views on a current political and philosophical controversy. We cannot believe that these acts fall within the meaning of "extreme and outrageous" conduct contemplated by the drafters of the Restatement.

Id. See also Price v. Viking Press, 625 F. Supp. 641, 12 Media L. Rep. 1689, 1696 (D. Minn. 1985) (plaintiff FBI agent had no claim for intentional infliction of emotional distress based on publication of city where plaintiff and his family lived, despite claim that this encouraged violent individuals to consider physically harming him and his family, when such information was publicly available).

[175]*Fry,* 300 N.W.2d 687 (report of fire that killed man and woman referred to fact that male victim was survived by wife and two children who were named in report); *Bridges,* 423 So. 2d 426 (photograph of partially nude woman fleeing after being held hostage by estranged husband not actionable). *But see* Armstrong v. H & C Communications, 575 So. 2d 280, 18 Media L. Rep. 1845 (Fla. Dist. Ct. App. 1991) (dismissing privacy claim but sustaining outrage claim by child's parents where television station broadcast closeup of child's skull in report about child's disappearance three years earlier).

[176]Doe v. Sarasota-Bradenton Television, 436 So. 2d 328, 9 Media L. Rep. 2074 (Fla. Dist. Ct. App. 1983) (dismissal, pursuant to *Cox Broadcasting,* of rape victim's action against television station that broadcast her name in connection with reports of assailant's trial).

[177]485 U.S. 46, 14 Media L. Rep. 2281 (1988).

infliction of emotional distress.[178] The plaintiff contended that he had suffered severe emotional distress from the publication of a parody ad that portrayed him as having sex with his mother in an outhouse while drunk.[179] The defendant admitted it was intended to cause distress.[180] The Supreme Court held that public figures and officials cannot recover damages for emotional distress unless they show that the defendant published a false statement of fact about them with constitutional actual malice.[181]

§4.9 DEFENSES

§4.9(A) Waiver, Consent, and Estoppel

Generally, the common law defenses of waiver, consent, and estoppel apply to private facts cases. If a plaintiff consents to be interviewed for a news article, some courts hold that he or she has waived the right to privacy with regard to everything told to the interviewer.[182] Other courts hold that disclosure of information by the plaintiff to a person known to be a reporter does not necessarily constitute consent by the plaintiff, although this would appear to be a knowing waiver.[183]

When the subject agrees to be interviewed but only on the condition that he or she remain anonymous or that certain information not be published, the consent or waiver defense may not be available, and the publisher may be liable for breach of confidentiality for printing information beyond the scope of the consent.[184] Consent need not be express, however; it can be implied from

---

[178]*Id.* at 46–47.
[179]*Id.* at 48–49.
[180]*Id.* at 53.
[181]*Id.* at 56.
[182]Buckley v. W.E.N.H. TV, 5 Media L. Rep. 1509 (D.N.H. 1979) (prison inmate participated in filmed interview at prison); Faucheux v. Magazine Mgmt., 5 Media L. Rep. 1697 (E.D. La. 1979) (husband-and-wife police officers' consent to be photographed for news story in local newspaper vitiated private facts claim based on same photograph appearing in "adult" men's magazine). However, in Barber v. Time, Inc., 159 S.W.2d 291, 296 (Mo. 1942), the fact that the plaintiff's photograph had appeared earlier in a newspaper did not provide a complete consent defense on the part of the magazine that reprinted the photo where the magazine assumed that the plaintiff had consented to the original publication but in fact had not. The court, however, struck the plaintiff's punitive damage award because the defendant had fairly assumed that consent had been given for the earlier photograph; therefore, no malice existed. *Id.*

[183]In Virgil v. Time, Inc. 527 F.2d 1122, 1125–26 (9th Cir. 1975), *cert. denied,* 425 U.S. 998 (1976), the Ninth Circuit, in reversing and remanding the defendant's summary judgment, held that a plaintiff's consensual interview with a reporter gathering information for a story on body surfing in which both public and private facts were discussed, did not as a matter of law make these facts public. However, the court also held that:

Talking freely to a member of the press, knowing the listener to be a member of the press, is not then in itself making public. Such communication can be said to anticipate that what is said will be made public since making public is the function of the press, and accordingly such communication can be construed as a consent to publicize. Thus, if publicity results it can be said to have been consented to.

Id. at 1127. In Hawkins v. Multimedia, 344 S.E.2d 145, 12 Media L. Rep. 1878 (S.C.), *cert. denied,* 479 U.S. 1012 (1986), the reporter conducted a brief telephone interview with the plaintiff, a teenage father, in compiling a story on teenage pregnancy. The plaintiff terminated the interview after a few minutes and the reporter did not obtain express permission to identify or quote him. The South Carolina Supreme Court held that merely demonstrating that the plaintiff knew he was talking to a reporter gathering information for a story is not enough to prevail on a consent defense. 344 S.E.2d at 146, 12 Media L. Rep. at 1879. *See also* Raible v. Newsweek, 341 F. Supp. 804, 809 (W.D. Pa. 1972) (although plaintiff agreed to be photographed with family in front of their house for "patriotic article," consent defense was jury question where photograph was actually published in unflattering article about "The Troubled American—A Special Report on the White Majority").

[184]In Poteet v. Roswell Daily Record, 584 P.2d 1310, 4 Media L. Rep. 1749 (N.M. Ct. App. 1978), the court found that a publisher's constitutional privilege to print newsworthy information was not abrogated

the conduct of the plaintiff, such as when a person seeks publicity, poses for a picture, or even performs an act in a public place.[185]

One court has held that gratuitous consent can be revoked at any time before the disclosure so long as the publisher is given adequate notice to stop publication.[186] If the consent is given by contract, however, many courts hold that it may not be revoked unilaterally by the plaintiff.[187] Waiver and estoppel are also available as defenses.[188]

§4.9(B) Defamation Privileges

Warren and Brandeis advocated that the common law privileges for defamation be extended to privacy claims,[189] and that view is widely accepted today.[190]

§4.9(C) The First Amendment

Because the private facts tort deals with punishing dissemination of the truth, it raises myriad First Amendment problems. These issues are discussed throughout this chapter, because the First Amendment has substantially modified the prima facie case for the private facts tort.

§4.10 REMEDIES

In contrast to the defamation plaintiff, a private facts plaintiff's remedies are not designed to cure damage to reputation but to compensate for the violation of a person's right to be let alone.[191] Accordingly, courts hold that retraction and correction statutes do not apply to private facts actions.[192]

---

by a reporter's promise to a prosecutor not to publish the name of a rape victim. *Id.* at 1312–14, 4 Media L. Rep. at 1750. See Chapter 14 regarding this issue.

[185]Holman v. Central Ark. Broadcasting Co., 610 F.2d 542 (8th Cir. 1979) (plaintiff's drunken tirade in jail cell in presence of news reporter and boisterous comments to reporter could be construed as consent to be interviewed); Neff v. Time, Inc., 406 F. Supp. 858 (W.D. Pa. 1976) (photograph of plaintiff with pants zipper down made with his consent because picture was taken with his active encouragement, participation, and knowledge that it would be published); Gill v. Hearst Pub'g Co., 40 Cal. 2d 224, 253 P.2d 441 (Cal. 1953) (couple photographed during romantic moment in public market).

[186]*Virgil*, 527 F.2d at 1127 ("[I]f consent is withdrawn prior to the act of publicizing, the consequent publicity is without consent."). However, an estoppel argument should succeed on such facts. Buchanan v. Foxfire Fund, 258 S.E.2d 751, 752 (Ga. Ct. App. 1979) (plaintiff's consent to publish certain materials held to be irrevocable contractual right where defendant had incurred expenses in reliance on employee's consent).

[187]LAW OF TORTS, *supra* note 4, §117, at 867.

[188]Rawls v. Conde Nast Pubns., 446 F.2d 313, 316–17 (5th Cir. 1971), *cert. denied,* 404 U.S. 1038 (1972).

[189]*The Right to Privacy, supra* note 1, at 216–17.

[190]Bichler v. Union Bank & Trust Co. of Grand Rapids, 745 F.2d 1006 (6th Cir. 1984) (en banc) (common law qualified privilege to report on matters of public interest extended to private facts action stemming from comments on person's private financial problems in connection with closing of dinner theater owned by that person); Senogles v. Security Benefit Life Ins. Co., 536 P.2d 1358, 1361–62 (Kan. 1975); LAW OF TORTS, *supra* note 4, §117, at 868. These common law privileges include the absolute privilege of a witness, In re Thiene, 115 A.2d 543 (N.J. 1955), and statements by an executive officer in performance of a duty, Carr v. Watkins, 177 A.2d 841 (Md. Ct. App. 1962). The privilege to report public proceedings is protected by *Cox Broadcasting,* which is discussed in greater detail *supra* §4.6(C)(i). The qualified privilege of a defendant to protect and further its own interest is also a defense to a private facts action. Wheeler v. P. Sorenson Mfg. Co., 415 S.W.2d 582 (Ky. 1967) (public disclosure of wages and deductions of employees in opposition to union drive); Shorter v. Retail Credit Co., 251 F. Supp. 329 (D.S.C. 1966) (reasonable investigation of consumer's credit). Such privileges are discussed at length in Chapter 2.

[191]*The Right to Privacy, supra* note 1, at 219; RESTATEMENT (SECOND) §652H.

[192]Kapellas v. Kofman, 1 Cal. 3d 20, 35, 459 P.2d 912 (Cal. 1969).

A private facts plaintiff, without proving special damages, can recover for purely emotional injury.[193] Punitive damages may be awarded to a plaintiff upon a proper showing,[194] although imposing punitive damages for publication of the truth raises substantial constitutional issues.[195] Warren and Brandeis suggested injunctive relief and criminal sanctions in certain limited cases; however, few cases deal with these remedies, which are frowned upon by courts because of their chilling effect on First Amendment rights.[196]

---

[193]RESTATEMENT (SECOND) §652H; *The Right to Privacy, supra* note 1, at 219.
[194]Diaz v. Oakland Tribune, 139 Cal. App. 3d 118, 135–36 (1983).
[195]Florida Star v. B.J.F., 491 U.S. 524, 530 n.5, 541 n.9, 16 Media L. Rep. 1801 (1989).
[196]*See supra* §4.6(C)(i) and (ii); Davis v. Forbes, Inc., 10 Media L. Rep. 1272, 1272–73 (N.D. Tex. 1983) (plaintiff could not show that magazine's publication of his name as one of "America's 400 wealthiest" people would disclose highly offensive private facts, and thus preliminary injunction barring such disclosure denied); Minneapolis Star & Tribune Co. v. Lee, 353 N.W.2d 213, 10 Media L. Rep. 2300 (Minn. Ct. App. 1984) (overturning trial court's order prohibiting news media from publishing details of juvenile proceedings obtained in open court); *The Right to Privacy, supra* note 1, at 219–20; *see also* Huskey v. National Broadcasting Co., 632 F. Supp. 1282, 1295–96 (N.D. Ill. 1986) (film of plaintiff had not yet been shown; court refused to strike plaintiff's claim for injunction, stating that such relief as pleaded was not improper). The entire issue of prior restraints is dealt with in Chapter 10.

CHAPTER 5

INTRUSION, TRESPASS, WIRETAPPING, AND RELATED PROBLEMS

§5.1 Introduction

This chapter deals with civil and criminal sanctions that are imposed on news gathering.[1] It discusses invasion of privacy by intrusion,[2] trespass,[3] conversion,[4] trespass to chattels,[5] wiretapping,[6] bugging,[7] eavesdropping,[8] and related problems.

§5.2 Elements of Intrusion

The Restatement (Second) of Torts sets forth the basic definition of intrusion, one of the four privacy torts: "One who intentionally intrudes, physically or otherwise, upon the solitude or seclusion of another or his private affairs or concerns, is subject to liability to the other for invasion of his privacy, if the intrusion would be highly offensive to a reasonable person."[9] Thus, the four elements of intrusion are (1) an intentional act (2) that intrudes (3) into the private affairs or concerns of another (4) that is highly offensive to a reasonable person.

---

[1] The closely related problem of bans on access to information, usually government controlled information, is discussed in Chapter 1. For a discussion of the history of invasion of privacy and of issues common to all privacy claims, see Chapter 4.
[2] See infra §5.2.
[3] See infra §5.3.
[4] See infra §5.4.
[5] See id.
[6] See infra §5.5.
[7] See id.
[8] See id.
[9] RESTATEMENT (SECOND) OF TORTS §652B (1977) [hereinafter RESTATEMENT (SECOND)]. This definition of intrusion has been adopted by numerous courts. See, e.g., Nelson v. Maine Times, 373 A.2d 1221, 1223, 2 Media L. Rep. 2011, 2012–13 (Me. 1977); Harkey v. Abate, 346 N.W.2d 74, 76 (Mich. Ct. App. 1983); McLain v. Boise Cascade Corp., 533 P.2d 343, 346 (Or. 1975); Froelich v. Werbin, 548 P.2d 482, 484 (Kan. 1976); Mark v. Seattle Times, 635 P.2d 1081, 1094, 7 Media L. Rep. 2209, 2219 (Wash. 1981), cert. denied, 457 U.S. 1124 (1982); Crump v. Beckley Newspapers, 320 S.E.2d 70, 85, 10 Media L. Rep. 2225, 2233 (W. Va. 1984); Phillips v. Smalley Maintenance Servs., 435 So. 2d 705, 708 (Ala. 1983). However, some jurisdictions do not recognize an intrusion claim. See, e.g., Howell v. New York Post Co., 612 N.E.2d 699, 703, 21 Media L. Rep. 1273, 1275 (N.Y. 1993) (New York right to privacy governed exclusively by §§50 and 51 of Civil Rights Law, which does not permit intrusion claim).

§5.2(A) Intentional Acts

The intrusive acts that constitute the heart of intrusion claims against the media—for example, wiretapping[10]—are not acts that ordinarily occur as a result of carelessness or negligence. Thus, the intentional act requirement has not been seriously discussed in the decided cases.

§5.2(B) Intrusive Acts

A number of acts have been held to be intrusive. These include forcing one's way into another's hotel room or home,[11] wiretapping,[12] and, in some circumstances, taking photographs.[13] It also was held to be intrusive for a "paparazzo" to, among other things, endanger Jacqueline Kennedy Onassis' child while he was riding his bicycle by jumping in front of him, coming "uncomfortably close" to Mrs. Onassis with a motorboat while she was swimming, and bribing doormen to keep track of her family's movements, all in an effort to obtain photographs of her and her children.[14]

However, it is not intrusive merely to gather information about someone,[15] to repeatedly try to interview someone over their objections,[16] or to conduct numerous interviews in an effort to uncover information about someone,[17] even if fraud and subterfuge are used to obtain such interviews.[18] It is not intrusive to make numerous threatening and harassing telephone calls to someone's home at odd hours.[19] However, a publication may be intrusive where it

---

[10] See *infra* §5.2(B) for examples of such acts.
[11] RESTATEMENT (SECOND) §652B, cmt. b. *see also infra* note 34 and accompanying text. *See generally* Annot., *Uninvited Entry Into Another's Living Quarters As Invasion of Privacy*, 56 A.L.R.3d 434 (1974).
[12] *See infra* §5.5.
[13] *See generally* Annot., *Taking Unauthorized Photographs As Invasion of Privacy*, 86 A.L.R.3d 374 (1978). A trespass has been found where a television camera crew, seeking to visit restaurants cited for health code violations, entered a public restaurant at lunch unannounced with cameras rolling. Le Mistral, Inc., v. Columbia Broadcasting Sys., 402 N.Y.S.2d 815, 3 Media L. Rep. 1913 (N.Y. App. Div. 1978); *contra* Dempsey v. National Enquirer, 702 F. Supp. 927, 931, 16 Media L. Rep. 1396, 1399 (D. Me. 1988) ("taking a photograph ... in a public place [restaurant] cannot constitute an invasion of privacy"). *See also* Stessman v. American Black Hawk Broadcasting Co., 416 N.W.2d 685, 687–88, 14 Media L. Rep. 2073, 2075 (Iowa 1987) (allegation that reporter photographed plaintiff over her objection while seated in restaurant stated claim for intrusion when it was unclear whether she was seated in public or private dining room).
[14] Galella v. Onassis, 487 F.2d 986, 991–92, 994–95 & n.12, 1 Media L. Rep. 2425, 2426, 2428–29 & n.12 (2d Cir. 1973).
[15] Nader v. General Motors Corp., 255 N.E.2d 765, 769 (N.Y. 1970) ("the mere gathering of information ... does not give rise to a cause of action"); *see also* Solis v. Southern Cal. Rapid Transit Dist., 164 Cal. Rptr. 343, 348–49 (Cal. Ct. App. 1980) (questions asked by uniformed investigator in hospital emergency room of accident victim without any objection from victim not intrusive).
[16] *Dempsey*, 702 F. Supp. at 931, 16 Media L. Rep. at 1399 (reporter's persistent attempts to photograph and interview plaintiff at home and at restaurant after plaintiff's refusals to be interviewed not intrusive). *See also infra* notes 30 and 41.
[17] *Nader*, 255 N.E.2d at 770.
[18] Ault v. Hustler Magazine, 860 F.2d 877, 882, 15 Media L. Rep. 2205, 2209 (9th Cir. 1988), *cert. denied*, 489 U.S. 1080 (1989); Rifkin v. Esquire Pub'g, 8 Media L. Rep. 1384, 1386 (C.D. Cal. 1982); Wolf v. Regardie, 553 A.2d 1213, 1218, 16 Media L. Rep. 1780, 1783 (D.C. 1989) (citing numerous cases); *see also* Chicarella v. Passant, 494 A.2d 1109, 1114 (Pa. Super. Ct. 1985) (no intrusion when insurance company investigator used pretext to obtain hospital records that did not contain sensitive information). *Contra* Noble v. Sears, Roebuck & Co., 109 Cal. Rptr. 269, 272–73 (Cal. Ct. App. 1973); Goodyear Tire & Rubber Co. v. Vandergriff, 184 S.E. 452 (Ga. Ct. App. 1935). There are also various state statutes making it a crime to impersonate public officials or other individuals. *See, e.g.,* State v. Cantor, 534 A.2d 83, 86, 14 Media L. Rep. 2103, 2104 (N.J. Super. Ct. App. Div. 1987), *cert. denied*, 540 A.2d 1274 (N.J. 1988); *Vandergriff*, 184 S.E. 452.
[19] *Nader*, 255 N.E.2d at 770 (but suggesting intentional infliction of emotional distress claim might be available). *Contra* Housh v. Peth, 133 N.E.2d 340, 344 (Ohio 1956). *See generally* Annot., *Unsolicited*

causes hundreds of harassing telephone calls,[20] but the simple publication of an article is not an intrusion, although it may be some other type of invasion of privacy.[21] The intrusion must also be substantial to be actionable.[22]

§5.2(C) Private Affairs

Like the private facts branch of invasion of privacy, intrusion requires a showing that the matters intruded upon were private.[23] There can be no intrusion into matters that are public.[24]

Thus, it is not an intrusion to photograph a house from a public street;[25] to photograph a couple in an affectionate pose in their booth at an open air market;[26] to videotape, through a two-way mirror, the activities of an undercover police officer and a model in a room at a massage parlor;[27] to photograph a couple standing at a Miami airline counter, next to boxes containing their Latin American purchases, for a magazine article on the favorable impact of such purchases on Miami's economy;[28] to walk up a driveway and film an

---

Mailing, Distribution, House Call, or Telephone Call As Invasion of Privacy, 56 A.L.R.3d 457 (1974) (cases discussing under what circumstances unsolicited mailing, distribution, house call or telephone call constitutes tort). If sufficiently outrageous, such telephone calls may constitute intentional infliction of emotional distress. *Nader*, 255 N.E.2d at 770. *See also infra* note 44 and accompanying text.

[20]Harms v. Miami Daily News, 127 So. 2d 715, 718 (Fla. Dist. Ct. App. 1961) (newspaper's publication of plaintiff's name and business telephone number, along with statement that plaintiff had sexy voice, presents jury question as to whether complaint stated claim for intrusion). *See also* Vescovo v. New Way Enters., 130 Cal. Rptr. 86, 88–89 (Cal. Ct. App. 1976) (classified advertisement describing young girl's mother as sexy young bored housewife and giving mother's first name and address was intrusion when people came to her home in response to ads). Both of these cases are discussed in Chapter 7. *See also infra* note 45 and accompanying text.

[21]Harris v. Easton Pub'g Co., 483 A.2d 1377, 1383–84, 11 Media L. Rep. 1209, 1211–12 (Pa. Super. Ct. 1984); Lovgren v. Citizens First Nat'l Bank of Princeton, 534 N.E.2d 987, 989–90, 16 Media L. Rep. 1214, 1216 (Ill. 1989); Reuber v. Food Chem. News, 925 F.2d 703, 718, 18 Media L. Rep. 1689, 1701 (4th Cir.), *cert. denied*, 111 S. Ct. 2814 (1991) (invasion of privacy requires positive act by defendant aside from publication, such as unlawfully obtaining information that encroaches on plaintiff's seclusion). *See also infra* §5.2(E) and *infra* note 154. Regarding private facts, *see generally* Chapter 4.

[22]Mark v. Seattle Times, 635 P.2d 1081, 1095, 7 Media L. Rep. 2209, 2220 (Wash. 1981) (no substantial intrusion when 13-second film clip shot from place open to public), *cert. denied*, 457 U.S. 1124 (1982); Froelich v. Werbin, 548 P.2d 482, 485 (Kan. 1976) (not substantial intrusion when sample of plaintiff's hair taken from trash container and not from hospital room or person); *Chicarella*, 494 A.2d at 1114 (no substantial intrusion when insurance company investigator used pretext to obtain hospital records that did not contain sensitive information); RESTATEMENT (SECOND) §652B, cmt. d.

[23]RESTATEMENT (SECOND) §652B, cmt. c and §652D, cmt. h; *Nader*, 255 N.E.2d at 769; Nelson v. Maine Times, 373 A.2d 1221, 1223, 2 Media L. Rep. 2011, 2012–13 (Me. 1977). Regarding private facts, *see generally* Chapter 4.

[24]Brewer v. Hustler Magazine, 749 F.2d 527, 529–30, 11 Media L. Rep. 1502, 1504 (9th Cir. 1984) (publication of plaintiff's photograph in sexually explicit magazine when plaintiff had already published picture in another forum); Smith v. National Broadcasting Co., 292 P.2d 600, 603 (Cal. Ct. App. 1956) (plaintiff made false report to police of escape of black panther, and radio program about incident broadcast several months later); Pierson v. News Group Pubns., 549 F. Supp. 635, 640 (S.D. Ga. 1982) (publisher photographed soldier during prisoner of war training; plaintiff had no reasonable expectation of privacy on military reservation); Tellado v. Time-Life Books, 643 F. Supp. 904, 907, 13 Media L. Rep. 1401, 1403 (D.N.J. 1986) (publication of photograph of plaintiff and other soldiers during combat mission in Vietnam).

[25]Jaubert v. Crowley Post-Signal, 375 So. 2d 1386, 1390–91, 5 Media L. Rep. 2084, 2087 (La. 1979); Wehling v. Columbia Broadcasting Sys., 721 F.2d 506, 509, 10 Media L. Rep. 1125, 1128 (5th Cir. 1983); Aisenson v. American Broadcasting Co., 269 Cal. Rptr. 379, 388, 17 Media L. Rep. 1881, 1887–88 (Cal. Ct. App. 1990) (no intrusion where television camera crew videotaped judge in front of his home when crew was across street and did not physically encroach on judge's property).

[26]Gill v. Hearst Pub'g Co., 253 P.2d 441, 444–45 (Cal. 1953) ("the photograph did not disclose anything . . . private, but rather only extended knowledge of the particular incident to a somewhat larger public than had actually witnessed it").

[27]Cassidy v. American Broadcasting Cos., 377 N.E.2d 126, 131–32, 3 Media L. Rep. 2449, 2452 (Ill. App. Ct. 1978) (plaintiff's status as policeman tantamount to implied consent to informing public about activities in discharging public duties).

[28]Fogel v. Forbes, Inc., 500 F. Supp. 1081, 1087, 6 Media L. Rep. 1941, 1944 (E.D. Pa. 1980).

individual who was inside of a pharmacy that was closed for the day;[29] to aggressively and possibly abrasively question someone on camera in front of a building after that person said he did not want to be filmed for television;[30] to publish information from a public record;[31] to photograph a plaintiff's activities on his property outside his home even though the photographers trespassed on the periphery of the plaintiff's property;[32] or to take an adhesive bandage from a trash container in a hospital's utility room to obtain samples of a patient's hair.[33]

It is an intrusion, however, to enter a hospital room or home and photograph someone.[34] Taking a photograph of a woman in a "fun house" when a jet of compressed air blew her skirt over her head and revealed her underwear was also held to be an intrusion.[35] This decision appears to be erroneous, because what was photographed was open to public view.[36]

Secretly photographing and tape-recording the activities of a medical "quack" in his home's den has been held to be an intrusion.[37] Photographing prisoners, however, is usually not intrusive.[38]

Overzealous shadowing and surveillance, where one tries to see what is not open to the public, is actionable,[39] although the cases that have found liability for such conduct have involved extreme examples of shadowing coupled

---

[29]Mark v. Seattle Times, 635 P.2d 1081, 1095, 7 Media L. Rep. 2209, 2220 (Wash. 1981), *cert. denied*, 457 U.S. 1124 (1982).

[30]Machleder v. Diaz, 538 F. Supp. 1364, 1367, 1374 (S.D.N.Y. 1982); *see also supra* note 16 and *infra* note 41.

[31]Cox Broadcasting Corp. v. Cohn, 420 U.S. 469, 496, 1 Media L. Rep. 1819, 1829 (1975) ("At the very least, the First and Fourteenth Amendments will not allow exposing the press to liability for truthfully publishing information released to the public in official court records."); Bisbee v. John C. Conover Agency, 452 A.2d 689, 691, 9 Media L. Rep. 1298, 1299 (N.J. Super. Ct. App. Div. 1982) (publishing information from public records about sale price of home, house's purchaser, and related information not intrusive); McNally v. Pulitzer Pub'g Co., 532 F.2d 69, 78–79 (8th Cir.) (publishing portions of psychiatric reports read in open court not intrusive), *cert. denied*, 429 U.S. 855 (1976). *See also* Chapter 4.

[32]McLain v. Boise Cascade Corp., 533 P.2d 343, 346 (Or. 1975). However, nominal damages of $250 for trespass were upheld. *Id.* at 344. Regarding trespass, *see infra* §5.3.

[33]Froelich v. Werbin, 548 P.2d 482, 485 (Kan. 1976). *Contra* Tennant Co. v. Advance Mach. Co., 355 N.W.2d 720, 725 (Minn. Ct. App. 1984). *See also infra* note 194.

[34]Miller v. National Broadcasting Co., 232 Cal. Rptr. 668, 678 (Cal. Ct. App. 1986) (reversing summary judgment for defendants where videotape was filmed inside plaintiff's apartment); Estate of Berthiaume v. Pratt, 365 A.2d 792, 795 (Me. 1976) (hospital bed); Barber v. Time, Inc., 159 S.W.2d 291, 295, 1 Media L. Rep. 1779, 1782 (Mo. 1942) (hospital room); DeMay v. Roberts, 9 N.W. 146, 149 (Mich. 1881) (home). *See also supra* note 11 and accompanying text.

[35]Daily Times Democrat v. Graham, 162 So. 2d 474, 478 (Ala. 1964).

[36]*Id.* The woman contended that she was unfamiliar with fun houses and did not know how compressed air jets worked. *Id.* at 476.

[37]Dietemann v. Time, Inc., 449 F.2d 245, 246, 1 Media L. Rep. 2417, 2419 (9th Cir. 1971). For a discussion of whether the ruse that the defendants used to gain entrance to the plaintiff's home affects this conclusion, see *infra* §5.2(E). *See also supra* note 18. This decision has been criticized. *See infra* note 267 and accompanying text. *Contra* McCall v. Courier Journal, 6 Media L. Rep. 1112, 1113 (Ky. Ct. App. 1980) (tape-recording conversation with attorney in his office), *rev'd on other grounds*, 623 S.W.2d 882, 7 Media L. Rep. 2118 (Ky. 1981), *cert. denied*, 456 U.S. 975 (1982). Regarding tape-recording, *see generally infra* §5.5.

[38]Huskey v. Dallas Chronicle, 13 Media L. Rep. 1057, 1058 (D. Or. 1986) (not intrusive); Cox Communications v. Lowe, 328 S.E.2d 384, 386, 11 Media L. Rep. 2314, 2315 (Ga. Ct. App.) (same), *cert. denied*, 474 U.S. 982 (1985); Haynick v. Zimlich, 498 N.E.2d 1095, 1100, 13 Media L. Rep. 2057, 2061 (Ohio C.P.) (same), *rereported*, 508 N.E.2d 195, 201 (Ohio C.P. 1986); Jenkins v. Winchester Star, 8 Media L. Rep. 1403, 1404 (W.D. Va. 1981) (same). *But see* Huskey v. National Broadcasting Co., 632 F. Supp. 1282, 1287, 12 Media L. Rep. 2105, 2107 (N.D. Ill. 1986) (may be intrusive).

[39]Nader v. General Motors Corp., 255 N.E.2d 765, 771 (N.Y. 1970); Pinkerton Nat'l Detective Agency v. Stevens, 132 S.E.2d 119, 123–24 (Ga. Ct. App. 1963); Souder v. Pendleton Detectives, 88 So. 2d 716, 718 (La. Ct. App. 1956). *See generally* Annot., *Investigations and Surveillance, Shadowing and Trailing, As Violation of Right of Privacy*, 13 A.L.R.3d 1025 (1967).

with other intrusive acts.[40] It is not intrusive, however, to follow people or to take pictures of them on public streets.[41]

§5.2(D) The "Highly Offensive to a Reasonable Person" Requirement

The law does not prohibit all intrusions, because almost all contact with other people is in a sense intrusive.[42] Like the private facts tort, the intrusion tort only prohibits acts that are highly offensive to a reasonable person.[43] A single or a few telephone calls would not be highly offensive, even in the dead of night,[44] but an endless series of calls, even during the day and at work, could be highly offensive.[45] One court has held that it is a jury question whether attendance at a mock "unwedding" ceremony on a hill by uninvited members of the media was highly offensive.[46] While it is not highly offensive to take an adhesive bandage from a trash container in a hospital's utility room to obtain a sample of a patient's hair,[47] it is a jury question as to whether it is highly offensive for the media to enter an apartment with a paramedic team.[48]

Surprisingly, despite its importance, the "highly offensive" requirement is seldom mentioned in the cases.[49]

§5.2(E) Publication of Information Obtained by the Media's Intrusion and the First Amendment

Unlike other types of invasion of privacy torts, publication of the information obtained is not an essential element of intrusion.[50] It is the act of intrusion, not a later publication, that is essential to an intrusion claim.[51]

The courts, however, are divided over whether liability for intrusion also makes one liable for any injury that results from the publication of information obtained by an intrusion. The leading intrusion case granting damages for

---

[40]Ellenberg v. Pinkerton's, Inc., 202 S.E. 2d 701, 704 (Ga. Ct. App. 1973).

[41]*Nader,* 255 N.E.2d at 769; Forster v. Manchester, 189 A.2d 147, 149–50 (Pa. 1963); Pemberton v. Bethlehem Steel, 502 A.2d 1101, 1117 (Md. Ct. Spec. App.), *cert. denied,* 508 A.2d 488 (Md.), *cert. denied,* 479 U.S. 984 (1986). *See also supra* notes 16 and 30.

[42]RESTATEMENT (SECOND) §652B, cmt. d and §652D, cmt. c; Nelson v. Maine Times, 373 A.2d 1221, 1224, 2 Media L. Rep. 2011, 2013 (Me. 1977).

[43]Cason v. Baskin, 20 So. 2d 243, 251 (Fla. 1944) (protection cannot extend to supersensitive or agoraphobic); *see also supra* §5.2(B). Corporations usually are not "persons" for these purposes. NOC, Inc. v. Schaefer, 484 A.2d 729, 730–31 (N.J. Super. Ct. Law. Div. 1984); *see also* Chapter 4.

[44]RESTATEMENT (SECOND) §652B, cmt. d. *See* Tollefson v. Safeway Stores, 351 P.2d 274 (Colo. 1960); Household Fin. Corp. v. Bridge, 250 A.2d 878 (Md. 1969); *see also supra* note 19 and accompanying text.

[45]Harms v. Miami Daily News, 127 So. 2d 715, 717 (Fla. Dist. Ct. App. 1961); Rugg v. McCarty, 476 P.2d 753, 755–56 (Colo. 1970); Summit Loans v. Pecola, 288 A.2d 114 (Md. 1972); *see also supra* note 20 and accompanying text.

[46]Rafferty v. Hartford Courant Co., 416 A.2d 1215, 1216, 6 Media L. Rep. 1668, 1669 (Conn. Super. Ct. 1980).

[47]*See supra* note 33 and accompanying text.

[48]Miller v. National Broadcasting Co., 232 Cal. Rptr. 668, 679 (Cal. Ct. App. 1986) (court must still make preliminary determination as to offensiveness). *Accord* Wolf v. Regardie, 553 A.2d 1213, 1219, 16 Media L. Rep. 1780, 1785 (D.C. 1989); *see also infra* note 139.

[49]This is also true of the "highly offensive" requirement in private facts cases. *See supra* §4.5(D).

[50]*Miller,* 232 Cal. Rptr. at 679; Dietemann v. Time, Inc., 449 F.2d 245, 249–50, 1 Media L. Rep. 2417, 2421 (9th Cir. 1971); Pearson v. Dodd, 410 F.2d 701, 704, 1 Media L. Rep. 1809, 1811 (D.C. Cir.), *cert. denied,* 395 U.S. 947 (1969); Fowler v. Southern Bell Tel. & Tel. Co., 343 F.2d 150, 156 (5th Cir. 1965); Oliver v. Pacific N.W. Bell Tel. Co., 632 P.2d 1295, 1298 (Or. Ct. App. 1981); NOC, Inc. v. Schaefer, 484 A.2d 729, 732 (N.J. Super Ct. Law Div. 1984); Phillips v. Smalley Maintenance Servs., 435 So. 2d 705, 709 (Ala. 1983); Froelich v. Adair, 516 P.2d 993, 996 (Kan. 1973); Hamberger v. Eastman, 206 A.2d 239, 242 (N.H. 1964); *see supra* notes 20 and 21.

[51]RESTATEMENT (SECOND) §652B, cmts. a, b. *See infra* §5.4(A).

publication is *Dietemann v. Time, Inc.*,[52] where two employees of *Life* magazine gained entrance to the plaintiff's home by falsely stating that they wanted medical treatment from him. They surreptitiously took pictures of the plaintiff and used a hidden radio to transmit their conversations with him to a tape recorder in a parked automobile occupied by another *Life* employee, an investigator for the California Department of Health, and an investigator for the Los Angeles District Attorney's Office. One of these photographs and certain portions of the tape-recorded information later were used in a *Life* magazine article about the plaintiff, his arrest for practicing medicine without a license, and his nolo contendere plea to that charge.[53]

The court rejected the media defendant's argument that no damages should be available for publication of the truthful article, holding that "[t]he First Amendment has never been construed to accord newsmen immunity from torts or crimes committed during the course of newsgathering."[54] Without citing any authority, the court then concluded that

> [a] rule forbidding the use of publication as an ingredient of damages would deny to the injured plaintiff recovery for real harm done to him without any countervailing benefit to the legitimate interest of the public in being informed. The same rule would encourage conduct by news media that grossly offends ordinary men.[55]

To the extent that *Dietemann* and the cases that follow it stand for the proposition that the First Amendment does not *absolutely* immunize the press from liability for all torts or crimes committed during news gathering, they are properly decided.[56] No one can seriously contend that the First Amendment allows a reporter to commit murder solely to get a good story.[57] However, to the extent that *Dietemann* and the cases that follow it have been interpreted to mean that the First Amendment has absolutely no bearing on whether particular conduct is a tort or a crime, such cases are wrongly decided.

At least one case decided before *Dietemann* contravenes its holding that damages for publication are available in an intrusion or trespass case. In *Costlow v. Cusimano*,[58] which *Dietemann* does not discuss, two children suffocated to death when they trapped themselves in a refrigerator at their family's residence. The defendant reporter arrived at the scene and, without permission,

---

[52] 449 F.2d 245, 1 Media L. Rep. 2417 (9th Cir. 1971). The balance of this section is based on an article by the author, *Added Damages for Publication Should Not Be Available in Intrusion-Trespass Cases Without Independent Justification*, 1 COMM. LAW. 3, at 6 (Summer 1983).

[53] 449 F.2d at 246–47, 1 Media L. Rep. at 2418–19.

[54] *Id.* at 249, 1 Media L. Rep. at 2420. While the statement quoted in the text is true, it goes too far in denying First Amendment protection to news gathering activities, as this section explains. *See also infra* §5.2(G)(iv).

[55] 449 F.2d at 250, 1 Media L. Rep. at 2421. Other cases have also followed this holding without analysis. *See, e.g.,* Belluomo v. KAKE TV & Radio, 596 P.2d 832, 842 (Kan. Ct. App. 1979); Prahl v. Brosamle, 295 N.W.2d 768, 781–82 (Wis. Ct. App. 1980).

[56] *See generally* Annot., *First Amendment As Immunizing Newsman From Liability for Tortious Conduct While Gathering News*, 28 A.L.R. FED. 904 (1976); Annot., *Intrusions by News-Gathering Entity As Invasion of Right of Privacy*, 69 A.L.R.4th 1059 (1989).

[57] *See* New York Times Co. v. United States, 403 U.S. 713, 727–48, 1 Media L. Rep. 1031, 1036–45 (1971) (Stewart, White, & Marshall, JJ., concurring); Branzburg v. Hayes, 408 U.S. 665, 684–85, 691, 1 Media L. Rep. 2617, 2625, 2627 (1972) (plurality opinion by Justice White) ("It would be frivolous to assert—and no one does in these cases—that the First Amendment, in the interest of securing news or otherwise, confers a license on either the reporter or his news sources to violate valid criminal laws. Although stealing documents or private wiretapping could provide newsworthy information, neither reporter nor source is immune from conviction for such conduct, whatever the impact on the flow of news.").

[58] 311 N.Y.S.2d 92 (N.Y. App. Div. 1970).

CH. 5   INTRUSION, TRESPASS, WIRETAPPING, AND RELATED PROBLEMS   191

photographed the premises and the deceased children. He then wrote an article using the photographs.[59]

The deceased children's family brought a trespass action. The court held that "since the tort of trespass is designed to protect interests in possession of property, damages for trespass are limited to consequences flowing from the interference with possession and not for separable acts more properly allocated under other categories of liability."[60]

More important than *Dietemann*'s failure to deal with this decision is its failure to adequately explain its own rationale. While the First Amendment is not an absolute barrier to the punishment of torts and crimes, it certainly places limits on what acts may be punished as torts and crimes. Simply because an act is a "crime" or a "tort" does not mean it is automatically without First Amendment protection.[61]

The cases that follow *Dietemann* demonstrate this. *Galella v. Onassis*,[62] which relies upon *Dietemann*,[63] often is cited for the proposition that the First Amendment does not protect against liability for crimes or torts committed while gathering news. Even so, in *Galella,* where a photographer was found to have unmercifully harassed Jacqueline Kennedy Onassis and her children to obtain their photographs, the court stated that "Mrs. Onassis was properly found to be a public figure and thus subject to news coverage.... Nonetheless, Galella's action went far beyond the reasonable bounds of news gathering."[64] Thus, even the *Galella* court recognized that a person's right to be free from intrusion is limited by the right to gather news.

Moreover, the *Galella* court implemented this recognition by modifying the trial court's injunction: It relaxed the restrictions on how close Galella could approach Mrs. Onassis and her family and lifted the trial court's ban on his surveillance and following of Mrs. Onassis and her children.[65] In so doing, the court reasoned that "[r]elief must be tailored to protect Mrs. Onassis from the 'paparazzo' attack which distinguishes Galella's behavior from that of other photographers; *it should not unnecessarily infringe on reasonable efforts* to 'cover' Mrs. Onassis."[66] Thus, while *Galella* stands for the proposition that the First Amendment cannot absolutely immunize the press from liability for

---

[59]*Id.* at 93.
[60]*Id.* at 97.
[61]*See, e.g.,* New York Times Co. v. Sullivan, 376 U.S. 254, 279–80, 1 Media L. Rep. 1527, 1537–38 (1964) (public officials can recover for libel only on showing that publication was made by media knowing that it was false or with reckless disregard as to its truthfulness); Cox Broadcasting Corp. v. Cohn, 420 U.S. 469, 493–95, 1 Media L. Rep. 1819, 1828–29 (1975) (private facts action in which defendant published name of rape victim in violation of state law dismissed on First Amendment grounds because states may not impose sanctions for publication of truthful information contained in official court records open to public inspection); Virginia State Bd. of Pharmacy v. Virginia Citizens Consumer Council, 425 U.S. 748, 762, 1 Media L. Rep. 1930, 1935 (1976) (Virginia statute making it a crime for any pharmacist to advertise price of prescription drugs struck down as violation of First Amendment); Martin v. Struthers, 319 U.S. 141, 149 (1943) (trespass statute unconstitutional under First Amendment); Allen v. Combined Communications Corp., 7 Media L. Rep. 2417, 2420 (Colo. Dist. Ct. 1981) (news gathering has qualified First Amendment protection from intrusion and trespass claims).
[62]487 F.2d 986, 1 Media L. Rep. 2425 (2d Cir. 1973).
[63]*Id.* at 995, 1 Media L. Rep. at 2429.
[64]*Id.* (citation omitted).
[65]*Id.* at 998, 1 Media L. Rep. at 2432.
[66]*Id.* (emphasis added). *See also id.* at 995, 1 Media L. Rep. at 2429, where the court recognized that Mrs. Onassis is subject to news coverage, and, more importantly, substantially reduced the injunction against the photographer's news gathering. *Compare id.* at 993, 998–99, 1 Media L. Rep. at 2427, 2432–33. Judge

all torts and crimes, it also holds that the First Amendment must be considered in determining what constitutes a tortious or criminal act during news gathering.

The cases following *Dietemann* often cite *Branzburg v. Hayes*[67] for the proposition that "the First Amendment does not guarantee the press a constitutional right of special access to information not available to the public generally."[68] From this premise it is argued that the First Amendment provides *no* protection in tort or criminal actions involving news gathering.

Not only does that conclusion not follow as a matter of logic, it totally ignores other statements made by the *Branzburg* court: "Nor is it suggested that news gathering does not qualify for First Amendment protection; without some protection for seeking out the news, freedom of the press could be eviscerated,"[69] and "as we have earlier indicated, news gathering is not without its First Amendment protections. . . . ."[70] Thus, *Branzburg* stands for the proposition that the First Amendment limits the media's liability for their actions while gathering news. While *Branzburg* does not establish an absolute privilege for all news gathering, like *Galella,* it recognizes that the First Amendment provides some protection for such activities.

Ultimately, *Dietemann* relies on the rationale that denying a plaintiff damages for publication would result in no "countervailing benefit to the legitimate interest of the public in being informed."[71] That bold conclusion, unsupported by logic or authority, cannot be accepted. It was obviously beneficial for the public to learn that the plaintiff in *Dietemann* was a "quack" who practiced medicine without a license.

Professor Alfred Hill has illustrated this point by postulating the following scenario: What damages are available if a pair of reporters, employing hidden camera and bugging devices, intrude upon a meeting of members of organized crime, discover conclusive proof that these individuals and the police, prosecutors, and other high government officials are engaging in major criminal activity, and then publish that information?[72] No public policy would be served by allowing damages for truthful publicity that results from such news gathering.[73] Indeed, this may well be a case where no damages should be permitted, even for the intrusion.[74] In any event, Professor Hill's hypothetical illustrates the point that the public's interest in obtaining accurate information must be considered before damages for publication may be recovered in a trespass or intrusion case.

Timbers' concurrence sets forth the modification of the injunction in a convenient table. *Id.* at 1001 (Timbers, J., concurring).

[67]408 U.S. 665, 1 Media L. Rep. 2617 (1972). *Dietemann* was decided in 1971, one year before *Branzburg.*
[68]*Id.* at 684, 1 Media L. Rep. at 2624.
[69]*Id.* at 681, 1 Media L. Rep. at 2623.
[70]*Id.* at 707, 1 Media L. Rep. at 2634.
[71]*Dietemann,* 449 F.2d at 250, 1 Media L. Rep. at 2421.
[72]Hill, *Defamation and Privacy Under the First Amendment,* 76 COLUM. L. REV. 1205, 1278–79 (1976).
[73]*Id.* at 1282. *See also* Cassidy v. American Broadcasting Cos., 377 N.E.2d 126, 131–32, 3 Media L. Rep. 2449, 2453 (Ill. App. Ct. 1978) (policeman has no invasion of privacy claim for secret videotaping through two-way mirror and subsequent television broadcast of his investigation into massage parlor, because "no right of privacy . . . can be said to exist with reference to the gathering and dissemination of news concerning [the] discharge of public duties").
[74]*See* RESTATEMENT (SECOND) §205(e).

How then should the balance be struck between a plaintiff's right to damage recovery and the right to gather news? *Costlow v. Cusimano*[75] suggests the proper rule: Damages for publication should be limited to any independent torts—e.g., defamation, false light, and private facts—that arise from the publication itself.[76] If publication of the information is independently improper, it will be actionable, and the plaintiff's rights are protected. If publication is not independently improper, however, the public's interest in obtaining accurate information is fulfilled by denying liability for damages resulting from the publication. In addition, the plaintiff might have the right to recover civil damages for the intrusion or trespass itself in proper cases, as well as the right to request criminal prosecutions of such activities.[77] Thus, publication damages should not be available in intrusion and trespass cases unless the publication itself gives rise to an independent tort.

§5.2(F) Possession and Ownership

Only people entitled to the possession of the premises invaded may bring an action for intrusion or trespass.[78] In one case, members of the media ignored a police sign stating "Do Not Enter, Crime Scene" that had been placed on the apartment door of accused "Son of Sam" killer David Berkowitz, and entered his apartment.[79] The court dismissed criminal trespass charges against the media because the police did not have a sufficient possessory interest in the premises for a trespass action.[80] The same rule applies in civil trespass[81] and conversion[82] actions.

§5.2(G) Defenses

§5.2(G)(i) Government Invitations

Only a handful of decisions address the issue of whether the media are immunized from liability for trespass, intrusion, and related torts when government officials invite or allow the media to accompany them during the officials'

---

[75]311 N.Y.S.2d 92 (N.Y. App. Div. 1970); *see supra* notes 58–60 and accompanying text. The Supreme Court has noted but not resolved this issue. Florida Star v. B.J.F., 491 U.S. 524, 535 n.8, 16 Media L. Rep. 1801, 1806 n.8 (1989).

[76]311 N.Y.S.2d at 95–96.

[77]*Id.* at 97.

[78]Lal v. CBS, Inc., 726 F.2d 97, 100, 10 Media L. Rep. 1276, 1278 (3d Cir. 1984) (owner who does not have possession of property because of tenant cannot maintain trespass action without injury to reversionary interest); Ellenberg v. Pinkerton's, Inc., 202 S.E.2d 701, 704 (Ga. Ct. App. 1973) (same); RESTATEMENT (SECOND) §§157, 158.

[79]People v. Berliner, 3 Media L. Rep. 1942, 1943 (N.Y. City Ct. 1978).

[80]*Id.* at 1943–44. The court also dismissed obstruction of justice charges because there was no claim that the media representatives engaged in intimidation, physical force, interference, or any other illegal act. *Compare* Wood v. Fort Dodge Messenger, 13 Media L. Rep. 1610, 1614 (Iowa Dist. Ct. 1986) (no trespass by media on farm because it was crime scene under sheriff's control and he had consented to media's presence).

[81]Prahl v. Brosamle, 295 N.W.2d 768, 778 (Wis. Ct. App. 1980); Miller v. National Broadcasting Co., 232 Cal. Rptr. 668, 682 (Cal. Ct. App. 1986).

[82]Liberty Lobby v. Pearson, 390 F.2d 489, 491 (D.C. Cir. 1967). *See also* Pearson v. Dodd, 410 F.2d 701, 706 n.23, 1 Media L. Rep. 1809, 1812 n.23 (D.C. Cir.), *cert. denied,* 395 U.S. 947 (1969) (ownership of U.S. senator's documents).

performance of their duties. The leading case on this issue is *Florida Publishing Co. v. Fletcher*,[83] where, at the invitation of the police and fire departments, members of the news media entered the plaintiff's "burned out" home.[84] At the fire marshal's request, one newspaper photographer took a picture of the silhouette left by the body of the plaintiff's deceased daughter after the body was removed from the house.[85] Copies of the photograph were included in the police and fire department files. The photographer's newspaper later published this photograph and other pictures taken by the photographer in conjunction with a story about the fire.[86] The plaintiff first learned of her daughter's death by reading the story and seeing her daughter's silhouette in the picture.[87]

The defendants supplied several affidavits from government officials and media representatives who stated that it was the common custom and practice for news media photographers to enter private property following a disaster.[88] The evidence also indicated that the entry was peaceful, caused no physical damage, and was at the invitation of government officers.[89] Upon this showing, the Florida Supreme Court upheld dismissal of the plaintiff's trespass and intrusion claims, reasoning that such custom and practice established implied consent.[90] Had the plaintiff objected to the media's entry onto her property, her implied consent would have immediately been terminated.[91] The *Fletcher* court recognized that the issue was one of first impression,[92] which indicates that the long-standing practice of the media's entry onto private property during emergencies had gained the general public's acceptance because it had not previously generated litigation.

In contrast, the court in *Green Valley School v. Cowles Florida Broadcasting*[93] reversed summary judgment for members of the media who, at the invitation of government investigators, accompanied the police when they executed a search warrant and made arrests at a private school at night.[94] Relying solely on the Florida District Court of Appeal's opinion in *Fletcher*,[95] the *Green Valley* court held that a government official's invitation to the media to accompany him onto private property did not establish a common usage and custom that immunized the media from tort liability, at least under the circumstances of that case.[96]

The *Green Valley* decision is not sound precedent since the only authority it relied on has been reversed. The result in *Green Valley*, however, would be consistent with *Fletcher* if the plaintiffs in *Green Valley* had explicitly objected

---

[83] 340 So. 2d 914, 2 Media L. Rep. 1088 (Fla. 1976), *cert. denied*, 431 U.S. 930 (1977).
[84] 340 So. 2d at 915, 2 Media L. Rep. at 1089.
[85] *Id.* at 915–16.
[86] *Id.* at 916.
[87] *Id.*
[88] *Id.* at 916–17, 2 Media L. Rep. at 1090.
[89] 340 So. 2d at 915, 2 Media L. Rep. at 1089.
[90] *Id.* at 917–18, 2 Media L. Rep. at 1092. *See also* Wood v. Fort Dodge Messenger, 13 Media L. Rep. 1610, 1614 (Iowa Dist. Ct. 1986).
[91] *Id.* at 918–19, 2 Media L. Rep. at 1092. *See also infra* §5.2(G)(ii).
[92] 340 So. 2d at 918, 2 Media L. Rep. at 1092.
[93] 327 So. 2d 810 (Fla. Dist. Ct. App. 1976).
[94] *Id.* at 813.
[95] 319 So. 2d 100 (Fla. Dist. Ct. App. 1975), *reversed*, 340 So. 2d 914, 2 Media L. Rep. 1088 (Fla. 1976), *cert. denied*, 431 U.S. 930 (1977).
[96] 327 So. 2d at 819 & n.15.

to the media's presence during the raid on their property.[97] Thus, in cases where government officials invite or consent to the media's presence, there should be liability only when the media are told not to go on or to leave someone's property by the possessor of the property; there should not be liability where the possessor of the property does not ask the media to leave.

Without citation or explanation, one court has asserted that such a rule is unsatisfactory because the circumstances of such situations may be distracting to the possessor, and the media's identity may be unknown.[98] If this position were followed, the media could never cover newsworthy events that transpire on private property unless they received explicit consent, which often will be unobtainable—in *Fletcher*, for example, the plaintiff was out of town.[99] It also is unlikely that members of the media will be unidentifiable, given the visible equipment needed for television and radio broadcasts and the need of the press to approach and question people about events and then transcribe those comments. Furthermore, absent a duty to object, plaintiffs would be permitted to avoid making an express objection to the media's presence but could file a lawsuit later on, claiming that they were "distracted" and did not "know" that the media were present. This would make it impossible for the media to shield themselves from open-ended liability, because they would not know they were at risk until it was too late to protect themselves by leaving.

In *Prahl v. Brosamle,* the court distinguished *Fletcher*.[100] In *Prahl,* a television cameraman accompanied the police when they charged onto the plaintiff's property to investigate a claim that shots from the property had been fired at four boys who were bicycling in the area.[101] Although the police had told the cameraman that "he could come forward when the situation was under control,"[102] the court emphasized the fact that no official requested the cameraman's assistance.[103] This distinction, however, based on the absence of any request for assistance from the government, is without merit. While the *Fletcher* court noted that the police asked a media photographer to take a picture on the plaintiff's property,[104] such assistance was in no way central to *Fletcher*'s holding, because the government's request came after the media were already present on the plaintiff's property.[105] An "intrusion" had occurred by the time the government requested assistance.

The request for assistance in *Fletcher* was not crucial to its holding for an additional reason. In *Fletcher,* a photographer assisted the government[106] by taking one of several photographs. If the government's request for assistance was essential to *Fletcher*'s holding, then the court would have shielded from

---

[97]Anderson v. WROC-TV, 441 N.Y.S.2d 220, 7 Media L. Rep. 1987 (N.Y. Sup. Ct. 1981). In *Anderson*, the plaintiffs objected to the media accompanying an animal control officer when he executed a search warrant at their home. The court struck the media defendant's *Fletcher* defenses because the plaintiff's objection eliminated any implied consent. *Id.* at 222–23, 7 Media L. Rep. at 1992.
[98]Prahl v. Brosamle, 295 N.W.2d 768, 780 (Wis. Ct. App. 1980).
[99]340 So. 2d 914, 915, 2 Media L. Rep. 1088, 1089 (Fla. 1976), *cert. denied,* 431 U.S. 930 (1977). *See also* Miller v. National Broadcasting Co., 232 Cal. Rptr. 668, 674 & n.4 (Cal. Ct. App. 1986).
[100]295 N.W.2d at 779.
[101]*Id.* at 772.
[102]*Id.* at 773.
[103]*Id.* at 780.
[104]340 So. 2d at 915–16, 2 Media L. Rep. at 1089.
[105]*Id.* at 915.
[106]*Id.* at 916.

liability only the acts necessary to the taking of that single photograph by one photographer. Instead, the *Fletcher* court dismissed all intrusion and trespass claims against all the media representatives that were present.[107] Thus, the result in *Fletcher* is not dependent on a showing that the government asked the media for assistance, as was ultimately recognized in *Prahl.*[108]

§5.2(G)(ii) Consent

Consent is a well-recognized defense in tort actions[109] and is also a defense in intrusion cases.[110] Consent can be implied from the plaintiff's failure to object to the media's presence;[111] failure to object may also constitute a waiver or estoppel.[112]

Various attempts have been made to overcome consent defenses, including claims that the consent was void because it was fraudulently obtained[113] and that it was revocable,[114] but such contentions have not been successful. A claim that a mental patient's consent was invalid because of his incompetence has been sustained, however.[115]

§5.2(G)(iii) Public Interest/Newsworthiness

One case has held that the public's interest in a public official's performance of his duties bars an intrusion claim against the media for filming his activities in a massage parlor through a two-way mirror.[116] Another case has reasoned that if a patient/plaintiff had contracted a contagious disease or a

---

[107]*Id.* at 916, 917, 919, 2 Media L. Rep. at 1089, 1090–91, 1092.

[108]On remand the trial court dismissed the suit on the basis of the implied consent defense. Apparently on the basis of new evidence that had not been in the record at the time of the appeal, the judge concluded that there was "a common and accepted custom in the State of Wisconsin and nationally for reporters and photographers to accompany public officers and firemen onto private premises where newsworthy events of general public interest such as crime, shootings, fires or storms have or are occurring, provided that (1) such entry can be made peacefully, without force or physical destruction; (2) there is no objection to such entry; and (3) such entry is made for purposes of newsgathering or the taking of news photographs." *Prahl v. Brosamle,* Case No. 152-062, Circuit Court, Dane County, Aug. 28, 1982 (Pekowsy, J.).
M. FRANKLIN, MASS MEDIA LAW—CASES AND MATERIALS 62 (4th ed. 1990). *See also* Higbee v. Times-Advocate, 5 Media L. Rep. 2372, 2372 (S.D. Cal. 1980) (no violation of constitutional right of privacy where newspaper photographer accompanied police on execution of search warrant at plaintiffs' home and where newspaper published photo of interior of plaintiffs' home); Moncrief v. Hanton, 10 Media L. Rep. 1620, 1622 (N.D. Ohio 1984) (no violation of constitutional right of privacy where media accompanied police on execution of search warrant and took pictures of one plaintiff handcuffed in his home).

[109]RESTATEMENT (SECOND) §§892–892D and 652F, cmt. b.

[110]Belluomo v. KAKE TV & Radio, 596 P.2d 832, 840–41 (Kan. Ct. App. 1979); Lal v. Columbia Broadcasting Sys., 726 F.2d 97, 100, 10 Media L. Rep. 1276, 1278 (3d Cir. 1984) (tenant's consent is complete defense to landlord's trespass action); Ault v. Hustler Magazine, 860 F.2d 877, 882–83, 15 Media L. Rep. 2205, 2209 (9th Cir. 1988) ("when a person agrees to be photographed for a newspaper, the photograph is not a private concern and its republication does not create a ground for liability"), *cert. denied,* 489 U.S. 1080 (1989).

[111]Machleder v. Diaz, 538 F. Supp. 1364, 1375 (S.D.N.Y. 1982). *See also supra* §5.2(G)(i).

[112]Rawls v. Conde Nast Pubns., 446 F.2d 313, 314–15, 317 (5th Cir. 1971), *cert. denied,* 404 U.S. 1038 (1972).

[113]*Belluomo,* 596 P.2d at 835, 836, 843 (jury verdict finding no fraud upheld).

[114]*Id.* at 844 (revocation of consent day after TV crew allowed to film in nonpublic areas of restaurant ineffective).

[115]Delan v. Columbia Broadcasting Sys., 445 N.Y.S.2d 898, 904–05, 7 Media L. Rep. 2453, 2456 (N.Y. Sup. Ct. 1981), *rev'd on other grounds,* 458 N.Y.S.2d 608, 614, 9 Media L. Rep. 1130 (N.Y. App. Div. 1983).

[116]Cassidy v. American Broadcasting Cos., 377 N.E.2d 126, 132, 3 Media L. Rep. 2449, 2453 (Ill. App. Ct. 1978) ("no right of privacy against intrusion can be said to exist with reference to the gathering and dissemination of news concerning discharge of public duties"). *See also* Truxes v. Kenco Enters., 119 N.W.2d 914, 919 (S.D. 1963) (photograph of postal employee taken with supervisor's consent).

CH. 5   INTRUSION, TRESPASS, WIRETAPPING, AND RELATED PROBLEMS   197

disease that was dangerous to others, no intrusion claim would exist even though she was photographed in her hospital room over her protest.[117] The scope of this defense remains to be determined.[118]

§5.2(G)(iv) The First Amendment and Criminal Trespass

In *Stahl v. State*,[119] the court considered the impact of the First Amendment on criminal trespass actions against the media.[120] In a 2-1 decision, the majority dismissed the First Amendment defense of media representatives who accompanied demonstrators onto the site of a nuclear generating plant that was under construction.[121] The majority reached this conclusion by repeating the inaccurate maxim that "[t]he First Amendment does not shield newspersons from liability for torts and crimes committed in the course of news-gathering."[122] This broad maxim cannot be correct, for the very purpose of the Constitution is to limit the scope of otherwise valid civil and criminal laws.[123]

The *Stahl* dissent noted that the demonstration was a newsworthy event, that the media had inadequate access to the demonstration because their designated viewing area was not close to the demonstration site, and that the public had a right to know the information the media were seeking because it related to the operation of government.[124] Against this, the state of Oklahoma argued that a conviction was necessary to protect public safety and property interests.[125]

As to the issue of public safety, the dissent reasoned that the nine newspeople involved always had been peaceful and never interfered with the police who arrested the demonstrators.[126] The dissent also suggested that the media's presence may have prevented a violent confrontation between the demonstrators and the police.[127] As to protecting property rights, the dissent observed that site owners had no reason to believe that the newspeople would damage the site or its facilities.[128] The dissent also indicated that the property involved had a quasi-public nature.[129]

Finally, the dissent stated that the property owners' purpose in restricting the media to the designated viewing area was "to limit press access based on

---

[117]Barber v. Time, Inc., 159 S.W.2d 291, 295, 1 Media L. Rep. 1779, 1782 (Mo. 1942). *See also supra* §5.2(E); Tureen v. Equifax, Inc., 571 F.2d 411, 416 (8th Cir. 1978) (collection and retention of insured's past insurance history served legitimate public interest).
[118]*Compare* the analogous issue in private facts cases in Chapter 4.
[119]665 P.2d 839, 9 Media L. Rep. 1945 (Okla. Crim. App. 1983), *cert. denied*, 464 U.S. 1069 (1984). The trial court's factual findings are set forth *id.* at 843–44, 9 Media L. Rep. at 1949.
[120]For a discussion of First Amendment principles and their impact on liability for intrusion by news gathering, *see supra* §5.2(E).
[121]665 P.2d at 840, 9 Media L. Rep. at 1945–46.
[122]*Id.* at 841, 9 Media L. Rep. at 1947. *See supra* §5.2(E).
[123]In an earlier case, Landmark Communications v. Virginia, 435 U.S. 829, 3 Media L. Rep. 2153 (1978), the Court stated:
A legislature appropriately inquires into and may declare the reasons impelling legislative action but the judicial function commands analysis of whether the specific conduct charged falls within the reach of the statute and if so whether the legislation is consonant with the Constitution. Were it otherwise, the scope of freedom of speech and of the press would be subject to legislative definition and the function of the First Amendment as a check on legislative power would be nullified.
435 U.S. at 844, 3 Media L. Rep. at 2159. *See supra* §5.2(E).
[124]665 P.2d at 847, 9 Media L. Rep. at 1952 (Brett. J., dissenting).
[125]*Id.*
[126]*Id.*
[127]*Id.* at 847–48.
[128]*Id.* at 848, 9 Media L. Rep. at 1953.
[129]665 P.2d at 841, 848, 9 Media L. Rep. at 1947, 1953.

their disapproval of the message the media would convey to the public."[130] Accordingly, the dissent concluded that the state's interests did not outweigh the media's right to gather news to inform the public about a newsworthy event.[131]

Since the state presented no real justification for enforcing its criminal trespass law in this case, the court had little reason to disregard the media's constitutional right to gather news,[132] which would have provided the public with information about a newsworthy issue.[133] Other courts properly have recognized that the First Amendment limits the scope of criminal trespass laws.[134]

§5.2(H) Damages

The damages recoverable in intrusion actions have not provoked much discussion,[135] apparently because plaintiffs usually have lost such cases or have received small awards.[136]

§5.2(I) Question of Law

It is for the court to determine, in the first instance, whether an intrusion claim can be sustained.[137] Whether an intrusion is highly offensive to a reasonable person may be a jury question,[138] although it is at least initially a question of law.[139]

§5.3 TRESPASS

What has been said concerning intrusion claims is generally applicable to trespass actions.[140] Indeed, in many of the cases already discussed, the plaintiffs sought recovery for intrusion and trespass.[141]

---

[130]*Id.* at 841, 849.

[131]*Id.* at 849, 9 Media L. Rep. at 1954.

[132]Branzburg v. Hayes, 408 U.S. 665, 681, 683–84, 1 Media L. Rep. 2617, 2623, 2625 (1972).

[133]*See generally* Note, *Press Passes and Trespasses: Newsgathering on Private Property*, 84 COLUM. L. REV. 1297, 1334–42 (1984) (arguing that competing interests must be weighed to determine whether First Amendment prevents punishment for trespass); Note, *And Forgive Them Their Trespasses: Applying the Defense of Necessity to the Criminal Conduct of the Newsgatherer*, 103 HARV. L. REV. 890 (1990).

[134]*See* Freedman v. New Jersey State Police, 343 A.2d 148, 151 (N.J. Super. Ct. Law. Div. 1975) (court applied state constitutional provision that afforded rights identical to First Amendment); People v. Rewald, 318 N.Y.S.2d 40, 45 (N.Y. 1971). *See also* State v. Shack, 277 A.2d 369, 375 (N.J. 1971) (conduct of defendants in seeking to visit farm workers in privacy of their living quarters and without farmer-employer's supervision beyond reach of trespass statute); Chapter 1. *Contra* Oak Creek v. King, 436 N.W.2d 285 (Wis. 1989) (4-3 decision upholding news gatherer's disorderly conduct conviction for refusal to leave site of air crash); State v. McCormack, 682 P.2d 742 (N.M. 1984) (free-lance photographer convicted of criminal trespass for following protesters past barricade).

[135]*See generally* RESTATEMENT (SECOND) §652H. On punitive damages, *see* Barber v. Time, Inc., 159 S.W.2d 291, 296, 1 Media L. Rep. 1779, 1782 (Mo. 1942). On damages for publication, *see supra* §5.2(E).

[136]*Barber*, 159 S.W.2d at 292, 1 Media L. Rep. at 1782 ($1,500 for actual damages and $1,500 for punitive damages); Dietemann v. Time, Inc., 449 F.2d 245, 245, 1 Media L. Rep. 2417, 2417 (9th Cir. 1971) ($1,000 in general damages); Le Mistral, Inc. v. Columbia Broadcasting Sys., 402 N.Y.S.2d 815, 818, 3 Media L. Rep. 1913, 1914 (N.Y. App. Div. 1978) ($1,200 in compensatory damages upheld, but $250,000 in punitive damages reversed because of evidentiary error).

[137]*Barber*, 159 S.W.2d at 295, 1 Media L. Rep. at 1782.

[138]*See* Harms v. Miami Daily News, 127 So. 2d 715, 718 (Fla. Dist. Ct. App. 1961) and cases cited therein.

[139]Gill v. Hearst Pub'g Co., 253 P.2d 441, 444 (Cal. 1953); Miller v. National Broadcasting Co., 232 Cal. Rptr. 668, 678 (Cal. Ct. App. 1986); *see also supra* note 48.

[140]*See supra* §5.2(G)(iv); *see generally supra* §5.2.

[141]*See, e.g.,* Pearson v. Dodd, 410 F.2d 701, 704, 1 Media L. Rep. 1809, 1811 (D.C. Cir.), *cert. denied*, 395 U.S. 947 (1969); Florida Pub'g Co. v. Fletcher, 340 So. 2d 914, 916, 2 Media L. Rep. 1088, 1090 (Fla. 1976), *cert. denied*, 431 U.S. 930 (1977); Machleder v. Diaz, 538 F. Supp. 1364, 1367 (S.D.N.Y. 1982).

Damages for trespass do not include recovery for damage to reputation or for emotional distress.[142] A trespass claim must allege actual injury to the plaintiff's property;[143] it cannot be based solely on claims for nominal and punitive damages.[144] In the media context, a plaintiff must show intent, reckless disregard, or specific damage attributable to trespass.[145]

§5.4 Conversion and Trespass to Chattels

What has been stated about intrusion and trespass is also generally applicable to actions against the media for conversion and trespass to chattels.[146] Problems in this area usually arise when documents have been copied and then turned over to the media.[147]

The theory of a conversion case is that the defendant so substantially interfered with the plaintiff's right to use his or her property that the defendant must be judicially forced to buy it.[148] If the defendant's interference with the plaintiff's property is not that substantial, then the plaintiff must sue for trespass to chattels[149] and may recover only damages for lost use of the property.[150] Nominal damages may be recovered in a conversion action, but only actual damages may be recovered in a trespass to chattels action.[151]

The mere copying of documents does not amount to conversion unless the information obtained has economic value and can be sold—for instance, trade secrets or scientific inventions.[152] The office records of a U.S. senator, including letters from constituents, are not such property and therefore cannot be converted.[153]

§5.4(A) Publication of Stolen Information

The mere publication of information is not an intrusion.[154] Thus, in *Pearson v. Dodd*,[155] the court refused to hold two newspaper columnists liable for

---

[142]Costlow v. Cusimano, 311 N.Y.S.2d 92, 97 (N.Y. App. Div. 1970); RESTATEMENT (SECOND) OF TORTS §162 (1965). *See also* Allen v. Combined Communications Corp., 7 Media L. Rep. 2417, 2420 (Colo. Dist Ct. 1981) (trespass claims against media must allege that media knew they were committing trespass or that they did so in reckless disregard of that fact, or that plaintiff suffered actual damage as result of trespass); *supra* §5.2(E). *But see Miller,* 232 Cal. Rptr. at 677 (emotional distress damages available if physical injury results to person or property).

[143]*See supra* note 142.

[144]*Id. But see* Prahl v. Brosamle, 295 N.W.2d 768, 781 (Wis. Ct. App. 1980) (allowing award of nominal damages without showing of actual injury to property).

[145]*Allen,* 7 Media L. Rep. at 2420; Magenis v. Fisher Broadcasting, 798 P.2d 1106, 1110, 18 Media L. Rep. 1229, 1232 (Or. Ct. App. 1990) (television station's allegedly unlawful trespass onto plaintiff's property does not by itself constitute intrusion; plaintiff must still show that trespass was highly offensive).

[146]*See supra* §§5.2(G)(iv) and 5.3; *see generally supra* §5.2.

[147]Pearson v. Dodd, 410 F.2d 701, 703, 1 Media L. Rep. 1809, 1810 (D.C. Cir.), *cert. denied,* 395 U.S. 947 (1969); Liberty Lobby v. Pearson, 390 F.2d 489, 490 (D.C. Cir. 1968).

[148]RESTATEMENT (SECOND) §222A; *Dodd,* 410 F.2d at 706–07.

[149]RESTATEMENT (SECOND) §217; *see Dodd,* 410 F.2d at 707, 1 Media L. Rep. at 1813.

[150]*Dodd,* 410 F.2d at 707, 1 Media L. Rep. at 1813.

[151]*Id.*

[152]*Id.* at 707–08, 1 Media L. Rep. at 1813–14. Nor does temporary removal of documents and subsequent printing of information contained in them constitute conversion. Harper & Row, Pubrs. v. Nation Enters., 723 F.2d 195, 201, 9 Media L. Rep. 2489, 2493 (2d Cir. 1983), *rev'd on other grounds,* 471 U.S. 539, 11 Media L. Rep. 1969 (1985).

[153]*Dodd,* 410 F.2d at 708, 1 Media L. Rep. at 1814.

[154]*See supra* note 21 and accompanying text, and *infra* note 155. Of course, the publication may be actionable under some other theory, such as defamation or private facts.

[155]410 F.2d 701, 1 Media L. Rep. 1809 (D.C. Cir.), *cert. denied,* 395 U.S. 947 (1969).

intrusion when they published articles based on confidential files that a U.S. senator's current and former staff had taken from his office without his permission.[156] The court also held that even the columnists' receipt of such documents with knowledge that they were removed without authorization was not actionable as an intrusion.[157] These two rules have been followed by other courts that have considered the issue.[158]

Although there is no civil liability for publication of information contained in stolen documents, so long as the media do not participate in the theft, the possibility of a criminal prosecution exists. The federal government may prosecute the interstate transportation of stolen property under federal criminal statutes.[159] These statutes only cover "goods, wares, merchandise, securities or money, of the value of $5,000 or more . . . ."[160] Thus, it is essential in such a case for the government to show that the information taken was a good, ware, or merchandise.

Documents that contain ideas and other information are not "goods, wares, or merchandise" unless they are " 'ordinarily a subject of commerce.' "[161] Similarly, intangible intellectual property, such as a computer program or a copyright interest, cannot constitute goods, wares, or merchandise within the meaning of the statutes.[162] In *In re Vericker,* since there was no evidence that

---

[156]*Id.* at 703, 1 Media L. Rep. at 1810. *See also* Liberty Lobby v. Pearson, 261 F. Supp. 726, 727 (D.D.C. 1966), *aff'd on other grounds,* 390 F.2d 489 (D.C. Cir. 1968) (" 'The courts may not review the manner in which a newspaper man obtains his information and may not restrain the publication of news merely because the person responsible for the publication obtained it in a manner that may perhaps be illegal or immoral.' " 390 F.2d at 493 n.1 (Wright, J., concurring) (quoting district court with approval)); McNally v. Pulitzer Pub'g Co., 532 F.2d 69, 79 n.14 (8th Cir.), *cert. denied,* 429 U.S. 855 (1976) (manner in which information is acquired not relevant in assessing whether publication of private facts is actionable but relevant in determining whether there has been intrusion); *see* Chapter 4, §§4.6(C)(i) and (ii).

[157]410 F.2d at 705, 1 Media L. Rep. at 1811–12, *cited with approval in* McNally v. Pulitzer Pub'g Co., 532 F.2d 69, 79 n.14 (8th Cir.), *cert. denied,* 429 U.S. 855 (1976). Aiding and abetting the *removal* of the documents may, however, be actionable, but participating in the secret copying of them is not. *See* 410 F.2d at 705 & n.20, 1 Media L. Rep. at 1811–12 & n.20; Branzburg v. Hayes, 408 U.S. 665, 696 n.36, 1 Media L. Rep. 2617, 2629 n.36 (1972) (both knowledge of crime and some affirmative act of concealment or participation required). Possessing the only known copies of documents that are the property of another may, however, subject the defendant to liability for conversion. FMC Corp. v. Capital Cities/ABC, 915 F.2d 300, 304, 18 Media L. Rep. 1195, 1199 (7th Cir. 1990) (ABC's retention of only known copies of documents that belonged to FMC, to exclusion of their owner, is equivalent of conversion; but ABC could retain copies of documents so that its First Amendment investigatory activities would not be chilled).

[158]Belluomo v. KAKE TV & Radio, 596 P.2d 832, 842 (Kan. Ct. App. 1979); Nicholson v. McClatchy Newspapers, 223 Cal. Rptr. 58, 63–64, 12 Media L. Rep. 2009, 2013–14 (Cal. Ct. App. 1986). *See also* Bilney v. Evening Star Newspaper Co., 406 A.2d 652, 657–58, 5 Media L. Rep. 1931, 1934–35 (Md. Ct. Spec. App. 1979) (media reliance on confidential source). The Supreme Court reached a similar result in Landmark Communications v. Virginia, 435 U.S. 829, 837–45, 3 Media L. Rep. 2153, 2156–59 (1978), which is discussed in Chapter 4. *See* Florida Star v. B.J.F., 491 U.S. 524, 535 n.8, 16 Media L. Rep. 1801, 1806 n.8 (1989). For a discussion of prior restraints in such situations, *see* New York Times Co. v. United States, 403 U.S. 713, 1 Media L. Rep. 1031 (1971), which is addressed in Chapter 10.

[159]18 U.S.C. §§2314, 2315 (1989).

[160]*Id.*

[161]In re Vericker, 446 F.2d 244, 246, 248 (2d Cir. 1971) (quoting United States v. Seagraves, 265 F.2d 876, 880 (3d Cir. 1959)) (holding in alleged theft and interstate transportation of FBI documents that FBI documents not ordinarily subject of commerce). *But see* Carpenter v. United States, 484 U.S. 19, 25–26, 14 Media L. Rep. 1853, 1856–57 (1987), where an evenly divided Court upheld the conviction of a newspaper reporter under securities statutes and unanimously upheld a conviction under mail and wire fraud statutes on grounds that the reporter misappropriated the newspaper's "property" right in its confidential business information—the nature and timing of columns dealing with securities—and used that information to tip stock traders; the Court observed that even though this property right was "intangible," it still was protected (distinguishing McNally v. United States, 483 U.S. 350 (1987)). *McNally* was later overruled by new legislation. *See* 18 U.S.C. §1346 (1989).

[162]United States v. Dowling, 473 U.S. 214, 217 (1985) (§2314 does not apply when individual is charged with stealing copyright interest rather than being charged with stealing material itself); United States v. Brown, 925 F.2d 1301, 1308 (10th Cir. 1991) (computer program is intangible intellectual property and does not constitute goods, wares, or merchandise within meaning of §§2314 and 2315).

"papers showing that individuals are or may have been engaging in criminal activity or what procedures are used by the FBI in tracking them down are ordinarily bought or sold in commerce," the unlawful taking of such documents did not violate the federal statutes prohibiting interstate transportation of stolen goods.[163]

The government has been successful, however, in prosecuting similar conduct under a federal statute that prohibits the theft or sale of "any record, voucher, money, or thing of value of the United States . . . ."[164] Prosecution under the federal espionage laws[165] is also possible in certain circumstances.[166]

Liability also may exist under state criminal statutes that prohibit the receipt of stolen property.[167] A conviction for this crime requires that there be (1) property (2) that has been stolen, (3) that the receiver knows is stolen, and (4) that was received with felonious intent.[168] The first requirement—property—may bar prosecutions based on documents containing information about government operations,[169] although prosecutions for the theft of the actual paper containing the information are possible.[170]

The second element—that the documents be stolen—requires that the documents be taken permanently to commit the common law crime of larceny.[171] Thus, temporarily using the documents—for example, copying them—is probably not larceny.[172]

The third element—proof that the receiver knew that the documents were stolen—is usually circumstantial.[173] Proof of surreptitious behavior by the person providing the documents to the media may simply indicate that the person who provides the information does not want his or her activities known for fear of retaliation, even though the person has a perfect right to release the information.[174]

The fourth element—receipt with felonious intent—has not received much attention.

---

[163]446 F.2d at 248. The court noted, however, that geophysical maps and documents describing procedures for manufacturing drugs were the subject of sales and therefore were "goods, wares or merchandise." *Id. See also* United States v. Greenwald, 479 F.2d 320, 322 (6th Cir.) (document containing chemical formulas are "goods, wares, or merchandise"), *cert. denied,* 414 U.S. 854 (1973).

[164]18 U.S.C. §641 (1989). *See* United States v. DiGilio, 538 F.2d 972, 975–76 (3d Cir. 1976) (photocopying of FBI files by FBI employee who used government equipment and supplies), *cert. denied,* 429 U.S. 1038 (1977). *See also* 18 U.S.C. §1905 (1989).

[165]18 U.S.C. §§793–98 (1989).

[166]For an excellent discussion of these laws, *see* Edgar & Schmidt, *The Espionage Statutes and Publication of Defense Information,* 73 COLUM. L. REV. 929 (1973); United States v. Morison, 844 F.2d 1057, 15 Media L. Rep. 1369 (4th Cir.) (upholding espionage indictment and conviction for releasing three photographs, classified as secret, to British defense magazine), *cert. denied,* 488 U.S. 908 (1988); United States v. Truong Dinh Hung, 629 F.2d 908 (4th Cir. 1980) (upholding conviction for transmission of classified information to representatives of socialist Vietnamese Republic during Paris negotiations), *cert. denied,* 454 U.S. 1144 (1982).

[167]*See generally* Annot., *Receipt of Public Documents Taken by Another Without Authorization As Receipt of Stolen Property,* 57 A.L.R.3d 1211 (1974) (discussing state cases where possessor of purloined public documents charged with having received stolen goods).

[168]*Id.* at 1211.

[169]*But see* CAL. PENAL CODE §146e (West 1988 & Supp. 1994), which was passed as a result of the decision in People v. Kunkin, 507 P.2d 1392, 1400 n.14 (Cal. 1973). This statute permits prosecution for unlawfully publishing the residential address of a peace officer.

[170]Annot., *supra* note 167, at 1215–16.

[171]Liability may also exist for receiving property with knowledge that it was embezzled, taken by false pretenses, or stolen. *Id.* at 1212.

[172]*Id.*

[173]*Id.*

[174]*Id.* at 1212–13 & n.11.

In the leading case of *People v. Kunkin*,[175] a newspaper was charged with receiving stolen property: a copy of a personnel roster for the California Bureau of Narcotics Enforcement,[176] which the newspaper later published under the headline "Know Your Local Narc."[177] The court assumed, without deciding, that the roster was "property" and that the defendants had "received" it.[178] Accordingly, the court focused its attention on whether the roster was stolen and whether the defendants knew it.[179]

After observing that "theft by larceny requires a specific intent permanently to deprive the rightful owner of his property,"[180] the court noted that Jerry Reznick, the government employee who provided the roster to the newspaper, had not sold the document to the newspaper; that he was to receive $20 for letting the newspaper look at it, although he was never paid; and that he insisted that he wanted to return the roster to the government when the newspaper was finished with it, but that he later had left his government job and therefore could not conveniently return the roster.[181] Based on this evidence, especially the last item, the court upheld the jury's findings that the roster was stolen.[182]

As to the newspaper's knowledge that the roster was stolen, the court stated that the newspaper did not know that Reznick was no longer employed by the government.[183] The government argued that knowledge that the roster was stolen could be inferred from various suspicious circumstances.[184] The court held that "[t]he Attorney General's list of suspicious circumstances confuses circumstances which might well serve to put a publisher on notice that official displeasure would result from publication of information released to him without authorization, with circumstances which should signal that the property tendered has been taken by theft by larceny."[185] Accordingly, it reversed the newspaper's conviction for receiving stolen property.[186]

The effect of the First Amendment was not discussed, and what its impact would be is uncertain;[187] however, liability probably would be permissible under a narrowly drawn statute that protected essential government interests.[188]

§5.4(B) Privilege to Disclose Illegal Acts

At least one case has noted that there appears to be a privilege for employees and agents to disclose their employers' wrongdoing to the media or others.[189]

---

[175] 507 P.2d 1392 (Cal. 1973).
[176] *Id.* at 1394.
[177] *Id.* at 1394–95.
[178] *Id.* at 1395.
[179] *Id.*
[180] 507 P.2d at 1396.
[181] *Id.* at 1397.
[182] *Id.*
[183] *Id.* at 1398.
[184] *Id.* at 1399 & n.13.
[185] 507 P.2d at 1399.
[186] *Id.* at 1399–1400. This decision is discussed in Sobel, *Government Documents as "Stolen Property": Reflections on the "Free Press" Case*, 48 L.A. B. BULL. 291 (1973).
[187] *See supra* §5.2(E).
[188] *See* Landmark Communications v. Virginia, 435 U.S. 829, 3 Media L. Rep. 2153 (1978), which is discussed in Chapter 4. *See also* Nimmer, *National Security Secrets v. Free Speech: The Issues Left Undecided in the Ellsberg Case*, 26 STANFORD L. REV. 311 (1974) (explores constitutional standard that balances national security and free speech).
[189] Pearson v. Dodd, 410 F.2d 701, 705 n.19, 1 Media L. Rep. 1809, 1811 n.19 (D.C. Cir.) (citing RESTATEMENT (SECOND) OF AGENCY §395, cmt. f (1958)), *cert. denied*, 395 U.S. 947 (1969). Even the fairly new tort of wrongful termination, developed to protect employees who are fired for whistle-blowing, recognizes this principle. *See, e.g.,* Tameny v. Atlantic Richfield Co., 610 P.2d 1330, 1336–37 (Cal. 1980).

§5.5 WIRETAPPING, BUGGING, AND EAVESDROPPING

Wiretapping, bugging, and eavesdropping may be actionable under a number of theories: federal constitutional law, federal statutory law, federal administrative regulations, state statutory law, or state common law.[190] Each raises several of the same problems: establishing when there is a reasonable expectation that a communication will be private; whether all parties to a conversation must consent to its being intercepted or overheard; and what devices must be used to intercept or overhear the conversation before there is a violation of the law.

§5.5(A) The Fourth Amendment

One possible basis for liability is the Fourth Amendment to the U.S. Constitution, which prohibits unreasonable searches and seizures without a search warrant based on probable cause.[191] While initially the Supreme Court required a physical intrusion or trespass into a protected space before a wiretapping or bugging could violate the Fourth Amendment,[192] the Court later rejected this analysis, holding that "the Fourth Amendment protects people—and not simply 'areas'—against unreasonable searches and seizures."[193] Thus, the Fourth Amendment may be a basis for liability for wiretapping, bugging, or other acts if the intrusion is into a protected area.[194]

The Fourth Amendment has been an impotent weapon against the media for at least two reasons. First, while it is possible to bring a civil action against federal officials for the violation of at least some federal constitutional rights,[195] it is unclear whether private parties who conspire with federal officials to violate such rights may also be civilly liable.[196] At least one court, however, has refused to impose liability on the media for such conspiracies.[197] Thus, the lack of governmental action usually will bar such actions against the media.[198]

---

[190]For an excellent discussion of these issues, *see* Middleton, *Journalists and Tape Recorders: Does Participant Monitoring Invade Privacy?* 2 COMM./ENT. 287 (1979) [hereinafter *Tape Recorders*].
[191]U.S. CONST. amend. IV.
[192]Olmstead v. United States, 277 U.S. 438 (1928).
[193]Katz v. United States, 389 U.S. 347, 353 (1967).
[194]*Id.* at 353, 361 (Harlan, J., concurring); *see* California v. Greenwood, 486 U.S. 35 (1989) (warrantless search of garbage left for collection outside curtilage of home does not violate Fourth Amendment); United States v. Hedrick, 922 F.2d 396, 400 (7th Cir. 1991) (garbage placed within residential curtilage for collection may be searched by police without warrant where garbage is placed in area "readily accessible" to public); Florida v. Riley, 490 U.S. 1014 (1989) (warrantless observation of greenhouse with naked eye from helicopter at height of 400 feet does not violate Fourth Amendment). *But see* State v. Hempele, 576 A.2d 793, 813 (N.J. 1990) (basing ruling on state constitution's counterpart to Fourth Amendment, court rejected *Greenwood*'s finding that police do not need search warrant to open and examine garbage left at curbside for collection). *See also supra* note 33.
[195]Bivens v. Six Unknown Named Agents of Fed. Bureau of Narcotics, 403 U.S. 388 (1971) (Fourth Amendment claims).
[196]Benford v. American Broadcasting Cos., 502 F. Supp. 1159, 1161–62, 6 Media L. Rep. 2489, 2491 (D. Md. 1980), *aff'd without opinion,* 661 F.2d 917 (4th Cir.), *cert. denied,* 454 U.S. 1060 (1981); Zerilli v. Evening News Ass'n, 628 F.2d 217, 223 n.11, 6 Media L. Rep. 1530, 1534–35 n.11 (D.C. Cir. 1980); Reuber v. United States, 750 F.2d 1039, 1054–56 (D.C. Cir. 1984). *Compare* Lugar v. Edmondson Oil Co., 457 U.S. 922, 939–42 (1982) (private party who invoked state prejudgment procedures resulting in public official's attachment of debtor's property was joint actor with public official).
[197]*Zerilli,* 628 F.2d at 222–24, 6 Media L. Rep. at 1534–35; *see also* In re Providence Journal, 820 F.2d 1342, 1350 (1st Cir. 1986) (as private parties, newspaper and its editor could not violate Fourth Amendment: "Absent a claim that a newspaper and the FBI were somehow conspiring to violate an individual's rights, the Fourth Amendment simply cannot be the predicate of a prior restraint."), *modified,* 820 F.2d 1354 (1st Cir. 1987) (en banc), *cert. dismissed,* 485 U.S. 693 (1988).
[198]*See also* Chapter 9 regarding civil rights conspiracies.

Second, in the Fourth Amendment area, the Supreme Court repeatedly has held that one party's consent to a recording or other interception of a conversation eliminates any Fourth Amendment violation.[199] Thus, participants in such conversations assume the risk that their conversations will be reproduced accurately,[200] even though those conversations take place in traditionally private surroundings[201] and even if one of the participants fails to disclose that he or she is wired for sound[202] or that he or she is no longer a friend.[203] These holdings seriously undercut the underlying reasoning of the common law decisions that reach a different result.[204]

Based on these decisions, Fourth Amendment claims against the media where a single party consents to the interception have been rejected.[205] Thus, the lack of government action, single party consent, or both usually will immunize the media from Fourth Amendment claims.

§5.5(B) Federal Statutes

§5.5(B)(i) Title III of the Omnibus Crime Control Act of 1968

The most important federal statute concerning wiretapping and bugging is Title III of the Omnibus Crime Control Act of 1968.[206] Title III prevents the intentional interception of or intentional attempts to intercept any wire or oral communications[207] with any electronic, mechanical, or other device.[208]

"Wire communications" are any foreign or interstate "aural transfers" by the use of wire, cable, or like connections in whole or part—for instance, telephone calls.[209] "Oral communications" are ones "uttered by a person exhibiting an expectation that such communication is not subject to interception under circumstances justifying such expectation, but such term does not include

---

[199]On Lee v. United States, 343 U.S. 747, 749 (1952) (agent overheard transmitted conversation from public part of laundry); Lopez v. United States, 373 U.S. 427, 430 (1963) (agent equipped with concealed recorder); Lewis v. United States, 385 U.S. 206, 207 (1966) (undercover agent in private home buying drugs); Hoffa v. United States, 385 U.S. 293, 296–98 (1966) (undercover agent who was defendant's "friend" admitted to hotel room); Osborn v. United States, 385 U.S. 323, 326 (1966) (secret tape-recording by policeman in lawyer's office); United States v. White, 401 U.S. 745, 747 (1971) (agent overheard conversation transmitted by informant who was in car with defendant).
[200]*Lopez,* 373 U.S. at 439.
[201]*Lewis,* 385 U.S. 206 (in home); Osborn v. United States, 385 U.S. 323 (1966) (at office).
[202]*On Lee,* 343 U.S. 747; *Hoffa,* 385 U.S. at 302–03; *Lopez,* 373 U.S. at 438–39.
[203]*White,* 401 U.S. at 749.
[204]*See infra* §5.5(E) and *supra* notes 199–203.
[205]Benford v. American Broadcasting Cos., 502 F. Supp. 1159, 1161, 6 Media L. Rep. 2489, 2491 (D. Md. 1980), *aff'd without opinion,* 661 F.2d 917 (4th Cir.), *cert. denied,* 454 U.S. 1060 (1981).
[206]18 U.S.C. §§2510–20 (1989) (Title III).
[207]*Id.* §2511(1)(a).
[208]*Id.* at (b). Whether extension phones are such devices still is unsettled. Annot., *Application to Extension Telephones of Title III of the Omnibus Crime Control and Safe Streets Act of 1968 (18 U.S.C.S. §§2510 et seq.) Pertaining to Interception of Wire Communications,* 58 A.L.R. FED. 594 (1982). Whether videotaped surveillance is prohibited by Title III is also unsettled. For a discussion of the split of authority on this issue, *see* United States v. Andonian, 735 F. Supp. 1469, 1472 (C.D. Cal. 1990) (finding Title III does not place restrictions on use of video surveillance).
[209]18 U.S.C. §2510(1). The proper classification of cordless telephone communications has generated a confusing body of law. Note, *Don't Touch That Dial: Radio Listening Under the Electronic Communications Privacy Act of 1986,* 63 N.Y.U. L. REV. 416, 430–31 & n.108, 435–37 (1988). Courts are split as to whether Title III applies to a spouse's recording of telephone conversations in their mutual home without the other spouse's knowledge or consent. For a discussion of these cases, see People v. Otto, 808 P.2d 234 (Cal. 1991).

any electronic communication."[210] Thus, the rules that apply to wire and oral communication are quite different; only the latter requires a reasonable expectation of privacy before it will be protected.

In addition to interception or attempts to intercept such communications, the intentional disclosure or use of the contents of such communications with knowledge or reason to know that the communications were obtained illegally also violates Title III.[211]

There are both criminal[212] and civil[213] penalties for the violation of Title III, and the content of any communication obtained in violation of Title III cannot be admitted into evidence in any federal or state proceeding.[214]

Attempts to use Title III against the media have met with little success.[215] Where the media have simply published information from others' wiretaps, they usually have not been found liable.[216] Where there is no reasonable expectation of privacy in an oral communication, Title III has not been violated.[217] The applicable statute of limitations may also provide a good defense.[218]

The most important exception to Title III is the single-party consent provision, which makes it lawful "for a person not acting under color of law to intercept a wire, oral, or electronic communication where such person is a party to the communication or where one of the parties to the communication has given prior consent to such interception . . . ."[219] This single-party consent provision precludes liability in many situations of importance to the media, such as where a reporter is wired for sound or where a reporter is filming

---

[210]18 U.S.C. §2510(2). *See* Holman v. Central Ark. Broadcasting Co., 610 F.2d 542, 545 n.3, 5 Media L. Rep. 2217, 2218 n.3 (8th Cir. 1979) (no expectation of privacy exists in jail or open field; expectation of privacy usually exists in home or office).

[211]18 U.S.C. §2511(1)(c), (d).

[212]*Id.* at (4), (5).

[213]*Id.* §2520 (in general, actual damages and violator's profits, or statutory damages of higher of $100 for each day of violation or $10,000; punitive damages; and reasonable attorneys' fees and court costs). *See generally* Annot., *Construction and Application of Provision of Omnibus Crime Control and Safe Streets Act of 1968 (18 U.S.C.S. §2520) Authorizing Civil Cause of Action by Person Whose Wire or Oral Communication Is Intercepted, Disclosed, or Used in Violation of Act,* 25 A.L.R. FED. 759 (1975).

[214]18 U.S.C. §2515.

[215]For cases where attempts were made to use Title III to block the media's access to court records, see Chapter 1. Members of the media also have used Title III against their antagonists. *See* Smith v. Nixon, 606 F.2d 1183 (D.C. Cir. 1979), *cert. denied,* 453 U.S. 912 (1981).

[216]In re Providence Journal Co., 820 F.2d 1342, 1349–50 (1st Cir. 1986) (Title III provided no basis for imposition of prior restraint against newspaper that published materials compiled from FBI electronic surveillance when FBI disclosed materials to newspaper as result of proper FOIA request), *modified,* 820 F.2d 1354 (1st Cir. 1987) (en banc), *cert. dismissed,* 485 U.S. 693 (1988); Smith v. Cincinnati Post & Times-Star, 475 F.2d 740, 741 (6th Cir. 1973) (where underlying recording lawful, newspaper did not violate Title III by publishing its contents); Zerilli v. Evening News Ass'n, 628 F.2d 217, 219–22, 6 Media L. Rep. 1530, 1531–33 (D.C. Cir. 1980) (where bugging by government occurred before effective date of Title III, disclosure of such communications to newspaper, which published such information, did not violate Title III). The First Amendment may also provide a complete defense even if Title III is violated. *See* Chapter 4.

[217]Holman v. Central Ark. Broadcasting Co., 610 F.2d 542, 544–45, 5 Media L. Rep. 2217, 2218 (8th Cir. 1979) (recording of jailed suspect's loud and boisterous comments to his attorney, which anyone in jail could hear). *But see* Boddie v. American Broadcasting Cos., 731 F.2d 333, 338–39, 10 Media L. Rep. 1923, 1927 (6th Cir. 1984) (where plaintiff consented to interview but refused to appear on camera and media secretly videotaped interview, question of fact as to plaintiff's expectation of privacy), *on remand,* 694 F. Supp. 1304 (1988).

[218]Brown v. American Broadcasting Co., 704 F.2d 1296, 1304–05 (4th Cir. 1983) (noting contrary decisions but holding cause of action for illegal surveillance accrues when plaintiff discovers interception). A two-year discovery rule now limits recovery of civil damages. 18 U.S.C. §2520(e).

[219]18 U.S.C. §2511(2)(d) (Supp. 1993). *See generally* Annot., *Interception of Telecommunication by or With Consent of Party As an Exception, Under 18 U.S.C.S. §2511(2)(c) and (d), to Federal Proscription of Such Interceptions,* 67 A.L.R. FED. 429, 448–50 (1984) (discussing cases concerning consent exception).

through a two-way mirror and has obtained the consent of one of the people being filmed.

The single-party consent provision, however, is subject to two important exceptions. It is inapplicable if a "communication is intercepted for the purpose of committing any criminal or tortious act in violation of the Constitution or laws of the United States or of any State."[220]

In an earlier version of this statute, single party consent was also destroyed if the interception was "for the purpose of committing any other injurious act."[221] The use of the term "injurious act" caused considerable confusion. Congress had not defined it,[222] and its legislative history shed little if any light on its meaning.[223] It seemed clear, though, that Congress did not intend to employ the literal meaning of the term, because "[a] perfectly legitimate act may often be injurious."[224] Thus it was held that Congress did not intend the term "to be read to embrace every act which disadvantages the [nonconsenting] party to [the] communication," because any other reading would nullify the exemption created by Section 2511(2)(d).[225]

Similarly, it was held that Congress intended to permit one party to record a conversation in order to protect oneself[226] or to obtain evidence for the police.[227] Similarly, an injurious act occurred only when the interception was made "with an intent to use that interception against the non-consenting party in some harmful way and in a manner in which the offending party had no right to proceed."[228] This interpretation of "injurious act" was consistent with the well-established "principle that criminal statutes [like Title III] must be strictly construed, to avoid ensaring behavior that is not clearly proscribed."[229]

Nevertheless, three cases brought against the media—*Benford v. American Broadcasting Cos.*,[230] *Brown v. American Broadcasting Cos.*,[231] and *Boddie v. American Broadcasting Co.*[232]—held that the media's purpose in such situations was a question of fact.[233] Neither the court that originated this rule nor

---

[220]18 U.S.C. §2511(2)(d) (Supp. 1993). Defamation would constitute such a tort. *Boddie*, 694 F. Supp. at 1308, 16 Media L. Rep. at 1103–04 (quoting legislative history), *aff'd*, 881 F.2d 267, 16 Media L. Rep. 2038 (6th Cir. 1989), *cert. denied*, 493 U.S. 1028 (1990); Brooks v. American Broadcasting Cos., 737 F. Supp. 431, 437, 17 Media L. Rep. 2041, 2046 (N.D. Ohio 1990), *aff'd in part and vacated in part*, 932 F.2d 495, 18 Media L. Rep. 2121 (6th Cir. 1991) (network's recording of conversation that took place on public street not violation of Title III because it did not violate state surveillance law). *See generally* Annot., *supra* note 219, at 450–55 (discussing cases concerning consent exception).

[221]18 U.S.C. §2511(2)(d) (1970).

[222]Moore v. Teflon Communications Corp., 589 F.2d 959, 965 & n.3 (9th Cir. 1978).

[223]Meredith v. Gavin, 446 F.2d 794, 798 & n.5 (8th Cir. 1971).

[224]*Id.* at 799.

[225]*Moore*, 589 F.2d at 966.

[226]*Id.*; By-Prod Corp. v. Armen-Berry Co., 668 F.2d 956, 959–60 (7th Cir. 1982); *Meredith*, 446 F.2d at 798–99 & n.5.

[227]United States v. Phillips, 540 F.2d 319, 325 (8th Cir.), *cert. denied*, 429 U.S. 1000 (1976). *See also* Wasserman v. Low, 691 P.2d 716, 723 (Ariz. Ct. App. 1984) (videotaping by television station of meeting with insurance agents to be turned over for use in administrative hearing not injurious act).

[228]*Meredith*, 446 F.2d at 799 (taping conversation for use at worker's compensation proceeding not injurious act); *Moore*, 589 F.2d at 966 (taping extortionate conversation not injurious act).

[229]Simpson v. Simpson, 490 F.2d 803, 809 (5th Cir.), *cert. denied*, 419 U.S. 897 (1974).

[230]502 F. Supp. 1159, 6 Media L. Rep. 2489 (D. Md. 1980), *aff'd without opinion*, 661 F.2d 917 (4th Cir.), *cert. denied*, 454 U.S. 1060 (1981).

[231]704 F.2d 1296 (4th Cir. 1983).

[232]731 F.2d 333, 10 Media L. Rep. 1923 (6th Cir. 1984), *on remand*, 694 F. Supp. 1304, 16 Media L. Rep. 1100 (N.D. Ohio 1988), *aff'd*, 881 F.2d 267, 16 Media L. Rep. 2038 (6th Cir. 1989), *cert. denied*, 493 U.S. 1028 (1990).

[233]*Benford*, 502 F. Supp. at 1162–63, 6 Media L. Rep. at 2491–92; *Brown*, 704 F.2d at 1305; *Boddie*, 731 F.2d at 338, 10 Media L. Rep. at 1927.

the two courts that followed it cited any authority or explained their holdings.[234] However, it was unlikely that, under the test for an "injurious act," the plaintiffs' cases could have survived summary judgment motions,[235] especially because plaintiffs have the burden of showing that the single-party consent exception does not apply.[236] In any event, Congress now has explicitly overruled these three cases by deleting the "injurious act" exception.[237]

A single-party consent exception also arises for "a person acting under color of law to intercept a wire, oral, or electronic communication, where such person is a party to the communication or one of the parties to the communication has given prior consent to such interception."[238] This exception is not limited by any requirement that there be no purpose to commit a criminal or tortious act.[239] In *Benford,* which appears to be the only case where the media have asserted this exception as a defense, the court held that for this exception to apply, "ABC would *at least* have to show that its only purpose in taping the meeting was to aid the congressional subcommittee."[240] Under this interpretation, even if the media are successful in asserting that they are acting under color of law, this exception is unlikely to offer them much protection, because it would be a rare case where the media's only purpose is to aid the government.

§5.5(B)(ii) 47 U.S.C. Section 605

Claims also may be brought against the media for violation of 47 U.S.C. Section 605,[241] which prohibits the interception and later disclosure of nonpublic radio[242] broadcasts—e.g., police, fire, and other emergency radio transmissions.[243] In what appears to be the only case under Section 605 involving the media—*United States v. Fuller*—the court refused to dismiss a criminal indictment against an individual for intercepting radio messages of police and fire agencies and disclosing them to a radio station.[244] The court rejected the defendant's First Amendment defense without providing any convincing reasons for

---

[234]*See supra* note 233.
[235]*See Boddie,* 731 F.2d at 339–40, 10 Media L. Rep. at 1928 (Wellford, J., concurring).
[236]*See* By-Prod Corp. v. Armen-Berry Co., 668 F.2d 956, 960 (7th Cir. 1982).
[237]S. REP. NO. 541, 99th Cong., 2d Sess. 15 (1986), *reprinted in* 1986 U.S.C.C.A.N. 3571–72; *Boddie,* 881 F.2d 267, 16 Media L. Rep. 2039 (also holding phrase "injurious act" unconstitutionally vague), *cert. denied,* 493 U.S. 1028 (1990).
[238]18 U.S.C. §2511(2)(c) (1989).
[239]*Id.*
[240]502 F. Supp. 1159, 1162, 6 Media L. Rep. 2489, 2491 (D. Md. 1980).
[241]*See generally* Annot., *What Constitutes an "Interception" of a Telephone or Similar Communication Forbidden by the Federal Communications Act [47 U.S.C.S. §605] or Similar State Statute,* 9 A.L.R.3d 423 (1966).
[242]Subscription television broadcasts are also protected by §605 because they are not for the use of the general public. Chartwell Communications Group v. Westbrook, 637 F.2d 459, 465, 6 Media L. Rep. 2368, 2373 (6th Cir. 1980); National Subscription Television v. S&H TV, 644 F.2d 820, 823–26, 7 Media L. Rep. 1399, 1401–04 (9th Cir. 1981). *See also* 28 U.S.C. §2511(4), (5) (1989) (outlining when interception of satellite transmission is Title III violation). *See generally* Richard P. Shafer, Annot., *Federal Legal Problems Arising From Subscription Television or "Pay TV" Broadcast Over the Air,* 61 A.L.R. FED. 809 (1983) (discussing federal cases relating to all federal legal problems arising from over-the-air subscription television) *and* Annot., *Criminal Liability for Unauthorized Interference With or Reception of Radio or Television Transmission,* 43 A.L.R.4th 991 (1986) (analyzing state and federal cases discussing criminal liability of individual for unauthorized interference with or reception of radio or television transmission).
[243]As indicated in the first sentence of §605(a), the limits on Title III, discussed *supra* §5.5(B)(i), are incorporated into §605. Edwards v. State Farm Ins. Co., 833 F.2d 535, 537–38 (5th Cir. 1987); Zerilli v. Evening News Ass'n, 628 F.2d 217, 221 & n.7, 6 Media L. Rep. 1530, 1533 & n.7 (D.C. Cir. 1980).
[244]202 F. Supp. 356, 356–57 (N.D. Cal. 1962).

the suppression of such newsworthy information that was available to anyone who wanted to listen.[245] The court also held that it could not determine whether the statutory exception "for the use of the general public" was met on the facts before it.[246]

The disclosure of nonpublic radio transmissions also may subject Federal Communications Commission (FCC) licensees and nonlicensees to criminal[247] and civil[248] liability.

§5.5(C) Federal Administrative Regulations

The FCC has prohibited the use of any devices required to be licensed by 47 U.S.C. Section 301[249] "for the purpose of overhearing or recording the private conversations of others unless such use is authorized by all of the parties engaging in the conversation."[250] There is an exception for such activities by law enforcement officers.[251]

Whether the FCC has the power to issue such regulations, especially because its regulations requiring all-party consent are more restrictive than Title III, does not appear to have been litigated.[252] The penalties for violating the FCC's rules and regulations appear to be too great or too small to have had much impact on such activities.[253]

Before recording telephone conversations for broadcast, licensees must inform all parties of their intention to broadcast the conversation.[254] If all parties are aware or can be presumed to be aware that the recording is being or is likely to be broadcast, however, no notice is necessary.[255] Apparently, this restriction is easily evaded by showing verbatim transcripts from the tape on the screen while they are read by a newsperson.[256]

---

[245]*Id.* at 357–59.

[246]*Id.* at 359. The court also rejected a defense based on the anti-censorship provisions of 47 U.S.C. §326 (1982). 202 F. Supp. at 360.

[247]Willful violation of §605 is punishable by a criminal fine up to $2,000, six months in jail, or both. 47 U.S.C. §605(e)(1) (1992). Violations that are also for "commercial advantage or private financial gain" may be punished by fines up to $100,000, five years in jail, or both. *Id.*

[248]A plaintiff can recover actual damages and any profits of the offender or statutory damages of not less than $1000 or more than $10,000, as well as reasonable attorneys' fees. 47 U.S.C. §605(e)(3)(C)(1).

[249]Such devices include low-power transmitters like wireless microphones. 47 C.F.R. §§15.4(f), 15.104, and 15.154 (1989).

[250]*Id.* §§2.701(a), 15.11(a), and 73.1206; Brooks v. American Broadcasting Cos., 737 F. Supp. 431, 437, 17 Media L. Rep. 2041, 2045 (N.D. Ohio 1990) (regulation does not apply to conversation between individual and reporter that takes place on public street because such conversation is not private), *aff'd in relevant part and vacated in part,* 932 F.2d 495, 18 Media L. Rep. 2121 (6th Cir. 1991).

[251]47 C.F.R. §§2.701(b), 15.11(b).

[252]*Tape Recorders, supra* note 190, at 315–16.

[253]Violation of §605 by any person is punishable by a criminal fine of up to $10,000, a year in jail, or both. 47 U.S.C. §501 (1982). Under certain circumstances, forfeiture penalties of $2,000 per day of violation up to a total of $5,000 may also be imposed by the FCC against nonlicensees who violate the federal communications law or FCC rules or regulations. *Id.* §503(b)(2)(B) and (b)(5) (1982 and Supp. 1987). In addition to 47 U.S.C. §501, broadcast licensees are subject to FCC-imposed forfeitures of $2,000 per day of violation up to a total of $20,000. 47 U.S.C. §503(b)(2)(A) (1982). They are also subject to a fine of up to $500 a day in criminal fines for violation of any FCC rule or regulation. *Id.* §502. In theory, broadcast licensees may also lose their FCC licenses for such violations. *Id.* §312 (1982 and Supp. 1987). *See also Tape Recorders, supra* note 190, at 315.

[254]47 C.F.R. §73.1206.

[255]*Id.*

[256]*Tape Recorders, supra* note 190, at 319. For a discussion of the related but ineffectual "beep tone" requirement, which can result in the loss of telephone service, see *id.* at 315–20.

§5.5(D) State Statutory Law

A number of states have passed statutes that deal with wiretapping, bugging, and eavesdropping;[257] no attempt will be made here to discuss all of those laws. Some jurisdictions require all parties to the communication to consent to its interception, but most do not.[258] Liability under such statutes has been avoided in a number of ways—because the communication is not confidential, because the equipment used does not violate the statute, because the statute has an exception for law enforcement officials, because the interception was not willful, or because of other statutory exceptions.[259]

Attempts to strike down more restrictive state wiretapping and bugging laws on grounds that they are federally preempted have not been successful.[260] Similarly, an attempt to strike down Florida's all-party consent statute on First Amendment grounds was unsuccessful.[261]

§5.5(E) State Common Law

Several courts[262] and other authorities[263] agree that a common law claim exists for intrusion by wiretapping or bugging. This tort is subject to the same restrictions that apply to other intrusion claims.[264]

---

[257]*See, e.g.,* CAL. PENAL CODE §§631–32 (West Supp. 1990); FLA. STAT. ANN. §§934.02–.28 (West Supp. 1990); GA. CODE ANN. §16-11-62 (1988); ILL. ANN. STAT. ch. 38, ¶¶14-2 to 14-9 (Smith-Hurd 1979 & Supp. 1989); MD. CODE ANN., CTS. & JUD. PROC. §10-402 (1989); MASS. GEN. LAWS ANN. ch. 272, §99 (West 1990); MICH. COMP. LAWS ANN. §§750.539(a)–539i (West 1968 & Supp. 1990); MONT. CODE ANN. §45-8-213 (1989); N.H. REV. STAT. ANN. §§570-A:1–:11 (1986 & Supp. 1990); OR. REV. STAT. §§165.535–.545 (1989); 18 PA. CONS. STAT. ANN. §5703 (Purdon Supp. 1988); VA. CODE §§19.2-61 to 19.2-70.3 (1983 & Supp. 1990); WASH. REV. CODE ANN. §§9.73.030–.250 (1988 & Supp. 1990).

[258]*Tape Recorders, supra* note 190, at 305.

[259]*Id.* at 304–09; Annot., *Construction and Application of State Statutes Authorizing Civil Cause of Action by Person Whose Wire or Oral Communication Is Intercepted, Disclosed, or Used in Violation of Statutes,* 33 A.L.R.4th 506 (1984); Annot., *Permissible Surveillance, Under State Communications Interception Statute, by Person Other Than State or Local Law Enforcement Officer or One Acting in Concert With Officer,* 24 A.L.R.4th 1208 (1983); Annot., *Validity, Construction, and Effect of State Legislation Making Wiretapping a Criminal Offense,* 74 A.L.R.2d 855 (1960). *See, e.g.,* Cassidy v. American Broadcasting Cos., 377 N.E.2d 126, 129, 3 Media L. Rep. 2449, 2451 (Ill. App. Ct. 1978) (camera not "eavesdropping" device within meaning of Illinois statute).

[260]People v. Conklin, 522 P.2d 1049, 1058 (Cal.), *appeal dismissed,* 419 U.S. 1064 (1974); People v. Broady, 158 N.E.2d 817, 823 (N.Y.), *appeal dismissed and cert. denied,* 361 U.S. 8 (1959); State v. Williams, 617 P.2d 1012, 1017–18 (Wash. 1980); Commonwealth v. Vitello, 327 N.E.2d 819, 839 (Mass. 1975). However, a state statute that is less stringent than the federal statute is preempted. State v. Farha, 544 P.2d 341, 348 (Kan. 1975), *cert. denied,* 426 U.S. 949 (1976); State v. Dowdy, 563 P.2d 425 (Kan. 1977).

[261]Shevin v. Sunbeam Television Corp., 351 So. 2d 723, 726–27, 3 Media L. Rep. 1312, 1314–15 (Fla. 1977), *appeal dismissed,* 435 U.S. 920 (1978); *see also* Oregon v. Knobel, 777 P.2d 985, 16 Media L. Rep. 2478 (Or. Ct. App. 1989) (rejecting First Amendment challenge to Oregon statute preventing surreptitious use of electronic or mechanical devices to intercept conversations). *But see* Gardner v. Bradenton Herald, 413 So. 2d 10, 8 Media L. Rep. 1251 (Fla.), *cert. denied,* 459 U.S. 865 (1982) (state statute making it unconstitutional to publish name of any person who was wiretapped before indictment unconstitutional).

[262]Fowler v. Southern Bell Tel. & Tel. Co., 343 F.2d 150, 156 (5th Cir. 1965); Hamberger v. Eastman, 206 A.2d 239, 241–42 (N.H. 1964); *see* Pacific Tel. & Tel. Co. v. Superior Ct., 465 P.2d 854 (Cal. 1970); LaCrone v. Ohio Bell Tel. Co., 182 N.E.2d 15, 16 (Ohio Ct. App. 1961); McDaniel v. Atlanta Coca-Cola Bottling Co., 2 S.E.2d 810, 816–17 (Ga. Ct. App. 1939) (bugging); Rhodes v. Graham, 37 S.W.2d 46, 47 (Ky. 1931) (wiretapping); Roach v. Harper, 105 S.E.2d 564, 568 (W. Va. 1958) (bugging); Billings v. Atkinson, 489 S.W.2d 858, 860 (Tex. 1973). *See generally* Annot., *Eavesdropping As Violating Right of Privacy,* 11 A.L.R.3d 1296 (1967) *and* Annot., *Eavesdropping on Extension Telephone As Invasion of Privacy,* 49 A.L.R.4th 430 (1986) (reviewing case law addressing whether civil action for damages or injunction will lie for eavesdropping); *but see* Bianco v. American Broadcasting Cos., 470 F. Supp. 182, 186–88 (N.D. Ill. 1979) (wiretapping and bugging claims based on Illinois Constitution dismissed because invasion of privacy provision only applied to government actions).

[263]RESTATEMENT (SECOND) §652(B), illus. 3; W. PROSSER & P. KEETON, HANDBOOK ON THE LAW OF TORTS §117, at 854 and nn. 55, 56 (5th ed. 1984).

[264]*See supra* §5.2.

The cases are split on whether single party consent to wiretapping or bugging is sufficient to make it lawful. The media have often won these cases,[265] but they have lost at least one of them, namely *Dietemann*.[266] The better view is that *Dietemann* is not sound authority because "the court's opinion ignores so many contrary opinions on the nature of electronic intrusion, the expectation of privacy in a place of business and the legality of participant monitoring under police supervision."[267]

---

[265]McCall v. Courier-Journal, 6 Media L. Rep. 1112, 1113 (Ky. Ct. App. 1980), *rev'd on other grounds*, 623 S.W.2d 882, 7 Media L. Rep. 2118 (Ky. 1981), *cert. denied*, 456 U.S. 975 (1982); Smith v. Cincinnati Post & Times-Star, 475 F.2d 740, 741 (6th Cir. 1973); Chaplin v. National Broadcasting Co., 15 F.R.D. 134, 140–41 (S.D.N.Y. 1953).
[266]Dietemann v. Time, Inc., 449 F.2d 245, 247, 1 Media L. Rep. 2417, 2418–19 (9th Cir. 1971).
[267]*Tape Recorders, supra* note 190, at 312. *See also* the criticism of *Dietemann supra* §5.2(E).

CHAPTER 6

APPROPRIATION AND THE RIGHT OF PUBLICITY

§6.1 Introduction

Two closely related concerns are present in the cases discussed in this chapter. First, there is the desire to protect noncelebrities from mental anguish caused by the unauthorized use of their names or likenesses. Second, there is the desire to protect the commercial value that celebrities have in their names or likenesses.

Of course, these concerns often overlap. For example, the noncelebrity's primary injury may be mental anguish, but there may also be some minimal economic value in the noncelebrity's name or likeness. Similarly, while a celebrity's main damages may be economic because of the commercial value of his or her name or likeness, there may also be some minimal damages available for mental anguish. It is this overlap that has led to much of the confusion in this area.[1]

To avoid this confusion, the privacy interest in freedom from injury to feelings and a celebrity's publicity interest in the pecuniary value of his or her name and likeness must be distinguished.[2] The former is referred to here as appropriation, and the latter is referred to as the right of publicity.

§6.2 Development of Appropriation and Publicity Law

Traditionally, the appropriation of someone's name or likeness has been viewed as one of four torts loosely grouped under the term "invasion of

---

[1]Crump v. Beckley Newspapers, 320 S.E.2d 70, 81–86, 10 Media L. Rep. 2225, 2232–36 (W. Va. 1984). These issues are discussed in greater detail below.

[2]Motschenbacher v. R.J. Reynolds Tobacco Co., 498 F.2d 821, 824 (9th Cir. 1974) ("[t]he gist of the cause of action in a privacy case is . . . injury to the feelings without regard to any effect . . . on . . . pecuniary interest;. . . . where the identity appropriated has a commercial value, the injury may be largely, or even wholly, of an economic or material nature"). *See, e.g.,* O'Brien v. Pabst Sales Co., 124 F.2d 167 (5th Cir. 1941), *cert. denied,* 315 U.S. 823 (1942), where the plaintiff, a football player, had brought suit under an invasion of privacy theory for the appropriation of his photograph, which was printed on calendars sold by the defendant. The majority held that the plaintiff had no cause of action for invasion of his privacy since he was only getting the publicity that public figures constantly seek. 124 F.2d at 170. The dissent argued that the athlete had really only sought to recover for the pecuniary value of his likeness and had merely pled the wrong theory of recovery. *Id.* at 170–71. *See also infra* notes 16 and 17; Gautier v. Pro-Football, 107 N.E.2d 485, 489–90 (N.Y. 1952) (concurring opinion) (contending that, while broadcast of plaintiff's trained animal act was use for "advertising purposes," such use did not invade plaintiff's right to be left alone and was therefore not actionable under New York privacy statute); Comment, *Lugosi v. Universal Pictures:*

privacy."[3] Under this view, the primary injury caused by the unauthorized use of someone's name or likeness is to the feelings of the person whose name or likeness is appropriated. The concept underlying an action for appropriation is that "the individual has a right personal to him to be let alone and, thus, to prevent others from invading his privacy, injuring his feelings, or assaulting his peace of mind."[4]

More recently, courts have realized that celebrity plaintiffs are, in reality, attempting to recover for the unauthorized use of their name or likeness without compensation rather than for the mental anguish caused by the wrongful use.[5] This right of publicity[6] has been defined as "a celebrity's right to the exclusive use of his or her name and likeness."[7] This right is usually asserted by or on behalf of celebrities and other public personalities, because the pecuniary value of a noncelebrity's name or likeness is minimal.[8]

The Restatement (Second) of Torts has attempted to strike some sort of middle ground between these two torts, stating that "[o]ne who appropriates to his own use or benefit the name or likeness of another is subject to liability to the other for invasion of his privacy."[9] Although labeling the wrong as an invasion of privacy, the Restatement defines the interest protected as "the interest of the individual in the exclusive use of his own identity, in so far as it is represented by his name or likeness, and in so far as the use may be of benefit to him or to others."[10] While the Restatement recognizes that the interest to be protected is a person's feelings, which are a personal right, it also indicates that this right is "in the nature of a property right, for the exercise of which an exclusive license may be given to a third person, which will entitle the licensee to maintain an action to protect it."[11] Thus, the Restatement, unfortunately, continues to treat these two torts as one.

Descent of the Right of Publicity, 29 HASTINGS L.J. 751, 752, 754 (1978); Gordon, *Right of Property in Name, Likeness, Personality and History,* 55 Nw. U. L. REV. 553 (1960).

[3] W. PROSSER & P. KEETON, HANDBOOK ON THE LAW OF TORTS 849–69 (5th ed. 1984). For a discussion of the history of invasion of privacy and of issues common to all privacy claims, see Chapter 4.

[4] Estate of Presley v. Russen, 513 F. Supp. 1339, 1353 (D.N.J. 1981).

[5] *Id.* at 1353.

[6] The right of publicity was first recognized in Haelan Labs. v. Topps Chewing Gum, 202 F.2d 866 (2d Cir.), *cert. denied,* 346 U.S. 816 (1953), a case involving two chewing gum manufacturers' dispute over the right to print certain baseball players' photographs on baseball cards. The plaintiff manufacturer asserted that it had acquired by contract the exclusive right to use the ballplayers' photographs. The court found that the defendant manufacturer had violated the baseball players' "right of publicity" that had been acquired by the plaintiff manufacturer:

> We think that, in addition to and independent of that right of privacy (which in New York derives from a statute), a man has a right in the publicity value of his photograph, *i.e.,* the right to grant the exclusive privilege of publishing his picture, and that such a grant may validly be made "in gross," *i.e.,* without an accompanying transfer of a business or of anything else. Whether it be labeled a "property" right is immaterial; for here, as often elsewhere, the tag "property" simply symbolizes the fact that courts enforce a claim which has pecuniary worth.
>
> This right might be called a "right of publicity." For it is common knowledge that many prominent persons (especially actors and ball-players), far from having their feelings bruised through public exposure of their likenesses, would feel sorely deprived that they no longer received money for authorizing advertisements, popularizing their countenances, displayed in newspapers, magazines, buses, trains and subways. This right of publicity would usually yield them no money unless it could be made the subject of an exclusive grant which barred any other advertiser from using their pictures.

Id. at 868. *Accord* Palmer v. Schonhorn Enters., 232 A.2d 458 (N.J. Super. Ct. Ch. Div. 1967). *See generally* Nimmer, *The Right of Publicity,* 19 LAW & CONTEMP. PROBS. 203 (1954).

[7] Martin Luther King, Jr., Ctr. for Social Change v. American Heritage Prods., 296 S.E.2d 697, 700, 8 Media L. Rep. 2377, 2378 (Ga. 1982); Price v. Hal Roach Studios, 400 F. Supp. 836, 843 (S.D.N.Y. 1975).

[8] *See infra* §6.3(B) and (F)(i).

[9] RESTATEMENT (SECOND) OF TORTS §652C (1977).

[10] *Id.* at cmt. a.

[11] *Id.* Some courts also do not treat the torts separately and instead treat the right of publicity as merely an element of damage in appropriation cases. Reeves v. United Artists, 572 F. Supp. 1231, 9 Media L. Rep.

Although the two torts are distinct, they are often alleged as alternate causes of action in the same case, and the elements and defenses available under either theory overlap to a great extent. Nevertheless, as will be seen below, characterizing a claim as one for appropriation or violation of the right of publicity can have important implications for the viability of such a claim.[12]

§6.3 THE CAUSE OF ACTION

§6.3(A) Plaintiffs

One of the main differences between the appropriation and publicity torts concerns possible plaintiffs. Since appropriation is primarily designed to protect the feelings and sensibilities of human beings rather than to safeguard property, business, or other pecuniary interests, most courts have denied legal entities, such as corporations and partnerships, the right to bring a cause of action for appropriation under an invasion of privacy theory.[13]

The right of such legal entities to bring a cause of action for invasion of their right of publicity is less clear. However, case and statutory law generally refuse to permit any legal person other than a human being to bring a publicity claim.[14]

A relative has no claim based on their relationship with someone whose rights were invaded.[15]

§6.3(B) Is Celebrity or Public Status Required?

On the one hand, since appropriation guards against injury to an individual's feelings and sensibilities, some courts hold that only private citizens may bring a cause of action for appropriation, reasoning that celebrities and other

---

2484 (N.D. Ohio 1983), aff'd, 765 F.2d 79, 11 Media L. Rep. 2181 (6th Cir. 1985); Brinkley v. Casablancas, 438 N.Y.S.2d 1004, 7 Media L. Rep. 1457 (N.Y. App. Div. 1981).

[12]The law in this area also has been strongly influenced by the New York privacy statute. N.Y. CIV. RIGHTS LAW §§50–51 (McKinney 1976). For a discussion of this law, see infra §6.5(A).

[13]See, e.g., Ion Equip. Corp. v. Nelson, 168 Cal. Rptr. 361 (Cal. Ct. App. 1980) (corporation); Maysville Transit Co. v. Ort, 177 S.W.2d 369 (Ky. 1943) (corporation); Rosenwasser v. Ogoglia, 158 N.Y.S. 56 (N.Y. App. Div. 1916) (partnership); Rosemont Enters. v. Random House, 294 N.Y.S.2d 122 (N.Y. Sup. Ct. 1968), aff'd, 301 N.Y.S.2d 948 (N.Y. App. Div. 1969) (corporation organized for purpose of preparing Howard Hughes' biography held to have no standing to assert Hughes' right of privacy even though corporation was assignee of right to commercially exploit Hughes' name; right held to be purely personal, enforceable only by Hughes). See also Chapter 3, §3.5(A) and Chapter 4.

[14]See Heinemann v. General Motors Corp., 342 F. Supp. 203, 209 (N.D. Ill. 1972), aff'd without opinion, 478 F.2d 1405 (7th Cir. 1973) (name of racing car has no right of publicity); University of Notre Dame du Lac v. Twentieth Century-Fox Film Corp., 256 N.Y.S.2d 301, 305 (N.Y. App. Div. 1965), aff'd, 207 N.E.2d 508 (N.Y. 1965) (educational institution not "living person" under New York statute); Rosenwasser, 158 N.Y.S. 56 (partnership has no statutory right of publicity); but see Bi-Rite Enters. v. Button Master, 555 F. Supp. 1188, 9 Media L. Rep. 1531 (S.D.N.Y.) (extending right of publicity beyond individuals to name of rock group), supplemental opinion, 578 F. Supp. 59 (S.D.N.Y. 1983). See also N.Y. CIV. RIGHTS LAW §50 (McKinney 1976) (prohibiting commercial use of name or picture of "any living person"); CAL. CIV. CODE §3344(a) (Deering 1990 Supp.) ("Any person who knowingly uses another's name, voice . . . ."). Nevertheless, legal entities may be able to obtain relief under related theories, e.g., trade name, trademark, or service mark infringement.

[15]See, e.g., Nelson v. Maine Times, 373 A.2d 1221, 2 Media L. Rep. 2011 (Me. 1977); Gleason v. Hustler Magazine, 7 Media L. Rep. 2183 (D.N.J. 1981) (citing numerous cases but noting contrary authority in Georgia). See also Chapter 3, §3.5(A) and Chapter 4. On the question of survival of a cause of action, see infra §6.6.

public figures have sought publicity and cannot complain when they receive it.[16] There is substantial contrary authority, however.[17]

On the other hand, since the right of publicity protects the commercial value of an individual's identity, many courts have indicated that such a cause of action can only be brought by a celebrity or other public figure, because the commercial value of a private citizen's identity would be minimal.[18] However, celebrities and other public figures do not have to have actually exploited their rights of publicity to bring publicity claims.[19] Other courts hold that private citizens can bring right of publicity claims.[20]

§6.3(C) Must the Use Be for Advertising or Trade Purposes?

Many cases have been brought pursuant to the New York privacy statute and statutes modeled on it that require the use to be for purposes of advertising or trade.[21] Most courts in these cases define use for the purpose of advertising as solicitation for patronage intended to directly promote the sale of some product or service.[22]

---

[16]*Bi-Rite Enters.*, 555 F. Supp. at 1197–98, 9 Media L. Rep. at 1537 (since plaintiffs were famous rock musicians they were public figures who had waived right to privacy and thus could not maintain action under New York privacy statute, California privacy statute, or Georgia or Illinois common law; they could, however, maintain action for invasion of right of publicity), *supplemental opinion,* 578 F. Supp. 59; *see also* Briscoe v. Reader's Digest Ass'n, 93 Cal. Rptr. 866, 869 n.5, 1 Media L. Rep. 1845, 1847 n.5 (Cal. 1971) ("By volunteering his services for public office the official (as opposed to the ordinary employee) waives much of his right to privacy."); *supra* note 2.

[17]Motschenbacher v. R.J. Reynolds Tobacco Co., 498 F.2d 821, 824 (9th Cir. 1974); Grant v. Esquire, Inc., 367 F. Supp. 876, 881 (S.D.N.Y. 1973); Brinkley v. Casablancas, 438 N.Y.S.2d 1004, 7 Media L. Rep. 1457 (N.Y. App. Div. 1981).

[18]Lerman v. Flynt Distrib. Co., 745 F.2d 123, 134, 10 Media L. Rep. 2497, 2504 (2d Cir. 1984), *cert. denied,* 471 U.S. 1054 (1985) ("Because the plaintiff must generally have developed a property interest with financial value in order to prove that he suffered damages, the right is most frequently invoked by public figures or celebrities."); Martin Luther King, Jr., Ctr. for Social Change v. American Heritage Prods., 296 S.E.2d 697, 703, 8 Media L. Rep. 2377, 2382 (Ga. 1982) ("while private citizens have the right of privacy, public figures have a similar right of publicity"); Delan v. CBS, Inc., 458 N.Y.S.2d 608, 615, 9 Media L. Rep. 1130, 1133 (N.Y. App. Div. 1983) ("Plaintiff has not demonstrated that he is in any fashion a public personality."); Cox v. Hatch, 761 P.2d 556, 564, 16 Media L. Rep. 1366, 1372–73 (Utah 1988) (workers' pictures with political candidate fungible with those of any other workers and therefore not actionable, because no showing that workers' names or likenesses had "intrinsic value"); *accord* Jackson v. Playboy Enters., 574 F. Supp. 10, 13, 9 Media L. Rep. 1575, 1577 (S.D. Ohio 1983); *see also* Ali v. Playgirl, 447 F. Supp. 723, 728–29, 3 Media L. Rep. 2540, 2543–44 (S.D.N.Y. 1978) (noting distinction); *see also supra* note 2.

[19]*See, e.g., Grant,* 367 F. Supp. at 880; Eastwood v. Superior Ct., 198 Cal. Rptr. 342, 10 Media L. Rep. 1073, 1076–77 (Cal. Ct. App. 1983); Palmer v. Schonhorn Enters., 232 A.2d 458, 462 (N.J. Super. Ct. Ch. Div. 1967). *See also infra* §6.6 on whether exploitation of this right before death is required for it to survive a celebrity's death.

[20]*Motschenbacher,* 498 F.2d at 824 n.11; Tellado v. Time-Life Books, 643 F. Supp. 904, 913, 13 Media L. Rep. 1401, 1408 (D.N.J. 1986); Cohen v. Herbal Concepts, 473 N.Y.S.2d 426, 431, 10 Media L. Rep. 1561, 1564 (N.Y. App. Div.), *aff'd,* 472 N.E.2d 307 (N.Y. 1984).

[21]*See, e.g.,* Valentine v. CBS, Inc., 698 F.2d 430, 9 Media L. Rep. 1249 (11th Cir. 1983); Arrington v. New York Times Co., 434 N.E.2d 1319, 8 Media L. Rep. 1351 (N.Y. 1982), *cert. denied,* 459 U.S. 1146 (1983); Gautier v. Pro-Football, 107 N.E.2d 485 (N.Y. 1952). *But see* Zacchini v. Scripps-Howard Broadcasting Co., 351 N.E.2d 454, 458, 2 Media L. Rep. 1199, 1201 (Ohio 1976) (citing cases where courts have not limited right solely to uses for purposes of trade and advertising but have extended right to any use constituting appropriation of defendant's exclusive rights to own identity), *rev'd on other grounds,* 433 U.S. 562, 2 Media L. Rep. 2089 (1977).

[22]*See, e.g.,* Rogers v. Grimaldi, 875 F.2d 994, 1004, 16 Media L. Rep. 1648, 1656 (2d Cir. 1989) (under Oregon law, use of celebrity's name in movie title closely related to context of movie not disguised advertisement for sale of goods or services or collateral commercial product); *Valentine,* 698 F.2d 430 (under Florida law, use of plaintiff's name in song lyrics not use for advertising or trade simply because it was included in publication for profit; defendants must have used plaintiff's name to directly promote product); *Arrington,* 434 N.E.2d 1319 (under New York statute, use of black youth's photograph to illustrate newspaper article not advertising use); *Gautier,* 107 N.E.2d 485 (under New York law, broadcast of plaintiff's live animal act during football game's intermission not use for advertising or trade purposes where broadcast did

While use for the "purposes of trade" is not as susceptible to ready definition, the courts generally hold that to prove trade purposes a plaintiff must present evidence of "commercial exploitation."[23] In addition, courts have applied the trade purposes requirement to exempt uses that would otherwise fall under the protection of the First Amendment.[24] The courts that apply the requirement in this fashion hold that care must be taken to avoid a conflict with the First Amendment in cases involving the free dissemination of thoughts, ideas, newsworthy events, and information concerning matters of public interest.[25] Accordingly, they hold that a use is for the purposes of trade only if there is no reasonable connection between the use and a matter of public interest, or if the use is infected with material fictionalization or falsification and takes such a form that the reader would reasonably believe the falsification.[26]

However, since there can be no tort in these jurisdictions unless this test is met, some decisions tend to be liberal in their interpretation of what constitutes "advertising purposes" or "purposes of trade."[27] The Restatement also

---

not solicit patronage); Heller v. Family Circle, 445 N.Y.S.2d 513, 8 Media L. Rep. 1031 (N.Y. App. Div. 1981) (use of plaintiff's laudatory letter in article adapted from book not advertisement in disguise).

[23]Vinci v. American Can Co., 591 N.E.2d 793 (Ohio Ct. App. 1990) (use of Olympic athletes' pictures on disposable drinking cups not actionable); Benavidez v. Anheuser Busch, Inc., 873 F.2d 102, 16 Media L. Rep. 1733 (5th Cir. 1989) (beer company's production of documentary on Hispanic Congressional Medal of Honor recipients shown at hospitality centers where company's logos were prominently displayed and free beer was distributed not commercial use); Mendonsa v. Time, Inc., 678 F. Supp. 967, 971, 15 Media L. Rep. 1017, 1020 (D.R.I. 1988) (plaintiff depicted in famous photograph of sailor kissing nurse on V-J Day in 1945 stated cause of action for invasion of privacy where plaintiff alleged magazine used picture without his consent in subsequent publications and in limited edition sale of photograph); Novel v. Beacon Operating Corp., 446 N.Y.S.2d 118 (N.Y. App. Div. 1982) (tenant could not recover damages for invasion of privacy against landlord for unauthorized entry into her apartment and taking of picture where no evidence of commercial exploitation adduced at trial); Compare Titan Sports v. Comics World Corp., 870 F.2d 85, 16 Media L. Rep. 1408 (2d Cir. 1989) (triable issue of fact as to whether fold-out posters in wrestling magazine's centerfold used for purposes of trade).

[24]See Stephano v. News Group Pubns., 474 N.E.2d 580, 585, 11 Media L. Rep. 1303, 1306 (N.Y. 1984) ("The [statutory] exception reflects Federal and State constitutional concerns for free dissemination of news and other matters of interest to the public."); Delan v. CBS, Inc., 458 N.Y.S.2d 608, 613, 9 Media L. Rep. 1130, 1133 (N.Y. App. Div. 1983); see also Davis v. High Soc'y Magazine, 457 N.Y.S.2d 308, 313, 9 Media L. Rep. 1164, 1167 (N.Y. App. Div. 1982), appeal dismissed, 58 N.Y.2d 1115 (1983) ("the use of a name or picture by the media in connection with a newsworthy item is protected by the First Amendment and is not considered a use for purposes of trade within the ambit of the Civil Rights Law").

[25]Arrington, 434 N.E.2d at 1322 (holding that liberal application of exception reflects federal and state constitutional concerns for free speech and press).

[26]See Finger v. Omni Pubns. Int'l, 566 N.E.2d 141, 18 Media L. Rep. 1555 (N.Y. 1990) (use of photograph of two adults and their six children to illustrate article on fertility not use for advertising or trade purposes; advertising or trade purposes limit to be strictly construed); Falwell v. Flynt, 797 F.2d 1270, 13 Media L. Rep. 1145 (4th Cir. 1986) (publication of advertisement parody did not constitute use of public figure's identity for purposes of trade where parody not reasonably believable, contained disclaimer, and was thus protected by First Amendment), rev'd on other grounds, 485 U.S. 46, 14 Media L. Rep. 2281 (1988); Ault v. Hustler Magazine, 13 Media L. Rep. 2232 (D. Or. 1987), aff'd in part and rev'd in part on other grounds, 860 F.2d 877, 15 Media L. Rep. 2205 (9th Cir. 1988), cert. denied, 489 U.S. 1080 (1989) (use of photo of antipornography activist for "Asshole of the Month" column not for purposes of trade because image not exclusively used for commercial gain; that magazine makes profit does not make every article commercial use); Lerman v. Flynt Distrib. Co., 745 F.2d 123, 10 Media L. Rep. 2497 (2d Cir. 1984), cert. denied, 471 U.S. 1054 (1985) (use of plaintiff's name in connection with movie on cover of porn magazine held not for purposes of trade where movie was of legitimate public interest and plaintiff failed to establish that use had no real relationship to article); Herink v. Harper & Row, Pubrs., 607 F. Supp. 657, 659–60, 11 Media L. Rep. 1927, 1928 (S.D.N.Y. 1985) (use of plaintiff's name as example in book on corporate management "newsworthy and informative" and therefore protected by First Amendment; not use for purposes of trade); Lopez v. Triangle Communications, 421 N.Y.S.2d 57, 5 Media L. Rep. 2039 (N.Y. App. Div. 1979) (article on grooming and makeup tips newsworthy even though brand names of products mentioned). See also infra §6.4(A)–(C). But see White v. Samsung Elecs. of Am., 971 F.2d 1395, 1396–97, 20 Media L. Rep. 1457, 1458 (9th Cir. 1992), cert. denied, 113 S. Ct. 2443 (1993) (2-1 decision holding that ad with robot on set of "Wheel of Fortune" game show that spoofed show's hostess, Vanna White, was not protected parody).

[27]See, e.g., Beverley v. Choices Women's Medical Ctr., 579 N.Y.S.2d 637, 19 Media L. Rep. 1724 (1991) (use of plaintiff's picture in calendar honoring significant contributions by American women published

permits recovery when a defendant makes use of the plaintiff's name or likeness, without consent and for his or her own purposes and benefit, even though the "use is not a commercial one, and even though the benefit sought to be obtained is not a pecuniary one."[28]

§6.3(D) What Must Be Used?

§6.3(D)(i) Names

The unauthorized use of a plaintiff's actual or legal name is actionable.[29] However, the unauthorized use of only part of a plaintiff's name usually is not actionable, because the plaintiff usually cannot be identified from such a brief reference.[30] Nevertheless, if the plaintiff is identifiable, the unauthorized use of a nickname, stage name, or other name by which the plaintiff is known or under which the plaintiff works professionally is actionable.[31] Liability has

---

by abortion clinic was for advertising purposes and thus actionable under New York statute where calendar contained clinic's logo, address, telephone number, and was distributed primarily to sources from whom clinic received medical referrals); *Mendonsa*, 678 F. Supp. 967 (magazine's attempt to sell famous photograph of sailor kissing nurse on V-J Day in 1945 in subsequent publications and in magazine's limited edition offered for sale for $1,600 clearly had commercial purpose apart from dissemination of news); *Davis*, 457 N.Y.S.2d at 313, 9 Media L. Rep. at 1167 (while true that §51 legislative history suggests it be read narrowly, "courts have broadly construed what constitutes commercial misappropriation of a person's name or picture under the statutes"); Almind v. Sea Beach Ry., 141 N.Y.S. 842 (N.Y. App. Div. 1913) (use by railway company of plaintiff's picture for purpose of teaching passengers safe way to enter and exit car held to be use for advertising, though not for trade); Jeppson v. United Television, 580 P.2d 1087, 3 Media L. Rep. 2513 (Utah 1978) (3-2 decision finding claim where plaintiff called by host "Dialing for Dollars" television program and conversation was broadcast). *See also* Zacchini v. Scripps-Howard Broadcasting Co., 351 N.E.2d 454, 458, 2 Media L. Rep. 1199, 1201 (Ohio 1976) (plaintiff whose performance as human cannonball was videotaped by television station reporter and shown on news program has right to publicity value of performance even if defendant's use of film was not commercial), *rev'd on other grounds*, 433 U.S. 562, 2 Media L. Rep. 2089 (1977).

[28]RESTATEMENT (SECOND) OF TORTS §652C, cmt. b (1977); *see also* CAL. CIV. CODE §3344(a) (Deering 1990 Supp.) (prohibiting use "in any manner, on or in products, merchandise, goods, or for purposes of advertising or selling, or soliciting purchases of, products, merchandise, goods or services"). The Restatement would allow liability if a defendant signs the plaintiff's name to a telegram sent to the governor of a state urging the governor to veto a bill without obtaining the plaintiff's consent, even though the defendant obtained no pecuniary gain from the use of the plaintiff's name and was not using the plaintiff's name for advertising purposes. *See, e.g.*, Hinish v. Meier & Frank Co., 113 P.2d 438 (Or. 1941).

[29]Zim v. Western Pub'g Co., 573 F.2d 1318, 4 Media L. Rep. 1467 (5th Cir. 1978) (applying Florida law, use of author's name on books without authorization); Flores v. Mosler Safe Co., 164 N.E.2d 853, 857 (N.Y. 1959) (cause of action alleging that defendant safe company reprinted in advertising circular news photo of burning building and accompanying new story mentioning plaintiff's name several times and relating how fire started by plaintiff's carelessness held to sufficiently allege violation of plaintiff's privacy right under New York civil rights law); Selsman v. Universal Photo Books, 18 A.D.2d 151, 152 (N.Y. App. Div. 1963) (use of plaintiff's name and picture in camera manual held to be for advertising purposes because it went beyond educational purpose and expounded virtues of camera). *But see* Hooker v. Columbia Pictures, 551 F. Supp. 1060 (N.D. Ill. 1982) (use of name of famous woodcarver for title of television series about police not actionable because plaintiff's name not used to appropriate reputation of woodcarver).

[30]Allen v. Gordon, 446 N.Y.S.2d 48, 8 Media L. Rep. 1124 (N.Y. App. Div.), *aff'd*, 437 N.E.2d 284 (N.Y. 1982) (use of name "Dr. Allen" not actionable); Luecke v. G.P. Putnam's Sons, 10 Media L. Rep. 1250, 1253 (S.D.N.Y. 1983) (use of plaintiff's first name, "Michelle," not actionable).

[31]Cher v. Forum Int'l, 692 F.2d 634, 8 Media L. Rep. 2484 (9th Cir. 1982) (unauthorized use of "Cher" actionable), *cert. denied*, 462 U.S. 1120 (1983); Adrian v. Unterman, 118 N.Y.S.2d 121 (N.Y. App. Div. 1952) (where famous fashion designer generally known by first name only, unauthorized use of surname actionable), *aff'd*, 118 N.E.2d 477 (N.Y. 1954); Hirsch v. S.C. Johnson & Son, 280 N.W.2d 129 (Wis. 1979) (unauthorized use of football player's nickname, "Crazylegs," to advertise pantyhose held actionable); *but see* Meeropol v. Nizer, 560 F.2d 1061, 1068, 2 Media L. Rep. 2269, 2273 (2d Cir. 1977) (plaintiffs, children of Julius and Ethel Rosenberg, had no claim because although their real names were used they were known by names of adoptive parents), *cert. denied*, 434 U.S. 1013 (1978); Geisel v. Poynter Prods., 295 F. Supp. 331 (S.D.N.Y. 1968) (court denied recovery for unauthorized use of name "Dr. Seuss," by which author was known, since New York's privacy statute does not protect against use of individual's assumed or trade name; plaintiff's actual legal name, Theodore Seuss Geisel, not used); *see also infra* note 36. For an extreme application of this concept, see Carson v. Here's Johnny Portable Toilets, 698 F.2d 831, 9 Media L. Rep.

§6.3(D)(ii) *Likenesses and Look-Alikes*

The unauthorized use of a plaintiff's photographic likeness is actionable.[33] Similarly, an unauthorized drawing or other artistic rendition of a plaintiff has been found to be actionable if the plaintiff is recognizable.[34]

Where the likeness of an individual has been portrayed by a look-alike model, liability has been found.[35] The plaintiff's likeness may be appropriated in a photograph, even though the plaintiff was not shown, if the surrounding circumstances sufficiently identify the plaintiff.[36] However, some courts have

---

1153 (6th Cir. 1983) (2-1 decision: use of phrase "Here's Johnny" to advertise portable toilets held actionable infringement of entertainer Johnny Carson's "name"). This decision has been criticized. C. Pesce, *The Likeness Monster: Should the Right of Publicity Protect Against Imitation?* 65 N.Y.U. L. REV. 782, 802–03 (1990).

[32]Bi-Rite Enters. v. Button Master, 555 F. Supp. 1188, 1198–99, 9 Media L. Rep. 1531, 1538 (S.D.N.Y. 1983) (unauthorized use of rock group's name on buttons held to violate group's right of publicity but *not* right of privacy since group members waived right when they became public figures; court held that groups that develop market value in their "persona" deserve as much protection as individuals); Winterland Concessions Co. v. Sileo, 528 F. Supp. 1201, 1208 (N.D. Ill. 1981) (unauthorized use of musical rock group names, e.g., "Judas Priest" and "Iron Maiden" on "bootleg" T-shirts held to violate groups' right of publicity), *aff'd in part, rev'd in part on other grounds sub nom.* Winterland Concessions Co. v. Trela, 735 F.2d 257 (7th Cir. 1984).

[33]Haelan Labs. v. Topps Chewing Gum, 202 F.2d 866 (2d Cir.) (unauthorized use by defendant manufacturer of baseball players' photographs on baseball cards violates plaintiffs' right of publicity), *cert. denied*, 346 U.S. 816 (1953); *see also* Cohen v. Herbal Concepts, 472 N.E.2d 307, 10 Media L. Rep. 1561 (N.Y. App. Div.) (finding triable issue of fact where plaintiffs' faces not visible in photograph but nude rears and sides were), *aff'd*, 472 N.E.2d 307 (1984); *but see* Diportanova v. New York News, 6 Media L. Rep. 1376 (1980) (plaintiffs not allowed to recover for invasion of right of privacy for unauthorized use of photograph of their house where house not identified as belonging to plaintiffs; not wrongful use of *plaintiffs'* photograph), *aff'd*, 440 N.Y.S.2d 535, 7 Media L. Rep. 1187 (N.Y. App. Div. 1981); *see also infra* note 36.

[34]Ali v. Playgirl, 447 F. Supp. 723, 3 Media L. Rep. 2540 (S.D.N.Y. 1978) (drawing in *Playgirl Magazine* depicting nude black man with unmistakable resemblance to boxer Muhammed Ali with caption identifying him as "The Greatest"); Jumez v. ABC Records, 3 Media L. Rep. 2324 (S.D.N.Y. 1978) (unauthorized use of guitarists' likenesses on record album).

[35]In Onassis v. Christian Dior-New York, 472 N.Y.S.2d 254, 10 Media L. Rep. 1859 (N.Y. Sup. Ct. 1984), the court held that the defendant's use of a Jacqueline Kennedy Onassis look-alike in a print advertisement violated the plaintiff's rights under New York Civil Rights Law §51. However, the court specifically excluded imitators of other performers or those who comment on or satirize others, as long as they not do so for trade or advertising purposes. *See also* Allen v. National Video, 610 F. Supp. 612, 624 (S.D.N.Y. 1985) (approving *Onassis* but holding that use of Woody Allen look-alike in print advertisement better addressed under federal Lanham Act because New York statute, unlike Lanham Act, requires proof that photograph in question created illusion of plaintiff's actual presence in advertisement); *accord* Allen v. Men's World Outlet, 679 F. Supp. 360, 366–67, 15 Media L. Rep. 1001, 1006–07 (S.D.N.Y. 1988) (declining to decide §51 issue because use of Woody Allen look-alike in magazine advertisement actionable under Lanham Act). *Compare* Tin Pan Apple v. Miller Brewing Co., 737 F. Supp. 826 (S.D.N.Y. 1990) (refusing to dismiss look-alike case brought under §51).

[36]In Motschenbacher v. R.J. Reynolds Tobacco Co., 498 F.2d 821 (9th Cir. 1974), the plaintiff, a world-renowned professional race car driver, consistently marked the cars he drove in a distinctive manner, making them readily identifiable as his: the cars were uniformly solid red with distinctive narrow white pinstriping with the plaintiff's racing number, "11," set in an oval background. The defendant used a picture of one of the plaintiff's cars, taken while the plaintiff was driving it in a race, to advertise its cigarettes. Although the plaintiff's facial features were not visible and the defendant had altered the photograph to change the plaintiff's car number from 11 to 71 and had added a sign to the plaintiff's car advertising the cigarettes, the white pinstriping, oval medallion, and red color of the plaintiff's car were clearly identifiable. *Id.* at 827.

The Ninth Circuit reversed a trial court ruling that held that there could be no liability since the person driving the plaintiff's car was not recognizable, holding that the plaintiff's "proprietary interest in his own identity" had been violated. *Id.* at 825. While the Ninth Circuit agreed that the plaintiff's "likeness" was not recognizable in the commercial, the "distinctive decorations" appearing on the car implied that the person driving the car was the plaintiff. *Id.* at 827. *Compare* Branson v. Fawcett Pubns., 124 F. Supp. 429 (E.D. Ill. 1954) (although plaintiff and friends recognized photograph of accident at race track as including plaintiff in car involved, it was not of and concerning plaintiff where there were no identifying marks on car).

strictly construed state statutory requirements that the plaintiff's "name, portrait or picture" must be used.[37]

§6.3(D)(iii) *Voice, Gestures, Mannerisms, or Live Shows*

Live stage shows and other productions in which celebrities are imitated in appearance, voice, gestures, or mannerisms have also been held to be actionable.[38] Nonetheless, the impersonation of a plaintiff's voice alone has been held to not be actionable.[39] There is case law[40] to the contrary, although the California and New York statutes do not provide a cause of action.[41]

§6.3(E) Fault

Some courts do not require a showing of a defendant's fault, holding that the truth or falsity of a communication is not at issue in cases involving a claim for infringement of the right of publicity or for appropriation.[42] Many other

---

[37] *See, e.g.,* Faloona v. Hustler Magazine, 607 F. Supp. 1341 (N.D. Tex. 1985) (use without consent of photo of nude children not actionable without use of names because children not identifiable), *aff'd,* 799 F.2d 1000 (5th Cir. 1986), *cert. denied,* 479 U.S. 1088 (1987); Wojtowicz v. Delacorte Press, 403 N.Y.S.2d 218, 219, 3 Media L. Rep. 1992 (N.Y. 1978) (no cause of action stated where plaintiffs and events in which they were involved portrayed in movie and books in sufficient detail that they were readily identifiable, because neither plaintiffs' names nor pictures were used); *see also supra* notes 30 and 32.

[38] Estate of Presley v. Russen, 513 F. Supp. 1339 (D.N.J. 1981); Price v. Worldvision Enters., 455 F. Supp. 252, 4 Media L. Rep. 1301 (S.D.N.Y. 1978) (more than permissible imitation of names and likenesses of Laurel and Hardy through impersonation of appearances, costumes, mannerisms, and voice similarities), *aff'd without opinion,* 603 F.2d 214 (2d Cir. 1979); Lombardo v. Doyle, Dane & Bernbach, 396 N.Y.S.2d 661, 2 Media L. Rep. 2321 (N.Y. App. Div. 1977) (imitation of famous bandleader's gestures and performance actionable under New York common law but not under New York statutory law, which must be strictly construed because it is penal statute); KGB, Inc. v. Giannoulas, 164 Cal. Rptr. 571 (Cal. Ct. App. 1980) (performer's rights in chicken character upheld). *But see* Groucho Marx Prods. v. Day & Night Co., 523 F. Supp. 485, 7 Media L. Rep. 2030 (S.D.N.Y. 1981), *rev'd on other grounds,* 689 F.2d 317, 319 n.2, 8 Media L. Rep. 2201, 2202 n.2 (2d Cir. 1982) (noting "defendants' substantial argument that their play is protected expression as a literary work, especially in light of the broad scope permitted parody in First Amendment law"); Nurmi v. Peterson, 16 Media L. Rep. 1606 (C.D. Cal. 1989) (under California statutory and common law, plaintiff's rights in character that plaintiff created not infringed by defendant's similar but not identical character).

[39] Tin Pan Apple v. Miller Brewing Co., 737 F. Supp. 826 (S.D.N.Y. 1990) (dismissing sound-alike claim brought under New York statute); Booth v. Colgate-Palmolive Co., 362 F. Supp. 343, 347 (S.D.N.Y. 1973) (court refused to extend protection for imitation of actress Shirley Booth's voice in television commercial without showing that plaintiff's name or likeness had also been used by defendants); Davis v. Trans World Airlines, 297 F. Supp. 1145 (C.D. Cal. 1969) (imitation of plaintiff's recorded performance of song did not violate plaintiff's privacy rights under California law). *See also* Sinatra v. Goodyear Tire & Rubber Co., 435 F.2d 711 (9th Cir. 1970) (imitation of plaintiff's vocal rendition of song did not constitute unfair competition), *cert. denied,* 402 U.S. 906 (1971).

[40] Midler v. Ford Motor Co., 849 F.2d 460, 15 Media L. Rep. 1620 (9th Cir. 1988) (imitation of famous actress' voice in plaintiff's commercial not actionable under California statute but actionable under California common law); Lahr v. Adell Chem. Co., 300 F.2d 256 (1st Cir. 1962) (imitation of famous actor's voice in defendant's commercial not actionable under New York statute but presented jury questions under New York common law of defamation and unfair competition). *See also* Motown Record Corp. v. George A. Hormel & Co., 657 F. Supp. 1236 (C.D. Cal. 1987).

[41] California Civil Code §3344 was amended in 1984 to provide liability for the unauthorized use of another's voice and signature. The New York privacy statute does not provide a cause of action, because it only protects against unauthorized use of a person's "name, portrait or picture," but a common law claim has been recognized. *See, e.g.,* Ali v. Playgirl, 447 F. Supp. 723, 728, 3 Media L. Rep. 2540, 2542 (S.D.N.Y. 1978); *but see infra* §6.5(A). *See also supra* note 39.

[42] *See* Zacchini v. Scripps-Howard Broadcasting Co., 433 U.S. 562, 2 Media L. Rep. 2089 (1977) (noting inapplicability in right of publicity case of actual malice test applied in false light actions); National Bank of Commerce v. Shaklee Corp., 503 F. Supp. 533, 539 (W.D. Tex. 1980) (constitutional actual malice requirement does not apply to right of privacy or appropriation cases because claim "does not depend upon any element of falsity"); *see also* Flores v. Master Safe Co., 164 N.E.2d 853, 196 N.Y.S.2d 975, 980–81 (N.Y. 1959) (proof of false endorsement not needed for violation of New York privacy statute).

courts have imposed such a fault requirement.[43] Some statutes also impose fault requirements.[44]

§6.3(F) Relief

§6.3(F)(i) Damages

The measure of damages to a plaintiff who successfully proves a violation of his or her right of publicity is usually the market value of the use to the user.[45] Courts may also award loss of income as damages where the unpermitted use will injure the future earning potential of the plaintiff's professional career.[46] In some cases[47] and under some state statutes,[48] plaintiffs may be awarded the user's profits. While the main damages for violation of a plaintiff's right to publicity are economic because of the commercial value of a plaintiff's identity, there may also be some damages available for mental anguish.[49]

---

[43]*See* Lerman v. Flynt Distrib. Co., 745 F.2d 123, 139–41, 10 Media L. Rep. 2497, 2508 (2d Cir. 1984), *cert. denied,* 471 U.S. 1054 (1985) (limited-purpose public figure held not entitled to obtain recovery under New York privacy statute; although plaintiff's name in magazine containing misidentified nude photographs were fictionalized or false, distributor of magazine did not act with actual malice); Maheu v. CBS, Inc., 247 Cal. Rptr. 304, 15 Media L. Rep. 1548 (Cal. Ct. App. 1988) (appropriation claim against publishers of *Citizen Hughes,* a best-selling biography of the late Howard Hughes, dismissed based on public interest in material and absence of allegation of actual malice); Cher v. Forum Int'l, 7 Media L. Rep. 2593 (C.D. Cal. 1982) (false claim of celebrity endorsement), *aff'd in part and rev'd in part,* 692 F.2d 634, 8 Media L. Rep. 2487 (9th Cir. 1982), *cert. denied,* 462 U.S. 1120 (1983); Davis v. High Soc'y Magazine, 457 N.Y.S.2d 308, 315, 9 Media L. Rep. 1164, 1168–69 (N.Y. App. Div. 1982) (plaintiff, a well-known female boxer, required to show actual malice before defendant could be held liable under New York statute for publishing picture of partially clad female boxer and erroneously captioning it as being plaintiff); Quezada By Delamota v. Daily News, 501 N.Y.S.2d 971, 975, 12 Media L. Rep. 2097, 2099 (N.Y. Sup. Ct. 1986) ("Given the close connection between privacy and defamation claims, particularly in the area of first amendment concerns, it is clear that a heightened degree of fault must be shown before section 51 sanctions can be imposed against a media defendant for a publication about a newsworthy event or a matter of public interest."). *See also* Pesce, *The Likeness Monster: Should the Right of Publicity Protect Against Imitation?* 65 N.Y.U. L. Rev. 782 (1990) (arguing that likelihood of consumer confusion standard needed).

[44]*See, e.g.,* Cal. Civ. Code §3344(a), (f) (requiring knowing use); Eastwood v. Superior Ct., 198 Cal. Rptr. 342, 346 n.6, 10 Media L. Rep. 1073, 1075 n.6 (Cal. Ct. App. 1983) (holding that §3344(d) as it pertains to news does not provide exemption from liability for infringement for knowing or reckless falsehood); Welch v. Mr. Christmas, 440 N.E.2d 1317, 454 N.Y.S.2d 971, 974–75, 8 Media L. Rep. 2366, 2368–69 (N.Y. 1982) (knowledge that use is unlawful required for punitive damages but not for compensatory damages or injunctive relief).

[45]*See, e.g.,* Clark v. Celeb Pub'g, 530 F. Supp. 979, 983, 8 Media L. Rep. 1261, 1263 (S.D.N.Y. 1981) (court, in determining award of $6,750 to be commercial value of plaintiff's identity for use of photo in advertisement in *Celeb* magazine, looked to amount plaintiff received for appearing as centerfold in *Penthouse* magazine); Alonso v. Parfet, 325 S.E.2d 152, 154 (Ga. 1985) ("[t]he measure of damages ... is the value of the benefit derived by the person appropriating the other's name or likeness"); *accord* Martin Luther King, Jr., Ctr. for Social Change v. American Heritage Prods., 296 S.E.2d 697, 703, 8 Media L. Rep. 2377, 2381–82 (Ga. 1982). *See generally* Hoffman, *The Right of Publicity—Heirs' Rights, Advertisers' Windfall, or Courts' Nightmare,* 31 DePaul L. Rev. 1, 13 (1982).

[46]*See, e.g.,* Douglass v. Hustler Magazine, 769 F.2d 1128, 1143–44, 11 Media L. Rep. 2264, 2275–76 (7th Cir. 1985), *cert. denied,* 475 U.S. 1094 (1986); Clark v. Celeb Pub'g, 530 F. Supp. 979, 984, 8 Media L. Rep. 1261, 1264 (S.D.N.Y. 1981).

[47]*See, e.g.,* Factors Etc. v. Pro Arts, 496 F. Supp. 1090, 1104 (S.D.N.Y. 1980) (plaintiff permitted under New York law to recover all defendant's profits from sales of infringing poster), *rev'd on other grounds,* 652 F.2d 278, 7 Media L. Rep. 1617 (2d Cir. 1981), *cert. denied,* 456 U.S. 927 (1982). *But see* Price v. Hal Roach Studios, 400 F. Supp. 836, 847 (S.D.N.Y. 1975) (court refused accounting of profits, applying New York law).

[48]*See, e.g.,* Cal. Civ. Code §§990(a), 3344(a) (Deering 1990 Supp.); Tenn. Stat. §47-25-1106(d) (1984); Wis. Stat. §895.50(1)(b) (1983).

[49]*See, e.g.,* National Bank of Commerce v. Shaklee Corp., 503 F. Supp. 533, 547–48 (W.D. Tex. 1980); Grant v. Esquire, Inc., 367 F. Supp. 876, 881 (S.D.N.Y. 1973).

The main damages awarded to a plaintiff who can successfully prove appropriation are for mental anguish.[50] The plaintiff is also usually entitled to recover special damages such as medical expenses and possibly loss of earning capacity.[51]

Punitive damages may be awarded in most states in appropriation and publicity suits.[52] Punitive damages may not be available under the Lanham Act, however.[53]

§6.3(F)(ii) Injunctions

Surprisingly, many courts have granted injunctions in these cases without any consideration of the First Amendment issues involved, probably as a result of the courts' dislike of the publications' contents.[54] In addition, several state appropriation and publicity statutes expressly provide for injunctive relief.[55] Failure to even consider the First Amendment, however, is plainly erroneous.[56]

§6.3(F)(iii) Attorneys' Fees

A few state statutes explicitly permit the recovery of attorneys' fees in appropriation and publicity suits.[57] Otherwise, relevant state law must be reviewed to determine the availability of attorneys' fees in these types of cases.[58]

§6.4 DEFENSES

§6.4(A) The First Amendment

The only U.S. Supreme Court case in this area is *Zacchini v. Scripps-Howard Broadcasting Co.*[59] In *Zacchini,* an entertainer brought suit against a television station when it filmed the entertainer's entire 15-second "human cannonball" act at a state fair and televised it that night on the local evening news. The entertainer sued the station for violation of his right of publicity

---

[50]See Vassiliades v. Garfinckel's, Brooks Bros., 492 A.2d 580, 594, 11 Media L. Rep. 2057, 2065–66 (D.C. 1985); Eick v. Perk Dog Food Co., 106 N.E.2d 742, 745 (Ill. App. Ct. 1952).

[51]*See, e.g.,* O'Brien v. Papa Gino's of Am., 780 F.2d 1067, 1076 (1st Cir. 1986); Manger v. Kree Inst. of Electrolysis, 233 F.2d 5 (2d Cir. 1956); Fairfield v. American Photocopy Equipment Co., 291 P.2d 194, 198–99 (Cal. Ct. App. 1955); Candebat v. Flanagan, 487 So. 2d 207, 12 Media L. Rep. 2149, 2153–54 (Miss. 1986).

[52]*See Shaklee Corp.,* 503 F. Supp. at 545; Clark v. Celeb Pub'g, 530 F. Supp. 979, 984, 8 Media L. Rep. 1261, 1264 (S.D.N.Y. 1981); *Candebat,* 487 So. 2d at 212, 12 Media L. Rep. at 2154. *See also* CAL. CIV. CODE §§990(a), 3344 (Deering 1989 Supp.); N.Y. CIV. RIGHTS LAW §51 (McKinney 1976); VA. CODE §8.01-40 (1977).

[53]Nurmi v. Peterson, 16 Media L. Rep. 1606, 1609 (C.D. Cal. 1989).

[54]*See, e.g.,* Ali v. Playgirl, 447 F. Supp. 723, 3 Media L. Rep. 2540 (S.D.N.Y. 1978) (nude drawing of famous boxer); Barrows v. Rozanky, 489 N.Y.S.2d 481 (N.Y. App. Div. 1985) (injunctive relief granted prohibiting sale of nude photos of "Mayflower Madam" taken by former lover); Onassis v. Christian Dior-New York, 472 N.Y.S.2d 254, 258, 10 Media L. Rep. 1859, 1861 (N.Y. Sup. Ct. 1984) (injunctive relief granted for use and distribution of commercial magazine advertisement containing picture of look-alike model). *But see* Hansen v. High Soc'y Magazine, 429 N.Y.S.2d 552, 6 Media L. Rep. 1618 (N.Y. App. Div. 1980) (injunction unwarranted for lack of irreparable harm).

[55]*See, e.g.,* FLA. STAT. §540.08 (1981); MASS. GEN. LAWS ANN. ch. 214, §3A (West 1982); N.Y. CIV. RIGHTS LAW §51 (McKinney 1976); TENN. STAT. §47-25-1106 (1984).

[56]For a discussion of prior restraints, see Chapter 10.

[57]*See, e.g.,* CAL. CIV. CODE §§990(a), 3344(a) (Deering 1990 Supp.); UTAH CODE ANN. §45-3-4 (1981); WIS. STAT. §895.50 (1983).

[58]Shakey's Inc. v. Covalt, 704 F.2d 426, 435 (9th Cir. 1983) ("[S]tate law governs the award of attorneys' fees in diversity actions.").

[59]433 U.S. 562, 2 Media L. Rep. 2089 (1977).

under Ohio law.[60] The Ohio Supreme Court ruled that the broadcast was protected by the First Amendment because it was about a matter of legitimate public interest.[61] The U.S. Supreme Court reversed, stating that it was "quite sure that the First and Fourteenth Amendments do not immunize the media when they broadcast a performer's entire act without his consent."[62]

The Court's decision turned on the fact that it was the performer's *entire* act that was televised, not just a portion of it.[63] The Court held that the First Amendment does not authorize the media to broadcast a performer's entire act without consent, just as the media could not televise a stage play, prize fight, or baseball game in its entirety without consent, because such a broadcast would go "to the heart of [the performer's] ability to earn a living as an entertainer."[64] The Court distinguished *Time, Inc. v. Hill*,[65] on which the defendant attempted to rely, since *Hill* involved the tort of false light, "an entirely different tort from the 'right of publicity.'"[66]

Similarly, the Court stated that if the television station had merely reported that the entertainer was performing at the fair and described or commented on his act, with or without showing his picture on television, "we would have a very different case."[67] Such commentary would certainly be immunized by the First Amendment.

The three dissenting justices strongly criticized the majority's "repeated incantation of a single formula: 'a performer's entire act'."[68] The dissent disagreed that the respondent's action was, as stated by the majority, comparable to a situation where a broadcaster made unauthorized commercial broadcasts

---

[60]*Id.*

[61]351 N.E.2d 454, 2 Media L. Rep. 1199 (Ohio 1976), *rev'd*, 433 U.S. 562, 2 Media L. Rep. 2089 (1977).

[62]433 U.S. at 575, 2 Media L. Rep. at 2094. *See also* Roberson v. Rochester Folding Box Co., 64 N.E. 442, 443 (N.Y. 1902) where, in the first New York case to reject a common law right of privacy, the court held that such a right could improperly infringe on the freedom of the press to publish newsworthy information. It also recognized that this novel right, if properly limited, could peacefully coexist with the First Amendment, stating that the legislature could "provide that no one should be permitted for his own selfish purpose to use the picture or the name of another for advertising purposes without his consent. In such event no embarrassment would result to the general body of law."; *and* Pavesich v. New England Life Ins. Co., 50 S.E. 68, 80 (Ga. 1905) where, in the first Georgia case to recognize a right of privacy, the court held, in resolving the conflict between the right of privacy and the First Amendment, that "[t]here is in the publication of one's picture for advertising purposes not the slightest semblance of an expression of an idea, a thought, or an opinion, within the meaning of the constitutional provision which guaranties [sic] to a person the right to publish sentiments on any subject."

[63]433 U.S. at 573 n.10, 576, 2 Media L. Rep. at 2093 n.10, 2094.

[64]*Id.* at 576, 2 Media L. Rep. at 2094 (" 'The rationale for [protecting the right of publicity] is the straightforward one of preventing unjust enrichment by the theft of good will. No social purpose is served by having the defendant get free some aspect of the plaintiff that would have market value and for which he would normally pay.' " (citations omitted)).

[65]385 U.S. 374, 1 Media L. Rep. 1791 (1967).

[66]433 U.S. at 571, 2 Media L. Rep. at 2092. The Court noted that the states' interest in providing a cause of action for each tort differs. In false light cases, the interest protected is that of reputation, with the same overtones of mental distress as in defamation cases. *Id.* at 573, 2 Media L. Rep. at 2093. By contrast, the states' interest in permitting a right of publicity is that of protecting the proprietary interest of the individual in his act and to encourage such entertainment, which the Court noted "is closely analogous to the goals of patent and copyright law, focusing on the right of the individual to reap the reward of his endeavors and having little to do with protecting feelings or reputation." *Id.* Furthermore, the Court noted that the two torts differ in the degree to which they intrude on dissemination of information to the public. In false light cases, the only way to protect the interest involved is to minimize publication of the damaging material. In right of publicity cases, however, the issue involves *who* gets to do the publishing. The Court also noted that the goal of any entertainer is to achieve widespread publication of his act as long as he gets the commercial benefit of such publication. *Id.*

[67]*Id.* at 569, 2 Media L. Rep. at 2090.

[68]*Id.* at 579, 2 Media L. Rep. at 2095 (Powell, J., dissenting). Justice Stevens expressed no opinion on the merits because he concluded that the case was not properly before the Court. *Id.* at 583, 2 Media L. Rep. at 2097.

of sporting events and theatrical performances and then kept the profits, stating that in the case before them, the broadcast was part of an "ordinary daily news program, consuming a total of 15 seconds. It is a routine example of the press' fulfilling the informing function so vital to our system."[69]

The dissent also argued that putting such limitations on the media had "disturbing implications" and would lead to media self-censorship.[70] Because the media may be unsure whether certain film footage might be held to portray an "entire act," they may decline coverage—even of newsworthy events—or may describe the event in "watered-down verbal reporting" that "is hardly the kind of news reportage that the First Amendment is meant to foster."[71]

Despite the outcome of *Zacchini,* and because of its narrow holding, numerous cases both before and after *Zacchini* recognize that there can be no cause of action for appropriation or violation of the right of publicity where the use is in connection with the publication of newsworthy information.[72] Some cases reach this result by finding that the use is not for advertising or trade purposes even though the media sell their publications for a profit;[73] others reach it by explicit reliance on the First Amendment.[74] In some statutes

---

[69] *Id.* at 580, 2 Media L. Rep. at 2096.

[70] *Id.*

[71] 433 U.S. at 580–81, 2 Media L. Rep. at 2096 (footnote omitted). The dissent would thus have begun at a different starting point than the majority—rather than asking whether the performer's entire act was filmed, the dissent focused on *what use* was made of the film. Where the film is used for a regular news broadcast, the dissent would find no liability absent a strong showing by the plaintiff that "the news broadcast was a subterfuge or cover for private or commercial exploitation." *Id.* at 581, 2 Media L. Rep. at 2096.

[72] *See, e.g.,* Gautier v. Pro-Football, 107 N.E.2d 485, 488 (N.Y. 1952); Creel v. Crown Pubrs., 496 N.Y.S.2d 219, 12 Media L. Rep. 1588 (N.Y. App. Div. 1985); Lutz v. Hoffman, 4 Media L. Rep. 2294, 2295 (E.D.N.Y. 1979); Brooks v. ABC, 737 F. Supp. 431, 17 Media L. Rep. 2041 (N.D. Ohio 1990).

[73] Murray v. New York Magazine Co., 267 N.E.2d 256, 258 (N.Y. 1971) (" 'A picture illustrating an article on a matter of public interest is not considered used for the purposes of trade or advertising within the prohibition of the statute . . . unless it has no real relationship to the article . . . or unless the article is an advertisement in disguise.' " (citation omitted)); Arrington v. New York Times Co., 434 N.E.2d 1319, 1322, 8 Media L. Rep. 1351, 1353 (N.Y. 1982) (quoting *Murray* with approval and then stating: "And this holds true though the dissemination of news and views is carried on for profit or that illustrations are added for the very purpose of encouraging sales of the publications."), *cert. denied,* 459 U.S. 1146 (1983). *See also* Leidholdt v. LFP, Inc., 860 F.2d 890, 895, 15 Media L. Rep. 2201, 2204 (9th Cir. 1988) ("The fact that Hustler Magazine is operated for profit does not extend a commercial purpose to every article within it."), *cert. denied,* 489 U.S. 1080 (1989); Martinez v. Democrat-Herald Pub'g Co., 669 P.2d 818, 10 Media L. Rep. 1340 (Or. Ct. App. 1983) (use of student's photograph in connection with article discussing drug use in junior high school held not actionable without proof that article conveyed extraordinary commercial benefit to publishers beyond that ordinarily obtained as result of dissemination of news); Jaubert v. Crowley Post-Signal, 375 So. 2d 1386, 1391, 5 Media L. Rep. 2084, 2087 (La. 1979) (photo of house published on newspaper's front page not actionable even though published for profit); *see also supra* §6.3(C); *but see* Ali v. Playgirl, 447 F. Supp. 723, 726–27, 3 Media L. Rep. 2540, 2542 (S.D.N.Y. 1978) (recognizing rule but finding it inapplicable).

[74] Ann-Margret v. High Soc'y Magazine, 498 F. Supp. 401, 6 Media L. Rep. 1774 (S.D.N.Y. 1980) (photograph from movie of partially nude actress published in "skin" magazine not actionable because of public interest); Freihofer v. Hearst Corp., 480 N.E.2d 349, 353, 12 Media L. Rep. 1056, 1058 (1985) ("the protection afforded by this statute to individuals does not apply to the publication of newsworthy matters or events"); Stephano v. News Group Pubns., 474 N.E.2d 580, 584–85, 11 Media L. Rep. 1303, 1306 (N.Y. 1984) ("[C]ourts have consistently held, from the time of its enactment, that [§§50 and 51] should not be construed to apply to publications concerning newsworthy events or matters of public interest. The exception reflects Federal and State constitutional concerns for free dissemination of news and other matters of interest to the public." (citations omitted)); Delan v. CBS, Inc., 458 N.Y.S.2d 608, 9 Media L. Rep. 1130 (N.Y. App. Div. 1983) (use of film clip of patient in state mental hospital not actionable under New York privacy statute; any other result would render statute unconstitutional); Cohn v. NBC, 414 N.Y.S.2d 906, 4 Media L. Rep. 2533 (N.Y. App. Div. 1979) (movie about former Senator Joseph McCarthy matter of public interest; former aides have no claim), *aff'd,* 408 N.E.2d 672, 6 Media L. Rep. 1398, *cert. denied,* 449 U.S. 1022 (1980); Spahn v. Julian Messner, Inc., 260 N.Y.S.2d 451, 453 (N.Y. App. Div. 1965) (publication of "news, history, biography, and other factual subjects of public interest" privileged), *aff'd,* 221 N.E.2d 543 (N.Y. 1966), *vacated and remanded for reconsideration,* 387 U.S. 239 (1967), *aff'd on remand,* 233 N.E.2d 840 (N.Y. 1967), *appeal dismissed,* 393 U.S. 1046 (1969); University of Notre Dame du Lac v. Twentieth

there are exceptions that recognize First Amendment values to a greater or lesser extent.[75]

§6.4(B) Fiction, Docudramas, and Biographies

The vast majority of courts hold, by various reasoning, that fictional works, docudramas, and biographies are not actionable as infringement of the right of publicity or as appropriation.[76] The leading case in the area of First Amendment protection for works of fiction is *Guglielmi v. Spelling-Goldberg Productions.*[77] *Guglielmi* was an action brought by the nephew of Rudolph Valentino who sought damages for the infringement of Valentino's right of publicity, which he allegedly inherited, due to a fictionalized movie of Valentino's life that had been televised.[78]

In a concurring opinion, joined by two other justices, Chief Justice Bird stated that the real issue for the court to decide was whether "the use of a deceased celebrity's name and likeness in a fictional film as exhibited on television constitutes an actionable infringement of that person's right of publicity."[79] A fourth justice also concurred, emphasizing that, while the facts of *Guglielmi* specifically involved the rights of an heir of a prominent person, "it seems clear that the principles [in the concurrence] similarly would apply to a suit brought by that [living prominent] person."[80] Thus, a majority of the California Supreme Court agreed that a right of publicity claim would be barred by the First Amendment where the work at issue is a fictionalized, albeit biographical, story of the plaintiff's life.

The court first noted that both entertainment and fiction are entitled to full First Amendment protection.[81] Second, in response to the nephew's argument that Valentino's name and likeness were used only because they increased the marketability of the film, the court stated that "[t]he First Amendment is not limited to those who publish without charge."[82] Finally, the court rejected the nephew's claim that the film was not entitled to First Amendment protection because it was fiction and thus false, stating that so long as a work is labeled as fiction, it cannot be false.[83]

Century-Fox Film Corp., 256 N.Y.S.2d 301 (N.Y. App. Div.) (movie where university was satirized protected by First Amendment), *aff'd,* 207 N.E.2d 508 (N.Y. 1965); New Kids on the Block v. News Am. Pub'g, 745 F. Supp. 1540, 18 Media L. Rep. 1089 (C.D. Cal. 1990) (use of plaintiffs' names to conduct opinion poll on who is most popular member of rock group protected by First Amendment even though callers charged for telephone calls via "900"-number system). *Compare* Paulsen v. Personality Posters, 299 N.Y.S.2d 501 (N.Y. Sup. Ct. 1968) (poster of comedian Pat Paulsen, who ran mock campaign for president, with legend "For President" protected by First Amendment) *with* Factors Etc. v. Pro Arts, 579 F.2d 215, 4 Media L. Rep. 1144 (2d Cir. 1978) (poster of Elvis Presley with legend "In Memory" not protected by First Amendment), *cert. denied,* 440 U.S. 908 (1979); *see also infra* §6.4(C).
[75]*Compare* CAL. CIV. CODE §990(n) *with* CAL. CIV. CODE §3344(d) (Deering 1990 Supp.).
[76]*See infra* note 84.
[77]160 Cal. Rptr. 352, 5 Media L. Rep. 2208 (Cal. 1979).
[78]The California Supreme Court affirmed the dismissal of the nephew's suit because, following its holding in Lugosi v. Universal Pictures, 160 Cal. Rptr. 323, 5 Media L. Rep. 2185 (Cal. 1979), the right of publicity "is not descendible and expires upon the death of the person so protected." *Guglielmi,* 160 Cal. Rptr. at 353, 5 Media L. Rep. at 2209. For a detailed discussion of this issue, *see infra* §6.6.
[79]160 Cal. Rptr. at 353, 5 Media L. Rep. at 2209 (Bird, C.J., concurring).
[80]*Id.* at 362, 5 Media L. Rep. at 2216 (Newman, J., concurring).
[81]*Id.* at 356–57, 5 Media L. Rep. at 2211–12.
[82]*Id.* at 357, 5 Media L. Rep. at 2212.
[83]*Id.* at 359, 5 Media L. Rep. at 2214 ("[T]he author who denotes his work as fiction proclaims his . . . indifference to 'the facts.' . . . All fiction, by definition, eschews an obligation to be faithful to historical

A number of other cases also hold that fictional works are protected by the First Amendment despite right of publicity or appropriation claims.[84] However, if a biography or other publication contains substantial falsifications, then there may be a cause of action for defamation or false light invasion of privacy.[85]

§6.4(C) Incidental Use

To be able to recover, the use of a plaintiff's identity must constitute more than a mere incidental mention or reference to it.[86] Whether a particular use is incidental is normally determined by assessing the relationship of the use in question to the main purpose and subject of the work at issue.[87] Essentially, the courts appear to be applying a de minimis test, coupled with a recognition that, as a practical matter, every use cannot be actionable.[88] The incidental publication of names or likenesses is not elevated to a commercial use simply because the defendant seeks to make a profit out of the sale of its publications or broadcasts.[89]

---

truth."). *See also* Hicks v. Casablanca Records, 464 F. Supp. 426, 4 Media L. Rep. 1497 (S.D.N.Y. 1978) (court, after recognizing existence of cause of action by heirs of Agatha Christie under New York law, held that fictional novel and movie concerning her unexplained 11-day disappearance protected by First Amendment).

[84]*See* Rogers v. Grimaldi, 875 F.2d 994, 16 Media L. Rep. 1648 (2d Cir. 1989) (if title of artistic work is related to its contents, First Amendment protects that use); Meeropol v. Nizer, 560 F.2d 1061, 1067, 2 Media L. Rep. 2269, 2273 (2d Cir. 1977), *cert. denied,* 434 U.S. 1013 (1978) ("Unauthorized biographical works are not subject to suits under §51 since they are viewed as legitimate dissemination of information on subjects of general interest."); Maheu v. CBS, 247 Cal. Rptr. 304, 15 Media L. Rep. 1548 (Cal. Ct. App. 1988) (fictional biography of Howard Hughes protected by First Amendment); Frosch v. Grosset & Dunlap, Inc., 427 N.Y.S.2d 828, 6 Media L. Rep. 1272 (N.Y. App. Div. 1980) (fictional biography of Marilyn Monroe protected by First Amendment).

[85]Bindrim v. Mitchell, 155 Cal. Rptr. 29, 5 Media L. Rep. 1113 (Cal. Ct. App.), *cert. denied,* 444 U.S. 984 (1979). This case was overruled on other grounds in McCoy v. Hearst Corp., 727 P.2d 711, 13 Media L. Rep. 2169 (Cal. 1986). Spahn v. Julian Messner, Inc., 233 N.E.2d 840, 842 (N.Y. 1967), *appeal dismissed,* 393 U.S. 1046 (1969); Davis v. High Soc'y Magazine, 457 N.Y.S.2d 308, 313–14, 9 Media L. Rep. 1164, 1167–68 (N.Y. App. Div. 1982); Sinatra v. Wilson, 2 Media L. Rep. 2008 (S.D.N.Y. 1977). *See generally* Chapters 2 and 3 on defamation and false light, respectively.

[86]Ladany v. William Morrow & Co., 465 F. Supp. 870, 4 Media L. Rep. 2153 (S.D.N.Y. 1978) (viewed in context of main purpose and subject of book about terrorist attack on Israeli Olympic team, incidental and isolated references to plaintiff not actionable even though use was fictional and plaintiff's name appeared on 13 different pages).

[87]RESTATEMENT (SECOND) OF TORTS §652C, cmt. d (1977). Marquette v. Warner Bros., 16 Media L. Rep. 1957 (N.Y. Sup. Ct. 1989) (three-second appearance of "Pee Wee" Marquette in film about Charles Parker held incidental and not actionable under New York Civil Rights Law §51); Delan v. CBS, Inc., 458 N.Y.S.2d 608, 613, 9 Media L. Rep. 1130, 1132 (N.Y. App. Div. 1983) (use of plaintiff's picture for approximately four seconds in 60-minute news documentary held to be incidental); University of Notre Dame du Lac v. Twentieth Century-Fox Film Corp., 256 N.Y.S.2d 301, 304 (N.Y. App. Div.) (references to university president on three pages of novel incidental, *aff'd,* 207 N.E.2d 508 (N.Y. 1965); Damron v. Doubleday, Doran & Co., 231 N.Y.S. 444 (N.Y. Sup. Ct. 1928) (mention of plaintiff's name once in book of 400 pages merely incidental), *aff'd,* 234 N.Y.S. 773 (N.Y. App. Div. 1929); Cox v. Hatch, 761 P.2d 556, 565–66, 16 Media L. Rep. 1366, 1373–74 (Utah 1988) (citing numerous cases; use of fungible pictures of company workers not actionable); Crump v. Beckley Newspapers, 320 S.E.2d 70, 86, 10 Media L. Rep. 2225, 2236 (W. Va. 1984) (where picture of any woman coal miner could have been used, use of plaintiff's picture not actionable).

[88]Merle v. Sociological Research Film Corp., 152 N.Y.S. 829 (N.Y. App. Div. 1915) (where plaintiff put name on building to advertise company and defendant merely took motion picture of building that included plaintiff's name on sign, plaintiff could not claim that defendant's use was anything more than incidental part of photograph of actual building, which did not add to value of photograph for trade or advertising); Shubert v. Columbia Pictures Corp., 72 N.Y.S.2d 851 (N.Y. Sup. Ct. 1947) (where motion picture showed view from city rooftop with plaintiff's name, "Shubert," prominently appearing on side of factory in foreground, use was incidental), *aff'd,* 80 N.Y.S.2d 274 (N.Y. App. Div. 1948).

[89]RESTATEMENT (SECOND) OF TORTS §652C, cmt. d; Fogel v. Forbes, Inc., 500 F. Supp. 1081, 1088–89, 6 Media L. Rep. 1941, 1946 (E.D. Pa. 1980) (use of photo of plaintiffs at airline counter with boxes of merchandise to illustrate article on Latin Americans' large purchases in Florida not actionable); Tropeano

§6.4(D) Advertisements of the Media's Contents

Where the plaintiff's name, photograph, or likeness is used to advertise a magazine, book, television broadcast, or other publication in which it originally had lawfully appeared, such later use is also lawful.[90]

§6.4(E) Federal Preemption

Appropriation and the right of publicity can collide with society's interest in free enterprise and free expression, and they may be preempted by the federal statutory monopolies of copyright and trademark. While the case law governing the federal preemption of state law affecting intellectual property has changed considerably over the years,[91] the Supreme Court's current position is that state regulation of intellectual property is preempted only when it conflicts with the objectives of federal law.[92]

The preemption rules of the Copyright Act of 1976[93] create a single system of federal protection for all "original works of authorship," published or unpublished, from the moment they are fixed in a tangible medium of expression.[94] Section 301(a) provides that any state law, whether based on common law or statute, is subject to federal preemption if (1) it creates "legal or equitable rights that are equivalent to any of the exclusive rights" of a federal

---

v. Atlantic Monthly Co., 400 N.E.2d 847, 5 Media L. Rep. 2526 (Mass. 1980) (use of plaintiff's photo in article about modern sexual and social mores not actionable); Nelson v. Maine Times, 373 A.2d 1221, 1224, 2 Media L. Rep. 2011, 2013 (Me. 1977) (use of Native American infant's photo in book review not actionable); *see also supra* §6.4(A) and *infra* §6.4(D). *Compare* Tellado v. Time-Life Books, 643 F. Supp. 904, 13 Media L. Rep. 1401 (D.N.J. 1986) (use of plaintiff's photo on publisher's letter and outside of envelope containing letter, which promoted books on Vietnam War that did not include plaintiff's photo, held sufficiently commercial to be actionable and outside scope of incidental use defense).

[90]Lerman v. Flynt Distrib. Co., 745 F.2d 123, 131, 10 Media L. Rep. 2497, 2501 (2d Cir. 1984) (magazine's republication of previous cover photos in advertisement not actionable), *cert. denied,* 471 U.S. 1054 (1985); Cher v. Forum Int'l, 692 F.2d 634, 639, 8 Media L. Rep. 2484, 2487 (9th Cir. 1982) (statement that interview was exclusive not actionable where interview had not previously been published and celebrity had given exclusive interviews to magazine before, but statement that celebrity told one magazine things she would not tell another false and thus actionable), *cert. denied,* 462 U.S. 1120 (1983); Guglielmi v. Spelling-Goldberg Prods., 160 Cal. Rptr. 352, 360, 5 Media L. Rep. 2208, 2215 (Cal. 1979) ("it is of no moment that the advertisement [for the film] may have increased the profitability of the film"); Lawrence v. A.S. Abell Co., 475 A.2d 448, 453, 10 Media L. Rep. 2001, 2005 (Md. 1984) ("it is acceptable to use extractions of past issues of a publication for advertising"); Booth v. Curtis Pub'g Co., 223 N.Y.S.2d 737, 1 Media L. Rep. 1784 (N.Y. App. Div.) (no tort where magazine used picture of actress as part of advertisement for magazine when picture had previously appeared in magazine with actress' consent), *aff'd,* 182 N.E.2d 812 (N.Y. 1962); Namath v. Sports Illustrated, 371 N.Y.S.2d 10, 1 Media L. Rep. 1843 (N.Y. App. Div. 1975) (use of football star's picture, which previously appeared with consent in magazine, to advertise subscriptions to magazine held to be incidental advertising of protected news medium), *aff'd,* 352 N.E.2d 584 (N.Y. 1976); *see also supra* §6.4(C).

[91]Sears, Roebuck & Co. v. Stiffel Co., 376 U.S. 225 (1964); Compco Corp. v. Day-Brite Lighting, 376 U.S. 234, 237 (1964) (holding that "when an article is unprotected by a patent or copyright, state law may not forbid others to copy that article"). *See also* Goldstein v. California, 412 U.S. 546, 570 (1973) (holding that where "Congress has drawn no balance; . . . it has left the area unattended, and no reason exists why the State should not be free to act."); Kewanee Oil Co. v. Bicron Corp., 416 U.S. 470 (1974) (holding that congressional failure to grant federal patent in no way preempts state power to protect trade secrets and inventions); Zacchini v. Scripps-Howard Broadcasting Co., 433 U.S. 562, 577, 2 Media L. Rep. 2089, 2095 (1977) (upholding policy of state law prohibiting infringement of right of publicity by reproduction of performer's act, reasoning that supremacy clause of "[t]he Constitution does not prevent [a state] from making a similar choice here in deciding to protect the entertainer's incentive in order to encourage the production of this type of work").

[92]*See, e.g.,* Bonito Boats v. Thunder Craft Boats, 489 U.S. 141 (1989) (Court held that its previous decisions "made it clear that the Patent and Copyright Clauses do not, by their own force *or by negative implication,* deprive the States of the power to adopt rules for the promotion of intellectual creation within their own jurisdictions" (emphasis added)); *Kewanee Oil Co.,* 416 U.S. at 479.

[93]17 U.S.C. §§101–810 (Supp. III 1979).

[94]*Id.* §301.

copyright[95] *and* (2) the state right is "within the subject matter of copyright" as defined in the Act.[96] Since the passage of Section 301, several courts presented with the issue of federal preemption of the right of privacy and the right of publicity have held, for various reasons, that there is no preemption.[97]

In *Midler v. Ford Motor Co.*,[98] the Ninth Circuit held that the use of a sound-alike to mimic singer Bette Midler's performance of a song infringed upon Midler's right of publicity and rejected a copyright preemption defense that had previously proved fatal to publicity claims in sound-alike cases.[99] The court reasoned that, because Midler claimed rights in her persona and did not seek damages for the defendant's use of the song, her claim was not preempted by federal copyright law[100]—that is, the court held that the right of publicity was not equivalent to a copyright, because it was not the defendant's mere performance of the song, but rather a performance in a manner intended to simulate the plaintiff, that infringed her right of publicity. Restricting only the imitation of a particular performance of a copyrighted work does not conflict with the broader right of the copyright holder to perform the work in nonimitative ways, the court held.[101] Moreover, the court held that the subject

---

[95]*Id.* §301(a). Some courts determine whether rights defined by state law are "equivalent" to federal copyrights by employing the "extra element" test. Harper & Row, Pubrs. v. Nation Enters., 723 F.2d 195, 200, 9 Media L. Rep. 2489, 2492 (2d Cir. 1983) ("[w]hen a right defined by state law [within the subject matter of copyright] may be abridged by an act which, in and of itself, would infringe one of the exclusive rights, the state law in question must be deemed preempted .... Conversely, when a state law violation is predicated upon an act incorporating elements beyond mere reproduction or the like, the rights involved are not equivalent and preemption will not occur"), *rev'd on other grounds*, 471 U.S. 539, 11 Media L. Rep. 1969 (1985); Baltimore Orioles v. Major League Baseball Players Ass'n, 805 F.2d 663, 678 n.26, 13 Media L. Rep. 1625, 1636 n.26 (7th Cir. 1986) (finding that baseball players' assertion of rights of publicity in televised baseball games is "equivalent" to exclusive right to perform embodied in federal copyright law and is therefore preempted), *cert. denied*, 480 U.S. 941 (1987). *See also* C. Pesce, *The Likeness Monster: Should the Right of Publicity Protect Against Imitation?* 65 N.Y.U. L. Rev. 782, 814 (1990) (arguing that extra element must qualitatively change nature of state right, not just its scope); Abrahms, *Copyright, Misappropriation and Preemption: Constitutional and Statutory Limits of State Law Protection*, 1983 Sup. Ct. Rev. 509.

[96]17 U.S.C. §301(a) (Supp. III 1979). A state right is within the "subject matter" of copyright if it protects "original works of authorship fixed in any tangible medium of expression." *Id.* §102(a). *See also id.* §103(b). Examples of work not "fixed in any tangible medium of expression," and thus not subject to possible federal copyright preemption, include extemporaneous speeches, live conversations (or interviews), and musical performances or dramatic sketches improvised or developed from memory without being recorded or written down. H.R. Rep. No. 1496, 94th Cong., 2d Sess. 131 (1976).

[97]Bi-Rite Enters. v. Button Master, 555 F. Supp. 1188, 1201, 9 Media L. Rep. 1531, 1540 (S.D.N.Y.) (federal preemption no bar to relief under right of publicity law since intangible proprietary interest does not constitute a writing), *supplemental opinion*, 578 F. Supp. 59 (S.D.N.Y. 1983); Factors Etc. v. Pro Arts, 496 F. Supp. 1090, 1097 (S.D.N.Y. 1980) (1976 Copyright Act not intended to preempt right of publicity), *rev'd on other grounds*, 652 F.2d 278 (2d Cir. 1981), *cert. denied*, 456 U.S. 927 (1982); *accord* Price v. Hal Roach Studios, 400 F. Supp. 836, 846 (S.D.N.Y. 1975). *Contra* Motown Record Corp. v. George A. Hormel & Co., 657 F. Supp. 1236, 1240 (C.D. Cal. 1987) (California Civil Code §3344 claim that singing group's tune and image were appropriated preempted by federal copyright law).

[98]849 F.2d 460, 15 Media L. Rep. 1620 (9th Cir. 1988).

[99]Sinatra v. Goodyear Tire & Rubber Co., 435 F.2d 711, 716 n.12 (9th Cir. 1970) (rejecting unfair competition claim on grounds of federal preemption where defendant, who used look-alike and sound-alike to imitate plaintiff in advertisements, owned copyright in music, lyrics, and arrangement of song closely identified with plaintiff), *cert. denied*, 402 U.S. 906 (1971); *Motown Record Corp.*, 657 F. Supp. at 1238–41 (publicity claim under California statute preempted by Copyright Act where basic act constituting alleged wrong—unauthorized use of plaintiff's composition by look-alike and sound-alike group—was same as that of copyright). *See also* Allen v. Men's World Outlet, 679 F. Supp. 360, 366–67, 15 Media L. Rep. 1001, 1005–07 (S.D.N.Y. 1988) (holding that dilution claim involving use of celebrity's picture "equivalent" to infringement of statutory right of publicity and thus could not be asserted because New York privacy statute preempts field).

[100]849 F.2d at 462–63, 15 Media L. Rep. at 1622–23. The court stated that if Midler were seeking to prevent the defendants from using the song, her claim would clash with federal copyright law and she would fail like the plaintiffs in previous sound-alike cases. *Id.*

[101]*Id.* at 462, 15 Media L. Rep. at 1621–22.

matter of the right of publicity cannot be the subject matter of copyright, because the intangible identity of the plaintiff does not constitute a "writing" subject to copyright protection.[102]

However, the dissenting opinion in *Carson v. Here's Johnny Portable Toilets*[103] argued that federal law may preempt some assertions of the right of publicity. Judge Cornelia Kennedy attacked the majority's position that the use of the phrase "Here's Johnny" violated entertainer Johnny Carson's right of publicity, because such an expansive reading of the right of publicity would create a common law monopoly that removes items, words, and acts from the public domain in direct violation of the federal policy that favors free enterprise.[104]

The dissent indicated that protection under the common law right of publicity would "run afoul of first amendment challenges" because it lacks the requirement of notice to the public of what is being removed from the public domain[105] and is not limited in duration, as are copyrights and patents.[106]

As the dissent noted, the federal copyright statute only protects original works that cement the author's particular expression of an idea or a concept in a tangible form. If federal law and policy do not protect phrases such as "Here's Johnny," which is not in and of itself an original combination of words, state law should also not protect them under a right of publicity, the dissent argued.[107]

Similarly, in *Baltimore Orioles v. Major League Baseball Players Association*,[108] the Seventh Circuit, in holding that professional baseball players had no right of publicity in certain telecasts of baseball games, concluded that their rights were preempted by federal copyright law.[109] The court found that both conditions required by Section 301(a) of the Copyright Act, copyrightability and equivalency, were met.[110] First, the court held that as soon as a performance is fixed in tangible form, federal copyright law preempts a right of publicity in that performance.[111] Telecasts, if broadcast and simultaneously recorded, do preempt the right of publicity because they are fixed in tangible form.[112]

---

[102]*Id.* *See also* Factors Etc. v. Pro Arts, 496 F. Supp. 1090, 1100 (S.D.N.Y. 1980) (holding that federal copyright law does not preempt post mortem assertion of infringement of state right of publicity because "extra element" of exploitation by celebrity before death made publicity right not equivalent to copyrights), *rev'd on other grounds,* 652 F.2d 278 (2d Cir. 1981), *cert. denied,* 456 U.S. 927 (1982).

[103]698 F.2d 831, 9 Media L. Rep. 1153 (6th Cir. 1983) (Kennedy, J., dissenting).

[104]*Id.* at 840, 9 Media L. Rep. at 1159–60.

[105]*Id.* at 841, 9 Media L. Rep. at 1160–61. For example, under copyright, trademark, and patent law, notice to the public is required in the form of filing with the appropriate government office. Members of the public are thus apprised of the nature and extent of what is being removed from the public domain and also of what may be the subject of infringement claims. On the other hand, the right of publicity provides only a limited notice to the public at best, especially if it is expanded beyond the protection of name, likeness, and actual performances to more subjective attributes such as phrases identified with individuals.

[106]The common law monopoly created by the right of publicity offers no protection against the monopoly existing for an indefinite time or even in perpetuity. Many jurisdictions, however, have limited by statute the length of time the right will last. *See infra* §6.6.

[107]698 F.2d at 841, 9 Media L. Rep. at 1161. The dissent thus concluded that "[a]part from the possibility of outright federal preemption, public policy requires that the public's interest in free enterprise and free expression take precedence over any interest Johnny Carson may have in a phrase associated with his person." *Id.*

[108]805 F.2d 663, 13 Media L. Rep. 1625 (7th Cir. 1986), *cert. denied,* 480 U.S. 941 (1987).

[109]805 F.2d at 676, 13 Media L. Rep. at 1634–35.

[110]*See infra* notes 111–13.

[111]805 F.2d at 675, 13 Media L. Rep. at 1634.

[112]*Id.* at 679 n.30, 13 Media L. Rep. at 1638 n.30 (holding that telecasts not fixed in tangible form include "games that are not broadcast or that are televised without being videotaped"). *Compare* Zacchini v.

Second, the court found that the right of publicity was equivalent to rights under federal copyright law that vest the exclusive right to publicly perform telecasts of the games in the players' employer.[113]

§6.4(F) Consent

There can be no liability where a plaintiff has consented to the use of his or her name or likeness.[114] In many states, by statute, such consent must be in writing.[115] Where consent for a use was originally obtained and the photograph was then substantially altered or used in a context other than that to which the plaintiff consented, the original consent may be invalid.[116] Where consent has been obtained, however, and the photograph has only been altered in a minor way, there can be no recovery.[117]

Consent is not lost by a disagreement over compensation,[118] and minors may not disaffirm consent given by their parents.[119] The courts appear to be split on whether consent can be revoked after the defendant has taken actions in reliance on the consent.[120]

§6.4(G) Privileges

The qualified and absolute privileges available in defamation actions[121] are also available in appropriation and right of publicity cases.[122]

Scripps-Howard Broadcasting Co., 433 U.S. 562, 2 Media L. Rep. 2089 (1977) (finding no conflict between federal copyright law and right of publicity where television station videotaped live performance of plaintiff being shot out of cannon and then broadcast it).

[113]805 F.2d at 677, 13 Media L. Rep. at 1635–36.

[114]Zim v. Western Pub'g, 573 F.2d 1318, 4 Media L. Rep. 1467 (5th Cir. 1978); O'Brien v. Pabst Sales Co., 124 F.2d 167 (5th Cir. 1941), cert. denied, 315 U.S. 823 (1942); Pierson v. News Group Pubns., 549 F. Supp. 635 (S.D. Ga. 1982); Cox v. Hatch, 761 P.2d 556, 562–63, 16 Media L. Rep. 1366, 1371 (Utah 1988); RESTATEMENT (SECOND) OF TORTS §652F, cmt. b (1977).

[115]N.Y. CIV. RIGHTS LAW §§50–51 (McKinney 1986); OKLA. STAT. ANN. tit. 21, §§839.1–.3; VA. CODE §§2.1-377 to 2.1-386 (1950); WIS. STAT. ANN. §895.50; NEB. REV. STAT. §§20-201 to 20-211, 25-840.01. Brinkley v. Casablancas, 438 N.Y.S.2d 1004, 7 Media L. Rep. 1457 (N.Y. App. Div. 1981) (poster manufacturer found liable for unauthorized publication of famous fashion model's picture on poster because there was no written consent). Compare CAL. CIV. CODE §3344(a) (Deering 1990 Supp.) (no requirement that consent be "written"). Moreover, some courts hold that a defendant may be liable in the absence of written consent even when the defendant had reason to believe written consent had been obtained. Welch v. Mr. Christmas, 440 N.E.2d 1317, 8 Media L. Rep. 2366 (N.Y. 1982); Brinkley, 438 N.Y.S.2d at 1004, 7 Media L. Rep. at 1457. See also Chapters 3, 4, and 5.

[116]Grant v. Esquire, Inc., 367 F. Supp. 876 (S.D.N.Y. 1973) (use of altered photograph of Cary Grant without consent held actionable).

[117]Sharman v. C. Schmidt & Sons, 216 F. Supp. 401 (E.D. Pa. 1963) (where plaintiff had given consent to use of his photograph in beer commercial and picture of beer glass and bottle were later superimposed on photograph, recovery denied because there was no substantial alteration of photograph); Dahl v. Columbia Pictures Corp., 166 N.Y.S.2d 708 (N.Y. Sup. Ct. 1957) (no recovery allowed where actress consented to use of her likeness and it was not substantially altered by defendant, although actress claimed use was in "objectionable and unflattering" manner), aff'd, 183 N.Y.S.2d 992 (N.Y. App. Div. 1959).

[118]Castagna v. Western Graphics Corp., 590 P.2d 291, 4 Media L. Rep. 2497 (Or. Ct. App. 1979).

[119]Faloona v. Hustler Magazine, 799 F.2d 1000, 1005, 13 Media L. Rep. 1354, 1356–57 (5th Cir. 1986) (decided under California law), cert. denied, 479 U.S. 1088 (1987); Shields v. Gross, 448 N.E.2d 108, 9 Media L. Rep. 1466 (N.Y. 1983).

[120]Revocation Allowed: Garden v. Parfumerie Rigaud, 271 N.Y.S. 187 (N.Y. Sup. Ct. 1933); State ex rel. La Follette v. Hinkle, 229 P. 317, 319 (Wash. 1924). Revocation Not Allowed: Alonso v. Parfet, 325 S.E.2d 152 (Ga. 1985). See also Chapter 4.

[121]See Chapter 2.

[122]Bond v. Pecout, 561 F. Supp. 1037 (N.D. Ill. 1983), aff'd without opinion, 734 F.2d 18 (7th Cir. 1984); McCall v. Courier-Journal & Louisville Times Co., 623 S.W.2d 882, 7 Media L. Rep. 2118 (Ky. 1981), cert. denied, 456 U.S. 975 (1982); Crump v. Beckley Newspapers, 320 S.E.2d 70, 80 n.5, 10 Media L. Rep. 2225, 2233 n.5 (W. Va. 1983) (citing numerous authorities). See also Chapters 3 and 4.

§6.5 STATUTES

§6.5(A) New York

After New York's highest court ruled that there was no common law right of privacy in that state,[123] the New York Legislature adopted the first statute in this area.[124] Sections 50 and 51 of the New York Civil Rights Law make it both a misdemeanor and a tort for any person, firm, or corporation to use another person's name, portrait, or picture without that person's written consent if the use is for advertising purposes or for the purposes of trade.[125]

In addition to authorizing injunctive or other equitable relief, Section 51 also provides for the recovery of actual damages for injuries sustained by reason of the unauthorized use. If it can be proven that the defendant knowingly used an individual's name, portrait or picture, the jury, in its discretion, may award exemplary damages.[126]

The New York statute does not discuss its impact on common law rights, and the state courts were once divided on whether New York recognized a nonstatutory right of privacy or publicity.[127] As a result, the federal courts in New York concluded that a common law right of publicity existed under New York law separate from the New York statute.[128] More recently, however, the Second Circuit followed newer New York state court decisions, holding that there is no common law right of publicity.[129]

Cases decided under New York law have had wide impact on the development of this area of law. Because the New York law was the first statute in this area, it was the model for the statutes of many other states,[130] and there has been a great deal of litigation over its terms.[131]

---

[123]Roberson v. Rochester Folding Box Co., 64 N.E. 442 (N.Y. 1902).
[124]On the history of New York's statute, see Shields v. Gross, 448 N.E.2d 108, 110, 9 Media L. Rep. 1466 (N.Y. 1983). For a more detailed history of privacy rights, see Chapter 4.
[125]N.Y. CIV. RIGHTS LAW §§50–51 (McKinney 1986).
[126]Id. §51. On the issue of consent under the statute, see supra §6.4(F). On the issue of post mortem uses under New York law, see infra §§6.6(C)(i) and (ii).
[127]Arrington v. New York Times Co., 434 N.E.2d 1319, 1321, 8 Media L. Rep. 1319, 1353 (N.Y. 1982) (" 'there exists no so-called common-law right to privacy' "), cert. denied, 459 U.S. 1146 (1983); Frosch v. Grossett & Dunlap, Inc., 75 A.D.2d 768, 768–69, 6 Media L. Rep. 1272 (N.Y. App. Div. 1980) (New York statutory right of privacy only extends to living persons; even assuming New York recognizes nonstatutory right of publicity and that such right is inheritable, free expression is so important that such right should not be extended to publication of literary work about deceased person). Contra Lombardo v. Doyle, Dane & Bernbach, 396 N.Y.S.2d 661, 664, 2 Media L. Rep. 2321, 2322 (N.Y. App. Div. 1977) ("while a cause of action under the Civil Rights Law is not assignable during one's lifetime and terminates at death, the right to publicity, i.e., the property right in one's name, photograph and image is under no such inhibition").
[128]Factors, Etc. v. Pro Arts, 579 F.2d 215, 220–22, 4 Media L. Rep. 1144, 1147–49 (2d. Cir. 1978) (descendible; no ruling on whether exploitation before death required), cert. denied, 440 U.S. 908 (1979); accord Hicks v. Casablanca Records, 464 F. Supp. 426, 429, 4 Media L. Rep. 1497, 1498 (S.D.N.Y. 1978); Price v. Hal Roach Studios, 400 F. Supp. 836 (S.D.N.Y. 1975) (descendible without exploitation before death).
[129]Pirone v. MacMillan, Inc., 894 F.2d 579, 585–86, 17 Media L. Rep. 1472, 1477 (2d Cir. 1990) (citing Stephano v. News Group Pubns., 474 N.E.2d 580, 584, 11 Media L. Rep. 1303, 1305–06 (N.Y. 1984)); Hurwitz v. United States, 884 F.2d 684 (2d Cir. 1989) (holding, in context of intrusion claim, that there is no separate common law right of publicity), cert. denied, 493 U.S. 1056 (1990); Allen v. Men's World Outlet, 679 F. Supp. 360, 367, 15 Media L. Rep. 1001, 1106–07 (S.D.N.Y. 1988) (rejecting earlier federal authorities that recognized separate common law right of publicity).
[130]FLA. STAT. ANN. §540.08 (West 1988); MASS. GEN. LAWS ANN. ch. 214, §3A (West 1989); NEB. REV. STAT. §§20-201 to 20-211 (1991); OKLA. STAT. ANN. tit. 21, §§839.1–2 (criminal) (West 1983 & Supp. 1994); R.I. GEN. LAWS §9-1-28 (1985); UTAH CODE ANN. §§45-3-1 to 45-3-6 (1993); VA. CODE §8.01-40 (Michie 1992); WIS. STAT. ANN. §895.50(2)(b) (West 1983).
[131]See, e.g., Brown v. American Broadcasting Co., 704 F.2d 1296, 1302 (4th Cir. 1983) (meaning of Virginia statute modeled on New York statute controlled by New York state court decisions). But see

§6.5(B) California

In California, California Civil Code Section 3344[132] creates civil liability for the knowing use of a person's name, photograph, likeness, voice, or signature without that individual's consent "in any manner, on or in products, merchandise, or goods, or for purposes of advertising or selling, or soliciting purchases of, products, merchandise, goods or services."[133]

Under Section 3344, a successful plaintiff is entitled to $750 or actual damages, whichever is greater, and the defendant's profits from the unauthorized use. Punitive damages are available, and the prevailing party shall recover reasonable attorneys' fees and costs.[134]

In an apparent effort to avoid First Amendment conflicts, Section 3344 provides certain exemptions from liability, including those for (1) uses in connection with news, public affairs, or sports broadcasts or political campaigns;[135] and (2) owners or employers of an advertising medium, including but not limited to newspapers, magazines, radio, and television networks and stations, cable television systems, billboards, and transit ads through which the advertising reaches the public, provided that the owners or employers did not have knowledge of the unauthorized use.[136]

"Photograph" is defined to mean "any photograph or photographic reproduction, still or moving, or any videotape or live television transmission, of any person, such that the person is *readily identifiable*."[137] A person is "readily identifiable" when "one who views the photograph with the naked eye can reasonably determine that the person depicted in the photograph is the same person who is complaining of its unauthorized use."[138]

If the photograph at issue includes more than one person who is readily identifiable, then all of the persons complaining of the use are to "be represented as individuals rather than solely as members of a definable group

---

Tropeano v. Atlantic Monthly Co., 400 N.E.2d 847, 848–49, 5 Media L. Rep. 2526, 2526–27 (Mass. 1980) (New York decisions not binding on application of Massachusetts statute modeled on New York statute).

[132] CAL. CIV. CODE §3344 (Deering 1990 Supp.).

[133] *Id.* §3344(a). While knowing use is a requirement under §3344(a), the courts agree that it is not a requirement under the common law. Fairfield v. American Photocopy Equip. Co., 291 P.2d 194, 197 (Cal. Ct. App. 1955) ("inadvertence or mistake is no defense"). *Accord* Motschenbacher v. R.J. Reynolds Tobacco Co., 498 F.2d 821, 826 n.16 (9th Cir. 1974); Eastwood v. Superior Ct., 198 Cal. Rptr. 342, 346 n.6, 10 Media L. Rep. 1073, 1075 n.6 (Cal. Ct. App. 1983). The heirs of deceased persons have similar but lesser rights. CAL. CIV. CODE §990 (Deering 1990 Supp.), discussed *infra* §6.6(A)(i).

[134] CAL. CIV. CODE §3344(a).

[135] *Id.* at (d). A similar exemption exists in §990(j). One case has held, however, that there is an exception to this exemption. In Eastwood v. Superior Court, 198 Cal. Rptr. 342, 10 Media L. Rep. 1073 (1983), actor Clint Eastwood sued the *National Enquirer* over an article indicating Eastwood and two women were involved in a "love triangle." The article was featured on the defendant's cover with pictures of Eastwood and the women. The defendant also advertised the article on television using a copy of the issue with Eastwood's name and picture on the cover. Eastwood claimed that the article was false in many respects and invaded his privacy, in part through the commercial use of his name, photograph, and likeness under both the common law and California Civil Code §3344. *Id.* at 345, 10 Media L. Rep. at 1074. The court stated that the use of Eastwood's name and likeness in the context of a news account, which was allegedly false but presented as true, provided the *Enquirer* "with a ready-made 'scoop'—a commercial advantage over its competitors which it would otherwise not have." *Id.* at 349, 10 Media L. Rep. at 1077. The court held that the news exemption from §3344 did not prevent liability for the publication of falsehoods with constitutional actual malice. *Id.* at 352, 10 Media L. Rep. at 1080. This decision seriously confuses two different torts: false light and the right of publicity. Eastwood had already pled a false light claim. *Id.* at 344, 10 Media L. Rep. at 1073–74. There was no reason or need to convert §3344 into a false light statute.

[136] CAL. CIV. CODE §3344(f); *id.* §990(l).

[137] *Id.* §3344(b); *id.* §990(i) (emphasis added).

[138] *Id.* §3344(b)(1). *See also id.* §990(i).

represented in the photograph."[139] A "definable group" includes but is not limited to a crowd at any sporting event, in any street, or in any public building; the audience at any theatrical or stage production; a glee club; or a baseball team.[140] Under the statute, individuals will be considered members of a definable group if they are represented in the photograph solely as a result of being present at the time the photograph was taken and were not singled out as individuals in any manner.[141]

Section 3344 was also specifically amended to add a section creating a rebuttable presumption that affects the burden of producing evidence, where the photograph or likeness being used is that of an employee of the user in an advertisement or other publication prepared by the user, and the use is incidental. The rebuttable presumption in favor of the user is that the failure to obtain consent of the employee was not a knowing use of the employee's photograph or likeness.[142]

Furthermore, Section 3344 provides that the use of an individual's name, voice, signature, photograph, or likeness in a commercial medium shall not constitute a use for which consent is required just because the material containing the use is commercially sponsored or contains paid advertising. The statute provides that it "shall be a question of fact" whether the use was so directly connected with the commercial sponsorship or with the paid advertising as to constitute a use for which consent is required.[143]

Finally, Section 3344 expressly provides that the statutory remedies are "cumulative and shall be in addition to any others provided for by law."[144] Thus, the statute makes clear that the statutory remedies complement but do not replace common law rights.

§6.5(C) The Lanham Act

Courts have recognized that right of publicity law bears some similarity to the law of trademarks and false advertising under the federal Lanham Act.[145]

For instance, a plaintiff may find protection against the unpermitted use of his or her name or picture in federal court under the false advertising prong of Lanham Act Section 43(a) if certain conditions are met.[146] However, the major feature found by most courts to distinguish a claim of right of publicity from a claim of false advertising is the element of falsity, which, while the sine qua non of false advertising,[147] is not a necessary element of the right of

---

[139]*Id.* §3344(b)(2).
[140]*Id.* This limitation does not appear in §990.
[141]CAL. CIV. CODE §3344(b)(3).
[142]*Id.* at (c).
[143]*Id.* at (e).
[144]*Id.* at (g); *id.* §990(m). On the issue of consent under the statute, *see supra* §6.4(F).
[145]15 U.S.C.S. §1125(a) (1993). Factors Etc. v. Creative Card Co., 444 F. Supp. 279, 283, 3 Media L. Rep. 1290, 1292 (S.D.N.Y. 1977), *aff'd*, 579 F.2d 215, 4 Media L. Rep. 1144 (2d Cir. 1978) (right of publicity "has more to do with unfair competition than it does with the right to be left alone"), *cert. denied*, 440 U.S. 908 (1979); Grant v. Esquire, Inc., 367 F. Supp. 876, 879 (S.D.N.Y. 1973) ("The 'right of publicity' is somewhat akin to the exclusive right of a commercial enterprise to the benefits to be derived from the goodwill and secondary meaning that it has managed to build up in its name.").
[146]Lanham Act §43(a), 15 U.S.C.S. §1125(a).
[147]*See* American Home Prods. Corp. v. Johnson & Johnson, 577 F.2d 160, 165 (2d Cir. 1978) (§43(a) proof submitted may include not only literal falsehoods but also proof of misleading "innuendo, indirect

publicity.[148] For this reason, courts have treated the two claims separately; proof of each claim is measured by its own set of requirements.[149]

Similarly, under certain circumstances, the unpermitted use in the sale of goods or services of a plaintiff's name or picture in which the plaintiff has acquired trademark or service mark rights may also be protected against infringement.[150] While courts have thus often commented on the resemblance of trademark and service mark law to the right of publicity,[151] most courts have noted their important differences.[152] Thus, a plaintiff may have valid claims for both the infringement of the right of publicity and trademark or service mark infringement, but proof of each count will again be determined according to each claim's separate test of requirements.[153]

§6.6 SURVIVAL OF THE CAUSE OF ACTION

Since invasion of the right of privacy is personal to the individual claiming that his or her name or likeness has been appropriated, most courts hold that

---

intimations, and ambiguous suggestions"); Parkway Baking Corp. v. Freihofer Baking Co., 255 F.2d 641, 649 (3d Cir. 1958) (injunctive relief granted on proof that advertisement has "tendency to deceive").

[148]Eastwood v. Superior Ct., 198 Cal. Rptr. 342, 348, 10 Media L. Rep. 1073, 1076–77 (Cal. Ct. App. 1983) ("[T]he appearance of an 'endorsement' is not the *sine qua non* of a claim for commercial appropriation [of the right of publicity]."); Flores v. Mosler Safe Co., 164 N.E.2d 853, 857 (N.Y. 1959) (proof of false endorsement not needed for violation of right of privacy under New York law); *see supra* §6.3(E).

[149]For instance, in Allen v. National Video, 610 F. Supp. 612 (S.D.N.Y. 1985), celebrity Woody Allen alleged infringement of his statutory and common law rights of publicity, and false advertising under Lanham Act §43(a), by the unpermitted use of a Woody Allen look-alike in an advertisement. The court, doubting whether a violation of the New York statutory right of publicity had occurred, granted summary judgment for Allen under §43(a), reasoning that it was violated because the defendant's advertisement created a likelihood of consumer confusion over whether the plaintiff "endorsed or was otherwise involved with [the defendant's] goods and services." *Id.* at 627. *Accord* Allen v. Men's World Outlet, 679 F. Supp. 360, 15 Media L. Rep. 1001 (S.D.N.Y. 1988). *But see* Pirone v. MacMillan, Inc., 894 F.2d 579, 581–85, 17 Media L. Rep. 1472, 1475–77 (2d Cir. 1990) (defendant's use of photographs of Babe Ruth in calendar not actionable under §43(a) or as infringement of common law right of publicity under New York law); Booth v. Colgate-Palmolive Co., 362 F. Supp. 343 (S.D.N.Y. 1973) (defendant's use of sound-alike in advertisement not actionable as infringement of right of publicity or as false endorsement under Lanham Act §43(a)).

[150]*See* In re Carson, 197 USPQ 554 (T.M.T.A.B. 1977) (name "Johnny Carson" held registerable as service mark for entertainment services where plaintiffs substantiated use of name as service mark with advertising of "Johnny Carson in Concert"). *Compare* In re Mancini, 219 USPQ 1047 (T.M.T.A.B. 1983) (distinguishing *In re Carson* on basis that "Boom Boom" not used as service mark of professional boxer "Boom Boom" Mancini because to constitute trademark or service mark infringement, defendant's use of mark must create likelihood of confusion as to sponsorship or approval). *See also Pirone,* 894 F.2d 579.

[151]*See supra* notes 149 and 150.

[152]Rogers v. Grimaldi, 875 F.2d 994, 1004, 16 Media L. Rep. 1648, 1656 (2d Cir. 1989) ("Because the right of publicity, unlike the Lanham Act, has no likelihood of confusion requirement, it is potentially more expansive than the Lanham Act."); Bi-Rite Enters. v. Button Master, 555 F. Supp. 1188, 9 Media L. Rep. 1531 (S.D.N.Y. 1983) (distinguishing trademark rights from right of publicity, noting distinct requirement of "likelihood of confusion" for trademark infringement); *Eastwood,* 198 Cal. Rptr. at 343, 10 Media L. Rep. at 1077 (holding that to prove claim for infringement of right of publicity, actor need not prove that his name was impressed with "secondary meaning" through prior commercial exploitation, a requirement of trademark protection for personal names); *but see* Lugosi v. Universal Pictures, 160 Cal. Rptr. 323, 328, 5 Media L. Rep. 2185, 2188 (Cal. 1979) (existence of post mortem right of publicity depends on whether plaintiff's name impressed during life with "secondary meaning").

[153]Estate of Presley v. Russen, 513 F. Supp. 1339, 1379–83 (D.N.J. 1981) (preliminary injunction based not on right of publicity claim but only on service mark, unfair competition, and Lanham Act claims); National Bank of Commerce v. Shaklee Corp., 503 F. Supp. 533, 541–42 (W.D. Tex. 1980) (damages for infringement of both rights); Hirsch v. S.C. Johnson & Son, 280 N.W.2d 129 (Wis. 1979). *But see Men's World Outlet,* 679 F. Supp. at 366–67, 15 Media L. Rep. at 1005–06 (holding that claim of dilution of trademark rights in celebrity's picture is "equivalent" of infringement of statutory right of publicity and thus could not be asserted because New York privacy statute "preempts" field).

the only person who may bring an action under the invasion of privacy theory is the individual, and such a cause of action terminates at the death of the individual.[154] The statutes of some states, however, provide that, in general, causes of action shall survive the death of the person bringing the action or on whose behalf the action was brought.[155]

On the other hand, there is profound disagreement as to whether the right of publicity is inheritable.[156] Many states have statutes that explicitly or implicitly create a statutory post mortem right of publicity that lasts for varying periods of time after the death of the individual.[157] In addition, courts have found that the common law of several states provides for survivability of the right of publicity.[158]

Those courts holding that the right of publicity is descendible emphasize the right of each individual to enjoy and pass to one's heirs the fruits of one's labors and the broader social goals, similar to those found in copyright and patent laws, of encouraging personal accomplishments from which others may benefit.[159]

In contrast, those courts holding against descendibility stress the personal nature of the right not to have others capitalize on one's name and likeness; the practical difficulties of judicial line-drawing that would arise if the right were recognized, such as determining how many years and how many generations the right survives, whether the right is taxable, and the worth one attaches to the right at death; and the inherent conflict with First Amendment interests.[160]

---

[154]Maritote v. Desilu Prods., 345 F.2d 418 (7th Cir.) (under Illinois law, heirs of Al Capone had no claim for invasion of his privacy by television show since right is personal and terminated at death), *cert. denied,* 382 U.S. 883 (1965); James v. Screen Gems, 344 P.2d 799 (Cal. Ct. App. 1959) (widow of Jesse James, Jr., had no cause of action for alleged wrongful portrayal of husband in movie); Gleason v. Hustler Magazine, 7 Media L. Rep. 2183 (D.N.J. 1981) (widow and children have no relational right of appropriation for publication of deceased husband's/father's photo); Shibly v. Time, Inc., 321 N.E.2d 791, 797 (C.P. Cuyahoga County 1974), *aff'd,* 341 N.E.2d 337 (Ohio Ct. App. 1975) (privacy claims are personal and do not survive death of plaintiff).

[155]*Survivability of Actions in General:* MICH. COMP. LAWS ANN. §600.2921 (West 1986) (all actions and claims survive death); OR. REV. STAT. §115.305 (1991) (all "causes of action or suit, by one person against another, survive to the personal representative of the former and against the personal representative of the latter"); S.D. CODIFIED LAWS ANN. §15-4-1 (1984) (all causes of action survive death); VA. CODE §8.01-25 (Michie 1992) (every cause of action, whether legal or equitable, survives death). *Compare* NEB. REV. STAT. §20-201 to 20-211 (1991) ("appropriation privacy rights" survive death of subject of any such invasion of privacy) *and* OKLA. STAT. tit. 21, §§839.1, 839.2 (West 1983 & Supp. 1994) (provides liability under right of privacy statute for unauthorized use of deceased person's name, portrait, or picture) *with* KY. STAT. §391.170 (Michie/Bobbs-Merrill 1984) (recognizing that "the traditional right of privacy terminates upon death of the person asserting it").

[156]*See infra* §6.6(A)–(D).

[157]*Explicit Statutes:* CAL. CIV. CODE §990 (Deering 1990 & Supp. 1994) (50 years); FLA. STAT. ANN. §540.08 (West 1988) (40 years); KY. STAT. §391.170 (Michie/Bobbs-Merrill 1984) (50 years); OKLA. STAT. tit. 12, §1448 (1993) (100 years); TENN. CODE ANN. §47-25-1107 (1988) (10 years); TEX. PROP. CODE §§26.001–26.015 (West 1994 Supp.) (50 years); VA. CODE §8.01-40 (Michie 1992) (20 years). *See also* NEB. REV. STAT. §§20-202, 20-208 (1991) (civil rights).

[158]*See infra* §§6.6(B)(i) and 6.6(D).

[159]Factors Etc. v. Pro Arts, 579 F.2d 215, 4 Media L. Rep. 1144 (2d Cir. 1978), *cert. denied,* 440 U.S. 908 (1979); Lugosi v. Universal Pictures, 160 Cal. Rptr. 323, 5 Media L. Rep. 2185 (Cal. 1979) (Bird, C.J., dissenting).

[160]Memphis Dev. Found. v. Factors Etc., 616 F.2d 956, 5 Media L. Rep. 2521 (6th Cir. 1980), *cert. denied,* 449 U.S. 953 (1980); *Lugosi,* 160 Cal. Rptr. 323. *See generally* Note, *An Assessment of the Commercial Exploitation Requirement As a Limit on the Right of Publicity,* 96 HARV. L. REV. 1703 (1983); Fletcher & Rubin, *The Descendibility of the Right of Publicity: Is There Commercial Life After Death?* 89 YALE L.J. 1125 (1980).

§6.6(A) California

§6.6(A)(i) Common Law

In *Lugosi v. Universal Pictures*,[161] the California Supreme Court established the rule that, together with *Guglielmi v. Spelling-Goldberg Productions*,[162] prohibits the descendibility of the right of publicity under California common law.[163]

In *Lugosi*, the widow and surviving son of actor Bela Lugosi brought an action against Universal Pictures seeking to recover the profits made by Universal in its licensing to commercial firms the use of the likeness of the character "Dracula" as portrayed by Lugosi in a film made for Universal.[164] The California Supreme Court held that the right to exploit a name and likeness is personal to the artist and must be exercised, if at all, by him during his lifetime.[165] Since the Court found that Lugosi did not commercially exploit his name and likeness during his life, it could not be exploited after his death by his heirs.[166]

In *Guglielmi*,[167] which was decided two days after *Lugosi*, however, the California Supreme Court perfunctorily held that an heir of actor Rudolph Valentino could not bring suit for damages for the infringement of Valentino's right of publicity since, citing *Lugosi*, the right of publicity "is not descendible and expires upon the death of the person so protected."[168] *Guglielmi* did not discuss whether an individual's commercial exploitation of his right during his lifetime would allow that right to descend to his heirs.

Later decisions have attempted to resolve the confusion created by *Lugosi* and *Guglielmi* by holding that the right of publicity is descendible if an individual commercially exploited the right before death. In *Groucho Marx Productions v. Day and Night Co.*,[169] the Second Circuit noted that *Lugosi*, as affirmed by *Guglielmi*, could be interpreted in three different ways: (1) the right of publicity was not descendible in California at all; (2) it was descendible only as to those items, e.g., T-shirts, where it had been exploited before death; or (3) it was descendible as to any item so long as it was exploited in some manner before death.[170] The Second Circuit rejected the last interpretation but did not have to choose between the first two, holding that the heirs had not inherited the Marx Brothers' rights of publicity because the play at issue did not use the names or likenesses of the Marx Brothers in connection with any product or service that the comedians promoted during their lives.[171]

---

[161] 160 Cal. Rptr. 323, 5 Media L. Rep. 2185 (Cal. 1979).
[162] 160 Cal. Rptr. 352, 5 Media L. Rep. 2208 (Cal. 1979).
[163] Groucho Marx Prods. v. Day & Night Co., 689 F.2d 317, 320–22, 8 Media L. Rep. 2201, 2203–05 (2d Cir. 1982); Eastwood v. Superior Ct., 198 Cal. Rptr. 342, 10 Media L. Rep. 1073, 1077 (Cal. Ct. App. 1983).
[164] 160 Cal. Rptr. at 325, 5 Media L. Rep. at 2185.
[165] *Id.* at 326, 5 Media L. Rep. at 2187.
[166] *Id.* at 328, 5 Media L. Rep. at 2188. The court suggested that had Lugosi established a business under the name of "Lugosi Horror Pictures" and sold T-shirts with his picture on them, this would have constituted the commercial exploitation of his name and likeness. *Id.* at 326–27, 5 Media L. Rep. at 2187.
[167] 160 Cal. Rptr. 352, 5 Media L. Rep. 2208 (1979).
[168] *Id.* at 353, 5 Media L. Rep. at 2209.
[169] 689 F.2d 317, 8 Media L. Rep. 2201 (2d Cir. 1982).
[170] *Id.* at 321–22, 8 Media L. Rep. at 2203–04.
[171] *Id.* at 323, 8 Media L. Rep. at 2205.

In *Acme Circus Operating Co. v. Kuperstock*,[172] the Eleventh Circuit, applying California law, held that the widow of a famous circus performer had inherited her husband's right of publicity since he had exploited it during his lifetime.[173] The court stated that "[w]e reject the possibility that the publicity interest never survives because such a strict interpretation would mean that much of the *Lugosi* majority opinion is pure dicta and surplusage."[174]

Whatever the correct answer under California common law, the California statutory right is inheritable.[175]

§6.6(A)(ii) Statutory Law

Section 990 of the California Civil Code legislatively overruled *Lugosi* and *Guglielmi*.[176] It provides for liability on the part of any person who uses "a deceased personality's name, voice, signature, photograph, or likeness, in any manner, on or in products, merchandise, goods, or for purposes of advertising or selling, or soliciting purchases of, products, merchandise, goods, or services, without prior consent."[177] The statute defines "deceased personality" as a "natural person whose name, voice, signature, photograph, or likeness has commercial value at the time of his or her death," whether or not that person used them for commercial purposes during their lifetime.[178]

Section 990 provides that the right it creates is a transferable property right during a personality's lifetime that may be inherited upon the death of the personality. If the right is not so transferred or devised, the statute sets forth in detail the individuals who would be entitled to inherit the right.[179]

As a prerequisite to recovery, any person claiming to be a successor-in-interest to the rights of the deceased personality under this section must register his or her claim with the California Secretary of State in the manner prescribed.[180] No recovery is allowed for damages that occur before registration.[181] The rights created by Section 990 expire 50 years after the death of the personality.[182]

The statute specifically exempts use of the deceased personality's name, voice, signature, photograph, or likeness in connection with news, public affairs, or sports broadcasts or political campaigns.[183] Section 990 also exempts any use of a deceased personality's name, voice, signature, photograph, or likeness in (1) a play, book, magazine, newspaper, musical composition, film, radio or television program, other than an advertisement or commercial

---

[172] 711 F.2d 1538, 9 Media L. Rep. 2138 (11th Cir. 1983).
[173] *Id.* at 1544–45, 9 Media L. Rep. at 2143.
[174] *Id.* at 1543, 9 Media L. Rep. at 2142.
[175] *See infra* §6.6(A)(ii).
[176] In *Lugosi*, the California Supreme Court had suggested that "[c]ertainly the Legislature by appropriate amendment to Civil Code Section 3344 . . . might recognize a right of action on behalf of the family or immediate heirs of persons such as Lugosi." The court itself, however, declined to do so. 160 Cal. Rptr. 323, 328, 5 Media L. Rep. 2185, 2188 (Cal. 1979). The California Legislature heeded this suggestion and enacted §990.
[177] CAL. CIV. CODE §990(a) (West 1990 Supp.).
[178] *Id.* §990(h).
[179] *Id.* at (b)–(d).
[180] *Id.* at (f).
[181] *Id.*
[182] CAL. CIV. CODE §990(g) (West 1990 Supp.).
[183] *Id.* at (j).

announcement not exempt under paragraph (4); (2) material that is of political or newsworthy value; (3) single and original works of fine art; and (4) an advertisement or commercial announcement for a use permitted by paragraph (1), (2), or (3).[184] Thus, Section 990 exempts many works that California Civil Code Section 3344 does not explicitly mention.[185]

§6.6(B) Tennessee

§6.6(B)(i) Common Law

In *State ex rel. Elvis Presley International Memorial Foundation v. Crowell*,[186] one in the long series of cases brought by Elvis Presley's heirs asserting his post mortem right of publicity, the Tennessee Court of Appeals disagreed with an earlier Sixth Circuit decision—*Memphis Development Foundation v. Factors, Etc.*[187]—that had held, under Tennessee common law, that the right of publicity was not inheritable.[188] The Sixth Circuit, in another Presley case heard a few weeks after the decision in *Crowell*, held that it was bound by *Crowell*'s ruling that, under Tennessee common law, the right of publicity was inheritable.[189]

§6.6(B)(ii) Statutory Law

Like the California Legislature, the Tennessee Legislature enacted legislation that overruled Tennessee common law as initially interpreted by the Sixth Circuit in *Memphis Development*.[190] The Personal Rights Protection Act of 1984 provides that "[e]very individual has a property right in the use of his name, photograph or likeness in any medium in any manner" that is "freely assignable and licensable," and which "shall not expire upon the death of the individual so protected, whether or not such rights were commercially exploited by the individual during the individual's lifetime, but shall be descendible to the executors, assigns, heirs, or devisees of the individual so protected."[191]

The Act provides that the right will last for ten years after death, even in the absence of any commercial use of the right.[192] However, the Act also provides a way of continuing the post mortem right beyond ten years by continuing to commercially exploit it. This right can be terminated by proof that the name, likeness, or image of the individual was not used for a period of two years after the initial ten-year period following the individual's death.[193]

---

[184]*Id.* at (n).
[185]*See* the discussion of §3344 *supra* §6.5(B). *See also supra* note 71.
[186]733 S.W.2d 89, 14 Media L. Rep. 1043 (Tenn. Ct. App. 1987).
[187]616 F.2d 956, 5 Media L. Rep. 2521 (6th Cir.), *cert. denied*, 449 U.S. 953 (1980). The court held that the right of publicity is not inheritable under Tennessee common law and that "[a]fter death the opportunity for gain shifts to the public domain, where it is equally open to all." *Id.* at 957–59, 5 Media L. Rep. at 2521–23.
[188]*Id.*
[189]Elvis Presley Enters. v. Elvisly Yours, 817 F.2d 104, 14 Media L. Rep. 1053 (6th Cir. 1987) (opinion designated "unpublished").
[190]*See supra* §6.6(B)(i).
[191]TENN. CODE ANN. §47-25-1103(a), (b) (1989).
[192]*Id.* §47-25-1104(a).
[193]*Id.* at (b)(2).

The Act provides for liability for the knowing use by any person of

> another individual's name, photograph, or likeness in any medium, in any manner directed to any person other than such individual, as an item for commerce for purposes of advertising products, merchandise, goods, or services, or for purposes of fund raising, solicitation of donations, purchases of products, merchandise, goods or services.[194]

Similar to California's Section 3344, the Tennessee Act provides an exception for group photographs where the individual complaining of the use is not represented as an individual but rather is represented solely as a member of a definable group.[195]

The remedies provided for by the Act include injunctions to prevent the unauthorized use of an individual's name, photograph, or likeness; and the impounding of any materials that have been made or used in violation of the individual's rights.[196] The court may also enjoin the use of "all plates, molds, matrices, masters, tapes, film negatives, or other articles by means of which such materials may be reproduced."[197] As part of a final judgment, the court may order the destruction of all of these materials and award actual damages.[198] The remedies provided for by the Act are in addition to any other remedies provided for by law.[199]

§6.6(C) New York

§6.6(C)(i) Common Law

New York law on the descendibility of the right of publicity was once uncertain, largely because of the uncertainty over whether New York law recognized a common law remedy in this area. While New York state courts had usually refused to recognize any nonstatutory right of publicity,[200] federal courts in New York had often held that the right of publicity lasted after death under New York common law.[201]

More recently, however, the Second Circuit held that the right of privacy and the right of publicity exist solely by virtue of the New York statute,[202] relying on a controlling New York Court of Appeals decision, *Stephens v. News Group Publications*.[203] The Second Circuit then concluded that, because New York state courts had indicated clearly that New York does not recognize any common law right of publicity, the New York Court of Appeals would reject the earlier federal authority to the contrary and hold that rights under the New York statute are not descendible.[204]

---

[194]*Id.* at (a).
[195]*Id.* at (b). For other exemptions in the Act, *see* §47-25-1107.
[196]TENN. CODE ANN. §47-25-1106(b) (1989).
[197]*Id.* at (a), (b).
[198]*Id.* at (c).
[199]*Id.* at (c)–(e).
[200]*See supra* note 127.
[201]*See supra* note 128.
[202]*See supra* note 129.
[203]474 N.E.2d 580, 584, 11 Media L. Rep. 1303, 1305–06 (1984).
[204]Pirone v. MacMillan, Inc., 894 F.2d 579, 17 Media L. Rep. 1472 (2d Cir. 1990). The Second Circuit acknowledged that there might be some ambiguity in *Stephano* but concluded that it was for the New York

§6.6(C)(ii) Statutory Law

New York's statute is expressly limited to "living person[s]," so rights under that statute are not descendible.[205]

§6.6(D) Other Jurisdictions

Other jurisdictions that have considered whether the right of publicity is descendible have reached opposite conclusions. In *Estate of Presley v. Russen*,[206] the court held that New Jersey recognizes the descendibility of the right of publicity[207] and granted an injunction to the estate of Elvis Presley against an entertainer who promoted and presented a theatrical production designed to simulate a stage performance by Elvis Presley.[208]

The Georgia Supreme Court reached the same conclusion in *Martin Luther King, Jr., Center for Social Change v. American Heritage Productions*.[209] There, the plaintiffs were attempting to halt the manufacture and sale by the defendant of plastic busts of Dr. Martin Luther King, Jr.[210] The Georgia Supreme Court addressed specific certified questions from the Eleventh Circuit regarding the "right of publicity"[211] and held that "the right of publicity survives the death of its owner and is inheritable and devisable."[212] The court also found "no reason to protect after death only those who took commercial advantage of their fame."[213]

The opposite conclusion was reached, however, by a federal court interpreting Ohio law in *Reeves v. United Artists*.[214] There, the widow of a boxer attempted to recover for the dramatization of her husband's life in the film *Raging Bull*. The court held that, under Ohio law, since the right of publicity is linked more closely to the right of privacy than to a property right, "the right of publicity, like the right of privacy, is not descendible."[215] Illinois law has

---

Court of Appeals or the New York Legislature to indicate that descendibility was recognized. *Id.* at 585–86, 17 Media L. Rep. at 1477.

[205] *Id.* at 585–86, 17 Media L. Rep. at 1477.

[206] 513 F. Supp. 1339 (D.N.J. 1981). *Contra* Gleason v. Hustler Magazine, 7 Media L. Rep. 2183 (D.N.J. 1981).

[207] 513 F. Supp. at 1354.

[208] *Id.* at 1382.

[209] 296 S.E.2d 697, 8 Media L. Rep. 2377 (Ga. 1982).

[210] *Id.* at 698–99, 8 Media L. Rep. at 2377–78.

[211] *Id.* at 699, 8 Media L. Rep. at 2378.

[212] *Id.* at 705, 8 Media L. Rep. at 2383. *See also* National Bank of Commerce v. Shaklee Corp., 503 F. Supp. 533 (W.D. Texas 1980) (holding, under Texas law, that action for use of decedent's name and likeness on front cover of special edition of decedent's book and inclusion of decedent's name in advertisement on back cover associating decedent with defendant did not abate following decedent's death while action was pending).

[213] 296 S.E.2d at 706, 8 Media L. Rep. at 2384 ("[t]he net result of following [cases that require exploitation] would be to say that celebrities and public figures have the right of publicity during their lifetimes (as others have the right of privacy), but only those who contract for bubble gum cards, posters and tee-shirts have a descendible right of publicity upon their deaths . . . . That we should single out for protection after death those entertainers and athletes who exploit their personae during life, and deny protection after death to those who enjoy public acclamation but did not exploit themselves during life, puts a premium on exploitation."). *But see* Sinkler v. Goldsmith, 623 F. Supp. 727 (D. Ariz. 1985) (court suggested that right of publicity would be descendible if right had been exploited during decedent's lifetime).

[214] 572 F. Supp. 1231, 9 Media L. Rep. 2484 (N.D. Ohio 1983), *aff'd*, 765 F.2d 79, 11 Media L. Rep. 2181 (6th Cir. 1985).

[215] *Id.* at 1235, 9 Media L. Rep. at 2487.

the same effect.[216] In Utah, the right of publicity is inheritable if it was exploited before death.[217] Washington does not recognize a descendible right of publicity.[218]

---

[216] Maritote v. Desilu Prods., 345 F.2d 418 (7th Cir.), *cert. denied,* 382 U.S. 883 (1965).
[217] Nature's Way Prods. v. Nature-Pharma, 736 F. Supp. 245, 251–53 (D. Utah 1990). *See generally* Annot., *Right to Publicize or Commercially Exploit Deceased Person's Name or Likeness As Inheritable,* 10 A.L.R.4th 1193 (1981).
[218] Joplin Enters. v. Allen, 795 F. Supp. 349, 351 (W.D. Wash. 1992).

CHAPTER 7

MEDIA LIABILITY FOR FALSE ADVERTISEMENTS AND OTHER SIMILAR STATEMENTS

§7.1 INTRODUCTION

This chapter discusses the media's liability for intentional, negligent, and innocent false statements in advertising and news stories, as well as for other intentional, negligent, and innocent statements that are not otherwise actionable, for example, defamation or invasion of privacy.[1] It discusses the media's liability to advertisers for the media's errors as well as the media's liability to readers or listeners for errors. It also discusses the related question of tort liability for publishing illegal advertisements.

§7.2 LIABILITY TO ADVERTISERS FOR ERRORS IN ADVERTISEMENTS

Each year the media print millions of lines of advertising and broadcast thousands of hours of advertising, which are worth millions of dollars.[2] Despite this, there are very few cases discussing the media's liability to advertisers for errors made by misprinting or incorrectly broadcasting advertisements.[3]

Advertisers' claims against the media are usually based on a breach of contract theory, although other theories may be available.[4] The clauses in many advertising contracts, which severely limit the media's liability for such errors, probably explain why advertisers seldom sue.[5] Also, most of the damage done by such incorrect advertising can be (and based on the paucity of decisions

---

[1]The cases discussed in this chapter primarily involve misrepresentation claims, although other types of claims are discussed. Defamatory statements are discussed in Chapter 2, and ones that invade privacy are discussed in Chapters 3–6. Imitation and incitement cases are discussed in Chapter 8.

[2]In 1990 alone, for example, advertising expenditures in newspapers totaled $32,281,000,000; in magazines, $6,803,000,000; in television, including cable, $28,405,000,000; and in radio, $8,726,000,000. ADVERTISING AGE, May 21, 1991, at 1.

[3]Annot., *Liability of Publisher for Mistake in Advertisement,* 10 A.L.R.2d 686 (1950) and supplements.

[4]*See, e.g.,* King Creations v. Conde Nast Pubns., 311 N.Y.S.2d 757 (N.Y. App. Div. 1970) (affirming dismissal of negligence claim against publisher for misprinting ad but allowing contract and disparagement of product claims to proceed).

[5]For examples of such clauses, *see* 1 AM. JUR. LEGAL FORMS 2d, *Advertising* §§12:78, 12:118 (1971) [hereinafter *Advertising*] *and* 4 ROSDEN, THE LAW OF ADVERTISING app. A (1991). However, errors in telephone directories have generated substantial litigation over the validity of such clauses, probably because corrections cannot be readily made to such directories. *See, e.g.,* Rozeboom v. Northwestern Bell Tel. Co., 358 N.W.2d 241 (S.D. 1984), which cites many of the leading cases on both sides; *see generally* Annot., *Liability of Telephone Company for Mistakes in or Omissions From its Directory,* 47 A.L.R.4th 882 (1986).

apparently is) readily remedied by prompt corrective advertising and by the advertisers' mitigation of their damages by, for example, explaining to customers that an error has been made. Care must be taken to make sure that advertising agencies, on behalf of advertisers, have not used insertion orders to disclaim liability.[6]

§7.3 LIABILITY TO READERS OR VIEWERS FOR FALSE ADVERTISEMENTS AND OTHER FALSE STATEMENTS

Much more common than the problems in the previous section are those that arise when a publisher publishes exactly what it received from an advertiser, but a reader or viewer contends that the advertisement was in some manner false.[7] As in the related area of imitation and incitement cases,[8] the two principal questions are whether the media owe a duty of care to readers and viewers and, if there is such a duty, what limits the First Amendment places on that duty.

§7.3(A) Intentional False Statements

There seems to be little doubt that the media can be liable if they publish advertisements that they know are false, i.e., if they engage in intentional misrepresentations.[9] The First Amendment does not prohibit punishment of intentional misrepresentations because such statements have such slight social value.[10] However, claims of intentional misrepresentation, conspiracy to de-

---

[6] CBS, Inc. v. Stokley-Van Kamp, Inc., 456 F. Supp. 539 (S.D.N.Y. 1977).

[7] In such situations, the media are often entitled to indemnification from advertisers because of clauses in their contracts with advertisers. For examples of such clauses see *Advertising, supra* note 5, §§12:76 and 12:117 *and* 4 ROSDEN, *supra* note 5.

[8] *See* Chapter 8.

[9] A number of cases recognize this explicitly or implicitly. First Equity of Fla. v. Standard & Poor's Corp., 670 F. Supp. 115, 119, 14 Media L. Rep. 1945, 1949 (S.D.N.Y. 1987) (dismissing negligence claim but allowing intentional misrepresentation claim to proceed), *dismissed,* 690 F. Supp. 256, 15 Media L. Rep. 1858 (S.D.N.Y. 1988), *aff'd,* 869 F.2d 175, 16 Media L. Rep. 1282 (2d Cir. 1989). *See also* Pittman v. Dow Jones & Co., 662 F. Supp. 921, 14 Media L. Rep. 1284 (E.D. La.) (plaintiff who claimed that *Wall Street Journal* advertisement falsely stated that deposits were backed by federal government had no cause of action; court observed that even though *Journal* made effort to investigate firm placing ad, newspaper was not aware of advertisement's falsities), *aff'd,* 834 F.2d 1171, 14 Media L. Rep. 2384 (5th Cir. 1987); Roman v. City of N.Y., 442 N.Y.S.2d 945, 948 (N.Y. Sup. Ct. 1981) (on summary judgment motion, no evidence of intentional misrepresentation by publisher of booklet about birth control); Demuth Dev. Corp. v. Merck & Co., 432 F. Supp. 990, 994–95, 3 Media L. Rep. 1092, 1095 (E.D.N.Y. 1977) (drug manufacturer has no claim against publisher of drug index even though publisher allegedly intentionally misrepresented toxicity of plaintiff's drug, because plaintiff did not rely on index; plaintiff's prima facie tort theory also rejected because of no showing on motion for summary judgment that defendant's *sole* intent was to injure plaintiff). *Compare* Advance Music Corp. v. American Tobacco Co., 53 N.Y.S.2d 337, 340–41 (N.Y. App. Div. 1945) (plaintiff contended that defendant's radio broadcast refused to say plaintiff's song was one of top ten songs in country; lower court held that only negligence was alleged and there was no claim for negligent misrepresentation in such circumstances; appellate court held that plaintiff had actually alleged intentional conduct and thus stated cause of action for prima facie tort), *rev'd on other grounds,* 70 N.E.2d 401 (N.Y. 1946) *with* Blatty v. New York Times Co., 728 P.2d 1177, 1183, 13 Media L. Rep. 1928, 1933 (Cal. 1986) (plaintiff claimed that newspaper falsely represented that plaintiff's novel did not meet sales criteria necessary to make newspaper's "best sellers" list; court held that there could be no liability for "injurious falsehood" absent showing that publication at issue was "of and concerning" plaintiff), *cert. denied,* 485 U.S. 934 (1988).

[10] Garrison v. Louisiana, 379 U.S. 64, 75, 1 Media L. Rep. 1548, 1552–53 (1964) (calculated falsehoods of such slight social value that they are not constitutionally protected). *See also* Gertz v. Robert Welch, Inc., 418 U.S. 323, 340, 1 Media L. Rep. 1633, 1640 (1974) ("there is no constitutional value in false statements

fraud, or other intentional torts cannot be based on the mere fact that the media broadcast or published advertisements or other information prepared by third parties.[11]

§7.3(B) Negligent False Statements

The more common cases involve claims that the media were negligent because they should have known that the items they published were false. The cases uniformly hold that the media owe no duty of care to readers or viewers in such situations;[12] that merely because someone puts the media on notice that certain advertisements are allegedly false, the media do not have to

---

of fact"); Virginia State Bd. of Pharmacy v. Virginia Citizens Consumer Council, 425 U.S. 748, 771, 1 Media L. Rep. 1930, 1938 (1976) ("Untruthful speech, commercial or otherwise, has never been protected for its own sake."). *But see* Philadelphia Newspapers v. Hepps, 475 U.S. 767, 778, 12 Media L. Rep. 1977, 1982 (1986) ("To provide 'breathing space' . . . for true speech on matters of public concern, the Court has been willing to insulate even *demonstrably* false speech from liability, and has imposed additional requirements of fault upon the plaintiff in a suit for defamation." (citation omitted)); *Gertz,* 418 U.S. at 339–41, 1 Media L. Rep. at 1640 ("The First Amendment requires that we protect some falsehood in order to protect speech that matters.").

[11]Hernandez v. Underwood, 7 Media L. Rep. 1535, 1536 (N.Y. Sup. Ct. 1981) ("What is alleged is merely that [defendant newspaper], by accepting this advertisement, aided the alleged conspirators in their plan. This is insufficient to impose liability on [defendant newspaper] for conspiracy to defraud . . . ." (citation omitted)); Goldstein v. Garlick, 318 N.Y.S.2d 370, 373 (N.Y. Sup. Ct. 1971) (summary judgment granted where all that was submitted to show conspiracy to engage in unfair competition was that newspaper defendants published advertisements).

[12]Jaillet v. Cashman, 189 N.Y.S. 743 (N.Y. Sup. Ct. 1921) (no negligence claim against ticker tape service that inaccurately reported effect of U.S. Supreme Court decision), *aff'd,* 194 N.Y.S. 947 (N.Y. App. Div. 1922), *aff'd per curiam,* 139 N.E. 714 (N.Y. 1923); Gutter v. Dow Jones, Inc., 490 N.E.2d 898, 12 Media L. Rep. 1999 (Ohio 1986) (newspaper publisher cannot be held liable for negligent misrepresentation in inaccurately reporting bonds' trading status); Yuhas v. Mudge, 322 A.2d 824, 825 (N.J. Super. Ct. App. Div. 1974) (no negligence claim against magazine for carrying advertisement for fireworks that injured plaintiff, despite claim that magazine was pseudo-scientific publication with " 'aura of authentativeness' " in public mind and purported duty to investigate inherently dangerous products); *Demuth Dev. Corp.,* 432 F. Supp. at 993–94, 3 Media L. Rep. at 1094 (publisher of drug index could not be sued for negligent misrepresentation); Suarez v. Underwood, 426 N.Y.S.2d 208, 211, 6 Media L. Rep. 1094, 1096 (N.Y. Sup. Ct. 1980) (summary judgment granted in favor of newspaper that carried allegedly false advertisements about hair implants because of "no showing of maliciousness, intent to harm, or recklessness without regard to the consequences"), *aff'd,* 449 N.Y.S.2d 438 (N.Y. App. Div. 1981); Libertelli v. Hoffman-La Roche, Inc., 7 Media L. Rep. 1734, 1735 (S.D.N.Y. 1981) (plaintiff who allegedly became addicted to Valium had no claim on theories of failure to warn or gross negligence against publisher of *Physician's Desk Reference* because she was unable to show "maliciousness, intent to harm, or recklessness without regard to the consequences"); *Roman,* 442 N.Y.S.2d 945 (allegations that Planned Parenthood negligently published booklet that falsely stated pregnancy is impossible after tubal ligation not actionable); Alm v. Van Nostrand Reinhold Co., 480 N.E.2d 1263 (Ill. App. Ct. 1985) (individual injured while following instructions in defendant's "how to" book has no cause of action based on negligent misrepresentation for failure to provide safe instructions and warnings; imposing duty on publishers to scrutinize and test all procedures in any of their publications would impermissibly infringe on public's right of free access to ideas as well as publishers' right to freely disseminate ideas); Pressler v. Dow Jones & Co., 450 N.Y.S.2d 884, 885, 8 Media L. Rep. 1680 (N.Y. App. Div. 1982) ("there was no basis for recovery for an allegedly negligent misstatement [by a newspaper] since no special relationship existed between the parties"); Langworthy v. Pulitzer Pub'g Co., 368 S.W.2d 385, 390 (Mo. 1963) ("No action for damages lies against a newspaper for merely inaccurate reporting when the publication does not constitute libel."); Gale v. Value Line, 640 F. Supp. 967, 13 Media L. Rep. 1198 (D.R.I. 1986) (negligence claim based on error in financial publication rejected); *Pittman,* 662 F. Supp. at 923, 14 Media L. Rep. at 1286 (rejecting claim against *Wall Street Journal* for false ad even though newspaper held in high esteem); *First Equity,* 670 F. Supp. at 118, 14 Media L. Rep. at 1948 (rejecting negligence claim against publisher of financial data); Walters v. Seventeen Magazine, 241 Cal. Rptr. 101, 102–03 (Cal. Ct. App. 1987) (rejecting negligence claim against magazine that published ad for tampons that allegedly caused toxic shock); Daniel v. Dow Jones & Co., 520 N.Y.S.2d 334, 14 Media L. Rep. 1995 (N.Y. Sup. Ct. 1987) (rejecting negligence claim against computerized news retrieval service); Annot., *Newspaper's Liability to Reader-Investor for Negligent but Nondefamatory Misstatement of Financial News,* 56 A.L.R.4th 1162 (1987). *See also* Yanase v. Automobile Club of S. Cal., 260 Cal. Rptr. 513, 17 Media L. Rep. 1085 (Cal. Ct. App. 1989) (publisher of travel guide not liable for crime at hotel because it made no representations on subject); Keenum v. Remington Arms Co., 15 Media L. Rep. 1447 (W.D. Okla. 1988) (no causation shown). *See also infra* §7.7.

arbitrate such disputes;[13] and that the media have no duty to investigate the truthfulness of advertisements.[14]

The result has been the same even if the theory against the media was not negligent misrepresentation, but some related theory.[15] The result has also been the same when the information was in a news story or some other nonadvertising context, such as an obituary.[16]

The following policy considerations justify these rules. First, these rules are consistent with the general rule that there is no liability for negligent misstatements that are broadcast to the world in general. As Professor Prosser stated:

> The spectre of unlimited liability, with claims devastating in number and amount crushing the defendant because of a momentary lapse from proper care, has haunted the courts. Thus attorneys, abstractors of title, inspectors of goods, accountants, surveyors, the operator of a ticker service, and a bank dealing with a non-depositor's check all have been held to be under no obligation to third parties.[17]

---

[13]For instance, in *Goldstein*, the court stated:
   They would have this court set forth a rule that once a newspaper received notice from a competitor . . . that an advertisement which was published was false or misleading that newspaper would publish that advertisement at its peril. This court does not agree. Such a rule would make a newspaper an arbiter of the conflicting claims of competing advertisers and would impose an intolerable burden upon newspapers and would, in the end, have a chilling effect on them since they would have to refuse many items submitted because of a possibility that publication would lead to liability. Nor should the onerous burden be placed upon newspapers under ordinary circumstances to conduct investigations in order to determine the effect of a questioned advertisement.
318 N.Y.S.2d at 375–76.
   [14]*Id.; Yuhas*, 322 A.2d at 825 ("We disagree, and hold that no such legal duty [to investigate advertisers] rests upon" defendant magazine); *Hernandez*, 7 Media L. Rep. at 1536 (allegations that newspaper was placed on notice that advertising was false "failed to state a cause of action against Newsday because a newspaper has no duty to investigate each of the advertisers who purchase space in its paper"); *Pressler*, 450 N.Y.S.2d at 885, 8 Media L. Rep. at 1680 ("a newspaper has no duty to investigate each of the advertisers who purchases space in its publication"(citation omitted)); *see also* Manual Enters. v. Day, 370 U.S. 478, 493 (1962) (Harlan, Stewart, JJ.) ("publishers cannot practicably be expected to investigate each of their advertisers").
   [15]Curry v. Journal Pub'g Co., 68 P.2d 168 (N.M. 1937) (negligent infliction of emotional distress claim dismissed), *overruled on other grounds*, Ramirez v. Armstrong, 673 P.2d 822 (N.M. 1983); Tumminello v. Bergen Evening Record, 454 F. Supp. 1156, 3 Media L. Rep. 2547 (D.N.J. 1978) (intentional and negligent infliction of emotional distress claims dismissed); Indiana Constr. Corp. v. Chicago Tribune Co., 648 F. Supp. 1419, 1421, 13 Media L. Rep. 1863, 1865 (N.D. Ind. 1986) (summary judgment entered for newspaper defendant on negligence theory that newspaper had duty "not to lose" advertisement).
   [16]MacKown v. Illinois Pub'g & Printing Co., 6 N.E.2d 526 (Ill. App. Ct. 1937) (no negligence claim against newspaper that printed story about dandruff remedy that allegedly did not work) (this case is the basis for RESTATEMENT (SECOND) OF TORTS §552, cmt. c, illus. 2 (1977)); *Tumminello*, 454 F. Supp. 1156 (no claim for intentional or negligent infliction of emotional distress based on news story that incorrectly reported that statute of limitations for murder was five years, allegedly causing accused murderer great emotional distress); *Roman*, 442 N.Y.S.2d 945 (no negligence claim for erroneous statements in booklet about birth control); *Daniel*, 520 N.Y.S.2d at 335, 14 Media L. Rep. at 1996 (report about company's restructuring); *Gutter*, 490 N.E.2d at 901, 12 Media L. Rep. at 2001–02 (no claim for negligent misrepresentation in inaccurate report of bonds' trading status). *See also Curry*, 68 P.2d 168 (no negligent infliction of emotional distress claim against newspaper for erroneous report that former governor had died); Decker v. Princeton Packet, 561 A.2d 1122, 1128–29, 16 Media L. Rep. 2194, 2199–200 (N.J. 1989) (same, except plaintiff was not public figure); Herrick v. Evening Express Pub'g Co., 113 A. 16 (Me. 1921) (mother whose son's picture published with incorrect statement that he had died had no negligence claim against newspaper publisher), *overruled on different facts*, Culbert v. Sampson's Supermkts., 444 A.2d 433 (Me. 1982); Rubinstein v. New York Post, 488 N.Y.S.2d 331, 333–35, 11 Media L. Rep. 1329, 1330–31 (N.Y. Sup. Ct. 1985) (because publication of names of those who have died is matter of public interest, publishing incorrect notice that plaintiff was dead does not give rise to liability for negligence or for intentional infliction of emotional distress).
   [17]W. PROSSER, HANDBOOK ON THE LAW OF TORTS §107, at 708 (4th ed. 1971) (ticker tape case in quote is Jaillet v. Cashman, 189 N.Y.S. 743 (N.Y. Sup. Ct. 1921)). *Accord Gutter*, 490 N.E.2d at 902, 12 Media L. Rep. at 2002; *Yuhas*, 322 A.2d at 825; Demuth Dev. Corp. v. Merck & Co., 432 F. Supp. 990, 993–94, 3 Media L. Rep. 1092, 1094–95 (E.D.N.Y. 1977); First Equity of Fla. v. Standard & Poor's Corp., 670 F. Supp. 115, 117–18, 14 Media L. Rep. 1945, 1947–48 (S.D.N.Y. 1987); *Roman*, 442 N.Y.S.2d at 948.

Second, the courts have recognized that requiring the media to investigate every ad they broadcast or print is unrealistic and impractical.[18] While in the aggregate the media receive substantial income from carrying advertising, the cost of any individual advertisement is usually relatively small.[19] Because of the enormous variety of advertising that the media carry, the relatively small amounts that they receive for any given ad, the high costs of attempting to determine the truthfulness of most ads, and the impossibility of determining the truthfulness of many ads, it is economically and practically impossible for the media to investigate the truthfulness of every ad.[20]

It has been argued that these problems can be solved by requiring the media to investigate only where they have received complaints putting them on notice that certain ads might be false. However, this argument has also been rejected, because the media cannot be expected to serve as judge and jury between competing clients.[21] Otherwise, when anyone complained about any ad, the media would have to censor it to avoid liability for publishing false ads.[22] The pernicious effect of such a rule is self-evident. Political rivals could stop each others' ads by simply telling the media that the ads were false, while business rivals would have a ready method to stop each other from advertising their products. The real loser in such a situation would be the public, which would be deprived of valuable information about innumerable subjects.[23]

Courts have also refused to grant injunctions against the media in false advertising cases because such injunctions are prior restraints.[24]

---

[18]*Yuhas,* 322 A.2d at 825 ("To impose the suggested broad legal duty [to investigate advertisements] upon publishers of national circulated magazines, newspapers and other publications, would not only be impractical and unrealistic, but would have a staggering adverse effect on the commercial world and our economic system."); *Hernandez,* 7 Media L. Rep. at 1536 ("Logically, a newspaper cannot vouch for every product and service advertised in its paper."); *Manual Enters.,* 370 U.S. at 493.

[19]*See, e.g.,* Vaill v. Oneida Dispatch Corp., 493 N.Y.S.2d 414, 417 (N.Y. Sup. Ct. 1985) (classified ad cost three dollars).

[20]*Supra* note 18; *see* Cardozo v. True, 342 So. 2d 1053, 1055, 2 Media L. Rep. 1635, 1637 (Fla. Dist. Ct. App.) (retail book seller accused of selling book with dangerous recipes; court noted impracticability and enormous economic burden of requiring book seller to retain experts to test every recipe in book), *cert. denied,* 353 So. 2d 674 (Fla. 1977); Alm v. Van Nostrand Reinhold Co., 480 N.E.2d 1263 (Ill. App. Ct. 1985) (requiring publishers to test all procedures in publications would impermissibly infringe on public's right of access to ideas and publishers' right to disseminate those ideas); *Vaill,* 493 N.Y.S.2d at 416 (rejecting negligence claim because it would so raise cost of ads that such ads would stop or be seriously curtailed); Walters v. Seventeen Magazine, 241 Cal. Rptr. 101, 103 (Cal. Ct. App. 1987) (noting enormous costs of testing staffs and effect on media's insurance rates if such liability was imposed).

[21]*Supra* note 13.

[22]*Id.*

[23]Merrill, *First Amendment Protection for Commercial Advertising: The New Constitutional Doctrine,* 44 U. CHI. L. REV. 205, 252–53 (1976) ("To impose liability in this context [false advertising] on a showing of mere negligence could deter the media from distributing any advertising related to the product, thereby depriving the public of a valuable source of commercial information."); Demuth Dev. Corp. v. Merck & Co., 432 F. Supp. 990, 993–94, 3 Media L. Rep. 1092, 1094 (E.D.N.Y. 1977) (rejecting negligence claim against publisher because of "the overriding societal interest in the untrammeled dissemination of knowledge" and "because of [such a claim's] manifestly chilling effect upon the right to disseminate knowledge"); Gutter v. Dow Jones, Inc., 490 N.E.2d 898, 901–02, 12 Media L. Rep. 1999, 2001–02 (Ohio 1986) (follows *Demuth*). *See also supra* note 20.

[24]Quinn v. Aetna Life & Casualty Co., 409 N.Y.S.2d 473, 479, 482, 4 Media L. Rep. 1049, 1053, 1055 (N.Y. Sup. Ct. 1978) (preliminary injunction denied and media dismissed from suit to enjoin publication of insurance company's ads complaining about high jury awards). This case was then removed to federal court, where the defendant was alleged to have improperly attempted to influence jurors to lower verdict amounts; the insurance company was granted judgment on the pleadings. Quinn v. Aetna Life & Casualty Co., 482 F. Supp. 22, 5 Media L. Rep. 1310 (E.D.N.Y. 1979), *aff'd,* 616 F.2d 38, 5 Media L. Rep. 2432 (2d Cir. 1980). Silverman v. Oliver, 5 Media L. Rep. 1971 (Mass. Super. Ct. 1979) (injunction against newspaper's publication of future ads for auctioneer denied as prior restraint); Rutledge v. Liability Ins. Indus., 487 F. Supp. 5, 8–9, 5 Media L. Rep. 1153, 1155 (W.D. La. 1979) (preliminary injunction denied plaintiffs' attorney who claimed that defendant insurance industry's advertisements resulted in lower damage awards; court ruled

One trial court did hold a newspaper liable for using the wrong telephone number in an advertisement concerning single adults.[25] This case is wrongly decided:[26] it has not been followed by any other court, it does not discuss any of the cases that are contrary to it, and the newspaper defendant had repeatedly defaulted.[27] One other case reaching a similar result suffers from similar defects.[28]

§7.3(C) Strict Liability

In some cases it has been contended that the media should be liable without a showing of fault—e.g., for strict products liability, failure to warn, or breach of warranty. Because such theories seek to impose liability without fault, they have been even less successful than the negligence theory discussed in the preceding section.[29]

---

that prior restraint not justified, holding that advertisements not "commercial speech" per se because they represented information and industry's position on matter of public concern). For a detailed discussion of prior restraints, see Chapter 10.

[25]Blinick v. Long Island Daily Press Pub'g Co., 323 N.Y.S.2d 853 (N.Y. Sup. Ct. 1971), *appeal dismissed,* 337 N.Y.S.2d 859 (N.Y. App. Term 1972).

[26]Daniel v. Dow Jones & Co., 520 N.Y.S.2d 334, 339, 14 Media L. Rep. 1995, 1999 (N.Y. Sup. Ct. 1987) ("The only New York case to the contrary, [*Blinick*], does not correctly follow the cases finding liability for negligent misstatements, incorrectly evaluates the public policies requiring a free press to publish thousands of advertisements, and has been 'rejected' in this state and elsewhere . . . . *Blinick's* holding of liability for negligence is simply wrong."); Merrill, *supra* note 23, at 252 n.247 ("Unusual procedural aspects make the case [*Blinick*] suspect."); Vaill v. Oneida Dispatch Corp., 493 N.Y.S.2d 414, 416 (N.Y. Sup. Ct. 1985) (rejects *Blinick*); Tatta v. News Group Pubns., 12 Media L. Rep. 2318, 2319 (N.Y. Sup. Ct. 1986) ("it is far from certain that the [*Blinick*] court would have reached the same result had defendant been permitted to contest liability"); Pittman v. Dow Jones & Co., 662 F. Supp. 921, 922, 14 Media L. Rep. 1284, 1285 (E.D. La. 1987) (rejects *Blinick* because higher New York courts have also rejected it); Pressler v. Dow Jones & Co., 450 N.Y.S.2d 884, 885, 8 Media L. Rep. 1680 (N.Y. App. Div. 1982) (court grants summary judgment to defendant publisher for negligent publication of newspaper advertisement without even mentioning *Blinick*).

[27]*Blinick,* 323 N.Y.S.2d at 854.

[28]Vescovo v. New Way Enters., 130 Cal. Rptr. 86 (Cal. Ct. App. 1976). The *Los Angeles Free Press* published an ad saying: "Hot Lips—Deep Throat Sexy young bored housewife Norma—[plaintiff's address]." Its successful demurrer to Norma's daughter's claims for invasion of privacy, intentional infliction of emotional distress, and negligent infliction of emotional distress was reversed. As to the first two claims, the court found that Norma's daughter had pled that the advertisement was published " 'with intent and design to injure, disgrace and aggrieve' " her. 130 Cal. Rptr. at 89 (quoting plaintiff's first amended complaint). This was found to be sufficient to *plead* these intentional causes of action. *Id.* However, without any citation of direct authority, consideration of any of the cases discussed in this chapter, and any appearance by the defendant publisher, the court also held that the third claim for negligent infliction of emotional distress was sufficiently pled. *Id.* at 90. Because of these defects, this latter holding is of doubtful validity and has not been followed. *See also* Harms v. Miami Daily News, 127 So. 2d 715, 716 (Fla. Dist. Ct. App. 1961) (reversing dismissal of intrusion claim based on newspaper's publication of *article* stating: "Wanna hear a sexy telephone voice? Call [plaintiff's telephone number at work] and ask for Louise [plaintiff]."). The defendant's alleged level of fault, e.g., intentional or negligent, is unclear from the opinion; only the former should be actionable. RESTATEMENT (SECOND) OF TORTS §652B (1977); *Vaill,* 493 N.Y.S.2d at 414 (rejects negligence claim for ad soliciting "male companionship"); *Tatta,* 12 Media L. Rep. at 2318 (rejects negligence claim for ad about "adult entertainment").

[29]In Walter v. Bauer, 439 N.Y.S.2d 821 (N.Y. Sup. Ct. 1981), *aff'd in relevant part,* 451 N.Y.S.2d 533 (N.Y. App. Div. 1982), the court stated:

Discovering Science 4 [a textbook] cannot be said to be a defective product, for the infant plaintiff was not injured by use of the book for the purpose for which it was designed, i.e., to be read. More importantly perhaps, the danger of plaintiff's proposed theory is the chilling effect it would have on the First Amendment—Freedoms of Speech and Press. Would any author wish to be exposed to liability for writing on a topic which might result in physical injury? e.g. How to cut trees; How to keep bees?

439 N.Y.S.2d at 822–23. Smith v. Linn, 563 A.2d 123, 126, 16 Media L. Rep. 2228, 2231 (Pa. Super. Ct. 1989) ("no appellate court in any jurisdiction has held a book to be a product"), *aff'd,* 587 A.2d 309 (Pa. 1991); Jones v. J.B. Lippincott Co., 694 F. Supp. 1216, 1217, 15 Media L. Rep. 2155, 2156 (D. Md. 1988) ("No case has extended [Restatement (Second) of Torts] Section 402A [on products liability] to the dissemination of an idea or knowledge in books or other published material. Indeed to do so could chill expression and publication which is inconsistent with fundamental free speech principles . . . ."); Libertelli v. Hoffman-

§7.3(D) Impact of the First Amendment

Much but not all[30] advertising involves commercial speech.[31] Since at least 1975, commercial speech has been protected by the First Amendment.[32] However, the scope of First Amendment protection is less than that available to noncommercial speech,[33] although exactly how much less is not settled.[34]

The lesser First Amendment protection available to commercial speech arguably means that media carrying ads that consist of commercial speech are entitled to limited First Amendment protection. However, an analysis of the Supreme Court's reasons for giving commercial speech less protection than that given to other protected speech demonstrates that the media are entitled to full First Amendment protection when they carry ads, even when the ads are commercial speech.

The Supreme Court has given two justifications for treating commercial speech differently from other speech. First, "[t]he truth of commercial speech, for example, may be more easily verifiable than, let us say, news reporting or political commentary, in that ordinarily the advertiser seeks to disseminate information about a specific product or service that he himself provides and presumably knows more about than anyone else."[35]

However true this may be as to advertisers, it has no application to the media,[36] which carry advertising on subjects as diverse as horse breeding, laser technology, and the cost of traveling to Nepal, as the review of any newspaper's classified ads will show. The media cannot be expected to be experts on everything about which they publish ads.[37]

The Supreme Court's other rationale for treating commercial speech differently is that "commercial speech may be more durable than other kinds. Since advertising is the *sine qua non* of commercial profits, there is little

---

La Roche, Inc., 7 Media L. Rep. 1734 (S.D.N.Y. 1981) (rejecting failure to warn theory); Lewin v. McCreight, 655 F. Supp. 282, 13 Media L. Rep. 2454 (E.D. Mich. 1987) (rejecting claim against publisher of book for failure to warn of defective ideas in book about metalsmithing). *See also* Cardozo v. True, 342 So. 2d 1053, 1057, 2 Media L. Rep. 1635, 1638 (Fla. Dist. Ct. App. 1977) (rejecting liability without fault based on implied warranty under Uniform Commercial Code); Chapter 8. *See generally* Phillips, *Product Misrepresentation and the First Amendment*, 18 IDAHO L. REV. 395 (1982). *But see infra* §7.4 concerning maps.

[30]*See, e.g.,* New York Times Co. v. Sullivan, 376 U.S. 254, 1 Media L. Rep. 1527 (1964) (allegedly libelous ad concerning police treatment of civil rights demonstrators).

[31]Commercial speech is discussed in greater detail in Chapter 11.

[32]Bigelow v. Virginia, 421 U.S. 809, 818, 1 Media L. Rep. 1919, 1922–23 (1975).

[33]Virginia State Bd. of Pharmacy v. Virginia Citizens Consumers Council, 425 U.S. 748, 770–72, 1 Media L. Rep. 1930, 1938–39 (1976); Zauderer v. Office of Disciplinary Counsel, 471 U.S. 626 (1985).

[34]*See* Chapter 11.

[35]*Virginia State Bd. of Pharmacy,* 425 U.S. at 771 n.24, 1 Media L. Rep. at 1938–39 n.24. *See* Central Hudson Gas & Elec. Corp. v. Public Serv. Comm'n of N.Y., 447 U.S. 557, 564 n.6, 6 Media L. Rep. 1497, 1500 n.6 (1980) ("[C]ommercial speakers have extensive knowledge of both the market and their products. Thus, they are well situated to evaluate the accuracy of their messages and the lawfulness of the underlying activity."). The validity of this rationale has been questioned. *See, e.g.,* Lin, *Corporate Image Advertising and the First Amendment,* 61 S. CAL. L. REV. 459, 488–89 (1988).

[36]Merrill, *supra* note 23, at 251 ("The media are generally more vulnerable to the chilling effects of governmental regulation of advertising because they . . . lack the advertisers' access to the facts about specific products and services."). *See also* Farber, *Commercial Speech and First Amendment Theory,* 74 Nw. U. L. REV. 372 (1979):

> [C]ommercial speech is not necessarily more verifiable than other speech. There may well be uncertainty about some quality of a product, such as the health effects of eggs. . . . On the other hand, political speech is often quite verifiable by the speaker. A political candidate knows the truth about his own past and his present intentions, yet misrepresentations on these subjects are immune from state regulation.

Id. at 385–86.

[37]*See supra* note 20.

likelihood of its being chilled by proper regulation and forgone entirely."[38] Again, however true this rationale may be as to advertisers, it has little to do with the realities that confront the media, where turning down any one ad, which generates only a small portion of any medium's total revenue, is far easier and cheaper than being a defendant in a lawsuit.[39]

Accordingly, given the enormous importance of economic information in our society,[40] the media's central role in disseminating such information to the public,[41] and the inapplicability to the media of the rationales for lessening the First Amendment protection of commercial speech, the media should be entitled to full First Amendment protection when they carry advertisements—whether commercial or noncommercial.

Many cases that have considered the impact of the First Amendment on the media's liability for publishing or broadcasting false advertising have not discussed the commercial speech issue, although there are exceptions to this.[42] The courts have concluded, however, that the First Amendment bars any recovery against the media for the negligent publication of false advertisements.[43]

---

[38]*Virginia State Bd. of Pharmacy,* 425 U.S. at 771 n.24, 1 Media L. Rep. at 1938–39 n.24. *See Central Hudson Gas & Elec. Corp.,* 447 U.S. at 564 n.6, 6 Media L. Rep. at 1500 n.6 ("[C]ommercial speech, the offspring of economic self-interest, is a hardy breed of expression that is not 'particularly susceptible to being crushed by overbroad regulation.'" (citation omitted)). This rationale has also been questioned. *See, e.g.,* Lin, *supra* note 35, at 489–93.

[39]Merrill, *supra* note 23, at 251 ("The media are generally more vulnerable to the chilling effects of governmental regulation of advertising because they have less financial interest than advertisers in the distribution of any particular type of advertising"). *See also* Hill, *Defamation and Privacy Under the First Amendment,* 76 COLUM. L. REV. 1205, 1223 (1976) ("Whatever the liability that may be incurred by the advertiser, it is far from certain that the media must stand on the same footing."); Redish, *The Value of Free Speech,* 130 U. PA. L. REV. 591 (1982):

[I]t is also incorrect to distinguish commercial from political expression on the ground that the former is somehow hardier because of the inherent profit motive. It could just as easily be said that we need not fear that commercial magazines and newspapers will cease publication for fear of governmental regulation, because they are in business for profit. Of course, the proper response to this contention is not *whether* they will publish, but *what* they will publish: fear of regulation might deter them from dealing with controversial subjects.

Id. at 633.

[40]Advertising, however tasteless and excessive it sometimes may seem, is nonetheless dissemination of information as to who is producing and selling what product, for what reason, and at what price. So long as we preserve a predominantly free enterprise economy, the allocation of our resources in large measure will be made through numerous private economic decisions. It is a matter of public interest that those decisions, in the aggregate, be intelligent and well informed. To this end, the free flow of commercial information is indispensable. And if it is indispensable to the proper allocation of resources in a free enterprise system, it is also indispensable to the formation of intelligent opinions as to how that system ought to be regulated or altered. Therefore, even if the First Amendment were thought to be primarily an instrument to enlighten public decisionmaking in a democracy, we could not say that the free flow of information does not serve that goal.

Virginia State Bd. of Pharmacy, 425 U.S. at 765, 1 Media L. Rep. at 1936.

[41]Gutter v. Dow Jones, Inc., 490 N.E.2d 898, 901, 12 Media L. Rep. 1999, 2002 (Ohio 1986) (negligent misrepresentation claim may not be maintained for allegedly inaccurate bonds' listing; "[the] right to publish free of liability is guaranteed by the First Amendment . . . and the overriding societal interest in the untrammeled dissemination of knowledge"). *See also supra* note 20.

[42]Quinn v. Aetna Life & Casualty Co., 409 N.Y.S.2d 473, 479, 4 Media L. Rep. 1049, 1053 (N.Y. Sup. Ct. 1978) (commercial speech in the form of ads published by the media is fully protected by the First Amendment). *See also* Smith v. Linn, 563 A.2d 123, 125–26, 16 Media L. Rep. 2228, 2230 (Pa. Super. Ct. 1989) (rejecting arguments that diet books are not about matter of public concern); Daniel v. Dow Jones & Co., 520 N.Y.S.2d 334, 340, 14 Media L. Rep. 1995, 2000 (N.Y. Sup. Ct. 1987) (news report on company's restructuring not commercial speech); Rutledge v. Liability Ins. Indus., 487 F. Supp. 5, 5 Media L. Rep. 1153 (W.D. La. 1979) (insurance industry ads about high jury awards not commercial speech).

[43]Pittman v. Dow Jones & Co., 662 F. Supp. 921, 923, 14 Media L. Rep. 1284, 1286 (E.D. La. 1987) ("The First Amendment strongly counsels against adoption of a rule establishing the kind of liability [negligent misrepresentation] plaintiffs seek."); Demuth Dev. Corp. v. Merck & Co., 432 F. Supp. 990, 993–94, 3 Media L. Rep. 1092, 1094 (E.D.N.Y. 1977) (imposing liability for negligent misrepresentation would have "manifestly chilling effect upon the right to disseminate knowledge"); *see infra* note 44.

Liability in such situations may only be imposed if at least constitutional actual malice—publishing a statement with knowledge that a statement is false or with substantial doubts as to its truthfulness—is shown.[44]

§7.4 LIABILITY FOR THE PUBLICATION OF MAPS

In what appears to be the first important map case, *De Bardeleben Marine Corp. v. United States,* the United States was sued for publishing a map used by mariners that failed to show the location of a pipeline.[45] While the court noted cases holding that the media are not responsible for the negligent publication of false information, it distinguished these cases, noting that, unlike ordinary publishers with their much smaller resources, the government, with its greater financial resources, was unlikely to be deterred from speaking because of possible liability for negligent statements.[46] The court also noted that, unlike book or magazine publishers, cartographers must know that their maps will be relied on by their purchasers.[47] Accordingly, it found that the government could be liable for negligent errors in its maps.[48]

The court then found, however, that the government was not liable, because it published weekly notices that had corrected the error sufficiently before the accident so that "a prudent shipowner-navigator would have reasonably received" the notice of correction.[49]

This decision's application has been limited to cases where the government is the defendant,[50] but other cases have held that nongovernment map publishers can be liable for publishing erroneous maps.[51] However, attempts

---

[44]Tumminello v. Bergen Evening Record, 454 F. Supp. 1156, 1159–60, 3 Media L. Rep. 2547, 2549 (D.N.J. 1978); Libertelli v. Hoffman-La Roche, Inc., 7 Media L. Rep. 1734, 1736 (S.D.N.Y. 1981); Merrill, *supra* note 23, at 252–53. *See also* First Equity of Fla. v. Standard & Poor's Corp., 690 F. Supp. 256, 258, 15 Media L. Rep. 1858, 1861 (S.D.N.Y. 1988).

[45]451 F.2d 140 (5th Cir. 1971); *see generally* McCowan, *Liability of the Chartmaker,* 47 INS. COUNS. J. 359 (1980); Fadely, *Liabilities of the United States for Negligent Charting,* 21 TORT & INS. L.J. 171 (1985).

[46]451 F.2d at 148. *See also* Reminga v. United States, 631 F.2d 449 (6th Cir. 1980) (Federal Aviation Administration required to use due care in publishing accurate charts); Murray v. United States, 327 F. Supp. 835 (D. Utah 1971), *modified on other grounds,* 463 F.2d 208 (10th Cir. 1972) (government negligent in publishing inaccurate information on runway lighting); Sullivan v. United States, 299 F. Supp. 621 (N.D. Ala. 1968), *aff'd,* 411 F.2d 794 (5th Cir. 1969) (government had duty to ascertain accuracy of information in chart relied on by pilots).

[47]451 F.2d at 148.

[48]*Id.* at 148–49.

[49]*Id.* at 149.

[50]First Equity of Fla. v. Standard & Poor's Corp., 670 F. Supp. 115, 117 n.4, 14 Media L. Rep. 1945, 1947 n.4 (S.D.N.Y. 1987).

[51]Aetna Casualty & Sur. Co. v. Jeppesen & Co., 642 F.2d 339, 343 (9th Cir. 1981) (upholding as "not clearly erroneous" district court's determination that airline map was defective product; court does not discuss any cases discussed in this chapter or its reasoning); Saloomey v. Jeppesen & Co., 707 F.2d 671, 676–77 (2d Cir. 1983) (because airline maps are mass produced, they are products, so cartographers are strictly liable for contents; court does not discuss any cases discussed in this chapter); Fluor Corp. v. Jeppesen & Co., 170 Cal. App. 3d 468, 474, 216 Cal. Rptr. 68 (Cal. Ct. App. 1985) (adopting *Saloomey*'s rationale). *Saloomey*'s rationale is untenable. Since most publications are mass produced, if mass production alone is sufficient to impose strict liability, almost all publishers would be strictly liable for the contents of their publications. *See supra* §7.3(C). Brocklesby v. United States, 767 F.2d 1288, 1294–95 (9th Cir. 1985), *cert. denied,* 474 U.S. 1101 (1986), also holds that cartographers are strictly liable for defective maps if they are mass produced. (*Brocklesby* refused to consider a First Amendment defense because it was not raised below. 767 F.2d at 1295 n.9.) *But see* Times Mirror Co. v. Sisk, 593 P.2d 924, 927 (Ariz. 1978) ("Although we have serious misgivings about whether this is a products liability case [map for airlines], we need not decide this issue . . . ."; publisher of instrument approach chart for planes not liable under strict liability and breach of warranty theories absent conclusive showing that chart was defective, unreasonably dangerous, and proximate cause of plane accident).

to extend the map cases to the publishers of other items, such as books, have been squarely rejected.[52]

§7.5 LIABILITY FOR ENDORSING ADVERTISED PRODUCTS

If a broadcaster or publisher explicitly endorses the products whose ads it carries,[53] an exception exists to the general rule that the media are not liable for negligently publishing false advertisements or other similar false statements.[54]

The leading case in this area is *Hanberry v. Hearst Corp.*, where the plaintiff alleged she was injured while wearing shoes that had slippery soles.[55] Among others, she sued the publisher of *Good Housekeeping* magazine because it had carried ads for her shoes, and those ads stated that the shoes had received the "Good Housekeeping's Consumers' Guaranty Seal."[56] With respect to such seals, *Good Housekeeping* stated: "We satisfy ourselves that products advertised in Good Housekeeping are good ones and that the advertising claims made for them in our magazine are truthful."[57] After noting that *Good Housekeeping* endorsed goods for its own economic benefit and with the purpose of inducing consumers to purchase goods it endorsed, the court held that the plaintiff had stated a claim for negligent misrepresentation, although not for breach of warranty or for strict products liability.[58]

A somewhat similar case is *Romanski v. Prairie Farmer*.[59] When the plaintiff farmers did not receive the prefabricated building they had ordered after seeing an ad in the defendant newspaper, they sued both the building's manufacturer and the newspaper.[60] As to the latter, the plaintiffs relied on the following alleged guarantee, which appeared in each issue of the defendant newspaper: "PRAIRIE FARMER refuses to publish dishonest advertising. We guarantee our cooperation to subscribers in obtaining fair treatment and reasonable adjustments from advertisers in case any misunderstandings arise, providing subscribers mention Prairie Farmer, when writing to advertisers."[61]

---

[52]*First Equity of Fla.*, 670 F. Supp. at 118 n.5, 14 Media L. Rep. at 1948 n.5; Smith v. Linn, 563 A.2d 123, 127, 16 Media L. Rep. 2228, 2231 (Pa. Super. Ct. 1989) ("In those cases [maps], extremely technical and detailed materials were involved, upon which a limited class of persons imposed absolute trust having reason to believe in their unqualified reliability. As such they took on the attributes of a product and are not protected by the first amendment."); Jones v. J.B. Lippincott Co., 694 F. Supp. 1216, 1217, 15 Media L. Rep. 2155, 2156 (D. Md. 1988) ("Courts have applied strict liability to the narrow area of published maps or charts.... The underlying theory for these rulings is the analogy of a nautical chart or an airline chart to other instruments of navigation such as a compass or radar finder which, when defective, will prove to be dangerous.").

[53]*See generally* Annot., Liability of Product Indorser or Certifier for Product-Caused Injury, 39 A.L.R.3d 181 (1971).

[54]Yuhas v. Mudge, 322 A.2d 824, 825 (N.J. Super. Ct. App. Div. 1974) (magazine publisher has no duty to investigate advertisements "unless it undertakes to guarantee, warrant or endorse the product"); Suarez v. Underwood, 426 N.Y.S.2d 208, 210, 6 Media L. Rep. 1094, 1096 (N.Y. Sup. Ct. 1980) (publisher has no duty to investigate advertisements unless it guarantees, warrants, or endorses advertised products); Libertelli v. Hoffman-La Roche, Inc., 7 Media L. Rep. 1734, 1735 (S.D.N.Y. 1981) (publisher has no legal duty to verify advertised claims unless it warrants or guarantees advertised product).

[55]81 Cal. Rptr. 519 (Cal. Ct. App. 1969).
[56]*Id.* at 521.
[57]*Id.*
[58]*Id.* at 524.
[59]371 N.E.2d 109 (Ill. App. Ct. 1977).
[60]*Id.* at 109–11.
[61]*Id.* at 110.

The court held that the first sentence was only a promise not to publish advertising that was known to be false.[62] The court rejected the plaintiffs' contention that the newspaper had obligated itself to police its advertisers, finding "[s]uch an interpretation would go far beyond what is customary, practicable, or even possible for a newspaper to do and far beyond what its quoted statement obligated it to do."[63] As to the second sentence, the court found that the newspaper had fully cooperated with the plaintiffs in trying to help them recover their money.[64]

These cases make it clear that the media can impose additional duties on themselves by making explicit guarantees about things that they advertise, so such statements should be carefully scrutinized before publication.

§7.6 STATUTORY LIABILITY FOR FALSE ADVERTISING

Various federal statutes prohibit false advertising;[65] the Federal Trade Commission Act is the most important of these.[66] Section 53 of the Act gives the Federal Trade Commission (FTC) the power to issue injunctions to restrain the use of such advertising.[67] However, a special exemption from these injunctions is provided for the press.[68] Similar protection is also given to the media where injunctive relief is sought against trademark infringement and other violations of the Lanham Act.[69]

---

[62]*Id.* at 111.
[63]*Id.* at 112.
[64]371 N.E.2d at 112.
[65]Many of these statutes are collected in 1 ROSDEN, THE LAW OF ADVERTISING §11.01[2] (1991); Note, *The Regulation of Advertising*, 56 COLUM. L. REV. 1018, 1097–98 (1956).
[66]15 U.S.C. §§41–77 (1989). *See generally* 2 KANWIT, FEDERAL TRADE COMMISSION, ch. 22 (1991); Annot., *What Constitutes False, Misleading, or Deceptive Advertising or Promotional Practices Subject to Action by Federal Trade Commission*, 65 A.L.R.2d 225 (1959).
[67]15 U.S.C. §53(a) (1989).
[68]*Id.* §53(c):
Exception of periodical publications
　Whenever it appears to the satisfaction of the court in the case of a newspaper, magazine, periodical, or other publication, published at regular intervals—
　(1) that restraining the dissemination of a false advertisement in any particular issue of such publication would delay the delivery of such issue after the regular time therefor, and
　(2) that such delay would be due to the method by which the manufacture and distribution of such publication is customarily conducted by the publisher in accordance with sound business practice, and not to any method or device adopted for the evasion of this section or to prevent or delay the issuance of an injunction or restraining order with respect to such false advertisement or any other advertisement,
the court shall exclude such issue from the operation of the restraining order or injunction.
See also Chapter 10 on prior restraints.
[69]15 U.S.C. §1114(2)(b) and (c) (1989):
(b) Where the infringement or violation complained of is contained in or is part of paid advertising matter in a newspaper, magazine, or other similar periodical or in an electronic communication as defined in section 2510(12) of Title 18, the remedies of the owner of the right infringed or person bringing the action under section 1125(a) of this title as against the publisher or distributor of such newspaper, magazine, or other similar periodical or electronic communication shall be limited to an injunction against the presentation of such advertising matter in future issues of such newspapers, magazines, or other similar periodicals or in future transmissions of such electronic communications. The limitations of this subparagraph shall apply only to innocent infringers and innocent violators.
(c) Injunctive relief shall not be available to the owner of the right infringed or person bringing the action under section 1125(a) of this title with respect to an issue of a newspaper, magazine, or other similar periodical or an electronic communication containing infringing matter or violating matter where restraining the dissemination of such infringing matter or violating matter in any particular issue of such periodical or in an electronic communication would delay the delivery of such issue or transmission of such electronic communication after the regular time for such delivery or transmission, and such delay would be due to the method by which publication and distribution of such periodical or transmission of such

Special provisions also limit the media's liability for financial penalties.[70] In recent years, the extension of First Amendment protection to commercial speech has been used to limit the relief obtained by the FTC in advertising cases.[71]

The most important restrictions on false advertising at the state level are statutes based on the Printers' Ink Model Statute, which was drafted in 1911 by *Printers' Ink* magazine.[72] However, many states exempt the media from liability for publishing false advertising unless they had actual knowledge of the falsity.[73] The constitutionality of such statutes has been upheld, at least where they provide that the media are only liable when they intentionally publish false advertising.[74] This is consistent with the First Amendment.[75]

Similarly, the Uniform Deceptive Trade Practices Act exempts the media from liability for publishing deceptive material if it is done "without knowledge of its deceptive character."[76] Thus, these laws are generally consistent with the common law rule that the media are not liable for negligently published false statements.[77]

---

electronic communication is customarily conducted in accordance with sound business practice, and not due to any method or device adopted to evade this section or to prevent or delay the issuance of an injunction or restraining order with respect to such infringing matter or violating matter.

[70]*Id.* §54(b):
Exception of advertising medium or agency
No publisher, radio-broadcast licensee, or agency or medium for the dissemination of advertising, except the manufacturer, packer, distributor, or seller of the commodity to which the false advertisement relates, shall be liable under this section by reason of the dissemination by him of any false advertisement, unless he has refused, on the request of the Commission, to furnish the Commission the name and post-office address of the manufacturer, packer, distributor, seller, or advertising agency, residing in the United States, who caused him to disseminate such advertisement. No advertising agency shall be liable under this section by reason of the causing by it of the dissemination of any false advertisement, unless it has refused, on the request of the Commission, to furnish the Commission the name and post-office address of the manufacturer, packer, distributor, or seller, residing in the United States, who caused it to cause the dissemination of such advertisement.

[71]*See, e.g.,* Standard Oil Co. v. Federal Trade Comm'n, 577 F.2d 653, 662–63, 4 Media L. Rep. 1459, 1466–67 (9th Cir. 1978) (cease and desist order enjoining *all* advertising creating misleading impression ordered modified to refer to challenged product only); National Comm'n on Egg Nutrition v. Federal Trade Comm'n, 570 F.2d 157, 164, 3 Media L. Rep. 2196, 2202 (7th Cir. 1977) (court modified order requiring future ads to specify medical experts' belief that eggs increased risk of heart disease because it interfered "unnecessarily with the effective presentation of the pro-egg position" and therefore was overly broad under First Amendment), *cert. denied,* 439 U.S. 821 (1978); Warner-Lambert Co. v. Federal Trade Comm'n, 562 F.2d 749, 758, 2 Media L. Rep. 2303, 2309 (D.C. Cir. 1977) (commission has "special responsibility [triggered by the First Amendment] . . . to order corrective advertising only if the restriction . . . is no greater than necessary to serve the interest involved"), *cert. denied,* 435 U.S. 950 (1978); Beneficial Corp. v. Federal Trade Comm'n, 542 F.2d 611, 619 (3d Cir. 1976) (First Amendment allows prior restraint on protected commercial speech to go no farther "than is reasonably necessary to accomplish the remedial objective of preventing the violation"), *cert. denied,* 430 U.S. 983 (1977). *But see* Grolier Inc. v. Federal Trade Comm'n, 699 F.2d 983, 988 (9th Cir.) (FTC given greater discretion in regulating commercial speech by door-to-door encyclopedia salespeople because of potential for abuse), *cert. denied,* 464 U.S. 891 (1983); United States v. Reader's Digest Ass'n, 662 F.2d 955, 965, 7 Media L. Rep. 1921, 1924 (3d Cir. 1981) (First Amendment does not require FTC to show actual deception to establish violation of consent decree), *cert. denied,* 455 U.S. 908 (1982); Jay Norris, Inc. v. Federal Trade Comm'n, 598 F.2d 1244, 1252 (2d Cir.) (requirement of written substantiation in mail order advertising not impermissible prior restraint under First Amendment), *cert. denied,* 444 U.S. 980 (1979). *See generally* Chapter 11 on commercial speech.

[72]Note, *supra* note 65, at 1058; State v. Beacon Pub'g Co., 42 P.2d 960, 963 (Kan. 1935); Comment, *Responsibility for Illness Caused by Defamation of Plaintiff,* 36 YALE L.J. 1148 (1927). For a list of such statutes, see 2 ROSDEN, THE LAW OF ADVERTISING §16.02 (1973); Note, *supra* note 65, at 1098–99.

[73]*Developments in the Law—Deceptive Advertising,* 80 HARV. L. REV. 1005, 1152 n.128 and accompanying text (1967); Note, *supra* note 65, at 1059–60, nn. 252–53; *see, e.g.,* CAL. BUS. & PROF. CODE §17502 (Deering 1976).

[74]Note, *supra* note 65, at 1063 n.277; *Beacon Pub'g Co.,* 42 P.2d at 964.

[75]*See supra* §7.3(D).

[76]UNIF. DECEPTIVE TRADE PRAC. ACT §4(a)(2), 7A U.L.A. 88 (1985) ("This Act [1964 Act] does not apply to . . . publishers, broadcaster, printers, or other persons engaged in the dissemination of information or reproduction of printed or pictorial matter who publish, broadcast, or reproduce material without knowledge of its deceptive character").

[77]*See supra* §7.3(B).

§7.7 LIABILITY FOR ADVERTISING ILLEGAL ACTS

Some cases have been brought on the theory that the media are liable for physical injuries that result when they publish an advertisement that offers illegal goods or services. In *Eimann v. Soldier of Fortune Magazine*,[78] the decedent's son and mother contended that she was killed by an assassin hired by her husband through an advertisement published by the defendant, *Soldier of Fortune* magazine (SOF).[79] The advertisement read: "EX-MARINES—67–69 'Nam Vets, Ex-DI, weapons specialist—jungle warfare, pilot, M.E., high risk assignments, U.S. or overseas. [phone number]."[80]

At the trial, which resulted in a jury verdict of $9.4 million for the plaintiffs, the assassin testified that 90 percent of the responses to the ad sought his help with illegal acts.[81] The Fifth Circuit reversed the jury's verdict and ordered the entry of judgment for the defendants, finding that they owed the plaintiffs no duty of care.[82]

In reaching this conclusion, the court noted that the gravity of the threatened harm was great, because it involved serious crimes—extortion and jailbreaks—and that the probability that the ads contributed to such harm was "more than a remote risk," because nine of SOF's some 2,000 classified ads printed between 1975 and 1984 had served as links in crimes.[83] Turning to the burden of preventing harm, the court noted that the ad at issue did not constitute a readily identifiable criminal solicitation, because it was fundamentally ambiguous.[84] To impose liability for publishing such ambiguous ads would be especially burdensome, because it "would open the doors 'to a liability in an indeterminate amount for an indeterminate time to an indeterminate class.'"[85] This would force the media to reject all ambiguous ads, which would cause an "economic crunch" on editorial content as a result of lost advertising revenue.[86]

After noting that many everyday activities, such as driving on freeways, pose substantial risks of great harm, the court concluded that "[g]iven the pervasiveness of advertising in our society and the important role it plays, we decline to impose on publishers the obligation to reject all ambiguous advertisements for products or services that might pose a threat of harm."[87]

The court did not reach the First Amendment issues in the case,[88] but it did rely on First Amendment cases to support its conclusion that publishers do not have a duty to reject all ambiguous advertisements and cited various cases involving commercial speech to highlight the important role that such

---

[78] 880 F.2d 830, 16 Media L. Rep. 2148 (5th Cir. 1989), *cert. denied*, 493 U.S. 1024 (1990). *But see* Norwood v. Soldier of Fortune Magazine, 651 F. Supp. 1397, 13 Media L. Rep. 2025 (W.D. Ark. 1987).
[79] 880 F.2d at 831, 16 Media L. Rep. at 2149.
[80] *Id.*
[81] *Id.*
[82] *Id.* at 831, 16 Media L. Rep. at 2151.
[83] *Id.* at 835, 16 Media L. Rep. at 2152–53.
[84] 880 F.2d at 835–36, 16 Media L. Rep. at 2153.
[85] *Id.* at 837, 16 Media L. Rep. at 2154 (citing Yuhas v. Mudge, 322 A.2d 824 (N.J. Super. Ct. App. Div. 1974)).
[86] *Id.* (citing Walters v. Seventeen Magazine, 241 Cal. Rptr. 101 (Cal. Ct. App. 1987)).
[87] *Id.* at 837–38, 16 Media L. Rep. at 2154–55. This duty analysis is similar to that in misrepresentation cases. *See supra* §7.3(B).
[88] 880 F.2d at 834 & n.1, 16 Media L. Rep. at 2151 & n.1.

communications have.[89] The court found this relevant in weighing the risks involved in publishing the ads against the burden of imposing a duty to reject all ambiguous ads.[90]

In a more recent SOF case, *Eimann* was distinguished on the grounds that the ad included somewhat different words, including "other special skills" and "all jobs considered" and on the basis of different jury instructions.[91] These word differences are not substantial, while the differences in jury instructions are irrelevant, because the Fifth Circuit in *Eimann* did not remand for a new trial—it dismissed the entire case. The defendant's First Amendment defense was rejected on the grounds that the ad was commercial speech.[92] Because the Supreme Court denied certiorari, the conflict between these cases remains unresolved.

---

[89] *Id.* at 836–37, 16 Media L. Rep. at 2153–54.

[90] *Id.*

[91] Braun v. Soldier of Fortune Magazine, 968 F.2d 1110, 1115–16, 1121, 20 Media L. Rep. 1777, 1781, 1786 (11th Cir. 1992), *cert. denied,* 113 S. Ct. 1028 (1993). The ad in *Braun* stated: "GUN FOR HIRE: 37 year old professional mercenary desires jobs. Vietnam Veteran. Discrete [sic] and very private. Body guard, courier, and other special skills. All jobs considered."

[92] *Id.* at 1116–20, 20 Media L. Rep. at 1782–85 ("we conclude that the First Amendment permits a state to impose upon a publisher liability for compensatory damages for negligently publishing a commercial advertisement where the ad on its face, and without the need for investigation, makes it apparent that there is a substantial danger of harm to the public." (footnote omitted)). *Compare supra* §7.3(D).

CHAPTER 8

IMITATION AND INCITEMENT

§8.1 INTRODUCTION

This chapter discusses the media's liability for broadcasting or publishing information that allegedly causes people to imitate or engage in dangerous or violent acts that they have seen, heard, or read about.[1] Section 8.2 discusses the cases that establish the general rule that the media are not liable for viewers' acts in such situations,[2] while Section 8.3 discusses the one imitation case in which the plaintiffs prevailed.[3] Section 8.4 discusses the reasons why the constitutional actual malice test is not the proper standard of fault in imitation cases.

§8.2 THE GENERAL RULE: NO MEDIA LIABILITY

The cases on point have involved a variety of facts, including:
(1) a plaintiff who allegedly was subliminally intoxicated and desensitized by watching 10 years of "violent" television programming that purportedly caused him to shoot his elderly neighbor to death;[4]

---

[1] The relevant cases will collectively be referred to as "imitation" cases, although this is a slight misnomer since some people who committed the illegal or dangerous acts were allegedly influenced by broadcasts but did not really imitate what they saw. *See* cases cited *infra* notes 3, 16, and 17 and text accompanying notes 16 and 17.

[2] Zamora v. Columbia Broadcasting Sys., 480 F. Supp. 199, 5 Media L. Rep. 2109 (S.D. Fla. 1979); Walt Disney Prods. v. Shannon, 276 S.E.2d 580, 7 Media L. Rep. 1209 (Ga. 1981); Olivia N. v. National Broadcasting Co. (Olivia N. II), 178 Cal. Rptr. 888, 7 Media L. Rep. 2359 (Cal. Ct. App. 1981), *cert. denied,* 458 U.S. 1108 (1982); DeFilippo v. National Broadcasting Co., 446 A.2d 1036, 8 Media L. Rep. 1872 (R.I. 1982); Bill v. Superior Ct., 187 Cal. Rptr. 625, 8 Media L. Rep. 2622 (Cal. Ct. App. 1982); Herceg v. Hustler Magazine, 814 F.2d 1017, 13 Media L. Rep. 2345 (5th Cir. 1987), *cert. denied,* 485 U.S. 959 (1988); McCollum v. CBS Inc., 249 Cal. Rptr. 187, 15 Media L. Rep. 2001 (Cal. Ct. App. 1988); Yakubowicz v. Paramount Pictures Corp., 536 N.E.2d 1067, 16 Media L. Rep. 1725 (Mass. 1989); Sakon v. Pepsico, 553 So. 2d 163, 17 Media L. Rep. 1277 (Fla. 1989); Watters v. TSR, Inc., 715 F. Supp. 819 (W.D. Ky. 1989), *aff'd on other grounds,* 904 F.2d 378 (6th Cir. 1990).

[3] Weirum v. RKO Gen., 539 P.2d 36 (Cal. 1975); *see also* Vance v. Judas Priest, 16 Media L. Rep. 2241 (Nev. Dist. Ct. 1989) (denying defendants' summary judgment motion where plaintiffs alleged that audio subliminal messages in record album caused decedents' suicides). *But see* Waller v. Osbourne, 763 F. Supp. 1144 (M.D. Ga. 1991) (granting summary judgment because of no showing of subliminal message).

[4] *Zamora,* 480 F. Supp. 199. Ronny Zamora's private suit against the networks followed his unsuccessful attempt to base his insanity defense in his criminal case on "involuntary subliminal television intoxication." Because Florida did not recognize irresistible impulse or diminished capacity as a defense, the trial judge refused to allow a psychologist to testify about the effect of television violence on adolescent viewers. Zamora v. State, 361 So. 2d 776 (Fla. Dist. Ct. App. 1978), *cert. denied,* 372 So. 2d 472 (Fla. 1979). Later, Zamora unsuccessfully sought to overturn his murder conviction in part on the ground that his counsel

(2) a plaintiff who, after watching a demonstration on television's "Mickey Mouse Club" about how to reproduce the sound of a tire coming off a car by putting a BB pellet inside a "large round balloon, filling the balloon with air, and rotating the BB inside the balloon," allegedly attempted to repeat the demonstration using a piece of lead twice the size of a BB and a "large skinny balloon" and was partially blinded when his balloon exploded and propelled the lead into his eye;[5]

(3) a plaintiff who was raped with a soda bottle on a San Francisco beach by minors who were allegedly imitating a scene from the television movie *Born Innocent,* in which a young girl in a juvenile home appears to be raped by other girls with a plunger while she is in the shower;[6]

(4) a 13-year-old who hung himself to death while allegedly imitating a segment of "The Tonight Show" in which a professional stuntman, after demonstrating how hangings are staged for movies, staged a mock hanging of Johnny Carson;[7]

(5) a plaintiff who alleged that, while walking down a street from a theater to a bus stop after attending the movie *Boulevard Nights,* she was shot by someone who had been attracted to the theater by the showing of this "violent" movie;[8]

(6) a 14-year-old who died while allegedly attempting to engage in autoerotic asphyxiation as described in a *Hustler Magazine* article entitled "Orgasm of Death;"[9] and

(7) a 19-year-old who shot and killed himself while listening to Ozzy Ozbourne music, which his parents claimed incited him to commit suicide.[10]

The plaintiffs in these cases have usually been minors, and they have often been joined in their lawsuits by their parents.[11] The defendants have usually been television broadcasters but have also included magazine publishers, movie producers, musicians, and others involved in the production and distribution of information.[12]

---

ineffectively assisted him by failing to object to the "prejudicial" presence of television cameras in the courtroom. His was the first criminal case televised in Florida. Zamora v. State, 422 So. 2d 325 (Fla. Dist. Ct. App. 1982). On subliminal messages, *see also Waller,* 763 F. Supp. 1144; *Watters,* 715 F. Supp. 819 (W.D. Ky. 1989); *Vance,* 16 Media L. Rep. 2241.

[5] *Walt Disney,* 276 S.E.2d 580. This case is discussed with approval in Moody, *Broadcast Negligence and the First Amendment,* 33 MERCER L. REV. 423 (1981).

[6] *Olivia N. II,* 178 Cal. Rptr. 888.

[7] DeFilippo v. National Broadcasting Co., 446 A.2d 1036, 8 Media L. Rep. 1872 (R.I. 1982). *See also* Sakon v. Pepsico, 553 So. 2d 163, 17 Media L. Rep. 1277 (Fla. 1989), which involved imitation of a commercial where young people rode their bicycles off a ramp and landed in a lake.

[8] Bill v. Superior Ct., 187 Cal. Rptr. 625, 8 Media L. Rep. 2622 (Cal. Ct. App. 1982). *See also* Yakubowicz v. Paramount Pictures Corp., 536 N.E.2d 1067, 16 Media L. Rep. 1725 (Mass. 1989), which involved a stabbing after a showing of the movie *The Warriors.*

[9] Herceg v. Hustler Magazine, 814 F.2d 1017, 13 Media L. Rep. 2345 (5th Cir. 1987), *cert. denied,* 485 U.S. 959 (1988).

[10] McCollum v. CBS Inc., 249 Cal. Rptr. 187, 15 Media L. Rep. 2001 (Cal. Ct. App. 1988). *See also* Waller v. Osbourne, 763 F. Supp. 1144 (M.D. Ga. 1991); Vance v. Judas Priest, 16 Media L. Rep. 2241 (Nev. Dist. Ct. 1989).

[11] *See, e.g., Zamora* v. Columbia Broadcasting Sys., 480 F. Supp. 199, 5 Media L. Rep. 2109 (S.D. Fla. 1979) (15-year-old and his parents); Walt Disney Prods. v. Shannon, 216 S.E.2d 580, 7 Media L. Rep. 1209 (Ga. 1981) (11-year-old); Olivia N. II, 178 Cal. Rptr. 888, 7 Media L. Rep. 2359 (Cal. Ct. App. 1981), *cert. denied,* 458 U.S. 1108 (1982) (nine-year-old); *DeFilippo,* 446 A.2d 1036 (parents of deceased 13-year-old in their roles as co-administrators of their son's estate, as individuals, and as his parents); *Bill,* 187 Cal. Rptr. 625 (minor and her mother); *Herceg,* 814 F.2d 1017 (plaintiffs sued over death of their 14-year-old son and brother); *Yakubowicz,* 536 N.E.2d 1067 (father as administrator of deceased son's estate).

[12] *See, e.g., Zamora,* 480 F. Supp. 199 (three major television networks); *Walt Disney,* 276 S.E.2d 580 (producer, syndicator, and broadcaster of television show); *Olivia N. II,* 178 Cal. Rptr. 888 (television network and television station); *DeFilippo,* 446 A.2d 1036 (television network, television station owner, and

Ordinarily, the plaintiffs have contended that their injuries resulted from specific broadcasts or publications, although in one case it was claimed that injury resulted from unspecified television broadcasts over a 10-year period.[13] The plaintiffs have also usually argued that they injured themselves by imitating the broadcasts or publications they saw[14] or that someone else injured them while imitating what that person had seen in the media.[15] Strictly speaking, however, some of these cases do not involve imitation. In one of them, the minor plaintiff contended that he could no longer control his murderous tendencies because he had seen too many "violent" television broadcasts.[16] In another case, the minor plaintiff contended that a movie's "violent" content attracted violent people to the vicinity of a movie theater where she was shot.[17]

In all of these cases the plaintiffs sought to impose a duty of care on the media using virtually every conceivable theory, including subliminal intoxication and intentional infliction of emotional distress,[18] adults as "Pied Pipers" who mislead children,[19] negligence and recklessness,[20] failure to warn,[21] implied misrepresentation,[22] attractive nuisance,[23] and strict product liability.[24] In each of these cases the injuries resulted in death or were otherwise quite severe.[25]

---

commercial sponsors of television broadcast); *Bill*, 187 Cal. Rptr. 625 (executive producer, producer, director, and production company of movie); *Herceg*, 814 F.2d 1017 (magazine publisher); *McCollum*, 249 Cal. Rptr. 187 (musician and record company); *Yakubowicz*, 536 N.E.2d 1067 (movie production company and theater).

[13]*Zamora*, 480 F. Supp. 199. *See also* Watters v. TSR, Inc., 715 F. Supp. 819 (W.D. Ky. 1989), *aff'd on other grounds*, 904 F.2d 378 (6th Cir. 1990), which involved five years of playing a game—Dungeons and Dragons.

[14]*Walt Disney*, 276 S.E.2d 580; *DeFilippo*, 446 A.2d 1036; *Herceg*, 814 F.2d 1017; *McCollum*, 249 Cal. Rptr. 187.

[15]*Olivia N. II*, 178 Cal. Rptr. 888.

[16]*Zamora*, 480 F. Supp. 199. *See also Watters*, 715 F. Supp. 819, which involved a claim that playing a game caused the plaintiff to lose control and commit suicide.

[17]Bill v. Superior Ct., 187 Cal. Rptr. 625, 8 Media L. Rep. 2622 (Cal. Ct. App. 1982). *See also* Yakubowicz v. Paramount Pictures Corp., 536 N.E.2d 1067, 16 Media L. Rep. 1725 (Mass. 1989).

[18]*Zamora*, 480 F. Supp. at 202 n.1, 5 Media L. Rep. at 2111 n.1. *See generally* Bernstein, *First Amendment Limits on Tort Liability for Words Intended to Inflict Severe Emotional Distress*, 85 COLUM. L. REV. 1749 (1985).

[19]Walt Disney Prods. v. Shannon, 276 S.E.2d 580, 583, 7 Media L. Rep. 1209, 1211–12 (Ga. 1981). The court found that the "Pied Piper" cases contained two elements:

(1) there must be an express or implied invitation extended to the child to do something posing a foreseeable risk of injury; and (2) the defendant must be chargeable with maintaining or providing the child with the instrumentality causing the injury. In this case, the first element is arguably present, but the second element is undisputably absent.

Id. The court indicated without explanation or citation of authority, however, that an adult's invitation to a child could alone be the basis for liability, at least in some situations, but only if "what the adult invited the child to do presented a clear and present danger that injury would in fact result." 276 S.E.2d at 583, 7 Media L. Rep. at 1212.

[20]Olivia N. II, 178 Cal. Rptr. 888, 890, 7 Media L. Rep. 2359, 2360 (Cal. Ct. App. 1981), *cert. denied*, 458 U.S. 1108 (1982); DeFilippo v. National Broadcasting Co., 446 A.2d 1036, 1038, 8 Media L. Rep. 1872, 1873 (R.I. 1982); Herceg v. Hustler Magazine, 814 F.2d 1017, 1019, 13 Media L. Rep. 2345, 2345–46 (5th Cir. 1987); McCollum v. CBS Inc., 249 Cal. Rptr. 187, 189, 15 Media L. Rep. 2001, 2002 (Cal. Ct. App. 1988).

[21]*DeFilippo*, 446 A.2d at 1038, 8 Media L. Rep. at 1873; *Bill*, 187 Cal. Rptr. at 626, 8 Media L. Rep. at 2623; Sakon v. Pepsico, 553 So. 2d 163, 167, 17 Media L. Rep. 1277, 1280–81 (Fla. 1989) (discusses issue at length).

[22]*Bill*, 187 Cal. Rptr. at 627, 8 Media L. Rep. at 2624.

[23]*Herceg*, 814 F.2d at 1019, 13 Media L. Rep. at 2345–46.

[24]*DeFilippo*, 446 A.2d at 1038; *Herceg*, 814 F.2d at 1019, 13 Media L. Rep. at 2345–46; *McCollum*, 249 Cal. Rptr. at 189, 15 Media L. Rep. at 2002. For a further discussion of products liability as a theory for suing the media, see Chapter 7.

[25]*See, e.g.*, Zamora v. Columbia Broadcasting Sys., 480 F. Supp. 199, 5 Media L. Rep. 2109 (S.D. Fla. 1979) (murder conviction); Walt Disney Prods. v. Shannon, 276 S.E.2d 580, 7 Media L. Rep. 1209 (Ga. 1981) (partial blindness); Olivia N. II, 178 Cal. Rptr. 888, 7 Media L. Rep. 2359 (Cal. Ct. App. 1981), *cert. denied*, 458 U.S. 1108 (1982) (rape); *DeFilippo*, 446 A.2d 1036 (death); *Bill*, 187 Cal. Rptr. 625 (gunshot wound); *Herceg*, 814 F.2d 1017 (death); *McCollum*, 249 Cal. Rptr. 187 (death); *Yakubowicz*, 536 N.E.2d 1067 (death).

Despite the many factual differences, the plaintiffs' ingenious legal theories, and the severity of the plaintiffs' injuries, the courts consistently have rejected such claims because they have found that the media owed the plaintiffs no duty of care, that recovery was barred by the First Amendment, or both.[26] These cases were usually dismissed as a result of pretrial motions.[27]

§8.2(A) No Duty of Care

There are several reasons why the media have been held to owe no duty of care in imitation cases. First, such a duty would make the media liable to an indeterminate class for an indeterminate period of time for an indeterminate amount.[28] Such limitless liability would deter the media from publishing or broadcasting anything except the most innocuous information for fear that they might be liable to someone for something. As one court has noted, the "deterrent effect of subjecting the television networks to negligence liability because of their programming choices would lead to self-censorship which would dampen the vigor and limit the variety of public debate."[29] Such a duty also would be contrary to the more general principle, illustrated by the doctrine of proximate cause, that liability should not be so unlimited that it crushes those on whom it is imposed.[30]

Second, there is no standard by which to evaluate whether the media have violated such a duty of care.[31] No one can tell how much "violent" television programming is too much or which program someone will choose to imitate. The very vagueness of this duty makes it impossible for anyone to act in conformity with it.[32]

Third, such a duty is inconsistent with the fundamental premise of our democratic society. As one commentator has noted:

---

[26]*See, e.g., Zamora,* 480 F. Supp. 199 (both); *Walt Disney,* 276 S.E.2d 580 (First Amendment); *Olivia N. II,* 178 Cal. Rptr. 888 (First Amendment); *DeFilippo,* 446 A.2d 1036 (First Amendment); *Bill,* 187 Cal. Rptr. 625 (both); *Herceg,* 814 F.2d 1017 (both); *McCollum,* 249 Cal. Rptr. 187 (both); *Yakubowicz,* 536 N.E.2d 1067 (First Amendment). *But see infra* §8.3.

[27]*See, e.g., Zamora,* 480 F. Supp. 199 (failure to state claim); *Walt Disney,* 276 S.E.2d 580 (summary judgment); *Olivia N. II,* 178 Cal. Rptr. 888 (judgment of nonsuit after plaintiff's opening statement); *DeFilippo,* 446 A.2d 1036 (summary judgment); *McCollum,* 249 Cal. Rptr. 187 (demurrer); *Bill,* 187 Cal. Rptr. 625 (summary judgment); *Yakubowicz,* 536 N.E.2d 1067 (summary judgment). *But see Herceg,* 814 F.2d 1017 (jury trial).

An earlier decision in the *Olivia N.* litigation, Olivia N. v. National Broadcasting Co., 141 Cal. Rptr. 511, 3 Media L. Rep. 1454 (1977), *cert. denied sub nom.* National Broadcasting Co. v. Niemi, 434 U.S. 1354 (1978), also set forth the applicable First Amendment principles but then held that, because the case had been assigned to a judge for trial when there was no pending summary judgment motion, it was error for the trial judge to deny the plaintiff her right to a jury trial by reviewing only the broadcast and then granting summary judgment on the grounds that the plaintiff could never prove incitement).

[28]*Zamora,* 480 F. Supp. at 202, 5 Media L. Rep. at 211 (citing Yuhas v. Mudge, 322 A.2d 824, 825 (N.J. Super. Ct. App. Div. 1974) (citing Ultramares Corp. v. Touche, Niven & Co., 174 N.E. 441 (N.Y. 1931))). For a further discussion of *Yuhas,* see Chapter 7.

[29]*Olivia N. II,* 7 Media L. Rep. at 2362 (citing New York Times Co. v. Sullivan, 376 U.S. 254, 279, 1 Media L. Rep. 1527, 1537 (1964)). *See also McCollum,* 249 Cal. Rptr. at 197, 15 Media L. Rep. at 2008–09; Gertz v. Robert Welch, Inc., 418 U.S. 323, 340, 1 Media L. Rep. 1633, 1640 (1974).

[30]*Zamora,* 480 F. Supp. at 201–02, 5 Media L. Rep. at 2111. *See also* Sakon v. Pepsico, 553 So. 2d 163, 166, 17 Media L. Rep. 1277, 1280 (Fla. 1989).

[31]*Zamora,* 480 F. Supp. at 202–03, 5 Media L. Rep. at 2112; *Sakon,* 553 So. 2d at 166–67, 17 Media L. Rep. at 1279–80.

[32]This also creates serious due process concerns. *See, e.g.,* Papachristou v. City of Jacksonville, 405 U.S. 156, 162 (1972) (vagrancy ordinance held void for vagueness because it failed to give person of ordinary intelligence fair notice that contemplated conduct was forbidden by statute); Connally v. General Constr. Co., 269 U.S. 385, 391 (1926) (minimum wage law found so uncertain as to deprive contractors of property without due process; statute must be sufficiently explicit to inform those subject to it what conduct will render them liable to its penalties).

The basic assumption of our form of government is that each citizen in a free society is deemed to have the judgment and responsibility to decide which theories and ideas to accept, not because we assume that everyone will exercise that judgment wisely or responsibly, but that we are, on the whole, far better off leaving these matters to the marketplace of ideas than to legislature, judge or jury.[33]

Other potential problems with such a duty of care remain to be explored,[34] as do several defenses to any such claims.[35]

Besides these general problems with such a duty, several of the specific theories asserted in imitation cases present additional difficulties. The theory that the media have a duty to warn viewers of the effects that a particular broadcast or publication may have on them has been rejected because there is no general duty to warn others that third parties may be dangerous, unless the dangerous person has made threats against an identifiable victim.[36] Such a general duty to warn is also unlikely to be effective because it would produce so many warnings from so many different people that few, if any, of the warnings would be heeded.[37]

The theory that the contents of a broadcast or a newspaper are a product, which would create a claim for strict product liability, has also been rejected.[38] No court appears to have ever adopted this theory for a media publication[39] and, not surprisingly, there is case law holding that the contents of a book are not a product.[40] The idea that a jury could weigh the risk of harm from a publication or broadcast against its utility, as is done with a tangible product like a lawn mower, is very dangerous to free speech: It amounts to nothing less than pure censorship, because the jury is being asked to determine the worth of an idea.[41]

For all of these reasons, the courts have properly concluded that the media owe no duty of care in imitation cases.[42]

§8.2(B) First Amendment Barriers

Even if it is assumed that the media owe a duty of care in imitation cases, the First Amendment is a virtually insurmountable barrier to recovery.[43] The

---

[33]Hoffman, *From Random House to Mickey Mouse: Liability for Negligent Publishing and Broadcasting*, 21 TORT & INS. L.J. 65, 81 (1985).

[34]*See, e.g., Zamora*, 480 F. Supp. at 202, 5 Media L. Rep. at 2112 (lack of causation).

[35]*Id.* (assumption of risk and contributory and comparative negligence); Walt Disney Prods. v. Shannon, 276 S.E.2d 580, 583 n.3, 7 Media L. Rep. 1209, 1211 n.3 (Ga. 1981) (assumption of risk and contributory negligence). Suicide is generally an independent intervening act that breaks the chain of causation. Watters v. TSR, Inc., 904 F.2d 378, 383–84 (6th Cir. 1990).

[36]Bill v. Superior Ct., 187 Cal. Rptr. 625, 631, 8 Media L. Rep. 2622, 2628–29 (Cal. Ct. App. 1982) (citing Johnson v. State of Cal., 73 Cal. Rptr. 240, 447 P.2d 352 (Cal. 1968)); Thompson v. County of Alameda, 167 Cal. Rptr. 70, 614 P.2d 728 (Cal. 1980) (county found not liable for failure to warn local police and neighborhood parents that it was releasing person from prison who had dangerous and violent propensities toward young children); Davidson v. City of Westminster, 185 Cal. Rptr. 252, 649 P.2d 894 (Cal. 1984) (police officers found to have no general duty to warn potential victims in vicinity about someone they were surveilling).

[37]*Bill*, 187 Cal. Rptr. at 628–29.

[38]Herceg v. Hustler Magazine, 565 F. Supp. 802, 803, 9 Media L. Rep. 1959, 1960 (S.D. Tex. 1983) (trial court held that magazine article was not product); *Watters*, 904 F.2d at 381 ("the doctrine of strict liability has never been extended to words or pictures."). For a further discussion of products liability as a theory for suing the media, see Chapter 7.

[39]*Herceg*, 565 F. Supp. at 803, 9 Media L. Rep. at 1960; *Watters*, 904 F.2d at 381. *See also* Chapter 7.

[40]*Herceg*, 565 F. Supp. at 803, 9 Media L. Rep. at 1960 (citing Cardozo v. True, 342 So. 2d 1053, 1056–57, 2 Media L. Rep. 1635 (Fla. Dist. Ct. App.), *cert. denied*, 353 So. 2d 674 (Fla. 1977)). For a further discussion of *Cardozo*, see Chapter 7.

[41]*See* Gertz v. Robert Welch, Inc., 418 U.S. 323, 339, 349–50, 1 Media L. Rep. 1633, 1639, 1643–44 (1974).

[42]Similar considerations have caused the courts to severely limit the media's liability in false advertising cases. *See* Chapter 7. *But see infra* §8.3.

[43]Zamora v. Columbia Broadcasting Sys., 480 F. Supp. 199, 203–07, 5 Media L. Rep. 2109, 2112–15

cases that have considered this issue have applied the First Amendment's clear and present danger[44] or incitement[45] test to determine whether there is any liability in imitation cases.

The incitement test was developed in cases where the government sought to punish speech that advocated the violent overthrow of government.[46] While speech that advocates the violent overthrow of government may at first blush seem far removed from speech that leads to imitation, these types of speech are closely related: They both raise the issue of the propriety of punishing speech, not because the speech is harmful in and of itself, but because it may cause its listeners to take action that is illegal or dangerous.

The courts have applied the incitement test because they have been concerned that a less stringent standard for liability in imitation cases "would place broadcasters in jeopardy for televising *Hamlet, Julius Caesar, Grimm's Fairy Tales;* more contemporary offerings such as *All Quiet on the Western Front,* and even *The Holocaust,* and indeed would render John Wayne a risk not acceptable to any but the boldest broadcasters."[47] Understandably, such liability is intolerable under the First Amendment because it "would invariably lead to self-censorship by broadcasters in order to remove any matter that may be emulated and lead to a law suit."[48] Thus, imposing liability in cases where the defendants' acts do not amount to incitement would allow the reactions of a few hypersensitive individuals to determine the information made available to everyone else.[49] In *Walt Disney,* for example, only one of the estimated 16 million viewers brought suit.[50]

(S.D. Fla. 1979); Walt Disney Prods. v. Shannon, 276 S.E.2d 580, 582–83, 7 Media L. Rep. 1209, 1210–12 (Ga. 1981); Olivia N. II, 178 Cal. Rptr. 888, 892–93, 7 Media L. Rep. 2359, 2362 (Cal. Ct. App. 1981), *cert. denied,* 458 U.S. 1108 (1982); DeFilippo v. National Broadcasting Co., 446 A.2d 1036, 1040–42, 8 Media L. Rep. 1872, 1875–77 (R.I. 1982); *Bill,* 187 Cal. Rptr. at 627–29, 8 Media L. Rep. at 2624–26; *Herceg,* 814 F.2d at 1021, 13 Media L. Rep. at 2346; McCollum v. CBS Inc., 249 Cal. Rptr. 187, 191–95, 15 Media L. Rep. 2001, 2004–07 (Cal. Ct. App. 1988); Yakubowicz v. Paramount Pictures Corp., 536 N.E.2d 1067, 1071–72, 16 Media L. Rep. 1725, 1728–29 (Mass. 1989); Watters v. TSR, Inc., 715 F. Supp. 819, 823 (W.D. Ky. 1989).

[44]Initially known as the "clear and present danger" test, based on Justice Holmes' famous example of falsely shouting "Fire!" in a theater (Schenck v. United States, 249 U.S. 47, 52 (1919)), this test has now evolved into a more stringent test commonly known as the "incitement" test (Brandenburg v. Ohio, 395 U.S. 444 (1969)). The incitement test consists of two parts: the court must be satisfied that (1) the speech was directed or intended to produce imminent lawless conduct, and (2) the speech was likely to produce such imminent conduct. Speech directed to action at some indefinite time in the future will not satisfy this test. Hess v. Indiana, 414 U.S. 105, 108 (1973).

[45]*Id.* But see infra §8.3.

[46]*See, e.g.,* Schenck v. United States, 249 U.S. 47 (1919); Frohwek v. United States, 249 U.S. 204 (1919); Debs v. United States, 249 U.S. 211 (1919).

[47]*Zamora,* 480 F. Supp. at 206, 5 Media L. Rep. at 2114–15.

[48]DeFilippo v. National Broadcasting Co., 446 A.2d 1036, 1041, 8 Media L. Rep. 1872, 1876 (R.I. 1982) (footnote omitted); *see also* McCollum v. CBS Inc., 249 Cal. Rptr. 187, 195, 15 Media L. Rep. 2001, 2007 (Cal. Ct. App. 1988).

[49]*Zamora,* 480 F. Supp. at 205, 5 Media L. Rep. at 2114 ("the right of the public to have broad access to programming and the right of the broadcaster to disseminate should not be inhibited by those members of the public who are particularly sensitive"); Bill v. Superior Ct., 187 Cal. Rptr. 625, 628–29, 8 Media L. Rep. 2622, 2625 (Cal. Ct. App. 1982) (expressing concern that a few sensitive and lawless individuals would be able to exercise "heckler's veto" over what others could see and hear); *McCollum,* 249 Cal. Rptr. at 197, 15 Media L. Rep. at 2008–09 ("it is not acceptable ... to impose a duty upon performing artists to limit and restrict their creativity in order to avoid the dissemination of ideas in artistic speech which may adversely affect emotionally troubled individuals"); Watters v. TSR, Inc., 715 F. Supp. 819, 822 (W.D. Ky. 1989) ("atrocities have been committed in the name of many of civilization's religions, intellectuals, and artists, yet the first amendment does not hold those whose ideas inspired the crimes to answer for such acts. To do so would allow the freaks and misfits of society to declare what the country can and cannot read, watch, and hear.").

[50]Walt Disney Prods. v. Shannon, 276 S.E.2d 580, 583 n.4, 7 Media L. Rep. 1209, 1212 n.4 (Ga. 1981); *DeFilippo,* 446 A.2d at 1041, 8 Media L. Rep. at 1876 ("as far as [the court was] aware" plaintiff was only viewer to imitate hanging).

Numerous arguments have been made in an effort to avoid applying the First Amendment to imitation cases, but each of them has been rejected. *Olivia N. II* is the leading case in this area because it discusses such issues at length.

In *Olivia N. II,* the court initially rejected any distinction between news, which the plaintiff admitted is protected by the First Amendment, and fiction, which the plaintiff argued is not protected by the First Amendment.[51] As the court recognized, such a distinction is too vague because it fails to recognize that " '[e]veryone is familiar with instances of propaganda through fiction. What is one [person's] amusement, teaches another's doctrine.' "[52] The court observed that it was well established that fictional works like *Born Innocent* were entitled to First Amendment protection.[53]

Similarly, the court held that the broadcast's First Amendment protection was not lessened because it was profitable or commercial.[54] This conclusion is sound, because First Amendment protection cannot realistically be limited to broadcasters and publishers that are unprofitable.[55]

The court also noted that the electronic media, like the print media, are entitled to First Amendment protection,[56] and that this result is not altered by the pervasiveness of the government's regulation of the electronic media.[57] Finally, the court rejected the argument that, since children have access to the electronic media, the only things that can be broadcast are things suitable for them; any other conclusion would mean that adults would only be able to watch programs suitable for children.[58] Accordingly, because of the First Amendment, liability may not be imposed in imitation cases unless the incitement test is met.[59]

Whether the incitement test is met is a question of law for the court.[60] The test must be construed to give broad protection against liability in imitation cases.[61]

---

[51]Olivia N. II, 178 Cal. Rptr. 888, 893, 7 Media L. Rep. 2359, 2362 (Cal. Ct. App. 1981).

[52]*Id.* (quoting Winters v. New York, 333 U.S. 507 (1948)).

[53]*Id.* at 891, 7 Media L. Rep. at 2361. *But see* Sakon v. Pepsico, 553 So. 2d 163, 166, 17 Media L. Rep. 1277, 1279 (Fla. 1989) (First Amendment is not absolute bar in imitation case involving commercial).

[54]178 Cal. Rptr. at 892, 7 Media L. Rep. at 2361.

[55]*See* New York Times Co. v. Sullivan, 376 U.S. 254, 265–66, 1 Media L. Rep. 1527, 1531–32 (1964) (Court, in rejecting argument that allegedly libelous statement deserved no constitutional protection because it was part of commercial advertisement, stated that fact that "the Times was paid ... is as immaterial in this connection as is the fact that newspapers and books are sold.").

[56]178 Cal. Rptr. at 892, 7 Media L. Rep. at 2361; *see also* Schad v. Borough of Mt. Ephraim, 452 U.S. 61, 65–66 (1981) (Court emphasized that "[e]ntertainment, as well as political and ideological speech, is protected; motion pictures, programs broadcast by radio and television, and live entertainment, such as musical and dramatic works, fall within the First Amendment guarantee.").

[57]178 Cal. Rptr. at 892, 7 Media L. Rep. at 2361.

[58]*Id.* at 892–93, 7 Media L. Rep. at 2362.

[59]*See* Hoffman, *From Random House to Mickey Mouse: Liability for Negligent Publishing and Broadcasting,* 21 TORT & INS. L.J. 65 (1985); Hilker, *Tort Liability of the Media for Audience Acts of Violence: A Constitutional Analysis,* 52 S. CAL. L. REV. 529 (1979) (concluding that media owe duty of care but that such duty is limited by incitement test). *But see* Weingarten, *Tort Liability for Nonlibelous Negligent Statements: First Amendment Considerations,* 93 YALE L.J. 744 (1984); Powell, *Products Liability and the First Amendment: The Liability of Publishers for Failure to Warn,* 59 IND. L.J. 503 (1984); Miller, *Media Liability for Injuries That Result From Television Broadcasts to Immature Audiences,* 22 SAN DIEGO L. REV. 377 (1985). *See generally* Annot., *Liability for Personal Injury or Death Allegedly Resulting From Television or Radio Broadcast,* 20 A.L.R.4th 327 (1983). For a debate on this issue between Prof. Harvey L. Zuckman and Floyd Abrams, *see Tort/Retort,* 1 COMM. LAW. 1 (1983).

[60]DeFilippo v. National Broadcasting Co., 446 A.2d 1036, 1041 & n.6, 8 Media L. Rep. 1872, 1875–76 & n.6 (R.I. 1982); Yakubowicz v. Paramount Pictures Corp., 536 N.E.2d 1067, 1071, 16 Media L. Rep. 1725, 1728 (Mass. 1989); *see also* McCollum v. CBS Inc., 249 Cal. Rptr. 187, 193, 15 Media L. Rep. 2001, 2005 (1988).

[61]*DeFilippo,* 446 A.2d at 1042, 8 Media L. Rep. at 1876–77.

In the cases reviewed above, a variety of plaintiffs sued the media on virtually every conceivable theory for injuries that allegedly resulted from the imitation or influence of what was broadcast or published. With the exception of *Weirum v. RKO General*,[62] the plaintiffs have lost every imitation case. Because of the stringent requirements of the incitement test, it is extremely unlikely that a plaintiff will prevail in a future imitation case.[63]

§8.3 THE EXCEPTION: INCITEMENT OF IMMINENT LAWLESS ACTION

The only imitation case in which the plaintiffs have prevailed is *Weirum v. RKO General*. In that wrongful death action, the decedent's wife and children sued two teenagers and a radio station for negligence. The decedent's car had been forced off the highway, resulting in his death, by the two minor defendants, who were driving separate automobiles and following a disc jockey's automobile to its next stop.[64]

The disc jockey, Donald Steele Revert, known professionally as "The Real Don Steele,"[65] worked for radio station KHJ, which had a large teenage following. In July 1970, KHJ launched a promotion entitled "The Super Summer Spectacular." Steele traveled from place to place in Los Angeles in a conspicuous red automobile, periodically apprising KHJ, in general, of his whereabouts and his intended destination; KHJ in turn broadcast this information.[66] The first person to rendezvous with Steele and fulfill a specified condition received a small cash prize ($5–$25)[67] and was briefly interviewed on the air by Steele.[68]

---

[62] 123 Cal. Rptr. 468, 539 P.2d 36 (Cal. 1975). This case is discussed *infra* §8.3.

[63] For an excellent discussion of the constitutional barriers to more direct regulation of violence in the media, e.g., by the Federal Communications Commission, *see* Krattenmaker & Powe, *Televised Violence: First Amendment Principles and Social Science Theory*, 64 VA. L. REV. 1123 (1978). *Contra* Albert, *Constitutional Regulation of Televised Violence*, 64 VA. L. REV. 1299 (1978). *See also* authorities cited in Hilker, *supra* note 59, at 530 n.11.

[64] 539 P.2d 36 (Cal. 1975); *see also* Vance v. Judas Priest, 16 Media L. Rep. 2241 (Nev. Dist. Ct. 1989) (denying defendants' summary judgment motion where plaintiffs alleged that audio subliminal messages in record album caused decedents' suicides). *But see* Waller v. Osbourne, 763 F. Supp. 1144 (M.D. Ga. 1991) (granting summary judgment in very similar case because of no showing of subliminal message). *Compare* Rubio v. Swiridoff, 211 Cal. Rptr. 338, 339–40 (Cal. Ct. App. 1985) (plaintiffs unsuccessfully argued that defendant, who had driven off at high speed after arguing with his girlfriend, who then followed him and collided with decedent's car, owed duty of care to decedent because defendant knew or should have known that everything girlfriend did that night was imitative of and in reaction to what he did; "for all practical purposes, he was in the driver's seat of both automobiles.").

[65] The court's frequent references to Steele as "The Real Don Steele" (*Weirum*, 539 P.2d at 38, 39, 40) leaves the reader with the uncomfortable feeling that the decision was influenced by the court's distaste for the content of KHJ's program. Content discrimination is plainly impermissible under the First Amendment. *See, e.g.*, Police Dep't of Chicago v. Mosely, 408 U.S. 92, 95 (1972) ("above all else, the First Amendment means that government has no power to restrict expression because of its message, its ideas, its subject matter, or its content").

[66] *Weirum*, 539 P.2d at 38.

[67] Fleming, *The Supreme Court of California, 1974–75*, 64 CAL. L. REV. 239, 617 n.2 (1976). This article contains an excellent discussion of *Weirum*.

[68] Excerpts of KHJ's broadcast, as quoted in the California Supreme Court's decision, include the following:

9:30 and The Real Don Steele is back on his feet again with some money and he is headed for the Valley. Thought I would give you a warning so that you can get your kids out of the street.

The Real Don Steele is out driving on—could be in your neighborhood at any time and he's got bread to spread, so be on the lookout for him.

The Real Don Steele is moving into Canoga Park—so be on the lookout for him. I'll tell you what will happen if you get to The Real Don Steele. He's got twenty-five dollars to give away if you can get it . . . and baby, all signed and sealed and delivered and wrapped up.

10:54—The Real Don Steele is in the Valley near the intersection of Topanga and Roscoe Boulevard, right by the Loew's Holiday Theater—you know where that is at, and he's standing there with a

Steele testified that he was aware that in the past vehicles had followed him from location to location and that he was aware that the same contestants sometimes appeared at consecutive stops.[69] There was no contention, however, that Steele himself had ever violated the speed limit in moving from location to location, nor was there any evidence that he knew others had disregarded highway safety while following him.[70]

The court stated that the primary question before it was whether KHJ owed the decedent a duty of care, and held that this determination was primarily a question of law; that the foreseeability of the risk is the primary consideration in determining whether there is a duty; and, somewhat contradictorily, that foreseeability is a question of fact for the jury.[71] The court felt that the accident was foreseeable "in the middle of a Los Angeles summer, a time when young people were free from the constraints of school and responsive to relief from vacation tedium."[72] Because money and a small measure of notoriety awaited the first person to arrive, the court upheld the jury's verdict that "[i]t was foreseeable that defendant's youthful listeners ... would race to arrive first at the next site and in their haste disregard the demands of highway safety."[73]

The court then noted that, while every act involves some conceivable danger, "[l]iability is imposed only if the risk of harm resulting from the act is deemed unreasonable—i.e., if the gravity and likelihood of the danger outweigh the utility of the conduct involved."[74] Applying this test, the court said that there was a grave danger inherent in the contest because of the risk of a high-speed automobile chase that would result in death or serious injury.[75]

In one paragraph, without citation of authority or explanation of its conclusion, the court then held that the First Amendment did not protect KHJ from liability.[76]

Weirum correctly approached this issue by trying to decide whether any duty was owed by the media and by then trying to determine the impact of the First Amendment on this issue.[77] However, *Weirum*'s conclusions, that there is a duty and that the First Amendment does not limit the media's liability in such situations, are both incorrect.

Instead of viewing foreseeability as only one of many elements to be considered in determining whether there is a duty, *Weirum* relied entirely on

---

little money he would like to give away to the first person to arrive and tell him what type car I helped Robert W. Morgan give away yesterday morning at KHJ. What was the make of the car. If you know that, split. Intersection of Topanga and Roscoe Boulevard—right nearby the Loew's Holiday Theater you will find The Real Don Steele. Tell him and pick up the bread.
Weirum, 539 P.2d at 38.

[69]*Id.* at 40.
[70]*Id.* at 38 n.2, 40.
[71]*Id.* at 39.
[72]*Id.* at 46.
[73]539 P.2d at 40. The court repeatedly refers to teenagers and KHJ's appeal to them, but it never explicitly rests its decision on the grounds that teenagers are careless drivers. Presumably this is because the majority of KHJ's audience were not teenagers and because the court was not prepared to create special liability where teenage drivers are involved. Fleming, *supra* note 67, at 625–27. Why then did the court repeatedly refer to teenagers? The obvious explanation is that the court felt such references were necessary to bolster its finding of liability even though it was not prepared to live with the implications of a special rule for teenagers.
[74]*Weirum*, 539 P.2d at 40.
[75]*Id.*
[76]*Id.*
[77]*See supra* §§8.2(A) and (B).

the issue of foreseeability to determine whether there was a duty.[78] However, the question of whether a duty exists, like the question of whether there is proximate cause, is ultimately a question of policy.[79] Foreseeability, like causation-in-fact in proximate cause cases, is only one factor to consider in determining such policy—other relevant factors include the social utility of the conduct compared to the risks it involves, the relative ability of the parties to avoid the risks involved, and the moral blame attached to the defendant's conduct.[80] Since *Weirum* does not consider any of these factors or any of the reasons other courts have held there is no such duty, its analysis of the duty question is unpersuasive.[81]

To justify its decision, the court did attempt to characterize KHJ's broadcast as generating a fierce competitive pursuit by automobile of Steele, but the facts do not support this characterization. Neither Steele's route nor his exact location were broadcast until after he had arrived at his next stop, so there was no attempt to generate a competitive pursuit of Steele.[82] In any event, liability for the negligent acts of third parties only attaches where there is a probability, not just a possibility, of harm.[83] The court does not even suggest there was any such probability.

KHJ correctly argued that imposing liability on it under these circumstances would mean that anyone who encouraged people to go to a location to buy anything would be liable for all accidents that occurred en route.[84] The court understandably was not prepared to go this far because of the limitless liability that would result. In its only attempt to avoid this result, the court sought to distinguish the case before it from all such "while-they-last" situations by mischaracterizing KHJ's actions as generating a "competitive scramble."[85]

Weirum simply is not the case the California Supreme Court wanted it to be. KHJ did not encourage teenagers to speed or to otherwise disregard traffic safety, its disc jockey did not speed or disregard traffic safety, and KHJ and Steele did not have any reason to believe that their actions were causing teenagers to speed or disregard traffic safety. Accordingly, *Weirum*'s holding that a media defendant is liable for the negligent acts of unrelated third parties,

---

[78]539 P.2d at 40–41. The discussion of the duty question presented here owes much to the excellent discussion in Fleming, *supra* note 67, at 617–33.

[79]W. PAGE KEETON ET AL., PROSSER & KEETON ON THE LAW OF TORTS §31, at 171–72 (5th ed. 1984).

[80]Fleming, *supra* note 67, at 622 (quoting Raymond v. Paradise Unified Sch. Dist., 31 Cal. Rptr. 847, 851–52 (1963)). There is another serious deficiency in the *Weirum* court's exclusive reliance on foreseeability. Since that court held that foreseeability is a jury question and makes foreseeability the sole test of whether there is a duty, 539 P.2d at 39, it effectively abdicated its responsibility to determine whether there is a duty. Not only is this contrary to the court's own statement that duty "is primarily a question of law" for a court, *id.*, such an approach is particularly inappropriate where constitutional rights are at stake and the courts must closely examine factual determinations made by juries. Herceg v. Hustler Magazine, 814 F.2d 1017, 1021, 13 Media L. Rep. 2345, 2349 (5th Cir. 1987); McCollum v. CBS Inc., 249 Cal. Rptr. 187, 195–96, 15 Media L. Rep. 2001, 2007–08 (1988). *See also* Bose Corp v. Consumers Union of U.S., 466 U.S. 485 (1984).

[81]*Weirum* does mention some of these other factors, 539 P.2d at 40, but it does not analyze them. It is undoubtedly true, as the court says, that high-speed automobile chases are dangerous and that different programming by KHJ could have avoided this particular danger. These are truisms that tell us little about what duty, if any, should be imposed, since every action entails some risk and not taking the action could avoid risk.

[82]Fleming, *supra* note 67, at 627–28; *see also supra* note 70.

[83]RESTATEMENT (SECOND) OF TORTS §302, cmt. d (1965).

[84]539 P.2d at 40–41.

[85]*Id.* Indeed, by trying, albeit unsuccessfully, to distinguish the case before it from "while-they-last" sales where there is no duty, the court implicitly recognized that KHJ owed the decedent no duty.

based on a showing that the defendant offered a small inducement to third parties to take action that might result in injury to others, even though that had never happened in the past, is untenable. It would justify the imposition of liability in almost any situation, since every act creates some risk that someone will somehow be injured.[86]

While *Weirum*'s rationale as to duty is unacceptable, its treatment of the First Amendment issue is nonexistent. *Weirum* never attempts to explain why the First Amendment did not limit KHJ's liability, except for its statement that "[t]he First Amendment does not sanction the infliction of physical injury merely because [it is] achieved by word, rather than act."[87]

What this statement has to do with *Weirum*'s facts is never explained by the court and is certainly not obvious. While it is true that *A*, who gets *B* to agree to kill *C*, cannot avoid responsibility for his criminal act by simply claiming that he only engaged in speech and that speech is protected by the First Amendment,[88] such a situation has nothing to do with the facts of *Weirum*.

The imitation cases that have considered *Weirum* and the First Amendment have explicitly or implicitly distinguished or rejected *Weirum*. Thus, in *Walt Disney*, the court said that "even assuming the correctness of the holding," *Weirum* only "constitute[s] authority for the proposition that a tort defendant can be held liable if the defendant incited ... a third party to commit a crime against the plaintiff."[89] Several other imitation cases contain similar statements.[90] Like *Walt Disney*, none of them endorses the result in *Weirum*, and their statements seem to be more of an easy way to dispose of *Weirum* than any holding that *Weirum* meets the incitement test.

Assuming, however, that *Weirum* should be viewed as a holding that the incitement test was met, was it correctly decided? Under *Brandenburg v. Ohio*,[91] the leading incitement case, a statement that allegedly causes illegal

---

[86]This is not to say that KHJ and Steele owed no duty under any circumstances. *See* Fleming, *supra* note 67, at 628–33, for a discussion of the three situations in which imposition of a duty might be appropriate, namely where a defendant (1) knows of the third parties' negligent propensities, (2) controls the third parties' conduct, or (3) provides the third parties with an instrumentality that is especially dangerous and causes the injury.

[87]539 P.2d at 40.

[88]Frohwerk v. United States, 249 U.S. 204, 206 (1919). Even when murder is the subject of discussion, however, such speech cannot be punished unless constitutional standards are met. United States v. Kelner, 534 F.2d 1020 (2d Cir.), *cert. denied*, 429 U.S. 1022 (1976); People v. Rubin, 158 Cal. Rptr. 488, 490–94 (1979), *cert. denied*, 449 U.S. 821 (1980).

[89]Walt Disney Prods. v. Shannon, 276 S.E.2d 580, 582 n.2, 7 Media L. Rep. 1209, 1211 n.2 (Ga. 1981). Unfortunately, *Walt Disney* and the four cases listed *infra* note 90 only consider *Weirum*'s holding on the First Amendment issue and do not address its analysis of the duty question. *But see* McCollum v. CBS Inc., 249 Cal. Rptr. 187, 196, 15 Media L. Rep. 2001, 2008 (1988) (in addressing duty analysis of *Weirum*, court stated that "[w]hat the conduct in *Weirum* and culpable incitement have in common, when viewed from the perspective of a duty analysis, is a very high degree of foreseeability of undue risk of harm to others. Under such circumstances, imposition of negligence liability does not offend the First Amendment.").

[90]Olivia N. II, 178 Cal. Rptr. 888, 893–94, 7 Media L. Rep. 2359, 2362–63 (Cal. Ct. App. 1981); DeFilippo v. National Broadcasting Co., 446 A.2d 1036, 1041 n.7, 8 Media L. Rep. 1872, 1876 n.7 (R.I. 1982); Bill v. Superior Ct., 187 Cal. Rptr. 625, 630–31, 8 Media L. Rep. 2622, 2626–27 (Cal. Ct. App. 1982). In Herceg v. Hustler Magazine, 814 F.2d 1017, 13 Media L. Rep. 2345 (5th Cir. 1987), the Fifth Circuit criticized *Weirum*, noting that the decision contains

no guidance for distinguishing between protected speech containing—or implying—dangerous ideas and speech so clearly and immediately dangerous and 'of such slight social value as a step to truth that any benefit that may be derived from [it] is clearly outweighed by the social interest in order and morality.'

Id. at 1024, 13 Media L. Rep. 2350 (quoting Chaplinsky v. New Hampshire, 315 U.S. 568, 572 (1942)).

[91]395 U.S. 444 (1969). *See also* NAACP v. Claiborne Hardware Co., 458 U.S. 886, 927–29 (1982).

acts is protected unless it "is directed to inciting or producing imminent lawless action and is likely to incite or produce such action."[92]

In *Hess v. Indiana*,[93] a more recent U.S. Supreme Court decision applying this test, the defendant had been convicted of disorderly conduct during a demonstration against the Vietnam War for saying within the hearing of a sheriff that "[w]e'll take the fucking street later" or "again."[94] This occurred after the sheriff and his deputies had cleared the street of demonstrators and while Hess was facing the crowd of demonstrators. Hess made his statement in a loud voice, though not louder than that of others, and did not appear to be speaking to any particular person or group; nor did he appear to be exhorting the crowd to return to the street.[95]

After noting that "at worst, [Hess' statement] amounted to nothing more than advocacy of illegal action at some indefinite future time,"[96] the Court quoted the *Brandenburg* incitement test, emphasizing its requirement that, for a statement to be actionable, it had to be "directed to inciting or producing *imminent* lawless action."[97] The Court then held that since Hess' statement was not directed to a particular person or group, it was not advocacy of action.[98] Moreover, since there was no evidence "that his words were intended to produce, and likely to produce, *imminent* disorder, those words could not be punished by the State."[99]

Similarly, in *Weirum,* which was solely a negligence case, there was no evidence that KHJ intended to cause harm. In addition, there was no evidence that KHJ's broadcasts were likely to produce imminent lawless action; indeed, there was no evidence that KHJ's broadcasts had ever caused any violations of the traffic laws or any injuries.[100] This is strong evidence that such injury was not likely. Injury was also unlikely since *Weirum* appears to be the only reported case where a radio contest allegedly caused a car accident, even though similar contests must have been run innumerable times and been heard by thousands, if not millions, of people.

Since there was no evidence that KHJ engaged in advocacy intended to *and* likely to produce *imminent* lawless action, the result in *Weirum* cannot be upheld under the incitement test.

§8.4 Rejection of the Constitutional Actual Malice Test

Only one case, *Walt Disney Productions v. Shannon*,[101] has discussed whether the constitutional actual malice test, set forth in *New York Times Co. v. Sullivan*[102] and its progeny, is applicable to imitation cases. The famous

---

[92] 395 U.S. at 447.
[93] 414 U.S. 105 (1973).
[94] *Id.* at 107.
[95] *Id.* at 106–07.
[96] *Id.* at 108.
[97] *Id.*
[98] 414 U.S. at 108–09.
[99] *Id.* at 109.
[100] 123 Cal. Rptr. 468, 472, 539 P.2d 36, 40 (Cal. 1975).
[101] 276 S.E.2d 580, 7 Media L. Rep. 1209 (Ga. 1981).
[102] 376 U.S. 254, 1 Media L. Rep. 1527 (1964). This case is discussed at length in Chapter 2.

Sullivan decision held that, in a libel action brought by a public official against his critics, the plaintiff must prove that the allegedly defamatory statements were uttered by the defendant with knowledge that they were false or with reckless disregard as to whether or not they were false.[103]

The court in *Walt Disney* rejected the application of the constitutional actual malice test in imitation cases.[104] In reaching this conclusion, it noted the *Sullivan* court's statement that the case before it had to be considered " 'against the background of a profound national commitment to the principle that debate on public issues should be uninhibited, robust, and wide-open.' "[105] *Walt Disney* then held that "[t]here is nothing in the content of what was broadcast in this television program [a demonstration of how to use a BB inside a balloon to reproduce the sound of a tire coming off an automobile] that would bring it within the scope of New York Times [Co. v. Sullivan]. Therefore, we hold that New York Times and its progeny are inapposite here."[106]

That conclusion is correct, but not for the reasons stated in *Walt Disney*. The important difference between *Walt Disney* and *Sullivan* is not that *Walt Disney* is about sound effects and *Sullivan* is about the civil rights movement: it is that *Walt Disney* has nothing to do with statements asserted to be false, while *Sullivan* is *only* about statements asserted to be false. *Sullivan*'s constitutional actual malice test is directed to the speaker's knowledge of the falsity of what the speaker said. That test cannot be applied to situations, like imitation cases, that do not involve any alleged falsity, because it would be impossible to determine in an imitation case whether the speaker acted with constitutional actual malice, i.e., knew that a statement was false or had substantial subjective doubts about its truthfulness.

The actual malice test is an important protection for free speech. Like the incitement test, however, it cannot be converted into a litmus test in every free speech case. It can only be used in certain areas, i.e., where the issue is whether the speaker knew his or her statements were false or had substantial doubts about their truthfulness.[107]

---

[103] 376 U.S. at 279–80.
[104] 276 S.E.2d at 581–82, 7 Media L. Rep. at 1210.
[105] *Id.* (quoting New York Times Co. v. Sullivan, 376 U.S. 254, 270, 1 Media L. Rep. 1527 (1964)).
[106] 276 S.E.2d at 582, 7 Media L. Rep. at 1210.
[107] *See, e.g.,* Chapters 2 and 3.

CHAPTER 9

APPLICABILITY OF GENERAL LAWS TO THE MEDIA

§9.1 INTRODUCTION

This chapter discusses whether various general laws apply to the media's news gathering and publishing activities, as distinct from their commercial activities.[1] It also discusses the First Amendment's impact on these laws.[2]

§9.2 FEDERAL ANTITRUST LAW

Numerous antitrust laws impact the media's commercial operations, but a discussion of those issues is beyond the scope of this chapter.[3]

§9.2(A) No Automatic Exemption

The media are not entitled to any automatic exemption from the federal antitrust laws.[4] The leading case on this issue is *Associated Press v. United States (Associated Press II),*[5] which involved restrictive covenants enforced against members of the Associated Press news organization. Associated Press' bylaws prohibited its members from selling news stories to nonmembers and otherwise limited the transfer of information outside of the organization.[6] Members were also given "veto power" to block competitors from becoming

---

[1] No attempt is made to provide an in-depth discussion of the scope of each of these laws, however.

[2] The focus of this chapter is on federal laws because of their nationwide impact and because that is where First Amendment issues usually have been raised. *See generally* R.J. BRINKMANN, FEDERAL LAWS AFFECTING NEWSPAPERS (1987).

[3] For antitrust cases concerning the media, *see* S.C. OPPENHEIM & C. SHIELDS, NEWSPAPERS AND THE ANTITRUST LAWS (1981); Annot., *Federal Antitrust Act as Applied to Publishers of Newspapers or Other Periodicals—Federal Cases,* 19 L. Ed. 2d 1530 (1968); Comment, *Antitrust Malaise in the Newspaper Industry: The Chains Continue to Grow,* 8 ST. MARY'S L.J. 160 (1976); Comment, *Individual and Chain Newspaper Conduct Versus the Antitrust Laws: What Boundaries Do the Traditional Means of Checking Economic Concentration Establish for the Newspaper Industry?* 14 GONZAGA L. REV. 819 (1979). For a good, current summary of the law in this area, *see* COMMUNICATIONS LAW (Practising Law Institute 1993) (annual publication).

[4] Sherman Act §§1–6, 8 (15 U.S.C. §§1–7 (1976)); Clayton Act §§2–8, 10–16, 26 (15 U.S.C. §§12–27 (1976)); Robinson-Patman Act §§2–4 (15 U.S.C. §§13–13b (1976)); Federal Trade Commission Act §5 (15 U.S.C. §45 (1976)).

[5] 326 U.S. 1, 1 Media L. Rep. 2269 (1944). For a discussion of *Associated Press I,* which involves federal labor law, *see* §9.5.

[6] 326 U.S. at 9, 1 Media L. Rep. at 2272.

members of the organization.[7] The Supreme Court held that these restrictions violated the Sherman Act.[8]

The Associated Press contended that, even if its conduct violated the antitrust laws, the First Amendment barred the application of the Sherman Act to media organizations. The Supreme Court rejected this claim, explaining that "[t]he fact that the publisher handles news while others handle food does not ... afford the publisher a peculiar constitutional sanctuary in which he can with impunity violate laws regulating his business practices."[9]

The Court also ruled that the clear and present danger doctrine[10] did not apply to antitrust actions because no restriction on the content of press reports was involved.[11] The Court then noted that, if anything, First Amendment principles would argue *in favor* of the Sherman Act's application, because "[f]reedom of the press from governmental interference under the First Amendment does not sanction repression of that freedom by private interests."[12]

Similarly, in *United States v. Lorain Journal Co.*,[13] the defendant owned the only daily newspaper in Lorain, Ohio. As the primary media outlet in the area,[14] the *Journal* had considerable market power. When a radio station began operating in Lorain, the *Journal* informed its advertisers that it would not carry any ads for merchants advertising with the radio station.[15] In response, the government sought an injunction to prevent the *Journal* from rejecting advertisements on this basis.[16]

The district court found a violation of the Sherman Act despite the *Journal*'s claim that a prohibitory injunction "forcing" it to run advertisements would constitute an impermissible prior restraint.[17] The court also recognized the importance of the First Amendment and reiterated the need for caution in restricting freedom of the press.[18] However, it noted that the newspaper's rejection of the advertisements was done with the clear intent to destroy a competing advertising medium.[19] It therefore concluded that "[t]his is a vice condemned by the Sherman Act and the evil may be restrained without affecting the operations of the *Journal* as an organ of opinion and without touching upon the legitimate conduct of its business affairs."[20]

The U.S. Supreme Court unanimously affirmed, holding that this injunction did not constitute an impermissible prior restraint because it only prevented the *Journal* from refusing advertisements for anticompetitive reasons.[21] How-

---

[7] *Id.* at 9–11.
[8] *Id.* at 19.
[9] *Id.* at 7 (citations omitted).
[10] *See, e.g.,* Schenck v. United States, 249 U.S. 47 (1919). *See also* Chapter 8.
[11] 326 U.S. at 7.
[12] *Id.* at 20.
[13] 92 F. Supp. 794 (N.D. Ohio 1950), *aff'd,* 342 U.S. 143, 1 Media L. Rep. 2697 (1951).
[14] The *Journal* reached 99% of the families in Lorain, Ohio, and had only limited competition from the other four newspapers serving the region. *Id.* at 796.
[15] *Id.*
[16] *Id.* at 795–96.
[17] *Id.* at 801.
[18] 92 F. Supp. at 800.
[19] *Id.* at 796 ("The record reveals a story of bold, relentless, and predatory commercial behavior.").
[20] *Id.* at 801.
[21] Lorain Journal Co. v. United States, 342 U.S. 143, 155, 1 Media L. Rep. 2697, 2701 (1951); *see also* Kansas City Star Co. v. United States, 240 F.2d 643, 666 (8th Cir.), *cert. denied,* 354 U.S. 923 (1957). A First Amendment challenge to the Federal Communications Commission (FCC) rules barring jointly owned newspapers and television stations in the same locality has been rejected for similar reasons. Federal

ever, the injunction did not limit the *Journal*'s right to accept or reject ads for other reasons.[22]

Thus, the antitrust laws may be applied to the media to prevent anticompetitive commercial conduct. However, the constitutionality of ordering the media to publish items they do not wish to publish is in doubt.[23] In addition, the antitrust laws cannot be used to regulate the content of the media or their methods of newsgathering.[24]

§9.2(B) The Newspaper Preservation Act's Constitutionality

Before the passage of the Newspaper Preservation Act of 1970 (NPA),[25] many struggling newspapers entered into joint operating agreements to enable them to operate more efficiently by sharing equipment and support staff.[26] Such arrangements generally had been thought to be exempt from the federal antitrust laws under the failing company doctrine.[27] However, in 1969, the Supreme Court held that joint operating agreements not only were per se violations of the federal antitrust laws but usually were not exempt from those laws under the failing company doctrine.[28] In response, Congress promptly passed the NPA to overrule this decision.[29]

The NPA creates a limited exception to the federal antitrust laws[30] for newspapers to engage in joint operating agreements[31] but specifically prohibits other anticompetitive acts.[32]

Communications Comm'n v. National Citizens Comm. for Broadcasting, 436 U.S. 775, 798–802 (1978); *see also* Marsh Media v. Federal Communications Comm'n, 798 F.2d 772, 776, 13 Media L. Rep. 1676, 1680 (D.C. Cir. 1986).

[22]*Lorain Journal Co.,* 342 U.S. at 157–59, 1 Media L. Rep. at 2702.

[23]For a discussion of attempts to gain access to the media, see Chapter 13.

[24]*See* Citizen Pub'g Co. v. United States, 394 U.S. 131, 139, 1 Media L. Rep. 2704, 2707 (1969); Safecard Servs. v. Dow Jones & Co., 537 F. Supp. 1137 (E.D. Va. 1982), *aff'd without opinion,* 705 F.2d 445 (4th Cir.), *cert. denied,* 464 U.S. 831 (1983); Hohensee v. Goon Squad, 171 F. Supp. 562, 568 (M.D. Pa. 1959).

[25]15 U.S.C. §§1801–04 (1970).

[26]Joint operating agreements, or "joint newspaper operating arrangements" as the NPA calls them, are, in essence, agreements where two or more newspapers have joint production facilities but have separate reporting and editorial staffs as well as separate editorial policies. 15 U.S.C. §1802(2).

[27]*See* Comment, *The Newspaper Preservation Act: An Ineffective Step in the Right Direction,* 12 B.C. INDUS. & COM. L. REV. 937, 939, 940 (1972). For a list of 22 such joint operating agreements entered into before 1966, *see* Comment, *The Newspaper Preservation Act,* 32 U. PITT. L. REV. 347, 347 n.3 (1971). For a review of the NPA's application, *see* Martel & Haydel, *Judicial Application of the Newspaper Preservation Act: Will Congressional Intent Be Relegated to the Back Page?* 1984 B.Y.U. L. REV. 123.

[28]*Citizen Pub'g Co.,* 394 U.S. at 135–39, 1 Media L. Rep. at 2705.

[29]Committee for an Indep. P-I v. Hearst Corp., 704 F.2d 467, 473–74, 9 Media L. Rep. 1489, 1494 (9th Cir.), *cert. denied,* 464 U.S. 892 (1983); City & County of Honolulu v. Hawaii Newspaper Agency, 7 Media L. Rep. 2495, 2496, 2498 (D. Haw. 1981).

[30]The NPA has also been held to preempt state antitrust laws to the extent they are contrary to it. Bay Guardian Co. v. Chronicle Pub'g Co., 344 F. Supp. 1155, 1160 (N.D. Cal. 1972).

[31]Any such agreement entered into before July 24, 1970, does not need the U.S. attorney general's approval, although at the time the arrangement was made "not more than one of the newspaper publications involved . . . [can have been] likely to remain or become a financially sound publication . . . ." 15 U.S.C. §1803(a). Any such agreement entered into after that date needs the attorney general's approval. 15 U.S.C. §1803(b). The applicable regulations are in 28 C.F.R. §48 (1983). Before approving such an agreement, the attorney general must find that "not more than one of the newspaper publications . . . is a publication other than a failing newspaper." 15 U.S.C. §1803(b). A "failing newspaper" is one "in probable danger of financial failure." 15 U.S.C. §1802(5). The NPA does not prohibit newspapers from entering into joint operating agreements without the attorney general's approval, but such agreements have no antitrust immunity. Newspaper Guild v. Levi, 539 F.2d 755, 757, 1 Media L. Rep. 2709, 2713 (D.C. Cir. 1976), *cert. denied,* 429 U.S. 1092 (1977).

[32]15 U.S.C. §1803(c).

Although at first glance the NPA would appear to enhance freedom of the press by preventing the number of newspapers from declining, challenges have been made to it on First Amendment grounds.[33] The plaintiffs in these cases have claimed that, by permitting some newspapers to operate jointly and giving them a competitive advantage, other newspapers would be driven out of the market, depriving the latter of their First Amendment rights.[34]

These First Amendment challenges have been rejected for two reasons.[35] First, a distinction has been drawn between regulations that directly control media content and those that cause only incidental economic effects on individual newspapers. As the Ninth Circuit explained:

> the Newspaper Preservation Act's antitrust exemption will not affect the *content* of speech of these smaller newspapers.... At most, the Act *may* affect the number of "readers" a newspaper has. But that the Act may have such an effect is no different, in our view, than any other economic regulation of the newspaper industry.[36]

Second, the courts have noted that passage of the federal antitrust laws was not required by the First Amendment; they were simply laws that Congress had adopted and that it could create exemptions to if it chose.[37]

§9.3 Civil Rights Law

Numerous attempts have been made to use the federal civil rights laws as a substitute for common law defamation or privacy claims or for other similar claims, as well as to force the media to publish or broadcast particular statements.[38] Such attempts to sue the media have almost never been successful.

§9.3(A) Section 1983

The most important of the federal civil rights laws is 42 U.S.C. Section 1983.[39] Its two essential requirements are that the defendant's act be "under color of state law" and that a federal right be infringed.[40]

---

[33]*Independent P-I,* 704 F.2d 467, 9 Media L. Rep. 1489; *Hawaii Newspaper Agency,* 7 Media L. Rep. 2495; *Bay Guardian Co.,* 344 F. Supp. 1155.

[34]*E.g., Bay Guardian Co.,* 344 F. Supp. at 1157.

[35]Other constitutional challenges to the NPA have also been rejected. *Independent P-I,* 704 F.2d at 481, 9 Media L. Rep. at 1501 (vagueness); *Hawaii Newspaper Agency,* 7 Media L. Rep. at 2498–99 (equal protection); *Bay Guardian Co.,* 344 F. Supp. at 1158 (equal protection).

[36]*Independent P-I,* 704 F.2d at 483, 9 Media L. Rep. at 1501.

[37]*Id.,* 9 Media L. Rep. at 1502 (noting also that NPA did not favor large newspapers over small newspapers because it was available to all papers no matter what their size); *Hawaii Newspaper Agency,* 7 Media L. Rep. at 2498; *Bay Guardian Co.,* 344 F. Supp. at 1158.

[38]For a discussion on attempts to force the media to publish or broadcast statements by others, see Chapter 13.

[39]"Every person who, under color of any statute, ordinance, regulation, custom, or usage, of any State or Territory, subjects or causes to be subjected, any citizen of the United States or other person within the jurisdiction thereof to the deprivation of any rights, privileges, or immunities secured by the Constitution and laws, shall be liable to the party injured." 42 U.S.C. §1983 (1978).

[40]Parratt v. Taylor, 451 U.S. 527, 535 (1981). The §1983 violation must also be the proximate cause of the plaintiff's injury. Mt. Healthy City Sch. Dist. v. Doyle, 429 U.S. 274, 284–87 (1977); Arnold v. International Business Machs. Corp., 637 F.2d 1350 (9th Cir. 1981).

§9.3(A)(i) The "Under Color of State Law" Requirement

The first requirement, "under color of state law" or its synonym, "state action,"[41] means that the defendant's act must be " 'fairly attributable to the State.' "[42] Because most media are owned privately rather than by the government, actions by the media ordinarily do not constitute state action.[43] Thus, the state action requirement usually presents an insurmountable barrier to Section 1983 claims against the media.

If private parties conspire with state or local officials to violate Section 1983, however, the state action requirement is then met and such private parties may be liable under Section 1983.[44] This rule has often been used in an attempt to meet the state action requirement in suits against the media. While such allegations are easily made, they usually have been found to be inadequately pled or to lack a factual foundation.[45]

§9.3(A)(ii) Federal Right Requirement and Defamation

The second requirement of a Section 1983 action is that a federal right be infringed.[46] Section 1983 protects rights created by the federal Constitution or by federal statute, but it does not protect against the violation of all legal rights.[47]

---

[41]"Under color of state law" is synonymous with the "state action" required to establish a violation of the Fourteenth Amendment. Rendell-Baker v. Kohn, 457 U.S. 830, 838 (1982).

[42]*Id.* at 838 (quoting Lugar v. Edmondson Oil Co., 457 U.S. 922, 937 (1982)). *Accord* United States v. Classic, 313 U.S. 299, 326 (1941); United States v. Screws, 325 U.S. 91, 111 (1945); Polk County v. Dodson, 454 U.S. 312, 317–20 (1981).

[43]Sheppard v. E.W. Scripps Co., 421 F.2d 555, 556 (6th Cir.), *cert. denied sub nom.* Strickland v. E.W. Scripps Co., 400 U.S. 941 (1970); Keen v. Philadelphia Daily News, 325 F. Supp. 929, 930 (E.D. Pa. 1971); Mimms v. Philadelphia Newspapers, 352 F. Supp. 862, 865 (E.D. Pa. 1972); Levitch v. Columbia Broadcasting Sys., 495 F. Supp. 649, 657 (S.D.N.Y. 1980); Prahl v. Brosamle, 295 N.W.2d 768, 774 (Wis. Ct. App. 1980); Jones v. Taibbi, 508 F. Supp. 1069, 1072 n.6, 7 Media L. Rep. 1225, 1227 n.6 (D. Mass. 1981); Manax v. McNamara, 660 F. Supp. 657, 664 (W.D. Tex. 1987), *aff'd,* 842 F.2d 808, 812, 15 Media L. Rep. 1655, 1657–59 (5th Cir. 1988); Provisional Gov't v. ABC, 11 Media L. Rep. 2107, 2110 (D.D.C. 1985) (broadcast license does not amount to state action); Wellman v. Williamson Daily News, 582 F. Supp. 1526, 1527–28 (S.D. W. Va. 1984), *aff'd without opinion,* 742 F.2d 1450 (4th Cir. 1984); Smith v. Butler, 507 F. Supp. 952, 954 (E.D. Pa. 1981); *see also* cases cited *infra* §9.3(B).

[44]Adickes v. S.H. Kress & Co., 398 U.S. 144, 150–52 (1970); Dennis v. Sparks, 449 U.S. 24, 27–28 (1980); United Steelworkers of Am. v. Phelps Dodge Corp., 883 F.2d 804, 806 (9th Cir. 1987) ("there must be some evidence of control by the private party over the actions of the state officials").

[45]Mattheis v. Hoyt, 136 F. Supp. 119, 124 (W.D. Mich. 1955); Cook v. Houston Post, 616 F.2d 791, 794 n.3 (5th Cir. 1980); Borduin v. Panax Corp., 7 Media L. Rep. 1645 (E.D. Mich. 1981); Darby v. Stender, 8 Media L. Rep. 1508, 1509 (D.N.J. 1982); Baker v. Burlington County Times, 9 Media L. Rep. 1967, 1967 (D.N.J. 1983); Hauptmann v. Wilentz, 570 F. Supp. 351, 383–84 (D.N.J. 1983), *aff'd,* 770 F.2d 1070 (3d Cir. 1985), *cert. denied,* 474 U.S. 1103 (1986); Pawelek v. Paramount Studios Corp., 571 F. Supp. 1082, 1084 (N.D. Ill. 1983); *Manax,* 660 F. Supp. at 665, *aff'd,* 842 F.2d at 810, 15 Media L. Rep. at 1656–57 (also holding plaintiff's allegations of Racketeer Influenced and Corrupt Organizations Act "enterprise" inadequate); Bowes v. Wisconsin Vocational Bd., 9 Media L. Rep. 2372, 2378 (Wis. Cir. Ct. 1983); May v. State of Mich., 10 Media L. Rep. 2454, 2455 (E.D. Mich. 1984); Denis v. Rhinelander, 11 Media L. Rep. 2141, 2144 (W.D. Mich. 1985). *Contra* Bergman v. Stein, 404 F. Supp. 287, 296 (S.D.N.Y. 1975) (issue briefly discussed); National Bar Ass'n v. Capital Cities, 10 Media L. Rep. 2317, 2326 (W.D.N.Y. 1984). This case is unsound because its reasoning would require denial of summary judgment in virtually all conspiracy cases. *See also* Phelps v. Wichita Eagle-Beacon, 886 F.2d 1262, 1270–71 (10th Cir. 1989) (case remanded for finding on conspiracy issue). Specificity is also required in pleading civil rights conspiracies. *See, e.g.,* Slotnick v. Garfinkle, 632 F.2d 163, 165–66 (1st Cir. 1980). *See infra* note 79. *But see* Leatherman v. Tarrant County Narcotics Intelligence & Coordination Unit, 113 S. Ct. 1160, 1163 (1993) (refusing to apply heightened pleading standard in civil rights action against municipality).

[46]*Supra* note 40.

[47]Maine v. Thiboutot, 448 U.S. 1, 4 (1980). The primary application of §1983 is to provide a remedy against state and local officials who violate the Fourteenth Amendment. Monroe v. Pape, 365 U.S. 167, 171 (1961), *overruled on other grounds,* Monell v. Department of Social Servs. of City of N.Y., 436 U.S. 658 (1978). Section 1983 does not apply to federal officials. Bivens v. Six Unknown Named Agents of FBI, 403 U.S. 388 (1971). See *infra* note 51.

Consistent with this rule and numerous lower court decisions,[48] the Supreme Court held in *Paul v. Davis*[49] that there is no federal right to a good reputation, reasoning that Section 1983 does not federalize every tort[50] and that the "stigma" to a person's reputation caused by defamation does not injure the kind of property or liberty interests protected by the Fourteenth Amendment.[51] Accordingly, the Court concluded that libel and slander claims cannot be brought under Section 1983.[52]

In reaching this conclusion, the Court drew a distinction between cases where the plaintiff's claim was simply for defamation and those where the plaintiff's claim was that he or she had lost some tangible legal right, usually a government job, *and* was defamed by the government in conjunction with the loss of a job or some other tangible legal right.[53] Only in the latter situation is a Section 1983 claim for defamation available.[54]

Thus, it is virtually impossible to state a Section 1983 claim against the media for defamation because, by themselves, defamatory statements do not infringe any federal right, and the media do not have the power to defame someone *and* deprive that person of a tangible legal right, such as a government-issued driver's license or job, that constitutes "property" or "liberty" under the Fourteenth Amendment. As a result, since *Paul,* claims against the media for defamation brought under Section 1983 have been unsuccessful.[55]

---

[48]*See, e.g., Mattheis,* 136 F. Supp. at 124; Hopkins v. Wasson, 329 F.2d 67, 68 (6th Cir.), *cert. denied,* 379 U.S. 854 (1964); Temple v. Pergament, 235 F. Supp. 242, 244 (D.N.J. 1964), *aff'd,* 343 F.2d 474 (3d Cir. 1965); Heller v. Roberts, 386 F.2d 832 (2d Cir. 1967); Morey v. Independent Sch. Dist., 312 F. Supp. 1257, 1262 (D. Minn. 1969), *aff'd per curiam,* 429 F.2d 428 (8th Cir. 1970); Gorman v. Lukowsky, 431 F.2d 971, 972 (6th Cir. 1970); Keen v. Philadelphia Daily News, 325 F. Supp. 929, 930 (E.D. Pa. 1971); Church v. Hamilton, 444 F.2d 105, 106 (3d Cir. 1971); Jervey v. Martin, 336 F. Supp. 1350, 1354 (W.D. Va. 1972); Mimms v. Philadelphia Newspapers, 352 F. Supp. 862, 865 (E.D. Pa. 1972); El-Em Band of Pomo Indians v. 49th Dist. Agric. Fair Ass'n, 359 F. Supp. 1044, 1046 (N.D. Cal. 1973); *see also* Martin v. Merola, 532 F.2d 191, 194–95 (2d Cir. 1976) (claim for violation of criminal defendants' right to fair trial by prosecutor's remarks to press dismissed as premature because state criminal trial had not taken place); Ellingburg v. Lucas, 518 F.2d 1196, 1197 (8th Cir. 1975). *But see* United States ex rel. Sabella v. Newsday, 315 F. Supp. 333, 334 (E.D.N.Y. 1970) (claim stated under §1983 against newspaper and district attorney who allegedly conspired to have newspaper employees falsely testify at criminal trial and fail to obey subpoena).

[49]424 U.S. 693 (1976) (plaintiff alleged he had been defamed by police flier about shoplifters that included his picture). *Accord* Siegert v. Gilley, 500 U.S. 226 (1991).

[50]424 U.S. at 699–701.

[51]*Id.* at 701–10. The Court noted that the same reasoning barred defamation actions against federal officials brought under the Fifth Amendment. *Id.* at 702 n.3. In some circumstances, actions based solely on the federal Constitution may be brought against federal officials. *Bivens,* 403 U.S. 388; Reuber v. United States, 750 F.2d 1039 (D.C. Cir. 1984) While it is unclear whether a *Bivens* claim is available against private parties for conspiring with federal officials, the courts have refused to allow such a claim for conspiracies between the media and federal officials. Zerilli v. Evening News Ass'n, 628 F.2d 217, 223 & n.11, 6 Media L. Rep. 1530, 1534–35 & n.11 (D.C. Cir. 1980); Manax v. McNamara, 660 F. Supp. 657, 664 (W.D. Tex. 1987), *aff'd,* 842 F.2d 808, 15 Media L. Rep. 1655 (5th Cir. 1988). *But see* Lugar v. Edmondson Oil Co., 457 U.S. 922 (1982) (right of action allowed against private party who used writ of attachment procedures including county sheriff to execute writ).

[52]424 U.S. at 698, 712.

[53]*Id.* at 701–10.

[54]*Id.* at 706, 710. *See also* Siegert v. Gilley, 500 U.S. 226, 232–33 (1991) (defamation claim cannot be brought under §1983 especially where defamation was not in connection with employment termination because plaintiff resigned and allegedly defamatory letter was written several weeks after termination); Bishop v. Wood, 426 U.S. 341, 348 (1976) (discharged policeman cannot claim damage to liberty interests where there was no public disclosure of reasons for discharge); Owen v. City of Independence, 445 U.S. 622, 632–33 n.13 (1980) (dismissal of government employee coupled with contemporaneous charges that impugned employee's honesty and integrity, even if charges did not cause discharge, actionable under §1983).

[55]Walker v. Cahalan, 542 F.2d 681, 683–84 (6th Cir. 1976), *cert. denied,* 430 U.S. 966 (1977); Cook v. Houston Post, 616 F.2d 791, 794 n.3 (5th Cir. 1980); Jenkins v. Winchester Star, 8 Media L. Rep. 1403, 1404 (W.D. Va. 1981); Smith v. Butler, 507 F. Supp. 952, 954 (E.D. Pa. 1981); Baker v. Burlington County Times, 9 Media L. Rep. 1967, 1968 (D.N.J. 1983); Duff v. Sherlock, 432 F. Supp. 423, 429 (E.D. Pa. 1977) (defamatory statement published in newspaper that plaintiff is alcoholic not actionable under §1983); Green v. DeCamp, 612 F.2d 368, 369–71 (8th Cir. 1980) (state legislative committee's release of defamatory report

§9.3(A)(iii) Federal Right Requirement and Privacy

Paul v. Davis also rejected the plaintiff's claim that his privacy had been invaded by the disclosure that he had been arrested for shoplifting.[56] The Court noted that a constitutional right of privacy as to certain "fundamental" rights—namely marriage, procreation, contraception, family relationships, child rearing and education, and unreasonable searches and seizures—had been recognized.[57] The Court refused to extend this privacy right beyond these areas, however, indicating that giving publicity to an arrest did not violate any constitutional right of privacy.[58]

In a 2-1 decision, an earlier case, *York v. Story*,[59] had found a violation of the constitutional right of privacy actionable under Section 1983, where a police officer ordered a female assault victim, over her objections, to let him take nude pictures of her in indecent poses, which he then circulated to other police officers.[60] Whether *York* survives *Paul* is unclear;[61] it does not fall within any of the constitutional privacy categories set forth in *Paul*. In any event, the courts,[62] including the Ninth Circuit, which decided *York*,[63] have

---

to media not actionable under §1983); *see also* Tsermengas v. Pontiac Press, 199 F. Supp. 557, 558 (E.D. Mich. 1961) (prisoner's claim that newspaper printed "false and defamatory" articles during his murder trial did not state cause of action). *But see* National Bar Ass'n v. Capital Cities, 10 Media L. Rep. 2317, 2322 (W.D.N.Y. 1984) (drawing untenable distinction between defamation and loss of rights through defamation).

[56] 424 U.S. 693, 713 (1976).
[57] *Id.*
[58] *Id.*
[59] 324 F.2d 450 (9th Cir. 1963), *cert. denied*, 376 U.S. 939 (1964).
[60] *Id.* at 452.
[61] Reilly v. Leonard, 459 F. Supp. 291, 299–300 (D. Conn. 1978) (no constitutional right of privacy where police distributed report stating that plaintiff murdered his mother; relying on *Paul*, court held that constitutional right of privacy prevents government regulation of certain areas of one's life but does not prevent unwarranted and unwanted publicity about one's affairs); J.P. v. DeSanti, 653 F.2d 1080, 1090 (6th Cir. 1981) (relying on *Paul* to conclude that disclosure of juveniles' social histories prepared for probation proceedings does not violate constitutional right of privacy); *see also* Katz v. United States, 389 U.S. 347, 350–51 (1967) ("[T]he protection of a person's general right to privacy—his right to be left alone by other people—is, like the protection of his property and his very life, left largely to the law of the individual States."). *Contra* Fadjo v. Coon, 633 F.2d 1172, 1176 (5th Cir. 1981) (constitutional right of privacy extends beyond areas set forth in *Paul* and is violated by disclosure of information alleged to be "the most private details" of plaintiff's life); Slayton v. Williams, 726 F.2d 631, 635 (10th Cir. 1984) (*Paul* does not bar claim against police for showing photographs of plaintiff "of a highly sensitive, personal, and private nature" where they were obtained during illegal search). *Fadjo* and *Slayton* have been limited to their facts. Davis v. Bucher, 853 F.2d 718, 721 (9th Cir. 1988).
[62] Travers v. Paton, 261 F. Supp. 110, 115 (D. Conn. 1966) (broadcaster's secret filming and broadcast of prisoner's parole hearing does not violate constitutional right of privacy; *York* distinguished on grounds that defendants' conduct there was "so shocking 'that our policy will not endure it' " (citation omitted)); Mimms v. Philadelphia Newspapers, 352 F. Supp. 862, 865 (E.D. Pa. 1972) (newspaper's publication of article entitled "Prisoners Walk All Over Us Half The Time" with plaintiff's photo did not violate constitutional right of privacy; *York* distinguished on grounds that "the conduct complained of [there] was so outrageous as to shock anyone's conscience"); Rosenberg v. Martin, 478 F.2d 520, 525 (2d Cir.), *cert. denied*, 414 U.S. 872 (1973) (no violation of constitutional right of privacy by police officer inflaming public through false statements to media because he did not cause plaintiff's conviction for murder; *York* distinguished on grounds that it should not be extended); Kipps v. Ewell, 391 F. Supp. 1285, 1290 (W.D. Va. 1975), *aff'd*, 538 F.2d 564 (4th Cir. 1976) (no violation of constitutional right to privacy where, after securing plaintiff's arrest, detective told press he was going to take well-deserved vacation and where press was given picture of plaintiff in prison garb; *York* distinguished on grounds there was no "gross abuse" in this case); Higbee v. Times-Advocate, 5 Media L. Rep. 2372 (S.D. Cal. 1980) (no violation of constitutional right of privacy where newspaper accompanied police on execution of search warrant at plaintiffs' home and where newspaper published photo of inside of plaintiffs' home; *York* distinguished on grounds that it involved "gross abuse" by defendants); Moncrief v. Hanton, 10 Media L. Rep. 1620, 1622 (N.D. Ohio 1984) (no violation of constitutional right of privacy where media accompanied police on execution of search warrant and took pictures of one plaintiff handcuffed in his home; *York* distinguished on grounds that photographs here "in no way compared to those in *York*").
[63] Baker v. Howard, 419 F.2d 376, 377 (9th Cir. 1969) (no violation of constitutional right of privacy where police released false and libelous report that indicated plaintiff had committed crime and that news media then broadcast; *York* distinguished on grounds that here offense was not "so flagrant that it calls for invocation of the constitution," and on further grounds that *York* did not, as this case did, involve defendants'

been careful to limit *York* to its facts and not extend it. Privacy claims against the media under Section 1983 have been quite unsuccessful.[64]

Similarly, the courts have concluded that claims for intentional or negligent infliction of emotional distress are not actionable under Section 1983 because no federal right is invaded.[65]

§9.3(B) Section 1985: State Action, Class-Based Animus, and Federal Rights

Claims against the media are also frequently brought under 42 U.S.C. Section 1985—and especially under its third paragraph.[66] To state a claim under Section 1985(3)[i]

First Amendment free press and free speech rights). No media defendant was involved in *York*. It is noteworthy that the author of *York* joined in the per curiam opinion in *Baker*. *See also Davis*, 853 F.2d at 721 (correction officer examined nude photographs of inmate's wife, showed them to two other inmates without permission, and later made derogatory comments about inmate's wife's anatomy; *York* distinguished because correction officer's "malefaction is simply not in [*York*'s] league").

[64]*Travers*, 261 F. Supp. 110; *Baker*, 419 F.2d 376; *Mimms*, 352 F. Supp. 862; *Higbee*, 5 Media L. Rep. 2372; Jenkins v. Winchester Star, 8 Media L. Rep. 1403 (W.D. Va. 1981); *Moncrief*, 10 Media L. Rep. 1620; Prahl v. Brosamle, 295 N.W.2d 768, 774 (Wis. Ct. App. 1980) (no violation of constitutional right to privacy where newscaster accompanied police on raid and broadcast film he shot; "An investigation reminiscent of the charge on San Juan hill is in no sense confidential."); *see also* McNally v. Pulitzer Pub'g Co., 532 F.2d 69, 76–78 (8th Cir. 1976) (even assuming that newspaper's publication of psychiatric report on criminal defendant violated constitutional right of privacy, such information already had been distributed in open court and thus further distribution absolutely privileged under Cox Broadcasting v. Cohn, 420 U.S. 469, 494–95 (1975)); Holman v. Central Ark. Broadcasting Co., 610 F.2d 542, 544 (8th Cir. 1979) (no §1983 claim for invasion of privacy where radio station recorded and broadcast statements of plaintiff, who was under arrest for drunken driving, because plaintiff's statements could be heard throughout police station (citing Cox Broadcasting Corp. v. Cohn, 420 U.S. 469 (1975))); Bergman v. Stein, 404 F. Supp. 287, 296–97 (S.D.N.Y. 1975); Dixon v. Pennsylvania Crime Comm'n, 67 F.R.D. 425, 429 (M.D. Pa. 1975). *See also* Smith v. Fairman, 98 F.R.D. 445, 448 (C.D. Ill. 1982) (prisoner may have right of privacy not to be filmed in cell); *contra* Jones/Seymour v. LeFebvre, 781 F. Supp. 355, 357 (E.D. Pa. 1991) (holding that *Smith* overruled by subsequent Supreme Court decision), *aff'd*, 961 F.2d 1567 (3d Cir. 1992). *Compare* Scheetz v. Morning Call, 946 F.2d 202, 19 Media L. Rep. 1385 (3d Cir. 1991) (recognizing constitutional privacy claim for disclosure of confidential information but holding there is no right of privacy in police reports), *cert. denied*, 112 S. Ct. 1171 (1992).

[65]Robinson v. McCorkle, 462 F.2d 111, 114 (3d Cir.), *cert. denied*, 409 U.S. 1042 (1972); Dear v. Rathje, 391 F. Supp. 1, 9 (N.D. Ill. 1975); Brainerd v. Potratz, 421 F. Supp. 836, 840 (N.D. Ill. 1976), *aff'd without opinion*, 566 F.2d 1177 (7th Cir. 1977); Whelehan v. County of Monroe, 558 F. Supp. 1093, 1111 n.10 (W.D.N.Y. 1983); *see also* Poirier v. Hodges, 445 F. Supp. 838, 843 (M.D. Fla. 1978) (interference with contractual relations not actionable under §1983).

[66]42 U.S.C. §1985 provides:

(1) Preventing officer from performing duty. [i] If two or more persons in any State or Territory conspire to prevent, by force, intimidation, or threat, any person from accepting or holding any office, trust, or place of confidence under the United States, or from discharging any duties thereof; or [ii] to induce by like means any officer of the United States to leave any State, district or place, where his duties as an officer are required to be performed, or [iii] to injure him in his person or property on account of his lawful discharge of the duties of his office, or while engaged in the lawful discharge thereof, or [iv] to injure his property so as to molest, interrupt, hinder or impede him in the discharge of his official duties;

(2) Obstructing justice; intimidating party, witness or juror. [i] If two or more persons in any State or Territory conspire to deter, by force, intimidation, or threat, any party or witness in any court of the United States from attending such court, or from testifying to any matter pending therein, freely, fully, and truthfully, or to injure such party or witness in his person or property on account of his having so attended or testified, or to influence the verdict, presentment, or indictment of any grand or petit juror in any such court, or to injure such juror in his person or property on account of any verdict, presentment, or indictment lawfully assented to by him, or of his being or having been such juror; or [ii] if two or more persons conspire for the purpose of impeding, hindering, obstructing, or defeating, in any manner, the due course of justice in any State or Territory, with intent to deny to any citizen the equal protection of the laws, or to injure him or his property for lawfully enforcing, or attempting to enforce, the right of any person, or class of persons, to the equal protection of the laws;

(3) Depriving persons of rights or privileges. [i] If two or more persons in any State or Territory conspire, or go in disguise on the highway or on the premises of another, for the purpose of depriving, either directly or indirectly, any person or class of persons of the equal protection of the laws, or of equal privileges and immunities under the laws, or for the purpose of preventing or hindering the constituted authorities of any State or Territory from giving or securing to all persons within such State or Territory

the plaintiff must allege and prove four elements: (1) a conspiracy; (2) for the purpose of depriving, either directly or indirectly, any person or class of persons of the equal protection of the laws, or of equal privileges and immunities under the laws; and (3) an act in furtherance of the conspiracy; (4) whereby a person is either injured in his person or property or deprived of any right or privilege of a citizen of the United States.[67]

In addition, after *Griffin v. Breckenridge*[68] was decided, it was widely believed that an allegation of state action was not necessary to state a claim under Section 1985(3)[i]. As a result, such a claim was frequently brought with a Section 1983 claim to avoid Section 1983's state action requirement.

In *United Brotherhood of Carpenters and Joiners of America v. Scott*,[69] however, the Supreme Court, in a 5-4 decision, held that, under Section 1985(3)[i], it must be "proved that the State is involved in the conspiracy or that the aim of the conspiracy is to influence the activity of the State,"[70] if the right infringed, there a First Amendment right, is the type of right protected only against government, not private, interference.[71] For most purposes, then, *Carpenters* reestablishes the state action requirement in Section 1985(3) cases, because the federal constitution is almost exclusively concerned with limiting government action; that requirement usually will bar suits against the media.[72]

In *Griffin*, the Court also held that, to state a claim under Section 1985(3)[i], the conspiracy must be motivated by "some racial, or perhaps otherwise class-based, invidious discriminatory animus."[73] In *Carpenters*, the Court limited this statement by holding that a conspiracy motivated by economic or commercial animus, there a conspiracy against workers who refused to join a union, is not actionable under Section 1985(3)[i],[74] but it refused to decide whether conspiracies motivated by political animus were actionable.[75]

---

the equal protection of the laws; or [ii] if two or more persons conspire to prevent by force, intimidation, or threat, any citizen who is lawfully entitled to vote, from giving his support or advocacy in a legal manner, toward or in favor of the election of any lawfully qualified person as an elector for President or Vice-President, or as a member of Congress of the United States; or to injure any citizen in person or property on account of such support or advocacy; in any case of conspiracy set forth in this section, if one or more persons engaged therein do, or cause to be done, any act in furtherance of the object of such conspiracy, whereby another is injured in his person or property, or deprived of having and exercising any right or privilege of a citizen of the United States, the party so injured or deprived may have an action for the recovery of damages, occasioned by such injury or deprivation, against any one or more of the conspirators.

42 U.S.C.S. §1985 (1989). Bracketed numbers for clauses have been inserted and are used in the discussion that follows.

[67]United Bhd. of Carpenters and Joiners of Am. v. Scott, 463 U.S. 825, 829 (1983). The §1985 violation must also be the proximate cause of the plaintiff's injury. Arnold v. International Business Machs. Corp., 637 F.2d 1350 (9th Cir. 1981).

[68]403 U.S. 88, 101 (1971).

[69]463 U.S. 825.

[70]*Id.* at 830.

[71]*Id.* at 833; *Griffin*, 403 U.S. at 105–6. *Accord* Bray v. Alexandria Women's Health Clinic, 113 S. Ct. 753 (1993). *See also* Roe v. Abortion Abolition Soc'y, 811 F.2d 931, 933 (5th Cir.), *cert. denied*, 484 U.S. 848 (1987) (§1985(3) "does not protect individuals against private efforts to encroach on constitutional shields, such as the first amendment that protects only against official conduct").

[72]*See Bray*, 113 S. Ct. at 764 (noting that only constitutional rights protected from private interference are right to be free from involuntary servitude and right to interstate travel; refusing to recognize abortion or privacy as constitutional rights protected from private interference); *supra* §9.3(A)(i); Dworkin v. Hustler Magazine, 12 Media L. Rep. 2162, 2164 (D. Wyo. 1986).

[73]403 U.S. at 102. *Accord Bray*, 113 S. Ct. at 759 (rejecting argument that class of women seeking abortion protected by §1985(3)).

[74]463 U.S. at 838.

[75]*Id.* at 835. *See* Annot., *What Occupational Groups May Be Deemed Entitled to Protection Under 42 U.S.C.S. §1985 Against Invidious Class-Based Discrimination*, 53 A.L.R. FED. 741 (1981) for cases concerning

Like the rejuvenated state action requirement, the class-based animus requirement will usually prevent successful suits against the media.[76]

The holding of *Paul*, that defamation and invasion of privacy claims are usually not actionable under Section 1983 because no federal right is infringed,[77] applies to Section 1985(3) suits.[78] In addition, the failure to adequately plead or demonstrate a conspiracy often leads to the dismissal of Section 1985 claims.[79]

Suits under the other parts of Section 1985—namely Sections 1985(1)[i]–[iv], 1985(2)[i] and [ii], and 1985(3)[ii]—are also possible. Section 1985(2)[ii] is limited by the same restrictions as Section 1985(3)[i], because both of these sections deal with equal protection violations.[80]

The other half of Section 1985(2)—Section 1985(2)[i]—which deals with conspiracies to deter "litigants, witnesses, and grand and petit jurors" by "force, intimidation, or threat" from participating in federal judicial proceedings; and conspiracies under the other half of Section 1985(3)—Section 1985(3)[ii]—"to prevent [citizens] by force, intimidation, or threat" from participating in federal elections, have no apparent application to the media, because the media's publishing activities will seldom if ever amount to "force, intimidation, or threat." For the same reason, the "force, intimidation, or threat" requirement of Sections 1985(1)[i] and [ii] should prevent successful suits against the media under those provisions.

The only remaining provisions of Section 1985—Sections 1985(1)[iii] and [iv]—do not require a showing of "force, intimidation, or threat."[81] With this in mind, two courts, both over dissents and with almost no analysis, have held that the simple defamation of many federal officials is actionable under Section 1985(1),[82] although the plaintiffs in both cases failed to overcome the defendants' First Amendment defenses.[83]

---

what sorts of class-based animus are sufficient under §§1985(2) and (3). As to media-related classes, *see id.* at 745–46.

[76]Manax v. McNamara, 660 F. Supp. 657, 665 (W.D. Tex. 1987), *aff'd*, 842 F.2d 808, 15 Media L. Rep. 1655 (5th Cir. 1988); McNally v. Pulitzer Pub'g Co., 532 F.2d 69, 74–75 (8th Cir. 1976); Hauptmann v. Wilentz, 570 F. Supp. 351, 385–86 (D.N.J. 1983); Moncrief v. Hauton, 10 Media L. Rep. 1620, 1622 (N.D. Ohio 1984).

[77]*See supra* §§9.3(A)(ii) and (iii).

[78]Mattheis v. Hoyt, 136 F. Supp. 119, 123, 124 (N.D. Mich. 1955); Travers v. Paton, 261 F. Supp. 110 (D. Conn. 1966); Holy Spirit Ass'n v. New York State Congress of Parents & Teachers, 408 N.Y.S.2d 261, 266 (N.Y. Sup. Ct. 1978); Johnston v. National Broadcasting Co., 356 F. Supp. 904, 909 (E.D.N.Y. 1973); Clark v. Solem, 628 F.2d 1120, 1121 (8th Cir. 1980); Smith v. Butler, 507 F. Supp. 952, 954 (E.D. Pa. 1981); *but see* Azar v. Conley, 456 F.2d 1382 (6th Cir. 1972) (slander could be integral part of §1985(3) conspiracy).

[79]*Mattheis*, 136 F. Supp. at 123, 124; Mimms v. Philadelphia Newspapers, 352 F. Supp. 862, 866 (E.D. Pa. 1972); *Butler*, 507 F. Supp. at 954; *Hauptmann*, 570 F. Supp. at 385, *aff'd*, 770 F.2d 1070 (3d Cir. 1985), *cert. denied*, 474 U.S. 1103 (1986). *But see* Windsor v. The Tennessean, 719 F.2d 155, 161 (6th Cir. 1983), *reh'g denied with opinion*, 726 F.2d 277 (6th Cir.), *cert. denied*, 469 U.S. 826 (1984). *See also* Brooks v. American Broadcasting Cos., 932 F.2d 495, 18 Media L. Rep. 2121 (6th Cir. 1991) (§1985 claim so vague and conclusory that dismissal is affirmed). *See also supra* note 45.

[80]*See supra* note 66. Kush v. Rutledge, 460 U.S. 719, 725–26 (1983). However, claims under §§1985(1)[i]–[iv], 1985(2)[i], and 1985(3)[ii] are actionable without an allegation of class-based animus. *Id.* at 724–26. To make out a cause of action under §1985(2), the plaintiff must have suffered an actual injury. Morast v. Lance, 807 F.2d 926, 930 (11th Cir. 1987).

[81]Stern v. United States Gypsum, 547 F.2d 1329, 1340–41 (7th Cir.), *cert. denied*, 434 U.S. 975 (1977).

[82]*Stern*, 547 F.2d at 1337–38; *Windsor*, 719 F.2d at 161 (6th Cir. 1983), *reh'g denied with opinion*, 726 F.2d 277, *cert. denied*, 469 U.S. 826. Only federal employees, who are not protected by civil service, may bring such claims, and they must show that they were intentionally defamed. *Windsor*, 726 F.2d at 278. *See generally* Annot., *Action Under 42 U.S.C.S. §1985(1) for Conspiracy to Defame or Otherwise Harm the Reputation of Federal Official*, 69 A.L.R. FED. 913 (1984).

[83]In *Stern*, the court recognized that the First Amendment right to petition the government barred the plaintiff's claim, which was based on the defendants' complaints to the plaintiff's supervisors at the Internal Revenue Service about his performance of an audit of the defendants. 547 F.2d at 1342–46. In *Windsor*, the

§9.3(C) Section 1986

Claims not actionable under Section 1985 are not actionable under Section 1986,[84] which provides a remedy for anyone who (1) knows that Section 1985 is about to be violated, (2) has the power to prevent or aid in preventing such violations, and (3) neglects or fails to do so.[85]

§9.3(D) Section 1981

Section 1981[86] prohibits racial discrimination, by the government and private parties, in the formation of contracts.[87]

In one of the few cases under Section 1981 against the media for publishing activities, the plaintiffs contended that a newspaper refused to print their wedding announcements on the "white" society page because they were black.[88] Anyone who wanted an announcement published filled out a questionnaire available from the newspaper,[89] and the newspaper then wrote and published stories, based on the questionnaires, on its "white" and "black" society pages.[90] The newspaper received no consideration for publishing such announcements, and it never promised on the questionnaires, nor anywhere else,

---

newspaper prevailed because the court held that, as a matter of constitutional law, the plaintiff had to prove that the newspaper made defamatory statements with constitutional actual malice and that he was collaterally estopped from doing so by the outcome of his state court defamation case. 719 F.2d at 162.

[84]*See Morast,* 807 F.2d at 930; Poirier v. Hodges, 445 F. Supp. 838, 847 (M.D. Fla. 1978) and cases cited therein; Petrone v. City of Reading, 541 F. Supp. 735, 741 (E.D. Pa. 1982) and cases cited therein; Hauptmann v. Wilentz, 570 F. Supp. 351, 387 (D.N.J. 1983); May v. State of Mich., 10 Media L. Rep. 2454, 2456 (E.D. Mich. 1984); Manax v. McNamara, 660 F. Supp. 657, 665 (W.D. Tex. 1987), *aff'd,* 842 F.2d 808, 15 Media L. Rep. 1655 (5th Cir. 1988).

[85]Section 1986 provides that:
Every person who, having knowledge that any of the wrongs conspired to be done, and mentioned in the preceding section, are about to be committed, and having power to prevent or aid in preventing the commission of the same, neglects or refuses so to do, if such wrongful act be committed, shall be liable to the party injured, or his legal representatives, for all damages caused by such wrongful act, which such person by reasonable diligence could have prevented; and such damages may be recovered in an action on the case; and any number of persons guilty of such wrongful neglect or refusal may be joined as defendants in the action, and if the death of any party be caused by any such wrongful act and neglect, the legal representatives of the deceased shall have such action therefor, and may recover not exceeding five thousand dollars damages therein, for the benefit of the widow of the deceased, if there be one, and if there be no widow, then for the benefit of the next of kin of the deceased. But no action under provisions of this section shall be sustained which is not commenced within one year after the cause of action has accrued.
42 U.S.C. §1986 (1978).

[86]Section 1981 provides:
(a) Statement of equal rights
All persons within the jurisdiction of the United States shall have the same right in every State and Territory to make and enforce contracts, to sue, be parties, give evidence, and to the full and equal benefit of all laws and proceedings for the security of persons and property as is enjoyed by white citizens, and shall be subject to like punishment, pains, penalties, taxes, licenses, and exactions of every kind, and to no other.

(b) Definition
For purposes of this section, the term "make and enforce contracts" includes the making, performance, modification, and termination of contracts, and the enjoyment of all benefits, privileges, terms, and conditions of the contractual relationship.

(c) Protection against impairment
The rights protected by this section are protected against impairment by nongovernmental discrimination and impairment under color of State law.
42 U.S.C. §1981 (1992).

[87]Patterson v. McClean Credit Union, 491 U.S. 164 (1989); Runyon v. McCrary, 427 U.S. 160, 168–71 (1976); McDonald v. Santa Fe Trail Transp. Co., 427 U.S. 273, 286–87 (1976); *see generally* Annot., Romualdo P. Eclavez, *Supreme Court's Views as to Constitutionality, Construction, and Application of 42 U.S.C.S. §1981,* 49 L. Ed. 2d 1349 (1976).

[88]Cook v. Advertiser Co., 458 F.2d 1119, 1120–21 (5th Cir. 1972).

[89]*Id.* at 1122–23.

[90]*Id.* at 1120–22.

that it would publish information from them.[91] The Fifth Circuit held that, under such circumstances, there was no contract between the plaintiffs and the defendant newspaper and, thus, there could be no violation of Section 1981.[92]

As a result, even though Section 1981 applies to the activities of private parties, it ordinarily will not regulate how the media gather the news or what they broadcast or publish.[93]

§9.3(E) Civil Rights Suits by the Media

With varying degrees of success, the media have used the federal civil rights laws against their antagonists.[94]

§9.4 FEDERAL ELECTION LAW

The Federal Election Campaign Act of 1971[95] requires every person who makes independent expenditures in excess of $250 a year to file a statement with the Federal Election Commission (FEC).[96] In addition, it is illegal for a corporation to make a contribution or expenditure in connection with any federal election or primary.[97]

The definition of "expenditures," however, excludes "any news story, commentary or editorial distributed through the facilities of any broadcasting station, newspaper, magazine or other periodical publication, unless such facilities are owned or controlled by any political party, political committee, or candidate."[98] The interpretation of these provisions has spawned several decisions.

In *Reader's Digest Association v. Federal Election Commission*,[99] a magazine sought to enjoin the FEC from investigating whether it violated the Act by making expenditures to distribute videotapes of a computer reenactment of Senator Edward Kennedy's car accident at Chappaquiddick to other members of the media.[100] The videotapes were prepared as part of a study for a *Reader's Digest* article on the accident and were distributed with the article.[101]

---

[91] *Id.*

[92] *Id.* Judge Wisdom concurred, emphasizing that there was no contract since the newspaper, in determining what to publish, was exercising its First Amendment right to decide what was newsworthy. *Id.* at 1124. The District Court had held that the First Amendment barred the plaintiff's claim. *Id.* at 1121. For a discussion of access to the media, see Chapter 13.

[93] Provisional Gov't v. ABC, 11 Media L. Rep. 2107, 2110 (D.D.C. 1985) (rejecting §1981 claims); Brooks v. American Broadcasting Cos., 932 F.2d 495, 18 Media L. Rep. 2121 (6th Cir. 1991) (same, noting that state action probably required for violations of some portions of §1981).

[94] *See, e.g.,* WSB-TV v. Lee, 842 F.2d 1266, 15 Media L. Rep. 1583 (11th Cir. 1988) (summary judgment for sheriff in journalists' §1983 lawsuit for interfering with news gathering reversed); Frissel v. Rizzo, 4 Media L. Rep. 2249, 2251 (3d Cir. 1979) (newspaper reader has no standing to sue city that withdrew ads from newspaper because it does not like newspapers' reporting, but newspaper could sue under §1983); Western Telecasters v. California Fed'n of Labor, 415 F. Supp. 30 (S.D. Cal. 1976) (television station's and employees' suit against union under §1985(3) dismissed because no showing of class-based animus); Hutchens v. Beckman, 521 F. Supp. 426, 429 (S.D. Ga. 1981) (newspaper publisher has no §1985(3) claim because newspaper publishers are not protected class); Matthes v. East Fishkill, 785 F.2d 43, 12 Media L. Rep. 1874 (2d Cir. 1986); *see also* Environmental Planning Council v. El Dorado Super. Ct., 36 Cal. 3d 188, 197, 680 P.2d 1086 (Cal. 1984) (newspaper that was target of private group's boycott effort could not claim that its constitutional rights were violated because no governmental action was involved).

[95] 2 U.S.C. §§431–55 (1993).

[96] *Id.* §434(c).

[97] *Id.* §441b(a). "Contribution or expenditure" is defined *id.* §441(b)(2).

[98] *Id.* §431(9)(B)(i). *See also* 11 C.F.R. §100.8(b)(2) (1993).

[99] 509 F. Supp. 1210, 7 Media L. Rep. 1053 (S.D.N.Y. 1981).

[100] *Id.* at 1211.

[101] *Id.* at 1212.

The FEC opposed the preliminary injunction on the grounds that *Reader's Digest*'s claims were not ripe and that it had adequate remedies at law under the Act, so equitable relief was unnecessary.[102] After noting that preenforcement review of administrative agency actions is often inappropriate,[103] the court held that such review was appropriate in the case because (1) *Reader's Digest* claimed it was intimidated by the FEC's investigation, (2) the express media exemption in the law apparently was meant to prevent even investigations of media activities by the FEC, and (3) First Amendment considerations favored relief because freedom of the press is substantially eroded by investigations of the press.[104]

The court then adopted a two-step analysis to determine whether an FEC investigation was appropriate. The court held that the FEC cannot investigate the substance of the media's activity until it demonstrates that the media exemption is inapplicable.[105] However, the FEC can investigate whether the media exemption applies, i.e., whether the media entity is owned by a political party, political committee, or political candidate; and whether the media entity is acting as the media in making the complained-of distribution of information.[106] Only if the press exemption is found not to apply may the FEC investigate whether a substantive violation has occurred.[107] Accordingly, the court held that initially the FEC should limit its investigation to the applicability of the media exemption.[108]

In *Federal Election Commission v. Phillips Publishing*,[109] the court adopted the *Reader's Digest* two-step analysis.[110] There, the FEC offered no evidence that the defendant was controlled by any political candidate or party,[111] nor was there any indication that the defendant's newsletter's solicitation of subscriptions, which emphasized the newsletter's opposition to Senator Edward Kennedy's presidential campaign, was anything but a normal and legitimate press function.[112] Accordingly, because there was no proof that the statutory exemption for the press did not apply, the court refused to require the defendant to answer interrogatories about its personnel and operations.[113]

In *Federal Election Commission v. Massachusetts Citizens for Life*,[114] the Supreme Court narrowed the reach of the media exemption. There, the nonprofit, incorporated Massachusetts Citizens for Life (MCFL) claimed that because it distributed a newsletter to contributors and noncontributors who expressed support for its goals, a "Special Election Edition" that expressly advocated election of certain candidates fell under the media exemption as a

---

[102]*Id.* at 1213.
[103]*Id.*
[104]509 F. Supp. at 1214.
[105]*Id.* at 1215.
[106]*Id.*
[107]*Id.*
[108]*Id.* at 1215–16.
[109]517 F. Supp. 1308, 7 Media L. Rep. 1825 (D.D.C. 1981).
[110]*Id.* at 1313.
[111]*Id.*
[112]*Id.* at 1309.
[113]*Id.* at 1314. *See also* Kay v. Federal Election Comm'n, 7 Media L. Rep. 1474 (D.D.C. 1981) (newspaper's publication of chart setting forth positions of major political candidates did not violate federal election law); Federal Election Comm'n v. Machinists Non-Partisan Political League, 655 F.2d 380, 386 (D.C. Cir.), *cert. denied*, 454 U.S. 897 (1981).
[114]479 U.S. 238 (1986).

"periodical publication."[115] The Court, without deciding whether the regular newsletter itself qualified for the media exemption,[116] concluded that "considerations of form," when taken in combination, will distinguish campaign flyers from regular publications, and that entities that publish newsletters are not automatically entitled to the media exemption.[117]

The Court concluded that the special edition did not qualify as an exempt periodical publication because it did not carry the regular newsletter masthead; was produced by a separate staff; was not distributed to the newsletters' regular audience, but to the public at large; and contained no volume and issue number identifying it as one in a series.[118] The Court distinguished *Phillips Publishing* and *Reader's Digest* on the basis that the media organizations in those cases were engaged in "the normal business activity of a press entity."[119] However, the Court held that, even though the media exemption did not apply, the Act's restrictions on independent spending, as applied to MCFL, were unconstitutional.[120]

§9.5 FEDERAL LABOR LAW

It is clear that the media have no First Amendment exemption from labor laws that are of general application.[121] Thus, in general, the National Labor Relations Act (NLRA)[122] and the Fair Labor Standards Act (FLSA)[123] may be applied to the media without violating the First Amendment.[124] However, particular applications of those laws may violate the First Amendment.

For example, an injunction against distribution of a newspaper because of FLSA violations is prohibited by the First Amendment.[125] Similarly, a National Labor Relations Board (NLRB) order that a newspaper resume publication of a reporter's column that had been suspended because of the reporter's union activities was unconstitutional.[126]

Nor may a newspaper be forced to engage in collective bargaining over ethical standards for employees, at least as to those "reasonable rules designed to prevent its employees from engaging in activities which may directly compromise their standing as responsible journalists and that of the publication for which they work as a medium of integrity."[127] Similarly, employees who help formulate editorial policy are exempt from the NLRA.[128] A media employer has no absolute First Amendment right to fire journalists because of their union

---

[115]*Id.* at 250.
[116]*Id.*
[117]*Id.* at 250–51.
[118]*Id.*
[119]479 U.S. at 251 n.5.
[120]*Id.* at 263.
[121]Associated Press v. NLRB (Associated Press I), 301 U.S. 103, 132–33, 1 Media L. Rep. 2689 (1937).
[122]29 U.S.C. §141 (1973).
[123]29 U.S.C. §§201–19 (1965).
[124]*Associated Press I,* 301 U.S. 103 (NLRA); Oklahoma Press Pub'g Co. v. Walling, 327 U.S. 186, 192 (1946) (FLSA); *see also* Mabee v. White Plains Pub'g Co., 327 U.S. 178, 184 (1946) (same).
[125]Sun Pub'g Co. v. Walling, 140 F.2d 445, 449–50 (6th Cir. 1944).
[126]Passaic Daily News v. NLRB, 736 F.2d 1543, 1556–59 (D.C. Cir. 1984).
[127]Newspaper Guild v. NLRB, 636 F.2d 550, 561 (D.C. Cir. 1980) (remanded to NLRB for further proceedings).
[128]Wichita Eagle & Beacon Pub'g Co. v. NLRB, 480 F.2d 52, 55–56 (10th Cir. 1973), *cert. denied,* 416 U.S. 982 (1974). *Accord* Walla Walla Union Bulletin v. NLRB, 631 F.2d 609 (9th Cir. 1980). *Compare Passaic Daily News,* 736 F.2d at 1549–51.

activities, however.[129] It is unsettled whether journalists have a First Amendment right not to pay compulsory union dues.[130]

Attempts to apply the antidiscrimination provisions of Title VII of the Civil Rights Act of 1964[131] to the media because of the way they publish advertisements—e.g., under headings for men or women—have failed.[132] The media do not meet the statutory definition of an "employment agency" when they publish these advertisements.[133] State laws have been applied to these advertisements, however.[134]

§9.6 FEDERAL SECURITIES LAW

As might be anticipated, the federal securities laws have been held to apply to the media in certain circumstances, because those laws seek to prevent false speech.

§9.6(A) Rule 10b-5

Only a handful of cases have been brought against the press under Section 10(b) of the Securities and Exchange Act of 1934 and its companion Rule 10b-5.[135] These cases generally fall into two categories.[136]

In the first category are cases involving claims that a newspaper published false information that influenced a purchase or sale of securities.[137] These cases have properly held that there can be no strict liability claims against the press in such situations,[138] that the press has no duty to investigate information that it is provided by others and then publishes,[139] and that, in any event, recovery cannot be had in such situations without a showing of scienter—i.e., "a mental state embracing intent to deceive, manipulate or defraud."[140]

---

[129]Associated Press I, 301 U.S. 103, 131 (1937) (5-4 decision); see also Press Co. v. NLRB, 118 F.2d 937, 942–43 (D.C. Cir. 1940), cert. denied, 313 U.S. 59 (1941). Similarly, federal antidiscrimination laws can be constitutionally applied to employees with editorial responsibilities. Hausch v. Donrey of Nev., 833 F. Supp. 822, 22 Media L. Rep. 1076 (D. Nev. 1993).

[130]Buckley v. A.F.T.R.A., 496 F.2d 305, 311 (2d Cir. 1974), cert. denied, 419 U.S. 1093 (1974) (issues concerning compulsory union membership and discipline not decided because they were initially for NLRB).

[131]42 U.S.C. §§2000e–2000e-15 (1978).

[132]Brush v. San Francisco Newspaper Printing Co., 315 F. Supp. 577 (N.D. Cal. 1970), aff'd per curiam, 469 F.2d 89 (9th Cir. 1972), cert. denied, 409 U.S. 943 (1973); Greenfield v. Field Enters., 47 FEP Cases 548 (N.D. Ill. 1972).

[133]42 U.S.C. §2003-3(b). An identical definition is used in 29 U.S.C. §623(e), concerning age discrimination.

[134]Pittsburgh Press v. Pittsburgh Comm'n on Human Relations, 413 U.S. 376, 1 Media L. Rep. 1908 (1973). For a discussion of the constitutional problems raised by such laws, see Chapter 11.

[135]15 U.S.C. §78j (1984) and 17 C.F.R. §240.10b-5 (1986), respectively. See generally Estreicher, Securities Regulation and the First Amendment, 24 GA. L. REV. 223 (1990).

[136]Additional cases brought against the media under §10(b) and Rule 10b-5 are discussed infra §§9.6(B) and (C).

[137]The closely related subject of the media's liability for false advertising is discussed in Chapter 7.

[138]Milberg v. Western Pac. R.R. Co., 51 F.R.D. 280, 282 (S.D.N.Y. 1970), appeal dismissed sub nom. Korn v. Franchard Corp., 443 F.2d 1301 (2d Cir. 1971). The same conclusion has been reached in false advertising cases. See Chapter 7.

[139]In re Republic Nat'l Life Ins. Corp., 387 F. Supp. 902, 905 (S.D.N.Y. 1975) (Standard & Poor's and Best had no duty to investigate or verify statistics given to them by other companies even though it made stock recommendations based on such statistics); Siclari v. Rio de Oro Mining Co., [1976–77 Transfer Binder] Fed. Sec. L. Rep. (CCH) ¶95,672 (S.D.N.Y. July 21, 1976). The same conclusion has been reached in false advertising cases. See Chapter 7.

[140]Siclari, [1976–77 Transfer Binder] Fed. Sec. L. Rep. (CCH) ¶95,672; Ernst & Ernst v. Hochfelder, 425 U.S. 185, 194 n.12 (1976). See also Reliance Ins. Co. v. Barron's, 442 F. Supp. 1341, 1353 (S.D.N.Y.

In the second category are cases where the federal securities laws have been used as a thinly veiled attempt to avoid the restrictions placed on libel actions. At least one court has indicated correctly that this practice should not be tolerated.[141]

There is no justification for allowing the securities laws to be used as a substitute for a libel action. No legitimate goal of the securities law is furthered by such claims. The courts that allow such claims are sentencing themselves to the unenviable task of deciding, on a case-by-case basis, whether each of the rules that apply to libel cases also apply to such securities claims. Finally, the media will be left with very hazy rules to follow in publishing stories, especially about the business world, which will inevitably result in self-censorship to avoid possible violations of the law.[142]

Such securities claims have also failed because the plaintiff has been unable to show that the media's false statements were, as required by Section 10(b), made "in connection with the [plaintiff's] purchase or sale of any security."[143] In addition, such claims have failed because the statements objected to were true,[144] were expressions of opinion,[145] or were not published with the scienter necessary in Rule 10b-5 actions.[146]

Such claims against the media are subject to First Amendment restrictions,[147] although, as a practical matter, the scienter requirement may obviate the need to decide First Amendment questions in most Rule 10b-5 cases brought against the media.[148]

§9.6(B) Scalping

"Scalping" has been defined by the Supreme Court as an investment adviser's "practice of purchasing shares of a security for his own account

---

1977). The elements of a 10b-5 claim are: a duty, false representations, scienter, and materiality. Chiarella v. United States, 445 U.S. 222 (1980); United States v. Gregg, 612 F.2d 43, 50 (2d Cir. 1979).

[141]*Reliance Ins. Co.,* 442 F. Supp. at 1353 ("Plaintiff's case, if it has one, is a libel action pure and simple. The securities laws, and particularly Rule 10b-5, were not developed with the intention of overlapping or reinforcing the law of libel, nor to inhibit the exercise of freedom of the press."). *See also* Hohensee v. Goon Squad, 171 F. Supp. 562, 568 (M.D. Pa. 1959) (reaching similar conclusion as to antitrust laws). Another court found it curious that no libel claim was brought with a 10b-5 claim, because the 10b-5 claim was really a disguised libel suit. Safeguard Servs. v. Dow Jones & Co., 537 F. Supp. 1137, 1141 n.5 (E.D. Va. 1982), *aff'd without opinion,* 705 F.2d 445 (4th Cir.), *cert. denied,* 464 U.S. 831 (1983).

[142]*See also* Chapter 2.

[143]*Safeguard Servs.,* 537 F. Supp. at 1141–43 (no causation). This requirement often will prevent 10b-5 claims from being used as vehicles for what really are libel claims.

[144]*Id.* at 1143.

[145]*Id.* at 1143–44; *see also* Milberg v. Western Pac. R.R. Co., 51 F.R.D. 280, 282 (S.D.N.Y. 1970) (estimate of earnings not actionable).

[146]Reliance Ins. Co. v. Barron's, 442 F. Supp. 1341, 1353 (S.D.N.Y. 1977).

[147]The Supreme Court has said that "[n]umerous examples could be cited of communications that are regulated without offending the First Amendment such as the exchange of information about securities." Ohralik v. Ohio State Bar Ass'n, 436 U.S. 447, 456 (1978). *See also* Curtis Pub'g Co. v. Butts, 388 U.S. 130, 152 (1967) ("Federal securities regulation [15 U.S.C. §77k] . . . are only some of the examples of our understanding that the right to communicate information of public interest is not 'unconditional.'"). Exactly what the Court meant by this dicta is unclear. Apparently, *Ohralik's* and *Butts'* statements about the securities laws mean nothing more than that federal securities laws are not unconstitutional simply because they regulate commercial speech. *See generally* Chapter 11 on commercial speech.

[148]Whether, like constitutional actual malice (see Chapter 2), scienter is also limited to statements made with knowledge that they are false or with substantial doubts as to their truthfulness, is unclear. Some cases have held that scienter does not include recklessness (e.g., Holmes v. Bateson, 583 F.2d 542, 552 n.11 (1st Cir. 1978)), but others have reached a contrary conclusion (e.g., Coleco Indus. v. Berman, 567 F.2d 569, 574 (3d Cir. 1977), *cert. denied,* 439 U.S. 830 (1978)). Even assuming that scienter means the same thing as constitutional actual malice, its application is different from the constitutional actual malice rule. Scienter

shortly before recommending that security for long-term investment and then immediately selling the shares at a profit upon the rise in the market price following the recommendation."[149] Several possible sanctions exist under the federal securities laws for such conduct. First, the Securities and Exchange Commission (SEC) may obtain an injunction under the Investment Advisers' Act of 1940[150] to compel an investment adviser to disclose the scalping and to provide other relief.[151]

Second, criminal sanctions are available for violations of Section 17(b) of the Securities Act of 1933,[152] which makes it unlawful for any person to, among other things, distribute any advertisement, newspaper, or article that, though not purporting to offer a security for sale, describes such a security and does not disclose that (1) the author of the advertisement, newspaper, or article has received consideration from an issuer, underwriter, or dealer for publishing such information and (2) does not disclose the amount of such consideration.[153] A criminal conviction under this disclosure statute has been upheld despite a First Amendment challenge.[154] In addition, an injunction to force disclosure of "consideration" may be permissible.[155] Whether there is an implied civil cause of action under Section 17 is not completely settled, but it is unlikely.[156]

Third, civil damages may be sought under Rule 10b-5. The Ninth Circuit's two decisions in *Zweig v. Hearst Corp.* deal with this problem at length. In *Zweig I,*[157] the issue was the liability of a newspaper publisher for its financial columnist-employee's scalping. The plaintiffs sought to hold the newspaper liable on a respondeat superior theory.[158] Alternatively, the plaintiffs argued that, even if the newspaper publisher was not liable on a respondeat superior theory, it was an error to grant the newspaper summary judgment based on the good-faith defense in Section 20(a) of the Securities and Exchange Act of 1934, commonly known as the "controlling person" provision.[159] While noting that there was a split in the circuit courts, the Ninth Circuit held that the

---

is broader than the constitutional actual malice rule because it applies regardless of whether the plaintiff is a public figure or public official. Scienter is also narrower because, for example, it need not be proven by the clear and convincing evidence (Herman & MacLean v. Huddleston, 459 U.S. 375, 387–90 (1983)) necessary in constitutional actual malice cases. *See* Chapter 2.

[149]Securities & Exch. Comm'n v. Capital Gains Research Bureau, 375 U.S. 180, 181 (1963). *Capital Gains* was distinguished in Lowe v. Securities and Exchange Commission, 472 U.S. 181 (1985) (publications that do not offer customized, personal advice are not covered by Investment Advisers Act). *See also* Note, *The Inadequacy of Rule 10b-5 to Address Outsider Trading by Reporters,* 38 STAN. L. REV. 1549, 1557 (1986) (concluding that *Lowe* effectively overruled *Capital Gains*). For a discussion of *Lowe, see infra* §9.6(C).

[150]15 U.S.C. §§80b-1 to 80b-21 (1984).

[151]*Capital Gains,* 375 U.S. at 182; Securities & Exch. Comm'n v. Blavin, 557 F. Supp. 1304, 1316 (E.D. Mich. 1983) (enjoining future violations and ordering disgorgement), *aff'd,* 760 F.2d 706 (6th Cir. 1985). For a discussion of this law, *see infra* §9.6(C).

[152]15 U.S.C. §77q(b) (1984).

[153]*Id.*

[154]United States v. Amick, 439 F.2d 351, 364–65 & n.19 (7th Cir.), *cert. denied sub nom.* Irving v. United States, 403 U.S. 918 (1970).

[155]Securities & Exch. Comm'n v. Wall Street Pub'g Inst., 851 F.2d 365, 376 (D.C. Cir. 1988), *cert. denied,* 489 U.S. 1066 (1989) (receipt of free text need not be disclosed, but receipt of free text in return for purchase of advertising space or reprints of articles can constitutionally be compelled).

[156]Blue Chip Stamps v. Manor Drug Stores, 421 U.S. 723, 733 n.6 (1975) (expressing "no opinion" on whether there is implied cause of action). In re Washington Pub. Power Supply Sys. Sec. Litig., 823 F.2d 1349 (9th Cir. 1987) (en banc) (no implied civil cause of action; reversing earlier contrary decision); Finkel v. Stratton Corp., 962 F.2d 169, 174–75 (2d Cir. 1992) (same).

[157]Zweig v. Hearst Corp., 521 F.2d 1129 (9th Cir.), *cert. denied,* 423 U.S. 1025 (1975).

[158]521 F.2d at 1131.

[159]*Id.*

newspaper had no respondeat superior liability and that its liability for its columnist's actions, if any, was as a controlling person under Section 20(a).[160]

Turning to the good-faith defense of Section 20(a), the court noted that (1) the newspaper had employed its columnist for a number of years; (2) the newspaper was unaware of the columnist's financial interest in the company he wrote about; (3) the newspaper never investigated employees' financial affairs without cause; (4) before the publication of the article in question the newspaper never received any complaints about its columnist employee; (5) after the newspaper received complaints about this employee, it suspended him and conducted an investigation; and (6) as a result of the investigation, the newspaper reinstated publication of the reporter's articles only after he agreed that he would not write about companies in which he had a financial interest.[161]

In this case of first impression, the court then held that to demonstrate good faith, a controlling person must show that it maintained and enforced a reasonable and proper system of supervision and internal control over controlled persons to prevent violations of Rule 10b-5.[162] The court noted, however, that newspapers should not be held to the same supervision standards as those applied to a broker-dealer, because

> [t]he practicalities of operating a large daily newspaper make it impossible for each item of news or reported interview to be rechecked by supervising editors. If the column or news story prepared and submitted by the columnist or reporter does not, on its face, reveal impropriety, the very nature of the newspaper business prohibits cross-checking.[163]

The court concluded that the facts set forth demonstrated the newspaper's good faith.[164]

In *Zweig II*,[165] the Ninth Circuit discussed the columnist's liability for scalping under Rule 10b-5. The court held that the columnist was a "quasi-insider" who owed a duty to his readers to disclose his stock ownership.[166] The court went on to hold that, even though the plaintiffs had agreed to purchase their stock months *before* the columnist's story was printed, the columnist could be liable to the plaintiffs under Rule 10b-5.[167]

There has been substantial discussion of *Zweig II* by commentators, and much of it is favorable.[168] *Zweig II*, however, has been criticized for giving the

---

[160]*Id.* at 1132–33. See Kelly, *Testing the Vicarious Liability of a Newspaper Publisher Under 10b-5—Zweig v. Hearst Corp.*, 1975 UTAH L. REV. 740, 749 (concluding that *Zweig I* correctly decided because, among other reasons, respondeat superior liability would "create an intolerable economic burden on a newspaper" since if "each affected person [were] able to recover a sizeable judgment, legitimate newspaper reporting could be severely inhibited"). See also Chapter 7, where similar considerations have limited recovery against the media for false advertising. However, the Ninth Circuit has now held that §20(a) supplements rather than supplants the common law, so liability based on a respondeat superior theory is still possible. Hollinger v. Titan Capital Corp., 914 F.2d 1564, 1577 (9th Cir. 1990) (en banc), *cert. denied*, 111 S. Ct. 1621 (1991).

[161]521 F.2d at 1133.
[162]*Id.* at 1134–35.
[163]*Id.* at 1135.
[164]*Id.* at 1136.
[165]Zweig v. Hearst Corp., 594 F.2d 1261 (9th Cir. 1979).
[166]*Id.* at 1267 n.9. The similar practice of an investment adviser telling a select group of its customers to buy a particular stock before publicly recommending it has also been held to be actionable. Courtland v. Walston & Co., 340 F. Supp. 1076 (S.D.N.Y. 1972).
[167]594 F.2d at 1270–71.
[168]*See* Ewald, *Securities Law: Financial Columnist's Duty and Liability Under Rule 10b-5*, 19 WASHBURN L.J. 382 (1980) (essentially summarizing *Zweig II* with approval); Haber, *A Financial Columnist's Duty to the Market Under Rule 10b-5: Civil Damages for Trading on a Misleading Investment Recommendation,*

plaintiffs, who already had agreed to purchase their stock before the column was published, a claim.[169]

Supreme Court cases narrowing the scope of Rule 10b-5 suggest that *Zweig II* might no longer be good law,[170] but circuit court decisions have concluded that this rule embraces a breach of fiduciary duty owed an employer even when the employee cannot be considered an "insider" or "quasi-insider" for Rule 10b-5 purposes.[171]

In *Carpenter v. United States*,[172] the Supreme Court considered whether a *Wall Street Journal* reporter violated Rule 10b-5 by using confidential information about the publication dates and contents of his influential column on stocks to make profits for himself.[173] There was no showing that the reporter altered the column's contents to influence stock prices; rather, the Court found that information about the contents and timing of articles in the column was the *Journal*'s confidential information.[174] However, the reporter's conviction under Rule 10b-5 was affirmed only by an equally divided Court,[175] so it is still unclear whether the "misappropriation" of such information violates Rule 10b-5.[176] The reporter's conviction for violation of the mail and wire fraud statutes was upheld by the Court, however.[177]

§9.6(C) Investment Advisers Act

The Investment Advisers Act of 1940 (IAA)[178] regulates the activities of "investment advisers," i.e.,

---

26 WAYNE L. REV. 1021 (1980) (agreeing with conclusion in *Zweig II* but arguing that it should have been reached on somewhat different grounds). The result in *Zweig II* was foreshadowed in Peskind, *Regulation of the Financial Press: A New Dimension to Section 10(b) and Rule 10b-5*, 14 ST. LOUIS U. L.J. 80 (1969).

[169]Gallichio, *The Ninth Circuit Expands the 10b-5 Net to Catch a Columnist—Zweig v. Hearst Corporation*, 29 DE PAUL L. REV. 287 (1979).

[170]L. LOSS, FUNDAMENTALS OF SECURITIES REGULATION 761–62 (1988) (querying whether *Zweig II* survives Chiarella v. United States, 445 U.S. 222 (1980)); Note, *The Inadequacy of Rule 10b-5 to Address Outside Trading by Reporters*, 38 STAN. L. REV. 1548 (1986) (concluding that *Zweig II* holding is in serious doubt as result of later Supreme Court decisions). *See also* Dirks v. Securities & Exch. Comm'n, 463 U.S. 646 (1983).

[171]United States v. Newman, 664 F.2d 12, *aff'd after remand*, 722 F.2d 729 (2d Cir. 1981), *cert. denied*, 464 U.S. 863 (1983) (employee owes employer duty under federal securities laws not to disclose confidential information); Securities & Exch. Comm'n v. Materia, 745 F.2d 197 (2d Cir. 1984), *cert. denied*, 471 U.S. 1053 (1985) (employee of financial printing firm breached fiduciary duty to employer by trading on information in tender offer documents in advance of their release). *See also* Securities & Exch. Comm'n v. Clark, 915 F.2d 439 (9th Cir. 1990) (agreeing with Second Circuit).

[172]484 U.S. 19, 14 Media L. Rep. 1853 (1987), *aff'g* United States v. Carpenter, 791 F.2d 1024, 12 Media L. Rep. 2169 (2d Cir. 1986).

[173]484 U.S. at 28.

[174]*Id.* at 23.

[175]*Id.* at 24–25.

[176]*See* Note, *Financial Reporters, the Securities Laws and the First Amendment: Where to Draw the Line*, 53 FORDHAM L. REV. 1036 (1985) (concluding that because newspaper owes no fiduciary duty to corporations about which it reports, misappropriation theory cannot be applied to reporters; however, author advocates that reporters be required to disclose holdings to SEC); Note, *The Inadequacy of Rule 10b-5 to Address Outsider Trading by Reporters*, 38 STAN. L. REV. 1549 (1986) (observing that enforcing reporter's duty to newspaper under Rule 10b-5 would result in incoherent approach to securities regulation but that newspapers should be required to publish daily notice that their reporters and other employees are allowed to trade stock in advance of forthcoming articles).

[177]484 U.S. at 24. *See also* Manax v. McNamara, 660 F. Supp. 657, 660–61 (W.D. Tex. 1987) (plaintiff who claimed that newspapers conspired with state officials to damage his reputation could not sustain cause of action for mail fraud; *Carpenter* distinguished as case where misappropriation of information involved actual, identifiable scheme to defraud that resulted in reputational injury to reporter's newspaper), *aff'd on other grounds*, 842 F.2d 808, 15 Media L. Rep. 1655 (5th Cir. 1988).

[178]15 U.S.C. §§80b-1 to 80b-21 (1984); *see generally* Annot., *Construction and Effect of Investment Advisers Act of 1940 as Amended (15 U.S.C. §§80b-1–80-b-21)*, 5 A.L.R. FED. 246 (1970) and Harroch, *The*

any person who, for compensation, engages in the business of advising others, either directly or through publications or writings, as to the value of securities or as to the advisability of investing in, purchasing, or selling securities, or who, for compensation and as part of a regular business, issues or promulgates analyses or reports concerning securities.[179]

Thus, on its face, the IAA appears to apply to virtually every writing that is produced as part of a regular business for compensation and that discusses securities.[180]

The IAA requires investment advisers, except those who fall within specified exemptions,[181] to register with the SEC[182] and to provide the SEC with substantial information.[183] Investment advisers must also maintain various records[184] and are prohibited from entering into a variety of transactions.[185]

Violations of the IAA can result in substantial penalties, including SEC lawsuits for injunctions,[186] loss of registration under the IAA,[187] and criminal sanctions.[188] Violations of the IAA also allow investors to cancel their contracts with investment advisers and to recover sums paid to them, although damage actions are not available.[189] Similar state laws also provide penalties for violations.[190]

Congress limited application of the IAA to the media by providing that "the publisher of any bona fide newspaper, news magazine or business or financial publication of regular and general circulation" is not an "investment adviser."[191] The scope of this exemption was thoroughly litigated in *Securities and Exchange Commission v. Lowe*.[192]

In *Lowe,* the SEC sought to enjoin Christopher Lowe's publication of investment advisory materials because he was not registered as an investment adviser; the SEC had revoked his previous registration and had barred him from associating with any investment adviser because of his previous criminal convictions for serious misconduct in connection with his investment advisory

---

Applicability of the Investment Advisers Act of 1940 to Financial and Investment Related Publications, J. CORP. L. 55 (1979).

[179] 15 U.S.C. §80b-2(11). The term "security" is defined *id.* §80b-2(18). There has been substantial litigation over the definition of a "security." *See, e.g.,* International Bhd. of Teamsters v. Daniel, 434 U.S. 1061 (1979).

[180] 7 L. LOSS & J. SELIGMAN, SECURITIES REGULATION ch. 7C(2)(a), 3345 (3d ed. 1991). Whether the authors of syndicated columns or the electronic media are covered by the IAA is unclear but unlikely. 1 A.L.I. FED. SEC. CODE §202(78) (1980); LOSS, *supra,* at 1398; Loomis, *The Securities Exchange Act of 1939 and the Investment Advisers Act of 1940,* 28 GEO. WASH. L. REV. 214, 245 n.97 (1959).

[181] 15 U.S.C. §80b-2(11) (1984).

[182] *Id.* §80b-3(a), (b); Harroch, *supra* note 178, at 547–59.

[183] 15 U.S.C. §80b-3(c)(1) (1984); 17 C.F.R. §279 (1978); Harroch, *supra* note 178, at 547–58 n.9.

[184] 15 U.S.C. §80b-4 (1984).

[185] *Id.* §§80b-5, 80b-6; Harroch, *supra* note 178, at 559–61.

[186] 15 U.S.C. §80b-9(e) (1984).

[187] *Id.* §80b-3(e).

[188] *Id.* §80b-17.

[189] *Id.* §80b-15; Transamerica Mortgage Advisers v. Lewis, 444 U.S. 11 (1979).

[190] *See, e.g.,* CAL. CORP. CODE §§25200–25246 (1977); N.Y. GEN. BUS. LAW §359eee (1987).

[191] 15 U.S.C. §80b-2(a)(11)(D) (1984).

[192] 556 F. Supp. 1359, 9 Media L. Rep. 1281 (E.D.N.Y. 1983), *rev'd,* 725 F.2d 892, 10 Media L. Rep. 1225 (2d Cir. 1984), *rev'd,* 472 U.S. 181 (1985). *See also* Securities & Exch. Comm'n v. Wall Street Transcript Corp., 422 F.2d 1371 (2d Cir.), *cert. denied,* 398 U.S. 958 (1970) (upholding SEC subpoena in investigation of whether publication was within bona fide newspaper exemption); Securities & Exch. Comm'n v. Wall Street Transcript Corp., 454 F. Supp. 559, 3 Media L. Rep. 2438 (S.D.N.Y. 1978) (finding same publication within bona fide newspaper exemption); Person v. New York Post Corp., 427 F. Supp. 1297, 1303 (E.D.N.Y. 1977), *aff'd,* 573 F.2d 1294 (2d Cir. 1977) ("The plain truth is that newspapers of general circulation like the Post are not meant to be subject to the Investment Advisers Act").

business.[193] The district court held that, so long as Lowe only gave impersonal investment advice—i.e., by publications, and not by telephone, individual letter, or in person—to deny him the right to register and then to use his failure to register as the basis for enjoining his publications would violate the First Amendment.[194] The district court also held that the SEC could require Lowe to disclose his criminal convictions and the SEC's previous order against him, but only after the SEC promulgated rules requiring such disclosures.[195]

The Second Circuit, in a 2-1 decision, reversed. With virtually no analysis, the majority held that Lowe's newsletters were not within the press exemption.[196] The majority then held that enjoining Lowe from distributing his publications was constitutionally permissible because he was a professional being denied a license just as a lawyer or doctor might be denied a license to practice his or her profession.[197]

The dissent properly recognized that Lowe's advice on securities through his publications no more made him a professional investment adviser than the publication of a magazine on good health constitutes the practice of medicine or the publication of a book on how to avoid probate constitutes the practice of law.[198] The dissent also properly rejected the majority's conclusion that Lowe's publications were commercial speech.[199] They were, of course, publications *about* commercial matters, but that is no more commercial speech than advertising the sale of political campaign buttons is political speech.

The dissent also correctly pointed out that a prior restraint, like the one sought by the SEC against Lowe, is almost never permissible, and that no showing had been made that this was one of those truly exceptional cases—where there is "the threat of grave and immediate danger to the security of the United States"—where a prior restraint would be permissible.[200]

The Supreme Court reversed.[201] Avoiding the constitutional issue, the majority decided the issue on statutory grounds, holding that the "bona fide" newspaper exclusion applied to Lowe's publication.[202] It found that Congress was interested in regulating the business of rendering "personalized" investment advice but did not seek to regulate the press through licensing

---

[193] 556 F. Supp. at 1363; 725 F.2d at 894–95; 472 U.S. at 185.

[194] 556 F. Supp. at 1369–70. To the same general effect is Securities & Exch. Comm'n v. Blavin, 557 F. Supp. 1304, 1310 (E.D. Mich. 1983), aff'd, 760 F.2d 706 (6th Cir. 1985).

[195] 556 F. Supp. at 1370–71. *See also* Securities & Exch. Comm'n v. Suter, 732 F.2d 1294, 10 Media L. Rep. 2159 (7th Cir. 1984) (upholding preliminary injunction requiring defendant to send SEC copies of each of his publications when they are distributed to anyone else).

[196] 725 F.2d at 898. A similarly erroneous conclusion was reached in *Suter,* 732 F.2d 1294, where the court concluded that the press exemption did not apply for no better reason than that the newsletters in question were directed to investors.

[197] 725 F.2d at 901–3. The majority gave scant attention to Lowe's First Amendment argument. *Id.* at 900–901. A comparable decision was rendered, under the Commodity Exchange Act's similar provisions (7 U.S.C. §2(ii) and (iv)), in Savage v. Commodity Futures Trading Comm'n, 548 F.2d 192, 197–98 (7th Cir. 1977).

[198] 725 F.2d at 903.

[199] *Id.* at 904. For a discussion of the commercial speech doctrine, see Chapter 11. For a discussion of constitutional issues involved in restrictions on the general advertising of securities, see Schoeman, *The First Amendment and Restrictions on Advertising of Securities Under the Securities Act of 1933,* 41 BUS. LAW. 377 (1986).

[200] 725 F.2d at 907. Prior restraints are discussed in Chapter 10.

[201] Securities & Exch. Comm'n v. Lowe, 472 U.S. 181 (1985).

[202] *Id.* at 211. *But see* Lee, *The Effects of Lowe on the Application of the Investment Advisers Act of 1940 to Impersonal Investment Advisory Opinions,* 42 BUS. LAW. 507 (1987) (author analyzes *Lowe's* rationale to observe that majority strongly intimated that First Amendment considerations dictated holding).

"nonpersonalized" publishing activities.[203] Lowe's newsletters were "bona fide" because they contained disinterested commentary and analysis, not individualized advice geared to specific portfolios or clients, and were circulated to the public at large on a "regular" basis as required by the Act.[204] The Court considered it immaterial that Lowe himself had an unsavory history, for the exemption described the publication, not the publisher.[205] It was also not crucial that the newsletters were not "regular" in the sense of consistent circulation; the test of regularity was met because the newsletters were not timed to specific market activity or to events affecting the securities industry.[206]

The justices who concurred in the result construed the bona fide publications exception to embrace only those publications containing general financial news, not those that were devoted primarily to providing investment advice or those that were personally tailored to individual clients.[207] In their view, the IAA applied to persons who sent out bulletins from time to time.[208] Finding Lowe's publications were covered by the IAA, the concurring justices reached the First Amendment issue and concluded that the statute was an impermissible prior restraint.[209] The IAA unconstitutionally prohibited legitimate disinterested advice, not just fraudulent, deceptive, or manipulative advice.[210] The government's fear that Lowe would publish misleading advice because of his past misconduct did not rise to the level required to outweigh First Amendment protections.[211]

§9.6(D) Proxy Solicitation

In *Long Island Lighting Co. v. Barbash*,[212] a utility sought to enjoin publication of a newspaper advertisement that advocated public ownership of the utility.[213] Granting summary judgment for the defendants, the district court found that the ad was not a proxy solicitation and that to interpret it to be one would create serious First Amendment problems.[214] The Second Circuit reversed, finding that the ad was capable of being interpreted to be a proxy solicitation, and allowed further discovery.[215] The Second Circuit did not reach the First Amendment issues.

---

[203] 472 U.S. at 204. *See also* Lee, *supra* note 202 (author concludes that *Lowe* means that most impersonal investment advisory publications can no longer be required to register under IAA before publishing and selling investment views).
[204] 472 U.S. at 206.
[205] *Id.*
[206] *Id.* at 209.
[207] *Id.* at 216. The majority suggested that "touts" and "tipsters" might not qualify for exemption if they offered personalized advice. *Id.* at 217 n.3.
[208] *Id.* at 220 n.5.
[209] 472 U.S. at 234–35.
[210] *Id.*
[211] *Id.* at 235 ("Our commercial speech cases have consistently rejected the proposition that such drastic prohibitions on speech may be justified by a mere possibility that the prohibited speech will be fraudulent."). *See also* Secretary of State of Md. v. J.H. Munson Co., 81 L. Ed. 2d 786, 800–801 n.12 (1984) ("Our cases make clear that a statute that requires such a 'license' for the dissemination of ideas is inherently suspect."); Schoeman, *Subscription Advisers, Blue Sky Registration and the First Amendment*, 33 BUS. LAW. 249 (1977); *but see* Underhill Assocs. v. Bradshaw, 674 F.2d 293, 296 (4th Cir. 1982).
[212] 625 F. Supp. 221 (E.D.N.Y.), *rev'd*, 779 F.2d 793 (2d Cir. 1985).
[213] 625 F. Supp. at 222.
[214] *Id.* at 226.
[215] 779 F.2d at 796.

§9.7 TAXATION

It is well-established that the First Amendment does not immunize newspapers or other media from being subjected to generally applicable taxes.[216] However, taxation of the media is not without constitutional limitations. Concern that taxation could be used as a tool of censorship by the government has existed since the early 1700s, when the English Parliament imposed taxes on newspapers with the intent of suppressing criticism of the Crown by limiting newspapers' circulation.[217] This historical framework has led modern courts to carefully scrutinize any taxes on the media to determine if the taxes infringe on the exercise of First Amendment rights.

In the first Supreme Court case dealing with media taxation, *Grosjean v. American Press,*[218] the Court was faced with a Louisiana state tax on advertisements that applied only to newspapers with circulations of more than 20,000 per week.[219] The Court immediately recognized the tax as a not-so-subtle attempt by then Louisiana Governor Huey Long to silence the larger newspapers, which had been critical of his administration: "[I]n the light of its history and of its present setting, [this tax] is seen to be a deliberate and calculated device in the guise of a tax to limit the circulation of information to which the public is entitled."[220] Consequently, the Court struck down the tax as an unconstitutional prior restraint.[221]

Similarly, in *Murdock v. Pennsylvania,*[222] the Supreme Court struck down a license tax imposed on door-to-door solicitors that had been applied to Jehovah's Witnesses seeking contributions.[223] The Court held that the government could not impose a tax as a precondition of exercising one's constitutional rights, noting that "[t]he power to tax the exercise of a privilege is the power to control or suppress its enjoyment."[224]

Forty years later, the Supreme Court decided another landmark case involving taxation of the media. In *Minneapolis Star & Tribune Co. v. Minnesota*

---

[216] *See, e.g.,* Grosjean v. American Press Co., 297 U.S. 233, 250, 1 Media L. Rep. 2685, 2689 (1936) ("[i]t is not intended by anything we have said to suggest that the owners of newspapers are immune from any of the ordinary forms of taxation for support of the government"); Minneapolis Star & Tribune Co. v. Minneapolis Comm'r of Revenue, 460 U.S. 575, 587 n.9 (1983) ("Indeed, our cases have consistently recognized that nondiscriminatory taxes on the receipts of income of newspapers would be permissible."); Arkansas Writers' Project v. Ragland, 481 U.S. 221, 229 (1987) ("a genuinely nondiscriminatory tax on the receipts of newspapers would be constitutionally permissible"). *See also* Publishers New Press v. Moysey, 141 F. Supp. 340 (S.D.N.Y. 1957) (upholding tax applied to all businesses, including newspapers, on ground that media subject to general laws); Alaska v. Journal Printing Co., 135 F. Supp. 169 (D. Alaska 1953) (upholding business license fee applied to all businesses, including newspapers, on ground that press not immune from generally applicable tax); Catholic Archdiocese of Denver v. Denver, 741 P.2d 333, 14 Media L. Rep. 1964 (Colo. 1987) (upholding application of retail sales tax to newspapers where no greater burden imposed than on other businesses).

[217] *See, e.g.,* the discussion in *Grosjean,* 297 U.S. at 244–49, 1 Media L. Rep. at 2687–88.
[218] 297 U.S. 233, 1 Media L. Rep. 2685 (1936).
[219] *Id.* at 240–41, 1 Media L. Rep. at 2685.
[220] *Id.* at 250, 1 Media L. Rep. at 2689.
[221] *Id.* at 251, 1 Media L. Rep. at 2689.
[222] 319 U.S. 105 (1943).
[223] *Id.* at 106–07, 117.
[224] *Id.* at 112. *Accord* Follett v. McCormick, 321 U.S. 573, 577 (1944). *Murdock* and *Follett* have been limited to situations involving a flat license tax that is a precondition to the exercise of constitutional rights. Jimmy Swaggart Ministries v. Board of Equalization of Cal., 493 U.S. 378 (1990). *Accord* Alaska v. Journal Printing Co., 135 F. Supp. 169 (D. Alaska 1953) (upholding business license fee applied to all businesses, including newspapers, and rejecting argument that *Murdock* made it unconstitutional to require any First Amendment interest to have license).

Commissioner of Revenue,[225] the Court invalidated, on First Amendment grounds, a Minnesota state tax on the cost of paper and ink products consumed in the production of a publication.[226] Before 1971, Minnesota's sales and use tax provisions exempted newspapers, but this tax exemption was eliminated in 1971 when the Minnesota Legislature adopted provisions taxing ink and paper used in publications.[227] The tax was later amended to exempt the first $100,000 worth of ink and paper consumed.[228] As a result of that exemption, "only a handful of publishers" paid any tax at all, and even fewer paid "any significant amount of tax."[229]

Unlike the statute in *Grosjean,* there was no evidence that the Minnesota Legislature adopted its special use tax on the media for any impermissible motive or to censor the media.[230] Nonetheless, the Supreme Court invalidated the special use tax on the grounds that its structure alone violated the First Amendment rights of the newspaper.[231]

As the Court explained, differential taxation of the media carries with it grave risks of government censorship:

> A power to tax differentially, as opposed to a power to tax generally, gives a government a powerful weapon against the taxpayer selected. When the State imposes a generally applicable tax, there is little cause for concern. We need not fear that a government will destroy a selected group of taxpayers by burdensome taxation if it must impose the same burden on the rest of its constituency. When the State singles out the press, though, the political constraints that prevent a legislature from passing crippling taxes of general applicability are weakened, and the threat of burdensome taxes become acute....
>
> *Differential taxation of the press, then, places such a burden on the interests protected by the First Amendment that we cannot countenance such treatment unless the State asserts a counterbalancing interest of compelling importance that it cannot achieve without differential taxation.*[232]

Following *Minneapolis Star,* a number of state courts[233] have evaluated the constitutionality of various taxing schemes applied to the media. In several cases, state tax schemes have been invalidated because they impermissibly differentiated between members of the media without demonstrating a compelling justification for such differential taxation[234] or because they targeted only

---

[225]460 U.S. 575, 9 Media L. Rep. 1369 (1983).
[226]*Id.* at 592–93, 9 Media L. Rep. at 1377.
[227]*Id.* at 577, 9 Media L. Rep. at 1370.
[228]*Id.* at 578, 9 Media L. Rep. at 1370.
[229]*Id.* at 591, 9 Media L. Rep. at 1376–77.
[230]460 U.S. at 580, 9 Media L. Rep. at 1371.
[231]The Court noted that "[w]e need not and do not impugn the motives of the Minnesota Legislature in passing the ink and paper tax," adding that "[i]llicit legislative intent is not the *sine qua non* of a violation of the First Amendment." *Id.* at 592, 9 Media L. Rep. at 1377. *Accord* City of Baltimore v. A.S. Abell Co., 145 A.2d 111 (Md. 1958).
[232]460 U.S. at 585, 9 Media L. Rep. at 1374 (footnote and citations omitted; emphasis added). The Court also made clear that the government's obvious need to raise revenues is not a sufficiently compelling interest to justify differential taxation. *Id.* at 586, 9 Media L. Rep. at 1374.
[233]The federal tax injunction act, 28 U.S.C.A. §1341 (1976), prohibits federal courts from enjoining state taxation "where a plain speedy and efficient remedy may be had in the courts of such State." *See, e.g.,* Advertiser Co. v. Wallace, 446 F. Supp. 677, 3 Media L. Rep. 2220 (M.D. Ala. 1978) (holding that federal district court had no jurisdiction to hear challenge to state tax statute on First Amendment grounds). For that reason, there are few federal court cases concerning the constitutionality of taxing the media.
[234]*See, e.g.,* Louisiana Life v. McNamara, 504 So. 2d 900 (La. Ct. App. 1987) (invalidating on federal constitutional grounds state sales tax that applied to magazines but not to newspapers); McGraw-Hill, Inc. v. State Tax Comm'n, 541 N.Y.S.2d 252 (N.Y. App. Div. 1989), *aff'd on opinion below,* 552 N.E.2d 163 (N.Y. 1990) (invalidating franchise tax formula favoring broadcasting over print media). *See also* Dow Jones & Co. v. Oklahoma, 787 P.2d 843, 16 Media L. Rep. 2049 (Okla. 1989) (invalidating tax that treated publications less favorably if they sold for more than 75 cents or were delivered by mail). *Accord* Oklahoma Broadcasters Ass'n v. Oklahoma Tax Comm'n, 789 P.2d 1312, 17 Media L. Rep. 1994 (Okla. 1990) (invalidating taxes on television broadcasters because various other media were exempt).

some publishers.[235] Other courts have refused to invalidate differential tax schemes, either on the ground that the differential tax schemes furthered compelling government interests[236] or because the courts found that *Minneapolis Star*'s holding did not apply to the particular tax scheme at issue.[237] These decisions cannot readily be reconciled.

In *Arkansas Writers' Project v. Ragland*,[238] the Supreme Court struck down an Arkansas statute that exempted all newspapers and certain special interest magazines from a sales tax but did not exempt general interest magazines. The Court held that the Arkansas tax statute was unconstitutional, because it differentiated between magazines based on their content, but left open the issue of whether the differential taxation of different media—e.g., newspapers and magazines—was also unconstitutional.[239]

This question was resolved in *Leathers v. Medlock*,[240] where the Supreme Court held that taxation of cable and satellite television without taxation of newspapers and magazines was not unconstitutional[241] because the press was

---

[235]Festival Enters. v. Pleasant Hill, 227 Cal. Rptr. 601 (Cal. Ct. App. 1986) (invalidating municipal "admissions tax" on entertainment events where plaintiffs' movie theaters were only businesses actually subject to tax); United Artists Communications v. City of Montclair, 257 Cal. Rptr. 124 (Cal. Ct. App.), *cert. denied*, 493 U.S. 918 (1989) (invalidating similar tax where 90% of tax would be borne by two movie theaters and two adult bookstores); City of Alameda v. Premier Communications Network, 202 Cal. Rptr. 684 (Cal. Ct. App.), *cert. denied*, 469 U.S. 1073 (1984) (invalidating city tax ordinance that imposed different tax burden on subscription television services than on many other businesses without advancing any compelling government interest). *Compare* Forbes v. City of Seattle, 785 P.2d 431 (Wash. 1990) (upholding tax on motion picture patrons but exempting patrons of nonprofit entities; *Festival Enterprises* and *United Artists* distinguished).

[236]*See, e.g.,* In re Assessment of Additional N.C. & Orange County Use Taxes Against Village Pub'g Corp., 322 S.E.2d 155 (N.C. 1984), *appeal dismissed for want of substantial federal question sub nom.* Village Pub'g Corp. v. North Carolina Dep't of Revenue, 472 U.S. 1001 (1985) (upholding exemption from tax for sale of newspapers door-to-door). Justices Brennan and White dissented from this dismissal. 472 U.S. at 1003. *See also* Chicago Tribune Co. v. Johnson, 477 N.E.2d 482 (Ill.), *appeal dismissed for want of substantial federal question,* 474 U.S. 915 (1985) (upholding state use tax that applied to printing presses but not other "manufacturing machinery").

[237]For example, in Thomson Newspapers v. Florence, 338 S.E.2d 324, 12 Media L. Rep. 1463 (S.C. 1985), the South Carolina Supreme Court reversed a lower court's decision that had held a city ordinance unconstitutional because it imposed a higher business license tax on newspapers than on any other businesses. In upholding the ordinance, the South Carolina Supreme Court held that *Minneapolis Star* was inapplicable because only newspapers were subject to the particular Minnesota statute in question, while the South Carolina law taxed all businesses. 338 S.E..2d at 325.

Similarly, in Times Mirror v. City of Los Angeles, 237 Cal. Rptr. 346, 14 Media L. Rep. 1289 (Cal. Ct. App. 1987), *appeal dismissed for want of substantial federal question,* 484 U.S. 1022 (1988), a California Court of Appeal upheld a city tax ordinance that differentially taxed different members of the media (for example, by imposing a cap on the amount of the tax paid by movie producers, while no limit was imposed on the tax paid by newspapers). The Court of Appeal distinguished *Minneapolis Star* on the ground that the Los Angeles tax was a "general" tax applied to all businesses and therefore was different from the Minneapolis tax on newspapers only. *See also* Redwood Empire Pub'g Co. v. California State Bd. of Equalization, 255 Cal. Rptr. 514, 16 Media L. Rep. 1257 (Cal. Ct. App. 1989) (statute exempted "newspapers" and "periodicals," i.e., publications issued at regular intervals of not more than three months; administrative regulation that excluded any such publications if more than 90% of their content was advertising upheld on commercial speech rationale).

[238]481 U.S. 227, 13 Media L. Rep. 2313 (1987).

[239]*Id.* at 232–33. *See also* Texas Monthly v. Bullock, 489 U.S. 1, 16 Media L. Rep. 1177 (1989) (invalidating statute granting tax exemption to religious periodicals as violation of First Amendment's Establishment Clause).

[240]111 S. Ct. 1438, 18 Media L. Rep. 1953 (1991).

[241]*Id.* at 1447, 18 Media L. Rep. at 1959. Since *Leathers,* several decisions have rejected attacks on differential taxation of the media. Maryland Pennysaver Group v. Maryland Comptroller, 594 A.2d 1142, 19 Media L. Rep. 1937 (Md. Ct. App. 1991) (not unconstitutional to deny "pennysavers" or shopper advertisers tax exemption available to "newspapers"); Sacramento Cable Television v. City of Sacramento, 286 Cal. Rptr. 470, 19 Media L. Rep. 1532 (Cal. Ct. App. 1991) (application of city's utility tax to cable television not unconstitutional); Gallagher v. Connecticut Comm'r of Revenue Servs., 602 A.2d 996, 19 Media L. Rep. 2140 (Conn. 1992) (publication primarily consisting of television listings not entitled to "newspaper" tax exemption; such denial not unconstitutional); Bancroft Info. Group v. Maryland Comptroller, 603 A.2d 1289, 20 Media L. Rep. 1016 (Md. Ct. Spec. App. 1992) (denial of "newspaper" tax exemption to bi-weekly not unconstitutional because denial based on frequency of publication, not content); Cox Cable Hampton Roads v. City of Norfolk, 410 S.E.2d 652, 19 Media L. Rep. 1656 (Va. 1991) (upholding, against First Amendment attack, application of city's utility tax to cable television even though only one cable system

not singled out for taxation, there was no evidence that the tax scheme was intended to infringe First Amendment rights, the tax did not burden only a limited number of the media, and the tax was not content-based.[242] The Court remanded an equal protection challenge to the different tax treatment of cable and satellite television services.[243]

At least one federal court has invalidated Internal Revenue Service (IRS) tax regulations on the grounds that the regulations were unconstitutionally vague.[244] After the IRS revised its regulations to eliminate the objectionable discretion, they were upheld.[245] In contrast, a state court refused to invalidate a city tax ordinance challenged as being unconstitutionally vague.[246]

Several states have statutes that exempt newspapers from sales or use taxes.[247] Interpretations of what constitutes a "newspaper" under these statutes vary.[248]

---

in city). *But see* Globe Newspaper Co. v. Massachusetts, 571 N.E.2d 617, 18 Media L. Rep. 2354 (Mass. 1991) (overturning tax that denied newspapers two tax exemptions available to all other manufacturers).

[242]*Id.* at 1444–45, 18 Media L. Rep. at 1957.

[243]*Id.* at 1447, 18 Media L. Rep. at 1959. *Compare* Satellink of Chicago v. City of Chicago, 523 N.E.2d 13 (Ill. App. Ct. 1988) (upholding equal protection challenge to municipal tax that applied to satellite television service but exempted cable television) *and* Cox Cable Hampton Roads v. City of Norfolk, 410 S.E.2d 652, 19 Media L. Rep. 1656 (Va. 1991) (overruling demurrer to equal protection claim that alleged that cable television and SMATV were virtually identical services) *with* Chesterfield Cablevision v. County of Chesterfield, 401 S.E.2d 678 (Va. 1991) (tax on cable television that exempted newspapers and broadcasters sustained against equal protection claim). Relying on *Leathers,* the Court also issued three other rulings. First, it vacated and remanded for further consideration, in light of *Leathers,* Florida Dep't of Revenue v. Magazine Publishers of Am., 565 So. 2d 1304 (Fla.), *vacated and remanded,* 111 S. Ct. 1614 (1991), which had held that a tax on secular magazines but not on newspapers was unconstitutional, but that the appropriate remedy was to eliminate the newspaper exemption rather than to invalidate the magazine tax. On remand, the Florida Supreme Court affirmed its earlier decision. Florida Dep't of Revenue v. Magazine Pubrs. of Am., 604 So. 2d 459, 20 Media L. Rep. 1502 (Fla. 1992). Second, the Court denied review in Newsweek v. Celauro, 789 S.W.2d 247, 18 Media L. Rep. 1134 (Tenn. 1990), *cert. denied,* 111 S. Ct. 1639 (1991) and Southern Living v. Celauro, 789 S.W.2d 251 (Tenn. 1990), *cert. denied,* 111 S. Ct. 1639 (1991), which had held that a tax scheme that exempted newspapers but not other publications was unconstitutional, apparently because the definition of "newspaper" was not content-neutral. Third, the Court denied review in Hearst Corp. v. Iowa Department of Revenue and Finance, 461 N.W.2d 295, 18 Media L. Rep. 1241 (Iowa 1990), *cert. denied,* 111 S. Ct. 1639 (1991), where a constitutional challenge to the exemption of newspapers from taxation was rejected.

[244]Big Mama Rag v. United States, 631 F.2d 1030, 1034 (D.C. Cir. 1980).

[245]National Alliance v. United States, 710 F.2d 868 (D.C. Cir. 1983).

[246]Times Mirror v. City of Los Angeles, 237 Cal. Rptr. 346, 14 Media L. Rep. 1289 (Cal. Ct. App. 1987), *appeal dismissed for want of substantial federal question,* 484 U.S. 1022 (1988) (rejecting claim that city business tax scheme that permitted city clerk to apportion taxes by whatever method clerk determined "necessary and desirable" was unconstitutional).

[247]*See, e.g.,* ARK. STAT. ANN. §84-1904(f) (1947) (gross receipts or gross proceeds from sale of newspapers); CAL. REV. & TAX CODE §6362 (West 1970) (newspapers or periodicals regularly issued); CONN. GEN. STAT. ANN. §12-412(6) (West 1986 Supp.) (magazine subscriptions and newspapers circulated among public); D.C. CODE ANN. §§47-2005(6), 47-2001(r) (1981) (newspapers and publications for religious, scientific, charitable, or educational purposes); FLA. STAT. §212.08(6) & (7)(e) (1985) (newspapers and magazine subscriptions); IND. CODE ANN. §6-2.5-5-17 (Burns 1984) (newspapers); IOWA CODE ANN. §422.45.9 (West 1986) (newspapers, free newspapers, or shoppers guides); MD. CODE ANN. TAX-GEN. §11-215 (1993) (printing and sales of newspapers of any and all types); MASS. GEN. LAWS ANN. ch. 64H, §6(m) (West 1969) (newspapers, magazines, certain books); MICH. STAT. ANN. §7.525(h) (Callaghan 1986) (newspapers and periodicals); MINN. STAT. ANN. §297A.25(i) (West 1986) (any publication regularly issued at average intervals excluding magazines and periodicals sold over counter); MISS. CODE ANN. §27-65-111(b) (1972) (daily or weekly newspapers); NEB. REV. STAT. §77-2704(d) (1985) (regularly issued newspapers); N.J. STAT. ANN. §54:32B-8(e) (West 1985) (newspapers, magazines, and periodicals); N.M. STAT. ANN. §§7-9-63, 7-9-64 (1978) (newspapers and magazines); N.Y. TAX LAW §115(a)(5) (McKinney 1986) (newspapers and periodicals); OHIO REV. CODE ANN. §5739.02(B)(4) (Page 1985) (newspapers; magazine subscriptions shipped by second class mail); OKLA. STAT. ANN. tit. 68, §1357(c) (West 1985) (newspapers and periodicals); S.C. CODE ANN. §12-35-550(7) (Law. Co-op. 1976) (newsprint paper; newspapers); S.D. CODIFIED LAWS ANN. §10-45-12.1 (1986 Supp.) (newspaper sales and subcriptions); TENN. CODE ANN. §§66-6-323, 67-6-329 (3) (1983) (newspapers); TEX. TAX. CODE ANN. §§151.319, 151.320 (Vernon 1982) (newspapers; magazine subscriptions entered as second class mail); UTAH CODE ANN. §59-15-4(b)(1) (1985) (newspapers); VT. STAT. ANN. tit. 32, §9741(15) (1981) (newspapers with at least 10% news of general interest); VA. CODE §58.1-608(13) (1950) (any daily or regularly issued publication excluding newsstand sales of same); WASH. REV. CODE ANN. §82.08.0253 (1981) (newspapers); W. VA. CODE §11-15-9 (1983) (sales of newspapers delivered by route carriers); WIS. STAT. ANN. §77.54(15) (West 1985) (newspapers and regularly issued periodicals); WYO. STAT. §39-6-405(xxi) (1977) (sale of newspapers).

[248]*Compare* Greenfield Town Crier v. Commissioner of Revenue, 433 N.E.2d 898, 8 Media L. Rep. 1626 (Mass. 1982) (holding that free publication distributed weekly that contains information on matters of

§9.8 "SON OF SAM" ANTIPROFIT STATUTES

The majority of states[249] and the federal government[250] have adopted "Son of Sam" victims' compensation statutes[251] that are intended to deprive convicted criminals of proceeds from selling their stories to the media by diverting those proceeds to the victims of the crimes depicted or recounted. These antiprofit statutes are premised on the theory that no criminal should be able to profit from crime,[252] and that to allow such profits would unjustly enrich wrongdoers.[253]

In general, these laws require all sums due an accused, indicted, or convicted criminal under media contracts allowing reenactment of the crime or compensating the alleged criminal for telling his or her own story to be placed in a state-administered escrow account.[254] The account is available as a fund to satisfy any money judgments won by victims of the crime in civil actions

---

public interest is "newspaper" under state tax exemption); Daily Record v. James, 629 S.W.2d 348, 8 Media L. Rep. 1581 (Mo. 1982) (advertising supplement inserted into and distributed with newspaper entitled to tax exemption for "newspapers" under state statute); *and* Sears, Roebuck & Co. v. State Tax Comm'n, 345 N.E.2d 893 (Mass. 1976) (advertising supplement inserted into and distributed with newspaper entitled to tax exemption as "newspaper" under state law) *with* Caldor, Inc. v. Heffernan, 440 A.2d 767, 7 Media L. Rep. 1747 (Conn. 1981) (preprinted advertising supplements inserted into and distributed with newspaper not entitled to tax exemption as "newspaper" under state law); Memphis Shoppers News v. Woods, 584 S.W.2d 196, 5 Media L. Rep. 1445 (Tenn. 1979) ("shopper" publication distributed free of charge not entitled to tax exemption as "newspaper" under state law); *and* Shoppers Guide Pub'n Co. v. Woods, 547 S.W.2d 561, 2 Media L. Rep. 1825 (Tenn. 1977) (free shoppers guide containing only advertisements, classified ads, and local announcements not entitled to tax exemption as "newspaper" under state law).

[249]Fasching v. Kallinger, 510 A.2d 694, 695 n.1 (N.J. Super. Ct. App. Div. 1986).
[250]18 U.S.C.A. §3671 (West 1985).
[251]The statutes generally are patterned after New York Executive Law §§621-632-a (McKinney 1982 and Supp. 1992), adopted in 1977 in the wake of the "Son of Sam" killings. For a general discussion of these statutes, *see* Note, *Criminals-Turned-Authors: Victim's Rights v. Freedom of Speech,* 54 IND. L.J. 443 (1979); Rothman, *In Cold Type: Statutory Approaches to the Problem of Offender As Author,* 71 CRIM. L. & CRIMINOLOGY 255 (1980); Note, *Alabama's Anti-Profit Statute: A Recent Trend in Victim Compensation,* 33 ALA. L. REV. 109 (1981); Note, *Publication Rights Agreements in Sensational Crime Cases: A Response to the Problem,* 68 CORNELL L. REV. 686 (1983); Snider, *My Life of Crime: Coming Soon to a Theater Near You,* CAL. LAW. 29 (April 1987); Roberts, *Criminals, Authors and Criminal Authors,* N.Y. TIMES, March 22, 1987, §7, at 1, col. 1.
[252]Snider, *supra* note 251, at 29.
[253]Note, *supra* note 251, 54 IND. L.J. at 443–44.
[254]Typical is the New Jersey statute, which provides, in pertinent part:
Every person, firm, corporation, partnership, association or other legal entity contracting with a person convicted or accused of a crime in this State or an agent, assignee, beneficiary, conservator, executor, guardian, representative, relative, friend, associate or conspirator of a person convicted or accused of a crime in this State, with respect to the reenactment of the crime, by way of a movie, book, magazine article, other literary expression, recording, radio or television presentation, live entertainment or presentation of any kind, or from the expression of the persons' thoughts, feelings, opinions or emotions regarding the crime, shall submit a copy of the contract to the [Violent Crimes Compensation Board] and shall pay over to the board all moneys which would otherwise, by the terms of the contract, be owing the person convicted or accused of a crime in this State or an agent, assignee, beneficiary, conservator, executor, guardian, representative, relative, friend, associate or conspirator of a person convicted or accused of a crime in this State. The board shall deposit these moneys in an interest bearing escrow account for the benefit of and payable to any victim of the convicted or accused person or the victim's representative, provided that the person is eventually convicted of the crime and that the victim or victim's representative brings, within five years of the date of the establishment of the escrow account, a civil action for damages resulting from the crime, or has already obtained a judgment for damages resulting from the crime against the person or an agent, assignee, beneficiary, conservator, executor, guardian, representative, relative, friend, associate or conspirator of a person convicted or accused of a crime in this State.
N.J. STAT. ANN. §52:4B-28 (1993). For a list of such statutes, *see* Children of Bedford v. Petromelis, 573 N.E.2d 541, 548–49 n.3, 18 Media L. Rep. 2255, 2261 n.3 (N.Y. 1991), *vacated and remanded,* 112 S. Ct. 859 (1992) (remanded for reconsideration in light of Simon & Schuster, Inc. v. New York State Crime Victims Bd., 112 S. Ct. 501 (1991)).

against the convicted criminal.[255] The fund may also be used as a source for the alleged criminal's defense costs and attorneys' fees.[256]

Victims generally are required to bring such civil actions within five years of the date of the crime or within five years of the time the escrow account is established.[257] Some statutes require the contracting party—the publisher—to place advances, royalties, or other compensation owed to the alleged criminal directly into the account.[258] Other statutes place no affirmative duties on publishers.[259]

The scope and constitutionality of these statutes has provoked substantial discussion by legal commentators.[260] Some commentators concluded that the statutes are subject to challenge on First Amendment grounds because they infringe on the accused person's right to express himself and publishers' rights to disseminate information to the public.[261] The statutes were also criticized for depriving an accused person of property without due process of law.[262]

The initial reported decisions did not address First Amendment issues.[263] At least one appellate court concluded, however, that New Jersey's statute could not be interpreted to reach publishers' own profits even though proceeds owed criminals were subject to forfeiture.[264]

While New York's highest court rejected First Amendment challenges to New York's Son of Sam law,[265] the U.S. Supreme Court shortly afterward reached just the opposite conclusion.[266] The Court rejected the argument that the Son of Sam law was one of general application, holding that instead the law

---

[255] *See, e.g.,* CAL. CIV. CODE §2225(4)(A) (West Supp. 1994) (beneficiary includes someone who "has or had a right to recover damages from the convicted felon for physical, mental, or emotional injury, pecuniary loss proximately caused by the convicted felon as a result of the crime for which the felon was convicted").

[256] *See, e.g.,* N.J. STAT. ANN. §52:4B-32 (Violent Crimes Compensation Board "shall make payments from an escrow account to a person accused of crime, upon the order of a court of competent jurisdiction, after a showing by the person that a reasonable amount of these moneys shall be used for the exclusive purpose of retaining legal representation at any stage of the criminal proceedings against the person, including the appeal process"). *But see* Note, *supra* note 251, 33 ALA. L. REV. at 119–20 (observing that Alabama statute contains no provision for payments from account to cover costs of legal representation).

[257] *See, e.g.,* N.Y. EXEC. LAW §632-a(4) (McKinney Supp. 1994).

[258] *See, e.g., id.* §632-a(1); N.J. STAT. ANN. §52:4B-28; Fasching v. Kallinger, 510 A.2d 694, 703 (N.J. Super. Ct. App. Div. 1986).

[259] *See, e.g.,* CAL. CIV. CODE §2225(e)(1) ("the Attorney General may bring an action to require proceeds received by a convicted felon to be held in an express trust"); Snider, *supra* note 251, at 30 (observing that California's law imposes no obligations on party paying felon but merely gives attorney general or crime victim cause of action to require felon to establish trust account).

[260] *See supra* note 251.

[261] *See* Note, *supra* note 251, 54 IND. L.J. 443; Note, *supra* note 251, 33 ALA. L. REV. 109; *see also* Note, *Compensating the Victim from the Proceeds of the Criminal Story: The Constitutionality of the New York Approach,* 14 COLUM. J.L. & SOC. PROBS. 93 (1978).

[262] *See supra* note 261.

[263] Barrett v. Wojtowicz, 414 N.Y.S.2d 350 (N.Y. App. Div. 1979); In re Johnsen, 430 N.Y.S.2d 904 (N.Y. Sup. Ct. 1979); United States v. MacDonald, 607 F. Supp. 1183 (D.N.C. 1985); Fasching v. Kallinger, 510 A.2d 694 (N.J. Super. Ct. App. Div. 1986).

[264] *Fasching,* 510 A.2d at 703. The court also held that crime victims could not bring a claim for unjust enrichment against publishers because they had no direct relationship with them and the publishers did not aid the criminals in any wrongdoing. *Id.* at 699–700. *See also* Collazo v. Kallinger, 11 Media L. Rep. 1509, 1511 (Pa. C.P. 1985) (relatives of murder victim failed to state cause of action for unjust enrichment against publisher that published account of murder because no injustice would result from publisher's retention of profits).

[265] Children of Bedford v. Petromelis, 573 N.E.2d 541, 18 Media L. Rep. 2255 (N.Y. 1991), *vacated and remanded,* 112 S. Ct. 859 (1992) (remanded for reconsideration in light of Simon & Schuster, Inc. v. New York State Crime Victims Bd., 112 S. Ct. 501 (1991)).

[266] Simon & Schuster, Inc. v. New York State Crime Victims Bd., 112 S. Ct. 501, 19 Media L. Rep. 1609 (1991).

was one that imposed penalties because of the content of speech.[267] The Court then held the law to be unconstitutional because it was not justified by a narrowly tailored and compelling state interest, noting that "[s]hould a prominent figure write his autobiography at the end of his career, and include in an early chapter a brief recollection of having stolen (in New York) a nearly worthless item as a youthful prank, the [New York] Board would control his entire income for five years...."[268] Thus, the New York law was not a narrowly tailored attempt to compensate crime victims from the profits of crime.[269]

§9.9 POSTAL RATES

For more than 100 years Congress has used its exclusive power over the postal system to grant subsidized second class postal rates to newspapers and other periodicals.[270] Publishers must meet several conditions before their publications may be granted the subsidized rates.[271]

The First Amendment, however, does not require that all publications be granted unconditional access to the mails, nor that they all enjoy access on the same financial terms.[272] Nevertheless, mindful of the possible censorship inherent in postal officials' power over subsidized access to the mails, courts have carefully scrutinized denials of second class rate status to ensure that First Amendment as well as due process rights are not overtly or covertly violated.[273]

This rule has been applied in a variety of cases.[274] For example, in *Hannegan v. Esquire, Inc.*,[275] the postmaster general revoked the second class

---

[267]*Id.* at 508–09, 19 Media L. Rep. at 1614–15.
[268]*Id.* at 512, 19 Media L. Rep. at 1617.
[269]*Id.* The Court also noted that it was not ruling on the constitutionality of Son of Sam laws that "may be quite different from New York's." *Id.* The New York law was amended in 1992 in response to the Supreme Court's decision. N.Y. EXEC. LAW §632-a (McKinney Supp. 1994).
[270]Lewis Pub'g Co. v. Morgan, 229 U.S. 288, 302 (1913). *See also* U.S. CONST. art. I, §8.
[271]39 C.F.R. §200.010–200.013 (1987).
[272]Enterprise, Inc. v. United States, 833 F.2d 1216, 1224, 14 Media L. Rep. 2153, 2160 (6th Cir. 1987) ("The first amendment is not violated merely because a content-neutral regulation raises the cost of one avenue of communication, or prevents the use of one mode of communication where others exist. This is especially true where the cost of the desired mode is artificially reduced through government subsidies."); Lewis Pub'g Co. v. Wyman, 182 F. 13, 16 (8th Cir. 1910), *aff'd*, 228 U.S. 610 (1913) (second class rate "was intended for newspapers and periodicals published for the dissemination of information of a public character or devoted to literature, the sciences, arts, or some special industry and circulated for the most part among bona fide subscribers, and not for publications designed principally for advertising purposes or for free circulation or circulation of nominal rates"). *See also* Hannegan v. Esquire, Inc., 327 U.S. 146, 155 n.18, 1 Media L. Rep. 2292 (1946) (observing that Congress may exclude obscene and fraudulent materials from mails); Jones v. North Carolina Prisoners' Union, 433 U.S. 119, 130–31 (1977) (prison officials permissibly denied prisoners' union right to send lower-priced bulk mailings to prison for distribution even though other groups, such as Jaycees, enjoyed privilege: "Since other avenues of outside informational flow by the Union remain available, the prohibition on bulk mailing, reasonable in the absence of First Amendment considerations, remains reasonable.").
[273]*See, e.g.,* Greenberg v. Bolger, 497 F. Supp. 756, 778 (E.D.N.Y. 1980) (regulation of mails by its nature regulates expression of ideas and information). *Compare Morgan,* 229 U.S. 288 (upholding requirement that information on newspaper's management, financial affairs, and circulation must be disclosed to obtain second class mail rates).
[274]*Contra* United States ex rel. Milwaukee Social Democratic Pub'g Co. v. Burleson, 255 U.S. 407 (1921), where the Court held that during World War I the postmaster general did not act unconstitutionally in revoking the second class permit held by a newspaper that the postmaster general believed had published false, pro-German articles intended to obstruct U.S. military operations and recruiting in violation of the Espionage Act. This is no longer sound authority. *See, e.g., Hannegan,* 327 U.S. at 156, 1 Media L. Rep. at 2297 ("grave constitutional questions are immediately raised once it is said that use of the mails is a privilege which may be extended or withheld on any grounds whatsoever") (citing *Burleson,* 255 U.S. 407, 421–23, 430–32, 437–38 (1921) (Brandeis, Holmes, JJ., dissenting)).
[275]327 U.S. 146, 1 Media L. Rep. 2292 (1946).

privilege held by *Esquire* magazine on grounds that the magazine's risque contents, even though not obscene, violated the statute's requirement that a second class periodical be published "for the dissemination of information of a public character, or devoted to literature, the sciences, arts, or some special industry,"[276] because the magazine's contents were "morally improper and not for the public welfare and the public good."[277] Holding that the postmaster general had not been clothed "with the power to supervise the tastes of the reading public of the country,"[278] the Supreme Court held that his content-based decision was impermissible censorship.[279]

Despite constitutional challenges, the rule that second class mailing privileges may be conditioned on a publication having a certain number of paid subscribers has been upheld.[280]

At least one court has concluded that, when a postal statute is facially content-neutral but indirectly requires a publisher to change its message or associations to receive reduced rates, the statute is unconstitutional.[281]

---

[276]*Id.* at 149, 1 Media L. Rep. at 2294.
[277]*Id.*
[278]*Id.* at 156, 1 Media L. Rep. at 2297.
[279]*Id.* at 158–59, 1 Media L. Rep. at 2297–98; *see also* Sunshine Pub'g Co. v. Summerfield, 184 F. Supp. 767, 772 (D.D.C. 1960) (court held that magazines exclusively about nudism were of public character or devoted to special industry, so they met statute's requirements, observing that even though such magazines "do not have the public acceptance given the ideas and way of life presented by 'Ladies' Home Journal' and 'House and Garden,' " they nevertheless deserved equal treatment by Postal Service).
[280]Enterprise, Inc. v. United States, 833 F.2d 1216, 14 Media L. Rep. 2153 (6th Cir. 1987); *see also* North Jersey Suburbanite v. State, 384 A.2d 831 (N.J. 1977) (same result in challenge to definition of "newspaper" in statute regulating who may carry legal notices).
[281]Spencer v. United States Postal Serv., 613 F. Supp. 990 (S.D. Ohio 1985) (making temporary injunction granted in Spencer v. Herdesty, 571 F. Supp. 444 (S.D. Ohio 1983), permanent); *see also* Greenberg v. Bolger, 497 F. Supp. 756, 777 (E.D.N.Y. 1980).

Chapter 10

PRIOR RESTRAINTS

§10.1 Introduction

This chapter discusses prior restraints, which are restrictions on speech or other expression before publication[1] and before an adequate judicial determination that the expression is not protected by the First Amendment.[2] The First Amendment protects expression, with a few possible exceptions,[3] from the imposition of any prior restraints by the government.[4]

§10.2 History and Nature of Prior Restraints

As the printing press developed in England, the church and then the state required licenses for all printed matter in order to stop scandalous or seditious matter from being disseminated; opposition to this interference with publication grew during the seventeenth century.[5] This licensing system expired in 1694, not so much from opposition to it as from frustration with its administration.[6] A century after the licensing system had lapsed, freedom of the press from

---

[1]*See* Nebraska Press Ass'n v. Stuart, 427 U.S. 539, 1 Media L. Rep. 1064 (1976); New York Times Co. v. United States, 403 U.S. 713, 1 Media L. Rep. 1031 (1971); Organization for a Better Austin v. Keefe, 402 U.S. 415, 1 Media L. Rep. 1021 (1971); Near v. Minnesota, 283 U.S. 697, 1 Media L. Rep. 1001 (1931); Kingsley Books v. Brown, 354 U.S. 436, 441–42, 1 Media L. Rep. 1111, 1113 (1957) (quoting Freund, *The Supreme Court and Civil Liberties,* 4 Vand. L. Rev. 533, 539 (1951)). *See also infra* notes 37–42.

[2]Southeastern Promotions v. Conrad, 420 U.S. 546, 1 Media L. Rep. 1140 (1975); Freedman v. Maryland, 380 U.S. 51, 1 Media L. Rep. 1126 (1965); Bantam Books v. Sullivan, 372 U.S. 58, 1 Media L. Rep. 1116 (1963); Joseph Burstyn, Inc. v. Wilson, 343 U.S. 495, 1 Media L. Rep. 1357 (1952).

[3]Pittsburgh Press Co. v. Pittsburgh Comm'n on Human Relations, 413 U.S. 376, 390, 1 Media L. Rep. 1908, 1914, *reh'g denied,* 414 U.S. 881 (1973). The Supreme Court has recognized that as to certain categories of speech, their "prevention and punishment . . . has never been thought to raise any Constitutional problem." Chaplinsky v. New Hampshire, 315 U.S. 568, 571–72 (1942). Speech that creates "a clear and present danger," Schenck v. United States, 249 U.S. 47, 52 (1919), " 'fighting' words," *Chaplinsky,* 315 U.S. at 572, and obscenity, Miller v. California, 413 U.S. 15, 1 Media L. Rep. 1441 (1973), are such categories of expression. *See also* Federal Communications Comm'n v. Pacifica Found., 438 U.S. 726, 3 Media L. Rep. 2553 (1978) (upholding FCC's regulation of "indecent speech"). Whether these exceptions apply in prior restraint cases is unclear. *See infra* note 27.

[4]Emerson, *The Doctrine of Prior Restraint,* 20 Law & Contemp. Probs. 648 (1955).

[5]W.E. Hocking, Freedom of the Press 3–4 (1947); Gold, *Does Equity Still Lack Jurisdiction to Enjoin a Libel or Slander?* 48 Brooklyn L. Rev. 231, 245 n.55 (1982). Under the Licensing Act of 1662, for example, not only were seditious and heretical books prohibited, but no one was allowed to print any material unless it was first duly licensed by the state. Books could not be imported or sold without a license, and printing presses and printers had to be registered. Emerson, *supra* note 4, at 650.

[6]Jeffries, *Rethinking Prior Restraint,* 92 Yale L.J. 409, 412 (1983). A detailed account of the licensing systems in England can be found in Emerson, *supra* note 4, at 650–52, and cases cited therein.

licensing had come to be seen as a right. Thus, Blackstone's famous passage equated freedom of the press with a rule against prior restraint:

> The liberty of the press is indeed essential to the nature of a free state; but this consists in laying no *previous* restraints upon publications, and not in freedom from censure for criminal matter when published. Every freeman has an undoubted right to lay what sentiments he pleases before the public; to forbid this is to destroy the freedom of the press, but if he publishes what is improper, mischievous, or illegal, he must take the consequence of his own temerity.[7]

The drafters of the First Amendment intended to prevent the establishment of any system of prior restraint similar to the English censorship system.[8]

For a time, Blackstone's passage was read with a focus on what was not protected: the "improper, mischievous, or illegal" speech. Thus, it was argued that, while the First Amendment was designed to prevent the establishment of a system of prior restraints similar to the English licensing system, it was not intended to prevent subsequent punishment of any publication.[9] The modern view, however, is to the contrary.[10]

Nearly 130 years after the adoption of the First Amendment, the Supreme Court, in its 1931 landmark decision, *Near v. Minnesota*,[11] first discussed the history and doctrine of prior restraints. In *Near*, a Minnesota statute provided for the abatement, as a public nuisance, of a "malicious, scandalous and defamatory newspaper, magazine or other periodical."[12] The statute authorized permanent injunctions preventing the operation of such nuisances, and also provided that "there shall be available the defense that the truth was published with good motives and for justifiable ends."[13]

The defendants in *Near* published a newspaper, *The Saturday Press,* on nine occasions in 1927 with articles critical of several public officials, the Jewish "race," and the members of the county grand jury.[14] The articles charged in substance that a Jewish gangster was in control of gambling, bootlegging, and racketeering in Minneapolis, and that law enforcement officers and agencies were not energetically performing their duties.[15] The defendants were prosecuted under the statute, and the newspaper was found to be a public nuisance.[16] The defendants claimed that the statute authorizing this injunction

---

[7]Jeffries, *supra* note 6, at 412–13 (quoting 4 W. BLACKSTONE, COMMENTARIES 152 (1916)).
[8]Near v. Minnesota, 283 U.S. 697, 714, 1 Media L. Rep. 1001, 1006 (1931).
[9]*Near,* 283 U.S. at 714.
[10]In Blackstone's view, any such speech could validly be made subject to criminal prosecution. Adopted as a construction of the First Amendment, this view would have imposed little or no substantive limit on governmental authority to suppress speech, so long as such suppression was done by subsequent punishment and not by prior restraint. . . . More modern observers usually look to the protective aspect of Blackstone's statement. They commonly cite him to confirm the doctrine of prior restraint as an independent bar to official regulation of speech, one applicable even to speech not otherwise protected under the First Amendment.
Jeffries, *supra* note 6, at 413. *See also* Z. CHAFEE, FREE SPEECH IN THE UNITED STATES 9 (1941).
[11]283 U.S. 697, 1 Media L. Rep. 1001 (1931). Indeed, *Near* marks the beginning of the Supreme Court's modern First Amendment decisions.
[12]*Id.* at 701–02, 1 Media L. Rep. at 1001.
[13]*Id.* at 702, 1 Media L. Rep. at 1001.
[14]*Id.* at 703–04, 1 Media L. Rep. at 1002.
[15]*Id.* at 704, 1 Media L. Rep. at 1002–03.
[16]The defendants were permanently enjoined from "producing, editing, publishing, circulating, having in their possession, selling or giving any publication whatsoever which is a malicious, scandalous or defamatory newspaper, as defined by law," and also "from further conducting said nuisance under the name and title of said *The Saturday Press* or any other name or title." 283 U.S. at 706, 1 Media L. Rep. at 1003.

was constitutionally invalid on its face;[17] the case reached the U.S. Supreme Court on appeal from the Minnesota Supreme Court.

In an opinion by Chief Justice Charles E. Hughes, five members of the Supreme Court struck down the law as an invalid prior restraint.[18] The Court found four aspects of the statute significant: First, "[t]he statute is not aimed at the redress of individual or private wrongs";[19] second, "[t]he statute is directed not simply at the circulation of scandalous and defamatory statements with regard to private citizens, but at the continued publication by newspapers and periodicals of charges against public officers of corruption, malfeasance in office, or serious neglect of duty. Such charges by their very nature create a public scandal";[20] third, "[t]he object of the statute is not punishment, in the ordinary sense, but suppression of the offending newspaper or periodical.... It is the continued publication of scandalous and defamatory matter that constitutes the business and the declared nuisance";[21] and fourth, "[t]he statute not only operates to suppress the offending newspaper or periodical, but to put the publisher under an effective censorship.... [R]esumption of publication is punishable as a contempt of court by fine or imprisonment."[22]

The Court reviewed the history of "previous restraints upon publications"[23] in both England and the colonial era in America, and quoted Blackstone and others who condemned prior restraints.[24] Although the Court noted that abuses of the liberty of the press are subject to punishment, and cited as examples of abuse publications that were libelous or that directly tended to prevent the proper discharge of judicial functions, it found that *Near* did not involve punishment of past speech but suppression and restraint of publication.[25] The Court also found that the rarity of prior restraint cases was evidence of the basic constitutional infirmity of such restraints.[26]

The Court stated that protection against prior restraints is not absolute: the press could be restrained from publishing obscenity; the sailing dates of transports, as well as the number or location of troops, during a war; and words that may have all the effect of force.[27] Such exceptions were not applicable in *Near*, however.

---

[17]*Id.* at 705, 1 Media L. Rep. at 1002.
[18]*Id.* at 723, 1 Media L. Rep. at 1010.
[19]*Id.* at 709, 1 Media L. Rep. at 1004. The statute was concerned with the detrimental effect on the general welfare of the distribution of scandalous matter.
[20]*Id.* at 710, 1 Media L. Rep. at 1005.
[21]283 U.S. at 711, 1 Media L. Rep. at 1005.
[22]*Id.* at 712, 1 Media L. Rep. at 1005.
[23]*Id.* at 713, 1 Media L. Rep. at 1006.
[24]*Id.* at 713–14, 1 Media L. Rep. at 1006.
[25]*Id.* at 715, 1 Media L. Rep. at 1007.
[26]"The fact that for approximately one hundred and fifty years there has been almost an entire absence of attempts to impose previous restraints upon publications relating to the malfeasance of public officers is significant of the deep-seated conviction that such restraints would violate constitutional right." 283 U.S. at 718, 1 Media L. Rep. at 1008.
[27]*Id.* at 716, 1 Media L. Rep. at 1007. Professor Emerson notes that these exceptions to the prior restraint rule were not carefully considered and served to confuse the opinion:

The war exception rests upon peculiar factors of obvious weight. But the Chief Justice made no attempt to explain why obscene or seditious utterances should be distinguished from "malicious, scandalous and defamatory" utterances. Certainly no such distinction can be based upon the appeal to history; on the contrary, the opposition to licensing plainly extended to prior restraint of allegedly seditious publications and probably to the obscene, too, so far as obscenity was then a ground for restraint.... It may be that the Chief Justice merely intended to make the traditional point that seditious and obscene publications were subject to subsequent punishment as exceptions to the First Amendment. In any event,

The Court concluded that "liberty of the press, historically considered and taken up by the Federal Constitution has meant, principally, although not exclusively, immunity from previous restraints or censorship."[28] The Court recognized that, during the colonial period, freedom from prior restraint was particularly cherished because it permitted criticism of public officers and charges of official misconduct; otherwise, the patriots would have been stifled in their efforts to inform their fellow subjects of their rights and the duties of rulers.[29] Public officials were not without some remedy: "Public officers whose character and conduct remain open to debate and free discussion in the press, find their remedies for false accusations in actions under libel laws providing for redress and punishment, and not in proceedings to restrain the publication of newspapers and periodicals."[30]

In a dissent joined by three others, Justice Pierce Butler concluded that the published statements in *Near* were so improbable as to compel a finding of falsity: "The articles themselves show malice."[31] The dissent also deemed the law a proper exercise of the state's police power because the publication in question had given rise to people arming themselves and shooting,[32] and thus the statute must "be deemed appropriate to deal with conditions existing in Minnesota."[33] Justice Butler found the publications unquestionably "constitute an abuse of the right of free press"[34] and questioned how obscenity, the publication of which could be restrained, could be distinguished from other types of speech that may not be restrained: "As that resulting from lewd publications constitutionally may be enjoined it is hard to understand why the one resulting from a regular business of malicious defamation may not."[35]

Two important aspects of the decision make *Near* a landmark case: (1) it is the first clear outline of the prior restraint doctrine, and (2) the Court struck down a statute that was not the equivalent of the seventeenth century censoring-licensing statutes that the doctrine was created to prevent, although in practice it had many similar aspects.[36]

---

the attempt to enumerate exceptions to the prior restraint rule was not carefully considered and can scarcely be said to have settled the issue.
Emerson, *supra* note 4, at 661. *But see infra* notes 66 and 67. For a discussion of the distinction between prior restraint and subsequent punishment, *see infra* §10.3.
[28]*Near,* 283 U.S. at 716, 1 Media L. Rep. at 1007.
[29]*Id.* at 718, 1 Media L. Rep. at 1008. On this point, James Madison is quoted at length: "And can the wisdom of this policy [prohibiting prior restraints] be doubted by any who reflect that to the press alone, checkered as it is with abuses, the world is indebted for all the triumphs which have been gained by reason and humanity over error and oppression." *Id.*
[30]*Id.* at 718–19, 1 Media L. Rep. at 1008. The Court went on to state that "[c]harges of reprehensible conduct, and in particular of official malfeasance, unquestionably create a public scandal, but the theory of the constitutional guarantee is that even a more serious public evil would be caused by authority to prevent publication." *Id.* at 722, 1 Media L. Rep. at 1009.
[31]*Id.* at 724, 1 Media L. Rep. at 1010 (Butler, J., dissenting).
[32]*Id.* at 731, 1 Media L. Rep. at 1013.
[33]283 U.S. at 732, 1 Media L. Rep. at 1013–14.
[34]*Id.* at 735, 1 Media L. Rep. at 1015.
[35]*Id.* at 737, 1 Media L. Rep. at 1016.
[36]No original approval of a publication was required. Only after a person had published "malicious, scandalous and defamatory" matter could he be enjoined. And the injunction did not prevent him from continuing to publish at all; it only restrained publishing a "malicious, scandalous and defamatory" newspaper. Thus, the publisher would be guilty of contempt and punished only as and when he committed subsequent offenses. Theoretically, therefore, the statute could hardly be said to set up prior restraint. On paper, it was a system for subsequent punishment by contempt procedure.
But in practice, the system was bound to operate as a serious prior restraint. Punishment could be summarily dispensed by a single official, without jury trial or the other protections of criminal procedure, for infraction of a loose and illusive mandate. Under such circumstances, any publisher seeking to avoid

Since *Near,* prior restraint cases have fallen into a "four-part typology"[37] set out by Professor Emerson.[38] The first and clearest category of prior restraint occurs in situations where a government regulation prevents any publication unless an official gives prior approval, i.e., licensing. The English licensing laws, censorship of motion pictures, or requirements of permits for public meetings serve as examples of this type of prior restraint.[39] The second category of prior restraint involves injunctions enforced by contempt proceedings.[40] The statute in *Near* illustrates this type of prior restraint. The third type involves legislative restraints—registration or certain taxation of newspapers or other media, for example.[41] Finally, the fourth type of prior restraint involves tests for holding political office or a position of influence, for example, the Taft-Hartley non-Communist affidavit.[42]

Regardless of the typology, the Supreme Court has repeatedly invalidated prior restraints no matter what the context.[43]

§10.3 Theory and Rationales

The Supreme Court, in *Pittsburgh Press Co. v. Pittsburgh Commission on Human Relations,*[44] explained its primary concern about prior restraints: "The special vice of a prior restraint is that communication will be suppressed, either directly or by inducing excessive caution in the speaker, before an adequate determination that it is unprotected by the First Amendment."[45]

---

prison would, in sheer self-protection, have to clear in advance any doubtful matter with the official wielding such direct, immediate, and unimpeded power to sentence. The judge would, in effect, become a censor.

Emerson, *supra* note 4, at 654.

[37]Jeffries, *supra* note 6, at 421.
[38]Emerson, *supra* note 4, at 655.
[39]*See, e.g.,* Joseph Burstyn, Inc. v. Wilson, 343 U.S. 495, 1 Media L. Rep. 1357 (1952) (statute requiring motion picture license); Kunz v. New York, 340 U.S. 290 (1951) (permit for worship on public streets); Niemotko v. Maryland, 340 U.S. 268 (1951) (permit for religious meetings in parks); Saia v. New York, 334 U.S. 558 (1948) (ordinance requiring police chief's prior approval for sound amplification equipment); Cantwell v. Connecticut, 310 U.S. 296 (1940) (license for religious solicitation); Lovell v. City of Griffin, 303 U.S. 444 (1938) (ordinance requiring city manager's prior permission to distribute literature of any kind). In Southeastern Promotions v. Conrad, 420 U.S. 546, 552–53, 1 Media L. Rep. 1140, 1142 (1975), the Court cited the following additional cases as ones involving prior restraints where officials denied use of a forum in advance of actual expression: Shuttlesworth v. City of Birmingham, 394 U.S. 147, 150–51 (1969); Staub v. City of Baxley, 355 U.S. 313, 322 (1958); Schneider v. State, 308 U.S. 147, 161–62 (1939); Hague v. Committee for Indus. Org., 307 U.S. 496 (1939). For a full discussion of such licensing restrictions, see Chapter 12. *See also* Bantam Books v. Sullivan, 372 U.S. 58, 1 Media L. Rep. 1116 (1963) (blacklists of publications circulated by government agency constituted prior restraint); Heller v. New York, 413 U.S. 483 (1973) (if only one copy of publication exists, it cannot be seized as evidence; it must be copied and original must be returned); Penthouse Int'l v. McAuliffe, 610 F.2d 1353, 5 Media L. Rep. 2531 (5th Cir.) (combination of facts from *Bantam Books* and *Heller*), *cert. dismissed,* 447 U.S. 931 (1980).

[40]New York Times Co. v. United States, 403 U.S. 713, 1 Media L. Rep. 1031 (1971) (per curiam) (for a detailed discussion of this case, *see infra* §10.6(A)); Oklahoma Pub'g Co. v. District Ct., 430 U.S. 308, 2 Media L. Rep. 1456 (1977); Nebraska Press Ass'n v. Stuart, 427 U.S. 539, 1 Media L. Rep. 1064 (1976); Organization for a Better Austin v. Keefe, 402 U.S. 415, 1 Media L. Rep. 1021 (1971). For a discussion of judicial gag orders, see *infra* §10.7. For a discussion of invasion of privacy and prior restraints, see *infra* §10.8.

[41]*See, e.g.,* Grosjean v. American Press Co., 297 U.S. 233, 1 Media L. Rep. 2685 (1936). For a discussion of taxation and the First Amendment, see Chapter 9.

[42]Emerson, *supra* note 4, at 656.

[43]*Keefe,* 402 U.S. at 419, 1 Media L. Rep. at 1022 (invalidating prior restraint based on invasion of privacy); *New York Times Co.,* 403 U.S. at 714, 1 Media L. Rep. at 1031 (invalidating prior restraint based on national security concerns); *Nebraska Press,* 427 U.S. at 561, 1 Media L. Rep. at 1072–73 (invalidating prior restraint of prejudicial pretrial publicity).

[44]413 U.S. 376, 1 Media L. Rep. 1908 (1973).

[45]*Id.* at 390, 1 Media L. Rep. at 1914.

Courts also fear that by allowing prior restraints before information can be published, the government can "foreclose timely expression and thereby destroy the immediacy of the speech."[46]

Traditional reasons for supporting the different treatment of prior restraints and subsequent punishment are that prior restraints (1) shut off expression before it can be heard, (2) are more likely to be overused because they are more easily obtained than criminal convictions, (3) lack the procedural protections of the criminal process, (4) require adjudication in the abstract without knowing precisely what will be said or what its impact will be, (5) prevent audiences from receiving any message, and (6) unduly extend state power over individuals.[47]

Professor Emerson has set forth a similar list of reasons:

> A system of prior restraint is in many ways more inhibiting than a system of subsequent punishment: It is more likely to bring under government scrutiny a far wider range of expression; it shuts off communication before it takes place; suppression by a stroke of the pen is more likely to be applied than suppression through a criminal process; the procedures do not require attention to the safeguards of the criminal process; the system allows less opportunity for public appraisal and criticism; [and] the dynamics of the system drive toward excesses, as the history of all censorship shows.[48]

Whatever reasons are given, courts have been quite hostile to prior restraints.[49]

One of the primary reasons given for prior restraints being more harmful than subsequent punishment is that a subsequent criminal prosecution is subject to numerous procedural safeguards not present when prior restraints are sought.

---

[46]Gold, *supra* note 5, at 243–44 n.47 (citing Carroll v. President & Comm'rs of Princess Anne, 393 U.S. 175, 182, 1 Media L. Rep. 1016, 1019 (1968); Bridges v. California, 314 U.S. 252, 269, 1 Media L. Rep. 1275, 1279 (1941)).

[47]Redish, *The Proper Role of the Prior Restraint Doctrine in First Amendment Theory*, 70 VA. L. REV. 53, 59 (1984).

[48]T. EMERSON, THE SYSTEM OF FREEDOM OF EXPRESSION 506 (1970). Gold has restated Emerson's earlier discussion of these principles:
Emerson . . . has identified the following distinguishing characteristics of a system of prior restraint:
  1. *Breadth:* All expression within the area controlled, including the innocent and borderline, is subject to governmental scrutiny. The system "is geared to universal inspection, not to scrutiny in particular cases. . . ." Emerson, *The Doctrine of Prior Restraint*, 20 Law & Contemp. Prob. 648, 656 (1955).
  2. *Timing and delay:* The communication either never reaches the public or is finally released when it may have become obsolete. *Id.* at 657.
  3. *Propensity toward an adverse decision:* A decision to restrain speech in advance is often reached more readily than a decision to punish after the fact as the former imposes less of a burden on the government. *Id.*
  4. *Procedure:* The initial decision to suppress rests on an administrative official, thus depriving the speaker of the procedural protections of a criminal prosecution or the benefits of a jury decision. *Id.*
  5. *Opportunity for public appraisal and criticism:* The licensing official operates away from public scrutiny, thereby increasing the chances of discrimination and other abuse. *Id.* at 658.
  6. *The dynamics of prior restraint:* The system itself creates and perpetuates "unintelligent, overzealous and usually absurd administration." *Id.*
  7. *Certainty and risk.* Society's interest in freedom of expression is undermined by implying a willingness to conform to official opinion and a fear of asserting unacceptable opinions. *Id.* at 659.
  8. *Effectiveness.* A system of prior restraint is "in general" more effectively enforced than a system of subsequent punishment. *Id.*
Gold, *supra* note 5, at 255 n.115. For Emerson's earlier statement of these principles, *see* Emerson, *supra* note 4, at 656–60.

[49]Barnett, *The Puzzle of Prior Restraint*, 29 STAN. L. REV. 539, 543 (1977) (citing Southeastern Promotions v. Conrad, 420 U.S. 546, 559, 1 Media L. Rep. 1140, 1144–45 (1975); Carroll v. President & Comm'rs of Princess Anne, 393 U.S. 175, 180–81, 1 Media L. Rep. 1016, 1018 (1968)).
Some commentators argue that these reasons are not valid, and that prior restraints have no more significant impact on First Amendment rights than the threat of subsequent punishment. *See* Barnett, *supra* note 49, at 549 (prior restraints preferable to subsequent punishment); Jeffries, *supra* note 6; Redish, *supra*

If a statute prohibits certain expression and the statute is violated, a prosecutor may decide that the expression did not sufficiently harm the community to justify prosecution. "Even if the prosecutor wants to proceed, he must contemplate the hurdles of the grand jury, the need for a unanimous trial jury, an error-free trial, the burden of proof beyond a reasonable doubt, and other protections extended to criminal defendants."[50]

Similarly, in *Nebraska Press Association v. Stuart*,[51] the Supreme Court stated:

> A criminal penalty or a judgment in a defamation case is subject to the whole panoply of protections afforded by deferring the impact of the judgment until all avenues of appellate review have been exhausted. Only after judgment has become final, correct or otherwise, does the law's sanction become fully operative.[52]

In addition, the double jeopardy provision in the Fifth Amendment prevents appeal by the government in criminal cases, while the government can appeal injunctive cases.[53]

Conversely, if someone disobeys an injunction, the judge is likely to begin contempt proceedings despite any lack of harm to the community. "The more certain the legal proceedings, the greater costs the person will incur by proceeding and the less likely he will be to engage in that conduct. The likelihood that the public will hear the speech is greatly reduced."[54] Thus, prior restraints are

---

note 47, at 59, 90. Professor Barnett argues that gag orders are preferable to subsequent punishment because they can prevent publication and thus the threat to the fairness of trial, and they can be more narrowly and precisely drawn than a statutory prohibition with its subsequent punishment. *See also* Blasi, *Toward a Theory of Prior Restraint: The Central Linkage*, 66 MINN. L. REV. 11, 27–49 (1981), in which Professor Blasi argues that both prior restraint injunctions and subsequent punishment cause an equal degree of self-censorship, delay, fear of bias, and personalization, so prior restraints have no more inhibiting effect than subsequent punishment. The Seventh Circuit has held that the attempt to differentiate prior restraints from subsequent punishment is "a distinction without a difference . . . ." Worrell Newspapers of Ind. v. Westhafer, 739 F.2d 1219, 1222, 10 Media L. Rep. 2088, 2090 (7th Cir. 1984), *aff'd without opinion,* 469 U.S. 1200 (1985). *Worrell* stated that the Supreme Court's decision in Smith v. Daily Mail Publishing Co., 443 U.S. 97, 5 Media L. Rep. 1305 (1979), eliminated the "semantic distinction" between prior restraints and subsequent punishment. *Worrell*, 739 F.2d at 1222, 10 Media L. Rep. at 2090. In *Daily Mail,* the Supreme Court stated only that "First Amendment protection reaches beyond prior restraints . . . . Whether we view the statute as a prior restraint or as a penal sanction for publishing lawfully obtained, truthful information is not dispositive because even the latter action requires the highest form of state interest to sustain its validity." 443 U.S. at 101–02, 5 Media L. Rep. at 1307 (citation omitted).

[50] M.A. FRANKLIN & D.A. ANDERSON, CASES AND MATERIALS ON MASS MEDIA LAW 59 (2d ed. 1982).
[51] 427 U.S. 539, 1 Media L. Rep. 1064 (1976).
[52] *Id.* at 559, 1 Media L. Rep. at 1072 (citing A. BICKEL, THE MORTALITY OF CONSENT 61 (1975)).
[53] J. NOWAK, R. ROTUNDA, & J. YOUNG, HANDBOOK ON CONSTITUTIONAL LAW 742 (1978).
[54] From the publisher's point of view there is a crucial difference between prior restraints and subsequent punishment statutes: the certainty of punishment. The "collateral bar rule" prevents a party who disobeys a court order from defending against resulting contempt charges by arguing that the order was unconstitutional or erroneous. A publisher faced with a restraining order knows he definitely will be held in contempt if he violates it. Subsequent punishment statutes, however, allow the publisher to weigh the importance of publishing against a *risk* of punishment rather than against the burden of the certain punishment that prior restraint imposes. In other words, under a subsequent punishment statute the publisher will consider not only the penalty itself but also the constitutionality of the statute and its popular support when considering publishing restricted information.

When the message to be published is not "time bound," *i.e.,* when swift dissemination is immaterial, this difference between prior restraint and subsequent punishment is inconsequential, since the publisher faced with a prior restraint will merely delay publication until he can appeal the order and receive adequate determination of its constitutionality. In a democratic government, however, even a delay of a day or two in publication may be crucial. The problems with a restraining order given just prior to elections are obvious. More generally, "damage can be particularly great when the prior restraint falls upon the communication of news and commentary on current events."

Comment, *First Amendment Standards for Subsequent Punishment of Dissemination of Confidential Government Information,* 68 CAL. L. REV. 83, 100–101 (1980) (footnotes omitted). For a discussion of the collateral bar rule, see *infra* §10.5.

a much more direct and immediate deterrent than the possibility of subsequent punishment.[55] The Supreme Court has explicitly recognized this.[56]

Even those who argue that prior restraints have no more significant an impact on free expression than subsequent punishment admit that, where the collateral bar rule is operative, prior restraint injunctions have a greater impact than the threat of subsequent punishment:[57]

> By virtue of this [collateral bar] rule, a newspaper or broadcast station subject to a gag order is placed in a trilemma of chilling effects unique to a prior restraint situation. It can comply with the order and take no legal steps, thereby accepting the suppression. It can appeal the order directly, but it must obey the interim restraint while it does so, which in the case of a daily newspaper will almost certainly result in the suppression of at least one day's coverage. Or it can publish in the face of the gag order, but only at the price of forfeiting its legal and constitutional objections to the order and thus, in all probability, embracing a contempt conviction. Where the collateral bar rule applies, then, a gag order is more chilling than subsequent punishment, and is very likely to stop the speech at least temporarily.[58]

Application of the collateral bar rule to the violation of injunctions is strikingly different from the procedures for punishing statutory violations, because one who violates a statute can defend in a criminal proceeding on the ground that the law is unconstitutional. If the collateral bar rule were abolished, the chilling effects of prior restraints might be reduced and an injunction would be less readily distinguishable from subsequent punishment for violation of a criminal statute, because in both cases the individual could violate the injunction and then defend on the basis of its unconstitutionality.[59]

§10.4 Presumptive Unconstitutionality and Heavy Burden of Justification

Prior restraints bear a heavy presumption of unconstitutionality.[60] The Supreme Court concluded in *Nebraska Press Association v. Stuart* that "prior restraints on speech and publication are the most serious and the least tolerable infringement on First Amendment rights."[61] A prior restraint has "an immediate and irreversible sanction. If it can be said that a threat of criminal or civil sanctions after publication 'chills' speech, prior restraint 'freezes' it at least for the time."[62] Consequently, a prior restraint on publication is "one of the most extraordinary remedies known to our jurisprudence."[63]

The heavy presumption against prior restraints can only be overcome, if at all, under rare and unusual circumstances. As the Supreme Court ruled in *Near v. Minnesota,* prior restraints may be justified "only in exceptional cases," such as the publication of troop movements during wartime.[64]

---

[55] Nebraska Press Ass'n v. Stuart, 427 U.S. 539, 559, 1 Media L. Rep. 1064, 1072 (1976).
[56] *Id.* at 559, 1 Media L. Rep. at 1072.
[57] Barnett, *supra* note 49, at 553; Jeffries, *supra* note 6, at 431.
[58] Barnett, *supra* note 49, at 553; *see also* Jeffries, *supra* note 6, at 432.
[59] Redish, *supra* note 47, at 94; *see infra* note 72.
[60] Organization for a Better Austin v. Keefe, 402 U.S. 415, 419, 1 Media L. Rep. 1021, 1022 (1971); Bantam Books v. Sullivan, 372 U.S. 58, 70, 1 Media L. Rep. 1116, 1121 (1963).
[61] 427 U.S. 539, 559, 1 Media L. Rep. 1064, 1072 (1976).
[62] *Id.*
[63] *Id.* at 562, 1 Media L. Rep. at 1073.
[64] Near v. Minnesota, 283 U.S. 697, 716, 1 Media L. Rep. 1001, 1007 (1931).

Prior restraints are not per se unconstitutional.[65] The Supreme Court has upheld prior restraints in certain cases involving administrative film censorship[66] as well as statutes enjoining the sale and distribution of obscene material.[67] However, the fact that only a handful of such cases exists illustrates the strength of the rule against prior restraints.

§10.5 THE COLLATERAL BAR RULE

The collateral bar rule provides that one who knowingly violates an injunction cannot defend against a later contempt citation on the ground that the injunction was invalid.[68] Under such a rule, once an injunction is issued against a party, that party must obey it until it is either stayed, vacated, or reversed on appeal.[69] Although the collateral bar rule has a long history in other contexts,[70] application of the rule in the First Amendment context (violations of injunctions against expression) has raised substantial controversy.[71] Commentators have noted that the collateral bar rule justifies a special First Amendment presumption against injunctions that restrain speech.[72]

The leading case in the First Amendment context is *Walker v. City of Birmingham*,[73] where an Alabama state court issued an injunction ordering protesters (Dr. Martin Luther King and a group of local Birmingham ministers)

---

[65]Southeastern Promotions v. Conrad, 420 U.S. 546, 558, 1 Media L. Rep. 1140, 1144 (1975).
[66]Times Film Corp. v. Chicago, 365 U.S. 43, 46 (1961). However, in Freedman v. Maryland, 380 U.S. 51, 52 & n.1, 1 Media L. Rep. 1126, 1126 & n.1 (1965), the Court modified *Times Film* by striking down a statute that required prior approval of motion pictures by a state board of censors before their exhibition. The Court held this statute to be unconstitutional because it impermissibly shifted the burden of proof onto the film's exhibitor rather than properly resting the burden on the party seeking to suppress the film. *Id.* at 58–60, 1 Media L. Rep. at 1128–29. *See also infra* note 195. *But see supra* note 27.
[67]In Kingsley Books v. Brown, 354 U.S. 436, 437, 1 Media L. Rep. 1111 (1957), the Supreme Court upheld a New York statute that enjoined the sale and distribution of material that previously had been judged obscene after a trial. However, in Bantam Books v. Sullivan, 372 U.S. 58, 59–60, 66, 1 Media L. Rep. 1116, 1116–17, 1119 (1963), the Court held unconstitutional a state commission that threatened prosecutions if the dissemination of "objectionable" books to minors did not stop. 372 U.S. at 59–60, 1 Media L. Rep. at 1116–17. The commission's operation was deficient because it did not operate under judicial supervision. *Id.* (citing Freedman v. Maryland, 380 U.S. 51, 1 Media L. Rep. 1126 (1965)). In *Freedman*, the Court required a censor to either issue a license or hold a judicial proceeding before or immediately after the denial of a license. The censor also had the burden of establishing a constitutionally acceptable reason for suppressing "obscene" books or magazines:

> *Freedman*'s preference for judicial evaluation of first amendment claims rests upon the most fundamental considerations—the inherent institutional differences between courts and administrative agencies . . . . First, long judicial tenure frees judges, in most cases, from direct political pressures. Judicial insulation encourages impartial decisionmaking; more importantly, it permits the court to take the "long view" of issues. Administrative bodies, particularly at a state level, are rarely so insulated; indeed, they are often seen primarily as political organs. Second, the role of the administrator is not that of the impartial adjudicator but that of the expert—a role which necessarily gives an administrative agency a narrow and restricted viewpoint. . . . Courts, on the other hand, do not suffer congenitally from this myopia; their general jurisdiction gives them a broad perspective which no agency can have. They deal daily with a wide variety of situations, and this fact goes far toward eliminating the deficiencies that come from excessive singlemindedness.

Monaghan, *First Amendment "Due Process,"* 83 HARV. L. REV. 518, 522–23 (1970); Gold, *supra* note 5, at 246 (citing Roth v. United States, 354 U.S. 476, 485, 1 Media L. Rep. 1375, 1378 (1957) *and* Marcus v. Search Warrants of Property, 367 U.S. 717, 729–31 (1961)).
[68]Barnett, *supra* note 49, at 552. The collateral bar rule is so named because the contempt proceeding is considered collateral to the court order. Rendleman, *Free Press-Fair Trial: Review of Silence Orders*, 52 N.C. L. REV. 127, 147 (1973).
[69]Barnett, *supra* note 49, at 552; Redish, *supra* note 47, at 93.
[70]*See* Cox, *The Void Order and the Duty to Obey*, 16 U. CHI. L. REV. 86 (1948); Watt, *The Divine Right of Government by Judiciary*, 14 U. CHI. L. REV. 409 (1947).
[71]Redish, *supra* note 47, at 93.
[72]*See* O. FISS, THE CIVIL RIGHTS INJUNCTION 30, 73 (1978) *and* Barnett, *supra* note 49, at 553. It is the collateral bar rule, at least in part, that makes injunctions as stifling as the historic licensing systems, which gave rise to the prior restraint doctrine. Blasi, *supra* note 49, at 21. *See also supra* note 59.
[73]388 U.S. 307 (1967).

not to violate an ordinance against parading without a permit. The protesters, unsuccessful in their attempt to obtain the required permit, went ahead with the march despite the injunction.[74] The state court refused to allow the protesters to challenge the permit ordinance at the contempt hearing, and Dr. King and the other leaders were convicted of criminal contempt.[75] The Supreme Court, in a 5-4 decision, upheld the criminal convictions because of the collateral bar rule.[76]

Even the Court acknowledged that its decision might appear to be a harsh application of the collateral bar rule because of the protesters' cause.[77] The Court indicated that the *Walker* demonstrators should have challenged the injunction's validity in court before violating it in the streets: "[R]espect for judicial process is a small price to pay for the civilizing hand of law."[78] The Court did acknowledge, however, that at least in the context of injunctions against expression, courts must be careful in applying the collateral bar rule and should not apply it if an injunction is "transparently invalid" or if delay or frustration is encountered in appellate efforts to contest its validity.[79]

A leading federal case applying the collateral bar rule to the media is *United States v. Dickinson (Dickinson I)*.[80] In *Dickinson I*, a federal judge ordered that " 'there shall be no reporting of the details of the evidence taken in this court today.' "[81] Two reporters violated the order and were subsequently convicted of contempt.[82] Although the Fifth Circuit found the gag order unconstitutional, it upheld the convictions because of the collateral bar rule.[83] The court then remanded the case to the trial judge to reconsider the fines he levied on each reporter, in light of its determination that the underlying order was unconstitutional.[84] The trial judge refused to alter the sentence, and the court of appeals affirmed in *United States v. Dickinson (Dickinson II)*.[85] *Dickinson I* recognized that the media presented special problems, but both the Court of Appeals and the District Court had been available and could have been contacted that day for relief, "thereby affording speedy and effective but *orderly* review of the injunction in question swiftly enough to protect the right to publish news while it was still 'news'."[86]

---

[74]*Id.* at 310–11.
[75]*Id.* at 311–12.
[76]388 U.S. 307. This ordinance was later found to be an unconstitutional restraint on free expression in a virtually identical case. Shuttlesworth v. City of Birmingham, 394 U.S. 147 (1969).
[77]The Court noted that "[o]ne may sympathize with the petitioners' impatient commitment to their cause." *Walker,* 388 U.S. at 321.
[78]388 U.S. at 321. The Court justified the collateral bar rule with the argument that "in the fair administration of justice no man can be judge in his own case, however exalted his station, however righteous his motives, and irrespective of his race, color, politics, or religion." *Id.* at 320–21.
[79]*Id.* at 315, 318. One commentator has noted that "the normal operation of the collateral bar rule can be sustained only so long as expedited appellate review allows an immediate opportunity to test the validity of an injunction against speech and only so long as that opportunity is genuinely effective to allow timely publication should the injunction ultimately be adjudged invalid." Jeffries, *supra* note 6, at 433.
[80]465 F.2d 496, 1 Media L. Rep. 1338 (5th Cir. 1972).
[81]*Id.* at 500, 1 Media L. Rep. at 1339.
[82]*Id.*
[83]The *Dickinson I* court relied upon *Walker,* concluding that: "Absent a showing of 'transparent invalidity' or patent frivolity surrounding the order, *it must be obeyed* until reversed by orderly review or disrobed of authority by delay or frustration in the appellate process, regardless of the ultimate determination of constitutionality, or lack thereof." *Id.* at 509–10, 1 Media L. Rep. at 1347.
[84]*Id.* at 514, 1 Media L. Rep. at 1350.
[85]476 F.2d 373 (5th Cir.), *cert. denied,* 414 U.S. 979 (1973).
[86]465 F.2d at 512, 1 Media L. Rep. at 1349. In recognizing the special problems presented by the media, *Dickinson I* stated:

There are certain other exceptions to the collateral bar rule. A defendant could challenge the jurisdiction of the issuing court during a contempt proceeding[87] if the court's assertion of jurisdiction was "frivolous and not substantial."[88] With *Walker*, the Supreme Court significantly expanded the exceptions to include frivolousness on the merits as well as to jurisdiction.[89]

The First Circuit amplified *Walker* in *In re Providence Journal Co.*[90] There, the *Providence Journal* obtained information from the Federal Bureau of Investigation (FBI) after the death of Raymond Patriarca, a reputed organized crime figure.[91] Patriarca's son filed suit seeking to enjoin the publication of this material. The District Court entered a temporary restraining order barring publication, and one day later, the *Providence Journal* published an article in violation of the order.[92] Patriarca's son filed a contempt motion but declined to litigate it, so the District Court appointed a special prosecutor to pursue it.[93] The court found the *Journal* and its executive editor guilty of criminal contempt.[94] The *Journal* appealed, and a panel of the First Circuit reversed.[95]

The First Circuit panel recognized that there is "an exception to the collateral bar rule for transparently invalid court orders."[96] The panel's opinion acknowledged, however, that the line between transparently invalid court orders and orders that are "merely invalid is, of course, not always distinct."[97] Sitting by designation, Judge John Wisdom wrote for the panel: "When, as here, the prior restraint impinges upon the right of the press to communicate news and involves expression in the form of pure speech—speech not connected with any conduct—the presumption of unconstitutionality is virtually

---

Where the thing enjoined is publication and the communication is "news", this condition presents some thorny problems. Timeliness of publication is the hallmark of "news" and the difference between "news" and "history" is merely a matter of hours. Thus, where the publishing of news is sought to be restrained, the incontestable inviolability of the order may depend on the immediate accessibility of orderly review. But in the absence of strong indications that the appellate process was being deliberately stalled—certainly not so in this record—violation with impunity does not occur simply because immediate decision is not forthcoming, even though the communication enjoined is "news." Of course the nature of the expression sought to be exercised is a factor to be considered in determining whether First Amendment rights can be effectively protected by orderly review so as to render disobedience to otherwise unconstitutional mandates nevertheless contemptuous. But newsmen are citizens, too.... They too may sometimes have to wait. They are not yet wrapped in an immunity or given the absolute right to decide with immunity whether a Judge's order is to be obeyed or whether an appellate court is acting promptly enough.

Id. at 511–12, 1 Media L. Rep. at 1348–49.
[87]Howat v. Kansas, 258 U.S. 181 (1922).
[88]United States v. Mine Workers (UMW), 330 U.S. 258, 293 (1947) (upholding fine imposed on union and its president for violating no-strike injunction). This defense may be more important than first appears, because the media are seldom parties to criminal cases where prior restraints often have been issued against them. *See infra* §10.7(A).
[89]Walker v. City of Birmingham, 388 U.S. 307, 315 (1967).
[90]820 F.2d 1342 (1st Cir. 1986), *modified*, 820 F.2d 1354, 14 Media L. Rep. 1029 (1st Cir. 1987) (en banc), *cert. dismissed*, 485 U.S. 693, 15 Media L. Rep. 1241 (1988). The Supreme Court dismissed the writ of certiorari for want of jurisdiction, holding that the special prosecutor lacked authority to represent the United States before the Supreme Court absent an authorization from the Solicitor General.
[91]The *Providence Journal* had requested the information under the Freedom of Information Act (FOIA) in 1986, but this request was refused by the FBI as an unwarranted invasion of personal privacy. 820 F.2d at 1344. The *Journal* filed an unsuccessful action seeking to compel disclosure under FOIA. *Id.* After Patriarca's death, the *Journal* renewed its FOIA request and the FBI provided the materials to it and other media. *Id.*
[92]*Id.* at 1345.
[93]*Id.*
[94]*Id.*
[95]*Id.* at 1344–45.
[96]820 F.2d at 1347.
[97]*Id.*

insurmountable."[98] The panel's opinion concluded that it was "patently clear" that the District Court's order failed to pass muster under *Nebraska Press,* was transparently invalid, and could not serve as a basis for the contempt citation.[99]

On rehearing, the First Circuit, sitting en banc, modified the panel's opinion by requiring the publisher,

> even when it thinks it is the subject of a transparently unconstitutional order of prior restraint, to make a good faith effort to seek emergency relief from the appellate court. If timely access to the appellate court is not available or if timely decision is not forthcoming, the publisher may then proceed and challenge the constitutionality of the order in the contempt proceedings.[100]

Several state courts have downplayed the impact of the collateral bar rule in free speech cases implicitly or explicitly.[101] The California Supreme Court, for example, has held that "[i]f ... it is ... finally determined that the order was issued without or in excess of jurisdiction ... violation of such void order constitutes no punishable wrong."[102]

While the collateral bar rule may still be the predominant rule,[103] doubt has been cast on its continued vitality with respect to injunctions on expression.[104]

§10.6 NATIONAL SECURITY

The Supreme Court has acknowledged that one of the few areas in which a prior restraint may be appropriate is protection of vital governmental information during a war.[105]

---

[98]*Id.* at 1348. He distinguished *Walker* because it involved speech coupled with conduct and the well-recognized state interest in regulating the use of streets and public forums. "[A] different result, or at a minimum a different analysis, would have been required had the *Walker* order restrained pure speech." *Id.*

[99]*Id.* at 1349–53.

[100]820 F.2d 1354, 1355, 14 Media L. Rep. 1029, 1030 (1st Cir. 1987), *cert. dismissed,* 485 U.S. 693, 15 Media L. Rep. 1241 (1988). The en banc court stated that its modification of the panel opinion provided "finer tuning ... to minimize the disharmony between respect for court orders and respect for free speech." *Id.* Requiring a publisher to make a record of its good faith effort to seek emergency appellate relief "is a price we should pay for the preference of court over party determination of invalidity." *Id.* The en banc court refused to punish the publisher, noting that there were only 8½ hours between the District Court's order and the deadline for publication. The court stated: "Not only are we left without a clear conviction that timely emergency relief was available within the restraints governing the publisher's decision making, but we would deem it unfair to subject the publisher to ... very substantial sanctions ... because of its failure to follow the procedure we have just announced." *Id.*

[101]Rendleman, *supra* note 68, at 153–54 nn.182–85 and cases cited therein; Cooper v. Rockford Newspapers, 365 N.E.2d 744, 2 Media L. Rep. 2288 (Ill. App. Ct. 1977); State v. Coe, 679 P.2d 353, 10 Media L. Rep. 1465 (Wash. 1984).

[102]In re Berry, 436 P.2d 273, 281 (Cal. 1968) (refusing to follow *Walker*).

[103]Redish, *supra* note 47, at 96 n.155.

[104]Barnett, *supra* note 49, at 554. Professor Barnett cites Nebraska Press Association v. Stuart, 427 U.S. 539, 1 Media L. Rep. 1064 (1976); Oklahoma Publishing Co. v. District Court, 430 U.S. 308, 2 Media L. Rep. 1456 (1977); and Cox Broadcasting Corp. v. Cohn, 420 U.S. 469, 1 Media L. Rep. 1819 (1975), in support of his observation that a gag order prohibiting publication of information disclosed in open court is transparently invalid. Barnett, *supra* note 49, at 555. Professor Barnett concludes that if the Supreme Court's caveat relating to "transparently invalid" orders in *Walker* has any real meaning, "it should follow that the collateral bar rule may not constitutionally be applied to prevent a publisher from relying on the constitutional infirmities of such an order as a defense to a charge of contempt." *Id.*

[105]Near v. Minnesota, 283 U.S. 697, 716, 1 Media L. Rep. 1001, 1007 (1931); *see also Nebraska Press,* 427 U.S. at 572, 590–95, 1 Media L. Rep. at 1077, 1084–86 (Brennan, J., concurring) (suggesting three exceptions to ban on prior restraints: (1) obscenity; (2) fighting words; and (3) disclosure of certain information during wartime).

§10.6(A) The "Pentagon Papers Case"

The leading case on prior restraints for national security reasons is *New York Times Co. v. United States*,[106] popularly called the "Pentagon Papers case." The United States sought to enjoin *The New York Times* and *The Washington Post* from publishing the contents of a classified study entitled "History of U.S. Decision-Making Process on Viet Nam Policy" (Pentagon Papers).[107] The government contended that publication of these materials could result in "grave and irreparable harm" to national security.[108]

The District Court for the Southern District of New York had declined to enjoin *The New York Times'* publication; the Second Circuit reversed.[109] In a short per curiam opinion, the Supreme Court noted that any system of prior restraints comes to the Court bearing a heavy presumption against its constitutional validity and that the government thus carries a heavy burden of showing justification for the imposition of such a restraint.[110] Since the government had failed to meet this burden, the Second Circuit's order was reversed.[111]

Each of the justices wrote a separate opinion. Justice Hugo Black, joined by Justice William Douglas, concurred and faulted the executive branch for forgetting "the essential purpose and history of the First Amendment."[112] They reiterated their absolutist position that the First Amendment precludes any governmental restraint.[113] Justice Douglas also filed a concurring opinion in which he pointed out that no statute barred publication by the press of the material at issue.[114]

Justice William Brennan filed a concurring opinion in which he observed that "never before has the United States sought to enjoin a newspaper from publishing information in its possession."[115] He stated that "[t]he First Amendment tolerates absolutely no prior judicial restraints of the press predicated upon surmise or conjecture that untoward consequences may result."[116]

Justice Potter Stewart, joined by Justice Byron White, filed a concurring opinion in which he stated: "I cannot say that disclosure of [the materials in

---

[106] 403 U.S. 713, 1 Media L. Rep. 1031 (1971).
[107] *Id.* at 714, 1 Media L. Rep. at 1031.
[108] *Id.* at 732, 1 Media L. Rep. at 1038.
[109] 444 F.2d 544 (2d Cir.), *rev'd*, 403 U.S. 713, 1 Media L. Rep. 1031 (1971). At the same time, *The Washington Post* had also acquired copies of the Pentagon Papers, and the government sought to enjoin its publication in the District Court for the District of Columbia. The Court of Appeals in that case eventually affirmed the District Court's denial of the government's motion for a preliminary injunction. United States v. Washington Post Co., 446 F.2d 1322, 1327 (D.C. Cir. 1971). When the Supreme Court heard arguments three days later, the Court reversed the judgment in the *New York Times* case and affirmed it in the *Washington Post* case. New York Times Co., 403 U.S. 713, 1 Media L. Rep. 1031 (1971).
[110] 403 U.S. at 714, 1 Media L. Rep. at 1031.
[111] *Id.*
[112] *Id.* at 715, 1 Media L. Rep. at 1032.
[113] "No one can read the history of the adoption of the First Amendment without being convinced beyond any doubt that it was injunctions like those sought here that Madison and his collaborators intended to outlaw in this Nation for all time." *Id.* at 719, 1 Media L. Rep. at 1033.
[114] *Id.* at 720, 1 Media L. Rep. at 1034.
[115] 403 U.S. at 725, 1 Media L. Rep. at 1035.
[116] *Id.* at 725–26, 1 Media L. Rep. at 1036 (footnote omitted). Although prior cases allowed a possible exception for enjoining the publication of critical information during wartime,
> only governmental allegation and proof that publication must inevitably, directly, and immediately cause the occurrence of an event kindred to imperiling the safety of a transport already at sea can support even the issuance of an interim restraining order. In no event may mere conclusions be sufficient.... Unless and until the government has clearly made out its case, the First Amendment commands that no injunction may issue.

Id. at 726–27, 1 Media L. Rep. at 1036.

question] will surely result in direct, immediate, and irreparable damage to our Nation or its people. That being so, there can under the First Amendment be but one judicial resolution of the issues before us."[117] Justice White, joined by Justice Stewart, also filed a concurring opinion in which he took a less absolute stand than Justices Black and Douglas: "I concur in today's judgments, but only because of the concededly extraordinary protection against prior restraints enjoyed by the press under our constitutional system. I do not say that in no circumstances would the First Amendment permit an injunction against publishing information about government plans or operations."[118]

Justice Thurgood Marshall filed a concurring opinion in which he relied heavily on the fact that Congress had expressly rejected proposed legislation that would have authorized the government to obtain the sort of injunction requested in this case.[119]

Chief Justice Warren Burger and Justices Harry Blackmun and John Harlan all dissented. They opposed the expedited hearing procedures, which they felt did not afford the Court sufficient time to fully contemplate and analyze the issues involved.[120]

Despite the separate opinions, five members of the Court agreed that an extraordinary showing must be made before a prior restraint can be issued to protect national security.[121] The result in the Pentagon Papers case indicates that a prior restraint based on national security grounds will almost never be permissible, the only exception being where the publication will indisputably and immediately cause serious harm equivalent to disclosure of troop transport schedules during a war.[122]

---

[117] *Id.* at 730, 1 Media L. Rep. at 1038.

[118] *Id.* at 730–31, 1 Media L. Rep. at 1038 (footnote omitted). Justice White agreed that the government had not satisfied its heavy burden that would warrant an injunction against publication in this case. In the first footnote of his opinion, Justice White lists several statutory prior restraints. He noted that, even though no injunction would issue, the government was not precluded from bringing a criminal action in response to the publications:
> Prior restraints require an unusually heavy justification under the First Amendment; but failure by the Government to justify prior restraints does not measure its constitutional entitlement to a conviction for criminal publication. That the government mistakenly chose to proceed by injunction does not mean that it could not successfully proceed in another way.

Id. at 733, 1 Media L. Rep. at 1039.

[119] *Id.* at 745–46, 1 Media L. Rep. at 1043–44.

[120] 403 U.S. at 752–59, 1 Media L. Rep. at 1046–49. Justice Harlan's dissenting opinion did reach the merits. In his view, the judiciary could review executive determinations to see if the matter lay within the scope of the president's foreign relations power, and the judiciary could properly insist that the determination of the consequences of disclosure of the subject matter be made by the head of the executive department concerned after personal consideration by that officer. "But in my judgment the judiciary may not properly go beyond these two inquiries and redetermine for itself the probable impact of disclosure on the national security." *Id.* at 757, 1 Media L. Rep. at 1048. Justice Harlan concluded:
> Pending further hearings in each case conducted under the appropriate ground rules, I would continue the restraints on publication. I cannot believe that the doctrine prohibiting prior restraints reaches to the point of preventing courts from maintaining the *status quo* long enough to act responsibly in matters of such national importance as those involved here.

Id. at 758–59, 1 Media L. Rep. at 1049.

Chief Justice Burger refused to reach the merits: "As I see it, we have been forced to deal with litigation concerning rights of great magnitude without an adequate record, and surely without time for adequate treatment either in the prior proceedings or in this Court." *Id.* at 751, 1 Media L. Rep. at 1046. Justice Blackmun agreed that the decision was too hurried. He rejected First Amendment absolutism and declared: "What is needed here is a weighing, upon properly developed standards, of the broad right of the press to print and of the very narrow right of the Government to prevent." *Id.* at 761, 1 Media L. Rep. at 1050. Justice Blackmun would have remanded the cases for orderly presentation of evidence from both sides. *Id.* at 761–62, 1 Media L. Rep. at 1050.

[121] *See* text accompanying *supra* notes 112–118; Medow, *The First Amendment and the Secrecy State: Snepp v. United States,* 130 U. PA. L. REV. 775, 793 (1982).

[122] Near v. Minnesota, 283 U.S. 697, 716, 1 Media L. Rep. 1001, 1007 (1931).

The parameters of this narrow exception to the ban on prior restraints were explored in *United States v. Progressive, Inc.*,[123] where the United States sought a temporary restraining order and preliminary injunction to prevent the defendant magazine from publishing an article containing allegedly restricted data about the construction and operation of hydrogen bombs, contending that publication of the data would irreparably impair national security.[124] The government also relied on Section 2274 of the Atomic Energy Act,[125] which prohibits anyone from communicating, transmitting, or disclosing any restricted data to any person "with reason to believe such data will be utilized to injure the United States or to secure an advantage to any foreign nation."[126] The statute defined "restricted data" to include all data concerning the design, manufacture, or utilization of atomic weapons.[127]

The court held that publication of a magazine article containing technical information that was not in the public domain concerning the manufacture and operation of the hydrogen bomb could properly be enjoined.[128] The court relied on dictum in *Near v. Minnesota,* which recognized a narrow area of national security interests that could outweigh the doctrine against prior restraints.[129] The court found that the government had met its burden under Section 2274 of the Atomic Energy Act and its burden of demonstrating "grave, direct, immediate and irreparable harm" to the United States, the test enunciated by Justices Stewart and White in the Pentagon Papers case.[130]

The *Progressive* court distinguished the Pentagon Papers case because (1) the study involved in that case concerned historical data relating to events occurring three to 20 years previously; (2) in the Pentagon Papers case, "no cogent reasons were advanced by the government as to why the article affected national security except that publication might cause some embarrassment to the United States;" and (3) most vitally, the Pentagon Papers case did not involve a statute that barred the publication, while Section 2274 of the Atomic Energy Act prohibited the communication, transmission, or disclosure of any restricted data under specified circumstances.[131]

---

[123] 467 F. Supp. 990, 4 Media L. Rep. 2377 (W.D. Wis. 1979), *dismissed without opinion,* 610 F.2d 819 (7th Cir. 1979).
[124] *Id.* at 991, 4 Media L. Rep. at 2377.
[125] 42 U.S.C. §§2011–2282 (1976).
[126] 467 F. Supp. at 994, 4 Media L. Rep. at 2380.
[127] 42 U.S.C. §2014(y) (1976).
[128] "[P]ublication of the technical information on the hydrogen bomb contained in the article is analogous to publication of troop movements or locations in time of war and falls within the extremely narrow exception to the rule against prior restraint." 467 F. Supp. at 996, 4 Media L. Rep. at 2381.
[129] *Id.* at 996, 4 Media L. Rep. at 2381; Near v. Minnesota, 283 U.S. 697, 716, 1 Media L. Rep. 1001, 1007 (1931) (footnote omitted) ("No one would question but that a government might prevent . . . the publication of the sailing dates of transports or the number and location of troops.").
[130] 467 F. Supp. at 996, 4 Media L. Rep. at 2381. The Court also noted it could find
no plausible reason why the public needs to know the technical details about hydrogen bomb construction to carry on an informed debate on this issue. Furthermore, the Court believes that the defendants' position in favor of nuclear non-proliferation would be harmed, not aided, by the publication of this article.
Id. at 994, 4 Media L. Rep. at 2380.
In Morland v. Sprecher, 443 U.S. 709, 5 Media L. Rep. 1393 (1979), the Supreme Court considered a similar case involving an injunction against the publication of the same information as in *Progressive* by another publication. There, the Supreme Court held that, although the injunction may have been an unconstitutional prior restraint, the publisher's long delay in filing for expedited appellate review of the injunction warranted denial of the petition for mandamus.
[131] 467 F. Supp. at 994, 4 Media L. Rep. at 2380; *see* Cheh, *The Progressive Case and the Atomic Energy Act: Waking to the Dangers of Government Information Controls,* 48 GEO. WASH. L. REV. 163 (1980);

The *Progressive* case is extremely unusual because it involves the hydrogen bomb and potential thermonuclear destruction; the court recognized its decision "is so difficult precisely because the consequences of error involve human life itself and on such an awesome scale."[132] While the *Progressive* court acknowledged the "notoriety" involved in issuing "the first instance of prior restraint against a publication in this fashion in the history of this country," it concluded that publication of technical information about the hydrogen bomb posed "grave, direct, immediate and irreparable harm to the United States" and thus fell "within the extremely narrow exception to the rule against prior restraint."[133] If anything, the *Progressive* case demonstrates just how narrow the exception to the ban on prior restraints really is.

§10.6(B) Government Contracts for Prepublication Approval

The government has been more successful when it has argued that national security considerations required enjoining disclosures by its employees or ex-employees. In *United States v. Marchetti*,[134] the government obtained an injunction against Victor Marchetti's publication of a book about the Central Intelligence Agency (CIA). Marchetti, a former CIA employee, had signed a contract upon joining the CIA in which he agreed not to divulge in any way any classified information, intelligence, or knowledge, except in the performance of his official duties, unless specifically authorized to do so in writing by the CIA Director.[135] The government sought an injunction to prevent Marchetti from publishing a book without submitting it to the Director for review.[136]

The Fourth Circuit held that the government could require CIA employees to sign secrecy agreements as a condition of employment, the agreements could require the employee to submit publications concerning the CIA to the Director for screening, and that the courts could enforce such agreements by injunctions.[137] The court also found that the government has a right to secrecy and that secrecy agreements with employees provide a reasonable means for government agencies to protect their internal secrets.[138]

An injunction cannot issue, however, if the employee seeks to reveal only unclassified information[139] or information, whether classified or not, that has already entered the public domain.[140] Under *Marchetti*, the CIA only had to

---

Note, *United States v. Progressive, Inc.: The Faustian Bargain and the First Amendment*, 75 Nw. U. L. Rev. 538 (1980).

[132] 467 F. Supp. at 995, 4 Media L. Rep. at 2381.

[133] *Id.* at 996, 4 Media L. Rep. at 2381.

[134] 466 F.2d 1309, 1 Media L. Rep. 1051 (4th Cir.), *cert. denied*, 409 U.S. 1063 (1972).

[135] *Id.* at 1312, 1 Media L. Rep. at 1052.

[136] *Id.* at 1311, 1 Media L. Rep. at 1051.

[137] *Id.* at 1316–18, 1 Media L. Rep. at 1055–57.

[138] [T]he Government's need for secrecy in this area [of foreign affairs] lends justification to a system of prior restraint against disclosure by employees and former employees of classified information obtained during the course of employment. One may speculate that ordinary criminal sanctions might suffice to prevent unauthorized disclosure of such information, but the risk of harm from disclosure is so great and maintenance of the confidentiality of the information so necessary that greater and more positive assurance is warranted. Some prior restraints in some circumstances are approvable of course.

Id. at 1316–17, 1 Media L. Rep. at 1056.

[139] 466 F.2d at 1313–17, 1 Media L. Rep. at 1053–56. *Accord* United States v. Snepp, 897 F.2d 138, 141–42, 17 Media L. Rep. 1579, 1581 (4th Cir. 1990).

[140] 466 F.2d at 1318, 1 Media L. Rep. at 1057. *Accord Snepp*, 897 F.2d at 141–42, 17 Media L. Rep. at 1581.

prove that the documents were classified; it did not have to show that the classification was proper.[141] The Fourth Circuit reversed this aspect of *Marchetti* three years later in *Alfred A. Knopf, Inc. v. Colby*.[142]

In a later Supreme Court decision, *Snepp v. United States*,[143] a former CIA employee had entered an agreement with the CIA not to divulge classified information without authorization and not to publish any information relating to the CIA without prepublication clearance.[144] After he left the CIA, Snepp published a book concerning certain CIA activities in South Vietnam; he did not submit the book to the CIA for prepublication review.[145]

The United States filed suit to enforce the agreement, seeking a declaration that Snepp had breached the contract, an injunction requiring him to submit future writings for prepublication review, and an order imposing a constructive trust for the government's benefit on all profits that Snepp might earn from publication of the book in violation of his fiduciary obligations to the CIA.[146] The District Court granted the requested relief, finding that Snepp had breached a valid agreement and a fiduciary obligation, and his breach had caused the United States "irreparable harm and loss."[147] The Fourth Circuit affirmed but concluded that the record did not support the imposition of a constructive trust.[148]

In a per curiam opinion, the Supreme Court reversed, insofar as the Fourth Circuit had refused to impose a constructive trust on Snepp's profits, and rejected Snepp's argument that the agreement was unenforceable as a prior restraint on protected speech: "The Government has a compelling interest in protecting both the secrecy of information important to our national security and the appearance of confidentiality so essential to the effective operation of our foreign intelligence service.... The agreement that Snepp signed is a reasonable means for protecting this vital interest."[149] The Court found that the agreement was not executed under duress and was an appropriate exercise of the CIA Director's statutory mandate to protect intelligence sources and methods from unauthorized disclosure.[150]

---

[141] 466 F.2d at 1317–18, 1 Media L. Rep. at 1056.

[142] 509 F.2d 1362 (4th Cir.), *cert. denied,* 421 U.S. 992 (1975). During those three years, Marchetti had written a book with John Marks, an ex-State Department employee who had also signed a secrecy agreement. Both authors sought prepublication clearance, and when it was refused by the CIA, they and their publisher brought suit. In *Knopf,* the Fourth Circuit reconsidered *Marchetti,* holding that items should only be suppressed "if they are found both to be classified and classifiable under Executive Order." *Id.* at 1367. It then remanded the case to the District Court for further proceedings. For a full discussion of *Knopf, see* Medow, *supra* note 121, at 785–88.

[143] 444 U.S. 507, 5 Media L. Rep. 2409 (1980).

[144] When Snepp left the CIA he signed a "termination secrecy agreement," which reaffirmed his promise never to reveal classified information. *Id.* at 508 n.1, 5 Media L. Rep. at 2409 n.1.

[145] *Id.* at 507, 5 Media L. Rep. at 2409.

[146] *Id.* at 508, 5 Media L. Rep. at 2410.

[147] *Id.* at 508–09, 5 Media L. Rep. at 2410.

[148] 444 U.S. at 509, 5 Media L. Rep. at 2410.

[149] *Id.* at 509 n.3, 1 Media L. Rep. at 2410 n.3. The agreement read:

Inasmuch as employment by the Government is a privilege not a right, in consideration of my employment by the CIA I undertake not to publish or participate in the publication of any information or material relating to the Agency, its activities or intelligence activities generally, either during or after the term of my employment by the Agency without specific prior approval by the Agency.

Snepp, 595 F.2d 926, 930 n.1, 4 Media L. Rep. 2313, 2314 n.1 (4th Cir. 1979), *rev'd in part,* 444 U.S. 507, 5 Media L. Rep. 2409 (1980).

[150] "Moreover, this Court's cases make clear that—even in the absence of an express agreement—the CIA could have acted to protect substantial government interests by imposing reasonable restraints on employee activities that in other contexts might be protected by the First Amendment." 444 U.S. at 509 n.3, 5 Media L. Rep. at 2410 n.3.

By publishing the book without submitting it to the CIA for prepublication clearance, Snepp breached his fiduciary obligation to the CIA. This breach of his obligation to submit the material—whether classified or not—for prepublication clearance irreparably harmed the United States government. The Court noted that a constructive trust was the appropriate remedy for breach of a fiduciary obligation.[151]

Justice Stevens, joined by Justices Brennan and Marshall, dissented on the grounds that the constructive trust was improperly granted and that the agreement was unconstitutional as a serious prior restraint on Snepp's ability to speak freely.[152]

In *Snepp*, the Court read the agreement literally and determined that it required prepublication submission of any publication containing CIA-related materials, but provided very little guidance as to what was to happen after an author submitted a publication.[153] In *Marchetti,* the Fourth Circuit was more explicit:

> Because we are dealing with a prior restraint upon speech, we think that the CIA *must act promptly* to approve or disapprove any material which may be submitted to it by Marchetti. Undue delay would impair the reasonableness of the restraint, and that reasonableness is to be maintained if the restraint is to be enforced. We should think that, in all events, *the maximum period* for responding after the submission of material for approval *should not exceed 30 days.*[154]

Marchetti placed the burden on the agent to seek judicial review if the CIA refused clearance.[155] In *Snepp,* however, the Supreme Court indicated, in a footnote, that if the parties could not resolve the issue, "the Agency would have borne the burden of seeking an injunction against publication."[156]

---

[151]A constructive trust . . . protects both the Government and the former agent from unwarranted risks. This remedy is the natural and customary consequence of a breach of trust. It deals fairly with both parties by conforming relief to the dimensions of the wrong. . . . The decision of the Court of Appeals would deprive the Government of this equitable and effective means of protecting intelligence that may contribute to national security.
Id. at 515–16, 5 Media L. Rep. at 2412–13.

[152]*Id.* at 520 n.9, 526 n.17, 5 Media L. Rep. at 2415 n.9, 2417 n.17. In view of the national interest in maintaining an effective intelligence service, however, Justice Stevens did not say that the restraint was intolerable. He did take issue with the Court's suggestion that publication of unreviewed material by a former CIA agent, even if no classified intelligence was involved, could be detrimental to vital national interests:
> I do not believe . . . the Agency has any authority to censor its employees' publication of unclassified information on the basis of its opinion that publication may be "detrimental to vital national interests" or otherwise "identified as harmful." . . . [E]ven if such a wide-ranging prior restraint would be good national security policy, I would have great difficulty reconciling it with the demands of the First Amendment.
Id. at 522, 5 Media L. Rep. at 2415–16.

[153]*See* Medow, *supra* note 121, at 783. *See also* Penguin Books USA v. Walsh, 756 F. Supp. 770, 18 Media L. Rep. 1856 (S.D.N.Y.) (applying *Snepp*), *appeal dismissed and judgment vacated,* 929 F.2d 69 (2d Cir. 1991).

[154]United States v. Marchetti, 466 F.2d 1309, 1317, 1 Media L. Rep. 1051, 1056 (4th Cir.), *cert. denied,* 409 U.S. 1063 (1972) (emphasis added). Under Freedman v. Maryland, 380 U.S. 51, 1 Media L. Rep. 1126 (1965), in which the Court ruled that prior review must have procedural safeguards and must be imposed only briefly in order to preserve the status quo, 30 days for CIA review may be too long. *See* Medow, *supra* note 121, at 784. Since *Snepp,* one court has upheld the CIA's censoring of portions of an article by an ex-agent because the documents were properly classified. McGeehee v. Casey, 7 Media L. Rep. 2270 (D.D.C. 1981). *See also* Agee v. Central Intelligence Agency, 500 F. Supp. 506, 6 Media L. Rep. 2006 (D.D.C. 1980) (enforcing CIA secrecy agreement). *But see* Stanford Univ. v. Sullivan, 773 F. Supp. 472, 19 Media L. Rep. 1345 (D.D.C. 1991) (federal contract confidentiality clause that bars university researchers from publishing or speaking about their government-funded research activities is unconstitutional prior restraint).

[155]466 F.2d at 1317, 1 Media L. Rep. at 1056.

[156]444 U.S. at 513 n.8, 5 Media L. Rep. at 2412 n.8 (citing, inter alia, Alfred A. Knopf, Inc. v. Colby, 509 F.2d 1362 (4th Cir.), *cert. denied,* 421 U.S. 992 (1975)).

After the Supreme Court's decision, Snepp submitted 19 manuscripts to the CIA for prepublication review. The parties were able to reach agreement on the first 18 manuscripts, but a disagreement over the last one resulted in further litigation in which Snepp sought to amend the injunction to place the burden on the government to seek judicial review if the parties were unable to agree on deletions from a submitted manuscript.[157] Snepp maintained that the Supreme Court's footnote, quoted above, overruled *Marchetti* and placed the burden of seeking review on the government.[158] The Fourth Circuit disagreed, holding that *Snepp* did not intend to overrule *Marchetti*.[159] Instead, the court offered what it deemed a "plausible interpretation" of this footnote: "While the language in the footnote arguably imposes on the CIA the burden of seeking an *injunction* by initiating a legal proceeding, such a requirement would not eliminate Snepp's burden to seek judicial review of the Agency's decision to withhold approval."[160]

The cases on secrecy agreements, therefore, indicate the following procedure: (1) all manuscripts with CIA-related information must be submitted for prepublication review; (2) within 30 days the CIA must complete its review; (3) if the CIA denies permission to publish, the author should institute an action for judicial review of the CIA's decision; and (4) the CIA may also file an action to enjoin the agent from publishing and to establish a constructive trust.[161]

§10.7 CRIMINAL AND OTHER TRIALS

In an effort to protect criminal defendants' Sixth Amendment fair trial rights, courts have attempted to restrain publicity by the media and by trial participants—e.g., lawyers, parties, and jurors. The former restraints are very disfavored, while the latter sometimes have been upheld.[162]

§10.7(A) Gag Orders on the Press

In *Nebraska Press Association v. Stuart*,[163] the Supreme Court unanimously struck down a prior restraint or gag order on publicity about a criminal jury trial. A mass murder in a small Nebraska town attracted widespread local and national news coverage, and the state trial court entered an order restraining the media from publishing or broadcasting accounts of (1) the existence or

---

[157] United States v. Snepp, 897 F.2d 138, 17 Media L. Rep. 1579 (4th Cir. 1990).
[158] *Id.* at 142, 17 Media L. Rep. at 1582.
[159] *Id.* at 142–43, 17 Media L. Rep. at 1583.
[160] *Id.*, 17 Media L. Rep. at 1582–83. According to the Fourth Circuit, the CIA would have the "option" to seek an injunction against publication, which would enhance its ability to enforce the secrecy agreement by resort to the contempt powers of the court. *Id.*
[161] Medow, *supra* note 121, at 788; *see Guidelines on Enforcing Predissemination Review Obligations,* 6 Media L. Rep. (BNA) 2261 (Dec. 9, 1980). Although "the First Amendment limits the extent to which the United States, *contractually or otherwise,* may impose secrecy requirements upon its employees and enforce them with a system of prior censorship," United States v. Marchetti, 466 F.2d 1309, 1313, 1 Media L. Rep. 1051, 1053 (4th Cir. 1972) (emphasis added), the key to these cases is that all of these former government agents voluntarily agreed to contractual provisions authorizing prepublication review. Medow, *supra* note 121, at 811–12; United States v. Snepp, 444 U.S. 507, 515–16, 5 Media L. Rep. 2409 (1980).
[162] *See infra* §§10.7(A) and (B).
[163] 427 U.S. 539, 1 Media L. Rep. 1064 (1976).

contents of the criminal defendant's confession, which had been introduced in open court at the arraignment; (2) statements made by the defendant to other persons; (3) the contents of a note written by the defendant on the night of the crime; (4) certain aspects of the medical testimony at the preliminary hearing; and (5) the identity of the victims of the alleged sexual assault and the nature of the assault.[164] The order also prohibited reporting the nature of the order itself.[165]

The petitioners applied to the Nebraska Supreme Court for a stay and an expedited appeal from that order.[166] The court balanced the presumption against prior restraints against the importance of the defendant's right to a fair trial and concluded that, because of the publicity surrounding the crime, the defendant's right was in jeopardy.[167] The court did narrow the order to only prohibit reporting of (1) the existence and nature of any confessions or admissions made by the defendant to law enforcement officers; (2) any confessions or admissions made by the defendant to any third parties, except members of the press; and (3) other facts "strongly implicative" of the defendant's guilt.[168] By its terms, the restraint expired when the jury was impaneled.[169]

The U.S. Supreme Court reversed.[170] Although earlier cases had established that the First Amendment affords protection against prior restraints on speech, none of these cases had involved an order entered to protect the defendant's right to a fair and impartial jury.[171] The Court discussed *Near v. Minnesota,* noting that "[t]he principles enunciated in *Near* were so universally accepted that the precise issue [of the invalidity of prior restraints] did not come before us again until *Organization For A Better Austin v. Keefe* . . . ."[172]

The Court also noted that

[t]he authors of the Bill of Rights did not undertake to assign priorities as between First Amendment and Sixth Amendment rights, ranking one as superior to the other . . . . if the authors of these guarantees, fully aware of the potential conflicts between them, were unwilling or unable to resolve the issue by assigning to one priority over the other, it is not for us to rewrite the Constitution by undertaking what they declined to do. It is unnecessary, after nearly two centuries, to establish a priority applicable in all circumstances.[173]

According to the Court, to determine whether such a restraint is proper in this type of case, a court

must examine the evidence before the trial judge when the order was entered to determine (a) the nature and extent of pretrial news coverage; (b) whether other measures would be likely to mitigate the effects of unrestrained pretrial publicity; and (c) how effectively a restraining order would operate to prevent the threatened danger. The precise terms of the restraining order are also important.[174]

---

[164]*Id.* at 543–44, 1 Media L. Rep. at 1066.
[165]*Id.*
[166]*Id.* at 544, 1 Media L. Rep. at 1066.
[167]*Id.* at 545, 1 Media L. Rep. at 1066.
[168]427 U.S. at 545, 1 Media L. Rep. at 1067.
[169]*Id.* at 543, 1 Media L. Rep. at 1066.
[170]*Id.* at 570, 1 Media L. Rep. at 1076.
[171]*Id.* at 556, 1 Media L. Rep. at 1071.
[172]*Id.* at 557, 1 Media L. Rep. at 1071.
[173]427 U.S. at 561, 1 Media L. Rep. at 1072–73.
[174]*Id.* at 562, 1 Media L. Rep. at 1073.

The Court's review of the record revealed that the trial judge was "justified in concluding that there would be intense and pervasive pretrial publicity concerning this case.... [and he could reasonably conclude that] publicity might impair the defendant's right to a fair trial."[175] The trial judge found only "a clear and present danger that pre-trial publicity *could* impinge upon the defendant's right to a fair trial."[176]

There was also little in the record that revealed a consideration of what alternative measures, short of an outright restraint on all publication, would have provided the defendant with a fair trial. The record did not support a finding that alternative measures would not have protected the defendant's rights; the Court instead identified several alternatives to a prior restraint.[177] As the Court emphasized, "pretrial publicity, even if pervasive and concentrated, cannot be regarded as leading automatically and in every kind of criminal case to an unfair trial."[178] The Court concluded that alternatives to a prior restraint might have mitigated the adverse effects of pretrial publicity, thereby making a prior restraint unnecessary.[179]

The Court also found that there were practical problems involved in managing and enforcing pretrial restraining orders, so it was unclear whether the prior restraint would even have protected the defendant's fair trial rights.[180]

To the extent that the order prohibited the recording of evidence adduced in open court, the order plainly violated settled principles.[181] The order's prohibition against reporting "implicative" information was also too vague and too broad to survive scrutiny under the First Amendment.[182] In addition, the

---

[175]*Id.* at 562–63, 1 Media L. Rep. at 1073.

[176]*Id.* at 563, 1 Media L. Rep. at 1073. The Court concluded: "[O]n the record now before us it is not clear that further publicity, unchecked, would so distort the views of potential jurors that 12 could not be found who would, under proper instructions, fulfill their sworn duty to render a just verdict on the evidence presented in open court." *Id.* at 569, 1 Media L. Rep. at 1075.

[177]*Id.* at 562–65, 1 Media L. Rep. at 1073–74. The Court cited various alternatives approved in Sheppard v. Maxwell, 384 U.S. 333, 357–62, 1 Media L. Rep. 1220, 1229–31 (1966), including (1) change of venue, (2) postponement of trial, (3) extensive voir dire, (4) clear jury instructions, and (5) sequestration of jurors. 427 U.S. at 564–65, 1 Media L. Rep. at 1073–74. A change of venue may also be accomplished by selecting a jury somewhere else and moving the jury to the trial location. *See, e.g.,* CAL. PENAL CODE §1036.7 (Deering Supp. 1993).

[178]427 U.S. at 565, 1 Media L. Rep. at 1074.

[179]*Id.* at 569, 1 Media L. Rep. at 1074. In United States v. McKenzie, 697 F.2d 1225 (5th Cir. 1983), the Fifth Circuit stated:

In addition to the scope of the Order [restraining the broadcast of a "60 Minutes" segment], the principal aspect of the proceedings below that disturbs us is the absence of any indication in the record that the alternatives to prior restraint (including a continuance or a further change in venue), which were so heavily emphasized in *Nebraska Press,* were considered by the district court. Specifically, we note that the case law in this circuit provides detailed procedures for evaluating the effect of pretrial publicity on potential jurors before and during voir dire, all designed to protect the defendants' right to a fair trial by an impartial jury .... There has been no express finding here, and we are unwilling to speculate about the correctness of such a finding, had it been made, that those procedures are likely to be inadequate to protect the defendants' constitutional rights .... This being so, we need not and do not reach the broader question of whether an injunction in the nature of the Order could ever constitutionally be issued.

697 F.2d at 1227 (citation omitted).

[180]427 U.S. at 565–67, 1 Media L. Rep. at 1074–75. These problems include limits on territorial and in personam jurisdiction as well as the difficulty of fashioning an order that is neither too broad nor too narrow. The Court also noted that, even without any news accounts being printed or broadcast, rumors concerning the criminal proceedings would spread through the small town where the trial was taking place. "[I]t is far from clear that prior restraint on publication would have protected [the defendant's] rights." *Id.* at 567, 1 Media L. Rep. at 1075.

[181]*Id.* at 568, 1 Media L. Rep. at 1075.

[182]*Id.* The Court concluded:

We reaffirm that the guarantees of freedom of expression are not an absolute prohibition under all circumstances, but the barriers to prior restraint remain high and the presumption against its use

Supreme Court noted that there may be significant jurisdictional problems with an order purporting to restrain publication at large by those who are not parties to the litigation in which the order is issued.[183]

Justice White filed a concurring opinion expressing his "grave doubt ... whether orders with respect to the press such as were entered in this case would ever be justifiable."[184] He felt that it would be wise not to issue a total ban on such restraints in the first case squarely presenting the issue, but stated that at some future point it might be advisable to "announce a more general rule and avoid the interminable litigation that our failure to do so would necessarily entail."[185] In his concurring opinion, Justice Lewis Powell emphasized "the unique burden that rests upon the party whether it be the State or a defendant, who undertakes to show the necessity for prior restraint on pretrial publicity."[186]

Justice Brennan, joined by Justices Stewart and Marshall, filed a concurring opinion in which he made very clear his view that the First Amendment would never permit an order restraining the press from reporting on the activities of the criminal justice system, given the adequate alternative tools available to state judges for protecting the Sixth Amendment rights of criminal defendants.[187]

Justice Stevens filed a concurring opinion in which he noted that he subscribed "to most of what Mr. Justice Brennan says and, if ever required to face the issues squarely, may well accept his ultimate conclusion."[188]

After *Nebraska Press,* the Supreme Court again rejected prior restraints in the form of court orders prohibiting the publication of information from a judicial proceeding, in *Oklahoma Publishing Co. v. District Court.*[189] In

---

continues intact. We hold that, with respect to the order entered in this case prohibiting reporting or commentary on judicial proceedings held in public, the barriers have not been overcome; to the extent that this order restrained publication of such material, it is clearly invalid. To the extent that it prohibited publication based on information gained from other sources, we conclude that the heavy burden imposed as a condition to securing a prior restraint was not met and the judgment of the Nebraska Supreme Court is therefore Reversed.

Id. at 570, 1 Media L. Rep. at 1076.

[183]*Id.* at 566 nn.9, 10, 1 Media L. Rep. at 1074–75 nn.9, 10. The Court noted the Nebraska Supreme Court's decision that "the District Court had no jurisdiction of the petitioners except by virtue of their voluntary submission to the jurisdiction of that court when they moved to intervene. Except for the intervention . . . the petitioners 'could have ignored the [restraining] order'." *Id.* at 566 n.9, 1 Media L. Rep. at 1074 n.9 (citation omitted).

[184]*Id.* at 570–71, 1 Media L. Rep. at 1076.

[185]472 U.S. at 571, 1 Media L. Rep. at 1076.

[186]*Id.* Justice Powell also stated:

[A] prior restraint properly may issue only when it is shown to be necessary to prevent the dissemination of prejudicial publicity that otherwise poses a high likelihood of preventing, directly and irreparably, the impanelling of a jury meeting the Sixth Amendment requirement of impartiality. This requires a showing that (i) there is a clear threat to the fairness of trial, (ii) such a threat is posed by the actual publicity to be restrained, and (iii) no less restrictive alternatives are available.

Id.

[187]Justice Brennan stated:

[T]here can be no prohibition on the publication by the press of any information pertaining to pending judicial proceedings or the operation of the criminal justice system, no matter how shabby the means by which the information is obtained. . . . an accused's right to a fair trial may be adequately assured through methods that do not infringe First Amendment values.

Id. at 588, 1 Media L. Rep. at 1083 (Brennan, J. concurring).

[188]*Id.* at 617, 1 Media L. Rep. at 1094.

[189]430 U.S. 308, 2 Media L. Rep. 1456 (1977). *Accord* Minneapolis Star & Tribune Co. v. Lee, 353 N.W.2d 213, 10 Media L. Rep. 2300 (Minn. Ct. App. 1984); KCST-TV Channel 39 v. Municipal Ct., 246 Cal. Rptr. 869, 16 Media L. Rep. 1026 (Cal. Ct. App. 1988) (order prohibiting television station from broadcasting drawing of defendant's face is unconstitutional prior restraint); In re Charlotte Observer, 921 F.2d 47, 18 Media L. Rep. 1365 (4th Cir. 1990) (order prohibiting publication of attorney's name, who was identified in open court as target of grand jury investigation, is unconstitutional prior restraint).

Oklahoma Publishing, the Court struck down a gag order prohibiting the press from publishing the name or picture of a minor involved in a pending juvenile proceeding.[190] The proceeding was held in open court with the media in attendance, even though a state statute provided that juvenile hearings were to be closed to the public unless specifically opened by court order.[191] The Court found that striking down this prior restraint was mandated by its decisions in *Nebraska Press* and *Cox Broadcasting Corp. v. Cohn.*[192] Where members of the press are present at a court hearing open to the public, they cannot be restrained from publishing information concerning the proceeding, even when a state statute requires that the proceeding ordinarily should be closed to the public.[193]

Since *Nebraska Press,* the courts that have considered prior restraints on the press' right to publish in the context of fair trial rights regularly have held such restraints to be unconstitutional.[194]

---

[190]430 U.S. at 311–12, 2 Media L. Rep. at 1458.

[191]*Id.* at 311, 2 Media L. Rep. at 1458.

[192]*Id.* at 310, 2 Media L. Rep. at 1457 (citing Nebraska Press Ass'n v. Stuart, 427 U.S. 539, 1 Media L. Rep. 1064 (1976) *and* Cox Broadcasting Corp. v. Cohn, 420 U.S. 469, 1 Media L. Rep. 1819 (1975)). *See also* Craig v. Harney, 331 U.S. 367, 1 Media L. Rep. 1310 (1947), in which the Court stated: "A trial is a public event. What transpires in the court room is public property. . . . Those who see and hear what transpired can report it with impunity." 331 U.S. at 374, 1 Media L. Rep. at 1313.

[193]430 U.S. at 310–11, 2 Media L. Rep. at 1457–58.

[194]Several federal decisions demonstrate this. In Goldblum v. National Broadcasting Corp., 584 F.2d 904, 4 Media L. Rep. 1718 (9th Cir. 1978), Judge Anthony M. Kennedy, writing for the court, rejected the argument of a plaintiff who claimed that NBC's planned broadcast of a docudrama relating to the Equity Funding scandal would inflame public opinion against him, jeopardize his release on parole, and threaten his constitutional rights to a fair jury in future criminal and civil trials. Judge Kennedy wrote:

> It is a fundamental principle of the first amendment that the press may not be required to justify or defend what it prints or says until after the expression has taken place . . . . A broadcaster or publisher should not, in circumstances such as those in this case, be required to make a sudden appearance in court and then to take urgent measures to secure appellate relief, all the while weighing the delicate question of whether or not refusal to comply with an apparently invalid order constitutes a contempt.

Id. at 907, 4 Media L. Rep. at 1720.

In CBS, Inc. v. United States District Court, 729 F.2d 1174, 10 Media L. Rep. 1529 (9th Cir. 1983), the court overturned an order prohibiting CBS from airing videotapes made by the government that appeared to show John Z. Delorean's involvement in a drug deal. In United States v. McKenzie, 697 F.2d 1225 (5th Cir. 1983), the court stayed a district court order prohibiting CBS from airing a "60 Minutes" segment about a crime where the order was unlimited geographically and in time. Justice White subsequently denied the criminal defendants' application to vacate this stay in Bonura v. CBS, Inc., 459 U.S. 1313 (1983). On remand, the district court limited the injunction to the Dallas metropolitan area and to the time period prior to jury selection. The Fifth Circuit again stayed the order. Chief Justice Burger, without written opinion, again denied the criminal defendants' application to vacate the stay. United States v. McKenzie, 735 F.2d 907, 909, 10 Media L. Rep. 1997, 1998 (5th Cir. 1984). In Hunt v. NBC, 872 F.2d 289, 10 Media L. Rep. 1434 (9th Cir. 1989), the Ninth Circuit affirmed the district court's denial of a criminal defendant's attempt, on grounds of prejudicial pretrial publicity, to enjoin NBC's broadcast of a docudrama entitled "Billionaire Boys Club."

Numerous state courts have reached the same result. In re A Minor, 537 N.E.2d 292, 301, 16 Media L. Rep. 1449, 1456 (Ill. 1989) (alleged safety concerns did not justify injunction against publication of name of juvenile charged with shooting); In re Summerville, 547 N.E.2d 513, 17 Media L. Rep. 1057 (Ill. App. Ct. 1989) (order forbidding public discussion of child custody case by parties and counsel unconstitutional prior restraint where no specific findings of clear and present danger of serious and imminent threat to fairness and integrity of trial); In re Guardianship of Kowalski, 16 Media L. Rep. 2018 (Minn. Ct. App. 1989) (emotional distress insufficient justification for prior restraint); State ex rel. Beacon Journal v. Kainrad, 348 N.E.2d 695, 2 Media L. Rep. 1123 (Ohio 1976) (pretrial order restraining media from publishing testimony during criminal trial is error); Arkansas Gazette v. Lofton, 598 S.W.2d 745, 6 Media L. Rep. 1535 (Ark. 1980) (order prohibiting press from referring to defendant as "Quapaw Quarter rapist" unconstitutional); KUTV, Inc. v. Conder, 668 P.2d 513, 9 Media L. Rep. 1825 (Utah 1983) (order prohibiting use of term "Sugarhouse rapist" and dissemination of any information about criminal defendant's past convictions during trial unconstitutional); State v. Coe, 679 P.2d 353, 10 Media L. Rep. 1465 (Wash. 1984) (order prohibiting television broadcast of accurate, legally obtained copies of tape recordings played in open court unconstitutional prior restraint); Florida Pub'g Co. v. Brooke, 576 So. 2d 842, 18 Media L. Rep. 1978 (Fla. Dist. Ct. App. 1991) (order barring publication of psychologist's letter about child, received from child's parents, is unlawful prior restraint). *See also* Gardner v. Bradenton Herald, 413 So. 2d 10, 8 Media L. Rep.

In *Nebraska Press,* Justices Brennan, Stewart, and Marshall squarely stated that all prior restraints in the fair trial context were unconstitutional. Justices White's and Stevens' concurrences indicated that they might join in such a holding in the future. Consequently, a number of commentators have concluded that there is, in fact, an absolute ban on prior restraints in this area:

> In view of the Court's language, and the cases it cites, the law now surely is that the freedom of the press to publish truthful reports of court proceedings that are open to the public is protected by the first amendment not only against prior restraints but against any subsequent legal sanction as well.[195]

Moreover, it is not clear that there is any conflict between the Sixth Amendment right to a fair trial and the First Amendment right to publish, because both rights are "limitations upon government, not upon citizens."[196] Because the media are not state actors, it is very doubtful that a criminal defendant's Sixth Amendment rights can ever warrant a prior restraint on the media.

The inability of the courts after *Nebraska Press* to enjoin the publication of information obtained in open court has led directly to attempts to close court proceedings to the press and the public; these attempts have been largely unsuccessful.[197]

1251 (Fla.) (Florida statute mandating criminal sanctions against newspaper that lawfully obtained names of wiretap subjects and published that information prior to indictment held unconstitutional), *cert. denied,* 459 U.S. 865 (1982); WXYZ, Inc. v. Hand, 658 F.2d 420, 7 Media L. Rep. 1817 (6th Cir. 1981) (statutory ban on publication of details of crime and names of victim and accused is unconstitutional prior restraint). *Contra* KUTV, Inc. v. Wilkinson, 686 P.2d 456, 10 Media L. Rep. 1749 (Utah 1984) (upholding prior restraint during criminal trial of defendant's alleged association with organized crime).

Several cases have also refused to restrain the publication of jurors' names. State ex rel. Chillicothe Gazette v. Court of Common Pleas, 442 N.E.2d 747, 9 Media L. Rep. 1018 (Ohio 1982) (trial court erred in issuing order prohibiting media from publishing names or addresses of prospective jurors learned in courtroom without giving adequate consideration to three-part test from *Nebraska Press*); Des Moines Register & Tribune Co. v. Osmundson, 248 N.W.2d 493, 2 Media L. Rep. 1321 (Iowa 1976) (trial judge's order prohibiting media from publishing jurors' names, addresses, and telephone numbers unconstitutional prior restraint where court order issued without sufficient evidence showing order necessary and without sufficient consideration of alternatives); Commonwealth v. Genovese, 487 A.2d 364, 11 Media L. Rep. 1388 (Pa. Super. Ct. 1985) (order prohibiting media from publishing jurors' names held to be unconstitutional prior restraint where no evidence of harassment of jurors and less restrictive alternatives not considered); KPNX Broadcasting Co. v. Superior Ct. of Maricopa County, 678 P.2d 431, 10 Media L. Rep. 1289 (Ariz. 1984) (court overturned order prohibiting television station from broadcasting sketches of jurors where risk that jurors' verdict would be rendered out of fear not grave; less restrictive alternatives available to guard against risk, and order was ineffective because newspapers not prohibited from publishing such sketches). *See also* Keene Pub'g Corp. v. Cheshire County Super. Ct., 406 A.2d 137, 5 Media L. Rep. 1626 (N.H. 1979) (order requiring counsel for newspaper to attend suppression hearing to advise client as to what information could not be published was unconstitutional implied gag order).

[195]Barnett, *supra* note 49, at 546; *see also* Swift, *Restraints on Defense Publicity in Criminal Jury Cases,* 1984 UTAH L. REV. 45, 52, 68 (1984); Portman, *The Defense of Fair Trial from Sheppard to Nebraska Press Association: Benign Neglect to Affirmative Action and Beyond,* 29 STAN. L. REV. 393, 409 n.72 (1977).

A prior restraint was upheld, however, in United States v. Noriega, 752 F. Supp. 1032, 18 Media L. Rep. 1348 (S.D. Fla. 1990), *aff'd sub nom.* In re Cable News Network, 917 F.2d 1543, 18 Media L. Rep. 1352, *stay and cert. denied,* 111 S. Ct. 451, 18 Media L. Rep. 1358 (1990), where the Cable News Network was enjoined from broadcasting tapes of an allegedly confidential conversation between a criminal defendant and his attorneys until the court could determine the merits of the defendant's contentions. After reviewing the tapes, the court vacated its restraining order. United States v. Noriega, 752 F. Supp. 1045, 18 Media L. Rep. 1537 (S.D. Fla. 1990). *See also supra* notes 66 and 67.

[196]CBS, Inc. v. United States Dist. Ct., 729 F.2d 1174, 1184, 10 Media L. Rep. 1529, 1536 (9th Cir. 1983) (Goodwin, J., concurring). Judge Reinhardt's concurring opinion completely agreed with Judge Goodwin's, and another panel of the Ninth Circuit has acknowledged that the state action doctrine may well bar prior restraints against the media in this context. *Hunt,* 872 F.2d at 296, 16 Media L. Rep. at 1440.

[197]*See* Chapter 1.

§10.7(B) Gag Orders on Trial Participants

Since the U.S. Supreme Court reversed the murder conviction of Dr. Sam Sheppard[198] because of prejudicial pretrial and trial publicity, trial courts have employed gag orders to prevent trial participants from speaking to the media or others. In *Sheppard,* the Supreme Court noted that the trial judge could have avoided a

> carnival atmosphere at trial ... since the courtroom and courthouse premises are subject to the control of the court.... More specifically, the trial court might well have proscribed extrajudicial statements by any lawyer, party, witness, or court official which divulged prejudicial matters ... or like statements concerning the merits of the case.[199]

Sheppard, however, did not involve First Amendment rights, and for a long time the Supreme Court did not rule on the propriety of gag orders or the standards to be used in assessing such orders on trial participants other than in dicta.[200] Without clear guidance from the Supreme Court, there was little agreement on the standard to be used in analyzing the constitutionality of such restraints. Courts generally held that gag orders were justified where the prospect of publicity was "reasonably likely" to interfere with the administration of justice or where publicity posed a "serious and imminent" threat or "clear and present danger" to the administration of justice.[201]

The precise tests used by the courts have included (1) a "reasonable likelihood" that prejudicial publicity "would make difficult the impaneling of an impartial jury and tend to prevent a fair trial;"[202] (2) that "before a trial court can limit defendants' and their attorneys' exercise of first amendment rights of freedom of speech, the record must contain sufficient specific findings by the trial court establishing that defendants' and their attorneys' conduct is a 'serious and imminent threat to the administration of justice';"[203] (3) a clear

---

[198]Sheppard v. Maxwell, 384 U.S. 333, 1 Media L. Rep. 1220 (1966).

[199]*Id.* at 358–61, 1 Media L. Rep. at 1229–31.

[200]In Nebraska Press Association v. Stuart, 427 U.S. 539, 564, 1 Media L. Rep. 1064, 1074 (1976), the Supreme Court cited to the above quotation from *Sheppard* in noting that trial courts may, under appropriate circumstances, limit the statements of various trial participants.

[201]Swift, *supra* note 195, at 45, 46 n.4; Todd, *A Prior Restraint by Any Other Name: The Judicial Response to Media Challenges of Gag Orders Directed at Trial Participants,* 88 Mich. L. Rev. 1171, 1177 n.34, 1178 n.49 (1990). *See also* Matheson, *The Prosecutor, the Press, and Free Speech,* 58 Fordham L. Rev. 865 (1990).

[202]United States v. Tijerina, 412 F.2d 661, 666 (10th Cir.), *cert. denied,* 396 U.S. 990 (1969). *Accord* In re Russell, 726 F.2d 1007, 1010–11, 10 Media L. Rep. 1359, 1361–62 (4th Cir. 1984), *cert. denied,* 469 U.S. 837 (1984). The Fourth Circuit upheld an order prohibiting any person notified by the government or defense that he or she might be called to testify from making extrajudicial statements either to the media or with the intent that the statements be publicly disseminated. The order proscribed statements relating to the testimony he or she might give, any of the parties or issues involved, or the events leading up to the prosecution. 726 F.2d at 1008–09, 10 Media L. Rep. at 1360–61. In an earlier case, the Fourth Circuit approved of an order dismissing a complaint filed by the media that sought to enjoin the district court's order prohibiting extrajudicial statements by lawyers, parties, witnesses, jurors, and court officials, the release of the names of prospective jurors, and photographing or sketching of jurors. The Fourth Circuit overruled the prohibition on "mingling" of trial participants and the media on sidewalks adjacent to the courthouse and suggested that the district court might reconsider the other portions of its order once a jury was impaneled. Central S.C. Chapter, Soc'y of Prof. Journalists v. Martin, 556 F.2d 706, 707–08, 2 Media L. Rep. 2146, 2147–48 (4th Cir. 1977), *cert. denied,* 434 U.S. 1022 (1978). *See also* KPNX Broadcasting Co. v. Superior Ct., 678 P.2d 431, 10 Media L. Rep. 1289 (Ariz. 1984) (restriction on court participants talking to press not a prior restraint).

[203]Chase v. Robson, 435 F.2d 1059, 1061 (7th Cir. 1970) (concluding that restraint constitutionally impermissible under either "serious and imminent threat" standard or "reasonable likelihood" standard).

and present danger to the administration of justice;[204] and (4) the three-part test of *Nebraska Press*.[205]

In *Levine v. United States District Court*,[206] a proceeding arising from the criminal espionage trial of Richard Miller, the trial court issued an order prohibiting the attorneys involved in the case from commenting on the "merits" of the case.[207] The Ninth Circuit held that this order was a prior restraint against counsel that could only be upheld if "(1) the activity restrained poses either a clear and present danger or a serious and imminent threat to a protected competing interest ... (2) the order is narrowly drawn ... and (3) less restrictive alternatives are not available ...."[208]

The Ninth Circuit then upheld the trial court's conclusion that a serious and imminent threat was posed by the "circus-like environment that surrounds highly publicized trials"—especially where the publicity is just before and during trial.[209] The court concluded, however, that the order was overbroad: "It is apparent that many statements that bear 'upon the merits to be resolved by the jury' present no danger to the administration of justice."[210] Finally, the

---

[204]CBS, Inc. v. Young, 522 F.2d 234, 240, 1 Media L. Rep. 1024, 1028 (6th Cir. 1975) (successful media challenge to order prohibiting trial participants and others from discussing case with media or public); United States v. Ford, 830 F.2d 596, 598–600, 14 Media L. Rep. 1901, 1903–04 (6th Cir. 1987) (order prohibiting congressman from making extrajudicial statements was prior restraint and had to meet "clear and present danger test" and pose "serious and imminent threat"). In *Ford*, the court had little difficulty in finding a "no discussion-of-the-case" order imposed on the defendant, an indicted U.S. congressman, overbroad and unjustified. 830 F.2d at 599–601, 14 Media L. Rep. at 1904–05. Similarly, the Sixth Circuit set aside, as an impermissible prior restraint, a bail condition prohibiting the defendant, who was convicted of tax evasion, from discussing his beliefs about his income taxes during his appeal. United States v. Krzyske, 836 F.2d 1013 (6th Cir.), *cert. denied*, 488 U.S. 832 (1988).

[205]427 U.S. 539, 562, 1 Media L. Rep. 1064, 1073 (1976). In Bailey v. Systems Innovation, 852 F.2d 93, 99–101, 15 Media L. Rep. 1756, 1762–63 (3d Cir. 1988), the trial court applied a local court rule, which limited the extrajudicial statements that counsel could make during litigation, to the parties. The local rule incorporated standards from the ABA Model Code of Professional Responsibility DR 7-107 that have been applied to counsel in numerous other jurisdictions. *Bailey* involved the parties' challenge to that rule as applied to the litigants and not to counsel. 852 F.2d at 97, 15 Media L. Rep. at 1760. Counsel have challenged variations of DR 7-107 as impermissible prior restraints. *See* Hirschkop v. Snead, 594 F.2d 356, 368, 4 Media L. Rep. 2599, 2605 (4th Cir. 1979) (Rule 7-107 of Virginia Code of Professional Responsibility not a prior restraint); Chicago Council of Lawyers v. Bauer, 522 F.2d 242, 248–49, 1 Media L. Rep. 1094, 1096–97 (7th Cir. 1975) (rules not prior restraints although they have "some elements similar to that which we have traditionally termed 'prior restraints'"), *cert. denied*, 427 U.S. 912 (1976). Although *Hirschkop* and *Chicago Council of Lawyers* applied different tests to these rules (reasonable likelihood and serious and imminent threat, respectively (*Hirschkop*, 594 F.2d at 370, 4 Media L. Rep. at 2607)), both courts concluded that parts of the rules were overbroad. *Hirschkop*, 594 F.2d at 371–74, 4 Media L. Rep. at 2608–10; *Chicago Council of Lawyers*, 522 F.2d at 252–59, 1 Media L. Rep. at 1099–1105. In Ruggieri v. Johns-Manville Prods. Corp., 503 F. Supp. 1036, 6 Media L. Rep. 2276 (D.R.I. 1980), the court held that a variation of DR 7-107, which adopted a "serious and imminent threat" test for pending criminal litigation and a "reasonable likelihood" standard for civil litigation, "makes no sense.... the standard in civil cases must necessarily be equal to or higher than that allowed for in criminal proceedings." 503 F. Supp. at 1040, 6 Media L. Rep. at 2277. The court adopted the "serious and imminent threat" standard. *Accord* Kemner v. Monsanto Co., 492 N.E.2d 1327, 1337 (Ill. 1986). The Supreme Court has now resolved this issue. *See infra* notes 224–230.

[206]764 F.2d 590, 11 Media L. Rep. 2289 (9th Cir. 1985), *cert. denied*, 476 U.S. 1158 (1986).

[207]*Id.* at 593, 11 Media L. Rep. at 2290–91.

[208]*Id.* at 595, 11 Media L. Rep. at 2292. In United States v. Lehder-Rivas, 667 F. Supp. 827, 828 (M.D. Fla. 1987), the district court cited *Levine* in vacating an order restraining the defendant and his attorney and agents from conducting surveys or studies of potential venire persons in the district. The court held that the government had failed to show that the survey posed an imminent threat to the administration of justice and held that the order amounted to an unconstitutional prior restraint. 667 F. Supp. at 829.

[209]764 F.2d at 598, 11 Media L. Rep. at 2295.

[210]*Id.* at 599, 11 Media L. Rep. at 2295–96. The Ninth Circuit listed subjects derived largely from Rule 3.6 of the Model Rules of Professional Conduct, the ABA Standards for Criminal Justice, and the Model Code of Professional Responsibility DR 7-107. *Id.* The court stated that it would be appropriate to proscribe statements relating to (1) the character, credibility, or reputation of a party; (2) the identity of a witness or expected testimony of a witness or party; (3) the contents of pretrial statements by a defendant or the failure to make such statements; (4) the identity, nature, or absence of physical evidence; (5) the strengths or weaknesses of either party's case; or (6) any other information the lawyer should reasonably know is likely

Ninth Circuit approved of the district court's findings that no less restrictive alternatives were available that would be effective or productive.[211]

After remand, the district court entered an amended restraining order that prohibited counsel from making extrajudicial statements to the news media on all of the subjects suggested by the Ninth Circuit in *Levine*.[212] The amended order was not challenged by counsel, but the Radio and Television News Association of Southern California claimed that the order, by effectively denying them access to trial participants, constituted an impermissible prior restraint on its members' news-gathering ability.[213]

The Ninth Circuit was not receptive to this argument:

> [T]he district court's order in this case is not directed toward the press at all. On the contrary, the media is free to attend all of the trial proceedings before the district court and to report anything that happens.... In fact, the press remains free to direct questions at trial counsel. Trial counsel simply may not be free to answer.[214]

In light of its conclusion that the media's interest in interviewing trial participants was "outside the scope of protection offered by the first amendment,"[215] the gag order was not subject to strict scrutiny as a prior restraint, but only needed to be reasonable and serve a legitimate governmental purpose.[216]

The Second Circuit has also held that gag orders on trial participants, when challenged by the media, are not prior restraints. In *In re Dow Jones & Co.*,[217] the appellant news agencies challenged a district court order that prohibited counsel and parties in the "Wedtech case" from making extrajudicial statements to the press.[218] The Second Circuit held that this order was not a prior restraint on the press: "[T]here is a substantial difference between a

---

to be inadmissible and would create a substantial risk of prejudice if disclosed. *Id.* at 599, 11 Media L. Rep. at 2296.

[211] *Id.* at 599–600, 11 Media L. Rep. at 2296–97. The court noted that voir dire would not eliminate prejudice caused by publicity during trial and would not "alleviate the harm to the integrity of the judicial process"; "jury instructions are often an ineffective remedy"; change of venue would have no impact in " 'curbing unwarranted statements by counsel' "; and sequestration of the jury was " 'an undesirable alternative. Jurors, especially in long trials, should not bear the brunt of counsel's transgressions'." *Id.* at 600, 11 Media L. Rep. at 2296–97.

[212] Radio & Television News Ass'n v. United States Dist. Ct., 781 F.2d 1443, 1444, 12 Media L. Rep. 1739, 1740 (9th Cir. 1986). *See supra* note 210.

[213] *Id.* at 1445, 12 Media L. Rep. at 1741.

[214] *Id.* at 1446, 12 Media L. Rep. at 1742 (citation omitted).

[215] *Id.* at 1447, 12 Media L. Rep. at 1743.

[216] *Id.* at 1447–48, 12 Media L. Rep. at 1743.

[217] 842 F.2d 603, 15 Media L. Rep. 1105 (2d Cir.), *cert. denied sub nom.* Dow Jones & Co. v. Simon, 488 U.S. 946, 15 Media L. Rep. 2159 (1988). *See also* In re New York Times Co., 878 F.2d 67, 16 Media L. Rep. 1877 (2d Cir. 1989) (trial court erred in prohibiting counsel in criminal prosecution from speaking with media during trial absent any showing of prejudice resulting from counsel's statements); State ex rel. Miami Herald Pub'g Co. v. McIntosh, 340 So. 2d 904, 906–07, 909–10, 2 Media L. Rep. 1328, 1329, 1331–32 (Fla. 1977) (gag order placed on all parties to trial but not media is abuse of discretion where jury sequestered and adequately admonished); NBC v. Cooperman, 501 N.Y.S.2d 405, 12 Media L. Rep. 2025 (N.Y. App. Div. 1986) (trial court order in criminal proceeding brought against two police officers prohibiting all counsel from communicating with media violated First Amendment); State ex rel. NBC v. Lake County Ct. of Common Pleas, 556 N.E.2d 1120, 17 Media L. Rep. 2209 (Ohio 1990) (invalidating gag order except as it applied to court personnel). Sometimes these orders are upheld, however. Mississippi Pubrs. Corp. v. Circuit Ct., 12 Media L. Rep. 1342 (Miss. 1985) (upholding order restraining counsel, law enforcement personnel, and court personnel from releasing statements about defendant's criminal record or reputation); Florida Freedom Newspapers v. McCrary, 520 So. 2d 32 (Fla. 1988) (upholding order prohibiting public comment on criminal case by prosecutor or law enforcement); In re T.R., 556 N.E.2d 439, 17 Media L. Rep. 2241 (Ohio), *cert. denied sub nom.* Dispatch Printing Co. v. Solove, 498 U.S. 958 (1990) (upholding order in child custody proceeding restricting comments by adult parties and their counsel).

[218] 842 F.2d at 606, 15 Media L. Rep. at 1107–08.

restraining order directed against the press—a form of censorship which the First Amendment sought to abolish from these shores—and the order here directed solely against trial participants and challenged only by the press. The distinction is critical."[219] The court focused on the fact that the district court order was directed solely at the trial participants and not at the press: although the order might limit the flow of information to the press, it did not prohibit the press from publishing any information in its possession.[220] "[W]e conclude that there is a fundamental difference between a gag order challenged by the individual gagged and one challenged by a third party; an order objected to by the former is properly characterized as a prior restraint, one opposed solely by the latter is not."[221] The Sixth Circuit has reached exactly the opposite conclusion.[222]

The Supreme Court has not solved this direct conflict among the circuit courts and was one vote shy of granting certiorari in *In re Dow Jones & Co.*[223]

While the Supreme Court has not resolved this conflict, it has provided some needed guidance on the constitutionality of restraints on the speech of trial participants. In *Gentile v. State Bar of Nevada*,[224] the Court considered the constitutionality of Nevada's Rule 177, which limited lawyers' statements about their pending cases.[225] In a 5-4 decision, the Court rejected the argument that a "clear and present danger" of "actual prejudice or an imminent threat" to the administration of justice must be shown.[226] Instead, the Court held that all that needed to be shown was a "substantial likelihood of material prejudice" to a fair trial.[227] The essential rationale for this holding was that lawyers involved in pending cases are officers of the court with special duties to the legal system.[228]

A different five-justice majority[229] held, however, that Nevada's Rule 177 was unconstitutionally vague because its safe harbor provisions, which specified what lawfully could be said, contradicted what Rule 177 prohibited.[230] Thus, Gentile won the battle but lost the war.

---

[219] *Id.* at 608, 15 Media L. Rep. at 1109–10.
[220] *Id.* at 609, 15 Media L. Rep. at 1110.
[221] *Id.*
[222] Although the news media are not directly enjoined from discussing the case, it is apparent that significant and meaningful sources of information concerning the case are effectively removed from them and their representatives.... A more restrictive ban upon freedom of expression in the trial context would be difficult if not impossible to find.
CBS, Inc. v. Young, 522 F.2d 234, 239, 1 Media L. Rep. 1024, 1027 (6th Cir. 1975).
[223] Dow Jones & Co. v. Simon, 488 U.S. 946, 15 Media L. Rep. 2159 (1988). Justices White, Brennan, and Marshall dissented from the denial of certiorari, recognizing this direct conflict.
[224] 111 S. Ct. 2720 (1991).
[225] *Id.* at 2723, 2741. Nevada's rule was almost identical to ABA Rule of Professional Conduct 3.6. *Id.*
[226] *Id.* at 2742. The Court rejected the argument that the standards of Nebraska Press Association v. Stuart, 427 U.S. 539 (1976), apply.
[227] 111 S. Ct. at 2745.
[228] *Id.* at 2744. The Court expressed no opinion on the duties of lawyers who are not participating in a case. *Id.* at 2743–44 n.5.
[229] Justice O'Connor was the decisive swing vote. *Id.* at 2720.
[230] *Id.* at 2731–32. For example, the safe harbor provisions provided that a lawyer "may state without elaboration . . . the general nature of the . . . defense." *Id.* at 2731. Gentile had been disciplined for holding a press conference in which he accused the undercover police of the same crimes—stealing drugs and money—that his client, the operator of a safety deposit vault, had been charged with. *Id.* at 2727–28. Gentile's client was ultimately acquitted on all counts by a jury. *Id.* at 2723.

§10.8 PRIVACY

In *Organization for a Better Austin v. Keefe*,[231] the Supreme Court struck down a state court injunction against distributing leaflets that allegedly invaded a real estate broker's privacy. The petitioners distributed leaflets that criticized the real estate broker's business practices as "blockbusting" and "panic peddling."[232] The Organization for a Better Austin (OBA) was a racially integrated group seeking "to 'stabilize' the racial ratio" in the Chicago neighborhood of Austin.[233] The OBA, after unsuccessfully attempting to dissuade Keefe from engaging in such practices in Austin, started distributing leaflets in a shopping center in Keefe's neighborhood that asked readers to call Keefe and urge him not to engage in such selling practices.[234] At Keefe's request, the trial court entered a temporary injunction enjoining the OBA "from passing out pamphlets, leaflets or literature of any kind, and from picketing, anywhere in the City of Westchester, Illinois."[235] The Illinois Appellate Court affirmed, sustaining the finding of fact that OBA's activities in Westchester invaded Keefe's right of privacy, caused him irreparable harm, and left him without an adequate remedy at law.[236]

The U.S. Supreme Court reversed, stating that "[n]o prior decisions support the claim that the interest of an individual in being free from public criticism of his business practices in pamphlets or leaflets warrants use of the injunctive power of a court."[237] Other courts generally have rejected prior restraints designed to protect privacy interests—especially after *Keefe*.[238]

---

[231] 402 U.S. 415, 1 Media L. Rep. 1021 (1971).

[232] *Id.* at 417, 1 Media L. Rep. at 1021–22.

[233] *Id.* at 416, 1 Media L. Rep. at 1021. Keefe's alleged tactics consisted of frightening white residents to move out, securing their listings, and then showing the vacated houses to blacks.

[234] *Id.* at 417, 1 Media L. Rep. at 1021–22.

[235] *Id.* at 417, 1 Media L. Rep. at 1022.

[236] 402 U.S. at 418, 1 Media L. Rep. at 1022.

[237] *Id.* at 419, 1 Media L. Rep. at 1022 (Justice Harlan dissented, but only on procedural grounds). The fact that the pamphlets might be characterized as "coercive" did not alter the result and did not remove them from the protection of the First Amendment. Citing Near v. Minnesota, 283 U.S. 697, 1 Media L. Rep. 1001 (1931), the Court declared, "Here as in that case, the injunction operates, not to redress alleged private wrongs, but to suppress, on the basis of previous publications, distribution of literature 'of any kind' in a City of 18,000." 402 U.S. at 418–19, 1 Media L. Rep. at 1022.

[238] In WXYZ, Inc. v. Hand, 658 F.2d 420, 7 Media L. Rep. 1817 (6th Cir. 1981), a state trial court judge issued a suppression order, pursuant to a Michigan statute, forbidding disclosure of the names of the victim and accused as well as the details of alleged sexual misconduct by a Catholic priest. The plaintiff broadcast an account of the incident and the name of the accused priest and subsequently sought an order restraining the trial judge from enforcing the suppression order and overturning the statute that permitted the order. The Sixth Circuit held that the statute constituted a "legislative determination that in every case involving certain sex offenses, there exists a sufficiently serious and imminent threat to the privacy interests of the persons involved to justify a suppression order." *Id.* at 427, 7 Media L. Rep. at 1822. In overturning the statute, the court held that "[d]eference to such legislative judgments is impossible when First Amendment rights are at stake." *Id. Accord* In re King World Prods., 898 F.2d 56, 17 Media L. Rep. 1531, 1534 (6th Cir. 1990) (overturning temporary restraining order that prevented broadcast of surreptitiously made videotape); Davis v. Forbes, 10 Media L. Rep. 1272 (N.D. Tex. 1983) (denying request to enjoin publication of *Forbes* magazine's list of 400 wealthiest men and women in America on privacy grounds).

In Commonwealth v. Wiseman, 249 N.E.2d 610 (Mass. 1969), *cert. denied*, 398 U.S. 960 (1970), on the other hand, a court modified and upheld a restraint against the showing of the movie *Titicut Follies* on privacy and contract grounds. The filmmaker had signed a contract with authorities that allowed him to film scenes in a correction facility for insane persons but required him to film only competent persons who executed releases. The court found that the filmmaker failed to take the necessary steps to ensure that he complied with these contractual requirements. The court also stated that "[t]here is a collective, indecent intrusion into the most private aspects of the lives of these unfortunate persons in the Commonwealth's custody." *Id.* at 615. Nonetheless, the court held that the film could be shown to judges, sociologists, legislators, and health care professionals with a legitimate interest in rehabilitation and mental care, but not

§10.9 DEFAMATION

Courts will not enjoin a slander or libel prior to publication:[239]

New York's Chancellor Walworth said that the power to enjoin a libel "cannot safely be entrusted to any tribunal consistently with the principles of a free government." This is in accord with the more recent line of Supreme Court cases holding such prior restraints to be presumptively unconstitutional.

The absoluteness of the rule is crucial. It forecloses the possibility of frequent lawsuits based upon a person's suspicion or fear that adverse commentary is about to be published. A more flexible rule would encourage inadequate reporting in an effort to keep knowledge of an impending derogatory article away from potential plaintiffs, thereby avoiding litigation.[240]

Some courts have approved injunctions that restrict defamatory speech after a trial has already established that the precise speech enjoined was defamatory.[241]

---

to the general public. *Id.* at 617–18. However, in Quinn v. Johnson, 381 N.Y.S.2d 875 (N.Y. App. Div. 1976), the court denied an injunction seeking to enjoin the broadcast of interviews of children at a state facility because the heavy burden of showing justification for a prior restraint was not met, even though there was a trespass. The court held that *Wiseman* was distinguishable because that case involved contract claims. *See also* Doe v. Roe, 345 N.Y.S.2d 560 (N.Y. App. Div.), *aff'd without opinion,* 307 N.E.2d 823 (N.Y. 1973), *cert. dismissed,* 420 U.S. 307 (1975) (granting preliminary injunction against publication of book authored by psychiatrist, which contained near-verbatim record of treatment of one of his patients, on breach of contract and privacy grounds); Ali v. Playgirl, 447 F. Supp. 723, 3 Media L. Rep. 2540 (S.D.N.Y. 1978) (granting request for preliminary injunction prohibiting further distribution of issue of *Playgirl Magazine,* which included nude likeness of former heavyweight champion, without consideration of First Amendment).

[239]Gold, *supra* note 5, at 231; *Near,* 283 U.S. at 713–14, 720, 1 Media L. Rep. at 1006, 1009; Sampson v. Murray, 415 U.S. 61, 91 (1974) (damage to reputation "falls far short of the type of irreparable injury which is a necessary predicate to the issuance of a temporary injunction"); Sunward Corp. v. Dun & Bradstreet, 568 F. Supp. 602, 609 (D. Colo. 1983), *aff'd in part and rev'd in part,* 811 F.2d 511 (10th Cir. 1987); Dworkin v. Hustler Magazine, 634 F. Supp. 727, 730, 12 Media L. Rep. 2162, 2164 (D. Wyo. 1986) (noting that order enjoining *Hustler* magazine from using name or likeness of Wyoming National Organization of Women members in "false" articles would constitute "massive injunctive relief" in violation of First Amendment constraints on prior restraints); Georgia Soc'y of Plastic Surgeons v. Anderson, 363 S.E.2d 140, 14 Media L. Rep. 2065 (Ga. 1987); Matchett v. Chicago Bar Ass'n, 467 N.E.2d 271, 10 Media L. Rep. 2131 (Ill. App. Ct. 1984), *cert. denied,* 471 U.S. 1054 (1985); Hajek v. Bill Mowbray Motors, 647 S.W.2d 253 (Tex. 1983); Marlin Firearms Co. v. Shields, 64 N.E. 163 (N.Y. 1902); Rosicrucian Fellowship v. Rosicrucian Fellowship Non-Sectarian Church, 245 P.2d 481, 495 (Cal. 1952), *cert. denied,* 345 U.S. 938 (1953); Northwestern Pac. R.R. v. Lumber & Sawmill Workers' Union, 189 P.2d 277, 282 (Cal. 1948); Orloff v. Los Angeles Turf Club, 180 P.2d 321, 325 (Cal. 1947); Brannon v. American Micro Distribs., 342 S.E.2d 301, 12 Media L. Rep. 2134 (Ga. 1986) (striking order enjoining company's former employee from disseminating false and misleading information to customers because of general rule that equity does not enjoin slander); Leonardini v. Shell Oil Co., 264 Cal. Rptr. 883, 904 (Cal. Ct. App. 1989) (holding that injunction unavailable in trade libel case where "statements [were] made in the context of a public debate before a governmental agency on a matter of public health"); Franklin Chalfont Assocs. v. Kalikow, 573 A.2d 550 (Pa. Super. Ct. 1990) (injunction against picketing developer and criticizing business practices was prior restraint); Corpus Christi Caller-Times v. Mancias, 794 S.W.2d 852, 17 Media L. Rep. 2204 (Tex. Ct. App. 1990). *See generally* Annot., *Injunction As Remedy Against Defamation of Person,* 47 A.L.R.2d 715 (1956).

[240]Brandreth v. Lance, 8 Paige 24 (N.Y. Ch. 1839).

[241]Advanced Training Sys. v. Caswell Equip. Co., 352 N.W.2d 1, 11 (Minn. 1984) (court approved of injunction entered after trial court and jury determined that matters to be enjoined were libelous and false and misleading commercial speech; court recognized general rule against enjoining allegedly libelous statements but noted that "courts have also upheld the suppression of libel, so long as the suppression is limited to the precise statements found libelous *after* a full and fair adversary proceeding."); Lemons v. Mycro Group Co., 667 F. Supp. 665, 667 (S.D. Iowa 1987) (citing Sunward Corp. v. Dun & Bradstreet, 568 F. Supp. 602 (D. Colo. 1983), for proposition that injunction may issue only upon showing of continuing or repetitive libelous or slanderous remarks); Retail Credit Co. v. Russell, 218 S.E.2d 54, 63 (Ga. 1975) (injunction against future speech held not to be prior restraint because jury had found statements to be false and defamatory and injunction limited to "exact allegations" found to be libelous); O'Brien v. University Community Tenants Union, 327 N.E.2d 753 (Ohio 1975) (court held that injunction against defamatory speech might be justified after judicial finding of defamation). *But see* Kramer v. Thompson, 947 F.2d 666 (3d Cir. 1991), *cert. denied,* 112 S. Ct. 2274 (1992) (reversing injunction where liability was based on directed rather than jury verdict and predicting that Pennsylvania Supreme Court would not follow these decisions).

§10.10 Business Interests: Trade Secrets, Trademarks, and Copyrights

Courts have issued injunctions to protect a business' trade secrets, but have been reluctant to issue prior restraints in other business situations.[242] Courts also have issued injunctions to restrain the improper use of registered copyrights.[243] Some courts have rejected such injunctions on First Amendment grounds, however.[244]

The courts have been willing to uphold injunctions against certain speech that unlawfully employs another's trademark to confuse consumers as to the source of the goods[245] or certain speech that is false and misleading commercial advertising.[246] This should not be surprising, given the holding of *Central Hudson Gas & Electric Corp. v. Public Service Commission,* where misleading commercial speech was held to be beyond the protection of the First Amendment.[247]

---

[242]*See* Bridge CAT Scan Assocs. v. Technicare Corp., 710 F.2d 940, 946 (2d Cir. 1983). However, the mere fact that speech may harm one's business interests does not warrant a prior restraint. *Leonardini,* 264 Cal. Rptr. 883 (holding that action seeking to enjoin alleged trade libel in context of public debate on public health issues not legally tenable because of First Amendment prohibition against prior restraints). In In re National Service Corp., 742 F.2d 859 (5th Cir. 1984), the Fifth Circuit overturned an order prohibiting a billboard company, which had furnished billboards to a plumbing company and had not been paid, from including warnings on the billboard stating that the plumbing company was in bankruptcy and did not pay its bills. The court held that the billboard company's message was "pure speech," that the order prohibiting the message was a prior restraint, and the "mere fact" that the plumbing company would be harmed by the speech "does not warrant a prior restraint." *Id.* at 862. *Accord* In re Stonegate Sec. Servs., 56 Bankr. Rep. 1014 (N.D. Ill. 1986).

[243]Injunctions restricting the unauthorized dissemination of copyrighted material present issues, such as the fair use doctrine, that go well beyond the scope of this work. Courts analyzing such injunctions often do not even discuss the topic of prior restraints. *See, e.g.,* Salinger v. Random House, 811 F.2d 90, 13 Media L. Rep. 1954 (2d Cir. 1987), *cert. denied,* 484 U.S. 890 (1987) (reversing denial of preliminary injunction with instructions to issue injunction prohibiting publication of biography of J.D. Salinger that quoted and closely paraphrased portions of Salinger's unpublished copyrighted letters). *But see* Belushi v. Woodward, 598 F. Supp. 36, 37, 10 Media L. Rep. 1870, 1871 (D.D.C. 1984) (denying request for injunction against further distribution of book about John Belushi containing one copyrighted photograph where court held that legal remedies would adequately compensate any injury to plaintiff and found that there was public interest in "promotion of free expression and robust debate"). Some federal courts have rejected the notion that injunctions under copyright law constitute prior restraints on protected speech. *See, e.g.,* Walt Disney Prods. v. Filmation Assocs., 628 F. Supp. 871, 878 n.6 (C.D. Cal. 1986). This is because of the view that "the Copyright Act itself embodies a permissible balance between First Amendment protections and the protection of a copyright holder's rights." *Id.* (citing Harper & Row, Pubrs. v. Nation Enters., 471 U.S. 539, 556, 11 Media L. Rep. 1969, 1977 (1985)); New Era Pubns. v. Henry Holt & Co., 873 F.2d 576, 584, 16 Media L. Rep. 1559, 1566 (2d Cir. 1989) (in affirming denial of injunction seeking to prohibit publication of biography of Church of Scientology founder on laches grounds, court stated: "We are not persuaded, however, that any first amendment concerns not accommodated by the Copyright Act are implicated in this action."), *cert. denied,* 493 U.S. 1094 (1990).

[244]Triangle Pubns. v. Knight-Ridder Newspaper, 445 F. Supp. 875, 883–84, 3 Media L. Rep. 2086, 2093 (S.D. Fla. 1978) (First Amendment bars copyright claim), *aff'd on other grounds,* 626 F.2d 1171, 6 Media L. Rep. 1734 (5th Cir. 1980); Time, Inc. v. Bernard Geis Assocs., 293 F. Supp. 130 (S.D.N.Y. 1968) (First Amendment fair use defense bars copyright claim); Denicola, *Trademarks As Speech: Constitutional Implications of the Emerging Rationales for the Protection of Trade Symbols,* 1982 Wis. L. Rev. 158 (1982).

[245]Dallas Cowboys Cheerleaders v. Pussycat Cinema, 604 F.2d 200, 205, 5 Media L. Rep. 1814, 1817 (2d Cir. 1979).

[246]*Id.* at 206, 5 Media L. Rep. at 1818 ("The propriety of a preliminary injunction where such relief is sought is so clear that courts have often issued an injunction without even mentioning the first amendment."); Vidal Sassoon, Inc. v. Bristol-Myers Co., 661 F.2d 272, 276 n.8 (2d Cir. 1981) ("The Lanham Act's content-neutral prohibition of false and misleading advertising does not arouse First Amendment concerns that justify alteration of the normal standard for preliminary injunctive relief."); *see also Nation Enters.,* 471 U.S. at 560–64, 11 Media L. Rep. at 1978–81 ("fair use" doctrine under copyright law did not shield publisher who copies segments of memoirs in order to "scoop" competing magazine's authorized publication of memoir excerpts).

[247]447 U.S. 557, 566, 6 Media L. Rep. 1497, 1501 (1980); *Vidal Sassoon,* 661 F.2d at 276 n.8; Charles of the Ritz Group v. Quality King Distribs., 832 F.2d 1317, 1324 (2d Cir. 1987). Regarding commercial speech, *see* Chapter 11.

The trademark owner acquires the right to prevent the goods bearing its mark from being confused with goods of another and to prevent its own trade from being diverted to those who use misleadingly similar marks.[248] The trademark owner does not obtain the right to enjoin all unauthorized uses of a mark by any person.[249]

Similarly, in *L.L. Bean, Inc. v. Drake Publishers*,[250] the First Circuit overturned an injunction that barred further publication of "L.L. Beam's Back-To-School Sex Catalog," which was a parody of the L.L. Bean catalog.[251] The court stated that "[t]he basis for the district court's injunction was that Bean's trademark had been tarnished by the parody in defendant's magazine. We think this was a constitutionally impermissible application of the anti-dilution statute."[252] The Court went on to note, however, that

> [t]he Constitution is not offended when the [Maine] anti-dilution statute is applied to prevent a defendant from using a trademark without permission in order to merchandise dissimilar products or services. Any residual effect on first amendment freedoms should be balanced against the need to fulfill the legitimate purpose of the anti-dilution statute.[253]

The court distinguished *Dallas Cowboys Cheerleaders v. Pussycat Cinema*,[254] which involved use of trademarks in an erotic film, by noting that the trademark use in *L.L. Bean* was an "editorial or artistic parody" used solely for noncommercial purposes.[255] The court noted that parody, although often inevitably offensive, enjoys an important role in society and is entitled to a full range of First Amendment protections.[256]

Finally, the court specifically declined to consider the constitutional limits that might be imposed on an anti-dilution statute where someone markets a product—for example, a T-shirt—whose principal purpose is to convey a message.[257] There is no clear consensus on this issue. The Eight Circuit upheld, in a 2-1 decision, an injunction against the marketing of T-Shirts, mugs, and other products bearing the words "Mutant of Omaha" and featuring a logo

---

[248]Power Test Petroleum Distribs. v. Calcu Gas, 754 F.2d 91, 97 (2d Cir. 1985); L.L. Bean, Inc. v. Drake Pubrs., 811 F.2d 26, 13 Media L. Rep. 2009 (1st Cir. 1987), *cert. denied and appeal dismissed*, 483 U.S. 1013 (1987).

[249]Lucasfilm v. High Frontier, 622 F. Supp. 931, 933–35 (D.D.C. 1985). *Lucasfilm* involved an attempt to enjoin various public interests groups from using its trademark, "Star Wars," to describe the Reagan administration's Strategic Defense Initiative. The court held that trademark laws "do not reach into the realm of public discourse to regulate the use of terms used outside the context of trade." *Id.* at 934.

[250]850 F.2d 26, 13 Media L. Rep. 2009 (1st Cir.), *cert. denied and appeal dismissed*, 483 U.S. 1013 (1987).

[251]The district court had denied L.L. Bean's motion for summary judgment on its trademark infringement, unfair competition, and deceptive trade practices claims, but granted summary judgment and an injunction based on Maine's trademark dilution law. *Id.* at 27, 13 Media L. Rep. at 2009. The district court ruled that the article "tarnished Bean's trademark by undermining the goodwill and reputation associated with the mark" and enjoined further publication or distribution of the "L.L. Beam Sex Catalog." *Id.*

[252]*Id.* at 30, 13 Media L. Rep. at 2012.

[253]*Id.* at 31, 13 Media L. Rep. at 2013.

[254]*See supra* note 245.

[255]811 F.2d at 31–32, 13 Media L. Rep. at 2013.

[256]*Id.* at 28, 33–34, 13 Media L. Rep. at 2010, 2014–15. *Accord* Cliffs Notes v. Bantam Doubleday Dell Pub'g Group, 886 F.2d 490, 493, 16 Media L. Rep. 2289, 2291 (2d Cir. 1989) ("[P]arody is a form of artistic expression, protected by the First Amendment."). In *Cliffs Notes,* the Second Circuit vacated an injunction against the publication of "Spy Notes," a parody of Cliffs Notes. *See also* Rogers v. Grimaldi, 875 F.2d 994, 997–98 (2d Cir. 1989) (case involving movie title; court "must construe the [Lanham] Act narrowly to avoid ... a conflict" with the First Amendment); Ocean Bio-Chem v. Turner Network Television, 741 F. Supp. 1546, 1553 (S.D. Fla. 1990) (use of business' name in fictional television show; "[w]hen First Amendment values are involved, the Lanham Act must be construed narrowly").

[257]811 F.2d at 32 n.4, 13 Media L. Rep. at 2014 n.4.

resembling the Mutual of Omaha logo, despite the fact that the district court found that the products were marketed primarily as a vehicle to express the artists' opposition to nuclear weapons.[258]

In *Tetley, Inc. v. Topps Chewing Gum*,[259] however, the court denied Tetley's request to enjoin the defendant from marketing "Wacky Packs" containing stickers reading "Petley Flea Bags" with letters and coloring similar to that used on Tetley tea bags.[260] The court noted that there were both obvious similarities and dissimilarities between the mark and the stickers: "This is because defendant's sticker is a broadly 'punned' adaptation of plaintiff's marks. The very broadness of the joke is a measure of the difference. . . ."[261] The court also noted that the products were sold in different noncompeting markets and that there was no evidence that anyone was actually confused as to the source of sponsorship of the "Petley" sticker.[262] The court also held that, although the defendant may have sought to satirize popular products "with the thought undoubtedly in mind that the more recognizable and popular the product . . . the more successful the particular sticker will be . . . there is no evidence that defendant . . . thought to realize that profit by means of confusion or contemplated injury to plaintiff's mark."[263]

§10.11 Student and Prison Newspapers

Newspapers and other publication that are published at government controlled institutions, e.g., schools and prisons, pose special prior restraint problems. These issues are discussed elsewhere.[264]

§10.12 Procedural Issues

In *Freedman v. Maryland*,[265] the Supreme Court held that a system of prior restraint "avoids constitutional infirmity only if it takes place under procedural safeguards designed to obviate the dangers of a censorship system."[266] In *Southeastern Promotions v. Conrad*, the Supreme Court reaffirmed the *Freedman* holding that

---

[258] Mutual of Omaha Ins. Co. v. Novak, 775 F.2d 247, 248–49 (8th Cir. 1985). The district court had held that Mutual of Omaha had made a sufficient showing of likelihood of confusion based on the strength of its mark, the obvious similarity between its mark and the plaintiff's designs, and the defendant's intent to associate his products with Mutual of Omaha. *Id.*

[259] 556 F. Supp. 785 (E.D.N.Y. 1983).

[260] *Id.* at 786, 796.

[261] *Id.* at 790. In *Cliffs Notes,* the Second Circuit held that parody need not be an "obvious joke . . . in order to be regarded as a parody. . . . parody may be sophisticated as well as slapstick. . . ." 886 F.2d at 495, 16 Media L. Rep. at 2293. The *Tetley* court also noted that the degree of similarity of products did not end with a comparison of the marks themselves. The stickers were not used as labels or packaging to sell other products, only became visible to consumers after the sticker's package was opened, were one of five stickers in a package, and clearly stated that they were satirical. 556 F. Supp. at 790.

[262] 556 F. Supp. at 790–91. The *Tetley* court distinguished Coca-Cola Co. v. Gemini Rising, 346 F. Supp. 1183 (E.D.N.Y. 1972), where the court enjoined the sale of a poster using the "Coca-Cola" logo and the message "Enjoy Cocaine," because in that case there was " 'factual proof that some persons of apparently average intelligence did attribute sponsorship to plaintiff and discontinued their use of plaintiff's product'." 556 F. Supp. at 792–93.

[263] 556 F. Supp. at 791.

[264] *See* Chapter 13, §13.5(B).

[265] 380 U.S. 51, 1 Media L. Rep. 1126 (1965).

[266] *Id.* at 58, 1 Media L. Rep. at 1128.

a system of prior restraint runs afoul of the First Amendment if it lacks certain safeguards: *First,* the burden of instituting judicial proceedings, and of proving that the material is unprotected, must rest on the censor. *Second,* any restraint prior to judicial review can be imposed only for a specified brief period and only for the purpose of preserving the status quo. *Third,* a prompt final judicial determination must be assured.[267]

Over the years, other procedural safeguards have been enunciated. In *National Socialist Party of America v. Village of Skokie,*[268] the Supreme Court reversed a ruling of the Illinois Supreme Court that denied a stay of an injunction and a request for an expedited appeal after the National Socialist Party of America was enjoined from parading through the village of Skokie, Illinois.[269] The Supreme Court held that "[i]f a State seeks to impose a restraint of this kind, it must provide strict procedural safeguards . . . including immediate appellate review . . . . Absent such review, the State must instead allow a stay."[270]

In *United States v. McKenzie,*[271] all of the judges for the Eastern District of Louisiana recused themselves from hearing a contempt proceeding.[272] A judge from another district then heard the contempt proceeding and found no contempt.[273] The private prosecutors, who had been appointed by all of the regular judges of the Eastern District, appealed. The Fifth Circuit held that, for purposes of the contempt proceeding, the visiting judge constituted the entire court for the Eastern District of Louisiana, so his dismissal of the contempt proceedings

> indicated that [the District Court for the Eastern District of Louisiana] did not wish the contempt proceeding to be pursued. The private prosecutors who derived their representation authority wholly from the district court for the Eastern District of Louisiana have had that authority wholly terminated by that same identical court.[274]

Another issue that sometimes arises in prior restraint cases is whether the court can order a party to turn over a copy of the materials it plans to disseminate so that the court may consider their contents before ruling on a request for a prior restraint. The district judge in *McKenzie* held that an order requiring CBS to turn over the script of the "60 Minutes" segment was unconstitutional.[275] Similarly, in *Goldblum v. National Broadcasting Corp.,*[276] Judge

---

[267]Southeastern Promotions v. Conrad, 420 U.S. 546, 560, 1 Media L. Rep. 1140, 1145 (1975) (citing Freedman v. Maryland, 380 U.S. 51, 58, 1 Media L. Rep. 1126, 1128 (1965)); Carroll v. President & Comm'rs of Princess Anne, 393 U.S. 175, 1 Media L. Rep. 1016 (1968) (temporary restraining order prohibiting members of white supremacist group from holding rally unconstitutional where order obtained without notice to other side and without using requisite procedural safeguards).
[268]432 U.S. 43, 2 Media L. Rep. 1993 (1977).
[269]*Id.* at 43–44, 2 Media L. Rep. at 1993.
[270]*Id.* at 44, 2 Media L. Rep. at 1993 (citations omitted).
[271]735 F.2d 907, 10 Media L. Rep. 1997 (5th Cir. 1984). See the discussion of this case *supra* note 194. In *McKenzie,* the District Court had cited CBS for contempt for failure to produce a copy of the script of a "60 Minutes" segment for in camera review by the court. The U.S. Justice Department declined to prosecute the contempt, and the District Court appointed private prosecutors to prosecute the criminal contempt. *Id.* at 910, 10 Media L. Rep. at 1999. All of the District Court judges disqualified themselves from hearing the contempt, and the Fifth Circuit appointed a District Court judge of the Eastern District as the "new" District Court. *Id.*
[272]*Id.* at 910, 10 Media L. Rep. at 1999.
[273]*Id.* at 910–11, 10 Media L. Rep. at 1999–2000.
[274]*Id.* at 911–12, 10 Media L. Rep. at 2000.
[275]*Id.* at 910, 10 Media L. Rep. at 1999.
[276]584 F.2d 904, 4 Media L. Rep. 1718 (9th Cir. 1978).

Anthony Kennedy wrote for the Ninth Circuit that a district court order requiring NBC to submit a film for review to assist the court in determining whether to issue an injunction enjoining the broadcast of the program "suffers the constitutional deficiencies of the application for an injunction. The order not only created a reasonable apprehension of an impending prior restraint, it was also a threatened interference with the editorial process. The district court's order was therefore void."[277] There is, however, at least one contrary decision.[278]

---

[277] Id. at 907, 10 Media L. Rep. at 1720.
[278] In re Capital Cities/ABC, 918 F.2d 140, 18 Media L. Rep. 1450 (11th Cir. 1990).

CHAPTER 11

COMMERCIAL SPEECH

§11.1 INTRODUCTION

This chapter addresses constitutional issues raised by laws that prohibit the publishing or broadcasting of commercial speech.[1] It describes (1) the tests for determining what constitutes "commercial speech,"[2] (2) the early evolution of the commercial speech doctrine in the U.S. Supreme Court,[3] (3) the four-part commercial speech test announced in *Central Hudson Gas & Electric Corp. v. Public Service Commission*[4] and the Court's application of that test,[5] and (4) later Supreme Court decisions, which have sometimes limited the protection afforded commercial speech.[6] This chapter also briefly discusses the law on specific types of advertising: liquor;[7] tobacco;[8] gambling and lotteries;[9] abortion, contraception, and family planning;[10] public utilities;[11] drug paraphernalia;[12] brothel and escort services;[13] housing and employment;[14] and professional advertising.[15]

§11.2 DEFINING COMMERCIAL SPEECH

The U.S. Supreme Court and lower courts have largely failed to come up with a workable definition of "commercial speech." The Supreme Court began by merely stating that "purely commercial advertising" was commercial speech.[16]

---

[1] The related issue of the media's liability for false advertisements and other similar statements is discussed in Chapter 7.
[2] *See infra* §11.2.
[3] *See infra* §11.3.
[4] 447 U.S. 557, 6 Media L. Rep. 1497 (1980).
[5] *See infra* §11.4.
[6] *See id.* (discussing Posadas de Puerto Rico v. Tourism Co., 478 U.S. 328, 13 Media L. Rep. 1033 (1986) and San Francisco Arts & Athletics v. United States Olympic Comm., 483 U.S. 522 (1987)).
[7] *See infra* §11.6(A).
[8] *See id.* at (B).
[9] *See id.* at (C).
[10] *See id.* at (D).
[11] *See id.* at (E).
[12] *See infra* §11.6(F).
[13] *See id.* at (G).
[14] *See id.* at (H).
[15] *See id.* at (I).
[16] Valentine v. Chrestensen, 316 U.S. 52, 54, 1 Media L. Rep. 1907, 1908 (1942). *Accord* Central Hudson Gas & Elec. Corp. v. Public Serv. Comm'n (Central Hudson), 447 U.S. 557, 562–63, 6 Media L. Rep. 1497, 1499–1500 (1980); Virginia Bd. of Pharmacy v. Virginia Citizens Consumer Council (Virginia Pharmacy), 425 U.S. 748, 771–72 n.24, 1 Media L. Rep. 1930, 1938–39 n.24 (1976).

Since then, the Court has generally relied on "common sense" in drawing the line between commercial and noncommercial speech, defining commercial speech as "speech which does 'no more than propose a commercial transaction.'"[17] The Court has rarely explained what this terse statement means or described what "common sense" differences it considers important.

The Court's most elaborate attempt to define commercial speech occurred in *Bolger v. Youngs Drug Products Corp.*[18] In that case, the Court outlined three factors to be considered in mixed speech cases, i.e., ones that contain elements of both commercial and noncommercial speech: whether the speech (1) is advertising, (2) makes reference to a specific product, and (3) is motivated by a desire for profits.[19] The Court in *Bolger* held that, considered alone, each of these factors was insufficient to render speech commercial, but that a combination of all of these factors provided "strong support" for concluding that speech is commercial.[20] However, the Court also explained that it was unnecessary that all three factors be present for speech to be commercial and refused to decide "whether reference to any particular product or service is a necessary element of commercial speech."[21]

Applying these three factors, the Court in *Bolger* found that pamphlets relating to condom use constituted commercial speech—despite the fact that they largely contained discussions of "important public issues" such as factual material about the use of condoms for family planning and venereal disease prevention—because the pamphlets (1) were "conceded to be advertisements," (2) referred to specific products, and (3) were economically motivated.[22]

Three years earlier, the Court in *Central Hudson* had reached a similar conclusion, holding that promotional advertising by an electric utility company discussing energy conservation was commercial speech.[23] The Court reasoned

---

[17]*Virginia Pharmacy*, 425 U.S. at 762, 1 Media L. Rep. at 1935 (quoting Pittsburgh Press Co. v. Pittsburgh Comm'n on Human Relations, 413 U.S. 376, 385, 1 Media L. Rep. 1908, 1912 (1973)); *Central Hudson*, 447 U.S. at 562, 6 Media L. Rep. at 1499; Ohralik v. Ohio State Bar Ass'n, 436 U.S. 447, 455–56 (1978). *Accord* Bolger v. Youngs Drug Prods. Corp., 463 U.S. 60, 66 (1983) ("core notion" of commercial speech is speech proposing commercial transaction).

As two commentators have noted, "[m]any of the commercial speech cases refer to the 'common sense differences' between commercial and noncommercial speech, as if further explication of these differences would be beneath the dignity of the Court." Kozinski & Banner, *Who's Afraid of Commercial Speech?* 76 VA. L. REV. 627, 634 (1990). The authors go on to state that a "close reading of the cases" reveals that the Court has found commercial speech different from noncommercial speech because (1) "commercial speech is more objective than noncommercial speech because its truth is more easily verifiable" and (2) since "commercial speech is engaged in for profit, it is claimed to be more durable than noncommercial speech." *Id.* They also contend that these two alleged differences are unsupportable. *Id.* at 634–38.

[18]463 U.S. at 68.

[19]*Id.* at 66–67.

[20]*Id.* at 67. The Court also said that, despite the presence of these three factors, speech advertising an activity that is itself protected by the First Amendment may not be "commercial speech." *Id.* at 67 n.14 (citing Murdock v. Pennsylvania, 319 U.S. 105 (1943) (advertising for religious book cannot be regulated as commercial speech) and Jamison v. Texas, 318 U.S. 413, 417 (1943) (handbills inviting public to attend religious meeting at which no admission would be charged cannot be regulated as commercial speech even though handbills contained advertising to sell religious books)).

[21]463 U.S. at 67 n.14. The Court acknowledged that commercial speech typically refers to a specific product or service, but stated that a generic reference to a product does not necessarily prevent speech from being labeled commercial. *Id.* at 66. For example, a company with sufficient market control or a trade association may be able to promote a product without referring to a specific brand name. *Id.* at 66–67 n.13.

[22]*Id.* at 67–68. The two "informational" pamphlets at issue were titled "Condoms and Human Sexuality" and "Plain Talk About Venereal Disease." The only reference to the contraceptive company was in the second pamphlet, at the bottom of the last page. *Id.* at 66. Despite its conclusion that the speech involved was commercial, the Court in *Bolger* held that, as applied, the federal statute at issue, which prohibited the unsolicited mailing of advertising for contraceptives, was unconstitutional. *Id.* at 67–68. *See infra* §11.6(D).

[23]447 U.S. 557, 6 Media L. Rep. 1497 (1980).

that, despite the "heavy presumption" against government regulation of ads conveying information of public concern, advertising that "links a product to a current public debate" may be commercial speech.[24]

Even though speaker motivation was a factor considered in *Bolger,* the Court has been inconsistent on whether motive should be considered in determining whether speech is commercial. In *Valentine v. Chrestensen,*[25] one of the first commercial speech cases that the Court decided, the majority indicated that the decisive factor in labeling speech commercial was whether a speaker's motive was to make a profit from the sale of commercial goods.[26]

The Court later came to the opposite conclusion in *New York Times Co. v. Sullivan,* where it rejected the plaintiff's argument that a newspaper advertisement placed by a civil rights group to solicit donations was commercial speech simply because the publisher's only motive was to make money.[27] Instead, the Court looked to the advertisement's content to determine its status as commercial or noncommercial.[28]

For several years after *Sullivan,* the Supreme Court appeared to define commercial speech solely by content. For example, the Court focused on the content of help-wanted ads to hold that they were "classic examples of commercial speech" that did "no more than propose a commercial transaction."[29] An abortion advertisement was protected speech, however, because it "did more than simply propose a commercial transaction. It contained factual material of clear 'public interest.' "[30]

While a majority of the Court appeared during this post-*Sullivan* period to reject profit motive as a factor in determining whether speech was commercial, there were indications that consideration of motive had not been completely discarded. In a footnote in *Virginia Board of Pharmacy v. Virginia Citizens Consumer Council (Virginia Pharmacy),* for example, Justice Harry Blackmun said that one reason commercial speech is not "wholly undifferentiable from other" protected speech is that "advertising is the *sine qua non* of

---

[24]*Id.* at 562 n.5, 6 Media L. Rep. at 1499–1500 n.5 ("[a] company has the full panoply of protections available to its direct comments on public issues, so there is no reason for providing similar constitutional protection when such statements are made in the context of commercial transactions."). *See also* Zauderer v. Office of Disciplinary Counsel, 471 U.S. 626, 687 n.7 (1985) (though statements about legal rights of Dalkon Shield victims would be "fully protected speech" in some contexts, such statements constituted commercial speech in attorney's newspaper ad).

[25]316 U.S. 52, 1 Media L. Rep. 1907 (1942).

[26]*Id.* at 54, 1 Media L. Rep. at 1908 (speaker's only motive was "pur[suit of] a gainful occupation"). *See also* Breard v. Alexandria, 341 U.S. 622 (1951) (upholding ordinance prohibiting door-to-door sales of magazine subscriptions based on speaker's economic motives and not magazines' content). *Compare* Murdock v. Pennsylvania, 319 U.S. 105 (1943) (upholding First Amendment right of Jehovah's Witnesses to sell religious materials door-to-door); Village of Schaumburg v. Citizens for a Better Env't, 444 U.S. 620, 630–32 (1980) (because charitable solicitation does more than inform economic decisions it is not purely commercial speech).

[27]376 U.S. 254, 1 Media L. Rep. 1527 (1964).

[28]*Id.* at 266, 1 Media L. Rep. at 1532 (speech at issue was not commercial because it "communicated information, expressed opinion, recited grievances, protested claimed abuses and sought financial support on behalf of a movement whose existence and objectives are matters of the highest public interest and concern").

[29]Pittsburgh Press Co. v. Pittsburgh Comm'n on Human Relations, 413 U.S. 376, 385, 1 Media L. Rep. 1908, 1912 (1973).

[30]Bigelow v. Virginia, 421 U.S. 809, 822, 1 Media L. Rep. 1919, 1924 (1975). Justice William Rehnquist, joined by Justice Byron White, disagreed with the majority's content-based approach. *Id.* at 831, 1 Media L. Rep. at 1927 (Rehnquist, J., dissenting ("[t]his was a proposal to furnish [abortion] services on a commercial basis, and since we have always refused to distinguish for First Amendment purposes on the basis of content, [an abortion service ad] is no different from an advertisement for a bucket shop operation or a Ponzi scheme").

commercial profits."[31] In the 1980 landmark *Central Hudson* case, a majority of the Court arguably affirmed Justice Blackmun's approach, stating that "expression related solely to the economic interests of the speaker and its audience" is commercial speech.[32]

In 1988, the Court clouded even further the issue of speaker motive. In *Riley v. National Federation of the Blind*,[33] the Court held that a regulation requiring professional fundraisers to disclose to potential donors the percentage of charitable contributions actually turned over to charity should *not* be examined under the "more deferential" commercial speech doctrine.[34] The state in *Riley* had argued that "even if charitable solicitations generally are fully protected," the regulatory provision at issue concerned only commercial speech, "because it relates only to the professional fundraiser's profit from the solicited contribution."[35] The Court disagreed:

> It is not clear that a professional's speech is necessarily commercial whenever it relates to that person's financial motivation for speaking.... *But even assuming, without deciding, that such speech in the abstract is merely "commercial," we do not believe that the speech retains its commercial character when it is inextricably intertwined with other fully protected speech.* Our lodestars in deciding what level of scrutiny to apply to a compelled statement must be the *nature of the speech taken as a whole....Thus, where, as here, the component parts of a single speech are inextricably intertwined, we cannot parcel out the speech applying one test to one phrase and another test to another phrase.* Such an endeavor would be both artificial and impractical. Therefore, we apply our test for fully protected expression.[36]

The following year, in *Board of Trustees v. Fox*,[37] the Court again indicated that speaker motive may be relevant to whether speech is commercial and stated that when a speaker seeks to "propose a commercial transaction," his or her speech is commercial.[38]

Lower court opinions largely reflect the Supreme Court's failure to articudlate a clear test for deciding whether speech is commercial or noncommercial. In *National Commission on Egg Nutrition v. Federal Trade Commission*, for example, the Seventh Circuit held that an egg industry advertisement stating that there is no scientific evidence that eating eggs increases the risk of high cholesterol and heart disease was commercial speech.[39] The court rejected the

---

[31]425 U.S. 748, 771 n.24, 1 Media L. Rep. 1930, 1938–39 n.24 (1976). *See also* In re Primus, 436 U.S. 412, 438 n.32 (1978) (line between commercial and noncommercial speech "based in part on the motive of the speaker and the character of the expressive activity").

[32]447 U.S. 557, 561, 6 Media L. Rep. 1497, 1499 (1980). Justice John Paul Stevens, however, noted that it was unclear whether this definition used the speech's subject matter or the speaker's motive as the "limiting factor." *Id.* at 579, 6 Media L. Rep. at 1507 (Stevens, J., concurring). Justice Stevens felt that a speaker's economic motive should not be used to qualify the constitutional protection afforded one's speech. *Id.* at 580, 6 Media L. Rep. at 1507.

According to one commentator, the Court has distinguished commercial advertising from commercially motivated speech that addresses noncommercial issues, although he admits that this distinction is not always clear. Lively, *The Supreme Court and Commercial Speech: New Words With an Old Message*, 72 MINN. L. REV. 289 (1987).

[33]487 U.S. 781 (1988).

[34]*Id.* at 795 (statute regulating solicitation of charitable contributions unconstitutional under strict scrutiny standard).

[35]*Id.*

[36]*Id.* (emphasis added).

[37]492 U.S. 469 (1989).

[38]*Id.* at 473–74 (citation omitted).

[39]570 F.2d 157, 3 Media L. Rep. 2196 (7th Cir. 1977), *cert. denied*, 439 U.S. 821, 4 Media L. Rep. 1560 (1978). For a critical review of the Seventh Circuit's holding in this case and a discussion of the difficulty in labeling such "advertisals," see Kozinski & Banner, *supra* note 17, at 638–48.

petitioner's contentions that the ads did not fit the *Virginia Pharmacy* paradigm of " 'speech that does no more than propose a commercial transaction' " and instead were "expressions of opinion on an important and controversial public issue."[40] The Seventh Circuit based its decision, in part, on its finding that the egg advertisements were not phrased as opinion, but instead were motivated by a desire for profit and were "made for the purpose of persuading people who read them to buy eggs."[41]

Other courts have reached contrary results concerning the issue of speaker motive in similar cases. For example, the initial holding in *R.J. Reynolds Tobacco Co.* was that speech could not be labeled commercial based solely on speaker motive, although a later decision to remand for more discovery left the definitional issue undecided.[42] In *Reynolds,* an administrative law judge (ALJ), faced with the sole issue of whether a Reynolds statement relating to cigarettes and heart disease was commercial speech, held that the ad was an "editorial" expressing Reynolds' "point of view on the issue of smoking and health" and thus was not commercial speech.[43] The ALJ's decision was later reversed and the case remanded by an FTC panel, which held that the ALJ should not have dismissed the complaint until further discovery was completed and that he could consider the various "messages, means, and motives of the advertisement" in determining whether it was commercial speech.[44]

---

[40]570 F.2d at 162–63 (petitioner was group formed by egg industry members to counteract "anti-cholesterol attacks on eggs").

[41]*Id.* at 163 (concluding that Supreme Court did not intend definition of commercial speech "to be narrowly limited to a mere proposal of a particular commercial transaction but [instead intended to] extend [the definition] to false claims as a to the harmlessness of the advertiser's product asserted for the purpose of persuading members of the reading public to buy the product"). *See also* Briggs & Stratton Corp. v. Baldridge, 728 F.2d 915 (7th Cir.), *cert. denied,* 469 U.S. 826 (1984) (companies' responses to questionnaires sent by several Arab countries to companies they suspected of violating boycott of Israel were commercial speech because speakers' motivation was solely economic; therefore, Export Administration Act, 50 U.S.C.A. §§2401–20 (1991), which prohibited companies from furnishing such information about their compliance with boycott, was constitutional); Association of Nat'l Advertisers v. Lungren, 809 F. Supp. 747, 752, 754 (N.D. Cal. 1992) (statute that regulates "green advertising," e.g., use of terms like "biodegradable," and "ozone friendly," is commercial speech because it applies only to representations that specific good possesses particular environmental attributes).

[42]51 Antitrust & Trade Reg. Rep. (BNA) No. 1277, at 219 (Aug. 4, 1986), *appeal docketed,* No. 9206 (FTC Aug. 7, 1986), *petition for stay of FTC remand of case for lack of jurisdiction and writ of mandamus docketed,* 5 Trade Reg. Rep. (CCH) No. 9206, §22,565, at 22,164 (July 1, 1988). The parties settled in May 1990. No. 9206 (FTC May 8, 1990).

[43]Trade Reg. Rep. [1983–87 Transfer Binder] FTC Complaints & Ords. (CCH) No. 9206, §22,386, at 23,467 (Aug. 6, 1986). Reynolds had placed a full-page ad in several leading newspapers and magazines discussing the results of a government-funded study designed to test various factors on coronary heart disease rates. The ad concluded that "the controversy over smoking and health remains an open one." The ad did not include any brand names, prices, or express promotional language. The ALJ dismissed the complaint because the Federal Trade Commission (FTC) only has jurisdiction over commercial speech, not speech that deserves full First Amendment protection. Further discovery, according to the ALJ, was "contrary to law and unacceptable" because the determination of whether speech is commercial is "customarily resolved by the courts on the basis of what is contained in the ads." 5 Trade Reg. Rep. (CCH) No. 9206, ¶22,522, at 22,182 (Apr. 11, 1988).

[44]5 Trade Reg. Rep. (CCH) No. 9206, §22,522, at 22,180 (Apr. 11, 1988). *See also* New York Pub. Interest Research Group v. Insurance Info. Inst., 531 N.Y.S.2d 1002, 1010–13 (N.Y. Sup. Ct. 1988), *aff'd,* 554 N.Y.S.2d 590 (N.Y. App. Div. 1990) (insurance information organization's ads describing current "Lawsuit Crisis" and need for tort reform not commercial speech because they did not intend to promote sales of insurance and did "not propose a commercial transaction"); New York City v. American Sch. Pubns., 505 N.Y.S.2d 594, 13 Media L. Rep. 1194 (N.Y. App. Div. 1986), *aff'd,* 509 N.E.2d 311, 14 Media L. Rep. 1153 (N.Y. 1987) (magazine containing (1) ads for defendant's school and (2) unrelated stories not commercial speech because publisher's intentions cannot be only factor used to determine if speech is commercial); Rutledge v. Liability Ins. Indus., 487 F. Supp. 5, 8, 5 Media L. Rep. 1153, 1155 (W.D. La. 1979) (insurance industry ad stressing loss prevention and legislative reform as best ways to cope with current insurance crisis not commercial speech despite advertisers' financial interests in sponsoring ad campaign because ads made "no attempt to sell insurance coverage; they propose no commercial transaction;" plaintiff, an attorney, had alleged ad was commercial speech because it attempted to improperly influence jurors to render lower damage awards).

In addition to speaker motivation, lower courts have considered other factors in determining whether to label speech commercial or noncommercial. For example, in *Ad World v. Township of Doylestown,* the Third Circuit held that a local weekly tabloid distributed without charge that carried extensive advertising and a few pages of consumer and community information was not commercial speech.[45] The court based its decision, in part, on the fact that the ratio of news and editorials to advertising was similar to large metropolitan newspapers.[46] Later in its opinion, however, the Third Circuit appeared to back away from this ratio approach, stating that "[t]he line between commercial and non-commercial speech for first amendment purposes cannot be drawn by some magic ratio of editorial to advertising content. The important question is whether the publication as a whole relates solely to the economic interest of the speaker and its audience."[47]

In *Minnesota Newspaper Association v. Postmaster General,* the court held that "[l]ists of (lottery) prizes awarded, which are ... prohibited by 18 U.S.C. section 1302, do not fit within the definition of commercial speech," although "a prize list contained within a lottery advertisement is commercial speech."[48] The court reasoned that prize lists have no "inherent claim ... to First Amendment protection."[49] Instead, it is the context of the prize list in an advertisement or a news report that determines the level of First Amendment protection it deserves.[50] As this and the other cases cited in this section demonstrate, however, the test for commercial speech remains unsettled.

---

[45] 672 F.2d 1136, 8 Media L. Rep. 1073 (3d Cir.), *cert. denied,* 456 U.S. 975 (1982). *Accord* Pacific Gas & Elec. Co. v. Public Utils. Comm'n, 475 U.S. 1, 8–9 (1986) (newsletter distributed by privately owned utility in its monthly billing statement that included political editorials, energy conservation tips, and other matters of public concern was not commercial speech).

[46] *Id.* at 1139.

[47] *Id.* (citation omitted). The Second Circuit later disagreed with *Ad World*'s holding that "the Supreme Court has limited commercial speech solely to product or service advertising." Securities & Exch. Comm'n v. Lowe, 725 F.2d 892, 900, 10 Media L. Rep. 1225, 1231 (2d Cir. 1984), *rev'd on other grounds,* 472 U.S. 181 (1985) (investment newsletter about economic and financial conditions is commercial speech despite fact it addressed commercial, political, social, and economic matters). Although it reversed the Second Circuit in *Lowe* on statutory grounds and held that the petitioners could not be enjoined from publishing the newsletter, the U.S. Supreme Court did not address the classification issue. *See also* Fargo Women's Health Org. v. Larson, 381 N.W.2d 176, 181 (N.D.), *cert. denied,* 476 U.S. 1108 (1986) (pro-life clinic's advertising for pregnancy testing services was commercial speech despite its assertion that ads were entitled to full First Amendment protection because they constituted political advocacy and testing services were free; "advertisers cannot, by merely including references to public issues or public debate," claim their speech is noncommercial); IDK, Inc. v. Clark County, 836 F.2d 1185, 1194–95 (9th Cir. 1988) (upholding regulation making it unlawful to operate and advertise "escort service" and rejecting escort service's assertion that more than commercial speech was impinged); Hornstein v. Hartigan, 676 F. Supp. 894, 895, 15 Media L. Rep. 1769 (C.D. Ill. 1988) (statute providing that no person may solicit ads to appear in any firefighters' publication without first obtaining state approval struck down, in part, because it regulated commercial and noncommercial speech; plaintiff was publisher of periodical, directed at lay audience, that covered fire safety and was distributed for free and funded solely by ads).

[48] 677 F. Supp. 1400, 1406–07, 15 Media L. Rep. 1292, 1297 (1987).

[49] *Id.* State courts too have wrestled with what constitutes commercial speech. In Loska v. Superior Court, 233 Cal. Rptr. 213, 219–20 (Cal. Ct. App. 1986), a California appellate court upheld the constitutionality of a municipal ordinance that prohibited offers to sell admission tickets to any assemblage in any public place, unless the sale was at an established ticket office, because it involved commercial speech. Two earlier California decisions reached different results. In Spiritual Psychic Science Church v. City of Azusa, 703 P.2d 1119, 1122 (Cal. 1988), the California Supreme Court held that fortune-telling for profit involves noncommercial speech because fortune-telling involves the passing of ideas between the teller and the client. Similarly, in Welton v. City of Los Angeles, 566 P.2d 1119 (Cal. 1976), the court held that selling maps of stars' homes did not constitute commercial speech.

[50] 677 F. Supp. at 1406–07, 15 Media L. Rep. at 1297.

§11.3 Early Evolution of the Commercial Speech Doctrine in the Supreme Court

The origins of the commercial speech doctrine are usually traced to the Supreme Court's 1942 decision in *Valentine v. Chrestensen*,[51] which involved a First Amendment challenge to a city ordinance prohibiting the distribution of "commercial and business advertising matter" in the streets.[52] In an opinion Justice William Douglas later characterized as "casual, almost off-hand,"[53] the Court upheld the ordinance's application to the distributor of a handbill that promoted submarine tours on one side and protested the city's denial of wharfage facilities on the other.[54] While noting that streets are proper places for disseminating information and opinions, the Court focused on the speaker's economic motivation and held that it was clear the Constitution imposed no restraint on the government respecting "purely commercial advertising."[55]

Three significant points stand out in *Chrestensen:* first, the unambiguous and still vital holding that commercial advertising of illegal activities is unprotected by the First Amendment,[56] which courts have frequently relied on to uphold restrictions on commercial speech promoting illegal products or services. As the Court later stated in *Central Hudson,* First Amendment interests are "altogether absent when the commercial activity itself is illegal and the restriction on advertising is incidental to a valid limitation on economic activity."[57]

Second, although several Supreme Court cases have read *Chrestensen* to imply that advertising for legal activities merits First Amendment protection,[58] this approach has been at least tempered by the Court's 1986 decision in *Posadas de Puerto Rico v. Tourism Co.,* which held that advertising for an admittedly legal activity could be banned by the government.[59]

Third, *Chrestensen* indicated that, to the extent commercial speech might merit protection, the interests served by the First Amendment should be weighed against the government's interest in the regulation.[60] As described below, this "balancing" approach figures prominently in later commercial speech cases.

---

[51]316 U.S. 52, 54, 1 Media L. Rep. 1907, 1908 (1942). Even before *Chrestensen,* the Supreme Court had rejected First Amendment challenges to advertising regulations, typically upholding such laws as legitimate government controls on economic activity based on a due process analysis. *See, e.g.,* Semler v. Oregon State Bd. of Dental Examiners, 294 U.S. 608 (1935) (upholding statutory prohibition on dental advertising); Packer Corp. v. Utah, 285 U.S. 105 (1932) (upholding prohibition of cigarette advertising on billboards).

[52]316 U.S. at 53 n.1, 1 Media L. Rep. at 1907 n.1 Many years later, the ordinance that *Chrestensen* upheld was held to be unconstitutional by the New York Court of Appeals, based on the Supreme Court's post-*Chrestensen* decision in *Virginia Pharmacy.* People v. Remeny, 355 N.E.2d 375 (N.Y. 1976).

[53]Cammarano v. United States, 358 U.S. 498, 514 (1959) (Douglas, J., concurring).

[54]316 U.S. at 53–55.

[55]*Id.* at 54. The Court summarily dismissed the political protest about wharfage facilities on the other side of the leaflet, finding that the protest had been placed there solely to evade the ordinance. *Id.* at 55.

[56]*Id.* at 54–55. *See also Central Hudson,* 447 U.S. 557, 566, 6 Media L. Rep. 1497, 1501 (1980) (for commercial speech to receive First Amendment protection it "at least must concern *lawful activity* and not be misleading").

[57]447 U.S. at 563–64, 6 Media L. Rep. at 1500 (citation omitted). *Accord* Bolger v. Youngs Drug Prods. Corp., 463 U.S. 60, 68 (1983) (for commercial speech to merit constitutional protection it must concern lawful activity).

[58]*See, e.g.,* Murdock v. Pennsylvania, 319 U.S. 105 (1943); Jamison v. Texas, 318 U.S. 413 (1943).

[59]478 U.S. 328, 13 Media L. Rep. 1033 (1986) (regulation prohibiting advertising for legal gambling activities constitutional).

[60]316 U.S. 52, 54, 1 Media L. Rep. 1907, 1908 (1942).

In 1964, the Supreme Court decided the seminal libel case of *New York Times Co. v. Sullivan,* which involved a newspaper's publication of an advertisement by a civil rights group.[61] The Court rejected the argument that, because the newspaper had been paid to print the advertisement, it was unworthy of First Amendment protection on the theory that it was unprotected commercial speech.[62]

In the 1970s, the Supreme Court began to reevaluate the commercial speech doctrine. In 1973, in *Pittsburgh Press Co. v. Pittsburgh Commission on Human Relations,* the Court upheld an injunction that prohibited the *Pittsburgh Press* from publishing want-ads under the headings of "Help Wanted—Men" or "Help Wanted—Women."[63] The injunction was based on a local ordinance that prohibited employment discrimination on the basis of sex.[64] In a 5-4 decision, the Court held that the want-ads were commercial speech.[65] The Court carefully finessed the newspaper's assertion that *Chrestensen* should be overruled by distinguishing that case on the grounds that the activity advertised in *Pittsburgh Press* was illegal.[66] Thus, the Court left open the possibility that commercial speech promoting legal activities might merit some First Amendment protection.[67]

Two years later, the Court took another step toward holding that commercial speech merited at least some First Amendment protection. In *Bigelow v. Virginia,* the Court invalidated a newspaper editor's conviction under a state statute that barred publication of material encouraging or promoting abortion services.[68] The editor in *Bigelow* published an advertisement in Virginia for an abortion referral agency in New York, where, unlike Virginia, abortions were then legal.[69]

After finding that the advertising was commercial speech deserving some First Amendment protection, the Court adopted a balancing test that weighed the First Amendment interests served by the speech's dissemination against the state's interest in suppressing it.[70] Rather than remand the case to the state court for such balancing, the Court itself determined that the Virginia statute

---

[61]376 U.S. 254, 1 Media L. Rep. 1527 (1964) (advertisement solicited donations for Committee to Defend Martin Luther King and the Struggle for Freedom in the South).

[62]*Id.* at 266, 1 Media L. Rep. at 1523.

[63]413 U.S. 376, 391, 1 Media L. Rep. 1908, 1914 (1973). One year before *Pittsburgh Press,* the Court upheld the Public Health Cigarette Smoking Act of 1969, 15 U.S.C.S. §§1331–41 (1993), which banned cigarette advertising in any electronic medium. Capital Broadcasting Co. v. Mitchell, 333 F. Supp. 582 (D.D.C. 1971), *aff'd mem. sub nom.* Capital Broadcasting Co. v. Acting Att'y Gen., 405 U.S. 1000 (1972). Although the district court largely based its decision on the unique nature of the electronic media, its holding indicated that the government may restrict truthful advertising of a legal product if it considers such advertising harmful. This notion was resurrected by the Supreme Court in 1986. *Posadas,* 478 U.S. at 344–45, 13 Media L. Rep. at 1040–41.

[64]413 U.S. at 378.

[65]*Id.* at 388–91.

[66]*Id.* at 388.

[67]Several justices were critical of *Chrestensen* around the time *Pittsburgh Press* was decided. *See* Lehman v. City of Shaker Heights, 418 U.S. 298, 314 n.6 (1974) (Brennan, J., dissenting) (questioning whether *Chrestensen* "retains continuing validity"); Dun & Bradstreet, Inc. v. Grove, 404 U.S. 898, 904–05 (1971) (Douglas, J., dissenting from denial of certiorari) (calling *Chrestensen* "ill-conceived").

[68]421 U.S. 809, 1 Media L. Rep. 1919 (1975).

[69]*Id.* at 812.

[70]*Id.* at 827–28, 1 Media L. Rep. at 1926. While not expressly overruling *Chrestensen,* the Court asserted that in *Chrestensen* it had merely affirmed a reasonable time, place, and manner restriction and had not immunized all commercial speech regulations from First Amendment challenge. *Id.* at 819–20, 1 Media L. Rep. at 1923.

served no legitimate state interest, because Virginia had no power to regulate the performance of abortions in New York on women from Virginia.[71]

Constitutional protection was finally expressly extended to pure commercial speech in the 1976 case of *Virginia Pharmacy*, which involved a challenge to a Virginia statute that prohibited pharmacists from advertising prescription drug prices.[72] This statute was challenged by drug customers who claimed a First Amendment right to receive all drug price information pharmacists desired to communicate.[73] After holding that consumers had standing to bring such a suit,[74] the Court stressed the importance of advertising to consumers: the poor, sick, and elderly, who typically lack the ability to comparison shop, as well as society as a whole, value such speech because it provides information regarding the price and availability of goods and services.[75]

Recognizing that it was squarely presented with the question of whether commercial speech merited First Amendment protection, the Court in *Virginia Pharmacy* stated: "Our question is whether speech which does 'no more than propose a commercial transaction,' . . . is so removed from any 'exposition of ideas' . . . that it lacks all protection. Our answer is that it is not."[76] The Court then discussed Virginia's justifications for enacting the statute—including the need to "maintain a high degree of professionalism on the part of licensed pharmacists"—but found that while it could not "discount the [state's] justifications entirely," such justifications could not survive the "close inspection" required by the First Amendment.[77] The Court went on to dismiss the balancing approach of *Bigelow* and *Pittsburgh Press* as constitutionally inappropriate:

> [T]he choice among these alternative approaches is not ours to make or the Virginia General Assembly's. *It is precisely this kind of choice,* between the dangers of suppressing information, and the dangers of its misuse if it is freely available, *that the First Amendment makes for us.*[78]

The Court then rejected as "highly paternalistic" the view that a state is better able than its citizens to determine what commercial information they should receive.[79] Such a view, according to the Court, is inconsistent with the

---

[71] *Id.* One important justification for the Court's holding in *Bigelow* was the public's need for commercial information. The Court also found that Virginia's regulation would unduly burden interstate commerce. *Id.* at 828–29, 1 Media L. Rep. at 1926–27.

[72] 425 U.S. 748, 1 Media L. Rep. 1930 (1976).

[73] *Id.* at 754.

[74] *Id.* at 763–64, 1 Media L. Rep. at 1935 (consumer's interest in "free flow of commercial information . . . may be as keen, if not keener by far, than his interest in the day's most urgent political debate").

Justice Rehnquist, the sole dissenter, strongly disagreed, contending that there is no right to receive information another seeks to disseminate. *Id.* at 782, 1 Media L. Rep. at 1942–43 (Rehnquist, J., dissenting). In a statement that foreshadowed his 1986 majority opinion in *Posadas,* Justice Rehnquist also said, "[u]nder the Court's opinion the way will be open not only for dissemination of price information but for active promotion of prescription drugs, liquor, cigarettes, and other products the use of which it has previously been thought desirable to discourage." *Id.* at 781, 1 Media L. Rep. at 1942 (Rehnquist, J., dissenting).

[75] *Id.* at 765, 1 Media L. Rep. at 1936. The Court reasoned that "[s]o long as we preserve a predominantly free enterprise economy," the "free flow of commercial information" is "indispensable" in encouraging enlightened economic decision-making by the public. Again, Justice Rehnquist disagreed. He viewed the public's need to make enlightened decisions as limited to "political, social, and other public issues, rather than the decision of a particular individual as to whether to purchase one or another kind of shampoo." *Id.* at 787, 1 Media L. Rep. at 1945 (Rehnquist, J., dissenting).

[76] *Id.* at 762, 1 Media L. Rep. at 1935 (citations omitted).

[77] 425 U.S. at 766–70, 1 Media L. Rep. at 1936–38.

[78] *Id.* at 770, 1 Media L. Rep. at 1938 (emphasis added).

[79] *Id.*

First Amendment principle that "people will perceive their own best interests if only they are well enough informed."[80]

Though adopting what has been referred to as a "per se approach" to commercial speech,[81] the Court softened the impact of *Virginia Pharmacy* in its famous footnote 24:

> There are commonsense differences between speech that does "no more than propose a commercial transaction," and other varieties. Even if the differences do not justify the conclusion that commercial speech is valueless ... they nonetheless suggest that a different degree of protection is necessary to insure that the flow of truthful and legitimate commercial information is unimpaired.[82]

A key reason cited by the Court for affording commercial speech less First Amendment protection was that it was unlikely that appropriate regulation would chill such speech.[83] The Court concluded that content-neutral time, place, and manner restrictions—as well as regulation of false and misleading advertisements and advertisements for illegal products or services—could be upheld, even where such restrictions on noncommercial speech would certainly be unconstitutional.[84] This left a gap in the "per se" approach that later enabled the Court to give much greater deference to state regulations than would otherwise appear possible under *Virginia Pharmacy*.

Supreme Court decisions immediately following *Virginia Pharmacy* are generally consistent with its basic thrust, holding that content-based restrictions

---

[80]*Id.* Thus, the Court concluded that a state may not "completely suppress the dissemination of concededly truthful information about entirely lawful activity, fearful of that information's effect upon its disseminators and its recipients." *Id.* at 773, 1 Media L. Rep. at 1939. As described below, this conclusion was effectively rejected 10 years later in Posadas de Puerto Rico v. Tourism Co., 478 U.S. 328, 13 Media L. Rep. 1033 (1986).

[81]Note, *Constitutional Protection of Commercial Speech,* 82 COLUM. L. REV. 720, 726 (1982) (under "per se approach," state cannot, consistent with First Amendment, "suppress truthful and nonmisleading advertising of lawful products"; courts, therefore, could not balance interests at stake when deciding whether commercial speech is protected).

[82]*Virginia Pharmacy,* 425 U.S. at 771 n.24, 1 Media L. Rep. at 1938–39 n.24 (citation omitted). In footnote 24, the Court also stated that the prohibition against prior restraints "may" be inapplicable to commercial speech because of its "hardiness." *Id.* The application of the prior restraint doctrine to commercial speech cases remains somewhat unclear. For example, in 1985 it was a concurring Justice White's view that, when commercial speech was at issue, prior restraints must be "narrowly tailored to advance a legitimate governmental interest," but were not "presumptively invalid," as is the case with fully protected speech. Lowe v. Securities & Exch. Comm'n, 472 U.S. 181, 235 (1985) (White, J., concurring). *See also* Fargo Women's Health Org. v. Larson, 381 N.W.2d 176, 180 (N.D.), *cert. denied,* 476 U.S. 1108 (1986) ("it is quite clear that prior restraints on commercial speech are allowed to an extent which would not be allowed toward other forms of protected speech"); Republic Entertainment v. Clark County, 672 P.2d 634 (Nev. 1983) (regulation prohibiting advertising of unlicensed or "sexually-oriented" escort services not unconstitutional prior restraint because it concerned only commercial speech related to activity state could regulate or prohibit). *Compare* Beneficial Corp. v. Federal Trade Comm'n, 542 F.2d 611, 619 (3d Cir. 1976), *cert. denied,* 430 U.S. 983 (1977) ("the remedy for the perceived violation can go no further in imposing a prior restraint on protected commercial speech than is reasonably necessary to accomplish the remedial objective of preventing the violation"). *See generally* Note, *Prior Restraints and Restrictions on Advertising After Virginia Pharmacy Board: The Commercial Speech Doctrine Reformulated,* 43 MO. L. REV. 64 (1978).

The Supreme Court has also held that the application of the overbreadth doctrine to such speech is "highly questionable." *See, e.g.,* San Francisco Arts & Athletics v. United States Olympic Comm., 483 U.S. 522, 536 n.15 (1987). *See also* Board of Trustees v. Fox, 492 U.S. 469, 481 (1989) ("overbreadth analysis does not normally apply to commercial speech"); Ohralik v. Ohio State Bar Ass'n, 436 U.S. 447, 462 n.20 (1978) (because commercial speech not as likely to be deterred as noncommercial speech, it "does not require the added protection afforded by the overbreadth approach"); Bates v. State Bar of Ariz., 433 U.S. 350, 380, 2 Media L. Rep. 2097, 2110 (1977) ("the justification for the application of overbreadth analysis applies weakly, if at all, in the ordinary commercial speech context").

The "void for vagueness" doctrine applies in commercial speech cases, although just how rigorously is not completely clear. Association of Nat'l Advertisers v. Lungren, 809 F. Supp. 747, 760–61 (N.D. Cal. 1992) (analyzing cases and applying doctrine where substantial criminal penalties were possible).

[83]425 U.S. at 771 n.24, 1 Media L. Rep. at 1938–39 n.24.

[84]*Id.*

on commercial speech are unconstitutional.[85] In the 1977 case of *Bates v. State Bar of Arizona,* for example, the Court held that an Arizona Supreme Court regulation that imposed a blanket ban on attorney advertising was unconstitutional.[86] The Court largely based its decision that attorneys could advertise the prices of their services on *Virginia Pharmacy* and held that it was not persuaded by the state's proffered interests in suppressing all attorney advertising.[87]

A lessening of the constitutional protection afforded commercial speech was evident, however, in the 1979 case of *Friedman v. Rogers,* which upheld provisions of the Texas Optometry Act forbidding the use of trade names, assumed names, or corporate names by optometrists.[88] The Court gave almost complete deference to the Texas Legislature's judgment that the use of trade names by optometrists was potentially misleading and deceptive; relying on footnote 24 of *Virginia Pharmacy,* the Court upheld the absolute prohibition as "necessary" to prevent a commercial message from being deceptive.[89] Going back to its holding in *Bigelow,* and in contrast with *Virginia Pharmacy,* the Court in *Friedman* stated:

> Because of the special character of commercial speech and the relative novelty of First Amendment protection for such speech, we act with caution in confronting First Amendment challenges to economic legislation that serves legitimate regulatory interests.[90]

Friedman thus marked a retreat from the protection of commercial speech. It upheld a state restriction based on the justification that less information, rather than more, best serves the public interest. This conclusion is at odds

---

[85]*See, e.g.,* Carey v. Population Servs. Int'l, 431 U.S. 678, 2 Media L. Rep. 1935 (1977) (holding unconstitutional statute prohibiting any "advertisement or display" of contraceptives, regardless of ad's potentially offensive nature to some recipients); Linmark Assocs. v. Township of Willingboro, 431 U.S. 85 (1977) (striking down local ordinance designed to prevent "white flight" by prohibiting posting of "For Sale" or "Sold" signs on residential property).

[86]433 U.S. 350, 2 Media L. Rep. 2097 (1977). As described below, the continued wisdom of the Court's ruling in *Bates*—that a blanket ban on attorney advertising is unconstitutional—was questioned by three dissenting judges in Shapero v. Kentucky Bar Association, 486 U.S. 466 (1988) (O'Connor, J., dissenting, joined by Rehnquist, C.J., and Scalia, J.).

[87]433 U.S. at 379, 2 Media L. Rep. at 2109. The Court said, however, that consistent with *Virginia Pharmacy*'s footnote 24, certain attorney advertising restrictions might be justified, given such advertising's potential to mislead an ignorant public. *Id.* at 383–84, 2 Media L. Rep. at 2110–11. For example, the Court said that the advertising must not be misleading or untruthful and that permissible limitations on attorney advertising might include reasonable time, place, and manner regulations; prohibitions against ads for illegal transactions; and bans on advertising in the electronic broadcast media. *Id.* at 384, 2 Media L. Rep. at 2111 (citations omitted). The Court also stated that it was specifically not ruling on advertising that described the "quality of service" provided by an attorney—or other items "not susceptible of measurement or verification"—as opposed to the price advertising at issue. *Id.* at 383, 2 Media L. Rep. at 211.

[88]440 U.S. 1, 4 Media L. Rep. 2213 (1979).

[89]*Id.* at 10, 4 Media L. Rep. at 2217. One year before *Friedman,* the Court, in In re Primus, 436 U.S. 412 (1978), overturned sanctions against an attorney cooperating with the American Civil Liberties Union (ACLU) who wrote to a prospective litigant, a victim of an unwanted sterilization operation, and offered the ACLU's free legal services. Emphasizing that the ACLU is a nonprofit organization and that the attorney's services were being offered without charge, the Court held that the attorney's solicitation was an expression of her political beliefs and associations that reflected her membership in the ACLU, an organization that pursues litigation as a vehicle for effective political expression and association. *Id.* at 428. Thus, the attorney's actions were entitled to First Amendment protection and could only be regulated by the government with "narrow specificity." *Id.* at 422, 426–32, 437–38 and n.32 (citations omitted).

At the same time it decided *In re Primus,* however, the Court held that a lawyer's in-person solicitation of automobile accident victims was not protected by the First Amendment. Ohralik v. Ohio State Bar Ass'n, 436 U.S. 447 (1978). Ohralik had offered his services on a contingent fee basis and had solicited employment in person. 436 U.S. at 449–52. The Court later held, however, that a certified public accountant's in-person solicitation of prospective clients was protected by the First Amendment. Edenfield v. Fane, 113 S. Ct. 1792, 21 Media L. Rep. 1321 (1993).

[90]440 U.S. at 11 n.9, 4 Media L. Rep. at 2217 n.9.

with *Virginia Pharmacy*'s stated dislike of paternalism as a justification for speech restrictions.

§11.4 *CENTRAL HUDSON*'S FOUR-PART TEST

The rationale of *Friedman* appeared to play a major role in the 1980 *Central Hudson* case,[91] one of the Supreme Court's most significant commercial speech decisions. In *Central Hudson,* the Court struck down a state regulation that absolutely banned any promotional advertising by electric utilities, but stated that an appropriately tailored regulation designed to suppress truthful information about a lawful activity would be permissible if the state could demonstrate a "substantial" interest in the regulation.[92]

Central Hudson flowed directly from *Friedman* and summarized commercial speech holdings since *Virginia Pharmacy* to create a four-part test that still serves as the standard for determining the constitutionality of commercial speech restrictions:

> At the outset, we must determine whether the expression is protected by the First Amendment. For commercial speech to come within that provision, it at least must *concern lawful activity and not be misleading.* Next, we ask whether the asserted *governmental interest is substantial.* If both inquiries yield positive answers, we must determine whether the regulation *directly advances the governmental interest* asserted, and whether *it is not more extensive than necessary* to serve that interest.[93]

Applying this test to the regulation before it, the Court first held that speech promoting electrical use was not inaccurate, nor did it promote an illegal activity.[94] Second, the Court found that substantial governmental interests existed in conserving electricity and promoting fair and efficient utility rates.[95] Third, the Court said that the advertising ban clearly served to further the state's interest in energy conservation.[96] Nevertheless, the regulation failed under the fourth prong because the advertising ban was more extensive than necessary: The Court found that the regulation suppressed speech about electrical services and devices that did not increase energy consumption.[97] In addition, no showing

---

[91] 447 U.S. 557, 6 Media L. Rep. 1497 (1980).

[92] *Id.* at 566, 6 Media L. Rep. at 1501.

[93] *Id.* (emphasis added). As it had done previously, the Court stressed consumers' need for commercial information. *Id.* at 567, 6 Media L. Rep. at 1501 ("[e]ven in monopoly markets, the suppression of advertising reduces the information available for consumer decisions and thereby defeats the purpose of the First Amendment").

[94] *Id.* at 566. *See also* Beneficial Corp. v. Federal Trade Comm'n, 542 F.2d 611, 617 (3d Cir. 1976), *cert. denied,* 430 U.S. 983 (1977) ("[w]hether particular advertising has a tendency to deceive or mislead is obviously an impressionistic determination more closely akin to a finding of fact than to a conclusion of law").

[95] 447 U.S. at 568–69, 6 Media L. Rep. at 1502.

[96] *Id.* at 569, 6 Media L. Rep. at 1502. The Court held that there was "an immediate connection" between advertising and the state's first asserted interest, reducing the demand for electricity. The link between advertising and the state's second asserted interest, the utilities' rate structure, however, was "at most, tenuous." *Id.*

In a statement that it would rely upon heavily in its 1986 decision in *Posadas,* the Court in *Central Hudson* noted that the utility company would not have contested the regulation unless it believed that advertising would increase its sales. *Id.*

[97] *Id.* at 570–71.

was made that a more limited restriction would not adequately serve the state's energy conservation interests.[98]

The Court in *Central Hudson* then articulated its reasons for permitting content-based regulation of commercial speech:

> Two features of commercial speech permit regulation of its content. First, commercial speakers have extensive knowledge of both the market and their products. Thus they are well-situated to evaluate the accuracy of their messages and the lawfulness of the underlying activity. In addition, commercial speech, the offspring of economic self-interest, is a hardy breed of expression that is not "particularly susceptible to being crushed by overbroad regulation."[99]

Thus, the Court held that a state may regulate the content and form of truthful commercial speech concerning a lawful activity as long as the regulation is no broader than necessary to serve a substantial state interest.[100]

Post-*Central Hudson* commercial speech decisions by the Supreme Court have applied the four-part test with inconsistent degrees of rigor. In *Metromedia, Inc. v. City of San Diego,* a plurality opinion authored by Justice White found that an ordinance permitting on-site commercial billboards but prohibiting all off-site commercial billboards and all noncommercial billboards was a constitutional regulation of commercial speech.[101] Although the plurality applied the four-part *Central Hudson* test, it did not place the burden of proof on the city.[102] Finding that there was "meager" evidence to support *Central Hudson*'s third prong—that the regulation must directly advance the government's interest—the plurality nonetheless upheld the billboard regulation.[103] The Court also showed great deference regarding *Central Hudson*'s fourth prong by finding that the city met the requirement that it could not achieve its goals by less intrusive regulations, despite the city's failure to offer any support for this conclusion.[104]

In 1982, the Court even dismissed an appeal for want of a substantial federal question in *Queensgate Investment Co. v. Liquor Control Commission,* which involved an unsuccessful challenge under *Central Hudson* to a state ban

---

[98]*Id.* at 569–71, 6 Media L. Rep. at 1502–03 (more limited restriction on "format and content" of utility advertising would, however, satisfy First Amendment concerns). As discussed *infra* §11.5, the Court in 1989 expressly held that, despite *Central Hudson*'s fourth prong, restrictions on commercial speech need not be the least restrictive means to achieve the government's ends. Board of Trustees v. Fox, 492 U.S. 469 (1989).

Justice Rehnquist, the sole dissenter in *Central Hudson,* stated that the state law was merely an economic regulation and that the speech involved, if it fell within the scope of the First Amendment at all, occupied a "significantly more subordinate position in the hierarchy of First Amendment values than the Court gives it today." 447 U.S. at 584, 6 Media L. Rep. at 1509 (Rehnquist, J., dissenting). According to one commentator, Justice Rehnquist's dissent in *Central Hudson* largely paralleled his majority opinion in the 1986 case of *Posadas.* Case Comment, *Posadas de Puerto Rico Associates v. Tourism Company: Rolling the Dice With Central Hudson,* 40 RUTGERS L. REV. 241, 280 (1987) ("*Posadas* has seriously weakened the *Central Hudson* test").

[99]447 U.S. at 564 n.6, 6 Media L. Rep. at 1500 n.6 (citation omitted).

[100]*Id.* at 564, 6 Media L. Rep. at 1500.

[101]453 U.S. 490 (1981). The regulation was ultimately held to be unconstitutional under the First and Fourteenth Amendments because of its ban on all noncommercial billboard advertising. *Id.* at 512–13.

[102]*Id.* at 507–08 (plurality simply accepted as substantial city's interest in promoting traffic safety and preserving aesthetic appearances).

[103]*Id.* at 509 (Court said it hesitated to disagree with local lawmakers' "accumulated common-sense judgments" that there is connection between billboards and traffic safety).

[104]*Id.* at 508 ("[i]f the city has a sufficient basis for believing that billboards are traffic hazards and are unattractive, then obviously the most direct and perhaps the only effective approach to solving the problems they create is to prohibit them").

on liquor permit holders' advertising of prices.[105] The Supreme Court appeared to affirm the importance of the Twenty-First Amendment in alcohol advertising cases.[106]

That same year, however, the Court, in *In re R.M.J.,*[107] applied *Central Hudson*'s four-part test with some rigor by holding state limits on attorney advertising that prohibited an attorney from (1) listing areas of his or her practice in language other than that specifically provided by state regulation, (2) listing the courts and states to which the attorney had been admitted to practice, and (3) mailing announcement cards to persons other than "lawyers, clients, former clients, personal friends, and relatives" to be unconstitutional.[108] The Court reasoned that since the advertising at issue, which did not comply with these rules, was not "inherently misleading," and that "experience" had not "proved that in fact such advertising is subject to abuse," it could not be banned.[109] The Court went on to find that the regulations at issue were an unconstitutional infringement on commercial speech because (1) the state had no "substantial interest" in prohibiting a lawyer from describing his or her areas of practice in a nonmisleading manner, even if that description varied from what the state regulation provided; (2) the state had no "substantial interest" in preventing a lawyer "from identifying the jurisdictions in which he is licensed to practice" and there was no finding that an attorney listing stating that he or she is a member of the bar of the U.S. Supreme Court could be misleading to the public; and (3) there were less restrictive alternatives available than completely banning attorney mailings to specified groups.[110]

The following year, in *Bolger v. Youngs Drug Products Corp.,* the Court again applied the *Central Hudson* test and found that a federal statute prohibiting unsolicited mailing of contraceptive advertisements was unconstitutional.[111] The regulation, the Court said, failed to significantly support the asserted governmental interests of shielding recipients from offensive material and helping parents control how their children are informed about birth control.[112]

---

[105]459 U.S. 807 (1982), *dismissing appeal from* 433 N.E.2d 138 (Ohio 1982) (per curiam) (applying *Central Hudson* test, Ohio Supreme Court had upheld regulation that only allowed (1) liquor license holders to advertise price of individual bottle or drink on their premises as long as such advertising was not visible from outside premises, and (2) media advertising of retail price of original containers if there was no reference to quantity price advantages).

[106]*See generally infra* §11.6(A).

[107]455 U.S. 191, 7 Media L. Rep. 2545 (1982).

[108]*Id.* at 205, 7 Media L. Rep. at 2551.

[109]*Id.* at 203, 7 Media L. Rep. at 2550.

[110]*Id.* at 204–06, 7 Media L. Rep. at 2551–52.

The same year as *Queensgate* and *In re R.M.J.,* the Court again held that commercial speech that promotes or encourages an illegal activity may be completely barred. Village of Hoffman Estates v. Flipside, Hoffman Estates, 455 U.S. 489 (1982). In that case, a retailer challenged the constitutionality of a municipal ordinance requiring (1) a license for the display of products relating to drug use, and (2) that the licensee keep records of purchasers of regulated materials. The Court rejected the suggestion that the municipality was improperly restricting noncommercial symbolic speech, noting that the ordinance only controlled the sale of substances in proximity to literature promoting illegal drugs and did not prohibit or regulate the sale of the literature itself. *Id.* at 496.

[111]463 U.S. 60 (1983).

[112]*Id.* at 71 n.20. The Court held that the government's interest in protecting recipients from offensive material carried "little weight." *Id.* at 71. Likewise, lower courts have held that trademarks are protected by the commercial speech doctrine even if some find them offensive. *See, e.g.,* Sambo's Restaurants v. Ann Arbor, 663 F.2d 686, 694–95 (6th Cir. 1981) (restaurant's use of trademark "Sambos," while perhaps offensive as "pernicious racial stereotype of blacks as inferior," was protected commercial speech, at least where there was no evidence that use of trademark affected government's goals of promoting "racial harmony and equality").

In *Bolger,* the Court also held that the government's interest in assisting children to discuss birth control with their parents was "undoubtedly substantial," but the regulation provided only "the most limited

In contrast to the plurality opinion in *Metromedia,* the Court in *Bolger* clearly stated that the party seeking to uphold a commercial speech restriction bears the burden of justifying the restriction.[113]

In 1985, in *Zauderer v. Office of Disciplinary Counsel,* the Supreme Court partially reversed a state ruling that disciplined an attorney for placing newspaper advertisements promoting his services for drunk driver and intrauterine contraceptive injury cases.[114] Citing *Central Hudson,* the Court held that a state may not discipline an attorney for soliciting business by advertisements containing "nondeceptive illustrations and legal advice."[115] The Court upheld the state's requirement that attorneys disclose certain fee information, however, reasoning that "an advertiser's rights are adequately protected as long as disclosure requirements are reasonably related to the State's interest in preventing deception of consumers."[116]

Thus, until 1986, when it decided *Posadas de Puerto Rico v. Tourism Co.,*[117] the Supreme Court applied the *Central Hudson* test with some rigor. Moreover, until 1986, the Court had not upheld a ban on truthful advertising since 1942, in *Chrestensen.*

§11.5 *POSADAS*—DIMINISHING PROTECTION FOR COMMERCIAL SPEECH

In the 1986 case of *Posadas de Puerto Rico v. Tourism Co.,* the Supreme Court, for the first time since *Chrestensen,* upheld a ban on truthful advertising for a legal product.[118] Relying on the *Central Hudson* test, the Court reasoned that if a state can prohibit the sale of a product, it can also ban or restrict advertising of that product.[119] Thus, the Court upheld a Puerto Rican statute that stated "[n]o gambling room shall be permitted to advertise or otherwise offer their facilities to the public of Puerto Rico."[120] A 1979 legislative memorandum had interpreted this advertising restriction to only prohibit any form of casino advertising that might be accessible to the Puerto Rican public.[121] Such advertisements were legal if they were not accessible to the Puerto Rican public.

---

incremental support" for that interest. 463 U.S. at 73. In addition, the Court held that the regulation failed *Central Hudson*'s fourth prong because it purged all mailboxes of material entirely suitable for adults. *Id.*

[113] 463 U.S. at 70. One possible justification for this different standard of review is that in *Bolger,* the speech at issue concerned a constitutionally protected activity. While the Court did not mention the importance of this distinction, it became a factor of "crucial" importance three years later in Posadas de Puerto Rico v. Tourism Co., 478 U.S. 328, 345–46, 13 Media L. Rep. 1033, 1041 (1986).

In 1984, in Capital Cities Cable v. Crisp, 467 U.S. 691, 10 Media L. Rep. 1873 (1984), the Court struck down an Oklahoma law that barred liquor advertising, because it was preempted by federal cable television laws. The Court did not reach the First Amendment issues.

The same year as *Crisp,* the Court declined to hear two other alcoholic beverage advertising cases. Dunagin v. City of Oxford, 718 F.2d 738, 10 Media L. Rep. 1001 (5th Cir. 1983) (en banc), *cert. denied,* 467 U.S. 1259 (1984). *Dunagin* was consolidated with a rehearing of the appeal in Lamar Outdoor Advertising v. Mississippi Tax Commission, 701 F.2d 314, 9 Media L. Rep. 1466, *reh'g granted,* 701 F.2d 336 (5th Cir. 1983). *See infra* §11.6(A).

[114] 471 U.S. 626 (1985).
[115] *Id.* at 629.
[116] *Id.* at 628 (there are "material differences between disclosure requirements and outright prohibitions on speech").
[117] *See infra* §11.5.
[118] 478 U.S. 328, 13 Media L. Rep. 1033 (1986).
[119] *Id.* at 336, 13 Media L. Rep. at 1041.
[120] *Id.* at 332, 13 Media L. Rep. at 1035. The Puerto Rico Legislature had legalized certain forms of casino gambling in licensed gambling rooms in 1948 to boost tourism. *Id.* at 331, 13 Media L. Rep. at 1035.
[121] *Id.* at 334, 13 Media L. Rep. at 1036.

The Supreme Court's five-justice majority opinion was authored by Chief Justice Rehnquist, a constant critic of commercial speech rights.[122] The majority said that the speech at issue passed the first prong of the *Central Hudson* test because it promoted a lawful act and was not fraudulent or misleading.[123] Next it assessed the strength of the government's interest in restricting the speech, deferentially holding that "[w]e have no difficulty in concluding that the Puerto Rico Legislature's interest in the health, safety and welfare of its citizens constitutes a 'substantial' government interest."[124]

Addressing *Central Hudson*'s third prong, the majority's summary answer to the question of whether the restriction directly advanced the government's interest was "clearly 'yes.' "[125] It rejected the plaintiff's argument that the regulation failed to directly advance the government's interest because it was under-inclusive, since certain types of gambling could still be advertised to Puerto Rican residents.[126]

The majority then held that it was "clear beyond peradventure" that the casino advertising regulation passed *Central Hudson*'s fourth prong, which requires that the advertising restriction be no more extensive than necessary to achieve the government's interest.[127] Adopting a highly deferential approach, the majority reasoned that an earlier narrowing construction of the regulation ensured that it would not affect casino advertising aimed at tourists and that it was up to the legislature to choose the policy it considered most effective to reduce the demand for casino gambling.[128]

The majority distinguished *Posadas* from the Court's earlier holdings in *Carey v. Population Services International*[129] and *Bigelow v. Virginia*,[130]

---

[122]For example, in both *Virginia Pharmacy* and *Central Hudson,* Justice Rehnquist was the sole dissenter. In *Virginia Pharmacy,* he stated that the issue of the public's interest in the free flow of commercial information concerns only state legislatures, not the Constitution. *Virginia Pharmacy,* 425 U.S. 748, 783–84, 1 Media L. Rep. 1930, 1942 (1976).

[123]478 U.S. at 340–41, 13 Media L. Rep. at 1039.

[124]*Id.* at 341, 13 Media L. Rep. at 1039 (excessive casino gambling, according to Puerto Rican legislature, would produce " 'the disruption of moral and cultural patterns, an increase in local crime, the fostering of prostitution, the development of corruption, and the infiltration of organized crime' ").

[125]*Id.*

[126]*Id.* Advertising for horse racing, cock fighting, and the lottery remained legal in Puerto Rico. The Court offered two reasons for its holding on this point. "First, whether other kinds of gambling are advertised in Puerto Rico or not the restrictions on advertising of casino gambling 'directly advance' the Legislature's interest in reducing demand for games of chance." *Id.* Second, the Court found that the governmental interest was to reduce casino gambling, not all games of chance. *Id. See also* Association of Nat'l Advertisers v. Lungren, 809 F. Supp. 747, 757 (N.D. Cal. 1992) (because *Posadas* accepted as adequate government's belief that advertising casino gambling increases demand for such gambling, "the California legislature's belief that uniform standards for frequently used environmental terms would promote the state's consumer protection goals, is clearly reasonable"). *Compare* Edenfield v. Fane, 113 S. Ct. 1792, 1800, 21 Media L. Rep. 1321, 1325 (1993) (mere speculation or conjecture will not justify restriction; government "must demonstrate that the harms it recites are real and that its restriction will in fact alleviate them to a material degree").

[127]*Id.* at 343, 13 Media L. Rep. at 1040.

[128]478 U.S. at 343–44, 13 Media L. Rep. at 1040. Justice Brennan, joined by Justices Marshall and Blackmun, severely criticized the majority's application of *Central Hudson. Id.* at 351, 13 Media L. Rep. at 1043 (Brennan, J., dissenting) ("no differences between commercial and other kinds of speech justify protecting commercial speech less extensively where, as here, the government seeks to manipulate private behavior by depriving citizens of truthful information concerning lawful activities").

In a separate dissent, Justice Stevens criticized the regulation in *Posadas* as discriminatory and "hopelessly vague and unpredictable." *Id.* at 359, 13 Media L. Rep. at 1047 (Stevens, J., dissenting). Justice Stevens also criticized the Puerto Rican regulatory scheme as imposing a prior restraint, because advertisers had to receive the approval of the Tourism Company for certain advertising. *Id.* at 361, 13 Media L. Rep. at 1048 (Stevens, J., dissenting). Because the appellant did not raise the prior restraint issue, the majority refused to rule on it. *Id.* at 348 n.11, 13 Media L. Rep. at 1042 n.11.

[129]431 U.S. 678, 2 Media L. Rep. 1935 (1977).

[130]421 U.S. 809, 1 Media L. Rep. 1919 (1975).

stating that in these cases—where the Court struck down a ban on contraceptive advertising and reversed a conviction for abortion clinic advertising—the underlying activity was constitutionally protected and could not have been prohibited by the state.[131] In contrast, the Puerto Rican legislature could have prohibited casino gambling altogether. The Court reasoned that the greater power to ban casino gambling necessarily included the lesser power to ban the advertising of casino gambling: "[I]t is precisely *because* the government could have enacted a wholesale prohibition of the underlying conduct that it is permissible for the government to take the less intrusive step of allowing the conduct, but reducing the demand through restrictions on advertising."[132] Thus, the Court seems to have added yet another dimension to the commercial speech doctrine—whether the underlying conduct is constitutionally protected.

Emphasizing the importance of this distinction, the Court noted that the power of states to regulate "products or activites deemed harmful, such as cigarettes, alcoholic beverages, and prostitution has varied from outright prohibition ... to legalization of the product or activity with restrictions on stimulation of its demand ...."[133] Chief Justice Rehnquist reasoned that "[t]he legislature could conclude, as it apparently did here, that residents of Puerto Rico are already aware of the risks of casino gambling, yet would nevertheless be induced by widespread advertising to engage in such potentially harmful conduct."[134]

The ultimate impact of *Posadas* on the constitutional protection of commercial speech is uncertain. Many scholars and commentators fear that the Court's decision represents a trend toward declining protection of commercial speech.[135] Some have gone so far as to view *Posadas* as precedent for the

---

[131]478 U.S. at 345, 13 Media L. Rep. at 1041.

[132]*Id.* at 346, 13 Media L. Rep. at 1041. The majority's holding that a state's "greater" power to ban an activity includes the "lesser" power to ban its advertising has subsequently been raised in lower courts with varying degrees of success in commercial speech and other contexts. *See, e.g.,* Astro Limousine Serv. v. Hillsborough County Aviation, 678 F. Supp. 1561, 1566 (M.D. Fla.), *aff'd,* 862 F.2d 877 (11th Cir. 1988) (relying on *Posadas* to hold that "the power to completely ban all other limousine operations includes the lesser power to limit advertising and solicitation and to grant a contractual privilege to another carrier"). *But see* Grant v. Meyer, 828 F.2d 1446, 1456 (10th Cir. 1987), *aff'd,* 486 U.S. 414 (1988) (overruling Colorado trial court's reliance on *Posadas,* in part, because speech at issue was not commercial and state's power to ban ballot initiatives entirely did not include lesser power to impose restrictions on use of initiative process).

[133]478 U.S. at 346, 13 Media L. Rep. at 1041.

[134]*Id.* at 344, 13 Media L. Rep. at 1040. The Court rejected the appellant's argument that the First Amendment required the legislature to reduce the demand for casino gambling not by suppressing advertising, "but by promulgating additional speech designed to *discourage* it." *Id.* In reaching its conclusion that the legislature did not need to employ "counter speech" as a less intrusive means of achieving its goals, the Court relied on Capital Broadcasting Co. v. Mitchell, 333 F. Supp. 582 (D.D.C. 1971), *aff'd mem. sub nom.* Capital Broadcasting Co. v. Acting Att'y Gen., 405 U.S. 1000 (1972) and Dunagin v. City of Oxford, 718 F.2d 738, 10 Media L. Rep. 1001 (5th Cir. 1983) (en banc), *cert. denied,* 467 U.S. 1259 (1984). In *Capital Broadcasting,* the district court held that "Congress had convincing evidence the [Cigarette] Labeling Act of 1965 had not materially reduced the incidence of smoking." 333 F. Supp. at 585. In *Dunagin,* the Fifth Circuit held that "[w]e do not believe that a less restrictive time, place, and manner restriction, such as a disclaimer warning of the dangers of alcohol, would be effective. The state's concern is not that the public is unaware of the dangers of alcohol. The concern instead is that advertising will unduly promote alcohol consumption despite known dangers." 718 F.2d at 75 (citation omitted).

[135]*See, e.g.,* Nutt, *Recent Development, Trends of First Amendment Protection of Commercial Speech,* 41 VAND. L. REV. 173, 175 (1988) (Court's deference to legislative judgment in *Posadas* "signals a retreat from first amendment protection of commercial speech and a willingness to encourage the governmental paternalism that this protection was intended to avoid"); Hovland & Wilcox, *The Future of Alcoholic Beverage Advertising,* COMM. & L. 5, 5 (April 1987) (*Posadas* "may further weaken the already tenuous status of advertisers' rights to free speech"); Trauth & Huffman, *The Commercial Speech Doctrine: Posadas Revisionism,* COMM. & L. 43, 43 (Feb. 1988) (Court is currently in process of "radically redefining" status of commercial speech); Lively, *The Supreme Court and Commercial Speech: New Words With an Old*

Court returning to the spirit, if not the actual holding, of *Chrestensen* and its progeny.[136]

In *Posadas,* the Court justified its holding that advertising for a legal activity can be banned by citing several lower court decisions restricting cigarette and liquor advertising.[137] Thus, *Posadas* might be read as paving the way for a ban on advertising alcohol and tobacco products. *Posadas* may be limited, however, by the Court's willingness to show unusual deference to the Puerto Rican legislature due to Puerto Rico's "unique cultural and legal history."[138]

The five-justice majority opinion in *Posadas* clearly runs contrary to the notion that the First Amendment prohibits government from paternalistically attempting to control behavior by limiting the public's access to information.[139] *Posadas* marks the first time the Court has been willing to uphold a law based on the government's concern that the public may react irrationally to truthful information concerning a lawful activity.[140]

Since *Posadas,* the Court has continued to address the issue of commercial speech. In the 1987 case of *San Francisco Arts & Athletics v. United States Olympic Committee,* the Court relied, in part, on commercial speech case law to hold that the First Amendment does not prohibit Congress from granting exclusive rights to the word "Olympic."[141] Largely reflecting *Posadas'* deferential approach, the Court held that an amateur athletic group could be prohibited from titling an athletic event the "Gay Olympic Games."[142] The Court acknowledged that although "many" promotional uses of the word "Olympic" will be commercial speech, "some uses may go beyond the 'strictly

---

Message, 72 MINN. L. REV. 289, 290 (1987) (Court in *Posadas* "retreated to a deferential standard of review reminiscent of . . . its abandoned view that commercial expression is unprotected").

One commentator believes that the Court "has adopted a hierarchy or dual standard for commercial speech." Case Comment, *supra* note 98, at 257 ("[d]ual-message commercial expression (i.e., speech that contains both commercial and noncommercial elements as opposed to "pure commercial expression"] like that in *Bigelow* and *Bolger* receives substantial first amendment protection, and the *Central Hudson* test is generally applied in accordance with its true tenor. In cases like *Metromedia* (and *Posadas*), pure commercial expression is accorded either a limited form of first amendment protection or none at all, and *Central Hudson* is applied in form, but not in substance"). The majority in *Posadas,* this commentator and others claim, only applied a rational basis test focusing on the "reasonableness" of the government's restrictions. *See, e.g., id.* at 271; Lively, *supra,* at 311. A dissenting Justice Brennan agreed with at least part of this analysis, stating that the majority in *Posadas* merely "tipp[ed] its hat" to *Central Hudson.* 478 U.S. at 352, 13 Media L. Rep. at 1044 (Brennan, J., dissenting).

[136]*See, e.g.,* Lively, *supra* note 135, at 301; Case Comment, *supra* note 98, at 275–76 (discussing *Posadas* and concluding Chief Justice Rehnquist "has never fully accepted the abrogation" of *Chrestensen*). The applicability of *Posadas* to state restrictions on commercial speech may be limited, however, if state courts hold that their state constitutions provide broader free speech protections than the Federal Constitution.

[137]478 U.S. at 347 n.10, 13 Media L. Rep. at 1041 n.10 (citing Capital Broadcasting Co. v. Mitchell, 333 F. Supp. 582 (D.D.C. 1971), *aff'd mem. sub nom.* Capital Broadcasting Co. v. Acting Att'y Gen., 405 U.S. 1000 (1972) (cigarette advertising); Dunagin v. City of Oxford, 718 F.2d 738, 10 Media L. Rep. 1001 (5th Cir. 1983) (en banc), *cert. denied,* 467 U.S. 1259 (1984) (liquor advertising); Queensgate Inv. Co. v. Liquor Control Comm'n, 433 N.E.2d 138 (Ohio), *appeal dismissed for want of substantial federal question,* 459 U.S. 807 (1982) (liquor advertising); Capital Cities v. Crisp, 699 F.2d 490 (10th Cir. 1983), *rev'd on other grounds sub nom.* Capital Cities Cable v. Crisp, 467 U.S. 691, 10 Media L. Rep. 1873 (1984) (liquor advertising)).

[138]478 U.S. at 339 n.6, 13 Media L. Rep. at 1038 n.6.

[139]First Nat'l Bank of Boston v. Bellotti, 435 U.S. 765, 792, 3 Media L. Rep. 2105, 2116 (1978) ("if there be any danger that the people cannot evaluate the information and arguments advanced [to them], it is a danger contemplated by the First Amendment"). *See also* Kleindienst v. Mandel, 408 U.S. 753, 762–63 (1972) (freedom of speech "necessarily protects the right to receive").

[140]478 U.S. at 349, 13 Media L. Rep. at 1042 (Brennan, J., dissenting).

[141]483 U.S. 522, 535–41 (1987). The statute at issue granted the U.S. Olympic Committee the right to prohibit certain commercial and promotional uses of the word "Olympic" and various Olympic symbols. The petitioner claimed that the statute violated the First Amendment because there was no requirement of a showing that a particular use was likely to cause confusion as to the sponsor of an event. *Id.* at 526–29.

[142]*Id.* at 535–41.

business' context."[143] Nonetheless, the Court dismissed the petitioner's claim that its use of "Olympic" was "intended to convey a political statement about the status of homosexuals in society."[144]

Two years later, the Court struck another blow to commercial speech by holding, in *Board of Trustees v. Fox*,[145] that governmental restrictions on commercial speech need not be the least restrictive means to achieve the government's goal.[146] Instead, the Court held that there must merely be a "reasonable" " ' 'fit' between the legislature's ends and the means chosen to accomplish those ends.' "[147] The Court in *Fox*, however, distinguished this reasonable fit test from the "rational basis" test used in equal protection cases by stating that, under the reasonable fit test, the *government* has the burden of establishing that its goals are "substantial, and the cost [is] to be carefully calculated."[148] Thus, the Court diluted the fourth prong of the *Central Hudson* test—whether the regulation at issue is not more extensive than necessary to serve that interest.[149]

The limited constitutional protection for commercial speech resulting from dilution of the *Central Hudson* test's fourth prong is apparent in the Supreme Court's *United States v. Edge Broadcasting* decision.[150] In *Edge Broadcasting*, the Court considered two federal statutes that prohibited the broadcasting of lottery advertising by stations located in states where lotteries were prohibited; the broadcaster was located in a nonlottery state near the border of a lottery state, and the bulk of its audience was in the lottery state.[151] The Court held that the statutes did not violate the broadcaster's First Amendment rights,[152] reasoning that the statutes' regulation of commercial speech was constitutional because there need only be, and there was, a reasonable fit between the regulation and the government's interest in prohibiting lottery advertising in states that prohibited lotteries.[153]

---

[143] *Id.* at 535.
[144] *Id.* at 537 n.16. The Court upheld the statute after applying *Central Hudson*'s four-part commercial speech test, which it stated was "substantially similar" to the time, place, and manner test articulated in *United States v. O'Brien*, 391 U.S. 367, 377 (1968), for symbolic speech. 483 U.S. at 537. For a criticism of the Court's ruling, see Case Note, *A Sad Time for the Gay Olympics: San Francisco Art & Athletics v. United States Olympic Committee, 107 S. Ct. 2971 (1987)*, 56 CINN. L. REV. 1487, 1489 (1988) (concluding "the Court disregarded the *no more extensive than necessary* analysis traditionally used" in commercial and expressive speech cases).
[145] 492 U.S. 469 (1989).
[146] *Id.* at 476–82.
[147] *Id.* at 480 (quoting Posadas de Puerto Rico v. Tourism Co., 478 U.S. 328, 341 (1986)). In *Fox*, the Court held that, on its face, a university's refusal to allow product demonstrations in campus dormitory rooms was constitutional, even though such demonstrations constituted commercial speech. The Court also held, however, that the issue of whether the university's rule, *as applied*, was unconstitutional was not yet ripe for resolution. *Id.* at 484–86.
[148] *Id.* at 480.
[149] Lower courts have applied *Fox* to hold that an advertising regulation may be constitutional even if it was not the least restrictive means to meet the government's ends. *See, e.g.,* Cramer v. Skinner, 931 F.2d 1020, 1034 (5th Cir.), *cert. denied*, 112 S. Ct. 298 (1991) (federal ban on certain airline flight ads enacted because of government's desire to promote certain airport upheld since reasonable fit existed between statute and government's goal); Adolph Coors Co. v. Brady, 944 F.2d 1543, 1551–54, 19 Media L. Rep. 1328, 1334–37 (10th Cir. 1991) (federal statute prohibiting disclosure of alcohol content information in certain beer advertising constitutional if such prohibition "results in a 'reasonable fit' between the legislature's goal and the means chosen to reach it").
[150] 113 S. Ct. 2696, 21 Media L. Rep. 1577 (1993).
[151] *Id.* at 2702, 21 Media L. Rep. at 1580.
[152] *Id.* at 2708, 21 Media L. Rep. at 1585.
[153] *Id.* at 2704–05, 21 Media L. Rep. at 1581–82. *See infra* notes 259–72 and accompanying text (discussing *Edge Broadcasting* in greater detail).

However, the fourth prong of the *Central Hudson* test still has some bite. In *City of Cincinnati v. Discovery Network*,[154] the Supreme Court struck down a city ordinance that prohibited distribution of commercial handbills on public property that was being used as a basis for removing news racks that contained free magazines, which consisted primarily of advertisements.[155] The Court held that there was not a reasonable fit between the city's legitimate interests in safety and aesthetics and the means chosen to serve those interests, because news racks containing newspapers were not banned.[156]

A slim majority of the Court in 1988 and in 1990, however, declined to limit constitutional protection for commercial speech, at least for attorney advertising. In *Shapero v. Kentucky Bar Association,* the Court held unconstitutional a state statute that categorically prohibited lawyers from soliciting legal business for pecuniary gain by sending truthful and nondeceptive letters to potential clients facing particular legal problems.[157] Writing for the majority,[158] Justice Brennan stated that lawyer solicitations for pecuniary gain that are not " 'false or deceptive' " and do not " 'concern unlawful activities' " may be restricted only " 'in the service of a substantial governmental interest.' "[159]

Since regulation of commercial speech " 'may extend only as far as the interests it serves,' " the Court in *Shapero* held that state rules designed to prevent the " 'potential for deception and confusion ... may be no broader than reasonably necessary to prevent' the perceived evil."[160] Thus, while the " 'unique features of in-person solicitation by lawyers ... justified a prophylactic rule prohibiting lawyers from engaging in such solicitation for pecuniary gain,' " these concerns are not present with written ads, in part because "[we] have never distinguished among various modes of written advertising to the general public."[161]

That the petitioner in *Shapero* targeted his letter to people known to need legal services did not render his letter unprotected, the Court reasoned, because "the First Amendment does not permit a ban on certain speech merely because it is more efficient."[162] Moreover, Justice Brennan wrote, "[t]he relevant

---

[154] 113 S. Ct. 1505, 21 Media L. Rep. at 1161 (1993).

[155] *Id.* at 1506–07, 21 Media L. Rep. at 1161–62.

[156] *Id.* at 1511–17, 21 Media L. Rep. at 1165–69. *See also infra* notes 170–75 and accompanying text.

[157] 486 U.S. 466 (1988). Shapero, an attorney, had applied to a state agency for approval of a letter he proposed to send to potential clients facing foreclosure suits. *Id.* at 469.

[158] Writing for the majority in *Shapero* in Parts I and II of that opinion was Justice Brennan, who was joined by Justices White, Marshall, Blackmun, Stevens, and Kennedy. In those two sections, the Court held that the regulation at issue violated the First Amendment. *Id.* at 469–78. In Part III, which discussed his finding that the advertising in question was not overreaching, Brennan was only joined by Justices Marshall, Blackmun, and Kennedy. *Id.* at 478–80. Brennan's opinion in Part III recognized, however, that the constitutionality of the regulation at issue, which was discussed in Parts I and II, did not turn on whether the particular speech at issue exhibited the evil of "overreaching" proscribed by the regulation. *Id.* at 478.

Justice White, joined by Justice Stevens, concurred with Parts I and II and Brennan's opinion but dissented from Part III, stating that the question of whether the petitioner's letter constituted overreaching should be left to state courts in the first instance. *Id.* at 480. Justice O'Connor, joined by Chief Justice Rehnquist and Justice Scalia, dissented. *Id.* at 480–91.

[159] *Id.* at 472 (citing Zauderer v. Office of Disciplinary Counsel, 471 U.S. 626, 638 (1985)). While a dissenting Justice O'Connor agreed with the majority that *Zauderer* supported its conclusion, she described *Zauderer* as "itself the culmination of a line of cases built on defective premises and flawed reasoning." *Id.* at 480 (O'Connor, J., dissenting). She also described Bates v. State Bar of Arizona, 433 U.S. 350, 2 Media L. Rep. 2097 (1977), as "an early experiment with the doctrine of commercial speech [which] ... has proved to be problematic in its application." 486 U.S. at 487.

[160] 486 U.S. at 475 (citations omitted).

[161] *Id.* (citation omitted). ("[i]n assessing the potential for overreaching and undue influence, the mode of communication makes all the difference").

[162] *Id.* at 473.

inquiry is not whether there exist potential clients whose 'condition' makes them susceptible to undue influence, but whether the mode of communication poses a serious danger that lawyers will exploit any such susceptibility."[163]

In 1990, the Supreme Court issued another decision in favor of attorney advertising. In *Peel v. Attorney Registration and Disciplinary Commission*,[164] the Court, in a 5-4 decision, held that an attorney's right to advertise his National Board of Trial Advocacy certification as a trial specialist on his letterhead was protected by the First Amendment.[165] The Court stated that such commercial speech is not

> an unverifiable opinion of ultimate quality of a lawyer's work or a promise of success ... but is simply a fact, albeit one with multiple predicates, from which a consumer may or may not draw an inference of the likely quality of an attorney's work in a given area of practice.[166]

Thus, the Court held that the ad was not "actually misleading."[167]

The Court in *Peel* then rejected the claim that the ad was "potentially misleading" and held that the state regulation at issue was "broader than reasonably necessary to prevent the perceived evil" of confusing the reader about the attorney's qualifications.[168] The Court stated:

> Even if we assume that petitioner's letterhead may be potentially misleading to some consumers, that potential does not satisfy the State's heavy burden of justifying a categorical prohibition against the dissemination of accurate factual information to the public.[169]

Moreover, two 1993 Supreme Court decisions indicate that the Court will still give substantial constitutional protection to commercial speech. First, in *City of Cincinnati v. Discovery Network*,[170] the district court had prevented enforcement of a city ordinance that prohibited distribution of commercial handbills on public property; the Court of Appeals for the Sixth Circuit affirmed.[171] The ordinance was being used as a basis for removing 62 news racks containing free magazines, which consisted primarily of advertisements for the respondents' services.[172] The ordinance was not applied to the rest of the city's 1,500–2,000 news racks containing newspapers.[173] In an opinion written by

---

[163]*Id.* at 482 (citation omitted). Justice O'Connor disagreed, emphasizing the "important differences between professional services and standardized consumer products" and concluding that "unsolicited legal advice was not analagous to the free samples that are often used to promote sales in other contexts." *Id.* at 493 (O'Connor, J., dissenting). Discussing the *Central Hudson* test, Justice O'Connor also said that the "government has more than ample justification for banning or strictly regulating most forms of price advertising" and "it is quite clear" states should be able to ban ads offering prices for " 'routine' " legal services. *Id.* (O'Connor, J., dissenting).
[164]496 U.S. 91 (1990).
[165]*Id.* at 111.
[166]*Id.* at 101.
[167]*Id.* at 106.
[168]*Id.* at 106–07. In a separate concurring opinion, Justices Marshall and Brennan stated that, while they believed the attorney's ad was "potentially misleading," the state could not ban such ads entirely, although it could require a disclaimer. *Id.* at 101–02.
[169]496 U.S. at 109 (citations omitted). The Court stated, however, that the state may be able to screen certifying organizations or require a "disclaimer" about the organization or "standards of specialty." *Id.* at 110. A dissenting Justice O'Connor would have deferred to the Illinois Supreme Court's determination that the ad was misleading and stated that, even if the ad was only potentially misleading, it could be absolutely banned. *Id.* at 120–25.
[170]113 S. Ct. 1505, 21 Media L. Rep. 1161 (1993).
[171]946 F.2d 464 (6th Cir. 1991).
[172]113 S. Ct. at 1506–07.
[173]*Id.* at 1507–09.

Justice John Paul Stevens for a six-member majority, the Court held that there was not a reasonable fit between the city's legitimate interests in safety and aesthetics and the means chosen to serve those interests, namely the ban on news racks containing commercial handbills, because news racks containing newspapers were not prohibited.[174] Further, the Court concluded that the law did not constitute a valid time, place, and manner restriction because it was not content-neutral.[175]

In a second 1993 decision, *Edenfield v. Fane*,[176] the Court affirmed summary judgment in favor of a certified public accountant (CPA) who challenged Florida's ban on in-person solicitation by CPAs.[177] The Court held that, as applied to a CPA's communication to potential clients of truthful, nondeceptive information proposing a lawful commercial transaction, the Florida ban violated the First Amendment.[178] In Justice Anthony Kennedy's opinion, written for an eight-member majority, the Court concluded that, although Florida's interests in protecting consumers from fraud or overreaching by CPAs and in maintaining CPAs' independence in auditing businesses and attesting to their financial statements were important, the prohibitions did not serve these interests directly or materially.[179] The Court distinguished in-person solicitation by lawyers, noting that "[u]nlike a lawyer, who is trained in the art of persuasion, a CPA is trained in a way that emphasizes independence and objectivity rather than advocacy."[180]

Thus, no consistent pattern has emerged in the Supreme Court's recent commercial speech cases. Instead, the Court's decisions appear to depend on the precise facts of the case before it. *Posadas* has not eliminated substantial First Amendment protection for commercial speech, however.

§11.6 SPECIFIC TYPES OF ADVERTISING

§11.6(A) Liquor

Unlike other types of commercial speech, regulation of liquor advertising involves a clash between two constitutional provisions. The First Amendment provides commercial advertising with some protection, while the Twenty-First Amendment grants states authority to regulate alcohol consumption within their borders.[181] The Supreme Court has not directly decided whether the

---

[174]*Id.* at 1511–15. *Compare* United States v. Edge Broadcasting, 113 S. Ct. 2696 (1993) (holding that regulation satisfied reasonable fit requirement). *See infra* notes 259–72 and accompanying text (discussing *Edge Broadcasting* in greater detail).
[175]113 S. Ct. at 1516–17. For a discussion of time, place, and manner restrictions, see Chapter 12.
[176]945 F.2d 1514 (11th Cir. 1991), *aff'd,* 113 S. Ct. 1792, 21 Media L. Rep. 1321 (1993).
[177]113 S. Ct. at 1804.
[178]*Id.* at 1797.
[179]*Id.* at 1799–1802.
[180]*Id.* at 1802–04.
[181]The Twenty-First Amendment states: "The transportation or importation into any State, Territory, or possession of the United States for delivery or use therein of intoxicating liquors, in violation of the laws thereof, is hereby prohibited." U.S. CONST. amend. XXI, §2 (adopted 1933). The framers of the Twenty-First Amendment intended to constitutionalize the principles of a statute that was designed to place the regulation of liquor transportation and sales within a state's police power, free from Commerce Clause restraints. Mandel, Note, *Liquor Advertising: Resolving the Clash Between the First and Twenty-First Amendments,* 59 N.Y.U. L. REV. 157, 166–68 (1984). The Twenty-First Amendment has been described as "unique in the constitutional scheme in that it represents the only express grant of power to the states, thereby creating a

Twenty-First Amendment limits the First Amendment's protection of commercial speech, though it has often found that the Twenty-First Amendment does not limit other constitutional guarantees.[182] Lower courts have relied on the Twenty-First Amendment, however, to limit the First Amendment protection afforded commercial speech[183] and other constitutional guarantees.[184] The impact of *Posadas* on this area of advertising remains unclear.[185]

The conflict between the First and Twenty-First Amendments was recognized in two Supreme Court cases upholding the right of state alcohol control boards to prohibit live or filmed sexual performances in establishments licensed to sell liquor.[186] The regulations at issue in both *New York State Liquor*

---

fundamental restructuring of the constitutional scheme as it relates to one product—intoxicating liquors." Castlewood Int'l Corp. v. Simon, 596 F.2d 638, 642 (5th Cir. 1979), *vacated and remanded sub nom.* Miller v. Castlewood Int'l Corp., 446 U.S. 949 (1980), *panel opinion reinstated,* 626 F.2d 1200 (5th Cir. 1980).

The impact of the Twenty-First Amendment on liquor advertising is unclear. *Compare* Annot., *Validity, Construction, and Effect of Statutes, Ordinances, or Regulations Prohibiting or Regulating Advertising of Intoxicating Liquors,* 20 A.L.R.4th 600, 605 (1983) ("[based] upon the states' regulatory power, coupled with the broad grant of power vested in the states by the Twenty-First Amendment, it would appear that liquor regulatory agencies have the power to allow advertising or forbid it altogether when it concerns alcoholic beverages") *with* Miller, *The First Amendment and Legislative Bars of Liquor and Cigarette Advertisements,* 85 COLUM. L. REV. 632, 633 (1985) ("bans on the advertising of potentially harmful substances such as liquor and cigarettes are unconstitutional because they violate the first amendment rights of those who receive commercial messages").

[182]*See, e.g.,* Capital Cities Cable v. Crisp, 467 U.S. 691, 712, 10 Media L. Rep. 1873, 1883 (1984) (Twenty-First Amendment does not override federal preemption doctrine); Larkin v. Grendel's Den, 459 U.S. 116 (1982) (Twenty-First Amendment may not impinge on Establishment Clause); California Retail Liquor Dealers Ass'n v. Midcal Aluminum, 445 U.S. 97, 106–17 (1980) (Twenty-First Amendment does not exempt state wine-pricing statute from scrutiny under federal antitrust laws); Craig v. Boren, 429 U.S. 190 (1976) (statute that differentiates between men and women regarding minimum age for beer purchase violates Equal Protection Clause); Wisconsin v. Constantineau, 400 U.S. 433 (1971) (statute that permits posting of excessive drinkers' names in retail liquor outlets violates Due Process Clause); Hostetter v. Idlewild Bon Voyage Liquor Corp., 377 U.S. 324, 331–32 (1964) ("absurd oversimplification" to conclude Twenty-First Amendment "somehow operated to 'repeal' the Commerce Clause wherever regulation of intoxicating liquors is concerned").

In some earlier Commerce Clause cases, however, the Supreme Court reached a different result. *See, e.g.,* Ziffrin, Inc. v. Reeves, 308 U.S. 132, 138 (1939) (state has broad power to regulate liquor manufacture, transportation, and sale "unfettered by the commerce clause"); Joseph S. Finch & Co. v. McKittrick, 305 U.S. 395 (1939) (state's power to regulate liquor importation not limited by Commerce Clause); State Bd. of Equalization v. Young's Market Co., 299 U.S. 59 (1936) (under Twenty-First Amendment, state can impose burdens on interstate commerce that would not otherwise be valid).

[183]*See infra* notes 192–208.

[184]*See, e.g.,* S & S Liquor Mart v. Pastore, 497 A.2d 729, 736–37, 12 Media L. Rep. 1236, 1240 (R.I. 1985) (alcoholic beverage advertising prohibition does not violate liquor retailers' rights under Equal Protection or Commerce clauses); Rhode Island Liquor Stores Ass'n v. Evening Call Pub'g Co., 497 A.2d 331, 337–38, 12 Media L. Rep. 1121, 1125–26 (R.I. 1985) (statute restricting alcoholic beverage advertising did not violate newspaper's rights under Commerce Clause); Memphis Pub'g Co. v. Leech, 539 F. Supp. 405, 408, 412–13 (W.D. Tenn. 1982) (statute requiring certain warnings in alcoholic beverage ads did not violate newspapers' rights under Equal Protection and Commerce clauses); Dunagin v. City of Oxford, 718 F.2d 738, 10 Media L. Rep. 1001 (5th Cir. 1983) (en banc), *cert. denied,* 467 U.S. 1259 (1984) (liquor advertising restrictions upheld against due process attack); Oklahoma Alcoholic Beverage Control Bd. v. Heublein Wines, Int'l, 556 P.2d 1158 (Okla. 1977) (Commerce Clause not violated by alcohol ad restrictions); Boscia v. Warren, 359 F. Supp. 900 (E.D. Wis. 1973) (statute prohibiting word "saloon" on liquor signs or ads does not violate due process or Ninth Amendment). *But see* Portwood v. Falls City Brewing Co., 318 S.W.2d 535 (Ky. 1958) (regulation prohibiting use of illuminated ads for alcoholic beverages has no rational relation to enforcement of state's alcoholic beverage laws).

[185]*See* Hovland & Wilcox, *The Future of Alcoholic Beverage Advertising,* 9 COMM. & L. 5, 13 (April 1987) ("precedential value" of *Posadas* "is still unclear, but certain factors evident in this and other cases seem determinant of regulation of commercial speech. The ability to withstand judicial scrutiny seems to rest on: (1) the nature of the product advertised; (2) the use and application of the *Central Hudson* test; (3) whether restrictions infringe on federal law; and (4) how strident they are in controlling in-state advertising").

[186]New York State Liquor Auth. v. Bellanca, 452 U.S. 714, 7 Media L. Rep. 1500 (1981) (per curiam) (statute that prohibited nude dancing in licensed liquor establishments upheld); California v. LaRue, 409 U.S. 109 (1972) (regulation prohibiting explicit sexual entertainment in licensed liquor establishments upheld). The U.S. Supreme Court also upheld against First Amendment attack a state statute that required nude dancers at entertainment establishments to wear "pasties" and a "G-string." Barnes v. Glen Theatre, 111 S. Ct. 2456, *on remand,* 941 F.2d 1212 (7th Cir. 1991). The Court, however, did not discuss the Twenty-First Amendment.

Authority v. Bellanca and *California v. LaRue* were found to constitute conditions on the sale of alcohol that only incidentally burdened commercial expression.[187] The Court also stated that the expression restricted by the challenged regulations in these two cases consisted of "gross sexuality" with little, if any, "communicative element."[188] Thus, while neither *Bellanca* or *LaRue* presented a head-on clash between the First and Twenty-First Amendments, they do imply that the Twenty-First Amendment might, in some manner, affect the First Amendment protection afforded commercial speech.

When the Court was first presented with a case directly raising the conflict between the First and Twenty-First Amendments in the commercial speech context, it provided very little guidance on how to resolve the conflict. In *Queensgate Investment Co. v. Liquor Control Commission*,[189] the Court summarily dismissed a challenge to an Ohio regulation that prohibited certain retail liquor permit holders from advertising, except at their premises, prices for a single bottle or drink of an alcoholic beverage but that permitted advertising of the retail price of original containers or packages of alcoholic beverages so long as no reference was made to price advantage.[190] Before reaching the issue of whether the First and Fourteenth Amendments were violated "by suppressing truthful information about a lawful activity," the Court dismissed this claim

---

[187]*Bellanca*, 452 U.S. at 716, 7 Media L. Rep. at 1501; *LaRue*, 409 U.S. at 118. Writing for the majority in *LaRue*, Justice Rehnquist stated:
While we agree that at least some of the performances . . . are within the limits of freedom of expression, the critical fact is that California has not forbidden these performances across the board. . . . [The conclusion] that certain sexual performances, and the dispensation of liquor by the drink ought not to occur at premises that have licenses was not . . . *irrational* . . . [g]iven the *added presumption in favor of validity of the state regulation in this area that the Twenty-First Amendment requires* . . . .
Id. at 118–19 (emphasis added).
Relying heavily on *LaRue* and using reasoning similar to that in its later decision in *Posadas*, the Court in *Bellanca* stated that "[t]he State's power to ban the sale of alcoholic beverages entirely includes the lesser power to ban the sale of liquor on premises where topless dancing occurs." 452 U.S. at 717, 7 Media L. Rep. at 1501.

[188]*Bellanca*, 452 U.S. at 716–17, 7 Media L. Rep. at 1501; *LaRue*, 409 U.S. at 117–18. Subsequent cases have distinguished *LaRue* on this basis. *See, e.g.,* Craig v. Boren, 429 U.S. 190, 207 (1976) (distinguishing *LaRue* because it consisted of conduct "more of gross sexuality than of communication"); Peto v. Cook, 364 F. Supp. 1, 3 (S.D. Ohio 1973) (same), *aff'd mem. sub nom.* Guggenheim v. Peto, 415 U.S. 943 (1974).

[189]433 N.E.2d 138 (Ohio) (per curiam), *appeal dismissed for want of substantial federal question*, 459 U.S. 807 (1982).

[190]*Id.* at 140. Summary dispositions are decisions on the merits, but they only bind lower courts regarding the "precise issue presented and necessarily decided." Mandel v. Bradley, 432 U.S. 173, 176 (1977) (per curiam).
The appellants in *Queensgate* had written and published a monthly newsletter that advertised drinks at special prices. The Ohio Supreme Court relied heavily on the Twenty-First Amendment to uphold the regulation, which prohibited several types of alcoholic beverage advertising but did not restrict nonprice ads by retailers or price advertising by nonretailers. 433 N.E.2d at 139 n.1.
Other courts have also held that it is permissible to prohibit ads containing alcoholic beverage pricing information. *See, e.g.,* Rhode Island Liquor Stores Ass'n v. Evening Call Pub'g Co., 497 A.2d 331, 12 Media L. Rep. 1121 (R.I. 1985); S & S Liquor Mart v. Pastore, 497 A.2d 729, 12 Media L. Rep. 1236 (R.I. 1985); On The Rox Liquors v. New York State Liquor Auth., 395 N.Y.S.2d 836 (N.Y. App. Div. 1977); House of Bacchus v. Sarafan, 357 N.Y.S.2d 318 (N.Y. App. Div. 1974); Rosenblum v. Al's Liquors, 276 N.Y.S.2d 846 (N.Y. App. Div. 1966).
Some New York courts have held that certain liquor ads that do not provide the exact price are permissible under that state's alcoholic beverage control law. *See, e.g.,* Anchor Liquors v. State Liquor Auth., 297 N.Y.S.2d 805 (N.Y. App. Div. 1969), *appeal dismissed,* 257 N.E.2d 43 (N.Y. 1970) (advertising whiskey "at cost" permissible under New York law); Samjack Liquors v. New York State Liquor Auth., 301 N.Y.S.2d 101, 102 (N.Y. App. Div. 1969) (liquor ad making such statements as "Full Quart At Fifth Price" and "Save Over $3.00 on Bot." does not violate New York law); Great Eastern Liquor Corp. v. New York State Liquor Auth., 255 N.E.2d 704 (N.Y. 1969) (liquor ad that did not provide exact prices but instead stated certain percentage savings permitted under New York law); Cohen v. New York State Liquor Auth., 275 N.Y.S.2d 484, 491 (N.Y. App. Div. 1966) (liquor advertisements giving "price ranges" by indicating that liquor is "priced under" certain amount permitted under New York law).

"for want of a substantial federal question" and left the challenged regulation intact.[191]

Two appellate courts have interpreted *Bellanca, LaRue,* and *Queensgate* to be a gloss on the commercial speech test announced in *Central Hudson* and have upheld state statutory prohibitions on liquor advertising. In *Oklahoma Telecasters Association v. Crisp,* the Tenth Circuit rejected claims by cable television franchisers and television broadcasters that a state constitutional and statutory ban on the broadcast of alcoholic beverage ads violated the First Amendment.[192] The court held that the Ohio Supreme Court's decision in *Queensgate*—that the Twenty-First Amendment "enhances" a state's authority to regulate commercial speech—was directly on point,[193] and proceeded to analyze the liquor advertising ban under the *Central Hudson* test. Reversing the trial court, the Tenth Circuit held that all four prongs of that test were satisfied.[194] The Supreme Court later reversed the Tenth Circuit, but only because the Oklahoma regulation was preempted by federal law.[195] The Court did not reach the issue of the Twenty-First Amendment's effect on the First Amendment.

In *Dunagin v. City of Oxford,* the Fifth Circuit employed the same reasoning as the Tenth Circuit in *Crisp* to uphold the constitutionality of Mississippi statutes that effectively banned most liquor ads originating from within the state on television, radio, newspapers, and billboards.[196] Again, *Bellanca, LaRue,* and *Queensgate* were relied on to hold that the Twenty-First Amendment tipped

---

[191]459 U.S. 807. The Liquor Control Commission in *Queensgate* had filed a motion to dismiss with the Supreme Court on the ground that the question presented was so insubstantial as not to warrant further argument. This motion was based on the assertion that the advertising prohibition was well within the scope of the state's powers under the Twenty-First Amendment. 433 N.E.2d at 139–41. According to one commentator, "*Queensgate* arguably stands for the proposition that the Twenty-First Amendment strengthens a state's regulatory authority over commercial advertising of alcoholic beverages." Mandel, *supra* note 181, at 174 & n.125.

[192]699 F.2d 490, 9 Media L. Rep. 1089 (10th Cir. 1983), *rev'd on other grounds sub nom.* Capital Cities Cable v. Crisp, 467 U.S. 691, 10 Media L. Rep. 1873 (1984). Three years later, the Tenth Circuit's holding in *Crisp* was relied on by the Supreme Court in Posadas de Puerto Rico v. Tourism Co., 478 U.S. 328, 343–44, 13 Media L. Rep. 1033, 1040 (1986).

[193]699 F.2d at 497, 9 Media L. Rep. at 1093. However, in Adolph Coors Co. v. Bentsen, 2 F.3d 355, 21 Media L. Rep. 2022 (10th Cir. 1993), the same court held unconstitutional a federal statute that prohibited stating the alcohol content of malt beverages unless state law required such a statement. The court held that while the government had a legitimate interest in preventing brewers from competing for customers by increasing the alcohol content of beverages, it had failed to show that factual statements of alcohol content would lead to such strength wars. *Id.* at 358–59, 21 Media L. Rep. at 2095–96.

[194]699 F.2d at 502, 9 Media L. Rep. at 1097–98. Although the speech did not promote illegal activity and was not misleading, the court held that (1) the state's interest in reducing alcohol consumption was substantial; (2) the regulation directly advanced the state's interest (noting that advertisers would not place the ads unless the ads increased sales and consumption); and (3) the statute was no more extensive than necessary, despite the fact that television and cable operators were completely prohibited from advertising alcoholic beverages. *Id.* at 501–02, 9 Media L. Rep. at 1098 ("[w]e again emphasize that the *Central Hudson* test is essentially a balancing test. When the Twenty-First Amendment is considered in addition to Oklahoma's substantial interest under its police power, the balance shifts in the state's favor, permitting regulation of commercial speech that might not otherwise be permissible").

[195]467 U.S. at 716. Enforcing the statute, the Court said, would thwart congressional and Federal Communications Commission (FCC) policy aimed at facilitating and encouraging "importation of distant broadcast signals." *Crisp,* 467 U.S. at 701–02, 708, 10 Media L. Rep. at 1878, 1881.

Two years after the Supreme Court reversed the Tenth Circuit in *Crisp,* an Oklahoma district court permanently enjoined the statute's enforcement on equal protection grounds. Oklahoma Broadcasters Ass'n v. Crisp, 636 F. Supp. 978, 12 Media L. Rep. 2379 (W.D. Okla. 1985) (advertising ban failed rational basis test because it divided media into out-of-state advertisers who could advertise alcoholic beverages to Oklahoma residents and in-state advertisers who could not).

[196]718 F.2d 738, 10 Media L. Rep. 1001 (5th Cir. 1983) (en banc), *cert. denied,* 467 U.S. 1259 (1984). In 1986, the Supreme Court in *Posadas* quoted the Fifth Circuit's opinion in *Dunagin* with approval. *Posadas,* 478 U.S. at 342, 13 Media L. Rep. at 1040.

the "balance" in favor of the challenged regulation.[197] A concurring judge in *Dunagin* was sharply critical of this approach, urging instead that the protectability of commercial speech under the First Amendment should remain unaffected by the Twenty-First Amendment.[198] Five of the thirteen judges in *Dunagin* would have struck down the Mississippi ordinances as violating the First Amendment under the *Central Hudson* test.[199]

The Ninth Circuit and the Supreme Courts of Rhode Island and Oklahoma have also upheld statutes that restrict alcohol advertising. In *Actmedia v. Stroh,*[200] the Ninth Circuit upheld a California statute that prohibited alcoholic beverage manufacturers from paying retail establishments to advertise their products.[201] The plaintiff, which was in the business of leasing advertising space on supermarket shopping carts, claimed that the statute violated its First Amendment right to engage in commercial speech.[202] The Ninth Circuit disagreed, holding that the defendants' application of the statute passed constitutional scrutiny under the *Central Hudson* test.[203] With regard to *Central Hudson*'s fourth prong, the court in *Actmedia* held that, because only *paid* advertising in *retail* stores was prohibited, the regulation at issue was no more extensive than necessary to achieve California's goals.[204]

Another statute that prohibited alcoholic beverage advertising was upheld a year earlier in *S & S Liquor Mart v. Pastore,* where the Rhode Island Supreme Court refused to overturn a state liquor control commissioner's decision to suspend the plaintiff's liquor license if he placed liquor price advertising in any in- or out-of-state publications.[205] The court stated that, while the Twenty-First Amendment must be read in conjunction with the rest of the Constitution and does not abrogate individual rights secured by the Fourteenth Amendment, a state statute that regulates alcoholic beverage sales is entitled to an "added presumption in favor of [its] validity."[206] The court in *S & S Liquor* also held

---

[197]718 F.2d at 750, 10 Media L. Rep. at 1011. "If there is any instance where a state can escape First Amendment constraint while prohibiting truthful advertising promoting lawful sales, it would be where the product being sold is intoxicating liquor." *Id.* at 743, 10 Media L. Rep. at 1005. The court frequently relied on the deferential approach taken by the plurality in Metromedia, Inc. v. City of San Diego, 453 U.S. 490 (1981), to uphold the ordinance under the *Central Hudson* test. 718 F.2d at 749–51, 10 Media L. Rep. at 1010–12.

[198]718 F.2d at 753–54, 10 Media L. Rep. at 1014 (Williams, J., concurring). Judge Williams, however, agreed with the majority's result based on the application of the *Central Hudson* test without reference to the Twenty-First Amendment.

[199]*Id.* at 755, 10 Media L. Rep. at 1015. *See also* Sterchi, *Restraints on Alcoholic Beverage Advertising: A Constitutional Analysis,* 60 NOTRE DAME L. REV. 779, 784–91 (1985) (arguing that courts in *Crisp* and *Dunagin* improperly applied standard for commercial speech because less restrictive alternatives existed). In 1989, however, the Supreme Court held that the least restrictive alternative doctrine does not apply to commercial speech. Board of Trustee v. Fox, 492 U.S. 469, 481–82 (1989).

[200]830 F.2d 957 (9th Cir. 1986).

[201]*Id.* at 964–68.

[202]*Id.* at 958, 965.

[203]*Id.* Discussing *Central Hudson*'s second prong, the Ninth Circuit deferentially noted that "there is little question that California has a 'substantial' interest in exercising its Twenty-First Amendment powers and regulating the structure of the alcoholic beverage industry in California." *Id.* at 965. The Ninth Circuit also held that the statute passed muster under *Central Hudson*'s third prong because it "directly advances California's interest in preventing vertical and horizontal integration of the alcoholic beverage industry and promoting temperance." *Id.* at 967. This holding is consistent with the arguments of proponents of advertising restrictions, who contend that advertisers glamorize drinking but fail to inform the public of the dangers of alcohol abuse. Younger, Comment, *Alcoholic Beverage Advertising on the Airwaves: Alternatives to a Ban or Counteradvertising,* 34 U.C.L.A. L. REV. 1139, 1141 (1987). Opponents of such restrictions argue that alcohol commercials merely develop brand loyalty and do not increase overall alcohol consumption. *Id.*

[204]830 F.2d at 967–68.

[205]497 A.2d 729, 12 Media L. Rep. 1236 (R.I. 1985).

[206]*Id.* at 732 (citations omitted). The Rhode Island Supreme Court went on to uphold the regulation under the *Central Hudson* test, relying on *Queensgate* and *Crisp* to find that the statute met the "critical" hurdle of directly advancing the state's interest in reducing liquor consumption. *Id.* at 734–35.

that the plaintiff had the burden of persuading the court that "a judicial veto of a legislative act on constitutional grounds" was warranted.[207]

Similarly, in *Oklahoma Alcoholic Beverage Control Board v. Burris,* the Oklahoma Supreme Court held that a ban on liquor advertising by retail sellers did not violate the First Amendment.[208] In reaching its conclusion, the court stated:

> The broad sweep of the twenty-first amendment ... gives the states near absolute power to regulate the liquor industry .... Wide latitude as to choice of the means to accomplish regulation is accorded the state regulatory agency. This latitude may include some regulation of rights granted by other portions of the United States Constitution most notably here, first amendment freedom of speech.[209]

Some cases decided before the Supreme Court's decision in *Posadas,* however, held that various types of restrictions on liquor advertising do violate the First Amendment's protection of commercial speech. For example, in *Michigan Beer & Wine Wholesalers Association v. Attorney General,* the court held that regulations prohibiting all off-premise advertising of prices of liquor, wine, and beer were unconstitutional restraints on commercial speech.[210] Relying on *Virginia Pharmacy* and *Bates,* the court reasoned that "[t]he free flow of information is 'indispensable' to a free enterprise economy such as ours which has at its heart strong and robust competition."[211] The court in *Michigan Beer & Wine* distinguished Michigan's ban on all off-premise price ads from *LaRue, Bellanca,* and *Crisp* on the grounds that the Michigan regulation at issue was "directly aimed at constitutionally-protected commercial speech. We therefore conclude that the Twenty-first Amendment does not require us to deal with restraints on freedom of speech any differently than we would if alcoholic beverages were not involved."[212]

Under somewhat different circumstances, a Tennessee district court upheld the commercial speech rights of the publisher and editor of two newspapers. In *Memphis Publishing Co. v. Leech,* the court held unconstitutional a statute that required certain newspapers to include a specified statement—which warned of the illegality and potential consequences of transporting liquor

---

[207]*Id.* at 734 (S & S Liquor could not demonstrate that "uncontrolled advertising of the price of liquor poses no threat to the legislative goal of alcoholic moderation or abstinence"). The same day it issued its decision in *S & S Liquor Mart,* the Rhode Island Supreme Court upheld another statutory provision that prohibited publication of liquor ads with price information. Rhode Island Liquor Stores Ass'n v. Evening Call Pub'g Co., 497 A.2d 331, 12 Media L. Rep. 1121 (R.I. 1985). Unlike the statute at issue in *S & S Liquor Mart,* which restrained liquor license holders from any off-premises advertising of alcoholic beverage prices, the regulation at issue in *Rhode Island Liquor Stores* prohibited the media from publishing liquor price information. *Id.* at 332. The plaintiff in *Rhode Island Liquor Stores,* a liquor retail trade organization, successfully obtained a permanent injunction against the defendant newspaper's publication of out-of-state liquor ads with price information. *Id.* at 338.

[208]626 P.2d 1316 (Okla. 1980) (appellee unsuccessfully attempted to overturn alcoholic beverage control board decision ordering him to remove sign reading "Beverage Mart" from his property).

[209]*Id.* at 1317. *See also* Boscia v. Warren, 359 F. Supp. 900 (E.D. Wis. 1973) (court dismissed complaint alleging that statute prohibiting tavern owner from calling his establishment "The Saloon" was unconstitutional restriction on commercial speech); Heir v. Degnan, 411 A.2d 194 (N.J. 1980) (state regulation prohibiting joint advertising by competing alcoholic beverage retailers violates commercial speech protection only insofar as nonprice advertising was prohibited).

[210]370 N.W.2d 328 (Mich. Ct. App. 1985), *cert. denied,* 479 U.S. 939 (1986).

[211]370 N.W.2d at 332. The court also noted that "the right to free speech encompasses not only the right to advertise, but also the reciprocal right of consumers to receive such advertising." *Id.* at 333.

[212]*Id.* at 335. The court also rejected the plaintiff's claim that *Queensgate* was controlling on how to apply *Central Hudson's* four-part test. Unlike the regulations at issue in *Queensgate,* which prohibited certain liquor license holders from advertising the price per bottle or drink, the statute at issue in *Michigan Beer & Wine* prohibited all off-premise price advertising by manufacturers, wholesalers, retailers, and out-of-state sellers. In addition, the Michigan restrictions applied to advertising of brands, not just prices. *Id.* at 330–31.

into Tennessee without a license—in any ads for alcoholic beverages sold by out-of-state retailers.[213] This statute, the court held, impermissibly intruded into the plaintiff's editorial discretion in accepting and preparing advertising copy and constituted an invalid restraint on commercial speech under the *Central Hudson* test.[214]

The year before *Leech*, in *Brooks v. State, Through Alcoholic Beverage Control Commission*, a Delaware court struck down a statute that prohibited price advertising of alcoholic beverages because it served no recognizable state interest and was an unconstitutional restraint on free speech.[215] The Delaware Superior Court reasoned that, while the Twenty-First Amendment may permit a total ban on alcohol sales, once a state opts to permit ads for such beverages, its advertising regulations are subject to some of the same constitutional freedoms as other commercial speech.[216] Thus, the constitutionality of restrictions on liquor advertising remains unsettled.

§11.6(B) Tobacco

The Supreme Court has not directly decided to what extent restrictions on tobacco advertising are constitutional since 1976, when *Chrestensen* was overruled in *Virginia Pharmacy* and commercial speech was afforded at least some First Amendment protection. Based on its most recent commercial speech decisions, it is unclear how the Court would view tobacco advertising under the *Central Hudson* test and also under *Posadas*, which cited approvingly a pre-*Virginia Pharmacy* decision upholding a ban on cigarette television ads.[217]

In that 1971 case, *Capital Broadcasting Co. v. Mitchell*, a three-judge district court held that cigarette ads on "any medium of electronic communication" could be banned by the Federal Communications Commission (FCC) without violating the First or Fifth Amendments.[218] The court provided two primary reasons for its decision. First, the court held that "product advertising" is less vigorously protected than other speech, and Congress could thus "prohibit the advertising of cigarettes in any media" based on either its power to supervise regulatory agencies or its power under the Interstate Commerce Clause.[219] Second, the court held that restrictions on broadcast media are more acceptable under the First Amendment than other speech restrictions because of the "unique" characteristics of such media, which require a court to balance broadcasters' editorial rights against the public's right of access to a scarce and powerful communication medium.[220]

---

[213] 539 F. Supp. 405, 8 Media L. Rep. 1601 (W.D. Tenn. 1982).

[214] *Id.* at 411–12. The statute did not, however, violate the plaintiff's First Amendment right to be free from impermissible restraints on newspaper revenue and circulation. *Id.* at 409.

[215] 442 A.2d 93 (Del. Super. Ct. 1981). Brooks had placed ads that included price information in a newspaper. *Id.* at 94.

[216] *Id.* at 96–97.

[217] Posadas de Puerto Rico v. Tourism Co., 478 U.S. 328, 344, 13 Media L. Rep. 1033, 1040 (1986) (citing Capital Broadcasting Co. v. Mitchell, 333 F. Supp. 582 (D.D.C. 1971), *aff'd mem. sub nom.* Capital Broadcasting Co. v. Acting Att'y Gen., 405 U.S. 1000 (1972)).

[218] 333 F. Supp. 582, 584 (D.D.C. 1971). 15 U.S.C.S. §1335 (1993) makes such advertisements unlawful.

[219] *Id.*

[220] *Id.* The district court added that the plaintiffs—six broadcasting corporations—were not precluded from speaking out on the question of cigarette smoking but were merely prevented from collecting revenues from others for broadcasting such messages. *Id.* Four years before *Capital Broadcasting*, a circuit court held that the FCC had authority to require radio and television stations carrying cigarette ads "to devote a

Few cases have discussed the issue of tobacco product advertising since *Capital Broadcasting*, and none was decided based on the Supreme Court's 1986 decision in *Posadas*. In *R.J. Reynolds Tobacco Co.*, the Federal Trade Commission (FTC) had filed a complaint against a tobacco company over its full-page newspaper and magazine advertisement stating that "the controversy over smoking and health remains an open one."[221] An administrative law judge had held that the ads did not constitute commercial speech and instead were editorials expressing Reynolds' point of view on the issue of smoking and health. This ruling was appealed, but the issue was never resolved because the case was settled.[222]

In *Federal Trade Commission v. Brown and Williamson Tobacco Corp.*,[223] the appellate court affirmed a district court's ruling that a tobacco manufacturer's ads, which included tar ratings, were misleading within the meaning of FTC regulations because the manufacturer's cigarettes delivered disproportionately more tar than other similarly rated cigarettes.[224] However, the court in *Brown* also held that an injunction that prohibited the manufacturer from advertising any tar number for its cigarettes without FTC approval was unenforceable because it was broader than reasonably necessary to prevent deception.[225]

Several bills have been presented to Congress to limit tobacco advertising. The Children's Health Protection Act of 1989 would have strictly limited "tobacco product advertising, promotion, and packaging" of all tobacco products in virtually all media, including newspapers, magazines, and billboards.[226] Under the terms of the proposed bill, "advertisement" includes "all newspapers and magazine advertisements and advertising inserts, billboards, posters, signs . . . and all other written material or other material used for promoting the sale or consumption of tobacco products to consumers."[227] Authors of the Children's Health Protection Act justified the statute based on several factors, including (1) "tobacco use is the largest preventable cause of illness and premature death in the United States," (2) "tobacco product advertising deceptively portrays the use of tobacco as socially acceptable and healthful," and (3) "the vast majority of new smokers are teenagers and younger."[228]

---

significant amount of broadcast time to presenting material against smoking" and that such a directive did not violate the First Amendment. Banzhaf v. Federal Communications Comm'n, 405 F.2d 1082 (D.C. Cir. 1968), *cert. denied sub nom.* Tobacco Inst. v. Federal Communications Comm'n, 396 U.S. 842 (1969). *See generally* Chapter 13.

[221]51 Antitrust & Trade Reg. Rep. (BNA) No. 1277, at 219, 221 (Aug. 4, 1986), *appeal docketed,* No. 9206 (FTC Aug. 7, 1986). The parties to this action agreed to a settlement in May 1990. No. 9206 (FTC May 8, 1990). *See also* the discussion of this case *supra* §11.2.

[222]*Id.*

[223]778 F.2d 35 (D.C. Cir. 1985) (Judges Bork and Scalia were two of the circuit judges hearing the case).

[224]*Id.* at 43.

[225]*Id.* at 45. For a discussion of cases dealing with tobacco advertising in the context of drug paraphernalia acts, see *infra* §11.6(F).

[226]H.R. 1493, 101st Cong., 1st Sess. (1989) (introduced by Rep. Mike Synar). The bill's advertising restrictions included (1) no pictures of anyone or anything but a single package of the product, no larger than actual size, with black print on a white background; and (2) no location in or on sports facilities or cars, boats, or sporting equipment or within 500 feet of any school attended by students under age 18. Promotional restrictions included (1) no sponsorship of athletic, music, artistic, or other events; and (2) generally no payment for the appearance of the tobacco product or its name or symbol in any movies, television shows, plays, or other entertainment. *Id.* §3.

[227]*Id.* §5.

[228]*Id.* §2. Other bills presented to the 101st Congress that, if passed, would have limited advertising for tobacco products, include the Protect Our Children From Cigarettes Act of 1989, H.R. 1250, 101st Cong., 1st Sess. §4(b) (1989) (banning promotion and certain advertising of tobacco products that "may be seen or heard by any person under the age of 18" as violations of Federal Trade Commission Act); the Internal

In 1986, Representative Synar introduced a bill, the Health Protection Act of 1986, which was very similar to his 1989 Children's Health Protection Act.[229] Although this bill ultimately was not passed, it was widely discussed, and scholars' predictions vary over whether the Supreme Court would find such a statute constitutional. Some, relying heavily on the Supreme Court's opinion in *Posadas*, predict that this or a similar statute would be upheld against First Amendment attack, reasoning that, as with the gambling activity at issue in *Posadas*, Congress has the power to prohibit the use of cigarettes on health and safety grounds.[230]

Others have predicted that the Court would scrutinize restrictions on tobacco advertising more carefully than gambling ad restrictions in *Posadas*.[231] Those predicting that the Court would narrowly interpret *Posadas* also point out that, while cigarettes are typically legal, casino gambling is an illegal activity in most states and is subject to extensive restrictions in Puerto Rico.[232]

It is clear, however, that *Posadas* took away one of the primary arguments of those opposed to tobacco advertising restrictions: truthful advertising of legal products can now be restricted to discourage unlawful conduct. The majority of the Court in *Posadas* even went so far as to specifically analogize between the gambling ad restraints at issue and restrictions on ads for harmful products such as cigarettes and liquor.[233]

A primary source of uncertainty surrounding the constitutionality of restrictions on tobacco advertising is how the four-part *Central Hudson* test would

---

Revenue Code of 1986 Amendment, H.R. 1544, 101st Cong., 1st Sess. (1989) (disallowing any deductions for advertising or other promotion expenses for sale of tobacco or tobacco products); Prohibiting Certain Cigarette Advertisements and Promotions, H.R. 3297, 101st Cong., 1st Sess. (1989) (making unlawful cigarette and little cigar ads appearing in publications with readerships primarily under age 21 that (1) suggest smoking is related to social success or sexual attraction, (2) depict individuals appearing to be under age 25, (3) depict smoking by well-known athletes, (4) depict smoking in association with stamina or athletic conditioning, *or* (5) depict as a smoker a celebrity having special appeal to youth); the Public Health Service Act Amendment—Tobacco Products, H.R. 3943, 101st Cong., 2d Sess. §3 (1990) (making it unlawful to engage in certain types of tobacco product advertising; providing for establishment of advisory committee to give advice on promulgation of regulations imposing restrictions on tobacco advertising; and allowing states and local governments to enact other such restrictions or tobacco acts); Proscribing Labels for Tobacco Packages and Advertising, H.R. 5041, 101st Cong., 2d Sess. §3 (1990) (restricting certain advertising for tobacco products); and the Tobacco Product Education and Health Protection Act of 1990, S. 2795, 101st Cong., 2d Sess. §3 (1990) (repealing federal preemption of state regulation of local tobacco advertising).

[229]H.R. 4972, 99th Cong., 2d Sess. (1986). Under this proposed statute, "[a]ll consumer sales promotion of tobacco products by manufacturers, packers, distributors, importers, or sellers of such products" would have been unlawful. *Id.* §3. The term "consumer sales promotion" included "all radio and television commercials, newspaper and magazine advertisements, billboards, [and] posters." *Id.* §5.

[230]*See* Comment, *Posadas de Puerto Rico Assocs. v. Tourism of Puerto Rico: A New Weapon in the Battle to Ban Tobacco Product Advertising*, 20 CONN. L. REV. 125, 126, 148 (1987) ("a ban on tobacco advertising would be seen as the next logical step in facing a tremendous health problem"); Welkowitz, *The Posadas Adventure: Commercial Speech Treading Water in Rough Constitutional Seas*, 196 N.Y. L.J. 47, at 5 (Sept. 5, 1986) (arguing that ban in *Posadas* limited only because evils it sought to control were limited, while smoking-related evils not so limited); Richards, *Clearing the Air About Cigarettes: Will Advertisers' Rights Go up in Smoke?*, 19 PAC. L.J. 1, 68 (1987) (logic of Congressman Synar's proposed anti-tobacco advertising bills "faulty," but such invalid logic has already condemned rights of gambling casino owners in Puerto Rico); Ross, *Pushing Puffing Post-Posadas*, 56 CINN. L. REV. 1461, 1484 (1988) (Congressman Synar's "proposed total ban on promotional tobacco advertising would be upheld under the current application of commercial speech standards").

[231]*See, e.g., Tobacco Advertising and Promotions: Hearings on H.R. 4972 before the Subcommittee on Health and the Environment of the House Comm. on Energy and Commerce*, 99th Cong., 2d Sess. 6 (1986) (statement of H. Monaghan—advertising foes have characterized *Posadas* as "routine fact-dependent application of *Central Hudson*"); Covington & Burling, Legal Memorandum, A Constitutional Analysis of Proposal to Ban or Restrict Tobacco Product Advertising, at 2 (July 18, 1986) (ban in *Posadas* did not substantively deprive residents of information concerning casino gambling but only screened residents from ads directed to them).

[232]*Hearings, supra* note 231, at 44 (statement of B. Neuborne).

[233]478 U.S. 328, 346, 13 Media L. Rep. 1033, 1041 (1986).

be applied. First, the Court would have to find that the ads at issue were not false or misleading and did not advertise an illegal activity. While the Court rarely invalidates advertising restrictions because they fail to pass muster under this first prong of *Central Hudson,* proponents of restrictions on tobacco advertising may point to *Friedman v. Rogers,* where the Supreme Court said "potentially deceptive" but truthful information may be restricted when it is "more likely to deceive the public than inform it."[234] The Court in *Friedman* also held that a "[s]tate rationally may wish to discourage while not prohibiting" altogether a certain practice.[235] Similarly, some argue that tobacco advertising restrictions would be constitutional because of the significant harms associated with normal use of the product.[236] These tobacco critics often claim that (1) tobacco advertisers' life-style messages overpower warnings required by the Surgeon General, and (2) tobacco ads are largely aimed at young people, a group the Court has allowed legislatures to shelter from certain communications.[237]

Under the second prong of the *Central Hudson* test, the government would probably have little difficulty establishing a substantial state interest, because smoking has been associated with 390,000 "unnecessary" deaths in the United States annually.[238]

The third prong of the *Central Hudson* test requires that the regulation "directly advances the governmental interests asserted."[239] In *Posadas,* the majority viewed the plaintiff's decision to sue to overturn the advertising restrictions as evidence that advertising would increase demand for gambling, and required no other proof.[240] The tobacco industry, however, argues that the purpose of its advertising is to induce brand loyalty, not to attract new smokers.[241]

Central Hudson's fourth prong requires a showing that the restriction is no more extensive than necessary to serve the government's interest. In *Posadas,* the majority adopted a highly deferential approach to this prong, stating that it was up to the legislature to determine whether "counter-speech" would be as effective as advertising restrictions.[242] Since *Posadas,* however, the Supreme Court has specifically held that a regulation on commercial speech need not

---

[234]440 U.S. 1, 13–15, 4 Media L. Rep. 2213, 2218 (1979) (upholding ban on optometrists advertising under trade names). *But see* Lowenstein, *"Too Much Puff": Persuasion, Paternalism, and Commercial Speech,* 56 CINN. L. REV. 1205, 1231 (1988) (words in many cigarette ads "*neither* truthful *nor* misleading. They are not truth-evaluative at all").

[235]440 U.S. at 13.

[236]*See, e.g.,* Comment, *supra* note 230, at 144 (citing S. WAGNER, CIGARETTE COUNTRY: TOBACCO IN AMERICAN HISTORY AND POLITICS 143 (1971)) ("[f]aced with mounting evidence supporting the dangers of smoking, tobacco producers have developed advertising schemes to conceal or minimize the dangers, such as associating smoking with 'sexual or social conquests and acts requiring physical stamina' ").

[237]Young people, some argue, cannot make an informed decision about smoking and are often induced by tobacco advertising to begin an addictive habit. *See, e.g.,* White, *The International Exploitations of Man's Known Weaknesses,* 9 HOUS. L. REV. 889, 902–03 n.140 (1972). In addition, tobacco advertising critics often point out that 90% of all smokers began smoking before they reached age 20, and 60% of all smokers began before age 13. Greenhouse, *Marlboro Man and the Domino Theory of Commercial Speech,* L.A. DAILY J. at 2 (Jan. 1, 1986). The logic of this argument appears to sweep too broadly, however. Binger, *Up in Smoke: Commercial Speech and a Tobacco Products Advertising Ban,* 54 TENN. L. REV. 703, 719 (1987) ("[t]o prohibit advertising of tobacco because it is unlawful for minors to purchase it, would suggest that like prohibitions could be placed on the advertising of alcohol, cars, adult magazines, and 'R' rated movies to achieve constitutional consistency").

[238]H.R. 1493, 101st Cong., 1st Sess. (1989).
[239]Central Hudson, 447 U.S. 557, 566, 6 Media L. Rep. 1497, 1501 (1980).
[240]478 U.S. 328, 342, 13 Media L. Rep. 1033, 1039 (1986).
[241]Covington & Burling, *supra* note 231, at 15–16 n.11.
[242]478 U.S. at 344, 13 Media L. Rep. at 1040.

be the least restrictive alternative, thus undermining the fourth prong of *Central Hudson*.[243]

At this time, the outcome of a First Amendment attack on an absolute ban on all cigarette advertising cannot be safely predicted.

§11.6(C) Gambling and Lotteries

The media's and others' ability to advertise activities related to lotteries, gambling, and similar games of chance has not only been severely restricted by the Supreme Court, but also by several federal statutes aimed at curtailing the dissemination of such information.[244] Thus, federal, state, and local governments are generally afforded great leeway in regulating advertising for lotteries and other gambling activities.

In the leading case in this area, *Posadas de Puerto Rico v. Tourism Co.,* the Supreme Court held that, despite the fact that certain types of gambling were legal in Puerto Rico, a Puerto Rican statute stating that "[n]o gambling room shall be permitted to advertise or otherwise offer their facilities" to Puerto Ricans was constitutional.[245] Thus, the Puerto Rican legislature was permitted to prohibit any form of casino advertising that might be accessible to its residents.

The sharply divided Court in *Posadas* held that the statute at issue survived *Central Hudson*'s first prong, because the advertising at issue promoted a lawful activity and was not fraudulent or misleading. Thus, an attempt to publish advertising for a local casino in a state where such gambling was unlawful would not survive scrutiny under *Central Hudson*.[246]

Importantly, Chief Justice Rehnquist, writing for the majority in *Posadas,* held that Puerto Rico's greater power to ban casino gambling altogether included the lesser power to ban advertising for casino gambling.[247] Thus, because gambling is not a constitutionally protected activity, and indeed the Court found it a "harmful" and highly regulated activity,[248] courts may rely on *Posadas* to uphold a ban on lottery or gambling advertising simply because the government has the ability to ban such activity completely.

Federal statutes forbid (1) the mailing of any publication containing any lottery advertising or lottery tickets[249] and (2) the broadcasting of lottery

---

[243]Board of Trustees v. Fox, 492 U.S. 469 (1989). *But see supra* notes 154–56.

[244]In addition, many states have adopted their own laws limiting the advertising of gambling and related activities. *See generally* Annot., *Constitutionality of Statutes Forbidding or Regulating Dissemination of Betting Odds or Other Gambling Information,* 47 A.L.R. 1135 (1927).

[245]478 U.S. at 332, 13 Media L. Rep. at 1035.

[246]*Id.* at 340–41, 13 Media L. Rep. at 1039. The Court in *Posadas* went on to give great deference to the Puerto Rican government, holding that the statute at issue also passed muster under *Central Hudson*'s second, third, and fourth prongs. *See supra* §11.5.

[247]478 U.S. at 346, 13 Media L. Rep. at 1041.

[248]*Id.,* 13 Media L. Rep. at 1040.

[249]18 U.S.C.S. §1302 (1979). As written, this statute encompasses the use of the mail to send lottery materials contained in "[a]ny newspaper, circular, pamphlet, or publication of any kind." *See, e.g.,* Horwitz v. United States, 63 F.2d 706 (5th Cir.), *cert. denied,* 289 U.S. 760 (1933) (advertising by radio broadcast that resulted in mail being used in furtherance of lottery prohibited). The punishment for a violation of §1302 is "not more than $1,000 or imprisonment not more than two years, or both."

The constitutionality of §1302 was upheld in In re Rapier, 143 U.S. 110, 133–34 (1892) (Congress' ability to establish postal system includes power to designate what may be carried in mails; "[t]he circulation of a newspaper is not prohibited, but the government declines itself to become an agent in the circulation of printed matter which it regards as injurious to the people"). *See also infra* note 250.

information on radio or television.[250] Since these two statutes were enacted, however, Congress has expressly exempted from them information about a state lottery disseminated by a newspaper, radio, or television station located in that state or another state that conducts such a lottery.[251]

Constitutional challenges to these laws have been mounted. In 1989, in *Frank v. Minnesota Newspaper Association,* the Supreme Court decided that a constitutional challenge to 18 U.S.C. Section 1302 was moot.[252] While both parties' appeals were waiting to be heard by the Court, Congress passed two laws limiting Section 1302's scope—the Charity Games Advertising Clarification Act of 1988[253] and the Indian Gaming Regulatory Act.[254] The more significant of the two laws, the Charity Games Advertising Clarification Act, was incorporated into 18 U.S.C. Section 1307, which allows the publication of gambling and similar ads (1) as long as they are not prohibited by the state where they are conducted, or (2) the gambling or similar activities are conducted by a nonprofit or governmental organization or are conducted as an occasional promotional activity "ancillary to the primary business" of that organization.[255]

In 1987, the trial court in *Minnesota Newspaper Association* held that, pursuant to Section 1302, it was permissible to ban lottery ads, but not news stories containing lists of prizes.[256] Both the newspaper association and the U.S. Postal Service appealed to the U.S. Supreme Court.

---

[250] 18 U.S.C.S. §1304 (1993). This statute applies to radio and television broadcasters licensed by the United States. Generally, 18 U.S.C. §§1302 and 1304 are aimed at materials concerning "any lottery, gift enterprise, or similar scheme offering prizes dependent in whole or in part upon lot or chance." 18 U.S.C. §1304. Postal regulations define lotteries as "[a]ny scheme or promotion, whether or not lawful under the laws of any state, which, upon payment of consideration, offers a prize dependent in whole or in part upon lot or chance." *Id.* Domestic Mail Manual §123.421, 39 C.F.R. §111.1 (1993). *See* Federal Communications Comm'n v. American Broadcasting Co., 347 U.S. 284 (1954) (radio and television "give-away" programs that distribute prizes to home listeners on basis of chance for correctly answering question not prohibited by §1304); Caples Co. v. United States, 243 F.2d 232 (D.C. Cir. 1957) (television "give-away" program based on game of bingo where viewers used cards obtained for free from stores handling sponsor's products not "lottery" under §1304); Post Pub'g Co. v. Murray, 230 F. 773 (1st Cir.), *cert. denied,* 241 U.S. 675 (1916) (newspaper ad offering prizes to persons identifying certain published photographs not unmailable under §1302 as lottery, gift enterprise, or game of chance).

The punishment for a knowing violation of §1304 is "not more than $1,000 or imprisoned not more than one year, or both." Other federal statutes give the Postal Service the power to investigate and act on fraudulent or deceptive ads carried in the mails, including ads that are not in compliance with 18 U.S.C. §§1302, 1304, and 1307. *See* 39 U.S.C.S. §§3001–05 (1993).

[251] 18 U.S.C.S. §1307 (1993). Section 1307 states, in part, that §§1301 and 1304 shall not apply to (1) an advertisement, list of prizes, or other information concerning a lottery conducted by a State acting under authority of State law which is —(A) contained in a publication published in that State or in a State which conducts such a lottery; or (B) broadcast by a radio or television station licensed to a location in that State or a State which conducts such a lottery; or (2) an advertisement, list of prizes, or other information concerning a lottery, gift, enterprise, or similar scheme . . . that is authorized or not otherwise prohibited by the State in which it is conducted and which is —(A) conducted by a not-for-profit organization or a governmental organization; or (B) conducted as a promotional activity by a commercial organization and is clearly occasional and ancillary to the primary business of that organization. Thus, §1307's exceptions do not affect newspapers in nonlottery states unless the lottery or similar scheme at issue meets the requirements of 18 U.S.C. §1307(2). Corresponding regulations with the same substantive restrictions on lottery advertising are contained in 47 C.F.R. pt. 73.1211 (1992) (FCC can revoke any station's license for violation of §1304).

[252] 490 U.S. 225, 16 Media L. Rep. 1511 (1989).

[253] 18 U.S.C.S. §1301 (1993). This act took effect on May 7, 1990.

[254] 18 U.S.C.S. §§1166 *et seq.* (1993). This act, now incorporated into 18 U.S.C. §1166 *et seq.* and 75 U.S.C. §§2701 *et seq.,* allowed all newspapers to accept advertisements for lotteries and games of chance conducted by Indian tribes.

[255] 18 U.S.C.S. §1306 (1993).

[256] 677 F. Supp. 1400, 1409, 15 Media L. Rep. 1292, 1300 (D. Minn. 1987), *vacated as moot and remanded,* 490 U.S. 225, 16 Media L. Rep. 1511 (1989). The trial court had applied the *Central Hudson* test to hold that §1302 did not violate the First Amendment's protection of commercial speech because the

Once Congress enacted the Charity Games Advertising Clarification Act and Indian Gaming Regulatory Act, however, the Postal Service agreed that Section 1302 did not apply to "non-commercial publishing of prize lists."[257] In light of this concession, the newspaper association agreed to drop its claim concerning advertising of lottery information.[258]

One year after the Supreme Court rendered its mootness decision in *Minnesota Newspaper Association,* a Virginia district court, in *Edge Broadcasting Co. v. United States,*[259] held that 18 U.S.C. Sections 1304 and 1307—which, read together, prohibit radio and television broadcast licensees located in nonlottery states from broadcasting lottery advertising in such states—did not apply to broadcasts of noncommercial lottery information.[260] The court then applied the *Central Hudson* test to determine how these statutes affected commercial speech and held that these statutes could not be applied to ads for the Virginia state lottery broadcast by a radio station located and licensed in the nonlottery state of North Carolina, when more than 90 percent of that station's listeners were in Virginia.[261] The district court held that the federal statutes, as applied to Edge Broadcasting, failed under the third prong of *Central Hudson*—whether the restriction directly advances the government's interests—because they were an ineffectual means of reducing lottery participation by the North Carolina residents in the radio station's service area, since these residents received most of their radio, newspaper, and television communication from Virginia-based media that could disseminate lottery advertising.[262]

In an unpublished per curiam opinion,[263] a divided Court of Appeals for the Fourth Circuit affirmed the district court's decision and held that the statutes were invalid as applied to Edge because they failed to directly advance any governmental interest.[264] The Supreme Court reversed,[265] concluding under the *Central Hudson* test that the statutes' regulation of commercial speech did not violate the First Amendment.[266]

---

statute directly advanced, by the least restrictive means, substantial governmental interests in prohibiting lotteries and in restricting the interstate growth of private lotteries. 677 F. Supp. at 1406, 15 Media L. Rep. at 1297. *See also* United States Postal Serv. v. C.E.C. Servs., 869 F.2d 184, 187 (2d Cir. 1989) (18 U.S.C. §1302, which prohibits sending mail concerning lotteries or similar games of chance, not facially unconstitutional).

The trial court in *Minnesota Newspaper Association* held, however, that the prohibition on news stories publishing lists of lottery prizes could not survive First Amendment scrutiny, because such publications did not involve commercial speech and the government could not establish that such prohibition was necessary to serve a compelling state interest. 677 F. Supp. at 1407, 15 Media L. Rep. at 1297–98 ("[p]rize lists have no inherent claim to First Amendment protection. It is the context of the prize list, in advertisements or news reports, that determines the level of protection").

[257]*Minnesota Newspaper Ass'n,* 490 U.S. at 227, 16 Media L. Rep. at 1512.
[258]*Id.*
[259]732 F. Supp. 633, 17 Media L. Rep. 1649 (E.D. Va. 1990), *aff'd,* 956 F.2d 263, 20 Media L. Rep. 1904 (4th Cir. 1992) (unpublished), *rev'd,* 113 S. Ct. 2696 (1993).
[260]732 F. Supp. at 635, 17 Media L. Rep. at 1650 (Edge Broadcasting asserted that it feared criminal prosecution for broadcasting *any* information about Virginia lottery, including news accounts of winning numbers and other announcements). *See also* New York State Broadcasters Ass'n v. United States, 414 F.2d 990, 997 (2d Cir. 1969), *cert. denied,* 396 U.S. 1061 (1970) (court held that §1304's phrase " 'information concerning any lottery' " referred only to information directly promoting "particular existing lottery" and did not prohibit broadcast of, for example, "an editorial for or against continuing the lottery experiment" in New York).
[261]732 F. Supp. at 638–42, 17 Media L. Rep. at 1652–55.
[262]*Id.* at 639–41, 17 Media L. Rep. at 1653–54.
[263]Edge Broadcasting Co. v. United States, 956 F.2d 263 (4th Cir. 1992).
[264]United States v. Edge Broadcasting, 113 S. Ct. 2696, 2702–03 (1993).
[265]*Id.* at 2708.
[266]*Id.*

The Court assumed, as had the lower courts, that the first *Central Hudson* factor, which requires that the commercial speech concern a lawful activity and not be misleading, was satisfied.[267] The Court next held that the government's substantial interest in supporting the policy of states that prohibited lotteries, while not interfering in the policy of states that permitted lotteries, satisfied *Central Hudson*'s second requirement of a substantial governmental interest.[268] The Court then concluded that the district court had erroneously considered, under *Central Hudson*'s third prong, whether the government's interest was directly advanced as applied to a single entity.[269] The Court stated that the third factor inquiry—whether the regulation directly advances the asserted governmental interest—should focus on its general application, and held that the statutes satisfied the third prong because they directly advanced the governmental interest by not favoring the policy of nonlottery states over that of lottery states.[270]

Finally, in analyzing the fourth prong—whether the regulation is more extensive than necessary to serve the governmental interest—the Court reiterated that the validity of the restriction should be judged by its relation to the interest to be advanced, not by the extent that it furthers the government's interest in an individual case, and held that there was a reasonable fit between the restrictions and the government's interests.[271] Because the Court found that the statutes were constitutional under *Central Hudson,* the Court did not reach the government's argument that the *Central Hudson* analysis is unnecessary because gambling does not implicate a constitutionally protected right and the greater power to prohibit gambling necessarily includes the lesser power to ban its advertisement.[272]

Another federal criminal statute, 18 U.S.C. Section 1084, limits the right to advertise and transmit information about gambling activities and focuses on the knowing use of a wire communication, including the telephone, for the transmission of wagering and betting information.[273] That statute, however, specifically excludes transmission of

> information for use in news reporting of sporting events or contests, or for the transmission of information assisting in the placing of bets or wagers on a sporting event or contest from a State or foreign country where betting on that sporting event or contest is legal into a State or foreign country in which such betting is legal.[274]

---

[267] *Id.* at 2702–03.
[268] *Id.* at 2703.
[269] 113 S. Ct. at 2704.
[270] *Id.*
[271] *Id.* at 2705.
[272] *Id.* at 2703.
[273] 18 U.S.C.S. §1084 (1979 & Supp. 1993). Specifically, subsection (a) of that statute concerns the knowing use of
> a wire communication facility for the transmission in interstate or foreign commerce of bets or wagers or information assisting in the placing of bets or wagers on any sporting event or contest, or for the transmission of a wire communication which entitles the recipient to receive money or credit as a result of bets or wagers, or for information assisting in the placing of bets or wagers . . .

The penalty for violating this section is "not more than $10,000 or imprisoned not more than two years, or both." 18 U.S.C. §1084(a).

[274] 18 U.S.C. §1084(b). *See* Kelly v. Illinois Bell Tel. Co., 325 F.2d 148, 151–52 (7th Cir. 1963) (use of telephone and telegraph company to receive and transmit racing and other news in publications sold and distributed to general public—through newsstands, agency news distributors, inside racetrack enclosures,

Thus, under Section 1084, the interstate transmission between one state that permits such wagering and another that does not is prohibited.[275] Several courts have upheld prosecutions under Section 1084 and found that the statute does not violate the First Amendment.[276]

There are also two other federal criminal statutes that prohibit the knowing interstate transportation of wagering paraphernalia.[277] As with some of the other statutes described above, however, there is an exception to enforcement of these statutes concerning the "carriage or transportation in interstate or foreign commerce of any newspaper or similar publication."[278] Several different types of publications containing sporting news and similar information have been found to be exempt pursuant to this provision.[279]

Thus, while news coverage of gambling and related activities is rather vigorously protected by both constitutional case law and exemptions in federal statutes, advertising for such activities is highly regulated, and courts are likely to give considerable deference to the government's efforts to restrict such advertising.

---

and to individual subscribers—did not violate 18 U.S.C. §1084; sports news service not "engaged in the business of betting or wagering").

Section 1084 also provides that if "any common carrier" is notified by a federal, state, or local law enforcement agency that "any facility furnished" by that carrier is being used for "transmitting or receiving gambling information" in violation of this statute, that common carrier shall "discontinue or refuse" to continue serving that subscriber. 18 U.S.C. §1084(d).

[275]*See, e.g.,* Martin v. United States, 389 F.2d 895 (5th Cir.), *cert. denied,* 391 U.S. 919 (1968) (§1084 not unconstitutional as applied to transmission of wagers from Texas to Nevada on theory that such application would defeat Nevada's policies, where wagering is legal); United States v. McDonough, 835 F.2d 1103 (5th Cir. 1988) (§1084 proscribes receiving bets on baseball and football games by telephone from Texas to Massachusetts, regardless of whether placing such bets in Massachusetts is state criminal offense).

[276]*See, e.g.,* Truchinski v. United States, 393 F.2d 627, 634 (8th Cir.), *cert. denied,* 393 U.S. 831 (1968) (§1084, which proscribes use of telephone for interstate transmission of information that assists in placing of bets on sporting events, not unconstitutional abridgement of freedom of speech); United States v. Kelly, 254 F. Supp. 9 (S.D.N.Y. 1966) (§1084 did not violate First Amendment where substantive evil sought to be curtailed was use of federally controlled means of communication to violate federal statute), *modified,* 395 F.2d 727 (2d Cir. 1968).

Several courts have also held that §1084 is not impermissibly vague. *See, e.g.,* Katz v. United States, 369 F.2d 130 (9th Cir.), *rev'd on other grounds,* 389 U.S. 347 (1966); United States v. Broadson, 390 F. Supp. 774, 780 (E.D. Wis. 1975); United States v. Smith, 209 F. Supp. 907, 918 (E.D. Ill. 1962). *See generally* Annot., *Validity and Construction of Federal Statute (18 U.S.C. §1084(a)) Making Transmission of Wagering Information a Criminal Offense,* 5 A.L.R. FED. 166 (1970); Annot., *Right or Duty to Refuse Telephone, Telegraph, or Other Wire Service in Aid of Illegal Gambling Operations,* 30 A.L.R.3d 1143 (1970).

[277]18 U.S.C.S. §§1952, 1953 (1984 & Supp. 1993). Section 1953(a) provides that

[w]hoever ... in the usual course of its business, knowingly carries or sends in interstate or foreign commerce any record, paraphernalia, ticket, ... writing, or other device used, or to be used, adapted, devised, or designed for use in (a) bookmaking; or (b) wagering pools with respect to a sporting event; or (c) in a numbers ... or similar game shall be fined not more than $10,000 or imprisoned for not more than five years or both.

Section 1952 states that "[w]hoever travels in interstate or foreign commerce or uses the mail or any facility in interstate or foreign commerce, with intent to—(1) distribute the proceeds of any unlawful activity .... (b) As used in this section ... 'unlawful activity' means (1) any business enterprise involving gambling ..."

[278]18 U.S.C. §1953(b)(3). Thus, if a publication is exempted under this provision, it is not subject to prosecution under §1952's "unlawful activity" language. As with other federal statutes described above, §§1952 and 1953 have survived First Amendment attack. *See, e.g.,* United States v. Mendelsohn, 896 F.2d 1183 (9th Cir. 1990) (§1953 not substantially overbroad because newspapers and "similar publications" exempted and all paraphernalia covered by statute easily identifiable).

[279]*See, e.g.,* United States v. Arnold, 380 F.2d 336 (4th Cir. 1967) (small weekly newsletter predicting results of upcoming football games and providing game schedules exempt under §1953(b)'s newspaper and "similar publications" provision); United States v. Kelly, 328 F.2d 227 (6th Cir. 1964) (publication exclusively covering horse racing news, results, and predictions exempt under newspaper or "similar publications" language of §1953(b) and was not wagering paraphernalia; Congress, cognizant of First Amendment concerns, did not intend to prohibit such publications); United States v. Azar, 243 F. Supp. 345 (S.D. Mich. 1964) ("tip sheet," publication designed to aid readers in search of winning choice in numbers game, fell within "any newspaper or similar publications" exception of §1953(b)); United States v. Kish, 303 F. Supp.

§11.6(D) Abortion, Contraception, and Family Planning

Bigelow v. Virginia[280] was the first Supreme Court case to suggest that a constitutional right to privacy protected some conduct involving abortion and contraception advertising. In that case, the conviction of a newspaper editor in Virginia for publishing ads for abortion services in New York was invalidated.[281] The Court announced a balancing test for determining whether the government interest in preventing the speech outweighed the constitutional interest in free speech[282] and then held that Virginia had no real interest in preventing the procurement of abortions in New York.[283]

Significantly, in ruling on the First Amendment question, the Court observed that the subject of the prohibited advertisement was of "clear 'public interest'," a factor that weighed heavily in favor of protecting the challenged speech.[284] This conclusion was reinforced by the Supreme Court's decisions in *Roe v. Wade*[285] and *Griswold v. Connecticut*,[286] after which courts have been unwilling to uphold regulatory bans on nonmisleading abortion advertisements.[287]

Courts have proven equally protective of contraceptive advertising. In *Carey v. Population Services International*,[288] a case in which the First Amendment issues were secondary, the Court ruled that the state could not constitutionally ban all "advertisement or display" of contraceptives.[289] Relying on *Virginia Pharmacy* and *Bigelow*, the Court concluded that a content-based restriction on nonmisleading commercial speech that promoted lawful transactions was unconstitutional, particularly where the information suppressed by the challenged statute "related to activity with which, at least in some respects, the

---

1212 (N.D. Ind. 1969) ("scratch sheet" allegedly used in connection with horse race bookmaking not "wagering paraphernalia" and instead falls within §1953(b)'s exemption for newspapers or "similar publications"). *See also Mendelsohn*, 896 F.2d 1183 (disk containing computer program to aid in sports bookmaking not exempted under "similar publication" language of §1953(b)).

In addition to these federal criminal statutes, the FTC has promulgated a rule regulating the use of games of chance promotions by food and gasoline retailers. 16 C.F.R. §419.1 (1982). In 1982, the FTC granted a "temporary" partial exemption, which is in effect indefinitely, that permits all marketers and users of games of chance to use the broadcast media without disclosing information about the full price and odds of winning. 48 Fed. Reg. 1046 (Jan. 10, 1983).

[280] 421 U.S. 809, 1 Media L. Rep. 1919 (1975). *See also supra* §11.3 and *supra* notes 68–71.
[281] 421 U.S. at 829, 1 Media L. Rep. at 1929.
[282] *See supra* note 70.
[283] *See supra* note 71.
[284] 421 U.S. at 822, 1 Media L. Rep. at 1924.
[285] 410 U.S. 113 (1973) (criminal abortion statute prohibiting abortions at any stage of pregnancy except to save life of mother unconstitutional invasion of individual's right to privacy).
[286] 381 U.S. 479 (1965) (state law forbidding (1) use of contraceptives and (2) any person from counseling about use of contraceptives unconstitutionally intruded on right to marital privacy found in "penumbra" of Constitution).
[287] *See, e.g.*, Meadowbrook Women's Clinic v. Minnesota, 557 F. Supp. 1172, 9 Media L. Rep. 1325 (D. Minn. 1983) (striking down ban on abortion ads that were not misleading and that contained information about lawful services and constitutionally protected conduct); Atlanta Coop. News Project v. United States Postal Serv., 350 F. Supp. 234 (N.D. Ga. 1972) (pre-*Roe v. Wade* decision holding statute prohibiting mailing of abortion information unconstitutional); Mitchell Family Planning v. City of Royal Oak, 335 F. Supp. 738 (E.D. Mich. 1972) (pre-*Roe v. Wade* decision holding advertising ban that failed to distinguish between legal and illegal abortions unconstitutional). Similarly, courts have held that bus companies may not ban abortion service advertising on their buses. *See* Chapter 13, §13.5(D).

Abortion advertising that is misleading can be prohibited, however. Fargo Women's Health Org. v. Larson, 381 N.W.2d 176, 182 (N.D. 1986), *cert. denied*, 476 U.S. 1108 (1986) (advertising using word "abortion" by medical clinic that was in fact pro-life and did not perform abortions and instead provided pregnancy tests and anti-abortion counseling services could be suppressed; such commercial speech "does not accurately inform the public about a lawful activity" and is more likely to deceive public than to inform it).

[288] 431 U.S. 678, 2 Media L. Rep. 1944 (1977).
[289] *Id.* at 701–02, 2 Media L. Rep. at 1944.

State could not interfere."[290] The Court rejected the state's asserted interest in protecting its citizens from offensive and embarrassing speech, reiterating its earlier holding that "[a]t least where obscenity is not involved ... the fact that protected speech may be offensive to some does not justify its suppression."[291]

Similarly, the Court in *Bolger v. Youngs Drug Products Corp.* held unconstitutional a federal postal law that prevented the unsolicited mailing of contraceptive promotional materials.[292] After first concluding that the speech in question was commercial, the Court applied the *Central Hudson* test and struck down the statute.[293] The Court rejected the government's asserted desire to protect recipients from embarrassment as sufficient justification for the law[294] and also found the government's apparent desire to aid parents in the upbringing of their children to be insufficient.[295]

§11.6(E) Public Utilities

The constitutionality of restrictions on public utility advertising was addressed extensively by the Supreme Court in *Central Hudson,* where the Court developed its four-part commercial test and held that a New York regulation completely banning promotional advertising by electric utilities was unconstitutional.[296] The New York Court of Appeals in *Central Hudson* had upheld the challenged regulation largely on the grounds that, given the "monopoly position" held by the public utility, its promotional advertising conveyed little useful information.[297] The Supreme Court rejected this analysis, noting that the existence of a natural monopoly in the market for electricity "provides no protection from competition with substitutes for that product."[298] Furthermore, the Court added, even where monopolies exist, "the suppression of advertising reduces the information available for consumer decisions and thereby defeats the purpose of the First Amendment."[299]

In a companion case, *Consolidated Edison Co. of New York v. Public Service Commission,* which involved a public utility's use of bill inserts to promote its support of nuclear power, the Court held that the speech was not commercial and that the state utility commission's order barring such mail inserts was unconstitutional.[300]

In 1986, a plurality of the Supreme Court in *Pacific Gas & Electric Co. v. Public Utilities Commission* again held that a public utility commission had

---

[290] *Id.*
[291] *Id.*
[292] 463 U.S. 60 (1983).
[293] *Id.* at 67. *See supra* §11.2.
[294] 463 U.S. at 72 ("[t]he short, though regular, journey from mail box to trash can ... is an acceptable burden, at least so far as the Constitution is concerned") (citation omitted).
[295] *Id. See also* Family Counseling Serv. v. Rust, 462 F. Supp. 74 (D. Nev. 1978) (Nevada law forbidding advertising of cost and availability of certified marriage counselors unconstitutional under *Bates*).
[296] 447 U.S. 557, 6 Media L. Rep. 1497 (1980). *See generally supra* §11.4.
[297] 390 N.E.2d 749 (N.Y. 1979), *rev'd,* 447 U.S. 557, 6 Media L. Rep. 1497 (1980).
[298] 447 U.S. at 568, 6 Media L. Rep. at 1502.
[299] *Id. See also* Jones, *Electric and Gas Utility Advertising: The First Amendment Legacy of Central Hudson,* 68 WASH. U. L. Q. 459, 462 (1982).
[300] 447 U.S. 530, 6 Media L. Rep. 1518 (1980). The utility commission had prohibited the utility from "using bill inserts to discuss political matters, including the desirability of future development of nuclear power." *Id.* at 532, 6 Media L. Rep. at 1519.

In a case addressing the same New York utility commission policy that was decided a year before *Central Hudson* and *Consolidated Edison,* the court held that the state could ban a power company's ads supporting nuclear power but could not ban ads for electric space heaters. Long Island Lighting v. New York Pub. Serv. Comm'n, 5 Media L. Rep. 1241 (E.D.N.Y. 1979).

violated a utility's First Amendment rights.[301] In that case, the Court held that the utility commission could not require a utility to allow consumer groups to use "extra space" in the utility's monthly billing statements to raise funds and communicate with customers.[302] The Court also held that the utility's newsletter did not constitute commercial speech because it "extends well beyond speech that proposes a business transaction ... and includes the kind of discussion of 'matters of public concern' that the First Amendment both fully protects and implicitly encourages."[303]

Tagline rules, which require utilities to include in their print, radio, and television ads a statement that the ad was paid for by either customers or shareholders, have also been successfully attacked.[304]

§11.6(F) Drug Paraphernalia

Courts have generally upheld federal, state, and local drug paraphernalia control laws against challenges that such ordinances violate the First Amendment,[305] although there are some exceptions.[306] In addition to upholding such

---

[301] 475 U.S. 1 (1986). A majority of the eight justices who heard the case (Justice Blackmun did not participate) agreed that the utility's First Amendment rights had been violated and remanded the case to the California Supreme Court for further proceedings. *Id.* at 21. Five separate opinions were filed by the justices. *Id.* at 21–39.

[302] 475 U.S. 1. The utility had been mailing a newsletter with its billing statements that included political editorials, feature stories on matters of public interest, and utility information. *Id.* at 5. For a discussion on access to the media, see generally Chapter 13.

[303] 475 U.S. at 8–9 (citations omitted).

[304] *See, e.g.,* Pacific Northwest Bell v. Davis, 608 P.2d 547, 5 Media L. Rep. 2443 (Or. Ct. App. 1979) (regulated utilities, news media, and ad organizations successfully challenged tagline rule on ground that it exceeded statutory limits of public utility commission authority); Kearns-Tribune v. Public Serv. Comm'n, 682 P.2d 858 (Utah 1984) (tagline requirements went beyond utility commission's statutory authority).

[305] *See, e.g.,* Village of Hoffman Estates v. Flipside, Hoffman Estates, 455 U.S. 489, 492 (1982) (municipal licensing ordinance applicable to businesses that sell merchandise "designed or marketed for use" with marijuana or other illegal drugs constitutional even if it regulates commercial speech and not merely commercial activity); Washington Merchantile Ass'n v. Williams, 733 F.2d 687 (9th Cir. 1984) (drug paraphernalia ban constitutional under *Central Hudson* test); Mid-Atlantic Accessories Trade Ass'n v. Maryland, 500 F. Supp. 834 (D. Md. 1980) (state drug paraphernalia act constitutional regardless of whether conduct banned—i.e., manufacture, distribution, and sale of drug paraphernalia—is labeled symbolic, commercial, or ordinary speech); Nova Records v. Sendak, 706 F.2d 782 (7th Cir. 1983) (drug paraphernalia statute sufficiently specific, despite lack of scienter requirement); Camille Corp. v. Phares, 705 F.2d 223 (7th Cir. 1983) (city drug paraphernalia law not constitutionally overbroad or vague); New England Accessories Trade Ass'n v. Nashua, 679 F.2d 1 (1st Cir. 1982) (rejecting argument, based on *Bigelow,* that state cannot ban promotion of activity outside state, noting that unlike abortions, ingestion of controlled substances illegal in all jurisdictions); Tobacco Accessories & Novelty Craftsmen Merchants Ass'n v. Treen, 681 F.2d 378 (5th Cir. 1982) (state drug paraphernalia act not overbroad or vague and did not violate First Amendment); New England Accessories Trade Ass'n v. Tierney, 528 F. Supp. 404 (D. Me. 1981), *aff'd,* 691 F.2d 35 (1st Cir. 1982) (same); World Imports v. Woodbridge Township, 493 F. Supp. 428 (D.N.J. 1980) (same); Pennsylvania Accessories Trade Ass'n v. Thornburgh, 565 F. Supp. 1568 (M.D. Pa. 1983) (same); Town Tobacconist v. Kimmelman, 462 A.2d 573 (N.J. 1983) (state drug paraphernalia act not unconstitutionally vague and must be upheld even if overbroad because that doctrine does not apply to commercial speech); Casbah, Inc. v. Thone, 651 F.2d 551, 564 (8th Cir. 1981), *cert. denied,* 455 U.S. 1005 (1982) (state drug paraphernalia act not unconstitutional or overbroad; court construed statute's ban on advertising, that "only in part" had purpose of promoting sale of drug paraphernalia, to forbid only that part of advertisement relating to drug paraphernalia and not remainder of ad); Murphy v. Matheson, 742 F.2d 564 (10th Cir. 1984) (state drug paraphernalia act not overbroad or vague); Kansas Rental Trade Coop. v. Stephan, 695 F.2d 1343 (10th Cir. 1982) (state drug paraphernalia act constitutional even if overbroad because commercial speech not protected by overbreadth doctrine); Weiler v. Carpenter, 695 F.2d 1348 (10th Cir. 1982) (state drug paraphernalia law constitutional); Florida Businessmen for Free Enter. v. Hollywood, 673 F.2d 1213 (11th Cir. 1982) (same); Bamboo Bros. v. Carpenter, 183 Cal. Rptr. 748 (Cal. Ct. App. 1982) (county drug paraphernalia ordinance not unconstitutionally vague); Levas & Levas v. Village of Antioch, 684 F.2d 446 (7th Cir. 1982) (same); Stoianoff v. Montana, 695 F.2d 1214 (9th Cir. 1983) (state drug paraphernalia act not unconstitutionally vague or overbroad); High Gear Toke Shop v. Beacom, 689 P.2d 624 (Colo. 1984) (same).

[306] *See, e.g.,* Opinion of Justices, 431 A.2d 152 (N.H. 1981) (striking down ban on ads that promote "in whole or in part" sale of objects designed or intended for use as drug paraphernalia because statute was not narrowly drawn as required by First Amendment; court recognized that similar statutory language had been upheld by other courts); Record Head Corp. v. Sachen, 682 F.2d 672 (7th Cir. 1982) (drug paraphernalia

ordinances as valid restrictions of commercial speech concerning illegal conduct, numerous courts have held that these ordinances are legitimate, incidental restrictions on otherwise protected noncommercial speech or that they do not affect speech at all.[307]

§11.6(G) Brothels and Escort Services

Courts have also generally upheld restrictions on advertising for brothels[308] and sexually oriented escort services.[309]

§11.6(H) Housing and Employment

Courts generally have upheld statutes that prohibit publication of discriminatory housing advertisements, but they have been inconsistent when ruling on the enforceability of laws restricting discriminatory employment advertising.

The only Supreme Court case in this area, *Pittsburgh Press Co. v. Pittsburgh Commission on Human Relations,* upheld the constitutionality of a local ordinance that prohibited publication of "help wanted" ads in "sex-designated columns except where the employer or advertiser is free to make hiring or employment referral decisions on the basis of sex."[310] Much of the five-justice majority opinion in that case—which applied to newspapers running the ads and the advertisers themselves—was predicated on the since-discredited notion that commercial speech is wholly unprotected by the First Amendment.[311] The Court in *Pittsburgh Press* said another justification for its holding was that the conduct being advertised—discriminatory employment—was illegal.[312]

Lower courts have often adopted the latter rationale as a basis for upholding statutes—including the Fair Housing Act of 1968[313]—that prohibit

---

ordinance unconstitutionally vague); High 01' Times v. Busbee, 621 F.2d 141, 6 Media L. Rep. 1617 (5th Cir. 1980) (drug paraphernalia statute overbroad); Record Museum v. Lawrence Township, 481 F. Supp. 768 (D.N.J. 1979) (drug paraphernalia ordinance unconstitutionally vague and indefinite). *See also* Windfaire, Inc. v. Busbee, 523 F. Supp. 868 (N.D. Ga. 1981) (certain provisions of state drug paraphernalia act prohibiting possession of drug-related objects void for vagueness, but statute's ban against certain advertising for drug-related products constitutional).

[307]*See, e.g., Weiler,* 695 F.2d at 1350; General Stores v. Bingaman, 695 F.2d 502, 504 (10th Cir. 1982); Lady Ann's Oddities v. Macy, 519 F. Supp. 1140, 1157 (W.D. Okla. 1981); Franza v. Carey, 478 N.Y.S.2d 873 (N.Y. App. Div. 1984); State v. Newman, 696 P.2d 856 (Idaho 1984); State v. Munson, 714 S.W.2d 515 (Mo. 1986).

[308]*See, e.g.,* Princess Sea Indus. v. Nevada, 635 P.2d 281, 7 Media L. Rep. 2474 (Nev. 1981), *cert. denied,* 456 U.S. 926 (1982) (lawful to ban ads soliciting prostitution in county where prostitution legal if ads appear in county where prostitution illegal, in spite of *Bigelow's* holding suggesting contrary result).
Prostitution itself—including face-to-face solicitation—is also not protected by the First Amendment. *See, e.g.,* State v. Johnson, 324 N.W.2d 447 (Wis. Ct. App. 1982); Wood v. United States, 498 A.2d 1140 (D.C. Ct. App. 1985). In Evenson v. Ortega, 605 F. Supp. 1115 (D. Ariz. 1985), the court held that, while the First Amendment did not protect advertising for prostitution, a local sheriff's department could run such ads as part of an undercover operation without a newspaper's consent or knowledge.

[309]Washington v. Clark County Liquor & Gaming Licensing Bd., 683 P.2d 31 (Nev. 1984); Republic Entertainment v. Clark County, 672 P.2d 634 (Nev. 1983); IDK, Inc. v. Clark County, 836 F.2d 1185 (9th Cir. 1988) (escort service regulation constitutional because, unlike speech in newspapers, expressive conduct arising from association of paid escorts and clients—to extent it constitutes expression and not commercial activity—did not merit full First Amendment protection).

[310]413 U.S. 376, 377–78, 1 Media L. Rep. 1908, 1909 (1973).

[311]*Id.* at 384–89, 1 Media L. Rep. at 1911–13.

[312]*Id.* at 389–90, 1 Media L. Rep. at 1913–14.

[313]42 U.S.C. §§3601–19 (1982). This statute makes it unlawful to
make, print, or publish, or cause to be made, printed or published any notice, statement, or advertisement, with respect to the sale or rental of a dwelling that indicates any preference, limitation, or discrimination

newspapers and others from publishing discriminatory housing ads.[314] The ethnic and racial diversity of human models appearing in newspaper housing ads has been litigated with some frequency. Generally, courts have held that virtually exclusive use of all white models violates the Fair Housing Act.[315]

Some courts addressing statutes that prohibit discriminatory employment ads have likewise upheld such statutes.[316] Other courts, however, have held that statutes restricting discriminatory employment ads are unenforceable, frequently due to First Amendment or due process concerns.[317]

§11.6(I) Professional Advertising

Courts have reached no consensus concerning the constitutional protection afforded advertising by various professionals. The holdings of the cases are

---

based on race, color, religion, sex, handicap, familial status, or national origin, or an intention to make any such preference, limitation or discrimination.
42 U.S.C. §3604(c). The Fair Housing Act was amended in 1988 to provide substantially more severe penalties against publishers and advertisers who use discriminatory ads in the sale, rental, or financing of housing. Fair Housing Amendments Act of 1988, P.L. 100-430. As amended, penalties of up to $10,000 may be imposed for a first offense if discriminatory classified or display ads are published. 42 U.S.C. §3612(g)(13). Prior to the 1988 amendment, the maximum penalty was $1,000.

[314]*See, e.g.,* United States v. Hunter, 459 F.2d 205 (4th Cir.), *cert. denied,* 409 U.S. 934 (1972) (federal Civil Rights Act prohibits newspapers from running housing ad stating that apartment for rent located in "white home"); Holmgrem v. Little Village Community Reporter, 342 F. Supp. 512 (N.D. Ill. 1971) (federal Civil Rights Act prohibits housing ads in newspaper directed to individuals speaking certain language); San Jose Country Club Apartments v. County of Santa Clara, 187 Cal. Rptr. 493 (Cal. Ct. App. 1982) (upholding ban on advertising for adult apartments based on housing ordinance prohibiting age or parenthood discrimination); Curtis v. Thompson, 840 F.2d 1291 (7th Cir. 1988) (applying *Central Hudson* test to hold that statute prohibiting soliciting sales of residential property once property owner has stated that he or she does not want to sell does not violate First Amendment). *But see* Penny Saver Pubns. v. Village of Hazel Crest, 905 F.2d 150, 17 Media L. Rep. 2057 (7th Cir. 1990) (court held (1) fair housing ordinance restricting publication of real estate sales and rentals unconstitutionally vague as applied to potential newspaper advertisers, and (2) plaintiff newspaper therefore entitled to almost $10,000 in damages based on lost revenues caused by potential advertisers' refusal to place housing ads). *See* Annot., *Validity, Construction, and Application of §804(c) of Civil Rights Act of 1968 (Fair Housing Act) (42 U.S.C.S. §3604(c)) Prohibiting Discriminatory Notice, Statement, or Advertisement With Respect to Sale or Rental of Dwelling,* 22 A.L.R. Fed. 359 (1975).

A somewhat different result was reached by the U.S. Supreme Court concerning allegedly discriminatory "For Sale" signs. Linmark Assocs. v. Township of Willingboro, 431 U.S. 85 (1977) (ordinance prohibiting "For Sale" and "Sold" signs violates First Amendment). *But see* City of Chicago v. Prus, 425 N.E.2d 426 (Ill. App. Ct. 1981) (upholding municipal ordinance that barred "For Sale" signs in certain neighborhoods).

[315]*See, e.g.,* Saunders v. General Servs. Corp., 659 F. Supp. 1042 (E.D. Va. 1987) (use of all-white models in marketing of real estate violates Fair Housing Act); Spann v. Colonial Village, 899 F.2d 24 (D.C. Cir. 1990) (reversing trial court, which held that, during period covered by applicable statute of limitations, exclusive use of white models in real estate advertising did not violate Fair Housing Act where there was no evidence of intent to indicate racial preference; appellate court remanded case for further proceedings, holding that plaintiffs' (black District of Columbia resident and two nonprofit corporations dedicated to ensure equality of housing opportunities) claims not time-barred and that corporation plaintiffs had standing to sue), *cert. denied,* 498 U.S. 980 (1990). *See also* Ragin v. New York Times Co., 726 F. Supp. 953, 17 Media L. Rep. 1945 (S.D.N.Y. 1989), *aff'd,* 923 F.2d 995, 18 Media L. Rep. 1666 (2d Cir. 1991), *cert. denied,* 116 L. Ed. 2d 54 (1991). *Contra* Housing Opportunities Made Equal v. Cincinnati Enquirer, 731 F. Supp. 801, 17 Media L. Rep. 1608 (S.D. Ohio 1990) (Fair Housing Act not violated because models of particular race not used in one advertisement or series of advertisements; also adopting First Amendment arguments of newspaper), *aff'd,* 943 F.2d 644 (6th Cir. 1991). *See* Comment, *Advertising for Apartheid: The Use of All White Models in Marketing Real Estate As a Violation of the Fair Housing Act,* 56 Cinn. L. Rev. 1–129, 140–41 (1988).

[316]*See, e.g.,* New York Human Rights Div. v. Binghamton Press, 415 N.Y.S.2d 523, 5 Media L. Rep. 1085 (N.Y. App. Div. 1979) ("patently discriminatory" sex-based employment ad proposed illegal transaction by virtue of discriminatory content and thus did not merit First Amendment protection).

[317]*See, e.g.,* New York Times Co. v. Commission on Human Rights, 361 N.E.2d 963, 2 Media L. Rep. 1435 (N.Y. 1977) (without deciding First Amendment issue presented, court held that newspaper ad concerning South African employment opportunities did not set forth, directly or indirectly, discriminatory conditions on employment and thus did not violate state's anti-discrimination laws); Pittsburgh Press v. Commonwealth, 376 A.2d 263, 2 Media L. Rep. 2337 (Pa. Commw. Ct.), *aff'd,* 396 A.2d 1187, 4 Media L. Rep. 2109 (Pa. 1979), *cert. denied,* 442 U.S. 942 (1979) (First Amendment violated by state statute that prohibited job seekers from specifying sex, age, race, or national origin in employment ad). *See* Annot., *Identification of*

fact-specific and often depend on whether the solicitations were made in writing or in person,[318] whether the ads were nondeceptive and fair,[319] and whether the ads were directed to specific groups of prospective clients.[320]

Not surprisingly, one of the most litigated areas is attorney advertising, which the Supreme Court has repeatedly addressed.[321] Other professionals—including doctors,[322] optometrists,[323] dentists,[324] accountants,[325] and others[326]—have also, with varying degrees of success, asserted that their advertisements and promotions are protected by the First Amendment.

Jobseekers by Race, Religion, National Origin, Sex, or Age, in "Situation Wanted" Employment Advertising As Violation of State Civil Rights Laws, 99 A.L.R.3d 154 (1980).

[318]*See* cases discussed *supra* note 89.

[319]*E.g.,* Bates v. State Bar of Ariz., 433 U.S. 350, 384 (1977) (restriction on attorney advertising might be justified if advertising is potentially misleading or untruthful).

[320]*See supra* notes 157–59 and accompanying text.

[321]*See, e.g.,* Peel v. Attorney Registration & Disciplinary Comm'n, 496 U.S. 91 (1990); Shapero v. Kentucky Bar Ass'n, 486 U.S. 466 (1988); Zauderer v. Office of Disciplinary Counsel, 471 U.S. 626 (1985); Ohralik v. Ohio State Bar Ass'n, 436 U.S. 447 (1978) (state could discipline attorney for personal solicitation of accident victims); In re Primus, 436 U.S. 412 (1978) (solicitation of prospective litigants by ACLU—which engages in litigation as form of political expression and association—protected by First Amendment); In re R.M.J., 455 U.S. 191, 7 Media L. Rep. 2545 (1982); *Bates,* 433 U.S. 350, 2 Media L. Rep. 2097. These cases are discussed *supra* §§11.3 and 11.4.

See generally Annot., *Advertising As Ground for Disciplining Attorney,* 30 A.L.R.4th 742 (1984); Drecksel, *Shapero v. Kentucky Bar Association and Targeted, Direct-Mail Solicitation by Lawyers: How Can States Protect Their Residents From Overreaching and Deceptive Solicitation?* 1989 UTAH L. REV. 521 (1989).

[322]*See, e.g.,* Health Sys. v. Virginia Bd., 424 F. Supp. 267, 2 Media L. Rep. 1107 (S.D. Va. 1976); Gregory v. Board of Chiropractic Examiners, 608 So. 2d 987 (La. 1992) (ban on chiropractors soliciting by mail patients involved in motor vehicle accidents unconstitutional).

[323]*See, e.g.,* Friedman v. Rogers, 440 U.S. 1, 4 Media L. Rep. 2213 (1979) (discussed *supra* §11.4); Louisiana Consumers League v. Louisiana State Bd. of Optometry Examiners, 557 F.2d 473 (5th Cir. 1977) (citing *Virginia Pharmacy* and *Bates,* court held that statute prohibiting price advertising of prescription eyeglasses, lenses, and frames violated First Amendment); Board of Medical Examiners v. Terminal Hudson Elecs., 140 Cal. Rptr. 757 (Cal. Ct. App. 1977) (same); Wall & Ochs, Inc. v. Hicks, 469 F. Supp. 873 (E.D.N.C. 1979) (statute prohibiting prescription eyeglass advertising unconstitutional).

[324]*See, e.g.,* Parker v. Kentucky Bd. of Dentistry, 818 F.2d 504 (6th Cir. 1987) (ban against dentists using terms such as "orthodontics," "brackets," and "braces" in advertisements unconstitutional); Parmley v. Missouri Dental Bd., 719 S.W.2d 745 (Mo. 1986) (statutes concerning specialty licenses for dentists did not violate First Amendment or Equal Protection Clause); Baker v. Registered Dentists of Okla., 543 F. Supp. 1177 (W.D. Okla. 1982) (statutory provisions prohibiting dentists from advertising on radio and television and in newspapers unconstitutional, but provisions prohibiting dentists from using trade names constitutional). *See also* Sell, *The First Amendment Protection of Commercial Speech and State Regulation of Advertising in the Dental Profession: Parker v. Kentucky Board of Dentistry, 818 F.2d 504 (6th Cir. 1987),* 56 CINN. L. REV. 1525 (1988).

[325]*See, e.g.,* Edenfield v. Fane, 113 S. Ct. 1792, 21 Media L. Rep. 1321 (1993) (ban on personal and telephone solicitation of clients by certified public accountants violates First Amendment); Comprehensive Accounting Serv. Co. v. Maryland State Bd. of Pub. Accountancy, 397 A.2d 1019 (Md. 1979) (statute prohibiting noncertified accountants from using words "accountant" and "accounting" in advertisements unconstitutional); Rhode Island Broadcasters Ass'n v. Michaelson, 4 Media L. Rep. 2224 (D.R.I. 1978) (court held that broadcasters had standing to challenge statute absolutely banning tax return preparers from advertising and that statute unconstitutional under *Virginia Pharmacy*); Moore v. California State Bd. of Accountancy, 831 P.2d 798 (Cal. 1992) (unlicensed accountant may not use term "accountant" unless term is further qualified to indicate that person has no state accountancy license or that services offered do not require such license), *cert. denied,* 113 S. Ct. 1364 (1993).

[326]*See, e.g.,* Kievlan v. Dahlberg Elecs., 144 Cal. Rptr. 585 (Cal. Ct. App. 1978), *appeal dismissed,* 440 U.S. 951 (1979) (hearing device manufacturer can be prohibited from advertising that product had effect on ear diseases or disorders because such ads were misleading).

CHAPTER 12

TIME, PLACE, AND MANNER RESTRICTIONS

§12.1 Introduction

This chapter sets forth the test for time, place, and manner restrictions on speech and the application of that test in a variety of situations. Many of the subjects discussed here overlap with those in other chapters, because the government often attempts to justify restrictions on speech as merely a restraint on the time, place, or manner of the speech.[1]

§12.2 The Test for Time, Place, and Manner Restrictions

Governmental regulation that is not primarily aimed at suppression of certain ideas and that does not require enforcement authorities or courts to base their decisions on the content of the speech at issue, but rather is aimed at regulating the circumstances under which people communicate, is generally referred to as "time, place, and manner" regulation. Under the established three-pronged test for determining the validity of such restrictions on speech in public forums, such regulations are valid provided that they (1) are justified without reference to the content of the regulated speech; (2) are narrowly tailored to serve a significant governmental interest; and (3) leave open ample alternative channels of communication for the information.[2] Such restrictions are often in the form of licenses, whose constitutionality is inherently suspect.[3]

§12.2(A) Content Neutrality and Standardless Discretion

The first requirement of any time, place, and manner restriction is that it must be content-neutral. Restrictions often fail because they exempt certain

---

[1] See especially Chapters 1, 5, 10, and 11.
[2] Frisby v. Schultz, 487 U.S. 474, 481 (1988); City of Renton v. Playtime Theatres, 475 U.S. 41, 47, 12 Media L. Rep. 1721, 1724 (1986); Regan v. Time, Inc., 468 U.S. 641, 648 (1984); Clark v. Community for Creative Non-Violence, 468 U.S. 288, 293 (1984); City Council of Los Angeles v. Taxpayers for Vincent, 466 U.S. 789, 804–05 (1984); United States v. Grace, 461 U.S. 171, 177 (1983); Perry Educ. Ass'n v. Perry Local Educators' Ass'n, 460 U.S. 37, 45 (1983); Heffron v. International Soc'y for Krishna Consciousness, 452 U.S. 640, 647–48, 7 Media L. Rep. 1489, 1492–93 (1981); Virginia State Bd. of Pharmacy v. Virginia Citizens Consumer Council, 425 U.S. 748, 771, 1 Media L. Rep. 1930, 1938 (1976). For a discussion of the public forum theory, see Chapter 13, §13.5(A).
[3] Secretary of State of Md. v. Joseph H. Munson Co., 467 U.S. 947, 964 n.12 (1984) ("that a statute that requires . . . a 'license' for the dissemination of ideas is inherently suspect"); Hornstein v. Hartigan, 676 F. Supp. 894, 15 Media L. Rep. 1769 (C.D. Ill. 1988) (requirement that any person who wants to solicit ads

speech and thus impermissibly discriminate between different types of speech based on content.[4] Very narrow exceptions to this rule may exist, however.[5]

The government may not give its officials standardless discretion to deny access to public forums, because such discretion constitutes a prior restraint that can be used to suppress speech with which the official disagrees.[6] Of course, the converse is true: an ordinance that does not grant such discretion cannot be successfully challenged on this ground.[7]

§12.2(B) "Narrowly Tailored to Serve a Significant Governmental Interest"

The second prong of time, place, and manner analysis has two parts. A valid time, place, and manner restriction must serve a significant or substantial governmental interest, and the regulation must be narrowly tailored to serve that interest so that it does not unduly restrict protected expression.

Generally speaking, "the significance of the governmental interest must be assessed in light of the characteristic nature and function of the particular

---

for firefighting or law enforcement magazines obtain license by showing they are "legitimate and bona fide" is unconstitutional).

[4]*See, e.g.,* Metromedia, Inc. v. City of San Diego, 453 U.S. 490 (1981) (plurality opinion) (ordinance restricting use of billboards invalid because it allowed greater freedom to commercial than to noncommercial billboards); Carey v. Brown, 447 U.S. 455 (1980) (statute barring picketing in residential neighborhoods not valid time, place, and manner regulation because it exempted labor picketing); Police Dep't of Chicago v. Mosley, 408 U.S. 92 (1972) (ordinance prohibiting picketing adjacent to school invalidated because labor picketing not prohibited); Grayned v. City of Rockford, 408 U.S. 104, 107 (1972) (same); *see also* Schad v. Borough of Mt. Ephraim, 452 U.S. 61, 74–77, 7 Media L. Rep. 1426, 1432–33 (1981) (invalidating zoning ordinance prohibiting live entertainment within community but permitting other commercial activities); Linmark Assocs. v. Township of Willingboro, 431 U.S. 85 (1977) (in striking down ordinance prohibiting "For Sale" signs in residential neighborhoods as excessive restriction, Court noted that ordinance was not content-neutral).

[5]*See* Consolidated Edison Co. v. Public Serv. Comm'n, 447 U.S. 530, 538, 6 Media L. Rep. 1518 (1980) ("governmental regulation based on subject matter has been approved in narrow circumstances," citing cases); *City of Renton,* 475 U.S. at 48, 12 Media L. Rep. at 1724 (city ordinance prohibiting adult movie theaters within 1,000 feet of residential zone, church, park, or school upheld; ordinance justified because it was not aimed at content of adult films but at secondary effects of films, such as crime); Young v. American Mini Theatres, 427 U.S. 50, 70–71, 1 Media L. Rep. 1151, 1158–59 (1976) (upholding zoning law restricting location of adult movie theaters; "the State may legitimately use the content of these materials [sexually explicit films] as the basis for placing them in a different classification from other motion pictures"); Action for Children's Television v. Federal Communications Comm'n, 852 F.2d 1332, 1343 n.18, 15 Media L. Rep. 1907, 1915–16 n.18 (D.C. Cir. 1988) (observing that FCC order requiring broadcasts containing indecent material to be "channeled" to certain times of day is "content-based regulation of speech" but could be permissible if precisely drawn).

[6]Forsyth County v. Nationalist Movement, 112 S. Ct. 2395, 20 Media L. Rep. 1268, 1269–70 (1992) (holding facially unconstitutional ordinance that gave county administrator standardless discretion to set fees, not to exceed $1000, for use of public property based on content of speech, i.e., whether it would cause hostility and thereby increase cost of police and other government services); City of Lakewood v. Plain Dealer Pub'g Co., 486 U.S. 750, 757–59, 15 Media L. Rep. 1482, 1483–84 (1988) (striking down ordinance giving mayor discretion to grant or deny news rack permits even though mayor had to give reasoning in writing and denial was subject to judicial review); Shuttlesworth v. City of Birmingham, 394 U.S. 147, 149 (1969) (invalidating ordinance that authorized city commission to refuse parade permit if "in its judgment the public welfare" so required); Staub v. City of Baxley, 355 U.S. 313 (1958) (ordinance authorizing mayor to deny permit required for solicitation of memberships in organizations, on basis of applicant's character or nature of organization, held facially invalid); Cantwell v. Connecticut, 310 U.S. 296, 302 (1940) (voiding statute that prohibited solicitation of funds by religious or charitable groups unless "public welfare council" had determined that group is "bona fide" and has "integrity"); Hague v. Committee for Indus. Org., 307 U.S. 496, 516 (1939) (finding facially invalid municipal ordinance permitting director of public safety to refuse permits required for assemblies in public streets or parks "on his mere opinion that such refusal will prevent 'riots, disturbances or disorderly assemblage' ").

[7]Poulos v. New Hampshire, 345 U.S. 395, 404 (1953) (ordinance "left to the licensing officials no discretion as to granting permits, no power to discriminate, no control over speech"); Cox v. New Hampshire, 312 U.S. 569, 576 (1941) ("licensing board was not vested with arbitrary power or an unfettered discretion").

forum involved."[8] Perhaps the most common governmental interest that has been recognized as a valid basis for time, place, and manner regulations is the state's interest in maintaining order in public places such as parks, schools, or streets.[9] The protection of a person's privacy in his or her home from unwanted intrusion is also a significant governmental interest.[10] Another accepted rationale for such regulations is the state's interest in preserving a desired quality of life for its citizens through regulation of the aesthetics of the environment, such as regulation of billboards or zoning of adult theaters.[11] The prevention of crime is also a significant governmental interest.[12]

Other governmental interests held by the Supreme Court to be substantial enough to justify time, place, and manner restrictions on expression include avoiding undue public pressure on the judiciary,[13] preserving integrated communities,[14] making counterfeiting of U.S. currency more difficult,[15] maintaining professionalism by licensed pharmacists,[16] and enhancing the parent-child bond by facilitating family discussions about birth control.[17]

Courts have rejected assertions that a governmental interest is substantial where the cost of ignoring the offending speech is very low, such as by throwing away an offensive mailing,[18] ignoring the early broadcast of election predictions,[19] or averting one's eyes from a defaced U.S. flag.[20] Lastly, in evaluating the significance of the governmental interest, courts will measure not only the importance of the interest as asserted in the case at hand, but also how the regulation at issue would affect parties not before the court. Where it appears that the government's stake in a particular case is not substantial, that interest may actually be substantial when considered in the context of all cases to which the regulation at issue might apply.[21]

---

[8]Heffron v. International Soc'y for Krishna Consciousness, 452 U.S. 640, 650–51, 7 Media L. Rep. 1489, 1493–94 (1981) (upholding regulations barring roving fundraisers at state fair).

[9]Clark v. Community for Creative Non-Violence, 468 U.S. 288, 298 (1984) (Lafayette Park, opposite White House); United States v. Grace, 461 U.S. 171, 181 (1983) (Supreme Court grounds); *Heffron,* 452 U.S. at 654, 7 Media L. Rep. at 1495 (state fair); Grayned v. City of Rockford, 408 U.S. 104, 119 (1972) (school); Cox v. Louisiana, 379 U.S. 559, 576 (1965) (streets); Cox v. New Hampshire, 312 U.S. 569, 574–76 (1941) (same).

[10]Frisby v. Schultz, 487 U.S. 474, 484 (1988); Martin v. City of Struthers, 319 U.S. 141, 144 (1943). *See also* Carey v. Brown, 447 U.S. 455, 471 (1980) (equal protection analysis).

[11]City of Renton v. Playtime Theatres, 475 U.S. 41, 54, 12 Media L. Rep. 1721, 1727 (1986) (city has substantial interest in "preserving the quality of life in the community at large"); City Council of Los Angeles v. Taxpayers for Vincent, 466 U.S. 789, 806 (1984) ("municipalities have a weighty, essentially esthetic interest in proscribing intrusive and unpleasant formats for expression"); Metromedia, Inc. v. City of San Diego, 453 U.S. 490, 507–08 (1981) (improving appearance of city is substantial governmental goal); Young v. American Mini Theatres, 427 U.S. 50, 71, 1 Media L. Rep. 1151, 1159 (1976) ("city's interest in attempting to preserve the quality of urban life is one that must be accorded high respect").

[12]Hynes v. Mayor of Oradell, 425 U.S. 610, 616–17 (1976) ("the Court has consistently recognized a municipality's power to protect its citizens from crime and undue annoyance by regulating soliciting and canvassing.").

[13]*Grace,* 461 U.S. at 183; Cox v. Louisiana, 379 U.S. 559, 562 (1965).

[14]Linmark Assocs. v. Township of Willingboro, 431 U.S. 85, 94–95 (1977).

[15]Regan v. Time, Inc., 468 U.S. 641, 656 (1984).

[16]Virginia State Bd. of Pharmacy v. Virginia Citizens Consumer Council, 425 U.S. 748, 766, 1 Media L. Rep. 1930, 1936–37 (1976).

[17]Bolger v. Youngs Drug Prods. Corp., 463 U.S. 60, 73 (1983).

[18]*Id.* at 72.

[19]Daily Herald Co. v. Munro, 838 F.2d 380, 388, 14 Media L. Rep. 2332, 2337–38 (9th Cir. 1988).

[20]Spence v. Washington, 418 U.S. 405, 412 (1974).

[21]Regan v. Time, Inc., 468 U.S. 641, 657–58 & n.12 (1984) (while *Time* magazine's use of reproductions of U.S. currency may be harmless, this might not be true of others using such reproductions); Clark v. Community for Creative Non-Violence, 468 U.S. 288, 296–97 (1984) (rule against sleeping in park serves to prevent such use by other than those, such as respondents, who wish to make only symbolic, limited demonstration); Heffron v. International Soc'y for Krishna Consciousness, 452 U.S. 640, 652–53, 7 Media

While the Supreme Court has frequently stated that a valid time, place, and manner regulation must be "narrowly tailored" to serve a significant governmental interest,[22] what this actually requires was the subject of some debate. Several courts read the Supreme Court opinions, particularly in cases involving limitations on residential solicitation, to require that municipalities use the *least restrictive means possible* to institute time, place, and manner regulations.[23] Under this interpretation, such regulations are invalid if there are means of achieving the state's goal that are less restrictive of the right of expression.[24] The Supreme Court has now held, however, that the state need not use the "least restrictive means" for a law to be "narrowly tailored."[25]

In applying the "narrowly tailored" test to time, place, and manner regulations, the Supreme Court has upheld a restriction on residential picketing that targets a particular house, holding that a complete prohibition of such activity was sufficiently narrow because this type of picketing intrudes upon residents in a particularly offensive way.[26] The Court also sustained a zoning regulation that concentrated adult theaters in one area, holding that the regulation was narrowly tailored because it applied only to those theaters (adult cinemas) that the community believed would have negative effects, rather than eliminating all types of entertainment.[27] Disclaiming an active role in reviewing practical decisions made by city officials, the Court noted, "the city should be allowed a reasonable opportunity to experiment with solutions to admittedly serious problems."[28] Similarly, the Court refused to second-guess the National Park Service when the Service allowed 24-hour demonstrations, but not sleeping, in Washington, D.C.'s, Lafayette Park. The Court found this policy to be narrowly tailored to preserve the park.[29]

On the other hand, the Court has rejected ordinances on the grounds of insufficiently narrow tailoring. Where a District of Columbia statute barred the carrying of signs on the sidewalk in front of the Supreme Court, the Court found that the regulation did not narrowly serve either the interest in order and

---

L. Rep. 1489, 1494–95 (1981) (state's ban on roving solicitation at state fairs must be considered not only as it applies to respondents but to all other groups who might take advantage of such opportunity).

[22]Frisby v. Schultz, 487 U.S. 474, 485 (1988) ("A statute is narrowly tailored if it targets and eliminates no more than the exact source of the 'evil' it seeks to remedy."); City of Renton v. Playtime Theatres, 475 U.S. 41, 47, 12 Media L. Rep. 1721, 1725 (1986) (regulation should be "designed to serve a substantial governmental interest"); *Clark*, 468 U.S. at 293 ("narrowly tailored to serve a significant governmental interest"); United States v. Grace, 461 U.S. 171, 177 (1983) ("narrowly tailored" (citing Perry Educ. Ass'n v. Perry Local Educators' Ass'n, 460 U.S. 37, 45 (1983))); *Heffron*, 452 U.S. at 647–48, 7 Media L. Rep. at 1492–93 ("serve a significant governmental interest" (citing Virginia State Bd. of Pharmacy v. Virginia Citizens Consumer Council, 425 U.S. 748, 771, 1 Media L. Rep. 1930, 1938 (1976))).

[23]City of Watseka v. Illinois Pub. Action Council, 796 F.2d 1547, 1553 (7th Cir. 1986), *aff'd*, 479 U.S. 1048 (1987); Cinevision Corp. v. City of Burbank, 745 F.2d 560, 569 (9th Cir. 1984), *cert. denied*, 471 U.S. 1054 (1985); Eastern Conn. Citizens Action Group v. Powers, 723 F.2d 1050, 1055 (2d Cir. 1983); Association of Community Orgs. for Reform Now v. City of Frontenac, 714 F.2d 813, 818 (8th Cir. 1983); New York City Unemployed & Welfare Council v. Brezenoff, 677 F.2d 232, 237 (2d Cir. 1982).

[24]This is an extremely difficult standard to meet. *City of Watseka*, 796 F.2d at 1564 (dissenting opinion) ("Adoption of 'less-restrictive-alternative' analysis imposes a high level of scrutiny and invariably leads to the invalidation of the statute because it is always possible to envisage alternative forms of regulation.").

[25]Ward v. Rock Against Racism, 491 U.S. 781, 798, *reh'g denied*, 492 U.S. 937 (1989) ("[W]e reaffirm today that a regulation of the time, place or manner of protected speech must be narrowly tailored to serve the government's legitimate content-neutral interests but that it need not be the least-restrictive or least-intrusive means of doing so."); *see infra* note 127.

[26]*Frisby*, 487 U.S. at 485–86.

[27]*City of Renton*, 475 U.S. at 52, 12 Media L. Rep. at 1725–26. *But see* Schad v. Borough of Mt. Ephraim, 452 U.S. 61, 7 Media L. Rep. 1426 (1981) (ordinance banning all live entertainment held unconstitutional); Erznoznik v. City of Jacksonville, 422 U.S. 205, 1 Media L. Rep. 1508 (1975) (ordinance barring all films containing nudity from drive-ins held unconstitutional).

[28]*City of Renton*, 475 U.S. at 52, 12 Media L. Rep. at 1725–26.

[29]Clark v. Community for Creative Non-Violence, 468 U.S. 288, 295 (1984).

decorum on Supreme Court grounds or the interest in avoiding the appearance that the Court could be swayed by public pressure.[30] Similarly, in two commercial speech cases, the Court found that barring the mailing of information on contraceptives to homes did not serve the goal of facilitating the parent-child bond,[31] and that forbidding "For Sale" signs did not narrowly serve the goal of preserving integrated communities by avoiding "blockbusting."[32]

§12.2(C) "Ample Alternative Means of Communication"

Even if a time, place, and manner regulation satisfies the first two requirements, it will not survive constitutional scrutiny unless it leaves open ample alternative means of communication.[33] Where the challenged ordinance leaves open other means of communication that are reasonably equivalent in function, however, the regulation is valid.[34] In deciding whether an alternative is "ample," courts will consider, in addition to functional equivalency, the relative cost of the alternatives[35] and the distance or effort involved in using them.[36]

---

[30]United States v. Grace, 461 U.S. 171, 182–83 (1983). *See also* Food & Commercial Workers v. IBP, Inc., 857 F.2d 422, 430–35 (7th Cir. 1988) (statute that prohibited "any form of picketing in which there are more than two pickets at any one time within either fifty feet of any entrance to the premises being picketed or within fifty feet of any other picket or pickets" and that barred "talking" to picketing targets facially overbroad; district court properly found that type of picketing prohibited did not present clear danger of violence; statute was not least restrictive means of preventing violence; and "anti-talking" provision impermissibly reached peaceful communications).

[31]Bolger v. Youngs Drug Prods. Corp., 463 U.S. 60, 73 (1983).

[32]Linmark Assocs. v. Township of Willingboro, 431 U.S. 85, 95–96 (1977).

[33]Meyer v. Grant, 486 U.S. 414, 424 (1988) ("Colorado's prohibition of paid petition circulators restricts access to the most effective, fundamental, and perhaps most economical avenue of political discourse, direct one-on-one communication. That it leaves open 'more burdensome' avenues of communication, does not relieve its burden on First Amendment expression."); Metromedia, Inc. v. City of San Diego, 453 U.S. 490, 515–17 (1981) (alternatives to banned outdoor billboards insufficient, inappropriate, and prohibitively expensive); Schad v. Borough of Mt. Ephraim, 452 U.S. 61, 75–77, 7 Media L. Rep. 1426, 1432–33 (1981) (no ample alternatives when ordinance barred all live entertainment); *Linmark Assocs.*, 431 U.S. at 92–94 (ordinance barring "For Sale" signs on houses struck down because alternatives of advertising, leafletting, or listing were more costly, involved less "autonomy," and were less likely to reach desired audience); Invisible Empire of Knights of Ku Klux Klan (Md. Chapter) v. Mayor, Board of Comm'rs, & Chief of Police of Thurmont, 700 F. Supp. 281 (D. Md. 1988) (town officials' denial of parade permit to KKK because it refused to allow blacks and non-Christians to march in parade violated First Amendment because nondiscrimination provision related to suppression of Klan's speech; "the condition was developed for the KKK and the KKK only" and, by effectively prohibiting Klan from holding parade, "does not leave open alternative means of communication for KKK"); Walnut Properties v. City of Whittier, 861 F.2d 1102 (9th Cir. 1988), *cert. denied*, 490 U.S. 1006 (1989) (affirming ruling that city ordinance prohibiting adult theater from operating within 1,000 feet of church was unconstitutional because ordinance failed to allow adequate alternative locations for such theaters); *see also infra* §12.4(D).

[34]Frisby v. Schultz, 487 U.S. 474, 483–84 (1988) (restriction on picketing in front of resident's home leaves ample alternatives of marching, door-to-door proselytizing, and distributing literature); Regan v. Time, Inc., 468 U.S. 641, 658 n.13 (1984) (magazine had ample alternatives in communicating editorial ideas other than employing banned color and size of reproductions of U.S. currency); Clark v. Community for Creative Non-Violence, 468 U.S. 288, 295 (1984) (ban on overnight sleeping in park left ample alternative means to communicate plight of homeless, such as symbolic constructs, signs, and demonstrations); City Council of Los Angeles v. Taxpayers for Vincent, 466 U.S. 789, 812 (1984) (right to speak and distribute literature on public property ample alternative to barred activity of posting signs on that property); Heffron v. International Soc'y for Krishna Consciousness, 452 U.S. 640, 649–54, 7 Media L. Rep. 1489, 1493–95 (1981) (alternatives to fundraising by ritual wandering, such as fundraising from fixed booth or wandering and speaking but not soliciting, ample).

[35]*Vincent*, 466 U.S. at 812 n.30 ("[T]he Court has shown special solicitude for forms of expression that are much less expensive than feasible alternatives and hence may be important to a large segment of the citizenry"); Martin v. City of Struthers, 319 U.S. 141, 146 (1943) ("Door to door distribution of circulars is essential to the poorly financed causes of little people."). *But see* Kovacs v. Cooper, 336 U.S. 77, 88–89 (1949) ("That more people may be more easily and cheaply reached by sound trucks . . . is not enough to call forth constitutional protection for what those charged with public welfare reasonably think is a nuisance when easy means of publicity are open.").

[36]City of Renton v. Playtime Theatres, 475 U.S. 41, 54–55, 12 Media L. Rep. 1721, 1726–27 (1986) (zoning regulation that barred adult theaters from all but 5% of city's land upheld because 5% constituted ample alternative means); *Heffron*, 452 U.S. at 655, 7 Media L. Rep. at 1495–96 (alternative to fundraising at state fair is to do it outside fairgrounds). *But see Schad*, 452 U.S. at 76, 7 Media L. Rep. at 1433

§ 12.3 TIME RESTRICTIONS

In deciding whether time restrictions are constitutional, "[t]he crucial question is whether the manner of expression is basically incompatible with the normal activity of a particular place at a particular time."[37] Thus, one could not "insist upon a street meeting in the middle of Times Square at the rush hour as a form of freedom of speech or assembly."[38]

Regulations on the time of expression occur in different contexts. Among the most common are regulations on the hours during which solicitors or canvassers may contact residents in their homes.[39] In the leading Supreme Court case on the First Amendment rights of solicitors, the Court struck down a city-wide ban on residential solicitation but noted approvingly that such ordinances are "aimed at the protection of the householders from annoyance, including intrusion upon the hours of rest."[40] Many municipalities have attempted to limit the times during which solicitors may approach residents, often restricting solicitation to 9 a.m. to 5 p.m., Monday to Saturday. Such ordinances have generally been struck down by the courts, at least if they ban canvassing before 9 p.m.[41] These courts have held that such regulations are not narrowly tailored to the asserted governmental goals, which are usually prevention of crime and protection of residents' peace, and instead point to the less restrictive means available to municipalities, such as requiring registration of solicitors, enforcing trespass laws, and asking those residents who do not want solicitors to post signs to that effect in front of their homes.[42]

Another common category of time restrictions is composed of ordinances that restrict the time of parades or demonstrations. A federal appellate court upheld a ban on rush-hour demonstrations in Washington, D.C.'s, Lafayette Park.[43] Similarly, another circuit court upheld a General Services Administration regulation that barred entry onto government property "after normal working hours" because of the federal interests in security and quiet.[44] One court, however, following the logic of the solicitation cases, overturned a ban on parades after 6 p.m., holding that the city's anticrime rationale applied only to parades held after dark.[45] In an unusual time regulation case, *Olivieri v. Ward*,[46] two separate groups sought to stage their rallies at the same time a third, larger

---

(borough-wide ban on live entertainment not saved by possible availability of such entertainment in other parts of county); Schneider v. New Jersey, 308 U.S. 147, 163 (1939) ("[O]ne is not to have the exercise of his liberty of expression in appropriate places abridged on the plea that it may be exercised in some other place.").

[37] Grayned v. City of Rockford, 408 U.S. 104, 116 (1972).
[38] Cox v. Louisiana, 379 U.S. 536, 554 (1965).
[39] Regulations on door-to-door solicitation are discussed more generally *infra* § 12.5(B).
[40] Martin v. City of Struthers, 319 U.S. 141, 144 (1943).
[41] New Jersey Citizen Action v. Edison Township, 797 F.2d 1250, 1254–62 (3d Cir. 1986), *cert. denied*, 479 U.S. 1103 (1987); City of Watseka v. Illinois Pub. Action Council, 796 F.2d 1547, 1555–58 (7th Cir. 1986), *aff'd*, 479 U.S. 1048 (1987); Wisconsin Action Coalition v. City of Kenosha, 767 F.2d 1248, 1257–58 (7th Cir. 1985); Association of Community Orgs. for Reform Now v. City of Frontenac, 714 F.2d 813, 818–20 (8th Cir. 1983). *Contra* Pennsylvania Alliance for Jobs & Energy v. Council of Munhall, 743 F.2d 182, 187–88 (3d Cir. 1984).
[42] *See supra* note 41.
[43] Quaker Action Group v. Morton, 516 F.2d 717, 733–34 (D.C. Cir. 1975).
[44] United States v. Christopher, 700 F.2d 1253, 1259–60 (9th Cir.), *cert. denied*, 461 U.S. 960 (1983).
[45] Beckerman v. City of Tupelo, 664 F.2d 502, 512 (5th Cir. 1981). *But see* Abernathy v. Conroy, 429 F.2d 1170, 1173–74 (4th Cir. 1970) (upholding ban on parades after 8 p.m.).
[46] 801 F.2d 602 (2d Cir. 1986), *cert. denied*, 480 U.S. 917 (1987).

rally was scheduled. The Second Circuit held that the opposing groups were entitled, albeit in a limited fashion, to conduct their rallies at the same time as the larger rally.[47]

Several other time restrictions have resulted in litigation. Courts have struck down the attempts of municipalities to severely limit the times when sound trucks may be used on city streets,[48] and time restrictions on the distribution of newspapers have also been overturned.[49]

In another case, *Carlin Communications v. Federal Communications Commission*,[50] Congress had criminalized any "dial-a-porn" service that did not forbid access to those under 18 years of age. The FCC then implemented this law by permitting such services if they limited their operations to 9 p.m. through 6 a.m. The Second Circuit ruled that this time restriction was invalid because it was not narrowly tailored to the governmental interest in preventing access by children: adults could not call in during the day, but children could easily call in at night. Further, the court found that there were less restrictive means to achieve the desired goal, such as using access codes or technical blocking of certain numbers.[51] On the other hand, the Fifth Circuit upheld a municipal regulation that limited the hours of adult bookstores to 10 a.m. to midnight, Monday through Saturday, finding that the legal period of 14 hours a day, six days a week did not impermissibly suppress the speech in question.[52]

The Supreme Court has held, in *Mills v. Alabama*,[53] that a statute prohibiting a newspaper from publishing an editorial on election day urging people to vote a certain way is unconstitutional. The Court noted that such political speech is clearly protected by the First Amendment, and that the statute did not really blunt the force of election-eve political attacks but merely shifted the cutoff date for replies to another date.[54]

§12.4 PLACE RESTRICTIONS

There are three types of public forums: traditional public, limited public, and nonpublic. The category into which a forum is placed substantially affects how much access to it is available.[55]

---

[47]*Id.* at 606–08.

[48]*Beckerman*, 664 F.2d at 516–17 (rationales for barring sound trucks apply only in nighttime hours; therefore, total ban from 6 p.m. to 9 a.m. not narrowly tailored); Reeves v. McConn, 631 F.2d 377, 383–85 (5th Cir. 1980) (city's restrictive policy on when sound trucks may operate not tailored to city's interest in preventing disruption of business and distraction of pedestrians and drivers). *See generally infra* §12.5(E).

[49]Schad v. Ocean Grove Camp Meeting Ass'n, 370 A.2d 449, 454–55, 2 Media L. Rep. 1354, 1357–59 (N.J. 1977), *overruled on other grounds sub nom.* State v. Celmer, 404 A.2d 1, 7 (N.J. 1979), *cert. denied*, 444 U.S. 951 (1979).

[50]749 F.2d 113 (2d Cir. 1984).

[51]*Id.* at 120–21. A 24-hour-a-day ban on all "indecent" programming on television and radio has also been struck down. Action for Children's Television v. Federal Communications Comm'n, 932 F.2d 1504 (D.C. Cir. 1991), *cert. denied*, 112 S. Ct. 1282 (1992).

[52]Star Satellite v. City of Biloxi, 779 F.2d 1074, 1079–80 (5th Cir. 1986); *see also* Federal Communications Comm'n v. Pacifica Found., 438 U.S. 726, 750, 3 Media L. Rep. 2553, 2562 (1978).

[53]384 U.S. 214, 1 Media L. Rep. 1334 (1966).

[54]*Id.* at 219–20, 1 Media L. Rep. at 1336. State courts have followed *Mills* in overruling similar statutes. Commonwealth v. Wadzinski, 422 A.2d 124, 132 (Pa. 1980) (Pennsylvania statute barring political advertisements in 48 hours before election, without reasonable notice to opponent, held unconstitutional under *Mills*); Town of Latana v. Pelczynski, 303 So. 2d 326, 326–28 (Fla. 1974) (voiding town ordinance prohibiting any charge or attack on candidate in seven days before election); KPOJ, Inc. v. Thornton, 456 P.2d 76, 77 (Or. 1969) (voiding Oregon statute that forbade electioneering on election day).

[55]For a detailed description of these three forums and their parameters, see Chapter 13, §13.5(A).

§12.4(A) Traditional Public Forums: Parks and Streets

Certain places—most notably public streets and parks—play a special role in time, place, and manner analysis. "In places which by long tradition or by government fiat have been devoted to assembly and debate, the rights of the state to limit expressive activity are sharply circumscribed."[56]

The classic expression of this notion is contained in Justice Owen Roberts' opinion in *Hague v. Committee for Industrial Organization:*

> Wherever the title of streets and parks may rest, they have immemorially been held in trust for the use of the public and, time out of mind, have been used for purposes of assembly, communicating thought between citizens, and discussing public questions. Such use of the streets and public places has, from ancient times, been a part of the privileges, immunities, rights and liberties of citizens. The privilege of a citizen of the United States to use the streets and parks for communication of views on national questions may be regulated in the interest of all; it is not absolute, but relative, and must be exercised in subordination to the general comfort and convenience, and in consonance with peace and good order; but it must not, in the guise of regulation, be abridged or denied.[57]

Even content-neutral regulations that restrict expression in such places will be closely scrutinized by the courts. The government must not unduly limit access to public forums; only the most minimal restrictions will be upheld in these places.[58]

§12.4(B) Nontraditional or Limited Forums: Public Property

With the expansion of the role of government in society, the number of government-owned or controlled buildings and open areas has multiplied. Because many of these places have some of the functional attributes of the traditional town square or park, they are treated by the courts as "limited purpose public forums." Free expression that is not inconsistent with the uses to which these places are regularly put may be abridged only under the circumstances discussed previously for traditional public forums. In considering these cases, "[t]he nature of a place, 'the pattern of its normal activities, dictate the kinds of regulations of time, place, and manner that are reasonable.' "[59]

One group of nontraditional public forums includes those places designed for discussion or debate. Once the state has opened property for use by the public for expressive activity, the Constitution forbids it from enforcing exclusions from the forum, even if the state was not required to create the forum in

---

[56]Perry Educ. Ass'n v. Perry Local Educators' Ass'n, 460 U.S. 37, 45 (1983). In Frisby v. Schultz, 487 U.S. 474, 480–81 (1988), the Court held that even streets in residential neighborhoods are public forums.

[57]307 U.S. 496, 515–16 (1939) (quoted approvingly in Shuttlesworth v. City of Birmingham, 394 U.S. 147, 152 (1969)). This overruled the Court's earlier decision that states have absolute control over public speaking and assembly on public property: "For the legislature absolutely or conditionally to forbid public speaking in a highway or public park is no more an infringement of the rights of a member of the public than for the owner of a private house to forbid it in his house." Davis v. Massachusetts, 167 U.S. 43, 47 (1897).

[58]United States v. Grace, 461 U.S. 171, 175–76 (1983) (federal law prohibiting display of banners on sidewalk outside Supreme Court held invalid); Jamison v. Texas, 318 U.S. 413 (1943) (ordinance prohibiting distribution of handbills on city streets held invalid); Lovell v. City of Griffin, 303 U.S. 444 (1938) (ordinance prohibiting pamphleteering on city streets without permission of police held invalid).

[59]Grayned v. City of Rockford, 408 U.S. 104, 116 (1972) (citation omitted).

the first place.[60] Examples of this sort of nontraditional, limited public forum include university meeting facilities,[61] school board meetings,[62] municipal theaters and auditoriums,[63] and the public areas surrounding some government buildings.[64]

A second group of nontraditional public forums includes those publicly owned places whose daily operations, although not dedicated primarily to discussion and debate, are not inconsistent with such use and will not be disrupted by certain forms of free expression. "If ... an area is not a public forum, but is one used by the government to perform some non-speech-related function, it may nevertheless be 'appropriate' for the exercise of First Amendment activities if that exercise does not interfere with the primary activity for which it is intended."[65] Under this analysis, courts have invalidated content-neutral restrictions on certain types of free expression in universities,[66] public libraries,[67] welfare centers,[68] bus terminals,[69] train stations,[70] and airports.[71]

---

[60]Perry Educ. Ass'n v. Perry Local Educators' Ass'n, 460 U.S. 37, 45 (1983). *See, e.g.,* Widmar v. Vincent, 454 U.S. 263, 267 (1981) (having created forum generally open for use by student groups, state university could not exclude student religious groups); City of Madison Joint Sch. Dist. v. Wisconsin Employment Relations Comm'n, 429 U.S. 167, 174–76 (1976) (although school board could have met in private session, it could not bar teachers from speaking at open board meeting at which public participation was permitted); Amato v. Wilentz, 753 F. Supp. 543, 18 Media L. Rep. 1985 (D.N.J. 1990), *rev'd on other grounds,* 952 F.2d 742 (3d Cir. 1991) (government cannot refuse to allow company to use courtroom for filming movie where it was previously used for filming and justification for refusal is disagreement with content of film). *Compare* Minnesota State Bd. for Community Colleges v. Knight, 465 U.S. 271, 280–82 (1984) (college administration policy-making session not public forum even though certain faculty members invited to attend).

[61]*Widmar,* 454 U.S. at 267. Colleges have also been held to be limited-purpose public forums. Hays County Guardian v. Supple, 969 F.2d 111, 118, 20 Media L. Rep. 1681, 1685 (5th Cir. 1992), *cert. denied,* 113 S. Ct. 1067 (1993).

[62]*City of Madison,* 429 U.S. at 174–76.

[63]Southeastern Promotions v. Conrad, 420 U.S. 546, 552, 1 Media L. Rep. 1140, 1142 (1975) (discretionary denial of access to city-owned theater for production of "Hair" invalid).

[64]Edwards v. South Carolina, 372 U.S. 229 (1963) (reversing breach of peace convictions for peaceful protest on state house grounds); United States v. Grace, 461 U.S. 171 (1983) (voiding statute barring display of banners on Supreme Court grounds).

[65]New York City Unemployed & Welfare Council v. Brezenoff, 677 F.2d 232, 237 (2d Cir. 1982) (analyzing regulations concerning welfare centers) (citation omitted).

[66]Widmar v. Vincent, 454 U.S. 263, 267 (1981) (meeting rooms for student groups). *But see* Grayned v. City of Rockford, 408 U.S. 104 (1972) (anti-noise ordinance could be used to prohibit noisy demonstration outside school while classes were in session).

[67]Brown v. Louisiana, 383 U.S. 131 (1966) (silent vigil in public library held constitutionally protected).

[68]Albany Welfare Rights Org. v. Wyman, 493 F.2d 1319, 1322–24 (2d Cir.), *cert. denied,* 419 U.S. 838 (1974) (complete ban on leafletting in welfare center invalid); *Brezenoff,* 677 F.2d at 238 (welfare office appropriate forum to reach welfare recipients on welfare issues).

[69]Wolin v. Port of N.Y. Auth., 392 F.2d 83 (2d Cir.), *cert. denied,* 393 U.S. 940 (1968) (ban on peaceful leafletting invalidated).

[70]Gannett Satellite Info. Network v. Metropolitan Transp. Auth., 745 F.2d 767, 773, 10 Media L. Rep. 2424, 2427 (2d Cir. 1984) (public areas of commuter railroad station appropriate forums for sale of newspapers through news racks); Wright v. Chief of Transit Police, 558 F.2d 67, 68–69, 2 Media L. Rep. 1980, 1982–83 (2d Cir. 1977) (ban on person-to-person sales of newspapers in subway stations could not be upheld in absence of showing that lesser restrictions would not adequately serve city's safety interest); Moskowitz v. Cullman, 432 F. Supp. 1263, 1266–67 (D.N.J. 1977) (publicly owned bus and train terminal is public forum for distribution of handbills).

[71]International Society for Krishna Consciousness v. Lee, 112 S. Ct. 2701, 20 Media L. Rep. 1297 (1992) (5-4 decision holding that airports are not public forums and using reasonableness test to uphold ban on in-person solicitation; by different 5-4 majority, striking down ban on distribution of literature in crowded airport terminals (relying on split decision in United States v. Kokinda, 497 U.S. 720 (1990), which upheld ban on solicitation on postal premises); Board of Airport Comm'rs v. Jews for Jesus, 482 U.S. 569, 575 (1987) (ordinance barring all "First Amendment Activities" in airport held invalid); United States S.W. Africa/Namibia Trade & Cultural Council v. United States, 708 F.2d 760, 774 (D.C. Cir. 1983) (ban on political advertisement in airport held invalid); International Soc'y for Krishna Consciousness v. Rochford, 585 F.2d 263 (7th Cir. 1978) (airport regulations restricting distribution of literature and solicitation of funds held invalid); Kuszynski v. City of Oakland, 479 F.2d 1130 (9th Cir. 1973) (per curiam) (ordinance restricting leafletting at airport held invalid).

§12.4(C) Public Property Not Regarded As a Public Forum

Property is not automatically deemed a public forum merely because it is owned by the government.[72] " 'The State, no less than a private owner of property, has power to preserve the property under its control for the use to which it is lawfully dedicated.' "[73] Thus, although postal mailboxes,[74] military bases,[75] prisons,[76] and certain public school facilities[77] are publicly owned property and are, under certain circumstances, open to the public, prohibitions on expressive activity at such places have been upheld where the banned First Amendment activity in question would have been inherently inconsistent with the operations of the public facility.[78]

§12.4(D) Private Property, Shopping Malls, and the Home

Governmental time, place, and manner restrictions on free expression generally regulate activities on public property.[79] Often, however, such regulations also affect private property. For instance, government regulations on adult theaters,[80] billboards on private property,[81] and magazines[82] have been upheld by the Supreme Court.

A more intriguing question is when private property may be deemed sufficiently public that the owner faces First Amendment barriers before he or she can restrict expressive activities on the property. Generally, the state is free to employ its police power to rid private property of unwelcome intruders, even if the intruders have entered the property for speech purposes.[83] As the Supreme Court noted in *Central Hardware Co. v. National Labor Relations Board*,[84] "[b]efore an owner of private property can be subjected to the commands of the first and fourteenth amendments, the privately owned property

---

[72]Perry Educ. Ass'n v. Perry Local Educators' Ass'n, 460 U.S. 37, 46 (1983); United States Postal Serv. v. Council of Greenburgh Civic Ass'ns, 453 U.S. 114, 129, 7 Media L. Rep. 1505, 1512 (1981).

[73]Greer v. Spock, 424 U.S. 828, 836 (1976) (quoting Adderly v. Florida, 385 U.S. 39, 47 (1966)).

[74]*Council of Greenburgh*, 453 U.S. at 116 (upholding federal law prohibiting deposit of "unstamped 'mailable matter' " in letterboxes).

[75]*Greer*, 424 U.S. 828 (army may ban partisan political speeches and require prior approval for distribution of literature on base even though base is open to public and nonpolitical speakers and entertainers had previously been invited); *but see* Flower v. United States, 407 U.S. 197 (1972) (per curiam) (overturning conviction of civilian for distribution of leaflets on avenue on military base on which military had abandoned right to exclude pedestrian traffic).

[76]Adderley v. Florida, 385 U.S. 39 (1966) (upholding trespass convictions of students who entered prison grounds to protest arrest of civil rights advocates); Jones v. North Carolina Prisoners' Labor Union, 433 U.S. 119 (1977) (prison officials may prohibit inmate-to-inmate solicitation to join prisoners' union).

[77]Perry Educ. Ass'n v. Perry Local Educators' Ass'n, 460 U.S. 37 (1983) (dissident union denied access to teachers' mailboxes in high school even though incumbent union permitted to use them); Connecticut State Fed'n of Teachers v. Board of Educ. Members, 538 F.2d 471 (2d Cir. 1976) (same).

[78]*See supra* notes 74–77.

[79]*See Perry Educ. Ass'n*, 460 U.S. at 45–46 (describing three categories of public property and applicable standards for restricting speech in each).

[80]City of Renton v. Playtime Theatres, 475 U.S. 41, 12 Media L. Rep. 1721 (1986); Young v. American Mini Theatres, 427 U.S. 50, 1 Media L. Rep. 1151 (1976). Regulation of adult theaters, however, is not open-ended. *See* Walnut Properties v. City of Whittier, 861 F.2d 1102 (9th Cir. 1988), *cert. denied*, 490 U.S. 1006 (1989) (affirming ruling that city ordinance prohibiting adult theater from operating within 1,000 feet of church unconstitutional because ordinance failed to allow adequate alternative locations for such theaters); *see also supra* §12.2(C).

[81]*See infra* §12.5(D).

[82]Regan v. Time, Inc., 468 U.S. 641 (1984) (prohibition on printing likenesses of U.S. currency).

[83]*See, e.g.,* Martin v. City of Struthers, 319 U.S. 141, 147 (1943) (discussing efficacy of enforcement of trespass laws in dealing with unwanted solicitors).

[84]407 U.S. 539 (1972).

must assume to some significant degree the functional attributes of public property devoted to public use."[85]

One kind of private property that falls into the public forum category is private property that has the functional attributes of a town. Thus, owners of "company towns" cannot restrict access to the towns by those who want to communicate with its residents.[86] Similar restrictions have been placed on owners of migrant labor camps.[87] In two decisions, the Supreme Court reversed an earlier decision that placed shopping malls in the same category,[88] but several state courts have held that their state constitutions prohibit owners of shopping malls from preventing canvassing.[89] A significant number of state courts, however, have reached the opposite result.[90]

Courts have given special attention to the rights of people in their homes.[91] In the interests of preventing burglary, fraud, or protecting privacy, the government may enact a "narrowly drawn ordinance, that does not vest in municipal officials the undefined power to determine what messages residents will hear."[92] For instance, criminal sanctions have been upheld when a potential communicator persists in contacting a resident at home after the resident has stated that he or she does not want to listen.[93] Nonetheless, the courts have generally been protective of the rights of solicitors and canvassers to call on residents at home.[94] The state may not prohibit all door-to-door canvassing on the grounds that such intrusions invade the homeowner's privacy and peace or on an anti-littering rationale.[95]

---

[85]*Id.* at 547.
[86]Marsh v. Alabama, 326 U.S. 501 (1946).
[87]Illinois Migrant Council v. Campbell Soup Co., 519 F.2d 391, 396–97 (7th Cir. 1975); Petersen v. Talisman Sugar Corp., 478 F.2d 73, 82–83 (5th Cir. 1973).
[88]Hudgens v. NLRB, 424 U.S. 507 (1976) *and* Lloyd Corp. v. Tanner, 407 U.S. 551 (1972), overruling Amalgamated Food Employees v. Logan Valley Plaza, 391 U.S. 308 (1968).
[89]Batchelder v. Allied Stores Int'l, 445 N.E.2d 590 (Mass. 1983); Alderwood Assocs. v. Washington Envtl. Council, 635 P.2d 108 (Wash. 1981); Robins v. Pruneyard Shopping Ctr., 592 P.2d 341 (Cal. 1979), *aff'd,* 447 U.S. 74, 82–85, 6 Media L. Rep. 1311, 1315–16 (1980) (also holding that enforced free speech access to private malls not unconstitutional deprivation of mall owner's property rights).
[90]Several states have followed the federal rule in holding that their state constitutions allow mall owners to exclude demonstrators. Jacobs v. Major, 407 N.W.2d 832 (Wis. 1987); Western Pa. Socialist Workers 1982 Campaign v. Connecticut Gen. Life Ins. Co., 515 A.2d 1331 (Pa. 1986); SHAD Alliance v. Smith Haven Mall, 488 N.E.2d 1211 (N.Y. 1985); Woodland v. Michigan Citizens Lobby, 378 N.W.2d 337 (Mich. 1985); Cologne v. Westfarms Assocs., 469 A.2d 1201 (Conn. 1984); State v. Felmet, 273 S.E.2d 708 (N.C. 1981). *See also* Judlo, Inc. v. Vons Cos., 259 Cal. Rptr. 624 (Cal. Ct. App. 1989) (grocery store could select which news racks to exclude from its property).
[91]Rowan v. Post Office Dep't, 397 U.S. 728, 737 ("The ancient concept that 'a man's home is his castle' into which 'not even the king may enter' has lost none of its vitality."); Martin v. City of Struthers, 319 U.S. 141, 148 (1943) (appropriate regulation "leaves the decision as to whether distributors of literature may lawfully call at a home where it belongs—with the homeowner himself").
[92]Hynes v. Mayor of Oradell, 425 U.S. 610, 617 (1976). *See also* Ad World v. Township of Doylestown, 672 F.2d 1136, 1140–41, 8 Media L. Rep. 1073, 1076 (3d Cir.), *cert. denied,* 456 U.S. 975 (1982) (noting there is "no evidence that accumulation [of newspapers at a residence] is so widespread that, even assuming a positive correlation with crime, it suggests more than a hypothetical or speculative increase in burglary").
[93]*Martin,* 319 U.S. at 148 ("A city can punish those who call at a home in defiance of the previously expressed will of the occupant."); City of Fredonia v. Chanute Tribune, 638 P.2d 347, 8 Media L. Rep. 1053 (Kan. Ct. App. 1981) (upholding conviction of newspaper distributor who continued to place newspapers on resident's front lawn after being asked not to). *Compare Ad World,* 672 F.2d at 1139–40, 8 Media L. Rep. at 1075–76 (ordinance that prohibited distribution of advertising material at residence or on residential mailbox without "affirmative request or consent" of occupant was unconstitutional violation of First Amendment when applied to publication that contained mostly advertising but had a few pages of consumer and community information).
[94]*See infra* §12.5(B).
[95]*Martin,* 319 U.S. 141; Van Nuys Pub'g Co. v. City of Thousand Oaks, 489 P.2d 809 (Cal. 1971), *cert. denied,* 405 U.S. 1042 (1972).

§12.5 MANNER RESTRICTIONS

This section deals with restrictions on particular manners or methods of communication.

§12.5(A) Handbills and Pamphlets

Different manners or methods of expression have received differing degrees of protection from the courts. The distribution of handbills or pamphlets in public forums is fully protected by the First Amendment. The leading case in this area is *Lovell v. City of Griffin*,[96] where the Supreme Court struck down a city ordinance that prohibited the distribution of any circulars without the prior permission of the city manager. The Court specifically held that pamphleteering was protected by the press clause of the First Amendment: "The liberty of the press is not confined to newspapers and periodicals. It necessarily embraces pamphlets and leaflets."[97] In protecting not only the printing of information but its dissemination, the Court stated: " 'Liberty of circulation is as essential [to freedom of the press] as liberty of publishing; indeed, without the circulation, the publication would be of little value.' "[98] The Court has emphasized that "pamphlets have proved most effective instruments in the dissemination of opinion,"[99] and that the freedom to distribute information to citizens "wherever [they] desire to receive it . . . is clearly vital to the preservation of a free society."[100] The essential holding of *Lovell* has been reaffirmed decade after decade by the Court.[101]

Like all free expression in public forums, the distribution of pamphlets is subject to reasonable time, place, and manner restrictions. The Court, in striking down the total leafletting ban in *Lovell*, hinted that a leafletting ordinance that targeted "disorderly conduct, the molestation of the inhabitants or the misuse or littering of the streets" might pass constitutional muster.[102] The Court has held, however, that preventing littering was not a significant enough governmental interest to justify a prohibition on leafletting.[103]

Courts generally will examine the facts about a forum in judging whether a ban on leafletting may be upheld. Where a military base is clearly open to the public, leafletting cannot be prohibited.[104] One court struck down a ban on distribution of pamphlets in a public hospital, holding that leafletting must be allowed in areas where it would not interfere with patient care.[105] Courts

---

[96]303 U.S. 444 (1938).
[97]*Id.* at 452.
[98]*Id.* (quoting Ex parte Jackson, 96 U.S. 727, 733 (1878)).
[99]Schneider v. New Jersey, 308 U.S. 147, 164 (1939) (citing Lovell v. City of Griffin, 303 U.S. 444 (1938)).
[100]Martin v. City of Struthers, 319 U.S. 141, 146–47 (1943).
[101]*See* Flowers v. United States, 407 U.S. 197, 198 (1972) (per curiam); Organization for a Better Austin v. Keefe, 402 U.S. 415, 419, 1 Media L. Rep. 1021, 1022 (1971); Talley v. California, 362 U.S. 60, 62 (1960); Jamison v. Texas, 318 U.S. 413, 416 (1943).
[102]Lovell v. City of Griffin, 303 U.S. 444, 451 (1938).
[103]*Schneider*, 308 U.S. at 162.
[104]*Flowers*, 407 U.S. at 197.
[105]Dallas Ass'n of Community Orgs. for Reform Now v. Dallas County Hosp. Dist., 670 F.2d 629, 632–35 (5th Cir.), *cert. denied*, 459 U.S. 1052 (1982).

have split over whether a ban on distributing leaflets to automobile drivers on city streets is constitutional.[106]

The Supreme Court has held that ordinances regulating the distribution of handbills that advertise a commercial product need not pass the same scrutiny as regulation of noncommercial handbills.[107] However, more recent cases[108] that explicitly give First Amendment protection to commercial speech cast doubt on those earlier holdings.[109]

§12.5(B) Door-to-Door Solicitation

The Supreme Court established early on that the freedom to spread one's message personally, by going from home to home, is protected by the First Amendment.[110] Indeed, this method of communication is entitled to "special solicitude" because of its low cost.[111] As the Court noted in *Martin v. City of Struthers*, "[d]oor to door distribution of circulars is essential to the poorly financed causes of little people."[112]

However, the right to seek out listeners in their homes must be balanced against the homeowner's right to privacy[113] and the municipality's interest in protecting its citizens from crime and undue annoyance.[114] Thus, a municipality is entitled to regulate door-to-door solicitation, as long as the ordinance is drawn with "narrow specificity."[115] The Supreme Court has held that municipalities may not absolutely prohibit canvassers from going door to door,[116] nor may they vest local officials with the discretion to grant or deny a permit, since this latter provision would allow content-based regulation.[117]

---

[106]*Compare* ACORN v. City of New Orleans, 606 F. Supp. 16, 22–24 (E.D. La. 1984) (ordinance banning solicitation of funds in roadway struck down as not narrowly tailored) *and* Houston Chronicle Pub'g Co. v. City of Houston, 620 S.W.2d 833, 7 Media L. Rep. 2043 (Tex. Civ. App. 1981) (same) *with* ACORN v. City of Phoenix, 798 F.2d 1260, 1268–70 (9th Cir. 1986) (given alternatives of pedestrian and door-to-door distribution, ban on leafletting drivers stopped at red lights narrowly drawn to meet traffic safety concerns) *and* State v. Horn, 643 P.2d 1338, 8 Media L. Rep. 1945 (Or. Ct. App. 1982) (criminal conviction of leafleteers of automobiles upheld).

[107]Breard v. City of Alexandria, 341 U.S. 622, 644–45 (1951); Valentine v. Chrestensen, 316 U.S. 52, 54, 1 Media L. Rep. 1907, 1908 (1942).

[108]*See* Virginia State Bd. of Pharmacy v. Virginia Citizens Consumer Council, 425 U.S. 748, 758, 1 Media L. Rep. 1930, 1933 (1976) (striking down ban on advertisements or prescription drug prices); Bigelow v. Virginia, 421 U.S. 809, 818–29, 1 Media L. Rep. 1919, 1922–27 (1975) (striking down ban on advertisements offering abortion services).

[109]New York v. Remeny, 355 N.E.2d 375 (N.Y. 1976) (striking down broad ban on commercial leafletting upheld in *Valentine*); State v. Bloss, 637 P.2d 1117 (Haw. 1981), *cert. denied,* 459 U.S. 824 (1982) (striking down broad ban on commercial leafletting); H&L Messengers v. City of Brentwood, 577 S.W.2d 444, 4 Media L. Rep. 2471 (Tenn. 1979) (same); *see also infra* §12.5(B).

[110]Lovell v. City of Griffin, 303 U.S. 444 (1938); Schneider v. New Jersey, 308 U.S. 147 (1939); Martin v. City of Struthers, 319 U.S. 141 (1943); Jamison v. Texas, 318 U.S. 413 (1943).

[111]City Council of Los Angeles v. Taxpayers for Vincent, 466 U.S. 789, 813 (1984).

[112]319 U.S. at 146.

[113]*See generally* Frisby v. Schultz, 487 U.S. 474, 484–85 (1988) (residential picketing); Carey v. Brown, 447 U.S. 455, 470–71 (1980) (same); Federal Communications Comm'n v. Pacifica Found., 438 U.S. 726, 748–49 (1978) (offensive radio broadcasts entering home); Rowan v. Post Office Dep't, 397 U.S. 728 (1970) (unwanted mailings to home); Breard v. City of Alexandria, 341 U.S. 622, 644–45 (1951) (residential peddlers); Gregory v. Chicago, 394 U.S. 111, 125–26 (1969) (Black, J., concurring) ("[T]he homes of men, sometimes the last citadel of the tired, the weary and the sick, can be protected by government from noisy, marching, tramping, threatening picketers and demonstrators.").

[114]Hynes v. Mayor of Oradell, 425 U.S. 610, 617 (1976).

[115]*Id.* at 620; Village of Schaumburg v. Citizens for a Better Env't, 444 U.S. 620, 632 (1980); *see* Schneider v. New Jersey, 308 U.S. 147, 161 (1939).

[116]*Village of Schaumberg,* 444 U.S. 620; *Hynes,* 425 U.S. 610; *Martin,* 319 U.S. 141.

[117]Secretary of State of Md. v. Joseph H. Munson Co., 467 U.S. 947, 964 n.12 (1984) ("that a statute that requires . . . a 'license' for the dissemination of ideas is inherently suspect"); *Schneider,* 308 U.S. 147; Lovell v. City of Griffin, 303 U.S. 444 (1938); *see supra* §12.2(A).

Municipalities often attempt to regulate door-to-door solicitation by restricting the hours during which canvassers may call on residents[118] or by requiring some sort of identification. While these identification requirements are acceptable, they may not be overly intrusive. The Third Circuit has invalidated an ordinance that required solicitors to be fingerprinted before being allowed to go door to door, characterizing such a requirement as stigmatizing and creating an "air of criminality."[119] Ordinances that required proof of the good character of the canvassers without being sufficiently specific as to how that requirement was to be met[120] and ordinances that barred convicted felons from canvassing, regardless of the nature or age of the felony,[121] have also been invalidated.

Although the Supreme Court has been clear about the protection to which door-to-door solicitation involving noncommercial speech is entitled, it has not yet provided a clear rule by which to judge solicitation ordinances that regulate purely commercial speech.[122] The Ninth Circuit has applied both the commercial speech test and a time, place, and manner analysis in rejecting a ban on in-person commercial solicitors.[123] A city ordinance that prohibited commercial door-to-door solicitation was upheld because the ordinance satisfied the test for the regulation of commercial speech.[124] However, nearly identical statutes have been held to be unconstitutional on state[125] or federal[126] constitutional grounds.

Nevertheless, the Supreme Court has held that the "least restrictive alternatives" test does not have to be met in a constitutional challenge to a university's ban on Tupperware parties in dormitory rooms, and then remanded the case for further proceedings.[127]

In any event, noncommercial door-to-door solicitation is not transformed into purely commercial speech solely because it involves a request for dona-

---

[118]*See supra* §12.3.

[119]New Jersey Citizen Action v. Edison Township, 797 F.2d 1250, 1265 (3d Cir. 1986), *cert. denied*, 479 U.S. 1103 (1987).

[120]Strasser v. Doorley, 432 F.2d 567 (1st Cir. 1970) (invalidating statute that required newsboys to register and wear identifying badge; registration could be refused if applicant was deemed not to be of good character); Wulp v. Corcoran, 454 F.2d 826 (1st Cir. 1972) (statute requiring prior registration of those wishing to sell newspapers on street held unconstitutional); Massachusetts Fair Share v. Town of Rockland, 610 F. Supp. 682 (D. Mass. 1985).

[121]Green v. Village of Schaumberg, 676 F. Supp. 870 (N.D. Ill. 1988).

[122]Some support for the argument that such a ban would be upheld is found in Metromedia, Inc. v. City of San Diego, 453 U.S. 490 (1981). There, in dicta, a majority of the justices suggested they would approve a ban on billboards that communicated only commercial speech. *See also* Breard v. City of Alexandria, 341 U.S. 622 (1951) (upholding conviction of residential solicitor of magazine subscriptions under statute banning door-to-door solicitation without prior consent of resident); *infra* notes 162 and 163.

[123]Projects 80's v. City of Pocatello, 942 F.2d 635 (9th Cir. 1991) (on remand for reconsideration in light of Board of Trustees of State Univ. of N.Y. v. Fox, 492 U.S. 469 (1989)).

[124]May v. People, 636 P.2d 672 (Colo. 1981); *see also* Commonwealth v. Sterlace, 391 A.2d 1066, 1067–68 (Pa. 1978) (upholding ordinance that barred placement of "advertising material" at residence without prior permission of resident as valid time, place, and manner restriction).

[125]City of Hillsboro v. Purcell, 761 P.2d 510 (Or. 1988) (ordinance overbroad because it prohibited all door-to-door solicitations for any purpose at any time).

[126]Ad World v. Township of Doylestown, 672 F.2d 1136, 8 Media L. Rep. 1073 (3d Cir.), *cert. denied*, 456 U.S. 975 (1982) (invalidating statute identical to that upheld in *Sterlace*, finding it insufficiently narrowly tailored); Chicago Tribune Co. v. Village of Downers Grove, 532 N.E.2d 821, 15 Media L. Rep. 2459 (Ill. 1988) (requirement that door-to-door solicitors of newspaper subscriptions comply with commercial solicitation registration ordinance held invalid under Equal Protection Clause and First Amendment); *see also supra* §12.5(A).

[127]*Fox*, 492 U.S. 469. *But see* American Future Sys. v. Pennsylvania State Univ., 688 F.2d 907 (3d Cir.), *cert. denied*, 459 U.S. 1093 (1982) (university may not censor contents of truthful commercial solicitation in common areas of dorms); *see also supra* note 25.

tions or the sale of an item, such as a bible. The Supreme Court has held that a state may not prohibit the distribution of handbills "merely because the handbills invite the purchase of books . . . or because the handbills seek in lawful fashion to promote the raising of funds."[128] The Court has cogently summarized the First Amendment interests at stake in such "commercial" solicitation:

> [C]haritable appeals for funds, on the street or door-to-door, involve a variety of speech interests—communication of information, the dissemination and propagation of views and ideas, and the advocacy of causes—that are within the protection of the First Amendment. Soliciting financial support is undoubtedly subject to reasonable regulation but the latter must be undertaken with due regard for the reality that solicitation is characteristically intertwined with informative and perhaps persuasive speech seeking support for particular views on economic, political or social issues, and for the reality that without solicitation the flow of such information and advocacy would likely cease.[129]

§12.5(C) News Racks and Vending Machines

The Supreme Court addressed the issue of government regulation of newspaper distribution through news racks (coin-operated newspaper vending machines) in *City of Lakewood v. Plain Dealer Publishing Co.*[130] This case provides some insight into the extent to which governments may constitutionally regulate news racks, but also leaves some important questions unanswered.

In *City of Lakewood,* a municipal ordinance required publishers to obtain annual permits for all news racks, giving the mayor the discretion to grant or deny permit applications and the authority to impose "such other terms and conditions" for the permits as he deemed "necessary and reasonable."[131] The plaintiff publisher made a facial challenge to the ordinance even though it had never applied for a permit. The Court found that two features of the Lakewood news rack licensing ordinance made the facial challenge appropriate: (1) the ordinance required publishers to apply for permits annually, allowing the mayor to use the content of already published speech in deciding whether to renew the license; and (2) the licensing system being challenged was "directed narrowly and specifically at expression or conduct commonly associated with expression: the circulation of newspapers."[132]

The Court struck down the ordinance because it allowed the mayor too much discretion in deciding whether to grant or deny a news rack permit.

---

[128] Jamison v. Texas, 318 U.S. 413, 417 (1943).
[129] Village of Schaumburg v. Citizens for a Better Env't, 444 U.S. 620, 632 (1980). *See also* Hynes v. Mayor of Oradell, 425 U.S. 610 (1976) (ordinance requiring identification permit for house-to-house solicitation of contributions struck down as unconstitutionally vague); Thomas v. Collins, 323 U.S. 516, 540–41 (1945) (any regulation of "collection of funds" may "not intrude upon the rights of free speech"); Murdock v. Pennsylvania, 319 U.S. 105 (1943) (sale of literature by itinerant evangelists entitled to First Amendment protection).
[130] 486 U.S. 750, 15 Media L. Rep. 1481 (1988). *See generally* Ball, *Extra! Extra! Read All About It: First Amendment Problems in the Regulation of Coin-Operated Newspaper Vending Machines,* 19 COLUM. J.L. & SOC. PROBS. 183 (1985) (analyzing conflict between First Amendment and states' police power to regulate and prohibit news racks).
[131] 486 U.S. at 753–54.
[132] *Id.* at 755–60, 15 Media L. Rep. at 1482–85. The Court also noted that "periodic licensing" could be required if governed by "neutral criteria." *Id.* at 760, 15 Media L. Rep. at 1486. *Compare* Gannett Satellite Info. Network v. Berger, 894 F.2d 61, 68–70, 17 Media L. Rep. 1302, 1306–09 (3d Cir. 1990) (upholding two and striking down one rule affecting news racks at Newark Airport based on how close a nexus there was between rule and expressive conduct).

While the ordinance required the mayor to state his reasons for a denial, the Court observed that the mayor could simply state: "This newsrack is not in the public interest."[133] The Court was not persuaded by the city's arguments that a denial would only be on the grounds of "health, safety or welfare."[134] Even though judicial review of permit decisions was provided, the Court noted that an appeal only was available from a denial of a permit and not from a permit for an undesirable location, and that the ordinance did not guarantee a prompt review.[135]

Significantly, the Court did not decide the overarching question of whether a city may completely prohibit news racks on public property.[136] Many lower federal and state courts have held that, because news racks are protected by the First Amendment, municipalities may not totally ban them from all public property.[137] Courts usually have rejected the argument that retail stores along city streets or other similar methods of distribution constitute adequate alternatives to news racks.[138] The courts are divided on whether ordinances that bar news racks from all residential areas are valid time, place, and manner regulations.[139]

The Supreme Court has held that "the well-settled time, place and manner test" should be applied to the regulation of news racks.[140] This confirms a burgeoning trend in the lower courts, which have ruled that news rack regulations are restrictions on free speech in a public forum and must be evaluated under the established three-part test.[141]

---

[133] 486 U.S. at 769, 15 Media L. Rep. at 1489.
[134] *Id.* at 770, 15 Media L. Rep. at 1490.
[135] *Id.* at 769–72, 15 Media L. Rep. at 1489–91.
[136] *Id.* at 762 n.7, 15 Media L. Rep. at 1486 n.7
[137] Multimedia Pub'g Co. v. Greenville-Spartanburg Airport Dist., 991 F.2d 154, 21 Media L. Rep. 1369 (4th Cir. 1993); Providence Journal Co. v. City of Newport, 665 F. Supp. 107, 15 Media L. Rep. 1545 (D.R.I. 1987); Remer v. City of El Cajon, 52 Cal. App. 3d 441, 125 Cal. Rptr. 116 (Cal. Ct. App. 1975); California Newspaper Pubrs. Ass'n v. City of Burbank, 51 Cal. App. 3d 50, 123 Cal. Rptr. 880 (Cal. Ct. App. 1975); Passaic Daily News v. City of Clifton, 491 A.2d 808, 11 Media L. Rep. 1962 (N.J. Super. Ct. Law Div. 1985). *See also* Southern N.J. Newspapers v. New Jersey Dep't of Transp., 542 F. Supp. 173 (D.N.J. 1982) (state law banning roadside signs on interstate and primary highway systems cannot constitutionally be applied to news racks); Philadelphia Newspapers v. Borough Council, 381 F. Supp. 228 (E.D. Pa. 1974) (borough ordinance and resolution generally prohibiting commercial use of sidewalks within borough, except for three-foot strip of sidewalk adjacent to certain premises within business district, cannot constitutionally be applied to news racks). *But see* Judlo, Inc. v. Vons Cos., 259 Cal. Rptr. 624 (Cal. Ct. App. 1989) (upholding supermarket's right to limit news racks).
[138] Chicago Newspaper Pubrs. Ass'n v. Wheaton, 697 F. Supp. 1464, 1470, 15 Media L. Rep. 2297 (N.D. Ill. 1988) ("[i]f private sellers are an adequate alternative channel under the Constitution, then an ordinance which is constitutional today becomes unconstitutional tomorrow, when those sellers close, relocate, or elect not to sell newspapers. The protection of the First Amendment cannot be so transitory."); *Providence Journal*, 665 F. Supp. at 117–18; *California Newspaper Pubrs.*, 51 Cal. App. 3d at 54; *Remer*, 52 Cal. App. 3d at 444. *Contra* Gannett Satellite Info. Network v. Berger, 716 F. Supp. 140, 154–55, 16 Media L. Rep. 2057, 2062–63 (D.N.J. 1989) (upholding ban on news racks at Newark Airport and finding that newsstands provided adequate alternatives), *aff'd in part and rev'd in part on other issues*, 894 F.2d 61, 17 Media L. Rep. 1306.
[139] Plain Dealer Pub'g Co. v. City of Lakewood, 794 F.2d 1139, 1147, 13 Media L. Rep. 1065, 1070–71 (6th Cir. 1986) (upholding residential ban), *aff'd in part on other grounds*, 486 U.S. 750, 15 Media L. Rep. 1481 (1988). *Contra Chicago Newspaper Pubrs.*, 697 F. Supp. at 1470, 15 Media L. Rep. at 2301 (ban on all residential news racks not least restrictive means of protecting "neighborhood aesthetics").
[140] *City of Lakewood*, 486 U.S. at 763, 15 Media L. Rep. at 1486–87.
[141] *See, e.g.*, Jacobsen v. Crivaro, 851 F.2d 1067, 15 Media L. Rep. 1958 (8th Cir. 1988); Gannett Satellite Info. Network v. Metropolitan Transp. Auth., 745 F.2d 767, 773, 10 Media L. Rep. 2424, 2427 (2d Cir. 1984); Miami Herald Pub'g Co. v. City of Hallandale, 734 F.2d 666, 673, 10 Media L. Rep. 2049, 2053 (11th Cir. 1984); *Chicago Newspaper Pubrs.*, 697 F. Supp. at 1466, 15 Media L. Rep. at 2297–98; *Providence Journal*, 665 F. Supp. at 112, 14 Media L. Rep. at 1549–50; City of Burlington v. New York Times Co., 532 A.2d 562, 564, 14 Media L. Rep. 1979, 1980–81 (Vt. 1987); Kash Enters. v. City of Los Angeles, 562 P.2d 1302, 1307, 2 Media L. Rep. 1716, 1719–20 (Cal. 1977).

Foreshadowing the Supreme Court's decision in *City of Lakewood,* a number of courts struck down local ordinances that required publishers to obtain licenses or permits for their news racks because the ordinances vested too much discretion in local officials.[142] Several courts have also struck down ordinances that require the securing of a license before news racks may be installed, on the grounds that such a requirement is an unconstitutional prior restraint.[143]

Other regulations of news racks have failed because they did not serve a significant governmental interest or were not narrowly tailored. For example, the Sixth Circuit rejected a provision that required a review of the designs of all news racks by a city architectural board, stating that the provision was not "narrowly tailored to serve a significant governmental interest."[144] A New Jersey court rejected a provision that barred placement of any news rack on the same side of the street and within 100 feet of another news rack selling the same publication, stating that the regulation "serves no substantial interest of [the city]."[145] The same court also rejected a provision that barred placement of news racks within 200 feet of any church, park, playground, schoolhouse, or any store selling newspapers, unless the church, school, or store waived the regulation.[146]

Some news rack regulations have been declared unconstitutional for failure to comply with due process requirements.[147] For the same reason, many courts have declared that it is unconstitutional for a city to summarily remove a publisher's news racks when there is no clear and imminent danger to persons

---

[142]*Miami Herald Pub'g Co.,* 734 F.2d at 674, 10 Media L. Rep. 2049 (issuance of license conditioned on compliance with all "applicable ordinances," leaving to discretion of city officials which ordinances applied and whether they had been violated); Gannett Satellite Info. Network v. Town of Norwood, 579 F. Supp. 108, 115 (D. Mass. 1984) (by-laws vested "virtually unbridled discretion" in town officials to grant or deny permits); News Printing Co. v. Borough of Totowa, 511 A.2d 139, 150, 13 Media L. Rep. 1072 (N.J. Super. Ct. Law Div. 1986) (ordinance vested city officials with "untoward discretion to deny licenses"); *City of Burlington,* 532 A.2d at 565, 14 Media L. Rep. at 1981 ("[The] ordinance leaves the task of setting standards entirely with the discretion of [city officials]."); New York News v. Metropolitan Transp. Auth., 753 F. Supp. 133, 18 Media L. Rep. 1808 (S.D.N.Y. 1990) (preliminary injunction issued to prevent city transit authority from using unfettered discretion to revoke permits of newspaper hawkers because of fear of illegal conduct by striking newspaper employees); Jacobsen v. Petersen, 728 F. Supp. 1415, 17 Media L. Rep. 2324 (D.S.D. 1990) (ordinances that required city's permission to put news racks on busy sidewalks violated First Amendment because of city's power to discriminate based on content); *see also supra* §12.2(A).

[143]*News Printing Co.,* 511 A.2d at 152, 13 Media L. Rep. at 1080–81; *Chicago Newspaper Pubrs.,* 697 F. Supp. at 1469, 15 Media L. Rep. at 2300; Minnesota Newspaper Ass'n v. City of Minneapolis, 9 Media L. Rep. 2116, 2123 (D. Minn. 1983); Gannett Co. v. City of Rochester, 330 N.Y.S.2d 648, 656 (N.Y. Sup. Ct. 1972). For a discussion of prior restraints, see generally Chapter 10.

[144]*City of Lakewood,* 794 F.2d at 1146, 13 Media L. Rep. at 1070, *aff'd in part on other grounds,* 486 U.S. 750, 15 Media L. Rep. 1481 (1988). *See also infra* note 154.

[145]*News Printing Co.,* 511 A.2d at 162, 13 Media L. Rep. at 1088–89.

[146]*Id.* at 160 n.4, 161–62, 13 Media L. Rep. at 1087 n.4, 1088 ("[T]he interest of Totowa from a regulatory standpoint cannot be treated as substantial for the balancing of competing interests under the First and Fourteenth Amendments when it lets private entities decide whether the regulation shall apply."). *Accord* Sebago, Inc. v. City of Alameda, 259 Cal. Rptr. 918, 16 Media L. Rep. 2377 (1989) (striking down ordinance barring placement of news racks containing adult newspapers in certain zoning districts or within 500 feet of residential area).

[147]Westchester Rockland Newspapers v. City of Yonkers, 5 Media L. Rep. 1777 (S.D.N.Y. 1979). The ordinance provided that the corporation counsel would determine when news racks were violating the ordinance and would notify the publisher. The publisher could correct the violation or challenge the violation finding, but the publisher was not given the right to examine the evidence on which the finding was based. Following an adverse decision by the corporation counsel, the publisher could appeal to an administrative board. The publisher had the burden of proof on appeal but was still not allowed to examine the city's evidence or cross-examine its witnesses. *Id.* at 1778. *See also Chicago Newspaper Pubrs.,* 697 F. Supp. at 1468, 15 Media L. Rep. at 2300 (ordinance did not require prompt decision by city officials and did not provide for prompt judicial review).

or property, especially in the absence of a narrowly drawn statute.[148] The California Supreme Court explained the constitutional danger involved:

> [The ordinance's] authorization of summary removal for *any* violation—no matter how minor—creates a very real risk that individual enforcement officers may consider a variety of extraneous factors, including the contents of a newsrack, in determining whether or not a particular rack should be removed from a public sidewalk.[149]

Some news rack regulations have been rejected because they imposed a burden only on First Amendment rights. For example, in *Plain Dealer Publishing Co. v. City of Lakewood,* the Sixth Circuit invalidated the city's requirement that publishers indemnify the city as a condition on access to streets and sidewalks for their news racks.[150] The court explained, "neither the bus nor the telephone companies are required to insure bus shelters or telephone equipment. Since the City cannot impose more stringent requirements on First Amendment rights than it does on others," the provision was unconstitutional.[151] Courts generally have struck down insurance and indemnification requirements in news rack ordinances, finding that municipalities can make no showing of any history of news rack-related claims to justify the provisions.[152]

Municipalities may restrict placement of news racks if they unreasonably interfere with pedestrian or vehicular traffic.[153] Courts have also upheld narrowly drawn regulations of the size, weight, appearance, and placement of news racks,[154] particularly ordinances that require owners of news racks to maintain them in a clean and neat condition.[155] Courts generally have struck down municipalities' attempts to circumscribe the placement of news racks pursuant to general statutes that bar street obstructions.[156]

---

[148]Miller Newspapers v. City of Keene, 546 F. Supp. 831, 835, 9 Media L. Rep. 1234 (D.N.H. 1982) (rejecting theory that city "has the inherent police power to impose, in its discretion, time, place, and manner restrictions on a case-by-case basis, without procedural due process protections otherwise accorded property rights and First Amendment interests"); City of New York v. American Sch. Pubns., 509 N.E.2d 311, 516 N.Y.S.2d 616, 616, 14 Media L. Rep. 1153 (1987) ("[I]t would be a violation of the First Amendment . . . to allow the City of New York, in the absence of local ordinance or regulation, to invoke judicial enforcement of its efforts to clear the City's sidewalks of defendant's bins installed for distribution of a free publication."); Jacobsen v. Filler, 15 Media L. Rep. 1705, 1707 (D. Ariz. 1988) ("In absence of an emergency justifying immediate seizure, Jacobsen was entitled to a hearing before the newsracks and other materials were seized."); Jacobsen v. Petersen, 728 F. Supp. 1415, 17 Media L. Rep. 2324 (D.S.D. 1990) (same).

[149]Kash Enters. v. City of Los Angeles, 562 P.2d 1302, 1313, 2 Media L. Rep. 1716, 1724–25 (Cal. 1977). However, the court noted, "[w]e have no doubt that the City of Los Angeles is constitutionally empowered to provide for the immediate seizure, without prior notice or hearing, of any newsrack that poses a danger to pedestrians or vehicles." *Id.* at 1314, 2 Media L. Rep. at 1725.

[150]794 F.2d 1139, 13 Media L. Rep. 1065 (6th Cir. 1986), *aff'd in part on other grounds,* 486 U.S. 750, 15 Media L. Rep. 1481 (1988).

[151]*Id.* at 1147, 13 Media L. Rep. at 1070–71; News Printing Co. v. Borough of Totowa, 511 A.2d 139, 158, 13 Media L. Rep. 1072, 1085 (N.J. Super. Ct. Law Div. 1986).

[152]Southern Conn. Newspapers v. Town of Greenwich, 11 Media L. Rep. 1051, 1055–56 (D. Conn. 1984); *News Printing Co.,* 511 A.2d 139, 13 Media L. Rep. 1072; Minnesota Newspaper Ass'n v. City of Minneapolis, 9 Media L. Rep. 2116 (D. Minn. 1983); Gannett Co. v. City of Rochester, 330 N.Y.S.2d 648 (N.Y. Sup. Ct. 1972). *But see* Jacobsen v. Harris, 869 F.2d 1172, 16 Media L. Rep. 1380 (8th Cir. 1989) (requirement that all users of city property, including news racks, carry insurance upheld).

[153]*Kash Enters.,* 562 P.2d 1302, 2 Media L. Rep. 1716; *News Printing Co.,* 511 A.2d 139, 13 Media L. Rep. 1072; Jacobsen v. Crivaro, 851 F.2d 1067, 15 Media L. Rep. 1958 (8th Cir. 1988).

[154]*Kash Enters.,* 562 P.2d 1302, 2 Media L. Rep. 1716 (size, weight, appearance, and placement regulations); *News Printing Co.,* 511 A.2d 139, 13 Media L. Rep. 1072 (maintenance, installation, location, and placement requirements); *Crivaro,* 851 F.2d 1067, 15 Media L. Rep. 1958 (size and placement regulations); Chicago Observer v. City of Chicago, 929 F.2d 325, 18 Media L. Rep. 1974 (7th Cir. 1991) (size regulations upheld; provision of ordinance forbidding news racks from carrying ads for businesses located more than 20 feet away also upheld). *See also supra* note 144.

[155]*Kash Enters.,* 562 P.2d 1302, 2 Media L. Rep. 1716; *News Printing Co.,* 511 A.2d 139, 13 Media L. Rep. 1072; Westchester Rockland Newspapers v. City of Yonkers, 5 Media L. Rep. 1777 (S.D.N.Y. 1979).

[156]Gannett Satellite Info. Network v. Town of Norwood, 579 F. Supp. 108, 114 (D. Mass. 1984); Gannett Satellite Info. Network v. City of Malden, 9 Media L. Rep. 2556, 2557 (D. Mass. 1983); Miller Newspapers

Many ordinances include provisions that require news rack owners to pay an annual fee.[157] As a general rule, a state may not raise revenue by imposing a licensing fee on First Amendment activity.[158] However, "a nominal fee may be imposed as a regulatory measure to defray the expenses of policing First Amendment activities."[159] Accordingly, courts have approved ordinances that require the payment of license or permit fees by news rack owners for the purpose of regulation, not revenue, where the fee constitutes an amount necessary to recover the administrative costs of the ordinance, including the expense of issuing the license and of inspecting and regulating the subject that it covers.[160] Administrative costs must be proven, however.[161]

Attempts have also been made to prohibit the distribution of newspapers because they were "commercial speech." These attempts have been rejected either because the speech is held not to be commercial[162] or because there was no justification for limiting such commercial speech.[163]

§12.5(D) Billboards and Other Signs

The Supreme Court has often addressed the validity of governmental regulation of billboards and other signs.[164] In doing so, the Court firmly

---

v. City of Keene, 546 F. Supp. 831, 9 Media L. Rep. 1234 (D.N.H. 1982); City of New York v. American School Pubns., 509 N.E.2d 311, 313, 516 N.Y.S.2d 616, 618, 14 Media L. Rep. 1153, 1155–56 (1987); Passaic Daily News v. City of Clifton, 491 A.2d 808, 811, 11 Media L. Rep. 1962, 1964 (N.J. Super. Ct. Law Div. 1985).

[157]*See, e.g., Crivaro*, 851 F.2d 1067, 15 Media L. Rep. 1958; Gannett Satellite Info. Network v. Metropolitan Transp. Auth., 745 F.2d 767, 10 Media L. Rep. 2424 (2d Cir. 1984); *News Printing Co.,* 511 A.2d 139, 13 Media L. Rep. 1072.

[158]*Crivaro*, 851 F.2d at 1071, 15 Media L. Rep. at 1961; *Metropolitan Transp. Auth.*, 745 F.2d at 774, 10 Media L. Rep. at 2428; Long v. City of Anaheim, 63 Cal. Rptr. 56, 62 (Cal. Ct. App. 1967). For a discussion of taxation, see generally Chapter 9, §9.7.

[159]Murdock v. Pennsylvania, 319 U.S. 105, 113–14 (1943) (footnote omitted); Cox v. New Hampshire, 312 U.S. 569, 577 (1941) (as applied to First Amendment activities, "[t]here is nothing contrary to the Constitution in the charge of a fee limited to the purpose stated"); Eastern Conn. Citizens Action Group v. Powers, 723 F.2d 1050, 1056 (2d Cir. 1983); Baldwin v. Redwood City, 540 F.2d 1360, 1372 (9th Cir. 1976), *cert. denied sub nom.* Leipzig v. Baldwin, 431 U.S. 913 (1977).

[160]*Crivaro*, 851 F.2d 1067, 15 Media L. Rep. 1958 ($10 per news rack); Jacobsen v. Harris, 869 F.2d 1172, 1173, 16 Media L. Rep. 1380, 1380 (8th Cir. 1979) (same). *But see Metropolitan Transp. Auth.,* 745 F.2d 767, 10 Media L. Rep. 2424 (holding that, given ample alternative means of distribution, fees for newspapers distributed through news racks in commuter train stations could lawfully be set "so high that they rendered newspaper rack sales economically unfeasible" and that government, acting as commercial enterprise, may charge fees).

[161]*News Printing Co.,* 511 A.2d at 157–58, 13 Media L. Rep. at 1084–85 (ordinance imposing $10 fee for news rack permit application and subsequent renewal unconstitutional prior restraint in absence of proof showing amount of fee was reasonable); Chicago Newspaper Pubrs. Ass'n v. Wheaton, 697 F. Supp. 1464, 1471–72, 15 Media L. Rep. 2297, 2303 (N.D. Ill. 1988) ($25 fee per news rack too high because city could not document that its administrative costs reached that level).

[162]Hays County Guardian v. Supple, 969 F.2d 111, 120, 20 Media L. Rep. 1681, 1687 (5th Cir. 1992), *cert. denied,* 113 S. Ct. 1067 (1993) (newspaper, which contains both commercial and noncommercial speech, entitled to full First Amendment protection because commercial and noncommercial speech are inextricably linked). *Accord* Ad World v. Township of Doylestown, 672 F.2d 1136, 8 Media L. Rep. 1073 (3d Cir.), *cert. denied,* 456 U.S. 975 (1983); Distribution Sys. v. Old Westbury, 19 Media L. Rep. 2071, 2077 (E.D.N.Y. 1992). *See also supra* note 122. *But see* Texas Review Soc'y v. Cunningham, 659 F. Supp. 1239 (W.D. Tex. 1987) (university rule prohibiting personal distribution of student newspapers containing advertising on campus but allowing distribution through unmanned news racks held constitutional).

[163]Cincinnati v. Discovery Network, 113 S. Ct. 1505 (1993) (ban on distribution by news racks of publications that constituted commercial speech unconstitutional where such distribution of newspapers was not banned).

[164]Boos v. Barry, 485 U.S. 312 (1988) (signs displayed within 500 feet of foreign embassy attacking that country); City Council of Los Angeles v. Taxpayers for Vincent, 466 U.S. 789 (1984) (temporary signs on public property); Metromedia, Inc. v. City of San Diego, 453 U.S. 490 (1981) (billboards); Linmark Assocs. v. Township of Willingboro, 431 U.S. 85 (1977) (residential "For Sale" signs).

established that such signs, even when used to convey wholly commercial messages, are protected by the First Amendment.[165]

In *Linmark Associates v. Township of Willingboro,* a unanimous Court struck down a municipal ordinance that prohibited the posting of "For Sale" and "Sold" signs in residential neighborhoods.[166] The Court held that the ordinance, aimed at stemming panic selling and preserving a racially integrated community, was an invalid time, place, and manner regulation because it failed to leave open adequate alternative channels for communication.[167] The Court also expressed doubt as to whether the ordinance was actually a time, place, or manner regulation since it was not content-neutral.[168] Although the Court acknowledged that the promotion of stable, integrated housing is a vital goal, it held that the township had failed to show that the ordinance was necessary to achieve that goal.[169]

In *Metromedia, Inc. v. City of San Diego,* the Court reviewed a city ordinance that substantially restricted the erection and use of outdoor advertising display signs.[170] The ordinance permitted on-site commercial advertising signs but virtually prohibited noncommercial signs, on-site or off, unless covered by a specified exception.[171] The Court struck down the regulation without agreeing on a rationale, and the four-justice plurality applied the four-part commercial speech test[172] and found that the ordinance satisfied constitutional requirements for regulating commercial speech.[173] With respect to noncommercial speech, however, the plurality held that, because the ordinance allowed some noncommercial speech, it must permit all types of noncommercial messages and could not permit communication of commercial information while prohibiting noncommercial speech.[174]

---

[165]*Linmark Assocs.,* 431 U.S. at 91–93; *Metromedia, Inc.,* 453 U.S. at 501 (plurality opinion of four justices); 453 U.S. at 524 (concurring opinion of two justices).

[166]431 U.S. at 86–87.

[167]*Id.* at 92–98.

[168]*Id.* at 93–94.

[169]*Id.* at 95. *Accord* Daugherty v. City of East Point, 447 F. Supp. 290, 296 (N.D. Ga. 1978); Greater Baltimore Bd. of Realtors v. Hughes, 596 F. Supp. 906, 924 (D. Md. 1984); Schoen v. Township of Hillside, 382 A.2d 704 (N.J. Super. Ct. Law Div. 1977); Mayor & City Council of Baltimore v. Crockett, 415 A.2d 606 (Md. Ct. Spec. App. 1980), *cert. denied,* 405 U.S. 967 (1981). For a case where panic selling was found to justify restrictions on such signs, *see* Barrick Realty v. City of Gary, 491 F.2d 161 (7th Cir. 1974); *see also* City of Chicago v. Louis Prus, 425 N.E.2d 426 (Ill. App. Ct. 1981) (ordering evidentiary hearing on issue).

[170]453 U.S. 490 (1981).

[171]*Id.* at 493–97.

[172]*See* Central Hudson Gas & Elec. Corp. v. Public Serv. Comm'n, 447 U.S. 557, 566, 6 Media L. Rep. 1497, 1501 (1980). For a discussion of commercial speech, see generally Chapter 11.

[173]453 U.S. at 507–12.

[174]*Id.* at 512–21. Lower courts have consistently struck down sign regulations that invert the constitutional preference for noncommercial over commercial speech. *See, e.g.,* Matthews v. Town of Needham, 764 F.2d 58 (1st Cir. 1985) (by-law prohibiting virtually all off-premises outdoor signs except those relating to premises); John Donnelly & Sons v. Campbell, 639 F.2d 6, 15–16, 7 Media L. Rep. 1132, 1133 (1st Cir. 1980), *aff'd,* 453 U.S. 916 (1981) (billboard regulations had excessive impact on noncommercial speech, limiting political signs to three weeks before elections); Jackson v. City Council of Charlottesville, 659 F. Supp. 470 (W.D. Va. 1987) (ordinance that virtually prohibited noncommercial and off-site commercial advertising while permitting on-site commercial advertising), *aff'd in part and vacated in part without opinion,* 840 F.2d 10 (4th Cir. 1988); National Advertising Co. v. City of Orange, 861 F.2d 246, 248 (9th Cir. 1988) (ordinance that prohibited commercial and noncommercial signs if they related to off-premises activity that had several exemptions, such as temporary political signs, unconstitutional because it regulated noncommercial billboards on basis of content); Norton Outdoor Advertising v. Village of Arlington Heights, 433 N.E.2d 198, 200–201, 8 Media L. Rep. 2018, 2019–20 (Ohio 1982) (ordinance banning all off-premises advertising signs and permitting only commercial on-premises signs); Metromedia v. Baltimore, 538 F. Supp. 1183, 8 Media L. Rep. 1762 (D. Md. 1982) (same); *see also* Community-Serv. Broadcasting v. Federal

In *City Council of Los Angeles v. Taxpayers for Vincent,* the Court upheld an ordinance that prohibited the posting of signs on public property, namely, utility poles.[175] The Court stated that aesthetic concerns were a significant enough governmental interest, sufficient to support a properly drawn time, place, and manner restriction on signs and, rejecting the argument that the city's utility poles constituted public forums for the placement of temporary signs, the Court ruled that, like any private property owner, the city could entirely exclude such signs.[176] The Court held that the ordinance was narrowly drawn to serve aesthetic interests and left open alternative avenues of expression.[177]

In *Boos v. Barry,* the Court struck down a provision of the District of Columbia Code that prohibited the display of any banner or placard within 500 feet of a building used for official purposes by a foreign government when the display was intended to bring that foreign government into "public odium."[178] The Court found that the ordinance was not a valid time, place, and manner regulation because it was content-based, and instead required that the ordinance be narrowly tailored to advance a *compelling* governmental interest.[179] The Court also expressed doubt that protecting the dignity of foreign diplomats constituted such an interest and held that, even if such an interest were compelling, the statute was not narrowly tailored to serve that interest, noting that the analogous federal statute that protects foreign dignitaries prohibited only the harassment or obstruction of foreign officials, leaving demonstrators free rein to picket.[180]

In addition to recognizing aesthetics as an important governmental interest, *Metromedia* and *Vincent* established that outdoor sign regulation is not unconstitutional merely because it is underinclusive: "Even if some visual blight remains, a partial, content-neutral ban may nevertheless enhance the city's appearance."[181] As *Vincent* emphasizes and most lower courts have held,

---

Communications Comm'n, 593 F.2d 1102, 1122, 4 Media L. Rep. 1257, 1273 (D.C. Cir. 1978) (en banc) (FCC regulation that affected only commercial broadcasters struck down on equal protection grounds). *Compare* City of Sunrise v. DCA Homes, 421 So. 2d 1084 (Fla. Dist. Ct. App. 1982) (distinguishing *Metromedia* and upholding limit of one off-site billboard per subdivision); Lamar Advertising v. City of Daytona Beach, 450 So. 2d 1145 (Fla. Dist. Ct. App. 1984) (distinguishing *Metromedia* and upholding ban on all off-site billboards in beach area of town but allowing on-site signs there). Relying on its state constitution, one court struck down an ordinance that regulated commercial but not nonnoncommercial advertising on billboards. Ackerley Communications v. Multnomah County, 696 P.2d 1140 (Or. Ct. App. 1985).

[175] 466 U.S. 789 (1984).
[176] *Id.* at 807–17.
[177] *Id.* at 805–07; *see also infra* note 181.
[178] 485 U.S. 312, 316 (1988).
[179] *Id.* at 321–22.
[180] 485 U.S. at 322–29. The *Boos* Court also considered a facial challenge to a second provision of the same ordinance, which banned all "congregations" within 500 feet of a foreign embassy. Aided by a limiting construction by the Court of Appeals, the Court upheld this provision of the ordinance. *Id.* at 331. Regarding picketing, *see* Frisby v. Schultz, 487 U.S. 474 (1988) (upholding ordinance banning demonstrators from targeting house in residential area for picketing). *Compare* State v. Hopf, 323 N.W.2d 746 (Minn. 1982) (upholding ban on billboards within 100 feet of school or church).
[181] *Vincent,* 466 U.S. at 811; *supra* note 177. *See also* Don's Porta Signs v. City of Clearwater, 829 F.2d 1051, 1052–54 (11th Cir. 1987), *cert. denied,* 485 U.S. 981 (1988) (ban on portable signs constitutional because it directly promoted aesthetic interests, although other types of signs may have contributed equally to problem); Lindsay v. City of San Antonio, 821 F.2d 1103 (5th Cir. 1987), *cert. denied,* 484 U.S. 1010 (1988) (city could attack visual blight piecemeal); Supersign of Boca Raton v. City of Ft. Lauderdale, 766 F.2d 1528 (11th Cir. 1985) (ordinance directly and effectively advanced city's interests in traffic safety and aesthetics although providing only partial solution).

however, a restriction on expression is not valid unless adequate alternative modes of communication remain.[182]

Dozens of billboard and outdoor advertising sign cases have been decided in the lower federal and state courts. While firm rules remain elusive, some trends have emerged. Several circuits, considering the plurality opinion together with the dissent in *Metromedia,* have held that a city may constitutionally ban all billboards other than those that are either noncommercial or that promote goods or services available on the site of the billboard.[183] More limited ordinances that severely limit the number of off-site billboards and ban off-site billboards in residential areas have been upheld.[184] Total bans and strict limitations on portable signs have also been upheld in some cases.[185] Ordinances that specifically regulate signs in front of topless bars[186] and on the sidewalk in front of the White House[187] have been upheld.

As in other contexts, a billboard ordinance that gives local officials significant enforcement discretion is unconstitutional.[188] Restrictions on the number of days that signs could be used have often been overturned,[189] but size restrictions have been upheld.[190]

---

[182]*Vincent,* 466 U.S. at 820. *See* Rzadkowolski v. Village of Lake Orion, 845 F.2d 653, 655 (6th Cir. 1988) (ordinance not shown to impede alternative avenues of communication); Wheeler v. Commissioner of Highways, 822 F.2d 586, 596 (6th Cir. 1987), *cert. denied,* 484 U.S. 1007 (1988) (Billboard Act left open ample alternatives for commercial and noncommercial communication). *Accord Lindsay,* 821 F.2d at 1111; National Advertising Co. v. City of Bridgeton, 626 F. Supp. 837, 842 (E.D. Mo. 1985).

[183]Georgia Outdoor Advertising v. City of Waynesville, 833 F.2d 43, 45 (4th Cir. 1987); Dills v. City of Marietta, 674 F.2d 1377, 1380–81 (11th Cir. 1982), *cert. denied,* 461 U.S. 905 (1983).

[184]*See, e.g., Rzadkowolski,* 845 F.2d 653 (content-neutral ordinance effectively limiting number of village billboards to one); Naegele Outdoor Advertising v. City of Durham, 844 F.2d 172, 173–74 (4th Cir. 1988) (city could properly rely on asserted aesthetic interest, although affected billboards were located in industrial or commercial areas); *Wheeler,* 822 F.2d at 591 (ordinance limited size and spacing of billboards and banned them from residential area); *City of Bridgeton,* 626 F. Supp. 837 (ordinance prohibiting off-site outdoor advertising signs); *City of Orange,* 861 F.2d at 248 (city could prohibit commercial billboards entirely "in the interest of traffic safety and aesthetics" and could ban them except where they related to activities on premises); Pigg v. State Dep't of Highways, 746 P.2d 961 (Colo. 1987) (tourist-related exception to restrictions on highway advertising, though content-based, sufficiently narrowly tailored to further important state interest); *compare* City of Lakewood v. Colfax Unlimited Ass'n, 634 P.2d 52 (Colo. 1981) (ban on political issue advertising struck down).

[185]*Don's Porta Signs,* 829 F.2d at 1052–54 (strict limitation on number and size of portable signs); *Lindsay,* 821 F.2d 1103 (ban on all new portable signs); Harnish v. Manatee County, 783 F.2d 1535, 1539–40 (11th Cir. 1986) (prohibition of portable signs); Mobile Sign v. Town of Brookhaven, 670 F. Supp. 68 (E.D.N.Y. 1987) (upholding limitation of total of six months at one location for portable sign). *But see City of Marietta,* 674 F.2d 1377 (time restrictions on display of portable signs held unconstitutional); Dills v. Cobb County, 755 F.2d 1473 (11th Cir. 1985) (per curiam) (ordinance requiring only portable signs to be located behind building setback line struck down); Signs, Inc. of Fla. v. Orange County, 592 F. Supp. 693, 697–98 (M.D. Fla. 1983) (ordinance that banned use of portable signs did not directly further state interest in traffic safety and aesthetics); Rhodes v. Gwinnett County, 557 F. Supp. 30 (N.D. Ga. 1982) (same).

[186]SDJ, Inc. v. City of Houston, 837 F.2d 1268 (5th Cir. 1988), *cert. denied sub nom.* MEF Enters. v. City of Houston, 489 U.S. 1052 (1989); Pennsylvania Alliance for Jobs & Energy v. Council of Munhall, 743 F.2d 182, 187 (3d Cir. 1984).

[187]White House Vigil v. Clark, 746 F.2d 1518 (D.C. Cir. 1984) (limitation on size, construction, and placement of signs on sidewalk in front of White House upheld as serving interests of preventing terrorism and providing unobstructed view to visitors).

[188]ACORN v. City of Tulsa, 835 F.2d 735 (10th Cir. 1987) (prohibition of signs in public park, except with permission of park board or superintendent); *see also* American Sign Rentals v. City of Orlando, 592 F. Supp. 85, 89 (M.D. Fla. 1983) (ordinance limiting use of portable trailer signs capriciously and unconstitutionally restricted free speech "under the pretext of traffic safety and aesthetics").

[189]Risner v. City of Wyoming, 383 N.W.2d 226 (Mich. Ct. App. 1985); City of Antioch v. Candidate's Outdoor Graphic Serv., 557 F. Supp. 52 (N.D. Cal. 1982).

[190]Donrey Communications v. City of Fayetteville, 660 S.W.2d 900 (Ark. 1983), *cert. denied,* 466 U.S. 959 (1984).

§12.5(E) Sound Trucks and Loudspeakers

In *Saia v. New York*,[191] the Supreme Court addressed the validity of an ordinance that prohibited sound trucks unless permission was received from the chief of police. Writing for a divided court, Justice Douglas stated: "Loudspeakers are today indispensable instruments of effective public speech. The sound truck has become an accepted method of political campaigning. It is the way people are reached."[192] Based on the conclusion that communication by loudspeaker is a mode of expression protected by the First Amendment, the Court held that the ordinance was unconstitutional as a prior restraint.[193]

Shortly after deciding *Saia,* however, the Court again confronted the amplified sound question. In *Kovacs v. Cooper,*[194] the Court affirmed the constitutionality of a municipal ordinance that prohibited sound trucks from broadcasting at a "loud and raucous volume" on public ways.[195] Since *Kovacs,* the Supreme Court has not decided a sound truck case, so the burden has fallen on lower courts to draw the line between liberty and order in this area.

Although an individual's First Amendment right to communicate by sound amplifier occupies a preferred position,[196] courts have held that it must be balanced against the state's competing interests in maintaining the safety of its roadways,[197] preventing the disruption of its commerce,[198] and protecting the tranquility of the community.[199] The Supreme Court has noted that "the ability of new technology to produce sounds more raucous than those of the human voice justifies time restrictions on the sound level, and on the hours and places of use, of sound trucks so long as the restrictions are reasonable and applied without discrimination."[200]

Unquestionably, an absolute ban on the use of sound amplification equipment in public places constitutes an impermissibly overbroad restriction.[201] Similarly, vague legislation that lacks explicit objective standards and permits arbitrary enforcement also will not pass constitutional muster.[202] To promote

---

[191]334 U.S. 558 (1948).

[192]*Id.* at 561.

[193]*Id.* at 559–60.

[194]336 U.S. 77 (1949).

[195]*Id.* at 89. The relationship between *Saia* and *Kovacs* was extensively debated in City of Lakewood v. Plain Dealer Publishing Co., 486 U.S. 750, 764–66, 784–85, 15 Media L. Rep. 1461, 1486–88, 1496–97 (1988).

[196]Beckerman v. City of Tupelo, 664 F.2d 502, 515 (5th Cir. 1981).

[197]Reeves v. McConn, 631 F.2d 377, 384 (5th Cir. 1980).

[198]*Id.* at 388.

[199]Phillips v. Township of Darby, 305 F. Supp. 763, 765 (E.D. Pa. 1969).

[200]Red Lion Broadcasting Co. v. Federal Communications Comm'n, 395 U.S. 367, 387, 1 Media L. Rep. 2053, 2061 (1969).

[201]Saia v. New York, 334 U.S. 558, 559–60 (1948); Beckerman v. City of Tupelo, 664 F.2d 502, 516 (5th Cir. 1981) (ban on use of sound equipment in residential zones and prohibition on operation of sound equipment between hours of 6:00 p.m. and 9:00 a.m. held unconstitutional); *Reeves,* 631 F.2d at 384–85 (ordinance prohibiting all sound amplification in downtown business district except for certain hours on Sunday, prohibiting all sound amplification except during nine hours of day, and prohibiting all sound amplification within 100 yards of schools, courthouses, and churches held unconstitutionally overbroad); United States Labor Party v. Rochford, 416 F. Supp. 204, 207 (N.D. Ill. 1975) (ban on use of loudspeakers in public held overbroad); Maldonado v. County of Monterey, 330 F. Supp. 1282, 1286 (N.D. Cal. 1971) (ban on use of loudspeakers on public roadways held unconstitutional); *Phillips,* 305 F. Supp. at 765 (prohibition on use of sound trucks held unconstitutionally overbroad). *See also* Weaver v. Jordan, 411 P.2d 289 (Cal.), *cert. denied,* 385 U.S. 844 (1966) (voiding citizen initiative that would have prohibited, in toto, subscription television business in California).

[202]United States Labor Party v. Pomerleau, 557 F.2d 410, 411–13 (4th Cir. 1977) (ordinance prohibiting sound amplifications over specified decibel level "at any point on the property line of use" held

an overriding state interest, however, the government may bar "loud and raucous" noise on public thoroughfares,[203] prohibit sound amplification above a specified volume or wattage and regulate sound quality,[204] prohibit amplification of words and sounds that are "obscene,"[205] and bar the use of sound amplification equipment that threatens to provoke a breach of the peace.[206]

§12.5(F) Anonymous Communications

The courts have recognized that, in certain contexts, free expression is facilitated if the speaker remains anonymous. The leading case in this area is *Talley v. California*,[207] where the Supreme Court invalidated a state ordinance that prohibited distribution of handbills that did not identify the author. The Court reviewed the long tradition of anonymous pamphlets challenging abusive government power and concluded that "identification and fear of reprisal might deter perfectly peaceful discussion of public matters of importance."[208]

The statute struck down in *Talley* was a broad one, barring the distribution of anonymous handbills regardless of the context. The Court expressly stated that its holding might not apply to a more limited ordinance.[209] This language has been cited by several courts in upholding statutes that only prohibit anonymous leaflets in the election context.[210] These courts have reasoned that the public's interest in knowing the possible bias of political commentators is of sufficient value to overcome the speculative disincentives to speech that disclosure might cause. The overwhelming majority of states, as well as the federal government, have such laws.[211] However, several courts have struck down these types of statutes, holding that, despite their being more narrowly drawn than the *Talley* ordinance, the logic of *Talley* is still controlling.[212]

---

unconstitutionally vague where investigators, in different instances, measured volume at varying distances from speaker); Jim Crockett Promotions v. City of Charlotte, 538 F. Supp. 1197, 1200 (W.D.N.C. 1982), *modified*, 706 F.2d 486 (4th Cir. 1983) (ordinance prohibiting sound amplification that exceeded prescribed decibel level for 10% of "any measurement period" held void for vagueness where "measurement period" not defined in ordinance).

[203]Kovacs v. Cooper, 336 U.S. 77, 89 (1949); *Reeves*, 631 F.2d at 386.

[204]Ward v. Rock Against Racism, 491 U.S. 781, *reh'g denied*, 492 U.S. 937 (1989) (court upheld city's regulation of volume, sound mix, and sound quality); *Reeves*, 631 F.2d at 386–87.

[205]*Reeves*, 631 F.2d at 386–87.

[206]Feiner v. New York, 340 U.S. 315, 321 (1951); Resident Advisory Bd. v. Rizzo, 503 F. Supp. 383, 401–02 (E.D. Pa. 1980).

[207]362 U.S. 60 (1960).

[208]*Id.* at 65.

[209]*Id.* at 64.

[210]United States v. Insco, 496 F.2d 204 (5th Cir. 1974); United States v. Scott, 195 F. Supp. 440 (D.N.D. 1961); State v. Acey, 633 S.W.2d 306 (Tenn. 1982); Moorefield v. Moore, 540 S.W.2d 873 (Ky. 1976); Canon v. Justice Ct., 393 P.2d 428 (Cal. 1964); *see also* Commonwealth v. Acquaviva, 14 Pa. D. & C.2d 285, *aff'd*, 145 A.2d 407 (Pa. Super. Ct. 1958).

[211]As of 1960, 36 states had statutes prohibiting the anonymous distribution of materials relating to elections. *Talley*, 362 U.S. at 70 n.2 (dissenting opinion). By 1975, 43 states and the federal government had such statutes. *Developments in the Law—Elections*, 88 HARV. L. REV. 1111, 1286–87 (1975). In 1976, the original federal statute, 18 U.S.C. §612, was repealed and 2 U.S.C. §441d was enacted. The newer statute requires that election advertising reveal whether it was authorized by the candidate or an authorized political committee. 2 U.S.C.S. §441d(1), (2) (1993). If unauthorized, the advertisement must so state and also reveal the name of the person who paid for it. 2 U.S.C. §441d(3).

[212]State v. North Dakota Educ. Ass'n, 262 N.W.2d 731 (N.D. 1978) (reversing conviction of publisher of newsletter); Wilson v. Stocker, 819 F.2d 943 (10th Cir. 1987); People v. White, 506 N.E.2d 1284 (Ill. 1987); State v. Fulton, 337 So. 2d 866 (La. 1976); Commonwealth v. Dennis, 329 N.E.2d 706 (Mass. 1975); People v. Duryea, 351 N.Y.S.2d 978 (N.Y. Sup. Ct. 1974), *aff'd*, 354 N.Y.S.2d 129 (N.Y. App. Div. 1974); *see also* Messerli v. State, 626 P.2d 81 (Alaska 1980) (remanded for factual review of likelihood of reprisals for those identified).

The effect of *Talley* is not limited to political literature. Other courts have applied *Talley*'s reasoning to invalidate a law that prohibited anonymous student publications,[213] to prohibit a regulation that required subscribers of a recording service to include their name and address in their recorded announcement,[214] and to invalidate statutes that required newspaper editorials to be signed by their authors.[215] Similarly, an ordinance that required advance disclosure of the names and addresses of those wishing to "exercise first amendment rights" at an air terminal was struck down.[216]

Several cases that addressed anonymity in the context of film and broadcasting have upheld regulations that require disclosure of the creators or recipients of such matter. Thus, a federal statute that requires those who wish to distribute films labeled by the State Department as "political propaganda" to register as foreign agents and to disclose the names of all exhibitors of the film has been upheld against First Amendment challenge.[217] In interpreting an FCC regulation that requires broadcast licensees to identify sponsors of political advertising, the District of Columbia Circuit noted that, while such a requirement was "apparently" constitutional, further intrusiveness, by way of identification requirements, could be "problematic."[218]

§12.5(G) Cable Television Distribution and Satellite Dishes

This section discusses restrictions on cable operators doing business in a certain area, e.g., a city or county.[219]

In *City of Los Angeles v. Preferred Communications* (*Preferred II*),[220] the Supreme Court decided that a trial was required to determine whether a city violated the First Amendment by refusing to issue a franchise to more than one cable television company.[221] The plaintiff, which was denied a franchise after it refused to participate in the auction to award a single franchise, contended that its rights as a First Amendment speaker were violated because there was sufficient excess physical and economic capacity in the city to accommodate more than one cable system.[222]

---

[213]Jacobs v. Board of Sch. Comm'rs, 490 F.2d 601 (7th Cir. 1973), *vacated on other grounds,* 420 U.S. 128 (1975).

[214]Huntley v. Public Util. Comm'n, 442 P.2d 685 (Cal. 1968) ("The First Amendment right to remain anonymous recognized in *Talley* clearly encompasses all forms of expression whether they be writing or . . . a recorded message over the telephone."); Figari v. New York Tel. Co., 303 N.Y.S.2d 245 (N.Y. App. Div. 1969) (same).

[215]Opinion of Justices, 306 A.2d 18 (Me. 1973); In re Opinion of Justices, 324 A.2d 211 (Del. 1974); People v. Mishkin, 234 N.Y.S.2d 342 (N.Y. App. Div. 1962), *aff'd,* 204 N.E.2d 209 (N.Y. 1964), *aff'd,* 383 U.S. 502 (1966).

[216]Rosen v. Port of Portland, 641 F.2d 1243, 1251 (9th Cir. 1981) ("The right of those expressing political, religious, social or economic views to maintain their anonymity is historic, fundamental, and all too often necessary.").

[217]Meese v. Keene, 481 U.S. 465, 14 Media L. Rep. 1385 (1987); Block v. Meese, 793 F.2d 1303, 13 Media L. Rep. 1209 (D.C. Cir. 1986).

[218]Loveday v. Federal Communications Comm'n, 707 F.2d 1443, 1459, 9 Media L. Rep. 1673, 1686–87 (D.C. Cir.), *cert. denied,* 464 U.S. 1008 (1983); *see* Southern Conn. Newspapers v. Town of Greenwich, 11 Media L. Rep. 1051, 1056 (D. Conn. 1984) (upholding requirement that news racks display name, address, and telephone number of distributors because, unlike *Talley,* ordinance did not compel disclosure of author of paper); Minnesota Newspaper Ass'n v. City of Minneapolis, 9 Media L. Rep. 2116, 2123–24 (D. Minn. 1983) (requirement that news racks identify distributor not grounds for voiding ordinance).

[219]Access to cable television is discussed in Chapter 13, §13.6.

[220]476 U.S. 488, 13 Media L. Rep. 2244 (1986).

[221]*Id.* at 494, 12 Media L. Rep. at 2247.

[222]*Id.* at 490–91, 12 Media L. Rep. at 2246.

In remanding the case for further proceedings, the Supreme Court noted that the city had presented factual arguments to justify its restrictions on cable franchises, but that the factual record had not been developed fully because the trial court had granted a motion to dismiss.[223] Accordingly, the Supreme Court declined to decide most of the First Amendment issues until the disputed factual issues were resolved.[224]

However, the Court did decide in *Preferred II* that, because cable television operators provide original programming or exercise editorial discretion over which stations or programs to include in their cable offerings, their activities "plainly implicate First Amendment interests."[225] It did not decide the extent of those First Amendment rights or the extent to which cable television activities may be regulated.[226]

Even so, recognizing that cable television requires use of public utility poles and public rights-of-way, the *Preferred II* Court suggested that cable television is subject to some sort of reasonable, non-content regulation, particularly on grounds that a municipality has an important interest in prohibiting forms of expression that are intrusive, nuisances, or a blight on the community.[227] This reference to reasonable time, place, and manner restrictions would allow local governments to impose reasonable regulations on a cable operator's use of the public ways, because regulation would be aimed directly at conduct involved in the physical occupation of rights-of-way, not the content of the cable operator's message.

Courts have just begun to chart the permissible scope of such cable regulation.[228] In evaluating cable regulation, courts have applied the test set forth in *United States v. O'Brien*,[229] which the Supreme Court cited in *Preferred II*.[230] That test provides that a governmental regulation on speech is justified if (1) it is within the constitutional power of government; (2) it furthers an important or substantial governmental interest that is unrelated to the suppression of free

---

[223]*Id.* at 493–94, 12 Media L. Rep. at 2247.
[224]*Id.* at 494, 12 Media L. Rep. at 2247.
[225]476 U.S. at 494, 12 Media L. Rep. at 2247.
[226]*Id.* at 496, 12 Media L. Rep. at 2248 (Blackmun, J., concurring).
[227]*Id.* at 495, 12 Media L. Rep. at 2247 ("Even protected speech is not equally permissible in all places and at all times.... Moreover, where speech and conduct are joined in a single course of action, the First Amendment values must be balanced against competing societal interests.") (citing City Council of Los Angeles v. Taxpayers for Vincent, 466 U.S. 789, 805–07 (1984); United States v. O'Brien, 391 U.S. 367, 376–77 (1968)).
[228]*See, e.g.,* Pacific W. Cable Co. v. City of Sacramento (Pacific West I), 798 F.2d 353, 355, 13 Media L. Rep. 1302, 1304 (9th Cir. 1986) (affirming denial of preliminary injunction sought by company denied cable franchise; even though cable activities implicated First Amendment interests, city "may regulate the noncommunicative aspects of cable broadcasting through reasonable time, place and manner restrictions," including cable franchise licensing requirement); Tele-Communications of Key W. v. United States, 757 F.2d 1330, 1338 (D.C. Cir. 1985) (public forum analysis involving time, place, and manner restrictions could be applied to case in which plaintiff alleged that there were no reasons why two cable companies could not simultaneously use cable rights-of-way); Group W Cable v. City of Santa Cruz, 679 F. Supp. 977, 980 (N.D. Cal. 1988) (city may adopt reasonable time, place, and manner regulations governing use of public facilities; because easements and rights-of-way must be regarded as limited public forum, regulations governing their use must be reasonable); Pacific W. Cable Co. v. City of Sacramento (Pacific West II), 672 F. Supp. 1322, 1332 (E.D. Cal. 1987) (exclusive franchise policy could not be justified as content-neutral time, place, and manner regulation because no alternative means of expression existed; "Defendants' single franchise policy results in plaintiff's cable television speech being restricted, in essence, to 'no time, no place and no manner.'"); Preferred Communications v. City of Los Angeles (Preferred I), 754 F.2d 1396, 1403–11 (9th Cir. 1985), *aff'd on narrower grounds,* 476 U.S. 488 (1986) (public access channels of cable television system not adequate substitute for right to operate cable system).
[229]391 U.S. 367 (1968).
[230]476 U.S. at 493, 12 Media L. Rep. at 2247.

expression; and (3) the incidental restriction on First Amendment is no greater than essential to further the governmental interest.[231]

Absent a firm pronouncement from the Supreme Court, the lower courts applying the *O'Brien* test have disagreed over the amount of First Amendment protection for cable television operators. Some courts have decided that cable television is akin to broadcast television because it requires the use of public rights-of-way and thus is subject to significantly more regulation than would be acceptable for the print media.[232] These cases, which adopt a broadcasting model of regulation, look to *Red Lion Broadcasting Co. v. Federal Communications Commission*,[233] in which the Supreme Court observed that, because the broadcast spectrum was limited, it constituted a scarce resource and governmental control was required to eliminate "the cacophony of competing voices" that otherwise would drown each other out.[234]

Courts testing cable television rules against the *Red Lion* rationale and the standards of *O'Brien* focus on the governmental interests that are claimed to justify substantial regulation even if it results in cable monopolies. Cable requires the use of public rights-of-way—both above and below the ground—to lay cable, and thus by its nature cable disrupts use of the public ways,[235] and physical and economic constraints may dictate that only a finite number of cable operations may exist, given present technology.[236] Some courts have also

---

[231] *O'Brien*, 391 U.S. at 377.

[232] *See, e.g.,* Community Communications Co. v. City of Boulder, 660 F.2d 1370, 1377, 7 Media L. Rep. 1993, 1998 (10th Cir. 1981), *cert. dismissed,* 456 U.S. 1001 (1982) (reversing grant of preliminary injunction enjoining city from limiting cable operator to certain territories; "The attributes of cable broadcasting technology indicate that the nearly absolute strictures against direct governmental regulation of newspapers' dissemination of information cannot be applied in wholesale fashion to cable operators. . . . A newspaper may reach its audience simply through the public streets or mails, with no more disruption to the public domain than would be caused by the typical pedestrian, motorist, or user of the mails. But a cable operator must lay the means of his medium underground or string it across poles in order to deliver his message."); Berkshire Cablevision of R.I. v. Burke, 571 F. Supp. 976, 986, 9 Media L. Rep. 2321, 2328 (D.R.I. 1983), *vacated on other grounds,* 773 F.2d 382 (1st Cir. 1985) (economic scarcity is sufficient rationale for regulation of cable); *see generally* Chapter 13, §13.2.

[233] 395 U.S. 367, 1 Media L. Rep. 2053 (1969).

[234] *Id.* at 376, 1 Media L. Rep. at 2057. In *Red Lion,* the Supreme Court upheld the FCC's "fairness doctrine," which required broadcasters to set aside time for the discussion of controversial public issues and to provide a "reasonable opportunity" for opposing viewpoints to be heard. *Id.* at 400–401, 1 Media L. Rep. at 2058. For a discussion of the fairness doctrine, see Chapter 13, §13.3.

[235] *See, e.g.,* Omega Satellite Prods. v. City of Indianapolis, 694 F.2d 119, 125 (7th Cir. 1982) ("If . . . municipal authorities must grant every applicant for a telephone or electric light franchise the right to use the streets on the same terms accorded corporations using the same, such streets must be rendered of little use for other purposes."); *City of Boulder,* 660 F.2d at 1370 ("a cable company must significantly impact the public domain in order to operate"); Preferred I, 754 F.2d 1396, 1406 (9th Cir. 1985) ("Cable television . . . requires the use of public facilities, and this provides a justification for some government regulation. The City has legitimate interests in public safety and in maintaining public thoroughfares."); Pacific West I, 798 F.2d 353, 355, 13 Media L. Rep. 1302, 1304 (9th Cir. 1986) ("Nothing in our earlier decision in *Preferred [I]* . . . requires that a municipality open its doors to all cable-television comers, regardless of size, shape, quality, qualifications or threat to the ultimate capacity of the system."); Erie Telecommunications v. City of Erie, 659 F. Supp. 580, 604 (W.D. Pa. 1987), *aff'd on other grounds,* 853 F.2d 1084 (3d Cir. 1988) ("The obvious distinction between cable and other forms of media is that passage through the streets is an incidental consequence of a radio or television station's or a newspaper's dissemination, whereas cable television's chosen means of dissemination utilizes the street as a conduit for speech.").

[236] *See, e.g.,* Central Telecommunications v. TCI Cablevision, 800 F.2d 711, 717 (8th Cir. 1986), *cert. denied,* 480 U.S. 910 (1987) ("natural monopoly" characteristics of relevant cable market justified city's offering of de facto exclusive franchise because there was room for only one operator at a time); *Omega Satellite Prods.,* 694 F.2d at 126 ("If a market has room for only one firm, it would be an effort worthy of King Canute to keep two firms in it."); *Berkshire Cablevision,* 571 F. Supp. at 986, 9 Media L. Rep. at 2328 ("[T]he economic realities of the cable industry . . . as a practical matter, create a 'natural monopoly' for the first cable operator to construct a cable system in a given service area."); Hopkinsville Cable TV v. Pennyroyal Cablevision, 562 F. Supp. 543, 547 (W.D. Ky. 1982) (because cable television system tends to be natural monopoly by nature, city may make conscious selection of firm to provide service); Carlson v.

applied *Red Lion*'s reasoning that the First Amendment right of cable viewers to receive information is a factor to consider in evaluating the regulatory scheme.[237]

Other courts have concluded, however, that cable television, which offers a virtually unlimited number of channels, is closer to newspaper publishing, and thus government regulation must be extremely limited. Relying on *Miami Herald Publishing Co. v. Tornillo*,[238] this line of cases adopts a print model for regulation.[239] Applying the *O'Brien* test, these courts have concluded that the governmental interests identified in the *Red Lion* line of authorities (physical and economic scarcity) are not sufficient to justify denial of a franchise to a particular would-be operator.[240]

Thus, the constitutional law regarding regulation of cable television is in flux[241] and marked by conflicting opinions. No clear rule yet exists.[242]

Attempts have also been made to use the Cable Communications Policy Act of 1984[243] as a basis for access to private property. In *Cable Investments v. Woolley*,[244] the Third Circuit rejected the argument that Section 541(a)(2)

Village of Union City, 601 F. Supp. 801, 810–11 (W.D. Mich. 1985) (because cable television is natural monopoly, city has interest in ensuring that cable operator who supplies service does so in way that serves public interest). *But see* Quincy Cable TV v. Federal Communications Comm'n, 768 F.2d 1434, 1450, 12 Media L. Rep. 1001, 1013 (D.C. Cir. 1985), *cert. denied sub nom.* Nat'l Ass'n of Broadcasters v. Quincy Cable TV, 476 U.S. 1169 (1986) ("[T]he Supreme Court has categorically rejected the suggestion that purely economic constraints on the number of voices available in a given community justify otherwise unwarranted intrusions into First Amendment rights.").

[237]*See, e.g., City of Boulder*, 660 F.2d at 1376 n.5, 7 Media L. Rep. at 1996 n.5 ("The First Amendment protects not only the right to disseminate, but also the public's interest in the receipt of diversified communications.... [T]he First Amendment interests of cable viewers cannot be left out of the equation for permissible regulation of cable companies."); *Central Telecommunications*, 800 F.2d at 717 (when there was economic capacity for only one cable speaker, city appropriately selected cable operator whose proposal "went further in advancing the First Amendment interest of the viewing public in the greatest variety of programming obtainable"); *Village of Union City*, 601 F. Supp. at 811 (revocation of franchise did not offend First Amendment; "government must have some authority . . . to see to it that optimum use is made of the cable medium in the public interest").

[238]418 U.S. 241, 258 (1974) (holding that "right to reply" statute (analogous to fairness doctrine applied to broadcasters in *Red Lion*) could not be applied to newspapers consistent with First Amendment). *See also Berkshire Cablevision*, 571 F. Supp. at 985, 9 Media L. Rep. at 2327 (newspaper, unlike cable television, "have historically operated free from any form of governmental control over their content").

[239]*See, e.g., Quincy Cable TV*, 768 F.2d at 1449–50, 12 Media L. Rep. at 1012 (even though physical disruption inherent in stringing coaxial cables might warrant regulation of installation, FCC "must carry" regulation requiring cable television operators to carry certain broadcast signals violated First Amendment; "the 'scarcity rationale' has no place in evaluating government regulation of cable television . . . since an essential precondition of that theory—physical interference and scarcity requiring an umpiring role for government—is absent"); *Preferred I*, 754 F.2d at 1403–11 (because it was alleged there was enough physical and economic capacity to accommodate more than one cable operator, *Tornillo* applied); Century Fed. v. City of Palo Alto, 648 F. Supp. 1465, 1472 (N.D. Cal. 1986) (because cable operators exercise editorial discretion, *Tornillo* rationale applied; economic constraints on number of cable speakers did not justify "unwarranted intrusions" into First Amendment rights). This issue is dealt with at length in Chapter 13.

[240]*See, e.g.,* Pacific West II, 672 F. Supp. 1322 (E.D. Cal. 1987) (granting declaratory judgment to would-be cable operator after jury found city's refusal to grant second franchise violated First Amendment because natural monopoly did not exist in market).

[241]An emerging issue is the extent to which cable operators may waive their First Amendment rights by entering into a franchise agreement. *See* Erie Telecommunications v. City of Erie, 853 F.2d 1084, 1098 (3d Cir. 1988) (by entering into release by which it released city from "any and all claims" arising out of franchise agreement, cable operator waived First Amendment claims).

[242]*See, e.g.,* Chicago Cable Communications v. Chicago Cable Comm'n, 678 F. Supp. 734, 744 (N.D. Ill. 1988) (Supreme Court "probably will recognize that the strict limits placed on the broadcast media by the physical constraints of the electromagnetic spectrum do not exist in the realm of cable television.... On the other hand, the Court will probably recognize that, at least in some instances, cable television possesses natural monopoly characteristics that warrants greater governmental regulation").

[243]47 U.S.C. §§521 *et seq.* (Supp. IV 1986).

[244]867 F.2d 151 (3d Cir. 1989).

of this Act gave a cable operator a statutory right of access to tenants in a multi-unit dwelling where the dwelling's owner had ordered the cable operator to remove its equipment.[245] Even where it was contended that the cable operator could use the existing easements of a telephone company to obtain access to apartment buildings, this argument has been rejected.[246] On the other hand, where cable operators have made this argument to obtain access to existing telephone and utility easements in planned residential communities where they have been granted franchises to operate, they have prevailed over the objections of the developers of those communities.[247]

Restrictions on the placement of satellite dishes have been upheld.[248]

§12.5(H) Telephones

A ban on the use of automatic telephone dialing machines to convey commercial speech, unless the recipient has requested or consented to the call or unless the call is preceded by a live operator who obtains consent, has been upheld.[249] However, there is contrary authority.[250]

---

[245]*Cable Investments*, 867 F.2d at 154–60. The court also rejected the same argument based on a Pennsylvania statute, the Pennsylvania Constitution, and the First Amendment. *Id* at 160–62. The court noted that any other result would raise serious constitutional problems about providing just compensation for the taking of private property. *Id.* at 159–60 (citing Loretto v. Teleprompter Manhattan CATV Corp., 458 U.S. 419 (1982)). *Accord* Media Gen. Cable of Fairfax v. Sequoyah Condominium Council of Co-Owners, 991 F.2d 1169, 1174 (4th Cir. 1993); Cable Holdings of Ga. v. McNeil Real Estate, 953 F.2d 600 (11th Cir.), *cert. denied,* 113 S. Ct. 182 (1992).

[246]Cable Assocs. v. Town & Country Mgmt. Corp., 709 F. Supp. 582 (E.D. Pa. 1989). *But see* Mumaugh v. Diamond Lake Area Cable TV Co., 456 N.W.2d 425 (Mich. Ct. App. 1990).

[247]Centel Cable Television Co. of Fla. v. Thomas J. White Dev. Corp., 902 F.2d 905 (11th Cir. 1990); Centel Cable Television Co. of Fla. v. Admiral's Cove Assocs., 835 F.2d 1359 (11th Cir. 1988); Cable TV Fund 14-A v. Property Owners Ass'n, Chesapeake Ranch Estates, 706 F. Supp. 422 (D. Md. 1989).

[248]Johnson v. City of Pleasanton, 982 F.2d 350 (9th Cir. 1992).

[249]Minnesota v. Casino Mktg. Group, 491 N.W.2d 882 (Minn. 1992), *cert. denied,* 113 S. Ct. 1648 (1993).

[250]Moser v. Federal Communications Comm'n, 826 F. Supp. 360 (D. Or. 1993). *But see* Destination Ventures v. Federal Communications Comm'n, 22 Media L. Rep. 1171 (D. Or. 1993) (federal law prohibiting "junk faxes" constitutional).

CHAPTER 13

ACCESS TO THE MEDIA

§13.1 Introduction

This chapter deals with the law concerning whether the media may be compelled to publish information against their wishes. First, the constitutional problems with mandated access are discussed.[1] Next, federal regulations that mandate access to the electronic media are discussed,[2] followed by a discussion of access to the print media.[3] Finally, access to government-controlled media[4] and access to cable television[5] are discussed.

§13.2 The Constitutionality of Government-Mandated Access to the Broadcast and Print Media

§13.2(A) Government-Mandated Access to the Broadcast Media

During the early days of broadcasting, when broadcasters operated without any legal limitation whatsoever, mutual interference on the airwaves made it difficult for anyone to be understood. In 1927, Congress enacted the Radio Act to create a scheme of federal regulation to impose order on this chaos, including creation of the Federal Radio Commission (FRC), which was empowered to license broadcasters.[6]

The FRC's licensing responsibilities were inherited by the Federal Communications Commission (FCC) with the passage of the Communications Act of 1934.[7] The purpose of the Communications Act was to make available to the nation a rapid, nationwide, and worldwide wire and communication service. The FCC was given authority to regulate broadcasting through renewable licenses issued to those serving the "public convenience, interest, or necessity."[8]

---

[1] *See infra* §13.2.
[2] *See infra* §13.3.
[3] *See infra* §13.4.
[4] *See infra* §13.5.
[5] *See infra* §13.6.
[6] Ch. 169, 44 Stat. 1162, 47 U.S.C. §81 (1927) (repealed 1934).
[7] Ch. 652, 48 Stat. 1064, 47 U.S.C. §§151–610 (1982).
[8] 47 U.S.C. §307(a).

In *NBC v. United States*,[9] the Supreme Court first announced the justification for FCC licensing: "[W]ith everybody on the air, nobody could be heard."[10] The Court noted that broadcast facilities "are not available to all who may wish to use them; the radio spectrum simply is not large enough to accommodate everybody. There is a fixed natural limitation upon the number of stations that can operate without interfering with one another."[11] This scarcity of frequencies justified having the government choose the few that would be allowed to broadcast. The denial of a broadcasting license was not a denial of free speech, the Supreme Court held, because the licensing scheme established by Congress was a proper exercise of its power over commerce and because the right to free speech does not encompass the right to use broadcast frequencies without a license.[12]

In addition to licensing, the FCC has imposed access regulations on the broadcast media. In 1969, in *Red Lion Broadcasting Co. v. Federal Communications Commission*,[13] the Supreme Court first dealt with the constitutionality of government-mandated access to the media. *Red Lion* involved a challenge to the FCC's Fairness Doctrine, which requires that a discussion of public issues be presented by broadcasters and that each side of those issues be given coverage.[14] In particular, the Court dealt with a corollary to the Fairness Doctrine, the personal attack rule, which requires that an individual whose honesty, character, integrity, or personal qualities are attacked in the course of a broadcast on a controversial issue of public importance must be offered a reasonable opportunity to respond to the attack.[15]

A Pennsylvania radio station owned by the Red Lion Broadcasting Company had carried a 15-minute broadcast in 1964 by the Reverend Billy James Hargis, who discussed a book by Fred J. Cook entitled *Goldwater—Extremist on the Right*.[16] In the broadcast, Hargis made a number of disparaging comments about Cook and his political affiliations.[17]

When Cook heard about the broadcast, he demanded free reply time; the station refused.[18] After an exchange of letters among Cook, Red Lion, and the FCC, the FCC concluded that the Hargis broadcast was a personal attack on Cook and that Red Lion had failed to meet its obligations under the Fairness Doctrine with respect to various issues, including Cook's right to reply time regardless of whether he could pay for it.[19] The Court of Appeals for the District of Columbia Circuit upheld the FCC's decision, and Red Lion petitioned the Supreme Court for certiorari.[20]

---

[9]319 U.S. 190 (1943).
[10]*Id.* at 212.
[11]*Id.* at 213.
[12]*Id.* at 226–27.
[13]395 U.S. 367 (1969).
[14]*Id.* at 369. The Fairness Doctrine is discussed in detail *infra* §13.3(C).
[15]395 U.S. at 373–75. The personal attack rule is discussed in detail *infra* f§13.3(D).
[16]395 U.S. at 371.
[17]Hargis stated that, among other things, Cook had been fired by a newspaper for making false charges against city officials; had worked for a communist-affiliated publication; had defended Alger Hiss; had attacked J. Edgar Hoover and the Central Intelligence Agency; and had written the book at issue "to smear and destroy Barry Goldwater." *Id.*
[18]*Id.* at 371–72.
[19]*Id.* at 372.
[20]395 U.S. at 367. *See* Red Lion Broadcasting Co. v. Federal Communications Comm'n, 381 F.2d 908 (D.C. Cir. 1967).

In affirming the Court of Appeals, the Supreme Court discussed the history of broadcast regulation at length. Recalling the chaos that existed until 1927, when the government began to allocate radio broadcast frequencies, the Court observed that "[w]ithout government control, the medium would be of little use because of the cacophony of competing voices, none of which could be clearly and predictably heard."[21] The Court concluded that government allocation of the scarce broadcast spectrum was in the public interest.[22] After deciding that the Fairness Doctrine and its component personal attack and political editorializing rules were a legitimate exercise of the authority Congress had given the FCC,[23] the Court turned its attention to a First Amendment challenge to such regulation.

Red Lion contended that the First Amendment precluded the government from requiring it to give equal time to opposing viewpoints.[24] While conceding that broadcasting is clearly a medium affected by a First Amendment interest,[25] the Court observed that the inherent characteristics of the broadcast spectrum, in particular the scarcity of frequencies, distinguished the broadcast medium from more traditional forms of communication.[26] The Court concluded that the goals of the First Amendment would be best served by upholding the regulation in question.[27] In so holding, it rejected claims that the Fairness Doctrine might lead to self-censorship on the part of broadcasters, concluding that historical evidence did not support such a view.[28] The Court also rejected the argument that changes in technology had eliminated any scarcity rationale for the regulations in question.[29]

While the Court was unsympathetic to the First Amendment interests of broadcasters in *Red Lion,* its next treatment of demands for access to the broadcast media, in *CBS v. Democratic National Committee,*[30] was more

---

[21] 395 U.S. at 376.
[22] *Id.*
[23] *Id.* at 385. The political editorializing rule is discussed in detail *infra* §13.3(E).
[24] 395 U.S. at 386.
[25] *Id.* (citing United States v. Paramount Pictures, 334 U.S. 131, 166 (1948)).
[26] *Id.* at 386–90.
[27] *Id.* at 390. According to *Red Lion,* the purpose of the First Amendment is to "preserve an uninhibited marketplace of ideas in which truth will ultimately prevail," thus producing "an informed public capable of conducting its own affairs . . . ." *Id.* at 390–92. In arriving at this conclusion, the Court emphasized that
> [t]here is nothing in the First Amendment which prevents the Government from requiring a licensee to share his frequency with others and to conduct himself as a proxy or fiduciary with obligations to present those views and voices which are representative of his community and which would otherwise, by necessity, be barred from the airwaves. . . . Because of the scarcity of radio frequencies, the Government is permitted to put restraint on licensees in favor of others whose views should be expressed on this unique medium. But the people as a whole retain their interest in free speech by radio and their collective right to have the medium function consistently with the ends and purposes of the First Amendment. It is the right of the viewers and listeners, not the right of the broadcasters, which is paramount.

Id. at 389–90 (citing Federal Communications Comm'n v. Sanders Bros. Radio Station, 309 U.S. 470, 475 (1940); Federal Communications Comm'n v. Allentown Broadcasting Corp., 349 U.S. 358, 361–62 (1955); 2 Z. CHAFEE, GOVERNMENT & MASS COMMUNICATIONS 546 (1947)).

[28] 395 U.S. at 392–95. The Court also observed that "if experience with the administration of these doctrines indicates that they have the net effect of reducing rather than enhancing the volume and quality of coverage, there will be time enough to reconsider the constitutional implications." *Id.* at 393. This statement was an important step in the FCC's ultimate abolition of the Fairness Doctrine. *See infra* §13.3(F).

[29] 395 U.S. at 396–401. The Court ended its discussion with an enigmatic footnote that indicated that, given its previous discussion, it was unnecessary to reach the argument that even if there was no longer a technological scarcity of frequencies limiting the number of broadcasters, such regulations would still be acceptable because freedom of speech or press is not abridged "by legislation directly or indirectly multiplying the voices and views presented to the public through time sharing, fairness doctrines, or other devices which limit or dissipate the power of those who sit astride the channels of communications with the general public." *Id.* at 401 n.28. *See infra* note 79.

[30] 412 U.S. 94 (1973).

sympathetic to their First Amendment concerns. The issue in that case was whether broadcasters could refuse to sell time to "responsible entities" for editorial advertisements.[31]

The Court's opinion in this case, authored by Chief Justice Warren Burger, was divided into four parts. The first part, where Chief Justice Burger was joined by four other justices, stated that, in evaluating the First Amendment interests of broadcasters, great weight should be given to the decisions of Congress and the FCC.[32]

The second part of the opinion, adopted by five justices in addition to Chief Justice Burger, concerned the Fairness Doctrine claim. It emphasized that Congress' intent in formulating the Communications Act was to permit private broadcasting to develop "the widest journalistic freedom consistent with its public obligations."[33] Recognizing that, under *Red Lion,* broadcasters act as public trustees, the Court nevertheless pointed out that, since it is physically impossible to provide time for all viewpoints, broadcasters must be allowed "significant journalistic discretion in deciding how best to fulfill the Fairness Doctrine obligations."[34] According to the Court, the broadcasters' refusal to accept the advertisements in question was within that discretion.[35]

The third part of Chief Justice Burger's opinion, which was joined by Justices Potter Stewart and William Rehnquist, dealt with the First Amendment claim. It concluded that the broadcasters' refusal to accept the ads did not constitute "state action," so analysis of the First Amendment was unnecessary.[36]

The concurring opinions concluded that the FCC's recognition of broadcaster freedom and discretion to make editorial decisions was consistent with the First Amendment[37] or found it unnecessary to reach the state action issue.[38]

---

[31]*Id.* at 99. The Democratic National Committee and the Business Executives' Move for Vietnam Peace each filed complaints with the FCC alleging that the networks' refusal to sell time for such ads violated both the Fairness Doctrine and the First Amendment. The FCC rejected these claims. Democratic Nat'l Comm., 25 F.C.C.2d 216 (1970); Business Executives' Move for Vietnam Peace, 25 F.C.C.2d 242 (1970). The FCC held that a broadcaster who meets public obligations to provide full and fair coverage of public issues is not required to accept editorial advertisements. *Democratic National Committee,* 25 F.C.C.2d at 226; *Vietnam Peace,* 25 F.C.C.2d at 246–47. The Court of Appeals reversed, holding that a broadcaster's fixed policy of refusing editorial advertisements violated the First Amendment. 412 U.S. at 97. *See* Business Executives' Move for Vietnam Peace v. Federal Communications Comm'n, 450 F.2d 642 (D.C. Cir. 1971).

[32]412 U.S. at 101–03.

[33]*Id.* at 110.

[34]*Id.* at 111. The Court noted and approved decisions by the FCC that "no private individual or group has a right to command the use of broadcast facilities." *Id.* at 113. Under the Fairness Doctrine, observed the Court,

broadcasters are responsible for providing the listening and viewing public with access to a balanced presentation of information on issues of public importance. The basic principle underlying that responsibility is "the right of the public to be informed, rather than any right on the part of the Government, any broadcast licensee or any individual member of the public to broadcast his own particular views on any matter . . . ."

Id. at 112–13 (quoting Report on Editorializing by Broadcast Licensees, 13 F.C.C. 1246, 1249 (1949)).

[35]*Id.*

[36]*Id.* at 118–20. The Court of Appeals had found that broadcasters are "instrumentalities of the government for First Amendment purposes" because they are granted use of part of the public domain and are thus regulated as fiduciaries of the people. 412 U.S. at 115. Justices Burger, Stewart, and Rehnquist disagreed, noting that the policy against accepting editorial advertising was that of the broadcasters, not of the FCC, and thus fell within the sphere of journalistic discretion left to licensees by Congress and the FCC. *Id.* at 118. These justices expressed concern that a finding that there was state action would subject nearly all editorial decisions of broadcasters to constitutional scrutiny. Doing this would erode the journalistic independence at the heart of the First Amendment. *Id.* at 120–21.

[37]412 U.S. at 145–46 (Stewart, J., concurring); *id.* at 147 (White, J., concurring and expressing discomfort with Chief Justice Burger's state action analysis).

[38]Justice Blackmun, joined by Justice Powell, wrote that a majority of the Court concluded that, even if there was state action, the First Amendment does not mandate that broadcasters accept editorial advertis-

Justice William Douglas, concurring in the judgment only, expressed his view that all content regulation of broadcasting, including the Fairness Doctrine, was impermissible under the First Amendment and that *Red Lion* had been improperly decided.[39]

The fourth part of the opinion, which was adopted by four justices in addition to Chief Justice Burger, evaluated whether broadcasters were required to accept the advertisements under the "public interest" standard of the Communications Act, which incorporates First Amendment principles. It noted that requiring broadcasters to sell time to any group desiring to purchase it would not serve the public interest in providing access to the marketplace of "ideas and experiences" since it would produce a system heavily weighted in favor of the affluent or those with access to wealth.[40] Such a right of access, according to the Court, could transfer the editorial discretion of broadcast licensees to the hands of private individuals who are not accountable to the government and are not the best judges of what the public ought to hear:

> For better or worse, editing is what editors are for; and editing is selection and choice of material. That editors—newspaper or broadcast—can and do abuse this power is beyond doubt, but that is no reason to deny the discretion Congress provided. Calculated risks of abuse are taken in order to preserve higher values. The presence of these risks is nothing new; the authors of the Bill of Rights accepted the reality that these risks were evils for which there was no acceptable remedy other than a spirit of moderation and a sense of responsibility—and civility—on the part of those who exercise the guaranteed freedoms of expression.[41]

Further, a right of access would enlarge government control over the broadcast media:

> Under a constitutionally commanded and Government supervised right of access system urged by respondents and mandated by the Court of Appeals, the Commission would be required to oversee far more of the day-to-day operations of broadcasters conduct .... Regimenting broadcasters is too radical a therapy for the ailment respondents complain of.[42]

The Court thus rejected any notion of a constitutionally required right of access and emphasized the importance of journalistic discretion in deciding what materials to include in a broadcast.

The next Supreme Court case dealing with government-mandated access to the broadcast media, *CBS v. Federal Communications Commission*,[43] involved

---

ing. Revising the right of access to the broadcast media is an ongoing process for Congress, the FCC, and the broadcasters themselves, the Court held, and "courts should not freeze this necessarily dynamic process into a constitutional holding." *Id.* at 132. In light of this conclusion, Justices Blackmun and Powell found that the state action issue was not outcome-determinative and thus declined to decide it. *Id.* at 148 (Blackmun, Powell, JJ., concurring).

In a dissenting opinion, Justice Brennan, joined by Justice Marshall, wrote that the challenged policy violates the First Amendment and "can serve only to inhibit, rather than to further our 'profound national commitment to the principle that debate on public issues should be uninhibited, robust, and wide-open.' " *Id.* at 172 (Brennan, J., dissenting) (quoting New York Times Co. v. Sullivan, 376 U.S. 254, 270 (1964)).

[39]412 U.S. at 148–70 (Douglas, J., concurring in judgment).

[40]*Id.* at 123. *Compare* Buckley v. Valeo, 424 U.S. 1 (1976) (First Amendment prevents limits on amount candidates can spend on their own campaigns).

[41]412 U.S. at 124–25.

[42]*Id.* at 126–27.

[43]453 U.S. 367 (1981) (decided together with ABC v. Federal Communications Comm'n and NBC v. Federal Communications Comm'n).

interpretation of the "reasonable access" provisions of Section 312(a)(7) of the Communications Act, which require broadcasters to provide "reasonable access" to candidates for federal office.[44] In October 1979, the Carter-Mondale campaign requested each of the three major television networks to provide time for a 30-minute program between 8:00 p.m. and 10:30 p.m. on certain days in December 1979. The time was intended for a documentary that outlined the record of the Carter administration, to be aired in conjunction with President Carter's formal announcement of his candidacy for reelection.[45] Each of the networks declined to sell the time sought.[46] The Carter-Mondale campaign filed a complaint with the FCC, which, in a 4-3 ruling, found that the networks' reasons for refusing to sell the time requested were "deficient" under the FCC's standards of reasonableness.[47] The Court of Appeals upheld the FCC's decision, and the networks sought Supreme Court review.[48]

The Supreme Court affirmed, holding that Section 312(a)(7) provides, to legally qualified individual candidates seeking federal elective office, an affirmative statutory right of reasonable access to the broadcast media that may be invoked by the candidates once a campaign has commenced.[49] The statute, according to the Court, does not merely codify previous "public interest" standards pursued by the FCC, but creates a special right of access in addition to general Fairness Doctrine requirements.[50] The Court held that the standards adopted by the FCC to implement Section 312(a)(7) were not arbitrary or capricious and that the FCC had not abused its discretion in finding that the networks had failed to grant the reasonable access required by Section 312(a)(7).[51]

Finally, the Court rejected claims by the networks that Section 312(a)(7) violated their First Amendment rights by unduly circumscribing their editorial discretion.[52] The Court acknowledged that it had never previously approved a general right of access to the media,[53] but pointed to its recognition, in previous cases, of the importance of permitting candidates a full opportunity to make their views known so that the electorate may make intelligent evaluations before reaching a decision on election day.[54] The Court ultimately returned to the central notion that it set forth in *Red Lion:* "It is the right of the viewers and listeners, not the right of the broadcasters, which is paramount. It is the purpose of the First Amendment to preserve an uninhibited marketplace of ideas in which truth will ultimately prevail, rather than to countenance monopo-

---

[44]This law is discussed in detail *infra* §13.3(B).

[45]453 U.S. at 371–72.

[46]CBS cited the large number of candidates for the Republican and Democratic presidential nominations and the potential disruption of regular programming that would result from requests to accommodate equal treatment; ABC stated that it would not yet sell political time for the 1980 presidential campaign; and NBC, noting the large number of potential requests, stated that it too was not prepared to sell time for the political programs as early as December 1979. *Id.* at 372–73.

[47]74 F.C.C.2d 631, 642 (1979).

[48]453 U.S. at 375–76.

[49]*Id.* at 379.

[50]*Id.*

[51]*Id.* at 393–94.

[52]*Id.* at 394.

[53]453 U.S. at 396 (citing Federal Communications Comm'n v. Midwest Video Corp., 440 U.S. 689 (1979); Miami Herald Pub'g Co. v. Tornillo, 418 U.S. 241 (1974); CBS v. Democratic Nat'l Comm., 412 U.S. 94 (1973)).

[54]*Id.* (citing Buckley v. Valeo, 424 U.S. 1, 52–53 (1976); Monitor Patriot Co. v. Roy, 401 U.S. 265, 272 (1971); Garrison v. Louisiana, 379 U.S. 64, 74–75 (1964)).

lization of that market ...."[55] Although conceding that "the broadcasting industry is entitled under the First Amendment to exercise 'the widest journalistic freedom consistent with its public [duties]',"[56] the Court concluded that Section 312(a)(7) represented an effort by Congress to assure that an important public resource was used in the public interest and that the statutory right of access at issue properly balanced the First Amendment rights of federal candidates, the public, and broadcasters.[57]

The Court has thus held that at least some forms of government-mandated access to the broadcast media are constitutional. This conclusion is largely based on the rationale that broadcast frequencies are scarce, so government regulation of them is permissible. However, the Court has rejected the claim that there is a constitutionally mandated right of access to the media.

§13.2(B) Government-Mandated Access to the Print Media

In stark contrast to *Red Lion* and its progeny[58] stands *Miami Herald Publishing Co. v. Tornillo*,[59] where the issue was the constitutionality of a state statute that granted political candidates a right to equal space to reply to criticism and attacks by newspapers.[60]

In *Tornillo,* the *Miami Herald* had printed editorials critical of Tornillo's candidacy for the Florida House of Representatives. A seldom-cited Florida statute provided that, if a candidate for nomination or election was attacked regarding his or her personal character or official record by any newspaper, the candidate had a right to demand that the newspaper print, free of cost to the candidate, any reply that the candidate chose to make to the newspaper's charges in as conspicuous a place and in the same kind of type as the charges that prompted the reply.[61] Tornillo demanded that the *Miami Herald* print his reply pursuant to this statute. The *Miami Herald* refused, and Tornillo brought suit seeking declaratory and injunctive relief as well as actual and punitive damages.[62]

The trial court held that the statute in question was an infringement on freedom of the press under the First and Fourteenth Amendments.[63] The Florida Supreme Court reversed, holding that free speech was enhanced and not abridged by the right-of-reply statute, which, in its view, furthered the " 'broad societal interest in the free flow of information to the public.' "[64] The newspaper appealed.

The opinion of the Supreme Court, written by Chief Justice Burger, discussed at length the contentions of the proponents of a right of access to newspapers. Access proponents asserted that changing economic realities in

---

[55]*Id.* at 395 (citing Red Lion Broadcasting Co. v. Federal Communications Comm'n, 395 U.S. 367, 390 (1969).
[56]*Id.* (quoting CBS v. Democratic Nat'l Comm., 412 U.S. 94, 110 (1973)).
[57]*Id.* at 397.
[58]*See supra* §13.2(A).
[59]418 U.S. 241 (1974).
[60]*Id.* at 243.
[61]FLA. STAT. ANN. §104.38 (West 1973).
[62]418 U.S. at 244.
[63]*Id.* at 245.
[64]*Id.* (quoting Tornillo v. Miami Herald Pub'g Co., 287 So. 2d 78, 82 (1973)).

the press and communications industry have led to a situation where the means of communication are not freely available to all, but are in the hands of a powerful few; that high entry barriers confront any individual or group seeking to enter the communications market; and that newspapers have become "big business."[65] Because the government is obligated to ensure that a variety of views reach the public, access proponents argued, these changes in the newspaper industry warrant greater government regulation in the form of a right of access to newspapers.[66]

Nevertheless, the Court unanimously rejected the claims of Tornillo and the proponents of government-mandated access. Noting that the core question in the case was whether editors and publishers could be compelled to publish that which " 'reason' tells them should not be published,"[67] the Court invalidated the Florida statute.

The Court first observed that the Florida statute could be characterized as exacting a penalty on the basis of the content of the newspaper, since the newspaper's choice of material to print could result (as it had in this case) in demands for free space by an aggrieved party, which would impose costs in time and materials as well as take up space that could be devoted to other matters.[68] Faced with such a possible penalty, the Court reasoned that coverage of political and electoral events might be blunted or reduced by newspapers choosing a "safe" course by avoiding all controversy.[69] A government-enforced right of access, the Court concluded, inescapably " 'dampens the vigor and limits the variety of public debate.' "[70]

Focusing on the sanctity of the editorial decision-making process, the Court further concluded:

> Even if a newspaper would face no additional costs to comply with a compulsory access law and would not be forced to forego publication of news or opinion by the inclusion of a reply, the Florida statute fails to clear the barriers of the First Amendment because of its intrusion into the function of editors. A newspaper is more than a passive receptacle or conduit for news, comment, and advertising. The choice of material to go into a newspaper, and the decisions made as to limitations on the size and content of the paper, and treatment of public issues and public officials—whether fair or unfair—constitute the exercise of editorial control and judgment. It has yet to be demonstrated how governmental regulation of this crucial process can be exercised consistent with First Amendment guarantees of a free press as they have evolved to this time.[71]

The Court reached this unanimous conclusion without even mentioning its decision in *Red Lion,* which upheld a right to reply to personal attacks aired over the broadcast media. Thus, although it has approved government-mandated access to the broadcast media, the Supreme Court has held that the editorial discretion of the print media cannot be limited through government

---

[65]"Chains of newspapers, national newspapers, national wire and news services, and one-newspaper towns, are the dominant features of a press that has become noncompetitive and enormously powerful and influential in its capacity to manipulate popular opinion and change the course of events." *Id.* at 249 (footnote omitted).

[66]*Id.* at 248–52.
[67]*Id.* at 256.
[68]418 U.S. at 256.
[69]*Id.* at 257.
[70]*Id.* (quoting New York Times v. Sullivan, 376 U.S. 254, 279 (1964)).
[71]*Id.* at 258 (footnote omitted).

regulations that impose a similar right of access. According to the Court, economic scarcity—e.g., the limited number of newspapers in most cities—is not the same as technological scarcity—e.g., the limited number of broadcast frequencies that exist.[72]

§13.2(C) The Supreme Court's Uneasy Dichotomy of the Print and Broadcast Media

As the preceding discussion makes clear, there is a sharp dichotomy of the Supreme Court's treatment of the print and broadcast media with respect to access regulations. Since it first addressed the issue of broadcast regulation, the Court has referred to physical limitations on the broadcast spectrum as the key factor in permitting government regulation of such media.[73] As the Court stated in *Red Lion*, "[b]ecause of the scarcity of radio frequencies, the Government is permitted to put restraints on licensees in favor of others whose views should be expressed on this unique medium."[74] With respect to newspapers and other print media, the Court has declined to impose such regulation because there is no inherent physical scarcity of such channels of communication, albeit economics limit the number of print media.[75]

This clear dichotomy of print and broadcast regulation cannot withstand scrutiny—there is no longer any realistic spectrum scarcity.[76] However, although the Supreme Court's own cases dealing with broadcast regulation clearly reflect the tensions inherent in its justification of broadcast regulation as the permissible allocation of a scarce public resource,[77] the Court has not been willing to reexamine the scarcity rationale,[78] nor has it been willing to inquire

---

[72]*Id.* at 257.

[73]NBC v. United States, 319 U.S. 190, 226–27 (1943) ("Freedom of utterance is abridged to many who wish to use the limited facilities of radio. Unlike other modes of expression, radio inherently is not available to all. That is its unique characteristic, and that is why, unlike other modes of expression, it is subject to governmental regulation.").

[74]395 U.S. 367, 390 (1969).

[75]*See, e.g.,* Federal Communications Comm'n v. League of Women Voters, 468 U.S. 364, 377 (1984).

[76]"[A]s of December 31, 1974, there were 7,785 radio stations on the air and 952 TV stations, serving nearly every part of the country. As of January 1, 1971, daily newspapers totalled only 1,749. And the broadcast spectrum is still not completely filled." Bazelon, *FCC Regulation of the Telecommunications Press,* 1975 DUKE L.J. 213, 224–25 (footnote omitted). By 1983, the number of daily newspapers had decreased to 1,730, while the number of commercial and educational radio stations had grown to nearly 10,000. Irving R. Kaufman, *Reassessing the Fairness Doctrine,* N.Y. TIMES, June 19, 1983, §6 (Magazine), at 17. "[M]any markets have a far greater number of broadcasting stations than newspapers." Telecommunications Research & Action Ctr. v. Federal Communications Comm'n, 801 F.2d 501, 509 n.4, 13 Media L. Rep. 1881, 1887 n.4 (D.C. Cir. 1986), *cert. denied,* 482 U.S. 919 (1987). For other commentators' rejection of the spectrum scarcity justification, *see, e.g.,* I. POOL, TECHNOLOGIES OF FREEDOM 151–56 (1983); Fowler & Brenner, *A Marketplace Approach to Broadcast Regulation,* 60 TEX. L. REV. 207, 221–26 (1982); *Leading Cases of the 1983 Term,* 98 HARV. L. REV. 87, 214 (1984) [hereinafter *Leading Cases*].

[77]*Compare* Red Lion Broadcasting Co. v. Federal Communications Comm'n, 395 U.S. 367 (1969) *and* CBS v. Federal Communications Comm'n, 453 U.S. 367 (1981) (emphasizing that public's right to know is paramount) *with* CBS v. Democratic Nat'l Comm., 412 U.S. 94 (1973) *and League of Women Voters,* 468 U.S. at 378–79 (emphasizing protected nature of editorial process and First Amendment guarantee of "the widest journalistic freedom consistent with [broadcasters'] public [duties]").

[78]In *League of Women Voters,* the Court held that Section 399 of the Public Broadcasting Act of 1967, which forbade any noncommercial educational station that received a grant from the Corporation for Public Broadcasting from engaging in editorializing, violated the First Amendment. While recognizing that Congress has the power to regulate broadcasting, the Court explicitly declined to consider whether spectrum scarcity still exists; it suggested that the task should be undertaken, if at all, by Congress or the FCC. 468 U.S. at 376 n.11. The Court's "staunch refusal to recognize the demise of spectrum scarcity underscores the conflict between the Court's continuing desire to limit government and its responsibility to protect freedom of expression." *Leading Cases, supra* note 76, at 213–14 (footnote omitted). Indeed, the Court has reaffirmed its belief in the scarcity rationale as recently as 1990. Metro Broadcasting v. Federal Communications

into underlying economic conditions that might justify regulation even in the absence of spectrum scarcity.[79]

If the Court does acknowledge that the spectrum scarcity rationale for broadcast regulation is no longer valid, as it ultimately must, it will then have to determine a direction for the constitutional jurisprudence of media access regulation. If it shifts from notions of spectrum scarcity to economic scarcity as the rationale for broadcast regulation, it will be difficult to sustain the position, taken in *Tornillo,* that the government may not mandate access to the print media.[80] On the other hand, if it abandons the spectrum scarcity rationale and fully embraces *Tornillo*'s rejection of an economic concentration rationale for access regulation, then any government-mandated access to the media would be constitutionally suspect. Despite the criticisms leveled at FCC access regulation, particularly in the area of the Fairness Doctrine,[81] many constitutional scholars, including strong advocates of freedom of the press, advise caution in deregulating all forms of broadcast communication.[82]

Comm'n, 497 U.S. 547, 566–67 (upholding FCC minority preference order), *reh'g denied,* 497 U.S. 1050 (1990).

[79]The enigmatic footnote 28 at the end of *Red Lion* noted but found it unnecessary to reach the argument that economic scarcity in the broadcast market was a sufficient justification for access regulation, even if technological scarcity no longer existed. 395 U.S. at 401 n.28; *see supra* note 29. To the extent that the realities of modern society and economics have concentrated power in the broadcast industry in the hands of a few individuals, some have argued that regulation is necessary to guarantee true freedom of expression. Emerson, *Toward a General Theory of the First Amendment,* 72 YALE L.J. 877, 902 (1963); *Leading Cases, supra* note 76, at 214–15 & n.59.

[80]For example, the arguments of the access proponents in *Tornillo* (*see supra* note 65 and accompanying text) focused heavily on economic concentration in the newspaper industry. If the scarcity rationale articulated in *Red Lion* and its progeny is actually based on economic realities, it is difficult to understand why the newspaper industry "does not constitute an equally appropriate occasion for access regulation." Bollinger, *Freedom of the Press and Public Access: Toward a Theory of Partial Regulation of the Mass Media,* 75 MICH. L. REV. 1, 10 (1976). At least one analysis has suggested that the Supreme Court's attempt to cling to the physical scarcity rationale as to broadcast frequencies long after changing conditions have eliminated any basis for such a doctrine is a result of the Court's desire to curb economic regulation in general and a fear of confronting the logical consequences of such an acknowledgment:

> The Court's desire to cabin the growth of the regulatory state may also shed light on its curious refusal to reconsider whether broadcasting outlets remain truly scarce. The Court has clung to the notion that access to broadcasting is chiefly impeded by a physical barrier, the finite spectrum of broadcasting frequencies, and has refrained from acknowledging the fundamental economic barriers to access. Perhaps the Court fears that such an acknowledgment—a recognition that economic concentration in the broadcasting industry, caused by underlying market forces, is what limits many people's opportunities to speak—could constitutionally justify, or even require, extensive governmental regulation of communications media in the interest of revitalizing the marketplace of ideas.

Leading Cases, supra note 76, at 212.

[81]As early as *Red Lion,* the Supreme Court acknowledged the argument of broadcast opponents that the Fairness Doctrine ultimately reduced the coverage of controversial public issues by forcing self-censorship on broadcasters. At that time, however, the Court stated that past experience had not demonstrated any such problem and that, if future experience with the administration of the Fairness Doctrine produced evidence of such effect, there would then be time to reconsider the constitutional implications of fairness regulations. *Red Lion,* 395 U.S. at 392–93; *see supra* note 28 and accompanying text. Various commentators attempted to evaluate the "chilling effect" of such regulation. Lang, *The Role of the Access Doctrine in the Regulation of the Mass Media: A Critical Review and Assessment,* 52 N.C. L. REV. 1, 70–71 (1973); Bollinger, *supra* note 80, at 29. While the *Red Lion* Court rejected such claims in the broadcasting context, the unanimous decision in *Tornillo* explicitly relied on this self-censorship argument in striking down the Florida statute as a violation of the First Amendment. Miami Herald Pub'g Co. v. Tornillo, 418 U.S. 241, 257 (1974). The FCC has now adopted this rationale in abolishing the Fairness Doctrine. *See infra* §13.3(F).

[82]"The greatest virtue of the F.C.C.'s regulation of Broadcast content," wrote Judge Irving R. Kaufman, "has always been the protection of minority views from the suppression or censorship by an entrenched majority." Kaufman, *supra* note 76, §6, at 17. Kaufman wrote that expanding technology, coupled with deregulation, may not be sufficient to produce a truly free marketplace of ideas or to protect the interests of disempowered minorities to express their views. "The sheer number of electronic communications outlets cannot guarantee robust debate if no signals pulsate to a different drum." *Id. See also* Ferris & Ballard, *Independent Political Action Groups: New Life for the Fairness Doctrine,* 36 VAND. L. REV. 929 (1983) (arguing that Fairness Doctrine provides effective check on potential political power of independent political action groups not accountable to political parties).

It has been suggested that the Supreme Court should acknowledge the demise of spectrum scarcity while maintaining two distinct regulatory regimes for the print and broadcast media.[83] This path, it is argued, would eliminate the doctrinal difficulties inherent in the Court's basing its current dichotomy on a false premise of spectrum scarcity while preserving the checks and balances of a mixed regulated/nonregulated system.[84] Whatever the policy advantages of such a proposal, there is certainly a substantial constitutional question as to whether, in the absence of spectrum scarcity, broadcast access regulation is constitutionally permissible.[85]

The proliferation of new communications technologies and regulatory regimes designed to respond to those technologies makes rationalizing the Court's current precedents necessary if the Court is to give any meaningful constitutional guidance to the shaping of the future regulatory milieu. Indeed, the rapid emergence of cable television and the proliferation of federal, state, and local attempts to regulate access to this new medium are already straining current constitutional doctrine in this area.[86]

§13.3 ACCESS REGULATIONS IMPOSED ON THE BROADCAST MEDIA

The FCC regulates access by the public to the broadcast media by means of five main rules: (1) the equal time/opportunities rule, (2) the reasonable access rule, (3) the Fairness Doctrine, (4) the personal attack rule, and (5) the political editorializing rule. This section discusses each of these rules.

§13.3(A) The Equal Time/Opportunities Rule

Broadly stated, the "equal time" or "equal opportunities" rule provides that if a broadcaster furnishes air time to a legally qualified candidate for any public office, it must afford an equal opportunity to obtain air time to all other such candidates.[87] The Supreme Court has said that the basic purpose of the statute is to encourage the "full and unrestricted discussion of political issues

---

[83]Bollinger, *supra* note 80, at 2–3.

[84]Professor Bollinger argues that an analysis of *Red Lion* and *Tornillo* demonstrates the need to maintain a partial regulatory structure for its own sake and that, despite the Court's improper focus on the indefensible notion of spectrum scarcity, differential treatment of the broadcast and print media is constitutionally justified by the advantages of such a system. *Id.* at 36. Access regulation of the broadcast media has both positive and negative impacts, as does laissez-faire operation of the print media. Bollinger suggests that allowing the two different systems to continue to coexist provides a necessary and effective check on the potential negative effects of either system. *Id.* at 32.

[85]"If spectrum scarcity has disappeared, broadcasting is now constitutionally indistinguishable from the more traditional forms of the press." *Leading Cases, supra* note 76, at 214 n.56. If so, then the Court's deference to Congress and the FCC in *League of Women Voters* is inappropriate; the Court is constitutionally required to undertake its own evaluation of the scarcity question. " '[D]eference to a legislative finding cannot limit judicial inquiry when First Amendment rights are at stake . . . . Were it otherwise, the scope of freedom of speech and of the press would be subject to legislative definition and the function of the First Amendment as a check on legislative power would be nullified.' " Federal Communications Comm'n v. League of Women Voters, 468 U.S. 364, 388 n.18 (1984) (quoting Landmark Communications v. Virginia, 435 U.S. 829, 843–44 (1978)).

[86]For a discussion of the courts' application of the *Red Lion* and *Tornillo* rationales to cable, *see infra* §13.6.

[87]This rule is codified at 47 U.S.C. §315(a). It states, in part:
If any licensee shall permit any person who is a legally qualified candidate for any public office to use a broadcasting station, he shall afford equal opportunities to all other such candidates for that office in the use of such broadcasting station: Provided, That such licensee shall have no power of censorship

by legally qualified candidates."[88] The Court also stated that Congress, in enacting the predecessor to the rule in the Radio Act of 1927, recognized broadcasting's potential importance as a medium of communication of political ideas, and "sought to foster its broadest possible utilization by encouraging broadcasting stations to make their facilities available to candidates for office without discrimination."[89]

§13.3(A)(i) What Constitutes a "Use"?

The meaning of "use" in Section 315(a) is central to the interpretation of that statute, because if there is no "use," the statute does not come into play. For 25 years after the Communications Act's inception, the FCC held that the equal time rule did not apply to candidates who appeared on newscasts, reasoning that since the candidate did not institute the coverage, no "use" of the facility had occurred.[90]

In 1959, however, in *Columbia Broadcasting System (Lar Daly)*,[91] the FCC held that the equal time rule applied to an appearance of a candidate on a regularly scheduled newscast.[92] This decision created a national furor, making Congress fear that this interpretation "would tend to dry up meaningful radio and television coverage of political campaigns."[93]

In response to *Lar Daly*, Congress added four exemptions to the equal time rule:

> Appearance by a legally qualified candidate on any:
> (1) bona fide newscast,
> (2) bona fide news interview,
> (3) bona fide news documentary (if the appearance of the candidate is incidental to the presentation of the subject or subjects covered by the news documentary), or
> (4) on-the-spot coverage of bona fide news events (including but not limited to political conventions and activities incidental thereto), shall not be deemed to be use of a broadcasting station within the meaning of this subsection. Nothing in the foregoing sentence shall be construed as relieving broadcasters, in connection with the presentation of newscasts, news interviews, news documentaries, and on-the-spot coverage of news events, from the obligation imposed upon them under this Act to operate in the public interest and to afford reasonable opportunity for the discussion of conflicting views on issues of public importance.[94]

---

over the material broadcast under the provisions of this section. No obligation is imposed under this subsection upon any licensee to allow the use of its station by any such candidate.
See generally The Law of Political Broadcasting and Cablecasting: A Political Primer, 69 F.C.C.2d 2209 (1978); Use of Broadcast and Cablecast Facilities by Candidates for Public Office, 34 F.C.C.2d 510 (1972); Licensee Responsibility as to Political Broadcasts, 15 F.C.C.2d 94 (1968). However, the rule does not create a private right of action for damages or for injunctive or other relief. Lamb v. Griffin Television, 804 F. Supp. 1430, 20 Media L. Rep. 1871 (W.D. Okla. 1992) (citing numerous cases). *See also infra* note 168.
[88]Farmers Educ. & Coop. Union v. WDAY, 360 U.S. 525, 529 (1959).
[89]*Id.*
[90]Allen H. Blondy, 40 F.C.C. 284, 14 Rad. Reg. (P & F) 1199 (1957); Use of Broadcast Facilities by Candidates for Public Office, FCC Public Notice 58-936 (§III-12), 105 CONG. REC. 14,459 (1959).
[91]18 Rad. Reg. (P & F) 238, *reconsideration denied,* 26 F.C.C. 715, 18 Rad. Reg. (P & F) 701 (1959).
[92]18 Rad. Reg. at 238.
[93]Chisholm v. Federal Communications Comm'n, 538 F.2d 349 (D.C. Cir.), *cert. denied,* 429 U.S. 890 (1976) (citing S. REP. No. 562, 86th Cong., 1st Sess. 10 (1959), *reprinted in* 1959 U.S.C.C.A.N. 2564, 2572).
[94]Pub. L. 86-274, §1, 73 Stat. 557, *amending* 47 U.S.C. §315 (1959).

These exemptions were added to further two objectives: (1) the right of the public to be informed through the broadcast of political events, and (2) the discretion of the broadcaster to select which events to broadcast.[95]

In determining whether a particular program falls within one of these exemptions, the FCC said:

> [T]he following considerations, among others, may be pertinent: (1) The format, nature, and content of the programs; (2) whether the format, nature, or content of the program has changed since its inception and, if so, in what respects; (3) who initiates the programs; (4) who produces and controls the program; (5) when the program was initiated; (6) is the program regularly scheduled; and (7) if the program is regularly scheduled, specify the time and day of the week when it is broadcast.[96]

Despite these four exemptions, in 1964 the FCC ruled that press conferences held by presidential candidates were not exempt from the equal time rule.[97] However, in 1976 the FCC determined that it had misinterpreted the legislative history of the 1959 exemptions to the equal time rule and held that presidential press conferences and press conferences of other candidates for political office that are broadcast live and in their entirety are exempt under the "bona fide news event" exemption to Section 315(a).[98] More recently, the FCC unanimously ruled that back-to-back interviews and speeches by major party candidates fit within the "bona fide news event" exception.[99]

The FCC has also ruled that debates between candidates for public office that do not include all candidates for the office are also exempt from Section 315(a) if such debates are arranged by nonbroadcasting organizations and are considered newsworthy by the broadcaster.[100] The Court of Appeals for the District of Columbia Circuit upheld this decision in *Chisholm v. Federal Communications Commission*[101] and has broadened the scope of the exemption for debates in subsequent decisions.[102] Thus, in 1984, that court affirmed an FCC decision that allows broadcasters themselves to conduct political debates without triggering the equal time rule,[103] and in 1987 the same court held that minority party presidential and vice presidential candidates could be excluded from debates without violating Section 315(a).[104]

---

[95]*Hearing on Political Broadcast—Equal Time Before the Subcommittee on Communications and Power of the House Committee on Interstate and Foreign Commerce*, 86th Cong., 1st Sess. 2 (1959).
[96]Public Notice, 24 F.C.C.2d 832, 838 (1970).
[97]CBS, Inc., 40 F.C.C. 395 (1964).
[98]Chisholm v. Federal Communications Comm'n, 538 F.2d 349, 354–55 (D.C. Cir. 1976). Specifically, the FCC found that its previous test, which granted a bona fide news event exemption only in instances where a candidate's appearance was "incidental to" some other newsworthy event, was not supported by the legislative history of the 1959 exemptions because the test had been removed from the legislation prior to its enactment. The proper test for a bona fide news event leaves the initial determination to the good faith judgment of broadcasters. *Id.*
[99]In re King Broadcasting Co., 6 F.C.C.R. 4998, 69 Rad. Reg. 2d (P & F) 1017 (1991). *See also* Harry A. Jessell, *FCC Liberalizes Equal-Time Exemption*, BROADCASTING, Aug. 5, 1991, at 26. The FCC hoped that the change would "foster 'innovative' programs featuring major party candidates by freeing stations from having to provide equal time to minor party candidates, if not major third-party ones." *Id.*
[100]*Chisholm*, 538 F.2d at 354–55.
[101]538 F.2d 349 (D.C. Cir. 1976).
[102]*See* cases cited *infra* notes 103–04.
[103]In re Geller, 95 F.C.C.2d 1236 (1983), *aff'd without opinion sub nom.* League of Women Voters Educ. Fund v. Federal Communications Comm'n, 731 F.2d 995 (D.C. Cir. 1984). The FCC found that third-party sponsorship is not an indispensable condition of impartiality and that a broadcaster-sponsored debate can be a bona fide news event. 95 F.C.C.2d at 1242–46.
[104]Johnson v. Federal Communications Comm'n, 829 F.2d 157 (D.C. Cir. 1987); *see also* DeYoung v. Patten, 898 F.2d 628, 17 Media L. Rep. 1638 (8th Cir. 1990) (holding that candidate for U.S. Senate had

§13.3(A)(ii) Who Is a "Legally Qualified Candidate"?

A "legally qualified candidate" is any person who publicly announces that he or she is a candidate for nomination or election to any local, county, state, or national office; and

> (1) Has qualified for a place on the ballot or
> (2) Is eligible under the applicable law to be voted for by sticker, by writing in his name on the ballot, or any other method, and
> > (i) has been duly nominated by a political party ... or
> > (ii) makes a substantial showing that he is a bona fide candidate ....[105]

Only an appearance by the actual candidate can trigger obligations under Section 315(a); appearances by friends, family, campaign managers, or other supporters do not require the broadcaster to give equal time to other candidates.[106] Political parties also do not have a claim to equal time.[107]

Appearances that do not fall under Section 315(a) may be governed by the Fairness Doctrine, however. In *Nicholas Zapple*,[108] the FCC ruled that noncandidate appearances do require the station to provide an opportunity for appearances by supporters of the other legally qualified candidates, absent unusual circumstances.[109] This rule is known as the Zapple Doctrine.

§13.3(A)(iii) The "No Censorship" Provision

In *Felix v. Westinghouse Radio Stations*,[110] the Third Circuit ruled that the "no censorship" provision of the equal time rule, which prohibits the broadcaster from censoring the candidates' statements, applies only to the candidates themselves and not to their spokespersons.[111] However, the Supreme Court later ruled that, since stations cannot control what the candidates say over the air, the broadcaster cannot be held responsible for their defamatory remarks; the candidate, however, may still be sued.[112]

§13.3(A)(iv) What Constitutes an "Equal Opportunity"?

While there is no obligation on the part of the broadcaster to afford the opposing candidate a broadcast at the exact time of day as the original broadcast, the station must consider the desirability of the time segment allotted as well as its length.[113] Thus, a broadcaster who offers one candidate time during the early morning and at noon while offering the opposing candidate time during early morning, noon, and evening hours has not fulfilled its obligation under the equal time rule.[114]

---

no right to be included in televised debate and that broadcaster would not be subject to requests for equal time).

[105] Public Notice, 24 F.C.C.2d 832, 836 (1970).
[106] CBS v. Federal Communications Comm'n, 454 F.2d 1018 (D.C. Cir. 1971).
[107] Felix v. Westinghouse Radio Stations, 186 F.2d 1 (3d Cir. 1950).
[108] 23 F.C.C.2d 707 (1970).
[109] *Id.* at 708. For a discussion of the Fairness Doctrine's current status, *see infra* §§13.3(C) and (F).
[110] 186 F.2d 1 (3d Cir. 1950).
[111] *Id.* at 3.
[112] Farmers Educ. & Coop. Union v. WDAY, 360 U.S. 525, 535 (1959).
[113] Public Notice, 24 F.C.C.2d 832, 869 (1970).
[114] *Id.*; Letter to D.L. Grace, 40 F.C.C. 297 (1958).

The Supreme Court has held, however, that providing equal time does not mean providing free air time. Broadcasters who provide air time to one candidate are not obligated to honor an opposing candidate's request for air time unless the candidate is willing to pay for the time.[115]

§13.3(B) The Reasonable Access Rule

The equal time rule could have a strangely perverse effect: By refusing all access to political candidates, a broadcaster could avoid any equal time obligations. Thus, the equal time rule could stifle the flow of information to the public rather than enhance it.

In response to concerns that broadcasters were not making enough time available to candidates and that candidates were being charged excessively high rates for the time they were permitted to purchase,[116] Congress enacted the reasonable access rule.[117] The Supreme Court later explained that, in enacting the rule, Congress " 'intended to increase [candidates'] accessibility to the media and to reduce the level of spending for its use.' ... 'so that they may better explain their stand on the issues, and thereby more fully and completely inform the voters.' "[118]

In *CBS v. Federal Communications Commission*,[119] the Supreme Court upheld the Carter-Mondale Presidential Committee's request for access to television air time pursuant to Section 312(a)(7), rejecting a claim that Section 312(a)(7) was unconstitutional.[120] The Court further held that it is within the FCC's power to determine when a campaign has begun and whether the obligations of Section 312(a)(7) have attached to a broadcaster.[121] Thus, access cannot be denied on the ground that broadcasters have not begun to sell air time for a campaign or because they believe it is too soon to recognize the existence of an election campaign.

---

[115]CBS v. Federal Communications Comm'n, 453 U.S. 367, 382 n.8 (1981); *see also* Paulsen v. Federal Communications Comm'n, 491 F.2d 887, 889 (9th Cir. 1974) (FCC does not require stations to donate time to candidates who cannot afford to buy time).

[116]Congress also addressed concerns about high rates and about the increasing cost of election campaigns generally by enacting 47 U.S.C. §315(b) (1972), which provides that the rates that broadcasters charge legally qualified candidates for 45 days before a primary or runoff election or for 60 days before a general or special election may not exceed the station's lowest unit charge for the same class and amount of time for the same period. At other times, the charge may not exceed that made for comparable use of the station by other users. Unlike the reasonable access rule, Section 315(b) provides no guarantee of access to broadcast time; it only entitles a candidate to certain rates once time is offered. Hernstadt v. Federal Communications Comm'n, 677 F.2d 893, 905 (D.C. Cir. 1980).

[117]Federal Campaign Election Act of 1971, 47 U.S.C. §312(a)(7) (1971). The rule provides that

[t]he Commission may revoke any station license or construction permit— ... (7) for willful or repeated failure to allow reasonable access to or to permit purchase of reasonable amounts of time for the use of a broadcasting station by a legally qualified candidate for Federal elective office on behalf of his candidacy.

See generally Commission Policy in Enforcing Section 312(a)(7) of the Communications Act of 1934, 68 F.C.C.2d 1079 (1983). *See also* Telecommunications Research & Action Ctr. v. Federal Communications Comm'n, 801 F.2d 501, 513, 13 Media L. Rep. 1881, 1890 (D.C. Cir. 1986), *cert. denied*, 482 U.S. 919 (1987) (reasonable access rule does not apply to teletext).

[118]CBS v. Federal Communications Comm'n, 453 U.S. 367, 379–80 (1981) (quoting *Federal Election Campaign Act of 1971: Hearings on S. 1., S. 382, and S. 956 before the Subcomm. on Communications of the Senate Comm. on Commerce*, 92d Cong., 1st Sess. 2 (1971) (remarks of Sen. Pastore) and S. REP. NO. 96, 92nd Cong., 1st Sess. 20 (1971)). For a more detailed discussion of this case, *see supra* §13.2(A).

[119]453 U.S. 367 (1981).

[120]*Id.* at 397. On the constitutionality of such rules, *see supra* §13.2(A).

[121]453 U.S. at 388.

In *Kennedy for President Committee v. Federal Communications Commission*,[122] the District of Columbia Circuit addressed the interplay between the equal time and reasonable access rules. The plaintiff argued that Senator Kennedy, as a candidate for president, should be given free air time to respond to a press conference given by President Carter.[123] Acknowledging that the equal time rule could not apply because the press conference was exempt from that rule, the plaintiff argued that Section 312(a)(7) bestowed a contingent right of access to free air time for federal political candidates.[124] The Court of Appeals rejected this argument, holding that Section 312(a)(7) cannot be used as a way to circumvent the exemptions in the equal time rule.[125] The Supreme Court has agreed, holding that the reasonable access rule only requires that candidates for federal office be given a reasonable opportunity to *pay* for air time and that broadcasters are under no obligation to donate time to a candidate.[126]

As explained by the *Kennedy* court, the difference between the equal time and reasonable access rules is quite simple. The equal time rule provides that whenever a broadcaster permits any candidate for any public office to "use" broadcast facilities, the broadcaster must afford an equal opportunity to any legally qualified rival of that candidate who seeks it: "[T]his right is contingent in nature; it does not come into fruition unless and until an opponent makes some 'use' of station facilities, but once that occurs it ripens, and the candidate becomes unconditionally entitled to equal opportunities, though to no more."[127]

By contrast, the reasonable access rule

> supplies a right of access by requiring broadcasters, on pain of license revocation, to make reasonable amounts of time available for use by legally qualified persons seeking federal elective office. This right is unconditional in the sense that no prior use by any opponent of that candidate is necessary. Irrefutably, reasonable access is for the asking if the candidate is willing to pay, and the amount he can be charged is carefully limited by law. The measure of the right remains constant, however, at "reasonable access."[128]

Thus, the right under the equal time rule is contingent on whether an opposing candidate has been given air time, whereas the reasonable access requirement confers an unconditional right to reasonable access. Under the equal time rule, the amount of access to which a candidate is entitled is measured by the amount of time given to the opposing candidate, while the time limitation under the access requirement is measured by what is "reasonable."[129] Finally, the equal time rule applies to any candidate for a public office, while the reasonable access requirement applies only to candidates for federal office.[130]

---

[122] 636 F.2d 432 (D.C. Cir. 1980).
[123] *Id.* at 435.
[124] *Id.* at 436–37.
[125] *Id.* at 449.
[126] *CBS*, 453 U.S. at 382 n.8 (citing Kennedy for President Comm. v. Federal Communications Comm'n, 636 F.2d 432, 446–50 (D.C. Cir. 1980) ("Section [312(a)(7)] entitled a candidate to free time only if and when a broadcaster refuses to sell a reasonable quantity of time.")).
[127] 636 F.2d at 448 (footnotes omitted).
[128] *Id.* (footnotes omitted).
[129] *Id.*
[130] *Id.*

§13.3(C) The Fairness Doctrine

The Fairness Doctrine imposes two duties on broadcasters: (1) the broadcaster must devote an adequate amount of time to controversial issues of public importance, and (2) the coverage must be fair in the sense that it accurately reflects opposing views.[131]

§13.3(C)(i) Development and Scope of the Doctrine

The Fairness Doctrine has evolved through policy statements and decisions of the FCC and its predecessor, the FRC, with help from the courts. The original statement of the Fairness Doctrine is usually attributed to a 1929 FRC case in which the Commission stated:

> [I]nsofar as a program consists of discussion of public questions, public interest requires ample play for the free and fair competition of opposing views and the Commission believes that the principle applies not only to addresses by political candidates but to all discussion of issues of importance to the public.[132]

The first "official" announcement of the Fairness Doctrine was made by the FCC in a 1949 report that stated:

> Broadcast licensees have an affirmative duty generally to encourage and implement the broadcast of all sides of controversial public issues over their facilities, over and beyond their obligation to make available on demand opportunities for the expression of opposing views. It is clear that any approximation of fairness in the presentation of any controversy will be difficult if not impossible of achievement unless the licensee plays a conscious and positive role in bringing about balanced presentation of the opposing viewpoints.[133]

The doctrine is described in 47 C.F.R. Section 73.1910: "The Fairness Doctrine is contained in Section 315(a) of the Communications Act of 1934, as amended, which provides that broadcasters have certain obligations to afford reasonable opportunity for the discussion of conflicting views on issues of public importance."[134]

This reference is misleading, however, because Congress has not passed a Fairness Doctrine law. Instead, as part of the 1959 amendments to Section 315(a), which created certain exemptions under the equal time rule,[135] Congress added the following language:

> Nothing in the foregoing sentence shall be construed as relieving broadcasters, in connection with the presentation of newscasts, news interviews, news documentaries, and on-the-spot coverage of news events, from the obligation imposed upon them under this Act to operate in the public interest and to afford reasonable opportunity for the discussion of conflicting views on issues of public importance.[136]

---

[131] Red Lion Broadcasting Co. v. Federal Communications Comm'n, 395 U.S. 367, 377 (1969).
[132] Great Lakes Broadcasting Co., 3 F.R.C. Ann. Rep. 32, 33 (1929), *rev'd on other grounds,* 37 F.2d 993 (D.C. Cir.), *cert. denied,* 281 U.S. 706 (1930).
[133] Editorializing by Broadcast Licensees, 13 F.C.C. 1246, 1251 (1949).
[134] 47 C.F.R. §73.1910 (1990).
[135] *See supra* text accompanying notes 91–95.
[136] 47 U.S.C. §315(a) (1981).

This amendment has subsequently been interpreted as congressional "recognition" of the doctrine.[137]

The next major event in the evolution of the doctrine, after the 1959 amendments, was the landmark decision of the U.S. Supreme Court in *Red Lion Broadcasting Co. v. Federal Communications Commission.*[138] The Court in *Red Lion* upheld the constitutionality of the Fairness Doctrine and its corollaries: the personal attack rule and the political editorializing rule.[139]

The Court recognized that the primary concern of Fairness Doctrine opponents was that the doctrine would have a "chilling effect" on speech, because broadcasters would stay away from controversial subjects to escape having to air opposing viewpoints.[140] The Court stated that this concern was speculative, that in the past the Fairness Doctrine had not had such an effect, and that "if experience with the administration of these doctrines indicates that they have the net effect of reducing rather than enhancing the volume and quality of coverage, there will be time enough to reconsider the constitutional implications."[141]

In 1974, the FCC published a report that discussed the efficacy of the Fairness Doctrine and gave guidelines for its application.[142] In answering the question of whether the Fairness Doctrine inhibited broadcast journalism, the FCC concluded in the Fairness Report that "[f]ar from inhibiting debate ... we believe that the doctrine has done much to expand and enrich it."[143]

In discussing a broadcaster's obligations under the doctrine, the FCC stated that it is up to the individual licensee to determine what constitutes "a reasonable amount of time" to be devoted to the discussion and consideration of public issues.[144] This great degree of discretion given to the broadcaster is an important aspect of the Fairness Doctrine, because it balances the right of the public to be informed against the general dislike of governmental regulation of the media. Thus, in *CBS v. Federal Communications Commission,*[145] the District of Columbia Circuit stated:

> The licensee may exercise wide latitude "in determining what subjects should be considered, the particular format of the programs devoted to each subject, the different shades of opinion to be presented, and the spokesmen for each point of view." The Commission's role in this area "is not to substitute its judgment for that of the licensee * * * but rather to determine whether the licensee can be said to have acted reasonably and in good faith."[146]

---

[137]Red Lion Broadcasting Co. v. Federal Communications Comm'n, 395 U.S. 367, 377 (1969); Telecommunications Research & Action Ctr. v. Federal Communications Comm'n, 801 F.2d 501, 517–18 (D.C. Cir. 1986). *See* text accompanying *infra* notes 180–92.

[138]395 U.S. 367 (1969). For a discussion of this case and its constitutional aspects, *see supra* §13.2(A).

[139]395 U.S. at 401. The Fairness Doctrine is applicable to political broadcasts, including campaign coverage, as long as the political broadcast is about a controversial issue of public importance. *See* Kennedy for President Comm. v. Federal Communications Comm'n, 636 F.2d 432 (D.C. Cir. 1980). The personal attack rule is discussed *infra* §13.3(D); the political editorializing rule is discussed *infra* §13.3(E).

[140]395 U.S. at 392–93.

[141]*Id.* at 393. For a discussion of the current status of the Fairness Doctrine, *see infra* §13.3(F).

[142]FEDERAL COMMUNICATIONS COMM'N, FAIRNESS DOCTRINE & PUBLIC INTEREST STANDARDS: FAIRNESS REPORT REGARDING HANDLING OF PUBLIC ISSUES, 39 Fed. Reg. 26,372 (1974) [hereinafter *Fairness Report*].

[143]*Id.* at 26,374.

[144]*Id.* at 26,375.

[145]454 F.2d 1018 (D.C. Cir. 1971).

[146]*Id.* at 1028–29 (citations omitted) (quoting Editorializing by Broadcast Licensees, 13 F.C.C. 1246 (1949) and APPLICABILITY OF THE FAIRNESS DOCTRINE IN THE HANDLING OF CONTROVERSIAL ISSUES OF PUBLIC IMPORTANCE, 29 Fed. Reg. 10,415 (1964)).

Furthermore, the FCC believes "that the public is best served by a system which allows individual broadcasters considerable discretion in selecting the manner of coverage, the appropriate spokesmen, and the techniques of production and presentation."[147]

Similarly, in determining what constitutes a "controversial issue of public importance," the FCC has left it up to the reasonable, good faith judgments of the broadcasters.[148] The FCC, however, has noted a number of considerations that should govern the broadcaster's decision, such as (1) the degree of media coverage, (2) the degree of attention the issue has received from government officials and other community leaders, and (3) the impact that the issue is likely to have on the community at large.[149] These judgments, according to the FCC, can be made only on a case-by-case basis.[150] Of course, it is not always easy to ascertain what issue is raised by a broadcast and whether it is a controversial issue of public importance.[151]

The FCC has also made it clear that broadcasters are not required to provide an "equal" opportunity for opposing views, recognizing that a perfect balance is unobtainable. Instead, the Fairness Doctrine requires "a balance in overall programming, in which the broadcasters must make an effort to round out their coverage with contrasting viewpoints."[152] Accordingly, the FCC and the courts have declined to establish mathematical ratios as guidelines for determining what constitutes a fair opportunity for opposing viewpoints.[153]

In addition, the FCC has stated that the licensee has wide discretion in choosing an appropriate spokesperson to present the contrasting viewpoint. It has warned, however, that

> [i]n providing for the coverage of opposing points of view, we believe that the licensee must make a reasonable allowance for presentations by genuine partisans who actually believe in what they are saying. The Fairness Doctrine does not permit the broadcaster "to preside over a 'paternalistic' regime," and it would clearly not be acceptable for the licensee to adopt a "policy of excluding partisan voices and always itself presenting views in a bland, inoffensive manner * * *."[154]

Until 1967, the Fairness Doctrine had been applied only to the airing of major social and political issues. Then, in *WCBS TV*,[155] the Fairness Doctrine was extended to commercials devoted in an obvious and meaningful way to the discussion of public issues. In that case, the FCC ruled that the Fairness Doctrine was applicable to the broadcast of cigarette commercials and that licensees who broadcast such commercials must make free time available for messages warning of the dangers of smoking.[156]

---

[147]*Fairness Report, supra* note 142, at 26,378.
[148]*Id.* at 26,376.
[149]*Id.*
[150]*Id.*
[151]*See, e.g.,* Green v. Federal Communications Comm'n, 447 F.2d 323 (D.C. Cir. 1971); National Broadcasting Co. v. Federal Communications Comm'n, 516 F.2d 1101 (D.C. Cir.), *cert. denied,* 424 U.S. 910 (1973).
[152]*Fairness Report, supra* note 142, at 26,376.
[153]*Id.* at 26,378; Democratic Nat'l Comm. v. Federal Communications Comm'n, 717 F.2d 1471 (D.C. Cir. 1983).
[154]*Fairness Report, supra* note 142, at 26,377–78 (quoting CBS, Inc., v. Democratic Nat'l Comm., 412 U.S. 94, 130 (1973) and Democratic Nat'l Comm., 25 F.C.C.2d 216, 222 (1970), respectively).
[155]8 F.C.C.2d 381 (1967), *aff'd sub nom.* Banzhaf v. Federal Communications Comm'n, 405 F.2d 1082 (D.C. Cir. 1968), *cert. denied,* 396 U.S. 842 (1969).
[156]405 F.2d at 1086–87.

In its Fairness Report, the FCC officially stated that "commercials" that consist of direct and substantial commentary on important public issues should be subject to the Fairness Doctrine requirements;[157] it declined, however to extend the doctrine to product advertising. In *Friends of the Earth v. Federal Communications Commission*,[158] the District of Columbia Circuit disagreed, holding that the Fairness Doctrine should apply to the advertising of large automobiles and that environmentalists should be entitled to present their opposing views, given the air pollution problems caused by those products.[159] This caused the FCC to shy away from its original ruling in *WCBS TV* and to divide commercials into different categories. Accordingly, the FCC asserted that the Fairness Doctrine would not apply to *commercial* advertising, i.e., the selling of products or services.[160]

§13.3(C)(ii) The Fairness Doctrine Compared With Other Broadcast Access Regulations

The Fairness Doctrine differs from the other rules discussed in this section in a number of ways. There are several important differences between the Fairness Doctrine and the equal time rule, perhaps the most important being that the equal time rule is limited to providing access for legally qualified candidates for public office, while the Fairness Doctrine applies to controversial *issues* of public importance. Furthermore, the Fairness Doctrine places an *affirmative duty* on the broadcaster to see that opposing views are presented. The equal time rule is not triggered unless a candidate seeks air time.

In addition, under the equal time rule, the licensee is under an obligation to provide the opposing candidate a specific amount of time equal to that provided to the original candidate. Under the Fairness Doctrine, however, the licensee is only required to use its reasonable good faith judgment as to what constitutes an overall balanced presentation of the controversial issue— equality is not required.[161]

Furthermore, the Fairness Doctrine, unlike the equal time rule, gives the broadcaster discretion in choosing the spokesperson to represent the contrasting views and in designing the formats of the program. Also, under the equal time rule, the broadcaster who has charged the first candidate for air time does not have to grant equal time to an opponent who is not willing or able to pay. By contrast, under the Fairness Doctrine, the broadcaster who has aired one view on a controversial issue supported by a sponsor ordinarily may not refuse to air the contrasting view on grounds that a paying sponsor for the second view cannot be found.[162]

Finally, the Fairness Doctrine imposes on the broadcaster a duty to "seek out" and broadcast information on controversial issues, while any obligation under the equal time rule arises only after time has been allotted to a political candidate.

---

[157]*Fairness Report, supra* note 142, at 26,380.
[158]449 F.2d 1164 (D.C. Cir. 1971).
[159]*Id.* at 1169.
[160]*Fairness Report, supra* note 142, at 26,381.
[161]Democratic Nat'l Comm. v. Federal Communications Comm'n, 717 F.2d 1471, 1478 (D.C. Cir. 1983).
[162]Cullman Broadcasting Co., 25 Rad. Reg. (P & F) 895, 897 (1963).

The major difference between the Fairness Doctrine and the reasonable access rule is that the Fairness Doctrine applies to issues, while the reasonable access rule applies to candidates for federal office. Moreover, the Fairness Doctrine places a burden on the broadcaster to allot time for the discussion of controversial issues, while the reasonable access rule only obligates the broadcaster to make time available for candidates who request access.

§13.3(D) The Personal Attack Rule

The personal attack rule is a corollary of the Fairness Doctrine and requires licensees to provide notice and an opportunity to reply whenever an attack is made upon the honesty, character, or integrity of an identified person or group during presentation of views on a controversial issue of public importance.[163]

The rule provides a list of exemptions to which the personal attack rule does not apply: (1) attacks on foreign groups or foreign public figures; (2) attacks made during uses by legally qualified candidates; (3) attacks made during broadcasts by legally qualified candidates, their spokespersons, or others associated with their campaign that are made on other candidates, their authorized spokespersons, or others associated with their campaigns; and (4) attacks made during bona fide newscasts, news interviews, and on-the-spot coverage of bona fide news events, including commentary and analysis on these programs.[164] The constitutionality of the personal attack rule was upheld in *Red Lion*.[165]

In contrast to the Fairness Doctrine's general requirements that licensees provide adequate coverage of issues of public importance and that the coverage fairly reflects differing viewpoints, the personal attack rule imposes more specific duties: The licensee must notify the person attacked within seven days, must provide a script or tape of the attack, and must take the initiative to offer a reasonable opportunity to reply over the licensee's facilities; furthermore, this offer must be extended directly to the person or group attacked.[166] Thus, the licensee lacks the control over spokesperson and format of the reply that it maintains under the Fairness Doctrine.

Another major aspect of the personal attack rule that distinguishes it from other rules discussed in this section is that there must be an attack upon the honesty, character, or integrity of a person. Because the personal attack rule was enacted to advance public debate of public issues and not to provide an avenue to vindicate private reputations, the rule applies only when the attack

---

[163] The rule provides in part:
(a) When, during the presentation of views on a controversial issue of public importance, an attack is made upon the honesty, character, integrity or like personal qualities of an identified person or group, the licensee shall, within a reasonable time and in no event later than one week after the attack, transmit to the persons or group attacked:
    (1) Notification of the date, time, and identification of the broadcast;
    (2) A script or tape (or an accurate summary if a script or tape is not available) of the attack; and
    (3) An offer of a reasonable opportunity to respond over the licensee's facilities.
47 C.F.R. §73.1920 (1990).
[164] *Id.*
[165] *See* discussion at text accompanying *supra* notes 138–41. On the constitutional questions, *see supra* §13.2.
[166] 47 C.F.R. §73.1920 (1990).

occurs "during the presentation of views on a controversial issue of public importance."[167] Moreover, there is no private right of action under the rule.[168]

As a corollary to the Fairness Doctrine, the licensee is given discretion in determining whether a violation of the personal attack rule has occurred: "The [FCC] will find a violation only where it determines that the licensee's actions and decisions have been unreasonable or in bad faith."[169]

§13.3(E) The Political Editorializing Rule

Another corollary to the Fairness Doctrine is the political editorializing rule, which is similar to the personal attack rule except that it applies only when the licensee itself endorses or opposes a legally qualified candidate for a public office. The rule provides:

> (a) Where a licensee, in an editorial, (1) Endorses or, (2) Opposes a legally qualified candidate or candidates, the licensee shall, within 24 hours after the editorial, transmit to, respectively, (i) The other qualified candidate or candidates for the same office or, (ii) The candidate opposed in the editorial, (A) Notification of the date and time of the editorial, (B) A script or tape of the editorial and (C) An offer of reasonable opportunity for the candidate or a spokesman of the candidate to respond over the licensee's facilities.[170]

§13.3(F) The Decline of Government-Mandated Access to the Broadcast Media: Demise of the Fairness Doctrine

The first step toward abandoning government-mandated access to the broadcast media occurred in 1981 when FCC Chairman Mark Fowler, as part of an aggressive deregulation program, recommended that the equal time rule, the reasonable access rule, and the Fairness Doctrine be abolished by Congress.[171] On June 14, 1981, the FCC voted 6-1 in favor of deregulating radio broadcasts and abandoned guidelines that had limited advertising to 18 minutes per hour and had reserved a minimum portion of air time for news and public affairs.[172] In June 1984, the FCC deregulated television in a similar fashion.[173]

The FCC's focus then shifted to the Fairness Doctrine. In 1984, the Supreme Court hinted that it was willing to reconsider the basis for its decision in *Red Lion*, stating that if the net effect of the Fairness Doctrine reduced rather than enhanced speech, it would reconsider the constitutional basis of its decision.[174]

The next year, the FCC released a report that outlined its comprehensive reexamination of the Fairness Doctrine.[175] The FCC concluded that the Fairness Doctrine lessens the amount of diverse views available to the public; inhibits

---

[167]*Id.*; Galloway v. Federal Communications Comm'n, 778 F.2d 16, 18 (D.C. Cir. 1985).
[168]Lechtner v. Brownyard, 679 F.2d 322 (3d Cir. 1982); Burt v. CBS, Inc., 769 F. Supp. 1012, 18 Media L. Rep. 2231 (S.D. Ohio 1991). *See also supra* note 87.
[169]Straus Communications v. Federal Communications Comm'n, 530 F.2d 1001, 1008 (D.C. Cir. 1976).
[170]47 C.F.R. §73.1930 (1990).
[171]*See, e.g., FCC Asks End of Fairness Doctrine*, N.Y. TIMES, Sept. 18, 1981, at C36, col. 1.
[172]46 Fed. Reg. 13,888 (1981).
[173]*See Report and Order, in* MM Docket No. 83-670, 98 F.C.C.2d 1076 (1984).
[174]Federal Communications Comm'n v. League of Women Voters, 468 U.S. 364, 378–79 n.12 (1984).
[175]FEDERAL COMMUNICATIONS COMM'N, GENERAL FAIRNESS DOCTRINE OBLIGATIONS OF BROADCAST LICENSEES, 50 Fed. Reg. 35,418 (1985).

the expression of unorthodox speech; places government in the intrusive and constitutionally disfavored role of scrutinizing program content; creates an opportunity for intimidation of the broadcasters by government officials; imposes unnecessary economic costs on broadcasters and the FCC; is not needed in light of the increase in the amount and type of information sources in the marketplace; and cannot be justified on the basis that it protects either broadcasters or the public from undue influence.[176]

The FCC concluded its report by stating that "far from serving its intended purpose, the doctrine has a chilling effect on broadcaster's speech."[177] Accordingly, the FCC "questioned the permissibility of the doctrine as a matter of both policy and constitutional law."[178] The FCC decided not to eliminate the Fairness Doctrine at that time, preferring instead to defer to Congress.[179]

One major reason that the FCC did not abolish the Fairness Doctrine then was that it was not convinced it had authority to do so. The FCC was uncertain whether the 1959 amendment to Section 315(a) of the Federal Communications Act, which recognized the Fairness Doctrine, was a codification of that doctrine by Congress.[180] If it was, then it would be outside the FCC's power to abolish the doctrine.

This question was answered by the District of Columbia Circuit in *Telecommunications Research & Action Center v. Federal Communications Commission*,[181] which held that the 1959 amendment was not a congressional codification of the Fairness Doctrine and thus was not a binding statutory obligation.[182] In so holding, the court gave the FCC power to abolish the Fairness Doctrine.

The court in *Meredith Corp. v. Federal Communications Commission*[183] then forced the FCC into action. In *Meredith,* the FCC held that a television station owned by the Meredith Corporation had violated the Fairness Doctrine by broadcasting advertisements that promoted a nuclear power plant without presenting opposing viewpoints.[184] In its ruling, the FCC refused to consider Meredith's constitutional challenge to the Fairness Doctrine, but on appeal, the D.C. Circuit held that the FCC was required to rule on Meredith's constitutional challenge, thereby guarding against premature or unnecessary constitutional adjudication by the courts.[185] This was true even though the "Commission's 1985 Fairness Report would appear to foreshadow its conclusion as to the constitutionality of this enforcement proceeding against Meredith."[186] The court also stated in a footnote that the FCC could determine "that the doctrine cannot be enforced because it is contrary to the public interest and thereby avoid the constitutional issue."[187] The court then reminded the FCC that it

---

[176]*Id.* at 35,418–53.
[177]*Id.* at 35,453.
[178]*Id.*
[179]*Id.*
[180]*Id.* at 35,451–52.
[181]801 F.2d 501, 13 Media L. Rep. 1881 (D.C. Cir. 1986), *cert. denied,* 482 U.S. 919 (1987).
[182]*Id.* at 517.
[183]809 F.2d 863 (D.C. Cir. 1987).
[184]*Id.* at 865–66.
[185]*Id.* at 872.
[186]*Id.*
[187]*Id.* at 872 n.10.

must make the decision and that a deferral to Congress was not an available option.[188]

On August 4, 1987, the FCC unanimously adopted a memorandum opinion and order that repealed the Fairness Doctrine.[189] In explaining the basis for the repeal, the FCC reiterated the findings set forth in its 1985 report:[190] the Fairness Doctrine inhibits free speech by discouraging broadcasters from making certain documentaries or taking controversial editorial stands.[191] This decision was subsequently upheld by the District of Columbia Circuit in *Syracuse Peace Council v. Federal Communications Commission.*[192] In abandoning the Fairness Doctrine, neither the FCC nor the circuit court made mention of the fate of the doctrine's corollaries: the personal attack rule and the political editorializing rule. In a September 1987 letter to the chairman of the House Commerce Committee, however, FCC Chairman Dennis Patrick made it clear that the FCC had not eliminated the personal attack or political editorializing rules, the Zapple Doctrine, or the application of the Fairness Doctrine to ballot issues or political campaigns.[193]

Despite the fact that the Fairness Doctrine appears to be dead, there have been aggressive campaigns by certain members of Congress to pass a Fairness Doctrine statute. One such bill, S. 742,[194] authored by Senator Ernest F. Hollings of South Carolina, was vetoed by President Reagan in June 1987 after being passed in a 59-31 vote by the Senate and in a 302-102 vote by the House of Representatives.[195] Hollings introduced another such bill, the Fairness in Broadcasting Act of 1991,[196] on January 15, 1991, and a companion bill was introduced in the House of Representatives on the same day.[197] No Fairness Doctrine law has been enacted, so its ultimate fate remains uncertain.

§13.4 Access to the Print Media

The print media have a broad right to decide what they will or will not publish,[198] but in some circumstances this right may be limited. In particular,

---

[188]809 F.2d at 873 n.11.
[189]In re Syracuse Peace Council, 2 F.C.C.R. 5043 (1987), *reconsideration denied,* 3 F.C.C.2d 2035 (1988).
[190]*See supra* note 175.
[191]*Id.* at 35,433.
[192]867 F.2d 654, 16 Media L. Rep. 1225 (D.C. Cir. 1989), *cert. denied,* 493 U.S. 1019 (1990). The court held that "the FCC's decision that the fairness doctrine no longer served the public interest was neither arbitrary, capricious, nor an abuse of discretion" and the commission would have terminated the doctrine based on public policy even if it had not believed the doctrine was unconstitutional. *Id.* at 669. *Accord* Arkansas AFL-CIO v. Federal Communications Comm'n, 11 F.3d 1430, 22 Media L. Rep. 1001 (8th Cir. 1993) (en banc) (following *Syracuse Peace Council*).
[193]D.M. GILLMOR ET AL., MASS COMMUNICATION LAW 817 (5th ed. 1990). Patrick noted that anyone wishing to challenge FCC policy in those areas could cite *Syracuse Peace Council* in support of their positions. Although it did not abandon the personal attack rule, in a report adopted the same day as its *Syracuse Peace Council* opinion the FCC stated its belief that the personal attack rule no longer serves the public interest. Inquiry into Section 73.1910 of the Commission's Rules and Regulations Concerning Alternatives to the General Fairness Doctrine Obligations of Broadcast Licensees, 2 F.C.C.R. 5272, ¶100 (1987).
[194]S. 742, 100th Cong., 1st Sess. (1987).
[195]133 CONG. REC. S3108 (daily ed. March 12, 1987) (introduced in Senate); 133 CONG. REC. S5232 (daily ed. April 21, 1987) (passed in Senate); 133 CONG. REC. H4160 (daily ed. June 3, 1987) (passed in House); 133 CONG. REC. S8438 (daily ed. June 23, 1987) (presidential veto).
[196]S. 217, 102d Cong., 1st Sess. (1991).
[197]H.R. 530, 102d Cong., 1st Sess. (1991).
[198]*See infra* §13.4(A).

courts have held that the print media may be required to accept a particular type of advertising because of the existence of a valid advertising contract.[199] Publication of advertisements has been compelled under the antitrust laws[200] when a newspaper's refusal to accept advertising constitutes a concerted action in restraint of trade or an attempt to maintain a monopoly. Newspapers may also be compelled to accept advertising under antidiscrimination laws, such as California's Unruh Civil Rights Act or the federal Ku Klux Klan Act of 1871.[201]

§13.4(A) The Publisher's General Right to Refuse Advertisements

Under *Miami Herald Publishing Co. v. Tornillo*,[202] publishers have a broad constitutional right to decide what they will or will not print.[203] This right stems from a concern that government-enforced access to the print media will chill public debate and intrude into the function of editors.[204] This broad right of editorial discretion extends to all contents of the print media, including advertising.[205]

Even before the Supreme Court's decision in *Tornillo*, numerous courts had ruled that a publication is not obligated by the First Amendment to carry advertising or other material that it does not wish to publish.[206] Similarly, decisions after *Tornillo* have adhered closely to its teachings.[207] In the case of

---

[199]*See id.* at (C).
[200]*See id.* at (B).
[201]*See id.* at (D).
[202]418 U.S. 241, 256–58, 1 Media L. Rep. 1898 (1974). This case is discussed in detail *infra* §13.3(B).
[203]*See also* Wooley v. Maynard, 430 U.S. 705 (1977) (invalidating New Hampshire law that required vehicle license plates to display ideological motto, noting that First Amendment absolutely prohibits government from compelling speech by unwilling person); Pacific Gas & Elec. v. Public Utils. Comm'n of Cal., 475 U.S. 1 (1986) (utility commission's order compelling utility to allow consumer group to place political material in billing envelopes impermissibly burdened utility's First Amendment rights); for a detailed discussion of this case, *see infra* §13.5(D).
[204]*Tornillo*, 418 U.S. at 257–58.
[205]"A newspaper is more than a passive receptable or conduit for news, comment and advertising." *Tornillo*, 418 U.S. at 258. "[A]ny such compulsion to publish that which " 'reason" tells [a newspaper] should not be published' is unconstitutional." *Id.* at 256.
[206]Associates & Aldrich Co. v. Times Mirror Co., 440 F.2d 133, 136 (9th Cir. 1971) (newspaper could not be forced to publish advertisement for X-rated movie exactly as submitted; "[W]e can find nothing . . . that allows us to compel a private newspaper to publish advertisements without editorial control of their content"); Chicago Joint Bd., Clothing & Textile Workers v. Chicago Tribune Co., 435 F.2d 470, 478 (7th Cir. 1970) (First Amendment does not require newspaper publisher to print striking union's editorial advertisement: "The [plaintiff's] right to free speech does not give it the right to make use of the defendants' printing presses and distribution systems without defendants' consent."), *cert. denied,* 402 U.S. 973 (1971). The only case to recognize a general duty on the part of a newspaper publisher to accept and publish advertisements is the obscure decision of Uhlman v. Sherman, 22 Ohio N.P. (n.s.) 225, 31 Ohio Dec. 54 (1919). The *Uhlman* court ruled that the publication of a newspaper was a business clothed with the public interest and that a publisher could be required to accept advertisements. Although *Uhlman* has not been expressly overruled, numerous courts consider it wrongly decided and have refused to follow it. Bloss v. Federated Pubns., 145 N.W.2d 800, 803 (Mich. Ct. App. 1966) (discussing other cases that have declined to follow *Uhlman*).
[207]Mississippi Gay Alliance v. Goudelock, 536 F.2d 1073 (5th Cir. 1976) (court upheld student newspaper's rejection of advertisement submitted by off-campus homosexual group); News & Sun-Sentinel Co. v. Board of County Comm'rs, 693 F. Supp. 1066, 1073, 14 Media L. Rep. 1477 (S.D. Fla. 1987) (court held unconstitutional county ordinance that required publishers of ads for regulated contracting services to include contractor's certificate of competency number because "cumulative burden which might be placed on publications by such legislation" pose unacceptable threat to free press); Person v. New York Post Corp., 427 F. Supp. 1297, 1301, 2 Media L. Rep. 1666 (E.D.N.Y.) (court denied injunction seeking to require newspaper to publish securities "tombstone advertisement" or to refrain from publishing similar ads, finding that injunction "ran squarely against the wall of freedom of the press"), *aff'd without opinion,* 573 F.2d 1294, 3 Media L. Rep. 1784 (2d Cir. 1977); Newspaper Printing v. Galbreath, 580 S.W.2d 777, 780, 5 Media L. Rep. 1065 (Tenn.) (court denied injunctive relief to plaintiff whose ad was rejected because it did

state-owned or sponsored print media, however, editors' First Amendment right to refuse advertisements may be more limited.[208]

§13.4(B) Antitrust Laws and the Publisher's Right to Refuse Advertisements

The First Amendment does not shield newspapers from the operation of generally applicable laws, including the antitrust laws.[209] A newspaper that violates antitrust laws in refusing to publish advertisements therefore risks being ordered to publish the advertisements.[210] More often than not, however, courts find that no antitrust violation has occurred.

Most cases concerning alleged antitrust violations by newspapers that refuse to accept advertisements involve the federal Sherman Act[211] or parallel state laws.[212]

§13.4(B)(i) Section 1 Violations

Under Section 1 of the Sherman Act, the court must make two principal findings in order to find a violation: (1) a combination, i.e., concerted action by two or more legal persons; and (2) an unreasonable restraint of trade.[213] The most difficult element to prove in a Section 1 action involving refusal to accept advertising is "concerted action."[214]

Section 1 violations have been found where a group of newspapers entered into an agreement to exclude from membership in the group and prohibit sale of news to newspapers in competition with group members,[215] where a

---

not conform to publisher's technical requirements, reasoning that "since the publisher may refuse to print at all, it may require that advertisements submitted to it for publication comply with such rules and regulations as the publisher deems proper"), *cert. denied,* 444 U.S. 870 (1979); Wisconsin Ass'n of Nursing Homes v. Journal Co., 285 N.W.2d 891 (Wis. Ct. App. 1979) (in dismissing suit by nursing home to require newspaper to publish ad responding to newspaper's investigative articles, court held that it did not have power under First Amendment to compel publication of news or advertising); Fernandez v. Progress Printing Co., 670 P.2d 611 (Okla. Ct. App. 1983) (court held that newspaper could reject ads from businesses that competed with businesses in newspaper's home town because newspaper has right to exercise discretion over who it deals with and plaintiff did not allege any unlawful discrimination); Citizen Awareness Regarding Educ. v. Calhoun County Pub'g, 406 S.E.2d 65, 68, 19 Media L. Rep. 1061 (W. Va. 1991) (court struck down injunction compelling newspaper to print paid political advertisement submitted by local political action committee, noting that "government can never compel a private newspaper to print anything without violating the First Amendment's guarantee of a free press").

[208]Access to government-sponsored media is discussed in detail *infra* §13.5.
[209]*See* Chapter 9.
[210]*See, e.g.,* Lorain Journal Co. v. United States, 342 U.S. 143 (1951); *infra* notes 223–26 and accompanying text.
[211]15 U.S.C. §§1–7 (West 1982 & Supp. 1988).
[212]*See, e.g.,* Marc's Restaurant v. CBS, 730 S.W.2d 582, 586 (Mo. Ct. App. 1987) (Missouri antitrust statute construed in accordance with Sherman Act).
[213]C. HILLS, ANTITRUST ADVISER 483 (1985) (citing Eastern States Retail Lumber Dealers Ass'n v. United States, 234 U.S. 600 (1914)); *see also* Northwest Wholesale Stationers v. Pacific Stationery & Printing Co., 472 U.S. 284, 294 (1985).
[214]*See, e.g.,* Walker v. Providence Journal Co., 493 F.2d 82 (1st Cir. 1974) (cessation of all advertising activity in response to newspaper's refusal to sell space did not establish collaboration between newspaper and advertiser); Diamond v. World News Corp., 542 F. Supp. 887, 888 (S.D.N.Y. 1982) (court rejected plaintiff's contention that agreement between defendant publication and tobacco advertisers not to publish anti-smoking pamphlet could be inferred from existence of refusal-to-deal policy); National Tire Wholesale v. Washington Post Co., 441 F. Supp. 81, 87 (D.C. Cir. 1977) (court held mere existence of advertising contracts between newspaper and wholesaler did not support inference that they had combined to restrict newspaper's dealings with wholesaler's competitor), *aff'd without opinion,* 595 F.2d 888 (D.C. Cir. 1979); America's Best Cinema Corp. v. Fort Wayne Newspapers, 347 F. Supp. 328, 332 (N.D. Ind. 1972) (newspapers operating under joint operating agreement are legally incapable of conspiring).
[215]Associated Press v. United States, 326 U.S. 1 (1945). *See generally* S. OPPENHEIM & C. SHIELDS, NEWSPAPERS AND THE ANTITRUST LAWS §38 (1981).

newspaper induced advertisers to cancel all advertising in the competitor's publication,[216] and where a newspaper refused to sell advertising to companies that charged a fee for providing real estate listings.[217]

§13.4(B)(ii) Section 2 Violations

Section 2 of the Sherman Act prohibits monopolization and attempted monopolization, whether unilateral or concerted. Two basic elements are necessary to prove a Section 2 violation: possession of monopoly power and the intentional acquisition or maintenance of such power.[218]

Antitrust violations generally are claimed when a newspaper refuses to accept advertisements, i.e., when it "refuses to deal" with the advertiser. Although as a general rule a business may refuse to deal with a potential customer,[219] if the refusal constitutes an attempt to create or maintain a monopoly, it violates Section 2.[220]

Section 2 does not require a monopoly publication to publish an advertisement when the refusal to deal does not affect a competitor.[221] Refusals to deal that have resulted in media liability for unilaterally refusing to publish advertising fall into two basic categories: (1) refusals to deal based on the advertiser using a competing publication, and (2) refusals to publish a competitor's advertisement.[222]

With respect to refusals to deal based on the advertiser using a competing publication, it is well established that a member of the media with monopoly power may not use access to advertising as a sword against competitors. In *Lorain Journal Co. v. United States*,[223] the leading antitrust case involving advertising practices of the print media, the Supreme Court affirmed a judgment that enjoined a newspaper from refusing to accept advertisements from customers who advertised on a competing radio station.[224] The Court found that the newspaper was using its monopoly power in the advertising market to destroy the threat of competition: the refusal forced the advertisers to boycott the radio station or lose their advertising space in the newspaper.[225] The Court ruled that such action violated Section 2 of the Sherman Act and rejected the publisher's

---

[216]Union Leader Corp. v. Newspapers of New Eng., 180 F. Supp. 125 (D. Mass. 1959), *modified and aff'd*, 284 F.2d 582 (1st Cir. 1960), *cert. denied*, 365 U.S. 833 (1961).

[217]Home Placement Serv. v. Providence Journal Co., 682 F.2d 274 (1st Cir. 1982); *see infra* notes 235–39 and accompanying text.

[218]United States v. Grinnell Corp., 384 U.S. 563, 570–71 (1966).

[219]United States v. Colgate & Co., 250 U.S. 300, 307 (1919); Great Atl. & Pac. Tea Co. v. Cream of Wheat, 227 F.2d 46, 48 (2d Cir. 1915); Official Airlines Guides v. Federal Trade Comm'n, 630 F.2d 920, 927–28 (2d Cir. 1980).

[220]Lorain Journal Co. v. United States, 342 U.S. 143, 156 (1951); *Colgate & Co.*, 250 U.S. at 307.

[221]Saxe, Bacon & Bolin, P.C. v. Martindale-Hubbell, Inc., 710 F.2d 87, 90 (2d Cir. 1983) (legal directory refused to publish advertisement for law firm; court held that refusal to publish ad was not intended to have anticompetitive effect on legal directory publishing, thus publication had right to exercise independent discretion as to parties with whom it would deal). *See also* Marc's Restaurant v. CBS, 730 S.W.2d 582, 586 (Mo. Ct. App. 1987) ("a radio station generally may choose among advertisers as a matter of business and editorial discretion"; court dismissed antitrust claim); Sagan v. Harvey, 1984-1 Trade Cas. (CCH) ¶65,778 (W.D. Pa. 1983) (refusal to publish political advertisement did not violate Section 2); America's Best Cinema Corp. v. Fort Wayne Newspapers, 347 F. Supp. 328, 333 (N.D. Ind. 1972) (refusal to publish advertisements for X-rated movies did not violate Section 2).

[222]*See, e.g., infra* note 223.

[223]342 U.S. 143 (1951).

[224]*Id.* at 157.

[225]*Id.* at 154–55.

contention that the injunction infringed on its First Amendment rights,[226] although this case was decided many years before *Tornillo*.

Nevertheless, even the fact that a newspaper occupies a monopolistic position in a given market does not of itself confer a right of access to its pages on would-be advertisers.[227] Although a monopoly newspaper's refusal to publish advertising may damage competitors, the courts have created an exemption from antitrust liability if the publisher has a legitimate business purpose for refusing to accept advertising, such as protecting its readers from misleading advertising,[228] countering competition by imposing unit rates,[229] safeguarding quality control,[230] or refusing to publish "undesirable" ads, e.g., those for adult films or escort services.[231]

For example, in *Homefinders of America v. Providence Journal Co.*,[232] the First Circuit held that there was no Sherman Act violation in a newspaper's refusal to publish advertisements for the plaintiff's property listing service where the ads were deceptive and had prompted complaints from the public.[233] The court found that the newspaper had a reasonable business justification for refusing the ads: "[W]e would hesitate long before holding that a newspaper,

---

[226]*Id.* See also Kansas City Star Co. v. United States, 240 F.2d 643 (8th Cir. 1957) (dominant newspaper's threat to refuse ads from those who also placed ads with competitors violated Section 2). The Eight Circuit declared, in response to the publisher's First Amendment argument, that "[p]ublishers of newspapers must answer for their actions in the same manner as anyone else. . . . Freedom to print does not mean freedom to destroy. To use the freedom of the press guaranteed by the First Amendment to destroy competition would defeat its own ends, for freedom to print news and express opinions as one chooses is not tantamount to having freedom to monopolize." 240 F.2d at 666.

[227]*See* Zimmerman v. Board of Pubns. of the Christian Reformed Church, 598 F. Supp. 1002 (D. Colo. 1984) (church publication's rejection of promissory note advertising in absence of assurance of advertiser's financial stability not unreasonable under Sherman Act); National Tire Wholesale v. Washington Post Co., 441 F. Supp. 81, 88 (D.D.C. 1977) (no Sherman Act violation established where newspaper refused to print advertisements for retail tire business with which it was not in competition); Person v. New York Post Co., 427 F. Supp. 1297, 1308 (E.D.N.Y.) (newspaper's refusal to print "tombstone" advertisement announcing securities offering by plaintiffs with whom it was not in competition did not constitute concerted refusal to deal under Sherman Act), *aff'd*, 573 F.2d 1294 (2d Cir. 1977); *see also* PMP Assocs. v. Globe Newspaper Co., 321 N.E.2d 915, 919 (Mass. 1975) (holding that newspaper's rejection of escort service advertisements not unfair trade practice under state statute; employing analysis used in antitrust cases); Marc's Restaurant v. CBS, 730 S.W.2d 582, 587 (Mo. Ct. App. 1987) (holding that radio station's failure to provide advertising for restaurant after placing it on waiting list did not violate state antitrust law analogous to Sherman Act).

[228]Staff Research Assocs. v. Tribune Co., 346 F.2d 372 (7th Cir. 1965) (newspaper's refusal to accept ads from employment agency unless ads were placed in certain classification did not violate antitrust laws; court found legitimate business reason of not misleading readers underlying such requirement).

[229]*See, e.g.,* Times-Picayune Pub'g Co. v. United States, 345 U.S. 594, 622 (1953) (publisher's refusal to publish ads that were not to be run in both morning and evening editions of newspapers did not violate Section 2, even though only competitor was evening newspaper; court noted that arrangement was motivated by "legitimate business aims").

[230]In Drinkwine v. Federated Publications, 780 F.2d 735 (9th Cir. 1985), *cert. denied*, 475 U.S. 1087 (1986), the Ninth Circuit held that a newspaper's refusal to publish brokered advertising did not violate Section 2 because it did not have any effect on consumers, competitors, or competition. The court concluded that the refusal to deal passed muster because it was motivated by legitimate business reasons, such as quality control and correction problems. The newspaper's desire to make more money did not render the refusal to deal illegitimate. *Id.* at 740.

[231]*See, e.g.,* America's Best Cinema Corp. v. Fort Wayne Newspapers, 347 F. Supp. 328, 332 (N.D. Ind. 1972) (newspaper's policy to reject all advertising from adult movie theaters did not violate antitrust laws); Adult Film Ass'n of Am. v. Times Mirror Co., 97 Cal. App. 3d 77, 81, 158 Cal. Rptr. 547 (Cal. Ct. App. 1979) (plaintiff claimed defendant's refusal to publish ads constituted interference with relationship between plaintiff and potential customers, but court held that liability cannot be imposed on newspaper for mere refusal to continue dealing with former customer); PMP Assocs. v. Globe Newspaper Co., 321 N.E.2d 915, 919 (Mass. 1975) (plaintiff claimed that defendant newspaper violated Massachusetts unfair trade practices statute by refusing to accept plaintiff's advertising for its escort service business; court recognized publisher's freedom to deal with whomever it chose and found no unfair trade practice).

[232]621 F.2d 441 (1st Cir. 1980).

[233]*Id.* at 443–44.

monopoly or not, armed with both the First Amendment and a reasonable business justification, can be ordered to publish advertising against its will."[234]

Two years later, in *Home Placement Service v. Providence Journal Co.*,[235] the First Circuit held that the newspaper violated both Sections 1 and 2 of the Sherman Act in refusing to accept advertisements for a similar property listing service.[236] The court found concerted action constituting a Section 1 violation because the newspaper would accept the plaintiff's ads only if the plaintiff agreed not to charge customers a fee for listings contained in those ads.[237] The court found a Section 2 violation because the newspaper was using its dominance in the newspaper advertising market to foreclose competition in the housing vacancy information market: "Because of its monopoly over rental listings in the general area where plaintiff was attempting to operate, the Journal's refusal to run ads where a fee was charged put plaintiff out of the rental referral business."[238] The court distinguished *Homefinders* by noting that there was no showing in *Home Placement* that the advertising was deceptive or had prompted complaints, and thus there was no reasonable business justification for the newspaper's refusal to accept the ads.[239] Although the *Home Placement* decision is one of the few that has actually found an antitrust violation from a publisher's refusal to print certain advertisements, the holding indicates that, despite the *Tornillo* Court's far-reaching rejection of a right of access, a publisher's refusal to accept advertising may constitute an antitrust violation, and a publisher, under certain circumstances, may be required to publish advertisements.

Courts are reluctant to apply antitrust laws to conduct protected by the First Amendment.[240] In light of this concept, known as the Noerr-Pennington Doctrine, and *Tornillo,* one could argue that federal antitrust laws cannot be used to compel publishers to print advertisements they do not want to print.

§13.4(C) Contractual Rights and the Publisher's Right to Refuse Advertisements

A newspaper's editorial discretion in rejecting advertisements may be limited by a contract.[241] Thus, a valid advertising contract is enforceable notwithstanding a newspaper's general right to reject advertisements.[242] Often,

---

[234]*Id.* at 444.
[235]682 F.2d 274 (1st Cir. 1982).
[236]*Id.* at 279–81.
[237]*Id.* at 279.
[238]*Id.* at 281.
[239]*Id.* at 277.
[240]Eastern R.R. Presidents Conf. v. Noerr Motor Freight, 365 U.S. 127, 140–41 (1961) (Sherman Act did not prohibit unethical, harmful, deceptive, and vicious publicity campaign waged by railroads against trucking industry to influence governmental action). *Accord* Mine Workers (UMW) v. Pennington, 381 U.S. 657, 670 (1965) (First Amendment "shields from the Sherman Act a concerted effort to influence public officials regardless of intent or purpose").
[241]Herald-Telephone v. Fatouros, 431 N.E.2d 171 (Ind. Ct. App. 1982) (court found contract to publish ad binding). The *Fatouros* court observed that "[w]hile a newspaper has a right to reject any ad it wishes, this right exists only until a contract is formed. Once the contract is entered into, the newspaper stands in the same position as any other business entity and may reject an ad only if it reserved the right to do so or has an equitable defense to specific performance." *Id.* at 175 (citation omitted).
[242]*Fatouros,* 431 N.E.2d at 176. For other cases suggesting, but not holding, that a valid advertising contract is enforceable, *see* Indiana Constr. Corp. v. Chicago Tribune Co., 648 F. Supp. 1419, 1422 (N.D. Ind. 1986) ("*[i]n the absence of a contractual obligation* a newspaper may refuse to print an advertisement,

however, a collision between editorial discretion and contractual obligation was averted by the court's finding that no valid contract existed.[243]

§13.4(D) Antidiscrimination Laws and the Publisher's Right to Refuse Advertisements

Although the Supreme Court's holding in *Tornillo*, that editorial discretion is protected "whether fair or unfair"[244] is broad,[245] private publishers' editorial discretion may be limited where their refusal to publish ads results in violation of an antidiscrimination law.

Since the publishing of a privately owned newspaper does not involve state action,[246] the Equal Protection Clause,[247] which affords relief for deprivation of constitutional rights under the color of state law, does not apply where a newspaper allegedly discriminates in its refusal to publish an advertisement.[248] Thus, absent specific statute authority, e.g., federal or state antidiscrimination

---

even if the refusal is the result of mere caprice, prejudice or malice") (emphasis added); Evenson v. Ortega, 605 F. Supp. 1115, 1117–18 (D. Ariz. 1985) ("unbridled editorial discretion" extends to commercial advertising except, inter alia, where refusal to advertise is breach of contract); Wisconsin Ass'n of Nursing Homes v. Journal Co., 285 N.W.2d 891, 894 (Wis. Ct. App. 1979) ("*[a]bsent contractual provisions . . .* first amendment protections do not embody any obligation on the part of a privately owned newspaper to publish anything which conflicts with its internal policies") (emphasis added).

[243]*See, e.g.,* Zimmerman v. Board of Pubns. of Christian Reformed Church, 598 F. Supp. 1002 (D. Colo. 1984) (religious magazine's historic dealings with church seeking to place ad did not give rise to implied contract to publish ad). *See also Indiana Constr. Corp.,* 648 F. Supp. at 1424 (mailroom clerk's signing of receipt for advertisement does not constitute acceptance of offer to advertise). The risk that a newspaper will unwittingly enter into a contract to publish particular advertisements is substantially diminished by the rule that a newspaper's own advertisements are not offers that may be accepted merely by sending a proposed advertisement to the publication. Brewster v. Ashland Pub'g Corp., 345 F. Supp. 35, 37 (W.D. Wis. 1972) (defendant's general advertising was not offer to plaintiff to enter into contract that would obligate defendant to accept plaintiff's paid advertisement); Chicago Joint Bd., Clothing & Textile Workers v. Chicago Tribune Co., 307 F. Supp. 422, 424 (N.D. Ill. 1969) (general advertising to public does not constitute offer to enter into contract), *aff'd,* 435 F.2d 470 (7th Cir. 1970), *cert. denied,* 402 U.S. 973 (1971); Marc's Restaurant v. CBS, 730 S.W.2d 582, 585 (Mo. Ct. App. 1987) (placement of would-be advertiser's name on waiting list did not signal mutuality of agreement to provide testimonial radio advertising).

[244]Miami Herald Pub'g Co. v. Tornillo, 418 U.S. 241, 259 (1974). For a general discussion of the publisher's right to reject advertisements, *see supra* §13.4(A).

[245]In Cook v. Advertiser Co., 458 F.2d 1119 (5th Cir. 1972), eight "Negro" class action plaintiffs sued an Alabama newspaper for refusing to print their wedding announcements on the paper's society page. The court held that the constitutional right of freedom of the press far outweighed the plaintiff's right against discrimination. The concurring opinion intimated, however, that the result might have been different had the case involved commercial advertisements. *Id.* at 1124. *Cook* is also discussed in Chapter 9, §9.3(D).

[246]While "[n]o precise method of determining the existence of state action exists," Sinn v. Daily Nebraskan, 638 F. Supp. 143, 148 (D. Neb. 1986), *aff'd,* 829 F.2d 662 (8th Cir. 1987), the publishing of private newspapers, and even of state university newspapers, consistently has been found not to involve state action, since the action of the publishing of these newspapers is not " 'fairly attributable' to the state," *id.* at 150. The *Sinn* court found that a student newspaper's refusal to publish sexual orientation in ads for roommates did not constitute state action: "Rejection of an advertisement is a constitutionally protected editorial decision in nowise diminished by state support or subsidization." *Id.* at 152. *See also* Wellman v. Williamson Daily News, 582 F. Supp. 1526, 1527 (S.D. W. Va. 1984) (publication of newspaper did not involve state action); Resident Participation of Denver v. Love, 322 F. Supp. 1100, 1105 (D. Colo. 1971) (private newspaper's refusal to carry classified advertisement manifests no element of state action and thus is not prohibited under First Amendment); Chicago Joint Bd., Clothing & Textile Workers v. Chicago Tribune Co., 435 F.2d 470, 477 (7th Cir. 1970) (newspaper publisher's rejection of labor union's editorial advertisement did not involve state action), *cert. denied,* 402 U.S. 973 (1971). *See also* Chapter 9, §9.3(A)(i).

[247]U.S. CONST. amend. XIV, §1.

[248]Since the Equal Protection Clause does not apply, private print media legally may discriminate against a class of persons unless a local antidiscrimination law prohibits them from doing so. *See, e.g.,* Loring v. Bellsouth Advertising & Pub'g Corp., 339 S.E.2d 372 (Ga. Ct. App. 1985), where the court found that a publisher had no duty to print an advertisement containing the words "gay male" and "lesbian"; "[A]ppellee, in publishing the yellow pages directory, is a private enterprise and does not perform an essential public service, and thus appellee has no statutory or common law duty to accept the advertising submitted by the appellant." *Id.* at 375. *See also* Pines v. Tomson, 206 Cal. Rptr. 866 (Cal. Ct. App. 1984), where the court affirmed an order that enjoined the defendants, publishers of the "Christian Yellow Pages" (CYP), from

laws, claims of discrimination have failed to prevail over the First Amendment's guarantee of freedom of the press.[249]

Decisions that involve such claims against the print media under the Ku Klux Klan Act of 1871[250] consistently have failed because the courts did not find the necessary "class based invidiously discriminatory animus" to constitute a violation of the Act.[251] For example, there was no showing of such class-based discrimination where the defendant newspapers adopted a policy rejecting all advertising from movie houses that habitually showed only adult films,[252] nor was there a showing of class-based discrimination where newspapers rejected "tombstone" advertisements announcing a securities offering.[253] Similarly, there was no class-based discrimination where a newspaper refused to print an advertisement that was "not in accordance with the newspaper's standards."[254]

§13.5 ACCESS TO GOVERNMENT-CONTROLLED MEDIA

The First Amendment prohibits the government from interfering with the free expression rights of the private media. What happens, however, when the media are government-sponsored or controlled?[255] Is the government, as publisher or broadcaster, subject to the same rules as the private publisher or broadcaster, or do different standards apply? This section discusses that issue.

---

refusing advertisements on the basis of religion. The CYP's policy had required advertisers to affirm that they were "born again Christians" before the CYP would publish their advertisements. Although this decision encroached on the publisher's editorial discretion, it was not challenged on First Amendment free speech grounds. *Id.* at 877–80.

[249]*See* Hatheway v. Gannett Satellite Info. Network, 459 N.W.2d 873, 18 Media L. Rep. 1458 (Wis. Ct. App. 1990) (dismissing plaintiff's claim that newspaper's refusal to accept ads containing words "gay" and "lesbian" violated Wisconsin's public accommodations act on ground that classified advertising section did not fall under act); Treanor v. Washington Post Co., 826 F. Supp. 568, 21 Media L. Rep. 1991 (D.D.C. 1993) (Americans with Disabilities Act does not require newspaper to publish review of disabled person's book because newspaper is not "public accommodation"); Note, *Exclusion and Access in Public Accommodations: First Amendment Limitations Upon State Law,* 16 PAC. L.J. 1047 (1985).

[250]42 U.S.C. §1985 (1981 & Supp. 1993). This law is discussed in detail in Chapter 9, §9.3(B).

[251]*See, e.g.,* Kops v. New York Tel. Co., 456 F. Supp. 1090, 1095 (S.D.N.Y. 1978) (in action alleging that telephone company's refusal to place attorneys' advertisement for legal services in telephone directory constituted conspiracy to deprive attorneys of their constitutional rights, court held that plaintiffs failed to establish requisite "class-based, invidiously discriminatory animus" to recover under Act), *aff'd,* 803 F.2d 213 (2d Cir. 1979).

[252]America's Best Cinema Corp. v. Fort Wayne Newspapers, 347 F. Supp. 328, 335 (N.D. Ind. 1972) (where stipulated that no racial discrimination involved in newspapers' adoption of policy to reject all advertising from adult movie theaters, and exhibitors of X-rated films presented nothing to show that newspapers' acts were based on some other invidiously discriminatory classification, exhibitors not deprived of equal protection under Ku Klux Klan Act).

[253]Person v. New York Post Corp., 427 F. Supp. 1297, 1305, 2 Media L. Rep. 1666 (E.D.N.Y.) (class of attorneys seeking to publicly finance antitrust litigation not recognized under Ku Klux Klan Act, which imposes civil liability on those who conspire to deny equal protection; recovery under Act for defendant newspapers' refusal to publish plaintiffs' "tombstone" advertisement also precluded because plaintiffs did not allege any invidiously discriminatory animus on part of newspaper, nor any intent to deny equal protection), *aff'd without opinion,* 573 F.2d 1294, 3 Media L. Rep. 1784 (2d Cir. 1977).

[254]Cyntje v. Daily News Pub'g Co., 551 F. Supp. 403, 405 (D.V.I. 1982) (in action brought by individual against newspaper for injunctive and monetary relief for failing to print several paid advertisements, court held that plaintiff, who did not prove that newspaper's refusal was based on invidiously discriminatory classification, failed to state legal claim).

[255]Government-sponsored media are those that are funded by the government or that the government controls or supervises. *See, e.g.,* Hazelwood School Dist. v. Kuhlmeier, 484 U.S. 260, 271 n.3, 14 Media L. Rep. 2081, 2086 n.3 (1988) (student newspapers produced as part of school curriculum are school-sponsored publications); Pittman v. Hutto, 594 F.2d 407 (4th Cir. 1979) (prison inmate newspapers are government-sponsored publications); *infra* note 334.

§13.5(A) The Public Forum Theory

To resolve disputes arising from the government's denial of access to its property or facilities for communication, the Supreme Court developed the public forum theory.[256] The Court has applied this theory to determine the extent to which the government may exercise control over the media it sponsors.

The foundation of the public forum theory lies with the Court's recognition that "the Government, 'no less than a private owner of property, has power to preserve the property under its control for the use to which it is lawfully dedicated.' "[257] Indeed, the Supreme Court recognizes that "[n]othing in the Constitution requires the Government freely to grant access to all who wish to exercise their right to free speech on every type of Government property without regard to the nature of the property or to the disruption that might be caused."[258]

Nevertheless, the government cannot deny all access to potential speakers or exercise unfettered editorial control over the content of the expression to be voiced on all government property. On the contrary, "[t]he existence of a right of access to public property and the standard by which limitations upon such a right must be evaluated differ *depending on the character of the property at issue.*"[259]

To determine the "character of the property at issue" in a systematic fashion, the Supreme Court has created three categories of forums. The scope of the government's editorial control over a particular forum and the speaker's corollary rights of access depend on whether the forum is (1) a traditional public forum; (2) a limited public forum; or (3) a nonpublic forum.[260]

The first type of forum, a "traditional public forum," is a place, such as a street or park, "which by long tradition or by government fiat [has] been devoted to assembly and debate."[261] "Because a principal purpose of traditional public fora is the free exchange of ideas,"[262] in these quintessential public fora "the rights of the [government] to limit expressive activity are sharply circumscribed."[263] "The government may not prohibit all communicative activity"[264] in a public forum, and "speakers can be excluded from a public forum only when the exclusion is necessary to serve a compelling state interest and the exclusion is narrowly drawn to achieve that interest."[265] The

---

[256]*See generally* Post, *Between Governance and Management: The History and Theory of the Public Forum,* 34 U.C.L.A. L. REV. 1713 (1987); Farber & Nowak, *The Misleading Nature of Public Forum Analysis: Content and Context in First Amendment Adjudication,* 70 VA. L. REV. 1219 (1984); Comment, *Access to State-Owned Communications Media—The Public Forum Doctrine,* 26 U.C.L.A. L. REV. 1410 (1979). This doctrine is also discussed in Chapter 12, particularly in §12.4.

[257]Cornelius v. NAACP Legal Defense & Educ. Fund, 473 U.S. 788, 800 (1985) (quoting Greer v. Spock, 424 U.S. 828, 836 (1976)).

[258]*Id.* at 800.

[259]Perry Educ. Ass'n v. Perry Local Educators' Ass'n, 460 U.S. 37, 44 (1983) (emphasis added).

[260]*See id.* at 45; *accord Cornelius,* 473 U.S. at 800.

[261]460 U.S. at 45; *accord Cornelius,* 473 U.S. at 800; *see* Hague v. Committee for Indus. Org., 307 U.S. 496, 515 (1939) (streets and parks "have immemorially been held in trust for the use of the public and, time out of mind, have been used for purposes of assembly, communicating thoughts between citizens, and discussing political questions").

[262]*Cornelius,* 473 U.S. at 800.

[263]*Perry,* 460 U.S. at 45.

[264]*Id.*

[265]*Id.* (citing Carey v. Brown, 447 U.S. 455, 461 (1980)); *see also* Frisby v. Schultz, 487 U.S. 474, 479–81 (1988); Boos v. Barry, 485 U.S. 312, 318 (1988); *Cornelius,* 473 U.S. at 800.

government may, however, "enforce regulations of the time, place, and manner of expression which are content-neutral, are narrowly tailored to serve a significant governmental interest, and leave open ample alternative channels of communication."[266]

The second type of forum, a "limited public forum," consists of "public property which the State has opened for use by the public as a place for expressive activity."[267] The limited public forum is "created by government designation of a place or channel of communication for use by the public at large for assembly and speech, for use by certain speakers, or for the discussion of certain subjects."[268] The government does not, however, create a public forum "by inaction or by permitting limited discourse, but only by *intentionally* opening a nontraditional forum for public discourse."[269]

In ascertaining whether the government intended to designate a place not traditionally open to assembly and debate as a public forum, the Court looks to the "policy and practice" of the government and examines "the nature of the property and its compatibility with expressive activity."[270] Once the government creates a limited public forum, its rights to impose constraints on the type of expression permitted in that forum are also restricted: "Although a state is not required to indefinitely retain the open character of the facility, as long as it does so it is bound by the same standards as apply in a traditional public forum."[271] In a limited public forum, as in a traditional public forum, "[r]easonable time, place and manner regulations are permissible, and a content-based prohibition must be narrowly drawn to effectuate a compelling state interest."[272]

The third type of forum, a "nonpublic forum," is "[p]ublic property which is not by tradition or designation a forum for public communication," and is governed by constitutional standards less rigorous than those governing the traditional and limited public forums.[273] In a nonpublic forum, the government, in addition to reasonable time, place and manner regulations, "may reserve the forum for its intended purposes, communicative or otherwise, as long as the regulation on speech is *reasonable* and not an effort to suppress expression merely because public officials oppose the speaker's view."[274]

---

[266]*Perry*, 460 U.S. at 45. *See generally* Chapter 12.

[267]*Cornelius*, 473 U.S. at 802; *Perry*, 460 U.S. at 45, 46 n.7.

[268]*Cornelius*, 473 U.S. at 802 (citing Perry Educ. Ass'n v. Perry Local Educators' Ass'n, 460 U.S. 37, 45, 46 n.7 (1983)).

[269]*Id.* at 802 (emphasis added).

[270]*Id.; see* Widmar v. Vincent, 454 U.S. 263, 267 (1981) (state university's express policy of making meeting facilities available to registered student groups evidenced clear intent to create public forum); Madison Joint Sch. Dist. v. Wisconsin Employment Relations Comm'n, 429 U.S. 167, 174 n.6 (1976) (forum for citizen involvement created by state statute providing for open school board meetings); Southeastern Promotions v. Conrad, 420 U.S. 546, 555 (1975) (public forum created when municipal auditorium and city-leased theater designed for and dedicated to expressive activities).

[271]Perry Educ. Ass'n v. Perry Local Educators' Ass'n, 460 U.S. 37, 46 (1983). "The Constitution forbids a State to enforce certain exclusions from a forum generally open to the public even if it was not required to create the forum in the first place." *Id.* at 45.

[272]*Id.* at 46 (citing Widmar v. Vincent, 454 U.S. 263, 269–70 (1981)).

[273]*Id.* at 46. The Court has recognized that the " 'First Amendment does not guarantee access to property simply because it is owned or controlled by the government.' " *Id.* (quoting United States Postal Serv. v. Council of Greenburgh Civic Ass'ns, 453 U.S. 114, 129 (1981)).

[274]*Id.* at 49 (emphasis added); *accord* Cornelius v. NAACP Legal Defense & Educ. Fund, 473 U.S. 788, 806 (1985) ("[c]ontrol over access to a nonpublic forum can be based on subject matter and speaker so long as the distinctions drawn are reasonable in light of the purpose served by the forum and are viewpoint neutral"). The rationale is that " '[t]he State, no less than a private owner of property, has power to preserve the property under its control for the use to which it is lawfully dedicated.' " *Perry*, 460 U.S. at 46 (quoting United States Postal Serv. v. Council of Greenburgh Civic Ass'ns, 453 U.S. 114, 129–30 (1981)).

However, "the existence of reasonable grounds for limiting access to a non-public forum will not ... save a regulation that is in reality a facade for viewpoint-based discrimination."[275]

Accordingly, which public forum category a court places a government medium in will ultimately determine the degree of editorial control that the government may exert over that medium and, correspondingly, the rights of those seeking access to that medium.[276]

§13.5(B) The Government As Publisher

The extent of the government's editorial control over publications that it sponsors is an issue that has arisen occasionally with prison inmate publications and more frequently with student publications. The courts' assessments of the competing interests involved—the First Amendment interests of the prisoners, students, or third parties wishing to speak versus the government's interests in exercising editorial control to maintain the appropriate environment in prisons and schools—have not always produced consistent results.

§13.5(B)(i) Prison Publications

For many years, the federal courts followed a "hands off" policy and did not interfere in prison affairs; some questioned whether prisoners retained any First Amendment rights while incarcerated.[277] Now, however, the courts readily acknowledge that although prison inmates do not retain a "full panoply of constitutional rights, normally enjoyed by those not convicted or incarcerated,"[278] incarceration does not "remove [prisoners] entirely from the purview of the first amendment."[279] "A prison inmate retains those rights that are not inconsistent with his status as a prisoner or with the legitimate penological objectives of the correction system."[280]

There are only a few cases decided in this area.[281] In *The Luparer v. Stoneman*,[282] the district court closely scrutinized the prison officials' restraint of articles in and the termination of an inmate publication.[283] The court held that once the government establishes a newspaper, prison officials cannot impose regulations broader than necessary to protect legitimate governmental

---

[275] *Cornelius*, 473 U.S. at 811.

[276] While all of the courts addressing access to government-sponsored media have not employed the public forum analysis, recent Supreme Court decisions indicate that this analysis will be controlling in future cases. *See, e.g.,* Hazelwood Sch. Dist. v. Kuhlmeier, 484 U.S. 260,14 Media L. Rep. 2081 (1988).

[277] *See* Comment, *First Amendment Rights of Prisoners: Freedom of the Prison Press*, 18 U.S.F. L. REV. 599, 599–600 (1984); *see also* Comment, *Public Forum Analysis and State Owned Publications: Beyond Kuhlmeier v. Hazelwood School District*, 55 FORDHAM L. REV. 243, 251–53 (1986); Note, *The First Amendment Rights of Prison Newspaper Editors*, 65 VA. L. REV. 1484 (1979).

[278] Pittman v. Hutto, 594 F.2d 407, 410 (4th Cir. 1979).

[279] *Id.* at 410; *see* Jones v. North Carolina Prisoners' Union, 433 U.S. 119, 129 (1977); Pell v. Procunier, 417 U.S. 817, 822 (1977); Procunier v. Martinez, 416 U.S. 396, 412 (1974).

[280] *Pittman*, 594 F.2d at 410 (citing Jones v. North Carolina Prisoners' Union, 433 U.S. 119, 129 (1977); Pell v. Procunier, 417 U.S. 817, 822 (1974); *and* Procunier v. Martinez, 416 U.S. 396, 412 (1974)).

[281] *See, e.g., Pittman*, 594 F.2d at 411–12; The Luparer v. Stoneman, 382 F. Supp. 495, 499–501 (D. Vt. 1974), *appeal dismissed,* 517 F.2d 1395 (2d Cir. 1975). *See also* Note, *supra* note 277, at 1485.

[282] 382 F. Supp. 495 (D. Vt. 1974), *appeal dismissed,* 517 F.2d 1395 (2d Cir. 1975).

[283] *Id.* at 500 (following Procunier v. Martinez, 416 U.S. 396 (1974)). In *Stoneman*, prison officials refused to publish the articles because they believed them to be "inflammatory," they "attack[ed] personalities, not issues," and "the circulation of the articles outside the prison might subject the state to defamation suits." *Id.* (footnotes omitted).

interests of prison security, order, or rehabilitation, nor can they impose a content-based prior restraint on publication of the paper unless it is necessary to protect those interests.[284] Since the articles and the publication did not threaten those interests, the court found that the restraint was unwarranted and therefore unconstitutional.[285]

However, in *Pittman v. Hutto*,[286] a district court denied relief to the plaintiff inmates whose publication was censored by prison officials because the officials believed the publication to be inflammatory and potentially disruptive.[287] The Fourth Circuit held that " 'it need only be shown that [prison officials'] concerns are reasonable in order for their reasonable prohibition on First Amendment ... rights to prevail.' "[288] The Fourth Circuit then affirmed the finding that the officials' actions were reasonable.[289]

Pittman was decided before *Perry* and *Cornelius* and does not analyze the editorial control issue under the public forum theory. Although the *Pittman* court found that "[t]he primary purpose of the prison publication [was] to be a forum for inmate discussion as well as a means of communication between inmates and the prison officials,"[290] it did not apply the compelling state interest standard that applies to traditional and limited purpose public forums—instead, it applied the "reasonableness" standard applicable to nonpublic forums.[291]

The different standards applied in *Pittman* and *Stoneman* essentially reflect developments in U.S. Supreme Court decisions on prisoners' rights. *Stoneman* followed *Procunier v. Martinez*,[292] where the Supreme Court held that censorship by prison officials had to further substantial state interests and limit First Amendment freedoms no more than necessary.[293] *Pittman* distinguished *Martinez* on the ground that it "dealt with a restriction on a prisoner's incoming and outgoing *personal* mail," thus involving more than "just the rights of the prisoner."[294] Concluding that the prison publication was "in effect a mass mailing," the *Pittman* court found that *Jones v. North Carolina Prisoners' Union*[295] was controlling.[296] In *Jones,* a prison inmate "labor union" brought

---

[284]*Id.* at 501. The court also held that "the state is not required to establish or support an inmate newspaper, and once it does so, it can withdraw its approval or support for any reason, except those impermissible under the first amendment." *Id.* at 499. However, "the objection of prison officials, or those in the Department of Corrections, to [the publication's] editorial content is not a permissible reason under the first amendment to prohibit its distribution." *Id.*

[285]*Id.* at 499–501.

[286]594 F.2d 407 (4th Cir. 1979).

[287]*Id.* at 412.

[288]*Id.* at 411–12 (quoting Jones v. North Carolina Prisoners' Union, 433 U.S. 119 (1977) (brackets in original).

[289]*Id.* at 412.

[290]*Id.* at 409, 411.

[291]594 F.2d at 411 (following Jones v. North Carolina Prisoners' Union, 433 U.S. 119 (1977). The *Jones* Court had expressly found that the prison was not a public forum even though certain other groups, such as Alcoholics Anonymous and the Boy Scouts, were permitted access. Jones v. North Carolina Prisoners' Union, 433 U.S. 119, 134, 136 (1977) (citing Greer v. Spock, 424 U.S. 828, 838 n.10 (1976)) ("prison may be no more easily converted into a public forum than a military base"). While the prison may not have been a public forum, the prison *publication* may have been. *See* Bailey v. Loggins, 32 Cal. 3d 912, 918, 654 P.2d 758 (Cal. 1982) ("*Jones* did not involve a prison newspaper, and nothing in that opinion indicates that a newspaper cannot serve as a forum for prisoner expression"). On the public forum doctrine, *see supra* §13.5(A).

[292]416 U.S. 396 (1974).

[293]*Id.* at 413.

[294]594 F.2d at 411.

[295]433 U.S. 119 (1977).

[296]594 F.2d at 411.

a civil rights action challenging various state prison regulations, including a ban on the delivery of packets of union publications mailed in bulk to individual inmates for redistribution to other inmates.[297] The *Pittman* court stated that, under *Jones,* "prison officials may limit first amendment rights, whether of speech or association, whenever they reasonably conclude that the exercise of such rights possesses the likelihood of disruption of prison order or stability or otherwise interferes with the penological objectives of the institution."[298]

The Supreme Court's later decision in *Thornburgh v. Abbott*[299] indicates that in future cases, regulations concerning prison publications will be analyzed under a "reasonableness" standard and not under the heightened scrutiny applied in *Stoneman*. In *Thornburgh,* a class of inmates and certain publishers challenged prison regulations that permitted prison officials to reject *incoming* publications found to be detrimental to institutional security.[300] The inmates and publishers asserted that the regulations violated their First Amendment rights under the heightened scrutiny standard enunciated in *Procunier v. Martinez*.[301] In *Martinez,* the Court had held that prison officials who wanted to censor a prisoner's mail had to show that the censorship furthered a "substantial governmental interest"—such as security or rehabilitation—"unrelated to the suppression of expression," and that the censorship was "no greater than is necessary or essential to the protection of [that interest]."[302]

The *Thornburgh* Court recognized that the language in *Martinez* could be (and had been) interpreted as establishing a standard of "strict" or "heightened" scrutiny, thus requiring prison officials to employ the "least restrictive alternative" to accomplish their objectives.[303] Following its earlier decision in *Turner v. Safley,*[304] however, the Court held that this standard "was not appropriate for ... regulations that are centrally concerned with the maintenance of order and security within prisons."[305] Instead, "the relevant inquiry is whether the actions of prison officials were 'reasonably related to legitimate penological interests.' "[306] The Court concluded that regulations affecting the sending of any information *to* a prisoner are valid if they meet this standard.[307]

---

[297]433 U.S. at 121.
[298]594 F.2d at 411.
[299]490 U.S. 401 (1989).
[300]*Id.* at 403.
[301]*Id.* The Court did recognize that "there is no question that publishers who wish to communicate with those who, through subscription, willingly seek their point of view have a legitimate First Amendment interest in access to prisoners." *Id.* at 408.
[302]*Martinez,* 416 U.S. 396, 413–14 (1974).
[303]490 U.S. at 409–10. The *Thornburgh* Court stated that "[w]e do not believe that *Martinez* should, or need be read as subjecting the decisions of prison officials to a strict 'least restrictive means' test.... *Martinez* required no more than that a challenged regulation be 'generally necessary' to a legitimate governmental interest." *Id.* at 411.
[304]482 U.S. 78 (1987).
[305]*Thornburgh,* 490 U.S. at 410 (footnote omitted). The Court, in distinguishing *Martinez,* emphasized the difference between incoming and outgoing information: "The implications of outgoing correspondence for prison security [at issue in *Martinez*] are of a categorically lesser magnitude than the implications of incoming materials." *Id.* at 413. For example, once inside the prison, disruption may result from prisoners observing particular material in the possession of others and drawing inferences about their sexual orientation, gang affiliation, or other beliefs. *Id.* at 412.
[306]*Id.* at 419 (quoting Turner v. Safley, 482 U.S. 79, 89 (1987)).
[307]*Id.* at 414. The Court went on to determine whether the regulations were "reasonable," applying the various factors set out in *Turner. Id.* at 414–19. The factors are (1) whether there is a "valid, rational connection" between the regulation and a legitimate and neutral governmental interest; (2) whether there are alternative means of exercising the asserted constitutional right that remain open to inmates; and (3) whether and the extent to which the accommodation of the asserted right will impact the prison guards, inmates, and

The Court limited the *Martinez* Court's heightened scrutiny test to regulations concerning *outgoing* correspondence.[308]

Turner and *Thornburgh* seem to indicate that regulations governing prison publications will be deemed valid if they are "reasonably related to legitimate penological interests."[309] Although the reasonableness standard is a less protective standard, prison officials still may not exercise unfettered editorial control over prison publications.[310]

In addition to the First Amendment, prison officials' editorial discretion may be further limited by state constitutions or statutes,[311] as illustrated by the California Supreme Court's decision in *Bailey v. Loggins*.[312] In *Bailey,* the inmate editor of the prison newspaper and others brought a mandamus action seeking to compel the publication of two articles in the paper and the establishment of narrower publication regulations and an expeditious review procedure.[313]

The trial court concluded that "the regulations in question were overbroad, and that regulations limiting the content of the newspaper were permissible only to protect institutional security" and issued a peremptory writ that mandated publication of the two articles and directed enactment of regulations " 'which limit censorship of articles to publications of matters which if published would reasonably be deemed a threat to security of the institution ...

---

prison resources. *See Turner,* 482 U.S. at 89–91. *See also* In re Malik, 552 N.Y.S.2d 182 (N.Y. App. Div. 1990) (inmate's First Amendment rights not violated by prison officials' decision to censor article from magazine to which inmate subscribed that had potential to incite disobedience to prison personnel and possibly cause hysteria and violence).

The Supreme Court has also held that a regulation prohibiting prisoners from receiving hardcover books from sources other than publishers, bookstores, and book clubs did not violate the inmates' First Amendment rights. The Court recognized the "obvious security problem" presented by such books, which are "especially serviceable for smuggling contraband into an institution," such as money, drugs, and weapons, which may be hidden in the bindings. Bell v. Wolfish, 441 U.S. 520, 550–51 (1979). It is unclear whether a similar rule would be upheld for softcover books. *See, e.g.,* Pratt v. Sumner, 807 F.2d 817, 819–20 (9th Cir. 1987) (acknowledging that neither Supreme Court nor Ninth Circuit had addressed constitutionality of total ban on felony prisoner's receipt of books, including all softcover legal materials, from sources other than publishers and bookstores).

[308]*Thornburgh,* 490 U.S. at 413; *see also* Martin v. Rison, 741 F. Supp. 1406, 1413–17 (N.D. Cal. 1990) (prison officials may constitutionally restrict inmate's ability to write and publish articles in local newspaper if such restrictions bear reasonable relationship to bona fide penological interest); Hendrix v. Evans, 715 F. Supp. 897, 902 (N.D. Ind. 1989) (court applied *Turner* factors and found that prisoners' First Amendment rights not violated by prohibition against publication and distribution—to general public—of leaflets regarding legislation affecting prisons).

[309]*Turner,* 482 U.S. at 89; *Martinez,* 416 U.S. 396, 413–14 (1974).

[310]The *Turner* Court emphasized that "[w]e have found it important to inquire whether prison regulations restricting inmates' First Amendment rights operated in a neutral fashion, without *regard to the content of the expression.*" 482 U.S. at 90 (emphasis added). However, the *Thornburgh* Court diluted this language, holding that some content-based censorship was necessary and thus permissible. Under *Thornburgh,* the prison officials may consider content, but " 'the regulation or practice in question must further an important or substantial government interest *unrelated to the suppression of expression.*' " 490 U.S. at 415 (quoting Procunier v. Martinez, 416 U.S. 396, 413 (1974) (footnote omitted; emphasis added).

[311]For example, the California Constitution's protection of speech-related activities is "more definitive and inclusive than is the first amendment." Robins v. Pruneyard Shopping Ctr., 23 Cal. 3d 899, 908, 592 P.2d 341 (Cal. 1979), *aff'd,* 447 U.S. 74, 6 Media L. Rep. 1311 (1980).

[312]32 Cal. 3d 907, 654 P.2d 758 (Cal. 1982).

[313]32 Cal. 3d at 910, 912. The articles concerned two lectures given at Soledad Prison, one by a professor at the Institute of Industrial Relations at the University of California, and the other by the governor's deputy legal affairs secretary. *Id.* at 911. The director of corrections rejected Bailey's request to publish the articles, concluding that they constituted an attack on the prison administration in violation of the regulations. *Id.* at 912. As described by the *Bailey* court, the regulations "provided generally that the newspaper should conform to good journalistic standards, be designed to appeal to all inmates, and avoid material offensive to racial, religious, or political groups." *Id.* The regulations also "prohibited the use of the newspaper to attack administration rules or policy, or to assert any grievance. They also banned the assumption of an editorial position on pending legislation, the attempt to elect or defeat any official, or an attack upon existing governmental policy." *Id.*

or which [describe] the making of any weapon, explosive, poison or destructive device.' "[314] The trial court also held that the existing appeals procedure was inadequate and mandated enactment of regulations to ensure the "expeditious review of censored articles for the prison newspaper."[315] The Court of Appeal affirmed the judgment.[316]

The California Supreme Court, in a 4-3 decision, affirmed the portion of the order directing publication of the two articles at issue and requiring that the Department of Corrections enact regulations to ensure expeditious review of administrative decisions to bar publication of particular articles.[317]

In the lead opinion, two justices observed that, although prison officials retain "greater powers to censor than would be appropriate outside the prison walls, [they] do not have total or arbitrary power, but must exercise [their] authority even-handedly and with sensitivity to the values protected by the First Amendment and corresponding California constitutional and statutory provisions [i.e., California Penal Code Section 2600]."[318] They also concluded that, where the prison administration intends a publication to operate as an institutional publication for the expression of prisoners' ideas and views, the publication is a limited public forum.[319] Thus, the state as publisher did not enjoy the same control over the content of the prison newspaper as a private publisher.[320]

Moreover, the lead opinion emphasized that the fact that the state finances the publication does not justify complete control over the publication's contents.[321] Accordingly, the prison administration could not censor newspapers "merely because it disagrees with the views presented, objects to inmate criticism of administration policy, or seeks to avoid discussion of controversial issues."[322] Instead, the administration must show that the restriction is necessary to achieve, and narrowly tailored to serve, valid penological objectives[323] or to achieve institutional security and ensure public safety.[324]

In his brief concurrence, Justice Newman agreed with the lead opinion's public forum analysis and explained that he read the lead opinion "as holding that, except when necessary to provide for reasonable security or reasonable

---

[314] *Id.* at 913 (discussing and quoting trial court's decision in part).
[315] *Id.* at 914 (quoting trial court's decision).
[316] *Id.*
[317] 32 Cal. 3d at 922 (lead opinion by Broussard, J., joined by Reynoso, J.); *id.* at 923 (Newman, J., Bird, C.J., concurring in judgment). *Bailey* consists of five separate opinions: a lead opinion by Justice Broussard and joined by Justice Reynoso, two separate concurring opinions by Justice Newman and Chief Justice Bird, a dissenting opinion by Justice Richardson, joined by Justice Mosk, and a separate dissenting opinion by Justice Kaus.
[318] *Id.* at 922. Chief Justice Bird concurred. Justice Newman also concurred, but only with respect to the California Constitution. *See infra* notes 325–28 and accompanying text.
[319] 32 Cal. 3d at 916.
[320] *Id.* at 918–19 (citing Miami Herald Pub'g Co. v. Tornillo, 418 U.S. 241, 255 (1974)) (contention that "the state as publisher enjoys the same total control over the content of the newspaper as a private publisher . . . overlooks the critical distinction between a government as publisher and a private publisher").
[321] *Id.* at 918.
[322] 32 Cal. 3d at 920.
[323] The lead opinion observed that since one purpose of the publication is "vocational training," the government could "insist on standards of good journalism—that articles be grammatically correct, that reporters verify their stories, that editorial opinions be distinguished from factual reporting, etc." *Id.* at 920 n.9. Likewise, since another purpose is "to present information of importance to the inmate community," the government "can also insist that the newspaper report announcements and events of interest to its readers." *Id.*
[324] *Id.* at 915 (citing CAL. PENAL CODE §2600 (West 1982)). Chief Justice Bird concurred, as did Justice Newman (although he limited his concurrence to the California Constitution). *See infra* notes 325–28 and accompanying text.

public protection, the Department of Corrections may not concretize provisions [such as those in the regulations prohibiting criticism of the administration]."[325] Justice Newman based his concurrence solely on Article I, sections 2(a) and 3 of the California Constitution, however, and not on the First Amendment and California Penal Code Section 2600, as did the lead opinion.[326]

Chief Justice Bird also concurred with the lead opinion's public forum analysis and the judgment, but wrote separately to emphasize two points. First, she noted that while the "majority opinion" refrained from "formally striking down any particular existing regulation," it would not be acceptable for the Department of Corrections to reissue regulations substantially similar to those already presented to the Court.[327] Second, the regulations subsequently promulgated "must comport with the First Amendment principles applicable to state publications generally (except as provided by [California Penal Code Section 2600])."[328]

Three justices dissented, criticizing the lead opinion primarily because in their view the prison newspaper was *not* a limited public forum.[329] Two justices also felt that inmates have neither constitutional nor statutory rights to publish their articles in such a newspaper.[330]

Courts interpreting *Bailey* have characterized its holding as follows: "[T]he state may censor newspapers in order to provide for the reasonable security of the institution and the reasonable protection of the public. It may also exercise control over the content of the newspaper to serve valid penological objectives, but censorship may not go beyond that which is necessary to achieve a legitimate penological objective."[331]

§13.5(B)(ii) School-Sponsored Publications

At one time the Supreme Court gave broad protection to students' free expression rights.[332] More recently, however, the Court has curtailed those

---

[325]*Id.* at 923 (Newman, J., concurring).
[326]*Id.*
[327]32 Cal. 3d at 923 (Bird, C.J., concurring).
[328]*Id.*
[329]*Id.* at 923–25 (Richardson, J., dissenting; Mosk, J., concurring in dissent) ("the department's regulations make clear the [publication] was never intended as a marketplace for the free expression of ideas, but primarily as a 'house organ' to be edited and printed *'as part of the education and vocational training programs . . .'* of the institution") (emphasis added); *id.* at 928 (Kaus, J., dissenting) ("the majority starts from an erroneous premise: That in permitting a 'newspaper' to be published the current Department of Correction's regulations create a 'forum for expression of ideas' ").
[330]*Id.* at 923 (Richardson, J., dissenting; Mosk, J., concurring in dissent). "Accordingly, prison authorities should have *broad* discretion to select among, and edit or reject, those articles submitted for publication without later being required to justify their actions on institutional, social or penological grounds." *Id.* These dissenters also would not require the Department of Corrections "to formulate elaborate review procedures directed at second-guessing prison-officials' discretionary decisions on publication matters." *Id.*
[331]In re Williams, 159 Cal. App. 3d 600, 607, 205 Cal. Rptr. 903 (Cal. Ct. App. 1984) (court concluded that prison publication regulations conformed to *Bailey* standard for limited scope publication functioning as public forum); *see also* Diaz v. Watts, 189 Cal. App. 3d 657, 665, 234 Cal. Rptr. 334 (Cal. Ct. App. 1987) (court analyzed opinions in *Bailey* and concluded that "at least five [out of seven] justices interpret the constitutional and statutory law as permitting broad discretionary control and censorship of prison newspapers by prison authorities based on their perceived need for prison security, public safety, and valid penological purposes"; court also scrutinized majority and dissenting opinions in *In re Williams,* which also analyzed *Bailey* opinions). In *Diaz,* inmates challenged the constitutionality of a prison regulation that prohibited, in part, articles that "attack any individual or serve as a vehicle for individual inmate complaints, as a substitute for the departmental inmate appeal process." The court upheld the regulations as a reasonable attempt to enhance prisoner rehabilitation through training and education. 189 Cal. App. 3d at 341.
[332]Tinker v. Des Moines Indep. Community Sch. Dist., 393 U.S. 503 (1969).

rights and correspondingly expanded the rights of school administrators[333] to censor school-sponsored publications[334]—at least if the publications are in elementary or high schools.[335]

Access to student publications has typically been analyzed by employing the forum theory;[336] access has usually been denied.[337]

§13.5(B)(ii)(a) Editorial Control. From 1969 to the mid-1980s, the seminal U.S. Supreme Court decision involving school officials' editorial control over student expression in student publications was *Tinker v. Des Moines Community Independent School District.*[338] In *Tinker,* school officials punished junior and senior public high school students for wearing black arm bands to school to protest the Vietnam war.[339] The Court held that the school officials' punishment violated the students' First Amendment rights.

---

[333]*See, e.g.,* Bethel Sch. Dist. No. 403 v. Fraser, 478 U.S. 675, 685 (1986) (court held that school district acted within its permissible authority in imposing sanctions on student who engaged in "lewd and indecent" speech during school election assembly); Hazelwood Sch. Dist. v. Kuhlmeier, 484 U.S. 260, 14 Media L. Rep. 2081 (1988).

[334]"School-sponsored" media are those produced as part of a school's curriculum or that parents or others "might reasonably perceive to bear the imprimatur of the school." *Hazelwood,* 484 U.S. at 271 n.3. Courts often apply different standards to determine the appropriate degree of control, if any, that constitutionally may be exerted over non-school-sponsored media. *Id.* at 271 n.3, 273 n.5. *Compare* Burch v. Barker, 861 F.2d 1149 (9th Cir. 1988) (school district's policy requiring high school students to submit *any* student-written material—regardless of whether material is school-sponsored—for approval before distribution was overly broad, content-based prior restraint) *and* Romano v. Harrington, 725 F. Supp. 687 (E.D.N.Y. 1989) (recognizing that school officials may exercise greater control over materials written for class than over materials voluntarily submitted for publication in extracurricular student paper) *with* Bystrom v. Fridley High School, 822 F.2d 747, 14 Media L. Rep. 1517 (8th Cir. 1987), *on remand,* 686 F. Supp. 1387 (D. Minn. 1987), *aff'd without opinion,* 855 F.2d 855 (8th Cir. 1988) (district's policy governing distribution of non-school-sponsored written material on high school premises not unconstitutional even though policy provided for prior review and approval by school officials) *and* Eisner v. Stamford Bd. of Educ., 440 F.2d 803 (2d Cir. 1971) (court approved school regulation that allowed broad prior review and censorship of non-school-sponsored student publications).

[335]The *Hazelwood* Court stated in a footnote that it was not deciding whether the same degree of deference was appropriate with respect to school-sponsored expressive activity at the college and university level. 484 U.S. at 571 n.7; *see* DiBona v. Matthews, 220 Cal. App. 3d 1329, 1346–48, 269 Cal. Rptr. 882 (1990) (distinguishing *Hazelwood* in action against college administrators for canceling drama class in which controversial play was to be performed). Earlier decisions also limited the control that could be exercised over college and university publications. Nicholson v. Board of Educ., Torrance Unified Sch. Dist., 682 F.2d 858, 863 n.4 (9th Cir. 1982) (quoting Schwartz v. Schuker, 298 F. Supp. 238, 242 (E.D.N.Y. 1969)) ("Different considerations govern application of the first amendment on the college campus and at lower level educational institutions. The activities of high school students, for example, may be more stringently reviewed than the conduct of college students, as the former are 'in a much more adolescent and immature stage of life and less able to screen fact from propaganda.' "); *Bystrom,* 822 F.2d at 750 (citing Stanley v. McGrath, 719 F.2d 279 (8th Cir. 1983)) (limiting decision to secondary schools, court noted that "[f]ew college students are minors, and colleges are traditionally places of virtually unlimited free expression"); *Eisner,* 440 F.2d at 808 n.5 ("Because of such factors as the larger size of university campuses and the tendency of students to spend a greater portion of their time there, the inhibitive effect of a similar policy statement [restricting distribution of written material] might be greater on the campus of an institution of higher education than on the premises of a secondary school and the justifications for such a policy might be less compelling in view of the greater maturity of the students there."); Antonelli v. Hammond, 308 F. Supp. 1329, 1336 (D. Mass. 1970) ("The university setting of college-age students being exposed to a wide range of intellectual experiences creates a relatively mature marketplace for the interchange of ideas so that the free speech clause of the First Amendment with its underlying assumption that there is positive social value in an open forum seems particularly appropriate."); *see generally* Papish v. Board of Curators, 410 U.S. 667 (1973) (per curiam); *see also* Tenhoff, *Censoring the Public University Press: A Constitutional Challenge,* 64 S. CAL. L. REV. 511 (1991) (arguing for broad freedom for college students); Comment, *Student Editorial Discretion, the First Amendment, and Public Access to the Campus Press,* 16 U.C. DAVIS L. REV. 1089 (1983).

[336]For a discussion of the forum theory, *see supra* §13.5(A).
[337]*See infra* §13.5(B)(ii)(b).
[338]393 U.S. 503 (1969).
[339]*Id.* at 504.

Tinker is significant because, for the first time, the Court declared that students do not "shed their constitutional rights to freedom of speech or expression at the schoolhouse gate."[340] The Court cautioned that, while students' expressive rights are to be "applied in light of the special characteristics of the school environment,"[341] "state-operated schools may not be enclaves of totalitarianism" where students are "confined to the expression of those sentiments that are officially approved."[342] The Court announced what became known as the *Tinker* standard: a prohibition against student expression could not stand unless the school administrators showed that "engaging in that forbidden conduct would 'materially and substantially interfere with the requirements of appropriate discipline in the operation of the school' "[343] or "inva[de] the rights of others."[344]

Although *Tinker* expanded students' rights of expression and circumscribed school officials' authority to restrict that expression, it did not expressly address the degree of editorial control that constitutionally could be imposed on student publications. The lower federal courts struggled with the issue and rendered a wide range of decisions.[345] At one end of the spectrum, the Seventh Circuit held that administrative censorship is a prior restraint and is per se unconstitutional.[346] Other courts took a less restrictive view but held that school officials could not exercise unfettered editorial control over school publications simply because the publication was funded or sponsored by the school.[347]

---

[340]*Id.* at 506.

[341]*Id.*

[342]*Id.* at 511.

[343]393 U.S. at 509 (quoting Burnside v. Byars, 363 F.2d 744, 749 (5th Cir. 1966)). The *Tinker* Court warned that the "undifferentiated fear or apprehension of disturbance is not enough to overcome the right to freedom of expression." *Id.* at 508.

[344]*Id.* at 513 ("conduct by the student, in class or out of it, which for any reason—whether it stems from time, place, or type of behavior—materially disrupts classwork or involves substantial disorder or invasion of the rights of others is, of course, not immunized by the constitutional guarantee of freedom of speech"). For a discussion of this criterion, *see, e.g.,* Note, *Administrative Regulation of the High School Press,* 83 MICH. L. REV. 625, 639–44 (1984).

[345]*See* Annot., *Validity Under Federal Constitution of Public School or State College Regulation of Student Newspapers, Magazines or Other Publications—Federal Cases,* 16 A.L.R. FED. 182 (1973 & 1990 Supps.); L.E. INGLEHART, PRESS LAW & PRESS FREEDOM FOR HIGH SCHOOL PUBLICATIONS (1986).

[346]Fujishima v. Board of Educ., 460 F.2d 1355 (7th Cir. 1972). In *Fujishima,* high school students challenged the constitutionality of a rule that, among other things, required students to submit all publications to the school superintendent for approval before distribution. The plaintiff students were disciplined for violating the rule by distributing their "underground" (i.e., non-school-sponsored) newspaper on campus. The Seventh Circuit held that "because [the rule] requires prior approval of publications, it is an unconstitutional prior restraint in violation of the First Amendment." *Id.* at 1357 (citing Near v. Minnesota, 283 U.S. 697 (1931); Tinker v. Des Moines Indep. Community Sch. Dist., 393 U.S. 503 (1969)). The Seventh Circuit reasoned that the *Tinker* standard "is properly a formula for determining when the requirements of school discipline justify *punishment* of students for exercise of their First-Amendment rights. It is not a basis for establishing a system of censorship and licensing designed to prevent the exercise of First Amendment rights." *Fujishima,* 460 F.2d at 1358.

[347]In the secondary school context, *see, e.g.,* Nicholson v. Board of Educ., Torrance Unified Sch. Dist., 682 F.2d 858 (9th Cir. 1982); Schiff v. Williams, 519 F.2d 257 (5th Cir. 1975); Reinecke v. Cobb County Sch. Dist., 484 F. Supp. 1252 (N.D. Ga. 1980); Gambino v. Fairfax County Sch. Bd., 429 F. Supp. 731 (E.D. Va.), *aff'd,* 564 F.2d 157 (4th Cir. 1977); Bayer v. Kinzler, 383 F. Supp. 1164 (E.D.N.Y. 1974), *aff'd,* 515 F.2d 504 (2d Cir. 1975); Koppell v. Levine, 347 F. Supp. 456 (E.D.N.Y. 1972); Korn v. Elkins, 317 F. Supp. 138 (D. Md. 1970); Zucker v. Panitz, 299 F. Supp. 613 (M.D. Ala. 1967), *dismissed as moot,* 402 F.2d 515 (5th Cir. 1968). *See generally* Note, *supra* note 344, at 625. In the college and university context, *see, e.g.,* Bazaar v. Fortune, 476 F.2d 570, *modified,* 489 F.2d 225 (5th Cir. 1973), *cert. denied,* 416 U.S. 995 (1974); Joyner v. Whiting, 477 F.2d 456 (4th Cir. 1973); Antonelli v. Hammond, 308 F. Supp. 1329, 1337 (D. Mass. 1970) ("The state is not necessarily the unrestricted master of what it creates and fosters. Thus, in cases concerning school supported publications or the use of school facilities, the courts have refused to recognize as permissible any regulations infringing free speech when not shown to be necessarily related to the maintenance of order and discipline within the educational process."); Lee v. Board of Regents, 306 F. Supp. 1097 (W.D. Wis. 1969), *aff'd,* 441 F.2d 1257 (7th Cir. 1971).

The Supreme Court finally addressed the issue in *Hazelwood School District v. Kuhlmeier*,[348] which arose when a public high school principal deleted two pages from a school-sponsored student newspaper that contained two "questionable" articles—one about pregnancy and the other about the impact of divorce on students.[349] The student editors brought suit for violation of their First Amendment rights.[350]

In analyzing the conflict between the school officials' exercise of editorial control and the students' First Amendment rights, the Court took note of the special characteristics of the school environment and of the concomitant limitations on students' rights in that environment.[351] With those limitations in mind, a five-justice majority rejected the Eighth Circuit Court of Appeals' holding that the student publication was a limited public forum for student expression, since "school officials did not evince either 'by policy or by practice' any intent to open the pages of [the newspaper] to 'indiscriminate use' by its student reporters and editors, or by the student body generally."[352] The Court determined instead that the school officials " 'reserve[d] the forum for its intended purpose[s],' as a supervised learning experience for journalism students."[353] Accordingly, the Court concluded that the newspaper was a nonpublic forum and that school officials were therefore entitled to regulate the contents of the newspaper in "any reasonable manner."[354]

After distinguishing *Tinker*, the Court announced that "educators do not offend the First Amendment by exercising control over the style and content of student speech in school sponsored expressive activities so long as their actions are *reasonably related to legitimate pedagogical concerns.*"[355] "It is

---

[348]484 U.S. 260, 14 Media L. Rep. 2081 (1988). The decision has received extensive scholarly treatment. *See, e.g.,* Abrams & Goodman, *End of an Era? The Decline of Student Press Rights in the Wake of Hazelwood School District v. Kuhlmeier,* 1988 DUKE L.J. 706 (1988); Buss, *School Newspapers, Public Forum, and the First Amendment,* 74 IOWA L. REV. 505 (1989); Hafen, *Hazelwood School District and the Role of First Amendment Institutions,* 1988 DUKE L.J. 685 (1988); Comment, *High School Newspapers and the Public Forum Doctrine: Hazelwood School District v. Kuhlmeier,* 74 VA. L. REV. 843 (1988); Note, *Hazelwood School District v. Kuhlmeier: Prior Restraint Doctrine Finds a Home in America's Public Schools,* 20 PAC. L.J. 395 (1989); Note, *A Lesson in School Censorship: Hazelwood v. Kuhlmeier,* 55 BROOK. L. REV. 291 (1989); Note, *The School as Publisher: Hazelwood School District v. Kuhlmeier,* 67 N.C. L. REV. 503 (1989).

[349]484 U.S. at 263.

[350]*Id.* at 264.

[351]A school "need not tolerate student speech that is inconsistent with its 'basic educational mission,' even though the government could not censor similar speech outside the school." *Id.* at 266 (quoting Bethel Sch. Dist. No. 403 v. Fraser, 478 U.S. 675, 685 (1986)). Furthermore, a school is "entitled to 'disassociate itself' from . . . speech . . . 'wholly inconsistent with the "fundamental values" of public school education.' " *Id.* (quoting Bethel Sch. Dist. No. 403 v. Fraser, 478 U.S. 675, 685–86 (1986)). *See also* Bethel Sch. Dist. No. 403 v. Fraser, 478 U.S. 675 (1986) (objectives of public education include "inculcation of fundamental values necessary to the maintenance of a democratic political system"); Board of Educ., Island Trees Union Free Sch. Dist. No. 26 v. Pico, 457 U.S. 853, 864 (1982) (opinion of Brennan, J., joined by Marshall & Stevens, JJ., announcing judgment of Court) (public schools have "legitimate and substantial community interest in promoting respect for authority and traditional values be they social, moral, or political").

[352]484 U.S. at 270 (quoting Perry Educ. Ass'n v. Perry Local Educators' Ass'n, 460 U.S. 37, 46–47 (1983)) (citations omitted). The Court looked to numerous factors in determining that the school did not intend for the paper to be a public forum: the newspaper was published as part of the school's journalism course; the newspaper's purpose was to impart journalistic skills to students; a faculty member taught the journalism course during school hours; the students received grades and academic credits; the school did not deviate in practice from its policy of publishing the newspaper as part of the course; and school officials reserved the authority to and did exercise editorial control over the paper. 484 U.S. at 268–70.

[353]*Id.* at 270 (quoting Perry Educ. Ass'n v. Perry Local Educators' Ass'n, 460 U.S. 37, 46 (1983)) (citations omitted).

[354]*Id.* (citing Perry Educ. Ass'n v. Perry Local Educators' Ass'n, 460 U.S. 37, 46–47 (1983)).

[355]*Id.* at 273 (emphasis added). In distinguishing *Tinker*, the Court held that the *Tinker* standard applied only to student expression that was "personal" and that "happen[ed] to occur on the school premises." *Id.* at

only when the decision to censor a school sponsored publication ... has no valid educational purpose that the First Amendment is so 'directly and sharply implicate[d]' as to require judicial intervention to protect constitutional rights."[356]

The *Hazelwood* Court did not determine outright that a student publication is not per se a limited public forum. Instead, in its fact-bound decision, the Court simply found that the Hazelwood school officials did not evince by their stated policy or practice "any intent to open the newspaper to 'indiscriminate use' by its student reporters and editors, or by the student body generally."[357] The Court also found that since the officials had reserved the forum for its intended purpose, as a supervised learning experience for journalism students, they were entitled to regulate the contents of the newspaper—a nonpublic forum—in any reasonable manner.[358]

While it appears at first blush that *Hazelwood* gives elementary and secondary school officials almost unlimited control over school-sponsored media, if future student plaintiffs can show that a school intended by "policy or practice" to open a school-sponsored publication to use by student reporters and editors or the student body generally, then the more constitutionally stringent standard for limited public forums should be applied.[359]

As in the prison context, the boundaries of school officials' editorial control may be further circumscribed by state constitutions or statutes. Students in California's public schools, for example, have such rights.[360] Finding that

---

271. In his dissenting opinion, Justice Brennan (joined by Justices Marshall and Blackmun) criticized the majority's departure from the *Tinker* standard and rejected their

> obscure tangle of three excuses to afford educators "greater control" over school-sponsored speech than the *Tinker* test would permit: the public educator's prerogative to control curriculum; the pedagogical interest in shielding the high school audience from objectionable viewpoints and sensitive topics; and the school's need to dissociate itself from student expression.

Id. at 282–83 (Brennan, J., dissenting). Justice Brennan felt that "[n]one of the excuses, once disentangled, supports the distinction the Court draws. *Tinker* fully addresses the first concern; the second is illegitimate; and the third is readily achievable through less oppressive means." *Id.* at 283 (Brennan, J., dissenting).

[356]*Id.* at 273 (quoting Epperson v. Arkansas, 393 U.S. 97, 104 (1968)) (footnote omitted). The *Hazelwood* Court explained at length the reasonable restrictions a school may impose on school-sponsored speech:

> Educators are entitled to exercise greater control over ... student expression to assure that participants learn whatever lessons the activity is designed to teach, that readers or listeners are not exposed to material that may be inappropriate for their level of maturity, and that the views of the individual speaker are not erroneously attributed to the school. ... In addition, a school must be able to take into account the emotional maturity of the intended audience in determining whether to disseminate student speech on potentially sensitive topics, which might range from the existence of Santa Claus in an elementary school setting to the particulars of teenage sexual activity in a high school setting. The school must retain the authority to refuse to associate the school with any position other than neutrality on matters of public controversy.

Id. at 271–72.

[357]484 U.S. at 270.

[358]*Id.*

[359]*See, e.g.,* Leuth v. St. Clair County Community College, 732 F. Supp. 1410, 1414–15 (E.D. Mich. 1990) (in action by former editor of college newspaper against college for omission of advertisement for Canadian drinking and nude dancing, district court distinguished *Hazelwood,* holding college newspaper was public forum for student expression); Rivera v. East Otero Sch. Dist. R-1, 721 F. Supp. 1189 (D. Colo. 1989) (overturning high school's content-based restriction on free nonstudent newspaper as prior restraint; rejecting argument that no fundamental right involved because school not public forum). *But see* Paye v. Gibraltar Sch. Dist., No. 90CV70444DT, 1991 U.S. Dist. LEXIS 16480 (E.D. Mich. 1991) (school district's prepublication review policy and confiscation of school publication did not violate supervising teachers' First Amendment rights because publication not intended to be limited public forum and administrators' actions reasonably related to pedagogical concerns).

[360]For a discussion of the development of student press rights in California, *see* Comment, *Prior Restraint and the Public High School Student Press: The Validity of Administrative Censorship of Student Newspapers Under the Federal and California Constitutions,* 20 Loy. L.A. L. Rev. 1055 (1987). *See also* 7 B. Witkin, Summary of California Law, Constitutional Law §§368–69 (9th ed. 1988).

the California Constitution[361] and the California Education Code[362] provide broader protection to students' free speech and press rights than the First Amendment, the California Court of Appeal, in *Leeb v. DeLong*,[363] ruled that school officials' discretion in censoring student publications was not subject to the mere reasonableness test established by *Hazelwood*.[364] Instead, the court followed *Bailey v. Loggins*[365] and found that the school-sponsored student newspaper, like the prison publication, was a limited public forum.[366] Accordingly, the court held that California school officials' ability to regulate expression is greatly reduced: they may restrict access to the forum only if the expression is inconsistent with the purpose for which it was created.[367]

§13.5(B)(ii)(b) Access. Although *Hazelwood* focused on school officials' editorial control over student expression, in essence the access rights of the *students* to the school-sponsored publication, the decision is instructive in determining the access rights of *nonstudents* to school-sponsored publications.

In *Planned Parenthood of Southern Nevada v. Clark County School District*,[368] for example, the Ninth Circuit followed *Hazelwood* in evaluating Planned Parenthood's challenge to the rejection of its advertisements for publication in the defendant school district's high school newspapers, yearbooks, and athletic event programs.[369] Using the *Hazelwood* forum analysis, the court determined that all three publications constituted nonpublic rather than limited public forums.[370] With respect to the newspapers and yearbooks, the court noted that the district's policy vested school principals with broad authority to control the publications' content, and that students produced both publications as part of the school curriculum.[371] Similarly, although the athletic programs were not published as part of the course curriculum, they too constituted nonpublic forums because the district's policy vested the principals with broad editorial

---

[361] Article I, Section 1(a) of the California Constitution guarantees that "[e]very person may freely speak, write and publish his or her sentiments on all subjects, being responsible for the abuse of this right. A law may not restrain or abridge liberty of speech or press."

[362] CAL. EDUC. CODE §48907 (West Supp. 1992).

[363] 198 Cal. App. 3d 47, 243 Cal. Rptr. 494 (Cal. Ct. App. 1988).

[364] *Id.* at 53–54.

[365] 32 Cal. 3d 912, 654 P.2d 758 (Cal. 1982). *See supra* notes 312–31 and accompanying text.

[366] 198 Cal. App. 3d at 56.

[367] *Id.* The court prohibited censorship of a student article unless there is a clear chance someone will prevail in a libel action. *Id.* at 62. *Compare Leeb with* Perumal v. Saddleback Valley Unified Sch. Dist., 243 Cal. Rptr. 545 (Cal. Ct. App.), *cert. denied*, 488 U.S. 933 (1988) (same panel that decided *Leeb* held that as long as school district maintained closed forum policy, it need not constitutionally recognize religious groups—such as plaintiffs'—as school-sponsored clubs; regulation that prohibited non-school-sponsored clubs from handing out flyers or advertising in yearbook constitutionally permissible).

[368] 941 F.2d 817 (9th Cir. 1991) (en banc).

[369] The court found that *Hazelwood* vitiated the precedential value of an earlier Ninth Circuit decision in which the court held that the student publication was a limited public forum. 941 F.2d at 827–28 (discussing San Diego Comm. Against Registration & Draft (CARD) v. Governing Bd., 790 F.2d 1471 (9th Cir. 1976)). In *San Diego CARD*, the school board rejected an anti-draft advertisement for student newspapers even though it accepted military recruitment ads. Finding that the newspapers were limited public forums, the court held that the board could not "allow presentation of one side of an issue, but prohibit the presentation of the other side." *San Diego CARD*, 790 F.2d at 1478. Hence, the court ruled that the board violated the First Amendment when it denied CARD access to the student papers. *Id.* The *Planned Parenthood* court did not, however, disturb the *CARD* court's alternative holding that, "assuming the school publications were nonpublic forums, the school engaged in impermissible viewpoint discrimination in accepting advertisements advocating military service but refusing CARD's advertisement offering an opposing point of view." 941 F.2d at 828 n.19 (citing San Diego Comm. Against Registration & Draft (CARD) v. Governing Bd., 790 F.2d 1471, 1481 (9th Cir. 1976)). *See also* Lee v. Board of Regents, 306 F. Supp. 1097 (W.D. Wis. 1969), *aff'd*, 441 F.2d 1257 (7th Cir. 1971) (court granted access to student newspaper by university employee's union that sought to place advertisement that discussed race relations and Vietnam).

[370] 941 F.2d at 823–29.

[371] *Id.* at 820–21, 823–29.

control over their content, and the programs played a role in the high schools' educational mission.[372]

The court held that the school district did not violate the First Amendment by rejecting Planned Parenthood's advertisements, because such advertisements would be controversial and would distract from the schools' educational mission.[373] Applying the nonpublic forum reasonableness standard, the Ninth Circuit held that the district's actions were reasonable and that it did not engage in viewpoint discrimination.[374]

Pre-*Hazelwood* courts also denied access to school-sponsored publications by nonstudents, focusing on the incompatibility of the exercise of editorial discretion with mandated access.[375]

§13.5(C) The Government As Broadcaster

In general, courts will not grant any more access to public broadcasting stations than they will to private commercial broadcasting stations.[376] The

---

[372] *Id.*
[373] *Id.* at 829–30.
[374] *Id.* Four judges (Norris, Hug, Pregerson, and Poole) dissented in a lengthy opinion authored by Judge Norris that attacked the majority's interpretation of the public forum analysis and *Hazelwood* and their application to the defendants' publications. The dissenters felt that the defendant school district had created a limited public forum for advertising in its publications because, in the past, the district had "sold space to every advertiser that came along," including those advertising casinos, bars, churches, political candidates, and the U.S. Army. *Id.* at 830 (Norris, J., dissenting). According to the dissenters, the majority disregarded the traditional public forum test, which "focuses on the degree to which government facilities are opened to the public," and instead announced a test by which the nature of the forum is determined "*solely* on the basis of whether government declares its intent to control content." *Id.* at 836 (Norris, J., dissenting). Thus, under the majority's test, "*so long as officials reserve for themselves broad discretion to control content, then they will be deemed to have 'intended' to create a nonpublic forum,* and their content-based exclusions will escape strict scrutiny." *Id.* (Norris, J., dissenting). "This test establishes as the law of our circuit a standard that is heresy in First Amendment jurisprudence." *Id.* (Norris, J., dissenting).

Finding that the publications were limited public forums, the dissenters concluded that the district's rejection of the Planned Parenthood advertisement must survive strict scrutiny to pass constitutional muster. Since the district's admitted "refusal to publish Planned Parenthood's ad was rooted in a desire to avoid controversy," it did not constitute a compelling state interest, because " 'avoidance of controversy is not a valid ground for restricting speech in a public forum.' " *Id.* at 831, 842 (Norris, J., dissenting) (quoting Cornelius v. NAACP Legal Defense & Educ. Fund, 473 U.S. 788, 811 (1985)). Moreover, the dissenters pointed out that the school administrators admitted that they had no legitimate basis for believing that the advertisement would have disrupted the educational programs. *Id.* (Norris, J., dissenting). Accordingly, the dissenters would have reversed and granted access to Planned Parenthood. *See also Recent Cases: First Amendment-Freedom of Speech—School District May Exclude Advertisement from School Newspapers (Planned Parenthood of Southern Nevada, Inc. v. Clark County School District, 9th Cir. 1991)*, 105 HARV. L. REV. 597 (1991) (criticizing majority's decision).

[375] *See, e.g.,* Mississippi Gay Alliance v. Goudelock, 536 F.2d 1073 (5th Cir. 1976), *cert. denied,* 430 U.S. 982 (1977). In *Goudelock,* an off-campus homosexual organization sought to place an advertisement in the state university newspaper that offered counseling, legal aid, and library use to students. Citing Miami Herald Publishing Co. v. Tornillo, 418 U.S. 241 (1974), the court upheld the editor's decision to deny access, ruling that the editor "had a right to take the position that the newspaper would not be involved . . . with off-campus homosexually-related activity." *Id.* at 1075–76. The dissent rejected the notion that the advertisements solicited criminal activity and described the case as a difficult question of competing First Amendment interests: the organization's right of access versus the editor's right of control. *Id.* at 1087. The dissent argued that *Tornillo* applied to private newspapers, not papers funded by student fees at public universities. Such funding raised a question of whether the editor's actions constituted state action. If there was state action, the dissent argued that the paper would be a public forum, and no person or group could be discriminated against based on the content of their message. *Id.* at 1080–81. *See also* Avins v. Rutgers State Univ. of N.J., 385 F.2d 151, 153 (3d Cir. 1967) (court held that law professor did not have right of access to university's law review because public access was incompatible with exercise of editorial discretion); Sinn v. Daily Nebraskan, 638 F. Supp. 143, 12 Media L. Rep. 2340 (D. Neb. 1986), *aff'd,* 829 F.2d 662 (8th Cir. 1987) (student newspaper's refusal to publish roommate advertisements containing description of sexual orientation of person placing ad not state action and was "constitutionally protected editorial decision not diminished by state financial support of the newspaper").

[376] For a general discussion of the federal regulation of public broadcasting under the Federal Communications Act of 1934 and the Public Broadcasting Act of 1967, *see* Comment, *First Amendment Claims Against Public Broadcasters: Testing the Public's Right to a Balanced Presentation,* 1989 DUKE L.J. 1386, 1386–99

most extensive discussion of this access issue arose out of the refusal of two public television stations to air the controversial program "Death of a Princess," which dramatized the public execution in 1977 of a Saudi Arabian princess and her lover for committing adultery.[377] The film sparked protests from the Saudi government when it was aired in London and created anxiety among Americans who feared for the safety of American citizens in Saudi Arabia if the film was shown in the United States.[378]

In *Muir II*,[379] a plurality of the Fifth Circuit held that viewers did not have a right to compel the stations to air "Death of a Princess" and refused to accept the argument that government-funded public broadcasters lost their editorial discretion.[380] Instead, the plurality found that the government, like other speakers, could participate in the "marketplace of ideas."[381] The plurality recognized that the broadcast media are subject to more control than the print media and discussed the historical "scarcity" rationale; the plurality stated, however, that the permissible degree of government regulation was the same whether the broadcaster was private or public.[382] The plurality dismissed the

---

(1989). *See generally* Annot., *Construction and Application of Public Broadcasting Act of 1967 As Amended (47 USCS §§396 et seq.) With Respect to Controlling Content of Public Television Programs*, 44 A.L.R. FED. 350 (1977 & 1991 Supp.); Annot., *State Regulation of Content of and Representation on Program Presented by "Public Broadcasting" Television or Radio Station*, 27 A.L.R.4th 375 (1984 & 1991 Supp.).

[377]In Muir v. Alabama Educational Television Commission (Muir I), 656 F.2d 1012 (5th Cir. 1981), the district court, in an unpublished decision, had denied injunctive relief and held that the station's viewers had no First Amendment right of access to public television. *Id.* at 1015. A panel of the Fifth Circuit affirmed, stating that "the naked fact of government ownership . . . is insufficient in itself to require denial of editorial freedom in this case to public broadcasters." *Id.* at 1019. The court held that public broadcast outlets are not public forums and explained that "[u]nlike public parks, bus terminals, airports, public libraries, shopping centers, and municipal auditoriums, public broadcast stations do not function and have not functioned as public access places." *Id.* at 1020, 1022. In Barnstone v. University of Houston, 514 F. Supp. 670 (S.D. Tex. 1980), *rev'd*, 660 F.2d 137 (5th Cir. 1981), the district court held that the First Amendment was designed to protect the people from government, not government from the people; therefore, the First Amendment's protection extended not to the station's editorial decisions but to "the right of viewers to be free of governmental control over the content of the programs presented to them." 514 F. Supp. at 688. The district court concluded that a government-owned and operated television station was a public forum that was required to cover significant political and social issues. *Id.* at 688–89. Bound by *Muir I*, another panel of the Fifth Circuit reversed this ruling. 660 F.2d at 137. The Court of Appeals then directed that both cases be consolidated and reheard en banc. Muir v. Alabama Educ. Television Comm'n/Barnstone v. University of Houston, 662 F.2d 1110 (5th Cir. 1981). Thus, in Muir v. Alabama Educational Television Commission (Muir II), 688 F.2d 1033 (5th Cir. 1982) (en banc), *cert. denied*, 460 U.S. 1023 (1983), the Fifth Circuit considered the consolidated appeals from *Muir I* and *Barnstone*.

[378]*See* Comment, *The Death of a Princess Cases: Television Programming by State-Owned Public Broadcasters and Viewers' First Amendment Rights*, 36 U. MIAMI L. REV. 779 (1982). The Fifth Circuit noted that other reasons also may have prompted the cancellation decision, such as a concern that the program was "in bad taste" and not balanced in a "responsible manner"; that audiences might believe the "docu-drama" was a true documentary; and that fund-raising activities for the University of Houston might be negatively affected. *Muir II*, 688 F.2d at 1037 n.5 (discussing University of Houston's reasons for canceling program).

[379]688 F.2d 1033.

[380]688 F.2d at 1040–41. *Muir II* was an en banc decision by 23 judges. The lead opinion was adopted by a total of 11 judges (one of whom wrote separately but concurred in the opinion). Two other judges authored concurrences, one of which was joined by three judges. Seven judges dissented.

[381]*Muir II*, 688 F.2d at 1038.

[382]*Id.* at 1039–40 ("[p]ublic television licensees are generally subjected to the same regulatory requirements as their commercial counterparts"; "the FCC, in its demand for unfettered licensee control over programming has made no distinction between private and public licensees"). The Fifth Circuit plurality determined that "[t]he picture which emerges from the regulatory scheme adopted by Congress is one which clearly shows broadcast licensees endowed with the privilege and responsibility of exercising free programming control of their broadcasts, yet also charged with the obligation of making programming decisions which protect the legitimate interests of the public." *Id.* The plurality further explained that "[t]he right to the free exercise of programming discretion is, for private licensees, not only statutorily conferred but also constitutionally protected." However, the lack of constitutional protection for public licensees "implies only that government could possibly impose restrictions on those licensees which it could not impose on private licensees." *Id.*

viewers' argument that the public had greater access rights to government-controlled media because the First Amendment did not protect the government, finding instead that "the lack of First Amendment protection does not result in the lessening of any of the statutory rights and duties held by the public licensees [nor] does [it] result in individual viewers gaining any greater right to influence the programming discretion of the public licensees."[383]

Finally, the plurality rejected the contention that a public television station is a public forum, reasoning that "Congress did not deem it necessary for viewers to be accorded a right of access to television broadcast stations in order for the public's First Amendment interests in this medium to be fully realized."[384] To the contrary, "Congress concluded that the First Amendment rights of public television viewers are adequately protected under a system where the broadcast licensee has sole programming discretion but is under an obligation to serve the public interest."[385]

The plaintiffs argued that they did not seek to create a public right of access to public television stations; instead, they contended that, even without a public right of access, the stations are public forums and thus could not make programming decisions based on the impact of the program.[386]

The plurality found this argument untenable, declaring that "[i]t is the right of public access which is the essential characteristic of a public forum and the basis which allows a speaker to challenge the state's regulation of the forum."[387] The plurality concluded that "[t]he gravamen of a speaker's public forum complaint is the invalid and discriminatory denial of his right of access to the forum. If a speaker does not have a right of access to a facility, that facility by definition is not a 'public forum' and the speaker is without grounds for challenge under the public forum doctrine."[388] The plurality also emphasized that the public television stations' decisions to cancel "Death of a Princess" were editorial by nature and could not properly be characterized as "censorship."[389]

---

[383] *Id.* at 1041.
[384] *Id.*
[385] *Id.*
[386] 688 F.2d at 1042–43.
[387] *Id.* at 1043.
[388] *Id.* (footnote omitted). The plurality observed that "[t]he pattern of usual activity for public television stations is the statutorily mandated practice of the broadcast licensee exercising sole programming authority," and "[t]he general invitation extended to the public is not to schedule programs, but to watch or decline to watch what is offered." *Id.* at 1041–42 (citing, inter alia, Columbia Broadcasting Sys. v. Democratic Nat'l Comm., 412 U.S. 94 (1973)) (noting that just because government facility specifically used for communication of information, it is not ipso facto a public forum; no public right of access to public broadcasting television station).
[389] *Id.* at 1045–47. The plurality noted that the public television stations did not forbid or curtail the right of any person to show or view the film. Instead, the state officials in charge of the stations "have simply exercised their statutorily mandated discretion and decided not to show a particular program at a particular time." *Id.* at 1047. "There is a clear distinction between a state's exercise of editorial discretion *over its own expression,* and a state's prohibition or suppression of the speech of another." *Id.* (footnote omitted, emphasis added). Seven judges dissented in *Muir II.* Judge Johnson, whose dissenting opinion was joined by four judges, stated that any decision by a public broadcaster not to show a program based on content was "presumptively unconstitutional." *Id.* at 1059. Two others, Judges Kravitch and Reavley, also expressed concern about public broadcasters making programming decisions based solely on "substantive content." *Id.* at 1053, 1060. These concerns find a voice in the recent public forum decisions holding that pure viewpoint-based discrimination is not allowed, even in nonpublic forums such as military bases or jails. Perry Educ. Ass'n v. Perry Local Educator's Ass'n, 460 U.S. 37, 46 (1983). For a discussion of the forum theory, *see supra* §13.5(A).

In a special concurrence to the plurality opinion—which is now considered to be the holding of *Muir II*—Judge Rubin disagreed with the plurality's application of the traditional public forum analysis to the public television station broadcasts and stated that "[t]he function [or mission] of a state agency operating an informational medium is significant in determining first amendment restrictions on its actions."[390] Examining the television stations in this light, Judge Rubin concluded that, while they "are operated by state agencies, neither station is designed to function as a marketplace of ideas, a medium open to all who have a message, whatever its nature."[391] Thus, "the state may regulate content in order to prevent hampering the primary function of the activity."[392] In Judge Rubin's view, judicial intervention is inappropriate unless the public licensee "adopt[s] or follow[s] *policies or practices* that transgress constitutional rights."[393] Accordingly, Judge Rubin agreed with the plurality that judicial intervention was neither required nor warranted for that *single* programming decision.[394]

As with their precursors,[395] *Muir II*'s progeny support the proposition that government funding does not enhance access rights to public broadcast outlets.[396]

---

[390] 688 F.2d at 1050 (Rubin, J., concurring). In Schneider v. Indian River Community College Found., 875 F.2d 1537 (11th Cir. 1989), the court regarded Judge Rubin's special concurrence as the holding of the *Muir II* court "[u]nder the principle that, absent a majority, the narrowest concurring opinion is the holding of the case." *Id.* at 1541 (citing Marks v. United States, 430 U.S. 188, 193 (1977)). *Accord* Chandler v. Georgia Pub. Telecommunications Comm'n, 917 F.2d 486, 488 & n.3, 18 Media L. Rep. 1314 (11th Cir. 1990), *cert. denied*, 112 S. Ct. 71 (1991).

[391] 688 F.2d at 1052 (Rubin, J., concurring). Judge Rubin relied on the various opinions in Board of Education, Island Trees Union Free School District No. 26 v. Pico, 457 U.S. 853 (1982), for the proposition that "the nature of the activity determines the strictures the first amendment places on governmental action." 688 F.2d at 1052 (Rubin, J., concurring).

[392] 688 F.2d at 1050 (Rubin, J., concurring).

[393] *Id.* (Rubin, J., concurring) (emphasis added).

[394] *Id.* at 1053 (Rubin, J., concurring).

[395] Several pre-*Muir* decisions also support the proposition that government funding does not enhance access rights to public broadcast outlets. *See, e.g.*, Gottfried v. Federal Communications Comm'n, 655 F.2d 297, 311–12 n.54 (D.C. Cir. 1981) (appellant sought revocation of several television stations' licenses for their failure to provide captioned programming to hearing impaired; court held that neither First Amendment nor Rehabilitation Act mandated unlimited access to broadcast outlets, stating that it could not accept position that First Amendment "requires all stations to make their programming accessible to all deaf persons all of the time"), *rev'd in part on other grounds*, 459 U.S. 498, 510–12, 9 Media L. Rep. 1185 (1983) (Supreme Court reversed part of appellate court's holding that stricter "public interest" license renewal standard should be applied to public licensee covered by §504 of Rehabilitation Act than to commercial licensee not covered by §504; FCC not required to evaluate public station's service to handicapped community by more stringent standard than that applicable to commercial stations); Community Serv. Broadcasting of Mid-Am. v. Federal Communications Comm'n, 593 F.2d 1102, 1104 (D.C. Cir. 1978) (en banc) (several government-funded educational broadcast stations challenged constitutionality of federal statute requiring such stations to make audio recordings of all broadcasts discussing issues of "public importance"; court found statute unconstitutional, holding that government had no more right to control content of noncommercial broadcasts than it did to interfere with commercial stations' programming decisions); Accuracy in Media v. Federal Communications Comm'n, 521 F.2d 288, 297, 4 Media L. Rep. 1257 (D.C. Cir. 1975) (Corporation for Public Broadcasting not required to provide programs with "strict adherence to objectivity and balance" but only to facilitate full development of programming toward that goal); State v. University of Me., 266 A.2d 863, 868–69 (Me. 1970) (state's police power and resulting right to control program offerings on state university's educational television system not enlarged by public funding of that system). *See generally* Canby, *The First Amendment and the State as Editor*, 52 Tex. L. Rev. 1123 (1974); Notes, *Editorial Discretion of State Public Broadcasting Licensees*, 82 Colum. L. Rev. 1161 (1982).

[396] *See, e.g.*, Chandler v. Georgia Pub. Telecommunications Comm'n, 917 F.2d 486, 488, 18 Media L. Rep. 1314 (11th Cir. 1990), *cert. denied*, 112 S. Ct. 71 (1991); Schneider v. Indian River Community College Found., 875 F.2d 1537, 1540–42 (11th Cir. 1989) (adopting Judge Rubin's analysis and holding that public college trustees' control of news programming content at college radio station did not curtail station employees' First Amendment rights because "station was not operated as a 'public access' broadcaster inviting the public to present programs and views over its facilities"); *see also* Comment, *First Amendment Claims Against Public Broadcasters: Testing the Public's Right to a Balanced Presentation*, 1989 Duke L.J. 1386

Courts have also given public broadcasters the same discretion as private stations in their coverage of political campaigns.[397] Similarly, a city may construct and operate a competing cable system without infringing on the First Amendment rights of the existing cable franchisee.[398]

§13.5(D) Other Government-Related Media

Questions of access to government-related media have arisen in a variety of contexts other than broadcast outlets and newspapers. Courts have also considered access issues with respect to other government-sponsored publications, such as state bar association journals and newsletters,[399] legislative services,[400] voter pamphlets,[401] and a city directory of public and private services and organizations.[402]

Courts have also addressed the rights of access to even less traditional government-related "media." In *Pacific Gas and Electric Co. v. Public Utilities Commission of California*,[403] for example, a California Public Utility

---

(1989). *See generally* Greater L.A. Council on Deafness v. Community Television of So. Cal., 719 F.2d 1017, 1024 (9th Cir. 1983) (First and Fifth Amendments do not impose on federal agencies that fund television programming constitutional duty of affirmative action to make television accessible to hearing impaired), *cert. denied sub nom.* Gottfried v. United States, 467 U.S. 1252 (1984).

[397]*See, e.g., Chandler,* 917 F.2d at 488 (court held that content-based decision not to include Libertarian candidate in debates on public television station between Democratic and Republican candidates for state lieutenant governor not viewpoint-restrictive and did not violate First Amendment—decision was "reasonable" and was " 'not an effort to suppress expression merely because public officials oppose the speaker's views' " (quoting Cornelius v. NAACP Legal Defense & Educ. Fund, 473 U.S. 788, 800 (1985))); DeYoung v. Patten, 898 F.2d 628, 633, 17 Media L. Rep. 2446 (8th Cir. 1990) (public television station not public forum; minority party candidate for U.S. Senate did not have First Amendment right to participate in televised candidates' debate and program televised on station, at least to any extent greater than limited right of access granted by equal time provision of Federal Communications Act); McGlynn v. New Jersey Pub. Broadcasting, 439 A.2d 54, 72, 7 Media L. Rep. 2446 (N.J. 1981) (decision of New Jersey Public Broadcasting Authority to exclude plaintiff candidates from program reasonable exercise of broad discretion vested in Authority to make editorial judgments in accordance with federal and state law requiring, inter alia, "fairness, balance and equity" in entirety of election coverage over course of campaign; therefore, no First Amendment violation).

[398]Warner Cable Communications v. City of Niceville, 911 F.2d 634 (11th Cir. 1990), *cert. denied,* 111 S. Ct. 2839 (1991). In *Warner,* a cable operator challenged an ordinance that permitted the city to issue revenue bonds for the purpose of constructing and operating a competing cable television system and to create an independent editorial commission. The Eleventh Circuit noted that " '[e]ven without First Amendment protection government may participate in the marketplace of ideas and contribute its own views to those of other speakers.' " 911 F.2d at 638 (quoting Muir v. Alabama Educ. Television Comm'n (Muir II), 688 F.2d 1033, 1038 (5th Cir. 1982)) (internal quotations omitted).

[399]*See, e.g.,* Barnard v. Chamberlain, 897 F.2d 1059 (10th Cir. 1990) (court determined that evidence supported finding that *Utah Bar Letter*—integrated state bar newsletter—was nonpublic forum and that refusal to publish plaintiff's article, which was critical of bar, was not impermissible viewpoint discrimination in violation of First Amendment); Estiverne v. Louisiana State Bar Ass'n, 863 F.2d 371, 16 Media L. Rep. 1481 (5th Cir. 1989) (*Louisiana State Bar Journal*—publication of bar association—published report on disciplinary proceedings against plaintiff and refused to publish his reply; court held that journal was nonpublic forum and refusal to publish reply was reasonable in light of magazine's purpose). *Contra* Radical Lawyers Caucus v. Pool, 324 F. Supp. 268, 269 (W.D. Tex. 1970) (court granted access to group of attorneys seeking to place ad in state's bar association publication; publication—acting as state—had not demonstrated compelling interest in denying access).

[400]Legi-Tech v. Keiper, 766 F.2d 728, 731, 11 Media L. Rep. 2482 (2d Cir. 1985) (court recognized limited right of access to state's legislative retrieval service by company providing computerized legislative information).

[401]Kaplan v. County of L.A., 894 F.2d 1076 (9th Cir.), *cert. denied,* 496 U.S. 907 (1990) (court held that pamphlet was limited public forum).

[402]Alaska Gay Coalition v. Sullivan, 578 P.2d 951, 3 Media L. Rep. 2297 (Alaska 1978) (city publication intended to provide vehicle for dissemination of information regarding area's public and private services and organizations was public forum; thus, city could not deny homosexual organization access to publication—i.e., delete its entry from publication—based solely on beliefs of group's members).

[403]475 U.S. 1 (1986) (plurality opinion). Justice Powell announced the judgment of the Court and delivered an opinion in which Chief Justice Burger and Justices Brennan and O'Connor joined. Chief Justice

Commission (CPUC) order that granted access to a utility company's billing envelopes was held to be unconstitutional by the Supreme Court.

In *Pacific Gas,* the CPUC granted a group named Toward Utility Rate Normalization (TURN) the right to place literature in the "extra space" of the utility company's billing envelopes.[404] The utility (Pacific Gas) regularly inserted its own newsletter, which contained political editorials and public interest stories as well as information about utility service, into the billing envelopes.[405] The CPUC held, however, that ratepayers, rather than Pacific Gas, "owned" the envelopes' extra space (space remaining after inclusion of the bill and required legal notices that would not result in any extra postage cost).[406] Since TURN had represented the interests of a "significant group" of ratepayers, the CPUC ordered that it be given access to that extra space.[407]

Justice Powell, writing for the plurality, vacated the CPUC's decision[408] because it infringed on Pacific Gas' First Amendment rights by compelling it to provide a forum for views other than its own.[409] Justice Powell relied heavily on *Miami Herald Publishing Company v. Tornillo,*[410] which held that Florida's "right of reply" statute abridged a newspaper's First Amendment rights. According to Justice Powell, CPUC's order, like the Florida statute, did not grant access to the general public; instead, it discriminated on the basis of a speaker's viewpoint.[411] "Access is limited to persons or groups—such as TURN—who disagree with appellant's views as expressed in [the Pacific Gas newsletter] .... Such one-sidedness impermissibly burdens appellant's own expression."[412]

Justice Powell dismissed the argument that ownership of the "extra space" was dispositive, stating that, regardless of ownership, the CPUC forced Pacific Gas to use its own property (the envelopes) to distribute TURN's message.[413] Justice Powell noted that the CPUC order might be valid if narrowly tailored to serve a compelling state interest[414] but found that the state's interest in fair and effective utility regulation could be achieved without violating Pacific Gas' First Amendment rights, "such as [by] awarding costs and fees."[415] Further, the CPUC order was not a valid time, place, or manner regulation because it was not content-neutral.[416]

Chief Justice Rehnquist, joined by Justice White and, in part, by Justice Stevens, dissented.[417] He did not find *Tornillo* to be controlling, because Florida's right-of-reply statute conditioned access on certain expressions *by the*

Burger filed a separate concurring opinion. Justice Marshall filed an opinion concurring in the judgment. Justice Rehnquist filed a dissenting opinion, in Part I of which Justices White and Stevens joined. Justice Stevens also filed a dissenting opinion. Finally, Justice Blackmun took no part in consideration of the case.

[404] *Id.* at 5.
[405] *Id.*
[406] *Id.* at 5–6.
[407] *Id.* at 6.
[408] 475 U.S. at 21.
[409] *Id.* at 9–18.
[410] 418 U.S. 241, 1 Media L. Rep. 1898 (1974). *Tornillo* is discussed at length *supra* §13.2(B).
[411] *Pacific Gas,* 475 U.S. at 14 ("[t]he order does not simply award access to the public at large; rather it discriminates on the basis of the viewpoints of the selected speakers").
[412] *Id.* at 13.
[413] *Id.* at 17.
[414] *Id.* at 19.
[415] *Id.* at 19–20.
[416] 475 U.S. at 20.
[417] *Id.* at 26 (Rehnquist, C.J., dissenting).

newspaper.[418] Pacific Gas, unlike the newspaper, "cannot prevent access by remaining silent or avoiding discussion of controversial subjects .... Accordingly the right of access should not be held to trigger heightened First Amendment scrutiny on the ground that it somehow might deter [Pacific Gas'] right to speak."[419]

Instead, Justice Rehnquist found *Pruneyard Shopping Center v. Robins*[420] analogous.[421] In *Pruneyard,* the Supreme Court upheld a state-created right of access to private shopping centers.[422] Justice Rehnquist noted that *Pruneyard* distinguished *Tornillo* on the ground that access to the shopping center would not dampen the vigor of public debate, as would access to a newspaper.[423] Since the CPUC did not inhibit Pacific Gas from expressing views in its own newsletter, Justice Rehnquist found *Pruneyard*'s reasoning applicable to the CPUC order.[424]

Plaintiffs have been somewhat more successful in enforcing access to other "public" facilities. For example, one court held that a city bus company could not deny an abortion rights group access to advertising space on its buses.[425] The court concluded that since the defendant created a public forum by allowing other political advertising to be displayed, it was impermissible to deny access to the abortion rights group.[426] Similarly, a district court held that the New York Metropolitan Transportation Authority, a public corporation, could not deny a plaintiff access to subway walls for an advertising poster depicting then-presidential candidate Walter Mondale.[427] After determining that the poster was political speech and subject to full First Amendment protection, the court concluded that since the Authority had created a public forum by accepting advertising of other commercial and political speech, it could not deny access to the plaintiff.[428] There are other similar decisions.[429]

§13.6 ACCESS TO CABLE TELEVISION

§13.6(A) Introduction

Over the past few decades, cable television has become a burgeoning new medium. Accompanying cable's growth has been intense debate over the

---

[418]*Id.* at 30–35.
[419]*Id.* at 31.
[420]447 U.S. 74, 6 Media L. Rep. 1311 (1980).
[421]*Pacific Gas,* 475 U.S. at 32 (Rehnquist, C.J., dissenting).
[422]447 U.S. at 79.
[423]475 U.S. at 28 (Rehnquist, C.J., dissenting).
[424]*Id.* at 31. Following *Pacific Gas,* other courts have also invalidated other "forced access" requirements. *See, e.g.,* Central Ill. Light Co. v. Citizens Util. Bd., 827 F.2d 1169 (7th Cir. 1987) (court held that "forced access" provisions in statute entitling Citizens Utility Board to solicit membership through enclosures in utility bills violated First Amendment); Mountain States Tel. & Tel. Co. v. District Ct., 778 P.2d 667 (Colo.) (court order requiring telephone company to include space in monthly billing envelopes for notices to customers of pending class action against telephone company brought by some customers held invalid), *cert. denied,* 493 U.S. 983 (1989).
[425]Coalition for Abortion Rights & Against Sterilization Abuse v. Niagara Frontier Transp. Auth., 584 F. Supp. 985 (W.D.N.Y. 1984).
[426]*Id.* at 989.
[427]Penthouse Int'l v. Koch, 599 F. Supp. 1338 (S.D.N.Y. 1984).
[428]*Id.* at 1349.
[429]Lebron v. Washington Metro. Area Transit Auth., 749 F.2d 893 (D.C. Cir. 1984) (court held artist could not be denied space in subway for political poster critical of President Reagan); United States S.W.

parameters of federal, state, and local cable regulation over, among other things, the public's access rights to cable and the concomitant editorial rights of cable operators.

The courts, legislators, and administrative entities such as the FCC have struggled in selecting an appropriate model of regulation for cable.[430] Some scholars and many cable operators argue that cable ought to be given the full First Amendment protection accorded to the print media under *Miami Herald Publishing Co. v. Tornillo;*[431] others stress cable's similarities to broadcasting and argue that cable, like broadcasting, needs government regulation.[432]

Courts have historically aligned cable with the broadcast media, thereby justifying government interference with cable operators' control over programming content and public access.[433] Only in recent years have the courts begun to ease away from the broadcasting model and move toward the print model in developing an independent analytical framework for determining the extent of permissible government regulation of cable.[434] Some scholars view the Cable Communications Policy Act of 1984[435] as a congressional resolution of these First Amendment issues and an accommodation of the competing interests.[436]

This section briefly discusses the historical development of cable regulation[437] and the sections of the Cable Act pertaining to public access to cable.

§13.6(B) The Historical Analogy to Broadcasting

The first cable television systems, known as community antenna television (CATV) systems, developed in the 1940s and 1950s to amplify and distribute television signals of good quality to areas where reception was poor or nonexistent.[438] In 1958, the FCC expressly disclaimed any jurisdiction over CATV systems and thus made no attempt to regulate the industry.[439] By 1959,

---

Afr./Namib. Trade & Cultural Council v. United States, 708 F.2d 760 (D.C. Cir. 1983) (Federal Aviation Administration's refusal to approve politically oriented advertisement as suitable for public display in various advertising areas of federally owned airports infringed in plaintiff's First Amendment rights); Planned Parenthood Ass'n/Chicago Area v. Chicago Transit Auth., 592 F. Supp. 544 (N.D. Ill. 1984), *aff'd*, 767 F.2d 1225 (7th Cir. 1985) (transit authority could not deny Planned Parenthood access to advertising space); *see also* American Council of the Blind v. Boorstin, 664 F. Supp. 811 (D.D.C. 1986) (Library of Congress' Program for the Blind and Physically Handicapped providing access to, inter alia, magazines in braille was nonpublic forum; thus, librarian's elimination of *Playboy* magazine from braille library, which was "viewpoint-based discrimination," impinged on freedom of expression under First Amendment).

[430] *See* D. BRENNER ET AL., CABLE TELEVISION & OTHER NONBROADCAST VIDEO (1990) [hereinafter *Cable Television*].

[431] 418 U.S. 241 (1974). *See also* G. SHAPIRO ET AL., CABLESPEECH viii (1983); Lee, *Cable Franchising & the First Amendment*, 36 VAND. L. REV. 867 (1983); Goldberg et al., *Cable Television, Government Regulation and the First Amendment*, 3 COMM. ENT. L.J. 577 (1981).

[432] *Cable Television*, supra note 430, at §6.03[1] n.4. Others argue that cable should be regulated under the telephone-common carrier model, *id.* (citing POOL, TECHNOLOGIES OF FREEDOM (1983); Nadel, *Electrifying the First Amendment*, 5 CARDOZO L. REV. 531 (1984)), or that cable should be treated as a hybrid and that each function it performs should be scrutinized under different constitutional analyses. *Id.* at n.5.1 (citing Myerson, *The First Amendment and the Cable Television Operator: An Unprotective Shield Against Public Access Requirements*, 4 COMM. ENT. L.J. 1, 25–26 (1981)).

[433] *See infra* §§13.6(B) and (C).

[434] *See* Preferred Communications v. City of L.A., 754 F.2d 1396 (9th Cir. 1985), *aff'd on other grounds*, 476 U.S. 488 (1986); Quincy Cable TV v. Federal Communications Comm'n, 768 F.2d 1434 (D.C. Cir. 1985), *cert. denied sub nom.* National Ass'n of Broadcasters v. Quincy Cable TV, 476 U.S. 1169 (1986).

[435] 47 U.S.C. §521 *et seq.* (1991).

[436] *Cable Television*, supra note 430, at §6.03[1].

[437] A detailed discussion of cable's development and the 1984 Cable Act is beyond the scope of this chapter.

[438] Clarksburg Pub'g Co. v. Federal Communications Comm'n, 225 F.2d 511, 517 n.16 (D.C. Cir. 1955).

[439] Frontier Broadcasting Co. v. Collier, 24 F.C.C. 251 (1958), *reconsideration denied*, In re Inquiry Into the Impact of Community Antenna Systems, TV Translators, TV "Satellite" Stations, and TV "Repeaters"

however, cable had grown to the point where the FCC could no longer ignore it. That year, the FCC found that CATV "related to interstate transmission" but nevertheless determined that it could not exercise its jurisdiction over CATV because CATV systems were neither common carriers nor broadcasters.[440] The FCC stated instead that it preferred to recommend legislation that would impose specific requirements on CATV.[441] Legislation was proposed but not enacted.[442]

In the following years the cable industry grew explosively, and the FCC gradually asserted its jurisdiction over cable by issuing rules that governed carriage of local signals and nonduplication of local programming.[443] The FCC's change in position was based on its finding that CATV systems were competing with broadcasters for their audience.[444] The FCC determined that it had the authority to regulate CATV to the extent that cable affected its broadcast regulatory duties.[445]

In 1968, in *United States v. Southwestern Cable Co.*,[446] the Supreme Court upheld the FCC's authority to regulate the retransmission of distant broadcast signals through cable systems.[447] The Court found that although cable systems were not specifically mentioned in the Communications Act of 1934, " '[u]nderlying the whole [Communications Act] is recognition of the rapidly fluctuating factors characteristic of the evolution of broadcasting and of the corresponding requirement that the administrative process possess sufficient flexibility to adjust itself to these factors.' "[448] The Court further reasoned that if the FCC was to perform with appropriate effectiveness certain of its other responsibilities—like providing a widely dispersed radio and television service—it must regulate cable.[449]

In reaching that conclusion, the Court recognized that cable systems had the capacity to help the FCC fulfill some of its most important goals but that, if unregulated, cable's rapid growth might instead interfere with those goals.[450] The Court thus upheld the FCC's authority to regulate CATV but restricted it "to that *reasonably ancillary* to the effective performance of the Commission's various responsibilities for the regulation of television broadcasting."[451] The

---

on the Orderly Development of Television Broadcasting, 26 F.C.C. 403 (1959) [hereinafter *CATV Report*]. In *Frontier Broadcasting Co.*, the FCC held that it did not have jurisdiction over CATV under the provisions of the 1934 Communications Act relating to common carriers. *CATV Report, supra*, at 427. Although it found "no present basis for asserting jurisdiction or authority over CATV's," *id.* at 431, the FCC noted that CATV could have an adverse impact on the development of broadcasting. Accordingly, the FCC advised as follows: "CATV systems should be required to obtain the consent of the stations whose signals they transmit and . . . they should be required to carry the signal of the local station (without degrading it) if the local station so requests." *Id.* at 441. The FCC then announced that since both of the steps would require changes in the Communications Act of 1934, it would recommend to Congress appropriate legislation. *Id.*

[440]CATV and TV Repeater Servs., 26 F.C.C. 403, 427–28 (1959). The Communications Act of 1934 limited the jurisdiction of the FCC to common carriers and broadcasters. *Id.*
[441]*Id.*
[442]*See Cable Television, supra* note 430, at §2.03[1][a].
[443]First Report and Order, Docket Nos. 14895 and 15233, 38 F.C.C. 683 (1965).
[444]*See* United States v. Southwestern Cable Co., 392 U.S. 157, 165 (1968) (quoting Rules re Microwave-Served CATV, 38 F.C.C. 683, 710–11 (1965)).
[445]Rules re Microwave-Served CATV, 38 F.C.C. 683, 713–15 (1965).
[446]392 U.S. 157 (1968).
[447]*Id.* at 178.
[448]*Id.* at 172–73 (quoting Federal Communications Comm'n v. Pottsville Broadcasting Co., 309 U.S. 134, 138 (1940)).
[449]*Id.* at 173.
[450]*Id.* at 175.
[451]392 U.S. at 178 (emphasis added).

Court announced that "[t]he Commission may, for these purposes, issue 'such rules and regulations and prescribe such restrictions and conditions, not inconsistent with law,' as 'public convenience, interest, or necessity requires.' "[452]

In *Black Hills Video Corp. v. Federal Communications Commission*,[453] for example, the Eighth Circuit rejected a cable operator's claim that his First Amendment rights were violated by the FCC's "must-carry" rules.[454] After citing *National Broadcasting Co. v. United States*,[455] where the Supreme Court held that the right of free speech did not include the right to use the airwaves without a license,[456] the *Black Hills Video* court held that the FCC's "effort to preserve local television by regulating CATVs has the same constitutional status under the First Amendment as regulation of the transmission of signals by the originating television stations."[457] The court noted that "[i]t is irrelevant to the Congressional power that the CATV systems do not themselves use the airwaves in their distribution systems" because the "crucial consideration is that they do use radio signals and that they have a unique impact upon, and relationship with, the television broadcast service."[458]

For nearly a decade following the *Black Hills Video* decision, the courts did not question the propriety of treating cable regulation the same as broadcast regulation for purposes of First Amendment analysis.[459] It was not until the landmark decision in *Home Box Office v. Federal Communications Commission*[460] that the courts began to reevaluate cable television's role in the telecommunications industry.

In *Home Box Office*, the District of Columbia Circuit considered the validity of an FCC regulation that limited the number and type of feature films and sports events that cable television systems and pay subscription broadcast stations could offer their subscribers.[461] The court found that the FCC did not have jurisdiction to promulgate the challenged regulation and therefore held it invalid.[462]

The court then went on to determine the proper standard of First Amendment analysis for cable television. It ruled that the First Amendment standard of analysis developed in *National Broadcasting Co. v. United States*[463] and affirmed in *Red Lion Broadcasting Co. v. Federal Communications Commission*,[464]

---

[452]*Id.* (quoting 47 U.S.C. §303(r)(1964)).
[453]399 F.2d 65 (8th Cir. 1968).
[454]*Id.* at 69. These rules provided that, on request, a CATV system must carry the programs of local and nearby stations and could not broadcast a program on the same day that a higher priority station on the system is broadcasting that program. They also provided for notice of an intent to commence service and an evidentiary hearing before transmitting a distant signal. *Id.* at 67–68.
[455]319 U.S. 190 (1943).
[456]*Id.* at 227.
[457]*Black Hills Video*, 399 F.2d at 69.
[458]*Id.* At the time of the *Black Hills Video* decision, cable television service was assumed to be secondary to broadcasting and virtually dependent on broadcast signals for its programming.
[459]*See, e.g.,* Southwest Pa. Cable TV v. Federal Communications Comm'n, 514 F.2d 1343, 1347 (D.C. Cir. 1975); Midwest Television v. Federal Communications Comm'n, 426 F.2d 1222, 1230 (D.C. Cir. 1970).
[460]567 F.2d 9 (D.C. Cir.) (per curiam), *cert. denied*, 434 U.S. 829 (1977).
[461]567 F.2d at 21.
[462]*Id.* at 18.
[463]319 U.S. 190 (1943); *see supra* notes 455–57 and accompanying text. In *National Broadcasting Co.*, the Court held that the First Amendment will tolerate a more intrusive regulation of the broadcast media than it will with regard to other forms of communication because of the physical limitations of the airwaves—only a limited number of voices or images can simultaneously be carried over the electromagnetic spectrum. *Id.* at 226. On whether this rationale has any continuing validity, *see supra* §13.2.(C).
[464]395 U.S. 367 (1969); *see supra* §13.2(A).

which allows for some degree of governmental regulation of the broadcast industry, could not be directly applied to cable television, reasoning that "since an essential precondition of that theory—physical interference and scarcity requiring an umpiring role for government—is absent," cable television was distinguishable from broadcast television.[465] The court made it clear, however, that the absence of the physical limitations of the electromagnetic spectrum did not automatically lead to the conclusion that no regulation of cable would be acceptable under the First Amendment.[466] The court was not willing to analogize cable television to the print media and adopt the standard of First Amendment protection set forth in *Tornillo*.[467]

Similarly, the Eighth Circuit Court of Appeals, when faced with evaluating the FCC's regulation of public access to cable, questioned the suitability of the historical analogy of cable to broadcasting.[468] In 1976, the FCC promulgated cable television access rules that required cable systems with over 3,500 subscribers to dedicate at least four channels for access use, including public access and leased access.[469] The regulations also required access to be provided by the cable operators on a nondiscriminatory, first come-first served basis.[470] The rules specifically prohibited cable operators from exercising any control over the content of access programming.[471]

The Eighth Circuit invalidated these regulations, finding that they impermissibly imposed common carrier responsibilities on cable operators.[472] The court held that the rules were not "reasonably ancillary" to the FCC's responsibilities for broadcast television and thus were beyond the FCC's jurisdiction.[473] The court concluded that congressional approval was required in order to expand the FCC's jurisdiction to include access requirements for cable systems.[474]

The Eighth Circuit also addressed the First Amendment issues in dicta.[475] The majority found that, in the context of public access requirements, the cable industry should be treated like the newspaper industry because, unlike broadcasting, it does not use public airwaves.[476] Referring to cable as a "private electronic 'publication,' " the court reasoned that, in light of *Tornillo,* a cable operator could not be compelled to provide access to the public.[477] The court also relied upon *Home Box Office v. Federal Communications Commission*,[478] which also analogized the First Amendment rights of cable operators to those

---

[465] *Home Box Office,* 567 F.2d at 45.
[466] *Id.* at 46.
[467] *Id. See* Miami Herald Pub'g Co. v. Tornillo, 418 U.S. 241 (1974). For a detailed discussion of *Tornillo, see supra* §13.2(B).
[468] Midwest Video Corp. v. Federal Communications Comm'n (Midwest II), 571 F.2d 1025 (8th Cir. 1978), *aff'd,* 440 U.S. 689 (1979). *Midwest II* was preceded by United States v. Midwest Video Corp. (Midwest I), 441 F.2d 1322 (8th Cir. 1971), *rev'd,* 406 U.S. 649 (1972), in which Midwest's challenge to the FCC's mandatory originator rule was upheld by the circuit court but struck down by the Supreme Court.
[469] *Midwest II,* 440 U.S. at 692–93 (citing 47 C.F.R. §76.254(a) (1977)).
[470] *Id.* at 694.
[471] *Id.* at 693–94 (citing 47 C.F.R. §76.256(b), (d) (1977)).
[472] *Midwest II,* 571 F.2d at 1050–52.
[473] *Id.* at 1050.
[474] *Id.*
[475] *Id.* at 1052–57. The court referred to the *Midwest II* case as "the first case raising First Amendment implications of a Commission effort to enforce unlimited public access requirements." *Id.* at 1053.
[476] *Id.* at 1056.
[477] *Midwest II,* 571 F.2d at 1055.
[478] 567 F.2d 9 (D.C. Cir.) (per curiam), *cert. denied,* 434 U.S. 829 (1977).

of the print media.[479] The Eighth Circuit concluded, as had the District of Columbia Circuit, that the economic scarcity of cable systems does not justify abridgement of a cable operator's First Amendment rights.[480] The court explained that:

> Though counsel said the reason lay in scarcity of broadcast frequencies, it appears to have escaped Commission attention that it is the scarcity of broadcast signals that *excuses* its limited regulatory intrusion on First Amendment and other rights of broadcasters. The Commission's notion that the absence of scarcity in the potential number of cables removes the limits on its authority has things backward. The absence of scarcity removes the *excuse* for intrusion.[481]

The Supreme Court affirmed the Eighth Circuit decision's jurisdictional ruling, holding that rules for mandatory access to cable did not fall within the FCC's statutory authority.[482] The Supreme Court conceded that in *CBS v. Democratic National Committee*[483] it had indicated that the FCC might have the flexibility to devise some kind of limited right of access in the future.[484] The Court felt, however that the particular cable access rules in controversy wrested precious editorial control from cable operators and imposed common carrier obligations on them without statutory authority.[485]

The Court declared that "[t]he Commission may not regulate cable systems as common carriers, just as it may not impose such obligations on television broadcasters."[486] "We think," added the Court, "authority to compel cable operators to provide common coverage of public-originated programs must come specifically from Congress."[487]

The Court declined to address the First Amendment issued raised in the Eighth Circuit's opinion, except to note that "it is not frivolous."[488] With this, the Supreme Court postponed a ruling on First Amendment standards for cable—standards that have yet to be articulated.

§13.6(C) Cable Access Requirements at the Local Level: Continuing the Analogy to Broadcasting

In the years following *Midwest II,* courts returned to analogizing cable to broadcasting. In *Community Communications Co. v. City of Boulder,*[489] the district court enjoined the City of Boulder from enforcing a legislative restriction on the authority of the Community Communications Company (CCC) to conduct its cable business in Boulder.[490]

---

[479] 567 F.2d at 43–46.
[480] *Midwest II,* 571 F.2d at 1055 (citing Home Box Office v. Federal Communications Comm'n, 567 F.2d 9, 46 (D.C. Cir.), *cert. denied,* 434 U.S. 829 (1977)).
[481] *Id.* at 1048.
[482] Midwest II, 440 U.S. 690, 708–09 (1978).
[483] 412 U.S. 94 (1973).
[484] *Midwest II,* 440 U.S. at 704–05 (citing Columbia Broadcasting Sys. v. Democratic Nat'l Comm., 412 U.S. 94, 122, 131 (1973)).
[485] *Id.*
[486] *Id.* at 709.
[487] *Id.*
[488] *Id.* at 709 n.19.
[489] 496 F. Supp. 823 (D. Colo. 1980), *rev'd,* 660 F.2d 1370, 7 Media L. Rep. 1993 (10th Cir. 1981), *cert. dismissed,* 456 U.S. 1001 (1982).
[490] 660 F.2d at 1372.

The Tenth Circuit reversed the injunction.[491] Recognizing that cable regulation is premised on the cable companies' need to use public street and rights of way to lay or string their cable, the court concluded that "government and cable operators are tied in a way that government and newspapers are not," because cable operators use public property and so need government permission before they disrupt the public domain.[492] The Tenth Circuit felt that it was inappropriate to adopt for cable the First Amendment principles governing newspapers, noting that while cable operators are entitled to First Amendment protection, Boulder's citizens have a significant First Amendment interest in the widest possible dissemination of information from diverse and antagonistic sources.[493] The court also concluded that economic scarcity justified regulation, distinguishing *Tornillo* on the ground that the government traditionally has not interfered with newspapers.[494] The court did stop short of equating the First Amendment rights of cable operators with those of broadcasters, however, and instead concluded that the creation of a natural monopoly is a constitutionally permissible rationale for cable regulation.[495]

With similar reasoning, a U.S. District Court in Rhode Island, in *Berkshire Cablevision v. Burke*,[496] upheld local regulations that required cable operators to construct an institutional/industrial network and to make several channels available for public access.[497] In *Berkshire Cablevision*, an applicant to develop and operate a cable system in Newport challenged the regulations on First Amendment grounds.[498] In refusing to declare the regulations unconstitutional, the court reviewed the judicial history of broadcasting and newspaper regulation, expressly disagreed with the analyses of the Eighth and District of Columbia Circuits in *Midwest II*[499] and *Home Box Office*,[500] and found that newspapers and cable were constitutionally distinguishable.[501] The court pointed out that, unlike newspapers, cable television does not have a history of being able to operate free from government control over its content.[502]

The court added that "government franchising of the cable television industry is virtually indispensable," noting, for example, that since "constructing a cable television system requires use of the public streets or telephone poles, the government has a substantial interest in limiting the number of cable operators who build cable systems."[503] The court further noted that due to the huge start-up costs involved in creating cable systems, there was a tendency for the first cable operator in an area to have a natural monopoly.[504]

---

[491]*Id.* at 1380.
[492]*Id.* at 1378.
[493]*Id.* at 1376 n.5.
[494]*Id.* at 1379.
[495]660 F.2d at 1379.
[496]571 F. Supp. 976 (D.R.I. 1983), *vacated as moot*, 773 F.2d 382 (1st Cir. 1985).
[497]571 F. Supp. at 992.
[498]*Id.* at 979–80.
[499]571 F.2d 1025 (8th Cir. 1978).
[500]567 F.2d 9 (D.C. Cir.) (per curiam), *cert. denied*, 434 U.S. 829 (1977).
[501]*Berkshire Cablevision*, 571 F. Supp. at 985.
[502]*Id.*
[503]*Id.; see also* Omega Satellite Prods. Co. v. City of Indianapolis, 694 F.2d 119 (7th Cir. 1982).
[504]571 F. Supp. at 986. The court observed:
While it is true that the Supreme Court has rejected economic scarcity as a basis for the regulation of newspapers, the lack of any access requirement for newspapers simply does not prevent a member of the general public from expressing his opinions *in that same medium,* which in such a case is print,

The *Community Communications* and *Berkshire Cablevision* decisions thus revived the analogy to broadcasting that the circuit courts in *Home Box Office* and *Midwest II* had rejected.

§13.6(D) The Cable Act: Legislative Recognition of Cable Regulation

In 1984, Congress enacted the Cable Communications Policy Act to clarify the power of local, state, and federal governments to regulate cable television.[505] The Act relies on the local franchising process as the primary means of cable regulation and limits the power that a franchise authority can exercise.

The Act also provides for mandatory and leased channel access requirements. Specifically, Section 531 of the Act authorizes the cable franchising authority to require cable operators to designate public education and government (PEG) channels to foster improved public rights of access to the cable medium. Section 531(b) authorizes the franchising authority to set the rules and procedures that govern use of the PEG channels, including rules under which the cable operator is and is not permitted to use the PEG channel capacity to provide other services. Further, the Act provides that the cable operator "shall not exercise any editorial control over any public, educational, or governmental use" of channel capacity provided under the section.[506] Determination of the eligibility for and entitlement to access to PEG channels is left to the franchising authority as well.[507]

Section 532 of the Act requires the designation of channels for commercial use "by persons unaffiliated with the [cable] operator."[508] The underlying goal is to "assure that the widest possible diversity of information sources are made available to the public ... in the manner consistent with growth and development of cable systems."[509]

§13.6(E) The Shift Away From the Cable/Broadcasting Analogy

After Congress passed the Cable Act, the judiciary rendered three decisions that questioned the validity of basing cable regulation on the broadcasting model. In *Quincy Cable TV v. Federal Communications Commission*,[510] the Court of Appeals for the District of Columbia reviewed FCC regulations that required cable operators, upon request and without compensation, to transmit

---

of course.... In contrast, a resident of Newport County who does not have seven million dollars to develop his own cable system is shut out of that medium with no way to express his ideas with the widely acknowledged power of the small screen.... The result is that *Red Lion,* the seminal case of contemporary communications law, retains its vitality in the high-tech world of cable television. To be sure, the scarcity rationale for governmental regulation here takes a somewhat different form, but the goal remains the same as in 1969: to *promote* the First Amendment by making a powerful communications medium available to as many of our citizens as is reasonably possible. For this court, at least, scarcity is scarcity—its particular source, whether "physical" or "economic," does not matter if its effect is to remove from all but a small group an important means of expressing ideas.

Id. at 986–87 (footnote omitted).
[505]*See* Pub. L. No. 98-549, 98 Stat. 2779 (1984), codified at 47 U.S.C. §§521 *et seq.* (1991).
[506]47 U.S.C. §531(e).
[507]*Id.* §531.
[508]*Id.* §532(b)(1).
[509]*Id.* §532(a).
[510]768 F.2d 1434 (D.C. Cir. 1985), *cert. denied sub nom.* National Ass'n of Broadcasters v. Quincy Cable TV, 476 U.S. 1169 (1986).

to their subscribers every over-the-air television broadcast signal that was " 'significantly viewed in the community' or otherwise considered local under the Commission's rules."[511] The owner of a variety of cable services challenged these "must-carry" rules as a violation of the First Amendment rights of cable operators, cable programmers, and the viewing public.[512]

The court noted that the original objective of these rules, which were promulgated in the mid-1960s, was to assure that the advent of cable "not undermine the financial viability of free, community-oriented television .... 'society's chosen instrument for the provision of video services.' "[513] The court began its analysis by noting that cable television warranted a standard of review distinct from that applied to broadcasters.[514] However, the court reasoned that, because the must-carry rules so clearly failed the ordinary "substantial government interest" test applicable to broadcasting, the court need not define the exact level of scrutiny applicable to cable.[515]

The *Quincy Cable* court then proceeded to assess the technological differences between broadcasting and cable and explained that, as "other courts have recognized, the 'scarcity rationale' has no place in evaluating government regulation of cable television."[516] The court did not find that certain attributes of cable—such as the fact that cable operators require use of a public right of way—justified the forgiving analysis traditionally applied to broadcasting, observing that "[n]o doubt a municipality has some power to control the placement of newspaper vending machines. But any effort to use that power as a basis for dictating what must be placed in such machines would surely be invalid."[517] The court similarly felt that arguments about economic scarcity lacked support since the scarcity was unproven and the existence of a monopoly, if it existed at all, may well have been attributable to government action.[518]

The court went on to assess the benefits and burdens of the must-carry rules. It found that by forcing distribution of a preselected package of programming, the must-carry rules were unduly intrusive and coerced speech.[519] Thus, the court found that the must-carry rules, like those at issue in *Tornillo,* placed substantial limitations on the operator's editorial discretion and were unconstitutional.[520]

After *Quincy Cable,* the FCC narrowed its must-carry rules,[521] but the revised rules were also struck down as a violation of the First Amendment.[522]

---

[511] 768 F.2d at 1437 (citing 47 C.F.R. §§76.57–76.61 (1984)).
[512] *Id.*
[513] *Id.* at 1440 (quoting Inquiry Into the Economic Relationship Between Broadcasting and Cable Television, 71 F.C.C.2d 632, 644 (1979)).
[514] *Id.* at 1448.
[515] *Id.*
[516] 768 F.2d at 1449.
[517] *Id.* (footnote omitted).
[518] *Id.* at 1450.
[519] *Id.* at 1452.
[520] *Id.* at 1453. In addition, as required under the *Home Box Office* test, the court found that the FCC had failed to prove that the problem the rules sought to cure—the destruction of free, local television—was an actual threat. *Id.* at 1457.
[521] Amendment of Part 76 of the Commission's Rules Concerning Carriage of Television Broadcast Signals by Cable Television Systems, FCC No. 86-357 (released Nov. 28, 1986), 51 Fed. Reg. 44,606 (1986), *modified by* No. 87-105 (released May 1, 1987), 52 Fed. Reg. 17,574 (1987).
[522] Century Communications Corp. v. Federal Communications Comm'n, 835 F.2d 292 (D.C. Cir. 1987), *clarified,* 837 F.2d 517, *cert. denied,* 436 U.S. 1032 (1988).

The District of Columbia Circuit again rejected the scarcity rationale: "Wire-carried media like cable, of course, have no such limitations."[523]

Similarly, in *Preferred Communications v. City of Los Angeles*,[524] a cable television company challenged the city's policy of auctioning off exclusive franchises to provide service in particular areas. The Ninth Circuit held that a city could not, consistent with the First Amendment, limit access to a given region to a single cable company when public utility facilities in that region were physically capable of accommodating more than one system.[525] The court expressly disagreed with the city's contention that the First Amendment standards applicable to broadcasting should apply to cable.[526]

The Ninth Circuit looked to *Black Hills Video Corp. v. Federal Communications Commission*,[527] which involved FCC efforts to regulate an early CATV system that merely transmitted the broadcasts of existing television stations, as the only case directly applying the physical scarcity rationale to cable.[528] The court noted that cable technology had evolved considerably since that time and that more recent decisions had expressly concluded that the scarcity rationale does not apply to cable.[529]

The Ninth Circuit also addressed the argument that cable is a natural monopoly, questioning the *Community Communications* and *Berkshire Cablevision* holdings that it is a monopoly. However, the court conceded that the conclusion that cable does not involve a scarce resource, as do the broadcast media, does not necessarily mean that all regulations are invalid.[530]

The court held that "[w]hile the City may promulgate reasonable time, place and manner regulations, it may not limit access under the circumstances set forth in the issue before us,"[531] adding that "[w]hile an outright ban would be viewpoint neutral, the City's action in the instant case creates an impermissible risk of covert discrimination based on the content of or the views expressed in the operator's proposed programming."[532]

When the Supreme Court reviewed this decision, it affirmed the Ninth Circuit on the narrow ground that the legal questions posed by the parties could not be decided, given the disputed factual assertions; the Court thus found that granting a motion to dismiss was improper.[533]

However, a Tenth Circuit decision, *Jones v. Wilkinson*,[534] albeit in a different context, has continued to analogize cable to broadcasting. In determining the constitutionality of the Utah Cable Television Programming Decency Act, the court reviewed the First Amendment standards for broadcasting, emphasizing that, in addition to the usual scarcity/public trust reasons, the greater

---

[523]835 F.2d at 295.
[524]754 F.2d 1396 (9th Cir. 1985), *aff'd on narrower grounds*, 476 U.S. 488 (1986).
[525]754 F.2d at 1411.
[526]*Id.* at 1403.
[527]399 F.2d 65 (8th Cir. 1968). *See supra* notes 453–58 and accompanying text.
[528]*Preferred Communications*, 754 F.2d at 1404.
[529]*Id.* (citing Omega Satellite Prods. Co. v. City of Indianapolis, 694 F.2d 119, 127 (7th Cir. 1982); Home Box Office v. Federal Communications Comm'n, 567 F.2d 9, 44–45 (D.C. Cir. 1977)).
[530]*Id.* at 1405.
[531]*Id.* at 1409.
[532]*Id.* (citation omitted).
[533]City of L.A. v. Preferred Communications, 476 U.S. 488, 493–94 (1986). For a further discussion of this case and media challenges to cable franchising regulation, *see* Chapter 12, §12.5(G).
[534]800 F.2d 989 (10th Cir. 1986).

constitutional leeway for governmental regulation of broadcasting stems from the pervasiveness of the medium: broadcasting intrudes into the home and is widely available to children.[535] Referring to the *Preferred* and *Community Communications* decisions, the court noted that the Supreme Court had yet to determine the First Amendment standards applicable to cable.[536] The court conceded that First Amendment regulations for cable were hard to justify on scarcity grounds,[537] but stressed cable's similarity to broadcasting in that both media rely on television receivers and offer a similar, often interchangeable product.[538] The court also noted that cable comes directly into the home, like broadcasting, and that, unlike newspapers, cable is frequently received without any advance warning of patently offensive material.[539] The court concluded that the rationale for regulating indecency in the broadcast media applied to cable as well,[540] stressing that even if cable is not scarce, as suggested by *Preferred,* its impact is similar to that of broadcasting.[541]

Thus, while the courts appear to be moving away from scarcity as a rationale for treating cable like broadcasting, other rationales are sometimes being used to justify such treatment, at least in some contexts, such as indecency. What First Amendment standards apply to cable is still unsettled, however. The Supreme Court has granted review of a case that may settle some of the issues in this area.[542]

---

[535]*Id.* at 999–1000 (citing Federal Communications Comm'n v. Pacifica Found., 438 U.S. 726 (1978)).
[536]*Id.* at 1000.
[537]*Id.* at 1001.
[538]*Id.* at 1004.
[539]800 F.2d at 1006.
[540]*Id.*
[541]*Id.* at 1004–06.
[542]Turner Broadcasting Sys. v. Federal Communications Comm'n, 819 F. Supp. 32, 21 Media L. Rep. 1993 (D.D.C. 1993), *appeal granted,* 114 S. Ct. 38 (1993). The issue in *Turner* is whether the must-carry provisions of the 1992 Cable Act are constitutional. In a 2-1 decision, the special three-judge district court held that they were. *See also* Daniels Cablevision v. United States, 835 F. Supp. 1, 21 Media L. Rep. 2225 (D.D.C. 1993) (ruling constitutionality of various other provisions of 1992 Cable Act).

Chapter 14

CONFIDENTIAL SOURCES AND RELATED PROBLEMS

§14.1 Introduction

This chapter discusses the constitutional, statutory, common law, and other bases for a reporter's right to refuse to divulge the identity of confidential sources, confidential information, or unpublished information. First, the U.S. Supreme Court's landmark decision in *Branzburg v. Hayes*,[1] which concerns reporters' First Amendment right to refuse to disclose their sources, is discussed. Second, the evolution of First Amendment protections and the growth of alternative sources of protection for reporters—including the Fifth Amendment, Department of Justice regulations, federal procedural rules, federal common law, and state law since *Branzburg*—are traced. Third, certain common issues—e.g., standing, waiver, sanctions, in camera inspection, and choice of law—are examined. Fourth, particular types of civil and criminal cases that raise reporter's privilege issues and cases involving "breach of promise" actions against journalists are discussed. Finally, the search and seizure issues arising out of *Zurcher v. Stanford Daily*[2] are examined.

§14.2 Branzburg v. Hayes

The first and only time the U.S. Supreme Court has directly considered whether the First Amendment affords reporters a testimonial privilege was in *Branzburg v. Hayes*[3] and its two companion cases, *In re Pappas*[4] and *United States v. Caldwell*.[5]

Branzburg began when Paul Branzburg, a Kentucky newspaper reporter, was summoned to testify before two separate grand juries that sought the identities of narcotics users and producers that Branzburg had interviewed

---

[1] 408 U.S. 665, 1 Media L. Rep. 2617 (1972).
[2] 436 U.S. 547, 3 Media L. Rep. 2377 (1978).
[3] *Branzburg* brought before the Supreme Court two judgments of the Kentucky court of appeals: Branzburg v. Pound, 461 S.W.2d 345 (1970), and Branzburg v. Meigs, an unreported case. The Supreme Court granted a writ of certiorari, 402 U.S. 942 (1971) and affirmed the judgments, 408 U.S. 665 (1972).
[4] 266 N.E.2d 297 (Mass. 1971) (ruling that newsperson had no privilege), *aff'd*, 408 U.S. 665 (1972).
[5] 311 F. Supp. 358 (N.D. Cal. 1970), *rev'd*, 434 F.2d 1081 (9th Cir. 1970), *cert. granted*, 402 U.S. 942 (1971), *rev'd*, 408 U.S. 665 (1972).

while writing news stories.[6] In 1969, Branzburg personally observed two residents of Jefferson County, Kentucky, synthesize hashish from marijuana, and he published a detailed account of that activity.[7] The county grand jury responded to the article by subpoenaing Branzburg and asking him the names of the hashish makers.[8] Although he appeared voluntarily, Branzburg refused to testify on the grounds of the First Amendment, the Kentucky Constitution, and the Kentucky reporter's privilege statute.[9] Branzburg's contentions were rejected by the trial court and the Kentucky Court of Appeals, and he was ordered to testify about all events he personally had observed.[10]

In 1971, Branzburg also interviewed dozens of drug users in Franklin County, Kentucky, and included his observations in another news story; in turn he was summoned by a Franklin County grand jury that was investigating drug sales.[11] Branzburg's motion to quash the subpoena on the grounds that disclosure of his confidences would "suppress vital First Amendment freedoms" was denied by the trial court, and he was ordered to answer questions pertaining to criminal acts that he had actually observed.[12] Following a second adverse decision in the Kentucky Court of Appeals, Branzburg sought review of both judgments in the U.S. Supreme Court.[13]

Branzburg's two companion cases also involved journalists who were summoned before grand juries and asked to divulge confidential information they had obtained in the course of producing news reports. In the first case, Paul Pappas, a television news reporter, gained entry to the New Bedford, Massachusetts, headquarters of the Black Panthers in July 1970, a period of serious civil disorder.[14] Two months later, Pappas was subpoenaed to appear before a county grand jury and was asked to disclose what he had seen and heard inside the headquarters and to identify the persons present.[15] The trial court rejected Pappas' contention that the First Amendment afforded him a privilege not to divulge such confidences.[16] Upon review, the Supreme Judicial Court of Massachusetts held that "there exists no constitutional newsman's privilege, either qualified or absolute, to refuse to appear and testify before a court or grand jury" and affirmed the denial of Pappas' motion to quash.[17]

In the second companion case, Earl Caldwell, a *New York Times* reporter assigned to cover black militant groups, was subpoenaed to appear before a federal grand jury that was investigating alleged criminal acts, including threats against the life of the president, conspiracy to assassinate, incitement to riot, and mail fraud.[18] The District Court denied Caldwell's motion to quash, but on First Amendment grounds it issued a protective order permitting him to withhold "confidential associations, sources or information" absent a showing

---

[6]408 U.S. at 667–71.
[7]*Id.* at 667.
[8]*Id.* at 668.
[9]*Id.*
[10]*Id.* at 668–69.
[11]408 U.S. at 669.
[12]*Id.* at 669–70 & n.5.
[13]*Id.* at 670–71.
[14]*Id.* at 672–75.
[15]*Id.* at 672–73.
[16]408 U.S. at 673.
[17]In re Pappas, 266 N.E.2d 297, 302–03 (Mass. 1971).
[18]408 U.S. at 675–77.

by the government of a "compelling and overriding national interest in requiring Mr. Caldwell's testimony which cannot be served by any alternative means."[19] After Caldwell still refused to even appear before the grand jury, he was held in contempt by the District Court.[20] On appeal, the Ninth Circuit found that the First Amendment provides a qualified testimonial privilege to reporters; therefore, not only was the scope of permissible interrogation limited, but Caldwell was privileged to refuse to appear before the grand jury at all, absent some special showing of necessity by the government.[21]

In the Supreme Court's 5-4 majority opinion,[22] Justice Byron White initially noted that the First Amendment had not been interpreted to confer upon the press any exemption from general laws.[23] In the specific context of criminal investigations by grand juries, he noted that the "great weight of authority" historically had refused to exempt journalists from the duty all citizens have to appear and testify.[24]

The majority declined to create a First Amendment testimonial privilege here because it believed that the burden on news gathering caused by requiring reporters to answer legitimate grand jury questions did not outweigh the public interest in law enforcement and effective grand jury proceedings; according to the Court, this holding imperiled only a small portion of those confidential relationships actually deserving of anonymity.[25] There was no evidence before the Court that requiring journalists to testify before grand juries would significantly impoverish the flow of news.[26] In addition, the majority feared that conferring First Amendment protection upon reporters' agreements to conceal information relating to crimes would create "a private system of informers operated by the press" that would be beyond legislative or judicial control.[27]

---

[19]United States v. Caldwell, 311 F. Supp. 358, 362 (N.D. Cal. 1970).

[20]408 U.S. at 678.

[21]*Id.* at 679.

[22]Chief Justice Burger and Justices Blackmun, Rehnquist, and Powell joined in Justice White's majority opinion. Justice Powell also filed a separate concurring opinion. The significance of his concurrence is discussed *infra* notes 34–37. Justices Brennan and Marshall joined in Justice Stewart's dissenting opinion. In a separate dissent, Justice Douglas argued that the First Amendment grants reporters an absolute privilege not to appear or testify before a grand jury "unless the reporter himself is implicated in a crime." 408 U.S. at 712 (Douglas, J., dissenting).

[23]408 U.S. at 683. Justice White pointed out that prior decisions permit general laws to be enforced against the press, *see id.* at 682–83, permit libel and slander actions against the press, *see id.* at 683–84, and refuse to grant the press special access to information unavailable to the general public, *see id.* at 684.

[24]*Id.* at 685. The Court noted that at common law, reporters were not relieved of the duty to testify about confidential information, *id.* at 685–86, based on the "ancient role" of the grand jury as an essential safeguard against "hasty, malicious and oppressive persecution," *id.* at 686–88 & n.23.

[25]*Id.* at 690–95. Because the grand jury inquiries are limited to criminal matters, the Court felt that the "vast bulk" of journalist-informant confidentiality agreements would be unaffected. *See id.* at 691. Of those affected, agreements concealing crimes or evidence of crimes are "hardly deserving of constitutional protection." *Id.* at 691–92.

[26]*Id.* at 693. Justice White described estimates of the deterrent effect as being "widely divergent" and "speculative." *Id.* at 693–94. He argued that, even in the face of the threat of grand jury subpoenas, informants "sincerely interested in furnishing evidence of crime" will continue to talk with reporters. *Id.* at 694–95. "From the beginning of our country the press has operated without constitutional protection for press informants and the press has flourished." *Id.* at 698–99. Later, Justice White also argued that any privilege short of an absolute privilege would fail to completely allay the suspicions of "sensitive" confidential sources, because the precise scope of its protection would be uncertain. *Id.* at 702–03.

In more recent cases, the Supreme Court has restated its reluctance to recognize a constitutional testimonial privilege without clear proof of any deterrent effect. *See* Cohen v. Cowles Media Co., 111 S. Ct. 2513, 18 Media L. Rep. 2273 (1991), *on remand,* 479 N.W.2d 387, 19 Media L. Rep. 1858 (Minn. 1992); University of Pa. v. Equal Empl. Opportunity Comm'n, 493 U.S. 182 (1990).

[27]408 U.S. at 697. Justice White distinguished such a system of informers from the system of informers operated by law enforcement officials on the grounds that, in the latter case, the decision to "unmask" an informer rests in public, not private, hands. *Id.* at 698.

The majority opinion rejected the conditional constitutional privilege proposed by the reporters[28] on the grounds that the grand jury's assessment of what information is relevant to its investigation should not be second-guessed[29] and that, in practice, the administration of a qualified privilege "would present practical and conceptual difficulties of a high order."[30] Justice White stressed that the Court's refusal to create a First Amendment reporter's privilege left Congress, state legislatures, state courts, and law enforcement officials free to fashion a reporter's privilege, either qualified or absolute, as they deemed appropriate.[31]

In concluding its analysis, the majority expressly recognized that "news gathering is not without its First Amendment protections."[32] The Court envisioned that, even after *Branzburg,* the judiciary could rely on the Constitution to protect journalists from grand jury actions undertaken other than in "good faith."[33]

Justice Lewis Powell provided the fifth vote essential to the majority opinion, but in addition to joining the majority opinion, he filed a separate concurring opinion to clarify the majority's "good faith" test and underscore that the Court's decision did not eliminate a journalist's constitutional right to safeguard sources from grand jury scrutiny.[34] According to Justice Powell, the majority rejected Caldwell's proposal—that the First Amendment should be interpreted to grant reporters a constitutional privilege to refuse to appear before a grand jury unless the government first meets certain preconditions[35]— and held instead that "[t]he newsman witness, like all other witnesses, will have to appear."[36] Only thereafter, during questioning by a grand jury, may the reporter seek a protective order.[37] Courts, then, on a case-by-case basis, should balance First Amendment interests against the public interest in obtaining the reporter's testimony concerning criminal conduct.

In dissent, Justice Potter Stewart contended that the Court's failure to shield relationships between journalists and their sources from an unbridled grand jury subpoena power would deter the acquisition and publication of

---

[28]Branzburg, Pappas, and Caldwell did not assert that the First Amendment afforded reporters an absolute privilege to never appear before a grand jury; rather, they argued that, before a journalist can be compelled to appear before a grand jury, the First Amendment requires the government to prove that three preconditions have been met: "that the reporter possesses information relevant to a crime the grand jury is investigating, that the information the reporter has is unavailable from other sources, and that the need for the information is sufficiently compelling to override the claimed invasion of First Amendment interests occasioned by the disclosure." *Id.* at 680.

[29]Justice White asserted that society's interest is best served by permitting grand juries to undertake extensive investigations in the manner they deem best, even when such investigations are based only on "tips" or "rumors." *See id.* at 701–02.

[30]*Id.* at 704. In the majority's view, implementing a qualified reporter's privilege would require courts to separate journalists into those eligible and ineligible for such constitutional protection, all to the detriment of the historically expansive definition of "the press" as including " 'every sort of publication which affords a vehicle of information and opinion.' " *Id.* (quoting Lovell v. City of Griffin, 303 U.S. 444 (1938)). Moreover, the majority warned that courts would be "embroiled" in complex factual and legal assessments of whether the need to enforce various laws served a "compelling" governmental interest. *Id.* at 705–06.

[31]*Id.* at 706. The Court noted that the U.S. Attorney General had already done this. *See id.* at 706–07 & n.41; *infra* §14.3(C). Many jurisdictions have accepted this invitation. *See infra* §14.3(H).

[32]408 U.S. at 707.

[33]*Id.* at 707–08.

[34]*Id.* at 709 (Powell, J., concurring).

[35]*See supra* note 28 (discussing reporters' version of "qualified" privilege). Justice Powell argued that such a no-appearance rule "would, as a practical matter, defeat . . . a fair balancing and the essential societal interest in the detection and prosecution of crime would be heavily subordinated." 408 U.S. at 710 n.* (Powell, J., concurring).

[36]*Id.*

[37]*Id.* at 710.

critical information and thereby impoverish the public dialogue, and that the reporter's right to gather news necessarily implies a right to a confidential relationship with news sources free from the threat of compulsory process by government officials.[38] Justice Stewart argued that the numerous authorities submitted to the Court proved that the lack of a testimonial privilege would impair the flow of information to the public; indeed, "*[n]o* such evidence contradicting the existence of such deterrent effects was offered [in the cases]."[39] The Court, according to Justice Stewart, shirked its duty to protect constitutional values when it demanded "elaborate empirical studies" and "scientific" proof of deterrence in a manner never before required in the First Amendment context.[40]

In addition, Justice Stewart maintained that a qualified First Amendment privilege for reporters was no less important than the well-established Fifth Amendment, Fourth Amendment, and common law limits on grand jury subpoena power.[41] Pointing to prior decisions that reconciled the public interest in the grand jury system with competing Fourth and Fifth Amendment interests, Justice Stewart criticized the majority for failing to strike "the proper balance" between the public interest in effective law enforcement and competing First Amendment interests[42] by refusing to transpose to the grand jury context the same safeguards that the Court required where other government investigations threatened First Amendment freedoms.[43]

Justice Stewart concluded that, before forcing a journalist to appear before a grand jury, the government should be required to demonstrate that (1) the reporter's information is "clearly relevant" to an alleged crime, (2) the information "cannot be obtained by alternate means," and (3) the government's interest in the information is "compelling and overriding."[44] Failure to require this preliminary showing would permit the government to harass the press.[45] Finally, Justice Stewart concluded that, although the application of this qualified testimonial privilege might prove difficult in practice, it is the function of courts to make hard choices.[46]

Branzburg kicked off a flurry of litigation and legislation to define a reporter's right to refuse to disclose information obtained while gathering news. The following sections detail that activity.

---

[38]*Id.* at 728–32 (Stewart, J., dissenting).

[39]*Id.* at 732–33. In related contexts, courts have recognized the dangers that exist to informants. John Z. v. Superior Ct., 2 Cal. Rptr. 2d 556 (Cal. Ct. App. 1991).

[40]*Id.* at 733–36. Justice Stewart explained that decisions in prior speech cases had been reached entirely "on the basis of common sense and available information." *Id.* at 733. It also seems obvious that most people who may engage in clandestine criminal acts will not invite reporters to observe them commit those acts if they know the reporters can be compelled to reveal their identities to law enforcement officials. *See also* Blasi, *The Newsman's Privilege: An Empirical Study,* 70 MICH. L. REV. 229 (1971); Osborn, *The Reporter's Confidentiality Privilege: Updating the Empirical Evidence After a Decade of Subpoenas,* 17 COLUM. HUM. RTS. L. REV. 57 (1985).

[41]408 U.S. at 737. Justice Stewart equated the public interest in democratic decision-making based on robust public debate—an interest secured by the First Amendment—with the interests protected by the Fifth Amendment, Fourth Amendment, and common law exemptions from grand jury testimony. *Id.* at 736–38.

[42]*Id.* at 738.

[43]*Id.* at 739–43. The specific safeguards identified by Justice Stewart include the requirement that the government prove that the information sought in an investigation is *clearly relevant* to a *compelling* governmental interest. *Id.* at 739–40.

[44]*Id.* at 743.

[45]*Id.* at 744 n.34. Justice Stewart worried that the Court's decision would encourage the government to conduct "fishing expedition[s]" and "to try to annex the press as an investigative arm, since any time government wants to probe relationships between the newsman and his source, it can, on virtually any pretext, convene a grand jury and compel the journalist to testify." *Id.*

[46]408 U.S. at 745–46.

§14.3 Sources of Protection

§14.3(A) The First Amendment and State Constitutions

Despite the Supreme Court's ruling in *Branzburg,* the federal courts of appeal, in later cases not involving grand juries, have held that the First Amendment protects the confidentiality of news sources.[47] The circuit courts have stressed the Supreme Court's recognition of a constitutional right to gather news[48] and have almost uniformly cited Justice Powell's concurring opinion, combined with the opinion of the four dissenters, as authority for the proposition that courts must balance the competing interests on a case-by-case basis to assess the journalist's duty to disclose.[49]

Acknowledging that *Branzburg* ruled out an absolute First Amendment privilege to refuse to reveal news sources, the Courts of Appeals for the District of Columbia,[50] First,[51] Second,[52] Third,[53] Fourth,[54] Fifth,[55] Eighth,[56] Ninth,[57] and Tenth[58] Circuits have recognized a *qualified* First Amendment privilege to withhold the identity of confidential sources in *civil* cases. The Seventh Circuit has yet to confront the issue; however a number of district courts in that circuit have concluded that such a First Amendment right exists.[59] Although no Eleventh Circuit decision has reached this question, the Fifth Circuit's *Miller* decision constitutes valid precedent in the Eleventh Circuit.[60] Only the Sixth Circuit has interpreted *Branzburg* to hold that there is no First Amendment reporter's privilege.[61]

Numerous circuit court decisions have confined *Branzburg* to criminal investigations by grand juries and have held that the case has limited applicability in civil cases, including libel suits against reporters,[62] civil rights cases,[63] civil contempt trials,[64] antitrust litigation,[65] and tort actions[66] involving journal-

---

[47]*See* cases cited *infra* notes 50–59.

[48]*Branzburg,* 408 U.S. at 681 ("without some protection for seeking out the news, freedom of the press could be eviscerated"); *id.* at 706 ("news gathering is not without its First Amendment protections").

[49]*E.g.,* Carey v. Hume, 492 F.2d 631, 636 (D.C. Cir.), *cert. dismissed,* 417 U.S. 938 (1974).

[50]*Id.*

[51]Bruno & Stillman, Inc. v. Globe Newspaper Co., 633 F.2d 583, 6 Media L. Rep. 205 (1st Cir. 1980).

[52]Baker v. F & F Inv., 470 F.2d 778 (2d Cir. 1972), *cert. denied,* 411 U.S. 966 (1973).

[53]Riley v. City of Chester, 612 F.2d 708 (3d Cir. 1979).

[54]United States v. Steelhammer, 561 F.2d 539 (4th Cir. 1977) (per curiam and en banc) (adopting dissenting panel opinion in United States v. Steelhammer, 539 F.2d 373 (4th Cir. 1976)).

[55]Miller v. Transamerican Press, 621 F.2d 721, 6 Media L. Rep. 1598 (5th Cir. 1980), *cert. denied,* 450 U.S. 1041 (1981).

[56]Cervantes v. Time, Inc., 464 F.2d 986, 1 Media L. Rep. 1751 (8th Cir. 1972), *cert. denied,* 409 U.S. 1125 (1973).

[57]Farr v. Pitchess, 522 F.2d 464 (9th Cir. 1975), *cert. denied,* 427 U.S. 912 (1976).

[58]Silkwood v. Kerr-McGee Corp., 563 F.2d 433, 3 Media L. Rep. 1987 (10th Cir. 1977).

[59]May v. Collins, 122 F.R.D. 535 (S.D. Ind. 1988); United States v. Lopez, 14 Media L. Rep. 2203 (N.D. Ill. 1987); Gulliver's Periodicals v. Charles Levy Circulating Co., 455 F. Supp. 1197 (N.D. Ill. 1978).

[60]Bonner v. City of Pritchard, 661 F.2d 1206 (11th Cir. 1981) (adopting as binding precedent all decisions of former Fifth Circuit decided before October 1, 1981).

[61]In re Grand Jury Proceedings, 810 F.2d 580, 13 Media L. Rep. 2049 (6th Cir. 1987).

[62]*See, e.g.,* Carey v. Hume, 492 F.2d 631 (D.C. Cir.), *cert. dismissed,* 417 U.S. 938 (1974); Bruno & Stillman, Inc. v. Globe Newspaper Co., 633 F.2d 583 (1st Cir. 1980); Miller v. Transamerican Press, 621 F.2d 721 (5th Cir. 1980), *cert. denied,* 450 U.S. 1041 (1981); Cervantes v. Time, Inc., 464 F.2d 986 (8th Cir. 1972), *cert. denied,* 409 U.S. 1125 (1973). On *Branzburg's* applicability in grand jury situations, *see infra* §14.6(A).

[63]*See, e.g.,* Baker v. F & F Inv., 470 F.2d 778 (2d Cir. 1972), *cert. denied,* 411 U.S. 966 (1973); Riley v. City of Chester, 612 F.2d 708 (3d Cir. 1979); *see also* May v. Collins, 122 F.R.D. 535 (S.D. Ind. 1988).

[64]*See, e.g.,* United States v. Steelhammer, 561 F.2d 539 (4th Cir. 1977).

[65]*See, e.g.,* McGraw-Hill, Inc. v. Arizona, 680 F.2d 5 (2d Cir.), *cert. denied,* 459 U.S. 909 (1982); *see also* Gulliver's Periodicals v. Charles Levy Circulating Co., 455 F. Supp. 1197 (N.D. Ill. 1978).

[66]*See, e.g.,* Silkwood v. Kerr-McGee Corp., 563 F.2d 433 (10th Cir. 1977).

ists as nonparty witnesses. Moreover, several courts of appeal have relied on this narrow view of *Branzburg* to extend the qualified reporter's privilege to criminal proceedings that do not involve grand juries.[67] The Sixth Circuit's *In re Grand Jury Proceedings*[68] decision stands alone among federal appellate court opinions in holding that, under *Branzburg,* there exists no First Amendment testimonial privilege for reporters in any setting, civil or criminal.[69]

At the state level, too, courts have addressed the issue of whether the First Amendment protects confidential relationships between reporters and their sources. Courts in 21 states have recognized a qualified reporter's privilege under the First Amendment.[70] Courts in 12 states have declared that the Constitution does not confer such a privilege on the press.[71]

---

[67]United States v. LaRouche Campaign, 841 F.2d 1176, 15 Media L. Rep. 1502 (1st Cir. 1988); United States v. Burke, 700 F.2d 70 (2d Cir.), *cert. denied,* 464 U.S. 816 (1983); United States v. Cuthbertson, 630 F.2d 139 (3d Cir. 1980), *cert. denied,* 449 U.S. 1126 (1981); Farr v. Pitchess, 522 F.2d 464 (9th Cir. 1975), *cert. denied,* 427 U.S. 912 (1976). *See also* United States v. Lopez, 14 Media L. Rep. 2203 (N.D. Ill. 1987). *But see* United States v. Cutler, 6 F.3d 67, 73, 21 Media L. Rep. 2075, 2080 (2d Cir. 1993) (indicating that *Burke* is limited to its facts); Karem v. Priest, 744 F. Supp. 136 (W.D. Tex. 1990) (refusing to extend privilege to criminal proceedings).

[68]810 F.2d 580 (6th Cir. 1987).

[69]*Id.* at 584–86. *See also Cutler,* 6 F.3d 67, 21 Media L. Rep. 2075 (questioning whether privilege applies to criminal proceedings).

[70]A First Amendment qualified privilege has been recognized in the following jurisdictions:
Alabama: Norandal U.S.A. v. Local Union Co. 7468, 13 Media L. Rep. 2167 (Ala. Civ. App. 1986).
California: Mitchell v. Superior Ct. (Synanon Church), 690 P.2d 625 (Cal. 1984).
Connecticut: Goldfeld v. Post Pub'g Co., 4 Media L. Rep. 1167 (Conn. Super. Ct. 1978); Connecticut State Bd. of Labor Relations v. Fagin, 370 A.2d 1095 (Conn. Super. Ct. 1976).
Delaware: Delaware v. McBride, 7 Media L. Rep. 1371 (Del. Super. Ct. 1981).
Florida: Tribune Co. v. Huffstetler, 489 So. 2d 722, 12 Media L. Rep. 2289 (Fla. 1986); Morgan v. State, 337 So. 2d 951 (Fla. 1976); Tribune Co. v. Green, 440 So. 2d 484 (Fla. Ct. App. 1983), *review denied,* 447 So. 2d 886 (Fla. 1984); Gadsden County Times v. Horne, 426 So. 2d 1234 (Fla. Ct. App.), *review denied,* 441 So. 2d 631 (Fla. 1983). *But see* Miami Herald Pub'g Co. v. Morejon, 561 So. 2d 577 (Fla. 1990) (holding that First Amendment privilege does not extend to reporter's eyewitness observations of event relevant to subsequent court proceeding); Carroll Contracting v. Edwards, 528 So. 2d 951 (Fla. Ct. App.) (questioning but not deciding whether First Amendment privilege applies to unpublished material that does not implicate confidential source), *review denied sub nom.* Citrus County Chronicle v. Carroll Contracting, 536 So. 2d 243 (Fla. 1988).
Idaho: In re Contempt of Wright, 700 P.2d 40 (Idaho 1985).
Illinois: In re Special Grand Jury Investig., 472 N.E.2d 450 (Ill. 1984) (citing First Amendment authority).
Iowa: Winegard v. Oxberger, 258 N.W.2d 847 (Iowa 1977), *cert. denied,* 436 U.S. 905 (1978).
Kansas: State v. Sandstrom, 581 P.2d 812 (Kan. 1978), *cert. denied,* 440 U.S. 929 (1979).
Louisiana: In re Ridenhour, 520 So. 2d 372, 15 Media L. Rep. 1022 (La. 1988).
Maine: In re Letellier, 578 A.2d 722 (Me. 1990) (adopting First Circuit's interpretation of First Amendment reporter's privilege). *But see* State v. Hohler, 543 A.2d 364 (Me. 1988) (holding that there is no qualified privilege for reporter to refuse to testify about nonconfidential, published information obtained from identified source).
Michigan: In re Photo Mktg. Ass'n, 327 N.W.2d 515 (Mich. Ct. App. 1982) (recognizing qualified First Amendment privilege for confidential information in civil cases). *But see* Marketos v. American Employers Ins. Co., 460 N.W.2d 272 (Mich. Ct. App. 1990) (refusing to recognize qualified First Amendment privilege for *nonconfidential* information in civil cases).
New Hampshire: New Hampshire v. Siel, 444 A.2d 499 (N.H. 1982).
New Jersey: State v. Boiardo, 414 A.2d 14 (N.J. 1980).
New York: O'Neill v. Oakgrove Constr., 523 N.E.2d 277 (N.Y. 1988).
North Carolina: North Carolina v. Smith, 13 Media L. Rep. 1940 (N.C. 1987).
Oklahoma: Taylor v. Miskovsky, 640 P.2d 959 (Okla. 1981).
Vermont: State v. St. Peter, 315 A.2d 254 (Vt. 1974).
Virginia: Brown v. Commonwealth, 204 S.E.2d 429 (Va.), *cert. denied,* 419 U.S. 966 (1974).
Washington: State v. Terwilliger, 11 Media L. Rep. 2463 (Wash. 1985).
West Virginia: State ex rel. Hudok v. Henry, 389 S.E.2d 188 (W. Va. 1989).

[71]Courts in the following jurisdictions have declined to find a First Amendment-based reporter's privilege:
Colorado: Pankratz v. District Ct., 609 P.2d 1101 (Colo. 1980).
Georgia: Vaughn v. State, 381 S.E.2d 30 (Ga. 1989).
Hawaii: In re Goodfader's Appeal, 367 P.2d 472 (Haw. 1961).
Kentucky: Kentucky's highest court declined to consider the question of a First Amendment privilege in Branzburg v. Pound, 461 S.W.2d 345 (Ky. 1970), *aff'd sub nom.* Branzburg v. Hayes, 408 U.S. 665

In Maryland, where the state's highest court at one time upheld a lower court ruling that no privilege applies where a reporter personally observes a crime being committed,[72] more recently refused to decide whether reporters possess a qualified *constitutional* privilege to withhold unpublished material obtained during the news-gathering process from prosecutorial summons.[73] In Texas, the state's highest criminal court has held that the First Amendment does not create a reporter's privilege as to alleged criminal conduct witnessed in a public place;[74] however, other Texas courts have held that a First Amendment reporter's privilege does exist in a civil context.[75]

Courts in 12 states have construed their respective state constitutions to provide a qualified privilege to journalists.[76] Courts in 10 states have found

---

(1972). However, that court later ruled that no reporter's privilege exists on any grounds. Lexington Herald-Leader v. Beard, 690 S.W.2d 374, 11 Media L. Rep. 1376 (Ky. 1984).

Massachusetts: Dow Jones & Co. v. Superior Ct., 303 N.E.2d 847 (Mass. 1973); In re Pappas, 266 N.E.2d 297 (Mass. 1971), *aff'd sub nom.* Branzburg v. Hayes, 408 U.S. 665 (1972).

Missouri: CBS, Inc. (KMOX-TV) v. Campbell, 645 S.W.2d 30 (Mo. Ct. App. 1982) (finding, inter alia, that U.S. Constitution does not permit reporter to refuse grand jury request for production of outtakes containing no confidential sources or information).

Nevada: Newburn v. Howard Hughes Medical Inst., 594 P.2d 1146, 1148 (Nev. 1979) ("Absent a statute, communications to a news reporter do not enjoy a privilege against use as evidence, and the reporter may be compelled to reveal information given to him in his professional capacity.").

New Mexico: Ammerman v. Hubbard Broadcasting, 572 P.2d 1258, 1265 (N.M. Ct. App.) ("The First Amendment does not grant a broadcaster any privilege, qualified or absolute, to refuse to reveal confidential information which is admittedly relevant to a court proceeding."), *cert. denied,* 572 P.2d 1257 (N.M. 1977), *cert. denied,* 436 U.S. 906 (1978).

Ohio: National Broadcasting Co. v. Court of Common Pleas, 556 N.E.2d 1120, 1126–27 (Ohio 1990) (finding that prior Ohio court cases holding that qualified First Amendment privilege exists seem inconsistent with *Branzburg*).

Oregon: State v. Buchanan, 436 P.2d 729 (Or.) (holding that there is no federal right to refuse to testify before grand jury), *cert. denied,* 392 U.S. 905 (1968).

Pennsylvania: In re Taylor, 193 A.2d 181, 184 (Pa. 1963) ("The language of [the United States and Pennsylvania] Constitution[s] is clear, and by no stretch of language can it protect or include under 'freedom of the press,' the non-disclosure of sources of information.").

Rhode Island: Outlet Communications v. Rhode Island, 588 A.2d 1050, 18 Media L. Rep. 1982 (R.I. 1991) (per curiam); Capuano v. Outlet Co., 579 A.2d 469 (R.I. 1990).

[72]Lightman v. State, 295 A.2d 212 (Md. 1972) (per curiam) (affirming Lightman v. State, 294 A.2d 149 (Md. Ct. Spec. App. 1972)), *cert. denied,* 411 U.S. 951 (1973).

[73]WBAL-TV Div., Hearst Corp. v. Maryland, 477 A.2d 776, 10 Media L. Rep. 2121 (Md. 1984).

[74]Ex parte Grothe, 687 S.W.2d 736, 10 Media L. Rep. 2009 (Tex. Crim. App. 1984), *cert. denied,* 474 U.S. 944 (1985). Federal district courts in Texas have issued conflicting opinions on whether the First Amendment reporter's privilege applies in state criminal proceedings. *Compare* Campbell v. Klevenhagen, 18 Media L. Rep. 2113 (S.D. Tex. 1991) (interpreting Fifth Circuit authority to require application of privilege in state criminal proceedings) *with* Karem v. Priest, 744 F. Supp. 136 (W.D. Tex. 1990) (refusing to extend privilege to state criminal proceedings).

[75]Channel Two Television Co. v. Dickerson, 725 S.W.2d 470 (Tex. Ct. App. 1987); Dallas Oil & Gas v. Mouer, 533 S.W.2d 70 (Tex. Ct. App. 1976).

[76]*California:* Mitchell v. Superior Ct. (Synanon Church), 690 P.2d 625 (Cal. 1984).

Florida: Florida v. Peterson, 7 Media L. Rep. 1090 (Fla. Cir. Ct. 1981); Coira v. Depoo Hosp., 4 Media L. Rep. 1692 (Fla. Cir. Ct. 1978).

Idaho: In re Contempt of Wright, 700 P.2d 40 (Idaho 1985).

Louisiana: In re Ridenhour, 520 So. 2d 372, 15 Media L. Rep. 1022 (La. 1988).

Maine: In re Letellier, 578 A.2d 722 (Me. 1990) (interpreting Maine Constitution to be consistent with First Amendment requirement that competing interests be balanced on case-by-case basis). *But see* State v. Hohler, 543 A.2d 364 (Me. 1988) (refusing to recognize reporter's privilege to refuse to testify concerning nonconfidential, published information obtained from identified source).

New Hampshire: New Hampshire v. Siel, 444 A.2d 499 (N.H. 1982); Opinion of Justices, 373 A.2d 644 (N.H. 1977).

New York: O'Neill v. Oakgrove Constr., 523 N.E.2d 277 (N.Y. 1988).

North Carolina: North Carolina v. Smith, 13 Media L. Rep. 1940 (N.C. 1987).

Ohio: Fawley v. Quirk, 11 Media L. Rep. 2336 (Ohio Ct. App. 1985).

Texas: Channel Two Television Co. v. Dickerson, 725 S.W.2d 470, 13 Media L. Rep. 2133 (Tex. Ct. App. 1987) (establishing qualified privilege in civil case pursuant to article I, §8 of Texas Constitution).

West Virginia: State ex rel. Hudok v. Henry, 389 S.E.2d 188 (W. Va. 1989).

Wisconsin: State v. Knops, 183 N.W.2d 93 (Wis. 1971); Amato v. Fellner, 4 Media L. Rep. 1552 (Wis. Ct. App. 1978).

that their respective state constitutions do not afford the press this privilege.[77] A constitutionally based reporter's privilege has been applied by state courts in both civil[78] and criminal[79] cases.

The Alaska Supreme Court has recognized a qualified reporter's privilege but did so without specifying the source of the privilege.[80] There are no reported decisions on this issue in Arizona,[81] Arkansas,[82] Indiana,[83] Minnesota,[84] Mississippi, Montana,[85] Nebraska,[86] North Dakota,[87] South Carolina, South Dakota, Tennessee,[88] Utah, or Wyoming.

Justice Powell's prescription that each claim of privilege should be judged by "the striking of a proper balance" between competing interests in the particular case[89] has become the law in the substantial majority of federal

---

[77]*Colorado:* Pankratz v. District Ct., 609 P.2d 1101 (Colo. 1980).
Georgia: Vaughn v. State, 381 S.E.2d 30 (Ga. 1989).
Kentucky: Lexington Herald-Leader v. Beard, 690 S.W.2d 374, 11 Media L. Rep. 1376 (Ky. 1984).
Michigan: Marketos v. American Employers Ins. Co., 460 N.W.2d 272, 281 (Mich. Ct. App. 1990) (holding that "nothing in the Michigan Constitution or its history . . . would lead us to conclude that its drafters intended to create a journalist's privilege as to nonconfidential materials").
Missouri: CBS, Inc. (KMOX-TV) v. Campbell, 645 S.W.2d 30 (Mo. Ct. App. 1982).
Nevada: Newburn v. Howard Hughes Medical Inst., 594 P.2d 1146, 1148 (Nev. 1979) ("Absent a statute, communications to a news reporter do not enjoy a privilege against use as evidence, and the reporter may be compelled to reveal information given to him in his professional capacity.").
Oregon: State v. Buchanan, 436 P.2d 729 (Or.), cert. denied, 392 U.S. 905 (1968).
Pennsylvania: In re Taylor, 193 A.2d 181 (Pa. 1963).
Rhode Island: Outlet Communications v. Rhode Island, 588 A.2d 1050, 18 Media L. Rep. 1982 (R.I. 1991) (per curiam).
Texas: Ex parte Grothe, 687 S.W.2d 736, 10 Media L. Rep. 2009 (Tex. Crim. App. 1984) (holding that article I, §8 of Texas Constitution does not create privilege whereby photojournalists may refuse to testify about alleged criminal activity witnessed in public place), cert. denied, 474 U.S. 944 (1985).

[78]*See* cases cited *supra* note 70.

[79]Courts in the following states have extended the qualified privilege to criminal cases:
Delaware: Delaware v. McBride, 7 Media L. Rep. 1371 (Del. Super. Ct. 1981).
Florida: Tribune Co. v. Huffstetler 489 So. 2d 722, 12 Media L. Rep. 2289 (Fla. 1986).
Idaho: In re Contempt of Wright, 700 P.2d 40 (Idaho 1985).
Illinois: In re Special Grand Jury Investig., 472 N.E.2d 450 (Ill. 1984) (citing First Amendment authority).
Kansas: State v. Sandstrom, 581 P.2d 812 (Kan. 1978), cert. denied, 440 U.S. 929 (1979).
Louisiana: In re Ridenhour, 520 So. 2d 372, 15 Media L. Rep. 1022 (La. 1988).
New Jersey: State v. Boiardo, 414 A.2d 14 (N.J. 1980). *But see supra* note 71.
North Carolina: North Carolina v. Smith, 13 Media L. Rep. 1940 (N.C. 1987).
Ohio: In re McAuley, 408 N.E.2d 697 (Ohio Ct. App. 1979).
Vermont: State v. St. Peter, 315 A.2d 254 (Vt. 1974).
Virginia: Brown v. Commonwealth, 204 S.E.2d 429 (Va.), cert. denied, 419 U.S. 966 (1974).
Washington: State v. Terwilliger, 11 Media L. Rep. 2463 (Wash. 1985).
Wisconsin: State v. Knops, 183 N.W.2d 93 (Wis. 1971).

[80]Nebel v. Mapco Petroleum, 10 Media L. Rep. 1871 (Alaska 1984).

[81]One Arizona court implied that a privilege not to disclose confidential information exists, but it did not identify the exact source of that privilege. Bartlett v. Superior Ct., 722 P.2d 346 (Ariz. Ct. App. 1986). In addition, the Arizona legislature has enacted a reporter's shield law. *See infra* §14.3(H).

[82]The state legislature has enacted a reporter's shield law. *See infra* §14.3(H).

[83]Indiana courts, however, have recognized a qualified reporter's privilege based on the state's shield law. Lipps v. State, 258 N.E.2d 622 (Ind. 1970); Jamerson v. Anderson Newspapers, 469 N.E.2d 1243 (Ind. Ct. App. 1984); *see also infra* §14.3(H).

[84]However, in Thompson v. State, 170 N.W.2d 101 (Minn. 1969), the Supreme Court of Minnesota, citing its earlier holding in State v. Kasherman, 224 N.W. 838, 838 (Minn. 1929) ("[i]t would be intolerable . . . if witnesses before a grand jury might delay its proceedings by requiring an affirmative ruling from the court upon the propriety of questions before answering them"), implied that a criminal defendant is entitled to know the identity of a reporter's confidential informants. 170 N.W.2d at 103.

[85]The state legislature has enacted a reporter's shield law. *See infra* §14.3(H).

[86]The state legislature has enacted a reporter's shield law. *See infra* §14.3(H).

[87]The state legislature has enacted a reporter's shield law. *See infra* §14.3(H).

[88]Although the Supreme Court of Tennessee has ruled out a qualified privilege based on common law, it has not yet confronted the question of whether a constitutionally based privilege exists. Austin v. Memphis Pub'g Co., 655 S.W.2d 146 (Tenn. 1983).

[89]Branzburg v. Hayes, 408 U.S. 665, 710 (1971) (Powell, J., concurring).

courts.[90] Most courts that have adopted Justice Powell's balancing approach[91] apply the three-prong test first outlined in *Garland v. Torre*,[92] namely: (1) Is the information highly material and relevant? (2) Can the information be obtained from an alternative source? and (3) Is there a compelling interest in the information?[93] Courts in the Tenth Circuit expressly add a fourth prong to this test: What is the nature of the underlying suit?[94]

Because the balancing approach is by nature a fact-specific inquiry, other courts have expressly declined to provide a definitive list of factors to be considered in the weighing process.[95] For example, in *United States v. Markiewicz*,[96] the court elected not to apply the *Garland* test and used a unique three-prong analysis—i.e., whether the testimony sought is relevant, not unduly cumulative, and not available from other sources—on the ground that "the test to be employed should be flexible."[97]

Exhaustion of alternative sources appears to be required in all cases. The party seeking disclosure must have exhausted every "reasonable" or "practical" alternative source.[98] What is "reasonable" ultimately depends on the particular facts and circumstances of each case. For example, where the party seeking disclosure is aware of specific people or a defined group of people who also may possess the information sought, the party must contact, interview, or depose those people before requiring the journalist to testify.[99] This principle holds even where as many as 60 depositions may be involved,[100] or where such additional discovery may prove "time-consuming, costly and unproductive."[101]

However, it would be unreasonable to require the party seeking disclosure to undertake further investigation where its knowledge of additional potential sources is "so imprecise as to afford [the party] no reasonable basis to know where to begin."[102] Moreover, some courts have held that the "exhaustion requirement" is colored by the nature of the information sought. For example,

---

[90]*See supra* notes 50–69.

[91]*See, e.g.,* Carey v. Hume, 492 F.2d 631 (D.C. Cir.), *cert. dismissed,* 417 U.S. 938 (1974); Miller v. Transamerican Press, 621 F.2d 721 (5th Cir. 1980), *cert. denied,* 450 U.S. 1041 (1981).

[92]259 F.2d 545 (2d Cir.), *cert. denied,* 358 U.S. 910 (1958). This case is discussed in detail *infra* §14.5(B).

[93]259 F.2d at 548–50.

[94]*See* Silkwood v. Kerr-McGee Corp., 563 F.2d 433 (10th Cir. 1977).

[95]*See* Bruno & Stillman, Inc. v. Globe Newspaper Co., 633 F.2d 583, 598 (1st Cir. 1980) (explaining that "[t]he task is one that demands sensitivity, invites flexibility, and defies formula"); United States v. Cuthbertson, 630 F.2d 139, 148 (3d Cir. 1980) (concluding that "we need not determine the precise factors the district court should consider and how it should weigh them in making its decision").

[96]732 F. Supp. 316 (N.D.N.Y. 1990).

[97]*Id.* at 320–21.

[98]*See, e.g.,* Zerilli v. Smith, 656 F.2d 705, 713 (D.C. Cir. 1981); Riley v. City of Chester, 612 F.2d 708, 717 (3d Cir. 1979); In re Williams, 766 F. Supp. 358, 369–71, 18 Media L. Rep. 2177, 2186–88 (W.D. Pa. 1991), *aff'd by equally divided court,* 963 F.2d 567, 20 Media L. Rep. 1232 (3d Cir. 1992); Liberty Lobby v. Rees, 111 F.R.D. 19, 22 (D.D.C. 1986). *See also infra* note 404.

[99]*See Zerilli,* 656 F.2d at 714–39; McGraw-Hill, Inc. v. Arizona, 680 F.2d 5, 8–9 (2d Cir. 1982); *Riley,* 612 F.2d at 717; *In re Williams,* 766 F. Supp. at 369–70; In re Special Grand Jury Investig. of Alleged Violation of Juvenile Ct. Act, 472 N.E.2d 450 (Ill. 1984) (holding that alternate sources had not been exhausted where only one of four witnesses had been called to testify); Sommer v. PMEC Assocs. & Co., 18 Media L. Rep. 2141, 2143 (S.D.N.Y. 1991); *Liberty Lobby,* 111 F.R.D. at 22.

[100]*See* Carey v. Hume, 492 F.2d 631, 639 (D.C. Cir. 1974).

[101]*See Zerilli,* 656 F.2d at 714–15. *See also* Shoen v. Shoen, 5 F.3d 1289, 1296, 21 Media L. Rep. 1961, 1964 (9th Cir. 1993) (written interrogatories do not satisfy exhaustion requirement where person can be deposed).

[102]*Carey,* 492 F.2d at 638–39. *Accord* Illinois v. Arya, 589 N.E.2d 832, 19 Media L. Rep. 2079 (Ill. App. Ct. 1992) (extensively reviewing numerous authorities on exhaustion and concluding that only those sources known or identified or likely to be known or identified need be exhausted).

in *United States v. Cuthbertson*,[103] the Third Circuit concluded that no alternative source could exist where film in the possession of a television network was the only recording of the information sought—verbatim statements of prospective witnesses.[104]

§14.3(B) The Fifth Amendment

While *Branzburg* limited the scope of First Amendment protection for the press, it did not restrict the use of the Fifth Amendment[105] as a mechanism for protecting a journalist's confidential sources.[106] The leading case in this area is *In re Seper*,[107] where the Ninth Circuit held that a newsperson possessed a Fifth Amendment privilege to refuse to disclose the identity of confidential informants.[108] Jerry Seper wrote news stories based on confidential information he had obtained from unidentified sources "close" to an ongoing Internal Revenue Service (IRS) audit of the United Liquor Company.[109] Following publication, United brought suit under 26 U.S.C. Section 7217[110] and attempted to depose the reporter as a nonparty witness.[111] At his deposition, Seper admitted that he had received the information from two IRS agents but refused to name them on the grounds that disclosure would incriminate him under 26 U.S.C. Section 7213(a)(3).[112] While the voluntary disclosure of incriminating facts waives the Fifth Amendment privilege, the Ninth Circuit held that Seper's deposition testimony did not reveal the scienter necessary for a conviction under Section 7213(a)(3); Seper therefore retained his Fifth Amendment privilege.[113]

Although *Seper* is somewhat unusual because a criminal penalty was provided for the publication of certain materials, the Fifth Amendment remains a valuable shield for reporters where other news gathering activities raise the specter of criminal prosecution. The Fifth Amendment may be invoked in civil as well as criminal proceedings[114] but can also be waived under certain circumstances[115] and can be overcome by a grant of immunity.[116]

---

[103]630 F.2d 139 (3d Cir. 1980).

[104]*Id.* at 148. *See also* United States v. Steelhammer, 539 F.2d 373, 376–77 (4th Cir. 1976) (reasoning that reporters could be compelled to testify, even where information sought could have been adduced from many other people, because information was not confidential).

[105]The Fifth Amendment provides, in relevant part, that "No person ... shall be compelled in any criminal case to be a witness against himself." U.S. CONST. amend. V.

[106]*See* In re Corrugated Container Antitrust Litig., 661 F.2d 1145, 1149 (7th Cir. 1981) (explaining that, in reaching its decision, *Branzburg* "in no way envisioned any narrowing of the Fifth Amendment"), *aff'd sub nom.* Pillsbury Co. v. Conboy, 459 U.S. 248 (1983).

[107]705 F.2d 1499 (9th Cir. 1983).

[108]*Id.* at 1502.

[109]*Id.* at 1500.

[110]Section 7431 creates a private right of action against any person who unlawfully discloses a tax return or return information.

[111]705 F.2d at 1500.

[112]*Id.* at 1501. Section 7213(a)(3) provides that it is a felony "for any person to whom any return or return information ... is disclosed in a manner unauthorized by this title thereafter willfully to print or publish ... any such return information."

[113]705 F.2d at 1502.

[114]Maness v. Meyers, 419 U.S. 449, 464 (1975); Kastigar v. United States, 406 U.S. 441, 444 (1972).

[115]Rogers v. United States, 340 U.S. 367 (1951).

[116]*See, e.g.,* In re Lewis, 384 F. Supp. 133 (C.D. Cal. 1974) (describing case in which court granted newsperson immunity and ordered him to provide information he had refused to give on basis of Fifth Amendment privilege against self-incrimination), *aff'd sub nom.* Lewis v. United States, 517 F.2d 236 (9th Cir. 1975).

§14.3(C) Department of Justice Guidelines

The U.S. Attorney General has adopted guidelines for issuing subpoenas to members of the press and for interrogating, indicting, or arresting journalists.[117] These guidelines are intended to shield reporters from "compulsory process, whether civil or criminal, which might impair the news gathering function" and are to be followed by all Department of Justice lawyers in all cases.[118]

In making the initial decision to subpoena a reporter, Section 50.10 requires that members of the Department balance First Amendment considerations against the public interest in effective law enforcement,[119] attempt to obtain the information sought from alternative sources,[120] and negotiate with the media to reconcile the competing interests.[121] The Attorney General's, Assistant Attorney General's, or U.S. Attorney's express authorization must be obtained in cases where a subpoena is thought to be necessary.[122]

The Attorney General will grant such authorization based, in part, on the nature of the underlying proceeding. In criminal cases, the lawyer seeking the subpoena should demonstrate that there are reasonable grounds to believe that a crime has occurred and that the information sought is essential to a successful investigation.[123] In civil cases, the issuance standard is that reasonable grounds exist for believing that the information sought is essential to the successful litigation of a case of substantial importance.[124]

Much of the debate surrounding Section 50.10 centers on whether the government's failure to abide by these guidelines renders the subpoena invalid. Section 50.10(n) expressly provides that "[t]he principles set forth in this section are not intended to create or recognize any legally enforceable right in any person." Consistent with this limitation, some courts have concluded that there is no burden on the government to show that it has adhered to interdepartmental policy statements or guidelines such as Section 50.10.[125] In contrast, other courts have held that the government "must" follow Section 50.10.[126] As one court explained, "[g]overnment agencies must follow their own regulations when important individual constitutional rights are affected even if such regulations are more rigid and strict than required by law."[127]

---

[117]28 C.F.R. §50.10 (1992).
[118]*Id.*
[119]*Id.* §50.10(a).
[120]*Id.* §50.10(b).
[121]*Id.* §50.10(c), (d).
[122]28 C.F.R. §50.10(e).
[123]*Id.* §50.10(f)(1).
[124]*Id.* §50.10(f)(2).
[125]In re Lewis, 384 F. Supp. 133, 137 (C.D. Cal. 1974), *aff'd on other grounds sub nom.* Lewis v. United States, 517 F.2d 236 (9th Cir. 1975); In re Shain, 978 F.2d 850, 20 Media L. Rep. 1930 (4th Cir. 1992).
[126]In re Williams, 766 F. Supp. 358, 371, 18 Media L. Rep. 2177, 2188 (W.D. Pa. 1991), *aff'd by equally divided court,* 963 F.2d 567, 20 Media L. Rep. 1232 (3d Cir. 1992); United States v. Blanton, 534 F. Supp. 295, 297 (S.D. Fla. 1982); Maurice v. National Labor Relations Bd., 7 Media L. Rep. 2221, 2224 (S.D. W. Va. 1981), *rev'd on other grounds,* 691 F.2d 182 (4th Cir. 1982).
[127]*Maurice,* 7 Media L. Rep. at 2224. *See also* United States v. Caceres, 440 U.S. 741, 751 n.14 (1979) (holding that government agencies have duty to obey their own internal procedures even where those procedures are more rigorous than otherwise required but refusing to exclude evidence because of agency's violation of its own rules).

§14.3(D) Federal Rules of Criminal Procedure

When served with a subpoena duces tecum in a criminal case pending in federal court, members of the press may argue that the subpoena fails to satisfy the requirements of Federal Rule of Criminal Procedure 17(c).[128] Rule 17 is not a discovery device; it instead allows litigants in criminal cases to procure admissible evidence in the possession of third parties for use during trial.[129] Thus, any items demanded from a journalist that are not relevant, material, and admissible in the underlying criminal proceeding are beyond the scope of Rule 17(c).[130]

Even if the subpoenaed materials fall within the scope of Rule 17(c), the moving party is not entitled to *pretrial* production and inspection unless it proves in addition that (1) the materials are not otherwise available before trial, (2) they are necessary in preparing for trial, and (3) the production request is made in good faith.[131]

The federal courts of appeals have disagreed as to whether this same *Nixon* test applies when production is limited to an in camera inspection of the materials by the court before trial. For example, the First Circuit has refined the *Nixon* test to require only three showings: relevancy, admissibility, and specificity.[132] According to the Third Circuit, the second and third elements of the *Nixon* test are inapplicable where production is only to the court.[133] In dicta, the Second Circuit has recommended that district courts undertake in camera inspections if there are "any reasonable grounds to believe that inspection ... would yield any probative evidence."[134]

When Rule 17(c) objections are joined with a claim of First Amendment privilege, the burden on the moving party is greater than in other cases. In *United States v. Burke*,[135] the Court of Appeals for the Second Circuit held that a journalist may be required to disclose confidential sources pursuant to Rule 17(c) "only upon a clear and specific showing that the information is: highly material and relevant, necessary or critical to the maintenance of the claim, and not obtainable from other available sources."[136]

---

[128]Rule 17(c) provides:
A subpoena may also command the person to whom it is directed to produce the books, papers, documents or other objects designated therein. The court on motion made promptly may quash or modify the subpoena if compliance would be unreasonable or oppressive. The court may direct that books, papers, documents or objects designated in the subpoena be produced before the court at a time prior to the trial or prior to the time when they are to be offered in evidence and may upon their production permit the books, papers, documents, or objects or portions thereof to be inspected by the parties and their attorneys.

[129]*See* Bowman Dairy Co. v. United States, 341 U.S. 214, 221 (1951) (holding "any document or other materials, admissible as evidence" subject to subpoena under Rule 17); United States v. Cuthbertson, 630 F.2d 139, 144 (3d Cir. 1980) ("Thus, rule 17(c) is designed as an aid for obtaining relevant evidentiary material that the moving party may use at trial."), *cert. denied*, 449 U.S. 1126 (1981).

[130]United States v. Paez, 13 Media L. Rep. 1973 (S.D. Fla. 1987).

[131]*See* United States v. Nixon, 418 U.S. 683 (1974); United States v. LaRouche Campaign, 841 F.2d 1176 (1st Cir. 1988); *Cuthbertson*, 630 F.2d 139.

[132]*See LaRouche*, 841 F.2d 1179–80.

[133]*See Cuthbertson*, 630 F.2d at 145.

[134]United States v. Burke, 700 F.2d 70, 78 n.9 (2d Cir.), *cert. denied*, 464 U.S. 816 (1983).

[135]700 F.2d 70 (2d Cir.), *cert. denied*, 464 U.S. 816 (1983).

[136]*Id.* at 77; *see also* United States v. Winans, 11 Media L. Rep. 1279, 1280 (S.D.N.Y. 1985) ("Where First Amendment issues are raised, the burden on the party seeking production is more demanding than usual."); United States v. Marcos, 17 Media L. Rep. 2005 (S.D.N.Y. 1990) (granting network's Rule 17(c) motion to squash because government failed to meet second element of *Burke* test—proving that material was necessary or critical to case).

At the state level, courts in Delaware,[137] Ohio,[138] and Vermont[139] have construed and applied analogous state rules of procedure.

§14.3(E) Federal Rules of Civil Procedure

Journalists who receive discovery requests for confidential information or the identity of informants in connection with civil litigation in the federal courts may turn to a number of provisions of the Federal Rules of Civil Procedure for protection. These include a Rule 26(b)(1) relevancy objection, a Rule 26(c) protective order, a Rule 26(d) scheduling order, a Rule 45(c)(3) motion to quash, and a Rule 45(c)(2)(B) objection to producing documents.

Rule 26 contains general provisions governing discovery. Pursuant to Rule 26(b)(1), civil litigants "may obtain discovery regarding any matter, not privileged, which is *relevant* to the subject matter involved in the pending action." In 1979, the Supreme Court admonished that the relevancy standard of Rule 26(b)(1) is heightened in cases where discovery implicates First Amendment interests.[140]

Rule 26(c) grants courts broad powers to halt or modify discovery requests in order to protect persons from unjust disclosures.[141] Under this provision, courts have balanced the hardship to the person seeking protection against the hardship to the party seeking discovery,[142] given more weight to interests that have a "distinctively social value," such as First Amendment interests,[143] and required litigants to seek the information from nonmedia sources first.[144] When

---

[137] In McBride v. State, 477 A.2d 174 (Del. 1984), the Supreme Court of Delaware upheld a trial court ruling that the criminal defendant's pretrial demand for production by a newspaper was beyond the scope of Superior Court Rule 17(c), because the defendant failed to show that the requested material was not "readily available from other sources." *Id.* at 180.

[138] In State v. Geis, 441 N.E.2d 803 (Ohio Ct. App. 1981), the court held that, where a Criminal Rule 17(c) motion to quash a subpoena duces tecum is joined with a claim of privilege under Ohio's shield law, the trial court *must* perform an in camera review of the requested materials in order to assure the confidentiality of the evidence. *See also* National Broadcasting Co. v. Court of Common Pleas, 556 N.E.2d 1120, 1127 (Ohio 1990) (explaining that press may rely on Criminal Rule 17(c) as adequate legal remedy for quashing "overbroad" subpoenas).

[139] In Vermont v. Blais, 6 Media L. Rep. 1537 (Vt. Dist. Ct. 1980), the court stated that federal cases construing Federal Rule of Criminal Procedure 17(c) are pertinent to questions raised under Vermont Rule of Criminal Procedure 17(c) and proceeded to apply the *Nixon* test. 6 Media L. Rep. at 1539.

[140] *See* Herbert v. Lando, 441 U.S. 153, 177 (1979); *id.* at 179–80 (Powell, J., concurring); Bruno & Stillman, Inc. v. Globe Newspaper Co., 633 F.2d 583, 596 (1st Cir. 1980) (observing "heightened sensitivity to any First Amendment implication that might result from the compelled disclosure of sources"); Solarex Corp. v. Arco Solar, 121 F.R.D. 163, 169–70 (E.D.N.Y. 1988), *aff'd,* 870 F.2d 642 (2d Cir. 1989).

[141] Rule 26(c) provides:
Upon motion by a party or by the person from whom discovery is sought, and for good cause shown, the court in which the action is pending or alternatively, on matters relating to a deposition, the court in the district where the deposition is to be taken may make any order which justice requires to protect a party or person from annoyance, embarrassment, oppression, or undue burden or expense, including one or more of the following: (1) that the disclosure or discovery not be had; (2) that the disclosure or discovery may be had only on specified terms and conditions, including a designation of the time or place; (3) that the discovery may be had only by a method of discovery other than that selected by the party seeking discovery; (4) that certain matters not be inquired into, or that the scope of the discovery be limited to certain matters; (5) that discovery be conducted with no one present except persons designated by the court; (6) that a deposition after being sealed be opened only by order of the court; (7) that a trade secret or other confidential research, development, or commercial information not be revealed or be revealed only in a designated way; and (8) that the parties simultaneously file specified documents or information enclosed in sealed envelopes to be opened as directed by the court.

[142] *See Solarex,* 121 F.R.D. at 169; *see also* Marrese v. American Academy of Orthopaedic Surgeons, 726 F.2d 1150, 1159 (7th Cir. 1984) (discussing Rule 26(c) motion brought by nonmedia professional association).

[143] *Solarex,* 121 F.R.D. at 169.

[144] *See* Solargen Elec. Motor Car Corp. v. American Motors Corp., 506 F. Supp. 546 (N.D.N.Y. 1981) (granting reporter's Rule 26(c) motion on grounds that party seeking discovery failed to explore alternative

First Amendment interests are found to outweigh the need for complete disclosure, the courts use a number of alternatives to complete disclosure "limited only by the needs of the situation and the ingenuity of court and counsel."[145]

Rule 26(d) empowers courts to control the sequence and timing of discovery "in the interests of justice." Under this rule, a reporter may request that sensitive discovery take place last or, at a minimum, only after the party seeking discovery first has resorted to nonconfidential sources.[146] The threshold for granting a Rule 26(d) motion to control the order and timing of discovery is lower than that for granting a Rule 26(c) motion to halt discovery.[147]

The issuing of civil subpoenas in federal court is governed by Rule 45 of the Federal Rules of Civil Procedure. Pursuant to Rule 45, the court may quash or modify a subpoena that is "unreasonable and oppressive." In *Los Angeles Memorial Coliseum Commission v. National Football League*,[148] the court explained that "[p]ersons who object to subpoenas on grounds of privilege thus have the alternative remedies under the Federal Rules of a motion to quash under Rule 45(b) or a motion for a protective order under Rule 26(c)."[149] The court in that case proceeded to use Rule 45 to quash subpoenas duces tecum that had been served on two nonparty journalists.[150]

Rule 45(c)(2)(B) entitles the person to whom a subpoena for documents or other tangible things is directed to lodge an objection to the production of any or all materials designated in the notice. The party objecting pursuant to Rule 45(c)(2)(B) need not petition the court for protection; instead, upon receiving such an objection, it is the duty of the party serving the subpoena to obtain an order compelling compliance with it.

§14.3(F) Federal Rules of Evidence

Rule 403 of the Federal Rules of Evidence empowers courts to exclude admittedly relevant evidence where its probative value is "substantially outweighed" by considerations of "needless presentation of cumulative evidence." In a number of cases, members of the press have successfully resisted the disclosure of confidential information, in part by asserting that the information sought merely duplicated or was cumulative to evidence available from nonconfidential sources.[151]

---

information sources); In re Consumers Union, 7 Media L. Rep. 2038 (S.D.N.Y. 1981) (granting publication's Rule 26(c) motion to quash on grounds that party seeking information failed to prove that no alternative source for information existed).

[145]C. WRIGHT & A. MILLER, FEDERAL PRACTICE & PROCEDURE §2043, at 307 (1970). Alternatives suggested by the courts include in camera inspections, redactions of the originals to remove confidential material, and limits on dissemination of produced material. *See* Bruno & Stillman, Inc. v. Globe Newspaper Co., 633 F.2d 583, 598 (1st Cir. 1980); *Marrese,* 726 F.2d at 1160.

[146]*See Bruno & Stillman,* 633 F.2d at 598; *Marrese,* 726 F.2d at 1161.

[147]*See Marrese,* 726 F.2d at 1159.

[148]89 F.R.D. 489 (C.D. Cal. 1981).

[149]*Id.* at 496 (citing Professor Moore for proposition that it makes no difference whether motion to resolve such issues is labeled as Rule 26(c) or Rule 45 motion).

[150]*Id.*

[151]United States v. Burke, 700 F.2d 70, 78 (2d Cir.) (refusing to override reporter's First Amendment privilege because any information thus derived would be "merely cumulative"), *cert. denied,* 464 U.S. 816 (1983); United States v. Marcos, 17 Media L. Rep. 2005, 2008 (S.D.N.Y. 1990) (quashing subpoena of network's materials because government failed to show that information sought was not merely cumulative); Liberty Lobby v. Rees, 111 F.R.D. 19, 22–23 (D.D.C. 1986) (refusing to compel disclosure of publisher's confidential source because disclosure would result in "cumulative evidence"); United States ex rel. Vuitton Et Fils S.A. v. Karen Bags, Inc., 600 F. Supp. 667, 671 (S.D.N.Y. 1985) (denying defendant's application for subpoena of network's materials where information sought likely to be "merely cumulative"); Dowd v.

For example, in *United States v. Burke*[152] and *United States ex rel. Vuitton Et Fils S.A. v. Karen Bags, Inc.*,[153] the courts determined that the litigants had no legitimate need to cull additional impeachment evidence from confidential press materials where substantial impeachment evidence already was available to them.[154] Similarly, in *In re Consumers Union*,[155] the court held that the publisher of *Consumer Reports* would not be required to produce unpublished material underlying certain automobile tests where a published article fully described those test results.[156] In contrast, in *Don King Productions v. Douglas*,[157] the court found that production of a reporter's audio tape would not be cumulative—despite the availability of "ear-witnesses"—because a record of the plaintiff's verbatim statements constituted critical demeanor evidence going to key substantive issues in the case.[158]

§14.3(G) Federal Common Law

In *Branzburg*, the Supreme Court dwelt on the principle that " 'the public ... has a right to every man's evidence,' except for those persons protected by a constitutional, common law or statutory privilege."[159] In the course of its opinion, the Court proceeded to deny journalists a *constitutional privilege* to refuse to appear before a grand jury.[160] Although federal common law at the time of *Branzburg* recognized no general reporter's testimonial privilege,[161] the question remained whether courts, in the wake of *Branzburg*, would grant the press a *common law privilege* wholly independent of the First Amendment.

In 1975 Congress enacted the Federal Rules of Evidence, Rule 501 of which governs evidentiary privileges in federal court.[162] The legislative history of Rule 501 suggests strongly that it was adopted, in part, to give courts in federal question and criminal cases the flexibility to develop a nonconstitu-

---

Calabrese, 577 F. Supp. 238, 240 (D.D.C. 1983) (denying motion to compel with respect to identity of two confidential sources whose testimony would be "cumulative evidence at best"); In re Consumers Union, 7 Media L. Rep. 2038, 2040 (S.D.N.Y. 1981) (granting publication's motion to quash where subpoenaed information would only be cumulative); United States v. Hubbard, 493 F. Supp. 202, 205 (D.D.C. 1979) (granting reporter's motion to quash where testimony would be "merely cumulative"). *But see* Don King Prods. v. Douglas, 131 F.R.D. 421, 424–26 (S.D.N.Y. 1990) (denying reporter's motion to quash because information sought was "noncumulative").

[152] 700 F.2d 70 (2d Cir.), *cert. denied,* 464 U.S. 816 (1983).
[153] 600 F. Supp. 667 (S.D.N.Y. 1985).
[154] *Burke,* 700 F.2d at 78; *Vuitton,* 600 F. Supp. at 671.
[155] 7 Media L. Rep. 2038 (S.D.N.Y. 1981).
[156] *Id.* at 2040.
[157] 131 F.R.D. 421 (S.D.N.Y. 1990).
[158] *Id.* at 424–26.
[159] 408 U.S. 665, 688, 1 Media L. Rep. 2617, 2626 (1972).
[160] *Id.* at 690–92.
[161] *See id.* at 693; *see also* United States v. Liddy, 354 F. Supp. 208, 214 (D.D.C. 1972) ("There can be little dispute that the common law recognized no privilege which would support a newspaper or reporter in refusing, upon proper demand, to disclose information received in confidence.") (footnoted omitted), *emerg. motions for stay denied,* 478 F.2d 586 (D.C. Cir. 1972).
[162] Federal Rule of Evidence 501 provides:
Except as otherwise required by the Constitution of the United States or provided by Act of Congress or in rules prescribed by the Supreme Court pursuant to statutory authority, the privilege of a witness, person, government, State, or political subdivision thereof shall be governed by the principles of the common law as they may be interpreted by the courts of the United States in the light of reason and experience. However in civil actions and proceedings, with respect to an element of a claim or defense as to which State law supplies the rule of decision, the privilege of a witness, person, government, State, or political subdivision thereof shall be determined in accordance with State law.

tional reporter's privilege.[163] Thus, the stage was set for the growth of a federal common law reporter's privilege "in the light of reason and experience."[164]

The Court of Appeals for the Third Circuit took the lead in creating a common law reporter's privilege based on Rule 501. Before its landmark 1979 decision in *Riley v. City of Chester*,[165] the Third Circuit had already held that the decision to grant or withhold an evidentiary privilege under Rule 501 is made by "a balancing of competing policies."[166] Therefore, in *Riley*, the court needed only to balance First Amendment interests against a civil litigant's need for disclosure to arrive at a federal common law reporter's privilege.[167] In short, *Riley* declared that, even if a reporter's privilege based on the First Amendment might be doubtful, a potent common law privilege that protects First Amendment interests could be founded on Rule 501. The principle of a federal common law reporter's privilege has also been approved by the Fourth Circuit[168] and some district courts.[169]

However, the Courts of Appeals for the First and Sixth Circuits have expressly rejected the notion of a reporter's privilege based on federal common law.[170] And although the federal law of privileges has sometimes been held to control in mixed law cases, i.e., in cases involving a federal question and one or more pendent state law claims,[171] there is no dispute that, to the extent such

---

[163]The privilege article of the Federal Rules of Evidence, as originally proposed by the Advisory Committee on Rules of Evidence and promulgated by the Supreme Court, limited the testimonial privileges that the federal courts could recognize to nine enumerated nonconstitutional privileges and to those well-established privileges based on the Constitution or federal statutes. *See* Proposed Federal Rules of Evidence 501–510, 56 F.R.D. 183, 230–56 (1973). This proposal wholly excluded any reporter's privilege.

In response to intense public criticism of the entire proposal, Congress rejected the Court's version of the rule, redrafted Rule 501, and adopted it in its current form. *See* S. Rep. No. 1277, 93d Cong., 2d Sess. 43 (1974), *reprinted in* 4 U.S.C.C.A.N. 7051, 7053–54, 7058 (1974). Congress' intent that Rule 501 serve as a basis for a common law reporter's privilege is clear. As Representative Hungate, the principal drafter of the Federal Rules of Evidence, commented: "[T]he Supreme Court's rules of evidence contained no rule of privilege for a newspaper person. The language of 501 [as adopted] permits the courts to develop a privilege for newspaper people on a case-by-case basis." 120 CONG. REC. H12253–54 (daily ed. Dec. 18, 1974).

For additional discussion of the adoption of Rule 501, *see* In re Grand Jury Impaneled Jan. 21, 1975, 541 F.2d 373, 379 & n.11 (3d Cir. 1976); Riley v. City of Chester, 612 F.2d 708, 714 (3d Cir. 1979); Trammel v. United States, 445 U.S. 40, 47 (1980).

[164]*See supra* note 162.

[165]612 F.2d 708 (3d Cir. 1979).

[166]*See In re Grand Jury*, 541 F.2d at 382 (citations omitted).

[167]*See Riley*, 612 F.2d at 713–15. The Third Circuit reaffirmed the concept of a common law reporter's privilege in later cases. United States v. CBS, 651 F.2d 189 (3d Cir. 1980), *cert. denied*, 454 U.S. 1056 (1981); United States v. Criden, 633 F.2d 346 (3d Cir. 1980), *cert. denied sub nom.* Schaffer v. United States, 449 U.S. 1113 (1981). *See also* In re Williams, 766 F. Supp. 358, 367–69, 18 Media L. Rep. 2177, 2185–86 (W.D. Pa. 1991) (applying Third Circuit's common law reporter's privilege), *aff'd by equally divided court*, 963 F.2d 567, 20 Media L. Rep. 1232 (3d Cir. 1992).

[168]United States v. Steelhammer, 561 F.2d 539 (4th Cir. 1977) (per curiam and en banc) (adopting dissenting panel opinion in United States v. Steelhammer, 539 F.2d 373, 377 (4th Cir. 1976) ("Under Federal Rules of Evidence 501, [reporters] should be afforded a common law privilege not to testify in civil litigation between private parties.")).

[169]*See* United States v. Vastola, 685 F. Supp. 917, 924 (D.N.J. 1988); Los Angeles Memorial Coliseum Comm. v. National Football League, 89 F.R.D. 489, 492, 496 (C.D. Cal. 1981).

[170]United States v. LaRouche Campaign, 841 F.2d 1176, 1178 n.4 (1st Cir. 1988) (rejecting network's "reliance upon a federal common law privilege wholly apart from the First Amendment"); In re Grand Jury Proceedings, 810 F.2d 580, 584 & n.6 (6th Cir. 1987) (declining to follow Third Circuit's decision in *Cuthbertson*).

[171]*See* von Bulow by Auersperg v. von Bulow, 811 F.2d 136, 141 (2d Cir.), *cert. denied sub nom.* Reynolds v. von Bulow by Auersperg, 481 U.S. 1015 (1987); Pinkard v. Johnson, 118 F.R.D. 517, 519–20 (M.D. Ala. 1987); *see also* S. REP. NO. 1277, 93d Cong., 2d Sess., *reprinted in* 1974 U.S.C.C.A.N. 7051, 7059 n.16 (explaining that Congress intended that federal privilege law apply to pendent state law claims in mixed law cases). *But see Los Angeles Memorial Coliseum*, 89 F.R.D. at 492 ("Thus, under Rule 501, when a civil action in federal court contains a combination of federal and state claims or defenses, federal courts should evaluate claims of privilege under both state and federal law."). *See also* Shaklee Corp. v.

a privilege does exist, it is inapplicable in federal court diversity suits governed by state privilege law.[172] Finally, it is clear that the common law reporter's privilege, like its First Amendment counterpart, is qualified and not absolute.[173]

§14.3(H) State Law

The legislatures of 29 states and the District of Columbia have enacted reporter's privilege statutes or "shield laws." A state-by-state analysis of these laws and of the more salient cases construing them, if any, follows. No reporter's shield law has been adopted in Connecticut,[174] Florida,[175] Hawaii, Idaho,[176] Iowa,[177] Kansas,[178] Maine,[179] Massachusetts,[180] Mississippi, Missouri,[181] New Hampshire,[182] North Carolina,[183] South Dakota, Texas, Utah, Vermont,[184] Virginia,[185] Washington,[186] West Virginia,[187] Wisconsin,[188] or Wyoming.

§14.3(H)(i) Alabama

The Alabama shield law[189] protects members of the press from the compulsory disclosure of the source of any published information in legal, tribunal, or legislative proceedings.

Gunnell, 110 F.R.D. 190, 192, 12 Media L. Rep. 2221 (N.D. Cal. 1986) (finding that where "state and federal claims are joined, but the evidence [sought to be disclosed] affects only the state claims the state law of privilege applies").

[172] In diversity cases, the *Erie* doctrine and Rule 501 require that state law govern substantive questions such as the testimonial privilege of a witness; therefore, federal common law is not authoritative in those instances. *See, e.g.,* Continental Cablevision v. Storer Broadcasting Co., 583 F. Supp. 427 (E.D. Mo. 1984); Williams v. American Broadcasting Cos., 96 F.R.D. 658 (W.D. Ark. 1983). For a further discussion of the choice-of-law question in diversity cases, *see infra* §14.4(G).

[173] *See, e.g.,* Riley v. City of Chester, 612 F.2d 708, 715 (3d Cir. 1979) (concluding that "journalists have a federal common law privilege, albeit qualified, to refuse to divulge their sources").

[174] Connecticut courts have recognized a qualified First Amendment privilege for reporters. *See supra* §14.3(A).

[175] Florida courts have recognized a qualified privilege under both the First Amendment and the state constitution. *See supra* §14.3(A).

[176] The Idaho Supreme Court has recognized a reporter's privilege under both the state and federal constitutions. *See supra* §14.3(A).

[177] The Iowa Supreme Court has recognized a First Amendment reporter's privilege. *See supra* §14.3(A).

[178] The Kansas Supreme Court has recognized a First Amendment reporter's privilege. *See supra* §14.3(A).

[179] In In re Letellier, 578 A.2d 722 (Me. 1990), the Supreme Judicial Court of Maine observed that "[a]lthough a reporter shield statute has been proposed in the Maine legislature from time to time, none has been enacted." *Id.* at 724 n.4.

[180] The Supreme Judicial Court of Massachusetts has noted the state legislature's "repeated failure to enact such a privilege." Promulgation of Rules Regarding Protection of Confidential News Sources, 479 N.E.2d 154, 167 (Mass. 1985).

[181] The court in CBS, Inc. (KMOX-TV) v. Campbell, 645 S.W.2d 30 (Mo. Ct. App. 1982), noted that although many states have created a statutory reporter's privilege, the Missouri legislature has not "seen fit to enact a Reporter's Shield Law." *Id.* at 31.

[182] The New Hampshire Supreme Court has recognized a reporter's privilege under both the state and federal constitutions. *See supra* §14.3(A).

[183] The North Carolina Supreme Court has recognized a reporter's privilege under both the state and federal constitutions. *See supra* §14.3(A).

[184] The Vermont Supreme Court has recognized a First Amendment reporter's privilege. *See supra* §14.3(A).

[185] The Virginia Supreme Court has recognized a First Amendment reporter's privilege. *See supra* §14.3(A).

[186] The Washington Supreme Court has recognized a First Amendment reporter's privilege. *See supra* §14.3(A).

[187] The West Virginia Supreme Court of Appeals has recognized a reporter's privilege under both the state and federal constitutions. *See supra* §14.3(A).

[188] The Wisconsin Supreme Court has recognized a reporter's privilege under the Wisconsin Constitution. *See supra* §14.3(A).

[189] ALA. CODE §12-21-142 (1986).

§14.3(H)(ii) Alaska

Under the Alaska shield law,[190] no reporter may be compelled to disclose the source of information obtained in the course of his or her duties as a reporter unless a court finds that the withholding of the testimony would be contrary to justice or the public interest. The privilege applies in all forums of the state of Alaska as well as in other settings where Alaska law is being applied. In cases where the reporter is a litigant, the statute bars the reporter who asserts the privilege from pleading or proving the source of withheld information.

§14.3(H)(iii) Arizona

Section 12-2237 of the Arizona shield law[191] provides that a journalist shall not be compelled to testify about or disclose the source of information procured for publication in "any proceeding whatever." Section 12-2214 establishes a number of requirements that a party seeking information must meet before subpoenaing a media witness and postpones the command of the subpoena where the witness desires a protective order. Although Section 12-2214 applies generally to civil and criminal proceedings, in contrast to Section 12-2237, it is inapplicable to subpoenas issued by a grand jury or magistrate during a criminal investigation.

According to one Arizona court, a party seeking disclosure has the initial (yet relatively light) burden of demonstrating compliance with the requirements of Section 12-2214 and, in turn, the party resisting disclosure has a heavier burden of bringing forth specific evidence that the opponent's efforts to obtain the information from alternative sources were deficient.[192]

§14.3(H)(iv) Arkansas

The Arkansas shield law[193] commands that, before a reporter shall be required to disclose the source of information for any article, it must be shown that the article was written or disseminated "in bad faith, with malice, and not in the interest of the public welfare."

The Arkansas Supreme Court interpreted the precursor to Section 16-85-510—Section 43-917[194]—to apply to both civil and criminal proceedings.[195] According to one federal court, the law shields only confidential sources and not outtakes.[196]

§14.3(H)(v) California

The California shield law's constitutional provision[197] prohibits any entity having the power to issue subpoenas from adjudging a journalist in contempt

---

[190] ALASKA STAT. §§09.25.150–.220 (1990 & Supp.).
[191] ARIZ. REV. STAT. ANN. §12-2237 (1982), §12-2214 (Supp. 1989).
[192] See Bartlett v. Superior Ct., 722 P.2d 346 (Ariz. Ct. App. 1986). See also Matera v. Superior Ct., 825 P.2d 971, 19 Media L. Rep. 2053 (Ariz. Ct. App. 1992) (holding that §12-2237 only applies to confidential sources or when disclosure would impede information gathering; does not protect author of book).
[193] ARK. STAT. ANN. §16-85-510 (1987).
[194] Id. §43-917 (Repl. 1977).
[195] See Saxton v. Arkansas Gazette Co., 569 S.W.2d 115 (Ark. 1978).
[196] See Williams v. American Broadcasting Cos., 96 F.R.D. 658 (W.D. Ark. 1983).
[197] CAL. CONST. art. I, §2(b).

for refusing to disclose unpublished information or a confidential source obtained in the course of newsgathering. The statutory provision[198] is nearly identical.

The California Supreme Court has outlined the parameters of the state's shield law in several major decisions[199] and has held that the shield law provides only an immunity from contempt, not a privilege.[200] As a result, the shield law does not bar the imposition of sanctions, other than contempt. Where a journalist is not a party, contempt is usually the only available sanction, so the shield law's protection is virtually absolute. Where a journalist is a party, the shield law only provides minimal protection because of the variety of other sanctions available.[201] Although the shield law may be overridden by a criminal defendant's constitutional right to a fair trial,[202] it is absolute in civil cases.[203] The law applies to unpublished materials, including photographs, even if not obtained in confidence, and to eyewitness observations of even public events.[204] The California Supreme Court has also recognized a reporter's privilege under the First Amendment and California Constitution in libel cases.[205]

§14.3(H)(vi) Colorado

The relatively complex Colorado shield law consists of two provisions.[206] Section 13-90-119 provides that, absent his or her express consent, no newsperson shall be compelled to disclose, be examined concerning refusal to disclose, or be subjected to any sanction in any judicial proceedings for refusal to disclose any information obtained or produced while acting in the capacity of a newsperson. Although this protection extends to nonconfidential as well as confidential information, it has a number of limitations. For example, the privilege does not apply in proceedings before the state's general assembly, nor does it protect a journalist's personal observation of certain crimes. Moreover, a litigant seeking disclosure who proves certain facts—i.e., relevancy of the information to a substantial issue in the case, lack of a reasonable alternative source, and a favorable balance of the competing interests, by a preponderance of the evidence—may subpoena a reporter. Finally, the Colorado law sets conditions on waiver of the privilege and expressly declines to preclude the issuance of search warrants in compliance with the federal Privacy Protection Act of 1980.[207] The provisions of Section 24-72.5-101 to -106 are parallel to those of Section 13-90-119.

---

[198]CAL. EVID. CODE §1070 (West Supp. 1988).
[199]New York Times Co. v. Superior Ct. (Sortomme), 796 P.2d 811, 18 Media L. Rep. 1145 (Cal. 1990); Delaney v. Superior Ct. (Kopetman), 789 P.2d 934 (Cal. 1990); Mitchell v. Superior Ct. (Synanon Church), 690 P.2d 625 (Cal. 1984).
[200]New York Times, 796 P.2d 811; Delaney, 789 P.2d 934.
[201]New York Times, 796 P.2d 811; Mitchell, 690 P.2d 625.
[202]Delaney, 789 P.2d 934.
[203]New York Times, 796 P.2d 811.
[204]Id.; Delaney, 789 P.2d 934.
[205]Mitchell, 690 P.2d 625.
[206]COLO. REV. STAT. §§13-90-119 and 24-72.5-101 to -106 (Supp. 1990). See People v. Henderson, 847 P.2d 239, 243–44 (Colo. Ct. App. 1993) (privilege applies to reporter pilot who assists police; exhaustion of alternate sources not shown).
[207]See infra §14.8.

§14.3(H)(vii) Delaware

Delaware's Reporter's Privilege[208] provides journalists an absolute privilege not to testify in nonadjudicative proceedings and a qualified privilege not to testify in adjudicative proceedings, if the journalist swears that doing so would violate a confidentiality pact or would substantially impair source relationships. Moreover, Section 4323 empowers a court to compel the journalist to testify as to the content, but not the source, of information where "the public interest in having the reporter's testimony outweighs the public interest in keeping the information confidential." The privilege does not apply to grand jury proceedings or to information obtained by a reporter's personal observations.

§14.3(H)(viii) District of Columbia

The District of Columbia's statute[209] protects "any person who is or has been employed by the news media in a news gathering or news disseminating capacity." It applies to unpublished information and to the identity of sources even if they have not been promised confidentiality. A court may order disclosure of information if it finds that there is clear and convincing evidence that the information sought "is relevant to a significant legal issue," that the information "could not, with due diligence, be obtained by any alternative means," and that there is an "overriding public interest in disclosure." Disclosure of a source's identity may not be ordered, however. Finally, the publication or disclosure of some otherwise protected material does not waive the protection against compelled disclosure of other protected information.

§14.3(H)(ix) Georgia

Georgia's shield law[210] confers on media personnel and entities a privilege against the disclosure of information and materials procured in the course of news gathering or dissemination. This privilege is qualified, however, and may be asserted only by a nonparty. The privilege is also subject to waiver and can be overcome by a showing that what is sought is material and relevant, cannot be reasonably obtained by alternative means, and is necessary to the proper preparation of the case of the party seeking disclosure.

§14.3(H)(x) Illinois

Under the Illinois shield law,[211] in libel and slander cases a court may not compel disclosure of information obtained by a reporter unless the court finds that there is no other source for the information and the plaintiff's need for disclosure in the particular case outweighs the public interest in maintaining the reporter's confidences. In other cases, the reporter may be divested of this privilege only if all alternative sources of information have been exhausted and disclosure is essential to protect the public interest.

---

[208] DEL. CODE ANN. tit. 10, §§4320–23 (1975).
[209] D.C. CODE §§16-4701 et seq. (1992).
[210] GA. CODE ANN. §24-9-30 (Supp. 1990).
[211] ILL. ANN. STAT. ch. 110, §§8-901 to -909 (Smith-Hurd 1984 & Supp. 1990).

The Illinois statute has been held to protect unpublished news photographs,[212] to shield reporters from testifying as to nonconfidential sources or information, and to require a balancing of interests consistent with the First Amendment.[213] Moreover, a reporter does not waive the right to refuse to disclose the identity of some sources by disclosing the identity of other sources.[214] In addition, the Illinois Supreme Court has ruled that the extent to which alternative information sources must be exhausted is not reducible to any "precise formula," but depends on the facts and circumstances of each particular case.[215]

§14.3(H)(xi) Indiana

Under the Indiana reporter's shield law,[216] an intricately defined class of media owners, officials, and employees is protected from compulsory disclosure of the source of information procured or obtained in the course of employment. This privilege applies "in any legal proceedings or elsewhere" and regardless of whether the information is published or unpublished. The statute has been held to provide an absolute privilege[217] personal to the reporter.[218]

§14.3(H)(xii) Kentucky

The Kentucky shield law[219] provides that no person may be forced to disclose the source of information published by a media entity with which the person is employed or connected. The privilege applies in any legal proceeding, including those before a grand jury, and in state, county, and city government proceedings.

Kentucky's highest court has held that the statute protects the source of information, but not the information itself,[220] and that it does not relieve persons from the duty to appear.[221] In a libel case, the plaintiff's need for information critical to issues in the case may override the journalist's privilege.[222] Publication of an informant's identity waives the privilege.[223]

§14.3(H)(xiii) Louisiana

Under Louisiana's reporter's privilege,[224] a broadly defined class of "reporters" is shielded from the compulsory disclosure of the source of informa-

---

[212]*See* Villeda v. Prairie Material Sales, 17 Media L. Rep. 2289 (Ill. Cir. Ct. 1990).
[213]People ex rel. Scott v. Silverstein, 412 N.E.2d 692 (Ill. App. Ct. 1980), *rev'd on other grounds,* 429 N.E.2d 483 (Ill. 1981).
[214]*Id.*
[215]In re Special Grand Jury Investig. of Alleged Violation of Juvenile Ct. Act, 472 N.E.2d 450 (Ill. 1984) (holding that alternate sources had not been exhausted where only one of four witnesses had been called to testify). *See also* Illinois v. Arya, 589 N.E.2d 832, 19 Media L. Rep. 2079 (Ill. App. Ct. 1992) (extensively reviewing numerous authorities on exhaustion and concluding that only those sources known or identified or likely to be known or identified need be exhausted).
[216]IND. CODE §34-3-5-1 (1988).
[217]Jamerson v. Anderson Newspapers, 469 N.E.2d 1243 (Ind. Ct. App. 1984).
[218]Hestand v. State, 273 N.E.2d 282 (Ind. 1971); Lipps v. State, 258 N.E.2d 622 (Ind. 1970).
[219]KY. REV. STAT. ANN. §421.100 (Michie/Bobbs-Merrill 1972).
[220]Branzburg v. Pound, 461 S.W.2d 345 (Ky. 1970), *aff'd sub nom.* Branzburg v. Hayes, 408 U.S. 665 (1972).
[221]Branzburg v. Meigs, 503 S.W.2d 748 (Ky. 1971), *aff'd sub nom.* Branzburg v. Hayes, 408 U.S. 665 (1972).
[222]Lexington Herald-Leader Co. v. Beard, 690 S.W.2d 374 (Ky. 1984).
[223]*Id.*
[224]LA. REV. STAT. ANN. §§45:1451–55 (West 1982 & Supp. 1990).

tion obtained while acting as a reporter. The privilege may be asserted in "any administrative, judicial or legislative proceedings or anywhere else"; however, a state trial court may revoke the privilege upon finding that disclosure is essential to the protection of the public interest. A media defendant in a defamation suit who raises the privilege together with a "good faith" defense must then bear the burden of proof on that defense.

The statute protects the identity of an informant, but not the information itself;[225] the information is protected by the federal and state constitutions.[226] To overcome the statutory privilege, a party seeking the source's identity must prove that disclosure is essential to the public interest; however, to overcome the constitutional privilege, a party must only show that disclosure is *necessary* to protect the public interest.[227] "Identity of an informant" includes not only the source's actual name but any information, such as place of employment, that would tend to identify the source.[228] An owner/publisher of a media entity qualifies as a "reporter" under the statute.[229]

§14.3(H)(xiv) Maryland

The Maryland shield law[230] bars judicial, legislative, and administrative organs of the government from forcing persons employed in a news-gathering or disseminating capacity to disclose the identity of an informant or any materials procured for communication to the public but ultimately not published. A court may order the journalist to divulge unpublished information only where there is "clear and convincing evidence" that the information is relevant to a significant legal issue, cannot be obtained by alternative means, and that disclosure will serve an overriding public interest. Moreover, the statute was amended in 1988 to provide that a reporter does not waive the privilege by disseminating to the public the source or information sought.

Maryland courts have held that Section 9-112 does not protect information about a crime obtained by the reporter through his or her personal observation,[231] and although the privilege applies in both civil and criminal proceedings[232] and to *any* source regardless of whether the source gave the information in confidence,[233] the Maryland shield law has no extraterritorial application.[234]

§14.3(H)(xv) Michigan

The Michigan shield law[235] now extends a privilege against the disclosure of the identity of an informant and of any unpublished material to persons

---

[225] Dumez v. Houma Mun. Fire & Police Civil Serv. Bd., 341 So. 2d 1206 (La. Ct. App. 1976), *cert. denied*, 344 So. 2d 667 (La. 1977).
[226] In re Ridenhour, 520 So. 2d 372, 15 Media L. Rep. 1022 (La. 1988).
[227] *Id.*
[228] In re Burns, 484 So. 2d 658 (La. 1986).
[229] Becnel v. Lucia, 420 So. 2d 1173 (La. Ct. App. 1982).
[230] MD. CTS. & JUD. PROC. CODE ANN. §9-112 (1989).
[231] Lightman v. State, 294 A.2d 149 (Md. Ct. Spec. App.), *aff'd*, 295 A.2d 212 (Md. 1972), *cert. denied*, 411 U.S. 951 (1973).
[232] Bilney v. Evening Star Newspaper Co., 406 A.2d 652 (Md. Ct. App. 1979).
[233] *Lightman*, 294 A.2d 149.
[234] In re State of Cal. ex rel. L.A., 471 A.2d 1141 (Md. Ct. App.), *cert. denied sub nom.* Rees v. L.A. County, 467 U.S. 1205 (1984).
[235] MICH. COMP. LAWS §767.5a(l) (1982 & Supp. 1990) and MICH. STAT. ANN. §28.945(l) (Callahan 1985 & Supp. 1990–91).

involved in broadcast as well as print media. The sole exception to the privilege is an investigation of a crime punishable by life imprisonment where it is shown that the information sought is essential and that alternative sources of the information have been exhausted.

One Michigan appellate court has held that the state's shield law applies only to the identities of informants and to unpublished confidential information and provides no protection for nonconfidential materials.[236]

§14.3(H)(xvi) Minnesota

The express purpose of Minnesota's Free Flow of Information Act[237] is "to insure and perpetuate, consistent with the public interest, the confidential relationship between the news media and its sources."[238] To that end, all state, county, and city government entities are prohibited from requiring a person engaged in news gathering and dissemination to divulge an informant, unpublished information, or notes, memoranda, tapes, films, and other data that would tend to identify the informant. A court may revoke this privilege only upon "clear and convincing" proof of three conditions: (1) the source has information clearly relevant to the commission of a felony, (2) the information cannot be obtained by alternative means less destructive of First Amendment rights, and (3) there is a compelling and overriding interest favoring disclosure. A court order revoking the privilege is immediately appealable to the appropriate court of appeals. Lastly, the privilege does not apply in a defamation action if the identity of the source will lead to relevant evidence on the issue of actual malice.

§14.3(H)(xvii) Montana

Under the Montana Media Confidentiality Act,[239] no media employee or entity may, without consent, be required to divulge or be examined concerning information or its source in any legal proceeding if the information was obtained in the course of news gathering or dissemination. The law further provides that no judicial, legislative, administrative, or other body having subpoena power may adjudge a reporter to contempt for refusing to disclose such a source or information. Testimony before the foregoing bodies does not constitute a waiver unless the journalist voluntarily agrees to waive the privilege.

§14.3(H)(xviii) Nebraska

Nebraska's Free Flow of Information Act[240] provides that no person engaged in news gathering or dissemination shall be required to reveal a news source or information, whether published or unpublished, so long as the information was received with an intent to communicate it to the public. The law expressly applies to any federal or state proceeding.

---

[236]Marketos v. American Employers Ins. Co., 460 N.W.2d 272 (Mich. Ct. App. 1990).
[237]MINN. STAT. §§595.021–.025 (1986).
[238]Id. §595.022.
[239]MONT. CODE ANN. §§26-1-901 to -903 (1989).
[240]NEB. REV. STAT. §§20-144 to -147 (1987).

§14.3(H)(xix) Nevada

Under the Nevada shield law,[241] no current or former journalist or employee of any newspaper or of any radio or television station may be required to reveal the identity of an informant or to disclose published or unpublished information gathered in the person's professional capacity for communication to the public. This law applies in judicial, legislative, and state administrative proceedings and in proceedings before local government bodies.

The Nevada shield law is fully applicable in libel actions.[242] The Nevada Supreme Court has held that the privilege is not absolute and is subject to waiver by the disclosure of a source and the attribution of remarks to that source; thus, during discovery, a defendant reporter can be compelled to testify as to matters revealed in a publication or broadcast.[243] Moreover, a libel defendant who asserts the privilege not to disclose certain information may not thereafter rely on it for a defense.[244] Finally, only the journalist who obtained the information in his or her professional capacity may assert the privilege, and the journalist must support the privilege claim by sworn affidavit.[245]

§14.3(H)(xx) New Jersey

The New Jersey Newspaperman's Privilege[246] confers on persons connected with or employed by news media for the purpose of news gathering or dissemination a privilege to refuse to disclose the source of information and news or information procured in the course of professional activities, whether disseminated or not. The broadcast media receive the benefit of this protection only if they maintain for inspection for one year an exact recording or transcript of the actual broadcast. The privilege is available to journalists in legal and quasi-legal proceedings or before any investigative body. Importantly, Section 2A:84A-21a(h) expressly exempts from protection "any situation in which a reporter is an eyewitness to, or participant in, any act involving physical violence or property damage."

Sections 2A:84A-21.1 to 21.8 set forth an elaborate procedure for resolving conflicts between a journalist's claim of privilege and a criminal defendant's Sixth Amendment right to a fair trial. Initially, the reporter must prove that he or she is connected with a media entity and that the subpoenaed materials were obtained in the course of professional activities. In turn, the defendant may overcome the privilege by proving by "clear and convincing evidence" that the privilege was waived, or by a "preponderance of evidence" that the materials are relevant to the defense, cannot be obtained in a less intrusive manner, bear heavily on the issue of guilt or innocence, and that the request is not oppressive. Upon finding that the defendant has overcome the privilege, the court must order an in camera inspection of the material to assess its admissibility, and must order production of any admissible information. If

---

[241] NEV. REV. STAT. ANN. §49.275 (Michie 1986).
[242] Newton v. National Broadcasting Co., 109 F.R.D. 522 (D. Nev. 1985).
[243] Las Vegas Sun v. Eighth Judicial Dist. Ct., 761 P.2d 849 (Nev. 1988); Newburn v. Howard Hughes Medical Inst., 594 P.2d 1146 (Nev. 1979).
[244] *Las Vegas Sun,* 761 P.2d 849.
[245] *Id.*
[246] N.J. STAT. ANN. §§2A:84A-21 to -21.8 (West 1993) and N.J. R. EVID. 37.

the defendant fails to prove a reasonable basis for his request, the court may award the reporter attorneys' fees and costs.

The New Jersey Supreme Court has held that the state's shield law is intended to protect confidential sources and information to the greatest extent permitted by the federal and state constitutions.[247] The statute provides an *absolute* privilege not to disclose sources, editorial processes, and other confidential information, even in libel suits.[248] In camera inspections are permissible only where there is no viable alternative for the preservation of competing constitutional rights, such as the right to a fair trial.[249] Communicating information or the identity of sources to third parties outside the course of newsgathering activities waives the privilege.[250] However, neither divulging the names of nonconfidential sources in response to a court order[251] nor publication of privileged information amounts to a waiver of the privilege.[252]

In *In re Woodhaven Lumber and Mill Work*,[253] the New Jersey Supreme Court was presented with its first opportunity to construe the "eyewitness exception" to the state's shield law. There, prosecutors seeking to obtain aerial photographs of a fire from three news photographers argued that the shield law did not protect the information because the newsmen were "eyewitnesses" to "an act involving property damage."[254] The court drew a distinction between the act of setting the fire, which would be covered by the exception, and its aftermath (the fire in progress), which would not be subject to the exception.[255] The court reasoned that if the reporter's privilege could be lost simply because a reporter witnessed the *consequences* of an act involving property damage, then the shield law would be eviscerated because there could be no principled basis upon which to shield a reporter who has gathered news at a crime or accident scene following the incident.[256]

§14.3(H)(xxi) New Mexico

The New Mexico shield law[257] provides that, unless essential to prevent injustice, no journalist or newscaster shall be required to disclose any unpublished information, or the source of any published or unpublished information, so long as such information was gathered for any medium of communication to the public. The statute extends to any legislative, judicial, executive, or administrative proceeding.

---

[247] In re Woodhaven Lumber & Mill Work, 589 A.2d 135, 18 Media L. Rep. 2049 (N.J. 1991); In re Farber, 394 A.2d 330 (N.J.), *cert. denied sub nom.* New York Times Co. v. New Jersey, 439 U.S. 997 (1978).
[248] Maressa v. New Jersey Monthly, 445 A.2d 376 (N.J.), *cert. denied*, 459 U.S. 907 (1982); Prager v. American Broadcasting Cos., 569 F. Supp. 1229 (D.N.J. 1983), *aff'd*, 734 F.2d 7 (3d Cir. 1984).
[249] State v. Boiardo, 414 A.2d 14 (N.J. 1980).
[250] In re Schuman, 552 A.2d 602 (N.J. 1989).
[251] Resorts Int'l v. New Jersey Monthly, 445 A.2d 395, 8 Media L. Rep. 1487 (N.J.), *cert. denied*, 459 U.S. 907 (1982).
[252] In re Woodhaven Lumber & Mill Work, 589 A.2d 135, 18 Media L. Rep. 2049 (N.J. 1991); *In re Schuman*, 552 A.2d 602. *See also* New Jersey v. Santiago, 593 A.2d 357, 19 Media L. Rep. 1214 (N.J. Super. Ct. App. Div. 1991) (eyewitness exception applies to attempted assault even though no one was hurt, but reporter cannot be compelled to testify to supply threshold showing that reporter actually witnessed something that falls within eyewitness exception).
[253] 589 A.2d 135, 18 Media L. Rep. 2049 (N.J. 1991).
[254] *Id.* at 136.
[255] *Id.* at 138.
[256] *Id.* at 143.
[257] N.M. Stat. Ann. §38-6-7 (Michie 1987).

In 1976, the New Mexico Supreme Court ruled that the provision is inapplicable to judicial proceedings because it represents a constitutionally invalid attempt by the state legislature to create a rule of evidence.[258] Six years later, that court promulgated New Mexico Supreme Court Rule 514,[259] which provides a reporter's privilege in judicial proceedings.

§14.3(H)(xxii) New York

The New York reporter's privilege[260] frees professional journalists and newscasters (and their supervisors and organizations) from being held in contempt by any court, the legislature, or other body having contempt powers for refusing to disclose any news or the source of any news they obtain in the course of gathering information for publication or broadcast.

Pursuant to amendments in 1990, the reporter's privilege to withhold *confidential* information is *absolute;* however, the privilege to withhold *nonconfidential* information is *qualified* and may be overridden by a "clear and specific" showing that the information is (1) highly material and relevant, (2) critical or necessary to the maintenance of a party's claim, defense, or proof of a material issue, and (3) not obtainable from any alternative source. Information obtained from the journalist in violation of this protection is inadmissible. Moreover, the statute prohibits the imposition of fines or imprisonment for any refusal to disclose such information. Finally, also in 1990, the state legislature incorporated a waiver provision into the statute providing that the privilege is waived if the journalist voluntarily discloses the information to any person who, in their own right, is not entitled to assert the privilege.

The New York statute has been construed to provide an absolute shield from contempt but not an absolute grant of immunity from all legal consequences.[261] New York courts historically have held that the statutory privilege shielded only information obtained under a "cloak of confidentiality" and, consequently, did not extend to nonconfidential sources or information.[262] The state legislature rejected this line of authority in 1990 by expressly extending the privilege to nonconfidential news.[263]

The statute may be overridden by a criminal defendant's Sixth Amendment interests.[264] It also benefits professional journalists and newscasters only and not those engaged in different fields of writing and research.[265]

Although the privilege clearly applies in defamation actions,[266] it does not shield confidential information generated strictly for purposes of the

---

[258]Ammerman v. Hubbard Broadcasting, 551 P.2d 1354 (N.M. 1976), *cert. denied,* 436 U.S. 906 (1978).
[259]N.M. STAT. ANN. §11-514 (Michie 1986).
[260]N.Y. CIV. RIGHTS LAW §79-h (Consol. 1982 & Supp. 1991).
[261]Sharon v. Time, Inc., 599 F. Supp. 538 (S.D.N.Y. 1984); Andrews v. Andreoli, 400 N.Y.S.2d 442 (N.Y. Sup. Ct. 1977).
[262]*See, e.g.,* Knight-Ridder Broadcasting v. Greenberg, 518 N.Y.S.2d 595 (N.Y. 1987); Nulty v. Pennzoil Co., 484 N.Y.S.2d 533, 11 Media L. Rep. 1647 (N.Y. App. Div. 1985); WBAI-FM v. Proskin, 344 N.Y.S.2d 393 (N.Y. App. Div. 1973); People v. Wolf, 333 N.Y.S.2d 299 (N.Y. App. Div. 1972).
Although before 1990 journalists who wanted to shield nonconfidential materials found no protection in the New York shield law, they could resort to the state and federal constitutions for such protection. O'Neill v. Oakgrove Constr., 523 N.E.2d 277 (N.Y. 1988) (prohibiting disclosure of nonconfidential photographs based on federal and state constitutions).
[263]N.Y. CIV. RIGHTS LAW §79-h(c).
[264]People v. Troiano, 486 N.Y.S.2d 991 (N.Y. Sup. Ct. 1985).
[265]People v. LeGrand, 415 N.Y.S.2d 252 (N.Y. App. Div. 1979).
[266]Oak Beach Inn Corp. v. Babylon Beacon, 464 N.E.2d 967 (N.Y. 1984), *cert. denied,* 469 U.S. 1158 (1985).

litigation;[267] nor, during trial, may a libel defendant rely on any confidential information that it refused to divulge.[268] The privilege is waived where the source renounces the confidentiality of the communication by disclosing his or her identity.[269]

§14.3(H)(xxiii) North Dakota

North Dakota's shield law[270] provides that, unless necessary to avoid a miscarriage of justice, no person engaged in news gathering and employed by or acting for a news organization shall be required to disclose information or the source of any information obtained in the course of gathering news. The privilege applies to "any proceeding or hearing."

The North Dakota Supreme Court has interpreted the privilege to apply to nonconfidential and confidential information, to both civil and criminal actions, and regardless of whether the news gatherer is or is not a party.[271] A specific finding that disclosure is the only means to obtain evidence is not required to overcome the privilege; the court simply must find that refusal to disclose would lead to a miscarriage of justice.[272]

§14.3(H)(xxiv) Ohio

Under the Ohio reporter's privilege,[273] Section 2739.04 shields broadcasters from the compulsory disclosure of the source of any information obtained in the course of news gathering in proceedings before any court, grand jury, state agency, or county or municipal body. Further, it requires radio and television stations to maintain, for a period of six months, a record of such information. Section 2739.12 protects newspaper reporters and press association employees from the compulsory disclosure of the source of any information obtained in the course of news gathering in proceedings before any court, grand jury, state agency, or county or municipal body.

The Ohio statute shields only the name of an informant, and not the information obtained by the journalist.[274] This privilege is qualified and not absolute—for example, a criminal defendant may override the privilege by establishing that the informant will provide evidence relevant to guilt or innocence.[275] Whether the statute bans in camera inspection of privileged materials in all cases or only in civil cases is unclear.[276]

---

[267] Westmoreland v. CBS, Inc., 9 Media L. Rep. 1521, 1523 (S.D.N.Y. 1983).
[268] Sands v. News Am. Pub'g, 560 N.Y.S.2d 416, 18 Media L. Rep. 1064 (N.Y. App. Div. 1990).
[269] Andrews v. Andreoli, 400 N.Y.S.2d 442 (N.Y. Sup. Ct. 1977).
[270] N.D. CENT. CODE §31-01-06.2 (1976).
[271] Grand Forks Herald v. District Ct., 322 N.W.2d 850 (N.D. 1982).
[272] *Id.*
[273] OHIO REV. CODE ANN. §§2739.04 and 2739.12 (Anderson 1981).
[274] State ex rel. National Broadcasting Co. v. Court of Common Pleas, 556 N.E.2d 1120 (Ohio 1990).
[275] In re McAuley, 408 N.E.2d 697 (Ohio Ct. App. 1979).
[276] *Compare* In re Rutti, 5 Media L. Rep. 1513 (Ohio Ct. App. 1979) (reading shield law to prohibit in camera inspections) *with* Weiss v. Thomson Newspapers, 8 Media L. Rep. 1258 (Ohio Ct. C.P. 1981) (finding that in camera inspections may be ordered only in criminal cases) *and* State v. Geis, 441 N.E.2d 803 (Ohio Ct. App. 1981) (encouraging use of such inspections in criminal case).

§14.3(H)(xxv) Oklahoma

The Oklahoma Newsman's Privilege[277] provides that no reporter shall be required to disclose unpublished information obtained in the course of news gathering for communication to the public or the source of published or unpublished information similarly obtained. However, a court can force a journalist to disclose such information upon a showing by "clear and convincing evidence" that the information is relevant to a significant issue in an action and cannot be obtained by alternative means. The application of the privilege is expressly confined to state proceedings. Moreover, the privilege does not apply in a defamation suit where the defendant journalist asserts a defense based on the content or source of the information he or she refuses to divulge.

In *Taylor v. Miskovsky*,[278] the Supreme Court of Oklahoma strictly construed the requirement that a party seeking disclosure prove that the information sought is relevant to a significant issue in the case. There, the plaintiff in a libel suit sought to obtain unpublished material from a reporter who, although employed by the defendant news organization, had no involvement in producing the allegedly defamatory articles.[279] Finding no evidence (much less "clear and convincing" evidence) that the material in question was relevant to the case, the Supreme Court reversed the trial court's orders, which had compelled disclosure and held the reporter in contempt.[280]

§14.3(H)(xxvi) Oregon

Under Oregon's Media Persons as Witnesses law,[281] legislative, executive, and judicial bodies, and any other authority having subpoena power, are prohibited from requiring a person connected with any medium of communication to the public to disclose unpublished information procured in the course of gathering news or the source of any published or unpublished information similarly obtained. Disclosure in other settings does not waive the privilege. However, the privilege does not apply in a defamation suit where the defendant journalist asserts a defense based on the content or source of the information he or she refuses to divulge.

The Oregon shield law has been held to bar disclosure in a libel suit where the defendant opted not to raise any defense based on the content or source of the information he withheld.[282] Moreover, the privilege has been construed to protect newspaper photographers.[283]

§14.3(H)(xxvii) Pennsylvania

The Pennsylvania shield law[284] provides that no person connected with a media entity for the purpose of gathering or publishing news shall be required

---

[277]OKLA. STAT. ANN. tit. 12, §2506 (West 1980).
[278]640 P.2d 959 (Okla. 1981).
[279]*Id.* at 960.
[280]*Id.* at 963.
[281]OR. REV. STAT. §§44.510–540 (1989).
[282]McNabb v. Oregonian Pub'g Co., 685 P.2d 458, 10 Media L. Rep. 2181 (Or. Ct. App.), *review denied,* 687 P.2d 797 (Or. 1984).
[283]McNeil v. Hupy, 18 Media L. Rep. 1238 (Or. Cir. Ct. 1990).
[284]42 PA. CONS. STAT. ANN. §5942 (Purdon 1985 & Supp. 1990).

to disclose the source of such news. The privilege applies "in any legal proceeding, trial or investigation before any government unit."[285] Radio and television stations may exercise the privilege only if they maintain for inspection, for one year, an exact recording or transcript of the actual broadcast or telecast.

The Pennsylvania Supreme Court has interpreted the shield law to confer an absolute privilege that is to be construed broadly.[286] The Pennsylvania shield law has withstood federal and state constitutional challenges,[287] and courts have construed it to bar the compulsory disclosure of a reporter's notes and tapes[288] as well as outtakes.[289] Moreover, all of a reporter's sources are privileged without reference to their confidentiality.[290] The Pennsylvania Supreme Court has held that a libel plaintiff may discover unpublished information to the extent that it does not reveal the identity of an informant.[291] Finally, a reporter's assertion of the privilege is not in itself sufficient ground for excluding the reporter's testimony as to the absence of malice in a defamation case.[292]

§14.3(H)(xxviii) Rhode Island

The Rhode Island Newsman's Privilege Act[293] provides that no person shall be required by any court, grand jury, or state agency to reveal confidential association or to disclose confidential information or the source of any confidential information received in his or her capacity as a journalist for any "accredited" news entity. The privilege does not apply to information made public by the journalist, to the source of allegedly defamatory information in a defamation case where the defendant asserts a defense based on that source, or to the source of information about proceedings required to be secret under Rhode Island law. A court may override the privilege if there is "substantial evidence" that disclosure is necessary to permit a felony prosecution or to prevent a threat to human life, and if such information or its source is not available from other witnesses.

The Rhode Island Supreme Court has construed the statutory privilege narrowly to apply only to information "given either in secret or in confidence to the news entity that claims the privilege."[294] Moreover, the court has held that a defamation defendant who pleads a good faith defense and testifies that the allegedly defamatory piece is based on a reliable confidential source is deemed to have waived the statutory privilege.[295]

---

[285] *Id.* §5942(A).
[286] Sprague v. Walter, 516 A.2d 706 (Pa. Super. Ct. 1986), *aff'd,* 543 A.2d 1078 (Pa.), *appeal dismissed,* 488 U.S. 988 (1988).
[287] Coughlin v. Westinghouse Broadcasting & Cable, 780 F.2d 340 (3d Cir. 1985), *cert. denied,* 476 U.S. 1187 (1986).
[288] Lal v. Columbia Broadcasting Sys., 726 F.2d 97 (3d Cir. 1984).
[289] Steaks Unlimited v. Deaner, 623 F.2d 264 (3d Cir. 1980).
[290] Altemose Constr. Co. v. Building & Constr. Trades Council of Phila., 443 F. Supp. 489 (E.D. Pa. 1977).
[291] Hatchard v. Westinghouse Broadcasting Co., 532 A.2d 346 (Pa. 1987).
[292] Sprague v. Walter, 516 A.2d 706 (Pa. Super. Ct. 1986), *aff'd,* 543 A.2d 1078 (Pa.), *appeal dismissed,* 488 U.S. 988 (1988).
[293] R.I. GEN. LAWS §§9-19.1-1 to 3 (1985).
[294] Outlet Communications v. Rhode Island, 588 A.2d 1050, 18 Media L. Rep. 1982 (R.I. 1991) (per curiam).
[295] Capuano v. Outlet Co., 579 A.2d 469 (R.I. 1990); *see also* Fischer v. McGowan, 585 F. Supp. 978 (D.R.I. 1984).

§14.3(H)(xxix) South Carolina

The South Carolina shield law,[296] which is applicable in judicial, legislative, and administrative proceedings, provides that any person, company, or entity engaged in gathering or disseminating news for the public has a qualified privilege against disclosure of information and documents. Disclosure may be compelled only if it can be shown by clear and convincing evidence that the information (1) is material and relevant to the controversy, (2) cannot be reasonably obtained through alternative means, and (3) is necessary for the case.[297] Finally, the law provides that publication of any information does not constitute a waiver of the qualified privilege against compelled disclosure.[298]

§14.3(H)(xxx) Tennessee

Under the Tennessee shield law,[299] a person who gathers information for publication or broadcast, regardless of whether that person is connected with a media entity or is independent, may not be required by a court, grand jury, the legislature, or any state agency to disclose that information or its source. A court may divest the journalist of this protection only upon proof "by clear and convincing evidence" that the information sought is clearly relevant to a probable illegality, the information cannot reasonably be obtained by alternative means, and a compelling and overriding public interest favors disclosure. An order of divestment is appealable to the court of appeals, which shall make an "independent determination" of the matter, according no presumption of correctness to the lower court's finding. Finally, the privilege does not protect the identity of the source of allegedly defamatory information in a defamation case where the defendant asserts a defense based on that source.

The Tennessee Supreme Court has held that application of the privilege is not contingent upon a finding that the information or its source was obtained in the course of a confidential journalist-informant relationship.[300] Moreover, the portion of the statute regarding appellate review of any order of divestment provides for an original hearing and disposition of factual, as well as legal, issues before the court of appeals and a direct appeal to the supreme court as a matter of right.[301]

§14.4 Common Issues

§14.4(A) Who Is Protected?

The issue of whether the reporter's privilege encompasses a particular individual or entity pervades privilege discussions regardless of the source of the testimonial privilege. Courts have held that the First Amendment reporter's privilege applies to a newspaper's restaurant reviewer,[302] an investigative

---

[296] S.C. Code Ann. §19-11-100 (Law. Co-op. Supp. 1993).
[297] Id. §19-11-100(B)(1)–(5).
[298] Id. at (C).
[299] Tenn. Code Ann. §24-1-208 (1980 & Supp. 1990).
[300] Austin v. Memphis Pub'g Co., 665 S.W.2d 146 (Tenn. 1983).
[301] State ex rel. Gerbitz v. Curriden, 738 S.W.2d 192 (Tenn. 1987).
[302] Equal Empl. Opportunity Comm'n v. McKellar Dev., 13 Media L. Rep. 1061 (N.D. Cal. 1986).

reporter making a documentary film,[303] and the publishers of a medical newsletter,[304] a consumer magazine,[305] a photography trade news periodical,[306] and an organization that rates and comments on the creditworthiness of companies.[307] In contrast, courts have held that there is no constitutional testimonial privilege for a political scientist,[308] an academic researcher,[309] or for the author of a book subpoenaed by a grand jury investigating alleged illegalities in the writing of the book.[310]

The Second Circuit has held that the First Amendment reporter's privilege does not extend to a person who gathers information for personal reasons unrelated to dissemination of information to the public.[311] In another case, the Second Circuit declined to decide whether a doctoral student employed as a waiter possessed a federal common law privilege not to disclose confidential information obtained in the course of writing a dissertation.[312] One district court declined to apply the First Amendment reporter's privilege to shield a researcher's study data from production because the information sought did not include the identity of any confidential source.[313]

With respect to state statutes, the decisions are not consistent.[314]

§14.4(B) Who Holds the Privilege?

The issue of who holds the privilege is a critical one, because possession determines who may waive it. Several courts have concluded that the journalist and not the informant holds the First Amendment privilege.[315] Under this view, the constitutional privilege remains intact regardless of a source's subsequent acts, such as signing a waiver,[316] and even if the party seeking disclosure is the source.[317]

---

[303]Silkwood v. Kerr-McGee Corp., 563 F.2d 433 (10th Cir. 1977).

[304]Apicella v. McNeil Labs., 66 F.R.D. 78 (E.D.N.Y. 1975).

[305]In re Consumers Union, 7 Media L. Rep. 2038 (S.D.N.Y. 1981).

[306]In re Photo Mktg. Ass'n, 327 N.W.2d 515 (Mich. Ct. App. 1982). In re Petroleum Prods. Antitrust Litig., 680 F.2d 5 (2d Cir.), *cert. denied sub nom.* Arizona v. McGraw-Hill, Inc., 459 U.S. 909 (1982).

[307]In re Scott Paper Co. Sec. Litig., 145 F.R.D. 366, 20 Media L. Rep. 2164 (E.D. Pa. 1992) (involving Standard & Poor's); In re Pan Am. Corp., 22 Media L. Rep. 1118, 1124 (S.D.N.Y. 1993) (rejecting argument that reporter's privilege does not apply because of Dun & Bradstreet v. Greenmoss Builders, 472 U.S. 749, 11 Media L. Rep. 2417 (1985)). *See also* Summit Technology v. Healthcare Capital Group, 19 Media L. Rep. 2180 (D. Mass. 1992) (investment analyst entitled to privilege).

[308]United States v. Doe, 460 F.2d 328 (1st Cir. 1972), *cert. denied sub nom.* Popkin v. United States, 411 U.S. 909 (1973).

[309]Wright v. Jeep Corp., 547 F. Supp. 871 (E.D. Mich. 1982).

[310]In re Grand Jury Matter (Gronowicz), 764 F.2d 983 (3d Cir. 1985), *cert. denied,* 474 U.S. 1055 (1986).

[311]von Bulow by Auersperg v. von Bulow, 811 F.2d 136 (2d Cir.), *cert. denied sub nom.* Reynolds v. von Bulow by Auersperg, 481 U.S. 1015 (1987). *See also* Shoen v. Shoen, 5 F.3d 1289, 1293, 21 Media L. Rep. 1961, 1964 (9th Cir. 1993) (following *von Bulow* but concluding that privilege applied to book author). *But see* Matera v. Superior Ct., 825 P.2d 971, 19 Media L. Rep. 2053 (Ariz. Ct. App. 1992) (state statute does not protect book author).

[312]In re Grand Jury Subpoena Dated Jan. 4, 1984, 750 F.2d 223 (2d Cir. 1984).

[313]*Wright,* 547 F. Supp. 871.

[314]Northside Sanitary Landfill v. Bradley, 462 N.E.2d 1321 (Ind. Ct. App. 1984) (state statute inapplicable to part-time journalist who did not obtain information in course of performing duties of journalist); People v. Von Villas, 13 Cal. Rptr. 62 (Cal. Ct. App. 1992) (free-lancer protected by state shield laws).

[315]United States v. Cuthbertson, 630 F.2d 139 (3d Cir. 1980), *cert. denied,* 449 U.S. 1126 (1981); United States v. Criden, 633 F.2d 346 (3d Cir. 1980), *cert. denied sub nom.* Schaeffer v. United States, 449 U.S. 1113 (1981); Los Angeles Memorial Coliseum Comm. v. National Football League, 89 F.R.D. 489 (C.D. Cal. 1981); Palandjian v. Pahlavi, 103 F.R.D. 410 (D.D.C. 1984).

[316]*Cuthbertson,* 630 F.2d 139; *Los Angeles Memorial Coliseum,* 89 F.R.D. 489. However, the *Criden* court limited its holding by explaining that, although the source does not hold the First Amendment privilege, that privilege is easily defeated in a criminal case where the informant has already disclosed the content of the conversation with the reporter. *Criden,* 633 F.2d 346.

[317]*See Palandjian,* 103 F.R.D. 410.

One court raised but declined to decide whether the First Amendment privilege is personal to the reporter or also extends to his or her employer, because the court was able to resolve a discovery dispute on alternative grounds.[318] However, the answer to this question is important where the reporter is willing to reveal material but the employer objects. Another court concluded that a reporter's former employer, a newspaper, could assert a constitutional privilege not to disclose confidential information in the reporter's old diary and notes despite the reporter's desire for disclosure.[319]

Whether a reporter holds a statutory privilege varies from state to state. For example, the New Jersey Supreme Court has held that the privilege arising under that state's shield law belongs to the reporter and not the source.[320] In contrast, the New York reporter's privilege evaporates where a confidential source subsequently reveals his or her identity.[321]

§14.4(C) Waiver

Waiver discussions focus on the types of conduct that can trigger waiver and on the scope of waiver. One federal court has held that only the journalist has the power to waive the federal constitutional and common law privilege.[322] Another court concluded that the First Amendment privilege is not waived even if the reporter discloses confidential information to third parties or refers to such information in a broadcast, because the "chilling effect" on the flow of information to the press and public of requiring reporters to divulge information is the same regardless of whether the information sought is confidential.[323] In examining waiver issues under the First Amendment reporter's privilege, one state court has held that a journalist waives any right to assert the constitutional privilege once he or she discloses confidential information to a third party outside of the news-gathering process "without imposing a stricture of confidentiality" upon the third party.[324] Importantly, the court expressly limited its decision to "the particular facts and circumstances" before it.[325]

Under state law, waiver largely is a function of whether the particular statutory language shields only the identity of confidential sources or both sources and confidential information. Under the Arkansas statute, a journalist does not waive the privilege by voluntarily disclosing the identity of a source to his or her employer and a third party.[326] Similarly, a reporter who discloses the identity of a source to a third party does not necessarily waive the protection of the Illinois statute.[327] New Jersey's Supreme Court has held that that state's absolute reporter's privilege against disclosure of confidences is not waived

---

[318]Bauer v. Brown, 11 Media L. Rep. 2168 (W.D. Va. 1985).
[319]United States v. Winans, 11 Media L. Rep. 1279 (S.D.N.Y. 1985).
[320]State v. Boiardo, 416 A.2d 793 (N.J. 1980).
[321]Andrews v. Andreoli, 400 N.Y.S.2d 442 (N.Y. Sup. Ct. 1977).
[322]Los Angeles Memorial Coliseum Comm. v. National Football League, 89 F.R.D. 489 (C.D. Cal. 1981).
[323]Altemose Constr. Co. v. Building & Constr. Trades Council of Phila., 443 F. Supp. 489 (E.D. Pa. 1977).
[324]*See* Wheeler v. Goulart, 593 A.2d 173, 175, 18 Media L. Rep. 2296, 2299 (D.C. Ct. App. 1991).
[325]*Id.*
[326]Saxton v. Arkansas Gazette, 569 S.W.2d 115 (Ark. 1978).
[327]People ex rel. Scott v. Silverstein, 412 N.E.2d 692, 6 Media L. Rep. 2141 (Ill. Ct. App. 1980), *rev'd on other grounds,* 429 N.E.2d 483 (Ill. 1981).

by disclosure (under court order) of nonconfidential sources or by assertion of a "good faith" defense in a libel suit.[328]

In contrast, a number of other states have held that their statutory privileges are more easily waived. For example, under Ohio law, the privilege is waived when the informant's identity is revealed, but only to the extent of the information disclosed.[329] The protection conferred by the Nevada shield law is waived by the voluntary disclosure of any significant part of a confidential matter[330] or, in a libel case, by the journalist's assertion of a defense based on confidential sources.[331]

§14.4(D) What Information and Materials Are Protected?

Generally, there is no protection for published materials—e.g., reporters can usually be compelled to authenticate quotes.[332] However, there is some support for the proposition that the First Amendment testimonial privilege protects the identity of sources and materials even if such information has become known or has been broadcast or published.[333] The New Jersey shield law also prohibits courts from forcing journalists to testify in criminal cases, even if the information sought has been published.[334]

Numerous courts have held that the qualified First Amendment privilege protects a journalist's unpublished materials, including notes, investigative reports, a manuscript, test results, photographs, outtakes, and memoranda.[335]

The scope of the privilege for unpublished materials under state shield laws varies from state to state. The California provisions provide immunity from contempt for failure to disclose unpublished information[336] or to produce the physical records containing that information.[337] This protection applies in civil[338] and criminal[339] cases. Minnesota's shield law protects a reporter's notes and interview transcripts.[340] Nevada's shield law protects all information and

---

[328]Resorts Int'l v. New Jersey Monthly, 445 A.2d 395, 8 Media L. Rep. 1487 (N.J.), *cert. denied,* 459 U.S. 907 (1982).
[329]State v. Geis, 441 N.E.2d 803 (Ohio Ct. App. 1981).
[330]Newburn v. Howard Hughes Medical Inst., 594 P.2d 1146 (Nev. 1979).
[331]Laxalt v. McClatchy, 116 F.R.D. 438, 14 Media L. Rep. 1199 (D. Nev. 1987). *See also supra* note 244.
[332]Nulty v. Pennzoil Co., 485 N.Y.S.2d 533, 11 Media L. Rep. 1647 (N.Y. App. Div. 1985); Maughan v. NL Indus., 524 F. Supp. 93 (D.D.C. 1981) (dictum).
[333]Altemose Constr. Co. v. Building & Constr. Trades Council of Phila., 443 F. Supp. 489 (E.D. Pa. 1977); Maurice v. National Labor Relations Bd., 7 Media L. Rep. 2221 (S.D. W. Va. 1981), *rev'd on other grounds,* 691 F.2d 182 (4th Cir. 1982); Parson v. Watson, 778 F. Supp. 214, 19 Media L. Rep. 1275 (D. Del. 1991) (citing other cases). *Contra* In re Shain, 978 F.2d 850, 20 Media L. Rep. 1930 (4th Cir. 1992).
[334]In re Schuman, 552 A.2d 602 (N.J. 1989).
[335]*See, e.g.,* Shoen v. Shoen, 5 F.3d 1289, 1293, 21 Media L. Rep. 1961, 1964 (9th Cir. 1993); United States v. LaRouche Campaign, 841 F.2d 1176, 15 Media L. Rep. 1502 (1st Cir. 1988); von Bulow by Auersperg v. von Bulow, 811 F.2d 136 (2d Cir.), *cert. denied sub nom.* Reynolds v. von Bulow by Auersperg, 481 U.S. 1015 (1987); United States v. Burke, 700 F.2d 70 (2d Cir.), *cert. denied,* 464 U.S. 816 (1983); United States v. Cuthbertson, 630 F.2d 139 (3d Cir. 1980), *cert. denied,* 449 U.S. 1126 (1981); Stickels v. General Rental Co., 750 F. Supp. 729, 18 Media L. Rep. 1644 (E.D. Va. 1990); Bauer v. Brown, 11 Media L. Rep. 2168 (W.D. Va. 1985); In re Consumers Union, 7 Media L. Rep. 2038 (S.D.N.Y. 1981); Loadholtz v. Fields, 389 F. Supp. 1299 (M.D. Fla. 1975); Hatch v. Marsh, 134 F.R.D. 300 (M.D. Fla. 1990). *But see supra* note 70.
[336]New York Times Co. v. Superior Ct. (Sortomme), 273 Cal. Rptr. 98, 18 Media L. Rep. 1145 (Cal. 1990); Mitchell v. Superior Ct. (Synanon Church), 690 P.2d 635 (Cal. 1984).
[337]Playboy Enters. v. Superior Ct. (Green), 201 Cal. Rptr. 207 (Cal. Ct. App. 1984).
[338]*See New York Times,* 273 Cal. Rptr. 98.
[339]Delaney v. Superior Ct. (Kopeteman), 789 P.2d 934 (Cal. 1990).
[340]Aerial Burials v. Minneapolis Star & Tribune, 8 Media L. Rep. 1653 (Minn. Dist. Ct. 1982).

material obtained in the news gathering process to the extent that such information or material is not disclosed in a publication or broadcast.[341] The Pennsylvania statute protects a reporter's notes in libel cases even if the source is known and even if the notes do not contain confidential information.[342]

Outtakes—portions of video and audio tapes not publicly broadcast—generally fall within the protection of a qualified First Amendment privilege.[343] However, according to some state courts, the First Amendment does not protect against the production of outtakes that contain no confidential information.[344] The Arkansas shield law protects only sources and not outtakes.[345] Pennsylvania's statute bars the compulsory disclosure of outtakes even in libel cases and even if the identity of the source is known.[346]

In *Herbert v. Lando*,[347] a libel plaintiff seeking to uncover proof of "actual malice" attempted to question a journalist about the state of mind of those who edited, produced, and published the allegedly libelous story; the journalist refused to respond to deposition questioning on the basis of a First Amendment "editorial privilege."[348] The U.S. Supreme Court rejected the journalist's position, reasoning that an inquiry into the journalist's mental processes might produce evidence material to an essential element of the plaintiff's case without necessarily placing any intolerable burden on the editorial process.[349] Thus, there exists no absolute First Amendment protection for such information obtained in the news gathering process.

§14.4(E) Sanctions for Failure to Disclose

The particular sanction a court may impose if a journalist refuses to obey an order of disclosure is often a function of the journalist's role in the case.

Where the reporter is the plaintiff or otherwise pursues a claim, refusal to disclose information has led to dismissal of the journalist's claims. In *Anderson v. Nixon*,[350] the plaintiff reporter refused to disclose the identity of sources having information highly material and relevant to a statute of limitations dispute; the court therefore decided the limitations question against the reporter and dismissed the suit.[351] *Dalitz v. Penthouse International*[352] involved a defendant publisher in a libel suit who filed a cross-complaint against the

---

[341] Las Vegas Sun v. Eighth Judicial Dist. Ct., 761 P.2d 849 (Nev. 1988).

[342] Lal v. Columbia Broadcasting Sys., 551 F. Supp. 356, 9 Media L. Rep. 1112 (E.D. Pa. 1982), *aff'd*, 726 F.2d 97 (3d Cir. 1984); Altemose Constr. Co. v. Building & Constr. Trades Council of Phila., 443 F. Supp. 489 (E.D. Pa. 1977).

[343] United States v. Cuthbertson, 630 F.2d 139 (3d Cir. 1980), *cert. denied*, 449 U.S. 1126 (1981); United States v. Smalley, 9 Media L. Rep. 1252 (N.D. Tex. 1983); United States v. Liddy, 354 F. Supp. 208 (D.D.C. 1972).

[344] CBS, Inc. v. Jackson, 578 So. 2d 698, 18 Media L. Rep. 2110 (Fla. 1991); CBS, Inc. (KMOX-TV) v. Campbell, 645 S.W.2d 30 (Mo. Ct. App. 1982). *But see* O'Neill v. Oakgrove Constr., 523 N.E.2d 277 (N.Y. 1988) (holding that qualified First Amendment reporter's privilege extends to nonconfidential material prepared or collected in course of news gathering).

[345] Williams v. American Broadcasting Cos., 96 F.R.D. 658 (W.D. Ark. 1983). *See also* Knight-Ridder Broadcasting v. Greenberg, 511 N.E.2d 1116 (N.Y. 1987) (modified by statutory amendment N.Y. CIV. RIGHTS LAW §79-h (amended 1990)).

[346] Steaks Unlimited v. Deaner, 623 F.2d 264 (3d Cir. 1980).

[347] 441 U.S. 153, 4 Media L. Rep. 2575 (1979). *See also infra* §14.5(B).

[348] 441 U.S. at 157.

[349] *Id.* at 169–75. However, a court can limit discovery because of First Amendment concerns. *Id.* at 177.

[350] 444 F. Supp. 1195, 3 Media L. Rep. 2051 (D.D.C. 1978). *See also infra* §14.5(A).

[351] 444 F. Supp. at 1200–1201.

[352] 214 Cal. Rptr. 254, 11 Media L. Rep. 2153 (Cal. Ct. App. 1985).

plaintiffs. The court first held that the publisher and its reporters would be treated as a "single entity" for purposes of the cross-complaint and then dismissed the cross-complaint as a sanction for the reporters' refusal to disclose their confidential sources, based on the finding that the need for disclosure was compelling and the information was relevant to the plaintiffs' defense against the cross-complaint.[353] Other courts have held that a reporter who places sources at issue by initiating a lawsuit waives the reporter's privilege and may be compelled to disclose the identity of those sources.[354]

In libel cases where the journalist or news entity is the defendant and the court concludes that no privilege is available, a variety of sanctions for refusal to obey an order requiring disclosure have been imposed. Courts have precluded the defendant from using the undisclosed sources as proof of responsibility[355] or have imposed a presumption that the defendant had no source whatsoever for an allegedly libelous article.[356] Where the reporter's refusal is "flagrant" or "willful," one court simply entered judgment in favor of the plaintiff and awarded damages.[357]

In contrast, the Idaho Supreme Court has held that the striking of media defendants' pleadings and the entry of a default judgment against them was unwarranted where, despite the defendants' refusal to disclose confidential information, the libel plaintiff had never proven an inability to obtain the information from alternative sources.[358] Moreover, courts have declined to punish media defendants who refuse to disclose information merely collateral to a plaintiff's case[359] or where a shield law prohibits courts from penalizing journalists for refusing to reveal confidential sources.[360]

Where a journalist is not a party, usually the only remedy available is contempt. Sometimes this sanction has been imposed where the court has determined that a criminal defendant's Sixth Amendment interests outweigh the reporter's First Amendment privilege.[361]

§14.4(F) Alternatives to Full Disclosure

The most common alternative to complete disclosure of confidential information is in camera production to the court. The controversy surrounding this alternative centers on whether the mere fact of disclosure, even if limited to a judge, produces the same "chilling effect" caused by full disclosure. In *In re Farber,* the New Jersey Supreme Court concluded that

---

[353]*Id.* at 258–61.
[354]Driscoll v. Morris, 111 F.R.D. 459 (D. Conn. 1986); Campus Communications v. Freedman, 374 So. 2d 1169 (Fla. Ct. App. 1979).
[355]Coronado Credit Union v. Koat, 656 P.2d 896, 9 Media L. Rep. 1031 (N.M. Ct. App. 1982); Greenberg v. CBS, Inc., 419 N.Y.S.2d 988, 5 Media L. Rep. 1470 (N.Y. App. Div. 1979).
[356]DeRoburt v. Gannett, 507 F. Supp. 860, 6 Media L. Rep. 2473 (D. Haw. 1981); Downing v. Monitor Pub'g Co., 415 A.2d 683, 6 Media L. Rep. 1193 (N.H. 1980).
[357]Georgia Communications Corp. v. Horne, 294 S.E.2d 725, 8 Media L. Rep. 2375 (Ga. Ct. App. 1982).
[358]Sierra Life Ins. Co. v. Magic Valley Newspapers, 623 P.2d 103 (Idaho 1980).
[359]Cervantes v. Time, Inc., 464 F.2d 986 (8th Cir. 1972), *cert. denied,* 409 U.S. 1125 (1973); Liberty Lobby v. Rees, 111 F.R.D. 19 (D.D.C. 1986); Dowd v. Calabrese, 577 F. Supp. 238 (D.D.C. 1983).
[360]Sprague v. Walter, 516 A.2d 706, 13 Media L. Rep. 1177 (Pa. Super. Ct. 1986), *aff'd,* 543 A.2d 1078 (Pa.), *appeal dismissed,* 488 U.S. 988 (1988).
[361]*See, e.g.,* United States v. Criden, 633 F.2d 346 (3d Cir. 1980), *cert. denied sub nom.* Schaeffer v. United States, 449 U.S. 1113 (1981); Karem v. Priest, 744 F. Supp. 136 (W.D. Tex. 1990); Delaney v. Superior Ct. (Kopetman), 789 P.2d 934 (Cal. 1990); Massachusetts v. Corsetti, 438 N.E.2d 805, 8 Media

inspection is no more than a procedural tool, a device to be used to ascertain the relevancy and materiality of [subpoenaed] material. Such an *in camera* inspection is not in itself an invasion of the statutory privilege. Rather it is a preliminary step to determine whether, and if so to what extent, the statutory privilege must yield to [competing] constitutional rights.[362]

Several other courts have also held that the requirements for in camera production are more lenient than for full disclosure.[363] A court need only find a reasonable probability or likelihood that the subpoenaed materials would reveal relevant evidence admissible at trial.[364]

The Supreme Court of Wisconsin has held that an in camera inspection should be ordered if a criminal defendant shows, by a preponderance of the evidence, that the information sought is relevant, material, and exculpatory, and that no reasonable alternative source for the information exists.[365] Similarly, the California Evidence Code expressly authorizes courts in that state to conduct in camera examinations of purportedly privileged information when necessary to rule on a claim of privilege.[366] In contrast, a Washington court ruled that the state's constitution, which grants reporters an *absolute* privilege against compulsory disclosure, prohibits even in camera inspections.[367]

Other alternatives to full disclosure include restricting disclosure to counsel,[368] postponing disclosure until late in the discovery process, identifying nonconfidential sources before confidential sources, and sealing deposition and court records.[369]

§14.4(G) Choice of Law

Complex choice of law questions arise in cases pending in federal court. The issues generally are twofold: (1) determining whether federal common law or state law is to be applied in assessing the validity of the asserted privilege; and (2) in instances where state law applies, determining which state's privilege law governs—the law of the state in which the federal court is sitting or the law of another state. This latter issue also arises in cases pending in state court.

Pursuant to Federal Rule of Evidence 501,[370] federal privilege law controls in federal criminal cases and civil lawsuits based on federal question jurisdiction.[371] In mixed law cases involving both a federal question and one or more

---

L. Rep. 2113 (Mass. 1982); In re Farber, 394 A.2d 330 (N.J.), *cert. denied sub nom.* New York Times Co. v. New Jersey, 439 U.S. 997 (1978).

[362] 394 A.2d at 337–38.

[363] United States v. LaRouche Campaign, 841 F.2d 1176 (1st Cir. 1988); United States v. Cuthbertson, 630 F.2d 139 (3d Cir. 1980), *cert. denied,* 449 U.S. 1126 (1981).

[364] *LaRouche,* 841 F.2d at 1179. *See also* United States v. Cutler, 6 F.3d 67, 21 Media L. Rep. 2075 (2d Cir. 1993) (ordering production without inspection).

[365] State ex rel. Green Bay Newspaper Co. v. Circuit Ct., 335 N.W.2d 367 (Wis. 1983).

[366] CAL. EVID. CODE §915 (Deering 1986).

[367] State v. Rinaldo, 673 P.2d 614 (Wash. Ct. App. 1983), *aff'd,* 689 P.2d 392 (Wash. 1984).

[368] Some courts have ordered that information about a confidential source was to be revealed only to the parties' attorneys. Miller v. Mecklenberg County, 11 Media L. Rep. 1836 (W.D.N.C. 1985); Hart v. Playboy Enters., 6 Media L. Rep. 2571 (D. Kan. 1981); *see also* Miller v. Transamerican Press, 621 F.2d 721 (5th Cir. 1980), *cert. denied,* 450 U.S. 1041 (1981) (on remand, advising district court to restrict information about informant's identity to counsel).

[369] Bruno & Stillman, Inc. v. Globe Newspaper Co., 633 F.2d 583, 598 (1st Cir. 1980).

[370] For the full text of this rule, see *supra* note 162.

[371] FED. R. EVID. 501; Lewis v. United States, 517 F.2d 236, 237 (9th Cir. 1975); Dillon v. San Francisco, 748 F. Supp. 722 (N.D. Cal. 1990); United Liquor Co. v. Gard, 88 F.R.D. 123, 125 (D. Ariz. 1980). *But*

pendent state law claims there is some dispute as to whether federal law governs or some combination of federal and state law controls.[372] In federal actions based solely on diversity of citizenship jurisdiction under 28 U.S.C. Section 1332, the *Erie* doctrine[373] and Rule 501 both mandate that state privilege law controls.[374]

Diversity actions sometimes present the second issue—which one of two or more states' privilege laws will apply.[375] Under the principle of *Klaxon Co. v. Stentor Electrical Manufacturing Co.*,[376] the choice of law rules of the forum state—i.e., the state in which the court confronting the discovery matter sits—control;[377] therefore, whether a journalist will be required to divulge his or her confidences is initially a function of the particular choice of law rules of the state in question. For example, in *Laxalt v. McClatchy*, the court held that Nevada's conflict of law rules required the application of Nevada's substantive law of privilege since Nevada was the *place* of the plaintiff's injury.[378]

---

see Riley v. City of Chester, 612 F.2d 708, 715 (3d Cir. 1979) (explaining that, although federal court in nondiversity civil case must follow federal privilege law, court retains flexibility to give state privilege law special consideration); Baker v. F & F Inv., 470 F.2d 778, 782 (2d Cir. 1972) (in federal question case, stating that state shield laws not conclusive but nonetheless reflected paramount First Amendment interest), *cert. denied,* 411 U.S. 966 (1973); Los Angeles Memorial Coliseum Comm. v. National Football League, 89 F.R.D. 489, 492 (C.D. Cal. 1981) (pointing out that, even in cases based "exclusively" on federal law, federal courts, in shaping federal common law of privilege, "traditionally" have sought guidance from state privilege law).

[372]The Central District of California has held that "under Rule 501, when a civil action in federal court contains a combination of federal and state claims or defenses, federal courts should evaluate claims of privilege under both state and federal law." *Los Angeles Memorial Coliseum,* 89 F.R.D. at 492. In contrast, the Second Circuit concluded that Congress intended that the federal law of privileges apply to both federal claims and pendent state law claims. von Bulow by Auersperg v. von Bulow, 811 F.2d 136, 144 (2d Cir. 1987); *see also* Pinkard v. Johnson, 118 F.R.D. 517, 519–20 (M.D. Ala. 1987) (holding that where evidence sought from reporter relevant to both federal and state claims, principles of federal privilege law govern).

In 1986, the Northern District of California found that where "state and federal claims are joined, but the evidence [sought to be disclosed] affects only the state claims the state law of privilege applies." Shaklee Corp. v. Gunnell, 110 F.R.D. 190, 192, 12 Media L. Rep. 2221 (N.D. Cal. 1986).

[373]The *Erie* doctrine holds that, in suits that are in federal court on the basis of diversity of citizenship, federal law governs procedural questions and state law governs substantive questions. Erie Ry. Co. v. Tompkins, 304 U.S. 64 (1938).

[374]Steaks Unlimited v. Deaner, 623 F.2d 264, 277 n.63 (3d Cir. 1980); Miller v. Transamerican Press, 621 F.2d 721, 724 (5th Cir. 1980); Cervantes v. Time, Inc., 464 F.2d 986, 989 n.5 (8th Cir. 1972); Don King Prods. v. Douglas, 131 F.R.D. 421, 423 (S.D.N.Y. 1990); May v. Collins, 122 F.R.D. 535, 538 (S.D. Ind. 1988); Laxalt v. McClatchy, 116 F.R.D. 438, 446, 14 Media L. Rep. 1199 (D. Nev. 1987); Shaklee Corp. v. Gunnell, 110 F.R.D. 190, 192, 12 Media L. Rep. 2221 (N.D. Cal. 1986); Coughlin v. Westinghouse Broadcasting & Cable, 603 F. Supp. 377 (E.D. Pa.), *aff'd,* 780 F.2d 340 (3d Cir. 1985), *cert. denied,* 476 U.S. 1187 (1986); Newton v. National Broadcasting Co., 109 F.R.D. 522, 528 (D. Nev. 1985); Continental Cablevision v. Storer Broadcasting, 583 F. Supp. 427, 431–32 (E.D. Mo. 1984); Fischer v. McGowan, 585 F. Supp. 978, 984 n.11 (D.R.I. 1984); Mazzella v. Philadelphia Newspapers, 479 F. Supp. 523, 526 (E.D.N.Y. 1979); Apicella v. McNeil Labs., 66 F.R.D. 78, 84 (E.D.N.Y. 1975); In re Cepeda, 233 F. Supp. 465, 467 (S.D.N.Y. 1964).

[375]Examples of these types of cases are those where a litigant seeks to depose an out-of-state journalist in the trial state or where a litigant seeks to depose a journalist in the journalist's own state that does not also happen to be the trial state. In criminal cases, the Uniform Act to Secure the Attendance of Witnesses From Without the State may apply. *See, e.g.,* Codey v. Capital Cities, 626 N.E.2d 636, 21 Media L. Rep. 2267 (N.Y. 1993) (where New Jersey to compel production of outtakes by New York television station to New Jersey grand jury, New Jersey courts should decide privilege issue).

[376]313 U.S. 487 (1941).

[377]*See Cervantes,* 464 F.2d at 989 n.5 (citing *Klaxon* for proposition that "a federal diversity court must apply the choice-of-law rules of the State in which it sits"); *Laxalt,* 116 F.R.D. at 446 (citing *Klaxon* for proposition that federal court sitting in Nevada must look to Nevada's conflict of law rule); *Newton,* 109 F.R.D. at 528 (same); *Continental Cablevision,* 583 F. Supp. at 432 (holding that *Klaxon* requires "a federal court sitting in diversity [to] apply the choice-of-law rules of the forum state"); Williams v. American Broadcasting Cos., 96 F.R.D. 658, 662 (W.D. Ark. 1983) (holding that, under *Klaxon,* federal court sitting in Arkansas must apply Arkansas choice-of-law rules); *Mazzella,* 479 F. Supp. at 526 (citing *Klaxon* for proposition that federal court sitting in New York must look to New York's conflict of law rules); *In re Cepeda,* 233 F. Supp. at 469 (explaining that, under *Klaxon,* "[i]t is clear that in a diversity case the Court sits as another state court and must apply the conflict of law rule of the state in which it sits").

[378]*Laxalt,* 116 F.R.D. at 446; *see also Newton,* 109 F.R.D. at 528.

Similarly, in *Williams v. American Broadcasting Cos.*, the court found that Arkansas choice of law rules, which mandate that evidentiary questions be determined by the law of the forum state, required the application of Arkansas privilege law.[379]

However, in *In re Cepeda,* the court held that New York's conflict of law rules mandated the use of California's privilege law where the testimony ultimately sought would be used in a California court and subject to California rules of admissibility.[380] Because Maryland's highest state court has held that that state's shield law "has no extraterritorial application,"[381] it is unclear what a federal court sitting outside of Maryland might do if it concluded that the choice of law rules of the forum state required the application of Maryland law.

§14.5 Civil Cases

§14.5(A) The Reporter As Plaintiff

Only a handful of reported cases chronicle instances in which the journalist is a plaintiff or makes a claim.[382] The central issue in such cases is whether the press may use the First Amendment to defeat efforts to uncover evidence relevant to the media's legal claims. Reporters have usually had their claims dismissed if they refused to disclose relevant information.[383] Some courts have concluded that a journalist may not assert this constitutional privilege when he or she is a plaintiff.[384] Similarly, others have concluded that the privilege is waived when the reporter puts the identity of his or her sources at issue[385] or that it is easily overridden by competing interests, such as the fair administration of justice.[386]

§14.5(B) The Reporter As Defendant

Reporter's privilege issues often arise in defamation actions where a member of the press is named as a defendant. In such cases, the ability of the media defendant to resist discovery on the basis of a privilege is often an issue. For example, *New York Times Co. v. Sullivan*[387] requires public officials and figures to show actual malice when suing a media defendant. Typically, evidence relevant to the actual malice issue is in the control of the defendant, in the form of outtakes, research material, and notes. Because a privilege to withhold that evidence could limit a plaintiff's ability to recover for defamation,

---

[379]96 F.R.D. at 662.
[380]233 F. Supp. at 470–71. *See also Mazzella,* 479 F. Supp. at 527 (holding that New York's choice of law principles required application of Pennsylvania privilege law).
[381]In re Cal.-County of L.A., 471 A.2d 1141 (Md.), *cert. denied,* 467 U.S. 1205 (1984).
[382]*See* cases cited *infra* notes 384–86.
[383]*Id.*
[384]Anderson v. Nixon, 444 F. Supp. 1195, 3 Media L. Rep. 2050 (D.D.C. 1978); Campus Communications v. Freedman, 374 So. 2d 1169 (Fla. Ct. App. 1979).
[385]Driscoll v. Morris, 111 F.R.D. 459 (D. Conn. 1986).
[386]Dalitz v. Penthouse Int'l, 214 Cal. Rptr. 254, 11 Media L. Rep. 2153 (Cal. Ct. App. 1985).
[387]376 U.S. 254 (1964).

some legislatures have limited the application of their shield law in defamation actions;[388] others have not.[389]

In the absence of a state shield law applicable to libel actions, federal and state constitutional protections can be relied upon.[390] One of the earliest decisions to address the dilemma was *Garland v. Torre*,[391] in which entertainer Judy Garland sued over an allegedly libelous newspaper article. Garland deposed the reporter in an attempt to discover the identity of the network executive who supplied the reporter with the substance of the statements.[392] After acknowledging that the compulsory disclosure of confidential sources may impose some limitation on news availability, the court nevertheless ordered the reporter to reveal the executive's identity because it was highly material and relevant, could not be obtained from alternative sources, and "went to the heart of the plaintiff's claim."[393]

In *Mitchell v. Superior Court*,[394] the California Supreme Court held that the defendant reporters in a libel action had a qualified constitutional privilege to withhold the identity of confidential sources and unpublished information from those sources, and that the following factors should be considered in deciding whether the privilege had been overcome: (1) the information sought must go to the heart of the plaintiff's claim—relevance is not enough; (2) discovery should be denied unless the person seeking it has exhausted all alternative sources of information; (3) the importance of the published information and the risk of harm to sources if they were revealed could bar any disclosure whatsoever; and (4) the plaintiff should be required to make a prima facie showing that the defamatory statements were false.[395] After finding that the plaintiffs had not made these showings, the court reversed the trial court's order compelling disclosure.[396] *Mitchell* properly balances the competing interests where confidential sources and related information are involved.

In *Herbert v. Lando*,[397] the U.S. Supreme Court considered whether the First Amendment also creates an editorial privilege for a reporter's or editor's unpublished work product. Specifically, *Herbert* involved an admitted public figure who sued the individual responsible for an allegedly defamatory broadcast and magazine article.[398] At a deposition, the media defendant claimed that

---

[388] *See, e.g.*, KY. REV. STAT. ANN. §421.100 (Michie/Bobbs-Merrill 1972). *See generally supra* §14.3(H).

[389] *See, e.g.*, IND. CODE §34-3-5-1 (1988) *and* N.J. STAT. ANN. §§2A:84A-21.1 to -21.8. *See also* Steaks Unlimited v. Deaner, 623 F.2d 264 (3d Cir.) (construing Pennsylvania's shield law), *cert. denied*, 449 U.S. 994 (1980); Coughlin v. Westinghouse Broadcasting & Cable, 603 F. Supp. 377 (E.D. Pa.) (same), *aff'd*, 780 F.2d 340 (3d Cir. 1985). *See generally supra* §14.3(H).

[390] *See generally supra* §14.3(A).

[391] 259 F.2d 545 (2d Cir.), *cert. denied*, 385 U.S. 910 (1958).

[392] *Id.* at 547.

[393] *Id.* at 548–50.

[394] 37 Cal. 3d 268 (Cal. 1984).

[395] *Id.* at 279–84. *See also* Dallas Morning News v. Garcia, 822 S.W.2d 675, 19 Media L. Rep. 2033 (Tex. Ct. App. 1991) (adopting similar test with special emphasis on need for plaintiff to establish falsity by something more than plaintiff's own testimony). This test can be met. Star Editorial v. United States Dist. Ct., 7 F.3d 856, 21 Media L. Rep. 2281 (9th Cir. 1993) (analyzing factors and holding that *Mitchell* test was met). Failure to object to a reporter testifying about confidential sources' reliability while refusing to disclose their identities waives any right to complain about this procedure. Desai v. Hersh, 954 F.2d 1408, 19 Media L. Rep. 1893 (7th Cir.), *cert. denied*, 113 S. Ct. 190 (1992). Similarly, where a libel plaintiff did not move to compel after the shield law was invoked, he could not complain that his discovery concerning actual malice was inadequate. Costello v. Ocean County Observer, 21 Media L. Rep. 2274, 2280 (N.J. Super. Ct. App. Div. 1993).

[396] *Id.*

[397] 441 U.S. 153 (1979). *See also supra* §14.4(D).

[398] 441 U.S. at 155–56.

the First Amendment protected it against any discovery request delving into the state of mind of editors, producers, or publishers.[399] The Court rejected the defendant's contention and refused to grant an editorial privilege for such unpublished information.[400] The Court emphasized that the evidence sought was critical to the plaintiff's case.[401]

However, courts have construed *Herbert* as being limited to libel cases involving public figures and officials and have relied on Justice Powell's concurring opinion in that case to recognize a qualified editorial privilege. For example, the First Circuit has interpreted *Herbert* to support the use of a fact-sensitive approach in balancing a libel plaintiff's need for information about the editorial process against First Amendment concerns.[402] Similarly, although it sustained a district court's order compelling a libel defendant to disclose the identity of a confidential informant, the Fifth Circuit required the lower court to impose strict limits on the scope of disclosure in order to protect important First Amendment interests.[403]

§14.5(C) The Reporter As Third Party

When subpoenaed as nonparty witnesses in civil litigation, journalists turn to the First Amendment, state constitutions, and state shield laws for protection against the compulsory disclosure of a source or information. In cases involving the qualified First Amendment privilege, courts often find in the reporter's favor because the party seeking information fails to establish one or more elements of the balancing test, usually exhaustion of alternative sources.[404] Where an absolute state constitutional privilege is recognized, constitutional challenges to it have failed.[405]

Where a state statute is available, the likelihood of the privilege being upheld is tied directly to whether the shield law is absolute[406] or qualified.[407] For example, in *Fisher v. McGowan*,[408] the court applied the Rhode Island reporter's privilege law. Based on its determination that the statute confers a nearly absolute protection to journalists, the litigant's motion to compel production by a nonparty reporter was denied.[409] The result would be different in a libel suit where the reporter is a defendant, because the Rhode Island statute does not apply "[t]o the source of any allegedly defamatory information in any

---

[399]*Id.* at 157.
[400]*Id.* at 158.
[401]*Id.* at 169.
[402]Bruno & Stillman, Inc. v. Globe Newspaper Co., 633 F.2d 583 (1st Cir. 1980).
[403]Miller v. Transamerican Press, 621 F.2d 721 (5th Cir. 1980), *cert. denied,* 450 U.S. 1041 (1981).
[404]*See, e.g.,* Shoen v. Shoen, 5 F.3d 1289, 1293, 21 Media L. Rep. 1961, 1964 (9th Cir. 1993) (written interrogatories do not satisfy exhaustion requirement where person can be deposed); In re Selcraig, 705 F.2d 789 (5th Cir. 1983); Zerilli v. Smith, 656 F.2d 705 (D.C. Cir. 1981); Riley v. City of Chester, 612 F.2d 708 (3d Cir. 1979); Baker v. F & F Inv., 470 F.2d 778 (2d Cir. 1972), *cert. denied,* 411 U.S. 996 (1973); Los Angeles Memorial Coliseum v. National Football League, 89 F.R.D. 489 (C.D. Cal. 1981); In re Consumers Union, 495 F. Supp. 582 (S.D.N.Y. 1980); Lamberto v. Bown, 326 N.W.2d 305, 8 Media L. Rep. 2525 (Iowa 1982). *See also supra* notes 98–104 and accompanying text.
[405]New York Times Co. v. Superior Ct. (Sortomme), 796 P.2d 811, 18 Media L. Rep. 1145 (Cal. 1990).
[406]*Id.*
[407]*Compare* Grand Forks Herald v. District Ct., 322 N.W.2d 850 (N.D. 1982) (finding that party seeking disclosure made sufficient showing to override North Dakota's qualified shield law) *with* Austin v. Memphis Pub'g Co., 655 S.W.2d 146 (Tenn. 1983) (quashing subpoena on grounds that litigant seeking information failed to meet requirements of Tennessee's qualified privilege).
[408]585 F. Supp. 978 (D.R.I. 1984).
[409]*Id.* at 987.

case where the defendant, in a civil action for defamation, asserts a defense based on the source of such information."[410]

§14.6 CRIMINAL CASES

§14.6(A) Grand Jury Subpoenas and Prosecutor Requests

Branzburg v. Hayes,[411] which arose in the grand jury context, established that the federal constitution does not permit reporters to refuse to appear before grand juries.[412] Moreover, the courts have usually interpreted *Branzburg* to mean that a journalist may not refuse, on First Amendment grounds, to identify a person that he or she, while in the course of gathering news, *personally* witnessed committing a crime.[413] However, where the grand jury asks the reporter questions that "might have something vaguely to do with conduct that might have criminal consequences"[414] rather than questions directly related to a crime, the First Amendment shields the reporter who refuses to answer from being held in contempt unless the state shows a "substantial connection" between the information sought and the criminal conduct under investigation.[415]

The courts are split with respect to the reporter's duty to testify about or produce evidence of crimes other than personal observations. Some courts have held that the First Amendment mandates a balancing of the competing interests to determine whether the journalist must answer grand jury questions or produce tangible evidence in his or her possession;[416] others have found that there is no First Amendment privilege to withhold any information sought by a grand jury.[417]

Whether a reporter will obtain protection in the grand jury context from a state shield law depends on the provisions of the particular statute. Certain state laws are expressly inapplicable to grand juries.[418] A Maryland court has interpreted that state's shield law to be inapplicable to a journalist's personal

---

[410]R.I. GEN. LAWS §9-19.1-3(b)(1) (1985).
[411]408 U.S. 665 (1972).
[412]*See supra* §14.2.
[413]*See, e.g.,* Bursey v. United States, 466 F.2d 1059, 1090–91 (9th Cir. 1972); In re Ziegler, 550 F. Supp. 530, 9 Media L. Rep. 1013 (W.D.N.Y. 1982); Miami Herald Pub'g Co. v. Morejon, 561 So. 2d 577, 17 Media L. Rep. 1921 (Fla. 1990); Vaughn v. State, 381 S.E.2d 30 (Ga. 1989); Lightman v. State, 294 A.2d 149 (Md. Ct. App.), *aff'd,* 295 A.2d 212 (Md. 1972), *cert. denied,* 411 U.S. 951 (1973); People v. Dan, 342 N.Y.S.2d 731 (N.Y. App. Div. 1973).
[414]466 F.2d at 1091.
[415]*Id.*
[416]*See, e.g.,* In re Lewis, 384 F. Supp. 133 (C.D. Cal. 1974), *aff'd sub nom.* Lewis v. United States, 517 F.2d 236 (9th Cir. 1975); In re John Doe Grand Jury Investig., 574 N.E.2d 373, 19 Media L. Rep. 1091 (Mass. 1991) (recognizing qualified privilege); Denk v. Iowa Dist. Ct., 20 Media L. Rep. 1454 (Iowa 1992) (same). *See also* Morgan v. State, 337 So. 2d 951, 1 Media L. Rep. 2589 (Fla. 1976) (recognizing privilege where grand jury leak being investigated). *But see* Roche v. Florida, 589 So. 2d 978, 19 Media L. Rep. 1632 (Fla. Dist. Ct. App. 1991) (qualified privilege overcome where reporter refused to disclose source of order terminating parental rights, which proceeding is closed by law), *cert. denied,* 113 S. Ct. 1027 (1993).
[417]In re Grand Jury Proceedings, 810 F.2d 580 (6th Cir. 1987); Tofani v. State, 465 A.2d 413 (Md. 1983). *See also* Scarce v. United States, 5 F.3d 397, 21 Media L. Rep. 1972 (9th Cir. 1993) (recognizing only narrow privilege), *cert. denied,* 114 S. Ct. 685 (1994). Indeed, the precise scope of the First Amendment protection available continues to divide the courts. In re Williams, 766 F. Supp. 358, 18 Media L. Rep. 2177 (W.D. Pa. 1991) (recognizing qualified First Amendment privilege in grand jury context), *aff'd by equally divided court,* 963 F.2d 567, 20 Media L. Rep. 1232 (3d Cir. 1992).
[418]*See, e.g.,* ARIZ. REV. STAT. ANN. §12-2214(D) (Supp. 1989); DEL. CODE ANN. tit. 10, §4320 (1975).

observation of a crime.[419] The "eyewitness" exception to the New Jersey law is limited to evidence of crimes involving violence and does not include testimony about nonviolent crimes, such as theft by deception.[420] In contrast, New York's highest court has ruled that the New York shield law allows journalists to refuse to disclose eyewitness observations of crimes even before grand juries.[421] Of course, a state reporter's shield law does not permit a reporter to refuse to testify before a federal grand jury.[422]

There is general agreement in the cases that journalists possess a qualified First Amendment privilege not to serve as prosecution witnesses in criminal proceedings outside the grand jury context; however, this privilege may be overridden by a showing of relevance, need, and lack of an alternative source for the information.[423] According to Massachusetts' highest court, this privilege is also overridden where the reporter's source is known and the information sought has been made public.[424] However, New Jersey's absolute shield law prohibits courts from forcing journalists to testify in criminal cases, even if the information sought was published.[425]

§14.6(B) Criminal Defendant Requests

When a criminal defendant subpoenas a reporter, additional constitutional questions arise due to the defendant's federal Sixth Amendment right to a fair trial. A court that recognizes a reporter's privilege must reconcile the competing interests and rights of the defendant to compel evidence against those of the press to withhold it, which involves balancing either the protection of the Sixth Amendment against that of a shield law[426] or the Sixth Amendment against the First Amendment.[427] Because of a criminal defendant's Sixth Amendment rights, he or she is more likely to overcome a reporter's privilege claim than are civil litigants.

Criminal defendants subpoena reporters to obtain a broad range of evidence, including alibi evidence,[428] material that might tend to reduce the charge,[429] impeachment evidence,[430] or evidence that shows misconduct by the police or prosecution.[431] An important concern in determining whether to enforce a

---

[419]Lightman v. State, 294 A.2d 149 (Md. Ct. App.), *aff'd,* 295 A.2d 212 (Md. 1972), *cert. denied,* 411 U.S. 951 (1973).
[420]In re Vrazo, 423 A.2d 695, 6 Media L. Rep. 2410 (N.J. Super. Ct. Law Div. 1980).
[421]Beach v. Shanley, 465 N.E.2d 304 (N.Y. 1984).
[422]In re Lewis, 384 F. Supp. 133 (C.D. Cal. 1974), *aff'd sub nom.* Lewis v. United States, 517 F.2d 236 (9th Cir. 1975).
[423]United States v. Blanton, 534 F. Supp. 295 (S.D. Fla. 1982); Tribune Co. v. Green, 440 So. 2d 484 (Fla. Ct. App. 1983); In re Wright, 700 P.2d 40 (Idaho 1985); WBAL-TV Div., Hearst Corp. v. Maryland, 477 A.2d 776, 10 Media L. Rep. 2121 (Md. 1984); People v. Korkala, 472 N.Y.S.2d 310 (N.Y. App. Div. 1984). *Contra* In re Grand Jury Proceedings, 810 F.2d 580 (6th Cir. 1987).
[424]Commonwealth v. Corsetti, 438 N.E.2d 805, 8 Media L. Rep. 2113 (Mass. 1982).
[425]In re Schuman, 552 A.2d 602 (N.J. 1989).
[426]*See, e.g.,* Delaney v. Superior Ct. (Kopetman), 789 P.2d 934 (Cal. 1990).
[427]*See, e.g.,* United States v. Cuthbertson, 630 F.2d 139 (3d Cir. 1980), *cert. denied,* 449 U.S. 1126 (1981).
[428]*See, e.g.,* Ex parte Grothe, 687 S.W.2d 738, 10 Media L. Rep. 2009 (Tex. Crim. App. 1984), *cert. denied,* 474 U.S. 944 (1985).
[429]New Hampshire v. Siel, 444 A.2d 499 (N.H. 1982).
[430]People v. Warden, 365 N.Y.S.2d 17 (N.Y. App. Div. 1975); Brown v. Commonwealth, 204 S.E.2d 429 (Va.), *cert. denied,* 419 U.S. 966 (1974).
[431]United States v. Orsini, 424 F. Supp. 229 (E.D.N.Y. 1976), *aff'd without opinion,* 559 F.2d 1206 (2d Cir.), *cert. denied,* 434 U.S. 997 (1977).

subpoena in these situations is whether the information, whatever its nature, is likely to affect the outcome or verdict in the particular case.[432] Courts have developed a variety of methods to determine whether the information sought by the defendant truly goes to the heart of his or her case, including in camera review of the material,[433] a hearing on the issue,[434] and voir dire examination.[435]

§14.7 BREACH OF PROMISE ACTIONS AGAINST REPORTERS

In a handful of reported cases, members of the press have been sued by news sources for reneging on promises of confidentiality. Plaintiffs in these cases have advanced a variety of legal theories, including breach of contract, promissory estoppel, negligence, fraudulent misrepresentation, invasion of privacy, and negligent and intentional infliction of emotional distress.

The only U.S. Supreme Court case in this area is *Cohen v. Cowles Media Co.*[436] In the closing days of the 1982 Minnesota gubernatorial race, Dan Cohen, an associate of the Republican gubernatorial candidate, provided information that discredited the Democratic candidate for lieutenant governor to several reporters in exchange for their express promises not to disclose him as the source of the information.[437] After concluding that the material was misleading and constituted a last-minute smear tactic, two news organizations elected to publish stories about the incident, including Cohen's identity.[438] On the same day that the news articles appeared, Cohen was fired by his employer.[439] He then successfully sued the news organizations for fraudulent misrepresentation and breach of contract.[440]

The Minnesota Supreme Court dismissed Cohen's contract claim on state law grounds, holding that, where a reporter promises to keep a source's identity confidential, the parties intended only a moral commitment, not a legally binding contract.[441] The court then proceeded, sua sponte, to consider whether the reporters' promises might be enforceable on a promissory estoppel theory. Based on its belief that imposing liability on the reporters would implicate the First Amendment and that First Amendment interests in this case outweighed

---

[432]Delaney v. Superior Ct. (Kopetman), 789 P.2d 934 (Cal. 1990) (effect on outcome of case); United States v. Burke, 700 F.2d 70 (2d Cir.) (request for evidence denied because it would have been cumulative), *cert. denied*, 464 U.S. 816 (1983); United States v. Cutler, 6 F.3d 67, 21 Media L. Rep. 2075 (2d Cir. 1993) (media's videotapes of defendant, charged with criminal contempt for violating order against talking to media, is "the only significant proof," but videotapes of interviews of government prosecutors need not be produced because only their statements that were broadcast could have affected trial and thus only those statements could be relevant to whether contemptor's statements adversely affected trial); United States v. DePalma, 466 F. Supp. 917 (S.D.N.Y. 1979) (lack of effect on trial determinative).

[433]United States v. CBS, 459 F. Supp. 832 (C.D. Cal. 1978); Washington v. Rinaldo, 689 P.2d 392 (Wash. 1984); Hammarley v. Superior Ct. (Sosa), 153 Cal. Rptr. 608 (Cal. Ct. App. 1979). *But see Cutler*, 6 F.3d 67, 21 Media L. Rep. 2075 (refusing to order in camera inspection). *See generally supra* §14.4(F).

[434]In re Farber, 394 A.2d 330 (N.J.), *cert. denied*, 439 U.S. 997 (1978).

[435]People v. Warden, 365 N.Y.S.2d 17 (N.Y. App. Div. 1975).

[436]457 N.W.2d 199, 17 Media L. Rep. 2176 (Minn. 1990), *rev'd only as to First Amendment issue*, 111 S. Ct. 2513, 18 Media L. Rep. 2273 (1991), *on remand*, 479 N.W.2d 387, 19 Media L. Rep. 1858 (Minn. 1992).

[437]457 N.W.2d at 200.

[438]*Id.* at 201.

[439]*Id.* at 202.

[440]*See infra* note 457.

[441]*Cohen*, 457 N.W.2d at 205. *Compare* Bindrim v. Mitchell, 155 Cal. Rptr. 29 (Cal. Ct. App.), *cert. denied*, 444 U.S. 984 (1979) (rejecting breach of contract claim) *with* Huskey v. NBC, 632 F. Supp. 1282, 12 Media L. Rep. 2105 (N.D. Ill. 1986) (refusing to dismiss breach of contract claim).

the common law interest in protecting a promise of anonymity, the court ultimately held that Cohen could not maintain a promissory estoppel action against the reporters.[442]

By a 5-4 vote,[443] the U.S. Supreme Court reversed, holding that the First Amendment does not prohibit a promissory estoppel action against a journalist for breach of a promise of confidentiality.[444] Writing for the majority, Justice Byron White reasoned that the state common law that authorizes promissory estoppel is a law of "general applicability" and that enforcement of that law against the press is not subject to stricter constitutional scrutiny than would be applied to any other person or organization.[445] In reaching these conclusions, Justice White distinguished promissory estoppel from libel laws, which do trigger special protections for the press, on the grounds that Cohen was not seeking damages for injury to his reputation but for breach of a promise.[446] Moreover, the Court stated that any burden on the publication of truthful information that may result from promissory estoppel actions against the media is "self-imposed" and "incidental."[447] In closing, Justice White observed that, upon remand, the Minnesota Supreme Court was free to construe its state constitution or common law to shield the press from such lawsuits.[448]

In dissent, Justice David Souter countered that, because the dispute in *Cohen* involved the "content of publication" and thereby placed legitimate constitutional interests at risk, Minnesota's promissory estoppel law was not a law of general application free from judicial scrutiny.[449] Justice Souter then reasoned that the only way to assess the propriety of promissory estoppel suits against journalists is to weigh the competing interests.[450] Based on his view that the public's right to know Cohen's identity was of paramount importance in this case, Justice Souter concluded that Minnesota's interest in enforcing the reporter's promise of anonymity did not outweigh the interest in unfettered publication of Cohen's name.[451]

In *Ruzicka v. Conde Naste Publications*,[452] the court concluded that the First Amendment permits news sources to sue the media for breach of contract but that it imposes a heightened burden of proof on plaintiffs; in particular, plaintiffs must prove "specific, unambiguous terms" of a contract and must provide "clear and convincing proof that the agreement was breached."[453]

---

[442] 457 N.W.2d at 205.
[443] Chief Justice Rehnquist and Justices Stevens, Scalia, and Kennedy joined in Justice White's majority opinion. Justices Marshall, Blackmun, O'Connor and Souter dissented.
[444] 111 S. Ct. at 2518–19.
[445] *Id.* at 2518.
[446] *Id.* at 2519.
[447] *Id.*
[448] *Id.* at 2520. On remand, the Minnesota Supreme Court upheld recovery on a promissory estoppel theory. 479 N.W.2d 387, 387, 19 Media L. Rep. 1858, 1858 (Minn. 1992).
[449] 111 S. Ct. at 2522 (Souter, J., dissenting).
[450] *Id.*
[451] *Id.* at 2523.
[452] 733 F. Supp. 1289 (D. Minn. 1990), *aff'd in part and remanded in part,* 939 F.2d 578, 19 Media L. Rep. 1048 (8th Cir. 1991).
[453] 733 F. Supp. at 1300. On remand, the trial court held that there was no viable promissory estoppel claim because the promise was not clear and definite enough and because it would be unjust to enforce such a vague promise. Ruzicka v. Conde Nast Pubns., 794 F. Supp. 303, 20 Media L. Rep. 1233 (D. Minn. 1992), *rev'd,* 499 F.2d 1319, 1322, 21 Media L. Rep. 1821, 1824 (8th Cir. 1993) (reversing summary judgment because scope of promises is question of fact).

In *Virelli v. Goodson-Todman Enterprises*,[454] which was decided before *Cohen*, a New York state appellate court held that a simple negligence theory was a "constitutionally insufficient basis" for holding a reporter liable for breaking her promise not to disclose the identity of news sources.[455] The court concluded that both the First Amendment and the New York Constitution mandated a standard of culpability higher than negligence in connection with publication of matters of public concern.[456]

The plaintiffs in *Cohen* and *Ruzicka* each brought fraudulent misrepresentation claims in addition to their breach of contract claims. The courts agreed that, to recover, the plaintiffs had to prove that the reporters did not intend to perform their promises at the time they were made.[457] Due to the lack of such evidence, the courts dismissed those claims.

Invasion of privacy causes of action against journalists who renege on a promise of confidentiality have been rejected under New York[458] and Pennsylvania[459] law but have been sustained under Illinois law.[460] Plaintiffs have also lost emotional distress causes of action in breach of promise lawsuits.[461]

§14.8 SEARCH AND SEIZURE OF PRESS FACILITIES

In *Zurcher v. Stanford Daily*,[462] the Supreme Court confronted the question of whether the Fourth Amendment required stricter procedures for issuing warrants to search premises occupied by the press as opposed to other places. The case arose after police searched the offices of a Stanford University student newspaper for photographs, negatives, and film that might help identify persons who had taken part in a violent campus demonstration.[463] The warrant was issued upon a finding of "just, probable and reasonable cause" for believing that the evidence sought was located in the place to be searched.[464] By a 5-3 vote,[465] the Court held that, although the Fourth Amendment must be applied with "scrupulous exactitude" where First Amendment interests are implicated,[466] the Constitution does not impose a general barrier against warrants to search newspaper premises, require resort to subpoenas, or demand prior notice and hearing before issuing such warrants.[467]

Congress responded to *Zurcher* by adopting the Privacy Protection Act of 1980,[468] which accomplishes two tasks. First, it makes unlawful certain

---

[454]536 N.Y.S.2d 571 (N.Y. App. Div. 1989).
[455]*Id.* at 575.
[456]*Id.* at 575–77.
[457]*Ruzicka*, 733 F. Supp. at 1301; Cohen v. Cowles Media Co., 457 N.W.2d 199, 201, 17 Media L. Rep. 2176 (Minn. 1990).
[458]*Virelli*, 536 N.Y.S.2d at 575.
[459]Morgan v. Celender, 780 F. Supp. 307, 19 Media L. Rep. 1862 (W.D. Pa. 1992).
[460]Huskey v. NBC, 632 F. Supp. 1281, 1285–92, 12 Media L. Rep. 2105 (N.D. Ill. 1986).
[461]*Ruzicka*, 733 F. Supp. 1289; Doe v. American Broadcasting Cos., 543 N.Y.S.2d 455 (N.Y. App. Div. 1989); *Virelli*, 536 N.Y.S.2d 571.
[462]436 U.S. 547, 3 Media L. Rep. 2377 (1978).
[463]*Id.* at 550–52.
[464]*Id.* at 551.
[465]The majority was composed of Chief Justice Burger and Justices Blackmun, Powell, Rehnquist, and White. Justices Marshall, Stevens, and Stewart dissented. Justice Brennan took no part in the decision.
[466]436 U.S. at 564.
[467]*Id.* at 567.
[468]42 U.S.C.S. §§2000aa *et seq.* (Supp. 1993). The Act took effect in 1981.

federal and state government conduct in connection with search and seizure of the work product materials of any person reasonably believed to have a purpose to disseminate a form of public communication to the public.[469] For example, under the Act, it is illegal for government officers and employees to search for or seize work product materials[470] and documentary materials[471] intended for public communication[472] in the absence of special circumstances.[473]

Second, the Act provides for a civil cause of action against the federal government, state governments, and state officers, and for the imposition of administrative sanctions against federal employees who violate it.[474] In *Minneapolis Star and Tribune Co. v. United States*,[475] the court awarded media litigants $3,000 in liquidated damages and over $80,000 in attorneys' fees against FBI agents who had conducted a seizure in violation of the Act.[476]

The Privacy Protection Act also directed the U.S. Attorney General to establish procedural requirements for the search and seizure of items in the possession of parties not suspected of a crime.[477] Accordingly, in 1981, the Department of Justice issued regulations[478] that prohibit federal officers and employees from using a search warrant to obtain "documentary materials"[479] in the possession of any disinterested third party unless (1) it appears that the use of a less intrusive alternative would substantially jeopardize the availability or usefulness of the materials sought and (2) the warrant application has been approved by an attorney for the government.[480] The Guidelines provide that federal agents who violate these requirements shall be subject to disciplinary action but that issues of compliance otherwise "may not be litigated" or used as grounds to suppress evidence.[481] In *Klitzman, Klitzman and Gallagher v. Krut*,[482] the Third Circuit held that the postal inspectors who searched the

---

[469] *Id.* §2000aa.

[470] "Work product" includes materials that (1) are prepared, produced or created in anticipation of communication to the public, (2) are possessed for purposes of communication to the public, and (3) include mental impressions, conclusions, opinions, or theories of the person who prepared, produced, or created the materials. Contraband is not included. *Id.* §2000aa-7.

[471] "Documentary materials" are those items upon which information is recorded, including written or printed matter, photographs, films, negatives, video and audio tapes, and magnetically or electronically recorded cards, tapes, or discs. *Id.* §2000aa-7(a). Contraband is not included. *Id.* §2000aa-7(b).

[472] Courts have limited the Act's protection to materials held for the purpose of dissemination to the public. *See, e.g.,* Doe v. Stephens, 851 F.2d 1457 (D.C. Cir. 1988) (finding that litigant's medical records did not fall within purview of Act because they were not intended to be communicated to public).

[473] In the case of work product materials, the government may conduct a search or seizure only if (1) there is probable cause to believe that the person in possession of the materials is involved in a crime related to the materials, or (2) immediate seizure is necessary to prevent death or serious bodily injury. 42 U.S.C. §2000aa(a). In addition to having the authority to search for and seize documentary materials under the foregoing conditions, the government may also search for and seize such materials where (1) there is reasonable cause to believe that notification in the form of a subpoena duces tecum would cause the alteration or concealment of the materials or (2) the materials have not been produced in response to a court order and all appellate remedies have been exhausted or further delay would threaten the interests of justice. *Id.* §2000aa(b). However, if the government claims that the interests of justice require a search warrant, then the person opposing the warrant must be given an adequate opportunity to show by affidavit why the materials are not subject to seizure. *Id.* §§2000aa(c).

[474] 42 U.S.C. §2000aa-6. Litigants who win suits under the Privacy Protection Act may recover a minimum of $1,000 in damages and reasonable attorneys' fees and costs. *Id.* §2000aa-6(f).

[475] 713 F. Supp. 1308 (D. Minn. 1989).

[476] *Id.* at 1309, 1315.

[477] 42 U.S.C. §§2000aa-11 and -12.

[478] Guidelines on Methods of Obtaining Documentary Materials Held by Third Parties (Guidelines), 28 C.F.R. §§59.1 to .6 (1989).

[479] *Compare* 28 C.F.R. §59.2(c) *with* 42 U.S.C. §2000aa-7(a).

[480] 28 C.F.R. §59.4(a).

[481] *Id.* §59.6.

[482] 744 F.2d 955 (3d Cir. 1984).

offices of a private law firm and seized 2,000 files, as well as the U.S. Attorneys who had approved the search, "should have been aware of, and followed" the Guidelines.[483] On that basis, the court ordered the government to return all seized materials to the searched law firm.[484]

Although the Privacy Protection Act applies equally to the state and federal governments, a number of states, including California,[485] Connecticut,[486] Illinois,[487] Louisiana,[488] Nebraska,[489] New Jersey,[490] Oregon,[491] Texas,[492] and Washington[493] responded to *Zurcher* with similar, and in some instances stricter, legislation. Colorado has explicitly rejected this approach.[494]

---

[483] *Id.* at 961.
[484] *Id.* at 962.
[485] CAL. PENAL CODE §1524(g) (Deering Supp. 1990).
[486] CONN. GEN. STAT. ANN. §§54-33i & 54-33j (West 1985).
[487] ILL. ANN. STAT. ch. 38, ¶108-3 (Smith-Hurd 1980).
[488] LA. REV. STAT. ANN. §15:42 (West Supp. 1990).
[489] NEB. REV. STAT. §29-813 (1989).
[490] N.J. STAT. ANN. §§2A:84A-21.9 to .13 (West Supp. 1990).
[491] OR. REV. STAT. §44.520(2) (1989).
[492] TEX. CRIM. PROC. CODE ANN. art. 18.01(e) (Vernon Supp. 1990).
[493] WASH. REV. CODE ANN. §10.79.015 (West 1990).
[494] *See supra* notes 206–07 and accompanying text.

TABLE OF CASES

Cases are referred to by chapter and footnote numbers, e.g., *4:* 45 indicates the case is cited in chapter 4, footnote 45. Alphabetization is letter-by-letter.

A

AAFCO Heating & Air Conditioning Co. v. Northwest Pub'g, 321 N.E.2d 580, 1 Media L. Rep. 1683 (Ind. Ct. App. 1974), *cert. denied,* 424 U.S. 913 (1976) *2:* 468

ABC
—In re (Hinckley), 537 F. Supp. 1168, 8 Media L. Rep. 1441 (D.D.C. 1982) *1:* 347–48
—In re, 10 Media L. Rep. 1828 (N.D. Ill. 1984), *application granted sub nom.* United States v. Wolfson, 10 Media L. Rep. 2047 (N.D. Ill. 1984) *1:* 346
—v. Cuomo, 570 F.2d 1080 (2d Cir. 1977) *1:* 541, 638

ABC Needlecraft Co. v. Dun & Bradstreet, 245 F.2d 775 (2d Cir. 1957) *2:* 536

Abernathy v. Conroy, 429 F.2d 1170 (4th Cir. 1970) *12:* 45

Accuracy in Media v. FCC, 521 F.2d 288, 4 Media L. Rep. 1257 (D.C. Cir. 1975) *13:* 395

Acey; State v., 633 S.W.2d 306 (Tenn. 1982) *12:* 210

Ackerley Communications v. Multnomah County, 696 P.2d 1140 (Or. Ct. App. 1985) *12:* 174

ACLU of Miss. v. Mississippi, 911 F.2d 1066, 18 Media L. Rep. 1056 (5th Cir. 1990) *1:* 305

Acme Circus Operating Co. v. Kuperstock, 711 F.2d 1538, 9 Media L. Rep. 2138 (11th Cir. 1983) *6:* 172–74

ACORN
—v. New Orleans, 606 F. Supp. 16 (E.D. La. 1984) *12:* 106
—v. Phoenix, 798 F.2d 1260 (9th Cir. 1986) *12:* 106
—v. Tulsa, 835 F.2d 735 (10th Cir. 1987) *12:* 188

Acquaviva; Commonwealth v., 14 Pa. D. & C.2d 285, *aff'd,* 145 A.2d 407 (Pa. Super. Ct. 1958) *12:* 210

Action for Children's Television v. FCC
—852 F.2d 1332, 15 Media L. Rep. 1907 (D.C. Cir. 1988) *12:* 5
—932 F.2d 1504 (D.C. Cir. 1991), *cert. denied,* 112 S. Ct. 1282 (1992) *12:* 51

Actmedia v. Stroh, 830 F.2d 957 (9th Cir. 1986) *11:* 200–204

Adams v. Frontier Broadcasting Co., 555 P.2d 556, 2 Media L. Rep. 1166 (Wyo. 1976) *2:* 670

Adderley v. Florida, 385 U.S. 39 (1966) *12:* 76, 78

Adickes v. S.H. Kress & Co., 398 U.S. 144 (1970) *9:* 44

Adolph Coors Co.
—v. Bentsen, 2 F.3d 355, 21 Media L. Rep. 2022 (10th Cir. 1993) *11:* 193
—v. Brady, 944 F.2d 1543, 19 Media L. Rep. 1328 (10th Cir. 1991) *11:* 149

Adrian v. Unterman, 118 N.Y.S.2d 121 (N.Y. App. Div. 1952), *aff'd,* 118 N.E.2d 477 (N.Y. 1954) *6:* 31

Adult Film Ass'n of Am. v. Times Mirror Co., 97 Cal. App. 3d 77, 158 Cal. Rptr. 547 (Cal. Ct. App. 1979) *13:* 231

Advanced Training Sys. v. Caswell Equip. Co., 352 N.W.2d 1 (Minn. 1984) *10:* 241

Advance Music Corp. v. American Tobacco Co., 53 N.Y.S.2d 337 (N.Y. App. Div. 1945), *rev'd,* 70 N.E.2d 401 (N.Y. 1946) *7:* 9

Advertiser Co. v. Wallace, 446 F. Supp. 677, 3 Media L. Rep. 2220 (M.D. Ala. 1978) *9:* 233

Ad World v. Township of Doylestown, 672 F.2d 1136, 8 Media L. Rep. 1073 (3d Cir.), *cert. denied,* 456 U.S. 975 (1982) *11:* 45–47; *12:* 92–93, 126, 162

Aerial Burials v. Minneapolis Star & Tribune, 8 Media L. Rep. 1653 (Minn. Dist. Ct. 1982) *14:* 340

Aetna Casualty & Sur. Co. v. Jeppesen & Co., 642 F.2d 339 (9th Cir. 1981) *7:* 51

Agee v. Central Intelligence Agency, 500 F. Supp. 506, 6 Media L. Rep. 2006 (D.D.C. 1980) *10:* 154

Age-Herald Pub'g Co. v. Waterman, 81 So. 621 (Ala. 1919) *2:* 6, 8

Agent Orange Prod. Liab. Litig., In re
—821 F.2d 139 (2d Cir.), *cert. denied,* 484 U.S. 953 (1987) *1:* 429, 438, 441, 457
—98 F.R.D. 539, 9 Media L. Rep. 2001 (E.D.N.Y. 1983) *1:* 426–27, 429, 436

Aguilar v. Universal City Studios, 219 Cal. Rptr. 819, 12 Media L. Rep. 1485 (Cal. Ct. App. 1985) *2:* 303

A.H. Belo Corp. v. Rayzor, 644 S.W.2d 71, 8 Media L. Rep. 2425 (Tex. Ct. App. 1982) *2:* 595

AIDS Counseling & Testing Ctrs. v. Group W Television, 903 F.2d 1000, 17 Media L. Rep. 1893 (4th Cir. 1990) *2:* 302

Aisenson v. ABC, 269 Cal. Rptr. 379, 17 Media L. Rep. 1881 (Cal. Ct. App. 1990) *5:* 25

Ajay Nutrition Foods v. Food & Drug Admin., 378 F. Supp. 210 (D.N.J. 1974), *aff'd,* 513 F.2d 625 (3d Cir. 1975) *2:* 307

Alameda, City of; v. Premier Communications Network, 202 Cal. Rptr. 684 (Cal. Ct. App.), *cert. denied,* 469 U.S. 1073 (1984) *9:* 235

Alarcon v. Murphy, 201 Cal. App. 3d 1, 248 Cal. Rptr. 26 (Cal. Ct. App. 1988) *4:* 72

Alaska v. Journal Printing Co., 135 F. Supp. 169 (D. Alaska 1953) *9:* 216, 224

Alaska Gay Coalition v. Sullivan, 578 P.2d 951, 3 Media L. Rep. 2297 (Alaska 1978) *13:* 402

Albany Welfare Rights Org. v. Wyman, 493 F.2d 1319 (2d Cir.), *cert. denied,* 419 U.S. 838 (1974) *12:* 68

Alderwood Assocs. v. Washington Envtl. Council, 635 P.2d 108 (Wash. 1981) *12:* 89

Alexander Grant & Co. Litig., In re, 820 F.2d 352, 14 Media L. Rep. 1370 (11th Cir. 1987) *1:* 428, 435

Alfego v. CBS, 7 Media L. Rep. 1075 (D. Mass. 1981) *3:* 60

Alfred A. Knopf, Inc. v. Colby, 509 F.2d 1362 (4th Cir.), *cert. denied,* 421 U.S. 992 (1975) *10:* 142, 156

Ali v. Playgirl, 447 F. Supp. 723, 3 Media L. Rep. 2540 (S.D.N.Y. 1978) *6:* 18, 34, 41, 54, 73; *10:* 238

Alim v. Superior Ct., 185 Cal. App. 3d 144, 229 Cal. Rptr. 58 (Cal. Ct. App. 1986) *4:* 98

Alioto v. Cowles Communications, 623 F.2d 616, 6 Media L. Rep. 1573 (9th Cir. 1980), *cert. denied,* 449 U.S. 1102 (1981) *2:* 448

Allen
—v. Combined Communications Corp., 7 Media L. Rep. 2417 (Colo. Dist. Ct. 1981) *5:* 61, 142–45
—v. Gordon, 446 N.Y.S.2d 48, 8 Media L. Rep. 1124 (N.Y. App. Div.), *aff'd,* 437 N.E.2d 284 (N.Y. 1982) *6:* 30
—v. Men's World Outlet, 679 F. Supp. 360, 15 Media L. Rep. 1001 (S.D.N.Y. 1988) *6:* 35, 99, 129, 149, 151, 153, 202
—v. National Video, 610 F. Supp. 612 (S.D.N.Y. 1985) *6:* 35, 149, 151

Alm v. Van Nostrand Reinhold Co., 480 N.E.2d 1263 (Ill. App. Ct. 1985) *7:* 12, 20, 22

Almind v. Sea Beach Ry., 141 N.Y.S. 842 (N.Y. App. Div. 1913) *6:* 27

Almy v. Kvamme, 387 P.2d 372 (Wash. 1963) *2:* 1, 215, 217

Alonso v. Parfet, 325 S.E.2d 152 (Ga. 1985) *6:* 45, 120

Altemose Constr. Co. v. Building & Constr. Trades Council of Phila., 443 F. Supp. 489 (E.D. Pa. 1977) *14:* 290, 323, 333, 342

Altman v. Amoco Oil Co., 406 N.E.2d 142 (Ill. App. Ct. 1980) *2:* 146

Amalgamated Food Employees v. Logan Valley Plaza, 391 U.S. 308 (1968) *12:* 88

Amato
—v. Fellner, 4 Media L. Rep. 1552 (Wis. Ct. App. 1978) *14:* 76
—v. Wilentz, 753 F. Supp. 543, 18 Media L. Rep. 1985 (D.N.J. 1990), *rev'd,* 952 F.2d 742 (3d Cir. 1991) *12:* 60

American Broadcasting Co., *see* ABC

American Broadcasting-Paramount Theatres v. Simpson, 126 S.E.2d 873 (Ga. Ct. App. 1962) *2:* 178, 308

American Council of the Blind v. Boorstin, 664 F. Supp. 811 (D.D.C. 1986) *13:* 429

American Future Sys. v. Pennsylvania State Univ., 688 F.2d 907 (3d Cir.), *cert. denied,* 459 U.S. 1093 (1982) *12:* 127

American Home Prods. Corp. v. Johnson & Johnson, 577 F.2d 160 (2d Cir. 1978) *6:* 147

American Sign Rentals v. Orlando, 592 F. Supp. 85 (M.D. Fla. 1983) *12:* 188

America's Best Cinema Corp. v. Fort Wayne Newspapers, 347 F. Supp. 328 (N.D. Ind. 1972) *13:* 214, 221, 231, 252

Amick
—v. Montross, 220 N.W. 51 (Iowa 1928) *2:* 197

—United States v., 439 F.2d 351 (7th Cir.), *cert. denied sub nom.* Irving v. United States, 403 U.S. 918 (1970)   *9:* 154

Ammerman v. Hubbard Broadcasting, 572 P.2d 1258 (N.M. Ct. App.), *cert. denied,* 572 P.2d 1257 (N.M. 1977), *cert. denied,* 436 U.S. 906 (1978)   *14:* 71, 258

Anchor Liquors v. State Liquor Auth., 297 N.Y.S.2d 805 (N.Y. App. Div. 1969), *appeal dismissed,* 257 N.E.2d 43 (N.Y. 1970)   *11:* 190

Anderson
—v. Cryovac, Inc., 805 F.2d 1, 13 Media L. Rep. 1721 (1st Cir. 1986)   *1:* 106, 122, 427–30, 439
—v. Dun & Bradstreet, 543 F.2d 732 (10th Cir. 1976)   *2:* 536
—v. Fisher Broadcasting Co., 712 P.2d 803 (Or. 1986)   *4:* 4, 6, 136
—v. Liberty Lobby, 477 U.S. 242, 12 Media L. Rep. 2297 (1986)   *2:* 460, 676
—v. Nixon, 444 F. Supp. 1195, 3 Media L. Rep. 2050 (D.D.C. 1978)   *14:* 350–51, 382–84
—v. WROC-TV, 441 N.Y.S.2d 220, 7 Media L. Rep. 1987 (N.Y. Sup. Ct. 1981)   *5:* 97

Andonian; United States v., 735 F. Supp. 1469 (C.D. Cal. 1990)   *5:* 208

Andrews v. Andreoli, 400 N.Y.S.2d 442 (N.Y. Sup. Ct. 1977)   *14:* 261, 269, 321

Angelico v. Louisiana, 593 F.2d 585, 5 Media L. Rep. 1026 (5th Cir. 1979)   *1:* 569

Angelotta v. ABC, 820 F.2d 806, 14 Media L. Rep. 1185 (6th Cir. 1987)   *3:* 18

Ann-Margret v. High Soc'y Magazine, 498 F. Supp. 401, 6 Media L. Rep. 1774 (S.D.N.Y. 1980)   *6:* 74

Anonymous
—v. Dun & Bradstreet, 3 Media L. Rep. 2376 (N.D. Ill. 1978), *aff'd,* 594 F.2d 867 (7th Cir. 1979)   *4:* 108
—State v., 479 A.2d 1244, 10 Media L. Rep. 2214 (Conn. Super. Ct. 1984)   *1:* 152, 154

Anselmi v. Denver Post, 552 F.2d 316, 2 Media L. Rep. 1530 (10th Cir.), *cert. denied,* 432 U.S. 911 (1977)   *2:* 644

Antioch, City of; v. Candidate's Outdoor Graphic Serv., 557 F. Supp. 52 (N.D. Cal. 1982)   *12:* 189

Antonelli v. Hammond, 308 F. Supp. 1329 (D. Mass. 1970)   *13:* 335, 347

Apicella v. McNeil Labs., 66 F.R.D. 78 (E.D.N.Y. 1975)   *14:* 304, 374

Appleby v. Daily Hampshire Gazette, 478 N.E.2d 721, 11 Media L. Rep. 2372 (1985)   *2:* 473–74

Appleyard v. Transamerican Press, 539 F.2d 1026 (4th Cir. 1976), *cert. denied,* 429 U.S. 1041 (1977)   *2:* 448, 586, 598

Application and Affidavit for Search Warrant, In re, 923 F.2d 324, 18 Media L. Rep. 1593 (4th Cir. 1991), *cert. denied,* 111 S. Ct. 2243 (1991)   *1:* 374

Arcand v. Evening Call Pub'g Co., 567 F.2d 1163, 3 Media L. Rep. 1748 (1st Cir. 1977)   *2:* 308

Arctic Co. v. Loudoun Times Mirror, 624 F.2d 518, 6 Media L. Rep. 1433 (4th Cir. 1980), *cert. denied,* 449 U.S. 1102 (1981)   *2:* 326

Arizona v. McGraw-Hill, Inc., *see* Petroleum Prods. Antitrust Litig., In re

Arkansas AFL-CIO v. FCC, 11 F.3d 1430, 22 Media L. Rep. 1001 (8th Cir. 1993)   *13:* 192

Arkansas Gazette v. Lofton, 598 S.W.2d 745, 6 Media L. Rep. 1535 (Ark. 1980)   *10:* 194

Arkansas Television Co. v. Tedder, 662 S.W.2d 174, 10 Media L. Rep. 1617 (Ark. 1983)   *1:* 144, 147–48

Arkansas Writers' Project v. Ragland, 481 U.S. 227, 13 Media L. Rep. 2313 (1987)   *9:* 216, 238–39

Armstrong v. H & C Communications, 575 So. 2d 280, 18 Media L. Rep. 1845 (Fla. Dist. Ct. App. 1991)   *4:* 175

Arnheiter v. Random House, 578 F.2d 804, 4 Media L. Rep. 1174 (9th Cir. 1978)   *2:* 325, 395

Arno v. Stewart, 54 Cal. Rptr. 392 (Cal. Ct. App. 1966)   *2:* 154

Arnold
—v. IBM, 637 F.2d 1350 (9th Cir. 1981)   *9:* 40, 46, 67
—United States v., 380 F.2d 336 (4th Cir. 1967)   *11:* 279

Arrington v. New York Times Co., 434 N.E.2d 1319, 8 Media L. Rep. 1351 (N.Y. 1982), *cert. denied,* 459 U.S. 1146 (1983)   *3:* 20, 40, 48, 94; *6:* 21–22, 25, 73, 127, 200

A.S. Abell Co. v. Kirby, 176 A.2d 340 (Md. 1961)   *2:* 270, 274

A.S. Abell Pub'g Co. v. Board of Regents of Univ. of Md., 514 A.2d 25, 13 Media L. Rep. 1359 (Md. Ct. Spec. App. 1986)   *1:* 304

Asay v. Hallmark Cards, 594 F.2d 692 (8th Cir. 1979)   *2:* 141, 520

Asbury Park Press v. Seaside Heights, 586 A.2d 870, 18 Media L. Rep. 2264 (N.J. Super. Ct. Law. Div. 1990)   *1:* 291

Ashby v. Hustler Magazine, 802 F.2d 856, 13 Media L. Rep. 1416 (6th Cir. 1986)   *2:* 466; *3:* 86

Ashpole v. Millard, 778 S.W.2d 169, 16 Media L. Rep. 2302 (Tex. Ct. App. 1989)   *1:* 457

Ashton v. Kentucky, 384 U.S. 195 (1966) *2:* 692

Assessment of Additional N.C. & Orange County Use Taxes Against Village Pub'g Corp., In re, 322 S.E.2d 155 (N.C. 1984), *appeal dismissed sub nom.* Village Pub'g Corp. v. North Carolina Dep't of Revenue, 472 U.S. 1001 (1985) *9:* 236

Associated Press
—v. Bell, 510 N.E.2d 313, 14 Media L. Rep. 1156 (N.Y. 1987) *1:* 150
—v. Bradshaw, 410 N.W.2d 577, 14 Media L. Rep. 1566 (S.D. 1987) *1:* 243, 261–62
—v. NLRB (Associated Press I), 301 U.S. 103, 1 Media L. Rep. 2689 (1937) *9:* 121
—v. United States, 326 U.S. 1, 1 Media L. Rep. 2269 (1944) *9:* 5–9, 11–12; *13:* 215
—v. United States Dist. Ct., 705 F.2d 1143, 9 Media L. Rep. 1617 (9th Cir. 1983) *1:* 307, 318, 365
—v. Walker, 388 U.S. 130, 1 Media L. Rep. 1568 (1967) *2:* 312, 340–47

Associates & Aldrich Co. v. Times Mirror Co., 440 F.2d 133 (9th Cir. 1971) *13:* 206

Association of Community Orgs. for Reform Now v. City of Frontenac, 714 F.2d 813 (8th Cir. 1983) *12:* 23, 41

Association of Nat'l Advertisers v. Lungren, 809 F. Supp. 747 (N.D. Colo. 1992) *11:* 41, 82, 126

Astri Inv. & Sec. Corp., In re, 88 Bankr. 730, 15 Media L. Rep. 1673 (D. Md. 1988) *1:* 265

Astro Limousine Serv. v. Hillsborough County Aviation, 678 F. Supp. 1561 (M.D. Fla.), *aff'd,* 862 F.2d 877 (11th Cir. 1988) *11:* 132

Atlanta Coop. News Project v. United States Postal Serv., 350 F. Supp. 234 (N.D. Ga. 1972) *11:* 287

Atlanta Journal & Const. v. Long, 369 S.E.2d 755, 15 Media L. Rep. 1821 (Ga. 1988), *modified,* 377 S.E.2d 150 (Ga. 1989) *1:* 447

Atlanta Prof. Firefighters v. Brown, 7 Media L. Rep. 2263 (N.D. Ga. 1981) *1:* 527–28

Ault v. Hustler Magazine, 13 Media L. Rep. 2232 (D. Or. 1987), *aff'd in part and rev'd in part,* 860 F.2d 877, 15 Media L. Rep. 2205 (9th Cir. 1988), *cert. denied,* 489 U.S. 1080 (1989) *3:* 63, 65; *5:* 18, 110; *6:* 26

Austin v. Memphis Pub'g Co., 655 S.W.2d 146 (Tenn. 1983) *14:* 88, 300, 407

Avins
—v. Rutgers State Univ. of N.J., 385 F.2d 151 (3d Cir. 1967) *13:* 375
—v. White, 627 F.2d 637 (3d Cir.), *cert. denied,* 449 U.S. 982 (1980) *2:* 259–60, 267, 396, 402

Avirgan v. Hall, 118 F.R.D. 252, 14 Media L. Rep. 2136 (D.D.C. 1987) *1:* 161, 279, 429

Azar
—v. Conley, 456 F.2d 1382 (6th Cir. 1972) *9:* 78
—United States v., 243 F. Supp. 345 (S.D. Mich. 1964) *11:* 279

B

Backus v. Look, 39 F. Supp. 662 (S.D.N.Y. 1941) *2:* 229

Bahr v. Statesman Journal Co., 624 P.2d 664 (Or. Ct. App. 1980) *4:* 109

Bailey
—v. Loggins, 32 Cal. 3d 912, 654 P.2d 758 (Cal. 1982) *13:* 291, 312–31, 365
—v. Systems Innovation, 852 F.2d 93, 15 Media L. Rep. 1756 (3d Cir. 1988) *10:* 205

Baker
—v. Burlington County Times, 9 Media L. Rep. 1967 (D.N.J. 1983) *9:* 45, 55
—v. F & F Inv., 470 F.2d 778 (2d Cir. 1972), *cert. denied,* 411 U.S. 966 (1973) *14:* 47, 52, 63, 90, 371, 404
—v. Howard, 419 F.2d 376 (9th Cir. 1969) *9:* 63
—v. Registered Dentists of Okla., 543 F. Supp. 1177 (W.D. Okla. 1982) *11:* 324
—United States v., 5 Media L. Rep. 1417 (W.D. Wash. 1979) *1:* 149

Baldwin v. Redwood City, 540 F.2d 1360 (9th Cir. 1976), *cert. denied sub nom.* Leipzig v. Baldwin, 431 U.S. 913 (1977) *12:* 159

Ball v. E.W. Scripps Co., 801 S.W.2d 684, 18 Media L. Rep. 1545 (Ky. 1990), *cert. denied,* 499 U.S. 976 (1991) *2:* 259–60, 268, 448, 702

Baltimore v. A.S. Abell Co., 145 A.2d 111 (Md. 1958) *9:* 231

Baltimore Orioles v. Major League Baseball Players Ass'n, 805 F.2d 663, 13 Media L. Rep. 1625 (7th Cir. 1986), *cert. denied,* 480 U.S. 941 (1987) *6:* 95, 108–9, 111–13

Baltimore Sun Co.
—In re, 841 F.2d 74, 14 Media L. Rep. 2379 (4th Cir. 1988) *1:* 525
—v. Goetz, 886 F.2d 60, 16 Media L. Rep. 2295 (4th Cir. 1989) *1:* 374, 376

Bamboo Bros. v. Carpenter, 183 Cal. Rptr. 748 (Cal. Ct. App. 1982) *11:* 305

Bancroft Info. Group v. Maryland Comptroller, 603 A.2d 1289, 20 Media L. Rep. 1016 (Md. Ct. Spec. App. 1992) *9:* 241

Bandido's, Inc. v. Journal Gazette Co., No. 57A03-9012-CV-00533, 1991 Ind. App. LEXIS 1653, 19 Media L. Rep. 1479 (Ind. Ct. App. 1991) *2:* 430

Bank of Am. Nat'l Trust & Sav. Ass'n v. Hotel Rittenhouse Assocs., 800 F.2d 339, 13 Media L. Rep. 1450 (3d Cir. 1986) *1:* 448, 455

Bantam Books v. Sullivan, 372 U.S. 58, 1 Media L. Rep. 1116 (1963) *10:* 2, 39, 60, 67

Banzhaf v. FCC, 405 F.2d 1082 (D.C. Cir. 1968), *aff'g* WCBS TV, 8 F.C.C.2d 381 (1967), *cert. denied sub nom.* Tobacco Inst. v. FCC, 396 U.S. 842 (1969) *11:* 220; *13:* 155–56

Barber v. Time, Inc., 159 S.W.2d 291, 1 Media L. Rep. 1779 (Mo. 1942) *4:* 56, 153, 158, 182; *5:* 11, 34, 117, 135–37

Barbieri v. News-Journal Co., 189 A.2d 773 (Del. 1963) *4:* 116

Barger v. Playboy Enters., 564 F. Supp. 1151, 9 Media L. Rep. 1656 (N.D. Cal. 1983), *aff'd,* 732 F.2d 163, 10 Media L. Rep. 1527 (9th Cir.), *cert. denied,* 469 U.S. 853 (1984) *2:* 306

Barnard v. Chamberlain, 897 F.2d 1059 (10th Cir. 1990) *13:* 399

Barnes v. Glen Theatre, 111 S. Ct. 2456, *on remand,* 941 F.2d 1212 (7th Cir. 1991) *11:* 186

Barnstone v. University of Houston, 514 F. Supp. 670 (S.D. Tex. 1980), *rev'd,* 660 F.2d 137 (5th Cir.), *reh'g granted sub nom.* Muir v. Alabama Educ. Television Comm'n/Barnstone v. University of Houston, 662 F.2d 1110 (5th Cir. 1981) *13:* 377

Barr v. Matteo, 360 U.S. 564 (1959) *2:* 522

Barrett v. Wojtowicz, 414 N.Y.S.2d 350 (N.Y. App. Div. 1979) *9:* 263

Barrick Realty v. City of Gary, 491 F.2d 161 (7th Cir. 1974) *12:* 169

Barron v. Florida Freedom Newspapers, 531 So. 2d 113, 15 Media L. Rep. 1901 (Fla. 1988) *1:* 277, 453–54

Barrows v. Rozanky, 489 N.Y.S.2d 481 (N.Y. App. Div. 1985) *6:* 54

Barry v. Time, Inc., 584 F. Supp. 1110, 10 Media L. Rep. 1809 (N.D. Cal. 1984) *2:* 579

Bartlett v. Superior Ct., 722 P.2d 346 (Ariz. Ct. App. 1986) *14:* 81, 192

Basarich v. Rodeghero, 321 N.E.2d 739 (Ill. App. Ct. 1974) *2:* 327

Basilius v. Honolulu Pub'g Co., 711 F. Supp. 548, 16 Media L. Rep. 1759 (D. Haw.), *aff'd,* 888 F.2d 1394 (9th Cir. 1989) *2:* 228

Batchelder v. Allied Stores Int'l, 445 N.E.2d 590 (Mass. 1983) *12:* 89

Bates
—v. Campbell, 2 P.2d 383 (Cal. 1931) *2:* 169
—v. State Bar of Ariz., 433 U.S. 350, 2 Media L. Rep. 2097 (1977) *11:* 82, 86–87, 159, 319, 321

Bauer v. Brown, 11 Media L. Rep. 2168 (W.D. Va. 1985) *14:* 318, 335

Baugh v. Judicial Inquiry & Review Comm'n, 907 F.2d 440, 17 Media L. Rep. 2092 (4th Cir. 1990) *4:* 82

Baum v. Gillman, 667 P.2d 41 (Utah 1983) *2:* 191

Bayer
—v. Kinzler, 383 F. Supp. 1164 (E.D.N.Y. 1974), *aff'd,* 515 F.2d 504 (2d Cir. 1975) *13:* 347
—v. Ralston Purina Co., 484 S.W.2d 473 (Mo. 1972) *4:* 26

Bay Guardian Co. v. Chronicle Pub'g Co., 344 F. Supp. 1155 (N.D. Cal. 1972) *9:* 30, 33–35, 37

Bazaar v. Fortune, 476 F.2d 570, *modified,* 489 F.2d 225 (5th Cir. 1973), *cert. denied,* 416 U.S. 995 (1974) *13:* 347

Bazemore v. Savannah Hosp., 155 S.E. 194 (Ga. 1930) *4:* 32

Beach v. Shanley, 465 N.E.2d 304 (N.Y. 1984) *14:* 417

Beacon Journal, State ex rel. v. Kainrad, 348 N.E.2d 695, 2 Media L. Rep. 1123 (Ohio 1976) *10:* 194

Beacon Pub'g Co.; State v., 42 P.2d 960 (Kan. 1935) *7:* 72, 74

Beard v. Akzona, Inc., 517 F. Supp. 128 (E.D. Tenn. 1981) *4:* 40

Beauharnais v. Pittsburgh Courier Pub'g Co., 243 F.2d 705 (7th Cir. 1957) *2:* 270, 275

Beckerman v. City of Tupelo, 664 F.2d 502 (5th Cir. 1981) *12:* 45, 48, 196, 201

Beckham; United States v., 789 F.2d 401, 12 Media L. Rep. 2073 (6th Cir. 1986) *1:* 353, 355, 358

Beckley Newspapers Corp. v. Hanks, 389 U.S. 81, 1 Media L. Rep. 1585 (1967) *2:* 425

Becnel v. Lucia, 420 So. 2d 1173 (La. Ct. App. 1982) *14:* 229

Beecher v. Montgomery Ward & Co., 517 P.2d 667 (Or. 1973) *2:* 2

Beef Indus. Antitrust Litig., In re, 589 F.2d 786 (5th Cir. 1979) *1:* 444

Bell
—v. Courier-Journal & Louisville Times Co., 402 S.W.2d 84 (Ky. Ct. App. 1966) *4:* 62
—v. Wolfish, 441 U.S. 520 (1979) *13:* 307
—United States v., 464 F.2d 667 (2d Cir.), *cert. denied,* 409 U.S. 901 (1972) *1:* 196, 207

Belli
—v. Orlando Daily Newspapers, 389 F.2d 579 (5th Cir. 1967), *cert. denied*, 393 U.S. 825 (1968) *2:* 135, 194
—v. Roberts Bros. Furs, 49 Cal. Rptr. 625 (Cal. Ct. App. 1966) *2:* 235
Belluomo v. KAKE TV & Radio, 596 P.2d 832 (Kan. Ct. App. 1979) *5:* 55, 110, 114, 158
Belo Broadcasting Corp. v. Clark, 654 F.2d 423, 7 Media L. Rep. 1841 (5th Cir. 1981) *1:* 326, 353, 356–57
Belushi v. Woodward, 598 F. Supp. 36, 10 Media L. Rep. 1870 (D.D.C. 1984) *10:* 243
Benavidez v. Anheuser Busch, Inc., 873 F.2d 102, 16 Media L. Rep. 1733 (5th Cir. 1989) *6:* 23
Bender v. Seattle, 664 P.2d 492, 9 Media L. Rep. 2101 *4:* 64
Beneficial Corp. v. FTC, 542 F.2d 611 (3d Cir. 1976), *cert. denied*, 430 U.S. 983 (1977) *7:* 71; *11:* 82, 94
Benford v. ABC, 502 F. Supp. 1159, 6 Media L. Rep. 2489 (D. Md. 1980), *aff'd*, 661 F.2d 917 (4th Cir.), *cert. denied*, 454 U.S. 1060 (1981) *5:* 196, 205, 230, 233–34, 240
Bennaly v. Hundred Arrows Press, 614 F. Supp. 969, 12 Media L. Rep. 1356 (D.N.M. 1985), *overruled*, 858 F.2d 618 *4:* 123–24
Berg v. Minneapolis Star & Tribune Co., 79 F. Supp. 957 (D. Minn. 1948) *4:* 51
Bergman v. Stein, 404 F. Supp. 287 (S.D.N.Y. 1975) *9:* 45, 64
Berkshire Cablevision of R.I. v. Burke, 571 F. Supp. 976, 9 Media L. Rep. 2321 (D.R.I. 1983), *vacated*, 773 F.2d 382 (1st Cir. 1985) *12:* 232, 236, 238; *13:* 496–98, 501–4
Berliner; People v., 3 Media L. Rep. 1942 (N.Y. City Ct. 1978) *5:* 79–80
Bernstein
—v. Dun & Bradstreet, 368 P.2d 780 (Colo. 1962) *2:* 180–81, 184
—v. NBC, 129 F. Supp. 817 (D.D.C.), *aff'd*, 232 F.2d 369 (D.C. Cir. 1955), *cert. denied*, 352 U.S. 945 (1956) *3:* 53; *4:* 25
Berry
—In re, 436 P.2d 273 (Cal. 1968) *10:* 102
—v. NBC, 480 F.2d 428 (8th Cir. 1973), *cert. dismissed*, 418 U.S. 911 (1974) *2:* 443–44; *3:* 86
Berthiaume, Estate of v. Pratt, 365 A.2d 792 (Me. 1976) *5:* 11, 34
Beruan v. French, 128 Cal. Rptr. 869 (Cal. Ct. App. 1976) *4:* 119
Bethel Sch. Dist. No. 403 v. Fraser, 478 U.S. 675 (1986) *13:* 333, 351

Beverley v. Choices Women's Medical Ctr., 579 N.Y.S.2d 637, 19 Media L. Rep. 1724 (N.Y. App. Div. 1988) *6:* 27
Bianco v. ABC, 470 F. Supp. 182 (N.D. Ill. 1979) *5:* 262
Bichler v. Union Bank & Trust Co. of Grand Rapids, 745 F.2d 1006, 10 Media L. Rep. 2393 (6th Cir. 1984) *3:* 8, 32, 44, 89; *4:* 190
Biederman's of Springfield v. Wright, 322 S.W.2d 892 (Mo. 1959) *4:* 40
Bigelow v. Virginia, 421 U.S. 809, 1 Media L. Rep. 1919 (1975) *7:* 32; *11:* 30, 68–71, 130, 280–84; *12:* 108
Big Mama Rag v. United States, 631 F.2d 1030 (D.C. Cir. 1980) *9:* 244
Bilder, State ex rel. v. Delavan, 334 N.W.2d 252, 9 Media L. Rep. 2294 (Wis. 1983) *1:* 449
Bill v. Superior Ct., 187 Cal. Rptr. 625, 8 Media L. Rep. 2622 (Cal. Ct. App. 1982) *8:* 1–2, 8, 11–12, 17, 21–22, 25–27, 36–37, 43, 49, 89–90
Billings v. Atkinson, 489 S.W.2d 858 (Tex. 1973) *5:* 262
Bilney v. Evening Star Newspaper Co., 406 A.2d 652, 5 Media L. Rep. 1931 (Md. Ct. Spec. App. 1979) *4:* 151; *5:* 158; *14:* 232
Binder v. Triangle Pubns., 275 A.2d 53 (Pa. 1971) *2:* 551, 565
Bindrim v. Mitchell, 155 Cal. Rptr. 29, 5 Media L. Rep. 1113 (Cal. Ct. App.), *cert. denied*, 444 U.S. 984 (1979) *2:* 303, 305; *6:* 85; *14:* 441
Bingaman, State ex rel. v. Brennan, 645 P.2d 982, 8 Media L. Rep. 1629 (N.M. 1982) *1:* 380
Bi-Rite Enters. v. Button Master, 555 F. Supp. 1188, 9 Media L. Rep. 1531 (S.D.N.Y.), *supplemental opinion*, 578 F. Supp. 59 (S.D.N.Y. 1983) *6:* 14, 16, 32, 97, 152
Birdsong; State v., 422 So. 2d 1135, 9 Media L. Rep. 1010 (La. 1982) *1:* 143, 146
Birmingham News Co. v. Roper, 4 Media L. Rep. 1075 (N.D. Ala. 1978) *1:* 305
Bisbee v. John C. Conover Agency, 452 A.2d 689, 9 Media L. Rep. 1298 (N.J. Super. Ct. App. Div. 1982) *4:* 126; *5:* 31
Bishop v. Wood, 426 U.S. 341 (1976) *9:* 54
Bivens v. Six Unknown Named Agents of FBI, 403 U.S. 388 (1971) *5:* 195; *9:* 45, 47, 51
Black Hills Video Corp. v. FCC, 399 F.2d 65 (8th Cir. 1968) *13:* 453–54, 457–58, 527
Blake v. Gannett Co., 529 So. 2d 595, 15 Media L. Rep. 1561 (Miss. 1988) *2:* 396
Blanton
—v. Equitable Bank Nat'l Ass'n, 485 A.2d 694 (Md. Ct. Spec. App. 1985) *2:* 683

—United States v., 534 F. Supp. 295 (S.D. Fla. 1982) *14:* 126, 423
Blatty v. New York Times Co., 42 Cal. 3d 1033, 728 P.2d 1177, 13 Media L. Rep. 1928 (Cal. 1986), *cert. denied,* 485 U.S. 934 (1988) *2:* 300, 688; *7:* 9
Blende v. Hearst Pubns., 93 P.2d 733 (Wash. 1939) *2:* 207
Blinick v. Long Island Daily Press Pub'g Co., 323 N.Y.S.2d 853 (N.Y. Sup. Ct. 1971), *appeal dismissed,* 337 N.Y.S.2d 859 (N.Y. 1972) *7:* 25–27
Block v. Meese, 793 F.2d 1303, 13 Media L. Rep. 1209 (D.C. Cir. 1986) *12:* 217
Blondy, 40 F.C.C. 284, 14 Rad. Reg. (P & F) 1199 (1957) *13:* 90
Bloss
—v. Federated Pubns., 145 N.W.2d 800 (Mich. Ct. App. 1966) *13:* 206
—State v., 637 P.2d 1117 (Haw. 1981), *cert. denied,* 459 U.S. 824 (1982) *12:* 109
Blount v. TD Pub'g Corp., 423 P.2d 421 (N.M. 1966) *4:* 134
Blovin v. Anton, 431 A.2d 489, 7 Media L. Rep. 1714 (Vt. 1981) *2:* 153
Blue Chip Stamps v. Manor Drug Stores, 421 U.S. 723 (1975) *9:* 156
Board of Airport Comm'rs v. Jews for Jesus, 482 U.S. 569 (1987) *12:* 71
Board of Educ., Island Trees Union Free Sch. Dist. No. 26 v. Pico, 457 U.S. 853 (1982) *13:* 351, 391
Board of Medical Examiners v. Terminal Hudson Elecs., 140 Cal. Rptr. 757 (Cal. Ct. App. 1977) *11:* 323
Board of Trustees v. Fox, 492 U.S. 469 (1989) *11:* 37–38, 82, 98, 145–48, 199, 243
Board of Trustees of State Univ. of N.Y. v. Fox, 492 U.S. 469 (1989) *12:* 25, 123, 127
Bock v. Plainfield Courier-News, 132 A.2d 523 (N.J. Super. Ct. App. Div. 1957) *2:* 583
Boddie v. ABC, 731 F.2d 333, 10 Media L. Rep. 1923 (6th Cir. 1984), *on remand,* 694 F. Supp. 1304, 16 Media L. Rep. 1100 (N.D. Ohio 1988), *aff'd,* 881 F.2d 267, 16 Media L. Rep. 2038 (6th Cir. 1989), *cert. denied,* 493 U.S. 1028 (1990) *5:* 217, 220, 232–35, 237
Boesky; United States v., 674 F. Supp. 1128, 14 Media L. Rep. 2105 (S.D.N.Y. 1987) *1:* 381
Boettger v. Loverro, 555 A.2d 1234, 16 Media L. Rep. 1467 (Pa. 1989), *vacated and remanded,* 493 U.S. 885 (1989), *aff'd,* 587 A.2d 712, 18 Media L. Rep. 2017 (1991) *4:* 107

Boiardo; State v., 414 A.2d 14 (N.J. 1980) *14:* 70, 78, 79, 249, 320
Bolen; United States v., 8 Media L. Rep. 1048 (S.D. Fla. 1981) *1:* 353
Bolger v. Youngs Drug Prods. Corp., 463 U.S. 60 (1983) *11:* 17–21, 57, 111–13, 292–95; *12:* 17–18, 31
Bon Air Hotel v. Time, Inc., 426 F.2d 858 (5th Cir. 1970) *2:* 670
Bond v. Pecaut, 561 F. Supp. 1037 (N.D. Ill. 1983), *aff'd,* 734 F.2d 18 (7th Cir. 1984) *3:* 89; *6:* 122
Bonito Boats v. Thunder Craft Boats, 489 U.S. 141 (1989) *6:* 92
Bonner v. City of Pritchard, 661 F.2d 1206 (11th Cir. 1981) *14:* 60, 90
Bonura v. CBS, Inc., 459 U.S. 1313 (1983) *10:* 194
Boos v. Barry, 485 U.S. 312 (1988) *12:* 164, 178–80; *13:* 265
Booth
—v. Colgate-Palmolive Co., 362 F. Supp. 343 (S.D.N.Y. 1973) *6:* 39, 149, 151
—v. Curtis Pub'g Co., 223 N.Y.S.2d 737, 1 Media L. Rep. 1784 (N.Y. App. Div.), *aff'd,* 182 N.E.2d 812 (N.Y. 1962) *6:* 90
Booth Newspapers
—v. Midland Circuit Judge, 377 N.W.2d 868, 12 Media L. Rep. 1519 (Mich. Ct. App. 1985), *appeal denied,* 384 N.W.2d 767 (Mich. 1986), *cert. denied,* 479 U.S. 1031 (1987) *1:* 446
—v. Twelfth Dist. Ct. Judge, 432 N.W.2d 400, 15 Media L. Rep. 2258 (Mich. Ct. App. 1988) *1:* 156
Borduin v. Panax Corp., 7 Media L. Rep. 1645 (E.D. Mich. 1981) *9:* 45
Borreca v. Fasi, 369 F. Supp. 906, 1 Media L. Rep. 2410 (D. Haw. 1974) *1:* 540
Boscia v. Warren, 359 F. Supp. 900 (E.D. Wis. 1973) *11:* 184, 209
Bose Corp. v. Consumers Union of U.S., 466 U.S. 485, 10 Media L. Rep. 1625 (1984), *reh'g denied,* 467 U.S. 1267 (1984) *1:* 106, 120; *2:* 240, 399, 459, 696–97; *8:* 80
Boston Mut. Life Ins. Co. v. Varone, 303 F.2d 155 (1st Cir. 1962) *2:* 544
Boswell v. Phoenix Newspapers, 730 P.2d 186, 13 Media L. Rep. 1785 (Ariz. 1986), *cert. denied,* 481 U.S. 1029 (1987) *2:* 612
Bowen v. Independent Pub'g Co., 96 S.E.2d 564, 566 (S.C. 1957) *2:* 130
Bowes
—v. Magna Concepts, 561 N.Y.S.2d 16, 18 Media L. Rep. 1303 (N.Y. App. Div. 1990) *2:* 148
—v. Wisconsin Vocational Bd., 9 Media L. Rep. 2372 (Wis. Cir. Ct. 1983) *9:* 45

Bowman Dairy Co. v. United States, 341 U.S. 214 (1951) *14:* 129
Boyd v. Thomson Newspaper Pub'g Co., 6 Media L. Rep. 1020 (W.D. Ark. 1980) *4:* 31
Boyer v. Pitt Pub'g Co., 188 A. 203 (Pa. 1936) *2:* 147
Boyles v. Mid-Florida Television Corp., 431 So. 2d 627 (Fla. Dist. Ct. App. 1983), *aff'd,* 467 So. 2d 282, 11 Media L. Rep. 1774 (Fla. 1985) *2:* 687
Bradshaw v. Swagerty, 563 P.2d 511 (Kan. Ct. App. 1977) *2:* 188–89
Brady
—v. Maryland, 373 U.S. 83 (1963) *1:* 368
—v. Ottaway Newspapers, 445 N.Y.S.2d 786, 8 Media L. Rep. 1671 (N.Y. App. Div. 1981) *2:* 307
Brainerd v. Potratz, 421 F. Supp. 836 (N.D. Ill. 1976), *aff'd,* 566 F.2d 1177 (7th Cir. 1977) *9:* 65
Braman v. Walthall, 225 S.W.2d 342 (Ark. 1949) *2:* 584
Brandenburg v. Ohio, 395 U.S. 444 (1969) *8:* 44, 91–92
Brandon v. Gazette Pub'g Co., 352 S.W.2d 92 (Ark. 1961) *2:* 556
Brandreth v. Lance, 8 Paige 24 (N.Y. Ch. 1839) *10:* 240
Brannon v. American Micro Distribs., 342 S.E.2d 301, 12 Media L. Rep. 2134 (Ga. 1986) *10:* 239
Branson v. Fawcett Pubns., 124 F. Supp. 429 (E.D. Ill. 1954) *4:* 20, 26, 51; *6:* 36
Branzburg
—v. Hayes, *see* Branzburg v. Meigs; Branzburg v. Pound; Pappas, In re
—v. Meigs, 503 S.W.2d 748 (Ky. 1971), *aff'd sub nom.* Branzburg v. Hayes, 408 U.S. 665, 1 Media L. Rep. 2617 (1972) *5:* 57, 67–70, 132, 157; *14:* 221
—v. Pound, 461 S.W.2d 345 (1970), *cert. granted,* 402 U.S. 942 (1971), *aff'd sub nom.* Branzburg v. Hayes, 408 U.S. 665, 1 Media L. Rep. 2617 (1972) *1:* 1, 162, 385, 477, 486; *5:* 57, 67–70, 132, 157; *14:* 1, 3, 6–16, 18, 20–46, 48, 71, 89, 159–61, 220, 411
Braun
—v. Flynt, 726 F.2d 245, 10 Media L. Rep. 1497 (5th Cir.), *cert. denied sub nom.* Chic Magazine v. Braun, 469 U.S. 883 (1984) *2:* 396; *3:* 50, 85–86, 90
—v. Soldier of Fortune Magazine, 968 F.2d 1110, 20 Media L. Rep. 1777 (11th Cir. 1992) *7:* 91, 92
Bray
—v. Alexandria Women's Health Clinic, 113 S. Ct. 753 (1993) *9:* 71–73

—v. Providence Journal Co., 220 A.2d 531 (R.I. 1966) *2:* 127, 554
Breard v. City of Alexandria, 341 U.S. 622 (1951) *11:* 26; *12:* 107, 113, 122, 162
Brents v. Morgan, 299 S.W. 967 (Ky. 1927) *4:* 40
Brewer
—v. Hearst Pub'g Co., 185 F.2d 846 (7th Cir. 1950) *2:* 272, 275
—v. Hustler Magazine, 749 F.2d 527, 11 Media L. Rep. 1502 (9th Cir. 1984) *5:* 24
—v. Memphis Pub'g Co., 626 F.2d 1238, 6 Media L. Rep. 2025 (5th Cir. 1980), *cert. denied,* 452 U.S. 962 (1981) *2:* 135, 436
Brewster v. Ashland Pub'g Corp., 345 F. Supp. 35 (W.D. Wis. 1972) *13:* 243
Brian W. v. Superior Ct., 574 P.2d 788, 3 Media L. Rep. 1993 (Cal. 1978) *1:* 240–47
Briarcliff Lodge Hotel v. Citizen-Sentinel Pub'g, 183 N.E. 193 (N.Y. 1932) *2:* 555
Bridge CAT Scan Assocs. v. Technicare Corp., 710 F.2d 940 (2d Cir. 1983) *10:* 242
Bridges v. California, 314 U.S. 252, 1 Media L. Rep. 1275 (1941) *10:* 45
Briggs & Stratton Corp. v. Baldridge, 728 F.2d 915 (7th Cir.), *cert. denied,* 469 U.S. 826 (1984) *11:* 41
Brink v. Griffith, 396 P.2d 793 (Wash. 1964) *3:* 10–11
Brinkley v. Casablancas, 438 N.Y.S.2d 1004, 7 Media L. Rep. 1457 (N.Y. App. Div. 1981) *6:* 11
Briscoe v. Readers Digest Ass'n, 4 Cal. 3d 529, 483 P.2d 34, 1 Media L. Rep. 1845 (Cal. 1971) *4:* 4, 117–19, 121, 143, 147, 158, 165–66; *6:* 16
Britton
—v. Koep, 470 N.W.2d 518, 19 Media L. Rep. 1208 (Minn. 1991) *2:* 325
—v. Winfield Pub. Library, 428 N.E.2d 650 (Ill. App. Ct. 1981) *2:* 148
Broadson; United States v., 390 F. Supp. 774 (E.D. Wis. 1975) *11:* 276
Broady; People v., 158 N.E.2d 817 (N.Y.), *appeal dismissed and cert. denied,* 361 U.S. 8 (1959) *5:* 260
Brocklesby v. United States, 767 F.2d 1288 (9th Cir. 1985), *cert. denied,* 474 U.S. 1101 (1986) *7:* 51
Brockman v. Detroit Diesel Allison Div., Gen. Motors Corp., 366 N.E.2d 1201 (Ind. Ct. App. 1977) *2:* 183, 186
Brodsky v. Journal Pub'g Co., 42 N.W.2d 855 (S.D. 1950) *2:* 3, 186
Brooklier; United States v., 685 F.2d 1162, 8 Media L. Rep. 2177 (9th Cir. 1982) *1:* 129–30, 138, 140–42, 225, 364

Brooks
—v. ABC, 737 F. Supp. 431, 17 Media L. Rep. 2041 (N.D. Ohio 1990), *aff'd in part and vacated in part,* 932 F.2d 495, 18 Media L. Rep. 2121 (6th Cir. 1991) *2:* 603; *5:* 220, 250; *6:* 72; *9:* 79
—v. State, Through Alcoholic Beverage Control Comm'n, 442 A.2d 93 (Del. Super. Ct. 1981) *11:* 215–16
Brown
—v. ABC, 704 F.2d 1296 (4th Cir. 1983) *5:* 218, 231, 233–34; *6:* 131
—v. Boney, 255 S.E.2d 784, 5 Media L. Rep. 1395 (N.C. Ct. App. 1979) *3:* 57
—v. Commonwealth, 204 S.E.2d 429 (Va.), *cert. denied,* 419 U.S. 966 (1974) *14:* 70, 78–79, 430
—v. Courier Herald Pub'g Co., 700 F. Supp. 534, 15 Media L. Rep. 2350 (S.D. Ga. 1988) *2:* 472–73
—v. Hartlage, 456 U.S. 45 (1982) *1:* 556
—v. Herald Co., 698 F.2d 949, 9 Media L. Rep. 1149 (8th Cir. 1983) *2:* 443
—v. Kelly Broadcasting Co., 771 P.2d 460, 16 Media L. Rep. 1625 (Cal. 1989) *2:* 540
—v. Louisiana, 383 U.S. 131 (1966) *12:* 67
—United States v., 925 F.2d 1301 (10th Cir. 1991) *5:* 162
Brown & Williamson Tobacco Corp.
—v. FTC, 710 F.2d 1165 (6th Cir. 1983), *cert. denied,* 465 U.S. 1100 (1984) *1:* 272, 275, 436, 449
—v. Jacobson
——713 F.2d 262, 9 Media L. Rep. 1936 (7th Cir. 1983) *2:* 179, 184, 193, 397, 599
——827 F.2d 1119, 14 Media L. Rep. 1497 (7th Cir. 1987), *cert. denied,* 485 U.S. 993 (1988) *2:* 446, 596
Brubaker v. Board of Educ., 502 F.2d 973 (7th Cir. 1974), *cert. denied,* 421 U.S. 965 (1975) *2:* 521
Brueggemeyer
—v. ABC, 684 F. Supp. 452, 15 Media L. Rep. 1449 (N.D. Tex. 1985) *3:* 85
—v. Associated Press, 609 F.2d 825, 5 Media L. Rep. 2369 (5th Cir. 1980) *2:* 289
Bruno & Stillman, Inc. v. Globe Newspaper Co., 633 F.2d 583, 6 Media L. Rep. 2057 (1st Cir. 1980) *2:* 397; *14:* 47, 51, 62, 90, 95, 140, 145–46, 369, 402
Brush v. San Francisco Newspaper Printing Co., 315 F. Supp. 577 (N.D. Cal. 1970), *aff'd,* 469 F.2d 89 (9th Cir. 1972), *cert. denied,* 409 U.S. 943 (1973) *9:* 132
Buchanan
—v. Foxfire Fund, 258 S.E.2d 751 (Ga. Ct. App. 1979) *4:* 186

—State v., 436 P.2d 729 (Or.), *cert. denied,* 392 U.S. 905 (1968) *14:* 71, 77
Buck v. Savage, 323 S.W.2d 363 (Tex. Civ. App. 1959) *2:* 204
Buckley
—v. AFTRA, 496 F.2d 305 (2d Cir. 1974), *cert. denied,* 419 U.S. 1093 (1974) *9:* 130
—v. Littell, 539 F.2d 882, 1 Media L. Rep. 1762 (2d Cir. 1976), *cert. denied,* 429 U.S. 1062 (1977) *2:* 259–60, 267–68
—v. New York Post Corp., 373 F.2d 175 (2d Cir. 1967) *2:* 644
—v. Valeo, 424 U.S. 1 (1976) *13:* 40, 54
—v. W.E.N.H. TV, 5 Media L. Rep. 1509 (D.N.H. 1979) *4:* 182
Buehl; Commonwealth v., 462 A.2d 1316, 9 Media L. Rep. 1896 (Pa. Super. Ct. 1983) *1:* 147
Bufalino
—v. Associated Press, 692 F.2d 266, 8 Media L. Rep. 2384 (2d Cir. 1982), *cert. denied,* 462 U.S. 1111 (1983) *2:* 336, 565–66
—v. Detroit Magazine, Nos. 125458, 125459, 1990 Mich. App. LEXIS 525, 18 Media L. Rep. 1491 (Mich. Ct. App. 1990) *2:* 394
Burak; State v., 431 A.2d 1246, 7 Media L. Rep. 1318 (Conn. Super. Ct. 1981) *1:* 106, 108, 112
Burch v. Barker, 861 F.2d 1149 (9th Cir. 1988) *13:* 334
Burke; United States v., 700 F.2d 70 (2d Cir.), *cert. denied,* 464 U.S. 816 (1983) *14:* 67, 90, 134–36, 151–52, 154, 335, 432
Burlington, City of; v. New York Times Co., 532 A.2d 562, 14 Media L. Rep. 1979 (Vt. 1987) *12:* 141–42
Burnett v. National Enquirer, 7 Media L. Rep. 1321 (Cal Super. Ct. 1981), *aff'd,* 193 Cal. Rptr. 206, 9 Media L. Rep. 1921 (Cal. Ct. App. 1983), *appeal dismissed,* 465 U.S. 1014 (1984) *2:* 8, 596, 600
Burney; State v., 276 S.E.2d 693, 7 Media L. Rep. 1411 (N.C. 1981) *1:* 210
Burns
—In re, 484 So. 2d 658 (La. 1986) *14:* 228
—v. McGraw-Hill Broadcasting Co., 659 P.2d 1351, 9 Media L. Rep. 1257 (Colo. 1983) *2:* 118
Burnside v. Byars, 363 F.2d 744 (5th Cir. 1966) *13:* 343
Burrascano v. Levi, 452 F. Supp. 1066 (D. Md. 1978), *aff'd,* 612 F.2d 1306 (4th Cir. 1979) *2:* 119–20
Bursey v. United States, 466 F.2d 1059 (9th Cir. 1972) *14:* 413–15
Burt v. CBS, Inc., 769 F. Supp. 1012, 18 Media L. Rep. 2231 (S.D. Ohio 1991) *13:* 168

Burton v. Crowell Pub'g Co., 82 F.2d 154 (2d Cir. 1936) *2:* 155

Bush v. Head, 97 P. 512 (Cal. 1908) *2:* 620

Business Executives' Move for Vietnam Peace v. FCC, 450 F.2d 642 (D.C. Cir. 1971) *13:* 31

Butterworth v. Smith, 494 U.S. 624 (1990) *4:* 82

Buzbee v. Journal Newspapers, 465 A.2d 426, 9 Media L. Rep. 2233 (1983) *1:* 148

Byers v. Meridian Printing Co., 95 N.E. 917 (Ohio 1911) *2:* 612

By-Prod Corp. v. Armen-Berry Co., 668 F.2d 956 (7th Cir. 1982) *5:* 226, 236

Bystrom v. Fridley High School, 822 F.2d 747, 14 Media L. Rep. 1517 (8th Cir. 1987), *on remand,* 686 F. Supp. 1387 (D. Minn. 1987), *aff'd,* 855 F.2d 855 (8th Cir. 1988) *13:* 334–35

C

Cable Assocs. v. Town & Country Mgmt. Corp., 709 F. Supp. 582 (E.D. Pa. 1989) *12:* 246

Cable Holdings of Ga. v. McNeil Real Estate, 953 F.2d 600 (11th Cir.), *cert. denied,* 113 S. Ct. 182 (1992) *12:* 245

Cable Investments v. Woolley, 867 F.2d 151 (3d Cir. 1989) *12:* 244–45

Cable News Network
—In re, *see* Noriega; United States v.
—v. ABC, 518 F. Supp. 1238, 7 Media L. Rep. 2053 (N.D. Ga. 1981) *1:* 543, 638

Cable TV Fund 14-A v. Property Owners Ass'n, Chesapeake Ranch Estates, 706 F. Supp. 422 (D. Md. 1989) *12:* 247

Caceres; United States v., 440 U.S. 741 (1979) *14:* 127

Cafferty v. Southern Tier Pub'g Co., 123 N.E. 76 (N.Y. 1919) *2:* 123

Cahill v. Hawaiian Paradise Park Corp., 543 P.2d 1356 (Haw. 1975) *2:* 481

Calder
—v. IRS, 890 F.2d 781, 17 Media L. Rep. 1283 (5th Cir. 1989) *1:* 305
—v. Jones, 465 U.S. 783, 10 Media L. Rep. 1401 (1984) *2:* 646–53, 672

Caldor, Inc. v. Heffernan, 440 A.2d 767, 7 Media L. Rep. 1747 (Conn. 1981) *9:* 248

Caldwell; United States v., 311 F. Supp. 358 (N.D. Cal. 1970), *rev'd,* 434 F.2d 1081 (9th Cir. 1970), *cert. granted,* 402 U.S. 942 (1971), *rev'd,* 408 U.S. 665 (1972) *14:* 5, 19

California
—v. Greenwood, 486 U.S. 35 (1989) *5:* 33, 194
—v. LaRue, 409 U.S. 109 (1972) *11:* 186–88

California ex rel. L.A., In re, 471 A.2d 1141 (Md. Ct. App.), *cert. denied sub nom.* Rees v. L.A. County, 467 U.S. 1205 (1984) *14:* 234

California for County of L.A., In re, 471 A.2d 1141 (Md.), *cert. denied,* 467 U.S. 1205 (1984) *14:* 381

California Newspaper Pubrs. Ass'n v. Burbank, 51 Cal. App. 3d 50, 123 Cal. Rptr. 880 (Cal. Ct. App. 1975) *12:* 137–38

California Retail Liquor Dealers Ass'n v. Midcal Aluminum, 445 U.S. 97 (1980) *11:* 182

Callahan v. Westinghouse Broadcasting Co., 363 N.E.2d 240, 2 Media L. Rep. 2226 (Mass. 1977) *2:* 461

Camille Corp. v. Phares, 705 F.2d 223 (7th Cir. 1983) *11:* 305

Cammarano v. United States, 358 U.S. 498 (1959) *11:* 53

Campbell
—v. Jacksonville Kennel Club, 66 So. 2d 495 (Fla. 1953) *2:* 189
—v. Klevenhagen, 18 Media L. Rep. 2113 (S.D. Tex. 1991) *14:* 74
—v. New York Evening Post, 157 N.E. 153 (N.Y. 1927) *2:* 559
—v. Seabury Press, 614 F.2d 395, 5 Media L. Rep. 2612 (5th Cir. 1980) *4:* 141, 157

Campo v. Paar, 239 N.Y.S.2d 494 (N.Y. App. Div. 1963) *2:* 225

Campus Communications v. Freedman, 374 So. 2d 1169 (Fla. Ct. App. 1979) *14:* 354, 382–84

Candebat v. Flanagan, 487 So. 2d 207, 12 Media L. Rep. 2149 (Miss. 1986) *6:* 51–52

Canon v. Justice Ct., 393 P.2d 428 (Cal. 1964) *12:* 210

Cantor; State v., 534 A.2d 83, 14 Media L. Rep. 2103 (N.J. Super. Ct. App. Div. 1987), *cert. denied,* 540 A.2d 1274 (N.J. 1988) *5:* 18

Cantrell
—v. ABC, 529 F. Supp. 746, 8 Media L. Rep. 1239 (N.D. Ill. 1981) *3:* 42, 85
—v. Forest City Pub'g Co., 419 U.S. 245, 1 Media L. Rep. 1815 (1974) *2:* 482, 488; *3:* 77–78, 92, 97–102

Cantwell v. Connecticut, 310 U.S. 296 (1940) *10:* 39; *12:* 6

Cape Pubns.
—v. Bridges, 423 So. 2d 426, 8 Media L. Rep. 2535 (Fla. Dist. Ct. App. 1982), *petition denied,* 431 So. 2d 988 (Fla.), *cert. denied,* 464 U.S. 893 (1983) *4:* 51, 155, 173, 175
—v. Hitchner, 549 So. 2d 1374, 16 Media L. Rep. 2337 (Fla.), *appeal dismissed,* 493 U.S. 929 (1989) *4:* 107

Capital Broadcasting Co.
—v. Acting Att'y Gen., *see* Capital Broadcasting Co. v. Mitchell
—v. Mitchell, 333 F. Supp. 582 (D.D.C. 1971), *aff'd mem. sub nom.* Capital Broadcasting Co. v. Acting Att'y Gen., 405 U.S. 1000 (1972) *11:* 63, 134, 137, 217–20
Capital Cities/ABC, In re, 918 F.2d 140, 18 Media L. Rep. 1450 (11th Cir. 1990) *10:* 278
Capital Cities/ABC's Application, In re, 913 F.2d 89, 18 Media L. Rep. 1049 (3d Cir. 1990) *1:* 106, 120, 222
Capital Cities Broadcasting Corp. v. Tenth Dist. Judge, 283 N.W.2d 779, 5 Media L. Rep. 2058 (Mich. Ct. App. 1979) *1:* 106–7
Capital Cities Cable v. Crisp, *see* Oklahoma Telecasters Association v. Crisp
Capital Cities Media v. Chester, 797 F.2d 1164 (3d Cir. 1986) *1:* 295
Capital Newspapers
—v. Brown, 429 N.Y.S.2d 749, 6 Media L. Rep. 1494 (N.Y. App. Div. 1980) *1:* 217
—v. Clyne, 418 N.E.2d 1111, 8 Media L. Rep. 1712 (N.Y. 1982) *1:* 217
—v. Lee, 530 N.Y.S.2d 872, 15 Media L. Rep. 1668 (N.Y. App. Div. 1988) *1:* 156
—v. Moynihan, 519 N.E.2d 825, 14 Media L. Rep. 2262 (N.Y. 1988) *1:* 259–60
Capital-Gazette Newspapers v. Stack, 445 A.2d 1038, 8 Media L. Rep. 1704 (Md.), *cert. denied*, 459 U.S. 989 (1982) *2:* 156
Caples Co. v. United States, 243 F.2d 232 (D.C. Cir. 1957) *11:* 249–50
Capobianco v. Pulitzer Pub'g Co., 812 S.W.2d 852, 18 Media L. Rep. 2290 (Mo. Ct. App. 1991) *2:* 146
Capra v. Thoroughbred Racing Ass'n, 787 F.2d 463 (9th Cir.), *cert. denied*, 479 U.S. 1017 (1986) *4:* 135
Capuano v. Outlet Co., 579 A.2d 469 (R.I. 1990) *14:* 71, 295
Cardillo v. Doubleday & Co., 518 F.2d 638 (2d Cir. 1975) *2:* 603
Cardozo v. True, 342 So. 2d 1053, 2 Media L. Rep. 1635 (Fla. Dist. Ct. App.), *cert. denied*, 353 So. 2d 674 (Fla. 1977) *7:* 20, 22, 29, 37; *8:* 40
Carey
—In re, 5 Media L. Rep. 1158 (N.Y. App. Div. 1979) *1:* 162, 387, 389
—v. Brown, 447 U.S. 455 (1980) *12:* 4, 10, 113; *13:* 264
—v. Evening Call Pub'g Co., 62 A.2d 327 (R.I. 1948) *2:* 165
—v. Hume, 492 F.2d 631 (D.C. Cir.), *cert. dismissed*, 417 U.S. 938 (1974) *14:* 47, 49–50, 62, 90–91, 100, 102

—v. Population Servs. Int'l, 431 U.S. 678, 2 Media L. Rep. 1935 (1977) *11:* 85, 129, 288–91
Carlin Communications v. FCC, 749 F.2d 113 (2d Cir. 1984) *12:* 50–51
Carlson v. Village of Union City, 601 F. Supp. 801 (W.D. Mich. 1985) *12:* 236–37
Carney v. Santa Cruz Women Against Rape, 271 Cal. Rptr. 30, 18 Media L. Rep. 1123 (Cal. Ct. App. 1990) *2:* 506
Caron v. Bangor Pub'g Co., 470 A.2d 782, 10 Media L. Rep. 1365 (Me. 1984), *cert. denied*, 467 U.S. 1241 (1984) *2:* 259–60, 267
Carpenter; United States v., 791 F.2d 1024, 12 Media L. Rep. 2169 (2d Cir. 1986), *aff'd*, 484 U.S. 19, 14 Media L. Rep. 1853 (1987) *5:* 161; *9:* 172–75, 177
Carpentier; United States v., 526 F. Supp. 292, 7 Media L. Rep. 2332 (E.D.N.Y. 1981) *1:* 307, 338
Carr v. Watkins, 177 A.2d 841 (Md. 1962) *4:* 190
Carroll v. President & Comm'rs of Princess Anne, 393 U.S. 175, 1 Media L. Rep. 1016 (1968) *10:* 45, 49, 267
Carroll City/County Hosp. v. Cox Enters., 256 S.E.2d 443, 444 (Ga. 1979) *2:* 234, 238
Carroll Contracting v. Edwards, 528 So. 2d 951 (Fla. Ct. App.), *review denied sub nom.* Citrus County Chronicle v. Carroll Contracting, 536 So. 2d 243 (Fla. 1988) *14:* 70
Carson
—In re, 197 USPQ 554 (T.M.T.A.B. 1977) *6:* 150–51
—v. Allied News Co., 529 F.2d 206 (7th Cir. 1976) *2:* 395, 398
—v. Here's Johnny Portable Toilets, 698 F.2d 831, 9 Media L. Rep. 1153 (6th Cir. 1983) *6:* 31, 103–5, 107
Carter v. Utah Power & Light Co., 800 P.2d 1095, 18 Media L. Rep. 1497 (Utah 1990) *1:* 427
Casbah, Inc. v. Thone, 651 F.2d 551 (8th Cir. 1981), *cert. denied*, 455 U.S. 1005 (1982) *11:* 305
Cason v. Baskin, 20 So. 2d 243 (Fla. 1944) *4:* 4, 22, 148; *5:* 43
Cassidy v. ABC, 377 N.E.2d 126, 3 Media L. Rep. 2449 (Ill. App. Ct. 1978) *5:* 27, 73, 116, 259
Casso v. Brand, 776 S.W.2d 551, 16 Media L. Rep. 1929 (Tex. 1989) *2:* 404, 677
Castagna v. Western Graphics Corp., 590 P.2d 291, 4 Media L. Rep. 2497 (Or. Ct. App. 1979) *6:* 118
Castlewood Int'l Corp. v. Simon, 596 F.2d 638 (9th Cir. 1979), *vacated and remanded sub*

Castlewood Int'l Corp.—*Contd.*
  nom. Miller v. Castlewood Int'l Corp., 446 U.S. 949 (1980), *panel opinion reinstated,* 626 F.2d 1200 (5th Cir. 1980) *11:* 181
Catalano v. Pechous, 419 N.E.2d 350, 6 Media L. Rep. 2511 (Ill. 1980), *cert. denied,* 451 U.S. 911 (1981) *2:* 548
Catalfo v. Jensen, 628 F. Supp. 1453, 12 Media L. Rep. 1867 (D.N.H. 1986) *2:* 222
Catholic Archdiocese of Denver v. Denver, 741 P.2d 333, 14 Media L. Rep. 1964 (Colo. 1987) *9:* 216
CBS
—(Lar Daly), 18 Rad. Reg. (P & F) 238, *reconsideration denied,* 26 F.C.C. 715, 18 Rad. Reg. (P & F) 701 (1959) *13:* 91–92
—40 F.C.C. 395 (1964) *13:* 97
—In re, 828 F.2d 958, 14 Media L. Rep. 1636 (2d Cir. 1987) *1:* 348, 363
—In re (Shannon), 540 F. Supp. 769, 8 Media L. Rep. 1833 (N.D. Ill. 1982) *1:* 346, 349–50
—v. Democratic Nat'l Comm., 412 U.S. 94 (1973) *13:* 30–42, 53, 56, 77, 154, 388, 483–84
—v. FCC, 453 U.S. 367 (1981) *13:* 43, 45–46, 48–57, 77, 106, 110–11, 115, 118–21, 125, 145–46
—v. Growe, 15 Media L. Rep. 2275 (D. Minn. 1988) *1:* 564
—v. Jackson, 578 So. 2d 698, 18 Media L. Rep. 2110 (Fla. 1991) *14:* 344
—v. Smith, 681 F. Supp. 794, 15 Media L. Rep. 1251 (S.D. Fla. 1988) *1:* 558–59, 564–65
—v. Stokley-Van Kamp, Inc., 456 F. Supp. 539 (S.D.N.Y. 1977) *7:* 6
—v. United States Dist. Ct.
——729 F.2d 1174, 10 Media L. Rep. 1529 (9th Cir. 1983) *10:* 194, 196
——765 F.2d 823, 11 Media L. Rep. 2285 (9th Cir. 1985) *1:* 185, 192–93
—v. Young, 522 F.2d 234, 1 Media L. Rep. 1024 (6th Cir. 1975) *10:* 204, 222
—United States v.
——497 F.2d 102, 19 Media L. Rep. 1351 (5th Cir. 1974) *1:* 568
——459 F. Supp. 832 (C.D. Cal. 1978) *14:* 429
——651 F.2d 189 (3d Cir. 1980), *cert. denied,* 454 U.S. 1056 (1981) *14:* 167
CBS (KMOX-TV) v. Campbell, 645 S.W.2d 30 (Mo. Ct. App. 1982) *14:* 71, 77, 181, 344
Cefalu v. Globe Newspaper, 391 N.E.2d 935, 5 Media L. Rep. 1940 (Mass. App. Ct. 1979), *cert. denied and appeal dismissed,* 444 U.S. 1060 (1980) *3:* 48

Celmer; State v., *see* Schad v. Ocean Grove Camp Meeting Ass'n
Centel Cable Television Co. of Fla.
—v. Admiral's Cove Assocs., 835 F.2d 1359 (11th Cir. 1988) *12:* 247
—v. Thomas J. White Dev. Corp., 902 F.2d 905 (11th Cir. 1990) *12:* 247
Central Hardware Co. v. NLRB, 407 U.S. 539 (1972) *12:* 84–85
Central Hudson Gas & Elec. Corp. v. Public Serv. Comm'n, 390 N.E.2d 749 (N.Y. 1979), *rev'd,* 447 U.S. 557, 6 Media L. Rep. 1497 (1980) *7:* 35, 38; *10:* 247; *11:* 4, 16–17, 23–24, 32, 56–57, 91–100, 239, 296–300; *12:* 172
Central Ill. Light Co. v. Citizens Util. Bd., 827 F.2d 1169 (7th Cir. 1987) *13:* 424
Central S.C. Chapter, Soc'y of Prof. Journalists v. Martin, 556 F.2d 706, 2 Media L. Rep. 2146 (4th Cir. 1977), *cert. denied,* 434 U.S. 1022 (1978) *1:* 568, 570; *10:* 202
Central Telecommunications v. TCI Cablevision, 800 F.2d 711 (8th Cir. 1986), *cert. denied,* 480 U.S. 910 (1987) *12:* 236–37
Century Communications Corp. v. FCC, 835 F.2d 292 (D.C. Cir. 1987), *clarified,* 837 F.2d 517, *cert. denied,* 436 U.S. 1032 (1988) *13:* 522–23
Century Fed. v. Palo Alto, 648 F. Supp. 1465 (N.D. Cal. 1986) *12:* 239
Cepeda
—In re, 233 F. Supp. 465 (S.D.N.Y. 1964) *14:* 370, 373, 376
—v. Cowles Magazine & Broadcasting, 328 F.2d 869 (9th Cir.), *cert. denied,* 379 U.S. 844, 13 L. Ed. 2d 50 (1964) *2:* 226
Certain Interested Individuals v. Pulitzer Pub'g Co. (Gunn II), 895 F.2d 460, 17 Media L. Rep. 1364 (8th Cir.), *cert. denied,* 498 U.S. 880 (1990) *1:* 377–78
Cervantes v. Time, Inc., 464 F.2d 986, 1 Media L. Rep. 1751 (8th Cir. 1972), *cert. denied,* 409 U.S. 1125 (1973) *14:* 47, 56, 62, 90, 359, 374, 377
Chagra; United States v., 701 F.2d 354, 9 Media L. Rep. 1409 (5th Cir. 1983) *1:* 106, 117, 163–67
Chambers v. Leiser, 86 P. 627 (Wash. 1906) *2:* 537
Chandler
—v. Florida, 449 U.S. 560, 7 Media L. Rep. 1041 (1981) *1:* 572, 574–75, 615–34
—v. Georgia Pub. Telecommunications Comm'n, 917 F.2d 486, 18 Media L. Rep. 1314 (11th Cir. 1990), *cert. denied,* 112 S. Ct. 71 (1991) *13:* 390, 396–97
Chang v. Michiana Telecasting Corp., 900 F.2d

1085, 17 Media L. Rep. 1768 (7th Cir. 1990) *2:* 223, 439, 446
Channel 10 v. Gunnarson, 337 F. Supp. 634 (D. Minn. 1972) *1:* 535
Channel Two Television Co. v. Dickerson, 725 S.W.2d 470, 13 Media L. Rep. 2133 (Tex. Ct. App. 1987) *14:* 75–76
Chaplin v. NBC, 15 F.R.D. 134 (S.D.N.Y. 1953) *5:* 265
Chaplinsky v. New Hampshire, 315 U.S. 568 (1942) *8:* 90; *10:* 3
Chappadeau v. Utica Observer-Dispatch, 341 N.E.2d 569, 1 Media L. Rep. 1693 (N.Y. 1975) *2:* 469
Chapski v. Copley Press, 442 N.E.2d 195, 8 Media L. Rep. 2403 (Ill. 1982) *2:* 145
Charles of the Ritz Group v. Quality King Distribs., 832 F.2d 1317 (2d Cir. 1987) *10:* 247
Charles Parker Co. v. Silver City Crystal Co., 116 A.2d 440 (Conn. 1955) *2:* 175, 186
Charlotte Observer, In re
—882 F.2d 850, 16 Media L. Rep. 2032 (4th Cir. 1989) *1:* 160, 278
—921 F.2d 47, 18 Media L. Rep. 1365 (4th Cir. 1990) *10:* 189
Charlottesville Newspapers v. Berry, 206 S.E.2d 267 (Va. 1974) *1:* 451
Chartwell Communications Group v. Westbrook, 637 F.2d 459, 6 Media L. Rep. 2368 (6th Cir. 1980) *5:* 242
Chase v. Robson, 435 F.2d 1059 (7th Cir. 1970) *10:* 203
Chaves v. Johnson, 335 S.E.2d 97 (Va. 1985) *2:* 241
Cher v. Forum Int'l, 7 Media L. Rep. 2593 (C.D. Cal. 1982), *aff'd in part and rev'd in part,* 692 F.2d 634, 8 Media L. Rep. 2484 (9th Cir. 1982), *cert. denied,* 462 U.S. 1120 (1983) *6:* 31, 43, 90
Chesterfield Cablevision v. County of Chesterfield, 401 S.E.2d 678 (Va. 1991) *9:* 243
Cheyenne K. v. Tuolomne County Super. Ct., 256 Cal. Rptr. 68, 16 Media L. Rep. 1411 (Cal. Ct. App. 1989) *1:* 238
Chiarella v. United States, 445 U.S. 222 (1980) *9:* 140, 170
Chicago v. Prus, 425 N.E.2d 426 (Ill. App. Ct. 1981) *11:* 314; *12:* 169
Chicago Cable Communications v. Chicago Cable Comm'n, 678 F. Supp. 734 (N.D. Ill. 1988) *12:* 242
Chicago Council of Lawyers v. Bauer, 522 F.2d 242, 1 Media L. Rep. 1094 (7th Cir. 1975), *cert. denied,* 427 U.S. 912 (1976) *10:* 205
Chicago Joint Bd., Clothing & Textile Workers v. Chicago Tribune Co., 307 F. Supp. 422 (N.D. Ill. 1969), *aff'd,* 435 F.2d 470 (7th Cir. 1970), *cert. denied,* 402 U.S. 973 (1971) *13:* 206, 243, 246
Chicago Newspaper Pubrs. Ass'n v. Wheaton, 697 F. Supp. 1464, 15 Media L. Rep. 2297 (N.D. Ill. 1988) *12:* 138–39, 141, 143, 147, 161
Chicago Observer v. Chicago, 929 F.2d 325, 18 Media L. Rep. 1974 (7th Cir. 1991) *12:* 144, 154
Chicago Tribune Co.
—v. Johnson, 477 N.E.2d 482 (Ill.), *appeal dismissed,* 474 U.S. 915 (1985) *9:* 236
—v. Village of Downers Grove, 532 N.E.2d 821, 15 Media L. Rep. 2459 (Ill. 1988) *12:* 126
Chicarella v. Passant, 494 A.2d 1109 (Pa. Super. Ct. 1985) *5:* 18, 22
Chic Magazine v. Braun, *see* Braun v. Flynt
Children of Bedford v. Petromelis, 573 N.E.2d 541, 18 Media L. Rep. 2255 (N.Y. 1991), *vacated and remanded,* 112 S. Ct. 859 (1992) *9:* 254, 265
Chillicothe Gazette, State ex rel. v. Court of Common Pleas, 442 N.E.2d 747, 9 Media L. Rep. 1018 (Ohio 1982) *10:* 194
Chisholm v. FCC, 538 F.2d 349 (D.C. Cir.), *cert. denied,* 429 U.S. 890 (1976) *13:* 93, 98, 100–101
Christopher; United States v., 700 F.2d 1253 (9th Cir.), *cert. denied,* 461 U.S. 960 (1983) *12:* 44
Church v. Hamilton, 444 F.2d 105 (3d Cir. 1971) *9:* 48
Church of Scientology
—v. Adams, 584 F.2d 893, 4 Media L. Rep. 1986 (9th Cir. 1978) *2:* 644
—v. Cazares, 638 F.2d 1272, 7 Media L. Rep. 1668 (5th Cir. 1981) *2:* 135
—v. Minnesota State Medical Ass'n Found., 264 N.W.2d 152, 3 Media L. Rep. 2177 (Minn. 1978) *2:* 224, 234, 238
Church of Scientology of Cal. v. Flynn, 744 F.2d 694 (9th Cir. 1984) *2:* 136
Chuy v. Philadelphia Eagles Football Club, 595 F.2d 1265, 4 Media L. Rep. 2537 (3d Cir. 1979) *2:* 135, 395
Cianci
—v. New Times Pub'g Co., 639 F.2d 54, 6 Media L. Rep. 1625 (2d Cir. 1980) *2:* 90, 259–60, 268, 579
—v. New Times Pub'g Co., 88 F.R.D. 562, 6 Media L. Rep. 2502 (S.D.N.Y. 1980) *1:* 427
—State v., 496 A.2d 139, 11 Media L. Rep. 2403 (R.I. 1985) *1:* 365
Cianfrani; United States v., 573 F.2d 835, 3

Cianfrani—*Contd.*
  Media L. Rep. 1961 (3d Cir. 1978) *1:* 124, 132
Cibenko v. Worth Pubrs., 510 F. Supp. 761, 7 Media L. Rep. 1298 (D.N.J. 1981) *3:* 12, 63
Cincinnati v. Discovery Network, 946 F.2d 464 (6th Cir. 1991), *aff'd,* 113 S. Ct. 1505, 21 Media L. Rep. 1161 (1993) *11:* 154–56, 170–75; *12:* 163
Cincinnati Gas & Elec. Co. v. General Elec. Co., 854 F.2d 900, 15 Media L. Rep. 2020 (6th Cir. 1988), *cert. denied,* 489 U.S. 1033 (1989) *1:* 265
Cinevision Corp. v. Burbank, 745 F.2d 560 (9th Cir. 1984), *cert. denied,* 471 U.S. 1054 (1985) *12:* 23
Cipollone v. Liggett Group, 785 F.2d 1108 (3d Cir. 1986), *on remand,* 113 F.R.D. 86 (D.N.J. 1986) *1:* 429, 440
Citizen Awareness Regarding Educ. v. Calhoun County Pub'g, 406 S.E.2d 65, 19 Media L. Rep. 1061 (W. Va. 1991) *13:* 207
Citizen Pub'g Co. v. United States, 394 U.S. 131, 1 Media L. Rep. 2704 (1969) *9:* 24, 28
Citrus County Chronicle v. Carroll Contracting, *see* Carroll Contracting v. Edwards
City of, *see* specific city
Civella; United States v., 493 F. Supp. 786, 6 Media L. Rep. 1744 (W.D. Mo. 1980) *1:* 157
C.L. v. Edson, 409 N.W.2d 417, 14 Media L. Rep. 1145 (Wis. Ct. App. 1987) *1:* 106, 121, 455
Clark
—v. ABC, 684 F.2d 1208, 8 Media L. Rep. 2049 (6th Cir. 1982), *cert. denied,* 460 U.S. 1040 (1983) *3:* 32
—v. Celeb Pub'g, 530 F. Supp. 979, 8 Media L. Rep. 1261 (S.D.N.Y. 1981) *6:* 45–46, 52
—v. Community for Creative Non-Violence, 468 U.S. 288 (1984) *12:* 2, 9, 21–22, 29, 34
—v. Pearson, 248 F. Supp. 188 (D.D.C. 1965) *2:* 134
—v. Solem, 628 F.2d 1120 (8th Cir. 1980) *9:* 78
—United States v., 475 F.2d 240 (2d Cir. 1973) *1:* 206
Clarksburg Pub'g Co. v. FCC, 225 F.2d 511 (D.C. Cir. 1955) *13:* 438
Classic; United States v., 313 U.S. 299 (1941) *9:* 42
Clean-Up '84 v. Heinrich, 759 F.2d 1511 (11th Cir. 1985) *1:* 557, 564–65
Cliffs Notes v. Bantam Doubleday Dell Pub'g Group, 886 F.2d 490, 16 Media L. Rep. 2289 (2d Cir. 1989) *10:* 256, 261
Clinton Community Hosp. Corp. v. Southern Md. Medical Ctr., 374 F. Supp. 450 (D. Md. 1974), *aff'd,* 510 F.2d 1037 (4th Cir.), *cert. denied,* 422 U.S. 1048 (1975) *3:* 27
Clyne; State v., 35 P. 789 (Kan. 1894) *2:* 8
CNA Fin. Corp. v. Teamsters Local 743, 515 F. Supp. 942 (N.D. Ill. 1981) *4:* 33
Coalition Against Police Abuse v. Superior Ct., 216 Cal. Rptr. 614 (Cal. Ct. App. 1985) *1:* 428
Coalition for Abortion Rights & Against Sterilization Abuse v. Niagara Frontier Transp. Auth., 584 F. Supp. 985 (W.D.N.Y. 1984) *13:* 425–26
Cobbs v. Chicago Defender, 31 N.E.2d 323 (Ill. App. Ct. 1941) *2:* 226
Coca-Cola Co. v. Gemini Rising, 346 F. Supp. 1183 (E.D.N.Y. 1972) *10:* 262
Codey v. Capital Cities, 626 N.E.2d 636, 21 Media L. Rep. 2267 (N.Y. 1993) *14:* 375
Coe; State v., 679 P.2d 353, 10 Media L. Rep. 1465 (Wash. 1984) *10:* 101, 194
Coffman v. Spokane Chronicle Pub'g Co., 117 P. 596 (Wash. 1911) *2:* 611
Cofield v. Advertiser Co., 486 So. 2d 434, 12 Media L. Rep. 2039 (Ala. 1986) *2:* 603
Cohen
—v. Cowles Media Co., 457 N.W.2d 199, 17 Media L. Rep. 2176 (Minn. 1990), *rev'd in part,* 111 S. Ct. 2513, 18 Media L. Rep. 2273 (1991), *on remand,* 479 N.W.2d 387, 19 Media L. Rep. 1858 (Minn. 1992) *14:* 26, 436–42, 444–51, 457
—v. Herbal Concepts, 473 N.Y.S.2d 426, 10 Media L. Rep. 1561 (N.Y. App. Div.), *aff'd,* 472 N.E.2d 307 (N.Y. 1984) *6:* 20, 33
—v. New York State Liquor Auth., 275 N.Y.S.2d 484 (N.Y. App. Div. 1966) *11:* 190
—v. New York Times Co., 138 N.Y.S. 206 (N.Y. App. Div. 1912) *2:* 152
Cohn v. NBC, 414 N.Y.S.2d 906, 4 Media L. Rep. 2533 (N.Y. App. Div. 1979), *aff'd,* 408 N.E.2d 672, 6 Media L. Rep. 1398 (N.Y.), *cert. denied,* 449 U.S. 1022 (1980) *2:* 302; *6:* 74
Coira v. Depoo Hosp., 4 Media L. Rep. 1692 (Fla. Cir. Ct. 1978) *14:* 76
Colaizzi v. Walker, 542 F.2d 969 (7th Cir. 1976), *cert. denied,* 430 U.S. 960 (1977) *2:* 523
Colbert v. World Pub'g Co., 747 P.2d 286, 14 Media L. Rep. 2188 (Okla. 1987) *3:* 83, 86
Coleco Indus. v. Berman, 567 F.2d 569 (3d Cir. 1977), *cert. denied,* 439 U.S. 830 (1978) *9:* 148

Coleman
—v. Collins, 384 So. 2d 229 (Fla. Dist. Ct. App. 1980) *2:* 471, 473
—v. MacLennan, 98 P. 281 (Kan. 1908) *2:* 277
—v. Newark Morning Ledger Co., 149 A.2d 193 (N.J. 1959) *2:* 563
Colgate & Co.; United States v., 250 U.S. 300 (1919) *13:* 219–20
Collazo v. Kallinger, 11 Media L. Rep. 1509 (Pa. C.P. 1985) *9:* 264
Cologne v. Westfarms Assocs., 469 A.2d 1201 (Conn. 1984) *12:* 90
Colon; People v., 521 N.E.2d 1075, 15 Media L. Rep. 1235 (N.Y.), *cert. denied,* 487 U.S. 1239 (1988) *1:* 221
Columbia Broadcasting Sys., *see* CBS
Combined Communications Corp.
—v. Boger, 689 F. Supp. 1065, 15 Media L. Rep. 2365 (W.D. Okla. 1988) *1:* 305
—v. Finesilver, 672 F.2d 818, 8 Media L. Rep. 1233 (10th Cir. 1982) *1:* 542, 638
Commercial Printing Co. v. Lee, 553 S.W.2d 270, 2 Media L. Rep. 2352 (Ark. 1977) *1:* 225
Committee for an Indep. P-I v. Hearst Corp., 704 F.2d 467, 9 Media L. Rep. 1489 (9th Cir.), *cert. denied,* 464 U.S. 892 (1983) *9:* 29, 33, 35–37
Commonwealth v., *see* name of other party
Community Communications Co. v. Boulder, 496 F. Supp. 823 (D. Colo. 1980), *rev'd,* 660 F.2d 1370, 7 Media L. Rep. 1993 (10th Cir. 1981), *cert. dismissed,* 456 U.S. 1001 (1982) *12:* 232, 235, 237; *13:* 489–95
Community-Serv. Broadcasting of Mid-Am. v. FCC, 593 F.2d 1102, 4 Media L. Rep. 1257 (D.C. Cir. 1978) *12:* 174; *13:* 395
Compco Corp. v. Day-Brite Lighting, 376 U.S. 234 (1964) *6:* 91
Complaint of Carter-Mondale Presidential Committee, Inc. against the ABC, CBS and NBC Television Networks, In re, 74 F.C.C.2d 631 (1979) *13:* 47
Comprehensive Accounting Serv. Co. v. Maryland State Bd. of Pub. Accountancy, 397 A.2d 1019 (Md. 1979) *11:* 325
Conklin
—v. Sloss, 150 Cal. Rptr. 121 (Cal. Ct. App. 1978) *4:* 119
—People v., 522 P.2d 1049 (Cal.), *appeal dismissed,* 419 U.S. 1064 (1974) *5:* 260
Conkwright v. Globe News Pub'g Co., 398 S.W.2d 385 (Tex. Civ. App. 1965) *2:* 272
Connally v. General Constr. Co., 269 U.S. 385 (1926) *8:* 32
Connecticut State Bd. of Labor Relations v. Fagin, 370 A.2d 1095 (Conn. Super. Ct. 1976) *14:* 70
Connecticut State Fed'n of Teachers v. Board of Educ. Members, 538 F.2d 471 (2d Cir. 1976) *12:* 77–78
Connell v. Hudson, 733 F. Supp. 465, 17 Media L. Rep. 1803 (D.N.H. 1990) *1:* 535
Connick v. Myers, 461 U.S. 138 (1983) *2:* 508; *4:* 138
Consolidated Edison Co. v. Public Serv. Comm'n, 447 U.S. 530, 6 Media L. Rep. 1518 (1980) *12:* 5
Consumers Power Co. Sec. Litig., In re, 109 F.R.D. 45 (E.D. Mich. 1985) *1:* 436
Consumers Union
—In re
——495 F. Supp. 582 (S.D.N.Y. 1980) *14:* 404
——7 Media L. Rep. 2038 (S.D.N.Y. 1981) *14:* 144, 151, 155–56, 305, 335
—v. Periodical Correspondents' Ass'n, 515 F.2d 1341 (D.C. Cir. 1975), *cert. denied,* 423 U.S. 1051 (1976) *1:* 539
Contakos; Commonwealth v., 453 A.2d 578, 9 Media L. Rep. 1038 (Pa. 1982) *1:* 209
Contemporary Mission v. New York Times Co., 842 F.2d 612, 15 Media L. Rep. 1180 (2d Cir.), *cert. denied sub nom.* O'Reilly v. New York Times Co., 488 U.S. 856 (1988) *2:* 127, 427
Contempt of Wright, In re, 700 P.2d 40 (Idaho 1985) *14:* 70, 76, 79
Continental Cablevision v. Storer Broadcasting Co., 583 F. Supp. 427 (E.D. Mo. 1984) *14:* 172, 370, 373
Continental Ill. Sec. Litig., In re, 732 F.2d 1302, 10 Media L. Rep. 1593 (7th Cir. 1984) *1:* 272, 427, 436
Continental Nut Co. v. Robert L. Berner Co., 345 F.2d 395 (7th Cir. 1965) *2:* 184
Converters Equip. Corp. v. Condes Corp., 258 N.W.2d 712 (Wis. 1977) *2:* 295
Conway v. United States, 852 F.2d 187, 15 Media L. Rep. 1967 (6th Cir.), *cert. denied,* 488 U.S. 943 (1988) *1:* 580, 637
Cook
—v. Advertiser Co., 458 F.2d 1119 (5th Cir. 1972) *9:* 88–92; *13:* 245
—v. Houston Post, 616 F.2d 791 (5th Cir. 1980) *9:* 45, 55
Cooper
—v. Alabama Farm Bureau Mut. Casualty Ins. Co., 385 So. 2d 630 (Ala. 1980) *2:* 482
—v. Rockford Newspapers, 365 N.E.2d 744, 2 Media L. Rep. 2288 (Ill. App. Ct. 1977) *10:* 101
Coopersmith v. Williams, 468 P.2d 739 (Colo. 1970) *2:* 534

Coordinated Pretrial Proceedings in Petroleum Prods. Antitrust Litig., In re, 101 F.R.D. 34, 10 Media L. Rep. 1300 (C.D. Cal. 1984) *1:* 427, 434, 445

Copley Press v. Superior Ct., 278 Cal. Rptr. 443, 18 Media L. Rep. 1800 (Cal. Ct. App.), *cert. denied,* 112 S. Ct. 304 (1991) *1:* 525

Corbitt; United States v., 879 F.2d 224, 16 Media L. Rep. 1993 (7th Cir. 1989) *1:* 381

Cordell v. Detective Pubns., 419 F.2d 989 (6th Cir. 1969) *4:* 28, 30

Corman v. Blanchard, 211 Cal. App. 2d 126, 27 Cal. Rptr. 327 (Cal. Ct. App. 1962) *2:* 115, 124, 167

Cormier v. Blake, 198 So. 2d 139 (La. Ct. App. 1967) *2:* 225

Cornelius v. NAACP Legal Defense & Educ. Fund, 473 U.S. 788 (1985) *13:* 257–58, 260–61, 274–75, 374, 397

Coronado Credit Union v. Koat, 656 P.2d 896, 9 Media L. Rep. 1031 (N.M. Ct. App. 1982) *14:* 355

Corpus Christi Caller-Times v. Mancias, 794 S.W.2d 852, 17 Media L. Rep. 2204 (Tex. Ct. App. 1990) *10:* 239

Correia v. Santos, 191 Cal. App. 2d 844, 13 Cal. Rptr. 132 (Cal. Ct. App. 1961) *2:* 201–2

Corrigan v. Bobbs-Merrill Co., 126 N.E. 260 (N.Y. 1920) *2:* 7, 304

Corrugated Container Antitrust Litig., In re, 661 F.2d 1145 (7th Cir. 1981), *aff'd sub nom.* Pillsbury Co. v. Conboy, 459 U.S. 248 (1983) *14:* 106

Corsetti; Commonwealth v., 438 N.E.2d 805, 8 Media L. Rep. 2113 (Mass. 1982) *14:* 424

Cortese; United States v., 568 F. Supp. 114, 9 Media L. Rep. 1912 (M.D. Pa. 1983) *1:* 129

Cosgrove Studio & Camera Shop v. Pane, 182 A.2d 751 (Pa. 1962) *2:* 2, 300

Costello v. Ocean County Observer, 21 Media L. Rep. 2274 (N.J. Super. Ct. App. Div. 1993) *14:* 395

Costlow v. Cusimano, 311 N.Y.S.2d 92 (N.Y. App. Div. 1970) *5:* 58–60, 75–77, 142–44

Cottman Transmission Sys.; State v., 542 A.2d 859, 15 Media L. Rep. 1644 (Md. Ct. Spec. App. 1988) *1:* 272

Coughlin v. Westinghouse Broadcasting & Cable, 603 F. Supp. 377 (E.D. Pa.), *aff'd,* 780 F.2d 340 (3d Cir. 1985), *cert. denied,* 476 U.S. 1187 (1986) *14:* 287, 374, 389

County of, *see* specific county

Courier-Journal v. Marshall, 828 F.2d 361, 14 Media L. Rep. 1561 (6th Cir. 1987) *1:* 428

Courier-Journal & Louisville Times Co. v. Peers, 747 S.W.2d 125, 15 Media L. Rep. 1051 (Ky. 1988) *1:* 106, 116, 429

Courtland v. Walston & Co., 340 F. Supp. 1076 (S.D.N.Y. 1972) *9:* 166

Couture; State v., 435 A.2d 369, 7 Media L. Rep. 1408 (Conn. Super. Ct. 1981) *1:* 148

Cowles Pub'g Co.
—v. Magistrate Ct., 800 P.2d 640, 18 Media L. Rep. 1273 (Idaho 1990) *1:* 156
—v. Murphy, 637 P.2d 966, 7 Media L. Rep. 2400 (Wash. 1981) *1:* 375

Cox
—v. Hatch, 761 P.2d 556, 16 Media L. Rep. 1366 (Utah 1988) *2:* 121; *6:* 18, 87, 114
—v. Lee Enters., 723 P.2d 238, 13 Media L. Rep. 1230 (Mont. 1986) *2:* 559
—v. Louisiana, 379 U.S. 559 (1965) *12:* 9, 13, 38
—v. New Hampshire, 312 U.S. 569 (1941) *12:* 7, 9, 159

Cox Broadcasting Corp. v. Cohn
——200 S.E.2d 127 (Ga. 1973) *4:* 59
——420 U.S. 469, 1 Media L. Rep. 1819 (1975) *2:* 572; *3:* 79–82; *4:* 4, 9, 19, 32, 38, 59–61, 65, 71–73, 105–6, 119, 121, 130, 137, 159–60, 176, 190; *5:* 31, 61; *9:* 64; *10:* 104

Cox Cable Hampton Roads v. City of Norfolk, 410 S.E.2d 652, 19 Media L. Rep. 1656 (Va. 1991) *9:* 241, 243

Cox Communications v. Lowe, 328 S.E.2d 384, 11 Media L. Rep. 2314 (Ga. Ct. App.), *cert. denied,* 474 U.S. 982 (1985) *5:* 38

Cox Enters.
—v. Gilreath, 235 S.E.2d 633, 3 Media L. Rep. 1031 (Ga. Ct. App. 1977) *2:* 221, 235, 238
—v. Holt, 678 F.2d 936, 8 Media L. Rep. 1701, *modified,* 691 F.2d 989 (11th Cir. 1982) *2:* 644

Craig
—v. Boren, 429 U.S. 190 (1976) *11:* 182, 188
—v. Harney, 331 U.S. 367, 1 Media L. Rep. 1310 (1947) *10:* 192
—v. Wright, 76 P.2d 248 (Okla. 1938) *2:* 544

Cramer v. Skinner, 931 F.2d 1020 (5th Cir.), *cert. denied,* 112 S. Ct. 298 (1991) *11:* 149

Crane v. Arizona Republic, 729 F. Supp. 698, 17 Media L. Rep. 1353 (C.D. Cal. 1989), *modified,* 972 F.2d 1511 (9th Cir. 1992) *2:* 406

Creel v. Crown Pubrs., 496 N.Y.S.2d 219, 12

Media L. Rep. 1588 (N.Y. App. Div. 1985) **6:** 72
Crellin v. Thomas, 247 P.2d 264 (Utah 1952) **2:** 209
Creswell v. Pruitt, 239 S.W.2d 165 (Tex. Civ. App. 1951) **2:** 537
Criden
—United States v., 633 F.2d 346 (3d Cir. 1980), *cert. denied sub nom.* Schaffer v. United States, 449 U.S. 1113 (1981) **14:** 167, 315–16, 361
—United States v. (Criden I), 648 F.2d 814, 7 Media L. Rep. 1153 (3d Cir. 1981) **1:** 308, 338–39, 342–43
—United States v. (Criden II), 675 F.2d 550, 8 Media L. Rep. 1297 (3d Cir. 1982) **1:** 129–35, 138
—United States v. (Criden III), 681 F.2d 919, 8 Media L. Rep. 2062 (3d Cir. 1982) **1:** 308, 325, 338, 344–45
Croton v. Gillis, 304 N.W.2d 820 (Mich. Ct. App. 1981) **2:** 186, 190
Crump v. Beckley Newspapers, 320 S.E.2d 70, 10 Media L. Rep. 2225 (W. Va. 1984) **2:** 540; **3:** 2, 10, 35–36, 41, 83, 89; **5:** 9; **6:** 1, 87, 122
Cubby, Inc. v. Compuserve, 776 F. Supp. 135, 19 Media L. Rep. 1525 (S.D.N.Y. 1991) **2:** 222
Cuevas; People v., 409 N.E.2d 1360 (N.Y. 1980) **1:** 202
Culbert v. Sampson's Supermkts., 444 A.2d 433 (Me. 1982) **7:** 16
Culliton v. Mize, 403 N.W.2d 853, 14 Media L. Rep. 1122 (Minn. Ct. App. 1987) **2:** 404
Cullman Broadcasting Co., 25 Rad. Reg. (P & F) 895 (1963) **13:** 162
Curry v. Journal Pub'g Co., 68 P.2d 168 (N.M. 1937), *overruled,* Ramirez v. Armstrong, 673 P.2d 822 (N.M. 1983) **7:** 15–16
Curtis v. Thompson, 840 F.2d 1291 (7th Cir. 1988) **11:** 314
Curtis Pub'g Co.
—v. Birdsong, 360 F.2d 344 (5th Cir. 1966) **2:** 135, 153
—v. Butts, 351 F.2d 702 (5th Cir. 1965), *aff'd,* 388 U.S. 130, 1 Media L. Rep. 1568 (1967) **2:** 36–44, 313, 315, 340–47, 489–97; **9:** 147
Cushman v. Day, 602 P.2d 327 (Or. Ct. App. 1979) **2:** 308
Cuthbertson v. CBS, Inc., 630 F.2d 139 (3d Cir. 1980), *cert. denied,* 449 U.S. 1126 (1981) **14:** 67, 90, 95, 103–4, 129, 131, 133, 315–16, 335, 343, 363, 427
Cutler; United States v., 6 F.3d 67, 21 Media L. Rep. 2075 (2d Cir. 1993) **14:** 67, 69, 364, 432–33
Cyntje v. Daily News Pub'g Co., 551 F. Supp. 403 (D.V.I. 1982) **13:** 254

D

Dacey
—v. Connecticut Bar Ass'n, 368 A.2d 125 (Conn. 1976), *appeal after remand,* 441 A.2d 49 (Conn. 1981) **2:** 461–62
—v. Florida Bar, 427 F.2d 1292 (5th Cir. 1970) **2:** 395
Dahl v. Columbia Pictures Corp., 166 N.Y.S.2d 708 (N.Y. Sup. Ct. 1957), *aff'd,* 183 N.Y.S.2d 992 (N.Y. App. Div. 1959) **6:** 117
Daily Gazette Co.
—v. Caryl, 380 S.E.2d 209, 16 Media L. Rep. 1908 (W. Va. 1989) **1:** 292
—v. Committee on Legal Ethics of W. Va. State Bar, 326 S.E.2d 705, 11 Media L. Rep. 1722 (W. Va. 1984) **1:** 289
—v. West Virginia Bd. of Medicine, 352 S.E.2d 66, 13 Media L. Rep. 2125 (W. Va. 1986) **1:** 290, 299
Daily Herald Co. v. Munro, 838 F.2d 380, 14 Media L. Rep. 2332 (9th Cir. 1988) **1:** 550, 558, 560–65; **12:** 19
Daily Record v. James, 629 S.W.2d 348, 8 Media L. Rep. 1581 (Mo. 1982) **9:** 248
Daily Times Democrat v. Graham, 162 So. 2d 474 (Ala. 1964) **4:** 58; **5:** 35, 36
Dalbec v. Gentleman's Companion, 828 F.2d 921, 14 Media L. Rep. 1705 (2d Cir. 1987) **2:** 469
Dalitz v. Penthouse Int'l, 214 Cal. Rptr. 254, 11 Media L. Rep. 2153 (Cal. Ct. App. 1985) **14:** 352–53, 382–83, 386
Dallas Ass'n of Community Orgs. for Reform Now v. Dallas County Hosp. Dist., 670 F.2d 629 (5th Cir.), *cert. denied,* 459 U.S. 1052 (1982) **12:** 105
Dallas Cowboys Cheerleaders v. Pussycat Cinema, 604 F.2d 200, 5 Media L. Rep. 1814 (2d Cir. 1979) **10:** 245–46, 254
Dallas Morning News
—v. Garcia, 822 S.W.2d 675, 19 Media L. Rep. 2033 (Tex. Ct. App. 1991) **14:** 395
—In re, 916 F.2d 205, 18 Media L. Rep. 1333 (5th Cir. 1990) **1:** 229
Dallas Oil & Gas v. Mouer, 533 S.W.2d 70 (Tex. Ct. App. 1976) **14:** 75
Dalton v. Meister, 188 N.W.2d 494 (Wis. 1971),

Dalton—*Contd.*
cert. denied, 405 U.S. 934 (1972) **2:** 583

D'Amario v. Providence Civic Center Auth., 639 F. Supp. 1538, 13 Media L. Rep. 1769 (D.R.I. 1986), *aff'd,* 815 F.2d 692 (1st Cir.), *cert. denied,* 484 U.S. 859 (1987) **1:** 548

Dameron v. Washington Magazine, 779 F.2d 736, 12 Media L. Rep. 1508 (D.C. Cir. 1985), *cert. denied,* 476 U.S. 1141 (1986) **2:** 398, 567–68

Damron v. Doubleday, Doran & Co., 231 N.Y.S. 444 (N.Y. Sup. Ct. 1928), *aff'd,* 234 N.Y.S. 773 (N.Y. App. Div. 1929) **6:** 87

Dan; People v., 342 N.Y.S.2d 731 (N.Y. App. Div. 1973) **14:** 413

Daniel v. Dow Jones & Co., 520 N.Y.S.2d 334, 14 Media L. Rep. 1995 (N.Y. Sup. Ct. 1987) **7:** 12, 16, 26, 42

Daniels v. Sanitarium Ass'n, 381 P.2d 652 (Cal. 1963) **2:** 293–94

Daniels Cablevision v. United States, 835 F. Supp. 1, 21 Media L. Rep. 2225 (D.D.C. 1993) **13:** 542

Danziger v. Hearst Corp., 107 N.E.2d 62 (N.Y. 1952) **2:** 560, 562

Darby v. Stender, 8 Media L. Rep. 1508 (D.N.J. 1982) **9:** 45

Daugherty v. City of East Point, 447 F. Supp. 290 (N.D. Ga. 1978) **12:** 169

Dauw v. Field Enters., 397 N.E.2d 41, 5 Media L. Rep. 1893 (Ill. App. Ct. 1979) **2:** 146

Davidson
—v. Rogers, 574 P.2d 624, 3 Media L. Rep. 2030 (Or. 1978) **2:** 612
—v. City of Westminster, 185 Cal. Rptr. 252, 649 P.2d 894 (Cal. 1984) **8:** 36

Davis
—v. Bucher, 853 F.2d 718 (9th Cir. 1988) **9:** 61, 63
—v. Costa-Gavras, 580 F. Supp. 1082, 10 Media L. Rep. 1257 (S.D.N.Y. 1984) **2:** 475
—v. Forbes, Inc., 10 Media L. Rep. 1272 (N.D. Tex. 1983) **4:** 196; **10:** 238
—v. Hearst, 116 P. 530 (Cal. 1911) **2:** 222
—v. High Soc'y Magazine, 457 N.Y.S.2d 308, 9 Media L. Rep. 1164 (N.Y. App. Div. 1982), *appeal dismissed,* 58 N.Y.2d 1115 (1983) **6:** 24, 27, 43, 85
—v. Littell, 398 F.2d 83, 85 (9th Cir. 1968), *cert. denied,* 393 U.S. 1018 (1969) **2:** 528
—v. Massachusetts, 167 U.S. 43 (1897) **12:** 57
—v. NBC, 320 F. Supp. 1070 (E.D. La. 1970), *aff'd,* 447 F.2d 981 (5th Cir. 1971) **2:** 225
—v. Schuchat, 510 F.2d 731, 738 (D.C. Cir. 1975) **2:** 586
—v. Trans World Airlines, 297 F. Supp. 1145 (C.D. Cal. 1969) **6:** 39

Dean
—v. Guard Pub'g Co.
——699 P.2d 1158 (Or. Ct. App. 1985) **3:** 83
——744 P.2d 1296, 14 Media L. Rep. 2100 (Or. Ct. App. 1987) **3:** 54
—United States v., 5 Media L. Rep. 2595 (S.D. Ga. 1980) **1:** 152

Dear v. Rathje, 391 F. Supp. 1 (N.D. Ill. 1975) **9:** 65

Deaton v. Delta Democrat Pub'g Co., 326 So. 2d 471 (Miss. 1976) **4:** 158

De Bardeleben Marine Corp. v. United States, 451 F.2d 140 (5th Cir. 1971) **7:** 45–48

Debs v. United States, 249 U.S. 211 (1919) **8:** 46

Decker v. Princeton Packet, 561 A.2d 1122, 16 Media L. Rep. 2194 (N.J. 1989) **7:** 16

Deese v. Collins, 133 S.E. 92 (N.C. 1926) **2:** 196

DeFalco v. Anderson, 506 A.2d 1280, 12 Media L. Rep. 2125 (N.J. Super Ct. App. Div. 1986) **2:** 140

DeFilippo v. NBC, 446 A.2d 1036, 8 Media L. Rep. 1872 (R.I. 1982) **8:** 2, 7, 11–12, 14, 20–21, 24–27, 43, 48, 50, 60–61, 89–90

Delan v. CBS, Inc., 445 N.Y.S.2d 898, 7 Media L. Rep. 2453 (N.Y. Sup. Ct. 1981), *rev'd,* 458 N.Y.S.2d 608, 9 Media L. Rep. 1130 (N.Y. App. Div. 1983) **5:** 115; **6:** 18, 24, 74, 87

Delaney v. Superior Ct. (Kopetman), 789 P.2d 934 (Cal. 1990) **14:** 199–200, 202, 204, 339, 361, 426, 432

Delaware v. McBride, 7 Media L. Rep. 1371 (Del. Super. Ct. 1981) **14:** 70, 79

De Libellis Farnosis, 77 Eng. Rep. 250 (1606) **2:** 280

DeMay v. Roberts, 9 N.W. 146 (Mich. 1881) **5:** 11, 34

Democratic Nat'l Comm.
—25 F.C.C.2d 216 (1970) **13:** 31, 154
—v. FCC, 717 F.2d 1471 (D.C. Cir. 1983) **13:** 153, 161

De Mott v. Amalgamated Meat Cutters, 320 P.2d 50 (Cal. Ct. App. 1958) **2:** 544

Dempsey v. National Enquirer
—687 F. Supp. 692, 15 Media L. Rep. 2193 (D. Me. 1988) **3:** 54
—702 F. Supp. 927, 16 Media L. Rep. 1396 (D. Me. 1988) **3:** 51; **5:** 13, 16, 30, 41

Demuth Dev. Corp. v. Merck & Co., 432 F. Supp. 990, 3 Media L. Rep. 1092 (E.D.N.Y. 1977) **7:** 9, 12, 17, 23, 43

Denis v. Rhinelander, 11 Media L. Rep. 2141 (W.D. Mich. 1985) **9:** 45

Denk v. Iowa Dist. Ct., 20 Media L. Rep. 1454 (Iowa 1992) **14:** 416

Dennis
—v. Sparks, 449 U.S. 24 (1980) *9:* 44
—Commonwealth v., 329 N.E.2d 706 (Mass. 1975) *12:* 212
Denny v. Mertz, 318 N.W.2d 141, 8 Media L. Rep. 1369 (Wis.), *cert. denied,* 459 U.S. 883 (1982) *2:* 466, 471, 473
DePalma; United States v., 466 F. Supp. 917 (S.D.N.Y. 1979) *14:* 432
DeRoburt v. Gannett Co.
—733 F.2d 701, 10 Media L. Rep. 1898 (9th Cir. 1984), *cert. denied,* 469 U.S. 1159 (1985) *2:* 529
—507 F. Supp. 860, 6 Media L. Rep. 2473 (D. Haw. 1981) *14:* 356
Desai v. Hersh, 954 F.2d 1408, 19 Media L. Rep. 1893 (7th Cir.), *cert. denied,* 113 S. Ct. 190 (1992) *14:* 395
Des Granges v. Crall, 149 P. 777 (Cal. Ct. App. 1915) *2:* 141
Des Moines Register & Tribune Co.
—v. Iowa Dist. Ct., 426 N.W.2d 142 (Iowa 1988) *1:* 156
—v. Osmundson, 248 N.W.2d 493, 2 Media L. Rep. 1321 (Iowa 1976) *1:* 525; *10:* 194
Destination Ventures v. FCC, 22 Media L. Rep. 1171 (D. Or. 1993) *12:* 250
Detroit Free Press
—v. Macomb Circuit Judge, 275 N.W.2d 482, 4 Media L. Rep. 2180 (Mich. 1979) *1:* 217
—v. Recorder's Ct. Judge, 294 N.W.2d 827, 6 Media L. Rep. 1586 (Mich. 1980) *1:* 212
Deupree v. Iliff, 860 F.2d 300, 15 Media L. Rep. 2225 (8th Cir. 1988) *2:* 247
Dexter's Hearthside Restaurant v. Whitehall Co., 508 N.E.2d 113, 14 Media L. Rep. 1664 (Mass. Ct. App. 1987) *2:* 302
DeYoung v. Patten, 898 F.2d 628, 17 Media L. Rep. 2446 (8th Cir. 1990) *13:* 104, 397
Diamond v. World News Corp., 542 F. Supp. 887 (S.D.N.Y. 1982) *13:* 214
Diaz
—v. Oakland Tribune, 139 Cal. App. 3d 118 (1983) *4:* 71, 131, 135, 137, 152, 194
—v. Watts, 189 Cal. App. 3d 657, 234 Cal. Rptr. 334 (Cal. Ct. App. 1987) *13:* 331
DiBona v. Matthews, 220 Cal. App. 3d 1329, 269 Cal. Rptr. 882 (1990) *13:* 335
Dickey v. CBS, Inc., 583 F.2d 1221, 4 Media L. Rep. 1353 (3d Cir. 1978) *2:* 434, 580
Dickinson
—United States v. (Dickinson I), 465 F.2d 496, 1 Media L. Rep. 1338 (5th Cir. 1972) *10:* 80, 86
—United States v. (Dickinson II), 476 F.2d 373 (5th Cir.), *cert. denied,* 414 U.S. 979 (1973) *10:* 85

Dickinson Newspapers v. Jorgensen, 338 N.W.2d 72, 9 Media L. Rep. 2063 (N.D. 1983) *1:* 152, 155
Didrichsons; United States v., 15 Media L. Rep. 1869 (W.D. Wash. 1988) *1:* 161, 279
Dietemann v. Time, Inc., 449 F.2d 245, 1 Media L. Rep. 2417 (9th Cir. 1971) *4:* 56; *5:* 37, 50, 52–55, 67–71, 136, 266
DiGilio; United States v., 538 F.2d 972 (3d Cir. 1976), *cert. denied,* 429 U.S. 1038 (1977) *5:* 164
Dillon v. San Francisco, 748 F. Supp. 722 (N.D. Cal. 1990) *14:* 371
Dills
—v. Cobb County, 755 F.2d 1473 (11th Cir. 1985) *12:* 185
—v. City of Marietta, 674 F.2d 1377 (11th Cir. 1982), *cert. denied,* 461 U.S. 905 (1983) *12:* 183, 185
Di Lorenzo v. New York News, 432 N.Y.S.2d 483, 6 Media L. Rep. 2136 (N.Y. App. Div. 1981) *2:* 611
Diplomat Elec. v. Westinghouse Elec. Supply Co., 378 F.2d 377 (5th Cir. 1967) *2:* 135
Diportanova v. New York News, 6 Media L. Rep. 1376 (1980), *aff'd,* 440 N.Y.S.2d 535, 7 Media L. Rep. 1187 (N.Y. App. Div. 1981) *6:* 33
Dirks v. Securities & Exch. Comm'n, 463 U.S. 646 (1983) *9:* 170
DiSalle v. P.G. Pub'g Co., 544 A.2d 1345, 15 Media L. Rep. 1873 (Pa. Super. Ct. 1988), *cert. denied,* 492 U.S. 906 (1989) *2:* 459
Dispatch Printing Co. v. Solove, *see* T.R., In re
Distribution Sys. v. Old Westbury, 19 Media L. Rep. 2071 (E.D.N.Y. 1992) *12:* 162
Diversified Mgmt. v. Denver Post, 653 P.2d 1103, 8 Media L. Rep. 2505 (Colo. 1982) *2:* 468
Dixon v. Pennsylvania Crime Comm'n, 67 F.R.D. 425 (M.D. Pa. 1975) *9:* 64
Dixson v. Newsweek, 562 F.2d 626, 3 Media L. Rep. 1123 (10th Cir. 1977) *2:* 221, 223
Dodrill v. Arkansas Democrat Co., 590 S.W.2d 840, 5 Media L. Rep. 1385 (Ark. 1979), *cert. denied,* 444 U.S. 1076 (1980) *3:* 83, 86
Doe
—v. ABC, 543 N.Y.S.2d 455 (N.Y. App. Div. 1989) *14:* 457
—v. District of Columbia, 697 F.2d 1115 (D.C. Cir. 1983) *1:* 405
—v. Doe, 941 F.2d 280, 19 Media L. Rep. 1705 (5th Cir. 1991) *2:* 548
—v. Florida Judicial Qualifications Comm'n, 748 F. Supp. 1520, 18 Media L. Rep. 1433 (S.D. Fla. 1990) *4:* 82

Doe—*Contd.*
—v. Roe
——345 N.Y.S.2d 560 (N.Y. App. Div.), *aff'd,* 307 N.E.2d 823 (N.Y. 1973), *cert. dismissed,* 420 U.S. 307 (1975) *10:* 238
——495 A.2d 1235, 12 Media L. Rep. 1219 (Me. 1985) *1:* 456
—v. Sarasota-Bradenton Fla. Television, 436 So. 2d 328, 9 Media L. Rep. 2074 (Fla. Dist. Ct. App. 1983) *4:* 97, 173, 176
—v. Stephens, 851 F.2d 1457 (D.C. Cir. 1988) *14:* 472
—v. Supreme Ct. of Fla., 17 Media L. Rep. 1405 (S.D. Fla. 1990) *4:* 82
—United States v., 460 F.2d 328 (1st Cir. 1972), *cert. denied sub nom.* Popkin v. United States, 411 U.S. 909 (1973) *14:* 308
Doherty; United States v., 675 F. Supp. 719, 14 Media L. Rep. 1406 (D. Mass. 1987) *1:* 526
Dombey v. Phoenix Newspapers, 724 P.2d 562, 13 Media L. Rep. 1282 (Ariz. 1986) *2:* 442
Dombrowski v. Pfister, 380 U.S. 479 (1965) *2:* 26
Don King Prods. v. Douglas, 131 F.R.D. 421 (S.D.N.Y. 1990) *14:* 151, 157–58, 374
Donovan
—In re, 801 F.2d 409, 13 Media L. Rep. 1233 (D.C. Cir. 1986) *1:* 162
—v. R.D. Andersen Constr. Co., 552 F. Supp. 249 (D. Kan. 1982) *1:* 527
Donrey Communications v. Fayetteville, 660 S.W.2d 900 (Ark. 1983), *cert. denied,* 466 U.S. 959 (1984) *12:* 190
Don's Porta Signs v. City of Clearwater, 829 F.2d 1051 (11th Cir. 1987), *cert. denied,* 485 U.S. 981 (1988) *12:* 177, 181, 185
Dorfman
—v. Meiszner, 430 F.2d 558, 1 Media L. Rep. 2396 (7th Cir. 1970) *1:* 569
—United States v., 690 F.2d 1230, 8 Media L. Rep. 2257 (7th Cir. 1982) *1:* 380
Dorman v. Aiken Communications, 398 S.E.2d 687, 18 Media L. Rep. 1394 (S.C. 1990) *4:* 96
Dorr v. C.B. Johnson, Inc., 660 P.2d 517 (Colo. Ct. App. 1983) *2:* 205, 628
Dorsey v. National Enquirer, 952 F.2d 250, 19 Media L. Rep. 1673 (9th Cir. 1991) *2:* 553
Douglas v. Wainwright, 714 F.2d 1532, 9 Media L. Rep. 2457 (11th Cir.), *vacated and remanded,* 468 U.S. 1206 (1984), *aff'd,* 739 F.2d 531 (11th Cir. 1984), *cert. denied,* 469 U.S. 1208 (1985) *1:* 213–15
Douglass v. Hustler Magazine, 769 F.2d 1128, 11 Media L. Rep. 2264 (7th Cir. 1985), *cert. denied,* 475 U.S. 1094 (1986) *2:* 596; *3:* 15, 51, 87; *6:* 46

Dowd v. Calabrese, 577 F. Supp. 238 (D.D.C. 1983) *14:* 151, 359
Dowdy; State v., 563 P.2d 425 (Kan. 1977) *5:* 260
Dow Jones & Co.
—In re, 842 F.2d 603, 15 Media L. Rep. 1105 (2d Cir.), *cert. denied sub nom.* Dow Jones & Co. v. Simon, 488 U.S. 946, 15 Media L. Rep. 2159 (1988) *10:* 217–21, 223
—v. Oklahoma, 787 P.2d 843, 16 Media L. Rep. 2049 (Okla. 1989) *9:* 234
—v. Simon, *see* In re Dow Jones & Co.
—v. Superior Ct., 303 N.E.2d 847 (Mass. 1973) *14:* 71
Dowling; United States v., 473 U.S. 214 (1985) *5:* 162
Downing v. Monitor Pub'g Co., 415 A.2d 683, 6 Media L. Rep. 1193 (N.H. 1980) *14:* 352
Drake; State v., 701 S.W.2d 604, 12 Media L. Rep. 1488 (Tenn. 1985) *1:* 147
Dresbach v. Doubleday & Co., 518 F. Supp. 1285, 7 Media L. Rep. 2105 (D.D.C. 1981) *2:* 162; *3:* 83; *4:* 4, 119, 121
Drinkwine v. Federated Pubns., 780 F.2d 735 (9th Cir. 1985), *cert. denied,* 475 U.S. 1087 (1986) *13:* 230
Driscoll v. Morris, 111 F.R.D. 459 (D. Conn. 1986) *14:* 354, 382–83, 385
Duff v. Sherlock, 432 F. Supp. 423 (E.D. Pa. 1977) *9:* 55
Dumez v. Houma Mun. Fire & Police Civil Serv. Bd., 341 So. 2d 1206 (La. Ct. App. 1976), *cert. denied,* 344 So. 2d 667 (La. 1977) *14:* 225
Dunagin v. City of Oxford, 718 F.2d 738, 10 Media L. Rep. 1001 (5th Cir. 1983), *cert. denied,* 467 U.S. 1259 (1984) *11:* 113, 134, 137, 183–84, 196–99
Dun & Bradstreet
—v. Greenmoss Builders, 472 U.S. 749, 11 Media L. Rep. 2417 (1985) *2:* 84, 93, 403, 464, 471, 473, 504–5; *14:* 303
—v. Grove, 404 U.S. 898 (1971) *11:* 67
—v. Robinson, 345 S.W.2d 34 (Ark. 1961) *2:* 186
Duncan v. WJLA-TV, 10 Media L. Rep. 1395 (D.D.C. 1984) *3:* 8, 32, 44
Dunn v. Gannett N.Y. Newspapers, 833 F.2d 446, 14 Media L. Rep. 1871 (3d Cir. 1987) *2:* 445
Dunnebacke v. Williams, 381 S.W.2d 909 (Tenn. 1964) *2:* 189, 195, 197
Duryea; People v., 351 N.Y.S.2d 978 (N.Y. Sup. Ct. 1974), *aff'd,* 354 N.Y.S.2d 129 (N.Y. App. Div. 1974) *12:* 212
Dworkin v. Hustler Magazine
—867 F.2d 1188, 16 Media L. Rep. 1113 (9th

Cir.), *cert. denied,* 493 U.S. 812 (1989)   *2:* 125, 507, 687
—634 F. Supp. 727, 12 Media L. Rep. 2162 (D. Wyo. 1986)   *2:* 222; *9:* 72; *10:* 239

E

Eadie v. Pole, 221 A.2d 547 (N.J. Super. Ct. App. Div. 1966)   *2:* 134
Eagle Printing Co. v. Delaney, 671 S.W.2d 883, 10 Media L. Rep. 2098 (Tex. Crim. App. 1984)   *1:* 162
Eason Pub'g v. Atlanta Gazette, 233 S.E.2d 232 (Ga. 1977)   *2:* 293–95
Eastern Airlines; United States v., 923 F.2d 241, 18 Media L. Rep. 1714 (2d Cir. 1991)   *1:* 377
Eastern Conn. Citizens Action Group v. Powers, 723 F.2d 1050 (2d Cir. 1983)   *12:* 23, 159
Eastern R.R. Presidents Conf. v. Noerr Motor Freight, 365 U.S. 127 (1961)   *13:* 240
Eastern States Retail Lumber Dealers Ass'n v. United States, 234 U.S. 600 (1914)   *13:* 213
Easter Seal Soc'y v. Playboy Enters., 530 So. 2d 643, 15 Media L. Rep. 2384 (La. Ct. App. 1988)   *3:* 51, 55
Easton v. Public Citizen, 19 Media L. Rep. 1882 (S.D.N.Y. 1991), *aff'd,* 969 F.2d 1043 (2d Cir. 1992)   *2:* 552, 570
Eastwood
—v. Cascade Broadcasting Co., 722 P.2d 1295, 13 Media L. Rep. 1136 (Wash. 1986)   *3:* 18, 113
—v. Superior Ct., 198 Cal. Rptr. 342, 10 Media L. Rep. 1073 (Cal. Ct. App. 1983)   *6:* 19, 44, 133, 135, 148, 152, 163
Eaves; United States v., 685 F. Supp 1243, 15 Media L. Rep. 1300 (N.D. Ga. 1988)   *1:* 352
Edenfield v. Fane, 945 F.2d 1514 (11th Cir. 1991), *aff'd,* 113 S. Ct. 1792, 21 Media L. Rep. 1321 (1993)   *11:* 89, 126, 156, 176–80, 318, 325
Edge Broadcasting Co.; United States v., 732 F. Supp. 633, 17 Media L. Rep. 1649 (E.D. Va. 1990), *aff'd,* 956 F.2d 263, 20 Media L. Rep. 1904 (4th Cir. 1992), *rev'd,* 113 S. Ct. 2696, 21 Media L. Rep. 1577 (1993)   *11:* 150–53, 156, 174, 259–72
Edmonds v. Delta Democrat Pub'g Co., 93 So. 2d 171 (Miss. 1957)   *2:* 679
Edward A. Sherman Pub'g Co. v. Goldberg, 443 A.2d 1252, 8 Media L. Rep. 1489 (R.I. 1982)   *1:* 243, 257–58

Edwards
—v. National Audubon Soc'y, 556 F.2d 113, 2 Media L. Rep. 1849 (2d Cir.), *cert. denied,* 434 U.S. 1002, 3 Media L. Rep. 1560 (1977)   *2:* 259–60, 267–68, 431, 574–78
—v. South Carolina, 372 U.S. 229 (1963)   *2:* 693; *12:* 64
—v. State Farm Ins. Co., 833 F.2d 535 (5th Cir. 1987)   *5:* 243
—United States v.
——672 F.2d 1289, 8 Media L. Rep. 1145 (7th Cir. 1982)   *1:* 353
——785 F.2d 1293, 12 Media L. Rep. 1997 (5th Cir. 1986)   *1:* 580, 637
——430 A.2d 1321, 7 Media L. Rep. 1324 (D.C. 1981), *cert. denied,* 455 U.S. 1022 (1982)   *1:* 172
——823 F.2d 111, 14 Media L. Rep. 1399 (5th Cir. 1987), *cert. denied sub nom.* Times-Picayune Pub'g Corp. v. Edwards, 485 U.S. 934 (1988)   *1:* 194, 278, 526
EEOC v. McKellar Dev., 13 Media L. Rep. 1061 (N.D. Cal. 1986)   *14:* 302
Eick v. Perk Dog Food Co., 106 N.E.2d 742 (Ill. App. Ct. 1952)   *6:* 50
Eimann v. Soldier of Fortune Magazine, 880 F.2d 830, 16 Media L. Rep. 2148 (5th Cir. 1989), *cert. denied,* 493 U.S. 1024 (1990)   *7:* 78–90
Eisner v. Stamford Bd. of Educ., 440 F.2d 803 (2d Cir. 1971)   *13:* 334–35
Elder; State v., 143 P. 482 (N.M. 1914)   *2:* 155
Ellenberg v. Pinkerton's, Inc., 202 S.E.2d 701 (Ga. Ct. App. 1973)   *5:* 40, 78
Ellingburg v. Lucas, 518 F.2d 1196 (8th Cir. 1975)   *9:* 48
Elliott v. Roach, 409 N.E.2d 661, 684 (Ind. Ct. App. 1980)   *2:* 582
Ellis
—v. Brockton Pub'g Co., 84 N.E. 1018 (Mass. 1908)   *2:* 616
—United States v., 8 Media L. Rep. 1868 (D. Mass. 1982)   *1:* 148
El-Em Band of Pomo Indians v. 49th Dist. Agric. Fair Ass'n, 359 F. Supp. 1044 (N.D. Cal. 1973)   *9:* 48
Elvis Presley Enters. v. Elvisly Yours, 817 F.2d 104, 14 Media L. Rep. 1053 (6th Cir. 1987)   *6:* 189
Elvis Presley Int'l Memorial Found. v. Crowell, 733 S.W.2d 89, 14 Media L. Rep. 1043 (Tenn. Ct. App. 1987)   *6:* 186
El Vocero de Puerto Rico v. Puerto Rico, 113 S. Ct. 2004, 21 Media L. Rep. 1440 (1993)   *1:* 82, 84, 156
Embrey v. Holly, 429 A.2d 251 (Md. Ct. Spec.

Embrey—Contd.

App. 1981), *rev'd in part,* 442 A.2d 966, 8 Media L. Rep. 1409 (Md. 1982) *2:* 154

England v. Automatic Canteen Co. of Am., 349 F.2d 989 (6th Cir. 1965) *2:* 146

Enterprise, Inc. v. United States, 833 F.2d 1216, 14 Media L. Rep. 2153 (6th Cir. 1987) *9:* 272, 280

Environmental Planning Council v. El Dorado Super. Ct., 36 Cal. 3d 188, 680 P.2d 1086 (Cal. 1984) *9:* 94

Epperson v. Arkansas, 393 U.S. 97 (1968) *13:* 356

Equal Employment Opportunity Comm'n, *see* EEOC

Erie Ry. Co. v. Tompkins, 304 U.S. 64 (1938) *14:* 373

Erie Telecommunications v. Erie, 659 F. Supp. 580 (W.D. Pa. 1987), *aff'd,* 853 F.2d 1084 (3d Cir. 1988) *12:* 235, 241

Ernst & Ernst v. Hochfelder, 425 U.S. 185 (1976) *9:* 140

Erznoznik v. Jacksonville, 422 U.S. 205, 1 Media L. Rep. 1508 (1975) *12:* 27

Estate of, *see* name of party

Estes v. Texas, 381 U.S. 532, 1 Media L. Rep. 1187 (1965) *1:* 11, 571, 573, 581–614

Estiverne v. Louisiana State Bar Ass'n, 863 F.2d 371, 16 Media L. Rep. 1481 (5th Cir. 1989) *13:* 399

Ettore v. Philco Television Broadcasting Corp., 229 F.2d 481 (3d Cir.), *cert. denied,* 351 U.S. 926 (1956) *2:* 230; *4:* 36

Evangelize China Fellowship, Inc. v. Evangelize China Fellowship, 146 Cal. App. 3d 440, 194 Cal. Rptr. 240 (Cal. Ct. App. 1983) *2:* 669

Evans

—v. Philadelphia Newspapers, 601 A.2d 330, 19 Media L. Rep. 1868 (Pa. Super. Ct. 1991) *2:* 624

—United States v., 16 Media L. Rep. 1174 (N.D. Ga. 1989) *1:* 358

Evenson v. Ortega, 605 F. Supp. 1115 (D. Ariz. 1985) *11:* 308; *13:* 242

Eversole v. Superior Ct., 195 Cal. Rptr. 816, 9 Media L. Rep. 2436 (Cal. Ct. App. 1983) *1:* 210

Ex parte, *see* name of party

Express News Corp., In re, 695 F.2d 807, 9 Media L. Rep. 1001 (5th Cir. 1982) *1:* 523

F

Faber v. Byrle, 229 P.2d 718 (Kan. 1951) *2:* 533

Factors Etc.

—v. Creative Card Co., 444 F. Supp. 279, 3 Media L. Rep. 1290 (S.D.N.Y. 1977), *aff'd,* 579 F.2d 215, 4 Media L. Rep. 1144 (2d Cir. 1978), *cert. denied,* 440 U.S. 908 (1979) *6:* 145

—v. Pro Arts

——579 F.2d 215, 4 Media L. Rep. 1144 (2d Cir. 1978), *cert. denied,* 440 U.S. 908 (1979) *6:* 74, 128, 201

——496 F. Supp. 1090 (S.D.N.Y. 1980), *rev'd,* 652 F.2d 278, 7 Media L. Rep. 1617 (2d Cir. 1981), *cert. denied,* 456 U.S. 927 (1982) *6:* 47, 97, 102, 159

Fadell v. Minneapolis Star & Tribune Co., 425 F. Supp. 1075, 2 Media L. Rep. 1961 (N.D. Ind. 1976), *aff'd,* 557 F.2d 107, 2 Media L. Rep. 2198 (7th Cir. 1977), *cert. denied,* 434 U.S. 966, 3 Media L. Rep. 1432 (1977) *2:* 325, 670, 675

Fadjo v. Coon, 633 F.2d 1172 (5th Cir. 1981) *9:* 61

Fairbanks Pub'g Co. v. Pitka, 376 P.2d 190 (Alaska 1962) *2:* 222, 481

Fairfield v. American Photocopy Equip. Co., 291 P.2d 194 (Cal. Ct. App. 1955) *6:* 51, 133

Faloona v. Hustler Magazine, 607 F. Supp. 1341 (N.D. Tex. 1985), *aff'd,* 799 F.2d 1000, 13 Media L. Rep. 1354 (5th Cir. 1986), *cert. denied,* 479 U.S. 1088 (1987) *3:* 50, 90; *4:* 48; *6:* 37, 119

Falwell v. Flynt, 797 F.2d 1270, 13 Media L. Rep. 1145 (4th Cir. 1986), *rev'd,* 485 U.S. 46, 14 Media L. Rep. 2281 (1988) *6:* 26

Family Counseling Serv. v. Rust, 462 F. Supp. 74 (D. Nev. 1978) *11:* 295

Farber

—In re, 394 A.2d 330 (N.J.), *cert. denied sub nom.* New York Times Co. v. New Jersey, 439 U.S. 997 (1978) *14:* 247, 361–62, 434

—v. Cornils, 487 P.2d 689 (Idaho 1971) *2:* 299

Fargo Women's Health Org. v. Larson, 381 N.W.2d 176 (N.D.), *cert. denied,* 476 U.S. 1108 (1986) *11:* 47, 82, 287

Farha; State v., 544 P.2d 341 (Kan. 1975), *cert. denied,* 426 U.S. 949 (1976) *5:* 260

Farmers Educ. & Coop. Union v. WDAY, Inc., 360 U.S. 525 (1959) *2:* 527; *13:* 88–89, 112

Farnsworth v. Hyde, 512 P. 1003 (Or. 1973) *2:* 155

Farr v. Pitchess, 522 F.2d 464 (9th Cir. 1975), *cert. denied,* 427 U.S. 912 (1976) *14:* 47, 57, 67, 90

Fasching v. Kallinger, 510 A.2d 694 (N.J. Super. Ct. App. Div. 1986) *9:* 249, 258, 263–64

Faucheux v. Magazine Mgmt. Co., 5 Media L. Rep. 1697 (E.D. La. 1979) *3:* 51, 90; *4:* 182

Fawcett Pubns. v. Morris, 377 P.2d 42 (Okla. 1962), *cert. denied and appeal dismissed,* 376 U.S. 513 (1964) *2:* 307

Fawley v. Quirk, 11 Media L. Rep. 2336 (Ohio Ct. App. 1985) *14:* 76

FCC
—v. ABC, 347 U.S. 284 (1954) *11:* 249–50
—v. Allentown Broadcasting Corp., 349 U.S. 358 (1955) *13:* 27
—v. League of Women Voters, 468 U.S. 364 (1984) *13:* 75, 77–78, 85, 174
—v. National Citizens Comm. for Broadcasting, 436 U.S. 775 (1978) *9:* 21
—v. Pacifica Found., 438 U.S. 726, 3 Media L. Rep. 2553 (1978) *10:* 3; *12:* 52, 113; *13:* 535
—v. Pottsville Broadcasting Co., 309 U.S. 134 (1940) *13:* 448
—v. Sanders Bros. Radio Station, 309 U.S. 470 (1940) *13:* 27

Federal Communications Comm'n, *see* FCC

Federal Election Comm'n
—v. Machinists Non-Partisan Political League, 655 F.2d 380 (D.C. Cir.), *cert. denied,* 454 U.S. 897 (1981) *9:* 113
—v. Massachusetts Citizens for Life, 479 U.S. 238 (1986) *9:* 114–20
—v. Phillips Pub'g, 517 F. Supp. 1308, 7 Media L. Rep. 1825 (D.D.C. 1981) *9:* 109–13

Federal Trade Comm'n, *see* FTC

Federated Pubns.
—v. Kurtz, 615 P.2d 440, 6 Media L. Rep. 1577 (Wash. 1980) *1:* 147–49
—v. Swedberg, 633 P.2d 74, 7 Media L. Rep. 1865 (Wash. 1981), *cert. denied,* 456 U.S. 984 (1982) *1:* 143, 145, 148

Feeney, State ex rel. v. District Ct. of Seventh Judicial Dist., 607 P.2d 1259, 6 Media L. Rep. 1174 (Wyo. 1980) *1:* 152

Feiner v. New York, 340 U.S. 315 (1951) *12:* 206

Felix v. Westinghouse Radio Stations, 186 F.2d 1 (3d Cir. 1950) *13:* 107

Fellows v. National Enquirer, 42 Cal. 3d 234, 721 P.2d 97, 13 Media L. Rep. 1305 (Cal. 1986) *2:* 688; *3:* 110; *4:* 37

Felmet; State v., 273 S.E.2d 708 (N.C. 1981) *12:* 90

Fenstermaker; Commonwealth v., 530 A.2d 414, 14 Media L. Rep. 1555 (1987) *1:* 373

Fernandes v. Tenbruggencate, 649 P.2d 1144, 8 Media L. Rep. 2577 (Haw. 1982) *2:* 127

Fernandez v. Progress Printing Co., 670 P.2d 611 (Okla. Ct. App. 1983) *13:* 207

Festival Enters. v. Pleasant Hill, 227 Cal. Rptr. 601 (Cal. Ct. App. 1986) *9:* 235

Figari v. New York Tel. Co., 303 N.Y.S.2d 245 (N.Y. App. Div. 1969) *12:* 214

Finger v. Omni Pubns. Int'l, 566 N.E.2d 141, 18 Media L. Rep. 1555 (N.Y. 1990) *6:* 26

Finkel v. Stratton Corp., 962 F.2d 169 (2d Cir. 1992) *9:* 156

Finley; United States v., 16 Media L. Rep. 1735 (N.D. Ill. 1989) *1:* 358

Firestone v. News-Press Pub'g Co., 538 So. 2d 457, 16 Media L. Rep. 1265 (Fla. 1989) *1:* 565, 567

First Amendment Coaliton v. Judicial Inquiry & Review Bd., 784 F.2d 467, 12 Media L. Rep. 1753 (3d Cir. 1986) *1:* 296–303

First Equity of Fla. v. Standard & Poor's Corp., 670 F. Supp. 115, 14 Media L. Rep. 1945 (S.D.N.Y. 1987), *dismissed,* 690 F. Supp. 256, 15 Media L. Rep. 1858 (S.D.N.Y. 1988), *aff'd,* 869 F.2d 175, 16 Media L. Rep. 1282 (2d Cir. 1989) *7:* 9, 12, 17, 44, 50, 52

First Indep. Baptist Church v. Southerland, 373 So. 2d 647 (Ala. 1979) *2:* 175

First Nat'l Bank of Boston v. Bellotti, 435 U.S. 765, 3 Media L. Rep. 2105 (1978) *11:* 139

Fischer v. McGowan, 585 F. Supp. 978 (D.R.I. 1984) *14:* 295, 374, 408–9

Fisher
—v. Larsen, 188 Cal. Rptr. 216 (Cal. Ct. App. 1982), *cert. denied,* 464 U.S. 959 (1983) *2:* 619
—v. Washington Post Co., 212 A.2d 335 (D.C. 1965) *2:* 274

Fitch v. Voit, 624 So. 2d 542, 21 Media L. Rep. 1863 (Ala. 1993) *4:* 32

Fitzgerald v. Penthouse Int'l, 525 F. Supp. 585, 7 Media L. Rep. 2385 (D. Md. 1981), *aff'd in part and rev'd in part,* 691 F.2d 666, 8 Media L. Rep. 2340 (4th Cir. 1982), *cert. denied,* 460 U.S. 1024 (1983) *2:* 395; *3:* 83

Fleck Bros. Co. v. Sullivan, 423 F.2d 155 (7th Cir. 1970) *2:* 184

Fleming v. Moore, 275 S.E.2d 632, 7 Media L. Rep. 1313 (Va. 1981) *2:* 179, 193

Fletcher v. San Jose Mercury News, 264 Cal. Rptr. 699, 17 Media L. Rep. 1321 (Cal. Ct. App. 1990), *cert. denied,* 111 S. Ct. 51 (1990) *2:* 424

Fleury v. Harper & Row, Pubrs., 698 F.2d 1022, 9 Media L. Rep. 1200 (9th Cir.), *cert. denied,* 464 U.S. 846 (1983) *2:* 639–40; *3:* 107

Flip Side v. Chicago Tribune Co., 564 N.E.2d 1244, 18 Media L. Rep. 1409 (Ill. App. Ct. 1990), *appeal denied,* 571 N.E.2d 147 (Ill. 1991) *2:* 156

Flores v. Mosler Safe Co., 164 N.E.2d 853, 196 N.Y.S.2d 975 (N.Y. 1959) *6:* 29, 42, 148

Florida
—v. Peterson, 7 Media L. Rep. 1090 (Fla. Cir. Ct. 1981) *14:* 76
—v. Riley, 490 U.S. 1014 (1989) *5:* 33, 194

Florida Businessmen for Free Enter. v. Hollywood, 673 F.2d 1213 (11th Cir. 1982) *11:* 305

Florida Dep't of Revenue v. Magazine Pubrs. of Am., 565 So. 2d 1304 (Fla.), *vacated and remanded,* 111 S. Ct. 1614 (1991), *aff'd,* 604 So. 2d 459, 20 Media L. Rep. 1502 (Fla. 1992) *9:* 243

Florida Freedom Newspapers v. McCrary, 520 So. 2d 32, 14 Media L. Rep. 2374 (Fla. 1988) *1:* 161; *10:* 217

Florida Pub'g Co.
—v. Brooke, 576 So. 2d 842, 18 Media L. Rep. 1978 (Fla. Dist. Ct. App. 1991) *10:* 194
—v. Fletcher, 319 So. 2d 100 (Fla. Dist. Ct. App. 1975), *rev'd,* 340 So. 2d 914, 2 Media L. Rep. 1088 (Fla. 1976), *cert. denied,* 431 U.S. 930 (1977) *5:* 83–92, 95, 97, 99–107, 141
—v. Morgan, 322 S.E.2d 233, 11 Media L. Rep. 1021 (Ga. 1984) *1:* 253

Florida Star v. B.J.F., 491 U.S. 524, 16 Media L. Rep. 1801 (1989) *4:* 38, 42, 70, 91–96, 98–104, 106–7, 163, 171, 195; *5:* 75, 158

Flower v. United States, 407 U.S. 197 (1972) *12:* 75, 78, 101, 104

Fluor Corp. v. Jeppesen & Co., 170 Cal. App. 3d 468, 216 Cal. Rptr. 68 (Cal. Ct. App. 1985) *7:* 51

Flynn
—v. Associated Press, 519 N.E.2d 1304, 15 Media L. Rep. 1265 (Mass. 1988) *2:* 627
—v. Higham, 197 Cal. Rptr. 145 (Cal. Ct. App. 1983) *2:* 687

Flynt v. Weinberger, 588 F. Supp. 57, 10 Media L. Rep. 1978 (D.D.C. 1984), *aff'd and vacated,* 762 F.2d 134, 11 Media L. Rep. 2118 (D.C. Cir. 1985) *1:* 536–38

FMC Corp. v. Capital Cities/ABC, 915 F.2d 300, 18 Media L. Rep. 1195 (7th Cir. 1990) *5:* 157

Fogel v. Forbes, Inc., 500 F. Supp. 1081, 6 Media L. Rep. 1941 (E.D. Pa. 1980) *3:* 46, 57, 110; *5:* 28; *6:* 89

Follett v. McCormick, 321 U.S. 573 (1944) *9:* 224

Food & Commercial Workers v. IBP, Inc., 857 F.2d 422 (7th Cir. 1988) *12:* 30

Forbes v. Seattle, 785 P.2d 431 (Wash. 1990) *9:* 235

Ford; United States v., 830 F.2d 596, 14 Media L. Rep. 1901 (6th Cir. 1987) *10:* 204

Foretich
—v. Advance Magazine Pubrs., 765 F. Supp. 1099, 18 Media L. Rep. 2280 (D.D.C. 1991) *2:* 450
—v. Glamour, 753 F. Supp. 955, 18 Media L. Rep. 1256 (D.D.C. 1990) *2:* 235

Forman v. Mississippi Pub'g Corp., 14 So. 2d 344 (Miss. 1943) *2:* 238

Forsher v. Bugliosi, 26 Cal. 3d 792, 608 P.2d 716, 6 Media L. Rep. 1097 (Cal. 1980) *2:* 133, 137; *4:* 119

Forster v. Manchester, 189 A.2d 147 (Pa. 1963) *5:* 30, 41

Forsyth County v. Nationalist Movement, 112 S. Ct. 2395, 20 Media L. Rep. 1268 (1992) *12:* 6

Fort; United States v., 14 Media L. Rep. 1942 (N.D. Ill. 1987) *1:* 498

Foster v. Turner Broadcasting, 844 F.2d 955, 15 Media L. Rep. 1225 (2d Cir.), *cert. denied,* 488 U.S. 994 (1988) *2:* 141

Fouts v. Fawcett Pubns., 116 F. Supp. 535 (D. Conn. 1953) *3:* 107

Fowler v. Southern Bell Tel. & Tel. Co., 343 F.2d 150 (5th Cir. 1965) *5:* 50, 262

Franceschina v. Morgan, 346 F. Supp. 833 (S.D. Ind. 1972) *1:* 530

Franchise Realty Interstate Corp. v. San Francisco Local Joint Exec. Bd. of Culinary Workers, 542 F.2d 1076 (9th Cir. 1976), *cert. denied,* 430 U.S. 940 (1977) *2:* 26, 144

Frank v. Minnesota Newspaper Ass'n, 490 U.S. 225, 16 Media L. Rep. 1511 (1989) *11:* 252, 257–58

Franklin v. Benevolent & Protective Order of Elks, 159 Cal. Rptr. 131, 5 Media L. Rep. 1977 (Cal. Ct. App. 1979) *2:* 327

Franklin Chalfont Assocs. v. Kalikow, 573 A.2d 550 (Pa. Super. Ct. 1990) *10:* 239

Franza v. Carey, 478 N.Y.S.2d 873 (N.Y. App. Div. 1984) *11:* 307

Frazier; State v., 440 A.2d 916, 7 Media L. Rep. 1854 (Conn. 1981), *cert. denied,* 458 U.S. 1112 (1982) *1:* 211

Fredonia, City of; v. Chanute Tribune, 638 P.2d 347, 8 Media L. Rep. 1053 (Kan. Ct. App. 1981) *12:* 93

Freedman
—v. Maryland, 380 U.S. 51, 1 Media L. Rep. 1126 (1965) *10:* 2, 66–67, 154, 265–67
—v. New Jersey State Police, 343 A.2d 148 (N.J. Super. Ct. Law Div. 1975) *1:* 529; *5:* 134

Freihofer v. Hearst Corp., 480 N.E.2d 349, 12 Media L. Rep. 1056 (1985) *6:* 74

Friedman v. Rogers, 440 U.S. 1, 4 Media L. Rep. 2213 (1979) *11:* 88–90, 234–35, 318

Friends of the Earth v. FCC, 449 F.2d 1164 (D.C. Cir. 1971) *13:* 158–59

Frisby v. Schultz, 487 U.S. 474 (1988) *12:* 2, 10, 22, 26, 34, 56, 113, 180; *13:* 265

Frissel v. Rizzo, 4 Media L. Rep. 2249 (3d Cir. 1979) *9:* 94

Froelich
—v. Adair, 516 P.2d 993 (Kan. 1973) *5:* 50
—v. Werbin, 548 P.2d 482 (Kan. 1976) *5:* 9, 22, 33, 47, 194

Frohwek v. United States, 249 U.S. 204 (1919) *8:* 46, 88

Frontier Broadcasting Co. v. Collier, 24 F.C.C. 251 (1958), *reconsideration denied sub nom.* In re Inquiry Into the Impact of Community CATV Report, 26 FCC 403 (1959) *13:* 439–41

Frosch v. Grosset & Dunlap, Inc., 427 N.Y.S.2d 828, 6 Media L. Rep. 1272 (N.Y. App. Div. 1980) *3:* 112; *6:* 84, 127, 200

Fry v. Ionia Sentinel Standard, 300 N.W.2d 687, 6 Media L. Rep. 2497 (Mich. Ct. App. 1980) *4:* 173, 175

FTC
—v. Brown & Williamson Tobacco Corp., 778 F.2d 35 (D.C. Cir. 1985) *11:* 223–25
—v. Standard Fin. Mgmt. Corp., 830 F.2d 404, 14 Media L. Rep. 1750 (1st Cir. 1987) *1:* 455

F.T.P. v. Courier-Journal & Louisville Times Co., 774 S.W.2d 444, 16 Media L. Rep. 1921 (Ky. App. 1989) *1:* 253

Fudge v. Penthouse Int'l, 840 F.2d 1012, 14 Media L. Rep. 2353 (1st Cir.), *cert. denied,* 488 U.S. 821 (1988) *3:* 51, 63

Fujishima v. Board of Educ., 460 F.2d 1355 (7th Cir. 1972) *13:* 346

Fuller; United States v., 202 F. Supp. 356 (N.D. Cal. 1962) *5:* 244–46

Fulton; State v., 337 So. 2d 866 (La. 1976) *12:* 212

Furgason v. Clausen, 785 P.2d 242, 18 Media L. Rep. 1369 (N.M. Ct. App. 1989) *2:* 326

Fyffe, Ohio ex rel. v. Pierce, 531 N.E.2d 673, 15 Media L. Rep. 2431 (Ohio 1988) *1:* 242

G

Gaare v. Melbostad, 242 N.W. 466 (Minn. 1932) *2:* 5

Gadsen County Times v. Horne, 426 So. 2d 1234 (Fla. Ct. App.), *review denied,* 441 So. 2d 631 (Fla. 1983) *14:* 70

Gaeta v. New York News, 465 N.E.2d 892, 10 Media L. Rep. 1966 (N.Y. 1984) *2:* 469

Gaetano v. Sharon Herald Co., 231 A.2d 753 (Pa. 1967) *2:* 1, 105, 215, 217, 232

Gale v. Value Line, 640 F. Supp. 967, 13 Media L. Rep. 1198 (D.R.I. 1986) *7:* 12

Galella v. Onassis, 487 F.2d 986, 1 Media L. Rep. 2425 (2d Cir. 1973) *5:* 14, 62–66

Gallagher v. Connecticut Comm'r of Revenue Servs., 602 A.2d 996, 19 Media L. Rep. 2140 (Conn. 1992) *9:* 241

Galloway v. FCC, 778 F.2d 16 (D.C. Cir. 1985) *13:* 167

Galvin v. New York, New Haven & Hartford Ry. Co., 168 N.E.2d 262 (Mass. 1960) *2:* 545

Gambino v. Fairfax County Sch. Bd., 429 F. Supp. 731 (E.D. Va.), *aff'd,* 564 F.2d 157 (4th Cir. 1977) *13:* 347

Gambrill v. Schooley, 48 A. 730 (Md. 1901) *2:* 172

Gambuzza v. Time, Inc., 239 N.Y.S.2d 466 (N.Y. App. Div. 1963) *2:* 127

Gang v. Hughes, 111 F. Supp. 27 (S.D. Cal.), *aff'd,* 218 F.2d 432 (9th Cir. 1954) *2:* 121

Gannett Co.
—v. DePasquale, 443 U.S. 368, 5 Media L. Rep. 1337 (1979) *1:* 7–27, 80–82, 86, 100–103, 106, 122, 125–26, 148, 197, 417
—v. Mark, 387 N.Y.S.2d 336, 2 Media L. Rep. 1189 (N.Y. App. Div. 1976) *1:* 187
—v. Rochester, 330 N.Y.S.2d 648 (N.Y. Sup. Ct. 1972) *12:* 143, 152
—v. State
——565 A.2d 895, 16 Media L. Rep. 2358 (Del. 1989) *1:* 106, 115, 117
——571 A.2d 735 (Del.), *cert. denied,* 495 U.S. 918 (1990) *1:* 526

Gannett Pac. Corp. v. Richardson, 580 P.2d 49, 3 Media L. Rep. 2575 (Haw. 1978) *1:* 152

Gannett River States Pub'g Co. v. Hand, 571 So. 2d 941, 18 Media L. Rep. 1516 (Miss. 1990) *1:* 106, 110, 115, 118

Gannett Satellite Info. Network
—v. Berger, 716 F. Supp. 140, 16 Media L. Rep. 2057 (D.N.J. 1989), *aff'd in part and rev'd in part,* 894 F.2d 61, 17 Media L. Rep. 1306 *12:* 132, 138
—v. City of Malden, 9 Media L. Rep. 2556 (D. Mass. 1983) *12:* 156
—v. Metropolitan Transp. Auth., 745 F.2d 767, 10 Media L. Rep. 2424 (2d Cir. 1984) *12:* 70, 141, 157–58, 160
—v. Town of Norwood, 579 F. Supp. 108 (D. Mass. 1984) *12:* 142, 156

Gannett Westchester Rockland Newspapers v. La Cava, 551 N.Y.S.2d 261, 18 Media L. Rep. 1397 (N.Y. App. Div. 1990) *1:* 151

Garden v. Parfumerie Rigaud, 271 N.Y.S. 187 (N.Y. Sup. Ct. 1933) *6:* 120

Gardner v. Bradenton Herald, 413 So. 2d 10, 8 Media L. Rep. 1251 (Fla.), *cert. denied,* 459 U.S. 865 (1989) *5:* 260; *10:* 194

Garland v. Torre, 259 F.2d 545 (2d Cir.), *cert. denied,* 385 U.S. 910 (1958) *14:* 92–93, 391–93

Garrett v. Estelle, 556 F.2d 1274, 2 Media L. Rep. 2265 (5th Cir. 1977), *cert. denied,* 438 U.S. 914 (1978) *1:* 520

Garrison v. Louisiana, 379 U.S. 64, 1 Media L. Rep. 1548 (1964) *2:* 6, 284, 291–92, 329–30, 400, 417, 423–25, 689–91; *7:* 10; *13:* 54

Gartner v. United States Info. Agency, 726 F. Supp. 1183 (S.D. Iowa 1989) *1:* 305

Gasbarro v. Lever Bros. Co., 490 F.2d 424 (7th Cir. 1973) *2:* 534

Gashgai v. Leibowitz, 703 F.2d 10 (1st Cir. 1983) *3:* 113

Gautier v. Pro-Football, 107 N.E.2d 485 (N.Y. 1952) *6:* 2, 21–22, 72

Gay v. Williams, 486 F. Supp. 12, 5 Media L. Rep. 1785 (D. Alaska 1979) *2:* 472–75

Gazette, Inc. v. Harris, 325 S.E.2d 713, 11 Media L. Rep. 1609 (Va. 1985) *2:* 214

Geis; State v., 441 N.E.2d 803 (Ohio Ct. App. 1981) *14:* 138, 276, 329

Geisel v. Poynter Prods., 295 F. Supp. 331 (S.D.N.Y. 1968) *6:* 31

Geisler v. Petrocelli, 616 F.2d 636, 6 Media L. Rep. 1023 (2d Cir. 1980) *2:* 144, 299; *3:* 30, 33–34

Geller, In re, 95 F.C.C.2d 1236 (1983), *aff'd sub nom.* League of Women Voters Educ. Fund v. FCC, 731 F.2d 995 (D.C. Cir. 1984) *13:* 103

General Motors Corp.; United States v., 352 F. Supp. 1071 (E.D. Mich. 1973) *1:* 371

General Stores v. Bingaman, 695 F.2d 502 (10th Cir. 1982) *11:* 307

Genovese; Commonwealth v., 487 A.2d 364, 11 Media L. Rep. 1388 (Pa. Super. Ct. 1985) *10:* 194

Gentile v. State Bar of Nev., 111 S. Ct. 2720 (1991) *10:* 224–30

George W. Prescott Pub'g Co. v. Register of Probate for Norfolk County, 479 N.E.2d 658, 11 Media L. Rep. 2331 (Mass. 1985) *1:* 454

Georgia Communications Corp. v. Horne, 294 S.E.2d 725, 8 Media L. Rep. 2375 (Ga. Ct. App. 1982) *14:* 357

Georgia Gazette Pub'g Co. v. Ramsey, 284 S.E.2d 386, 7 Media L. Rep. 2249 (Ga. 1981) *1:* 426

Georgia Outdoor Advertising v. Waynesville, 833 F.2d 43 (4th Cir. 1987) *12:* 183

Georgia Soc'y of Plastic Surgeons v. Anderson, 363 S.E.2d 140, 14 Media L. Rep. 2065 (Ga. 1987) *10:* 239

Georgia Television Co.
—v. Napper, 365 S.E.2d 275, 14 Media L. Rep. 2382 (Ga. 1988) *1:* 636
—v. State, 363 S.E.2d 528, 14 Media L. Rep. 2143 (Ga. 1988) *1:* 636

Gerbitz, State ex rel. v. Curriden, 738 S.W.2d 192 (Tenn. 1987) *14:* 301

Gertz v. Robert Welch, Inc.
—418 U.S. 323, 1 Media L. Rep. 1633 (1974) *2:* 9, 13, 59–85, 89, 92–93, 106, 213–14, 240, 259–60, 268, 313, 316, 326, 349–59, 396, 401, 408, 410–14, 460, 463–65, 501–3, 587–93, 597; *3:* 72–74, 76, 109; *7:* 10; *8:* 29, 41
—680 F.2d 527, 8 Media L. Rep. 1769 (7th Cir. 1982), *cert. denied,* 459 U.S. 1226 (1983) *2:* 599

Gibler v. Houston Post Co., 310 S.W.2d 377 (Tex. 1958) *2:* 175

Gilbert v. Medical Economics Co., 665 F.2d 305 (10th Cir. 1981) *4:* 134, 161

Gill
—v. Curtis Pub'g Co., 38 Cal. 2d 273, 239 P.2d 630 (Cal. 1952) *3:* 50; *4:* 6, 47
—v. Hearst Pub'g Co., 40 Cal. 2d 224, 253 P.2d 441 (Cal. 1953) *3:* 50; *4:* 6, 45–47, 185; *5:* 26, 139

Gleason v. Hustler Magazine, 7 Media L. Rep. 2183 (D.N.J. 1981) *6:* 15, 154, 206

Globe Newspaper Co.
—In re
——729 F.2d 47, 10 Media L. Rep. 1433 (1st Cir. 1984) *1:* 163, 168–71
——920 F.2d 88, 18 Media L. Rep. 1401 (1st Cir. 1990) *1:* 525
—v. Commonwealth, 556 N.E.2d 356, 17 Media L. Rep. 2195 (Mass. 1990) *1:* 191
—v. Massachusetts, 571 N.E.2d 617, 18 Media L. Rep. 2354 (Mass. 1991) *9:* 241
—v. Pokaski, 868 F.2d 497, 16 Media L. Rep. 1385 (1st Cir. 1989) *1:* 162, 318, 384, 390–91
—v. Superior Ct., 449 U.S. 894 (1980) *1:* 49
—v. Superior Ct., 423 N.E.2d 773, 7 Media L. Rep. 1626 (Mass. 1981), *rev'd,* 457 U.S. 596, 8 Media 1689 (1982) *1:* 45–48, 50–58

Gnapinsky v. Goldyn, 128 A.2d 697 (N.J. 1957) *2:* 3, 209

Gobin v. Globe Pub'g Co., 649 P.2d 1239, 8 Media L. Rep. 2191 (Kan. 1982) *2:* 162

Godbehere v. Phoenix Newspapers, 783 P.2d

781, 17 Media L. Rep. 1925 (Ariz. 1989) *3:* 19, 56
Goldblum v. NBC, 584 F.2d 904, 4 Media L. Rep. 1718 (9th Cir. 1978) *10:* 194, 276–77
Golden Bear Distrib. Sys. of Tex. v. Chase Revel. Inc., 708 F.2d 944, 9 Media L. Rep. 1857 (5th Cir. 1983) *2:* 284, 396
Golden Palace v. NBC, 386 F. Supp. 107 (D.D.C. 1974), *aff'd,* 530 F.2d 1094 (D.C. Cir. 1976) *2:* 295
Goldfeld v. Post Pub'g Co., 4 Media L. Rep. 1167 (Conn. Super. Ct. 1978) *14:* 70
Goldstein
—v. California, 412 U.S. 546 (1973) *6:* 91
—v. Garlick, 318 N.Y.S.2d 370 (N.Y. Sup. Ct. 1971) *7:* 11, 13, 21
Goldwater v. Ginzburg, 414 F.2d 324, 1 Media L. Rep. 1737 (2d Cir. 1969), *cert. denied,* 396 U.S. 1049 (1970) *2:* 448, 461, 598
Golub v. Esquire Pub'g, 508 N.Y.S.2d 188, 13 Media L. Rep. 1687 (N.Y. App. Div. 1986) *2:* 135
Gonzales v. Atlanta Constitution, 4 Media L. Rep. 2146 (N.D. Ill. 1979) *2:* 644
Goodfader's Appeal, In re, 367 P.2d 472 (Haw. 1961) *14:* 71
Good Gov't Group v. Superior Ct., 586 P.2d 572, 4 Media L. Rep. 2082 (Cal. 1978), *cert. denied,* 441 U.S. 961 (1979) *2:* 252, 269
Goodrich v. Waterbury Republican-Am., 448 A.2d 1317, 8 Media L. Rep. 2329 (Conn. 1982) *3:* 60, 83
Goodrow v. New York Am., 252 N.Y.S. 140 (N.Y. App. Div. 1931) *2:* 227
Goodyear Tire & Rubber Co. v. Vandergriff, 184 S.E. 452 (Ga. Ct. App. 1935) *5:* 18
Gore Newspapers Co. v. Reasbeck, 363 So. 2d 609, 4 Media L. Rep. 1751 (Fla. Dist. Ct. App. 1978) *1:* 124
Gorman v. Lukowsky, 431 F.2d 971 (6th Cir. 1970) *9:* 48
Gottfried
—v. FCC, 655 F.2d 297 (D.C. Cir. 1981), *rev'd in part,* 459 U.S. 498, 9 Media L. Rep. 1185 (1983) *13:* 395
—v. United States, *see* Greater L.A. Council on Deafness v. Community Television of So. Cal.
Goudy v. Dayton Newspaper, 237 N.E.2d 909, 914 (Ohio Ct. App. 1967) *2:* 481
Gough v. Tribune-Journal Co., 275 P.2d 663 (Idaho 1954) *2:* 619
Grace; United States v., 461 U.S. 171 (1983) *12:* 2, 9, 13, 22, 30, 58, 64
Grady v. Blair, 529 F. Supp. 370, 7 Media L. Rep. 2543 (N.D. Ill. 1981) *1:* 527–28
Grafton, Village of v. ABC, 435 N.E.2d 1131 (Ohio Ct. App. 1980) *2:* 567
Graham v. Today's Spirit, 468 A.2d 454, 10 Media L. Rep. 1337 (Pa. 1983) *2:* 232, 234
Grand Forks Herald v. District Ct., 322 N.W.2d 850 (N.D. 1982) *14:* 271–72, 407
Grand Jury, In re, 528 So. 2d 51, 15 Media L. Rep. 1963 (Fla. Dist. Ct. App. 1988) *1:* 162
Grand Jury Impaneled Jan. 21, 1975, In re, 541 F.2d 373 (3d Cir. 1976) *14:* 163, 166
Grand Jury Investig., In re, 587 F.2d 598, 4 Media L. Rep. 1713 (3d Cir. 1978) *1:* 115, 162
Grand Jury Investig. by Curran, In re, 561 A.2d 974, 16 Media L. Rep. 2238 (Conn. App. Ct. 1989) *1:* 162, 389
Grand Jury Investig. Spring Term 1988, In re, 543 So. 2d 757, 16 Media L. Rep. 1169 (Fla. Dist. Ct. App. 1989) *1:* 297
Grand Jury Matter (Gronowicz), In re, 764 F.2d 983 (3d Cir. 1985), *cert. denied,* 474 U.S. 1055 (1986) *14:* 310
Grand Jury Presentment, In re, 548 So. 2d 721, 16 Media L. Rep. 2204 (Fla. Dist. Ct. App. 1989) *1:* 162, 387
Grand Jury Proceedings, In re, 810 F.2d 580, 13 Media L. Rep. 2049 (6th Cir. 1987) *14:* 61, 90, 170, 417, 423
Grand Jury Subpoena Dated Jan. 4, 1984, In re, 750 F.2d 223 (2d Cir. 1984) *14:* 312
Granger v. Time, Inc., 568 P.2d 535, 3 Media L. Rep. 1021 (Mont. 1977) *2:* 307
Grant
—v. Esquire, Inc., 367 F. Supp. 876 (S.D.N.Y. 1973) *6:* 17, 19, 49, 116, 145
—v. Meyer, 828 F.2d 1446 (10th Cir. 1987), *aff'd,* 486 U.S. 414 (1988) *11:* 132
—v. Reader's Digest Ass'n, 151 F.2d 733 (2d Cir.), *cert. denied,* 326 U.S. 797 (1945) *2:* 119–20
Grayned v. City of Rockford, 408 U.S. 104 (1972) *1:* 472; *12:* 4, 9, 37, 59, 66
Great Atl. & Pac. Tea Co. v. Cream of Wheat, 227 F.2d 46 (2d Cir. 1915) *13:* 219
Great Eastern Liquor Corp. v. New York State Liquor Auth., 255 N.E.2d 704 (N.Y. 1969) *11:* 190
Greater Baltimore Bd. of Realtors v. Hughes, 596 F. Supp. 906 (D. Md. 1984) *12:* 169
Greater L.A. Council on Deafness v. Community Television of So. Cal., 719 F.2d 1017 (9th Cir. 1983), *cert. denied sub nom.* Gottfried v. United States, 467 U.S. 1252 (1984) *13:* 396
Great Falls Tribune Co., State ex rel. v. Montana Eighth Dist. Ct., 777 P.2d 345, 16 Media L. Rep. 2155 (Mont. 1989) *1:* 189

Great Lakes Broadcasting Co., 3 F.R.C. Ann. Rep. 32 (1929), *rev'd,* 37 F.2d 993 (D.C. Cir.), *cert. denied,* 281 U.S. 706 (1930) *13:* 132

Grecco; State v., 455 A.2d 485, 8 Media L. Rep. 2645 (N.J. Super. Ct. App. Div. 1982) *1:* 350

Green
—v. DeCamp, 612 F.2d 368 (8th Cir. 1980) *9:* 55
—v. FCC, 447 F.2d 323 (D.C. Cir. 1971) *13:* 151
—v. Village of Schaumburg, 676 F. Supp. 870 (N.D. Ill. 1988) *12:* 121
—State v., 395 So. 2d 532, 7 Media L. Rep. 1025 (Fla. 1981) *1:* 641

Green Acres Trust v. London, 688 P.2d 617 (Ariz. 1984) *2:* 520

Green Bay Newspaper Co., State ex rel. v. Circuit Ct., 335 N.W.2d 367 (Wis. 1983) *14:* 365

Greenbelt Coop. Pub'g Ass'n v. Bresler, 398 U.S. 6, 1 Media L. Rep. 1589 (1970) *2:* 156–57, 239, 259–60, 267, 395, 422, 424, 427, 695

Greenberg
—v. Bolger, 497 F. Supp. 756 (E.D.N.Y. 1980) *9:* 273, 281
—v. CBS, Inc., 419 N.Y.S.2d 988, 5 Media L. Rep. 1470 (N.Y. App. Div. 1979) *14:* 355

Greenfield v. Field Enters., 47 FEP Cases 548 (N.D. Ill. 1972) *9:* 132

Greenfield Town Crier v. Commissioner of Revenue, 433 N.E.2d 898, 8 Media L. Rep. 1626 (Mass. 1982) *9:* 248

Greensboro News Co., In re
—(Greensboro News I), 727 F.2d 1320, 10 Media L. Rep. 1239 (4th Cir.), *cert. denied,* 469 U.S. 829 (1984) *1:* 226
—(Greensboro News II), 727 F.2d 1326, 10 Media L. Rep. 1462 (4th Cir. 1984) *1:* 227–28

Green Valley School v. Cowles Fla. Broadcasting, 327 So. 2d 810 (Fla. Dist. Ct. App. 1976) *5:* 93–94

Greenwald; United States v., 479 F.2d 320 (6th Cir.), *cert. denied,* 414 U.S. 854 (1973) *5:* 163

Greenwood v. Wolchik, 544 A.2d 1156, 14 Media L. Rep. 2277 (Vt. 1988) *1:* 373

Greer
—v. Columbus Monthly Pub'g Corp., 448 N.E.2d 157, 8 Media L. Rep. 2129 (Ohio Ct. App. 1982) *2:* 261
—v. Spock, 424 U.S. 828 (1976) *12:* 73, 75, 78; *13:* 257, 291

Gregg; United States v., 612 F.2d 43 (2d Cir. 1979) *9:* 140

Gregoire v. G.P. Putnam's Sons, 81 N.E.2d 45 (N.Y.), *reh'g denied,* 83 N.E.2d 152 (N.Y. 1948) *2:* 229

Gregory
—v. Board of Chiropractic Examiners, 608 So. 2d 987 (La. 1992) *11:* 322
—v. Chicago, 394 U.S. 111 (1969) *12:* 113
—v. McDonnell Douglas Corp., 552 P.2d 425 (Cal. 1976) *2:* 241, 262

Grein v. La Poma, 340 P.2d 766 (Wash. 1959) *2:* 193

Greyhound Sec. v. Greyhound Corp., 207 N.Y.S.2d 383 (N.Y. App. Div. 1960) *2:* 125

Grice v. Holk, 108 So. 2d 359 (Ala. 1959) *2:* 168–69

Griffin v. Breckenridge, 403 U.S. 88 (1971) *9:* 68, 71, 73

Grimes v. Carter, 50 Cal. Rptr. 808 (Cal. Ct. App. 1966) *2:* 687; *3:* 39

Grimsley v. Guccione, 703 F. Supp. 903, 16 Media L. Rep. 1659 (M.D. Ala. 1988) *3:* 51

Grinnell Communications Corp., State ex rel. v. Love, 406 N.E.2d 809, 6 Media L. Rep. 1615 (Ohio 1980) *1:* 579, 635

Grinnell Corp.; United States v., 384 U.S. 563 (1966) *13:* 218

Griswold v. Connecticut, 381 U.S. 479 (1965) *11:* 286

Grolier Inc. v. Federal Trade Comm'n, 699 F.2d 983 (9th Cir.), *cert. denied,* 464 U.S. 891 (1983) *7:* 71

Grosjean v. American Press Co., 297 U.S. 233, 1 Media L. Rep. 2685 (1936) *9:* 216–21; *10:* 41

Grothe, Ex parte, 687 S.W.2d 736, 10 Media L. Rep. 2009 (Tex. Crim. App. 1984), *cert. denied,* 474 U.S. 944 (1985) *14:* 74, 77, 428

Groucho Marx Prods. v. Day & Night Co., 523 F. Supp. 485, 7 Media L. Rep. 2030 (S.D.N.Y. 1981), *rev'd,* 689 F.2d 317, 8 Media L. Rep. 2201 (2d Cir. 1982) *6:* 38, 163, 169–71

Group W Cable v. Santa Cruz, 679 F. Supp. 977 (N.D. Cal. 1988) *12:* 228

Grove v. Dun & Bradstreet, 438 F.2d 433 (3d Cir.), *cert. denied,* 404 U.S. 898 (1971) *2:* 402

Gruschus v. Curtis Pub'g Co., 342 F.2d 775 (10th Cir. 1965) *2:* 297; *4:* 28, 30

Grzelak v. Calumet Pub'g Co., 543 F.2d 579 (7th Cir. 1975) *2:* 184, 675

Guardianship of Kowalski, In re, 16 Media L. Rep. 2018 (Minn. Ct. App. 1989) *10:* 194

Guccione v. Hustler Magazine, 800 F.2d 298, 13 Media L. Rep. 1316 (2d Cir. 1986), *cert. denied*, 479 U.S. 1091 (1987) *2:* 604

Guggenheim v. Peto, *see* Peto v. Cook

Guglielmi v. Spelling-Goldberg Prods., 160 Cal. Rptr. 352, 5 Media L. Rep. 2208 (Cal. 1979) *6:* 77–83, 90, 167–68

Guinn v. Texas Newspapers, 738 S.W.2d 303, 16 Media L. Rep. 1024 (Tex. Ct. App. 1987), *cert. denied*, 488 U.S. 1041 (1989) *2:* 336

Gulliver's Periodicals v. Charles Levy Circulating Co., 455 F. Supp. 1197 (N.D. Ill. 1978) *14:* 47, 59, 65, 90

Gurney; United States v., 558 F.2d 1202, 3 Media L. Rep. 1081 (5th Cir. 1977), *cert. denied*, 435 U.S. 968 (1978) *1:* 162, 387, 525–26

Gustin v. Evening Press Co., 137 N.W. 674 (Mich. 1912) *2:* 126

Gutter v. Dow Jones, Inc., 490 N.E.2d 898, 12 Media L. Rep. 1999 (Ohio 1986) *7:* 12, 16–17, 23, 41

Guzzino; United States v., 766 F.2d 302, 11 Media L. Rep. 2215 (7th Cir. 1985) *1:* 355

H

Haberstroh v. Crain Pubns., 545 N.E.2d 295, 16 Media L. Rep. 2423 (Ill. App. Ct. 1989) *2:* 146

Haelan Labs. v. Topps Chewing Gum, 202 F.2d 866 (2d Cir.), *cert. denied*, 346 U.S. 816 (1953) *6:* 6, 33

Hagler v. Democrat-News, 699 S.W.2d 96, 99 (Mo. Ct. App. 1985) *3:* 56

Hague v. Committee for Indus. Org., 307 U.S. 496 (1939) *10:* 39; *12:* 6, 57; *13:* 261

Hajek v. Bill Mowbray Motors, 647 S.W.2d 253 (Tex. 1983) *10:* 239

Halkin, In re, 598 F.2d 176, 4 Media L. Rep. 2025 (D.C. Cir. 1979) *1:* 398, 400–402, 416

Hall v. Salisbury Post, 372 S.E.2d 711, 15 Media L. Rep. 2329 (N.C. 1988) *4:* 4, 6

Haller; United States v., 837 F.2d 84, 14 Media L. Rep. 2166 (2d Cir. 1988) *1:* 106, 110, 117–18, 122, 159, 382

Halquist v. Department of Corrections, 783 P.2d 1065, 17 Media L. Rep. 1250 (Wash. 1989) *1:* 522

Hamberger v. Eastman, 206 A.2d 239 (N.H. 1964) *5:* 50, 262

Hamilton v. Nance, 74 S.E. 627 (N.C. 1912) *2:* 200

Hammarley v. Superior Ct. (Sosa), 153 Cal. Rptr. 608 (Cal. Ct. App. 1979) *14:* 433

Hanberry v. Hearst Corp., 81 Cal. Rptr. 519 (Cal. Ct. App. 1969) *7:* 55–58

H&L Messengers v. City of Brentwood, 577 S.W.2d 444, 4 Media L. Rep. 2471 (Tenn. 1979) *12:* 109

H & M Assocs. v. City of El Centro, 109 Cal. App. 3d 399, 167 Cal. Rptr. 392 (Cal. Ct. App. 1980) *3:* 39; *4:* 34

Hanna; State v., 378 S.E.2d 640, 17 Media L. Rep. 1411 (W. Va. 1989) *1:* 636

Hannegan v. Esquire, Inc., 327 U.S. 146, 1 Media L. Rep. 2292 (1946) *9:* 272, 274–79

Hansen
—v. High Soc'y Magazine, 429 N.Y.S.2d 552, 6 Media L. Rep. 1618 (N.Y. App. Div. 1980) *6:* 54
—v. Stoll, 636 P.2d 1236, 8 Media L. Rep. 1204 (Ariz. Ct. App. 1981) *2:* 308

Hardge-Harris v. Pleban, 741 F. Supp. 764 (E.D. Mo. 1990)

Hardin v. Santa Fe Reporter, 745 F.2d 1323, 11 Media L. Rep. 1026 (10th Cir. 1984) *2:* 449

Hargan v. Purdy, 20 S.W. 432 (Ky. 1892) *2:* 201

Hargrove v. Oklahoma Press Pub'g Co., 265 P. 635 (Okla. 1928) *2:* 130

Harkey v. Abate, 346 N.W.2d 74 (Mich. Ct. App. 1983) *5:* 9

Harms v. Miami Daily News, 127 So. 2d 715 (Fla. Dist. Ct. App. 1961) *5:* 20, 45; *7:* 28

Harnish v. Manatee County, 783 F.2d 1535 (11th Cir. 1986) *12:* 185

Harper & Row, Pubrs. v. Nation Enters., 723 F.2d 195, 9 Media L. Rep. 2489 (2d Cir. 1983), *rev'd*, 471 U.S. 539, 11 Media L. Rep. 1969 (1985) *5:* 152; *6:* 95; *10:* 243, 246

Harrelson (El Paso Times); United States v., 713 F.2d 1114, 9 Media L. Rep. 2113 (5th Cir. 1983), *cert. denied*, 465 U.S. 1041 (1984) *1:* 524

Harris
—v. Curtis Pub'g Co., 121 P.2d 761 (Cal. Ct. App. 1942) *2:* 130
—v. Easton Pub'g Co., 483 A.2d 1377, 11 Media L. Rep. 1209 (Pa. Super. Ct. 1984) *4:* 39; *5:* 21, 154

Harrison
—v. Luse, 760 F. Supp. 1394 (D. Colo.), *aff'd*, 951 F.2d 1259 (10th Cir. 1991) *2:* 680
—v. Washington Post, 391 A.2d 781 (D.C. 1978) *4:* 52–54

Hart v. Playboy Enters., 6 Media L. Rep. 2571 (D. Kan. 1981) *14:* 368

Harte-Hanks Communications v. Connaughton, 491 U.S. 657, 16 Media L. Rep. 1881 (1989) *2:* 46, 426, 428–30, 448, 698–701

Hartmann
—v. American News Co., 171 F.2d 581 (7th Cir. 1948), *cert. denied,* 337 U.S. 907 (1949) *2:* 224
—v. Winchell, 73 N.E.2d 30 (N.Y. 1947) *2:* 173
Harwood Pharmacal Co. v. NBC, 174 N.E.2d 602 (N.Y. 1961) *2:* 300
Hastings; United States v., 695 F.2d 1278, 8 Media L. Rep. 2617 (11th Cir.), *cert. denied,* 461 U.S. 931 (1983) *1:* 580, 637
Hatch v. Marsh, 134 F.R.D. 300 (M.D. Fla. 1990) *14:* 335
Hatchard v. Westinghouse Broadcasting Co., 532 A.2d 346 (Pa. 1987) *14:* 291
Hatheway v. Gannett Satellite Info. Network, 459 N.W.2d 873, 18 Media L. Rep. 1458 (Wis. Ct. App. 1990) *13:* 249
Haub v. Friermuth, 82 P. 571 (Cal. Ct. App. 1905) *2:* 141
Hauptmann v. Wilentz, 570 F. Supp. 351 (D.N.J. 1983), *aff'd,* 770 F.2d 1070 (3d Cir. 1985), *cert. denied,* 474 U.S. 1103 (1986) *9:* 45, 76, 79, 84
Hausch v. Donrey of Nev., 833 F. Supp. 822, 22 Media L. Rep. 1076 (D. Nev. 1993) *9:* 129
Hawkins
—v. Justin, 311 N.W.2d 465 (Mich. Ct. App. 1981) *2:* 626
—v. Multimedia, 344 S.E.2d 145, 12 Media L. Rep. 1878 (S.C.), *cert. denied,* 479 U.S. 1012 (1986) *4:* 170, 183
Haycox v. Dunn, 104 S.E.2d 800 (Va. 1958) *2:* 533
Hayden v. Bracy, 744 F.2d 1338 (8th Cir. 1984) *2:* 153
Hayes; Commonwealth v., 414 A.2d 318, 6 Media L. Rep. 1273 (Pa.), *cert. denied,* 449 U.S. 992 (1980) *1:* 143, 148
Haynes v. Alfred A. Knopf, Inc., 8 F.3d 1222, 21 Media L. Rep. 2161 (7th Cir. 1993) *2:* 609
Haynick v. Zimlich, 498 N.E.2d 1095, 13 Media L. Rep. 2057 (Ohio C.P.), *rereported,* 508 N.E.2d 195 (Ohio C.P. 1986) *5:* 38
Hays v. American Defense Soc'y, 169 N.E. 380 (N.Y. 1929) *2:* 130
Hays County Guardian v. Supple, 969 F.2d 111, 20 Media L. Rep. 1681 (5th Cir. 1992), *cert. denied,* 113 S. Ct. 1067 (1993) *12:* 61, 162
Hayward v. Watsonville Register-Pajaronian & Sun, 265 Cal. App. 2d 255, 71 Cal. Rptr. 295 (Cal. Ct. App. 1965) *2:* 567
Hazelwood Sch. Dist. v. Kuhlmeier, 484 U.S. 260, 14 Media L. Rep. 2081 (1988) *13:* 255, 276, 333–35, 348–50, 352–59, 369–70, 374
Health Sys. v. Virginia Bd., 424 F. Supp. 267, 2 Media L. Rep. 1107 (S.D. Va. 1976) *11:* 322
Hearst Corp.
—v. Cholakis, 386 N.Y.S.2d 892, 2 Media L. Rep. 2085 (N.Y. App. Div. 1976) *1:* 124
—v. Iowa Dep't of Revenue and Fin., 461 N.W.2d 295, 18 Media L. Rep. 1241 (Iowa 1990), *cert. denied,* 111 S. Ct. 1639 (1991) *9:* 243
—v. State, 484 A.2d 292, 11 Media L. Rep. 1195 (Md. Ct. Spec. App. 1984) *1:* 106, 115
Heath v. Playboy Enters., 732 F. Supp. 1145 (S.D. Fla. 1990) *4:* 48, 72
Hedrick; United States v., 922 F.2d 396 (7th Cir. 1991) *5:* 33, 194
Heffron v. International Soc'y for Krishna Consciousness, 452 U.S. 640, 7 Media L. Rep. 1489 (1981) *12:* 2, 8–9, 21–22, 34, 36
Heinemann v. General Motors Corp., 342 F. Supp. 203 (N.D. Ill. 1972), *aff'd,* 478 F.2d 1405 (7th Cir. 1973) *6:* 14
Heir v. Degnan, 411 A.2d 194 (N.J. 1980) *11:* 209
Heller
—v. Family Circle, 445 N.Y.S.2d 513, 8 Media L. Rep. 1031 (N.Y. App. Div. 1981) *6:* 22
—v. New York, 413 U.S. 483 (1973) *10:* 39
—v. Roberts, 386 F.2d 832 (2d Cir. 1967) *9:* 48
Heltzel; State v., 552 N.E.2d 31 (Ind. 1990) *4:* 101
Hempele; State v., 576 A.2d 793 (N.J. 1990) *5:* 33, 194
Henderson
—v. Ripperger, 594 P.2d 251 (Kan. Ct. App. 1979) *2:* 191
—People v., 847 P.2d 239 (Colo. Ct. App. 1993) *14:* 206
Hendrix v. Evans, 715 F. Supp. 897 (N.D. Ind. 1989) *13:* 308
Henry
—v. Collins, 380 U.S. 356 (1965) *2:* 424
—v. Halliburton, 690 S.W.2d 775, 11 Media L. Rep. 2185 (Mo. 1985) *2:* 248
Herald Ass'n
—v. Ellison, 419 A.2d 323, 6 Media L. Rep. 1638 (Vt. 1980) *1:* 143, 148
—v. Judicial Conduct Bd., 544 A.2d 596, 15 Media L. Rep. 1078 (Vt. 1988) *1:* 297
Herald Co.
—In re, 734 F.2d 93, 10 Media L. Rep. 1673 (2d Cir. 1984) *1:* 129–30, 136–39

—v. McNeal, 511 F. Supp. 269, 7 Media L. Rep. 1248 (E.D. Mo. 1981) *1:* 391–92
—v. Tormey, 537 N.Y.S.2d 978, 16 Media L. Rep. 1702 (N.Y. Sup. Ct.), *aff'd,* 544 N.Y.S.2d 750 (N.Y. App. Div.) *appeal denied,* 547 N.E.2d 103 (N.Y. 1989) *1:* 263
—v. Weisenberg, 455 N.Y.S.2d 413, 8 Media L. Rep. 2450 (N.Y. App. Div. 1982), *aff'd,* 452 N.E.2d 1190 (N.Y. 1983) *1:* 291
Herald Mail Co., State ex rel. v. Hamilton, 267 S.E.2d 544, 6 Media L. Rep. 1343 (W. Va. 1980) *1:* 143, 146, 148, 150
Herald-Telephone v. Fatouros, 431 N.E.2d 171 (Ind. Ct. App. 1982) *13:* 241–42
Herbert v. Lando
—441 U.S. 153 (1979) *14:* 140, 347–49, 397–401
—603 F. Supp. 983, 11 Media L. Rep. 1692 (S.D.N.Y. 1985), *aff'd in part and rev'd in part,* 781 F.2d 292, 12 Media L. Rep. 1593 (2d Cir.), *cert. denied,* 476 U.S. 1182 (1986) *2:* 138, 141, 606
Herceg v. Hustler Magazine
—814 F.2d 1017, 13 Media L. Rep. 2345 (5th Cir. 1987), *cert. denied,* 485 U.S. 959 (1988) *8:* 2, 9, 11–12, 14, 20, 23–27, 43, 80, 89–90
—565 F. Supp. 802, 9 Media L. Rep. 1959 (S.D. Tex. 1983) *8:* 38–40
Herink v. Harper & Row, Pubrs., 607 F. Supp. 657, 11 Media L. Rep. 1927 (S.D.N.Y. 1985) *6:* 26
Herman & MacLean v. Huddleston, 459 U.S. 375 (1983) *9:* 148
Hernandez v. Underwood, 7 Media L. Rep. 1535 (N.Y. Sup. Ct. 1981) *7:* 11, 14, 18
Hernstadt v. FCC, 677 F.2d 893 (D.C. Cir. 1980) *13:* 116
Herrick v. Evening Express Pub'g Co., 113 A. 16 (Me. 1921) *7:* 16
Herrmann v. Newark Morning Ledger Co., 140 A.2d 529 (N.J. Super. Ct. App. Div. 1958) *2:* 119–20, 130
Hess v. Indiana, 414 U.S. 105 (1973) *8:* 44–45, 93–99
Hestand v. State, 273 N.E.2d 282 (Ind. 1971) *14:* 218
Hicks v. Casablanca Records, 464 F. Supp. 426, 4 Media L. Rep. 1497 (S.D.N.Y. 1978) *6:* 83, 128, 201
Higbee v. Times-Advocate, 5 Media L. Rep. 2372 (S.D. Cal. 1980) *5:* 108; *9:* 62, 64
High v. Supreme Lodge of the World, 7 N.W.2d 675 (Minn. 1943) *2:* 204, 207
High Ol' Times v. Busbee, 621 F.2d 141, 6 Media L. Rep. 1617 (5th Cir. 1980) *11:* 306

High Gear Toke Shop v. Beacom, 689 P.2d 624 (Colo. 1984) *11:* 305
Hill v. Hayes, 240 N.Y.S.2d 286 (N.Y. App. Div. 1963), *aff'd,* 207 N.E.2d 604 (N.Y. 1965), *rev'd sub nom.* Time, Inc. v. Hill, 385 U.S. 374, 1 Media L. Rep. 1791 (1967) *2:* 36; *3:* 52, 57, 66–67, 78, 83, 91, 93–96; *4:* 38, 140; *6:* 65
Hillery v. Procunier, 364 F. Supp. 196 (N.D. Cal. 1973) *1:* 468
Hillsboro v. Purcell, 761 P.2d 510 (Or. 1988) *12:* 125
Hinerman v. Daily Gazette Co., 423 S.E.2d 560, 20 Media L. Rep. 2169 (W. Va. 1992) *2:* 702
Hinish v. Meier & Frank Co., 113 P.2d 438 (Or. 1941) *6:* 28
Hirsch v. S.C. Johnson & Son, 280 N.W.2d 129 (Wis. 1979) *6:* 31, 153
Hirschkop v. Snead, 594 F.2d 356, 4 Media L. Rep. 2599 (4th Cir. 1979) *10:* 205
Hoffa v. United States, 385 U.S. 293 (1966) *5:* 199, 202
Hoffman v. Washington Post Co., 433 F. Supp. 600, 3 Media L. Rep. 1143 (D.D.C. 1977), *aff'd,* 578 F.2d 442, 3 Media L. Rep. 2546 (1978) *2:* 124, 276
Hoffman Estates v. Flipside, Hoffman Estates, 455 U.S. 489 (1982) *11:* 110, 305
Hohensee v. Goon Squad, 171 F. Supp. 562 (M.D. Pa. 1959) *9:* 24, 141
Hohler; State v., 543 A.2d 364 (Me. 1988) *14:* 70, 76
Holden v. Pioneer Broadcasting Co., 365 P.2d 845 (Or. 1961), *cert. denied and appeal dismissed,* 370 U.S. 157 (1962) *2:* 612
Hollinger v. Titan Capital Corp., 914 F.2d 1564 (9th Cir. 1990), *cert. denied,* 111 S. Ct. 1621 (1991) *9:* 160
Hollman v. Brady, 233 F.2d 877 (9th Cir. 1956) *2:* 209
Holman v. Central Ark. Broadcasting Co., 610 F.2d 542, 5 Media L. Rep. 2217 (8th Cir. 1979) *4:* 185; *5:* 210, 217; *9:* 64
Holmes v. Bateson, 583 F.2d 542 (1st Cir. 1978) *9:* 148
Holmgrem v. Little Village Community Reporter, 342 F. Supp. 512 (N.D. Ill. 1971) *11:* 314
Holy Spirit Ass'n v. New York State Congress of Parents & Teachers, 408 N.Y.S.2d 261 (N.Y. Sup. Ct. 1978) *9:* 78
Holy Spirit Ass'n for Unification of World Christianity v. New York Times Co., 424 N.Y.S.2d 165, 399 N.E.2d 1185, 5 Media L. Rep. 2219 (N.Y. 1979) *2:* 549, 551

Home Box Office v. FCC, 567 F.2d 9 (D.C. Cir.), *cert. denied,* 434 U.S. 829 (1977) *13:* 460–62, 465–67, 478–80, 500, 520, 529

Homefinders of Am. v. Providence Journal Co., 621 F.2d 441 (1st Cir. 1980) *13:* 232–34

Home Placement Serv. v. Providence Journal Co., 682 F.2d 274 (1st Cir. 1982) *13:* 217, 235–39

Honig v. Nashville Banner, 10 Media L. Rep. 2139 (Tenn. Ct. App. 1984) *4:* 64

Honolulu Advertiser v. Takao, 580 P.2d 58, 4 Media L. Rep. 1423 (Haw. 1978) *1:* 364

Honolulu, City and County of; v. Hawaii Newspaper Agency, 7 Media L. Rep. 2495 (D. Haw. 1981) *9:* 29, 33, 35, 37

Hood v. Naeter Bros. Pub'g Co., 562 S.W.2d 770 (Mo. Ct. App. 1978) *4:* 104

Hooker v. Columbia Pictures, 551 F. Supp. 1060 (N.D. Ill. 1982) *6:* 29

Hopf; State v., 323 N.W.2d 746 (Minn. 1982) *12:* 180

Hopkins v. Wasson, 329 F.2d 67 (6th Cir.), *cert. denied,* 379 U.S. 854 (1964) *9:* 48

Hopkinsville Cable TV v. Pennyroyal Cablevision, 562 F. Supp. 543 (W.D. Ky. 1982) *12:* 236

Horn; State v., 643 P.2d 1338, 8 Media L. Rep. 1945 (Or. Ct. App. 1982) *12:* 106

Hornstein v. Hartigan, 676 F. Supp. 894, 15 Media L. Rep. 1769 (C.D. Ill. 1988) *11:* 47; *12:* 3

Horwitz v. United States, 63 F.2d 706 (5th Cir.), *cert. denied,* 289 U.S. 760 (1933) *11:* 249

Hostetter v. Idlewild Bon Voyage Liquor Corp., 377 U.S. 324 (1964) *11:* 182

Hotchner v. Castillo-Puche, 551 F.2d 910, 2 Media L. Rep. 1545 (2d Cir.), *cert. denied,* 434 U.S. 834, 8 Media L. Rep. 1128 (1977) *2:* 249, 253, 265, 432, 449

Houchins v. KQED, 438 U.S. 1, 3 Media L. Rep. 2521 (1978) *1:* 14, 460, 499–518

Household Fin. Corp. v. Bridge, 250 A.2d 878 (Md. 1969) *5:* 19, 44

House of Bacchus v. Sarafan, 357 N.Y.S.2d 318 (N.Y. App. Div. 1974) *11:* 190

Housh v. Peth, 133 N.E.2d 340 (Ohio 1956) *5:* 19, 44

Housing Opportunities Made Equal v. Cincinnati Enquirer, 731 F. Supp. 801, 17 Media L. Rep. 1608 (S.D. Ohio 1990), *aff'd,* 943 F.2d 644 (6th Cir. 1991) *11:* 315

Houston Chronicle Pub'g Co.
—v. Dean, 792 S.W.2d 273, 17 Media L. Rep. 2071 (Tex. Ct. App. 1990) *1:* 160, 278
—v. Hardy, 678 S.W.2d 495, 10 Media L. Rep. 1841 (Tex. Civ. App. 1984), *cert. denied,* 470 U.S. 1052 (1985) *1:* 426, 435

—v. Houston
——531 S.W.2d 177 (Tex. Civ. App. 1975), *writ of error refused,* 536 S.W.2d 559 (Tex. 1976) *1:* 287
——620 S.W.2d 833, 7 Media L. Rep. 2043 (Tex. Civ. App. 1981) *12:* 106

—v. McMaster, 598 S.W.2d 864, 6 Media L. Rep. 1363 (Texas Ct. Crim. App. 1980) *1:* 188

—v. Shaver, 630 S.W.2d 927, 8 Media L. Rep. 1314 (Tex. Crim. App. 1982) *1:* 142

Howard v. Des Moines Register, 283 N.W.2d 289, 5 Media L. Rep. 1667 (Iowa 1979), *cert. denied,* 445 U.S. 904 (1980) *4:* 105, 160

Howat v. Kansas, 258 U.S. 181 (1922) *10:* 87

Howell v. New York Post Co., 612 N.E.2d 699 (N.Y.), 21 Media L. Rep. 1273 (N.Y. 1993) *3:* 20; *5:* 9

Hrlsky v. Globe Democrat Pub'g Co., 152 S.W.2d 119 (Mo. 1941) *2:* 127

Hruby v. Kalina, 424 N.W.2d 130, 15 Media L. Rep. 1559 (Neb. 1988) *2:* 206

H.S. Gere & Sons v. Frey, 509 N.E.2d 271, 14 Media L. Rep. 1791 (Mass. 1987) *1:* 455–56

Hubbard
—v. Journal Pub'g Co., 368 P.2d 147 (N.M. 1962) *4:* 62
—United States v.
——493 F. Supp. 202 (D.D.C. 1979) *14:* 151
——650 F.2d 293, 6 Media L. Rep. 1909 (D.C. Cir. 1980) *1:* 354, 359–63

Hudgens v. NLRB, 424 U.S. 507 (1976) *12:* 88

Hudok, State ex rel. v. Henry, 389 S.E.2d 188 (W. Va. 1989) *14:* 70, 76, 78

Hughes v. New Eng. Newspaper Pub'g Co., 43 N.E.2d 657 (Mass. 1942) *2:* 301

Hughes County Action No. JUV 90-3, In re, 452 N.W.2d 128, 17 Media L. Rep. 1513 (S.D. 1990) *1:* 243, 258, 262

Hunt
—v. Liberty Lobby, 720 F.2d 631, 10 Media L. Rep. 1097 (11th Cir. 1983) *2:* 284, 425, 498, 598
—v. NBC, 872 F.2d 289, 10 Media L. Rep. 1434 (9th Cir. 1989) *10:* 194, 196

Hunter; United States v., 459 F.2d 205 (4th Cir.), *cert. denied,* 409 U.S. 934 (1972) *11:* 314

Huntley v. Public Util. Comm'n, 442 P.2d 685 (Cal. 1968) *12:* 214

Hurley v. Northwest Pub'g, 273 F. Supp. 967 (D. Minn. 1967), *aff'd,* 398 F.2d 346 (8th Cir. 1968) *2:* 441

Hurwitz v. United States, 884 F.2d 684 (2d Cir. 1989), *cert. denied,* 493 U.S. 1056 (1990) *6:* 129, 202
Huskey
—v. Dallas Chronicle, 13 Media L. Rep. 1057 (D. Or. 1986) *5:* 38
—v. NBC, 632 F. Supp. 1282, 12 Media L. Rep. 2105 (N.D. Ill. 1986) *4:* 57, 196; *5:* 38; *14:* 441, 460
Hustler Magazine v. Falwell, 485 U.S. 46, 14 Media L. Rep. 2281 (1988) *2:* 250, 688; *3:* 64, 69; *4:* 136, 177–81
Hutchens v. Beckhan, 521 F. Supp. 426 (S.D. Ga. 1981) *9:* 94
Hutchinson v. Proxmire, 443 U.S. 111, 5 Media L. Rep. 1279 (1979) *2:* 323, 367, 369–75, 672
Huyen v. Driscoll, 479 N.W.2d 76 (Minn. 1991) *2:* 245
Hyde v. Columbia, 637 S.W.2d 251 (Mo. Ct. App. 1982), *cert. denied,* 459 U.S. 1226 (1983) *4:* 98, 104
Hynes v. Mayor of Oradell, 425 U.S. 610 (1976) *12:* 12, 92, 114–16, 129

I

IDK, Inc. v. Clark County, 836 F.2d 1185 (9th Cir. 1988) *11:* 47, 309
Illinois v. Arya, 589 N.E.2d 832, 19 Media L. Rep. 2079 (Ill. App. Ct. 1992) *14:* 102, 215
Illinois Migrant Council v. Campbell Soup Co., 519 F.2d 391 (7th Cir. 1975) *12:* 87
Immuno AG v. Moor-Jankowski, 567 N.E.2d 1270, 18 Media L. Rep. 1625 (N.Y.), *cert. denied,* 111 S. Ct. 2261 (1991) *2:* 245
Indiana Constr. Corp. v. Chicago Tribune Co., 648 F. Supp. 1419, 13 Media L. Rep. 1863 (N.D. Ind. 1986) *7:* 15; *13:* 242–43
Industrial Equip. Co. v. Emerson Elec. Co., 554 F.2d 276 (6th Cir. 1977) *2:* 481
Information Control Corp. v. Genesis One Computer Corp., 611 F.2d 781 (9th Cir. 1980) *2:* 262
Inquiry into the Impact of Community CATV Report, In re, *see* Frontier Broadcasting Co. v. Collier
In re, *see* name of party
Insco; United States v., 496 F.2d 204 (5th Cir. 1974) *12:* 210
Interception of Wire and Oral Communications (Kattar), In re, 682 F. Supp. 669, 15 Media L. Rep. 1355 (D.N.H. 1988) *1:* 380
International Bhd. of Teamsters v. Daniel, 434 U.S. 1061 (1979) *9:* 179

International Prods. Corp. v. Koons, 325 F.2d 403 (2d Cir. 1963) *1:* 402
International Soc'y for Krishna Consciousness
—v. Lee, 112 S.Ct. 2701, 20 Media L. Rep. 1297 (1992) *12:* 71
—v. Rochford, 585 F.2d 263 (7th Cir. 1978) *12:* 71
Invisible Empire of Knights of Ku Klux Klan (Md. Chapter) v. Mayor, Board of Comm'rs, & Chief of Police of Thurmont, 700 F. Supp. 281 (D. Md. 1988) *12:* 33
Ion Equip. Corp. v. Nelson, 168 Cal. Rptr. 361 (Cal. Ct. App. 1980) *4:* 34; *6:* 13
Iowa Freedom of Info. Council
—In re, 724 F.2d 658, 10 Media L. Rep. 1120 (8th Cir. 1983) *1:* 265, 267, 270
—v. Wifvat, 328 N.W.2d 920, 9 Media L. Rep. 1194 (Iowa 1983) *1:* 143, 147–50
Irving v. United States, *see* Amick; United States v.
ITT Telecom Prods. Corp. v. Dooley, 214 Cal. App. 3d 307, 262 Cal. Rptr. 773 (Cal. Ct. App. 1989) *2:* 518
Itzkovitch v. Whitaker, 39 So. 499 (La. 1905) *3:* 42

J

Jackson
—Ex parte, 96 U.S. 727 (1878) *12:* 97
—v. City Council of Charlottesville, 659 F. Supp. 470 (W.D. Va. 1987), *aff'd in part and vacated in part,* 840 F.2d 10 (4th Cir. 1988) *12:* 174
—v. Longcope, 476 N.E.2d 617, 11 Media L. Rep. 2282 (Mass. 1985) *2:* 602
—v. Playboy Enters., 574 F. Supp. 10, 9 Media L. Rep. 1575 (S.D. Ohio 1983) *3:* 51; *6:* 18
Jacobellis v. Ohio, 378 U.S. 184 (1964) *3:* 4
Jacobs
—v. Board of Sch. Comm'rs, 490 F.2d 601 (7th Cir. 1973), *vacated,* 420 U.S. 128 (1975) *12:* 213
—v. Major, 407 N.W.2d 832 (Wis. 1987) *12:* 90
Jacobsen
—v. Crivaro, 851 F.2d 1067, 15 Media L. Rep. 1958 (8th Cir. 1988) *12:* 141, 144, 153–54, 157–58, 160
—v. Filler, 15 Media L. Rep. 1705 (D. Ariz. 1988) *12:* 148
—v. Harris, 869 F.2d 1172, 16 Media L. Rep. 1380 (8th Cir. 1989) *12:* 152, 160
—v. Petersen, 728 F. Supp. 1415, 17 Media L. Rep. 2324 (D.S.D. 1990) *12:* 142, 148

Jacova v. Southern Radio & Television Co., 83 So. 2d 34 (Fla. 1955) *4:* 54
Jaillet v. Cashman, 189 N.Y.S. 743 (N.Y. Sup. Ct. 1921), *aff'd,* 194 N.Y.S. 947 (N.Y. App. Div. 1922), *aff'd,* 139 N.E. 714 (N.Y. 1923) *7:* 12, 17
Jamerson v. Anderson Newspapers, 469 N.E.2d 1243 (Ind. Ct. App. 1984) *14:* 83, 217
James
—v. Garrett Co., 353 N.E.2d 834 (N.Y. 1976) *2:* 147
—v. Screen Gems, 344 P.2d 799 (Cal. Ct. App. 1959) *3:* 28; *6:* 154
Jamison v. Texas, 318 U.S. 413 (1943) *11:* 20, 58; *12:* 58, 101, 110, 128
J & C, Inc. v. Combined Communications Corp., 14 Media L. Rep. 2162 (Ky. Ct. App. 1987) *3:* 27
Janklow
—v. Newsweek, 788 F.2d 1300, 12 Media L. Rep. 1961 (8th Cir.), *cert. denied,* 479 U.S. 883 (1986) *2:* 139
—v. Viking Press, 378 N.W.2d 875, 12 Media L. Rep. 1534 (S.D. 1985) *2:* 580
Jaubert v. Crowley Post-Signal, 375 So. 2d 1386, 5 Media L. Rep. 2084 (La. 1979) *5:* 25; *6:* 73
Jay Norris, Inc. v. FTC, 598 F.2d 1244 (2d Cir.), *cert. denied,* 444 U.S. 980 (1979) *7:* 71
J.D.C., In re, 594 A.2d 70, 19 Media L. Rep. 1040 (D.C. 1991) *1:* 243, 258
Jenkins v. Winchester Star, 8 Media L. Rep. 1403 (W.D. Va. 1981) *5:* 38; *9:* 55, 64
Jennings v. Telegram-Tribune Co., 164 Cal. App. 3d 119, 210 Cal. Rptr. 485, 11 Media L. Rep. 1419 (Cal. Ct. App. 1985) *2:* 549
Jenoff v. Hearst Corp., 644 F.2d 1004, 7 Media L. Rep. 1081 (4th Cir. 1981) *2:* 326
Jensen v. Times Mirror Co., 634 F. Supp. 304, 12 Media L. Rep. 2137 (D. Conn. 1986), *on reconsideration certified for appeal,* 647 F. Supp. 1525, 13 Media L. Rep. 2160 (D. Conn. 1986) *3:* 113
Jeppson v. United Television, 580 P.2d 1087, 3 Media L. Rep. 2513 (Utah 1978) *6:* 27
Jersawitz v. Hanberry, 783 F.2d 1532, 12 Media L. Rep. 1842 (11th Cir. 1986), *cert. denied,* 479 U.S. 883 (1986) *1:* 498
Jervey v. Martin, 336 F. Supp. 1350 (W.D. Va. 1972) *9:* 48
Jim Crockett Promotions v. Charlotte, 538 F. Supp. 1197 (W.D.N.C. 1982), *modified,* 706 F.2d 486 (4th Cir. 1983) *12:* 202
Jimmy Swaggart Ministries v. Board of Equalization of Cal., 493 U.S. 378 (1990) *9:* 224
John v. Tribune Co., 24 Ill. 2d 437, 181 N.E.2d 105 (Ill.), *cert. denied,* 371 U.S. 877 (1962) *2:* 145
John Doe Grand Jury Investig., In re, 574 N.E.2d 373, 19 Media L. Rep. 1091 (Mass. 1991) *14:* 416
John Donnelly & Sons v. Campbell, 639 F.2d 6, 7 Media L. Rep. 1132 (1st Cir. 1980), *aff'd,* 453 U.S. 916 (1981) *12:* 174
Johnsen, In re, 430 N.Y.S.2d 904 (N.Y. Sup. Ct. 1979) *9:* 263
Johnson
—v. Adams, 629 F. Supp. 1563, 12 Media L. Rep. 1973 (E.D. Tex. 1986) *1:* 542, 638
—v. California, 73 Cal. Rptr. 240, 447 P.2d 352 (Cal. 1968) *8:* 36
—v. FCC, 829 F.2d 157 (D.C. Cir. 1987) *13:* 104
—v. Harcourt, Brace, Jovanovich, Inc., 118 Cal. Rptr. 370 (Cal. Ct. App. 1974) *4:* 129
—v. Lexington Herald-Leader, 9 Media L. Rep. 1365 (Ky. Ct. App. 1983) *3:* 49, 54
—v. Pleasanton, 982 F.2d 350 (9th Cir. 1992) *12:* 248
—Commonwealth v., 455 A.2d 654, 9 Media L. Rep. 1649 (Pa. Super. Ct. 1982) *1:* 225
—State v., 324 N.W.2d 447 (Wis. Ct. App. 1982) *11:* 308
Johnson Newspaper Corp. v. Melino, 547 N.Y.S.2d 915, 17 Media L. Rep. 1060 (N.Y. App. Div. 1989), *aff'd,* 564 N.E.2d 1046, 18 Media L. Rep. 1551 (N.Y. 1990) *1:* 304
Johnston
—v. Cartwright, 355 F.2d 32 (8th Cir. 1966) *2:* 520
—v. Corinthian Television Corp., 583 P.2d 1101, 3 Media L. Rep. 2518 (Okla. 1978) *2:* 327
—v. NBC, 356 F. Supp. 904 (E.D.N.Y. 1973) *9:* 78
John Z. v. Superior Ct., 2 Cal. Rptr. 2d 556 (Cal. Ct. App. 1991) *14:* 39
Jolly v. Valley Pub'g Co., 388 P.2d 139 (Wash. 1964) *2:* 541
Jones
—v. Herald Post Co., 18 S.W.2d 972 (Ky. 1929) *3:* 43, 53
—v. J.B. Lippincott Co., 694 F. Supp. 1216, 15 Media L. Rep. 2155 (D. Md. 1988) *7:* 29, 52
—v. North Carolina Prisoners' Labor Union, 433 U.S. 119 (1977) *9:* 272; *12:* 76, 78; *13:* 279–80, 288, 291, 295, 297
—v. Palmer Communications, 440 N.W.2d 884, 16 Media L. Rep. 2137 (Iowa 1989) *2:* 326, 506, 677; *3:* 17
—v. Taibbi, 508 F. Supp. 1069, 7 Media L. Rep. 1225 (D. Mass. 1981) *9:* 43
—v. Wilkinson, 800 F.2d 989 (10th Cir. 1986) *13:* 534–41

—People v.
——391 N.E.2d 1335, 5 Media L. Rep. 1262 (N.Y. 1979), *cert. denied,* 444 U.S. 946 (1979) *1:* 202
——422 N.Y.S.2d 999, 7 Media L. Rep. 2096 (N.Y. App. Div. 1981) *1:* 211
Jones/Seymour v. LeFebvre, 781 F. Supp. 355 (E.D. Pa. 1991), *aff'd,* 961 F.2d 1567 (3d Cir. 1992) *9:* 64
Joopanenko v. Gavagan, 67 So. 2d 434 (Fla. 1953) *2:* 130
Joplin Enters. v. Allen, 795 F. Supp. 349 (W.D. Wash. 1992) *6:* 218
Joseph Burstyn, Inc. v. Wilson, 343 U.S. 495, 1 Media L. Rep. 1357 (1952) *10:* 2, 39
Joseph S. Finch & Co. v. McKittrick, 305 U.S. 395 (1939) *11:* 182
Journal Newspapers v. State, 456 A.2d 963, 9 Media L. Rep. 1392 (Md. Ct. Spec. App.), *aff'd,* 465 A.2d 426, 9 Media L. Rep. 2233 (Md. 1983) *1:* 144, 147–48, 150
Journal Pub'g Co. v. Mechem, 801 F.2d 1233, 13 Media L. Rep. 1391 (10th Cir. 1986) *1:* 523
Joy v. North, 692 F.2d 880 (2d Cir. 1982), *cert. denied,* 460 U.S. 1051 (1983) *1:* 427, 429
Joyner v. Whiting, 477 F.2d 456 (4th Cir. 1973) *13:* 347
J.P. v. DeSanti, 653 F.2d 1080 (6th Cir. 1981) *9:* 61
J.S., In re, 438 A.2d 1125, 7 Media L. Rep. 2402 (Vt. 1981) *1:* 254–56
Judicial Conference Guidelines, In re, 18 Media L. Rep. 1270 (1990) *1:* 576
Judlo, Inc. v. Vons Cos., 259 Cal. Rptr. 624 (Cal. Ct. App. 1989) *12:* 90, 137
Julian v. American Business Consultants, 155 N.Y.S.2d 1, 137 N.E.2d 1 (N.Y. 1956) *2:* 270, 273
Jumez v. ABC Records, 3 Media L. Rep. 2324 (S.D.N.Y. 1978) *6:* 34
Jungherr v. San Francisco Unified Sch. Dist. Bd. of Educ., 923 F.2d 743 (9th Cir.), *cert. denied,* 112 S. Ct. 51 (1991) *2:* 682
Justice v. Belo Broadcasting, 472 F. Supp. 145 (N.D. Tex. 1979) *4:* 30

K

Kahn v. Bower, 284 Cal. Rptr. 244, 19 Media L. Rep. 1236 (Cal. Ct. App. 1991) *2:* 259–60, 268, 320, 338, 685
Kalian v. People Acting Through Community Effort, 408 A.2d 608, 5 Media L. Rep. 2174 (R.I. 1979) *3:* 20, 48, 94
Kanarek v. Bugliosi, 108 Cal. App. 3d 327, 166 Cal. Rptr. 526, 6 Media L. Rep. 1864 (Cal. Ct. App. 1980) *2:* 235–36
Kansas City Star Co.
—In re, 666 F.2d 1168, 7 Media L. Rep. 2353 (8th Cir. 1981) *1:* 380
—v. Fossey, 630 P.2d 1176, 7 Media L. Rep. 2250 (Kan. 1981) *1:* 144–45, 148, 150
—v. United States, 240 F.2d 643 (8th Cir.), *cert. denied,* 354 U.S. 923 (1957) *9:* 21; *13:* 226
Kansas Rental Trade Coop. v. Stephan, 695 F.2d 1343 (10th Cir. 1982) *11:* 305
Kapellas v. Kofman, 1 Cal. 3d 20, 459 P.2d 912 (Cal. 1969) *2:* 615; *3:* 16, 108; *4:* 143, 192
Kaplan
—v. County of L.A., 894 F.2d 1076 (9th Cir.), *cert. denied,* 496 U.S. 907 (1990) *13:* 401
—v. Newsweek, 10 Media L. Rep. 2142 (N.D. Cal. 1984), *aff'd,* 776 F.2d 1053, 12 Media L. Rep. 1277 (9th Cir. 1985) *2:* 135
Karaduman v. Newsday, 416 N.E.2d 557, 6 Media L. Rep. 2345 (N.Y. 1980) *2:* 223, 225
Karem v. Priest, 744 F. Supp. 136 (W.D. Tex. 1990) *14:* 67, 74, 90, 361
Kash Enters. v. Los Angeles, 562 P.2d 1302, 2 Media L. Rep. 1716 (Cal. 1977) *12:* 141, 144, 149, 153–55
Kasherman; State v., 224 N.W. 838 (Minn. 1929) *14:* 84
Kassell v. Gannett Co., 875 F.2d 935, 16 Media L. Rep. 1814 (1st Cir. 1989) *2:* 467, 482
Kastigar v. United States, 406 U.S. 441 (1972) *14:* 114
Katz
—v. Katz, 514 A.2d 1374, 13 Media L. Rep. 1296 (Pa. Super. Ct. 1986), *appeal denied,* 527 A.2d 542 (Pa. 1987) *1:* 454
—v. United States, 369 F.2d 130 (9th Cir.), *rev'd,* 389 U.S. 347 (1966) *5:* 33, 41, 193–94; *9:* 61; *11:* 276
Kay v. Federal Election Comm'n, 7 Media L. Rep. 1474 (D.D.C. 1981) *9:* 113
KCST-TV Channel 39 v. Municipal Ct., Ariz., 246 Cal. Rptr. 869, 16 Media L. Rep. 1026 (Cal. Ct. App. 1988) *1:* 568; *10:* 189
Kearns-Tribune Corp.
—v. Lewis, 685 P.2d 515, 10 Media L. Rep. 1737 (Utah 1984) *1:* 144, 146, 148–50
—v. Public Serv. Comm'n, 682 P.2d 858 (Utah 1984) *11:* 304
—v. Utah Bd. of Corrections, 2 Media L. Rep. 1353 (D. Utah 1977) *1:* 519
Kee v. Armstrong, Byrd & Co., 182 P. 494 (Okla. 1919) *2:* 164

Keen v. Philadelphia Daily News, 325 F. Supp. 929 (E.D. Pa. 1971) *9:* 43, 48

Keene Pub'g Corp.
—v. Cheshire County Super. Ct., 406 A.2d 137, 5 Media L. Rep. 1626 (N.H. 1979) *1:* 143; *10:* 194
—v. Keene Dist. Ct., 380 A.2d 261, 3 Media L. Rep. 1595 (N.H. 1977) *1:* 152, 154

Keenum v. Remington Arms Co., 15 Media L. Rep. 1447 (W.D. Okla. 1988) *7:* 12

Keeton v. Hustler Magazine, 465 U.S. 770, 10 Media L. Rep. 1405 (1984) *2:* 231–32, 238, 641, 654–57, 659–67

Kelly
—v. Hoffman, 74 A.2d 922 (N.J. Super. Ct. App. Div. 1950) *2:* 273
—v. Illinois Bell Tel. Co., 325 F.2d 148 (7th Cir. 1963) *11:* 153, 274
—v. Johnson Pub'g Co., 160 Cal. App. 2d 718, 325 P.2d 659 (Cal. Ct. App. 1958) *2:* 298, 301; *4:* 30
—v. Schmidberger, 806 F.2d 44 (2d Cir. 1986) *2:* 144
—v. William Morrow & Co., 186 Cal. App. 3d 1625, 231 Cal. Rptr. 497 (Cal. Ct. App. 1986) *2:* 512
—United States v.
——328 F.2d 227 (6th Cir. 1964) *11:* 279
——254 F. Supp. 9 (S.D.N.Y. 1966), *modified,* 395 F.2d 727 (2d Cir. 1968) *11:* 276

Kelner; United States v., 534 F.2d 1020 (2d Cir.), *cert. denied,* 429 U.S. 1022 (1976) *8:* 88

Kemner v. Monsanto Co., 492 N.E.2d 1327 (Ill. 1986) *10:* 205

Kennedy v. Cannon, 182 A.2d 54 (Md. Ct. App. 1962) *2:* 520

Kennedy for President Comm. v. FCC, 636 F.2d 432 (D.C. Cir. 1980) *13:* 122–30, 139, 165

Kentucky Utils. Co.; United States v., 124 F.R.D. 146 (E.D. Ky. 1989) *1:* 436, 438, 457

Kerley; United States v., 753 F.2d 617, 11 Media L. Rep. 1572 (7th Cir. 1985) *1:* 580, 637

Kewanee Oil Co. v. Bicron Corp., 416 U.S. 470 (1974) *6:* 91–92

K.F., In re, 559 A.2d 663, 16 Media L. Rep. 1984 (Vt. 1989) *1:* 256

KFGO Radio v. Rothe, 298 N.W.2d 505, 6 Media L. Rep. 2217 (N.D. 1980) *1:* 287

KFMB-TV Channel 8 v. Municipal Ct., 271 Cal. Rptr. 109, 17 Media L. Rep. 2294 (Cal. Ct. App. 1990) *1:* 640, 642

KGB, Inc. v. Giannoulas, 164 Cal. Rptr. 571 (Cal. Ct. App. 1980) *6:* 38

Khaury v. Playboy Pubns., 430 F. Supp. 1342 (S.D.N.Y. 1977) *3:* 107

Kievlan v. Dahlberg Elecs., 144 Cal. Rptr. 585 (Cal. Ct. App. 1978), *appeal dismissed,* 440 U.S. 951 (1979) *11:* 326

Kilgore v. Younger, 30 Cal. 3d 770, 640 P.2d 793, 8 Media L. Rep. 1886 (Cal. 1982) *2:* 563

Kimball v. Post Pub'g Co., 85 N.E. 103 (Mass. 1908) *2:* 562

Kimberlin v. Quinlan, 145 F.R.D. 1 (D.D.C. 1992) *1:* 278

Kimmerle v. New York Evening Journal, 186 N.E. 217 (N.Y. 1933) *2:* 2, 109

King Broadcasting Co., In re, 6 F.C.C.R. 4998, 69 Rad. Reg. 2d (P & F) 1017 (1991) *13:* 99

King Creations v. Conde Nast Pubns., 311 N.Y.S.2d 757 (N.Y. App. Div. 1970) *7:* 4

Kingsley Books v. Brown, 354 U.S. 436, 1 Media L. Rep. 1111 (1957) *10:* 1, 67

King World Prods., In re, 898 F.2d 56, 17 Media L. Rep. 1531 (6th Cir. 1990) *10:* 238

Kinsey v. Macur, 165 Cal. Rptr. 608 (Cal. Ct. App. 1980) *3:* 36; *4:* 39

Kipps v. Ewell, 391 F. Supp. 1285 (W.D. Va. 1975), *aff'd,* 538 F.2d 564 (4th Cir. 1976) *9:* 62

Kirkman v. Westchester Newspapers, 24 N.Y.S.2d 860 (N.Y. App. Div. 1941), *aff'd,* 39 N.E.2d 919 (N.Y. 1942) *2:* 293–94

Kish; United States v., 303 F. Supp. 1212 (N.D. Ind. 1969) *11:* 279

Klaxon Co. v. Stentor Elec. Mfg. Co., 313 U.S. 487 (1941) *14:* 376–77

Kleindienst v. Mandel, 408 U.S. 753 (1972) *11:* 139

Kleir Advertising v. Premier Pontiac, 921 F.2d 1036, 18 Media L. Rep. 1529 (10th Cir. 1990) *2:* 182

Klitzman, Klitzman & Gallagher v. Krut, 744 F.2d 955 (3d Cir. 1984) *14:* 482–84

Klos v. Zahorik, 84 N.W. 1046 (Iowa 1901) *2:* 271

Knight v. Neodesha Police Dep't, 620 P.2d 837 (Kan. Ct. App. 1980) *2:* 186

Knight-Ridder Broadcasting v. Greenberg, 511 N.E.2d 1116 (N.Y. 1987) *14:* 262, 345

Knight Pub'g Co., In re, 743 F.2d 231, 10 Media L. Rep. 2379 (4th Cir. 1984) *1:* 104, 217

Knops; State v., 183 N.W.2d 93 (Wis. 1971) *14:* 76, 79

Knudsen v. Kansas Gas & Elec. Co., 807 P.2d 71, 18 Media L. Rep. 1900 (Kan. 1991) *2:* 395

KOIN-TV, State ex rel. v. Olsen, 711 P.2d 966,

12 Media L. Rep. 1625 (Or. 1985) *1:* 447
Kokinda; United States v., 497 U.S. 720 (1990) *12:* 71
Kooistra; United States v., 796 F.2d 1390, 13 Media L. Rep. 1175 (11th Cir. 1986) *1:* 106, 119, 159, 382
Koppell v. Levine, 347 F. Supp. 456 (E.D.N.Y. 1972) *13:* 347
Kops v. New York Tel. Co., 456 F. Supp. 1090 (S.D.N.Y. 1978), *aff'd,* 803 F.2d 213 (2d Cir. 1979) *13:* 251
Koral Sales v. Dun & Bradstreet, 389 F. Supp. 985 (E.D. Wis. 1975) *2:* 536
Korean Air Lines Disaster, In re, 597 F. Supp. 621, 10 Media L. Rep. 2494 (D.D.C. 1984) *1:* 428
Korkala; People v., 472 N.Y.S.2d 310 (N.Y. App. Div. 1984) *14:* 423
Korn
—v. Elkins, 317 F. Supp. 138 (D. Md. 1970) *13:* 347
—v. Franchard Corp., *see* Milberg v. Western Pac. R.R. Co.
Korry v. International Tel. & Tel. Corp., 444 F. Supp. 193 (S.D.N.Y. 1978) *2:* 202–3, 585
Koster v. Chase Manhattan Bank, 93 F.R.D. 471, 8 Media L. Rep. 1155 (S.D.N.Y. 1982) *1:* 426
Kovach v. Maddux, 238 F. Supp. 835, 1 Media L. Rep. 2367 (M.D. Tenn. 1965) *1:* 539
Kovacs v. Cooper, 336 U.S. 77 (1949) *12:* 35, 194–95, 203
KPNX Broadcasting Co. v. Maricopa County Super. Ct., 678 P.2d 431, 10 Media L. Rep. 1289 (Ariz. 1984) *1:* 106, 122, 568; *10:* 194, 202
KPOJ, Inc. v. Thornton, 456 P.2d 76 (Or. 1969) *12:* 54
Kraisinger v. Liggett, 592 P.2d 477 (Kan. Ct. App. 1979) *2:* 582
Kramer v. Thompson, 947 F.2d 666 (3d Cir. 1991), *cert. denied,* 112 S. Ct. 2274 (1992) *10:* 241
Krause v. Rhodes, 535 F. Supp. 338 (N.D. Ohio 1979), *aff'd,* 671 F.2d 212, 8 Media L. Rep. 1130 (6th Cir.), *cert. denied,* 459 U.S. 823 (1982) *1:* 428, 438, 457
Kruse v. Rabe, 79 A. 316 (N.J. 1911) *2:* 545
Krzyske; United States v., 836 F.2d 1013 (6th Cir.), *cert. denied,* 488 U.S. 832 (1988) *10:* 204
KSTP Television, In re, 504 F. Supp. 360, 6 Media L. Rep. 2249 (D. Minn. 1980) *1:* 325, 354
Kunkin; People v., 507 P.2d 1392 (Cal. 1973) *5:* 169, 175–86

Kunz v. New York, 340 U.S. 290 (1951) *10:* 39
Kush v. Rutledge, 460 U.S. 719 (1983) *9:* 80
Kuszynski v. Oakland, 479 F.2d 1130 (9th Cir. 1973) *12:* 71
KUTV, Inc.
—v. Conder
——635 P.2d 412, 7 Media L. Rep. 1915 (Utah 1981) *1:* 277
——668 P.2d 513, 9 Media L. Rep. 1825 (Utah 1983) *10:* 194
—v. Wilkinson, 686 P.2d 456, 10 Media L. Rep. 1749 (Utah 1984) *10:* 194

L

LaCrone v. Ohio Bell Tel. Co., 182 N.E.2d 15 (Ohio Ct. App. 1961) *5:* 262
La Crosse Tribune, State ex rel. v. Circuit Ct., 340 N.W.2d 460, 10 Media L. Rep. 1041 (Wis. 1983) *1:* 225
Ladany v. William Morrow & Co., 465 F. Supp. 870, 4 Media L. Rep. 2153 (S.D.N.Y. 1978) *6:* 86
Ladone v. Lerner, 521 N.Y.S.2d 760, 14 Media L. Rep. 2110 (N.Y. App. Div. 1987) *1:* 641
Lady Ann's Oddities v. Macy, 519 F. Supp. 1140 (W.D. Okla. 1981) *11:* 307
La Follette, State ex rel. v. Hinkle, 229 P. 317 (Wash. 1924) *6:* 120
Lahr v. Adell Chem. Co., 300 F.2d 256 (1st Cir. 1962) *6:* 40
Lakewood, City of
—v. Colfax Unlimited Ass'n, 634 P.2d 52 (Colo. 1981) *12:* 184
—v. Plain Dealer Pub'g Co., 486 U.S. 750, 15 Media L. Rep. 1481 (1988) *12:* 6, 130–36, 140, 195
Lal v. CBS, 551 F. Supp. 356, 9 Media L. Rep. 1112 (E.D. Pa. 1982), *aff'd,* 726 F.2d 97, 10 Media L. Rep. 1276 (3d Cir. 1984) *5:* 78, 110; *14:* 288, 342
Lamar Advertising v. Daytona Beach, 450 So. 2d 1145 (Fla. Dist. Ct. App. 1984) *12:* 174
Lamar Outdoor Advertising v. Mississippi Tax Comm'n, 701 F.2d 314, 9 Media L. Rep. 1466 (5th Cir.), *reh'g granted,* 701 F.2d 336 (5th Cir. 1983) *11:* 113
Lamb v. Griffin Television, 804 F. Supp. 1430, 20 Media L. Rep. 1871 (W.D. Okla. 1992) *13:* 87
Lambert v. Dow Chem. Co., 215 So. 673 (La. 1968) *4:* 21
Lamberto v. Bown, 326 N.W.2d 305, 8 Media L. Rep. 2525 (Iowa 1982) *14:* 404

Landmark Communications v. Virginia, 435 U.S. 829, 3 Media L. Rep. 2153 (1978) *4:* 78–82; *5:* 123, 158, 188; *13:* 84

Lane v. Arkansas Valley Pub'g Co., 675 P.2d 747, 9 Media L. Rep. 1726 (Colo. Ct. App.), *cert. denied,* 467 U.S. 1252 (1984) *2:* 154

Langford v. Vanderbilt Univ., 287 S.W.2d 32 (Tenn. 1956) *4:* 62

Langworthy v. Pulitzer Pub'g Co., 368 S.W.2d 385 (Mo. 1963) *2:* 186; *7:* 12

Larkin v. Grendel's Den, 459 U.S. 116 (1982) *11:* 182

LaRouche v. NBC, 780 F.2d 1134, 12 Media L. Rep. 1585 (4th Cir.), *cert. denied,* 479 U.S. 818 (1986) *2:* 681

LaRouche Campaign; United States v., 841 F.2d 1176, 15 Media L. Rep. 1502 (1st Cir. 1988) *14:* 67, 90, 131–32, 170, 335, 363–64

Lashlee v. Sumner, 570 F.2d 107 (6th Cir. 1978) *2:* 624

Laskowski v. County of Nassau, 394 N.Y.S.2d 442 (N.Y. App. Div. 1977) *2:* 220

Lasky v. ABC, 631 F. Supp. 962, 13 Media L. Rep. 1379 (S.D.N.Y. 1986) *2:* 130

Las Vegas Sun v. Eighth Judicial Dist. Ct., 761 P.2d 849 (Nev. 1988) *14:* 243–45, 331, 341

Latana, Town of; v. Pelczynski, 303 So. 2d 326 (Fla. 1974) *12:* 54

Lauderback v. ABC, 741 F.2d 193, 10 Media L. Rep. 2241 (8th Cir. 1984), *cert. denied,* 469 U.S. 1190 (1985) *2:* 251, 259–60, 264, 267, 674

Lavdati v. Stea, 117 A. 422 (R.I. 1922) *2:* 5

Lawrence
—v. A.S. Abell Co., 475 A.2d 448, 10 Media L. Rep. 2001 (Md. 1984) *6:* 90
—v. Evans, 573 So. 2d 695, 18 Media L. Rep. 1524 (Miss. 1990) *2:* 135
—v. Moss, 639 F.2d 634, 6 Media L. Rep. 2377 (10th Cir.), *cert. denied,* 451 U.S. 1031 (1981) *2:* 396

Laxalt v. McClatchy
—622 F. Supp. 737, 12 Media L. Rep. 1377 (D. Nev. 1985) *2:* 684
—116 F.R.D. 438, 14 Media L. Rep. 1199 (D. Nev. 1987) *14:* 331, 374, 377–78

Layne v. Tribune Co., 146 So. 234 (Fla. 1933) *2:* 5, 224

League of Women Voters Educ. Fund v. FCC, *see* Geller, In re

Leatherman v. Tarrant County Narcotics Intelligence & Coordination Unit, 113 S. Ct. 1160 (1993) *9:* 45

Leathers v. Medlock, 111 S. Ct. 1438, 18 Media L. Rep. 1953 (1991) *9:* 240–43

Lebron v. Washington Metro. Area Transit Auth., 749 F.2d 893 (D.C. Cir. 1984) *13:* 429

Lechtner v. Brownyard, 679 F.2d 322 (3d Cir. 1982) *13:* 168

Ledger-Enquirer Co. v. Brown, 105 S.E.2d 229 (Ga. 1958) *2:* 127

Lee
—v. Board of Regents, 306 F. Supp. 1097 (W.D. Wis. 1969), *aff'd,* 441 F.2d 1257 (7th Cir. 1971) *13:* 347, 369
—v. Dong-A Ilbo, 849 F.2d 876, 15 Media L. Rep. 1593 (4th Cir. 1988), *cert. denied,* 489 U.S. 1067 (1989) *2:* 571
—v. Weston, 402 N.E.2d 23 (Ind. Ct. App. 1980) *2:* 297, 301

Leeb v. DeLong, 198 Cal. App. 3d 47, 243 Cal. Rptr. 494 (Cal. Ct. App. 1988) *13:* 363–64, 366–67

Legi-Tech v. Keiper, 766 F.2d 728, 11 Media L. Rep. 2482 (2d Cir. 1985) *1:* 293, 295; *13:* 400

LeGrand; People v., 415 N.Y.S.2d 252 (N.Y. App. Div. 1979) *14:* 265

Lehder-Rivas; United States v., 667 F. Supp. 827 (M.D. Fla. 1987) *10:* 208

Lehman v. Shaker Heights, 418 U.S. 298 (1974) *11:* 67

Leidholdt v. LFP, Inc., 860 F.2d 890, 15 Media L. Rep. 2201 (9th Cir. 1988), *cert. denied,* 489 U.S. 1080 (1989) *4:* 37; *6:* 73

Leininger v. New Orleans Item Pub'g Co., 101 So. 411 (La. 1924) *2:* 554

Leipzig v. Baldwin, *see* Baldwin v. Redwood City

Leiserson v. San Diego, 229 Cal. Rptr. 22 (Cal. Ct. App. 1986) *1:* 535

Le Mistral, Inc., v. CBS, 402 N.Y.S.2d 815, 3 Media L. Rep. 1913 (N.Y. App. Div. 1978) *5:* 13, 136

Lemons v. Mycro Group Co., 667 F. Supp. 665 (S.D. Iowa 1987) *10:* 241

Lent v. Huntoon, 470 A.2d 1162, 9 Media L. Rep. 2547 (Vt. 1983) *2:* 187

Leonardini v. Shell Oil Co., 264 Cal. Rptr. 883 (Cal. Ct. App. 1989) *10:* 239, 242

Lerette v. Dean Witter Org., 131 Cal. Rptr. 592 (Cal. Ct. App. 1976) *2:* 518

Lerman v. Flynt Distrib. Co., 745 F.2d 123, 10 Media L. Rep. 2497 (2d Cir. 1984), *cert. denied,* 471 U.S. 1054 (1985) *2:* 395, 591; *3:* 86; *6:* 18, 26, 43, 90

Lesher Communications v. Superior Ct., 274 Cal. Rptr. 154, 18 Media L. Rep. 1331 (Cal Ct. App. 1990) *1:* 525

Lester v. Powers, 596 A.2d 65 (Me. 1991) *2:* 245

Letellier, In re, 578 A.2d 722 (Me. 1990) *14:* 70, 76, 179

Leuth v. St. Clair County Community College, 732 F. Supp. 1410 (E.D. Mich. 1990) *13:* 359

Levas & Levas v. Village of Antioch, 684 F.2d 446 (7th Cir. 1982) *11:* 305

Leverton v. Curtis Pub'g Co., 192 F.2d 974 (3d Cir. 1951) *3:* 8, 32, 44; *3:* 32

Levine
—v. CMP Pubns., 738 F.2d 660, 10 Media L. Rep. 2337 (5th Cir. 1984), *reh'g denied,* 753 F.2d 1341 (1985) *2:* 396, 572, 638
—v. United States Dist. Ct., 764 F.2d 590, 11 Media L. Rep. 2289 (9th Cir. 1985), *cert. denied,* 476 U.S. 1158 (1986) *10:* 206–11

Levitch v. CBS, 495 F. Supp. 649 (S.D.N.Y. 1980) *9:* 43

Lewin v. McCreight, 655 F. Supp. 282, 13 Media L. Rep. 2454 (E.D. Mich. 1987) *7:* 29

Lewis
—In re, 384 F. Supp. 133 (C.D. Cal. 1974), *aff'd sub nom.* Lewis v. United States, 517 F.2d 236 (9th Cir. 1975) *14:* 116, 125, 371, 416, 422
—v. Baxley, 368 F. Supp. 768, 1 Media L. Rep. 2525 (M.D. Ala. 1973) *1:* 539
—v. Coursolle Broadcasting of Wis., 377 N.W.2d 166, 12 Media L. Rep. 1641 (Wis. 1985) *2:* 339
—v. Hayes, 132 P. 1022 (Cal. 1913) *2:* 199
—v. Time, Inc., 83 F.R.D. 455, 5 Media L. Rep. 1790 (E.D. Cal. 1979), *aff'd,* 710 F.2d 549, 9 Media L. Rep. 1984 (9th Cir. 1983) *2:* 223, 241, 247, 263, 481
—v. United States
——*see* Lewis, In re
——385 U.S. 206 (1966) *5:* 199, 201

Lewis Pub'g Co.
—v. Morgan, 229 U.S. 288 (1913) *9:* 270
—v. Wyman, 182 F. 13 (8th Cir. 1910), *aff'd,* 228 U.S. 610 (1913) *9:* 272

Lexington Herald-Leader
—v. Beard, 690 S.W.2d 374, 11 Media L. Rep. 1376 (Ky. 1984) *14:* 71, 77, 222–23
—v. Meigs, 660 S.W.2d 658, 9 Media L. Rep. 2153 (Ky. 1983) *1:* 106, 122, 225
—v. Tackett, 601 S.W.2d 905, 6 Media L. Rep. 1436 (Ky. 1980) *1:* 211

Libertelli v. Hoffman-La Roche, Inc., 7 Media L. Rep. 1734 (S.D.N.Y. 1981) *7:* 12, 29, 44, 54

Liberty Lobby
—v. Anderson
——746 F.2d 1563, 11 Media L. Rep. 1001 (D.C. Cir. 1984), *vacated,* 477 U.S. 242 (1986) *2:* 603
——No. 81-2240, 1990 U.S. Dist. LEXIS 19587, 19 Media L. Rep. 1011 (D.D.C. 1990) *2:* 439
—v. Dow Jones & Co., 838 F.2d 1287, 14 Media L. Rep. 2249 (D.C. Cir.), *cert. denied,* 488 U.S. 825 (1988) *2:* 572
—v. Pearson, 261 F. Supp. 726 (D.D.C. 1966), *aff'd,* 390 F.2d 489 (D.C. Cir. 1968) *5:* 82, 147, 156
—v. Rees, 111 F.R.D. 19 (D.D.C. 1986) *14:* 98–99, 151, 359

Liddy; United States v., 354 F. Supp. 208 (D.D.C. 1972), *emerg. motions for stay denied,* 478 F.2d 586 (D.C. Cir. 1972) *14:* 161, 343

Liebel v. Montgomery Ward & Co., 62 P.2d 667 (Mont. 1936) *2:* 206

Life Printing & Pub'g Co. v. Field, 58 N.E.2d 307 (Ill. App. Ct. 1944) *2:* 5

Lightman v. State, 294 A.2d 149 (Md. Ct. Spec. App.), *aff'd,* 295 A.2d 212 (Md. 1972), *cert. denied,* 411 U.S. 951 (1973) *14:* 72, 231, 233, 413, 419

Lindsay v. San Antonio, 821 F.2d 1103 (5th Cir. 1987), *cert. denied,* 484 U.S. 1010 (1988) *12:* 177, 181–82, 185

Lininger v. Knight, 226 P.2d 809 (Colo. 1951) *2:* 221

Linmark Assocs. v. Township of Willingboro, 431 U.S. 85 (1977) *11:* 85, 314; *12:* 4, 14, 32–33, 164–69

Linn v. United Plant Guard Workers, 383 U.S. 53 (1966) *2:* 400, 427, 591, 596

Lipps v. State, 258 N.E.2d 622 (Ind. 1970) *14:* 83, 218

Litman v. Massachusetts Mut. Life Ins. Co., 739 F.2d 1549 (11th Cir. 1984) *2:* 510

Littlefield v. Fort Dodge Messenger, 481 F. Supp. 919 (N.D. Iowa 1978), *aff'd,* 614 F.2d 581, 5 Media L. Rep. 2325 (8th Cir.), *cert. denied,* 445 U.S. 945 (1980) *2:* 135, 162, 396, 596

Littlejohn v. BIC Corp., 851 F.2d 673, 15 Media L. Rep. 1841 (3d Cir. 1988) *1:* 427, 430, 457

Little Rock Newspapers v. Dodrill, 660 S.W.2d 933, 10 Media L. Rep. 1063 (Ark. 1983) *2:* 599, 601

Live Oak Pub'g Co. v. Cohagan, 286 Cal. Rptr. 198 (Cal. Ct. App. 1991) *2:* 513, 703

L.L. Bean, Inc. v. Drake Pubrs., 850 F.2d 26, 13 Media L. Rep. 2009 (1st Cir.), *cert. denied and appeal dismissed,* 483 U.S. 1013 (1987) *10:* 248, 250–53, 255–57

Lloyd
—v. Harris, 194 N.W. 101 (Minn. 1923) *2:* 201
—United States ex rel. v. Vincent, 520 F.2d

Lloyd—Contd.
1272 (2d. Cir.), *cert. denied,* 423 U.S. 937 (1975) *1:* 196, 198–201
Lloyd Corp. v. Tanner, 407 U.S. 551 (1972) *12:* 88
Lloyds v. United Press Int'l, 311 N.Y.S.2d 373 (N.Y. Sup. Ct. 1970) *2:* 394
Loadholtz v. Fields, 389 F. Supp. 1299 (M.D. Fla. 1975) *14:* 335
Locke v. Gibbons, 299 N.Y.S. 188 (N.Y. Sup. Ct. 1937), *aff'd,* 2 N.Y.S.2d 1015 (N.Y. App. Div. 1938) *2:* 171, 173
Locricchio v. Evening News Ass'n, 476 N.W.2d 112, 20 Media L. Rep. 1065 (Mich. 1991), *cert. denied,* 112 S. Ct. 1267 (1992) *2:* 139, 704
Logan v. District of Columbia, 447 F. Supp. 1328, 3 Media L. Rep. 2094 (D.D.C. 1978) *2:* 603; *3:* 59, 86; *4:* 68, 70
Lombardo v. Doyle, Dane & Bernbach, 396 N.Y.S.2d 661, 2 Media L. Rep. 2321 (N.Y. App. Div. 1977) *6:* 38, 127, 200
Long
—v. Anaheim, 63 Cal. Rptr. 56 (Cal. Ct. App. 1967) *12:* 158
—v. Arcell, 618 F.2d 1145, 6 Media L. Rep. 1430 (5th Cir. 1980), *cert. denied,* 449 U.S. 1083 (1981) *2:* 440
Long Island Lighting Co.
—v. Barbash, 625 F. Supp. 221 (E.D.N.Y.), *rev'd,* 779 F.2d 793 (2d Cir. 1985) *9:* 212–15
—v. New York Pub. Serv. Comm'n, 5 Media L. Rep. 1241 (E.D.N.Y. 1979) *11:* 300
Lopez
—United States v., 14 Media L. Rep. 2203 (N.D. Ill. 1987) *14:* 47, 59, 67, 90
—v. Triangle Communications, 421 N.Y.S.2d 57, 5 Media L. Rep. 2039 (N.Y. App. Div. 1979) *6:* 26
—v. United States, 373 U.S. 427 (1963) *5:* 199, 200, 202
Lorain Journal Co.; United States v., 92 F. Supp. 794 (N.D. Ohio 1950), *aff'd,* 342 U.S. 143, 1 Media L. Rep. 2697 (1951) *9:* 13–21; *13:* 210, 220, 222–25
Lorentz v. RKO Radio Pictures, 155 F.2d 84 (9th Cir.), *cert. denied,* 329 U.S. 727 (1946) *2:* 122, 167
Loretto v. Teleprompter Manhattan CATV Corp., 458 U.S. 419 (1982) *12:* 245
Loring v. Bellsouth Advertising & Pub'g Corp., 339 S.E.2d 372 (Ga. Ct. App. 1985) *13:* 248
Los Angeles v. Preferred Communications (Preferred II), 476 U.S. 488, 13 Media L. Rep. 2244 (1986) *12:* 220–27, 230; *13:* 533
Los Angeles City Council v. Taxpayers for Vincent, 466 U.S. 789 (1984) *12:* 2, 11, 34–35, 111, 164, 175–77, 181–82, 227
Los Angeles Fire & Police Protective League v. Rodgers, 86 Cal. Rptr. 623 (Cal. Ct. App. 1970) *2:* 310
Los Angeles Free Press v. Los Angeles, 88 Cal. Rptr. 605 (Cal. Ct. App. 1970), *cert. denied,* 401 U.S. 982 (1971) *1:* 533
Los Angeles Memorial Coliseum Comm. v. National Football League, 89 F.R.D. 489 (C.D. Cal. 1981) *14:* 148–50, 169, 315–16, 322, 371–72, 404
Loska v. Superior Ct., 233 Cal. Rptr. 213 (Cal. Ct. App. 1986) *11:* 49
Louisiana Consumers League v. Louisiana State Bd. of Optometry Examiners, 557 F.2d 473 (5th Cir. 1977) *11:* 323
Louisiana Life v. McNamara, 504 So. 2d 900 (La. Ct. App. 1987) *9:* 234
Louisville Times Co. v. Emrich, 66 S.W.2d 73 (Ky. 1933) *2:* 301
Loveday v. FCC, 707 F.2d 1443, 9 Media L. Rep. 1673 (D.C. Cir.), *cert. denied,* 464 U.S. 1008 (1983) *12:* 218
Lovell v. City of Griffin, 303 U.S. 444 (1938) *10:* 39; *12:* 58, 96–99, 102, 110, 117; *14:* 30
Lovett v. Caddo, 584 So. 2d 1197, 19 Media L. Rep. 1670 (La. Ct. App. 1991) *2:* 472–73
Lovgren v. Citizens First Nat'l Bank of Princeton, 534 N.E.2d 987, 16 Media L. Rep. 1214 (Ill. 1989) *3:* 83; *5:* 21, 154
Lowe
—v. Brown, 235 P. 272 (Or. 1925) *2:* 4
—v. DeHoog, 193 S.W. 969 (Mo. 1917) *2:* 200
—v. SEC, 472 U.S. 181 (1985) *9:* 149; *11:* 82
Lowenschuss v. West Pub'g Co., 542 F.2d 180 (3d Cir. 1976) *2:* 553
Lucasfilm v. High Frontier, 622 F. Supp. 931 (D.D.C. 1985) *10:* 249
Ludtke v. Kuhn, 461 F. Supp. 86, 4 Media L. Rep. 1625 (S.D.N.Y. 1978) *1:* 545, 638
Luecke v. G.P. Putnam's Sons, 10 Media L. Rep. 1250 (S.D.N.Y. 1983) *6:* 30
Lugar v. Edmondson Oil Co., 457 U.S. 922 (1982) *5:* 196; *9:* 42, 45, 47, 51
Lugosi v. Universal Pictures, 160 Cal. Rptr. 323, 5 Media L. Rep. 2185 (Cal. 1979) *6:* 78, 152, 159–62, 164–66, 176
Luparer v. Stoneman, 382 F. Supp. 495 (D. Vt. 1974), *appeal dismissed,* 517 F.2d 1395 (2d Cir. 1975) *13:* 281–85
Luster v. Retail Credit Co., 575 F.2d 609 (8th Cir. 1978) *2:* 225, 584
Lutz v. Hoffman, 4 Media L. Rep. 2294 (E.D.N.Y. 1979) *6:* 72

Lyles v. State, 330 P.2d 734 (Okla. Crim. App. 1958)   *1:* 635
Lynch v. Republic Pub'g Co., 243 P.2d 636 (Wash. 1952)   *2:* 619

M

Mabee v. White Plains Pub'g Co., 327 U.S. 178 (1946)   *9:* 124
MacConnell v. Mitten, 638 P.2d 689 (Ariz. 1981)   *2:* 241
MacDonald; United States v., 607 F. Supp. 1183 (D.N.C. 1985)   *9:* 263
Machleder v. Diaz
—538 F. Supp. 1364 (S.D.N.Y. 1982)   *5:* 16, 30, 41, 111, 141
—618 F. Supp. 1367, 12 Media L. Rep. 1193 (S.D.N.Y. 1985), *aff'd in part and rev'd in part,* 801 F.2d 46, 13 Media L. Rep. 1369 (2d Cir. 1986), *cert. denied,* 479 U.S. 1088 (1987)   *3:* 12, 38, 47, 54, 58–61, 83
MacKown v. Illinois Pub'g & Printing Co., 6 N.E.2d 526 (Ill. App. Ct. 1937)   *7:* 16
MacLeod v. Tribune Pub'g Co., 343 P.2d 36 (Cal. 1959)   *2:* 130–32
MacRae v. Afro-Am. Co., 172 F. Supp. 184 (E.D. Pa. 1959), *aff'd,* 274 F.2d 287 (3d Cir. 1960)   *2:* 124, 134, 147
Madison v. Yunker, 589 P.2d 126, 4 Media L. Rep. 1337 (Mont. 1978)   *2:* 612
Madison Joint Sch. Dist. v. Wisconsin Employment Relations Comm'n, 429 U.S. 167 (1976)   *12:* 60, 62; *13:* 270
Magenis v. Fisher Broadcasting, 798 P.2d 1106, 18 Media L. Rep. 1229 (Or. Ct. App. 1990)   *3:* 108, 113; *5:* 145
Maheu
—v. CBS, Inc., 247 Cal. Rptr. 304, 15 Media L. Rep. 1548 (Cal. Ct. App. 1988)   *6:* 43, 84
—v. Hughes Tool Co., 569 F.2d 459, 3 Media L. Rep. 1847 (9th Cir. 1977)   *2:* 599
Mahnke v. Northwest Pubns., 124 N.W.2d 411 (Minn. 1963)   *2:* 615
Maidman v. Jewish Pubns., 355 P.2d 265 (Cal. 1960)   *2:* 539, 543
Maine v. Thiboutot, 448 U.S. 1 (1980)   *9:* 47
Makofsky v. Cunningham, 576 F.2d 1223 (5th Cir. 1978)   *2:* 135
Maldonado v. County of Monterey, 330 F. Supp. 1282 (N.D. Cal. 1971)   *12:* 201
Malik, In re, 552 N.Y.S.2d 182 (N.Y. App. Div. 1990)   *13:* 307
Maloof v. Post Pub'g Co., 28 N.E.2d 458 (Mass. 1940)   *2:* 226
Manale v. New Orleans Dep't of Police, 673 F.2d 122 (5th Cir. 1982)   *2:* 135
Manax v. McNamara, 660 F. Supp. 657 (W.D. Tex. 1987), *aff'd,* 842 F.2d 808, 15 Media L. Rep. 1655 (5th Cir. 1988)   *9:* 43, 45, 51, 76, 84, 177
Mancini, In re, 219 USPQ 1047 (T.M.T.A.B. 1983)   *6:* 150–51
Mandel v. Bradley, 432 U.S. 173 (1977)   *11:* 190–91
Maness v. Meyers, 419 U.S. 449 (1975)   *14:* 114
Manger v. Kree Inst. of Electrolysis, 233 F.2d 5 (2d Cir. 1956)   *6:* 51
Mann v. State's Attorney for Montgomery County, 468 A.2d 124, 10 Media L. Rep. 1114 (Md. Ct. App. 1983)   *1:* 498
Manual Enters. v. Day, 370 U.S. 478 (1962)   *7:* 14, 18
Maple Properties v. Superior Ct., *see* Okun v. Superior Ct.
Marchesi v. Franchino, 387 A.2d 1129 (Md. 1978)   *2:* 541
Marchetti; United States v., 466 F.2d 1309, 1 Media L. Rep. 1051 (4th Cir.), *cert. denied,* 409 U.S. 1063 (1972)   *10:* 134–42, 154–55, 161
Marcone v. Penthouse Int'l, 533 F. Supp. 353, 8 Media L. Rep. 1444 (E.D. Pa. 1982), *rev'd,* 754 F.2d 1072, 11 Media L. Rep. 1577 (3d Cir.), *cert. denied,* 474 U.S. 864 (1985)   *2:* 183–84; *2:* 601
Marcos; United States v., 17 Media L. Rep. 2005 (S.D.N.Y. 1990)   *14:* 136, 151
Marc's Restaurant v. CBS, 730 S.W.2d 582 (Mo. Ct. App. 1987)   *13:* 212, 221, 227, 243
Marcus v. Search Warrants of Property, 367 U.S. 717 (1961)   *10:* 67
Maressa v. New Jersey Monthly, 445 A.2d 376 (N.J.), *cert. denied,* 459 U.S. 907 (1982)   *14:* 248
Marion County Sheriff's Merit Bd. v. Peoples Broadcasting Corp., 547 N.E.2d 235, 17 Media L. Rep. 1521 (Ind. 1989)   *1:* 304
Maritote v. Desilu Prods., 345 F.2d 418 (7th Cir.), *cert. denied,* 382 U.S. 883 (1965)   *4:* 30; *6:* 154, 216
Mark v. Seattle Times, 635 P.2d 1081, 7 Media L. Rep. 2209 (Wash. 1981), *cert. denied,* 457 U.S. 1124 (1982)   *5:* 9, 22, 29
Marketos v. American Employers Ins. Co., 460 N.W.2d 272 (Mich. Ct. App. 1990)   *14:* 70, 77, 236
Markiewicz; United States v., 732 F. Supp. 316 (N.D.N.Y. 1990)   *14:* 96–97
Marks v. United States, 430 U.S. 188 (1977)   *13:* 390

Marlin Firearms Co. v. Shields, 64 N.E. 163 (N.Y. 1902) *10:* 239
Marquette v. Warner Bros., 16 Media L. Rep. 1957 (N.Y. Sup. Ct. 1989) *6:* 87
Marrero v. Hialeah, 625 F.2d 499 (5th Cir. 1980), *cert. denied,* 450 U.S. 913 (1981) *2:* 520
Marrese v. American Academy of Orthopaedic Surgeons, 726 F.2d 1150 (7th Cir. 1984) *14:* 142, 145–47
Marsh v. Alabama, 326 U.S. 501 (1946) *12:* 86
Marsh Media v. FCC, 798 F.2d 772, 13 Media L. Rep. 1676 (D.C. Cir. 1986) *9:* 21
Martin
—v. Merola, 532 F.2d 191 (2d Cir. 1976) *9:* 48
—v. Municipal Pubns., 510 F. Supp. 255 (E.D. Pa. 1981) *3:* 54
—v. Outboard Marine Corp., 113 N.W.2d 135 (Wis. 1962) *2:* 170, 187
—v. Rison, 741 F. Supp. 1406 (N.D. Cal. 1990) *13:* 308
—v. City of Struthers, 319 U.S. 141 (1943) *5:* 61; *12:* 10, 35, 40, 83, 91, 93, 95, 100, 110, 112, 116
—v. United States, 389 F.2d 895 (5th Cir.), *cert. denied,* 391 U.S. 919 (1968) *11:* 275
—United States v., 746 F.2d 964, 10 Media L. Rep. 2465 (3d Cir. 1984) *1:* 350
Martinez v. Democrat-Herald Pub'g Co., 669 P.2d 818, 10 Media L. Rep. 1340 (Or. Ct. App. 1983) *6:* 73
Martin Luther King, Jr. Ctr. for Social Change v. American Heritage Prods., 296 S.E.2d 697, 8 Media L. Rep. 2377 (Ga. 1982) *6:* 7, 18, 45, 209–13
Martin Marietta Corp. v. Evening Star Newspaper Co., 417 F. Supp. 947 (D.D.C. 1976) *2:* 482
Maryland Pennysaver Group v. Maryland Comptroller, 594 A.2d 1142, 19 Media L. Rep. 1937 (Md. Ct. App. 1991) *9:* 241
Mashburn v. Collin, 355 So. 2d 879, 3 Media L. Rep. 1673 (La. 1977) *2:* 261
Mason v. Sullivan, 271 N.Y.S.2d 314 (N.Y. App. Div. 1966) *2:* 207–8
Massachusetts v. Corsetti, 438 N.E.2d 805, 8 Media L. Rep. 2113 (Mass. 1982) *14:* 361
Massachusetts Fair Share v. Town of Rockland, 610 F. Supp. 682 (D. Mass. 1985) *12:* 120
Masson v. New Yorker Magazine
—111 S. Ct. 2419, 18 Media L. Rep. 2241 (1991) *2:* 445, 450–51, 607–9
—960 F.2d 896, 20 Media L. Rep. 1009 (9th Cir. 1992) *2:* 609

Matchett v. Chicago Bar Ass'n, 467 N.E.2d 271, 10 Media L. Rep. 2131 (Ill. App. Ct. 1984), *cert. denied,* 471 U.S. 1054 (1985) *10:* 239
Matera v. Superior Ct., 825 P.2d 971, 19 Media L. Rep. 2053 (Ariz. Ct. App. 1992) *14:* 192, 311
Mathis v. Philadelphia Newspapers, 455 F. Supp. 406 (E.D. Pa. 1978) *2:* 565
Mattheis v. Hoyt, 136 F. Supp. 119 (N.D. Mich. 1955) *9:* 45, 48, 78–79
Matthes v. East Fishkill, 785 F.2d 43, 12 Media L. Rep. 1874 (2d Cir. 1986) *9:* 94
Matthews v. Town of Needham, 764 F.2d 58 (1st Cir. 1985) *12:* 174
Mattice v. Wilcox, 42 N.E. 270 (N.Y. 1895) *2:* 150
Mattox v. News Syndicate Co., 176 F.2d 897 (2d Cir.), *cert. denied,* 338 U.S. 858 (1949) *2:* 231
Mattson v. Chronicle Pub'g Co., 509 N.E.2d 150, 14 Media L. Rep. 1185 (Ill. App. Ct. 1987) *2:* 551
Mau v. Rio Grande Oil, 28 F. Supp. 845 (N.D. Cal. 1939) *4:* 36
Maughan v. NL Indus., 524 F. Supp. 93 (D.D.C. 1981) *14:* 328
Maurice v. NLRB, 7 Media L. Rep. 2221 (S.D. W. Va. 1981), *rev'd,* 691 F.2d 182 (4th Cir. 1982) *14:* 126–27, 333
May
—v. Collins, 122 F.R.D. 535 (S.D. Ind. 1988) *14:* 47, 59, 63, 90, 374
—v. Michigan, 10 Media L. Rep. 2454 (E.D. Mich. 1984) *9:* 45, 84
—v. People, 636 P.2d 672 (Colo. 1981) *12:* 124
Mayor & City Council of Baltimore v. Crockett, 415 A.2d 606 (Md. Ct. Spec. App. 1980), *cert. denied,* 405 U.S. 967 (1981) *12:* 169
Maysville Transit Co. v. Ort, 177 S.W.2d 369 (Ky. 1943) *4:* 33, 69, 70; *6:* 13
Mazzella v. Philadelphia Newspapers, 479 F. Supp. 523 (E.D.N.Y. 1979) *14:* 374, 377, 380
Mazzetti v. United States, 518 F.2d 781 (10th Cir. 1975) *1:* 569
McAndrew v. Scranton Republican Pub'g Co., 72 A.2d 780 (Pa. 1950) *2:* 130
McAuley, In re, 408 N.E.2d 697 (Ohio Ct. App. 1979) *14:* 79, 275
McBride
—v. Merrell Dow Pharmaceuticals, 800 F.2d 1208, 13 Media L. Rep. 1386 (D.C. Cir. 1986) *2:* 459
—v. State, 477 A.2d 174 (Del. 1984) *14:* 137
McCabe
—v. Kevin Jenkins & Assocs., 531 F. Supp.

648, 8 Media L. Rep. 1802 (E.D. Pa. 1982) *2:* 644
—v. Village Voice, 550 F. Supp 525, 8 Media L. Rep. 2580 (E.D. Pa. 1982) *4:* 146
McCall v. Courier-Journal & Louisville Times Co., 6 Media L. Rep. 1112 (Ky. Ct. App. 1980), *rev'd,* 623 S.W.2d 882, 7 Media L. Rep. 2118 (Ky. 1981), *cert. denied,* 456 U.S. 975 (1982) *2:* 580; *3:* 12, 14, 23, 83–84, 89; *5:* 37, 265; *6:* 122
McCammon & Assocs. v. McGraw-Hill Broadcasting Co., 716 P.2d 490, 12 Media L. Rep. 1846 (Colo. Ct. App. 1986) *3:* 83
McClatchy Newspapers v. Superior Ct.
—189 Cal. App. 3d 961, 234 Cal. Rptr. 702, 13 Media L. Rep. 2281 (Cal. Ct. App. 1987) *2:* 524, 552
—751 P.2d 1329, 15 Media L. Rep. 1529 (Cal. 1988) *1:* 162, 387
McCollum v. CBS Inc., 249 Cal. Rptr. 187, 15 Media L. Rep. 2001 (Cal. Ct. App. 1988) *8:* 2, 10, 12, 14, 20, 24–27, 29, 43, 48–49, 60, 80, 89
McCormack
—v. Oklahoma Pub'g Co., 613 P.2d 737 (Okla. 1980) *3:* 14, 23
—State v., 682 P.2d 742 (N.M. 1984) *5:* 134
McCoy
—v. Hearst Corp., 727 P.2d 711, 13 Media L. Rep. 2169 (Cal. 1986), *cert. denied,* 481 U.S. 1041 (1987) *2:* 303, 305, 421; *6:* 85; *14:* 441
—v. Providence Journal Co., 190 F.2d 760 (1st Cir.), *cert. denied,* 342 U.S. 894 (1951) *1:* 292, 295
McCracken v. Evening News Ass'n, 141 N.W.2d 694 (Mich. 1966) *2:* 565
McDaniel v. Atlanta Coca-Cola Bottling Co., 2 S.E.2d 810 (Ga. Ct. App. 1939) *5:* 262
McDonald
—v. Nugent, 98 N.W. 506 (Iowa 1904) *2:* 199
—v. Santa Fe Trail Transp. Co., 427 U.S. 273 (1976) *9:* 87
—v. Smith, 472 U.S. 479 (1985), *on remand,* Smith v. McDonald, 895 F.2d 147, 17 Media L. Rep. 1499 (4th Cir. 1990) *2:* 519
McDonough; United States v., 835 F.2d 1103 (5th Cir. 1988) *11:* 275
McGeehee v. Casey, 7 Media L. Rep. 2270 (D.D.C. 1981) *10:* 154
McGlynn v. New Jersey Pub. Broadcasting, 439 A.2d 54, 7 Media L. Rep. 2446 (N.J. 1981) *13:* 397
McGraw-Hill, Inc.
—v. Arizona, 680 F.2d 5 (2d Cir.), *cert. denied,* 459 U.S. 909 (1982) *14:* 65, 90, 99

—v. State Tax Comm'n, 541 N.Y.S.2d 252 (N.Y. App. Div. 1989), *aff'd,* 552 N.E.2d 163 (N.Y. 1990) *9:* 234
McGuire v. Adkins, 226 So. 2d 659 (Ala. 1969) *2:* 1
McKenzie; United States v.
—697 F.2d 1225 (5th Cir. 1983) *10:* 179, 194
—735 F.2d 907, 10 Media L. Rep. 1997 (5th Cir. 1984) *10:* 194, 271–75
McKinney v. Avery Journal, 393 S.E.2d 295, 18 Media L. Rep. 1204 (N.C. Ct. App. 1990) *2:* 472–73
McLain v. Boise Cascade Corp., 533 P.2d 343 (Or. 1975) *5:* 9, 32
McLaughlin v. Fisher, 24 N.E. 60 (Ill. 1890) *2:* 165
McLinn, In re, 739 F.2d 1395 (9th Cir. 1984) *3:* 107
McNabb v. Oregonian Pub'g Co., 685 P.2d 458, 10 Media L. Rep. 2181 (Or. Ct. App.), *review denied,* 687 P.2d 797 (Or. 1984) *14:* 282
McNally
—v. Pulitzer Pub'g Co., 532 F.2d 69 (8th Cir.), *cert. denied,* 429 U.S. 855 (1976) *5:* 31, 141, 147–57; *9:* 64, 76
—v. United States, 483 U.S. 350 (1987) *5:* 161
—v. Yarnall, 764 F. Supp. 853 (S.D.N.Y. 1991) *2:* 520
McNamara
—v. Freedom Newspapers, 802 S.W.2d 901, 18 Media L. Rep. 1679 (Tex. Ct. App. 1991) *4:* 55, 58
—v. Goldan, 87 N.E. 440 (N.Y. 1909) *2:* 169
McNeil v. Hupy, 18 Media L. Rep. 1238 (Or. Cir. Ct. 1990) *14:* 283
McNutt v. New Mexico State Tribune Co., 538 P.2d 804 (N.M. Ct. App.), *cert. denied,* 540 P.2d 248 (N.M. 1975) *4:* 162
Meadowbrook Women's Clinic v. Minnesota, 557 F. Supp. 1172, 9 Media L. Rep. 1325 (D. Minn. 1983) *11:* 287
Mecham; State v., 15 Media L. Rep. 2151 (Ariz. Super. Ct. 1988) *1:* 162, 388
Media Gen. Cable of Fairfax v. Sequoyah Condominium Council of Co-Owners, 991 F.2d 1169 (4th Cir. 1993) *12:* 245
Medico v. Time, Inc., 643 F.2d 134, 6 Media L. Rep. 2529 (3d Cir.), *cert. denied,* 454 U.S. 836 (1981) *2:* 557, 565, 580
Meeropol v. Nizer, 560 F.2d 1061, 2 Media L. Rep. 2269 (2d Cir. 1977), *cert. denied,* 434 U.S. 1013 (1978) *2:* 398, 432; *4:* 24; *6:* 31, 84
Meese v. Keene, 481 U.S. 465, 14 Media L. Rep. 1385 (1987) *12:* 217

Meetze v. Associated Press, 95 S.E.2d 606 (S.C. 1956) *4:* 162
MEF Enters. v. Houston, *see* SDJ, Inc. v. Houston
Megarry v. Norton, 290 P.2d 571 (Cal. Ct. App. 1955) *2:* 155
Mehau v. Gannett Pac. Corp., 658 P.2d 312, 9 Media L. Rep. 1337 (Haw. 1983) *2:* 475
Meiners v. Moriarity, 563 F.2d 343 (7th Cir.) *2:* 325
Melton v. Bow, 247 S.E.2d 100 (Ga.), *cert. denied,* 439 U.S. 985 (1978) *2:* 162
Melvin v. Reid, 112 Cal. App. 285, 297 P. 91 (Cal. Ct. App. 1931) *4:* 24, 111–16, 158
Memphis Dev. Found. v. Factors Etc., 616 F.2d 956, 5 Media L. Rep. 2521 (6th Cir. 1980), *cert. denied,* 449 U.S. 953 (1980) *6:* 160, 187–88
Memphis Pub'g Co.
—In re, 887 F.2d 646, 16 Media L. Rep. 2384 (6th Cir. 1989) *1:* 233–36
—v. Leech, 539 F. Supp. 405, 8 Media L. Rep. 1601 (W.D. Tenn. 1982) *11:* 184, 213–14
—v. Nichols, 569 S.W.2d 412, 4 Media L. Rep. 1573 (Tenn. 1978) *2:* 147, 187
Memphis Shoppers News v. Woods, 584 S.W.2d 196, 5 Media L. Rep. 1445 (Tenn. 1979) *9:* 248
Mendelsohn; United States v., 896 F.2d 1183 (9th Cir. 1990) *11:* 278–79
Mendonsa v. Time, Inc., 678 F. Supp. 967, 15 Media L. Rep. 1017 (D.R.I. 1988) *6:* 23, 27
Mendoza v. Gallup Indep. Co., 764 P.2d 492, 15 Media L. Rep. 2319 (N.M. Ct. App. 1988) *2:* 115
Mercury Motors Express v. Smith, 393 So. 2d 545 (Fla. 1981) *2:* 485
Meredith v. Gavin, 446 F.2d 794 (8th Cir. 1971) *5:* 223–24, 226, 228
Meredith Corp. v. FCC, 809 F.2d 863 (D.C. Cir. 1987) *13:* 183–88
Merle v. Sociological Research Film Corp., 152 N.Y.S. 829 (N.Y. App. Div. 1915) *6:* 88
Merola
—In re, 415 N.Y.S.2d 992, 5 Media L. Rep. 1033 (N.Y. App. Div.), *aff'd,* 393 N.E.2d 1038, 5 Media L. Rep. 1371 (1980), *cert. denied,* 448 U.S. 910 (1980) *1:* 123
—v. Warner, 427 N.Y.S.2d 808, 6 Media L. Rep. 1250 (N.Y. App. Div. 1980) *1:* 149
Messerli v. State, 626 P.2d 81 (Alaska 1980) *12:* 212
Metro Broadcasting v. FCC, 497 U.S. 547, *reh'g denied,* 497 U.S. 1050 (1990) *13:* 78

Metromedia, Inc.
—v. Baltimore, 538 F. Supp. 1183, 8 Media L. Rep. 1762 (D. Md. 1982) *12:* 174
—v. San Diego, 453 U.S. 490 (1981) *11:* 101–4, 197; *12:* 4, 11, 33, 122, 162, 164–65, 170–71, 173–74
Metter v. Los Angeles Examiner, 35 Cal. App. 2d 304, 95 P.2d 491 (Cal. Ct. App. 1939) *4:* 30, 51
Meyer v. Grant, 486 U.S. 414 (1988) *12:* 33
Miami Herald Pub'g Co.
—v. Chappell, 403 So. 2d 1342, 7 Media L. Rep. 1956 (Fla. Dist. Ct. App. 1981) *1:* 173, 180–83
—v. Hallandale, 734 F.2d 666, 10 Media L. Rep. 2049 (11th Cir. 1984) *12:* 141–42
—v. Lewis, 426 So. 2d 1, 8 Media L. Rep. 2281 (Fla. 1982) *1:* 143, 146, 148–50
—v. Marko, 352 So. 2d 518, 3 Media L. Rep. 1542 (Fla. 1977) *1:* 162, 387, 389–90
—v. Morejon, 561 So. 2d 577, 17 Media L. Rep. 1921 (Fla. 1990) *14:* 70, 413
—v. State, 363 So. 2d 603, 4 Media L. Rep. 1681 (Fla. Dist. Ct. App. 1978) *1:* 186
—v. Tornillo, 418 U.S. 241, 1 Media L. Rep. 1898 (1974) *12:* 238; *13:* 59–60, 62–72, 80–81, 84, 86, 202, 204–5, 244, 320, 375, 410, 431, 467
—State ex rel. v. McIntosh, 340 So. 2d 904, 2 Media L. Rep. 1328 (Fla. 1977) *1:* 181; *10:* 217
Miami Valley Broadcasting Corp., Ohio ex rel. v. Kessler, 413 N.E.2d 1203, 6 Media L. Rep. 2341 (Ohio 1980) *1:* 640
Michigan Beer & Wine Wholesalers Ass'n v. Attorney General, 370 N.W.2d 328 (Mich. Ct. App. 1985), *cert. denied,* 479 U.S. 939 (1986) *11:* 210–12
Michigan Microtech v. Federated Pubns., 466 N.W.2d 717, 18 Media L. Rep. 2131 (Mich. Ct. App. 1991) *2:* 135, 467
Michigan United Conservation Clubs v. CBS News, 485 F. Supp. 893, 5 Media L. Rep. 2566 (W.D. Mich. 1980), *aff'd,* 665 F.2d 110, 7 Media L. Rep. 2331 (6th Cir. 1981) *2:* 307; *3:* 29, 31, 35
Mick v. American Dental Ass'n, 139 A.2d 570 (N.J. Super. Ct. App. Div.), *cert. denied,* 141 A.2d 318 (N.J. 1958) *2:* 537, 539
Middlebrooks v. Curtis Pub'g Co., 281 F. Supp. 1 (D.S.C. 1968), *aff'd,* 413 F.2d 141 (4th Cir. 1969) *4:* 23
Midland Pub'g Co., In re, 362 N.W.2d 580, 11 Media L. Rep. 1337 (Mich. 1984) *1:* 152
Midler v. Ford Motor Co., 849 F.2d 460, 15 Media L. Rep. 1620 (9th Cir. 1988) *6:* 40, 98, 100–101

Mid-America Food Serv. v. ARA Serv., 578 F.2d 691 (8th Cir. 1978) *2:* 135

Mid-Atlantic Accessories Trade Ass'n v. Maryland, 500 F. Supp. 834 (D. Md. 1980) *11:* 305

Mid-Florida Television v. Boyles, 467 So. 2d 282, 11 Media L. Rep. 1774 (Fla. 1985) *2:* 180

Midwest Glass Co. v. Stanford Dev. Co., 339 N.E.2d 274 (Ill. App. Ct. 1975) *3:* 39

Midwest Television v. FCC, 426 F.2d 1222 (D.C. Cir. 1970) *13:* 459

Midwest Video Corp.
—v. FCC (Midwest II), 571 F.2d 1025 (8th Cir. 1978), *aff'd,* 440 U.S. 689 (1979) *13:* 468–77, 480–82, 484–88, 499
—United States v. (Midwest I), 441 F.2d 1322 (8th Cir. 1971), *rev'd,* 406 U.S. 649 (1972) *13:* 468

Mihalik v. Duprey, 417 N.E.2d 1238, 7 Media L. Rep. 1258 (Mass. App. Ct. 1981) *2:* 140

Milberg v. Western Pac. R.R. Co., 51 F.R.D. 280 (S.D.N.Y. 1970), *appeal dismissed sub nom.* Korn v. Franchard Corp., 443 F.2d 1301 (2d Cir. 1971) *9:* 138, 145

Miles v. Perry, 529 A.2d 199, 14 Media L. Rep. 1985 (Conn. App. Ct. 1987) *2:* 162, 467

Milkovich v. Lorain Journal Co., 497 U.S. 1, 17 Media L. Rep. 2009 (1990) *2:* 89, 239, 242–43, 253–54; *3:* 62, 64

Miller
—v. California, 413 U.S. 15, 1 Media L. Rep. 1441 (1973) *4:* 58; *10:* 3
—v. Castlewood Int'l Corp., *see* Castlewood Int'l Corp. v. Simon
—v. Mecklenberg County, 11 Media L. Rep. 1836 (W.D.N.C. 1985) *14:* 368
—v. NBC
——157 F. Supp. 240 (D. Del. 1957) *4:* 25
——232 Cal. Rptr. 668 (Cal. Ct. App. 1986) *5:* 11, 34, 48, 50, 81, 99, 139, 142–44
—v. Nestande, 192 Cal. App. 3d 191, 237 Cal. Rptr. 359, 14 Media L. Rep. 1233 (Cal. Ct. App. 1987) *2:* 404
—v. News Syndicate Co., 445 F.2d 356 (2d Cir. 1971) *2:* 432
—v. Transamerican Press, 621 F.2d 721, 6 Media L. Rep. 1598 (5th Cir.), *modified on reh'g,* 628 F.2d 932, 6 Media L. Rep. 2252 (5th Cir. 1980), *cert. denied,* 450 U.S. 1041 (1981) *2:* 395; *14:* 47, 55, 62, 90–91, 368, 374, 403
—United States v., 579 F. Supp. 862, 10 Media L. Rep. 1321 (S.D. Fla. 1984) *1:* 348

Miller Newspapers v. City of Keene, 546 F. Supp. 831, 9 Media L. Rep. 1234 (D.N.H. 1982) *12:* 148, 156

Mills v. Alabama, 384 U.S. 214, 1 Media L. Rep. 1334 (1966) *1:* 557; *12:* 53–54

Milwaukee Social Democratic Pub'g Co., United States ex rel. v. Burleson, 255 U.S. 407 (1921) *9:* 274

Mimms v. Philadelphia Newspapers, 352 F. Supp. 862 (E.D. Pa. 1972) *9:* 43, 48, 62, 64, 79

Mine Workers (UMW) v. Pennington, 381 U.S. 657 (1965) *13:* 240

Mine Workers (UMW); United States v., 330 U.S. 258 (1947) *10:* 88

Minneapolis Star and Tribune Co.
—v. Lee, 353 N.W.2d 213, 10 Media L. Rep. 2300 (Minn. Ct. App. 1984) *4:* 196; *10:* 189
—v. Minnesota Comm'r of Revenue, 460 U.S. 575 (1983) *9:* 216, 225–32, 237
—v. United States, 713 F. Supp. 1308 (D. Minn. 1989) *14:* 475–76

Minnesota v. Casino Mktg. Group, 491 N.W.2d 882 (Minn. 1992), *cert. denied,* 113 S. Ct. 1648 (1993) *12:* 249

Minnesota Newspaper Ass'n
—v. Minneapolis, 9 Media L. Rep. 2116 (D. Minn. 1983) *12:* 143, 152, 218
—v. Postmaster General, 677 F. Supp. 1400, 15 Media L. Rep. 1292 (D. Minn. 1987), *vacated and remanded,* 490 U.S. 225, 16 Media L. Rep. 1511 (1989) *11:* 48–50, 256

Minnesota State Bd. for Community Colleges v. Knight, 465 U.S. 271 (1984) *12:* 60

Minor, In re
—537 N.E.2d 292, 16 Media L. Rep. 1449 (Ill. 1989) *1:* 243, 258; *10:* 194
—595 N.E.2d 1052, 20 Media L. Rep. 1372 (Ill. 1992) *1:* 258

Minot Daily News v. Holum, 380 N.W.2d 347, 12 Media L. Rep. 1812 (N.D. 1986) *1:* 152

Mintz v. Director, Dep't of Motor Vehicles, 691 F.2d 507, 9 Media L. Rep. 1301 (9th Cir. 1982), *cert. denied,* 460 U.S. 1071 (1983) *1:* 533

Mishkin; People v., 234 N.Y.S.2d 342 (N.Y. App. Div. 1962), *aff'd,* 204 N.E.2d 209 (N.Y. 1964), *aff'd,* 383 U.S. 502 (1966) *12:* 215

Miskovsky v. Oklahoma Pub'g Co., 654 P.2d 587, 7 Media L. Rep. 2607 (Okla. 1982) *2:* 158

Mississippi Gay Alliance v. Goudelock, 536 F.2d 1073 (5th Cir. 1976), *cert. denied,* 430 U.S. 982 (1977) *13:* 207, 375

Mississippi Pubrs. Corp.
—v. Circuit Ct., 12 Media L. Rep. 1342 (Miss. 1985) *10:* 217
—v. Coleman, 515 So. 2d 1163, 14 Media L. Rep. 2005 (Miss. 1987) *1:* 147, 156

Mitchell
—v. Random House, 865 F.2d 664, 16 Media L. Rep. 1207 (5th Cir. 1989) *3:* 18
—v. Superior Ct. (Synanon Church), 37 Cal. 3d 268, 690 P.2d 625 (Cal. 1984) *14:* 70, 76, 199, 201, 205, 336, 394–96
—United States v.
——386 F. Supp. 639 (D.D.C. 1974) *1:* 316
——397 F. Supp. 186 (D.D.C. 1975), *rev'd*, 551 F.2d 1252, 2 Media L. Rep. 1097 (D.C. Cir. 1976), *rev'd*, 435 U.S. 589, 3 Media L. Rep. 2074 (1978) *1:* 317, 341
Mitchell Family Planning v. Royal Oak, 335 F. Supp. 738 (E.D. Mich. 1972) *11:* 287
Mobile Sign v. Town of Brookhaven, 670 F. Supp. 68 (E.D.N.Y. 1987) *12:* 185
Mock v. Chicago, Rock Island & Pac. R.R. Co., 454 F.2d 131 (8th Cir. 1972) *2:* 516
Moffit v. Willis, 459 So. 2d 1018 (Fla. 1984) *1:* 539
Mokhiber v. Davis, 537 A.2d 1100, 14 Media L. Rep. 2313 (D.C. 1988) *1:* 427, 430, 448
Moloney v. Tribune Pub'g Co., 613 P.2d 1179, 6 Media L. Rep. 1426 (Wash. Ct. App. 1980) *4:* 64
Molt v. Public Indem. Co., 161 A. 346 (N.J. 1932) *2:* 171
Moncrief v. Hanton, 10 Media L. Rep. 1620 (N.D. Ohio 1984) *5:* 108; *9:* 62, 64, 76
Monell v. Department of Social Servs. of City of N.Y., 436 U.S. 658 (1978) *9:* 47
Monitor Patriot Co. v. Roy, 401 U.S. 265, 1 Media L. Rep. 1619 (1971) *2:* 325, 330–33, 395, 417, 695; *13:* 54
Monroe v. Pape, 365 U.S. 167 (1961) *9:* 47
Montesano v. Donrey Media Group, 668 P.2d 1081, 9 Media L. Rep. 2266 (Nev. 1983), *cert. denied*, 466 U.S. 959 (1984) *4:* 106, 119
Montgomery Ward & Co. v. Skinner, 25 So. 2d 572 (Miss. 1946) *2:* 308
Moore
—v. Allied Chem. Corp., 480 F. Supp. 364 (E.D. Va. 1979) *2:* 225
—v. Big Picture Co., 828 F.2d 270, 14 Media L. Rep. 1865 (5th Cir. 1987) *3:* 36
—v. California State Bd. of Accountancy, 831 P.2d 798 (Cal. 1992), *cert. denied*, 113 S. Ct. 1364 (1993) *11:* 325
—v. P.W. Pub'g Co., 209 N.E.2d 412 (Ohio 1965), *cert. denied*, 382 U.S. 978 (1966) *2:* 184, 186
—v. Teflon Communications Corp., 589 F.2d 959 (9th Cir. 1978) *5:* 222, 225–26, 228
—v. Washington, 311 N.Y.S.2d 310 (N.Y. App. Div. 1970) *2:* 298
Moorefield v. Moore, 540 S.W.2d 873 (Ky. 1976) *12:* 210

Morast v. Lance, 807 F.2d 926 (11th Cir. 1987) *9:* 80, 84
Morey v. Independent Sch. Dist., 312 F. Supp. 1257 (D. Minn. 1969), *aff'd*, 429 F.2d 428 (8th Cir. 1970) *9:* 48
Morgan
—v. Celender, 780 F. Supp. 307, 19 Media L. Rep. 1862 (W.D. Pa. 1992) *14:* 459
—v. Foretich, 528 A.2d 425, 14 Media L. Rep. 1342 (D.C. 1987) *1:* 270
—v. State, 337 So. 2d 951, 1 Media L. Rep. 2589 (Fla. 1976) *14:* 70, 416
Moricoli v. Schwartz, 361 N.E.2d 74 (Ill. App. Ct. 1977) *2:* 210
Morison; United States v., 844 F.2d 1057, 15 Media L. Rep. 1369 (4th Cir.), *cert. denied*, 488 U.S. 908 (1988) *5:* 166
Morland v. Sprecher, 443 U.S. 709, 5 Media L. Rep. 1393 (1979) *10:* 130
Morris v. National Fed'n of the Blind, 13 Cal. Rptr. 336 (Cal. Ct. App. 1961) *2:* 613
Morrison
—v. NBC, 227 N.E.2d 572 (N.Y. 1967) *2:* 2
—v. Richie & Co., 39 Scot. L. Rep. 432 (1902) *2:* 166
Morrissey v. William Morrow & Co., 739 F.2d 962, 10 Media L. Rep. 2305 (4th Cir. 1984), *cert. denied*, 469 U.S. 1216 (1985) *2:* 238, 631–32
Moser v. FCC, 826 F. Supp. 360 (D. Or. 1993) *12:* 250
Mosesian v. McClatchy Newspapers, 285 Cal. Rptr. 430, 19 Media L. Rep. 1815 (Cal. Ct. App. 1991), *cert. denied*, 112 S. Ct. 1946 (1992) *2:* 407
Moskowitz v. Cullman, 432 F. Supp. 1263 (D.N.J. 1977) *12:* 70
Motown Record Corp. v. George A. Hormel & Co., 657 F. Supp. 1236 (C.D. Cal. 1987) *6:* 40, 97, 99
Motschenbacher v. R.J. Reynolds Tobacco Co., 498 F.2d 821 (9th Cir. 1974) *4:* 26; *6:* 2, 17, 20, 36, 133
Mounsey; State v., 5 Media L. Rep. 2387 (Wash. Ct. App. 1979) *1:* 211
Mountain States Tel. & Tel. Co. v. District Ct., 778 P.2d 667 (Colo.), *cert. denied*, 493 U.S. 983 (1989) *13:* 424
Mt. Healthy City Sch. Dist. Bd. of Educ. v. Doyle, 429 U.S. 274 (1977) *1:* 527; *9:* 40, 46
Mouzin; United States v., 559 F. Supp. 463, 9 Media L. Rep. 1357 (C.D. Cal. 1983) *1:* 346
Moyer v. Amador Valley Joint Union High Sch. Dist., 275 Cal. Rptr. 494, 18 Media L. Rep. 1602 (Cal. Ct. App. 1990) *2:* 245, 259–60, 267

Table of Cases

Mr. Chow of N.Y. v. Ste. Jour Azur, 759 F.2d 219, 11 Media L. Rep. 1713 (2d Cir. 1985) **2:** 261

Muir
—v. Alabama Educ. Television Comm'n (Muir I), 656 F.2d 1012 (5th Cir. 1981), *reh'g granted sub nom.* Muir v. Alabama Educ. Television Comm'n/Barnstone v. University of Houston, 662 F.2d 1110 (5th Cir. 1981) **13:** 377
—v. Alabama Educ. Television Comm'n (Muir II), 688 F.2d 1033 (5th Cir. 1982), *cert. denied*, 460 U.S. 1023 (1983) **13:** 377–94, 398

Mulherin v. Globe Oil Co., 328 S.E.2d 406 (Ga. Ct. App. 1985) **2:** 482

Multimedia Pub'g Co. v. Greenville-Spartanburg Airport Dist., 991 F.2d 154, 21 Media L. Rep. 1369 (4th Cir. 1993) **12:** 137

Multimedia WMAZ v. State, 353 S.E.2d 173, 13 Media L. Rep. 2069 (Ga. 1987) **1:** 640

Mumaugh v. Diamond Lake Area Cable TV Co., 456 N.W.2d 425 (Mich. Ct. App. 1990) **12:** 246

Munson; State v., 714 S.W.2d 515 (Mo. 1986) **11:** 307

Murdock v. Pennsylvania, 319 U.S. 105 (1943) **9:** 222–24; **11:** 20, 26, 58; **12:** 129, 159

Murphy v. Matheson, 742 F.2d 564 (10th Cir. 1984) **11:** 305

Murray
—v. Bailey, 613 F. Supp. 1276, 11 Media L. Rep. 1369 (N.D. Cal. 1985) **2:** 484
—v. New York Magazine Co., 267 N.E.2d 256 (N.Y. 1971) **6:** 73
—v. United States, 327 F. Supp. 835 (D. Utah 1971), *modified*, 463 F.2d 208 (10th Cir. 1972) **7:** 46

Mutual of Omaha Ins. Co. v. Novak, 775 F.2d 247 (8th Cir. 1985) **10:** 258

Myers v. Boston Magazine Co., 403 N.E.2d 376, 6 Media L. Rep. 1241 (1980) **2:** 261

N

NAACP
—v. Button, 371 U.S. 415 (1963) **2:** 20
—v. Claiborne Hardware Co., 458 U.S. 886 (1982) **8:** 91

Nader
—v. DeToledano, 408 A.2d 31, 5 Media L. Rep. 1550 (D.C. 1979), *cert. denied*, 444 U.S. 1078 (1980) **2:** 482
—v. General Motors Corp., 255 N.E.2d 765 (N.Y. 1970) **5:** 15–17, 19, 23, 30, 39, 41, 44

Naegele Outdoor Advertising v. City of Durham, 844 F.2d 172 (4th Cir. 1988) **12:** 184

Naked City v. Chicago Sun-Times, 395 N.E.2d 1042, 5 Media L. Rep. 1806 (Ill. App. Ct. 1979) **2:** 127

Namath v. Sports Illustrated, 371 N.Y.S.2d 10, 1 Media L. Rep. 1843 (N.Y. App. Div. 1975), *aff'd*, 352 N.E.2d 584 (N.Y. 1976) **6:** 90

Nance v. Flaugh, 253 S.W.2d 207 (Ark. 1952) **2:** 224

Nash v. Keene Pub'g Co., 498 A.2d 348, 12 Media L. Rep. 1025 (N.H. 1985) **2:** 327

Natchez Times Pub'g Co. v. Dunigan, 72 So. 2d 681 (Miss. 1954) **2:** 130

National Advertising Co.
—v. Bridgeton, 626 F. Supp. 837 (E.D. Mo. 1985) **12:** 182, 184
—v. Orange, 861 F.2d 246 (9th Cir. 1988) **12:** 174, 184

National Ass'n for the Advancement of Colored People, *see* NAACP

National Alliance v. United States, 710 F.2d 868 (D.C. Cir. 1983) **9:** 245

National Ass'n of Broadcasters v. Quincy Cable TV, *see* Quincy Cable TV v. FCC

National Ass'n of Gov't Employees v. National Fed'n of Fed. Employees, 844 F.2d 216 (5th Cir. 1988) **2:** 681

National Bank of Commerce v. Shaklee Corp., 503 F. Supp. 533 (W.D. Tex. 1980) **4:** 29; **6:** 42, 49, 52, 153, 212

National Bar Ass'n v. Capital Cities, 10 Media L. Rep. 2317 (W.D.N.Y. 1984) **9:** 45, 55

National Bonding Agency v. Demeson, 648 S.W.2d 748 (Tex. Ct. App. 1983) **4:** 133

National Broadcasting Co., *see* NBC

National Comm'n on Egg Nutrition v. FTC, 570 F.2d 157, 3 Media L. Rep. 2196 (7th Cir. 1977), *cert. denied*, 439 U.S. 821, 4 Media L. Rep. 1560 (1978) **7:** 71; **11:** 39–41

National Found. for Cancer Research v. Council of Better Business Bureaus, 705 F.2d 98, 9 Media L. Rep. 1915 (4th Cir.), *cert. denied*, 464 U.S. 830 (1983) **2:** 259–60, 267

Nationalist Socialist Party of Am. v. Village of Skokie, 432 U.S. 43, 2 Media L. Rep. 1993 (1977) **10:** 268–70

National Service Corp., In re, 742 F.2d 859 (5th Cir. 1984) **10:** 242

National Subscription Television v. S&H TV, 644 F.2d 820, 7 Media L. Rep. 1399 (9th Cir. 1981) **5:** 242

National Tire Wholesale v. Washington Post Co., 441 F. Supp. 81 (D.C. Cir. 1977), *aff'd*, 595 F.2d 888 (D.C. Cir. 1979) **13:** 214, 227

Nation Magazine v. United States Dep't of Defense, 762 F. Supp. 1558, 19 Media L. Rep. 1257 (S.D.N.Y. 1991)   *1:* 538

Nature's Way Prods. v. Nature-Pharma, 736 F. Supp. 245 (D. Utah 1990)   *6:* 217

NBC
—In re (Jenrette), 653 F.2d 609, 7 Media L. Rep. 1193 (D.C. Cir. 1981)   *1:* 308, 326, 338–39, 41
—In re (Myers), 635 F.2d 945, 6 Media L. Rep. 1961 (2d Cir. 1980)   *1:* 308, 327, 338–40, 351–52
—In re (Presser II), 828 F.2d 340, 14 Media L. Rep. 1417 (6th Cir. 1987)   *1:* 367
—v. Cleland, 697 F. Supp. 1204, 15 Media L. Rep. 2265 (N.D. Ga. 1988)   *1:* 565
—v. Colburg, 699 F. Supp. 241, 16 Media L. Rep. 1267 (D. Mont. 1988)   *1:* 565–66
—v. Communications Workers of Am., 860 F.2d 1022, 16 Media L. Rep. 1356 (11th Cir. 1988)   *1:* 542, 638
—v. Cooperman, 501 N.Y.S.2d 405, 12 Media L. Rep. 2025 (N.Y. App. Div. 1986)   *10:* 217
—v. FCC, 516 F.2d 1101 (D.C. Cir.), cert. denied, 424 U.S. 910 (1973)   *13:* 151
—v. Niemi, *see* Olivia N. v. NBC
—v. United States, 319 U.S. 190 (1943)   *13:* 9–12, 73, 455–56, 463
—v. United States Dep't of Justice, 735 F.2d 51, 10 Media L. Rep. 1866 (2d Cir. 1984)   *1:* 380
—State ex rel. v. Lake County Ct. of Common Pleas, 556 N.E.2d 1120, 17 Media L. Rep. 2209 (Ohio 1990)   *10:* 217; *14:* 71, 138, 274

Near v. Minnesota, 283 U.S. 697, 1 Media L. Rep. 1001 (1931)   *10:* 1, 8–9, 11–26, 28–35, 64, 105, 122, 129, 237, 239; *13:* 346

Nebel v. Mapco Petroleum, 10 Media L. Rep. 1871 (Alaska 1984)   *14:* 80

Nebraska Press Ass'n v. Stuart, 427 U.S. 539, 1 Media L. Rep. 1064 (1976)   *1:* 3; *10:* 1, 40, 43, 51–52, 55–56, 61–63, 104–5, 163–88, 191, 200, 205, 226

Neff v. Time, Inc., 406 F. Supp. 858 (W.D. Pa. 1976)   *4:* 55, 185

Neiman-Marcus v. Lait, 13 F.R.D. 311 (D.N.Y. 1952)   *2:* 307–8

Neish v. Beaver Newspapers, 581 A.2d 619, 18 Media L. Rep. 1251 (Pa. Super. Ct. 1990) *3:* 56

Nelson
—v. Associated Press, 667 F. Supp. 1468, 14 Media L. Rep. 1577 (S.D. Fla. 1987)   *2:* 472–73
—v. Globe Int'l, 626 F. Supp. 969, 12 Media L. Rep. 1785 (S.D.N.Y. 1986)   *3:* 88

—v. Maine Times, 373 A.2d 1221, 2 Media L. Rep. 2011 (Me. 1977)   *5:* 9, 23, 42; *6:* 15, 89

Nemeroff v. Abelson, 704 F.2d 652, 9 Media L. Rep. 1427 (2d Cir. 1983)   *2:* 683

Nero v. Hyland, 386 A.2d 846, 3 Media L. Rep. 2367 (N.J. 1978)   *1:* 305

Nevada Indep. Broadcasting Corp. v. Allen, 664 P.2d 337, 9 Media L. Rep. 1769 (1983) *2:* 596, 616, 619

New Bedford Standard-Times Pub'g Co. v. Clerk of Third Dist. Ct., 387 N.E.2d 110, 4 Media L. Rep. 2393 (Mass. 1979)   *1:* 391–92

Newburn v. Howard Hughes Medical Inst., 594 P.2d 1146 (Nev. 1979)   *14:* 71, 77, 243, 330

Newell v. Field Enters., 415 N.E.2d 434, 6 Media L. Rep. 2450 (Ill. App. Ct. 1980)   *2:* 559

New Eng. Accessories Trade Ass'n
—v. Nashua, 679 F.2d 1 (1st Cir. 1982)   *11:* 305
—v. Tierney, 528 F. Supp. 404 (D. Me. 1981), aff'd, 691 F.2d 35 (1st Cir. 1982)   *11:* 305

New Era Pubns. v. Henry Holt & Co., 873 F.2d 576, 16 Media L. Rep. 1559 (2d Cir. 1989), cert. denied, 493 U.S. 1094 (1990) *10:* 243

New Hampshire v. Siel, 444 A.2d 499 (N.H. 1982)   *14:* 70, 76, 429

New Jersey v. Santiago, 593 A.2d 357, 19 Media L. Rep. 1214 (N.J. Super. Ct. App. Div. 1991)   *14:* 252

New Jersey Citizen Action v. Edison Township, 797 F.2d 1250 (3d Cir. 1986), cert. denied, 479 U.S. 1103 (1987)   *12:* 41, 119

New Jersey Div. of Youth & Family Servs. v. J.B., 576 A.2d 261, 17 Media L. Rep. 2183 (N.J. 1990)   *1:* 253

New Kids on the Block v. News Am. Pub'g, 745 F. Supp. 1540, 18 Media L. Rep. 1089 (C.D. Cal. 1990)   *6:* 74

Newman
—v. Graddick, 696 F.2d 796, 9 Media L. Rep. 1104 (11th Cir. 1983)   *1:* 265–66, 268–69
—State v., 696 P.2d 856 (Idaho 1984)   *11:* 307
—United States v., 664 F.2d 12, aff'd after remand, 722 F.2d 729 (2d Cir. 1981), cert. denied, 464 U.S. 863 (1983)   *9:* 171

New Mexico Press Ass'n, State ex rel. v. Kaufman, 648 P.2d 300, 8 Media L. Rep. 1713 (N.M. 1982)   *1:* 209, 640

News Am. Div., Hearst Corp. v. State, 447 A.2d 1264, 8 Media L. Rep. 2088 (Md. 1982)   *1:* 106, 117

News & Observer Pub'g Co. v. State, 322 S.E.2d 133 (N.C. 1984) *1:* 305

News & Sun-Sentinel Co. v. Board of County Comm'rs, 693 F. Supp. 1066, 14 Media L. Rep. 1477 (S.D. Fla. 1987) *13:* 207

Newsday
—In re, 895 F.2d 74, 17 Media L. Rep. 1385 (2d Cir.) *cert. denied*, 496 U.S. 931 (1990) *1:* 374, 376
—v. Goodman, 552 N.Y.S.2d 965, 17 Media L. Rep. 1725 (N.Y. App. Div. 1990) *1:* 525

News Group Boston v. Massachusetts, 568 N.E.2d 600, 18 Media L. Rep. 2102 (Mass. 1991) *1:* 241

Newsome; State v., 426 A.2d 68, 7 Media L. Rep. 1308 (N.J. Super. Ct. App. Div. 1981) *1:* 636

Newson v. Henry, 443 So. 2d 817, 10 Media L. Rep. 1421 (Miss. 1983) *2:* 183

Newspaper Guild
—v. Levi, 539 F.2d 755, 1 Media L. Rep. 2709 (D.C. Cir. 1976), *cert. denied*, 429 U.S. 1092 (1977) *9:* 31
—v. NLRB, 636 F.2d 550 (D.C. Cir. 1980) *9:* 127

Newspaper Printing v. Galbreath, 580 S.W.2d 777, 5 Media L. Rep. 1065 (Tenn.), *cert. denied*, 444 U.S. 870 (1979) *13:* 207

Newspapers of New Eng. v. Clerk-Magistrate, 531 N.E.2d 1261, 16 Media L. Rep. 1457 (Mass. 1988), *cert. denied*, 490 U.S. 1066 (1989) *1:* 375

News Printing Co. v. Borough of Totowa, 511 A.2d 139, 13 Media L. Rep. 1072 (N.J. Super. Ct. Law Div. 1986) *12:* 142–46, 151–55, 157, 161

Newsweek v. Celauro, 789 S.W.2d 247, 18 Media L. Rep. 1134 (Tenn. 1990), *cert. denied*, 111 S. Ct. 1639 (1991) *9:* 243

Newton
—v. Family Fed. Sav. & Loan Ass'n, 616 P.2d 1213 (Or. Ct. App. 1980) *2:* 172, 187
—v. NBC
——677 F. Supp. 1066, 14 Media L. Rep. 1914 (D. Nev. 1987), *rev'd*, 930 F.2d 662, 18 Media L. Rep. 1001 (9th Cir. 1990), *cert. denied*, 112 S. Ct. 192 (1991) *2:* 447, 596, 703
——109 F.R.D. 522 (D. Nev. 1985) *14:* 242, 374, 377–78

New York
—v. Cordero, 541 N.Y.S.2d 417, 16 Media L. Rep. 1732 (N.Y. App. Div.), *aff'd*, 551 N.E.2d 103 (N.Y. 1989) *1:* 202
—v. Remeny, 355 N.E.2d 375 (N.Y. 1976) *12:* 109

New York, City of; v. American Sch. Pubns., 505 N.Y.S.2d 594, 13 Media L. Rep. 1194 (N.Y. App. Div. 1986), *aff'd*, 509 N.E.2d 311, 516 N.Y.S.2d 616, 14 Media L. Rep. 1153 (N.Y. 1987) *11:* 44; *12:* 148, 156

New York City Unemployed & Welfare Council v. Brezenoff, 677 F.2d 232 (2d Cir. 1982) *12:* 23, 65, 68

New York Human Rights Div. v. Binghamton Press, 415 N.Y.S.2d 523, 5 Media L. Rep. 1085 (N.Y. App. Div. 1979) *11:* 316

New York News v. Metropolitan Transp. Auth., 753 F. Supp. 133, 18 Media L. Rep. 1808 (S.D.N.Y. 1990) *12:* 142

New York Pub. Interest Research Group v. Insurance Info. Inst., 531 N.Y.S.2d 1002 (N.Y. Sup. Ct. 1988), *aff'd*, 554 N.Y.S.2d 590 (N.Y. App. Div. 1990) *11:* 44

New York State Broadcasters Ass'n v. United States, 414 F.2d 990 (2d Cir. 1969), *cert. denied*, 396 U.S. 1061 (1970) *11:* 260

New York State Liquor Auth. v. Bellanca, 452 U.S. 714, 7 Media L. Rep. 1500 (1981) *11:* 186–88

New York Times Co.
—In re
——828 F.2d 110, 14 Media L. Rep. 1625 (2d Cir. 1987), *cert. denied*, 485 U.S. 977 (1988) *1:* 129, 318, 380
——834 F.2d 1152, 14 Media L. Rep. 2013 (2d Cir. 1987), *cert. denied*, 485 U.S. 977 (1988) *1:* 379
——878 F.2d 67, 16 Media L. Rep. 1877 (2d Cir. 1989) *10:* 217
——9 Media L. Rep. 2077 (N.D. Ga. 1983) *1:* 370
—v. Commission on Human Rights, 361 N.E.2d 963, 2 Media L. Rep. 1435 (N.Y. 1977) *11:* 317
—v. Connor, 365 F.2d 567 (5th Cir. 1966) *2:* 441, 643
—v. Demakos, 529 N.Y.S.2d 97, 15 Media L. Rep. 1524 (N.Y. App. Div. 1988) *1:* 159, 382
—v. New Jersey, *see* Farber, In re
—v. Sullivan, 376 U.S. 254, 1 Media L. Rep. 1527 (1964) *2:* 12–17, 19–22, 24–35, 62, 91, 144, 277, 296, 299–300, 311, 314, 328, 400, 416, 441, 452, 461, 486–87, 493, 675, 693–94; *4:* 98; *5:* 61; *7:* 30; *8:* 29, 55, 102–3, 105; *11:* 27–28, 61–62; *13:* 38, 70; *14:* 387
—v. Superior Ct. (Sortomme), 273 Cal. Rptr. 98, 796 P.2d 811, 18 Media L. Rep. 1145 (Cal. 1990) *14:* 199–201, 203–4, 336, 338, 405
—v. United States, 403 U.S. 713, 1 Media L. Rep. 1031 (1971) *5:* 57, 158; *10:* 1, 40, 43, 106–20

N.H.B., In re, 769 P.2d 844 (Utah Ct. App. 1989) *1:* 253

Nichols v. Gamso, 315 N.E.2d 770 (N.Y. 1974) *1:* 297

Nicholson
—v. Board of Educ., Torrance Unified Sch. Dist., 682 F.2d 858 (9th Cir. 1982) *13:* 335, 347
—v. McClatchy Newspapers, 177 Cal. App. 3d 509, 223 Cal. Rptr. 58 (Cal. Ct. App. 1986) *4:* 82, 98, 101; *5:* 158

Niemotko v. Maryland, 340 U.S. 268 (1951) *10:* 39

Nigris, In re, 577 A.2d 1292, 18 Media L. Rep. 1422 (N.J. Super. Ct. App. Div. 1990) *1:* 280

Nixon
—v. Warner Communications, 435 U.S. 589, 3 Media L. Rep. 2074 (1978) *1:* 99, 306, 309–37
—United States v., 418 U.S. 683 (1974) *14:* 131

Noble v. Sears, Roebuck & Co., 109 Cal. Rptr. 269 (Cal. Ct. App. 1973) *5:* 18

NOC, Inc. v. Schaefer, 484 A.2d 729 (N.J. Super. Ct. Law. Div. 1984) *5:* 43, 50

Nodar v. Galbreath, 462 So. 2d 803, 11 Media L. Rep. 1521 (Fla. 1984) *2:* 403

Norandal U.S.A. v. Local Union Co. 7468, 13 Media L. Rep. 2167 (Ala. Civ. App. 1986) *14:* 70

Noriega; United States v., 752 F. Supp. 1032, 18 Media L. Rep. 1348 (S.D. Fla. 1990), *aff'd sub nom.* In re Cable News Network, 917 F.2d 1543, 18 Media L. Rep. 1352, *stay and cert. denied,* 111 S. Ct. 451, 18 Media L. Rep. 1358 (1990) *10:* 195

North Carolina v. Smith, 13 Media L. Rep. 1940 (N.C. 1987) *14:* 70, 76, 78–79

North Dakota Educ. Ass'n; State v., 262 N.W.2d 731 (N.D. 1978) *12:* 212

North Jersey Suburbanite v. State, 384 A.2d 831 (N.J. 1977) *9:* 280

Northrop Corp.; United States v., 746 F. Supp. 1002, 17 Media L. Rep. 2262 (C.D. Cal. 1990) *1:* 366

Northside Sanitary Landfill v. Bradley, 462 N.E.2d 1321 (Ind. Ct. App. 1984) *14:* 314

Northwestern Pac. R.R. v. Lumber & Sawmill Workers' Union, 189 P.2d 277 (Cal. 1948) *10:* 239

Northwest Pubns. v. Anderson, 259 N.W.2d 254, 3 Media L. Rep. 1302 (Minn. 1977) *1:* 307, 365

Northwest Wholesale Stationers v. Pacific Stationery & Printing Co., 472 U.S. 284 (1985) *13:* 213

Norton Outdoor Advertising v. Village of Arlington Heights, 433 N.E.2d 198, 8 Media L. Rep. 2018 (Ohio 1982) *12:* 174

Norwood v. Soldier of Fortune Magazine, 651 F. Supp. 1397, 13 Media L. Rep. 2025 (W.D. Ark. 1987) *7:* 78

Nova Records v. Sendak, 706 F.2d 782 (7th Cir. 1983) *11:* 305

Novel v. Beacon Operating Corp., 446 N.Y.S.2d 118 (N.Y. App. Div. 1982) *6:* 23

November v. Time, Inc., 194 N.E.2d 126 (N.Y. 1963) *2:* 148

Nulty v. Pennzoil Co., 484 N.Y.S.2d 533, 11 Media L. Rep. 1647 (N.Y. App. Div. 1985) *14:* 262, 332

Nurmi v. Peterson, 16 Media L. Rep. 1606 (C.D. Cal. 1989) *6:* 38, 53

Nusbaum v. Newark Morning Ledger Co., 206 A.2d 185 (N.J. Super. Ct. App. Div. 1965), *cert. denied,* 209 A.2d 138 (N.J. 1965) *2:* 554

O

Oak Beach Inn Corp. v. Babylon Beacon, 464 N.E.2d 967 (N.Y. 1984), *cert. denied,* 469 U.S. 1158 (1985) *14:* 266

Oak Creek v. King, 436 N.W.2d 285, 16 Media L. Rep. 1273 (Wis. 1989) *1:* 535; *5:* 134

Oberman v. Dun & Bradstreet, 586 F.2d 1173, 4 Media L. Rep. 2137 (7th Cir. 1978) *2:* 545

O'Brien
—v. Pabst Sales Co., 124 F.2d 167 (5th Cir. 1941), *cert. denied,* 315 U.S. 823 (1942) *6:* 2, 114
—v. Papa Gino's of Am., 780 F.2d 1067 (1st Cir. 1986) *6:* 51
—v. University Community Tenants Union, 327 N.E.2d 753 (Ohio 1975) *10:* 241
—v. Williamson Daily News, 735 F. Supp. 218, 18 Media L. Rep. 1037 (E.D. Ky. 1990), *aff'd,* 931 F.2d 893 (6th Cir. 1991) *2:* 306
—United States v., 391 U.S. 367 (1968) *11:* 144; *12:* 227, 229, 231

Ocala Star-Banner Co. v. Damron, 401 U.S. 295, 1 Media L. Rep. 1624 (1971) *2:* 325, 330, 337

Ocean Bio-Chem v. Turner Network Television, 741 F. Supp. 1546 (S.D. Fla. 1990) *10:* 256

O'Connor v. Field, 41 N.Y.S.2d 492 (N.Y. App. Div. 1943) *2:* 617

Oden v. Cahill, 398 N.E.2d 1061 (Ill. App. Ct. 1979) *4:* 108

Official Airlines Guides v. FTC, 630 F.2d 920 (2d Cir. 1980) *13:* 219

Ogden v. Association of U.S. Army, 177 F. Supp. 498 (D.D.C. 1959) *2:* 230

Ohralik v. Ohio State Bar Ass'n, 436 U.S. 447 (1978) *9:* 147; *11:* 17, 82, 89, 318, 321

Oklahoma Alcoholic Beverage Control Bd.
—v. Burris, 626 P.2d 1316 (Okla. 1980) *11:* 208–9
—v. Heublein Wines, Int'l, 556 P.2d 1158 (Okla. 1977) *11:* 184

Oklahoma Broadcasters Ass'n
—v. Crisp, 636 F. Supp. 978, 12 Media L. Rep. 2379 (W.D. Okla. 1985) *11:* 183, 195
—v. Oklahoma Tax Comm'n, 789 P.2d 1312, 17 Media L. Rep. 1994 (Okla. 1990) *9:* 234

Oklahoma Hosp. Ass'n v. Oklahoma Pub'g Co., 748 F.2d 1421, 11 Media L. Rep. 1325 (10th Cir. 1984), *cert. denied,* 473 U.S. 905 (1985) *1:* 446

Oklahoma Press Pub'g Co. v. Walling, 327 U.S. 186 (1946) *9:* 124

Oklahoma Pub'g Co.
—v. District Ct., 430 U.S. 308, 2 Media L. Rep. 1456 (1977) *4:* 74–77, 106; *10:* 40, 104, 189–93
—v. Givens, 67 F.2d 62 (10th Cir. 1933) *2:* 224

Oklahoma Telecasters Association v. Crisp, 699 F.2d 490, 9 Media L. Rep. 1089 (10th Cir. 1983), *rev'd sub nom.* Capital Cities Cable v. Crisp, 467 U.S. 691, 10 Media L. Rep. 1873 (1984) *11:* 113, 137, 182–83, 192–95

Okun v. Superior Ct., 29 Cal. 3d 442, 629 P.2d 1369 (Cal.), *cert. denied sub nom.* Maple Properties v. Superior Ct., 454 U.S. 1099 (1981) *2:* 147, 168

Old Dominion Branch No. 496, Nat'l Ass'n of Letter Carriers v. Austin, 418 U.S. 264 (1974) *2:* 89, 143, 239, 259–60, 267, 425, 591

Oliver
—In re, 333 U.S. 257 (1948) *1:* 11
—v. Pacific N.W. Bell Tel. Co., 632 P.2d 1295 (Or. Ct. App. 1981) *5:* 50

Olivia N.
—v. NBC (Olivia N. I), 141 Cal. Rptr. 511, 3 Media L. Rep. 1454 (1977), *cert. denied sub nom.* NBC v. Niemi, 434 U.S. 1354 (1978) *8:* 27
—v. NBC (Olivia N. II), 178 Cal. Rptr. 888, 7 Media L. Rep. 2359 (Cal. Ct. App. 1981), *cert. denied,* 458 U.S. 1108 (1982) *8:* 2, 11–12, 15, 20, 25–27, 29, 43, 51–54, 56–58, 89–90

Olivieri v. Ward, 801 F.2d 602 (2d Cir. 1986), *cert. denied,* 480 U.S. 917 (1987) *12:* 46–47

Ollman v. Evans, 750 F.2d 970, 11 Media L. Rep. 1433 (D.C. Cir. 1984), *cert. denied,* 471 U.S. 1127, 11 Media L. Rep. 2015 (1985) *2:* 26, 241, 247, 254–58

Olmstead v. United States, 277 U.S. 438 (1928) *5:* 192

O'Loughlin v. Patrolmen's Benevolent Ass'n, 576 N.Y.S.2d 858, 19 Media L. Rep. 1735 (N.Y. App. Div. 1991) *2:* 259–60, 267

Omega Satellite Prods. Co. v. Indianapolis, 694 F.2d 119 (7th Cir. 1982) *12:* 235–36; *13:* 503, 529

Onassis v. Christian Dior-New York, 472 N.Y.S.2d 254, 10 Media L. Rep. 1859 (N.Y. Sup. Ct. 1984) *6:* 35, 54

O'Neill v. Oakgrove Constr., 523 N.E.2d 277 (N.Y. 1988) *14:* 70, 76, 78, 262, 344

Oneonta Star v. Mogavero, 434 N.Y.S.2d 781, 6 Media L. Rep. 2271 (N.Y. App. Div. 1980) *1:* 149

On Lee v. United States, 343 U.S. 747 (1952) *5:* 199, 202

On The Rox Liquors v. New York State Liquor Auth., 395 N.Y.S.2d 836 (N.Y. App. Div. 1977) *11:* 190

Opinion of Justices
—373 A.2d 644 (N.H. 1977) *14:* 76
—431 A.2d 152 (N.H. 1981) *11:* 306
—In re
——306 A.2d 18 (Me. 1973) *12:* 215
——324 A.2d 211 (Del. 1974) *12:* 215

Opinion of Justices to the Senate, 392 N.E.2d 849, 5 Media L. Rep. 2059 (Mass. 1979) *1:* 539

Oregon v. Knobel, 777 P.2d 985, 16 Media L. Rep. 2478 (Or. Ct. App. 1989) *5:* 261

Oregonian Pub'g Co.
—v. O'Leary, 736 P.2d 173, 14 Media L. Rep. 1019 (Or. 1987) *1:* 160
—v. United States Dist. Ct., 920 F.2d 1462, 18 Media L. Rep. 1504 (9th Cir. 1990), *cert. denied sub nom.* Wolsky v. Oregonian Pub'g Co., 111 St. Ct. 2809 (1991) *1:* 159, 366, 382
—State ex rel. v. Deiz, 613 P.2d 23, 6 Media L. Rep. 1369 (Or. 1980) *1:* 261

O'Reilly v. New York Times Co., *see* Contemporary Mission v. New York Times Co.

Organization for a Better Austin v. Keefe, 402 U.S. 415, 1 Media L. Rep. 1021 (1971) *10:* 1, 40, 43, 60, 231–37; *12:* 101

Orloff v. Los Angeles Turf Club, 180 P.2d 321 (Cal. 1947) *10:* 239

Orr v. Argus-Press Co., 586 F.2d 1108, 4 Media L. Rep. 1593 (6th Cir. 1978), *cert. denied,* 440 U.S. 960, 4 Media L. Rep. 2536 (1979) *2:* 259–60, 267, 270, 277, 395

Orsini; United States v., 424 F. Supp. 229 (E.D.N.Y. 1976), aff'd, 559 F.2d 1206 (2d Cir.), *cert. denied,* 434 U.S. 997 (1977) *14:* 431
Ortiz v. Valdescastilla, 478 N.Y.S.2d 895, 10 Media L. Rep. 2193 (N.Y. App. Div. 1984) *2:* 475
Osborn v. United States, 385 U.S. 323 (1966) *5:* 199, 201
Osmond v. EWAP, Inc., 200 Cal. Rptr. 674 (Cal. Ct. App. 1984) *2:* 225
Ostrowe v. Lee, 175 N.E. 505 (N.Y. 1931) *2:* 172, 216, 218
Otto; People v., 808 P.2d 234 (Cal. 1991) *5:* 209
Outlet Communications v. Rhode Island, 588 A.2d 1050, 18 Media L. Rep. 1982 (R.I. 1991) *14:* 71, 77, 294
Owen
—v. Carr, 497 N.E.2d 1145 (Ill. 1986) *2:* 241
—v. Independence, 445 U.S. 622 (1980) *9:* 54
Owens v. Scott Pub'g Co., 284 P.2d 296 (Wash. 1955), *cert. denied,* 350 U.S. 968 (1956) *2:* 6
Oziel v. Superior Ct., 273 Cal. Rptr. 196, 18 Media L. Rep. 1113 (Cal. Ct. App. 1990) *1:* 375

P

Pacific & S. Co., In re, 361 S.E.2d 159, 14 Media L. Rep. 1764 (Ga. 1987) *1:* 358
Pacific Gas & Elec. Co. v. Public Utils. Comm'n of Cal., 475 U.S. 1 (1986) *11:* 45, 301–3; *13:* 203, 403–9, 411–19, 421, 423–24
Pacific Northwest Bell v. Davis, 608 P.2d 547, 5 Media L. Rep. 2443 (Or. Ct. App. 1979) *11:* 304
Pacific Packing Co. v. Bradstreet Co., 139 P. 1007 (Idaho 1914) *2:* 536
Pacific Tel. & Tel. Co. v. Superior Ct., 465 P.2d 854 (Cal. 1970) *5:* 262
Pacific W. Cable Co.
—v. Sacramento (Pacific West I), 798 F.2d 353, 13 Media L. Rep. 1302 (9th Cir. 1986) *12:* 228, 235
—v. Sacramento (Pacific West II), 672 F. Supp. 1322 (E.D. Cal. 1987) *12:* 228, 240
Packer Corp. v. Utah, 285 U.S. 105 (1932) *11:* 51
Paez; United States v., 13 Media L. Rep. 1973 (S.D. Fla. 1987) *14:* 130
Pageau; United States v.
—526 F. Supp. 1221 (N.D.N.Y. 1981) *1:* 160, 278

—535 F. Supp. 1031, 8 Media L. Rep. 1270 (N.D.N.Y. 1982) *1:* 346
Palandjian v. Pahlavi, 103 F.R.D. 410 (D.D.C. 1984) *14:* 315, 317
Palko v. Connecticut, 302 U.S. 319 (1937) *2:* 491
Palm Beach Newspapers
—v. Cook, 434 So. 2d 355 (Fla. Dist. Ct. App. 1983) *1:* 186
—v. Early, 334 So. 2d 50 (Fla. Dist. Ct. App. 1976), *cert. denied and appeal dismissed,* 354 So. 2d 351, 3 Media L. Rep. 2183 (Fla. 1977), *cert. denied,* 439 U.S. 910, 4 Media L. Rep. 1592 (1978) *2:* 157
—v. Nourse, 413 So. 2d 467, 8 Media L. Rep. 1606 (Fla. Dist. Ct. App. 1982) *1:* 158
—State v., 395 So. 2d 544, 7 Media L. Rep. 1021 (Fla. 1981) *1:* 568, 640
Palmer v. Schonhorn Enters., 232 A.2d 458 (N.J. Super. Ct. Ch. Div. 1967) *6:* 6, 19
Palmisano v. Modernismo Pubns., 470 N.Y.S.2d 196, 10 Media L. Rep. 1093 (N.Y. App. Div. 1983) *3:* 50
Pan Am Corp., In re, 22 Media L. Rep. 1118 (S.D.N.Y. 1993) *14:* 307
Pankratz v. District Ct., 609 P.2d 1101 (Colo. 1980) *14:* 71, 77
Pantos v. City & County of San Francisco, 198 Cal. Rptr. 489, 10 Media L. Rep. 1279 (Cal. Ct. App. 1984) *1:* 525
Papachristou v. Jacksonville, 405 U.S. 156 (1972) *8:* 32
Papish v. Board of Curators, 410 U.S. 667 (1973) *13:* 335
Pappas, In re, 266 N.E.2d 297 (Mass. 1971), *aff'd sub nom.* Branzburg v. Hayes, 408 U.S. 665, 1 Media L. Rep. 2617 (1972) *14:* 4, 17, 71
Paramount Pictures; United States v., 334 U.S. 131 (1948) *13:* 25
Parker v. Kentucky Bd. of Dentistry, 818 F.2d 504 (6th Cir. 1987) *11:* 324
Parkman v. Hastings, 531 S.W.2d 481 (Ark. 1976) *2:* 170–71
Parkway Baking Corp. v. Freihofer Baking Co., 255 F.2d 641 (3d Cir. 1958) *6:* 147
Parmley v. Missouri Dental Bd., 719 S.W.2d 745 (Mo. 1986) *11:* 324
Parratt v. Taylor, 451 U.S. 527 (1981) *9:* 40, 46
Parson v. Watson, 778 F. Supp. 214, 19 Media L. Rep. 1275 (D. Del. 1991) *14:* 333
Pasadena Star-News v. Superior Ct., 249 Cal. Rptr. 729 (Cal. Ct. App. 1988) *4:* 162
Passaic Daily News
—v. City of Clifton, 491 A.2d 808, 11 Media L. Rep. 1962 (N.J. Super. Ct. Law Div. 1985) *12:* 137, 156

—v. NLRB, 736 F.2d 1543 (D.C. Cir. 1984) *9:* 126, 128
Pastet v. Jackson Newspapers, 17 Media L. Rep. 1776 (Conn. Super. Ct. 1990) *2:* 606
Patterson
—v. McClean Credit Union, 491 U.S. 164 (1989) *9:* 87
—v. Renstrom, 195 N.W.2d 193 (Neb. 1972) *2:* 626
—v. Tribune Co., 146 So. 2d 623 (Fla. Dist. Ct. App. 1962), *cert. denied,* 153 So. 2d 306 (1963) *4:* 67
Patuxent Pub'g Corp. v. State, 429 A.2d 554, 7 Media L. Rep. 1349 (Md. Ct. Spec. App. 1981) *1:* 106–7
Paul v. Davis, 424 U.S. 693 (1976) *9:* 49–54, 56–58, 61
Paulsen
—v. FCC, 491 F.2d 887 (9th Cir. 1974) *13:* 115
—v. Personality Posters, 299 N.Y.S.2d 501 (N.Y. Sup. Ct. 1968) *6:* 74
Pavesich v. New Eng. Life Ins. Co., 50 S.E. 68 (Ga. 1905) *4:* 4, 6; *6:* 62
Pawelek v. Paramount Studios Corp., 571 F. Supp. 1082 (N.D. Ill. 1983) *9:* 45
Paye v. Gibraltar Sch. Dist., No. 90CV70444DT, 1991 U.S. Dist. LEXIS 16480 (E.D. Mich. 1991) *13:* 359
Pearson
—v. Dodd, 410 F.2d 701, 1 Media L. Rep. 1809 (D.C. Cir.), *cert. denied,* 395 U.S. 947 (1969) *5:* 50, 82, 189
—v. Fairbanks Pub'g Co., 413 P.2d 711 (Alaska 1966) *2:* 277
Peay v. Curtis Pub'g Co., 78 F. Supp. 305 (D.D.C. 1948) *3:* 7, 32, 44
Pechter v. Lyons, 441 F. Supp. 115, 3 Media L. Rep. 1445 (S.D.N.Y. 1977) *1:* 288
Peck v. Tribune Co., 214 U.S. 185 (1909) *2:* 9, 118–20
Peel v. Attorney Registration & Disciplinary Comm'n, 496 U.S. 91 (1990) *11:* 164–69, 321
Peisner v. Detroit Free Press, 242 N.W.2d 775 (Mich. Ct. App. 1976) *2:* 678–79
Pell v. Procunier, 417 U.S. 817, 1 Media L. Rep. 2379 (1974) *1:* 14, 459, 461–62, 464–78, 482–89; *13:* 279–80
Pemberton v. Bethlehem Steel, 502 A.2d 1101 (Md. Ct. Spec. App.), *cert. denied,* 508 A.2d 488 (Md.), *cert. denied,* 479 U.S. 984 (1986) *5:* 30, 41
Penguin Books USA v. Walsh, 756 F. Supp. 770, 18 Media L. Rep. 1856 (S.D.N.Y.), *appeal dismissed and judgment vacated,* 929 F.2d 69 (2d Cir. 1991) *10:* 153

Pennsylvania Accessories Trade Ass'n v. Thornburgh, 565 F. Supp. 1568 (M.D. Pa. 1983) *11:* 305
Pennsylvania Alliance for Jobs & Energy v. Council of Munhall, 743 F.2d 182 (3d Cir. 1984) *12:* 41, 186
Penny Saver Pubns. v. Village of Hazel Crest, 905 F.2d 150, 17 Media L. Rep. 2057 (7th Cir. 1990) *11:* 314
Penry v. Dozier, 49 So. 909 (Ala. 1909) *2:* 163–64
Penthouse Int'l
—v. Koch, 599 F. Supp. 1338 (S.D.N.Y. 1984) *13:* 427–28
—v. McAuliffe, 610 F.2d 1353, 5 Media L. Rep. 2531 (5th Cir.), *cert. dismissed,* 447 U.S. 931 (1980) *10:* 39
Penwell v. Taft Broadcasting Co., 469 N.E.2d 1025, 10 Media L. Rep. 1550 (Ohio Ct. App. 1984) *4:* 54
People v., *see* name of other party
Perez; People v., 417 N.Y.S.2d 487, 5 Media L. Rep. 1590 (N.Y. App. Div. 1979) *1:* 106, 119
Permitting Media Coverage for an Indefinite Period, In re, 539 A.2d 976, 15 Media L. Rep. 1473 (R.I. 1988) *1:* 578
Perry v. CBS, 499 F.2d 797 (7th Cir.), *cert. denied,* 419 U.S. 883 (1974) *2:* 407
Perry Educ. Ass'n v. Perry Local Educators' Ass'n, 460 U.S. 37 (1983) *12:* 2, 56, 60, 72, 77–79; *13:* 259–60, 263–68, 271–74, 352–54, 389
Person v. New York Post Corp., 427 F. Supp. 1297, 2 Media L. Rep. 1666 (E.D.N.Y.), *aff'd,* 573 F.2d 1294, 3 Media L. Rep. 1784 (2d Cir. 1977) *9:* 192; *13:* 207, 227, 253
Perumal v. Saddleback Valley Unified Sch. Dist., 243 Cal. Rptr. 545 (Cal. Ct. App.), *cert. denied,* 488 U.S. 933 (1988) *13:* 367
Peters; United States v., 754 F.2d 753, 11 Media L. Rep. 1513 (7th Cir. 1985) *1:* 232, 318, 393
Petersen v. Talisman Sugar Corp., 478 F.2d 73 (5th Cir. 1973) *12:* 87
Peto v. Cook, 364 F. Supp. 1 (S.D. Ohio 1973), *aff'd mem. sub nom.* Guggenheim v. Peto, 415 U.S. 943 (1974) *11:* 188
Petroleum Prods. Antitrust Litig., In re, 680 F.2d 5 (2d Cir.), *cert. denied sub nom.* Arizona v. McGraw-Hill, Inc., 459 U.S. 909 (1982) *14:* 306
Petrone v. Reading, 541 F. Supp. 735 (E.D. Pa. 1982) *9:* 84
Pettengill v. Booth Newspapers, 278 N.W.2d 682, 5 Media L. Rep. 1326 (Mich. Ct. App. 1979) *2:* 584

Petty v. General Accident Fire & Life Ins. Corp., 365 F.2d 419 (3d Cir. 1966) *2:* 515
Pfeifly v. Henry, 112 A. 768 (Pa. 1921) *2:* 164
P.G. Pub'g Co. v. Commonwealth, 566 A.2d 857, 16 Media L. Rep. 2433 (Pa. Super. Ct. 1989) *1:* 374
Phantom Touring v. Affiliated Pubns., 953 F.2d 724, 19 Media L. Rep. 1786 (1st Cir.), *cert. denied,* 112 S. Ct. 2942 (1992) *2:* 261
Phelps v. Wichita Eagle-Beacon, 886 F.2d 1262 (10th Cir. 1989) *9:* 45
Philadelphia Newspapers
—v. Borough Council, 381 F. Supp. 228 (E.D. Pa. 1974) *12:* 137
—v. Hepps, 475 U.S. 767, 12 Media L. Rep. 1977 (1986) *2:* 90, 285–88, 292; *7:* 10
—v. Jerome, 387 A.2d 425, 3 Media L. Rep. 2185 (Pa. 1978), *appeal dismissed,* 443 U.S. 913, 5 Media L. Rep. 1304 (1979) *1:* 123
Phillips
—v. Evening Star Newspaper Co., 424 A.2d 78, 6 Media L. Rep. 2191 (D.D.C. 1980), *cert. denied,* 451 U.S. 989 *2:* 467
—v. Smalley Maintenance Servs., 435 So. 2d 705 (Ala. 1983) *5:* 9, 50
—v. Township of Darby, 305 F. Supp. 763 (E.D. Pa. 1969) *12:* 199, 201
—United States v., 540 F.2d 319 (8th Cir.), *cert. denied,* 429 U.S. 1000 (1976) *5:* 227
Phoenix Newspapers
—v. Choisser, 312 P.2d 150 (Ariz. 1957) *2:* 561
—v. Church, 537 P.2d 1345 (Ariz. Ct. App. 1975), *cert. denied and appeal dismissed,* 425 U.S. 908 (1976) *2:* 223, 484
—v. Superior Ct., 680 P.2d 166, 10 Media L. Rep. 1659 (Ariz. 1984) *1:* 186
Phoenix Printing Co. v. Robertson, 195 P. 487 (Okla. 1921) *2:* 151
Photo Mktg. Ass'n, In re, 327 N.W.2d 515 (Mich. Ct. App. 1982) *14:* 70, 306
Phyfer v. Fiona Press, 12 Media L. Rep. 2211 (N.D. Miss. 1986) *2:* 506
Pickering v. Board of Educ., 391 U.S. 563 (1968) *1:* 527
Pierce v. Capital Cities Communications, 576 F.2d 495, 3 Media L. Rep. 2259 (3d Cir.), *cert. denied,* 439 U.S. 861 (1978) *2:* 121
Pierson v. News Group Pubns., 549 F. Supp. 635 (S.D. Ga. 1982) *5:* 24; *6:* 114
Pietrafeso v. DPI, Inc., 757 P.2d 1113, 15 Media L. Rep. 1736 (Colo. Ct. App. 1988) *2:* 140
Pigg v. State Dep't of Highways, 746 P.2d 961 (Colo. 1987) *12:* 184
Pigman v. Evansville Press, 537 N.E.2d 547, 16 Media L. Rep. 1688 (Ind. Ct. App. 1989) *1:* 162, 385
Pillsbury Co. v. Conboy, *see* Corrugated Container Antitrust Litig., In re
Pines v. Tomson, 206 Cal. Rptr. 866 (Cal. Ct. App. 1984) *13:* 248
Pinkard v. Johnson, 118 F.R.D. 517 (M.D. Ala. 1987) *14:* 171, 372
Pinkerton Nat'l Detective Agency v. Stevens, 132 S.E.2d 119 (Ga. Ct. App. 1963) *5:* 16, 39
Pioneer Hi-Bred Int'l v. Holden's Found. Seeds, 105 F.R.D. 76 (N.D. Ind. 1985) *1:* 428
Pirone v. MacMillan, Inc., 894 F.2d 579, 17 Media L. Rep. 1472 (2d Cir. 1990) *6:* 129, 149–51, 202, 204–5
Pittman
—v. Dow Jones & Co., 662 F. Supp. 921, 14 Media L. Rep. 1284 (E.D. La.), *aff'd,* 834 F.2d 1171, 14 Media L. Rep. 2384 (5th Cir. 1987) *7:* 9, 12, 26, 42–43
—v. Hutto, 594 F.2d 407 (4th Cir. 1979) *13:* 255, 278–81, 286–91, 294, 296, 298
Pittsburgh Press Co.
—v. Commonwealth, 376 A.2d 263, 2 Media L. Rep. 2337 (Pa. Commw. Ct.), *aff'd,* 396 A.2d 1187, 4 Media L. Rep. 2109 (Pa. 1979), *cert. denied,* 442 U.S. 942 (1979) *11:* 317
—v. Pittsburgh Comm'n on Human Relations, 413 U.S. 376, 1 Media L. Rep. 1908, *reh'g denied,* 414 U.S. 881 (1973) *9:* 134; *10:* 3, 44–45; *11:* 17, 29, 63–66, 310–12
Plain Dealer Pub'g Co. v. City of Lakewood, 794 F.2d 1139, 13 Media L. Rep. 1065 (6th Cir. 1986), *aff'd in part,* 486 U.S. 750, 15 Media L. Rep. 1481 (1988) *12:* 139, 144, 150–51, 154
Planned Parenthood Ass'n/Chicago Area v. Chicago Transit Auth., 592 F. Supp. 544 (N.D. Ill. 1984), *aff'd,* 767 F.2d 1225 (7th Cir. 1985) *13:* 429
Planned Parenthood of S. Nev. v. Clark County Sch. Dist., 941 F.2d 817 (9th Cir. 1991) *13:* 368–74
Planned Protective Serv. v. Gorton, 245 Cal. Rptr. 790 (Cal. Ct. App. 1988) *2:* 685
Plaquemines Comm'n Council Parish v. Delta Dev. Co., 472 So. 2d 560, 11 Media L. Rep. 2353 (La. 1985) *1:* 425
Playboy Enters. v. Superior Ct. (Green), 201 Cal. Rptr. 207 (Cal. Ct. App. 1984) *14:* 337
PMP Assocs. v. Globe Newspaper Co., 321 N.E.2d 915 (Mass. 1975) *13:* 227, 231
Poirier v. Hodges, 445 F. Supp. 838 (M.D. Fla. 1978) *9:* 65, 84
Police Dep't of Chicago v. Mosley, 408 U.S. 92 (1972) *8:* 65; *12:* 4

Polk County v. Dodson, 454 U.S. 312 (1981) *9:* 42
Polygram Records v. Superior Ct., 170 Cal. App. 3d 543, 216 Cal. Rptr. 252, 11 Media L. Rep. 2363 (Cal. Ct. App. 1985) *2:* 154
Popkin v. United States, *see* Doe; United States v.
Porten v. University of San Francisco, 64 Cal. App. 3d 825, 134 Cal. Rptr. 839 (Cal. Ct. App. 1976) *4:* 40
Porter v. Eyster, 294 F.2d 613 (4th Cir. 1961) *2:* 545
Portwood v. Falls City Brewing Co., 318 S.W.2d 535 (Ky. 1958) *11:* 184
Posadas de Puerto Rico v. Tourism Co., 478 U.S. 328, 13 Media L. Rep. 1033 (1986) *11:* 6, 59, 63, 80, 113, 118–21, 123–28, 131–35, 137–38, 140, 146, 183, 192, 196, 217, 233, 240, 242, 245–48
Posner; United States v., 594 F. Supp. 930, 11 Media L. Rep. 1560 (S.D. Fla. 1984) *1:* 364
Post-Newsweek Stations, In re
—722 F.2d 325, 10 Media L. Rep. 1087 (6th Cir. 1983) *1:* 355
—370 So. 2d 764, 5 Media L. Rep. 1039 (Fla. 1979) *1:* 617
Post-Newsweek Stations-Conn. v. Travelers Ins. Co., 510 F. Supp. 81, 6 Media L. Rep. 2540 (D. Conn. 1981) *1:* 547
Post-Newsweek Stations, Fla. v. State, 474 So. 2d 344, 12 Media L. Rep. 1039 (Fla. Dist. Ct. App. 1985), *approved,* 510 So. 2d 896 (Fla. 1987) *1:* 161
Post-Tribune Pub'g Co., State ex rel. v. Porter Super. Ct., 412 N.E.2d 748, 6 Media L. Rep. 2300 (Ind. 1980) *1:* 172
Post Pub'g Co. v. Murray, 230 F. 773 (1st Cir.), *cert. denied,* 241 U.S. 675 (1916) *11:* 249–50
Poteet v. Roswell Daily Record, 584 P.2d 1310, 4 Media L. Rep. 1749 (N.M. Ct. App. 1978) *4:* 73, 184
Potts v. Dies, 132 F.2d 734 (D.C. Cir. 1942), *cert. denied,* 319 U.S. 762 (1943) *2:* 272, 275
Poughkeepsie Newspapers v. Rosenblatt, 463 N.E.2d 1222, 10 Media L. Rep. 1560 (N.Y. 1984) *1:* 142
Poulos v. New Hampshire, 345 U.S. 395 (1953) *12:* 7
Powers
—v. Carvalho, 368 A.2d 1242 (R.I. 1977) *2:* 543
—v. Durgin-Snow Pub'g Co., 144 A.2d 294 (Me. 1958) *2:* 155
—United States v., 622 F.2d 317, 6 Media L. Rep. 1161 (8th Cir.), *cert. denied,* 449 U.S. 837 (1980) *1:* 203–5
Power Test Petroleum Distribs. v. Calcu Gas, 754 F.2d 91 (2d Cir. 1985) *10:* 248
P.R., In re, 637 P.2d 346, 7 Media L. Rep. 2277 (Colo. 1981) *1:* 162
Prager v. ABC, 569 F. Supp. 1229 (D.N.J. 1983), *aff'd,* 734 F.2d 7 (3d Cir. 1984) *14:* 248
Prahl v. Brosamle
—295 N.W.2d 768 (Wis. Ct. App. 1980) *5:* 55, 81, 98, 144; *9:* 43, 64
—Case No. 152–062, Circuit Court, Dane County (1982) *5:* 108
Pratt v. Sumner, 807 F.2d 817 (9th Cir. 1987) *13:* 307
Pratt & Whitney Can. v. United States, 14 Cl. Ct. 268, 15 Media L. Rep. 1033 (Cl. Ct. 1988) *1:* 427, 452
Preferred Communications v. Los Angeles (Preferred I), 754 F.2d 1396 (9th Cir. 1985), *aff'd,* 476 U.S. 488 (1986) *12:* 228, 235, 239; *13:* 434, 524–26, 528–32
Presley, Estate of v. Russen, 513 F. Supp. 1339 (D.N.J. 1981) *6:* 4–5, 38, 153, 206–8
Press Co. v. NLRB, 118 F.2d 937 (D.C. Cir. 1940), *cert. denied,* 313 U.S. 59 (1941) *9:* 129
Press-Enterprise Co.
—v. Superior Ct., 691 P.2d 1026, 1032 (Cal. 1984) *1:* 95
—v. Superior Ct. (Press-Enterprise I), 464 U.S. 501, 10 Media L. Rep. 1161 (1984) *1:* 59–68, 83, 106, 118, 223–24
—v. Superior Ct. (Press-Enterprise II), 478 U.S. 1, 13 Media L. Rep. 1001 (1986) *1:* 13, 16, 21, 27, 74–97, 104–5, 162–63
Pressler v. Dow Jones & Co., 450 N.Y.S.2d 884, 8 Media L. Rep. 1680 (N.Y. App. Div. 1982) *7:* 12, 14, 26
Price
—v. Hal Roach Studios, 400 F. Supp. 836 (S.D.N.Y. 1975) *6:* 7, 47, 97, 128, 201
—v. Viking Penguin, 881 F.2d 1426, 16 Media L. Rep. 2169 (8th Cir. 1989), *cert. denied,* 493 U.S. 1036 (1990) *2:* 139, 579
—v. Viking Press, 625 F. Supp. 641, 12 Media L. Rep. 1689 (D. Minn. 1985) *4:* 174
—v. Worldvision Enters., 455 F. Supp. 252, 4 Media L. Rep. 1301 (S.D.N.Y. 1978), *aff'd,* 603 F.2d 214 (2d Cir. 1979) *6:* 38
Pridonoff v. Balokovich, 228 P.2d 6 (Cal. 1951) *2:* 613
Primus, In re, 436 U.S. 412 (1978) *11:* 31, 89, 318, 321
Princess Sea Indus. v. Nevada, 635 P.2d 281, 7 Media L. Rep. 2474 (Nev. 1981), *cert. denied,* 456 U.S. 926 (1982) *11:* 308

Pring v. Penthouse Int'l
—695 F.2d 438, 8 Media L. Rep. 2409 (10th Cir. 1982), *cert. denied,* 462 U.S. 1132 (1983)   *2:* 259–60, 267, 305; *3:* 30
—7 Media L. Rep. 1101 (D. Wyo. 1981)   *2:* 393
Privitera v. Town of Phelps, 435 N.Y.S.2d 402, 6 Media L. Rep. 2470 (N.Y. App. Div. 1981)   *2:* 196
Procunier v. Martinez, 416 U.S. 396 (1974)   *13:* 279–80, 283, 292–93, 302, 305, 309–10
Progressive, Inc.; United States v., 467 F. Supp. 990, 4 Media L. Rep. 2377 (W.D. Wis. 1979), *dismissed,* 610 F.2d 819 (7th Cir. 1979)   *10:* 123–24, 126, 128–33
Projects 80's v. City of Pocatello, 942 F.2d 635 (9th Cir. 1991)   *12:* 123
Providence Journal Co.
—In re, 820 F.2d 1342 (1st Cir. 1986), *modified,* 820 F.2d 1354, 14 Media L. Rep. 1029 (1st Cir. 1987), *cert. dismissed,* 485 U.S. 693, 15 Media L. Rep. 1241 (1988)   *5:* 197, 216; *10:* 90–100
—v. Newport, 665 F. Supp. 107, 15 Media L. Rep. 1545 (D.R.I. 1987)   *12:* 137–38, 141
—v. Newton, 723 F. Supp. 846, 17 Media L. Rep. 1033 (D.R.I. 1989)   *4:* 82
Provisional Gov't v. ABC, 11 Media L. Rep. 2107 (D.D.C. 1985)   *9:* 43, 93
Pruneyard Shopping Ctr. v. Robins, 447 U.S. 74, 6 Media L. Rep. 1311 (1980)   *13:* 420, 422
Public Citizen v. Liggett Group, 858 F.2d 775, 15 Media L. Rep. 2129 (1st Cir. 1988), *cert. denied,* 488 U.S. 1030 (1989)   *1:* 106, 116, 429, 434, 437–38, 441, 443–44, 457
Publicker Indus. v. Cohen, 733 F.2d 1059, 10 Media L. Rep. 1777 (3d Cir. 1984)   *1:* 265, 271–76, 450
Publishers New Press v. Moysey, 141 F. Supp. 340 (S.D.N.Y. 1957)   *9:* 216
Pulitzer Pub'g Co.
—State ex rel. v. Lohmar, 633 S.W.2d 195, 8 Media L. Rep. 1417 (Mo. Ct. App. 1982)   *1:* 106, 122
—United States ex rel., 635 F.2d 676, 6 Media L. Rep. 2232 (8th Cir. 1980)   *1:* 225

Q

Quaker Action Group v. Morton, 516 F.2d 717 (D.C. Cir. 1975)   *12:* 43
Queensgate Inv. Co. v. Liquor Control Comm'n, 433 N.E.2d 138 (Ohio), *appeal dismissed,* 459 U.S. 807 (1982)   *11:* 105, 137, 189–91
Quezada By Delamota v. Daily News, 501 N.Y.S.2d 971, 12 Media L. Rep. 2097 (N.Y. Sup. Ct. 1986)   *6:* 43
Quincy Cable TV v. FCC, 768 F.2d 1434, 12 Media L. Rep. 1001 (D.C. Cir. 1985), *cert. denied sub nom.* Nat'l Ass'n of Broadcasters v. Quincy Cable TV, 476 U.S. 1169 (1986)   *12:* 236, 239; *13:* 434, 510–20
Quinn
—v. Aetna Life & Casualty Co.
——482 F. Supp. 22, 5 Media L. Rep. 1310 (E.D.N.Y. 1979), *aff'd,* 616 F.2d 38, 5 Media L. Rep. 2432 (2d Cir. 1980)   *7:* 24, 42
——409 N.Y.S.2d 473, 4 Media L. Rep. 1049 (N.Y. Sup. Ct. 1978)   *7:* 24
—v. Johnson, 381 N.Y.S.2d 875 (N.Y. App. Div. 1976)   *10:* 238

R

Raboya v. Shrybman & Assocs., 777 F. Supp. 58, 19 Media L. Rep. 1669 (D.D.C. 1991)   *2:* 194
Radical Lawyers Caucus v. Pool, 324 F. Supp. 268 (W.D. Tex. 1970)   *13:* 399
Radio & Television News Ass'n v. United States Dist. Ct., 781 F.2d 1443, 12 Media L. Rep. 1739 (9th Cir. 1986)   *10:* 212–16
Rafferty v. Hartford Courant Co., 416 A.2d 1215, 6 Media L. Rep. 1668 (Conn. Super. Ct. 1980)   *5:* 46
Raffoul; United States v., 826 F.2d 218, 14 Media L. Rep. 1534 (3d Cir. 1987)   *1:* 106, 109–11, 113–14
Ragin v. New York Times Co., 726 F. Supp. 953, 17 Media L. Rep. 1945 (S.D.N.Y. 1989), *aff'd,* 923 F.2d 995, 18 Media L. Rep. 1666 (2d Cir. 1991), *cert. denied,* 116 L. Ed. 2d 54 (1991)   *11:* 315
Raible v. Newsweek, 341 F. Supp. 804 (W.D. Pa. 1972)   *4:* 183
Rainey v. Shaffer, 456 N.E.2d 1328 (Ohio Ct. App. 1983)   *2:* 626
Rancho La Costa v. Superior Ct., 165 Cal. Rptr. 347, 6 Media L. Rep. 1351 (Cal. Ct. App. 1980), *cert. denied,* 450 U.S. 902 (1981)   *2:* 108, 394
Rankin v. Phillippe, 211 A.2d 56 (Pa. Super. Ct. 1965)   *2:* 537
Rapid City Journal Co.
—v. Circuit Ct. (Tice), 283 N.W.2d 563, 5 Media L. Rep. 1706 (S.D. 1979)   *1:* 225
—v. Circuit Ct. of Eighth Judicial Cir. (Bradenburg), 286 N.W.2d 125, 5 Media L. Rep. 2365 (S.D. 1979)   *1:* 152
Rapier, In re, 143 U.S. 110 (1892)   *11:* 249

Rawlins v. Hutchinson Pub'g Co., 543 P.2d 988 (Kan. 1975) *4:* 121

Rawls v. Conde Nast Pubns., 446 F.2d 313 (5th Cir. 1971), *cert. denied,* 404 U.S. 1038 (1972), *reh'g denied,* 405 U.S. 969 (1972) *4:* 26, 188; *5:* 112

Ray v. Time, Inc., 452 F. Supp. 618 (W.D. Tenn. 1976), *aff'd,* 582 F.2d 1280 (6th Cir. 1978) *2:* 602

Raymond v. Paradise Unified Sch. Dist., 31 Cal. Rptr. 847 (1963) *8:* 79, 80

Read
—v. News-Journal Co., 474 A.2d 119, 10 Media L. Rep. 1399 (Del. 1984) *2:* 509–10
—v. Phoenix Newspapers, 819 P.2d 939, 19 Media L. Rep. 1563 (1991) *2:* 289

Reader's Digest Ass'n
—v. Federal Election Comm'n, 509 F. Supp. 1210, 7 Media L. Rep. 1053 (S.D.N.Y. 1981) *9:* 99–108
—v. Superior Ct., 37 Cal. 3d 244, 690 P.2d 610, 11 Media L. Rep. 1065 (Cal. 1984) *2:* 431
—United States v., 662 F.2d 955, 7 Media L. Rep. 1921 (3d Cir. 1981), *cert. denied,* 455 U.S. 908 (1982) *7:* 71

Reardon v. News-Journal Co., 164 A.2d 263 (Del. 1960) *2:* 127

Reaves v. Foster, 200 So. 2d 453 (Miss. 1967) *2:* 156, 158

Rebozo v. Washington Post Co., 637 F.2d 375, 6 Media L. Rep. 2505 (5th Cir.), *cert. denied,* 454 U.S. 964 (1981) *2:* 339, 395

Record Head Corp. v. Sachen, 682 F.2d 672 (7th Cir. 1982) *11:* 306

Record Museum v. Lawrence Township, 481 F. Supp. 768 (D.N.J. 1979) *11:* 306

Red Bank Register v. Board of Educ., 501 A.2d 985, 12 Media L. Rep. 1860 (N.J. Super. Ct. App. Div. 1985) *1:* 291

Redco Corp. v. CBS, Inc., 758 F.2d 970, 11 Media L. Rep. 1861 (3d Cir.), *cert. denied,* 474 U.S. 843 (1985) *2:* 156, 266, 289–90, 688

Red Lion Broadcasting Co. v. FCC, 381 F.2d 908 (D.C. Cir. 1967), *aff'd,* 395 U.S. 367 (1969) *12:* 200, 233–34; *13:* 13–29, 55, 74, 77, 79–81, 84, 86, 131, 137–41, 165, 464, 504

Redwood Empire Pub'g Co. v. California State Bd. of Equalization, 255 Cal. Rptr. 514, 16 Media L. Rep. 1257 (Cal. Ct. App. 1989) *9:* 237

Reece v. Grissom, 267 S.E.2d 839 (Ga. Ct. App. 1980) *2:* 168

Reed
—v. Northwestern Pub'g Co., 530 N.E.2d 474, 15 Media L. Rep. 2233 (Ill. 1988) *2:* 327, 484, 487
—v. Real Detective Pub'g Co., 162 P.2d 133 (Ariz. 1945) *4:* 28

Rees v. L.A. County, *see* California ex rel. L.A., In re

Reeves
—v. ABC, 719 F.2d 602, 9 Media L. Rep. 2289 (2d Cir. 1983) *2:* 558
—v. McConn, 631 F.2d 377 (5th Cir. 1980) *12:* 48, 197–98, 201, 203–5
—v. United Artists, 572 F. Supp. 1231, 9 Media L. Rep. 2484 (N.D. Ohio 1983), *aff'd,* 765 F.2d 79, 11 Media L. Rep. 2181 (6th Cir. 1985) *6:* 11, 214–15

Regan v. Time, Inc., 468 U.S. 641 (1984) *12:* 2, 15, 21, 34, 82

Register Div. of Freedom Newspapers v. County of Orange, 205 Cal. Rptr. 92 (Cal. Ct. App. 1984) *1:* 305

Reilly
—v. Leonard, 459 F. Supp. 291 (D. Conn. 1978) *9:* 61
—v. McKnight, 439 N.Y.S.2d 727, 7 Media L. Rep. 1445 (N.Y. App. Div. 1981), *aff'd,* 430 N.E.2d 922 (N.Y. 1981) *1:* 364

Reinecke v. Cobb County Sch. Dist., 484 F. Supp. 1252 (N.D. Ga. 1980) *13:* 347

Reininger v. Prickett, 137 P.2d 595 (Okla. 1943) *2:* 537

Reiter; United States v., 7 Media L. Rep. 1927 (D. Md. 1981) *1:* 346

Reliance Ins. Co. v. Barron's
—428 F. Supp. 200, 2 Media L. Rep. 1641 (S.D.N.Y. 1977) *1:* 426
—442 F. Supp. 1341 (S.D.N.Y. 1977) *9:* 140–41, 146

Remeny; People v., 355 N.E.2d 375 (N.Y. 1976) *11:* 52

Remer v. City of El Cajon, 52 Cal. App. 3d 441, 125 Cal. Rptr. 116 (Cal. Ct. App. 1975) *12:* 137–38

Reminga v. United States, 631 F.2d 449 (6th Cir. 1980) *7:* 46

Rendell-Baker v. Kohn, 457 U.S. 830 (1982) *9:* 41–42

Renton, City of; v. Playtime Theatres, 475 U.S. 41, 12 Media L. Rep. 1721 (1986) *12:* 2, 5, 11, 22, 27–28, 36, 80

Renwick v. News & Observer Pub'g Co., 312 S.E.2d 405, 10 Media L. Rep. 1443 (N.C.), *cert. denied,* 469 U.S. 858 (1984) *3:* 6, 18, 20, 48, 94

Reporters Comm. for Freedom of the Press, In re, 773 F.2d 1325, 12 Media L. Rep. 1073 (D.C. Cir. 1985) *1:* 432–33

Republic Entertainment v. Clark County, 672 P.2d 634 (Nev. 1983) *11:* 82, 309

Republic Nat'l Life Ins. Corp., In re, 387 F. Supp. 902 (S.D.N.Y. 1975) *9:* 139

Resident Advisory Bd. v. Rizzo, 503 F. Supp. 383 (E.D. Pa. 1980) *12:* 206

Resident Participation of Denver v. Love, 322 F. Supp. 1100 (D. Colo. 1971) *13:* 246

Resorts Int'l v. New Jersey Monthly, 445 A.2d 395, 8 Media L. Rep. 1487 (N.J.), *cert. denied,* 459 U.S. 907 (1982) *14:* 251, 328

Retail Credit Co. v. Russell, 218 S.E.2d 54 (Ga. 1975) *10:* 241

Reuber
—v. Food Chem. News, 925 F.2d 703, 18 Media L. Rep. 1689 (4th Cir.), *cert. denied,* 111 S. Ct. 2814 (1991) *2:* 437; *4:* 150; *5:* 21
—v. United States, 750 F.2d 1039 (D.C. Cir. 1984) *5:* 196; *9:* 45, 47, 51

Rewald; People v., 318 N.Y.S.2d 40 (N.Y. 1971) *5:* 134

Reynolds v. von Bulow by Auersperg, *see* von Bulow by Auersperg v. von Bulow

Rhode Island Broadcasters Ass'n v. Michaelson, 4 Media L. Rep. 2224 (D.R.I. 1978) *11:* 325

Rhode Island Liquor Stores Ass'n v. Evening Call Pub'g Co., 497 A.2d 331, 12 Media L. Rep. 1121 (R.I. 1985) *11:* 184, 190, 207

Rhodes
—v. Graham, 37 S.W.2d 46 (Ky. 1931) *5:* 262
—v. Gwinnett County, 557 F. Supp. 30 (N.D. Ga. 1982) *12:* 185

Rhynas v. Adkisson, 159 N.W. 877 (Iowa 1916) *2:* 6

Richmond Newspapers
—v. Lipscomb, 362 S.E.2d 32, 14 Media L. Rep. 1953 (Va. 1987), *cert. denied,* 486 U.S. 1023 (1988) *2:* 327
—v. Virginia, 448 U.S. 555, 6 Media L. Rep. 1833 (1980) *1:* 28–44, 181, 195, 197, 222, 264, 301

Rickbeil v. Grafton Deaconess Hosp., 23 N.W.2d 247 (N.D. 1946) *2:* 218

Ridenhour, In re, 520 So. 2d 372, 15 Media L. Rep. 1022 (La. 1988) *14:* 70, 76, 79, 226–27

Rifkin v. Esquire Pub'g, 8 Media L. Rep. 1384 (C.D. Cal. 1982) *3:* 36; *5:* 18

Riley
—v. City of Chester, 612 F.2d 708 (3d Cir. 1979) *14:* 47, 53, 63, 90, 98–99, 163, 165, 167, 173, 371, 404
—v. National Federation of the Blind, 487 U.S. 781 (1988) *11:* 33–36

Rinaldi
—v. Holt, Rinehart & Winston, 366 N.E.2d 1299, 2 Media L. Rep. 2169 (N.Y. 1977) *2:* 90
—v. Viking Penguin, 438 N.E.2d 377, 7 Media L. Rep. 1202 (N.Y. 1981) *2:* 225

Rinaldo; State v., 673 P.2d 614 (Wash. Ct. App. 1983), *aff'd,* 689 P.2d 392 (Wash. 1984) *14:* 367

Rinsley v. Brandt, 446 F. Supp. 850 (D. Kan. 1977), *aff'd,* 700 F.2d 1304, 9 Media L. Rep. 1225 (10th Cir. 1983) *2:* 259–60, 267, 289, 625; *3:* 58–59, 63, 65, 83, 85

Risner v. City of Wyoming, 383 N.W.2d 226 (Mich. Ct. App. 1985) *12:* 189

Ritzmann v. Weekly World News, 614 F. Supp. 1336, 12 Media L. Rep. 1178 (N.D. Tex. 1985) *3:* 28

Rivera v. East Otero Sch. Dist. R-1, 721 F. Supp. 1189 (D. Colo. 1989) *13:* 359

R.M.J., In re, 455 U.S. 191, 7 Media L. Rep. 2545 (1982) *11:* 107–10, 321

Roach v. Harper, 105 S.E.2d 564 (W. Va. 1958) *5:* 262

Roberson v. Rochester Folding Box Co., 64 N.E. 442 (N.Y. 1902) *4:* 4, 6; *6:* 62, 123

Roberts v. Dover, 525 F. Supp. 987, 7 Media L. Rep. 2296 (M.D. Tenn. 1981) *3:* 84–86

Robins v. Pruneyard Shopping Ctr., 23 Cal. 3d 899, 592 P.2d 341 (Cal. 1979), *aff'd,* 447 U.S. 74, 6 Media L. Rep. 1311 (1980) *12:* 89; *13:* 311

Robinson v. McCorkle, 462 F.2d 111 (3d Cir.), *cert. denied,* 409 U.S. 1042 (1972) *9:* 65

Roche v. Florida, 589 So. 2d 978, 19 Media L. Rep. 1632 (Fla. Dist. Ct. App. 1991), *cert. denied,* 113 S. Ct. 1027 (1993) *14:* 416

Roe
—v. Abortion Abolition Soc'y, 811 F.2d 931 (5th Cir.), *cert. denied,* 484 U.S. 848 (1987) *9:* 71
—v. Wade, 410 U.S. 113 (1973) *11:* 285

Rogers
—v. Grimaldi, 875 F.2d 994, 16 Media L. Rep. 1648 (2d Cir. 1989) *6:* 22, 84, 152; *10:* 256
—v. United States, 340 U.S. 367 (1951) *14:* 115

Romaine v. Kallinger, 537 A.2d 284, 15 Media L. Rep. 1209 (N.J. 1988) *3:* 55; *4:* 4, 37, 121, 136

Roman v. New York City, 442 N.Y.S.2d 945 (N.Y. Sup. Ct. 1981) *7:* 9, 12, 16–17

Romano v. Harrington, 725 F. Supp. 687 (E.D.N.Y. 1989) *13:* 334

Romanski v. Prairie Farmer, 371 N.E.2d 109 (Ill. App. Ct. 1977) *7:* 59–64

Ronwin v. Shapiro, 657 F.2d 1071, 7 Media L. Rep. 2100 (9th Cir. 1981) *2:* 530, 553

Rosahn, In re, 671 F.2d 690, 8 Media L. Rep. 1187 (2d Cir. 1982) *1:* 162

Rosanova v. Playboy Enters., 580 F.2d 859, 4 Media L. Rep. 1550 (5th Cir. 1978) *2:* 438

Rosemont Enters. v. Random House, 294 N.Y.S.2d 122 (N.Y. Sup. Ct. 1968), aff'd, 301 N.Y.S.2d 948 (N.Y. App. Div. 1969) *6:* 13

Rosen v. Port of Portland, 641 F.2d 1243 (9th Cir. 1981) *12:* 216

Rosenbaum, Estate of v. New York City, 21 Media L. Rep. 1987 (E.D.N.Y. 1993) *1:* 279

Rosenberg v. Martin, 478 F.2d 520 (2d Cir.), *cert. denied,* 414 U.S. 872 (1973) *9:* 62

Rosenblatt v. Baer, 383 U.S. 75, 1 Media L. Rep. 1558 (1966) *2:* 87, 105, 309, 320–22, 324–25, 338–39, 406, 424–25

Rosenbloom v. Metromedia, 403 U.S. 29, 1 Media L. Rep. 1597 (1971) *2:* 47–58, 422, 461, 499–500; *3:* 70–71

Rosenblum v. Al's Liquors, 276 N.Y.S.2d 846 (N.Y. App. Div. 1966) *11:* 190

Rosenthal; United States v., 763 F.2d 1291, 11 Media L. Rep. 2237 (11th Cir. 1985) *1:* 380

Rosenwasser v. Ogoglia, 158 N.Y.S. 56 (N.Y. App. Div. 1916) *6:* 13–14

Roshto v. Hebert, 439 So. 2d 428 (La. 1983) *4:* 4, 120–21

Rosicrucian Fellowship v. Rosicrucian Fellowship Non-Sectarian Church, 245 P.2d 481 (Cal. 1952), *cert. denied,* 345 U.S. 938 (1953) *10:* 239

Ross
—v. Burns, 612 F.2d 271 (6th Cir. 1980) *4:* 173–74
—v. Gore, 48 So. 2d 412 (Fla. 1950) *2:* 613
—v. Midwest Communications, 870 F.2d 271, 16 Media L. Rep. 1463 (5th Cir. 1989), *cert. denied,* 493 U.S. 935 (1989) *4:* 22, 137, 161

Rossi v. Milwaukee, 7 Media L. Rep. 2265 (E.D. Wis. 1981) *1:* 527–28

Roth
—v. Greensboro News Co., 6 S.E.2d 882 (N.C. 1940) *2:* 5, 7
—v. United States, 354 U.S. 476, 1 Media L. Rep. 1375 (1957) *10:* 67

Rouch v. Enquirer & News of Battle Creek
—398 N.W.2d 245, 13 Media L. Rep. 2201 (Mich. 1986) *2:* 540
—487 N.W.2d 205, 20 Media L. Rep. 2265 (Mich. 1992) *2:* 704

Rovinsky v. McKaskle, 722 F.2d 197, 10 Media L. Rep. 1183 (5th Cir. 1984) *1:* 217, 222

Rovira v. Boget, 148 N.E. 534 (N.Y. 1925) *2:* 134

Rowan v. Post Office Dep't, 397 U.S. 728 (1970) *12:* 91, 113

Rozeboom v. Northwestern Bell Tel. Co., 358 N.W.2d 241 (S.D. 1984) *7:* 5

Rubin; People v., 158 Cal. Rptr. 488 (1979), *cert. denied,* 449 U.S. 821 (1980) *8:* 88

Rubinstein v. New York Post, 488 N.Y.S.2d 331, 11 Media L. Rep. 1329 (N.Y. Sup. Ct. 1985) *7:* 16

Rubio v. Swiridoff, 211 Cal. Rptr. 338 (Cal. Ct. App. 1985) *8:* 64

Rugg v. McCarty, 476 P.2d 753 (Colo. 1970) *5:* 20, 45

Ruggier v. Johns-Manville Prods. Corp., 503 F. Supp. 1036, 6 Media L. Rep. 2276 (D.R.I. 1980) *10:* 205

Ruiz-Estrella; United States v., 481 F.2d 723 (2d Cir. 1973) *1:* 206, 208

Runyon v. McCrary, 427 U.S. 160 (1976) *9:* 87

Rushford v. New Yorker Magazine, 846 F.2d 249, 15 Media L. Rep. 1841 (4th Cir. 1988) *1:* 427, 430–31

Russell
—In re, 726 F.2d 1007, 10 Media L. Rep. 1359 (4th Cir. 1984), *cert. denied,* 469 U.S. 837 (1984) *10:* 202
—v. Miami Herald Pub'g Co., 570 So. 2d 979, 18 Media L. Rep. 2036 (Fla. Dist. Ct. App. 1990) *4:* 108

Rust Communications Group v. 70 State Street Travel Serv., 504 N.Y.S.2d 927, 13 Media L. Rep. 1063 (N.Y. App. Div. 1986) *2:* 487

Rutledge
—v. Liability Ins. Indus., 487 F. Supp. 5, 5 Media L. Rep. 1153 (W.D. La. 1979) *7:* 24, 42; *11:* 44
—v. Phoenix Newspapers, 715 P.2d 1243, 12 Media L. Rep. 1969 (Ariz. Ct. App. 1986) *4:* 4, 6, 171

Rutti, In re, 5 Media L. Rep. 1513 (Ohio Ct. App. 1979) *14:* 276

Ruzicka v. Conde Naste Pubns., 733 F. Supp. 1289 (D. Minn. 1990), *aff'd in part and remanded in part,* 939 F.2d 578, 19 Media L. Rep. 1048 (8th Cir. 1991), *remanded,* 794 F. Supp. 303, 20 Media L. Rep. 1233 (D. Minn. 1992), *rev'd,* 499 F.2d 1319, 21 Media L. Rep. 1821 (8th Cir. 1993) *14:* 452–53, 457, 461

R.W. Page Corp. v. Lumpkin, 292 S.E.2d 815, 8 Media L. Rep. 1824 (Ga. 1982) *1:* 157

Ryan
—v. Brooks, 634 F.2d 726, 6 Media L. Rep. 2155 (4th Cir. 1980) *2:* 433, 435
—v. Hearst Pub'g, 100 P.2d 24 (Wash. 1940) *2:* 3, 301
—People v., 806 P.2d 935, 19 Media L. Rep.

Ryan—Contd.
1074 (Colo.), *cert. denied,* 112 S. Ct. 177 (1991) *2:* 689

Ryder v. Time, Inc., 557 F.2d 824, 2 Media L. Rep. 1221 (D.C. Cir. 1976) *2:* 396

Rzadkowolski v. Village of Lake Orion, 845 F.2d 653 (6th Cir. 1988) *12:* 182, 184

S

Sabella v. Newsday, 315 F. Supp. 333 (E.D.N.Y. 1970) *9:* 48

Sacramento Bee v. United States Dist. Ct., 656 F.2d 477, 7 Media L. Rep. 1929 (9th Cir. 1981), *cert. denied,* 456 U.S. 983 (1982) *1:* 218–20

Sacramento Cable Television v. Sacramento, 286 Cal. Rptr. 470, 19 Media L. Rep. 1532 (Cal. Ct. App. 1991) *9:* 241

Saenz v. Playboy Enters., 841 F.2d 1309, 15 Media L. Rep. 1043 (7th Cir. 1988) *2:* 140, 447

Safecard Servs. v. Dow Jones & Co., 537 F. Supp. 1137 (E.D. Va. 1982), *aff'd,* 705 F.2d 445 (4th Cir.), *cert. denied,* 464 U.S. 831 (1983) *9:* 24, 141, 143–45

Sagan v. Harvey, 1984-1 Trade Cas. (CCH) ¶65,778 (W.D. Pa. 1983) *13:* 221

Saia v. New York, 334 U.S. 558 (1948) *10:* 39; *12:* 191–93, 201

St. Amant v. Thompson, 390 U.S. 727, 1 Media L. Rep. 1586 (1968) *2:* 400, 418–20, 425, 439, 695

St. Peter; State v., 315 A.2d 254 (Vt. 1974) *14:* 70, 78, 79

Sakon v. Pepsico, 553 So. 2d 163, 17 Media L. Rep. 1277 (Fla. 1989) *8:* 2, 7, 21, 30–31, 53

Salinger v. Random House, 811 F.2d 90, 13 Media L. Rep. 1954 (2d Cir. 1987), *cert. denied,* 484 U.S. 890 (1987) *10:* 243

Sally v. Brown, 295 S.W. 890 (Ky. 1927) *2:* 199

Saloomey v. Jeppesen & Co., 707 F.2d 671 (2d Cir. 1983) *7:* 51

Sambo's Restaurants v. Ann Arbor, 663 F.2d 686 (6th Cir. 1981) *11:* 112

Samjack Liquors v. New York State Liquor Auth., 301 N.Y.S.2d 101 (N.Y. App. Div. 1969) *11:* 190

Sampson v. Murray, 415 U.S. 61 (1974) *10:* 239

San Bernardino County v. Superior Ct., 283 Cal. Rptr. 332, 19 Media L. Rep. 1545 (Cal. Ct. App. 1991) *1:* 241, 243, 253, 258

Sanders; United States v., 611 F. Supp. 45, 11 Media L. Rep. 1666 (S.D. Fla. 1985) *1:* 346

San Diego Comm. Against Registration and Draft (CARD) v. Governing Board, 790 F.2d 1471 (9th Cir. 1976) *13:* 369

Sands v. News Am. Pub'g, 560 N.Y.S.2d 416, 18 Media L. Rep. 1064 (N.Y. App. Div. 1990) *14:* 268

S & S Liquor Mart v. Pastore, 497 A.2d 729, 12 Media L. Rep. 1236 (R.I. 1985) *11:* 184, 190, 205–7

Sandstrom; State v., 581 P.2d 812 (Kan. 1978), *cert. denied,* 440 U.S. 929 (1979) *14:* 70, 79

S & W Seafoods Co. v. Jacor Broadcasting of Atlanta, 390 S.E.2d 228, 17 Media L. Rep. 1340 (Ga. Ct. App. 1989) *2:* 250

San Francisco Arts & Athletics v. United States Olympic Comm., 483 U.S. 522 (1987) *11:* 6, 82, 141–44

San Francisco Bay Guardian v. Superior Ct., 21 Cal. Rptr. 2d 464, 21 Media L. Rep. 1791 (Cal. Ct. App. 1993) *2:* 115

San Jose Country Club Apartments v. County of Santa Clara, 187 Cal. Rptr. 493 (Cal. Ct. App. 1982) *11:* 314

San Jose Mercury-News v. Municipal Ct., 638 P.2d 655, 7 Media L. Rep. 2522 (Cal. 1982) *1:* 74, 91, 152

San Juan Star Co., In re, 662 F.2d 108, 7 Media L. Rep. 2144 (1st Cir. 1981) *1:* 399, 403–5

Santiesteban v. Goodyear Tire & Rubber Co., 306 F.2d 9 (5th Cir. 1962) *4:* 40

Santos; People v., 551 N.E.2d 1245 (N.Y. 1990) *1:* 200

Sassone v. Elder, 626 So.2d 345, 22 Media L. Rep. 1049 (La. 1993) *2:* 138

Sattelink of Chicago v. Chicago, 523 N.E.2d 13 (Ill. App. Ct. 1988) *9:* 243

Satterfield v. McLellan Stores Co., 2 S.E.2d 709 (N.C. 1939) *2:* 218

Saucer v. Giroux, 54 Cal. App. 732, 202 P. 887 (Cal. Ct. App. 1921) *2:* 301

Sauerhoff v. Hearst Corp., 388 F. Supp. 117 (D. Md. 1974), *vacated,* 538 F.2d 588 (4th Cir. 1976) *2:* 194; *2:* 210

Saunders v. General Servs. Corp., 659 F. Supp. 1042 (E.D. Va. 1987) *11:* 315

Savage v. Commodity Futures Trading Comm'n, 548 F.2d 192 (7th Cir. 1977) *9:* 197

Saxbe v. Washington Post Co., 417 U.S. 843, 1 Media L. Rep. 2314 (1974) *1:* 14, 460–61, 463–64, 479–481, 490–97

Saxe, Bacon & Bolin, P.C. v. Martindale-Hubbell, Inc., 710 F.2d 87 (2d Cir. 1983) *13:* 221

Saxton v. Arkansas Gazette Co., 569 S.W.2d 115 (Ark. 1978) *14:* 195, 326

Scarce v. United States, 5 F.3d 397, 21 Media L. Rep. 1972 (9th Cir. 1993) *14:* 417

Schad
—v. Borough of Mt. Ephraim, 452 U.S. 61, 7 Media L. Rep. 1426 (1981) *8:* 56; *12:* 4, 27, 33, 36
—v. Ocean Grove Camp Meeting Ass'n, 370 A.2d 449, 2 Media L. Rep. 1354 (N.J. 1977), *overruled sub nom.* State v. Celmer, 404 A.2d 1 (N.J. 1979), *cert. denied,* 444 U.S. 951 (1979) *12:* 49
Schaefer v. Lynch, 406 So. 2d 185, 7 Media L. Rep. 2302 (La. 1981) *2:* 140
Schaeffer v. Zekman, 554 N.E.2d 988, 17 Media L. Rep. 1931 (Ill. App. Ct. 1990) *2:* 186
Schaffer v. United States, *see* Criden; United States v.
Schaumburg, Village of; v. Citizens for a Better Env't, 444 U.S. 620 (1980) *11:* 26; *12:* 115–116, 129
Scheetz v. Morning Call, 946 F.2d 202, 19 Media L. Rep. 1385 (3d Cir. 1991), *cert. denied,* 112 S. Ct. 1171 (1992) *9:* 64
Schelette; United States v., 854 F.2d 359 (9th Cir. 1988) *1:* 381
Schenck v. United States, 249 U.S. 47 (1919) *8:* 44, 46; *9:* 10; *10:* 3
Scherer v. Morrow, 401 F.2d 204 (7th Cir. 1968), *cert. denied,* 393 U.S. 1084 (1969) *2:* 522
Schermerhorn v. Rosenberg, 426 N.Y.S.2d 274, 6 Media L. Rep. 1376 (N.Y. App. Div. 1980) *2:* 126, 128
Schiavone Constr. Co. v. Time, Inc., 735 F.2d 94, 10 Media L. Rep. 1831 (3d Cir. 1984) *2:* 223
Schiff v. Williams, 519 F.2d 257 (5th Cir. 1975) *13:* 347
Schneider
—v. Indian River Community College Found., 875 F.2d 1537 (11th Cir. 1989) *13:* 390, 396
—v. New Jersey, 308 U.S. 147 (1939) *10:* 39; *12:* 36, 99, 103, 110, 115, 117
Schoen v. Township of Hillside, 382 A.2d 704 (N.J. Super. Ct. Law Div. 1977) *12:* 169
Schultz v. Newsweek, 668 F.2d 911, 7 Media L. Rep. 2552 (6th Cir. 1982) *2:* 673
Schulze v. Coykendall, 545 P.2d 392 (Kan. 1976) *2:* 141
Schuman, In re, 552 A.2d 602 (N.J. 1989) *14:* 250, 252, 334, 425
Schuster v. U.S. News & World Report, 459 F. Supp. 973, 4 Media L. Rep. 1911 (D. Minn. 1978), *aff'd,* 602 F.2d 850, 5 Media L. Rep. 1773 (8th Cir. 1979) *2:* 306, 569, 674
Schwartz v. United States Dep't of Justice, 435 F. Supp. 1203, 3 Media L. Rep. 1335 (D.D.C. 1977), *aff'd,* 596 F.2d 888 (D.C. Cir. 1979) *1:* 294
Sciandra v. Lynett, 187 A.2d 586 (Pa. 1963) *2:* 556
Scott
—People ex rel. v. Silverstein, 412 N.E.2d 692, 6 Media L. Rep. 2141 (Ill. Ct. App. 1980), *rev'd,* 429 N.E.2d 483 (Ill. 1981) *14:* 213, 327
—United States v., 195 F. Supp. 440 (D.N.D. 1961) *12:* 210
Scott Paper Co. Sec. Litig., In re, 145 F.R.D. 366, 20 Media L. Rep. 2164 (E.D. Pa. 1992) *14:* 307
Scott-Taylor, Inc. v. Stokes, 229 A.2d 733 (Pa. 1967) *2:* 151
Screws; United States v., 325 U.S. 91 (1945) *9:* 42
SDJ, Inc. v. Houston, 837 F.2d 1268 (5th Cir. 1988), *cert. denied sub nom.* MEF Enters. v. Houston, 489 U.S. 1052 (1989) *12:* 186
Seagraves; United States v., 265 F.2d 876 (3d Cir. 1959) *5:* 161
Sealed Documents, In re, 15 Media L. Rep. 1983 (D.D.C. 1988) *1:* 373–74, 377
Search Warrant for Second Floor Bedroom, In re, 489 F. Supp. 207, 6 Media L. Rep. 1420 (D.R.I. 1980) *1:* 376
Search Warrant for Secretarial Area Outside Office of Thomas Gunn, In re (Gunn I), 855 F.2d 569, 15 Media L. Rep. 1969 (8th Cir. 1988), *cert. denied,* 488 U.S. 1009 (1989) *1:* 373, 379
Search Warrants Issued on May 21, 1987, In re, 18 Media L. Rep. 1095 (D.D.C. 1990) *1:* 373, 380
Search Warrants Issued on June 11, 1988, In re, 710 F. Supp. 701, 16 Media L. Rep. 1602 (D. Minn. 1989) *1:* 373, 377–78
Sears, Roebuck & Co.
—v. State Tax Comm'n, 345 N.E.2d 893 (Mass. 1976) *9:* 248
—v. Stiffel Co., 376 U.S. 225 (1964) *6:* 91
—v. Ulman, 412 A.2d 1240 (Md. 1980) *2:* 626
Seattle Times Co.
—v. County of Benton, 661 P.2d 964, 9 Media L. Rep. 1541 (Wash. 1983) *1:* 238, 243
—v. Eberharter, 713 P.2d 710, 12 Media L. Rep. 1794 (Wash. 1986) *1:* 375–76
—v. Ishikawa, 640 P.2d 716, 8 Media L. Rep. 1041 (Wash. 1982) *1:* 157
—v. Rhinehart, 467 U.S. 20, 10 Media L. Rep. 1705 (1984) *1:* 394, 396–97, 406–25
—v. United States Dist. Ct., 845 F.2d 1513, 15 Media L. Rep. 1273 (9th Cir. 1988) *1:* 163

Sebago, Inc. v. City of Alameda, 259 Cal. Rptr. 918, 16 Media L. Rep. 2377 (1989) *12:* 146

SEC
—v. Blavin, 557 F. Supp. 1304 (E.D. Mich. 1983), *aff'd,* 760 F.2d 706 (6th Cir. 1985) *9:* 151, 194
—v. Capital Gains Research Bureau, 375 U.S. 180 (1963) *9:* 149, 151
—v. Clark, 915 F.2d 439 (9th Cir. 1990) *9:* 171
—v. Lowe, 556 F. Supp. 1359, 9 Media L. Rep. 1281 (E.D.N.Y. 1983), *rev'd,* 725 F.2d 892, 10 Media L. Rep. 1225 (2d Cir. 1984), *rev'd,* 472 U.S. 181 (1985) *9:* 192–211; *11:* 47
—v. Materia, 745 F.2d 197 (2d Cir. 1984), *cert. denied,* 471 U.S. 1053 (1985) *9:* 171
—v. Suter, 732 F.2d 1294, 10 Media L. Rep. 2159 (7th Cir. 1984) *9:* 195–96
—v. Wall Street Pub'g Inst., 851 F.2d 365 (D.C. Cir. 1988), *cert. denied,* 489 U.S. 1066 (1989) *9:* 155
—v. Wall Street Transcript Corp.
——422 F.2d 1371 (2d Cir.), *cert. denied,* 398 U.S. 958 (1970) *9:* 192
——454 F. Supp. 559, 3 Media L. Rep. 2438 (S.D.N.Y. 1978) *9:* 192
Secretary of State of Md. v. Joseph H. Munson Co., 467 U.S. 947 (1984) *9:* 211; *12:* 3, 117
Securities & Exch. Comm'n, *see* SEC
Seegmiller v. KSL, Inc., 626 P.2d 968, 7 Media L. Rep. 1012 (Utah 1981) *2:* 540
Seegrist, In re, 539 A.2d 799, 15 Media L. Rep. 1329 (Pa. 1988) *1:* 173
Selcraig, In re, 705 F.2d 789 (5th Cir. 1983) *14:* 404
Selleck v. Globe Int'l, 212 Cal. Rptr. 838 (Cal. Ct. App. 1985) *3:* 43
Sellers
—v. Henry, 329 S.W.2d 214 (Ky. 1959) *4:* 134
—v. Time, Inc., 423 F.2d 887 (3d Cir.), *cert. denied,* 400 U.S. 830 (1970) *2:* 151, 167
Semler v. Oregon State Bd. of Dental Examiners, 294 U.S. 608 (1935) *11:* 51
S.E.N. v. R.L.B., 699 P.2d 875, 11 Media L. Rep. 2278 (Alaska 1985) *1:* 453
Senogles v. Security Benefit Life Ins. Co., 536 P.2d 1358 (Kan. 1975) *4:* 190
Sentinel Star v. Edwards, 387 So. 2d 367, 6 Media L. Rep. 1603 (Fla. Ct. App. 1980) *1:* 277
Seper, In re
—705 F.2d 1499 (9th Cir. 1983) *14:* 107–9, 111–13
—810 F.2d 580 (6th Cir. 1987) *14:* 68–69, 90

Sexton
—v. American News Co., 133 F. Supp. 591 (N.D. Fla. 1955) *2:* 224
—v. Ryder Truck Rental, 320 N.W.2d 843 (Mich. 1982) *2:* 635
Shack; State v., 277 A.2d 369 (N.J. 1971) *5:* 134
SHAD Alliance v. Smith Haven Mall, 488 N.E.2d 1211 (N.Y. 1985) *12:* 90
Shain, In re, 978 F.2d 850, 20 Media L. Rep. 1930 (4th Cir. 1992) *14:* 125, 333
Shakey's Inc. v. Covalt, 704 F.2d 426 (9th Cir. 1983) *6:* 58
Shaklee Corp. v. Gunnell, 110 F.R.D. 190, 12 Media L. Rep. 2221 (N.D. Cal. 1986) *14:* 171, 372, 374
Shapero v. Kentucky Bar Ass'n, 486 U.S. 466 (1988) *11:* 86, 157–63, 320–21
Sharjah Inv. Co. v. P.C. Telemart, 107 F.R.D. 81, 11 Media L. Rep. 2383 (S.D.N.Y. 1985) *1:* 434
Sharman v. C. Schmidt & Sons, 216 F. Supp. 401 (E.D. Pa. 1963) *2:* 512; *6:* 117
Sharon v. Time, Inc., 599 F. Supp. 538, 11 Media L. Rep. 1153 (S.D.N.Y. 1984) *2:* 334–35; *14:* 261
Shaw v. Killingsworth, 106 So. 138 (Ala. 1925) *2:* 197
Shaw Cleaners & Dyers v. Des Moines Dress Club, 245 N.W. 231 (Iowa 1932) *2:* 180, 185–86
Shenandoah Pub'g House v. Fanning, 368 S.E.2d 253, 15 Media L. Rep. 1659 (Va. 1988) *1:* 453, 455
Shenkman v. O'Malley, 157 N.Y.S.2d 290 (N.Y. App. Div. 1956) *2:* 533
Shepard; State v., 438 A.2d 125, 7 Media L. Rep. 1140 (Conn. 1980) *1:* 210
Sheppard
—v. E.W. Scripps Co., 421 F.2d 555 (6th Cir.), *cert. denied sub nom.* Strickland v. E.W. Scripps Co., 400 U.S. 941 (1970) *9:* 43
—v. Maxwell, 384 U.S. 333, 1 Media L. Rep. 1220 (1966) *10:* 177, 198–200
Sheridan Newspapers v. City of Sheridan, 660 P.2d 785, 9 Media L. Rep. 2393 (Wyo. 1983) *1:* 287
Sherman; United States v., 581 F.2d 1358, 4 Media L. Rep. 1433 (9th Cir. 1978) *1:* 523
Sherrill v. Knight, 569 F.2d 124, 3 Media L. Rep. 1514 (D.C. Cir. 1977) *1:* 534
Shevin v. Sunbeam Television Corp., 351 So. 2d 723, 3 Media L. Rep. 1312 (Fla. 1977), *appeal dismissed,* 435 U.S. 920 (1978) *5:* 261

Shibly v. Time, Inc., 321 N.E.2d 791 (C.P. Cuyahoga County 1974), *aff'd,* 341 N.E.2d 337 (Ohio Ct. App. 1975) *6:* 154

Shields v. Gross, 448 N.E.2d 108, 9 Media L. Rep. 1466 (N.Y. 1983) *6:* 119, 124

Shifflet v. Thomson Newspapers, 431 N.E.2d 1014, 8 Media L. Rep. 1199 (Ohio 1982) *1:* 190; *4:* 108

Shiras v. Britt, 589 S.W.2d 18, 5 Media L. Rep. 2020 (Ark. 1979) *1:* 143

Shoen v. Shoen, 5 F.3d 1289, 21 Media L. Rep. 1961 (9th Cir. 1993) *14:* 101, 311, 335, 404

Shoppers Guide Pub'n Co. v. Woods, 547 S.W.2d 561, 2 Media L. Rep. 1825 (Tenn. 1977) *9:* 248

Shor v. Billingsley, 158 N.Y.S.2d 476 (N.Y. Sup. Ct.), *aff'd,* 169 N.Y.S.2d 416 (N.Y. App. Div. 1957) *2:* 175

Shorter v. Retail Credit Co., 251 F. Supp. 329 (D.S.C. 1966) *4:* 190

Shubert v. Columbia Pictures Corp., 72 N.Y.S.2d 851 (N.Y. Sup. Ct. 1947), *aff'd,* 80 N.Y.S.2d 274 (N.Y. App. Div. 1948) *6:* 88

Shuttlesworth v. Birmingham, 394 U.S. 147 (1969) *10:* 39, 76; *12:* 6, 57

Sible v. Lee Enters., 729 P.2d 1271, 13 Media L. Rep. 1738 (Mont. 1986), *cert. denied,* 483 U.S. 1011 (1987) *2:* 421

Sibley v. Holyoke-Telegram Pub'g Co., 461 N.E.2d 823, 10 Media L. Rep. 1557 (Mass. 1984) *2:* 560

Siclari v. Rio de Oro Mining Co., Fed. Sec. L. Rep. (CCH) 95,672 (S.D.N.Y. July 21, 1976) *9:* 139–40

Sidis v. F-R Pub'g Corp., 113 F.2d 806 (2d Cir.), *cert. denied,* 311 U.S. 711 (1940) *4:* 116, 128, 147

Siegert v. Gilley, 500 U.S. 226 (1991) *9:* 49, 54

Sierra Life Ins. Co. v. Magic Valley Newspapers, 623 P.2d 103 (Idaho 1980) *14:* 358

Sigma Delta Chi v. Speaker, Md. House of Delegates, 310 A.2d 156, 1 Media L. Rep. 2375 (Md. 1973) *1:* 639

Signs, Inc. of Fla. v. Orange County, 592 F. Supp. 693 (M.D. Fla. 1983) *12:* 185

Silberg v. Anderson, 50 Cal. 3d 205, 786 P.2d 365 (Cal. 1990) *2:* 515–16

Silkwood v. Kerr-McGee Corp., 563 F.2d 433, 3 Media L. Rep. 1987 (10th Cir. 1977) *14:* 47, 58, 66, 90, 94, 303

Silsdorf v. Levine, 449 N.E.2d 716, 9 Media L. Rep. 1815, *cert. denied,* 464 U.S. 831 (1983) *2:* 251, 265

Silverman v. Oliver, 5 Media L. Rep. 1971 (Mass. Super. Ct. 1979) *7:* 24

Silvester v. ABC, 839 F.2d 1491, 15 Media L. Rep. 1138 (11th Cir. 1988) *2:* 437

Simmons Ford, Inc. v. Consumers Union of U.S., 516 F. Supp. 742, 17 Media L. Rep. 1776 (S.D.N.Y. 1981) *2:* 605

Simon & Schuster, Inc. v. New York State Crime Victims Bd., 112 S. Ct. 501, 19 Media L. Rep. 1609 (1991) *9:* 254, 265–69

Simonson v. United Press Int'l, 654 F.2d 478, 7 Media L. Rep. 1737 (7th Cir. 1981) *2:* 289, 325

Simpson v. Simpson, 490 F.2d 803 (5th Cir.), *cert. denied,* 419 U.S. 897 (1974) *5:* 229

Sinatra
—v. Goodyear Tire & Rubber Co., 435 F.2d 711 (9th Cir. 1970), *cert. denied,* 402 U.S. 906 (1971) *6:* 39, 99
—v. Wilson, 2 Media L. Rep. 2008 (S.D.N.Y. 1977) *6:* 85

Sinkler v. Goldsmith, 623 F. Supp. 727 (D. Ariz. 1985) *6:* 213

Sinn v. Daily Nebraskan, 638 F. Supp. 143, 12 Media L. Rep. 2340 (D. Neb. 1986), *aff'd,* 829 F.2d 662 (8th Cir. 1987) *13:* 246, 375

Sioux Falls Argus Leader v. Young, 455 N.W.2d 864, 18 Media L. Rep. 1044 (S.D. 1990) *1:* 106, 122

Sipple v. Chronicle Pub'g Co., 154 Cal. App. 3d 1040, 201 Cal. Rptr. 665, 10 Media L. Rep. 1690 (Cal. Ct. App. 1984) *4:* 48–49, 146

Skeoch v. Ottley, 377 F.2d 804 (3d Cir. 1967) *2:* 481

Slaughter v. Valleydale Packers, 94 S.E.2d 260 (Va. 1956) *2:* 485

Slayton v. Williams, 726 F.2d 631 (10th Cir. 1984) *9:* 61

Slocum; United States v., 464 F.2d 1180 (3d Cir. 1972) *1:* 206

Slotnick v. Garfinkle, 632 F.2d 163 (1st Cir. 1980) *9:* 45

Small v. ABC, 10 Media L. Rep. 2391 (N.D. Iowa 1984) *2:* 141

Smalley; United States v., 9 Media L. Rep. 1252 (N.D. Tex. 1983) *14:* 343

Smith
—v. Butler, 507 F. Supp. 952 (E.D. Pa. 1981) *9:* 43, 55, 78–79
—v. Cincinnati Post & Times-Star, 475 F.2d 740 (6th Cir. 1973) *5:* 216, 265
—v. Daily Mail Publishing Co., 443 U.S. 97, 5 Media L. Rep. 1305 (1979) *4:* 83–90, 101; *10:* 49
—v. Doss, 37 So. 2d 118 (Ala. 1948) *4:* 32, 116
—v. Esquire, Inc., 494 F. Supp. 967, 6 Media L. Rep. 1825 (D. Md. 1980) *3:* 113

Smith—*Contd.*

—v. Fairman, 98 F.R.D. 445 (C.D. Ill. 1982)   *9:* 64

—v. Fielden, 326 S.W.2d 476 (Tenn. 1959)   *2:* 205

—v. Hatch, 271 Cal. App. 2d 39, 76 Cal. Rptr. 350 (Cal. Ct. App. 1969)   *2:* 514, 517

—v. Levitt, 227 F.2d 855 (9th Cir. 1955)   *2:* 4

—v. Linn, 563 A.2d 123, 16 Media L. Rep. 2228 (Pa. Super. Ct. 1989), *aff'd,* 587 A.2d 309 (Pa. 1991)   *7:* 29, 42, 52

—v. McMullen, 589 F. Supp. 642, 10 Media L. Rep. 2250 (S.D. Tex. 1984)   *2:* 135

—v. NBC, 138 Cal. App. 2d 807, 292 P.2d 600 (Cal. Ct. App. 1956)   *4:* 25; *5:* 24

—v. Nixon, 606 F.2d 1183 (D.C. Cir. 1979), *cert. denied,* 453 U.S. 912 (1981)   *5:* 215

—State ex rel. v. District Ct. of Eighth Judicial Dist., 654 P.2d 982, 8 Media L. Rep. 2608 (Mont. 1982)   *1:* 144–45, 148, 150

—United States v.

——209 F. Supp. 907 (E.D. Ill. 1962)   *11:* 276

——787 F.2d 111, 12 Media L. Rep. 1935 (3d Cir. 1986)   *1:* 222

Smith (Appeal of Patriot News Co.); United States v., 776 F.2d 1104, 12 Media L. Rep. 1345 (3d Cir. 1985)   *1:* 318, 370

Snepp

—v. United States, 595 F.2d 926, 4 Media L. Rep. 2313 (4th Cir. 1979), *rev'd in part,* 444 U.S. 507, 5 Media L. Rep. 2409 (1980)   *10:* 143–52, 156, 161

—United States v., 897 F.2d 138, 17 Media L. Rep. 1579 (4th Cir. 1990)   *10:* 139–40, 157–61

Society of Prof. Journalists

—v. Briggs, 675 F. Supp. 1308, 14 Media L. Rep. 2273 (D. Utah 1987)   *1:* 455

—v. Bullock, 743 P.2d 1116, 14 Media L. Rep. 1737 (Utah 1987)   *1:* 173, 183

—v. Secretary of Labor, 616 F. Supp. 569, 11 Media L. Rep. 2474 (D. Utah 1985), *appeal dismissed,* 832 F.2d 1180, 14 Media L. Rep. 1827 (10th Cir. 1987)   *1:* 280–86

Solarex Corp. v. Arco Solar, 121 F.R.D. 163 (E.D.N.Y. 1988), *aff'd,* 870 F.2d 642 (2d Cir. 1989)   *14:* 140, 142–43

Solargen Elec. Motor Car Corp. v. American Motors Corp., 506 F. Supp. 546 (N.D.N.Y. 1981)   *14:* 144

Solis v. Southern Cal. Rapid Transit Dist., 164 Cal. Rptr. 343 (Cal. Ct. App. 1980)   *5:* 15

Sommer v. PMEC Assocs. & Co., 18 Media L. Rep. 2141 (S.D.N.Y. 1991)   *14:* 99

Sorensen v. Wood, 243 N.W. 82 (Neb. 1932), *appeal dismissed,* 290 U.S. 599 (1933)   *2:* 175

Souder v. Pendleton Detectives, 88 So. 2d 716 (La. Ct. App. 1956)   *5:* 16, 39

Southard v. Forbes, Inc., 588 F.2d 140, 4 Media L. Rep. 2019 (5th Cir.), *cert. denied,* 444 U.S. 832 (1979)   *2:* 135

South Carolina Press Ass'n, Ex parte, 314 S.E.2d 321, 10 Media L. Rep. 1495 (S.C. 1984)   *1:* 152

Southeastern Promotions v. Conrad, 420 U.S. 546, 1 Media L. Rep. 1140 (1975)   *10:* 2, 39, 49, 65, 267; *12:* 63; *13:* 270

Southern Air Transport v. ABC, 670 F. Supp. 38, 14 Media L. Rep. 1683 (D.D.C. 1987), *on reconsideration,* 678 F. Supp. 8, 14 Media L. Rep. 2345 (D.D.C. 1988)   *3:* 27

Southern Conn. Newspapers v. Town of Greenwich, 11 Media L. Rep. 1051 (D. Conn. 1984)   *12:* 152, 218

Southern Living v. Celauro, 789 S.W.2d 251 (Tenn. 1990), *cert. denied,* 111 S. Ct. 1639 (1991)   *9:* 243

Southern N.J. Newspapers v. New Jersey Dep't of Transp., 542 F. Supp. 173 (D.N.J. 1982)   *12:* 137

South Pac. Terminal Co. v. Interstate Commerce Comm'n, 219 U.S. 498 (1911)   *1:* 106, 122

Southwestern Cable Co.; United States v., 392 U.S. 157 (1968)   *13:* 444, 446–52

Southwestern Pub'g Co. v. Horsey, 230 F.2d 319 (9th Cir. 1956)   *2:* 618–19

Southwest Pa. Cable TV v. FCC, 514 F.2d 1343 (D.C. Cir. 1975)   *13:* 459

Spahn v. Julian Messner, Inc., 260 N.Y.S.2d 451 (N.Y. App. Div. 1965), *aff'd,* 221 N.E.2d 543 (N.Y. 1966), *vacated and remanded,* 387 U.S. 239, *reaff'd,* 233 N.E.2d 840 (N.Y. 1967), *appeal dismissed,* 393 U.S. 1046 (1969)   *3:* 52, 95; *6:* 74, 85

Spann v. Colonial Village, 899 F.2d 24 (D.C. Cir. 1990), *cert. denied,* 111 S. Ct. 508 (1990)   *11:* 315

Spears Free Clinic and Hosp. for Poor Children v. Maier, 261 P.2d 489 (Colo. 1953)   *2:* 238, 625

Special Grand Jury, In re, 674 F.2d 778, 8 Media L. Rep. 1422 (9th Cir. 1982)   *1:* 162, 385–86, 388

Special Grand Jury Investig., In re, 472 N.E.2d 450 (Ill. 1984)   *14:* 70, 79, 99, 215

Speer v. Ottoway Newspapers, 828 F.2d 475, 14 Media L. Rep. 1601 (8th Cir. 1987), *cert. denied,* 485 U.S. 970 (1988)   *2:* 487

Spence

—v. Funk, 396 A.2d 967, 4 Media L. Rep. 1981 (Del. 1978)   *2:* 170, 187–88, 599

—v. Washington, 418 U.S. 405 (1974)   *12:* 20

Spencer
—v. Herdesty, 571 F. Supp. 990 (S.D. Ohio 1985) *9:* 281
—v. United States Postal Serv., 613 F. Supp. 990 (S.D. Ohio 1985) *9:* 281
Sperry Rand Corp. v. Hill, 356 F.2d 181 (1st Cir.), *cert. denied,* 384 U.S. 973 (1966) *4:* 48
Spiritual Psychic Science Church v. City of Azusa, 703 P.2d 1119 (Cal. 1988) *11:* 49
Sprague v. Walter, 516 A.2d 706, 13 Media L. Rep. 1177 (Pa. Super. Ct. 1986), *aff'd,* 543 A.2d 1078, 15 Media L. Rep. 1625 (Pa.), *appeal dismissed,* 488 U.S. 988 (1988) *2:* 482; *14:* 286, 292, 360
Spring; People v., 200 Cal. Rptr. 849 (Cal. Ct. App. 1984) *1:* 636
Staff Research Assocs. v. Tribune Co., 346 F.2d 372 (7th Cir. 1965) *13:* 228
Stahl v. State, 665 P.2d 839, 9 Media L. Rep. 1945 (Okla. Crim. App. 1983), *cert. denied,* 464 U.S. 1069 (1984) *5:* 119, 121–22, 124–31
Standard & Poor's Corp. v. Commodity Exchange, 541 F. Supp. 1273, 8 Media L. Rep. 1755 (S.D.N.Y. 1982) *1:* 270
Standard Oil Co. v. FTC, 577 F.2d 653, 4 Media L. Rep. 1459 (9th Cir. 1978) *7:* 71
Stanford Univ. v. Sullivan, 773 F. Supp. 472, 19 Media L. Rep. 1345 (D.D.C. 1991) *10:* 154
Stanley v. McGrath, 719 F.2d 279 (8th Cir. 1983) *13:* 335
Star Editorial v. United States Dist. Ct., 7 F.3d 856, 21 Media L. Rep. 2281 (9th Cir. 1993) *14:* 395
Starobin v. Northridge Lakes Dev. Co., 287 N.W.2d 747 (Wis. 1980) *2:* 196
Star Satellite v. Biloxi, 779 F.2d 1074 (5th Cir. 1986) *12:* 52
State v., *see* name of other party
State Bd. of Equalization v. Young's Mkt. Co., 299 U.S. 59 (1936) *11:* 182
State ex rel., *see* name of party
State-Record Co., In re, 917 F.2d 124, 18 Media L. Rep. 1286 (4th Cir. 1990) *1:* 307
Staub v. City of Baxley, 355 U.S. 313 (1958) *10:* 39; *12:* 6
Stauffer Communications
—State v., 592 P.2d 891 (Kan. 1979) *4:* 97
—v. Mitchell, 789 P.2d 1153, 17 Media L. Rep. 1739 (Kan. 1990) *1:* 242
Steaks Unlimited v. Deaner, 623 F.2d 264 (3d Cir.), *cert. denied,* 449 U.S. 994 (1980) *2:* 392; *14:* 289, 346, 374, 389
Steelhammer; United States v.
—539 F.2d 373 (4th Cir. 1976) *14:* 54, 64, 90, 104, 168
—561 F.2d 539 (4th Cir. 1977) *14:* 47, 54
Steinle v. Lollis, 307 S.E.2d 230, 10 Media L. Rep. 1255 (S.C. 1983) *1:* 152
Stepanian v. Addis, 699 F.2d 1046 (11th Cir. 1983) *2:* 522
Stephano v. News Group Pubns., 474 N.E.2d 580, 11 Media L. Rep. 1303 (N.Y. 1984) *6:* 24, 74, 129, 202–4
Stephens v. Van Arsdale, 608 P.2d 972, 6 Media L. Rep. 1142 (Kan. 1980) *1:* 391–92
Sterlace; Commonwealth v., 391 A.2d 1066 (Pa. 1978) *12:* 124
Stern v. United States Gypsum, 547 F.2d 1329 (7th Cir.), *cert. denied,* 434 U.S. 975 (1977) *9:* 81–83
Stessman v. American Black Hawk Broadcasting Co., 416 N.W.2d 685, 14 Media L. Rep. 2073 (Iowa 1987) *5:* 13
Stetson; Commonwealth v., 427 N.E.2d 926, 7 Media L. Rep. 2342 (Mass. 1981) *1:* 209
Stevens
—v. New York Racing Ass'n, 665 F. Supp. 164, 14 Media L. Rep. 1641 (E.D.N.Y. 1987) *1:* 546
—v. Wilber, 300 P. 329 (Or. 1931) *2:* 196
Stevenson v. Baltimore Baseball Club, 243 A.2d 533 (Md. 1968), *overruled,* 387 A.2d 1129 (Md. 1978) *2:* 535
Stickels v. General Rental Co., 750 F. Supp. 729, 18 Media L. Rep. 1644 (E.D. Va. 1990) *14:* 335
Stoianoff v. Montana, 695 F.2d 1214 (9th Cir. 1983) *11:* 305
Stone
—In re, 703 P.2d 1319, 11 Media L. Rep. 2209 (Colo. Ct. App. 1985) *1:* 524
—v. Essex County Newspapers, 330 N.E.2d 161 (Mass. 1975) *2:* 336, 461, 598
—v. University of Md. Medical Sys., 855 F.2d 178, 15 Media L. Rep. 2375 (4th Cir. 1988) *1:* 458
Stonegate Sec. Servs., In re, 56 Bankr. Rep. 1014 (N.D. Ill. 1986) *10:* 242
Storer Communications, In re (Presser I), 828 F.2d 330, 14 Media L. Rep. 1429 (6th Cir. 1987) *1:* 369
Strada v. Connecticut Newspapers, 477 A.2d 1005, 10 Media L. Rep. 2165 (Conn. 1984) *2:* 140
Straitwell v. National Steel Corp., 869 F.2d 248, 16 Media L. Rep. 1329 (4th Cir. 1989) *2:* 538
Strasser v. Doorley, 432 F.2d 567 (1st Cir. 1970) *12:* 120
Straus Communications v. FCC, 530 F.2d 1001 (D.C. Cir. 1976) *13:* 169

Street v. NBC, 645 F.2d 1227, 7 Media L. Rep. 1001 (6th Cir.), *cert. dismissed,* 454 U.S. 1095 (1981) *2:* 407

Strickland v. E.W. Scripps Co., *see* Sheppard v. E.W. Scripps Co.

Strickler v. NBC, 167 F. Supp. 68 (S.D. Cal. 1958) *4:* 36

Stromberg v. California, 283 U.S. 359 (1931) *2:* 112

Strutner v. Dispatch Printing Co., 442 N.E.2d 129, 8 Media L. Rep. 2344 (Ohio Ct. App. 1982) *4:* 156

Stuempges v. Parke, Davis & Co., 297 N.W.2d 252 (Minn. 1980) *2:* 585

Suarez
—v. Underwood, 426 N.Y.S.2d 208, 6 Media L. Rep. 1094 (N.Y. Sup. Ct. 1980), *aff'd,* 449 N.Y.S.2d 438 (N.Y. App. Div. 1981) *7:* 12, 54
—United States v., 880 F.2d 626, 16 Media L. Rep. 2283 (2d Cir. 1989) *1:* 383

Subpoena to Testify Before Grand Jury Directed to Custodian Records, In re, 864 F.2d 1559, 16 Media L. Rep. 1165 (11th Cir. 1989) *1:* 106, 117–18, 162, 385, 390

Sullivan
—v. Pulitzer Broadcasting Co., 709 S.W.2d 475, 12 Media L. Rep. 2187 (Mo. 1986) *3:* 18, 20, 48, 94
—v. United States, 299 F. Supp. 621 (N.D. Ala. 1968), *aff'd,* 411 F.2d 794 (5th Cir. 1969) *7:* 46
—v. Warner Bros. Theatres, 109 P.2d 760 (Cal. Ct. App. 1941) *2:* 122

Summerville, In re, 547 N.E.2d 513, 17 Media L. Rep. 1057 (Ill. App. Ct. 1989) *10:* 194

Summit Hotel Co. v. NBC, 8 A.2d 302 (Pa. 1939) *2:* 9

Summit Loans v. Pecola, 288 A.2d 114 (Md. 1972) *5:* 20, 45

Summit Technology v. Healthcare Capital Group, 19 Media L. Rep. 2180 (D. Mass. 1992) *14:* 307

Sun Pub'g Co. v. Walling, 140 F.2d 445 (6th Cir. 1944) *9:* 125

Sunrise, City of; v. DCA Homes, 421 So. 2d 1084 (Fla. Dist. Ct. App. 1982) *12:* 174

Sunshine Pub'g Co. v. Summerfield, 184 F. Supp. 767 (D.D.C. 1960) *9:* 279

Sunward Corp. v. Dun & Bradstreet, 568 F. Supp. 602 (D. Colo. 1983), *aff'd in part and rev'd in part,* 811 F.2d 511 (10th Cir. 1987) *10:* 239, 241

Supersign of Boca Raton v. Ft. Lauderdale, 766 F.2d 1528 (11th Cir. 1985) *12:* 177, 181

Susan A. v. Sonoma County, 3 Cal. Rptr. 2d 27, 19 Media L. Rep. 1889 (1991) *2:* 520

Swagman v. Swift & Co., 152 N.W.2d 562 (Mich. Ct. App.), *remanded,* 387 N.W.2d 912 (Mich. 1967) *2:* 190, 202

Sweenek v. Pathe News, 16 F. Supp. 746 (E.D.N.Y. 1936) *4:* 142

Sweeney v. Sengstacke Enters., 536 N.E.2d 823, 16 Media L. Rep. 1506 (Ill. App. Ct. 1989) *2:* 145

Swindall; United States v., 16 Media L. Rep. 1990 (N.D. Ga. 1989) *1:* 372

Syracuse Peace Council
—v. FCC, 867 F.2d 654, 16 Media L. Rep. 1225 (D.C. Cir. 1989), *cert. denied,* 493 U.S. 1019 (1990) *13:* 192
—In re, 2 F.C.C.R. 5043 (1987), *reconsideration denied,* 3 F.C.C.2d 2035 (1988) *13:* 189

T

Talley v. California, 362 U.S. 60 (1960) *12:* 101, 207–9, 211

Tallman; State v., 537 A.2d 422, 15 Media L. Rep. 1344 (Vt. 1987) *1:* 106, 115, 122, 141, 147, 151

Tameny v. Atlantic Richfield Co., 610 P.2d 1330 (Cal. 1980) *5:* 189

Taskett v. King Broadcasting Co., 546 P.2d 81, 1 Media L. Rep. 1716 (Wash. 1976) *2:* 598

Tatta v. News Group Pubns., 12 Media L. Rep. 2318 (N.Y. Sup. Ct. 1986) *7:* 26, 28

Tavoulareas
—v. Piro
——759 F.2d 90, 11 Media L. Rep. 1777 (D.C. Cir. 1985), *vacated in part,* 817 F.2d 762, 13 Media L. Rep. 2377 (D.C. Cir.), *cert. denied sub nom.* Tavoulareas v. Washington Post Co., 484 U.S. 870 (1987) *2:* 136, 424, 481
——93 F.R.D. 11 (D.D.C. 1981) *2:* 222
—v. Washington Post Co., *see* Tavoulareas v. Piro

Taylor
—In re, 193 A.2d 181 (Pa. 1963) *14:* 71, 77
—v. Gumpert, 131 S.W. 968 (Ark. 1910) *2:* 195
—v. KTVB Inc., 525 P.2d 984 (Idaho 1974) *4:* 54, 165, 167–69
—v. Miskovsky, 640 P.2d 959 (Okla. 1981) *14:* 70, 78, 278–80
—v. Murray, 204 S.E.2d 747 (Ga. 1974) *2:* 635
—v. State, 438 N.E.2d 275, 8 Media L. Rep. 2287 (Ind. 1982), *cert. denied,* 459 U.S. 1149 (1983) *1:* 238

—v. West Pub'g Co., 693 F.2d 837 (8th Cir. 1982) *2:* 553

Telecommunications Research & Action Ctr. v. FCC, 801 F.2d 501, 13 Media L. Rep. 1881 (D.C. Cir. 1986), *cert. denied,* 482 U.S. 919 (1987) *13:* 76, 117, 137, 181–82

Tele-Communications of Key W. v. United States, 757 F.2d 1330 (D.C. Cir. 1985) *12:* 228

Tellado v. Time-Life Books, 643 F. Supp. 904, 13 Media L. Rep. 1401 (D.N.J. 1986) *5:* 24–25; *6:* 20, 89

Temple v. Pergament, 235 F. Supp. 242 (D.N.J. 1964), *aff'd,* 343 F.2d 474 (3d Cir. 1965) *9:* 48

Tennant Co. v. Advance Mach. Co., 355 N.W.2d 720 (Minn. Ct. App. 1984) *5:* 33, 44, 194

Terwilliger; State v., 11 Media L. Rep. 2463 (Wash. 1985) *14:* 70, 78–79

Tetley, Inc. v. Topps Chewing Gum, 556 F. Supp. 785 (E.D.N.Y. 1983) *10:* 259–63

Texaco, In re, 84 Bankr. 14, 15 Media L. Rep. 1201 (Bankr. S.D.N.Y. 1988) *1:* 161, 279, 429

Texas Monthly v. Bullock, 489 U.S. 1, 16 Media L. Rep. 1177 (1989) *9:* 239

Texas Review Soc'y v. Cunningham, 659 F. Supp. 1239 (W.D. Tex. 1987) *12:* 162

Thiene, In re, 115 A.2d 543 (N.J. 1955) *4:* 190

Thomas v. Collins, 323 U.S. 516 (1945) *12:* 129

Thompson
—v. County of Alameda, 167 Cal. Rptr. 70, 614 P.2d 728 (Cal. 1980) *8:* 36
—v. State, 170 N.W.2d 101 (Minn. 1969) *14:* 84
—v. Upton, 146 A.2d 880 (Md. 1958) *2:* 180
—United States v., 17 Media L. Rep. 1004 (D.C. Cir. 1989) *1:* 345

Thomson v. Cash, 377 A.2d 135, 3 Media L. Rep. 1095 (N.H. 1977) *1:* 427

Thomson Newspapers v. Florence, 338 S.E.2d 324, 12 Media L. Rep. 1463 (S.C. 1985) *9:* 237

Thornburgh v. Abbott, 490 U.S. 401 (1989) *13:* 299–301, 303, 305–8

Thornhill v. Alabama, 310 U.S. 88 (1940) *2:* 111, 113; *4:* 141

Tijerina; United States v., 412 F.2d 661 (10th Cir.), *cert. denied,* 396 U.S. 990 (1969) *10:* 202

Time, Inc.
—v. Bernard Geis Assocs., 293 F. Supp. 130 (S.D.N.Y. 1968) *10:* 244
—v. Firestone, 424 U.S. 448, 1 Media L. Rep. 1665 (1976) *2:* 68, 159–61, 360–66, 465; *3:* 70

—v. Hill, *see* Hill v. Hayes
—v. Johnston, 448 F.2d 378 (4th Cir. 1971) *2:* 259–60, 267, 407
—v. Pape, 401 U.S. 279, 1 Media L. Rep. 1627 (1971) *2:* 454–59, 695
—v. Ragano, 427 F.2d 219 (5th Cir. 1970) *2:* 396

Times Film Corp. v. Chicago, 365 U.S. 43 (1961) *10:* 66

Times Mirror Co.
—v. Los Angeles, 237 Cal. Rptr. 346, 14 Media L. Rep. 1289 (Cal. Ct. App. 1987), *appeal dismissed,* 484 U.S. 1022 (1988) *9:* 237, 246
—v. Sisk, 593 P.2d 924 (Ariz. 1978) *7:* 51
—v. Superior Ct., 198 Cal. App. 3d 1420, 244 Cal. Rptr. 556 (Cal. Ct. App.), *modified,* 199 Cal. App. 3d 1099e (Cal. Ct. App. 1988), *cert. dismissed,* 489 U.S. 1094 (1989) *4:* 98, 104, 135, 158

Times Newspapers v. McDonnell Douglas Corp., 387 F. Supp. 189, 1 Media L. Rep. 2346 (C.D. Cal. 1974) *1:* 161, 278

Times-Mirror Co. v. United States, 873 F.2d 1210, 16 Media L. Rep. 1513 (9th Cir. 1989) *1:* 375–76

Times-Picayune Pub'g Co.
—v. Edwards, *see* Edwards; United States v.
—v. Lee, 15 Media L. Rep. 1713 (E.D. La. 1988) *1:* 540
—v. United States, 345 U.S. 594 (1953) *13:* 229

Times-Union v. Harris, 423 N.Y.S.2d 263, 5 Media L. Rep. 2153 (N.Y. App. Div. 1979), *appeal dismissed,* 407 N.E.2d 1349 (N.Y. 1980) *1:* 158

Times Pub'g Co.
—v. Florida Dep't of Corrections, 375 So. 2d 304, 5 Media L. Rep. 1510 (Fla. Dist. Ct. App.), *modified,* 375 So.2d 307, 5 Media L. Rep. 1861 (Fla. Dist. Ct. App. 1979) *1:* 498
—v. Penick, 433 So. 2d 1281, 9 Media L. Rep. 2185 (Fla. Dist. Ct. App. 1983) *1:* 191

Times World Corp., In re, 373 S.E.2d 484, 15 Media L. Rep. 2210 (Va. Ct. App. 1988) *1:* 106, 122, 232

Tinker v. Des Moines Indep. Community Sch. Dist., 393 U.S. 503 (1969) *13:* 332, 338–44, 346, 355

Tinley v. Davis, 609 P.2d 1252 (N.M. 1980) *2:* 482

Tin Pan Apple v. Miller Brewing Co., 737 F. Supp. 826 (S.D.N.Y. 1990) *6:* 35, 39

Titan Sports v. Comics World Corp., 870 F.2d 85, 16 Media L. Rep. 1408 (2d Cir. 1989) *6:* 23

Tobacco Accessories & Novelty Craftsmen Merchants Ass'n v. Treen, 681 F.2d 378 (5th Cir. 1982) *11:* 305
Tobacco Inst. v. FCC, *see* Banzhaf v. FCC
Tofani v. State, 465 A.2d 413 (Md. 1983) *14:* 417
Tokmakian v. Fritz, 67 A.2d 834 (R.I. 1949) *2:* 153
Tollefson v. Safeway Stores, 351 P.2d 274 (Colo. 1960) *5:* 19, 44
Toomey v. Farley, 138 N.E.2d 221 (N.Y. 1956) *2:* 130
Tornillo v. Miami Herald Pub'g Co., 287 So. 2d 78 (1973) *13:* 64
Torres; United States v., 602 F. Supp. 1458, 11 Media L. Rep. 1661 (N.D. Ill. 1985) *1:* 327, 346, 352
Township of, *see* name of township
Town Tobacconist v. Kimmelman, 462 A.2d 573 (N.J. 1983) *11:* 305
T.R., In re, 556 N.E.2d 439, 17 Media L. Rep. 2241 (Ohio), *cert. denied sub nom.* Dispatch Printing Co. v. Solove, 498 U.S. 958 (1990) *1:* 238, 253; *10:* 217
Trachtman v. Anker, 563 F.2d 512, 3 Media L. Rep. 1041 (2d Cir.), *cert. denied,* 435 U.S. 925 (1978) *1:* 531–32
Trammel v. United States, 445 U.S. 40 (1980) *14:* 163
Transamerica Mortgage Advisers v. Lewis, 444 U.S. 11 (1979) *9:* 189
Travers v. Paton, 261 F. Supp. 110 (D. Conn. 1966) *9:* 62, 64, 78
Treanor v. Washington Post Co., 826 F. Supp. 568, 21 Media L. Rep. 1991 (D.D.C. 1993) *13:* 249
Triangle Pubns. v. Knight-Ridder Newspapers, 445 F. Supp. 875, 3 Media L. Rep. 2086 (S.D. Fla. 1978), *aff'd,* 626 F.2d 1171, 6 Media L.Rep. 1734 (5th Cir. 1980) *10:* 244
Tribune Co.
—v. D.M.L., 566 So. 2d 1333, 18 Media L. Rep. 1076 (Fla. Dist. Ct. App. 1990) *1:* 173
—v. Green, 440 So. 2d 484 (Fla. Ct. App. 1983), *review denied,* 447 So. 2d 886 (Fla. 1984) *14:* 70, 423
—v. Huffstetler, 489 So. 2d 722, 12 Media L. Rep. 2289 (Fla. 1986) *14:* 70, 79
Tribune Newspapers West v. Superior Ct., 218 Cal. Rptr. 505 (Cal. Ct. App. 1985) *1:* 238, 248–52
Triggs v. Sun Printing & Pub'g Ass'n, 71 N.E. 739 (N.Y. 1904) *2:* 155
Trinidad v. Stettin, 5 Media L. Rep. 1171 (S.D. Fla. 1979) *1:* 635
Troiano; People v., 486 N.Y.S.2d 991 (N.Y. Sup. Ct. 1985) *14:* 264
Troman v. Wood, 340 N.E.2d 292 (Ill. 1975) *2:* 466
Tropeano v. Atlantic Monthly Co., 400 N.E.2d 847, 5 Media L. Rep. 2526 (Mass. 1980) *6:* 89, 131
Troy Pub'g Co. v. Dwyer, 494 N.Y.S.2d 537, 12 Media L. Rep. 1306 (N.Y. App. Div. 1985) *1:* 162
Truchinski v. United States, 393 F.2d 627 (8th Cir.), *cert. denied,* 393 U.S. 831 (1968) *11:* 276
Truong Dinh Hung; United States v., 629 F.2d 908 (4th Cir. 1980), *cert. denied,* 454 U.S. 1144 (1982) *5:* 166
Truxes v. Kenco Enters., 119 N.W.2d 914 (S.D. 1963) *5:* 116
Tsermengas v. Pontiac Press, 199 F. Supp. 557 (E.D. Mich. 1961) *9:* 55
Tsokalas v. Partill, 756 F. Supp. 89, 18 Media L. Rep. 1737 (D. Conn. 1991) *1:* 568
Tucker v. News Pub'g Co., 397 S.E.2d 499, 18 Media L. Rep. 1684 (Ga. Ct. App. 1990) *4:* 154
Tumminello v. Bergen Evening Record, 454 F. Supp. 1156, 3 Media L. Rep. 2547 (D.N.J. 1978) *7:* 15–16, 44
Tureen v. Equifax, Inc., 571 F.2d 411 (8th Cir. 1978) *5:* 117
Turner v. Safley, 482 U.S. 78 (1987) *13:* 304, 306–10
Turner Broadcasting Sys. v. FCC, 819 F. Supp. 32, 21 Media L. Rep. 1993 (D.D.C. 1993), *appeal granted,* 114 S. Ct. 38 (1993) *13:* 542
Twiggar v. Ossining Printing & Pub'g Co., 146 N.Y.S. 529 (N.Y. App. Div. 1914), *appeal dismissed,* 116 N.E. 1080 (N.Y. 1917) *2:* 149

U

Uhl v. CBS, 476 F. Supp. 1134, 5 Media L. Rep. 1801 (W.D. Pa. 1979) *3:* 113
Uhlman v. Sherman, 22 Ohio N.P. (n.s.) 225, 31 Ohio Dec. 54 (1919) *13:* 206
Ukiah Daily Journal v. Superior Court, 211 Cal. Rptr. 673, 11 Media L. Rep. 1676 (Cal. Ct. App. 1985) *1:* 230–32
Ultramares Corp. v. Touche, Niuen & Co., 174 N.E. 441 (N.Y. 1931) *8:* 28
Underhill Assocs. v. Bradshaw, 674 F.2d 293 (4th Cir. 1982) *9:* 211
Unelko Corp. v. Rooney, 912 F.2d 1049, 17 Media L. Rep. 2317 (9th Cir. 1990), *cert. denied,* 111 S. Ct. 1586 (1991) *2:* 245, 250

TABLE OF CASES 585

Union Leader Corp. v. Newspapers of New Eng., 180 F. Supp. 125 (D. Mass. 1959), *modified and aff'd*, 284 F.2d 582 (1st Cir. 1960), *cert. denied*, 365 U.S. 833 (1961)   *13:* 216

United Artists Communications v. City of Montclair, 257 Cal. Rptr. 124 (Cal. Ct. App.), *cert. denied*, 493 U.S. 918 (1989)   *9:* 235

United Bhd. of Carpenters and Joiners of Am. v. Scott, 463 U.S. 825 (1983)   *9:* 67, 69–71, 74, 75

United Liquor Co. v. Gard, 88 F.R.D. 123 (D. Ariz. 1980)   *14:* 371

United Press Int'l, In re, 106 B.R. 323, 16 Media L. Rep. 2401 (D.D.C. 1989)   *2:* 228, 579

United States v., *see* name of other party

United States Labor Party
—v. Pomerleau, 557 F.2d 410 (4th Cir. 1977)   *12:* 202
—v. Rochford, 416 F. Supp. 204 (N.D. Ill. 1975)   *12:* 201

United States Postal Serv.
—v. C.E.C. Servs., 869 F.2d 184 (2d Cir. 1989)   *11:* 256
—v. Council of Greenburgh Civic Ass'ns, 453 U.S. 114, 7 Media L. Rep. 1505 (1981)   *12:* 72, 74, 78; *13:* 273, 274

United States S.W. Africa/Namibia Trade & Cultural Council v. United States, 708 F.2d 760 (D.C. Cir. 1983)   *12:* 71; *13:* 429

United Steelworkers of Am. v. Phelps Dodge Corp., 883 F.2d 804 (9th Cir. 1987)   *9:* 44

University of Me.; State v., 266 A.2d 863 (Me. 1970)   *13:* 395

University of Notre Dame du Lac v. Twentieth Century-Fox Film Corp., 256 N.Y.S.2d 301 (N.Y. App. Div.), *aff'd*, 207 N.E.2d 508 (N.Y. 1965)   *4:* 27; *6:* 14, 74, 87

University of Pa. v. EEOC, 493 U.S. 182 (1990)   *14:* 26

Upton v. Times-Democrat Pub'g Co., 28 So. 970 (La. 1901)   *2:* 7

U.S. Healthcare v. Blue Cross of Greater Phila., 898 F.2d 914, 17 Media L. Rep. 1681 (3d Cir.), *cert. denied*, 498 U.S. 813 (1990)   *2:* 422

Utah State Farm Bureau Fed'n v. National Farmers Union Serv. Corp., 198 F.2d 20 (10th Cir. 1952)   *2:* 224

V

Vaill v. Oneida Dispatch Corp., 493 N.Y.S.2d 414 (N.Y. Sup. Ct. 1985)   *7:* 19–20, 22, 26, 28

Valentine
—v. CBS, Inc., 698 F.2d 430, 9 Media L. Rep. 1249 (11th Cir. 1983)   *4:* 64; *6:* 21–22
—v. Chrestensen, 316 U.S. 52, 1 Media L. Rep. 1907 (1942)   *11:* 16, 25–26, 51–52, 54–56, 60; *12:* 107

Valley Broadcasting Co. v. United States Dist. Ct. (Spilotro), 798 F.2d 1289, 13 Media L. Rep. 1347 (9th Cir. 1986)   *1:* 327, 351

Vance v. Judas Priest, 16 Media L. Rep. 2241 (Nev. Dist. Ct. 1989)   *8:* 1, 3–4, 10, 64

Vandenburg v. Newsweek, 441 F.2d 378 (5th Cir. 1971), *cert. denied*, 404 U.S. 864 (1971)   *2:* 395, 437

Van Nuys Pub'g Co. v. Thousand Oaks, 489 P.2d 809 (Cal. 1971), *cert. denied*, 405 U.S. 1042 (1972)   *12:* 95

Van Straten v. Milwaukee Journal, 447 N.W.2d 105, 16 Media L. Rep. 2408 (Wis. Ct. App. 1989), *cert. denied*, 110 S. Ct. 2626 (1990)   *4:* 141

Various Search Warrants, In re, 441 N.W.2d 255, 16 Media L. Rep. 1534 (Wis. Ct. App. 1989)   *1:* 376

Varnish v. Best Medium Pub'g Co., 405 F.2d 608 (2d Cir. 1968), *cert. denied*, 394 U.S. 987 (1969)   *2:* 432; *3:* 45, 52

Vassiliades v. Garfinckel's, Brooks Bros., 492 A.2d 580, 11 Media L. Rep. 2057 (D.C. 1985)   *4:* 157; *6:* 50

Vastola; United States v., 685 F. Supp. 917 (D.N.J. 1988)   *14:* 169

Vaughn v. State, 381 S.E.2d 30 (Ga. 1989)   *14:* 71, 77, 413

Vegod Corp. v. ABC, 25 Cal. 3d 763, 603 P.2d 14, 5 Media L. Rep. 2043 (Cal. 1979), *cert. denied*, 449 U.S. 886 (1980)   *2:* 390–91

Venn v. Tennessean Newspapers, 201 F. Supp. 47 (M.D. Tenn. 1962), *aff'd*, 313 F.2d 639 (6th Cir.), *cert. denied*, 374 U.S. 830 (1963)   *2:* 273–74

Vericker, In re, 446 F.2d 244 (2d Cir. 1971)   *5:* 161, 163

Vermont v. Blais, 6 Media L. Rep. 1537 (Vt. Dist. Ct. 1980)   *14:* 139

Vescovo v. New Way Enters., 130 Cal. Rptr. 86 (Ct. App. 1976)   *5:* 20, 45; *7:* 28

Vidal Sassoon, Inc. v. Bristol-Myers Co., 661 F.2d 272 (2d Cir. 1981)   *10:* 246–47

Village of, *see* name of village

Village Pub'g Corp. v. North Carolina Dep't of Revenue, *see* Assessment of Additional N.C. & Orange County Use Taxes Against Village Pub'g Corp., In re

Villeda v. Prairie Material Sales, 17 Media L. Rep. 2289 (Ill. Cir. Ct. 1990)   *14:* 212

Vinci v. American Can Co., 591 N.E.2d 793 (Ohio Ct. App. 1990)   *6:* 23

Virelli v. Goodson-Todman Enters., 536 N.Y.S.2d 571 (N.Y. App. Div. 1989) *14:* 454–56, 458, 461

Virgil
—v. Sports Illustrated, 424 F. Supp. 1286 (S.D. Cal. 1976) *4:* 126, 134, 146
—v. Time, Inc. 527 F.2d 1122 (9th Cir. 1975), cert. denied, 425 U.S. 998 (1976) *4:* 183, 186

Virginia State Bd. of Pharmacy v. Virginia Citizens Consumer Council, 425 U.S. 748, 1 Media L. Rep. 1930 (1976) *5:* 61; *7:* 10, 33, 35, 38, 40; *11:* 16–17, 31, 72–80, 82–84, 122; *12:* 2, 9, 16, 22, 108

Vitale v. National Lampoon, 449 F. Supp. 442, 3 Media L. Rep. 2223 (E.D. Pa. 1978) *2:* 394

Vitello; Commonwealth v., 327 N.E.2d 819 (Mass. 1975) *5:* 260

Vogel v. Bushnell, 221 S.W. 819 (Mo. Ct. App. 1920) *2:* 293–94

von Bulow by Auersperg v. von Bulow, 811 F.2d 136 (2d Cir.), cert. denied sub nom. Reynolds v. von Bulow by Auersperg, 481 U.S. 1015 (1987) *14:* 171, 311, 335, 372

Voneye v. Turner, 240 S.W.2d 588 (Ky. 1951) *4:* 40

Von Villas; People v., 13 Cal. Rptr. 62 (Cal. Ct. App. 1992) *14:* 314

Vrazo, In re, 423 A.2d 695, 6 Media L. Rep. 2410 (N.J. Super. Ct. Law Div. 1980) *14:* 420

Vuitton Et Fils S.A., United States ex rel. v. Karen Bags, Inc., 600 F. Supp. 667 (S.D.N.Y. 1985) *14:* 151, 153–54

VV Pub'g Corp., In re, 577 A.2d 412, 17 Media L. Rep. 2256 (N.J. 1990) *1:* 243, 258

W

Wadzinski; Commonwealth v., 422 A.2d 124 (Pa. 1980) *12:* 54

Waechter v. Carnation Co., 485 P.2d 1000 (Wash. Ct. App. 1971) *2:* 190

Wainman v. Bowler, 576 P.2d 268, 3 Media L. Rep. 2044 (Mont. 1978) *2:* 309

Waldbaum v. Fairchild Pub'g, 627 F.2d 1287, 5 Media L. Rep. 2629 (D.C. Cir.), cert. denied, 449 U.S. 898 (1980) *2:* 395

Walker
—v. Associated Press, 417 P.2d 486 (Colo. 1966) *2:* 628
—v. Birmingham, 388 U.S. 307 (1967) *10:* 73–79, 83, 89, 98, 102, 104
—v. Cahalan, 542 F.2d 681 (6th Cir. 1976), cert. denied, 430 U.S. 966 (1977) *9:* 55
—v. Providence Journal Co., 493 F.2d 82 (1st Cir. 1974) *13:* 214
—v. Tucker, 295 S.W. 138 (Ky. 1927) *2:* 5

Walkon Carpet Corp. v. Klaprodt, 231 N.W.2d 370 (N.D. 1975) *2:* 582

Wall & Ochs, Inc. v. Hicks, 469 F. Supp. 873 (E.D.N.C. 1979) *11:* 323

Walla Walla Union Bulletin v. NLRB, 631 F.2d 609 (9th Cir. 1980) *9:* 128

Waller
—v. Georgia, 467 U.S. 39, 10 Media L. Rep. 1714 (1984) *1:* 12–13, 69–73, 127, 213
—v. Osbourne, 763 F. Supp. 1144 (M.D. Ga. 1991) *8:* 1, 3–4, 10, 64

Walnut Properties v. City of Whittier, 861 F.2d 1102 (9th Cir. 1988), cert. denied, 490 U.S. 1006 (1989) *12:* 33, 80

Walt Disney Prods.
—v. Filmation Assocs., 628 F. Supp. 871 (C.D. Cal. 1986) *10:* 243
—v. Shannon, 276 S.E.2d 580, 7 Media L. Rep. 1209 (Ga. 1981) *8:* 2, 5, 11–12, 14, 19, 25–27, 35, 43, 50, 89, 101, 104–6

Walter
—v. Bauer, 439 N.Y.S.2d 821 (N.Y. Sup. Ct. 1981), aff'd in part, 451 N.Y.S.2d 533 (N.Y. App. Div. 1982) *7:* 29
—v. Duncan, 153 N.Y.S.2d 916 (N.Y. App. Div. 1956) *2:* 206

Walters
—v. Kansas City Star Co., 406 S.W.2d 44 (Mo. 1966) *2:* 146
—v. Seventeen Magazine, 241 Cal. Rptr. 101 (Cal. Ct. App. 1987) *7:* 12, 20, 22, 85

Wampler; State v., 569 P.2d 46, 3 Media L. Rep. 1639 (Or. Ct. App. 1977), cert. denied, 436 U.S. 960 (1978) *1:* 635

Wandt v. Hearst's Chicago Am., 109 N.W. 70 (Wis. 1906) *2:* 131

Ward
—v. Painters' Local Union, 252 P.2d 253 (Wash. 1953) *2:* 537
—v. Rock Against Racism, 491 U.S. 781, reh'g denied, 492 U.S. 937 (1989) *12:* 25, 127, 204

Warden; People v., 365 N.Y.S.2d 17 (N.Y. App. Div. 1975) *14:* 430, 435

Warford v. Lexington Herald-Leader Co., 789 S.W.2d 758, 17 Media L. Rep. 1785 (Ky. 1990), cert. denied, 111 S. Ct. 754 (1991) *2:* 450

Warner Cable Communications v. Niceville, 911 F.2d 634 (11th Cir. 1990), cert. denied, 111 S. Ct. 2839 (1991) *13:* 398

Warner-Lambert Co. v. Federal Trade Comm'n, 562 F.2d 749, 2 Media L. Rep. 2303 (D.C. Cir. 1977), cert. denied, 435 U.S. 950 (1978) *7:* 71

Washington
—v. Clark County Liquor & Gaming Licensing Bd., 683 P.2d 31 (Nev. 1984) *11:* 309
—v. Rinaldo, 689 P.2d 392 (Wash. 1984) *14:* 433
Washington Merchantile Ass'n v. Williams, 733 F.2d 687 (9th Cir. 1984) *11:* 305
Washington Post Co.
—In re, 807 F.2d 383, 13 Media L. Rep. 1793 (4th Cir. 1986) *1:* 159, 186, 318
—v. Keogh, 365 F.2d 965 (D.C. Cir. 1966), *cert. denied,* 385 U.S. 1011 (1967) *2:* 671
—v. Kleindiest, 494 F.2d 994 (D.C. Cir. 1974) *1:* 479
—v. Robinson, 935 F.2d 282, 18 Media L. Rep. 2027 (D.C. Cir. 1991) *1:* 159, 366, 382
—United States v., 446 F.2d 1322 (D.C. Cir. 1971) *10:* 109
Washington Pub. Power Supply Sys. Sec. Litig., In re, 823 F.2d 1349 (9th Cir. 1987) *9:* 156
Waskow v. Associated Press, 462 F.2d 1173 (D.C. Cir. 1972) *2:* 473, 475
Wasser v. San Diego Union, 236 Cal. Rptr. 772 (Cal. Ct. App. 1987) *4:* 119
Wasserman v. Low, 691 P.2d 716 (Ariz. Ct. App. 1984) *5:* 227
Watseka, City of; v. Illinois Pub. Action Council, 796 F.2d 1547 (7th Cir. 1986), *aff'd,* 479 U.S. 1048 (1987) *12:* 23–24, 41
Watson
—v. Cronin, 384 F. Supp. 652 (D. Colo. 1974) *1:* 533
—v. Wannamaker, 57 S.E.2d 477 (S.C. 1950) *2:* 218
Watters v. TSR, Inc., 715 F. Supp. 819 (W.D. Ky. 1989), *aff'd,* 904 F.2d 378 (6th Cir. 1990) *8:* 1–2, 4, 13, 16, 35, 38–39, 43, 49
WBAI-FM v. Proskin, 344 N.Y.S.2d 393 (N.Y. App. Div. 1973) *14:* 262
WBAL-TV Div., Hearst Corp. v. Maryland, 477 A.2d 776, 10 Media L. Rep. 2121 (Md. 1984) *14:* 73, 423
WCBS TV, *see* Banzhaf v. FCC
Weaver v. Jordan, 411 P.2d 289 (Cal.), *cert. denied,* 385 U.S. 844 (1966) *12:* 201
Webb v. Call Pub'g Co., 180 N.W. 263 (Wis. 1920) *2:* 617
Webbe; United States v., 791 F.2d 103, 12 Media L. Rep. 2193 (8th Cir. 1986) *1:* 358
Webster Groves Sch. Dist. v. Pulitzer Pub'g Co., 898 F.2d 1371, 17 Media L. Rep. 1633 (8th Cir. 1990) *1:* 270
Wehling v. CBS, 721 F.2d 506, 10 Media L. Rep. 1125 (5th Cir. 1983) *2:* 289; *5:* 25
Wehringer v. Newman, 400 N.Y.S.2d 533, 3 Media L. Rep. 1708 (N.Y. App. Div. 1978) *2:* 276
Weiler v. Carpenter, 695 F.2d 1348 (10th Cir. 1982) *11:* 305, 307
Weinberg v. Pollock, No. CV 89 02 77 735, 1991 Conn. Super LEXIS 1435, 19 Media L. Rep. 1442 (Conn. Super. Ct. 1991) *2:* 245
Weiner
—v. Doubleday & Co., 549 N.E.2d 453, 17 Media L. Rep. 1165 (N.Y. 1989), *cert. denied,* 495 U.S. 930 (1990) *2:* 506
—v. Superior Ct., 130 Cal. Rptr. 61 (Cal. Ct. App. 1976) *3:* 113
Weingarten v. Block, 102 Cal. App. 3d 129, 5 Media L. Rep. 2585 (Cal. Ct. App.), *cert. denied,* 449 U.S. 899 (1980) *2:* 339
Weirum v. RKO Gen., 123 Cal. Rptr. 468, 539 P.2d 36 (Cal. 1975) *8:* 1, 3, 62, 64–66, 68–76, 78, 80–81, 84–85, 87, 89–90, 100
Weiss v. Thomson Newspapers, 8 Media L. Rep. 1258 (Ohio Ct. C.P. 1981) *14:* 276
Welch v. Mr. Christmas, 440 N.E.2d 1317, 454 N.Y.S.2d 971, 8 Media L. Rep. 2366 (N.Y. 1982) *6:* 44, 115
Welfare of K., In re, 269 N.W.2d 367, 4 Media L. Rep. 1539 (Minn. 1978) *1:* 238, 243
Weller v. Home News Pub'g Co., 271 A.2d 738 (N.J. Super. Ct. Law Div. 1970) *3:* 28
Wellman v. Williamson Daily News, 582 F. Supp. 1526 (S.D. W. Va.), *aff'd,* 742 F.2d 1450 (4th Cir. 1984) *9:* 43; *13:* 246
Welton v. Los Angeles, 566 P.2d 1119 (Cal. 1976) *11:* 49
Werber v. Klopfer, 272 A.2d 631 (Md. 1971) *2:* 154
Werner
—v. Southern Cal. Associated Newspapers, 216 P.2d 825 (Cal. 1950) *2:* 612
—v. Times-Mirror Co., 193 Cal. App. 2d 111, 14 Cal. Rptr. 208 (Cal. Ct. App. 1961) *3:* 108; *4:* 30
Westchester Rockland Newspapers
—v. Leggett, 399 N.E.2d 518, 5 Media L. Rep. 2009 (N.Y. 1979) *1:* 158, 173–79, 382
—v. Marbach, 413 N.Y.S.2d 411, 4 Media L. Rep. 2256 (N.Y. App. Div. 1979) *1:* 161, 278
—v. Yonkers, 5 Media L. Rep. 1777 (S.D.N.Y. 1979) *12:* 147, 155
Western Broadcast Co. v. Times Mirror Co., 14 Cal. App. 2d 120, 57 P.2d 977 (Cal. Ct. App. 1936) *2:* 121–22
Western Pa. Socialist Workers 1982 Campaign v. Connecticut Gen. Life Ins. Co., 515 A.2d 1331 (Pa. 1986) *12:* 90
Western Telecasters v. California Fed'n of Labor, 415 F. Supp. 30 (S.D. Cal. 1976) *9:* 94

Westinghouse Broadcasting Co.
—v. Dukakis, 409 F. Supp. 895 (D. Mass. 1976) *1:* 542, 638
—v. National Transp. Safety Bd., 8 Media L. Rep. 1177 (D. Mass. 1982) *1:* 535
Westmoreland v. CBS, Inc.
—752 F.2d 16, 11 Media L. Rep. 1013 (2d Cir. 1984), *cert. denied,* 472 U.S. 1017 (1985) *1:* 580, 637
—9 Media L. Rep. 1521 (S.D.N.Y. 1983) *14:* 267
WFMJ Broadcasting Co., In re, 566 F. Supp. 1036, 9 Media L. Rep. 1622 (N.D. Ohio 1983) *1:* 348
WHC, Inc. v. Tri-State Road Boring, 468 So. 2d 764 (La. Ct. App. 1985) *2:* 470
Wheeler
—v. Commissioner of Highways, 822 F.2d 586 (6th Cir. 1987), *cert. denied,* 484 U.S. 1007 (1988) *12:* 182, 184
—v. Dell Pub'g Co., 300 F.2d 372 (7th Cir. 1962) *2:* 229
—v. Goulart, 593 A.2d 173, 18 Media L. Rep. 2296 (D.C. Ct. App. 1991) *14:* 324–25
—v. Green, 593 P.2d 777, 5 Media L. Rep. 1132 (Or. 1979) *2:* 394, 402
—v. P. Sorenson Mfg. Co., 415 S.W.2d 582 (Ky. 1967) *4:* 190
Whelehan v. County of Monroe, 558 F. Supp. 1093 (W.D.N.Y. 1983) *9:* 65
White
—v. Fawcett Pubns., 324 F. Supp. 403 (W.D. Mo. 1971) *3:* 113
—v. Fraternal Order of Police, 909 F.2d 512, 17 Media L. Rep. 2137 (D.C. Cir. 1990) *2:* 137, 558, 565–66; *4:* 141
—v. Samsung Elecs. of Am., 971 F.2d 1395, 20 Media L. Rep. 1457 (9th Cir. 1992), *cert. denied,* 113 S. Ct. 2443 (1993) *6:* 26
—v. Valenta, 44 Cal. Rptr. 241 (Cal. Ct. App. 1965) *2:* 613
—People v., 506 N.E.2d 1284 (Ill. 1987) *12:* 212
—United States v., 401 U.S. 745 (1971) *5:* 199, 203
White House Vigil v. Clark, 746 F.2d 1518 (D.C. Cir. 1984) *12:* 187
Wichita Eagle & Beacon Pub'g Co. v. NLRB, 480 F.2d 52 (10th Cir. 1973), *cert. denied,* 416 U.S. 982 (1974) *9:* 128
Wideman v. Garbarino, 770 P.2d 320, 16 Media L. Rep. 1253 (Ariz. 1989) *1:* 241
Widmar v. Vincent, 454 U.S. 263 (1981) *12:* 60–61, 66; *13:* 270, 272
Wiemer v. Rankin, 790 P.2d 347, 17 Media L. Rep. 1753 (Idaho 1990) *2:* 506
Wilder v. Johnson Pub'g Co., 551 F. Supp. 622, 9 Media L. Rep. 1145 (E.D. Va. 1982) *2:* 167
Wilk v. American Medical Ass'n, 635 F.2d 1295 (7th Cir. 1980) *1:* 437
Williams
—In re
——766 F. Supp. 358, 18 Media L. Rep. 2177 (W.D. Pa. 1991), *aff'd,* 963 F.2d 567, 20 Media L. Rep. 1232 (3d Cir. 1992) *14:* 98–99, 126, 167, 417
——159 Cal. App. 3d 600, 205 Cal. Rptr. 903 (Cal. Ct. App. 1984) *13:* 331
—v. ABC, 96 F.R.D. 658 (W.D. Ark. 1983) *14:* 173, 196, 345, 377, 379
—v. New York Times, 462 So. 2d 38, 11 Media L. Rep. 1364 (Fla. Dist. Ct. App. 1984) *4:* 159
—v. Stafford, 589 P.2d 322, 4 Media L. Rep. 2073 (Wyo. 1979) *1:* 172
—State v.
——459 A.2d 641, 9 Media L. Rep. 1585 (N.J. 1983) *1:* 146, 152–53
——617 P.2d 1012 (Wash. 1980) *5:* 260
Willie Nelson Music Co. v. Comm'r, 85 T.C. 914, 12 Media L. Rep. 1657 (T.C. 1985) *1:* 451
Willis v. Capital Cities Communications, 13 Media L. Rep. 1683 (D. Kan. 1986) *2:* 680
Wilson
—v. American Motors Corp., 759 F.2d 1568, 11 Media L. Rep. 2008 (11th Cir. 1985) *1:* 427, 452–53, 455
—v. Scripps-Howard Broadcasting Co., 642 F.2d 371, 7 Media L. Rep. 1169 (6th Cir.), *cert. granted,* 454 U.S. 962 (1981) *and cert. dismissed,* 454 U.S. 1130 (1981) *2:* 283–84, 396
—v. Stocker, 819 F.2d 943 (10th Cir. 1987) *12:* 212
Winans; United States v., 11 Media L. Rep. 1279 (S.D.N.Y. 1985) *14:* 136, 319
Windfaire, Inc. v. Busbee, 523 F. Supp. 868 (N.D. Ga. 1981) *11:* 306
Windsor v. The Tennessean, 719 F.2d 155 (6th Cir. 1983), *reh'g denied with opinion,* 726 F.2d 277 (6th Cir.), *cert. denied,* 469 U.S. 826 (1984) *9:* 79, 82–83
Winegard
—v. Larsen, 260 N.W.2d 816 (Iowa 1977) *3:* 38, 40, 57
—v. Oxberger, 258 N.W.2d 847 (Iowa 1977), *cert. denied,* 436 U.S. 905 (1978) *14:* 70
Wineholt v. Westinghouse Elec. Corp., 476 A.2d 217, 10 Media L. Rep. 2005 (Md. Ct. Spec. App.), *cert. denied,* 483 A.2d 38 (Md. 1984) *2:* 181, 186
Winterland Concessions Co.

—v. Sileo, 528 F. Supp. 1201 (N.D. Ill. 1981), *aff'd in part, rev'd in part sub nom.* Winterland Concessions Co. v. Trela, 735 F.2d 257 (7th Cir. 1984) *6:* 32
—v. Trela, *see* Winterland Concessions Co. v. Sileo
Winters
—v. Morgan, 576 P.2d 1152, 3 Media L. Rep. 2021 (Okla. 1978) *2:* 186
—v. New York, 333 U.S. 507 (1948) *8:* 51
Wisconsin v. Constantineau, 400 U.S. 433 (1971) *11:* 182
Wisconsin Action Coalition v. Kenosha, 767 F.2d 1248 (7th Cir. 1985) *12:* 41
Wisconsin Ass'n of Nursing Homes v. Journal Co., 285 N.W.2d 891 (Wis. Ct. App. 1979) *13:* 207, 242
Wisconsin State Journal, State ex rel. v. Circuit Ct., 389 N.W.2d 73, 12 Media L. Rep. 2320 (Wis. Ct. App. 1986) *1:* 173
Wiseman; Commonwealth v., 249 N.E.2d 610 (Mass. 1969), *cert. denied,* 398 U.S. 960 (1970) *10:* 238
WJW-TV v. Cleveland, 686 F. Supp. 177, 15 Media L. Rep. 1351 (N.D. Ohio 1988), *vacated as moot,* 878 F.2d 906, 16 Media L. Rep. 2328 (6th Cir.), *cert. denied,* 493 U.S. 819 (1989) *1:* 539
Wojtowicz v. Delacorte Press, 403 N.Y.S.2d 218, 3 Media L. Rep. 1992 (N.Y. 1978) *6:* 37
Wolf
—v. Regardie, 553 A.2d 1213, 16 Media L. Rep. 1780 (D.C. 1989) *4:* 48, 126, 162; *5:* 18, 48, 139
—People v., 333 N.Y.S.2d 299 (N.Y. App. Div. 1972) *14:* 262
Wolfson, United States v., *see* ABC, In re
Wolin v. Port of N.Y. Auth., 392 F.2d 83 (2d Cir.), *cert. denied,* 393 U.S. 940 (1968) *12:* 69
Wolsky v. Oregonian Pub'g Co., *see* Oregonian Pub'g Co. v. United States Dist. Ct.
Wolston v. Reader's Digest Ass'n, 443 U.S. 157, 5 Media L. Rep. 1273 (1979) *2:* 44, 64, 66, 68, 368, 376–89, 405
Wood
—v. Fort Dodge Messenger, 13 Media L. Rep. 1610 (Iowa Dist. Ct. 1986) *5:* 80, 90–91
—v. Hustler Magazine, 736 F.2d 1084, 10 Media L. Rep. 2113 (5th Cir. 1984), *cert. denied,* 469 U.S. 1107 (1985) *2:* 642; *3:* 28, 83
—v. United States, 498 A.2d 1140 (D.C. Ct. App. 1985) *11:* 308
Woodhaven Lumber & Mill Work, In re, 589 A.2d 135, 18 Media L. Rep. 2049 (N.J. 1991) *14:* 247, 252–56
Woodland v. Michigan Citizens Lobby, 378 N.W.2d 337 (Mich. 1985) *12:* 90
Woods v. Evansville Press Co., 791 F.2d 480, 12 Media L. Rep. 2179 (7th Cir. 1986) *2:* 241
Wooley v. Maynard, 430 U.S. 705 (1977) *13:* 203
World Imports v. Woodbridge Township, 493 F. Supp. 428 (D.N.J. 1980) *11:* 305
World-Wide Volkswagen Corp. v. Woodson, 444 U.S. 286 (1980) *2:* 651
World Pub'g Co.
—v. Minahan, 173 P. 815 (Okla. 1918) *2:* 222
—v. Mullen, 61 N.W. 108 (Neb. 1894) *2:* 123
Worrell Newspapers of Ind. v. Westhafer, 570 F. Supp. 1447, 9 Media L. Rep. 2222 (S.D. Ind. 1983), *rev'd,* 739 F.2d 1219, 10 Media L. Rep. 2088 (7th Cir. 1984), *aff'd,* 469 U.S. 1200 (1985) *1:* 371; *10:* 49
WPIX Inc. v. League of Women Voters, 595 F. Supp. 1484, 10 Media L. Rep. 2433 (S.D.N.Y. 1984) *1:* 544, 638
Wright
—In re, 700 P.2d 40 (Idaho 1985) *14:* 423
—v. Chief of Transit Police, 558 F.2d 67, 2 Media L. Rep. 1980 (2d Cir. 1977) *12:* 70
—v. Jeep Corp., 547 F. Supp. 871 (E.D. Mich. 1982) *14:* 309, 313
WSB-TV v. Lee, 842 F.2d 1266, 15 Media L. Rep. 1583 (11th Cir. 1988) *9:* 94
Wulp v. Corcoran, 454 F.2d 826 (1st Cir. 1972) *12:* 120
WXYZ, Inc. v. Hand, 658 F.2d 420, 7 Media L. Rep. 1817 (6th Cir. 1981) *1:* 210; *4:* 97; *10:* 194, 238
Wynberg v. National Enquirer, 564 F. Supp. 924, 8 Media L. Rep. 2398 (C.D. Cal. 1982) *2:* 604

Y

Yagman, In re, 796 F.2d 1165, 13 Media L. Rep. 1545 (9th Cir. 1986), *cert. denied,* 484 U.S. 963 (1987) *2:* 639
Yakubowicz v. Paramount Pictures Corp., 536 N.E.2d 1067, 16 Media L. Rep. 1725 (Mass. 1989) *8:* 1–2, 8, 11–12, 17, 25–27, 43, 60
Yanase v. Automobile Club of S. Cal., 260 Cal. Rptr. 513, 17 Media L. Rep. 1085 (Cal. Ct. App. 1989) *7:* 12
Yerkie v. Post-Newsweek Stations, Mich., 470 F. Supp. 91, 4 Media L. Rep. 2566 (D. Md. 1979) *2:* 276

Yeste v. Miami Herald Pub'g Co., 451 So. 2d 491, 10 Media L. Rep. 2298 (Fla. Dist. Ct. App. 1984) *1:* 305

Yetman v. English, 811 P.2d 323 (Ariz. 1991) *2:* 252

Yiamouyiannis v. Consumers Union of U.S., 619 F.2d 932, 6 Media L. Rep. 1065 (2d Cir.), *cert. denied,* 499 U.S. 839 (1980) *2:* 395, 673

Yonkers Bd. of Educ.; United States v., 747 F.2d 111, 10 Media L. Rep. 2521 (2d Cir. 1984) *1:* 639

York v. Story, 324 F.2d 450 (9th Cir. 1963), *cert. denied,* 376 U.S. 939 (1964) *9:* 59, 60, 62–63

Yorty v. Chandler, 13 Cal. App. 3d 467, 91 Cal. Rptr. 709 (Cal. Ct. App. 1970) *2:* 116, 156, 158

Young v. American Mini Theatres, 427 U.S. 50, 1 Media L. Rep. 1151 (1976) *12:* 5, 11, 80

Yuhas v. Mudge, 322 A.2d 824 (N.J. Super. Ct. App. Div. 1974) *7:* 12–14, 17–18, 54, 84–85; *8:* 28

Z

Zacchini v. Scripps-Howard Broadcasting Co., 351 N.E.2d 454, 2 Media L. Rep. 1199 (Ohio 1976), *rev'd,* 433 U.S. 562, 2 Media L. Rep. 2089 (1977) *6:* 21, 27, 42, 59–64, 66–71, 91, 112

Zamora
—v. CBS, 480 F. Supp. 199, 5 Media L. Rep. 2109 (S.D. Fla. 1979) *8:* 1–2, 4, 11–13, 16, 18, 25–28, 30–31, 34–35, 43, 47, 49
—v. State, 422 So. 2d 325 (Fla. Dist. Ct. App. 1982) *8:* 4

Zapple, 23 F.C.C.2d 707 (1970) *13:* 108–9

Zauderer v. Office of Disciplinary Counsel, 471 U.S. 626 (1985) *7:* 33; *11:* 24, 114–16, 159, 321

Zenith Radio Corp. v. Matsushita Elec. Indus., 529 F. Supp. 866 (E.D. Pa. 1981) *1:* 435

Zerangue v. TSP Newspapers, 814 F.2d 1066, 13 Media L. Rep. 2438 (5th Cir. 1987) *2:* 406, 442

Zerilli
—v. Evening News Ass'n, 628 F.2d 217, 6 Media L. Rep. 1530 (D.C. Cir. 1980) *5:* 196–97, 216, 243; *9:* 45, 47, 51
—v. Smith, 656 F.2d 705 (D.C. Cir. 1981) *14:* 98–99, 101, 404

Zetes v. Richman, 447 N.Y.S.2d 889 (N.Y. App. Div. 1982) *2:* 474

Ziegler, In re, 550 F. Supp. 530, 9 Media L. Rep. 1013 (W.D.N.Y. 1982) *14:* 413

Ziffrin, Inc. v. Reeves, 308 U.S. 132 (1939) *11:* 182

Zim v. Western Pub'g Co., 573 F.2d 1318, 4 Media L. Rep. 1467 (5th Cir. 1978) *6:* 29, 114

Zimmerman v. Board of Pubns. of Christian Reformed Church, 598 F. Supp. 1002, 11 Media L. Rep. 1545 (D. Colo. 1984) *2:* 638; *13:* 227; *13:* 227, 243

Zito v. American Fed'n of Musicians, 401 N.Y.S.2d 929 (N.Y. App. Div. 1978) *2:* 537, 539

Zucker v. Panitz, 299 F. Supp. 613 (M.D. Ala. 1967), *dismissed as moot,* 402 F.2d 515 (5th Cir. 1968) *13:* 347

Zurcher v. Stanford Daily, 436 U.S. 547, 3 Media L. Rep. 2377 (1978) *14:* 2, 462–64, 466–67

Zuschek v. Whitmoyer Labs, 430 F. Supp. 1163 (E.D. Pa. 1977), *aff'd,* 571 F.2d 573 (3d Cir. 1978) *2:* 534

Zweig
—v. Hearst Corp. (Zweig I), 521 F.2d 1129 (9th Cir.), *cert. denied,* 423 U.S. 1025 (1975) *9:* 157–64
—v. Hearst Corp. (Zweig II), 594 F.2d 1261 (9th Cir. 1979) *9:* 165–68, 170

INDEX

This index is alphabetized word-by-word (i.e., Fair trial precedes Fairness Doctrine).

A

Abortion advertising   342–43, 371, 457
"Abscam" cases and media right of access   35–36, 38
Absolute privilege defense
   appropriation and right of publicity   228
   defamation   121–22
   reporter's privilege   505, 509, 511
Abuse of conditional privilege   124
Access by media (*see* News gathering)
Access to media   407–67
   advertising, publisher's right to refuse   431–32
      school newspapers and publications   450–51
   antitrust law and publisher's right to refuse advertising   432–35
   broadcast media
      government-controlled or -sponsored media   451–55
      government-mandated access   407–13
   cable television   457–67
   constitutionality of government-mandated access   407–17
   deregulation of access to broadcast media   428–30
   equal time/opportunities rule (*see* Equal time)
   Fairness Doctrine   408–13, 415–17, 420, 423–27
      demise of doctrine   428–30
   FCC regulation   417–30
   government-controlled or -sponsored media   437–57
      broadcasting   451–55
      print media   440–51
   payment for   426
   personal attack rule   427–28
   political editorializing rule   428
   print media   430–37
      government-mandated access   413–15
      prison newspapers and publications   440–45
      reasonable access rule   421–22
         comparison to Fairness Doctrine   427
      student newspapers and publications   445–51
Accountants, solicitation of clients   356
Act of State doctrine   122
Actual injury (*see also* Defamation)
   trespass   199
Actual malice (*see also* Defamation)
   emotional distress   182
   false light   150–52
   imitation and incitement   266–67
Administrative proceedings
   access rights   30–32
   defamation
      absolute privilege   121–22
      accurate summary privilege   124–27
Adult bookstores   383
Adult theatres   379–80, 386, 434, 437
Advertising (*see also* Appropriation and right of publicity; Commercial speech; False advertising)
   antitrust law   270–71
   publisher's right to refuse   431–32
      antidiscrimination laws   436–37
      antitrust law   432–35
      contractual rights   435
   securities offering   285, 437
   student newspapers and publications   450–51
Alabama shield laws   486
Alaska shield laws   487
American Bar Association Fair Trial-Free Press Guidelines   15
Anonymity
   interviewee   182
   time, place, and manner restrictions   400–401
Antidiscrimination laws (*see* Discrimination)

591

Anti-dilution statutes and prior restraints   330
Antitrust law   269–72
   advertising, publisher's right to refuse   432–35
Apology and defamation   132
Appellate review of defamation cases   139–40
Appropriation and right of publicity   211–39
   absolute privilege defense   228
   advertising of media's contents   225
   advertising purposes test   214–16
   alternate causes of action   213
   attorney fee awards   220
   biographies   223–24
   California statutes   230–31
      survival of cause of action   234–36
   cause of action   213–20
      advertising or trade purposes test   214–16
      alternate causes   213
      celebrity or public status requirement   213–14
      fault, showing of   218–19
      plaintiffs   213–14
      relief   219–20
      survival   232–39
      unauthorized uses   216–18
   celebrity or public status requirement   213–14
   consent defense   228
   Copyright Act, preemption of state statutes   225–28
   damages   219–20
   de minimis test   224
   death of plaintiff, survival of cause of action   232–39
   defenses   220–28
      advertising of media's contents   225
      consent   228
      federal preemption   225–28
      fictional works, docudramas, and biographies   223–24
      First Amendment protection   215, 220–24
      incidental use   224
      privileges   228
   definitions   211–12
   development of law   211–13
   distinguishing between torts   211–13
   docudramas   223–24
   fault, showing of   218–19
   federal preemption   225–28
   fictional works   223–24
   First Amendment defense   215, 220–24
   gestures, unauthorized use   218
   incidental use defense   224
   injunctions   220
   Lanham Act   231–32
   likenesses, unauthorized use   217–18
   look-alikes, unauthorized use   217–18
   mannerisms, unauthorized use   218
   names, unauthorized use   216–17
   New York statutes   229
      survival of cause of action   237–38
   plaintiffs   213–14
   privilege defense   228
   public status requirement   213–14
   punitive damages   220
   qualified privilege defense   228
   relief   219–20
   Restatement (Second) of Torts   212
   standing   213–14
   state statutes   229–31
      federal preemption   225–28
      survival of cause of action   234–39
   survival of cause of action   232–39
      state statutes   234–39
   Tennessee statutes, survival of cause of action   236–37
   trade purposes test   214–16
   use for advertising or trade purposes   214–16
   voices, unauthorized use   218
Arizona shield laws   487
Arkansas shield laws   487, 501, 503
Arraignments, access rights   17
Atomic Energy Act   313
Attorneys
   advertising   348–49, 354–55, 375–76
   gag orders on   323–26
Attorneys' fees
   appropriation action, recovery   220
   defamation   137–38
   indigent criminal's defense, right of access to documents regarding payment   41
   right of publicity action, recovery   220
Audiotapes used in criminal proceedings, access rights   33–42
Authentication of quotes   502

B

Bail and related hearings, closure to media   18–19
Bar association journals and newsletters   455
Betting (*see* Gambling)
Biased reporting, effect on privilege   126
Billboards   379, 386, 395–98
Biographies, appropriation and right of publicity   223–24
Brandeis article on right to privacy   157–60, 166–67, 183–84
Branzburg and confidential sources   469–73

Breach of contract
  breach of promise actions against reporters 512–14
  false advertising, media liability to advertisers 241–42
Broadcasting (*see* Cable television; Radio broadcasts; Televised broadcasts)
Brothels, advertising restrictions 374
Bugging (*see* Wiretapping and eavesdropping)
Burden of proof (*see also* Defamation)
  false light 145, 149
Business entities
  defamation 100
  private facts actions 162

C

Cable Communications Policy Act 404, 464
Cable television 457–67
  city-operated cable system 455
  distribution 401–5
  indecency, regulation 466–67
  local regulation 462–64
  monopoly issue 466
  "must-carry" rules 464–67
  public access channels 463–64
  public education and government (PEG) channels 464
  taxation 293–94
California
  appropriation and right of publicity statutes 230–31
  Evidence Code 505
  prison publications 443–45
  shield laws 487–88, 502, 508
Campaign contribution law 280–82
Candidates (*see* Elections)
Cartoons and defamation 84
Causes of action (*see also* Survival of cause of action)
  appropriation 213–20
    survival of cause of action 232–39
  defamation, elements of claim 78–79
  false light, elements of claim 144–52
  imitation and incitement 257–58
  intrusion, elements of claim 185
  private facts actions, elements of claim 163–80
  right of publicity 213–20
    survival of cause of action 232–39
Celebrities (*see* Appropriation and right of publicity; Public officials and figures)
Censorship
  candidates' statements 420
  prisoners' mail 441–43
Charity Games Advertising Clarification Act 367–68
Chastity, defamatory statements concerning 90
Children's Health Protection Act 363
Choice of law determining reporter's privilege 505–7
CIA material, prior restraint on disclosure 314–17
Cigarette advertising 362–66
Civil actions (*see* Causes of action)
Civil proceedings (*see* Court proceedings)
Civil records, access rights 42–49
  discovery materials 42–47
  divorce records 48
  sealed records 48–49
  settlement records 48
Civil rights laws 272–80, 283
Civil rights suits by media 280
Civil rules
  Federal Rules of Civil Procedure and confidential sources 482–83
  state rules of procedure as source of reporter's privilege 482
Class actions
  access rights 29
  defamation 102
Classified information 310–17
Clear and convincing evidence of actual malice 116
Closed judicial proceedings (*see also* Court proceedings) 1–30
Collateral bar rule, prior restraints 306–10
"Color of state law" requirement, Section 1983 273
Colorado shield laws 488
Commercial speech 335–76
  abortion clinic advertising 342–43, 371
  brothel advertising 374
  casino advertising 349–51
  Central Hudson test 346–49
  contraceptive advertising 348–49, 371–72, 381
  definition 335–40
  door-to-door solicitation 390
  drug paraphernalia advertising 373–74
  escort service advertising 374, 434
  history 341–46
  liquor advertising 347–48, 356–62
  lottery advertising 353, 366–70
  motive 337–39
  "per se" approach 344
  Posadas case and impact 349–56
  public utility advertising 372–73
  ratio of editorial-to-advertising test 340
  reasonable fit test 353, 356
  time, place, and manner restrictions 344, 356, 389, 396
  tobacco advertising 362–66

Commercials, coverage under Fairness
    Doctrine 425–26
Common law
  access rights (*see* Court proceedings; News
      gathering)
  confidential sources 484–86
  defamation 69–70
  New York law on right of publicity 237
Communicable diseases, defamatory statement
    that person has 89
Communications Act 407, 459
  recognition of Fairness Doctrine 423–24
Community antenna television (CATV) (*see*
    Cable television)
"Company towns" 387
Compensatory damages (*see* Damages)
Concerts, access rights 57
Conditional privilege, defamation 123–28
Confidential sources 469–516
  alternatives to disclosure 504–5
  Branzburg and companion U.S. Supreme
      Court decisions 469–73
  breach of promise actions against
      reporters 512–14
  choice of law determining privilege
      505–7
  civil cases 474–75, 477, 507–10
  common law as source of protection
      484–86
  criminal cases 469–77
  discovery requests 482–83
  employer's right to assert privilege
      500–501
  exhaustion of alternative sources 478
  Federal Rules of Civil Procedure as source
      of protection 482–83
  Federal Rules of Criminal Procedure as source
      of protection 481–82
  Federal Rules of Evidence as source of
      protection 483–85, 505–6
  Fifth Amendment as source of
      protection 479
  First Amendment as source of
      protection 474–79
  grand jury proceedings, reporters as
      witnesses 470–73, 510–11
  in camera production 504–5, 512
  Justice Department guidelines as source of
      protection 480
  libel actions, effect of refusal to disclose
      503–4, 507–9
  material and information covered 502–3
  notes of reporter 502–3, 507
  outtakes 503, 507
  persons and entities covered 499–500
  protective orders 482–83
  qualified privilege to withhold identity 474,
      486, 508–9
  material and information covered 502
  relevancy standard for discovery
      requests 482
  sanctions for reporter's refusal to obey order
      to disclose source 503–4
  scheduling orders 483
  scope of protection 499–503
  sources of protection 474–79
  state constitutions as sources of
      protection 474–79, 505
  state laws as source of protection 486–99
  state rules of procedure as source of
      protection 482
  subpoenas
    criminal proceedings 511–12
    Federal Rules of Civil Procedure 483
    Federal Rules of Criminal Procedure 481
    grand jury proceedings 470–73, 510–11
    Justice Department guidelines 480
  unpublished materials 502–3, 508–9
  waiver of privilege 500–502
  who holds the privilege 500–501
Conflicts of laws
  defamation 134
  jurisdiction over reporter's privilege 507
Consent defense
  appropriation 228
  defamation 121
  intrusion 196
  private facts actions 182–83
  right of publicity 228
  wiretapping and eavesdropping, single party
      consent 204–7, 210
Conspiracy, Section 1985 actions 277
Constitutional issues
  commercial speech (*see* Commercial speech)
  defamation 70–78
  Fairness Doctrine 424
  government-mandated access to media
      407–17
  Newspaper Protection Act 271–72
  personal attack rule 427
  reporter's privilege (*see* Confidential sources)
  right of access
    administrative proceedings 30–32
    court proceedings (*see* Court proceedings)
Contempt
  prior restraints 301–10
  sanction for failure to disclose source 504
Context and defamation 79–90, 95
Contraceptive advertising 348–49, 371–72,
    381
Contract breach (*see* Breach of contract)
Controlling person under Section 20 of Securities
    Act of 1933 285–86
Conversion and trespass to chattels 199–202

damages 199
 privilege to disclose illegal acts 202
 publication of stolen information 199–202
Copying documents (*see also* Records)
 theft involved 199–202
Copyrights 329–31
 Copyright Act, preemption of state statutes 225–28
Corporations (*see* Business entities)
Correction
 defamatory statements, effect on damages 131–32
 disclosure of private facts 183
Countersuits, defamation 137–38
Court buildings, access rights 59
Court proceedings
 access rights 1–30
 common law right of access 11
  records and evidence 32–39
  standard of review 12
 confidential sources and reporter's privilege 474–75, 477, 507–10
 constitutional right of access 2–11
  civil pretrial and trial proceedings 29–30
  class actions 29
  Gannett Co. v. DePasquale 2–3, 13–14, 16, 18–19
  Globe Newspaper Co. v. Superior Court 5–6, 31
  juvenile proceedings 26–28
  preliminary hearing 8–11
  Press-Enterprise I 6–7, 21, 24–25, 29
  Press-Enterprise II 8–11, 13, 16–17
  pretrial suppression hearings 7–8, 13–16
  Richmond Newspapers v. Virginia 4–5, 14, 16, 21, 31–32
  standard of review 12
  voir dire 6–7, 21, 24–26
  Waller v. Georgia 7–8
 criminal cases (*see* Criminal proceedings)
 defamatory statements
  absolute privilege 121–22
  accurate summary privilege 124–27
 disclosure of information obtained as part of news gathering 168–71
 electronic coverage 60–66
 gag orders 317–26
 hearing requirements for closure 11–12
 motion requirements for closure 11–12
 notice requirements for closure 12
 prior restraints 317–26
 procedural requirements for closure 11–13
 sidebar conferences, access rights 24
 televised coverage 60–66
 transcripts of closed proceedings 12

voir dire, access rights 21
Credit reporting agencies and conditional privilege 123
Crime scenes, access rights 55
Criminal charges as slander per se 88–89
Criminal libel 139
Criminal penalties
 disclosure of confidential information 168–71
 securities violations 285, 288
Criminal proceedings
 access rights 2–28
  "Abscam" cases and 35–36, 38
  bail and related hearings 18–19
  depositions 18
  electronic coverage 60–66
  expungement, effect 42
  grand jury records 41
  indictments 40–41
  indigent criminal's defense, right of access to documents regarding payment 41
  juvenile proceedings 26–28
  juvenile rape victims 5–6
  mental competency hearings 19–21
  particular reporter, no right to bar access 42
  posttrial hearings 21
  preliminary hearings 8–11, 17–18
  pre-sentence reports 41
  pretrial suppression hearings 7–8, 13–16
  prior restraints 317–26
  records of criminal proceedings 33–42
  search warrants 39–40
  societal interests in open proceedings 14
  state courts 15
  televised coverage 60–66
  trials 21–28
   hijacking cases 23
   juvenile proceedings 26–28
   prior restraints 317–26
   sex crime cases 23–24
   voir dire 6–7, 21, 24–26
  voir dire 6–7, 21, 24–26
  Watergate affair 33–35, 38
 confidential sources and reporter's privilege 469–77, 510–12
 federal rules (*see* Federal Rules of Criminal Procedure)
 Sixth Amendment right (*see* Sixth Amendment rights)
Criminal records, access rights 33–42
Criminal rules of procedure (*see* Federal Rules of Criminal Procedure)
Criminal trespass and First Amendment rights 197–98
Criminals, antiprofit statutes 295–97

D

Damages (*see also* Punitive damages)
   appropriation 219–20
   conversion and trespass to chattels 199
   defamation (*see* Defamation)
   intrusion 198
   private facts actions 184
   publication in intrusion case 189–93
   right of publicity 219–20
   securities violations 285
   trespass 199
Death (*see* Survival of cause of action)
Deceptive advertising (*see* False advertising)
Defamation 69–140
   absolute privilege 121–22
      conditional absolute privilege 124–27
      consent 121
      public officials and figures 104
      publication required by law 122
   abuse of conditional privilege 124
   actual damages 75, 77, 79
   actual injury, defined 129–30
   actual malice 71–78, 98–99, 102–5, 109–16, 119–20
      appellate review 139–40
      clear and convincing evidence 116, 137
      conditional privilege, effect 124
      definition 112–15
      misinterpretation 115–16
      neutral report privilege 128
      private figures 117
      punitive damages 129–30
      reporter's privilege not to disclose confidential sources 503
   administrative proceedings, statements made during, covered by absolute privilege 121–22
   apology, effect on damages 132
   appellate review 139–40
   assumption of risk 110
   attorneys' fees 137–38
   biased reporting, effect on privilege 126
   burden of proof 78, 99, 130
      common law 69
   cartoons 84
   chastity, statements concerning 90
   class actions 102
   clear and convincing evidence of actual malice 116, 137
   colloquium 85
   common law 69–70
   conditional absolute privilege 124–27
   confidential sources, effect of refusal to disclose 503–4, 507–9
   conflicts of laws 134
   consent to publication creates absolute privilege 121
   corporations 100
   correction and retraction, effect on damages 131–32
   countersuits 137–38
   credit reporting agencies, whether conditional privilege applies 123
   criminal charges as 88–89
   criminal libel 139
   damages 75, 79, 85, 92–93, 100, 128–33
      apology, effect 132
      correction and retraction, effect 131–32
      Gertz's effect 128–30
      incremental harm doctrine 130–31
      legislative reform 133
      loss of political office 132
      matter of public concern 120–21
      mitigation 130–32
      private figures 116–17
      proposed legislation 133
      public figures 105
   deceased persons 100
   defamatory content 79–90
   definitions
      actual injury 129–30
      actual malice 112–15
      defamation 80
      public official 103
   disclaimers in fictitious works, effect 101
   dismissal 137
   disparagement 89–90
   distinguishing slander from libel 86–88
   editions of books, newspapers, etc., effect on suits 93
   editorials 95
   elements of claims 78–79
   epithets 84
   executive proceedings, statements made during, covered by absolute privilege 121–22
   fact vs. opinion 93–97
      test to determine 95–97
   fair comment privilege 97–98
   false light
      compared to 142
      principles of defamation applied to 154–55
      separate claim from 142–44
   falsity 98–99
   fault 75, 78, 102–20
   Federal Communications Act, required broadcasts 122
   federal rights, Section 1983 action 273–74
   fictitious works 101
   First Amendment issues 70–78

foreign government proceedings and privilege 127
government entities 100, 102, 104
government proceedings and privilege 124–27
gross negligence 112
groups of more than 25 people 101–2
headlines 81
humor 84
hyperbole 84, 93
identification and 100
implied meaning of statements 82
incremental harm doctrine 130–31
inducement and innuendo 85
injunctive relief 133
injury to reputation, requirement 85
innocent construction rule 83
insults 84
interested party privilege 123
jokes 84
judicial proceedings, statements made during, covered by absolute privilege 121–22
jurisdiction 135–37
legislative proceedings, statements made during, covered by absolute privilege 121–22
libel 85–88
libel-proof plaintiffs 130–31
loss of political office, damages 132
malicious prosecution 138
matter of public concern 120–21
meaning and context 79–90, 95
misconduct 89–90
misinterpretation 115–16
mitigation of damages 130–32
National Association of Broadcasters model statute 118
negligence 116–17
  gross negligence 112
neutral report privilege 127–28
newspaper editions, effect 93, 133–34
nominal damages 128
opinion 93–97
per quod libel 86–88
per se libel 86–88
per se slander 86–90
personal jurisdiction 135–37
plaintiffs 99–102
  libel-proof plaintiffs 130–31
pleading to contain all defamatory words 83
press conferences and privilege 126
presumed damages 128–30
prior restraints 133, 328
privacy interests and 79

private figures 76–77, 116–17
  actual malice 117
  damages 116–17
privileged statements 79
  absolute privilege 121–27
  biased reporting, effect on privilege 126
  conditional privilege 123–28
  disclosure of private facts, applicability 183
  fair comment 97–98
  public officials and absolute privilege 104
  reporting privilege 127–28
public officials and figures 71–78, 102–15
  absolute privilege 104, 122
  access to media for rebuttal 110–11
  assumption of risk 110–11
  compensatory damages for public figures 105
  criticism of doctrine 110–11
  definition of public official 103
  general-purpose public figures 105–9
  involuntary public figures 109, 111
  limited-purpose public figures 105–9
  mention of public official status, whether required 104
  nonmedia defendants 109–10
  official conduct 103–4
  passage of time, effect 110
  types of public figures 105
  voluntary public figures 105–9
publication 90–93
  absolute privilege, when required by law 122
  individual liability 91
  republication 92, 124
  single publication rule 92–93, 133–34
punitive damages 75, 77–78, 119, 128–30, 140
purposes of law 79
qualified privilege 123–28
  absolute privileges with conditions 124–27
  abuse 124
  excessive publication 124
  general circulation publications 123
  interested party privilege 123
  newsletters of organizations 123
  related causes of action 138–39
  relatives cannot bring action 100
  reporter's privilege not to disclose sources 503–4, 507–9
  reporting privilege 127–28
  republication 92, 124
    reporting privilege 127–28
  respondeat superior 118–19
  retraction, effect on damages 131–32

Defamation—Contd.
  reviews of books, movies, restaurants, etc. 95
  Section 1983, federal rights 273–74
  Section 1985, federal rights 278
  single instance rule 83–84
  single publication rule 92–93, 133–34
  slander 85–90
  "small and all" rule 102
  special damages 79, 83, 87–88, 128
  statistics on litigation outcomes 140
  statute of limitations 93, 133–34
  strict liability 69, 78, 90, 92, 101, 117–18, 124
  summary judgments 137, 140
  survivorship of suits 100
  truth and 71, 93–99, 139
  unfit for office or occupation, statements about person 89
  venereal disease, statements that person has 89
  vicarious liability 118–19
  waiver of First Amendment defense 119–20
  wire service defense 117
Defendants
  gag orders on 323–26
  reporters as, confidential sources involved in case 507–9
Defenses
  appropriation 220–28
  intrusion 193–98
  private facts actions 182–83
  right of publicity 220–28
  waiver of First Amendment defense to defamation 119–20
  wire service defense 117
Definitions
  actual injury 129–30
  actual malice 112–15
  appropriation 211–12
  commercial speech 335–40
  defamation 80
  false light 141–42
  government-sponsored media 437 n.255
  legally qualified candidate 420
  news 176
  oral communications 204
  public official 103
  right of publicity 212
  wire communications 204
Delaware shield laws 489
Demonstrations, restrictions 382–83
Denial of broadcast license 408
Department of Justice (*see* Justice Department)
Depositions
  civil cases, closure 30, 43–44
  criminal cases, closure 18

Deregulation of access to broadcast media 428–30
Directories, city 455
Disaster scenes, access 55–56
Disclaimers, effect on defamation 101
Disclosure (*see also* Confidential sources; News gathering; Private facts actions)
  public record information 166–68
  publicity of private facts 163–64
  securities 285–87
Discovery (*see also* Depositions)
  confidential sources, requests for 482–83
  materials, access rights in civil cases 42–47
Discrimination
  civil rights laws 272–80, 283
  employment discrimination 283, 374–75
  newspaper advertising 436–37
Diseases, defamatory statement that person has 89
Dismissal of defamation suits 137
Disparagement 89–90
Distribution
  cable television 401–5
  newspaper distribution and news rack ordinances 391–95
  political propaganda 401
District of Columbia shield laws 489
Diversity actions over reporter's privilege 505–7
Divorce case records, access rights 48
Docudramas, appropriation and right of publicity 223–24
Door-to-door solicitation 382, 387, 389–91
Drug paraphernalia advertising 373–74
Due process violations
  news racks, removal 393–94
  televised court proceedings 60–66

E

Eavesdropping (*see* Wiretapping and eavesdropping)
Editions of books, newspapers, etc., effect on defamation suits 93, 133–34
Editorials 95–96
  anonymity of authors 401
  commercial speech, ratio of editorial-to-advertising test 340
  election eve, restrictions 383
  endorsement of or opposition to candidates by broadcast media 428
  equal space for reply 413–15
Elections
  Congressional action seeking delay of projection broadcasts 58

editorials on election eve, restrictions 383
equal space for candidate's reply to
    editorials 408–13
equal time, access by candidates to broadcast
    media 408–13, 417–21
  comparison to Fairness Doctrine 426
  "equal opportunity" requirements
    420–21
  "legally qualified candidate,"
    defined 420
  newscast appearances 418
  "no censorship" provision 420
exit polls of voters 57–59
federal campaign law 280–82
loss of political office, damages 132
"official conduct" requirement,
    applicability 104
political activities, access rights 56–57
political editorializing, endorsement of or
    opposition to candidates by broadcast
    media 428, 430
public broadcasting and political
    campaigns 455
reasonable access rule, candidates seeking
    access to broadcast media 421–22
statements during campaigns, whether
    defamatory 95
voter pamphlets 455
Electronic coverage of court proceedings
    60–66
Eleventh Amendment 122
Emergency radio transmissions,
    interception 207–8
Emotional distress
  breach of promise actions against
    reporters 512, 514
  damages for appropriation of plaintiff's
    identity 219–20
  disclosure of private facts 181–82
  Section 1983 276
  trespass 199
Employers (*see also* Respondeat superior)
  right to assert privilege not to disclose
    confidential sources 500–501
Employment discrimination 283, 374–75
Endorsements
  candidates endorsed by broadcast media,
    political editorializing rule 428, 430
  media liability for advertised products
    250–51
Environmental aesthetics, restrictions 379,
    397
Epithets and defamation 84
Equal protection violations 278
Equal space for reply to editorials 413–15
Equal time 408–13, 417–21
  comparison to Fairness Doctrine 426

"equal opportunity" requirements
    420–21
"legally qualified candidate," defined 420
newscast appearances 418
"no censorship" provision 420
Escort service advertising 374, 434
Espionage laws, prosecution under 201
Estoppel (*see also* Defenses)
  promissory estoppel applied to breach
    of promise actions against
    reporters 512–13
Evidence
  access rights (*see* Records)
  clear and convincing evidence of actual
    malice 116
  defamation, burden of proof (*see* Defamation)
  Federal Rules of Evidence as source of
    protection for confidential
    sources 483–85, 505–6
Executions, access rights 49–54
Executive proceedings and defamation
  absolute privilege 121–22
  accurate summary privilege 124–27
Exemplary damages (*see* Punitive damages)
Exhaustion of alternative sources and disclosure
    of confidential sources 478
Exit polls of voters 57–59
Expungement of records
  disclosure of information from record
    172
  hearings, access rights 21
  no access after 42

F

Fair comment privilege 97–98
Fair Housing Act 374–75
Fair Labor Standards Act (FLSA) 282
Fair trial, free press (*see* Court proceedings;
    Criminal proceedings; Sixth
    Amendment rights)
Fairness Doctrine 408–13, 415–17, 420,
    423–27
  commercials, coverage 425–26
  comparison to equal time rule and reasonable
    access rule 426–27
  comparison to personal attack rule 427
  comparison with other broadcast access
    regulations 426–27
  demise of doctrine 428–30
  development and scope 423–26
  legislation introduced in Congress 430
False advertising 241–54
  advertisers, media liability to 241–42
  breach of contract, media liability to
    advertisers 241–42

False Advertising—Contd.
    endorsement of advertised products, media
        liability 250–51
    federal statutes 251–52
    Federal Trade Commission Act,
        applicability 251–52
    First Amendment protection, media liability
        to readers or viewers 247–49
    illegal acts, media liability for
        advertising 253–54
    injunctions under federal statutes 251
    intentional false statements, media liability
        to readers or viewers 242–43
    Lanham Act, applicability 251
        right of publicity action 231–32
    maps, media liability for publication
        249–50
    negligent false statements, media liability
        to readers or viewers 243–46
    Printers' Ink Model Statute 252
    readers or viewers, media liability to
        242–49
        First Amendment protection 247–49
        intentional false statements 242–43
        negligent false statements 243–46
        strict liability 246
    refusal to accept 434
    right of publicity action 231–32
    state statutes 252
    statutory liability 251–52
    strict liability, media liability to readers or
        viewers 246
    Uniform Deceptive Trade Practices Act,
        applicability 252
False light 141–55
    actual malice 150–52
    burden of proof 145, 149
    defamation
        compared to 142
        principles applied to 154–55
        separate claim from 142–44
    definition 141–42
    elements of claim 144–52
    First Amendment's fault requirements
        150–52
    group of plaintiffs 145
    "highly offensive" requirement 146–48
    identification of plaintiffs 144–45
    opinion 149
    oral statements 146
    plaintiffs 144–45
    private figures 150–52
    public officials and figures 150–52
    publicity 145–46
    showing of falsity 149
    truth as defense 149
Falsity (see also False advertising; Fraud)
    defamatory statements 98–99

Fault
    defamation 75, 78, 102–20
    disclosure of private facts 180
Fax use (see Telemarketing)
FCC (see Federal Communications
    Commission)
Federal Communications Act
    required broadcasts 122
Federal Communications Commission (FCC)
    (see also Fairness Doctrine)
    access regulations 417–30
    cable television regulation 458–62
    deregulation of access to broadcast
        media 428–30
    licensing authority 407–8
    wiretapping and eavesdropping
        regulation 208
Federal Election Campaign Act of 1971
    280
Federal preemption
    appropriation 225–28
    right of publicity 225–28
Federal Radio Commission 407
Federal rights
    Section 1983 273–76
    Section 1985 278
Federal Rules of Civil Procedure and confidential
    sources 482–83
Federal Rules of Criminal Procedure
    confidential sources 481–82
    Rule 53, challenges to 65–66
Federal Rules of Evidence and confidential
    sources 483–85, 505–6
Federal Trade Commission Act
    false advertising, applicability to 251–52
Fees (see also Attorneys' fees)
    news racks 395
Fictional works
    appropriation and right of publicity
        223–24
    defamation possibility 101
    fictionalized accounts 161
    imitation and incitement, First Amendment
        protection 261
Fiduciary duty, securities law 287
Fifth Amendment and confidential sources 479
Films for adults only (see Adult theatres)
Fire, police, and emergency radio transmissions,
    interception 207–8
First Amendment rights
    appropriation defense 215, 220–24
    cable television 459–67
    confidential sources (see Confidential sources)
    criminal trespass 197–98
    defamation (see Defamation)
    false advertising, media liability to readers
        or viewers 247–49

false light and fault 150–52
imitation and incitement, protection against media liability 259–62
intrusion and 189–93
  criminal trespass 197–98
judicial proceedings, access to (*see* Court proceedings; *specific type of court proceeding*)
news gathering (*see* News gathering)
prior restraints (*see* Prior restraints)
private facts actions 183
reporter's privilege (*see* Confidential sources)
right of publicity defense 215, 220–24
taxation 291–94
"For sale" signs, prohibition 381, 396
Foreign government proceedings and privilege 127
Fourth Amendment rights
  search and seizure of press facilities 514–16
  wiretapping and eavesdropping 203–4
Franchise authority for cable television 463–66
Fraud
  breach of promise actions against reporters 512, 514
  securities sales 283–84
Free press (*see* News gathering)
Freedom of Information Act (FOIA) 66

G

Gag orders (*see* Prior restraints)
Gambling
  advertising 349–51, 366–70
  transmission of betting information 369–70
  transport of wagering paraphernalia 370
General circulation publications and conditional privilege 123
Georgia shield laws 489
Gestures, unauthorized use 218
Gossip (*see* Private facts actions)
Government buildings (*see* Government property)
Government contracts for prepublication approval 314–17
Government entities (*see also* Administrative proceedings; Court proceedings; Executive proceedings; Legislative proceedings; Records)
  defamation 100, 102, 104
  invitation from, defense to intrusion 193–96
Government in the Sunshine Act 66
Government property

limited purpose public forum 385–86, 438–39, 444–45, 449–50
prosecution for theft of 201
public forum theory 438–40
Government-controlled or sponsored media 437–57
  broadcasting 451–55
  definition of government-sponsored media 437 n.255
  print media 440–51
  prison newspapers and publications 440–45
  student newspapers and publications 445–51
Government-mandated access to media 407–17
Grand juries
  proceedings 18
  records, access rights 41
  reporters as witnesses 470–73, 510–11
Groups of more than 25 people
  defamation and 101–2
  false light and 145

H

Habeas corpus proceedings 21
Handbills 388–89, 391, 400
Harassment (*see* Intrusion)
Headlines and defamation 81
Health Protection Act 364
Hearings
  administrative proceeding, access rights 30–32
  court proceeding, access rights 11–12
  posttrial hearings in criminal proceedings, access rights 21
  preliminary hearings (*see* Pretrial proceedings)
"Help wanted" ads 374–75
"Highly offensive" requirement
  false light 146–48
  intrusion 189
  private facts action 174–75
Hijacking cases, access rights 23
Hospitals 388
Housing advertising 374–75, 435
Humor and defamation 84
Hyperbole 84, 93

I

IAA (*see* Investment Advisers Act)
Identification
  defamation and 100
  false light and 144–45

Identification—*Contd.*
  names, newsworthiness 179–80
  rape victim's identity disclosed in news story 169–71
Illegal acts, media liability for advertising 253–54
Illinois shield laws 489–90, 501
Imitation and incitement 255–67
  actual malice test 266–67
  cause of action 257–58
  duty of care 258–59
  examples of cases 255–56
  fictional works, First Amendment protection 261
  First Amendment protection 259–62
  foreseeability of risk 263–65
  incitement of imminent lawless action 262–66
  liability of media 255–62
    duty of care not found 258–59
    First Amendment protection 259–62
    incitement of imminent lawless action 262–66
Impersonations 218
Implications as defamatory statements 82
In camera production 504–5, 512
Incitement (*see* Imitation and incitement)
Incremental harm doctrine and defamation 130–31
Indecency, regulation on cable television 466–67
Indian Gaming Regulatory Act 367–68
Indiana shield laws 490
Indictments, access rights 40–41
Inducement and innuendo, defamatory meaning 85
Infliction of emotional distress (*see* Emotional distress)
Informant's identity, refusal to disclose (*see* Confidential sources)
Injunctions (*see also* Prior restraints)
  appropriation 220
  defamation 133
  false advertising, federal statutes 251
  right of publicity 220
Innocent construction rule 83
Inspection of records (*see* Records)
Insults, defamation 84
Intellectual property, theft of 199–200
Intentional torts
  emotional distress 181–82
  false advertising, media liability to readers or viewers 242–43
  intrusion 186
Interception of police, fire, and emergency radio transmissions 207–8
Interested party privilege 123
Intervention, objection to protective orders 47

Interviews (*see* News gathering)
Intrusion (*see also* Trespass; Wiretapping and eavesdropping) 185–98
  consent defense 196
  criminal trespass and First Amendment rights 197–98
  damages 198
  defenses 193–98
  elements 185
  First Amendment rights and 189–93
  "highly offensive" requirement 189
  intentional acts 186
  interviews 186
  intrusive acts 186–87
  invitation from government officials 193–96
  possession and ownership 193
  private affairs 187–89
  public interest defense 196–97
  publication of information obtained by 189–93
  questions of law or fact 198
  Restatement (Second) of Torts 185
Invasion of privacy (*see* Appropriation and right of publicity; False light; Intrusion; Private facts actions)
Investment advisers 284–90
Investment Advisers Act (IAA) 285, 287–90
Invitation from government officials, defense to intrusion 193–96

J

Jails, access rights 49–54
Joint operating agreements, antitrust violations 271–72
Jokes and defamation 84
Judicial proceedings (*see* Court proceedings)
Judicial records (*see* Records)
Jurisdiction (*see also* Federal Communications Commission)
  defamation 135–37
  reporter's privilege 505–7
Jurors
  interviews regarding verdicts or deliberations 54
  misconduct, hearings regarding 21
  selection (*see* Voir dire)
Justice Department
  guidelines for reporters' privilege 480
  regulations for search and seizure of press facilities 515
Juveniles (*see also* Student newspapers and publications)
  disclosure of identity of juvenile offenders 168–69

imitation and incitement   256
proceedings, access rights   26–28
rape victims, closed judicial proceedings
    5–6

K

Kentucky shield laws   490
Ku Klux Klan Act   431, 437

L

Labor law   282–83
Lanham Act
    false advertising, applicability to   251
    right of publicity, applicability to   231–32
Law enforcement officers (*see* Police)
Leafletting (*see* Handbills)
Least restrictive means, time, place, and manner
    restrictions   380, 390
Legislative proceedings
    access rights   56–57
    accurate summary privilege   124–27
    defamatory statements made during, absolute
        privilege   121–22
Liability
    advertisers, media liability to for false
        advertising   241–42
    endorsements, media liability for endorsement
        of advertised products   250–51
    false advertising (*see* False advertising)
    imitation and incitement   255–62
    maps, media liability for publication
        249–50
    readers, media liability to for false
        advertising   242–49
    viewers, media liability to for false
        advertising   242–49
Libel (*see* Defamation)
Licensing laws   303
    FCC authority   407–8
    news racks   391–93
Likenesses (*see also* Appropriation and right
    of publicity; False light)
    Lanham Act, right of publicity action
        231–32
    unauthorized use   217–18
Limited-purpose public forums   384–85,
    438–39, 444–45, 449–50
Limited-purpose public figures   105–9
Liquor advertising   347–48, 356–62
Litigation (*see* Causes of actions; Court
    proceedings; Defamation)
Littering laws   387–88
Look-alikes, unauthorized use   217–18

Lottery advertising   353, 366–70
Loudspeakers (*see* Sound trucks)
Louisiana shield laws   490–91

M

Mail
    censorship of prisoners' mail   441–43
    rates   297–98
Malice (*see also* Actual malice; Defamation)
    disclosure of private facts   180
Malicious prosecution, defamation actions   138
Manner restrictions (*see* Time, place, and manner
    restrictions)
Mannerisms, unauthorized use   218
Maps, media liability for publication   249–50
Maryland shield laws   491, 507, 510–11
Meaning and defamation   79–90, 95
Meetings, public
    defamation and accurate summary
        privilege   124–27
    governmental   66–67
Mental anguish (*see* Emotional distress)
Mental competency hearings in criminal
    proceedings, access rights   19–21
Michigan shield laws   491–92
Migrant laborer interviews   55
Military operations, access rights   56
Mine safety hearings, access rights   30–31
Minnesota shield laws   492, 502
Minors (*see* Juveniles)
Misconduct
    defamatory remarks about   89–90
    juror's misconduct, hearings regarding   21
Misleading advertising (*see* False advertising)
Montana shield laws   492
Motion requirements
    defamation, summary judgments   137
    pretrial (*see* Pretrial proceedings)
Motive and commercial speech   337–39
Movies, adult (*see* Adult theatres)
Municipal ordinances (*see* Time, place, and
    manner restrictions)
Music concerts, access rights   57
"Must-carry" rules, cable television   464–67

N

Names (*see also* Appropriation and right of
    publicity)
    Lanham Act, right of publicity action
        231–32
    newsworthiness   179–80
    unauthorized use   216–17
National Association of Broadcasters model
    statute on defamation   118

National Labor Relations Act (NLRA) 282
National security 56, 310–17
Nebraska shield laws 492
Negligence
   breach of promise actions against
      reporters 512, 514
   defamation 116–17
      gross negligence 112
   false statements, media liability to readers
      or viewers 243–46
Neutral report privilege 127–28
Nevada shield laws 493, 502
New Jersey shield laws 493–94, 501–2, 511
New Mexico shield laws 494–95
New York
   appropriation and right of publicity
      statutes 229
         survival of cause of action 237–38
   conflict of law rules 507
   shield laws 495–96, 501, 511
News gathering (*see also* Confidential
      sources) 1–67
   administrative proceedings 30–32
   anonymity of interviewee 182
   bail hearings 18–19
   civil records 42–49
   civil trials 29–30
   court buildings 59
   crime scenes 55
   criminal proceedings 2–28
   criminal records 33–42
   disaster scenes 55–56
   disclosure of confidential sources (*see*
      Confidential sources)
   electronic coverage of court proceedings
      60–66
   exit polls of voters 57–59
   intrusive acts (*see* Intrusion)
   jails 49–54
   juror interviews 54
   juvenile proceedings 26–28
   legislative proceedings 56–57
   mental competency hearings 19–21
   migrant laborer interviews 55
   military operations 56
   open meetings laws 66–67
   political activities 56–57
   prisoner interviews 49–54
   public employee interviews 54–55
   public records laws 66–67
   sporting facilities 57
   student newspaper reporters, restrictions 55
   televised coverage of court proceedings
      60–66
News rack ordinances 391–95
Newscasts
   appearances, equal time 418

personal attack rule 427
Newsletters of organizations and conditional
      privilege 123
Newspaper distribution 391–95
Newspaper editions, effect on defamation
      suits 93, 133–34
Newspaper editorials (*see* Editorials)
Newspaper Preservation Act (NPA) 271–72
Newsworthiness defense 175–80, 196–97
Noerr-Pennington Doctrine 435
Noncelebrities (*see* Appropriation and right
      of publicity; Private figures)
Nonpublic forums 438–39, 448
   time, place, and manner restrictions
      384–85
North Dakota shield laws 496
Notes of reporters, protection against
      disclosure 502–3, 507
Notice requirements, court proceeding closure
      to media 12
Nuisance, prior restraints 300–301

O

Obscene speech (*see also* Pornography) 400
   indecency, regulation on cable
      television 466–67
   prior restraints 307
Occupationally unfit, defamatory statements that
      person is 89
Ohio shield laws 496, 502
Oklahoma shield laws 497
"Olympic," restrictions on use of word
      352–53
Omnibus Crime Control Act of 1968 204
Open meetings and records laws (*see* Meetings,
      public; Records)
Open trials (*see* Court proceedings)
Opinion
   defamatory statements 93–97
   false light 149
Opposition to candidates by broadcast media,
      political editorializing rule 428, 430
Oral communications
   false light 146
   private facts 163
   slander (*see* Defamation)
Oregon shield laws 497
Organizational newsletters and conditional
      privilege 123
Outtakes, protection from disclosure 503, 507

P

Pamphleteering (*see* Handbills)
Parades, restrictions 382–83

Parks, public forum 384, 438
Parodies, prior restraints 330–31
Parties to actions (*see* Defendants; Plaintiffs)
Partnerships (*see* Business entities)
Passage-of-time exception and privacy 172–74
Penalties (*see* Criminal penalties; Sanctions)
Pennsylvania shield laws 497–98, 503
"Pentagon Papers case" 311–14
Per quod libel 86–88
Per se libel 86–88
Per se slander 86–90
Personal attack rule 427–28, 430
Photographs
    false light (*see* False light)
    intrusive acts (*see* Intrusion)
    private facts actions 161, 165–66
Picketing at private residences 380
Place and manner restrictions (*see* Time, place, and manner restrictions)
Plaintiffs
    appropriation 213–14
    defamation 99–102
        libel-proof plaintiffs 130–31
    false light 144–45
    gag orders on 323–26
    private facts actions 160–63
    reporters as, confidential sources involved in case 503–4, 507
    right of publicity 213–14
    standing (*see* Standing)
Plea hearings (*see* Pretrial proceedings)
Pleadings to include all defamatory words 83
Police
    eavesdropping or bugging exemption 208
    radio transmissions by, interception 207–8
Political activities (*see also* Elections)
    access rights 56–57
    distribution of political propaganda 401
    meetings and accurate summary privilege 126
    statements during campaigns, whether defamatory 95
Political editorializing rule 428, 430
Polling places, exit polls 57–59
Pornography
    adult bookstores 383
    adult theatres 379–80, 386
Possession of property, requirement for trespass action 193
Postal rates 297–98
Posttrial hearings in criminal proceedings 21
Preemption (*see* Federal preemption)
Preliminary hearings (*see* Pretrial proceedings)
Presidential debates 419
Presidential Recordings and Materials Preservation Act of 1974 35

Press conferences
    accurate summary privilege 126
    equal time rules 419
Pretrial proceedings, access rights 2–3, 7–11
    civil proceedings 29–30
    criminal proceedings 17–18
        bail and related hearings 18–19
        mental competency hearings 19–21
    societal interests in open proceedings 14
    state courts 15
    suppression hearings 7–8, 13–16
Print media
    access to 430–37
    advertising, publisher's right to refuse 431–32
    government as publisher 440–51
    government-mandated access 413–15
    libel (*see* Defamation)
Printers' Ink Model Statute 252
Prior restraints 299–333
    collateral bar rule 306–10
    criminal trials, gag orders 317–26
    defamation 133, 328
    government contracts for prepublication approval 314–17
    history 299–303
    presumptive unconstitutionality 306–7
    prison newspapers and publications 331, 440–41
    procedural issues 331–33
    student newspapers 331
    taxation 291, 303
    theory and rationales 303–6
    time, place, and manner restrictions 378
    trade secrets, trademarks, and copyrights 329
    trials, gag orders 317–26
Prisoners and prisons
    access rights 49–54
    censorship of mail 441–43
    intrusion 188
    prison newspapers and publications 440–45
        prior restraints 331, 440–41
        state laws 443–45
    privacy rights in prison 166
Privacy (*see also* Appropriation and right of publicity; Intrusion; Private facts actions; Time, place, and manner restrictions)
    common law right of access to records and evidence vs. 38
    defamation and 79
    federal rights, Section 1983 275–76
    historical background 157–60
    prior restraints 327
Privacy Protection Act 514–16

Private facts actions 157–84
  breach of promise actions against reporters 512, 514
  business entities or corporations as plaintiffs 162
  consent defense 182–83
  criminal liability for disclosure of confidential information 168–71
  damages 184
  deceased plaintiffs 162
  defenses 182–83
  definition of "news" 176
  elements of claims 163–80
  emotional distress 181–82
  expunged records 172
  fault standard 180
  fictionalized accounts 161
  gossip 164
  "highly offensive" requirement 174–75
  historical background 159–60
  identification of plaintiff by name 179–80
  infliction of emotional distress 181–82
  issues of legitimate public concern 175–80
  judicial proceedings, disclosure of information as part of news gathering 168–71
  malice 180
  newsworthiness 175–80
  oral communications 163
  passage of time, effect on disclosure 172–74
  photographs 161, 165–66
  plaintiffs 160–63
  prisons, whether private or public places 166
  privileges 183
  public figures 177–79
  public record information as basis for suit 166–68
  publicity 163–64
  punitive damages 184
  questions of law or fact on newsworthiness 175–76
  relatives bringing actions 162, 178
  remedies 183–84
  republication 165
  Restatement (Second) of Torts 160, 164, 166–67, 175, 177–78
  retraction not applicable 183
  survivorship 162
  truth 163
  unauthorized disclosure by government of confidential information 171–72
  waiver of right to privacy 182
  Warren-Brandeis article on right to privacy 157–60, 166–67, 183–84
Private figures
  defamation 76–77
  false light 150–52
Private property 386–87, 396
  real estate advertising 374–75, 435
  solicitation (*see* Door-to-door solicitation)
Privilege defense
  appropriation and right of publicity 228
  defamation (*see* Defamation)
  disclosure of illegal acts 202
  reporter's privilege not to disclose confidential sources (*see* Confidential sources)
Professional advertising (*see also* Accountants; Attorneys) 375–76
Professionally unfit, defamatory statements that person is 89
Promissory estoppel applied to breach of promise actions against reporters 512–13
Prosser on right to privacy 158, 175
Prostitutes and escort service advertising 374, 434
Protective orders (*see also* Discovery)
  confidential sources 482–83
Proxy solicitations 290
Public disclosure of private facts (*see* Private facts actions)
Public education and government (PEG) channels on cable television 464
Public employees
  contracts for prepublication approval 314–17
  interviews 54–55
Public figures (*see* Public officials and figures)
Public forums 384–86
  government property 438–40
Public interest defense
  defamation 120–21
  intrusion 196–97
  private facts actions 175–80
Public meetings (*see* Meetings, public)
Public officials and figures
  defamation 71–78, 102–15
    absolute privilege for statements made by public officials 122
    fair comment privilege 97–98
    unfit for office 89
  false light 150–52
  invitation from government officials, defense to intrusion 193–96
  private facts disclosure 177–79
  tests for holding public office 303
Public places
  public forums 384–86
  government property 438–40
  time, place, and manner restrictions 379
Public/private concern distinction for defamation 120–21
Public records (*see* Records)

Public television 451–55
Public transportation advertising 457
Public utilities
  access to space in utility billing envelopes 456
  advertising 372–73
Publication of defamatory statements 90–93, 122
Publicity (*see also* Appropriation and right of publicity)
  false light 145–46
  private facts 163–64
Publisher's right to assert privilege not to disclose confidential sources 500–501
Punitive damages
  appropriation 220
  defamation 75, 77–78, 119, 128–30, 140
  private facts actions 184
  right of publicity 220
  trespass 199

Q

Qualified privilege defense (*see* Confidential sources; Defamation; Privilege defense)
Quasi-judicial proceedings, access rights 30–32
Questions of law or fact
  intrusion 198
  newsworthiness 175–76
Quotes, authentication 502

R

Racial discrimination 279
Radio Act 407, 418
Radio broadcasts
  commercials, coverage under Fairness Doctrine 425–26
  constitutionality of government-mandated access 407–13
  court proceedings 60–66
  defamatory statements 86
    rebroadcast 93
  deregulation of access 428–30
  equal time 408–13, 415–21
  interception of police, fire, and emergency transmissions 207–8
Rape trials, access to 5–6, 23–24
Rape victims
  closed judicial proceedings when victims are juveniles 5–6
  disclosure of identity in news story 169–71
Real estate advertising 374–75, 435
Reasonable access rule, candidates seeking access to broadcast media 421–22
  comparison to Fairness Doctrine 427
Records
  conversion and trespass to chattels 199
  court records and evidence, access rights (*see also* Transcripts) 32–49
    civil records 42–49
    common law right 32–36
    criminal records 33–42
  expungement (*see* Expungement of records)
  Freedom of Information Act (FOIA) 66
  Government in the Sunshine Act 66
  Presidential Recordings and Materials Preservation Act of 1974 35
  private facts actions based on information in public records 166–68
  public records laws 66–67
  unauthorized disclosure by government of confidential information 171–72
Relatives bringing suit
  defamation 100
  private facts actions 162, 178
Relevancy standard for discovery requests of confidential sources 482
Remedies (*see also* Attorneys' fees; Damages; Injunctions)
  appropriation 219–20
  private facts actions 183–84
  right of publicity 219–20
Reporters' privilege (*see* Confidential sources)
Republication
  defamatory statements 92, 124
  private facts 165
  Section 1983, federal rights 273–74
Reputation
  impairment to (*see* Defamation)
  personal attack rule, access to broadcast media 427–28
  trespass 199
Research material, protection against disclosure 502–3, 507
Residential picketing 380
Respondeat superior
  defamation 118–19
  securities violations 285–86
Restatement (Second) of Torts
  appropriation and publicity 212, 215–16
  intrusion 185
  privacy 160, 164, 166–67, 175
    newsworthiness 177
    public figures 177–78
Restraints on access to information (*see* News gathering)
Restrictive orders (*see* Prior restraints)

Retraction
  defamatory statements, effect on damages   131–32
  disclosure of private facts   183
Reviews of books, movies, restaurants, etc.   95
Rhode Island shield laws   498, 509
Right of publicity (*see* Appropriation and right of publicity)
Right-of-reply statutes   408–13, 456
Rule 10b-5   283–87

S

Sales and use tax   292–94
Sanctions
  Privacy Protection Act   515
  reporter's refusal to obey order to disclose source   503–4
Satellite dishes (*see* Cable television)
Satire and prior restraints   330–31
Scalping, securities sales   284–87
Scenes of crisis, access rights   55–56
Scheduling orders to protect confidential sources   483
School-sponsored publications (*see* Student newspapers and publications)
Sealed civil records, access rights   48–49
Search and seizure of press facilities   514–16
Search warrants, access rights   39–40, 514
Secrecy agreements and prior restraints   314–17
Section 1981   279–80
Section 1983   272–76
Section 1985   276–78
Section 1986   279
Securities advertising   437
Securities law   283–90
  Investment Advisers Act   287–90
  proxy solicitations   291
  scalping   284–87
Sentencing, access rights
  hearings   21
  pre-sentence reports   41
Settlement documents, access rights   48
Sex crimes (*see* Rape)
Sex discrimination   374
Sherman Act   269–72, 432–35
Shield laws (*see* Confidential sources)
Shopping malls   386–87, 457
Sidebar conferences, access rights   24
Signs (*see also* Billboards)
  "for sale" signs, prohibition   381, 396
Single instance rule   83–84
Single party consent to wiretapping and eavesdropping   204–7, 210
Single publication rule   92–93, 133–34
Sixth Amendment rights
  access to judicial proceeding   2–4, 24
  pretrial suppression hearing   7–8, 13
  televised proceedings   60–66
  voir dire, criminal proceeding   7
  prior restraint of gag orders   317–26
  reporter's failure to disclose source   504, 511
Slander (*see* Defamation)
Societal interests in open criminal proceedings   14
Solicitation at private homes (*see* Door-to-door solicitation)
Solicitation of clients   375–76
  accountants, in-person solicitation   356
  attorney advertising   348–49, 354–55
"Son of Sam" antiprofit statutes   295–97
Sound trucks   383, 399–400
Sources of information (*see* Confidential sources)
South Carolina shield laws   499
Sovereign immunity   122
Special damages
  appropriation of plaintiff's identity   219–20
  defamation (*see* Defamation)
Sporting facilities, access rights   57
Standing
  appropriation   213–14
  right of publicity   213–14
State action and Section 1985   276–78
State bar association journals and newsletters   455
State constitutions as sources of protection for confidentiality of news sources   474–79
State courts
  civil proceedings, access rights   30
  pretrial criminal proceedings, public access rights   15, 19
  televised proceedings   60–66
State interests in government-controlled or sponsored media (*see* Government-controlled or sponsored media)
State laws (*see also specific state*)
  appropriation   229–31
    federal preemption   225–28
    survival of cause of action   234–39
  confidential sources   486–99, 509
    constitutions as sources of protection   474–79
    defamation action limitation   507–8
    grand jury proceedings   510–11
    rules of procedure as source of protection   482
  defamation
    confidential sources involved in case   507–9

conflicts of laws 134
  fault by broadcasters 118
  innocent construction rule 83
  jurisdiction 135–37
  libel vs. slander 86
election polls, delay of broadcast 58
false advertising 252
federal preemption (*see* Federal preemption)
open meeting and public records laws 66–67
prison publications 443–45
right of publicity 229–31
  federal preemption 225–28
  survival of cause of action 234–39
right-of-reply statutes 408–13, 456
rules of procedure and confidential sources 482
search and seizure of press facilities 516
securities violations involving investment advisers 288
student publications 449–50
taxation 291–94
victim's compensation 295–97
wiretapping and eavesdropping 209–10
Statistics on outcomes in defamation suits 140
Statute of limitations
  defamation 93, 133–34
  Omnibus Crime Control Act of 1968 205
Stolen information, publication 199–202
Strict liability
  defamation (*see* Defamation)
  false advertising, media liability to readers or viewers 246
Student newspapers and publications 445–51
  access 450–51
  advertising 450–51
  editorial control 446–50
  prior restraints 331
  reporters, restrictions 55
  state laws 449–50
Subpoena of reporters (*see* Confidential sources)
Subway advertising 457
Suits (*see* Causes of action; Court proceedings; Defamation)
Summary judgments, defamation 137, 140
Suppression hearings (*see* Pretrial proceedings)
Surveillance, intrusive 188
Survival of cause of action
  appropriation and right of publicity 232–39
  defamation 100
  private facts actions 162

T

Tagline rules 373
Taped evidence used in criminal proceedings,
  access rights 33–42
Taxation 291–94
Telemarketing 387, 405
Telephone, "dial-a-porn" service 383, 405
Televised broadcasts (*see also* Cable television)
  commercials, coverage under Fairness Doctrine 425–26
  constitutionality of government-mandated access 407–13
  court proceedings, coverage 60–66
  defamatory statements 86, 91
    fault by broadcasters 118
    rebroadcast 93
  deregulation of access 428–30
  equal time 408–13, 415–21
  public television 451–55
Tennessee
  Personal Rights Protection Act 236–37
  right of publicity statutes, survival of cause of action 236–37
  shield laws 499
Testimonial privilege of reporters (*see* Confidential sources)
Third parties, reporters as 509–10
Time, place, and manner restrictions 377–405
  ample alternative means 381
  anonymous communications 400–401
  billboards (*see* Billboards)
  commercial speech 344, 356, 389, 396
  content neutral test 377–78, 384–85, 396–97
  criminal activities 379, 382
  door-to-door solicitation 382, 387, 389–91
  environmental aesthetics 379, 397
  handbills 388–89, 391, 400
  least restrictive means 380, 390
  limited purpose public forums 384–85, 438–39
  littering laws 387–88
  manner restrictions 388–405
  "narrowly tailored to serve significant governmental interest" 378–81
  news racks 391–95
  newspaper editorials, anonymity of authors 401
  nontraditional public forums 384–85, 438–39
  parades and demonstrations 382–83
  picketing at private residences 380
  place restrictions 383–87
  prior restraint 378
  privacy in own home 379, 382, 387, 389
  private property 386–87, 396
  public forums 384–86
  public places 379

Time restrictions—*Contd.*
  residential picketing   380
  sound trucks   383, 399–400
  test   377–81
  time of expression   382–83
  traditional public forums   384
  vending machines   391–95
  zoning regulation   380
Title VII, Civil Rights Act of 1964   283
Tobacco advertising   362–66
"Tombstone" advertising for securities offering   437
Trade secrets   199, 329–31
Trademarks   329–31
Traditional public forums   438
  time, place, and manner restrictions   384, 439
Transcripts
  closed court proceedings   12, 24
  inspection and copying   38
Transport of wagering paraphernalia   370
Trespass (*see also* Conversion and trespass to chattels; Intrusion)   198–202
  criminal trespass and First Amendment rights   197–98
  damages   199
Trials, access rights
  civil proceedings   29–30
  criminal proceedings   21–28
Truth
  defamation   71, 93–99, 139
  false light   149
  private facts actions   163
Truthful advertising, whether protected commercial speech (*see* Commercial speech)
Twenty-First Amendment   347–48, 356–62

U

Unauthorized disclosure by government of confidential information   171–72
"Under color of state law" requirement, Section 1983   273
Uniform Deceptive Trade Practices Act, applicability to false advertising   252
Union activities and dues   282–83
Unpublished materials, protection against disclosure   502–3, 508–9
Utilities (*see* Public utilities)

V

Vending machines, time, place, and manner restrictions   391–95

Venereal diseases, defamatory statements that person has   89
Vicarious liability and defamation   118–19
Victims of crime
  compensation statutes   295–97
  disclosure of private facts   178 (*see also* Rape victims)
Videotapes
  criminal proceedings, access rights   33–42
  outtakes, protection from disclosure   503, 507
Violence (*see* Imitation and incitement)
Voices (*see also* Appropriation and right of publicity)
  impersonations   218
  unauthorized use   218
Voir dire, access rights   6–7, 21, 24–26
Voluntariness and public/private figures
  defamation   105–9
  disclosure of private facts   177–78
Voting (*see* Elections)

W

Waiver (*see also* Defenses)
  reporter's privilege not to disclose confidential sources   500–502
Warren-Brandeis article on right to privacy   157–60, 166–67, 183–84
Washington Constitution and reporter's privilege   505
Watergate affair and media right of access   33–35, 38
Wire service defense and defamation   117
Wiretapping and eavesdropping   203–10
  definitions of wire and oral communications   204
  FCC regulation   208
  federal statutes   204–8
  Fourth Amendment rights   203–4
  interception of police, fire, and emergency radio transmissions   207–8
  intrusive act   186
  single party consent   204–7, 210
  state laws   209–10

Z

Zapple Doctrine   420, 430
Zoning regulation   380

About the Author

Rex S. Heinke is a litigation partner in the Los Angeles office of Gibson, Dunn & Crutcher, where he specializes in media law issues as well as related intellectual property and entertainment law issues. He received his B.A. from the University of Witwatersrand in 1971 and his J.D. from the Columbia University School of Law in 1975. From 1975–76 he clerked for the Honorable Frederick J.R. Heebe, Chief Judge, Eastern District of Louisiana. He then joined Gibson, Dunn & Crutcher. He has lectured and written extensively on freedom of the press, freedom of speech, and intellectual property issues for a variety of organizations.